The Marketing Book

The Chartered Institute of Marketing/Butterworth-Heinemann Marketing Series is the most comprehensive, widely used and important collection of books in marketing and sales currently available worldwide.

As the CIM's official publisher, Butterworth-Heinemann develops, produces and publishes the complete series in association with the CIM. We aim to provide definitive marketing books for students and practitioners that promote excellence in marketing education and practice.

The series titles are written by CIM senior examiners and leading marketing educators for professionals, students and those studying the CIM's Certificate, Advanced Certificate and Postgraduate Diploma courses. Now firmly established, these titles provide practical study support to CIM and other marketing students and to practitioners at all levels.

The Chartered
Institute of Marketing

Formed in 1911, The Chartered Institute of Marketing is now the largest professional marketing management body in the world with over 60 000 members located worldwide. Its primary objectives are focused on the development of awareness and understanding of marketing throughout UK industry and commerce and in the raising of standards of professionalism in the education, training and practice of this key business discipline.

Books in the series

Forthcoming

The Marketing Book

Fourth edition

Edited by
MICHAEL J. BAKER

Published in association with The Chartered Institute of Marketing

OXFORD   AUCKLAND   BOSTON   JOHANNESBURG   MELBOURNE   NEW DELHI

Butterworth-Heinemann
Linacre House, Jordan Hill, Oxford OX2 8DP
225 Wildwood Avenue, Woburn, MA 01801-2041
A division of Reed Educational and Professional Publishing Ltd

 A member of the Reed Elsevier plc group

First published 1987
Reprinted 1987, 1990 (twice)
Second edition, 1991
Reprinted 1992, 1993
Third edition, 1994
Reprinted 1995, 1997
Fourth edition 1999

British Library Cataloguing in Publication Data
A catalogue record for this book is available from the British Library

ISBN 0 7506 4114 2

Printed and bound in Great Britain by The Bath Press, Bath

FOR EVERY TITLE THAT WE PUBLISH, BUTTERWORTH-HEINEMANN
WILL PAY FOR BTCV TO PLANT AND CARE FOR A TREE.

Contents

Illustrations

Tables

Contributors

Michael J. Baker, TD, BA, BSc(Econ), Cert ITP, DBA, DipM, FCIM, FCAM, FRSA, FSCOTVEC, FRSE, FAM has been the Foundation Professor of Marketing at the University of Strathclyde since the inception of the department in 1971. He served as Dean of the Strathclyde Business School from 1978 to 1984, Deputy Principal of the University from 1984 to 1991 and Senior Adviser to the Principal 1991–1994. He has served as Chairman of SCOTBEC, the Chartered Institute of Marketing and the Marketing Education Group, as a Governor of the CAM Foundation and Member of the ESRC and UGC. He is the author/editor of more than twenty books of which the best known are *Marketing* (Macmillan, 6th edition, 1996), *Dictionary of Marketing and Advertising* (Macmillan, 3rd edition, 1998), and *Marketing Strategy and Management* (Macmillan, 3rd edition, 1999). A member of numerous editorial boards he is also the Founding Editor of the *Journal of Marketing Management*. He has extensive international experience and has held Visiting Professorships in Australia, Canada, Egypt, France, Hong Kong, New Zealand and Qatar as well as acting as a consultant to numerous international companies.

Keith Blois, BA, PhD is Fellow in Industrial Marketing at Templeton College, Oxford and is a member of the School of Management Studies, Oxford University. His particular interests are in relationship marketing in organizational markets, productivity in service industries, marketing research for high technology products and the role of marketing in non-capitalist economies. Publications include papers on industrial marketing, marketing of services, industrial economies and economic theory. His current research interests are: the impact of new manufacturing technologies on marketing strategy; productivity in service organizations; and marketing in non-capitalist economies. He was previously Reader in Marketing at Loughborough University of Technology. He has taught and researched in China, Thailand, Australia and Eastern Europe. He is also a Past President of the European Marketing Academy.

Douglas Brownlie is Professor of Marketing, Department of Marketing, School of Management, University of Stirling. He teaches and researches in marketing subjects in the Department of Marketing at the University of Stirling. He has previously held similar positions at the University of Strathclyde, the University of Glasgow and University College Cork. Before working in education his background was in engineering and marketing including a period in the steel industry.

David Carson is Professor of Marketing at the University of Ulster, Northern Ireland. His research interests lie in marketing for SMEs and quality of marketing in service industries. He has published widely in both of these areas. He has wide business experience both in consultancy and directorship roles. He is editor of the *European Journal of Marketing*, a category one international academic journal with a world-wide circulation. He is Chair of the Academy of Marketing UK, the foremost representative body of marketing academics in the UK and Ireland. He is also a Fellow of the Chartered Institute of Marketing (CIM) and a member of the CIM Academic Senate. He has been a Visiting Professor at numerous universities in Australia, New Zealand, Hong Kong and Bahrain.

Martin Charter is a management consultant specializing in 'business and the environment' who has worked with a range of international 'blue chip' private and public sector companies in environmental training, planning and exhibitions. He is also currently working as the Co-ordinator of The

Centre for Sustainable Design, and as the Co-ordinator of the Surrey and Hampshire Environmental Business Association (SHEBA). He is the editor of *The Journal of Sustainable Design* and European Editor of *The Journal of Corporate Environmental Strategy*. He is also a Director of Epsilon Press, who specialize in environmentally-related on-line publishing. He has previously worked as the Marketing and Development Director of The Earth Centre and as a founding Director of the consultancy KPH Environmental Management and Marketing, and also of the Green publisher Interleaf. He edited one of Interleaf's key publications *Greener Marketing* in 1992, and has also edited the 1999 second edition. He was the founding editor of the journal *Greener Management International* and is the author of a number of environmentally-related articles and reports. He has an MBA from Aston University and is a fellow of the Royal Society of Arts. He is a member of the Chartered Institute of Marketing and a former research fellow of the University of Southampton. He has also lectured widely on environmental marketing and green business issues.

Martin Christopher is Professor of Marketing and Logistics Systems at Cranfield School of Management, where he is Head of the Marketing and Logistics Faculty and Chairman of the Cranfield Centre for Logistics and Transportation. In addition, he is Deputy Director of the School of Management responsible for Executive Development Programmes. His interests in marketing and logistics strategy are reflected in his consultancy and management development activities. In this connection he has worked for major international companies in North America, Europe, the Far East and Australasia. In addition, he is a non-executive director of a number of companies. As an author, he has written numerous books and articles and is on the editorial advisory board of a number of professional journals in the marketing and logistics area. He is co-editor of *The International Journal of Logistics Management* and his recent books have focused upon relationship marketing, customer service and logistics strategy. He has held appointments as Visiting Professor at the University of British Columbia, Canada, the University of New South Wales, Australia and the University of South Florida, USA. Professor Christopher is a Fellow of the Chartered Institute of Marketing and of the Institute of Logistics Management, on whose Council he sits. In 1987 he was awarded the Sir Robert Lawrence medal of the Institute of Logistics and Distribution Management for his contribution to the development of logistics education in Great Britain.

Keith Crosier, BSc, MSc, DipCAM is Honorary Research Fellow in the Department of Marketing at the University of Strathclyde, where he was previously Director of the Honours Programme and Director of Teaching. After a degree in earth sciences, he unaccountably embarked on a career in marketing communications, starting as a copywriter in the in-house promotional unit of a multinational pharmaceutical company. After seven years with various responsibilities for advertising, publicity and sales promotion with Olivetti in London and New York, he came home to spend two years as executive assistant to the managing director of a small, family-owned electronic engineering firm. A mid-career master's degree in management studies at Durham University Business School converted him to academe, first as Director of the Diploma in Management Studies at what is now Teesside University. Moving to Strathclyde as a Research Fellow, studying the consumer movement, he stayed on to lecture in his managerial specialism. Periodic consultancy and four years as a monthly columnist for a Scottish professional magazine kept him in touch with developments in the marketing communications business. During the early nineties, he experienced as a regular visiting lecturer the excitement and challenges attending the emergence of organized management education in Poland. He was until 1998 Vice Chairman of the Marketing Education Group, now the Academy of Marketing. He is Assistant Editor of *Marketing Intelligence and Planning*.

Adamantios Diamantopoulos, BA, MSc, PhD, MCIM is Professor of Marketing and Business Research at Loughborough University Business School and the Nestlé Visiting Professor of Consumer Marketing at Lund University, Sweden. He was previously Professor of International Marketing at the European Business Management School, University of Wales Swansea, where he headed the Marketing Group. Other past academic posts include full-time appointments at the University of Edinburgh and the University of Strathclyde, and Visiting Professorships at the University of Miami, Vienna University of Economics and Business, and Université Robert Schuman (Strasbourg). His main research interests are in pricing, sales forecasting, marketing research and international marketing and he is the author of some 160 publications in these areas. His work has appeared, among others, in the *International Journal of Research in Marketing, Journal of International Marketing, International Journal of Forecasting* and *Industrial Marketing Management*. He has presented his research at more than 60 international conferences and has been the recipient of several Best Paper Awards. He sits on the editorial review boards of seven marketing journals, is a founder member of the Consortium for International Marketing Research (CIMaR), Associate Editor of the *International Journal of Research in Marketing*, and a referee for several academic journals, professional associations and funding bodies.

Bill Donaldson, BA, PhD, MCIM is Senior Lecturer in Marketing at the Strathclyde Graduate Business School and Academic Manager for the Strathclyde International MBA programme. He had more than ten years' experience in marketing positions, with three different companies, before joining Strathclyde in December 1983 and was awarded his PhD in 1993 for his thesis: 'An inquiry into the relative importance of customer service in the marketing of industrial products.' Author of *Sales and Management: Theory and Practice* (Macmillan, 2nd edition, 1998), he has several publications on customer service and the characteristics of customer-driven organizations. His current research interests continue in the area of sales operations, customer service and relationship marketing. He has taught sales operations at undergraduate level and a specialist class in managing customer relations. In addition to undergraduate and MBA teaching he has experience in training and consultancy with a number of leading companies. He is currently a Chartered Marketer and senior examiner for the new Institute of Professional Sales.

Peter Doyle is Professor of Marketing and Strategic Management at the University of Warwick. Previously he has taught at the London Business School, INSEAD, and Bradford University. He has also been Visiting Professor at Stanford, University of Hawaii and the University of South Carolina. He graduated with a first in economics from Manchester University and took a PhD in industrial administration from Carnegie-Mellon University, USA. His research interests are in marketing modelling and strategic planning. Publications include six books and numerous articles in leading journals, including *Journal of Marketing Research, Management Science, Journal of Business, Journal of Marketing, Journal of the Operational Research Society* and the *Economic Journal*. He is on the editorial boards of the *European Journal of Marketing, Journal of Business Research, International Journal of Advertising, International Journal of Research in Marketing* and the *Journal of Marketing Management* and he is a member of the Industry and Employment and International Activities Committees of the ESRC. He also acts as a consultant on international marketing and strategy with a number of companies including IBM, Shell, ICI, Unilever, 3M, Hewlett Packard, British Telecom and Marks and Spencer.

Sean Ennis is a lecturer in marketing at the University of Strathclyde in Glasgow. He graduated from the Dublin Institute of Technology with a BSc management degree. He received his master's degree in business studies from University College Dublin and his PhD from Dublin City University. He has worked in the newspaper industry, marketing research and marketing consultancy. He has served as Vice Chairman (Education) for the Marketing Institute of Ireland and participated actively on the re-design of their education programmes. His recently completed PhD examined the marketing planning practices of indigenous companies within the electronics sector in the Republic of Ireland. He has published in a number of journals including the *European Management Journal, The International Journal of Retail, Distribution and Consumer Research, The Irish Marketing Review* and *De Qualitate*. His research interests include marketing and the entrepreneurship interface, retailing, international channel management and supply chain management. He is currently a member of a research group within the marketing department that is actively researching the issue of competitiveness within Scotland. He is also actively involved in the Centre for Entrepreneurship and Marketing.

Martin Evans, BA, MA, MIDM, MMRS, FCIM is Royal Mail/Mail Marketing Professor of Marketing and Director of the Bristol Business School Research Unit in Marketing. He has previously held professorial posts at the Universities of Portsmouth and Glamorgan, and other academic positions at Cardiff Business School and Newcastle Polytechnic. Industrial experience was with Hawker Siddeley and then as a consultant to a variety of organizations for over 25 years. He has published over 100 papers plus eight books, mostly in the areas of marketing research and information, consumer behaviour and direct marketing – which is now his main (but not only) research interest. He founded the Direct Marketing Research Consortium which is a grouping of collaborative researchers at the Universities of Cardiff, Glamorgan, Bath and Portsmouth.

Keith Fletcher is Founding Dean and Professor of Management at the School of Management, University of East Anglia in Norwich. He has previously held posts at Strathclyde Graduate Business School and has research interests in IT in Marketing, with a particular interest in the development of database marketing and virtual relationships. He has published a text book and various chapters on IT and marketing, as well as numerous articles on his research interests in database marketing. He would be pleased to discuss interactive and database marketing, or other related academic issues, with any interested individuals.

Gordon R. Foxall is Professor of Consumer Behaviour and Honorary Professor in Psychology at Keele University. Prior to this appointment, he was Distinguished Research Professor at Cardiff Business School, University of Wales. He graduated first at the University of Salford where he won the Final Year Course Prize for Social Science. His master's degree, in management economics, is from the same university. He is also a graduate of the University of Birmingham (PhD in industrial economics and business studies) and of the University of Strathclyde (PhD in psychology), and holds a higher doctorate of the University of Birmingham (DSocSc). He is the author of some fifteen books on consumer behaviour and related themes, including the critically-acclaimed *Consumer Psychology in Behavioural Perspective* (Routledge, London and New York, 1990) and the best-selling text *Consumer Psychology for Marketing*, co-authored with Ron Goldsmith (Routledge, London and New York, 1994). In addition, he has authored over 250 refereed articles, chapters and papers on consumer behaviour and marketing. His previous professorial appointments have been at the Universities of Strathclyde and Birmingham; he has also held posts at Cranfield University and the University of Newcastle-upon-Tyne. He has held visiting appointments at the Universities of Michigan, Guelph, South Australia and Manchester. Professor Foxall's research interests lie in the psychological theory of consumer behaviour, consumer innovativeness, and micro-micro analysis of intra-firm behaviour.

Jim Hamill is Reader in International Marketing at the University of Strathclyde, Glasgow and Director of the Scottish Exporters Virtual Community. Author of numerous articles on Internet marketing, his main research interests include the role of the Internet in the internationalization of small- and medium-sized companies. Currently Internet Editor of the International Marketing Review, his ten-module 'Internet and International Marketing' online course is available on the Scottish Exporters Virtual Community web site at http://www.sevc.com

Susan Hart, is a Professor of Marketing at the University of Strathclyde. After working in industry in France and the UK, she joined the University of Strathclyde as a researcher. She completed her PhD on the subject of product management and has published widely on subjects such as the contribution of marketing to competitive success, and product design and development in the manufacturing industry. Current research interests are in the development of new products and innovation, the contribution of marketing to company success, loyalty marketing, and accounting for marketing performance.

Gerard Hastings is Professor of Social Marketing and Head of the Department of Marketing at the University of Strathclyde. The Department was rated as excellent in both research and teaching in the UK Government's latest assessment exercises. Professor Hastings' research interests are in social marketing, and he is the founder and Director of the Centre for Social Marketing (CSM). CSM is a self-funded research unit which investigates the applicability of marketing ideas to the solution of health and social problems as well as monitoring the potentially harmful effects of commercial marketing. Current funders include the Cancer Research Campaign, The Home Office and the Health Education Board for Scotland. Professor Hastings has published widely in such journals as *The British Medical Journal, The British Dental Journal, The Journal of Advertising* and *The European Journal of Marketing*. He has served as a non-executive director of Forth Valley Health Board and SACRO, was a member of the OECD Expert Committee on Social Marketing and a consultant to the Home Office Drugs Prevention Initiative. He is currently on the Editorial Boards of *Health Promotion International, The Journal of the Institute of Health Education, The Health Education Journal* and *Social Marketing Quarterly*.

Dale Littler is Head of School and Professor of Marketing at the Manchester School of Management at UMIST. He is the author of several books and of many papers and articles, mainly in the area of marketing and technological innovation, consumer behaviour and strategic marketing. He has undertaken extensive work on information and communications technologies as a principal researcher on the ESRC Programme on Information and Communications Technologies. He has been a member of the ESRC Research Grants Board and the Executive Committee of the British Academy of Management, and is currently a member of the Academic Senate of the Chartered Institute of Marketing.

Lynn MacFadyen is Research Officer and currently registered for a PhD at the University of Strathclyde, examining the influence of tobacco marketing communications on young people's smoking behaviour. Her main research interests, within the Centre for Social Marketing (CSM), are social marketing and societal marketing issues, particularly the marketing activities of the tobacco industry. She is also interested in tobacco control and smoking cessation and prevention initiatives. Her other interests include the use of Social Marketing to reduce misuse of over-the-counter medicines, reduce impulse confectionery sales and improve clean indoor air on public transport.

Malcolm McDonald, MA(Oxon), MSc, PhD, FCIM, FRSA is Professor of Marketing Strategy, Chairman of the Cranfield Marketing Planning Centre and Deputy Director of the Cranfield School of Management. He is a graduate in English Language and Literature from Oxford University, in Business Studies from Bradford University Management Centre and has a PhD from the Cranfield Institute of Technology. He has extensive industrial experience, including a number of years as Marketing Director of Canada Dry. During the past twenty years he has run seminars and workshops on marketing planning in the UK, Europe, India, the Far East, Australasia and the USA. He has written thirty books, including the best-seller *Marketing Plans: How to Prepare Them, How to Use Them* (Butterworth-Heinemann, fourth edition, 1999) and many of his papers have been published. His current interests centre around IT in marketing, the development of expert systems in marketing, and key account management.

Peter J. McGoldrick is the Professor of Retailing in the Manchester School of Management at UMIST. He has authored, edited or co-edited over 200 books, chapters and articles on aspects of retail strategy or consumer behaviour. He is the UMIST Director of the International Centre for Retail Studies. A major research interest has been the area of retail pricing with grants from the ESRC and the Office of Fair Trading. An extension of this work has been the measurement of how shoppers judge value, supported by a series of grants from the Department of Trade and Industry. Another major theme is electronic service delivery systems, work funded by EPSRC, BA, BT and Microsoft. He is Director of the Manchester Retail Research Forum, comprising senior executives or directors from 16 blue chip companies – they help establish the research agenda for the Centre, as well as sponsoring and facilitating a range of studies into key areas of retailing strategy.

Arthur Meidan, BSc(Econ), MBA, PhD, FCIM is Professor of Marketing at the School of Management, University of Sheffield. He has spent over twenty-five years in management teaching, instructing, consulting and researching. He is the author of many articles, monographs and textbooks including *The Appraisal of Managerial Performance* (American Marketing Association, 1981), *Marketing Applications of Operational Research Techniques* (MCB University Press, 1981), *Bank Marketing Management* (Macmillan, 1984), *Industrial Salesforce Management* (Croom Helm, 1986) and *Cases in Marketing of Services* (with L. Moutinho, Addison-Wesley, 1994). His research interests are in marketing of financial services and tourism. Professor Meidan has published over seventy refereed academic journals and conference proceedings in Britain and elsewhere and has consulted and taught post-experience courses, particularly on marketing of financial services and tourism, in Europe, Asia, America and Australia.

Luiz Moutinho, BA, MA, PhD, FCIM is Professor of Marketing, University of Glasgow Business School. He completed his PhD at the University of Sheffield in 1982 and held posts at Cardiff Business School, University of Wales College of Cardiff, Cleveland State University, Ohio, USA, Northern Arizona University, USA and California State University, USA, as well as visiting Professorship positions in New Zealand and Brazil. Between 1987 and 1989 he was the Director of the Doctoral Programmes at the Confederation of Scottish Business Schools and at the Cardiff Business School between 1993 and 1996. He is currently the Director of the Doctoral Programme at the University of Glasgow Business School. In addition to publishing fifteen books and presenting papers at many international conferences, he also has had a vast number of articles published in international journals. He is also a member of the Editorial Board of several international academic journals. He has been a full Professor of Marketing since 1989 and was appointed in 1996 to the Foundation Chair of Marketing at the University of Glasgow Business School.

Stanley J. Paliwoda, BA, MSc, PhD, FCIM, MIEx is Professor and Chair of Marketing at the University of Calgary, Alberta, Canada and Visiting Professor in Marketing at the Warsaw School of Economics, Poland. He has a master's degree from Bradford University, a PhD from Cranfield and was previously with the University of Manchester Institute of Science and Technology. His interests are primarily in international marketing focusing on market entry strategy, business-to-business marketing strategy and marketing relationship management. He is a fellow of the Chartered Institute of Marketing, a chartered marketer, a professional member of the Institute of Export and a former examiner for their International Marketing professional examinations. He is the author of seventeen books, some of which have been translated into Spanish and Chinese. Books include *International Marketing*, now in its third edition with Butterworth-Heinemann, 1998; *Investing in Eastern Europe*, Addison-Wesley/EIU Books, 1995; and *The International Marketing Reader*, Routledge, 1995 (with John K. Ryans Jr). He is founding author of *The Journal of East–West Business* published by Haworth Press, New York; Canadian editor of the *Journal of Marketing Management* and is on the editorial board of eleven other journals including: *International Marketing Review; Asia-Pacific International Journal of Marketing; Journal of Global Marketing; Journal of Euromarketing; International Business Review; Journal of Qualitative Market Research.*

Adrian Palmer is Professor of Tourism Marketing at the University of Ulster. Before joining academia he held marketing management positions within the travel industry. In recent years he has published extensively on the subject of relationship marketing and customer loyalty in publications which include *European Journal of Marketing*, *Journal of Marketing Management*, *Journal of Services Marketing*, *International Business Review* and *Annals of Tourism Research*. He is a member of the editorial review board for *Journal of Marketing Management*, *European Journal of Marketing* and *Journal of Vacation Marketing*. He is a Fellow of the Chartered Institute of Marketing and a Chartered Marketer. During his academic career he has spent time teaching abroad and giving guest lectures in a number of countries, including the United States, Australia, the Far East, India and Eastern Europe.

Ken Peattie is a Senior Lecturer in Strategic Management at Cardiff Business School, which he joined in 1986. Before becoming a lecturer he worked as a systems and business analyst for an American paper multinational, and as a strategic planner within the UK electronics industry. He is the author of *Environmental Marketing Management: Meeting the Green Challenge* (Pitman, 1995) and *Green Marketing* (Pitman, 1992), and he has written a number of journal articles and book chapters on the implications of environmentally-related issues for corporate and marketing strategies, and on the greening of management education. His books have been translated into several languages including Japanese, Swedish and Chinese. His other research interests include innovations in sales promotion; the use of social marketing in the prevention of skin cancer; and the implementation of strategic planning systems.

Sue Peattie is a Senior Lecturer in Statistics and Marketing at the University of Glamorgan Business School, which she joined in 1986. Previous to this she worked as a systems analyst in industry for five years and then completed an Economics Masters at Simon Fraser University in Vancouver. Her research interests and publications concentrate on innovations within sales promotions, in particular sales promotion competitions, and social marketing.

Nigel F. Piercy, PhD holds the Sir Julian Hodge Chair of Marketing and Strategy at Cardiff Business School, in Cardiff University. He has also been Visiting Professor at Texas Christian University; the University of California, Berkeley; Columbia Graduate School of Business; the Fuqua School of Business, Duke University; and the Athens Laboratory of Business Administration. He worked in retailing and industry before becoming an academic, and is an active consultant and workshop speaker, having worked with executives in a variety of organizations in the UK, the USA, Europe, Slovenia, Greece, Hong Kong, Malaysia, South Africa and Zimbabwe. He has published widely on marketing and management topics, including papers in the *Journal of Marketing*, the *Journal of the Academy of Marketing Science*, the *Journal of World Business*, and *Marketing Management*. His work focuses mainly on the role of process, information and structure in achieving the implementation of effective market strategy, and this is reflected in his most recent managerial books: *Market-Led Strategic Change: Transforming the Process of Going to Market* (Butterworth-Heinemann, 1997) and *Tales From The Marketplace: Stories of Revolution, Reinvention and Renewal* (Butterworth-Heinemann, 1999).

Martine Stead is Senior Researcher at the Centre for Social Marketing (CSM) at the University of Strathclyde, having joined in 1992 with a BA (Hons) in English and a background in health promotion and the media. Her research interests include social marketing theory and practice, health communication, development and evaluation of mass media interventions, health inequalities, smoking cessation and drugs prevention. She is currently involved in a major Home Office evaluation of a 3-year drugs prevention intervention in the north-east of England. She has published in the *British Medical Journal* and the *Health Education Journal* and is on the editorial board of *Social Marketing Quarterly*.

Peter W. Turnbull is Professor of Marketing and a member of the marketing faculty in the University of Birmingham Business School. He is a well-known researcher and writer in the field of industrial and international marketing. His books include *International Marketing and Purchasing* (Macmillan, 1981), *Strategies for International Industrial Marketing* (John Wiley, 1986), *Research in International Marketing* and *Managing Business Relationships* (Wiley, 1998). Additionally, he has written numerous articles for scholarly management journals. He has lectured widely in Western Europe and North America and has acted as consultant to a number of national and international companies.

Keith Ward is Visiting Professor of Financial Strategy at Cranfield School of Management. He studied economics at Cambridge and then qualified as both a chartered accountant and a cost and management accountant. He has worked both in the City and abroad as a consultant and held senior financial positions in manufacturing and trading companies (the last being as Group Financial Director of Sterling International). He then joined Cranfield School of Management and progressed to Head of the Finance and Accounting Group and Director of the Research Centre in Competitive Performance. His research interests are primarily in the fields of financial strategy, strategic management accounting and accounting for marketing activities. He is the author of *Corporate Financial Strategy, Strategic Management Accounting, Financial Management for Service Companies* and *Financial Aspects of Marketing*, as well as co-authoring *Management Accounting for Financial Decisions*. He has also published numerous articles and contributed to several other books, including as editor.

John Webb is currently the Director of the MSc in Marketing at Strathclyde University. After a first degree in optics, and research into visual psychophysics, he was an arts administrator in the UK and the USA for seven years. He read for an MBA in 1981 and was a freelance business consultant for two years before joining the Department of Marketing at Strathclyde University as a Teaching Company Associate. He was awarded his PhD in 1987 and appointed to a lectureship in the same year. His research interests concern the role of technology in business administration, marketing and the arts, and international marketing research. He has taught in Singapore, Hong Kong, Malaysia, the Czech Republic, the People's Republic of China, and France. He is the author of *Understanding and Designing Marketing Research*.

Robin Wensley is Professor of Strategic Management and Marketing at Warwick Business School and was Chair of the School from 1989 to 1994, and elected Chair of the Faculty of Social Studies in 1997. He was previously with RHM Foods, Tube Investments and London Business School and was visiting professor twice at UCLA and the University of Florida. He became Chair of the Council of the Tavistock Institute of Human Relations in 1998, having been a member since 1992. He is a member of the Senate of the Chartered Institute of Marketing and was a Board member of the ESRC Research Grants Board from 1991 to 1995. He has been involved with consultancy and management development with many major companies including British Telecom, Philips N.V., ICL, IBM, Glaxo, Nestlé, Dynacast and Jardine Pacific. His research and consultancy interests include marketing strategy and planning, investment decision making and the assessment of competitive advantage. In this regard he has published a number of books and articles in the *Harvard Business Review*, the *Journal of Marketing* and the *Strategic Management Journal* and has worked closely with other academics and practitioners both in Europe and the USA. He is joint editor of the *Journal of Management Studies* and has twice won the annual Alpha Kappa Psi Award for the most influential article in the US *Journal of Marketing*.

Preface to the fourth edition

Five years have now passed since the appearance of the third edition which was published at the height of what was then perceived to be 'Marketing's mid-life crisis'. Clearly, the appearance of a fourth edition would seem to confirm that marketing is both alive and well, and marching into a new millennium with resolution and confidence.

Superficially, it is often hard to distinguish the new edition of the book from the one that preceded it. At first sight, this may appear to be the case with this present edition which actually contains two chapters less than its predecessor. However, as closer inspection will reveal, very substantial changes have been made. Indeed, in reviewing them, I felt a certain kinship with the publishers of local newspapers who are sometimes caricatured as being concerned solely which 'hatches, matches and dispatches'.

Comparison of the third and fourth editions indicates that 11 authors' names are missing but 13 new ones (A Baker's dozen) have taken their place. Since 1995 six distinguished authors have retired – Jack Bureau, Don Cowell, John Lidstone, Peter Spillard, Michael Thomas and John Winkler. However, with the exception of Peter Spillard's review of *Organization for Marketing* new authors have taken the place of the old. As for other dispatches, these were largely the victims of the strictures of my publisher, Tim Goodfellow, when discussing my plans for the fourth edition, who advised me that *The Marketing Book* could not continue to try and emulate the universe and expand for ever. Accordingly, in order to make room for new material, some of the old had to go.

In order to set a good example the editor dropped his own chapter on *The Pursuit of Quality* on the grounds that such advice was clearly redundant, given the content of the many chapters which preceded it. Similarly, the chapters by John Saunders (*Marketing and Competitive Success*) and Steve Parkinson (*Computers in Marketing*) have also become part of the accepted wisdom of marketing and so able to give way to newer topics not contained in earlier editions.

Further economies were achieved by merging the former Chapter 5 *Strategic Marketing Planning* and Chapter 6 *Developing the Marketing Plan* into a single new chapter *Strategic Marketing Planning: Theory and Practice* by Malcolm McDonald, the lead author of the two original chapters. Similarly, the old Chapter 27 *International Marketing – The Main Issues* by Simon Majaro was dropped and incorporated with the old Chapter 28 *International Marketing – Getting Started* by Stan Paliwoda into a single new Chapter 23 – *International Marketing – The Issues* by Stan Paliwoda.

The final 'casualty' from the earlier edition was David Birks, whose chapter on *Market Research* was possibly too original in its scope and treatment for a mainstream text.

So much for the dispatches. What about the matches? With the retirals mentioned earlier the opportunity was taken to invite several new authors to contribute to this edition. As with other entries to *The Marketing Book* the basic criterion adopted was to invite persons who are recognised as the authors of definitive contributions (textbooks etc.) on the subject in question. On this basis the new Chapter 14 on *Pricing* is by Adamantios Diamantopoulos of Loughborough University. Chapter 15 on *Selling and Sales Management* is by Bill Donaldson of the Strathclyde Graduate Business School, while Chapter 13 on *New Product Development* is by Susan Hart, Professor of Marketing at the University of Strathclyde. Chapter 29 *The Marketing of Services* is by Adrian Palmer of the University of Ulster, while Chapter 20 *Controlling Marketing* is by Keith Ward. Finally, the new chapter on *Marketing Research* has been contributed by John Webb, a colleague at Strathclyde University and author of a best-selling text on the subject.

Given the structuring and reorganization of the content of the third edition a limited opportunity remained to introduce some new material. So what 'hatches' did the editor choose to include within the parsimonious limitations given to him by the publishers?

To begin with, the editor was considerably exercised by the fact that over 90 per cent of people in employment worked for organizations with fewer than 200 employees. Faced with this fact it seemed obvious that special consideration should be given to the smaller company. As a result, Professor David Carson, of the University of Ulster, was invited to contribute Chapter 27 *Marketing for Small-to-Medium Enterprises*. Without doubt this chapter will make a significant contribution to redressing the balance between the large and small organization's role in the marketplace.

Next, information technology in general and the Internet in particular have assumed an increasingly important role in the field of business and management. To that end I invited my colleagues at Strathclyde, Jim Hamill and Sean Ennis, to contribute Chapter 30 *The Internet: The Direct Route to Growth and Development*.

A third area which has seen significant growth in recent years is the area of social marketing. My own university has had a major commitment to this sub-field for many years now and the contribution by my colleagues Lynn MacFadyen, Martine Stead and Gerard Hastings of the Centre for Social Marketing provides an excellent overview and introduction to this topic.

Finally, the 1980s and 1990s have seen a continuing shift in the balance of power on the supply side from manufacturers to retailers. In recognition of this Peter J. McGoldrick of Manchester University has contributed Chapter 28 on the subject of *Retailing*.

In addition to the changes summarized above, all the remaining authors have undertaken a thorough review and revision of their contribution. Taken together, it is the editor's opinion that this book represents the most up-to-date and authoritative overview of marketing principles and practices based on the knowledge and expertise of the UK's pre-eminent marketing scholars. It has been a great privilege for me to orchestrate this distillation of the best of British marketing. If it meets with your approval then much of the credit must go to my secretary, June Peffer, who is certainly well known to all of the contributors, and without whose efforts this book could never have survived through four editions. For any faults I accept total responsibility.

Michael J. Baker
University of Strathclyde
February 1999

Part One
Organization and Planning for Marketing

CHAPTER 1

One more time – what is marketing?

MICHAEL J. BAKER

The enigma of marketing is that it is one of man's oldest activities and yet it is regarded as the most recent of the business disciplines.

Michael J. Baker, *Marketing: Theory and Practice*, 1st Edn, Macmillan, 1976

Introduction

As a discipline, marketing is in the process of transition from an art which is practised to a profession with strong theoretical foundations. In doing so it is following closely the precedents set by professions such as medicine, architecture and engineering, all of which have also been practised for thousands of years and have built up a wealth of descriptive information concerning the art which has both chronicled and advanced its evolution. At some juncture, however, continued progress demands a transition from description to analysis, such as that initiated by Harvey's discovery of the circulation of the blood. If marketing is to develop it, too, must make the transition from art to applied science and develop sound theoretical foundations, mastery of which should become an essential qualification for practice.

Adoption of this proposition is as threatening to many of today's marketers as the establishment of the British Medical Association was to the surgeon-barber. But, today, you would not dream of going to a barber for medical advice.

Of course, first aid will still be practised, books on healthy living will feature on the best-sellers list and harmless potions will be bought over the counter in drug stores and pharmacies. This is an amateur activity akin to much of what passes for marketing in British industry. While there was no threat of the cancer of competition it might have sufficed, but once the Japanese, Germans and others invade your markets you are going to need much stronger medicine if you are to survive. To do so you must have the courage to face up to the reality that aggressive competition can prove fatal, quickly; have the necessary determination to resist rather than succumb, and seek the best possible professional advice and treatment to assist you. Unfortunately, many people are unwilling to face up to reality. Even more unfortunate, many of the best minds and abilities are concentrated on activities which support the essential functions of an economy, by which we all survive, but have come to believe that these can exist by themselves independent of the manufacturing heart. Bankers, financiers, politicians and civil servants all fall into this category. As John Harvey-Jones pointed out so eloquently in the 1986 David Dimbleby lecture, much of our wealth is created by manufacturing industry and much of the output of service industries is dependent upon manufactured products for its continued existence. To assume service industries can replace manufacturing as the heart and engine of economic growth is naive, to say the least.

But merely to increase the size of manufacturing industry will not solve any of our current problems. Indeed, the contraction and decline of our manufacturing industry is not directly attributable to government and the City – it is largely due to the incompetence of industry itself. Those that survive will undoubtedly be the fittest and *all* will testify to the importance of marketing as an essential requirement for continued success.

However, none of this preamble addresses the central question 'What is marketing?' save perhaps to suggest that it is a newly emerging discipline inextricably linked with manufacturing. But this latter link is of extreme importance because in the evangelical excess of its original statement in the early 1960s, marketing and production were caricatured as antithetically opposed to one another. Forty years later most marketers have developed sufficient self-confidence not to feel it necessary to 'knock' another function to emphasize the importance and relevance of their own. So, what is marketing?

Marketing is both a managerial orientation – some would claim a business philosophy – and a business function. To understand marketing it is essential to distinguish clearly between the two.

Marketing as a managerial orientation

Management . . . the technique, practice, or science of managing or controlling; the skilful or resourceful use of materials, time, etc.

Collins Concise English Dictionary

Ever since people have lived and worked together in groups there have been managers concerned with solving the central economic problem of maximizing satisfaction through the utilization of scarce resources. If we trace the course of economic development we find that periods of rapid growth have followed changes in the manner in which work is organized, usually accompanied by changes in technology. Thus from simple collecting and nomadic communities we have progressed to hybrid agricultural and collecting communities accompanied by the concept of the division of labour. The division of labour increases output and creates a need for exchange and enhances the standard of living. Improved standards of living result in more people and further increases in output accompanied by simple mechanization which culminates in a breakthrough when the potential of the division of labour is enhanced through task specialization. Task specialization leads to the development of teams of workers and to more sophisticated and efficient mechanical devices and, with the discovery of steam power, results in an industrial revolution. A major feature of our own industrial revolution (and that of most which emulated it in the nineteenth century) is that production becomes increasingly concentrated in areas of natural advantage, that larger production units develop and that specialization increases as the potential for economies of scale and efficiency are exploited.

At least two consequences deserve special mention. First, economic growth fuels itself as improvements in living standards result in population growth which increases demand and lends impetus to increases in output and productivity. Second, concentration and specialization result in producer and consumer becoming increasingly distant from one another (both physically and psychologically) and require the development of new channels of distribution and communication to bridge this gap.

What of the managers responsible for the direction and control of this enormous diversity of human effort? By and large, it seems safe to assume that they were (and are) motivated essentially by (an occasionally enlightened) self-interest. Given the enormity and self-evident nature of unsatisfied demand and the distribution of purchasing power, it is unsurprising that most managers concentrated on making more for less and that to do so they pursued vigorously policies of standardization and mass production. Thus the first half of the twentieth century was characterized in the advanced industrialized economies of the West by mass production and mass consumption – usually described as a production orientation and a consumer society. But changes were occurring in both.

On the supply side the enormous concentration of wealth and power in super-corporations had led to legislation to limit the influence of cartels and monopolies. An obvious consequence of this was to encourage diversification. Second, the accelerating pace of technological and organizational innovation began to catch up with and even overtake the natural growth in demand due to population increases. Faced with stagnant markets and the spectre of price competition, producers sought to stimulate demand through increased selling efforts. To succeed, however, one must be able to offer some tangible benefit which will distinguish one supplier's product from another's. If all products are perceived as being the same then price becomes the distinguishing feature and the supplier becomes a price taker, thus having to relinquish the important managerial function of exercising control. Faced with such an impasse the real manager recognizes that salvation (and control) will be achieved through a policy of *product differentiation*. Preferably this will be achieved through the manufacture of a product which is physically different in some objective way from competitive offerings but, if this is not possible, then subjective benefits must be created through service, advertising and promotional efforts.

With the growth of product differentiation and promotional activity social commentators began to complain about the materialistic nature of society and question its value. Perhaps the earliest manifestation of the consumerist movement of the 1950s and 1960s is to be found in Edwin Chamberlin and Joan Robinson's articulation of the concept of imperfect competition in

the 1930s. Hitherto, economists had argued that economic welfare would be maximized through perfect competition in which supply and demand would be brought into equilibrium through the price mechanism. Clearly, as producers struggled to avoid becoming virtually passive pawns of market forces they declined to accept the 'rules' of perfect competition and it was this behaviour which was described by Chamberlin and Robinson under the pejorative title of 'imperfect' competition. Shades of the 'hidden persuaders' and 'waste makers' to come.

The outbreak of war and the reconstruction which followed delayed the first clear statement of the managerial approach which was to displace the production orientation. It was not to be selling and a sales orientation, for these can only be a temporary and transitional strategy in which one buys time in which to disengage from past practices, reform and regroup and then move on to the offensive again. The Americans appreciated this in the 1950s, the West Germans and Japanese in the 1960s, the British, belatedly in the late 1970s (until the mid-1970s nearly all our commercial heroes were sales people, not marketers – hence their problems – Stokes, Bloom, Laker). The real solution is marketing.

Marketing myopia – a watershed

If one had to pick a single event which marked the watershed between the production/sales approach to business and the emergence of a marketing orientation then most marketing scholars would probably choose the publication of Theodore Levitt's article entitled 'Marketing myopia' in the July–August 1960 issue of the *Harvard Business Review*.

Building upon the trenchant statement 'The history of every dead and dying "growth" industry shows a self-deceiving cycle of bountiful expansion and undetected decay', Levitt proposed the thesis that declining or defunct industries got into such a state because they were product orientated rather than customer orientated. As a result, the concept of their business was defined too narrowly. Thus the railroads failed to perceive that they were and are in the *transportation* business, and so allowed new forms of transport to woo their customers away from them. Similarly, the Hollywood movie moguls ignored the threat of television until it was almost too late because they saw themselves as being in the cinema industry rather than the *entertainment* business.

Levitt proposes four factors which make such a cycle inevitable:

1   A belief in growth as a natural consequence of an expanding and increasingly affluent population.
2   A belief that there is no competitive substitute for the industry's major product.
3   A pursuit of the economies of scale through mass production in the belief that lower unit cost will automatically lead to higher consumption and bigger overall profits.
4   Preoccupation with the potential of research and development (R&D) to the neglect of market needs (i.e. a technology push rather than market pull approach).

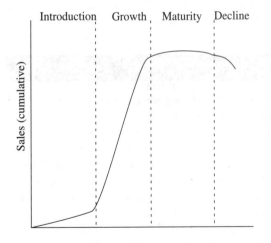

Figure 1.1   The product life cycle

Belief number two has never been true but, until very recently, there was good reason to subscribe to the other three propositions. Despite Malthus's gloomy prognostications in the eighteenth century the world's population has continued to grow exponentially; most of the world's most successful corporations see the pursuit of market share as their primary goal, and most radical innovations are the result of basic R&D rather than product engineering to meet consumer needs. Certainly the dead and dying industries which Levitt referred to in his analysis were entitled to consider these three factors as reasonable assumptions on which to develop a strategy.

In this, then, Levitt was anticipating rather than analysing but, in doing so, he was building upon perhaps the most widely known yet most misunderstood theoretical construct in marketing – the concept of the product life cycle (PLC).

The PLC concept draws an analogy between biological life cycles and the pattern of sales growth exhibited by successful products. In doing so it distinguishes four basic stages in the life of the product: introduction; growth; maturity; and decline (see Figure 1.1).

Thus at birth or first introduction to the market a new product initially makes slow progress as people have to be made aware of its existence and only the bold and innovative will seek to try it as a substitute for the established product which the new one is seeking to improve on or displace. Clearly, there will be a strong relationship between how much better the new product is, and how easy it is for users to accept this and the speed at which it will be taken up. But, as a generalization, progress is slow.

However, as people take up the new product they will talk about it and make it more visible to non-users and reduce the perceived risk seen in any innovation. As a consequence, a contagion or bandwagon effect will be initiated as consumers seek to obtain supplies of the new product and producers, recognizing the trend, switch over to making the new product in place of the old. The result is exponential growth.

Ultimately, however, all markets are finite and sales will level off as the market becomes saturated. Thereafter sales will settle down at a level which reflects new entrants to the market plus replacement/repeat purchase sales which constitutes the mature phase of the PLC. It is this phase which Levitt rightly characterizes as self-deceiving. Following the pangs of birth and introduction and the frenetic competitive struggle when demand took off, is it surprising that producers relax and perhaps become complacent when they are the established leaders in mature and profitable markets? But consumers, like producers, are motivated by self-interest rather than loyalty and will be quite willing to switch their allegiance if another new product comes along which offers advantages not present in the existing offering. Recognition of this represents a market opportunity for other innovators and entrepreneurs which they will seek to exploit by introducing their own new product and so initiating another new PLC while bringing to an end that of the product to be displaced.

The import of the PLC is quite simple, but frequently forgotten – *change is inevitable*. Its misunderstanding and misuse arise from the fact that people try to use it as a specific predictive device. Clearly, this is as misconceived as trying to guess the identity of a biological organism from the representation of a life cycle curve which applies equally to gnats and elephants.

Life cycles and evolution

As noted earlier, the PLC concept is based upon biological life cycles and this raises the question as to whether one can further extend the analogy from the specific level of the growth of organisms and products to the general case of the evolution of species and economies. At a conceptual level this seems both possible and worth while.

Consider the case of a very simple organism which reproduces by cell division placed into a bounded environment – a sealed test tube containing nutrients necessary for the cell's existence. As the cell divides the population will grow exponentially, even allowing for the fact that some cells will die for whatever reason, up

to the point when the colony reaches a ceiling to further growth imposed by its bounded environment. What happens next closely parallels what happens in product life cycles, industry life cycles and overall economic cycles – a strong reaction sets in. Discussing this in a biological context, Derek de Solla Price cites a number of ways in which an exponentially growing phenomenon will seek to avoid a reduction in growth as it nears its ceiling. Two of these, 'escalation', and 'loss of definition', seem particularly relevant in an economic context.

In the case of escalation, modification of the original takes place at or near the point of inflection and '. . . a new logistic curve rises phoenix-like on the ashes of the old'. In other words, the cell modifies itself so that it can prosper and survive despite the constraints which had impeded its immediate predecessor. In marketing, such a phenomenon is apparent in a strategy of product rejuvenation in which either new uses or new customers are found to revitalize demand.

In many cases, however, it is not possible to 'raise the ceiling' through modification and the cell, or whatever, will begin to oscillate wildly in an attempt to avoid the inevitable (the 'hausse' in the economic cycle which precedes crisis and depression). As a result of these oscillations the phenomenon may become so changed as to be unrecognizable, i.e. it mutates or diversifies and recommences life in an entirely new guise. Alternatively, the phenomenon may accept the inevitable, smoothing out the oscillations and settling in equilibrium at a stable limit or, under different circumstances, slowly decline to nothing.

Over time, therefore, civilizations (and economies) rise and fall but the overall progression is upwards and characterized by periods of rapid development and/or stability when conditions are favourable and of decline when they are not. Observation would also seem to suggest that not only is change inevitable but that its pace is accelerating.

While it is often difficult to analyse the major causes and likely effect of major structural change when one is living in the midst of it, it seems likely that future historians will regard the 1960s and 1970s as a period of hausse in our economic and social evolution. Certainly economic forecasters are inclined in this direction through their interest in 'the long wave' or Kondratieff cycle in economic development. Similarly, management writers of the standing of Drucker talk of 'turbulence' while Toffler speaks of the third wave which will bring about Galbraith's post-industrial society.

And what has this to do with marketing? Quite simply, everything. For the past two hundred years the advanced industrial economies have prospered because the nature of demand has been basic and obvious and entrepreneurs have been able to devote their energies to producing as much as possible for as little as possible. But, in a materialistic society, basic demand for standardized and undifferentiated products has become saturated and the ability to off-load surpluses onto Third World developing economies is limited by their inability to pay for these surpluses. Product differentiation and an emphasis upon selling provide temporary respite from the imbalance but the accelerating pace of technological change rapidly outruns these. Indeed, in the short run the substitution of technology for unskilled and semi-skilled labour has resulted in a rich working population, with much higher discretionary purchasing power than ever before, and a poor, unemployed and aging sector with limited or no discretionary purchasing power at all.

All the indications would seem to point to the fact that we are in an age of transition from one order to another. In terms of personal aspirations many people are growing out of materialism and want, in Maslow's terminology, to 'self-actualize' or 'do their own thing'. As a consequence we are moving towards a post-industrial, post-mass consumption society which is concerned with quality not quantity and the individual rather than the mass. To cope with this we need a complete rethink of our attitudes to production, distribution and consumption and it is this which marketing offers.

Marketing starts with the market and the consumer. It recognizes that in a consumer democracy money votes are cast daily and that to win those votes you need to offer either a better product at the same price or the same product at a lower price than your competitors. Price is objective and tangible but what is 'a better product'? Only one person can tell you – the consumer. It follows, therefore, that a marketing orientation starts and ends with consumers and requires one to make what one can sell rather than struggle to sell what one can make. But marketing is not a philanthropic exercise in which producers give away their goods. Indeed, the long-run interest of the consumer requires that they do not, for otherwise as with eating the seed corn, we will eventually finish up with nothing at all. Producers are entitled to profits and the more value they add and the greater the satisfaction they deliver, the more the customer will be prepared to pay for this greater satisfaction. Marketing therefore is all about mutually satisfying exchange relationships for which the catalyst is the producer's attempt to define and satisfy the customer's need better.

Marketing misunderstood

The emphasis thus far, and of the chapter as a whole, has been upon the need for a new approach to managing production and distribution in response to major environmental changes. The solution proposed is the adoption of a marketing orientation which puts the customer at the beginning rather than the end of the production–consumption cycle. To do so requires a fundamental shift of attitude on the part of all those concerned with production and consumption. Unfortunately, while this concept seems both simple and obvious to those who have subscribed to it there is ample evidence that it is widely misunderstood and hence misapplied.

In 1970, Charles Ames drew attention to this in an article in the *Harvard Business Review* entitled 'Trappings versus substance in industrial marketing'. The thesis of this was that industrial companies that complained marketing was not working for them as it appeared to do so for the consumer good companies had only themselves to blame as they had not understood the substance of the marketing concept but had merely adopted some of its superficial trappings. At worst, they had merely changed the name of their personnel from 'sales' to 'marketing'.

More recently in the *Journal of Marketing Management* (1985), Stephen King diagnosed at least four different misinterpretations of marketing in the UK as follows:

1   *Thrust marketing* – this occurs when the sales managers change their name to marketing managers. But the emphasis is still upon selling what we can make with an emphasis upon price and cost cutting but little attention to fitness for purpose, quality and value for money. In other words, it ignores what the customer really wants.

2   *Marketing department marketing* – indicated by the establishment of a bolt-on specialized department intended to remedy the lack of customer understanding. Some improvement followed in markets where change was slow and gradual but it did not address the critical areas where radical innovation was called for. A sort of 'fine tuning' of the customer service function but based on existing products and customers.

3   *Accountants marketing* – prevalent where chief executive officers have no direct experience of selling or marketing and concentrate upon short-term returns to the neglect of long-run survival. This approach was pungently criticized by Hayes and Abernathy in their 1980 *Harvard Business Review* article 'Managing our way to economic decline', which has been echoed many times since. Accountants marketing neglects investment in R&D, manufacturing and marketing and leads to a vicious downward spiral.

4   *Formula marketing* – in which control is seen as more important than innovation. This emphasizes sticking to the tried and true and reflects a risk-averse strategy. It appears professional (many MBAs) and concentrates on managing facts and information but its

consumer research bias tends to tell you more about the past than the future.

Failure of these approaches suggests. that *real* marketing has four essential features:

1   Start with the customer.
2   A long-run perspective.
3   Full use of *all* the company's resources.
4   Innovation.

The marketing function

From the foregoing it is clear that without commitment to the concept there is little likelihood that the marketing *function* will be executed effectively. It is also clear that the size and nature of the marketing function will vary enormously according to the nature of the company or organization and the markets which it serves.

Basically, the marketing function is responsible for the management of the marketing mix which, at its simplest, is summarized by the four Ps of product, price, place and promotion. While much more elaborate formulations containing a dozen or more elements are to be found in the marketing textbooks such fine distinctions are not central to the present inquiry into the nature of marketing. As a function marketing has as many quirks and mysteries as research and development, finance and production but the important point to establish here is that the adoption of a marketing orientation does not mean nor require that the marketing function should be seen as the largest or the most important. In fact, in a truly marketing-orientated organization the need for a specialized marketing function is probably far less than it is in a sales- or production-dominated company. Appreciation of this fact would do much to disarm the resistance of other functional specialists who equate the adoption of a marketing orientation with a diminution in their own organizational status and influence.

Ideally, of course, such functional divisions would not exist. Perhaps, if everyone were marketing orientated would they disappear to our continuing competitive advantage?

During the late 1980s and early 1990s there was considerable evidence to suggest that the marketing orientation had become so widely accepted that commentators were beginning to question the need for a separate marketing function to assume responsibility for it. Marketing's 'mid-life crisis' caused more than a frisson of anxiety amongst marketing academics and practitioners alike!

In retrospect it seems that the collapse of communism in the late 1980s had a significant effect on managerial perceptions of marketing and highlighted the need to reconsider its role and function. During the years following World War II, politics and economics were dominated by the 'super powers' – the USA and the Soviet Union – each of which represented a quite different ideology and approach to economic organization – capitalism and communism. An essential difference between the two is that the former believes in and encourages competition in free markets while the latter is founded on central control and an absence of competition in the marketplace.

The fall of the Berlin Wall and the disintegration of the Soviet Union which followed it would seem to confirm the view that competition is necessary to encourage change and progress. But the collapse of communism created the kind of dilemma addressed by Chamberlin and Robinson in the 1930s which led to the articulation of the theory of imperfect competition. Prior to this economists had focused analysis on the polar opposites of monopoly (no competition) and perfect competition with only limited attention given to intermediate conditions such as oligopoly. Clearly, there are many degrees of competition in the real world which lie between the polar extremes and it was these that came to be designated as imperfect.

The analogy may be extended if one considers communism to represent monopoly and the 'free' market as perfect competition. It was against this background that the dominant model of competition post-1950 was modelled on the

United States and gave rise to what we now distinguish as the marketing management paradigm immortalized in Levitt's (1960) article, 'Marketing myopia', McCarthy's 4Ps and Kotler's seminal (1967) *Marketing Management: Analysis, Planning and Control*. Because of its primacy few gave much attention to free markets subject to varying degrees of regulation despite the fact that these probably, like imperfect competition, represented the majority. All that was to change in 1989!

In a penetrating analysis entitled *Capitalisme contre Capitalisme* Michel Albert (1991) pointed out that there is no single, monolithic definition of capitalism just as there is no single model of competition. Dussart (1994) elaborated on this and contrasted the American, Friedmanite model of unfettered competition practised in the USA and UK (Anglo-Saxon competition) with a modified form to be found in many social democracies in which a degree of market control is exercised by the state to moderate the excesses of big business. This Alpine/Germanic model of competition is strongly associated with most West European economies, and also with Japan and the 'tiger' economies of South East Asia, most of which have achieved a consistently better economic performance than the USA and UK since 1950.

The essential difference between the Anglo-Saxon/marketing management approach and the Alpine/Germanic style of competition is that the former takes a short-term, zero-sum adversarial view based on one-off transactions while the latter adopts a long-term perspective which promotes win–win relationships.

Relationship marketing

According to Möller and Halinen-Kaila (1997) relationship marketing or RM is the 'hot topic' of the marketing discipline during the 1990s, but 'the rhetoric is often characterized more by elegance than by rigorous examination of the actual contents' (p. 2/3). The debate raises at least four critical questions:

1   Will RM replace the traditional marketing management school?
2   Will RM make marketing management theory obsolete?
3   Is RM a completely new theory, or does it derive from older traditions?
4   Do we need different theories of RM depending on the type of exchange relationships?

Möller and Halinen-Kaila seek to answer these questions. In doing so they stress the need to look back as well as forward and link new ideas with existing knowledge. They see the current interest in RM as deriving from four basic sources – marketing channels, business-to-business marketing (interorganizational marketing), services marketing and direct and database marketing (consumer marketing).

The dominant marketing management paradigm founded on the manipulation of the mix began to be questioned in the 1970s as it provided an inadequate explanation of the marketing of services. Such a challenge was unsurprising given that services had become the largest sector in the advanced industrial economies. Specifically, services marketing calls for recognition of both buyer and seller in the exchange process. Developments in information technology during the 1980s made it possible to both model and operationalize individual relationships through the use of databases.

However, the different research approaches are derived from different perspectives and conceptual frames of reference and provide only partial explanations which have yet to be synthesized and integrated into a holistic metatheory. Metatheory is derived from meta analysis which follows one of two closely related approaches – profiling or typology development. The latter tends to be abstract, the former descriptive, and it is this procedure which is followed by Möller and Halinen-Kaila who develop a detailed comparison matrix in which they examine the four traditions specified earlier across a number of dimensions, as illustrated in Table 1.1. While the authors acknowledge that such a matrix glosses over many details, none the less it

provides useful generalizations of the ways in which the different research traditions handle exchange relationships. To reduce the complexity of their comparison matrix with its four traditions, the authors collapse these into two categories – consumer and interorganizational relationships – and summarize their salient characteristics as in Table 1.1.

Although relationships are recognized as existing on a continuum in terms of closeness/involvement of the parties, the definition of the two categories is seen as helpful in 'anchoring' the ends of this continuum. This distinction is reinforced when one considers the different viewpoint or perspective taken in terms of the underlying assumptions on which consumer and interorganizational relationships have been evaluated – the former following a market perspective, the latter a network/systemic perspective.

In identifying two distinct streams of thought within the RM literature Möller and Halinen-Kaila recognize that they may be 'swimming against the fashionable stream of RM as the general marketing theory rhetoric!' (p. 16). If so, they are not alone as Mattsson (1997) is clearly of a similar opinion as is the author for, otherwise, he would have promoted an alternative perspective. That said, by adopting the Möller and Halinen-Kaila approach and identifying the key characteristics of the different schools of thought, it becomes possible to recognize both similarities and differences in much the same way that the concepts of pure competition and monopoly enabled the emergence of a theory of imperfect competition which reflects messy reality rather than theoretical purity. As Möller and Halinen-Kaila point out, the key managerial challenge in both forms of RM is how to manage a portfolio of exchange relationships. Within the domain of consumer or 'limited' relationship marketing, numerous approaches and techniques have evolved which are highly relevant to addressing this problem. Indeed, with the developments in information technology in recent years many of these have become of practical rather than theoretical

Table 1.1 Comparison matrix of research approaches to marketing exchange relationships

Research Tradition / Characteristics	Database and Direct Consumer Marketing	Services Marketing	Channel Relationships	Interaction and Networks
Basic Goals	Enhance marketing efficiency through better targeting of marketing activities, especially marketing communications – channels and messages. Strong managerial emphasis, integrated marketing communications (IMC) an important agenda.	Explain and understand services marketing relationships and services management. Managerial goal: enhance the efficiency of managing customer encounters and customer relationships through managing the perceived quality of the service offer and relationship.	Theoretical goal: explain governance structures and dyadic behaviour in the channel context. Normative goal: determine efficient relational forms between channel members.	Three interrelated sets of goals: (i) Understand and explain interorganizational exchange behaviour and relationship development at a dyadic level in a network context; (ii) understand how nets of relationships between actors evolve, and (iii) understand how markets function and evolve from a network perspective. Managerial goal: gain a more valid view of reality through network theory.
View of Relationship	Organization-personal customer relationships, often distant and generally comprising discrete transactions over time, handled through customized mass communication.	Personal customer relationships attended by service personnel and influenced through other marketing activities. Earlier a strong focus on the service encounter, later expanded to include the life cycle of relationships.	Interorganizational business relationships characterized by economic exchange and use of power. Actors are dependent on each other and behave reciprocally.	Relationships exist between different types of actors: firms, government and research agencies, individual actors. Not only goods, but all kinds of resources are exchanged through relationships. Relationships are seen as vehicles for accessing and controlling resources, and creating new resources.
Questions Asked	How to provide value for the customer, how to develop loyal customers, how to adapt marketing activities along the customer's life cycle, how to retain customers?	How to provide value and perceived quality for the customer, how to manage service encounters, how to create and manage customer relationships?	What forms of governance are efficient for what types of channel relationships? How is the use of power related to relationship efficiency? How can the more dependent party safeguard against the dominant party? In what way is the dyadic relationship contingent on the larger channel context?	How are relationships created and managed; how do nets of relationships evolve, how can an actor manage these relationships and create a position in a net?
Disciplinary Background	No disciplinary background; driven by information technology, marketing communication applications, and consultants.	No clear disciplinary background: early phase a response to 'traditional marketing management', later consumer behaviour applications, human resource perspective and general management outlook. Empirically- and theory-driven with heavy managerial orientation.	Primarily theory-driven; attempts to combine the economic and political aspects (power, dependency) of channels. The tradition relies on transaction cost theory, relational law, social exchange theory, political economy, power and conflict in organizational sociology.	Both empirically- and theory driven; earlier influenced by channels research, organizational buying behaviour, resource dependency theory, social exchange theory and institutional economics; later by institutional economics, dynamic industrial economics, organizational sociology and resource-based theory.
World View and	Pragmatic – no explicit assumptions; implicitly assumes competitive mar-	Primarily the management perspective; dyadic interactive relationship but cus-	Both parties can be active and reciprocally interdependent; the basic interest is in	Depending on the research goals, the relationship perspective can be

Assumptions about Relationships	kets of customers; S-O-R view with feedback: the marketer is active, plans the offers and communications on the basis of customer status (profile) and feedback. Relatively weak dependency between buyer and seller, as the goods exchanged are relatively substitutable and many buyers and sellers exist.	tomers often seen as objects; i.e., the marketer is generally the active party. Interdependence between the seller and the customer varies from weak to relatively strong. The basic service is often relatively substitutable, but the service relationship can be differentiated and individualized.	economic exchange and its efficiency. The relationship is unique, its substitutability depends on the availability of alternative buyers and sellers and the amount of switching costs related to relationship-specific investments.	dyadic, focal firm or network type. Any actor can be active, actors are generally seen as subjects. There is often relatively strong interdependency between actors, caused by heterogeneity of resources which makes substitution difficult.
Topics/ Concepts Important for RM	Customer retention, share of customer, database as a device for managing direct communications, integrated use of channels.	Service encounters, experience & expectations, service & relationship quality, life-time value of the customer, internal marketing, empowerment of personnel.	Bases of power, uses of power and conflict behaviour, interdependence, goal congruity, decision domains, environmental influence on dyadic behaviour, transaction-specific investments, switching costs, dyadic governance, dyad outcomes: efficiency, satisfaction, relational norms.	Interaction processes, adaptation and investments into relationships, phases of relationships, actor bonds, resource ties, activity chains and relationship outcomes; nets and networks of relationships; network dynamics and embeddedness.
Level/Unit of Analysis and Contextuality	Individual consumer, a group of consumers (segment); in applications customers are practically always aggregated into groups (segments). No conscious assumptions about the contextuality of the customer relationship; the competitive situation is the general contextuality perspective.	Individual customer, group or segment, service provider–client relationship. Little emphasis on contextuality, sometimes the history of a relationship is emphasized – generally handled through 'experience'; generally implicit assumption about the market as the dominant environmental form.	Firm, dyadic relationship in the channel context. Contingency perspective: dyadic behaviour and efficient forms of governance are dependent on the channel context. Well developed 'environment' theory.	Actor (organization, person), dyadic relationship, net of relationships. Transactions are episodes in the long-term relationship. The emphasis is on the embeddedness of relationships in nets and networks, and their history – no understanding of the present situation without history. Time is an essential phenomenon.
Time Orientation, Focus on Structure vs. Process	Rhetoric emphasizes the long-term view, no published tools for handling long-term issues of relationships. The focus is on the content of a customer profile, little emphasis/conceptual effort on tackling the dynamism of customer development.	Earlier emphasis on short-term encounters, now shifting to a more enduring relational perspective. The process aspect is evident, but empirical research is primarily on the content of relationship characteristics.	Emphasis on efficient forms of channel relationships ranging from market-like transactions to long-term reciprocal relationships. Theoretically dynamic, but the majority of empirical research is static; the focus is on structure not process.	Dynamic perspective, focus on both structure (content) and processes (how dyads, nets, and networks evolve).
Methodological Orientation	No conscious methodology, primarily cross-sectional analysis of survey data and customer databases.	Divided methodology; North American emphasis on explanation through hypothesis testing by multivariate analysis; Nordic emphasis on understanding through qualitative research.	Hypothetical – deductive reasoning, explanation through hypothesis testing by multivariate analysis.	Divided methodology, European emphasis (IMP Group) on understanding through historical case analysis; North American emphasis on explanation through hypothesis testing by multivariate analysis (this is primarily limited to dyads).

Source: Möller and Halinen-Kaila, 1997, p. 10.

interest. We should not lightly discard these methods.

In the domain of interorganizational relationships their complexity is likely to limit the extent to which 'packaged' solutions may be applied. While useful generalizations will have an important role to play, the situation-specific nature of most problems will continue to require decision-makers to use experience and judgement in coming up with effective solutions.

Summary

In this introductory chapter we have attempted to trace the evolution of exchange relationships and provide at least a partial answer to the question 'What is marketing?' In the process we have established that exchange is at the very heart of human development in both economic and social terms. Until recently, however, the desirability of enhancing consumer satisfaction through the provision of more and better goods and services has been so self-evident that little consideration has been given as to how to define 'more' and 'better', or the processes by which such evaluations are made. As Adam Smith observed in his *Wealth of Nations* (1776), 'Consumption is the sole end and purpose of production'. Having stated the obvious the remainder of his great work is devoted wholly to issues of improving supply with no consideration of demand *per se*.

As we have seen, it is only with the stabilization of populations in advanced economies, and the continuous and accelerating improvements in productivity attributable to technological innovation, that a preoccupation with supply side problems has given way to demand side considerations. Modern marketing, dating from the 1950s, reflects this transition. But, as we have attempted to show, the marketing management model which emerged was itself a purely transitional response to managing the changing balance between sellers and buyers. Initially, the marketing management model was concerned with what sellers needed to do to retain control over the transaction, with consumers seen as passive participants in the process. With the evolution of service dominated economies, so the balance of power changed and supply was now seen to be subservient to demand and consumer sovereignty.

The problem with this latter perspective is that it still sees exchange as a zero-sum game. The only difference now is that buyers are winners and sellers are losers. At the time of writing (mid-1998) the dangers of this adversarial approach to exchange are readily apparent, especially in the manufacturing sector where the greatest potential for growth and added value exists. If buyers continue to demand lower and lower prices, eventually sellers will go out of business, competition will disappear and choice will be severely restricted. Inevitably, consumer welfare will decline as the economies of the world move into ever-deepening recession. What is needed is a proper appreciation of the true marketing concept of exchange based upon *mutually satisfying relationships* in which both parties get what they want – a true win–win situation. In our view, implementation of this concept/orientation demands the existence of a marketing function and the management of the marketing mix. The remainder of *The Marketing Book* draws on the expertise of leading thinkers and practitioners to see how we might achieve this desired state.

References

Albert, M. (1991) *Capitalisme contre Capitalisme*, Seuil, L'Historie Immédiate, Paris.

Ames, C. (1970) Trappings versus substance in industrial marketing, *Harvard Business Review*, July–August, 93–103.

Dussart, C. (1994) 'Capitalism versus Capitalism', in Baker, M. J. (ed.) *Perspectives on Marketing Management*, Vol. 4, John Wiley & Sons, Chichester.

Hayes, R. and Abernathy, W. (1980) Managing our way to economic decline, *Harvard Business Review*, July–August, 67–77.

King, S. (1985) Has marketing failed or was it never really tried?, *Journal of Marketing Management*, **1**(1), Summer, 1–19.

Kotler, P. (1967) *Marketing Management: Analysis, Planning and Control*, Prentice-Hall, Englewood Cliffs, NJ.

Levitt, T. (1960) Marketing myopia, *Harvard Business Review*, July–August, 45–60.

Mattsson, L. -G. (1997) 'Relationship marketing' and the 'markets-as-networks approach' – a comparative analysis of two evolving streams of research, *Journal of Marketing Management*, **13**, 447–61.

Möller, K. and Halinen-Kaila, A., (1997) 'Relationship Marketing: Its Disciplin-ary Roots and Future Directions', Helsinki School of Economics and Business Administration, Helsinki: *Working Papers*, W–194.

Further reading

Baker, M. J. (2000) 'Marketing – Philosophy or Function?', Chapter 1 in Baker, M. J. (ed.) *Encyclopedia of Marketing*, 2nd edn, ITP, London.

CHAPTER 2

The basics of marketing strategy

ROBIN WENSLEY

Marketing strategy sometimes claims to provide an answer to one of the most difficult questions in our understanding of competitive markets: how to recognize and achieve an economic advantage which endures. In attempting to do so, marketing strategy, as with the field of strategy itself, has had to address the continual dialectic between analysis and action, or in more common managerial terms, between strategy formulation and strategic implementation.

Strategy: from formulation to implementation

From the late 1960s to the mid-1980s at least, management strategy seemed to be inevitably linked to issues of product-market selection and hence to marketing strategy. Perhaps ironically this was not primarily or mainly as a result of the contribution of marketing scholars or indeed practitioners. The most significant initial contributors, such as Bruce Henderson and Michael Porter, were both to be found at or closely linked to the Harvard Business School, but were really informed more by particular aspects of economic analysis: neo-marginal economics[1] and industrial organizational economics respectively. However in various institutions the marketing academics were not slow to recognize what was going on and also to see that the centrality of product-market choice linked well with the importance attached to marketing. This expansion of the teaching domain had a much less significant impact on the research agenda and activity within marketing itself, where the focus continued to underplay the emerging importance of the competitive dimension (Day and Wensley, 1983). Hence the relatively atheoretical development continued into the process of codification of this new area, most obviously in the first key text by Abell and Hammond (1979), which was based on a, by then, well established second year MBA option at Harvard.[2]

In retrospect this period was the high point for the uncontested impact of competitive market related analysis on strategic manage-

---

[1] Labelling the intellectual pedigree for Bruce Henderson and the Boston Consulting Group is rather more difficult than for Michael Porter. This is partly because much of the approach developed out of consulting practice (cf. Morrison and Wensley, 1989) in the context of a broad rather than focused notion of economic analysis. Some of the intellectual pedigree for the approach can be found in Henderson and Quant (1958) – this Henderson was at Harvard also – but some basic ideas such as dynamic economies of scale have a much longer pedigree (see, for instance, Jones, 1926).

[2] The book itself is clearly influenced by the work related to the Profit Impact of Market Strategy (PIMS) project, as well as work in management consultancies such as McKinsey, ADL and, perhaps most importantly, Boston Consulting Group, whose founder, Bruce Henderson, had close links with Derek Abell. The MBA course itself started in 1975 with a broad notion of 'filling the gap' between what was seen then as the marketing domain and the much broader area of business policy, so encompassing issues relating to R&D, distribution and competitive costs. The course itself was a second year elective and rapidly expanded to four sections with a major commitment on development and case writing in 1976 and 1977.

ment practice. With the advantage of hindsight, it is clear that a serious alternative perspective was also developing, most obviously signalled by Peters and Waterman (1982), which was to have a very substantial impact on what was taught in strategic management courses and what was marketed by consultancies. It was also a significant book in the sense that, although not widely recognized as so doing, it also attempted to integrate to some extent earlier work by other relevant academics such as Mintzberg (1973), Pettigrew (1973) and Weick (1976) .

As the decade progressed, it was inevitable that at least to some degree each side recognized the other as a key protagonist. Perhaps one of the most noteworthy comments is that in which Robert Waterman challenged the value of a Michael Porter based analysis of competition. Waterman (1988) argued that the Porter approach does not work because 'people get stuck in trying to carry out his ideas'[3] for three reasons:

1 There is usually no single, easily identified competitor.
2 Business is a positive sum game: at one level firms compete fiercely, at another level they help each other.
3 Competitors are human: they are neither dumb nor superhuman.[4]

Equally, the economists have not taken such attacks lying down: more recently Kay (1993) attempted to wrest back the intellectual dominance in matters of corporate strategy and Porter (1990) extended his domain to the nation-state itself.

The story, of course, has also become complicated in other ways, many of which are outside the scope of this chapter. In terms of key perspectives, Tom Peters has become more and more polemical about the nature of success,[5] C. K. Prahalad has, with Gary Hamel, refined his original notion of dominant logic to reflect in general terms the importance of transferable capabilities and technological interdependencies in the development of strategic advantage[6] and, of course, Peter Senge (1992) reiterated the importance of information structures and Hammer and Champy (1993) introduced a 'new' approach labelled business process analysis.

In terms of the disciplinary debate, what was originally broadly a debate between economists and sociologists, now also involves psychologists, social anthropologists and, if they are a distinct discipline, systems theorists.

However, the key change in emphasis has been the one from analysis to process, from formulation to implementation. Perhaps the single most important contributor to this change has been Henry Mintzberg, who has developed over the period an extensive critique of, what he calls the 'Design School' in strategic management, culminating in his 1994 book. In this he even challenges the notion of planning in strategy:

Thus we arrive at the planning school's grand fallacy: because analysis is not synthesis, strategic planning is not strategy formation. Analysis may precede and support synthesis, by defining the parts that can be combined into wholes. Analysis may follow and elaborate synthesis, by decomposing and formalising its consequences. But analysis cannot substitute for synthesis. No amount of elaboration will ever enable formal procedures to forecast discontinuities, to inform managers who are detached from their operations, to create novel strategies. Ultimately the term 'strategic planning' has proved to be an oxymoron. (p. 321)

Whilst his approach and indeed critique of strategy analysis is itself rather polemical and overstated,[7] there is little doubt that the general

---

[3] It is noteworthy that the very representation of the five-forces diagram for instance is one which emphasizes that the firm is under pressure from all sides.

[4] This is a particular and rather colourful way of representing the notion of 'rational expectations' (Muth, 1961; Simon, 1979) in economics to which we will return later in this chapter.

[5] Indeed to the extent of arguing in a recent interview that innovative behaviour now depends on ignoring rather than exploiting market evidence (Kelly, 1997).

[6] For instance, see Bettis and Prahalad (1995), Prahalad and Hamel (1990) and Prahalad and Bettis (1989).

[7] In fact Mintzberg himself goes on to argue three roles for 'corporate planning': (1) a more refined approach in traditional contexts, (2) a focus on techniques which emphasize the uncertain and emergent nature of strategic phenomena and/or (3) a more creative and intuitive form of strategic planning (see Wensley, 1996).

emphasis in strategic management has shifted significantly towards implementation and away from formulation and planning.

The nature of the competitive market environment

As our analysis of marketing strategy has developed over the last 25 years, so our representation of the marketing context has also changed.

As an example, Figure 2.1 is an overhead which the author used 25 years ago in describing the nature of the marketing context. A number of major omissions are clear. In particular there is no recognition of competitors and distribution is clearly seen as a solely logistical function. In addition, consumers are very much represented as 'at a distance'.

More recently marketing has recognized much more explicitly this further range of issues including the key role of competition and the

importance of a longer term so-called relationship perspective, particularly in the context of customers. On top of this, various entities in the distribution chain are now clearly seen as very active intermediaries rather than just passive logistics agents.

However, the development of this more complex dynamic representation of the competitive market – which can be seen broadly in the marketing strategy triangle of the 3Cs (see Figure 2.2): customers, competitors and channels – also implies a more fluid and complex context for systematic modelling purposes.

Customers, competitors and channels

The early more static model of the nature of the competitive market, which informed many of the still current and useful tools of analysis, was both positional and non-interactive. It was assumed that the market backcloth, often

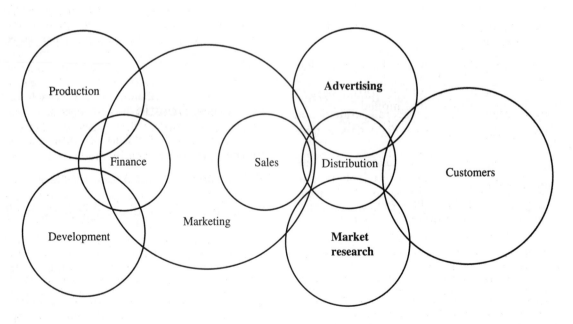

Figure 2.1   An overhead describing the nature of the marketing context (25 years old)

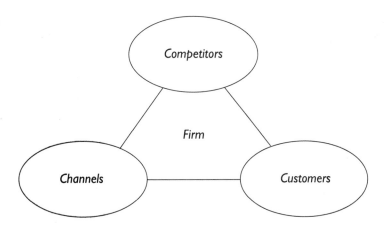

Figure 2.2   The marketing strategy triangle of the 3Cs

referred to as the product-market space, remained relatively stable and static so that at least in terms of first order effects, strategies could be defined in positional terms. Similarly, the general perspective, strongly reinforced by representations such as that in Figure 2.1, was that actions by the firm would generally not create equivalent reactions from the relatively passive 'consumers'. This perspective on the nature of marketing, which might be fairly labelled the 'patient' perspective (Wensley, 1990), is to be found rather widely in marketing texts and commentaries despite the continued espousal of slogans such as 'the customer is king'.

With the adoption of the more interactive and dynamic perspective implied in the 3Cs approach the nature of strategy becomes much more complex. At the same time we must be wary of the temptation to continue to apply the old tools and concepts without considering critically whether they are appropriate in new situations. They represent in general a special or limiting case which quite often requires us to distort the nature of the environment that we are attempting to characterize. The key question as to how far this distortion is, as our legal colleagues would say, material, is another but frequently unresolved matter. This notion of materiality is really linked to impact on actions rather than just understanding and the degree to

which in practice particular forms of marketing strategy analysis encourage actions which are either sub-optimal or indeed dysfunctional.

Lacking further experimental or research evidence on this question, this chapter is mainly written around the assumption that we need to recognize in using these simplifying approaches that (i) the degree to which they actually explain the outcomes of interest will be limited, particularly when it is a direct measure of individual competitive performance, and (ii) the ways in which the underlying assumptions can cause unintentional biases.

The evolution of analysis, interpretation and modelling in marketing strategy from customers to competitors to channels

Given that the underlying representation of the competitive market environment has changed, so, not surprisingly, have our processes of analysis, interpretation and modelling. Initially the key focus was on customer based positioning studies in particular product markets. Such work remains a key component in the analysis of much market research data but from the marketing strategy perspective, we need to recognize that the dimensionality of the analysis has often been rather low, indeed in some situations little more than a single price dimension which has been seen as highly correlated with an equivalent quality dimension.[8]

The increased emphasis on the analysis of competitors has also required us to make certain compromises. One, of course, relates to the balance between what might be termed public information, legitimate inference and private information. The other to the fact that our colleagues in business strategy now give emphasis to two rather different perspectives on the nature of competitive firms, one essentially based on similarities (strategic groups: McGee and Thomas, 1986) the other on differences (resource based perspective: Wernerfeld, 1984, 1995a). Sound competitor analysis should at least enable us to avoid making inconsistent assumptions, particularly in the context of public data, like, for instance, assuming that we will be able to exploit an opportunity which is known to all, without a significant amount of competitive reaction.

Finally there is the question of channels or, in more general terms, supply chains. The issue of retailers in particular as independent and significant economic intermediaries rather than just logistical channels to the final consumer has been an important consideration in consumer marketing at least since the 1970s. Similarly in industrial markets the issue of the supply chain and the central importance of some form of organization and coordination of the various independent entities within the chain has been seen as an increasingly important strategic issue. Both these developments have meant that any strategic marketing analysis needs to find ways to evaluate the likely impact of such independent strategies pursued by intermediaries, although in many cases our tools and techniques for doing this remain rather limited and often rely on no more than an attempt to speculate on what might be their preferred strategic action.

Beyond this there has been an attempt to resolve the underlying problem with the espousal of what has become known as relationship marketing. It is outside the remit of this chapter to provide a full overview but from a strategic viewpoint there are two important issues that need to be emphasized. The first is that a recognition of the relatively stable pattern of transaction relationship within, particularly, most industrial markets, often described as the 'markets as networks' perspective, is not necessarily the same as the more prescriptive, notion of the need to manage such relationships. Mattsson (1997) provides a very useful comparison and evaluation of the similarities and differences between the two approaches, which we will discuss later. The second is that whilst the relationship perspective rightly moves our attention away from individual transactions towards patterns of interaction over longer time periods, it often seems to assume that the motivations of each party are symmetric. In practice in both consumer (Fournier *et al.*, 1998) and industrial markets (Harland and Wensley, 1997) this may prove to be a very problematic assumption.

Codification of marketing strategy analysis as three strategies, four boxes and five forces

What can now be regarded as 'traditional' marketing strategy analysis was developed primarily in the 1970s. It was codified in various ways, including the strategic triangle developed by Ohmae (1982) as reproduced in Figure 2.3, but perhaps more memorably, the most significant elements in the analysis can be defined in terms of the three generic strategies, the four boxes (or perhaps more appropriately strategic contexts), and the five forces.

These particular frameworks also represent the substantial debt that marketing strategy

[8] There are undoubtedly good reasons for adopting such a low dimensionality approach in the name of either stability, which is clearly a critical issue if strategic choices are going to be made in this context, and/or a hierarchy of effects in

which strategic choices at this level dominate later more complex choices in a higher dimension perceptual space, but it is often doubtful whether either or both of these rationales are based on firm empirical evidence in many situations.

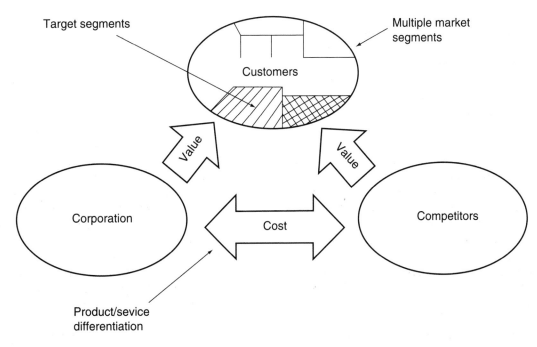

Target segments

Multiple market
segments

Customers

Value

Value

Corporation

Cost

Competitors

Product/sevice
differentiation

Source: Ohmae (1982: 92)

Figure 2.3 The strategic triangle

owes to economic analysis; the three strategies and the five forces are directly taken from Michael Porter's influential work, which derived from his earlier work in industrial organization economics. The four contexts model was initially popularized by the Boston Consulting Group under Bruce Henderson, again strongly influenced by micro-economic analysis. Whilst each of these approaches remains a significant component in much marketing strategy teaching (see Morrison and Wensley, 1981), we also need to recognize some of the key considerations and assumptions which need to be considered in any critical application.

The three strategies

It could reasonably be argued that Porter really reintroduced the standard economic notion of scale to the distinction between cost and differ-

entiation to arrive at the three generic strategies of focus, cost and differentiation. Indeed in his later formulation of the three strategies they really became four in that he suggested, rightly, that the choice between an emphasis on competition via cost or differentiation can be made at various scales of operation.

With further consideration it is clear that both of these dimensions are themselves not only continuous but also likely to be the aggregate of a number of relatively independent elements or dimensions. Hence scale is in many contexts not just a single measure of volume of finished output but also of relative volumes of sub-assemblies and activities which may well be shared. Even more so in the case of 'differentiation', where we can expect that there are various different ways in which any supplier attempts to differentiate their offerings. On top of this, a number of other commentators, most particularly

John Kay (1993), have noted that not only may the cost-differentiation scale be continuous rather than dichotomous but it also might not be seen as a real dimension at all. At some point this could become a semantic squabble but there clearly is an important point that many successful strategies are built around a notion of good value for money rather than a pure emphasis on cost or differentiation at any price. Michael Porter (1980) might describe this as a 'middle' strategy but rather crucially he has consistently claimed that there is a severe danger of getting 'caught in the middle'. In fact it might be reasonable to assume that in many cases being in the middle is the best place to be: after all, Porter has never presented significant systematic evidence to support his own assertion (cf. Wensley, 1994)

The four contexts

The four boxes (contexts) model relates to the market share/market growth matrix originally developed by the Boston Consulting Group (BCG) under Bruce Henderson. Although there have inevitably been a whole range of different matrix frameworks which have emerged since the early days, the BCG one remains an outstanding exemplar not only because of its widespread popularity and impact (nowadays even university vice-chancellors have been heard to use terms such as 'cash cow'), but because there was an underlying basic economic logic in its development. Many other similar frameworks just adopted the rather tautologous proposition that one should invest in domains which were both attractive and where one had comparative advantage!

The market growth/market share matrix however still involved a set of key assumptions which were certainly contestable. In particular alongside the relatively uncontroversial one that in general the growth rate in markets tends to decline, there were the assumptions that it was in some sense both easier to gain market share in higher growth rate markets, and also that the returns to such gains were likely to be of longer duration.

This issue can be seen as assumptions about

first the cost and then the benefit of investment in market share and has been discussed and debated widely in marketing over the last twenty years (see Jacobson and Aaker, 1985; Jacobson, 1994). The general conclusion would appear to be that:

(i)   Market share as an investment is not on average under-priced, and may well be over-priced.

(ii)   The cost of gaining market share is less related to the market growth rate and much more to the relationship between actual growth rates and competitors' expectations.

(iii) Much of the benefit attributed to market share is probably better interpreted as the result of competitive advantages generated by more specific resources and choices in marketing or other corporate areas.

On this basis, it would seem that the bias implied in the BCG matrix towards investment in market share at the early stages of market growth is not really justified, particularly when one takes into account that at this stage in market development many investments are likely to be somewhat more risky as well. If, however, a focus on market share position does encourage companies to place greater emphasis on the marketing fundamentals for a particular business then it could well be justified but as very much a means to an end rather than the solution itself.

More generally, the matrix as an analytical device suffers from some of the problems which we illustrated for the three strategies approach: an analysis which is essentially based on extreme points when in practice many of the portfolio choices are actually around the centre of the diagram. This implies that any discrimination between business units needs to be on the basis of much more specific analysis rather than broad general characteristics.

The five forces

The five forces analysis was originally introduced by Michael Porter to emphasize the extent to which the overall basis of competition was much wider than just the rivalries between established competitors in a particular market. Whilst not exactly novel as an insight, particularly to suggest that firms also face competition from new entrants and substitutes, it was presented in a very effective manner and served to emphasize not only the specific and increasing importance of competition as we discussed, but also the extent to which competition should be seen as a much wider activity within the value chain, as Porter termed it, although it might now more likely be seen as the supply chain. Actually, of course, the situation is a little more complex than this: Porter used the term value chain when in essence he was concentrating more on the chain of actual costs. Whilst ex post from an economic point-of-view there is no difference between value and cost, it is indeed the process of both competition and collaboration between various firms and intermediaries which finally results in the attribution of value throughout the relevant network. In this sense, as others have recognized, a supply chain is an intermediate organization form where there is a higher degree of cooperation between the firms within the chain and a greater degree of competition between the firms within different chains. In this context Porter's analysis has tended to focus much more clearly on the issue of competition rather than cooperation. Indeed at least in its representational form it has tended to go further than this and focus attention on the nature of the competitive pressures on the firm itself rather than interaction between the firm and other organizations in the marketplace.

The search for theory: rules for success amidst diversity

As we have suggested above, the codification of marketing strategy was based on three essential schema. This schemata, whilst based on some valid theoretical concepts, did not really provide a systematic approach to the central question: the nature of sustained economic performance in the competitive marketplace. Whilst such an objective was clearly recognized in the so-called search for sustainable competitive advantage (Day and Wensley, 1988), there remained some central concerns as to whether such a notion was realistic given the dynamic and uncertain nature of the competitive marketplace (Dickinson, 1992).

Ever since the economists of the 1930s, particularly Chamberlain and/or Robinson, depending on one's cultural heritage, it had been recognized that a competitive model based on homogeneous firms was inappropriate. Whilst their approach was broadly based on the heterogeneous nature of demand, more recently this has been extended to the wider issue of firm heterogeneity itself, in the development of the so-called 'resource based view of the firm', to which we will return later, with the emphasis on the differential portfolio of assets or resources which are owned by any one firm.

This very observation has itself raised questions for any attempt to derive relatively simple rules for strategic success beyond the self-evident tautologies such as exploit your distinctive capabilities[9] but the issue is compounded when we consider the heterogeneity of the demand side as well. In some developments

---

[9] I have intentionally forsworn using the term 'core competencies' because, as discussed above, I believe some of the work in this area represents a genuine attempt to identify transferable advantages residing either in organizational routines or technological synergies. However, it must be said that many actual applications of the 'core competencies approach' do fall well short of a rigorous definition such as provided by Bogner and Thomas (1994):

Firms with core competencies are more than just highly adept at executing core skill sets. In addition they have built appropriate cognitive traits which include:
1 Recipes and organisational routines for approaching ill-structured problems.
2 Shared value systems which direct action in unique situations, and
3 Tacit understandings of the interactions of technology, organisational dynamics and product markets.

of the resource based view such heterogeneity is included in the asset base of the firm, much as the rationale for the downward sloping demand curve in the original Robinson analysis was at least partly an implicit assumption about consumer response. It is perhaps clearer to try and retain a distinction between advantages as a result of access to or ownership of resources[10] which can be transformed into marketable offerings and advantages which are purely of the form of preferential access to a particular market itself.

A more useful way of looking at demand side heterogeneity is from the user[11] perspective directly. Arguably, from its relatively early origins, marketing, or at least the more functional focused study of marketing management, has been concerned with managerially effective ways of responding to this heterogeneity, particularly in terms of market segmentation. Indeed it would be reasonable to suggest that without a substantial level of demand heterogeneity, there would be little need for marketing approaches as they are found in most of our textbooks. Whilst there remains a substantial debate about the degree to which this market-based heterogeneity is indeed 'manageable' from a marketing perspective (cf. Wensley, 1995; Saunders, 1995), to which we will partly return later in this chapter, our concern at the moment is merely to recognize the substantial degree of heterogeneity and consider the degree to which such diversity on both the supply and demand side facilitates or negates the possibility of developing robust 'rules for success'.

To address this question, we need to consider the most useful way of characterizing the competitive market process. This is clearly a substantial topic in its own right, with proponents of various analogies or metaphors including game theory, sports games and military strategy. One key generic issue is the determining nature of the rule structure, which decreases as we move along the spectrum, or, in more technical language, the rules become more endogenously rather than exogenously determined. The most endogenous systems are to be found in the evolutionary ecology analogy which, since the original work by Hannan and Freeman (1977), has been recognized as being of interest in the strategy field.

It is undeniable that in the field of ecology we observe wide diversity in terms of both species and habitat, but there are two further critical aspects which must inform any attempt to transfer this analogy into the field of strategy. The first is the interactive relationship between any species and its habitat, nicely encapsulated in the title of the book by Levins and Leowontin (1985): *The Dialectical Biologist*. Particularly in the context of strategy it is important to recognize that the habitat (for which read market domain) evolves and develops at least as fast as the species (for which, rather more problematically, read the individual firm).[12]

The second aspect addresses directly our question of 'rules for success'. How far can we identify, particularly through the historical record, whether there are any reliable rules for success for particular species characteristics? Of course, it is very difficult to address this question without being strongly influenced by hindsight and most observations are seen as contentious. However, Stephen Jay Gould (1987, 1990) has perhaps most directly considered this issue in his various writings, particularly the analysis of the Burgess Shale, and come to the uncompromising conclusion that it is difficult if not impossible to recognize any species features or characteristics that provided a reliable ex ante rule for success.

---

[10] The notion that, in terms of strategic actions, it is not the narrow notion of ownership of resources but the broader one of influence over their disposition that is important owes much more to the 'network' perspective, which is another key influence on the current developments in strategy but rather outside the scope of this chapter, than the strict resource-based view.

[11] Again I will avoid terms such as customer or consumer and focus attention on defining the individual or group concerned purely in terms of product or service usage.

[12] For a much more developed discussion of the application of such notions as species to competitive strategy at the firm level see McKelvey (1982).

It would seem that we should at least be very cautious in any search for rules for success amidst a world of interactive diversity. Hence we should hardly be surprised that marketing strategy analysis does not provide for consistent and sustainable individual success in the competitive market-place. However, we do have a set of theoretical frameworks and practical tools which at least allow us to represent some of the key dynamics of both customer and competitive behaviour in a way which ensures we avoid errors of inconsistency or simple naiveté.

As we have discussed above, most analysis in marketing strategy is informed by what are essentially economic frameworks and so tend to focus attention on situations in which both the competitive structure of the market and the nature of consumer preferences are relatively well established. As we move our attention to more novel situations these structures tend to be at best indeterminate and therefore the analytical frameworks less appropriate. We encounter the first of many ironies in the nature of marketing strategy analysis. It is often least applicable in the very situations in which there is a real opportunity for a new source of economic advantage based on a restructuring of either or both the competitive environment and consumer preferences.

Models of competition: game theory versus evolutionary ecology

To develop a formal approach to the modelling of competitive behaviour we need to define:

1   The nature of the arena in which the competitive activity takes place.
2   The structure or rules which govern the behaviour of the participants.
3   The options available in terms of competitor behaviour (when these consist of a sequence of actions through time, or over a number of 'plays', then they are often referred to in game theory as strategies).

In this section, however, we particularly wish to contrast game theory approaches which in many ways link directly to the economic analysis to which we have already referred and analogies from evolutionary biology which raise difficult questions about the inherent feasibility of any systematic model building at the level of the individual firm.

Game theory models of competition

A game theory model[13] is characterized by a set of rules which describe: (1) the number of firms competing against each other, (2) the set of actions that each firm can take at each point in time, (3) the profits that each firm will realize for each set of competitive actions, (4) the time pattern of actions: whether they occur simultaneously or one firm moves first? And (5) the nature of information about competitive activity – who knows what, when? The notion of rationality also plays a particularly important role in models of competitive behaviour. Rationality implies a link between actions and intentions but not common intentions between competitors. Models describing competitive activity are designed to understand the behaviour of 'free' economic agents. Thus, these models start with an assumption of 'weak' rationality – the agents will take actions that are consistent with their longer-term objectives. The models also assume a stronger form of rationality – the intentions of the agents can be expressed in terms of a number of economic measures of outcome states such as profit, sales, growth, or market share objectives.

Do the results of game theory models indicate how firms should act in competitive situations? Do the models describe the evolution of competitive interactions in the real world? These questions have spawned a lively debate among management scientists concerning the

---

[13] A wider and comprehensive review of the application of game theory to marketing situations can be found in Moorthy (1985).

usefulness of game theory models.[14] Kadane and Larkey suggested that game theory models are conditionally normative and conditionally descriptive. The results do indicate how firms should behave given a set of assumptions about the alternatives, the payoffs, and the properties of an 'optimal' solution (the equilibrium). Similarly, game theory results describe the evolution of competitive strategy but only given a specific set of assumptions.

The seemingly unrealistic and simplistic nature of the competitive reactions incorporated in game theory models and nature of the equilibrium concept has led some marketers to question the managerial relevance of these models (Dolan, 1981). However, all models involve simplifying assumptions and game theory models, whilst often highly structured, underpin most attempts to apply economic analysis to issues of competition among a limited number of firms.

In this context, industrial organization (IO) economics provides one way of extending basic game theory approaches by examining the nature of competitive behaviour when assumptions about homogeneous firms and customers are relaxed. This branch of economics recognizes that not all firms are alike and that customers also differ. The dominant IO paradigm is known as structure-conduct-performance (SCP).

This paradigm suggests that a firm's performance is the result of competitive interactions (conduct in the marketplace) and that conduct is determined by the structure of the industry in which the firm competes. Conduct is the decisions made by individual firms such as price, building capacity, advertising, and investing in R&D. Structure is measured by properties of the industry (the set of firms using similar technologies) such as number and size of firms (concen-

tration), advertising intensity, capital intensity, concentration of suppliers and customers, the degree to which products are differentiated (demand is inelastic), and barriers to entry. Thus, the IO paradigm identifies a set of industry conditions that ultimately affect the competitive behaviour and performance of firms.

IO economists, especially Richard Caves (1980) and Michael Porter (1981), redirected the development of IO theory to strategic management issues. The concepts of strategic groups and mobility barriers are key elements in this new IO perspective. As Richard Caves (1984) indicates, 'the concepts of strategic groups and mobility barriers do not add up to a tight formal model. Rather, they serve to organise predictions that come from tight models and assist in confronting them with empirical evidence – a dynamised add-on to the traditional structure-conduct-performance paradigm'.

The concept of strategic groups was first articulated by Hunt (1972), based on his study of the US major household appliance industry. Hunt suggested that not all firms within an industry compete vigorously against each other. The most vigorous competition occurs between firms in a 'strategic' group which use similar approaches to attract customers – similar product line breadth, the product benefits offered, and distribution channels. Porter (1979) generalized Hunt's observation to other industries and concluded that an industry could consist of groups of firms, each group composed of firms that have similar strategies and would be defined as 'strategic groups'.

The concept of 'mobility barriers' generalized the notion of entry barriers to include strategic groups (Caves and Porter, 1977). Mobility barriers are the potential costs incurred by a firm in one strategic group that

---

[14] For an historical perspective see Joseph B. Kadane and Patrick D. Larkey, Subjective Probability and the Theory of Games, *Management Science*, 28 (February), 1982, 113–20; Reply to Professor Harsanyi, *Management Science*, 28 (February), 1982, 124; The Confusion of Is and Ought in Games Theoretic Contexts, *Management Science*, 29 (December), 1983, 1365–79; J.C. Harsanyi, Subjective Prob-

ability and the Theory of Games: Comments on Kadane and Larkey's Paper, *Management Science*, 28 (February), 1982, 124–5; Rejoinder to Professors Kadane and Larkey, *Management Science*, 28 (February), 1982, 124–4; Martin Shubik, Comment on 'The Confusion of Is and Ought in Game Theoretic Contexts', *Management Science*, 29 (December), 1983, 1380–3.

wishes to reposition itself into another strategic group. Thus, mobility barriers provide a deterrence to firms attempting to shift their strategic position within an industry. These mobility barriers also characterized the competitive advantage of firms within a strategic group over firms outside the group. The existence of strategic groups explains differing levels of firm performance (independent of size) within an industry.

Evolutionary ecological analogies

Evolutionary ecology has also emerged as a popular analogy for understanding the types of market-based strategies pursued by companies (Coyle, 1986; Lambkin and Day, 1989). These analogies have been previously used to describe both the nature of the competitive process itself (Henderson, 1983) as well as the notion of 'niche' strategy (Hofer and Schendel, 1977). Organizational theorists and sociologists have adopted an ecological model, describing the growth of a species in an ecology, to describe the types of firms in an environment.

r- and k-Strategies

From an ecological perspective, there is an upper limit on the population of a species in a resource environment. When the population of a species is small, the effects of the carrying capacity are minimal and the growth is an exponential function of the natural growth rate. The carrying capacity only becomes important when the population size is large relative to the carrying capacity. The parameters of the standard growth model have been used to describe two alternatives strategies: r-strategies and k-strategies. r-Strategies enter a new resource space (product-market space) at an early stage when few other organizations are present, while k-strategies join later when there are a larger number of organizations in the environment. Once a particular type of organization established itself in an environment, it resists change due to the development of vested interest within the organization. The number of firms in an environment at one point in time, referred to as the population density, is a proxy for the intensity of competition.

Based on this perspective, the nature of the firms and competition in an environment, the initial entrants into an environment are usually r-strategist-small, new firms that are quick to move and not constrained by the inherent inertia confronting firms established in other environments. While r-strategists are flexible, they are also inefficient due to their lack of experience. After several r-strategists have entered a new environment, established organizations, k-strategists, overcome their inertia, enter the environment, and exploit their advantage of greater efficiency based on extensive experience. The characteristics of the environment and particularly the viable niches that emerge determine whether these successive entrants can coexist.

A niche is defined as the specific combination of resources that is needed support a species or type of organization. Niche width indicates whether this combination of resource is available over a broad range of the resource source space or whether it is only available in a narrow range of the space. A generalist is able to operate in a broad range while a specialist is restricted to a narrow range. The nature of the environment favours either generalist or specialists.

Environments are described by two dimensions: variability and frequency of environmental change. In a highly variable environment, changes are dramatic, and fundamentally different strategic responses are required for survival. In contrast, strategic alterations are not required to cope with low variability. A specialist strategy in which high performance occurs in a narrow portion of the environment is surprisingly more appropriate when environmental changes are dramatic and frequent. Under these conditions, it is unlikely that a generalist would have sufficient flexibility to cope with the wide range of environmental conditions it would face, whilst the specialist can at least out-perform it in a specific environment.[15] A generalist strategist is most appropriate in an environment characterized by infrequent, minor changes because this environment allows the generalist to exploit its large-scale efficiencies.

Generic strategies

Thus the ecological analogy broadly suggests, contingent on the population density and nature of the environment, the following generic strategies:

1 *r-specialist:* small organizations that focus on exploiting first mover advantages, rather than on efficiency.
2 *r-generalists:* larger and established organizations that can exploit the new opportunity simply by minor expansion and modification of their existing activities.
3 *k-specialists:* small and probably new organizations that trade based on greater efficiency in exploiting a stable narrow area. They can often survive because the area they focus on is seen as marginal by other competitors or they are protected by captive demand.
4 *k-generalists:* large established organizations, with the advantage of experience in closely related areas, which can compete efficiently on a large scale.

Comparing the key elements in different models of competition[16]

The strategic groups and mobility barriers in the industrial organization economics approach recognize the critical asymmetries between competing firms. It identifies three methods by which firms can isolate themselves from competition: (1) differentiation, (2) cost efficiency and (3) collusion, although the latter issue has tended to be ignored. The developments within the IO paradigm have therefore tended to usefully focus on the nature and significance of various mechanisms for isolating the firm from its competition. The evolutionary ecological analogy, on the other hand, focuses on the notion of scope with the general distinction between specialists and generalists. The ecological approach also raises interesting questions about the form, level and type of 'organization' that we are considering. In particular we need to recognize most markets as forms of organization in their own right – as those who have argued the 'markets as networks' approach have done – and question how far we can justify an exclusive focus on the firm as the key organization unit. Finally, the analogy raises more directly the concern about the interaction between various different units (species) and their evolving habitat. The marketplace, like the habitat, can become relatively unstable and so both affect and be affected by the strategies of the individual firms.

As we have suggested, any analogy is far from perfect, as we would expect. The limitations are as critical as the issues that are raised because they give us some sense of the bounds within which the analogy itself is likely to be useful. Extending it outside these bounds is likely to be counter-productive and misleading.

The organization economics approach in practice tends to neglect the interaction between cost and quality. We have already suggested that while the notion 'focus' within this analogy is an attempt to recognize this problem, it is only

---

[15] For a more detailed discussion of this analysis see Lambkin and Day (1989), as well as an introduction to more complex strategy options involving polymorphism and portfolios. Achrol (1991) also develops this approach further with some useful examples.

[16] In this analysis we have left out two other generic types of competitive analogy which are commonly used: sports games and military conflict. Whilst in general these can both be illuminating and informative, they represent in many ways intermediate categories between game theory and evolutionary ecology.

The sports game approach focuses on the relationship between prior planning and the action in the game itself (including the degree of coordination between the various individual players), the interaction between competitive response within different time periods (play, game, season), the multiple routes to success, but the general evidence is that it is necessary to compete on more than one dimension,

partially successful because it transfers a characteristic of any successful competitive strategy to
one particular type only. We must further consider the extent to which we can reasonably reli-
ably distinguish between the various forms of
mixed strategies over time and the extent to
which the strategic groups themselves remain
stable.

The limitations of analogies from evolutionary ecology are more in terms of the questions that are not answered than those where the
answers are misleading. The nature of 'competition' is both unclear and complex, there is confusion as to the level and appropriate unit of
analysis, and the notion of 'niche' which has
become so current in much strategy writing
overlooks the fact that by definition every
species has one.[17]

Characterizing marketing strategy in terms of differentiation in time and space

Central to any notion of competition from a
marketing strategy viewpoint is the issue of

differentiation in time and space. Marketing is
not about the idealized world of some economic
models where competition takes place between
a multitude of homogeneous small firms in an
environment in which a market clearing price is
set instantaneously in each time period. Of
course, much of economics has evolved in
various ways – some systematic and some
rather ad hoc – to develop different and more
complex theories and models about the nature
of firm competition, and indeed many of the
tools and techniques that we discussed above
owe much of their development to particular
economists. We will return to some of these
developments shortly but need first to consider in more detail the central notion of differentiation.

What makes a real market interesting is
that (i) the market demand is heterogeneous,
(ii) the suppliers are differentiated and (iii) there
are processes of feedback and change through
time. Clearly these three elements interact
significantly, yet in most cases we find that to
reduce the complexity in our analysis and
understanding we treat each item relatively

and that success rapidly encourages imitation. Within the
sports game analogy, we recognize the key role of 'rules' and
particularly changes in rules as a means of influencing competitive strategies.

The military analogies raise the related issue of which
happens in competitive situations when the rules themselves are neither well codified nor necessarily fully
accepted combined with the fact that there is no analogy to
the referee in the sports game context. Perhaps most useful
from the point of view of competitive strategy is the focus on
the balance between clarity and confusion in one's intentions and the general notion of signalling. It is important to
avoid becoming over-committed to a particular approach
because one's intentions can be read unambiguously by the
enemy; on the other hand, a sense of direction is required
to maintain internal cohesion and morale. The military
perspective also reinforces the multiple time periods of
the sports game competitive analogy. In most military
conflicts it is assumed that the problems can be overcome
with enough resources and effort but then this degree of
commitment could prove too much from a wider perspective, and hence the old adage of winning the battle but not
the war.

In terms of limitations, sports game analogies – or
at least the ones in most common currency, which tend to
be games of position such as American football rather than
games of flow such as soccer – focus on a simple territorial

logic and a well-defined and unchanging set of rules
(Kierstead, 1972). They also presume a high degree of
control over the activities of individual players. Conversely, military analogies inevitably focus on conflict,
and again, in their most popular manifestations, direct
and immediate conflict. The physical terrain often occupies
a critical role in the analysis of competitive dispositions
and there is a focus on the nature of external factors, as
opposed to internal organization and control, and supply
logistics.

[17] Frequently, business commentators link the concept of
a niche to a competitive exclusion principle that no two
species (identical organisms or companies) can occupy the
same niche or compete in the same manner). Ecologists are
quite critical of this concept of a niche:

A niche, then, in either meaning is a description of the
ecology of the species and there is absolutely no justification
for supposing that each area has a number of pigeon-holes
into which species can be fitted until the community is full.
The most unfortunate result of using the term niche is to predispose the minds of readers into thinking that species
occupy exclusive compartments in communities and, therefore, competition leads to displacement because there is no
room for two species in one niche. We have already seen that
competition does not lead to displacement in a number of
representative examples (Pontin, 1982).

independently. For instance in most current treatments of these issues in marketing strategy we would use some form of *market segmentation* schema to map heterogeneous demand, some notion of the *resource based view* of the firm to reflect the differentiation amongst suppliers and some model of market evolution such as the *product life cycle* to reflect the nature of the time dynamic.

Such an approach has two major limitations which may act to remove any benefit from the undoubted reduction of analytical complexity. First it assumes implicitly that this decomposition is reasonably first order correct: that the impact of the individual elements is more important than their interaction terms. To examine this assumption critically we need some alternative form of analysis and representation such as modelling the phenomena of interest as the co-evolution of firms and customers in a dynamic phase space, which allows for the fact that time and space interact. A particular difficulty in this representation would appear to be how we introduce what might be termed learning behaviour into the system. To use biologists' language, it is clear that, unlike species evolution, we must recognize that the process of adaptation has strong Lamarckian characteristics in that changes and adaptation can take place in direct response to the environment rather than purely Darwinian in that they can only result from random mutation and then selection.

Second, it assumes that the ways of representing the individual elements that we use, in particular market segmentation and product life cycle concepts, are in fact robust representations of the underlying phenomena. In terms of the adequacy of each element in its own terms, we need to look more closely at the ways in which individual improvements may be achieved and finally we might wish to consider whether it would be better to model partial interactions, say, between two elements only rather than the complete system.

The various ways of modelling the market space: imperfect competition, product-markets and networks

When we come to the question of the modelling and representation of the market space, we again face a range of forms from simple to complex. In economic terms, perhaps the simplest form lies in the developments, discussed above, heralded by both Chamberlin and Robinson when they originally and independently developed the notion of imperfect or monopolistic competition. It was, with hindsight, not a dramatic move, but it remains a crucial insight that there is no reason why the demand curve should be horizontal except in the particular logic of perfect competition. To make the demand curve downward sloping would be to recognize the possibility of some form of price differentiation between suppliers in the market.

How then do we characterize the nature of the market space?

To move beyond the traditional economist notion of each firm facing a separate downward sloping but non-interacting demand curve, we need to develop a way of characterizing the nature of the space in which the firms compete. For convenience we will call this the market space and we will focus on the issue of what might be called the dimensionality of competition. In the limits the traditional imperfect competition model assumes that N firms compete in N dimensional space, that is that they do not interact, whereas the direct competition of the traditional economic model implies competition in N = 1 dimension only.

Differentiation in space: issues of market segmentation

The analysis of spatial competition has of course a long history, back at least to the classical

Hotelling model of linear competition such as that faced by the two ice-cream sellers on the sea-front. The basic Hotelling model however did capture the two critical issues in spatial competition: the notion of a space dimension which separated the various competitive suppliers as well as the fact that these suppliers themselves would have some degree of mobility. In traditional economic terms Hotelling was interested in establishing the equilibrium solution under these two considerations whereas in marketing we are often more concerned with the impact and likelihood of particular spatial moves although some notion of the stable long term equilibrium, if it exists, is obviously important. The Hotelling model provides us with the basic structure of spatial competition: a definition of the space domain, some model of the relationship between the positioning of the relevant suppliers within this space and their relative demands.

In marketing, the competitive space is generally characterized in terms of market segmentation. Market segmentation has, of course, received considerable attention in both marketing research and practice. There is by now a very large body of empirical work in the general field of market segmentation but even so there remain some critical problems. In particular:

1   We have evidence that the cross-elasticities with respect to different marketing mix elements are likely to be not only of different orders but actually imply different structures of relationship between individual product offerings.

2   Competitive behaviour patterns, which after all in a strict sense determine the nature of the experiment from which the elasticities

can be derived, seem to be, to use a term coined by Leeflang and Wittick (1993), 'out of balance' with the cross-elasticity data itself.[18]

The recent empirical evidence therefore raises severe questions about the commonly accepted notion of customer segmentation itself. Despite various caveats in the textbooks, there is a strong tendency to present segmentation as if:

(i)   There is little difference between customer segmentation and brand differentiation.

(ii)   'Closeness' of brands in terms of substitution can be represented in a two-dimensional diagram.

As a result of these two simplifying assumptions the notion of positioning has been given considerable emphasis (indeed in some cases, such as Ries and Trout (1981), almost exclusive concern) as a more strategic perspective on brand and product competition. Hence, it is asserted, we can make strategic statements about the positioning of the brand or product within its marketplace and leave more tactical marketing mix decisions to be taken within this strategic context.

Yet attempts to aggregate the specific evidence for cross-elasticities suggest that the patterns of interaction cannot be reduced in this way (or at least such reduction only explains a limited amount of the overall variance). This has led to the suggested use of overall indicators of competitive 'clout' and 'vulnerability' (Cooper and Nakanishi, 1988) as a better means of presenting aggregate results. Whilst this form of representation is also low dimensional, it bears little relationship to those we might encounter

---

[18] This, of course, raises questions about the nature and causes of this imbalance. Leeflang and Wittick, in their original approach, were particularly interested in the notion that forms of conjoint analysis could be used to determine the underlying customer trade-off matrix which is, of course, only partly revealed in the empirical customer elasticities (because individual customers can only respond to the actual offerings that are available) and which is 'assumed' (with some degree of bias and error) by individual competitors in determining their competitive actions and reactions. More recently they have argued that much of the managerial behaviour they observe could be explained by the imbalance in incentive structures in that management will rarely get criticized for reacting to competitive moves!

in more traditional maps generated from multi-dimensional scaling of attitude data. We can also argue even more radically that the search for any general form of intermediate and hence more 'strategic' representation of the market in these terms is basically flawed and that so-called 'tactical' marketing-mix decisions are the very essence of practical strategy. So far, we unfortunately have limited empirical evidence: there is undoubtedly a case that both the longevity of popular brands and the stability of individual purchase patterns (see early work by Ehrenberg (1972) and more recently Ehrenberg and Uncles (1995)) might suggest that any positional changes in competitive space are not only difficult to predict but also likely to be infrequent.

Beyond this the topic of market segmentation is covered in much greater depth elsewhere in this book. For the purposes of this chapter we wish to concentrate on the specific question as to how far segmentation provides us with an appropriate definition of the space within which competition evolves. In this sense the key questions are, as we discussed above, about the dimensionality of the space concerned, the stability of the demand function and the degree of mobility for individual firms (or more correctly individual offerings) in terms of repositioning.

These are in practice very difficult questions to deal with for two critical reasons:

(i)   The nature of the choice process is such that for many offerings, individual consumers choose from a portfolio of items rather than merely make exclusive choices, and, hence, in principle it is difficult to isolate the impact of one offering from the others in the portfolio.

(ii) The dimensions of the choice space are often inferred from the responses to current offerings and therefore it is difficult to distinguish between the effects of current offerings and some notion of an underlying set of preference structures.

Segmentation and positioning

In principle we can describe the nature of spatial competition in a market either in demand terms or in supply terms. Market segmentation represents the demand perspective on structure whilst competitive positioning represents the supply perspective.

Market segmentation takes as its starting point assumptions about the differing requirements that individual customers have with respect to bundles of benefits in particular use situations. Most obviously in this context it is an 'ideal' approach in that it is effectively assumed that each customer can/does specify their own ideal benefit bundle and their purchase choice in the relevant use situation is based on proximity to this ideal point. In consumer psychology this is equivalent to an assumption that individuals have strong and stable preferences.

The competitive positioning approach uses consumer judgements, normally on an aggregate basis to the similarities and differences between specific competitive offerings. In principle this provides an analytical output roughly equivalent to the spatial distribution in the Hotelling model. Such an analysis can also be used to provide an estimate of the dimensionality of the discriminant space but in many situations for ease of presentation the results are presented in a constrained 2D format. Equally benefit segmentation studies can be used along with techniques such as factor analysis to try and arrive at an estimate of the dimensionality of the demand side.

We can be reasonably certain that the attitude space for customers in any particular market is generally, say, $N > 3$: factor analytical studies might suggest at least four or five and that of competitive offerings is of at least a similar order. Indeed in the latter case, if we considered the resource-based view of the firm very seriously we might go for a dimensionality as high as the number of competitors.

Of more interest from a strategy point-of-view is a relatively parsimonious view as to how we represent what happens in terms of actual purchase behaviour through time. Although there is relatively little high quality empirical and indeed theoretical work in this area so far, there are intriguing results to suggest that the dimensionality of this space can be effectively much reduced although we may still then have problems with some second order effects in terms of market evolution. There have been a number of attempts to apply segmentation analysis to behavioural data with much less information as to attitudes or intention. In one of the more detailed of such studies, Chintagunta (1994) suggested that the dimensionality of the revealed competitive space was two dimensional but even this might be really an overestimate. In his own interpretation of the results he focuses on the degree to which the data analysis reveals interesting differences in terms of brand position revealed by individual purchase patterns through time.

In fact, on closer inspection it is clear that we can achieve a high level of discrimination with the one-dimensional map where there are two distinct groupings, and one intermediate brand and one 'outlier' brand. It is significant that these groupings are neither brand nor pack-sized based, but a mixture.[19] In fact the only result in moving from the one dimensional to the two dimensional analysis, is that one brand has become less discriminated. Hence it would appear that we can rather surprisingly reduce the effective competitive space to a single dimension with the possibility of only some second order anomalies.

In terms of second order anomalies, we can also consider some of the issues raised by so-called 'compromise effect' in choice situations where the choice between two alternatives depends on other, less attractive, alternatives. In an intriguing paper Wernerfeld (1995b) argues that this effect can be systematically explained by the notion that consumers draw inferences about their own personal valuations from the portfolio of offerings. However it may be that a compromise effect can also be seen as the result of mapping an N > 1 attribute and preference space on to an N = 1 set of purchase decisions.

A simple model of spatial competition might therefore be one in which a considerable amount of competition can be seen as along a single dimension, in circumstances in which multiple offerings are possible, and where there is no reason to believe a priori that individual offerings will be grouped either by common brand or specification, with a fixed entry cost for each item and a distribution of demand which is multi-modal. To this extent it may actually be true that the very simplifications that we criticized in Porter's three strategies approach may be reasonably appropriate in building a first order model of competitive market evolution. In the short run, following the notion of 'clout' and 'vulnerability', we might expect changes in position in this competitive dimension could be a function of a whole range of what might often be seen as tactical as well as strategic marketing actions.

We must now consider, however, in more detail how we might incorporate a longer-term time dimension.

Differentiation in time: beyond the PLC – characterizing the nature of competitive market evolution

The product life cycle remains an oft used model to represent the nature of time effects in product markets. It has the advantage that it does represent the most simple form of path development for any product (introduction, growth, maturity, decline), but, as has been widely recognized, this remains a highly stylized representation of the product sales pattern for most products during their lifetime. Whilst it is reasonably clear that it is difficult if not impossible to propose a better generic time pattern, any such pattern is subject to considerable distortion as a result of interactions with changes in

[19] (a) Surf 32 and Wisk 32 and Wisk 64; (b) Tide 64, Tide 96, Tide 128; (c) one 'intermediate', Era Plus 64; (d) one outlier, Surf 64.

technology as well as both customer and competitor behaviour.

It would seem that this is an area in which we lack some important research evidence. It is currently not only difficult to provide any advice on the reduced set of likely patterns (given that we know that the single pattern is relatively infrequent), but also to provide any advice on the most significant contingencies and interactions. Anecdotal evidence might suggest that the most important positive moderating effects (those which shift the sales level upwards) are to be found in the case of new uses amongst customers encouraged by supplier behaviour whilst the most common causes of downward moderation is to be found in competitive reaction. However a cynic might suspect this was another case of attribution bias and that we need more systematic and rigorous research.

Beyond this, more recent research on the process of market evolution has attempted to incorporate some insights from another area, evolutionary ecology. In particular work on the extensive Disk-drive database, which gives quarterly data on all disk drive manufacturers, has allowed Christiansen (1997) and Freeman (1997) to look at the ways in which at the early stages in the market development, the existence of competitive offerings seems to encourage market growth whereas of course at later stages the likelihood of firm exit increases with firm density. Other computer-related industries have also provided the opportunity for empirical work on some of the issue relating to both the impact of standardization, modularization and the nature of generation effects (Sanchez, 1995), although in the latter case it must be admitted that the effects themselves can sometimes be seen as marketing actions in their own right.

Much of the market shift towards standardization as it evolves can be seen as analogous to more recent work on the mathematics of chaos, and, in particular, questions about the nature of boundaries between domains of chaos and those of order – often labelled the phenomena of complexity (Cohen and Stewart, 1995). Whether

we can use such models to provide a better understanding of the nature of market evolution beyond the basic analogy remains an important question for empirical research, which we consider further when we look at the so-called markets-as-network perspective.

Research in marketing strategy: fallacies of free lunches and the nature of answerable research questions

Distinguishing between information about means, variances and outliers

As we indicated at the start of this chapter, much research in marketing strategy attempts to address what is in some senses an impossible question: what is the nature of a successful competitive marketing strategy? Such a question presumes the equivalent of a free lunch: we research to find the equivalent of a universal money machine. Before we explore this issue further we need to establish a few basic principles. The competitive process is such that:

(i)   Average performance can only produce average results which in the general nature of a competitive system means that success is related to above average and sometimes even outlier levels of performance.

(ii) The basic principle of rational expectations is that we can expect our competitors to be able on average to interpret any public data to reveal profitable opportunities as well as we can. In more direct terms it means that on average competitors are as clever or as stupid as stupid as we are. A combination of public information and the impact of basic rational expectations approaches therefore means that the route to success cannot lie in simply exploiting public information in an effective manner, although such a strategy may enable a firm to improve its own performance.

(iii)   As we have discussed above, the basis of individual firm or unit performance is a complex mix of both firm, competitor and market factors. We therefore can expect that any attempt to explain performance will be subject to considerable error given that it is difficult if not impossible to identify an adequate range of variables which cover both the specifics of the firm's own situation and the details of the market and competitor behaviour.

For these reasons research in marketing strategy, as in the strategy field as a whole, has almost always tended to be in one of the two categories:

(a)   Database, quantitative analysis which has relied on statistical and econometric approaches to produce results which indicate certain independent variables which on average correlate with performance. As McCloskey and Ziliak (1996) indicated more generally in econometric work, there is a danger that we often confuse statistical significance for what they term economic significance. This notion of economic significance can from a managerial perspective be decomposed into two elements: first the extent to which the relationship identified actually relates to a significant proportion of the variation in the dependent variable and second the extent to which even if it does this regularity actually enables one to produce a clear prescription for managerial action.

(b)   Case study based research on selected firms, often based on the notion of some form of outliers such as those that perform particularly well. Here the problems are the extent to which the story which is told about the particular nature of the success concerned can be used to guide action in other organizations. In practice this often results in managerial prescriptions that are rather tautological and at the same time non-discriminating.

We will now consider examples of both types of this research.

Market share and ROI: the 10 per cent rule in practice

One of the most famous results from the PIMS (Profit Impact of Market Strategy) database was that first reported by Bob Buzzell, Brad Gale and Ralph Sultan in the *Harvard Business Review* in 1976 under the title 'Market Share: A Key to Profitability'. They reported on the relationship between ROI and market share on a cross-sectional basis within the then current PIMS database. Although over the years estimates of the R^2 of this relationship have varied, it generally shows a value around 10 per cent up to a maximum of 15 per cent. We can start by simulating the original data that was used (Figure 2.4).

Figure 2.4 is a scatter plot of 500 datapoints (notional observations) where the relationship between the two implied variables is actually the equivalent of an R^2 of 0.12 or 12 per cent[20]. In their original article Buzzell, Gale and Sultan 'removed' much of the variation by calculating cohort means. We can do the same and also use more typical modern computer generated graphics to represent the results (Figure 2.5).

The cohort mean approach, although now not commonly used in strategy research of this sort, will show, as above, some deviations from the straight line trend at sample sizes such as 500 but as samples get even larger the deviations get, on average, even smaller: indeed some text-

---

[20] Because of the statistical nature of the data distribution in the PIMS database (the fact that it is not strictly normal), it is only possible to simulate a dataset which has either the right range or the right slope within the correct proportion of variance explained. This simulation is based on the right range of values so that the extreme points are estimated correctly. As a result, however, the actual slope is underestimated (see Wensley, 1997a, 1997b; Roberts, 1997).

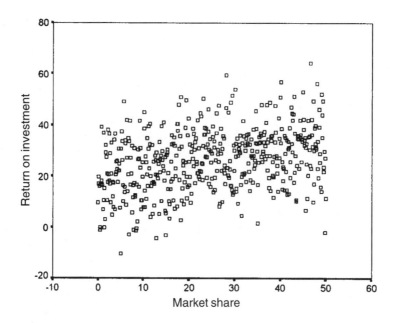

Figure 2.4   A scatter plot of 500 databases (notional observations)

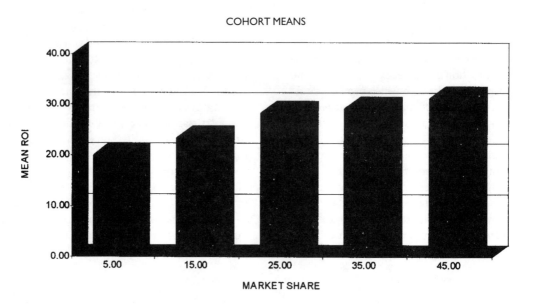

Figure 2.5   Cohort means

book representations of the results go as far as merely illustrating the trend with no deviations at all. Hence in the process of producing a clearer message from the data we have nearly eliminated nine-tenths of the variability in our performance variable.

How does one explain the 'unexplained' 90 per cent?

If we return to the scatter diagram and treat it as if it represented the current performance of 500 business units within a single corporate portfolio in terms of the relationship between return on investment (ROI) and market share, then we can see some of the problems that arise when we try and make managerial evaluations. The first set of problems relate to the nature of the data itself and the way in which the axes are measured. In most analysis of this sort, and in the PIMS data as we discussed above, the data is essentially cross-sectional, that is, it is either annual or averaged out over a longer fixed period. It therefore excludes any lead or lag effects and also compensates for particular one-off effects only to the extent that they are already discounted from the input data which is normally based on management accounts. The nature of the axes in a standard market share/ROI analysis is a problem in that they are both ratios. There are very considerable advantages that accrue from using ratios in this situation: most obviously the fact that it is possible to plot on the same graph units of very different absolute sizes, but we do then have the problem of measurement errors in both the numerator and denominator for both axes.

Finally, the basic data is also inevitably limited in the extent to which it can measure the specifics of any particular business unit situation. Using basic financial and accounting data we cannot take into account issues such as effectiveness as well as the degree of integration in terms of marketing and other activities.

However we must also put this overall critique of 'market share/return' analysis in con-

text. We should not underestimate the original impact of the 'market share' discovery. Even if it only 'explains' around 10 per cent of financial performance, this is still a considerable achievement. The problem is that, as we have seen, even at this level we face difficult interpretation problems. In the end, one perhaps concludes that its greatest impact was merely that it legitimized debate and discussion about key competitive market assumptions in any strategy dialogue.

Getting to management action: the additional problem of economics

Even if we can identify the source of a particular success or indeed the cause of a particular failure it is a big jump to assuming that suitable action can be taken at no cost or even at a   cost which is justified by the subsequent benefits.

We therefore need to overlay our notion of practical significance with one of economic significance: a factor or set of factors which explain a significant proportion of success can also be used as a decision rule for subsequent successful management action. This is a big jump. To return to the market share/ROI relationship, even if we conclude that there is a significant correlation between market share and profitability, we have to make two further assumptions to justify an economic rule of 'investing' in market share. First we have to move from the more general notion of 'correlation' or 'explanation' to the much more specific one of 'causation' and, second, we have to assume that, whatever its benefits, market share is somehow underpriced. If our first assumption is correct then broadly it can only be underpriced if either our competitors, both current and potential, have a different view or, for some unspecified reason, happen to value the asset (market share) significantly lower than we do. In fact in specific situations this latter assumption may be rather less unlikely than it at first appears: our competitors could indeed value the benefits differently given their differing portfolio of assets and market positions but it all depends on the specifics and the details of the individual situation rather than the general.

In the end, it is likely that the continued search for general rules for strategic success via statistical analysis and large databases will prove illusory. This does not make the research effort worthless, we merely have to be realistic about what can and cannot be achieved. After all, the in-depth case study narrative approach, which we will consider shortly, often results in another type of economic rule: the truth which is virtually impossible to apply. Perhaps the best example is to be found in Peters and Waterman's original work. Amongst many memorable criteria for success to be found in *In Search of Excellence* was that undeniable one: the achievement of simultaneous 'loose-tight' linkages. To those who thought that this might seem contradictory Peters and Waterman (1982) provided the helpful observation that:

These are the apparent contradictions that turn out in practice not to be contradictions at all. (p. 320)

The Honda case: interpreting success

One of the best known examples of a case history which has been interpreted to generate a number of marketing strategy lessons is the case of Honda and their entry into the American motor cycle market. The various interpretations and a set of comparative commentaries are to be found in a set of articles in the *California Management Review* (Mintzberg, 1996a).

In summary, the original consultancy study conducted for the UK government by the Boston Consulting Group interpreted the success that Honda enjoyed in the USA, particularly at the expense of the UK imports as the result of substantial economies of scale for their small bikes based on the Cub model, along with a market entry strategy to identify and exploit a new segment and set of customers. Richard Pascale, on the other hand, interviewed rather later a number of the key executives who had worked for

American Honda at the time and they told a story which suggested the whole operation was very much on a shoestring and the final success was down to a number of lucky breaks including a buyer from Sears persuading them to let him sell their small model bikes when they were really trying, and failing, to break into the big bike market.

The debate recorded in the *California Management Review* certainly illustrated how the same story can be interpreted in very different ways. It also emphasizes the problem that learning from the undoubted final success that Honda achieved can be very problematic: even perhaps for Honda itself. It would seem that in many ways one of the underlying dilemmas for Honda, as indeed for any new market entrant, was that, if they took the existing market structure as fixed and given, then the possibilities for them were remote; on the other hand market knowledge could only really hint at possibilities for new market structures.

In the end, Michael Goold (1996), who worked for BCG at the time, concludes that:

The (BCG) report does not dwell on how the Honda strategy was evolved and on the learning that took place. However, the report was commissioned for industry in crisis, with a brief of identifying commercially viable alternatives. The perspective required was managerial, not historical. And for most executives concerned with strategic management the primary interest will always be what should we do now?

Presumably the (Mintzberg) recommendation would be 'try something, see if it works and learn from your experience'; indeed there is some suggestion that one should specifically try probable non-starters. For the manager such advice would be unhelpful even irritating. 'Of course we should learn from experience' he will say, 'But we have neither the time nor the money to experiment with endless, fruitless non-starters'. Where the manager needs help is in what he should try to make work. This surely is exactly where strategic management thinking should endeavour to be useful.

Whilst Mintzberg (1996b) comments:

How then did BCG's clients actually learn from this report? And what lessons did BCG itself take from this particular bit of history? Did it take a good look at its own performance – do some analysis about the impact of its own analysis?

British motorcycle and parts exports to the United States collapsed to US$10 million in 1976, the year after the report was published. So much for the result of this practical managerial perspective. I believe that managers who have neither the time nor the money to experiment are destined to travel the road of the British motorcycle industry. How in the world can anyone identify those 'endless, fruitless non-starters' in advance? To assume such an ability is simply arrogance, and would, in fact, have eliminated many, if not most of the really innovative products we have come to know.

In the terms of our previous analysis we could argue that Goold is focusing attention on the 10 per cent that can be explained analytically whilst Mintzberg is arguing not only that the 90 per cent is much more important but, much more importantly, that a realization of specific causes of success can be achieved through processes such as learning. This is in practice a strong assertion about the efficacy of learning processes in organizations that others might dispute.[21]

In a further and more recent commentary on the whole debate about the Honda study, Mair (1999) argues that:

'the weaker hypothesis is therefore that Honda seeks ways to make apparent contradictory polarities in strategic management concepts mutually compatible. A strong hypothesis is that Honda has found ways to make the polarities mutually supportive, so that they are in fact positively rather than negatively correlated.

This suggests that . . . an appropriate paradigm under which the strategy industry could learn from Honda would be to analyse and reconstruct how Honda does not choose between the polar positions of the dichotomies of strategic management but synthesises them in its strategy making. This . . . would of course include analysis of the problems that arise when Honda fails to implement such an approach, notably the apparent over-domination of

---

[21] Perhaps most obviously James March, who in a number of contributions has argued that notions such as forgetting and foolishness are in fact much more important.

the product led aspects of strategy as revealed by the crisis in the 1990s'.

The recourse to processes, people and purpose in marketing as well as strategy as a whole

More recently in marketing strategy, as in strategy as a whole, there has been a move away from analysis based on real substantive recommendations for management action towards a concern more for processes, people and purposes rather than structure, strategies and systems. This change in emphasis was particularly introduced by Bartlett and Ghoshal (1995) in their influential *Harvard Business Review* article.

Whilst this shift can be seen as a reasonable response to our lack of substantive generalizable knowledge about the nature of successful marketing strategies in a competitive marketplace, as we have discussed above, it should also be seen as one which itself has rather limited evidence to support it. In marketing strategy in particular, two areas can be identified where this trend has been very evident and we will look critically at both of these: the shift towards a focus on networks and relationship marketing, and the increased emphasis on marketing processes within the firm.

Markets as networks

It is clear, as Easton (1990) has indicated, that actual firm relationships must be seen on a spectrum between outright competition at one end and collusion at the other. At the very least, such a self-evident observation raises the issue of the firm (or business unit) as the basic, and often only, unit of analysis: in certain circumstances we might more appropriately consider an informal coalition of such firms as the key unit:

Earlier, the border of the company was seen as the dividing line between co-operation and conflict – co-operation within the company and conflict in relation to all external units. The corresponding means for co-ordination are hierarchy and the market mechanism. The existence of relationships makes this picture much more diffuse. There are great opportunities for co-operation with a lot of external units forming, for example, coalitions. Thus, it is often more fruitful to see the company as a part of a network instead of a free and independent actor in an atomistic market. (Hakansson, 1987, p. 13)

However, the recognition that there is a network of relationships is merely the first step. Approaches need to be developed for the analysis of the network. Hakansson has, for instance, suggested that the key elements of any network are actors, activities and resources. He also suggests that the overall network is bound together by a number of forces including functional interdependence, as well as power, knowledge and time-related structure.

There is a danger in confusing a detailed descriptive model with a simple but robust predictive one, let alone one which aids the diagnostic process. The basic micro-economic framework which underlies the 'competitive advantage' approach, central to much marketing strategy analysis, should not be seen as an adequate description of the analytical and processual complexities in specific situations. It is a framework for predicting the key impacts of a series of market mediated transactions: at the very least outcomes are the joint effect of decisions themselves and the selection process. In this sense the only valid criticisms of the application of such a model is that either the needs of the situation are not met by the inherent nature of the model or that the model fails to perform within its own terms.

Relationship marketing

Equally we may wonder how far the new found concern for relationship marketing is indeed new at all. The recognition that customers faced switching costs and that therefore the retention of existing customers was clearly an effective economic strategy is certainly not new. One can therefore sympathize with Baker (1992) when he commented:

For example, the propositions that companies need to understand the industry infrastructure and/or that working closely with customers is likely to improve product development success rates have been known and accepted many years now and are embedded in the curricula of most business schools. (p. 88)

on the book by Regis McKenna (1992) on *Relationship Marketing*.

More recently, Mattsson (1997) has considered much more critically the relationship between the underlying approaches in the 'markets as networks' and relationship marketing perspectives. He rightly observed that much of the problem lay in the various different approaches claiming to represent relationship marketing:

My conclusion is that if we take the limited view of relationship marketing, we come close to the first extreme position stated in the beginning of this article: relationship marketing and the network perspective have very little in common. Some relationship marketing aspects are even contradictory to basic views in the network perspective. Relationship marketing in its limited interpretation is just a marketing strategy aimed to increase customer loyalty, customer satisfaction and customer retention. Relationship marketing is aided by modern information technology that makes it possible to individualise communication with customers in a mass market. In that sense relationship marketing is just a basic application of the marketing management thinking.

However, let us consider the extended view that the relationship marketing means true interaction between the parties over time, a relatively high mutual dependency between seller and buyer and a major concern for how individual relationships are interconnected in nets and networks. Then we will come much closer to my second initial position that relationship marketing and the network perspective have much to gain from more research interaction and mutual awareness than what is presently the case. Relationship marketing research would benefit from the following aspects of network perspective research: more focus on embeddedness of actors and relationships, more consideration of the buyer's point of view, more descriptive studies on interaction and relationships over time, more concern at the meso and macro levels in the governance structure, more use of longitudinal research methods, including case studies.

Obviously, both relationship marketing and the network perspective must become increasingly aware of, and contribute to, research developments in a broader social science framework where the focus is on the function of relationships between economic actors.

It may well be that the relationship marketing movement will have a rather similar impact on marketing as the market share once did in the 1970s and early 1980s. As such the renewed emphasis on the nature of the customer relationship, which is self-evidently important in industrial markets, will encourage retail marketers to take their customers more seriously, even to regard them as intelligent and rational agents. To do so, however, would also acknowledge severe scepticism about the various developments in relationship marketing such as 'loyalty' cards and one-to-one targeting.

However, it may also be true that the relationship and network perspective will in the longer run change our perception of the critical strategic questions faced by firms as they and their 'markets' evolve and develop. Easton *et al.* (1993), for instance, suggest that the notion of competition and markets is really only appropriate at specific stages in the life cycle of the firm or business unit. Indeed, their approach could be taken further to suggest that at the time when there is significant indeterminacy in terms of competitor and customer choice, this way of characterizing strategic choice is, of itself, of limited either theoretical or practical value. Almost by definition the product technology and market structure need to be relatively stable for such strategic choices to be formulated, yet by this stage the feasible choice set itself may be very restricted.[22]

Emergent or enacted environments

The notion of emergent phenomena has itself emerged as a key concept in organizational strategy. Much of the credit for this must go to Mintzberg (1994) but ironically his analysis of the concept itself has been rather limited. Indeed in his more recent work, he has tended to define the nature of emergent phenomena in a rather idiosyncratic manner:

Much as planners can study and interpret patterns in the organization's own behavior to identify its emergent strategies, so too can they study and interpret patterns in the external environment to identify possible opportunities and threats (including as already noted, the patterns of competitors' actions in order to identify their strategies). (p. 375)

This implies that emergent phenomena are such that they can be related ex post to intentions or actions through time of the individual actors. However a more common use of the term emergence incorporates some notion of interpretation at different levels of aggregation. After all, for instance, as a number of authors have previously commented, markets themselves are emergent phenomena. It was originally Adam Smith's insight that each actor in a market following their own interest could under certain conditions create an overall situation of welfare maximization: in this sense the invisible hand was much more effective than any attempts at local or even global optimization.

Others have paid much greater attention to the nature of emergent properties, but we also need to recognize a further distinction between what have been termed 'emergent' and 'enacted' environments. In a number of relevant areas, such as information systems, there is no overall agreement on the nature of the differences (see Mingers, 1995) but in the absolute an emergent environment is one in which there are a set of rules but they are generally undetermining of the outcome states or at least the only way in which an outcome state can be predicted is by a process of simulation, whereas an enacted environment is one in which the nature of the environment is itself defined by the cognitive patterns of the constituents.

This distinction is particularly important when we consider the notion of 'markets-as-networks' as a perspective for understanding

---

[22] The argument is, of course, rather more complicated than this and relates to the previous debate between Child (1972) and Aldrich (1979) on the more general issue of strategic choice.

the nature of competitive market phenomena. If we understand the nature of the phenomena we are trying to understand as essentially emergent then there remains considerable value in attempting to model the relevant structure of rules or relationships that characterize the environment.[23] If on the other hand, we are more inclined to an enactive view of the relationship between organizations and their environment, we need to consider the degree to which the structure of the network is not more than a surface phenomenon resulting itself from other deeper processes: in this analysis we need to consider the phenomena that Giddens (1979) identifies in terms of 'structuration'. In this process agents and organizations are simultaneously both creators of structures but also have their action constrained by these structures.

However, even if we are willing to give a relatively privileged ontological status to the detailed network structure in a particular context, we may still face insurmountable problems in developing high levels of regularities from a more detailed analysis. As Cohen and Stewart (1995) assert:

We've argued that emergence is the rule rather than the exception, and that there are at least two distinct ways for high level rules to emerge from low-level rules – simplexity and complicity.[24] Can we write down the equations for emergence? The short answer is no . . . Essentially what is needed is a mathematical justification for the belief that simple high-level rules not only can, but usually do, emerge from complex interactions of low-level rules. By 'emerge' we mean that a detailed derivation of the high-level rules from

the low-level ones would be so complicated that it could never be written down in full let alone understood. (p. 436)

It seems that whilst Cohen and Stewart warn convincingly of the dangers of drowning in the detail of low-level rules, they give only limited useful advice as to the practical nature of the alternatives. There has recently been a spate of interest in mathematical approaches under the general title of 'Complexity'. In the context of the economics of forms of market organization, perhaps the most obvious is that due to Kaufmann (1995):[25]

Organisations around the globe were becoming less hierarchical, flatter, more decentralised, and were doing so in the hopes of increased flexibility and overall competitive advantage. Was there much coherent theory about how to decentralise, I wondered. For I was just in the process of finding surprising new phenomena, that hinted at the possibility of a deeper understanding of how and why flatter, more decentralised organisations – business, political or otherwise – might actually be more flexible and carry an overall competitive advantage. (pp. 245–6)

Kaufmann goes on to discuss the logic of what he calls a 'patch' structure in which at various levels the form of organization involves a series of relatively autonomous sub-units which under certain conditions are more effective at achieving a system wide performance maxima compared with the more extreme options which he terms rather controversially, the fully integrated 'Stalinist' system, or the fully autonomous 'Italian leftist' system!

---

[23] Actually even this statement incorporates another critical assumption. As Mingers (1995) notes in commenting on assumptions about the nature of social systems and the degree to which they can be seen as self-producing (autopoietic), even those who develop such an analysis define the nature of the organizations and their environment in unexpected ways: 'Luhmann . . . in conceptualising societies as autopoietic . . . [sees them] as constituted not by people but by communications. Societies and their component subsystems are networks of communicative events, each communication being triggered by a previous one and leading in turn to another . . . People are not part of society but part of its environment.' (p. 211)

[24] Cohen and Stewart use specific meanings for both 'sim-

plexity' and 'complicity' which roughly describe phenomena where in the former case similar low-level rules create high-level similar structures whereas in the latter case 'totally different rules converge to produce similar features and so exhibit the same large scale structural patterns' (p. 414). As they emphasize, in the case of complicity one of the critical effects is the way in which 'this kind of system . . . *enlarges the space of the possible*' (original emphasis).

[25] With a fine, if unintentional sense of irony, the chapter in Kauffmann's book which addresses these questions has the same title as the Peters and Waterman classic *In Search of Excellence*. Interestingly, however, Kauffmann is drawing a distinction between the 'lesser' criteria of 'excellence' compared with 'optimality'!

However despite the fact that some of these general notions are now to be seen in the mainstream of strategic management thought (see Stacey, 1995), we should remain cautious. Horgan (1997) in a recent commentary suggests that we should be cautious of the likely advances to be made in the field that he has dubbed 'chaoplexity':

So far, chaoplexologists have created some potent metaphors, the butterfly effect, fractals, artificial life, the edge of chaos, self-organised criticality. But they had not told us anything about the world that is both concrete and truly surprising, either in a negative, or in a positive sense. They have slightly extended the borders of our knowledge in certain areas, and they have more sharply delineated the boundaries of knowledge elsewhere. (p. 226)

Marketing processes

Not surprisingly, the 1990s has also seen a renewed interest in the marketing process and particularly in the nature of the processes which support the development of a marketing orientation. This approach has been encouraged by the renewed attempts to model the nature of marketing orientation due to both Narver and Salter (1990) and Kohli and Jaworski (1990). In essence the shift is one that Herb Simon (1979) recognized in his original distinction between substantive and procedural rationality in which he suggested that it was an appropriate response to the problem of bounded rationality to focus attention more on the appropriate process for arriving at a particular choice rather than developing a general analytical approach to make that choice in any particular situation.

Much empirical research, in particular that based on key informant surveys, has been undertaken to establish the extent to which various operational measures of marketing orientation are correlated with commercial success. On top of this there has been work to establish some of the possible antecedents for such orientation including measures related to the accumulation and organizational dispersion of market research data. The results remain somewhat

contradictory but it seems likely that some level of association will finally emerge although whether it will achieve the minimum 10 per cent target which we considered earlier is rather another question.[26]

On top of this, we need to address more fundamental questions about the underlying logic of procedural rationality in this context. As we have suggested above, it is reasonable to argue that some consideration in any marketing context of each element in the 3Cs (customers, competitors and channels) must surely be seen as sensible. How far such a process should be routinized within a particular planning or decision making schema is another matter. Much of the writing in the area of marketing orientation suggests that the appropriate mechanisms and procedures are unproblematic, yet everyday experience in organizations suggests that achieving effective response to the market is difficult and indeed maybe not susceptible to programmed responses.

Rumelt's observations on the Honda debate – three explanations: economics, adaptability and intention

In our overall assessment of the nature of marketing strategy, it is perhaps appropriate to revisit the Honda debate. Rumelt in his own commentary on the debate suggests that actually successful strategies in most circumstances require aspects of all three elements: economic logic, organizational adaptability and managerial intention. As he argues, it is perhaps important to avoid too much emphasis on which element is more important and rather to recognize that each type of explanation is really addressing a different question. The nature of economics is that it inevitably explains the successes and failures after the event but it may give little guidance as to what informed and

---

[26] It is worth noting that even for samples of only 50, we can roughly speaking achieve a significant result, using the 'normal' criterion, and yet only have about 5 per cent of the variability 'explained'.

motivated the prior actions which is much more the domain of intention. Finally some form of adaptive behaviour is inevitably required when the competitive market context is evolving and changing.

Rather controversially, however, in the context of this chapter, Rumelt (1996) ends his discussion with the comment:

My own view is that the process/emergent school is right about good process being non-linear. A great deal of business success depends on generating new knowledge and on having the capabilities to react quickly and intelligently to this new knowledge. Thus peripheral vision and swift adaptation are critical. At the same time, I believe that the design school is right about the reality of forces like scale economies, accumulated experience, and the cumulative development of core competencies over time. These are strong forces and are not simply countered. But my own experience is that coherent strategy based upon analyses and understandings of these forces is much more often imputed than actually observed. Finally, I believe that strategic thinking is a necessary but greatly over-rated element in business success. If you know how to design great motorcycle engines, I can teach you all you need to know about strategy in a few days. If you have a PhD in strategy, years of labour are unlikely to give you ability to design great new motorcycle engines.

Conclusions: the limits of relevance and the problems of application

The study and application of marketing strategy therefore reflects a basic dilemma. The key demand in terms of application is to address the causes of individual firm or unit success in the competitive marketplace, yet we can be reasonably confident from a theoretical perspective that such knowledge is not systematically avail-

able because of the nature of the competitive process itself. In this way, the academic study of marketing strategy remains open to the challenge that it is not relevant to marketing practice. Yet to represent the problem solely in this way is to privilege one particular notion of the nature and use of academic research in marketing as well as the relationship between research and practice.[27] Recognizing the limits to our knowledge in marketing strategy may also help in a constructive way to define what can and cannot be achieved by more investigation and research.

There are a number of areas in which we can both improve our level of knowledge and provide some guidance and assistance in the development of strategy. First, we can identify some of the generic patterns in the process of market evolution which give some guidance as to how we might think about and frame appropriate questions to be asked in the development of marketing strategy. Such questions would be added to those we are used to using in any marketing management context such as the nature of the (economic) value added to the customer based on market research evidence and analysis. Recently it has been suggested in strategy that such additional questions are most usefully framed around questions of imitation and sustainability but rather as Dickinson (1992) argues[28] this really assumes sustainability is a serious option. It may be more appropriate to frame such additional questions around the more general patterns of market evolution: standardization, maturity of technology, stability of current networks, rather than attempt to address the unanswerable question of sustainability directly.

When it comes to the generics of success, we face an even greater problem. By definition any

---

[27] The issue of the relationship between theory and practice and the notion of relevance as the intermediary construct between the two is of course itself both problematic in general (Brownlie, 1998) as well as open to a range of further critical questions, particularly with respect to the institutional structures that have been developed and sustained on the assumption of the divide itself (Wensley, 1997c) and

therefore at some level represent interest in maintaining the divide but in the name of bridging it!

[28] Of course such a view about sustainability is also very much in tune with both Schumpeterian views about the nature of economic innovation and the general Austrian view about the nature of the economic system (Wensley, 1982; Jacobson, 1992).

approach which really depends on analysis of means or averages leaves us with a further dilemma: not only does any relative 'usable' explanation only provide us with a very partial picture where there are many unexplained outcomes, but also the very notion of a publicly available 'rule for success' in a competitive market is itself contradictory except in the context of a possible temporary advantage.[29] We can try and resolve the problem by looking at the behaviour of what might be called successful outliers but here we face a severe issue of interpretation. As we have seen, as we might expect the sources of such success are themselves ambiguous and often tautological: we often end up really asserting either that to be successful one needs to be successful or that the route to success is some ill-defined combination of innovation, effectiveness and good organization.

It may well be that the best we can do with such analysis is to map ways in which the variances of performance change in different market contexts: just like our finance colleagues we can do little more than identify the conditions under which variances in performance are likely to be greater and therefore through economic logic the average performance will increase to compensate for the higher risks.

Finally, we may need to recognize that the comfortable distinction between marketing management, which has often been framed in terms of the more tactical side of marketing and marketing strategy, is not really sustainable. At one level all marketing actions are strategic: we have little knowledge as to how specific even brand choices at the detailed level impact or not on the broad development of a particular market so we are hardly in a position to label some choices as strategic in this sense and others as not. On the other hand, the knowledge that we

already have and are likely to develop in the context of the longer-term evolutionary patterns for competitive markets will not really also enable us to engage directly with marketing managerial actions and choices at the level of the firm: the units of both analysis and description are likely to be different. In our search for a middle way which can inform individual practice it may well be that some of the thinking tools and analogies that we have already developed will prove useful, but very much as means to an end rather than solutions in their own right.

References

Abell, D. and Hammond, J. (1979) *Strategic Marketing Planning: Problems and Analytical Approaches*, Prentice-Hall, Englewood Cliffs, NJ.

Achrol, R. S (1991) Evolution of the Marketing Organisation: New Forms for Turbulent Environments, *Journal of Marketing*, **55**(4), 77–93.

Aldrich, H. E. (1979) *Organizations and Environments*, Prentice-Hall, Englewood Cliffs, NJ.

Baker, M. (1992) Book Review, *Journal of Marketing Management*, **9**, 97–98.

Bartlett, C. A. and Ghoshal, S. (1995) Changing the Role of Top Management: Beyond Systems to People, *Harvard Business Review*, **73**(3), May-June, 132–142.

Bettis, R. A. and Prahald, C. K. (1995) The Dominant Logic: Retrospective and Extension, *Strategic Management Journal*, **16**, 5–14.

Bogner, W. and Thomas, H. (1994) Core Competence and Competitive Advantage: A Model and Illustrative Evidence from the Pharmaceutical Industry, in G. Hamel and A. Heene (eds), *Competence Based Competition*, Wiley, Chichester.

Brownlie, D. (1998) Marketing Disequilibrium: On Redress and Restoration, in D. Brownlie, M. Saren, R. Wensley and R. Whittington (eds), *Rethinking Marketing*, Sage, London.

Buzzell, R. D., Gale, B. T. and Sultan, R. G. M.

---

[29] Indeed it would appear that in very rapid response markets such as currency markets this temporal advantage is itself measured only in seconds: it is reasonable to assume it is somewhat longer in product and service markets!

(1975) Market Share – A Key to Profitability, *Harvard Business Review*, **53**, Jan.–Feb., 97–106.

Caves, R. E. (1980) Industrial Organization, Corporate Strategy and Structure, *Journal of Economic Literature*, **43**, March, 64–92.

Caves, R. E. (1984) Economic Analysis and the Quest for Competitive Advantage, *American Economic Association Papers and Proceedings*, May, 130.

Caves, R. E. and Porter, M. E. (1977) From Entry Barriers to Mobility Barriers: Conjectural Decisions and Contrived Deterrence to New Competition, *Quarterly Journal of Economics*, **91**, May, 241–262.

Child, J. (1972) Organisational Structure, Environment and Performance: The Role of Strategic Choice, *Sociology*, **6**, 1–22.

Chintagunta, P. (1994) Heterogeneous Logic Model Implications for Brand Positioning, *Journal of Marketing Research*, **XXXI**, May, 304–311.

Christensen, C. M. (1997) *The Innovator's Dilemma*, Harvard Business School Press, Boston.

Cohen, J. and Stewart, I. (1995) *The Collapse of Chaos*, Penguin Books, USA.

Cooper, L. and Nakanishi, M. (1988) *Market Share Analysis: Evaluating Competitive Marketing Effectiveness*, Kluwer Academic Press, Boston.

Coyle, M. L. (1986) Competition in Developing Markets: The Impact of Order of Entry, Faculty of Management Studies Paper, University of Toronto, June.

Day, G. S. and Wensley, R. (1983) Marketing Theory with a Strategic Orientation, *Journal of Marketing*, Fall, 79–89.

Day, G. S. and Wensley, R. (1988) Assessing Advantage: A Framework for Diagnosing Competitive Superiority, *Journal of Marketing*, **52**, April, 1–20.

Dickinson, P. R. (1992) Toward a General Theory of Competitive Rationality, *Journal of Marketing*, **56**(1), Jan., 68–83.

Dolan, R. J. (1981) Models of Competition: A Review of Theory and Empirical Findings, in B. M. Enis and K. J. Roering (eds), *Review of Marketing*, American Marketing Association, Chicago, 224–234.

Easton, G. (1990) Relationship Between Competitors, in G. S. Day, B. Weitz and R. Wensley (eds), *The Interface of Marketing and Strategy*, JAI Press, Connecticut.

Easton, G., Burell, G., Rothschild, R. and Shearman, C. (1993) *Managers and Competition*, Blackwell, Oxford.

Ehrenberg, A. S. C. (1972) *Repeat Buying: Theory and Applications*, North-Holland, London.

Ehrenberg, A. S. C. and Uncles, M. (1995) Dirichlet-Type Markets: A Review, Working Paper, November.

Freeman, J. (1997) Dynamics of Market Evolution, *European Marketing Academy. Proceedings of the 26th Annual Conference*, May.

Fournier, S., Dobscha, S. and Mick, D. G. (1998) Preventing the premature death of Relationship Marketing, *Harvard Business Review*, Jan.-Feb., 42–50.

Giddens, A. (1979) *Central Problems in Social Theory: Action, Structure and Contradiction in Social Analysis*, London, Macmillan.

Goold, M. (1996) Learning, planning and strategy: extra time, *California Management Review*, **38**(4), 100–102.

Gould, S. J. (1987) *Time's Arrow, Time's Cycle: Myth and Metaphor in the Discovery of Geological Time*, Harvard University Press, Cambridge MA.

Gould, S. J. (1990) *Wonderful Life: the Burgess Shale and the Nature of History*, Hutchinson Radius, London.

Hakansson, H. (1987) *Industrial Technological Development: A Network Approach*, Croom Helm, London.

Hammer, M. and Champy, J. (1993) *Reengineering the Corporation: A Manifesto for Business Revolution*, London, Brealey.

Hannan, M. T. and Freeman, J. (1977) The Population Ecology of Organizations, *American Journal of Sociology*, **82**(5), 929–963.

Harland, C. and Wensley, R. (1997) Strategising Networks or Playing with Power: Understanding Interdependence in Both Industrial and Academic Networks, Working Paper presented at Lancaster/Warwick Conference on New Forms of Organization, Warwick, April.

Henderson, B. (1980) Strategic and Natural Competition, *BCG Perspectives*, 231.

Henderson, B. D. (1983) The Anatomy of Competition, *Journal of Marketing*, **2**, 7–11.

Henderson, J. M. and Quant, R. E. (1958) *Microeconomic Theory: A Mathematical Approach*, McGraw Hill, New York.

Hofer, C. W. and Schendel, D. (1977) *Strategy Formulation: Analytical Concepts*, West Publishing, St Paul, MN.

Horgan, J. (1997) *The End of Science*, Broadway Books, New York.

Hunt, M. S. (1972) Competition in the Major Home Appliance Industry, 1960–1970. Unpublished doctoral dissertation, Harvard University.

Jacobson, R. (1992) The 'Austrian' School of Strategy, *Academy of Management Review*, (Oct.).

Jacobson, R. (1994) The Cost of the Market Share Quest, Working Paper, Seattle: University of Washington.

Jacobson, R. and Aaker, D. (1985) Is Market Share All That It's Cracked Up To Be? *Journal of Marketing*, **49**(4), Fall, 11–22.

Jones, H. J. (1926) *The Economics of Private Enterprise*, Pitman and Sons, London.

Kaufmann, S. (1995) *At Home in the Universe*, Oxford University Press, New York.

Kay, J. (1993) *Foundations of Corporate Success*, Oxford University Press, Oxford,

Kelly, K. (1997) Peters Provocations, *Wired*, December, 204–210.

Kohli, A. K. and Jaworski, B. J. (1990) Market Orientation: The Construct, Research Propositions and Managerial Implications, *Journal of Marketing*, **54**(2), April, 1–18.

Kotler, P. (1991) Philip Kotler Explores the New Marketing Paradigm, *Marketing Science Institute Review*, Spring.

Kierstead, B. S. (1972) Decision Taking and the Theory of Games, in C. F. Carter and J. L. Ford (eds), *Uncertainty and Expectation in Economics:*

Essays in Honour of G. L. Shackle, Blackwell, Oxford.

Lambkin, M. and Day, G. (1989) Evolutionary Processes in Competitive Markets: Beyond the Product Life Cycle, *Journal of Marketing*, July, **53**(3), 4–20.

Leeflang, P. S. H. and Wittick, D. (1993) Diagnosing Competition: Developments and Findings, in G. Laurent, G. L. Lillien and B. Pras (eds), *Research Traditions in Marketing*, Kluwer Academic, Norwell, MA.

Levins, R. and Leowontin, R. (1985) *The Dialectical Biologist*, Harvard University Press, Cambridge, MA.

Mair, A. (1999) The Business of Knowledge: Honda and the Strategy Industry, *Journal of Management Studies* (forthcoming).

Mattsson, L.-G. (1997) 'Relationship Marketing' and the 'Markets-as-Networks Approach' – A Comparative Analysis of Two Evolving Streams of Research, *Journal of Marketing Management*, **13**, 447–461.

McCloskey, D. N. and Ziliak, S. T. (1996) The Standard Error of Regressions, *Journal of Economic Literature*, XXXIV (March), 97–114.

McGee, J. and Thomas, H. (1986) Strategic Groups: Theory, Research and Taxonomy, *Strategic Management Journal*, **7**, 141–160.

McKelvey, B. (1982) *Organisational Systematics: Taxonomy, Evolution, Classification*, University of California Press, Berkeley, CA.

McKenna, R. (1992) *Relationship Marketing*, Century Business.

Mingers, J. (1995) *Self-Producing Systems*, Plenum Press, New York.

Mintzberg, H. (1973) *The Nature of Managerial Work*, Harper and Row, New York.

Mintzberg, H. (1994) *The Rise and Fall of Strategic Planning*, Prentice-Hall, Englewood Cliffs, NJ.

Mintzberg, H. (1996a) CMR Forum: the Honda Effect Revisited, *California Management Review*, **38**(4), 78–79.

Mintzberg, H. (1996b) Reply to Michael Goold, *California Management Review*, **38**(4), 96–99.

Moorthy, J. S. (1985) Using Game Theory to Model Competition, *Journal of Marketing*

Research, **22** (August), 262–282.

Morrison, A. and Wensley, R. (1981) A Short History of the Growth/Share Matrix: Boxed Up or Boxed In? *Journal of Marketing Management*, **7**(2), April, 105–129.

Muth, J. F. (1961) Rational Expectations and the Theory of Price Movements, *Econometrica*, 29 July.

Narver, J. C. and Slater, S. F. (1990) The effect of market orientation on business profitability, *Journal of Marketing*, October, **54**(4), 20–35.

Ohmae, K. (1982) *The Mind of the Strategist*, McGraw-Hill, London.

Peters, T. J. and Waterman, R. H. (1982) *In Search of Excellence*, Harper and Row, New York.

Pettigrew, A. M. (1973) *The Politics of Organisational Decision Making*, Tavistock, London.

Pontin, A. J. (1982) *Competition and Coexistence*, Pitman-Longman, London.

Porter, M. E. (1979) The Structure Within Industries and Companies' Performance, *Review of Economics and Statistics*, **61**, May, 214–227.

Porter, M. E. (1980) *Competitive Strategy*, Free Press, New York.

Porter, M. E. (1981) The Contribution of Industrial Organization to Strategic Management, *Academy of Management Review*, **6**, 609–620.

Porter, M. E. (1985) *Competitive Advantage*, Free Press, New York.

Porter, M. E. (1990) *The Competitive Advantage of Nations*, Free Press, New York.

Prahalad, C. K. and Bettis, R. A. (1989) The Dominant Logic: A New Linkage Between Diversity and Performance, *Strategic Management Journal*, **10**(6), 523–552.

Prahalad, C. K. and Hamel, G. (1990) The Core Competence of the Corporation, *Harvard Business Review*, May-June, 79–91.

Ries, A. and Trout, J. (1981) *Positioning: The Battle for your Mind*, McGraw-Hill, London.

Roberts, K. (1997) Explaining Success – Hard Work, Not Illusion, *Business Strategy Review*, **8**(2), 75–77.

Rumelt, R. P. (1996) The Many Faces of Honda, *Californian Management Review*, **38**(4), 103–111.

Sanchez, R. (1995) Strategic Flexibility in Product Competition, *Strategic Management Journal*, **16** (Special Issue), 135–159.

Saunders, J. (1995) Invited Response to Wensley, *British Journal of Management*, **6** (Special Issue), S89–S91.

Senge, P. (1992) *The Fifth Discipline: The Art and Practice of the Learning Organization*, Century Business, London.

Simon, H. A. (1979) Rational Decision Making in Business Organizations, *American Economic Review*, September.

Stacey, R. D. (1995) The Science of Complexity: An Alternative Perspective for Strategic Change Processes, *Strategic Management Journal*, **16**(6), September.

Waterman, R. H. (1988) *The Renewal Factor*, Bantam Books, London.

Weick, K. E. (1976) Educational Organizations as Loosely Coupled Systems, *Administrative Science Quarterly*, **21**, 1–19.

Wensley, R. (1982) PIMS and BCG: New Horizon or False Dawn, *Strategic Management Journal*, **3**, 147–153.

Wensley, R. (1990) The Voice of the Consumer?: Speculations on the Limits to the Marketing Analogy, *European Journal of Marketing*, **24**(7), 49–60.

Wensley, R. (1994) Strategic Marketing: A Review, in M. J. Baker (ed), *The Marketing Book*, 3rd edn, Butterworth–Heinemann, Oxford, pp. 33–53.

Wensley, R. (1995) A Critical Review of Research in Marketing, *British Journal of Management*, **6** (Special Issue), December, S63–S82.

Wensley, R. (1996) Book Review: Henry Mintzberg and Kevin Kelly, *BAM Newsletter*, Spring, 4–7.

Wensley, R. (1997a) Explaining Success: The Rule of Ten Percent and the Example of Market Share, *Business Strategy Review*, **8**(1), Spring, 63–70.

Wensley, R. (1997b) Rejoinder to 'Hard Work, Not Illusion', *Business Strategy Review*, **8**(2), Summer, 77.

Wensley, R. (1997c) Two Marketing Cultures in Search of the Chimera of Relevance, Keynote address at joint AMA and AM seminar 'Marketing without borders', Manchester, July 7.

Wernerfeld, B. (1984) A Resource-based View of the Firm, *Strategic Management Journal*, **5**(2), 171–180.

Wernerfeld, B. (1995a) The Resource-based View of the Firm: Ten Years After, *Strategic Management Journal*, **16**, 171–174.

Wernerfeld, B. (1995b) A Rational Reconstruction of the Compromise Effect, *Journal of Consumer Research*, **21**, March, 627–633.

CHAPTER 3

Strategic marketing planning: theory and practice

MALCOLM McDONALD

Summary

In order to explore the complexities of developing a strategic marketing plan, this chapter is written in three sections.

The first describes the strategic marketing planning process itself and the key steps within it.

The second section provides guidelines for the marketer which will ensure that the input to the marketing plan is customer focused and considers the strategic dimension of all of the relationships the organization has with its business environment.

The final section looks at the barriers which prevent organizations from reaping the benefits which stem from a well-considered strategic marketing plan.

Introduction

Although it can bring many hidden benefits, like the better coordination of company activities, a strategic marketing plan is mainly concerned with competitive advantage – that is to say, establishing, building, defending and maintaining it.

In order to be realistic, it must take into account the organizations' existing competitive position, where it wants to be in the future, its capabilities and the competitive environment it faces. This means that the marketing planner must learn to use the various available processes and techniques which help to make sense of external trends, and to understand the organization's traditional ways of responding to these.

However, this poses the problem regarding which are the most relevant and useful tools and techniques, for each has strengths and weaknesses and no individual concept or technique can satisfactorily describe and illuminate the whole picture. As with a jigsaw puzzle, a sense of unity only emerges as the various pieces are connected together.

The links between strategy and performance have been the subject of detailed statistical analysis by the Strategic Planning Institute. The PIMS (Profit Impact of Market Strategy) project identified from 2600 businesses, six major links (Buzzell, 1987). From this analysis, principles have been derived for the selection of different strategies according to industry type, market conditions and the competitive position of the company.

However, not all observers are prepared to

take these conclusions at face value. Like strategy consultants Lubatkin and Pitts (1985), who believe that all businesses are unique, they are suspicious that something as critical as competitive advantage can be the outcome of a few specific formulae. For them, the PIMS perspective is too mechanistic and glosses over the complex managerial and organizational problems which beset most businesses.

What is agreed, however, is that strategic marketing planning presents a useful process by which an organization formulates its strategies, *providing it is adapted* to the organization and its environment.

I The marketing planning process

Most managers accept that some kind of procedure for marketing planning is necessary. Accordingly they need a system which will help them to think in a structured way and also make explicit their intuitive economic models of the business. Unfortunately, very few companies have planning systems which possess these characteristics. However, those that do tend to follow a similar pattern of steps.

Figure 3.1 illustrates the several stages that have to be gone through in order to arrive at a marketing plan. This illustrates the difference between the process of marketing planning and the actual plan itself, which is the output of the process.

Experience has shown that a marketing plan should contain:

- A mission statement.
- A financial summary.
- A brief market overview.
- A summary of all the principal external factors which affected the company's marketing performance during the previous year, together with a statement of the company's strengths and weaknesses vis-à-vis the competition. This is what we call SWOT

(strengths, weaknesses, opportunities, threats) analyses.
- Some assumptions about the key determinants of marketing success and failure.
- Overall marketing objectives and strategies.
- Programmes containing details of timing, responsibilities and costs, with sales forecasts and budgets.

Each of the stages illustrated in Figure 3.1 will be discussed in more detail later in this chapter. The dotted lines joining up stages 5–8 are meant to indicate the reality of the planning process, in that it is likely that each of these steps will have to be gone through more than once before final programmes can be written.

Although research has shown these marketing planning steps to be universally applicable, the degree to which each of the separate steps in the diagram needs to be formalized depends to a large extent on the size and nature of the company. For example, an undiversified company generally uses less formalized procedures, since top management tends to have greater functional knowledge and expertise than subordinates, and because the lack of diversity of operations enables direct control to be exercised over most of the key determinants of success. Thus, situation reviews, the setting of marketing objectives, and so on, are not always made explicit in writing, although these steps have to be gone through.

In contrast, in a diversified company, it is usually not possible for top management to have greater functional knowledge and expertise than subordinate management, hence planning tends to be more formalized in order to provide a consistent discipline for those who have to make the decisions throughout the organization.

Either way, there is now a substantial body of evidence to show that formalized planning procedures generally result in greater profitability and stability in the long term and also help to reduce friction and operational difficulties within organizations.

Where marketing planning has failed, it has generally been because companies have placed too much emphasis on the procedures themselves and the resulting paperwork, rather than on generating information useful to and consumable by management. But more about reasons for failure later. For now, let us look at the marketing planning process in more detail, starting with the marketing audit.

the external and internal factors that have affected a company's commercial performance over a defined period.

Given the growing turbulence of the business environment and the shorter product life cycles that have resulted, no one would deny the need to stop at least once a year at a particular point in the planning cycle to try to form a reasoned view of how all the many external and internal factors have influenced performance.

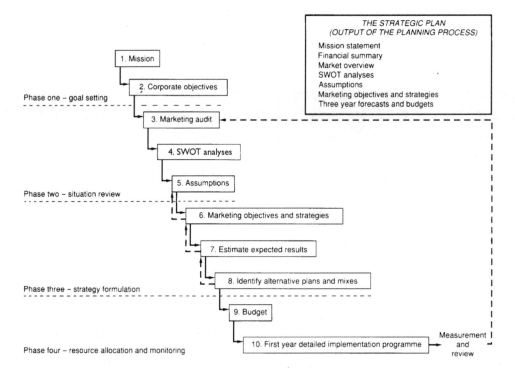

Figure 3.1   The ten steps of the strategic marketing planning process

What is a marketing audit?

Any plan will only be as good as the information on which it is based, and the marketing audit is the means by which information for planning is organized. There is no reason why marketing cannot be audited in the same way as accounts, in spite of its more innovative, subjective nature. A marketing audit is a systematic appraisal of all

Sometimes, of course, a company will conduct a marketing audit because it is in financial trouble. At times like these, management often attempts to treat the wrong symptoms, most frequently by reorganizing the company. But such measures are unlikely to be effective if there are more fundamental problems which have not been identified. Of course, if the company survived for long enough, it might eventually solve its problems through a process of elimination.

Essentially, though, the argument is that the problems have first to be properly defined. The audit is a means of helping to define them.

Two kinds of variable

Any company carrying out an audit will be faced with two kinds of variable. There is the kind over which the company has no direct control, for example economic and market factors. Second, there are those over which the company has complete control, the operational variables, which are usually the firm's internal resources.

This division suggests that the best way to structure an audit is in two parts, external and internal. Table 3.1 shows areas which should be investigated under both headings. Each should be examined with a view to building up an information base relevant to the company's performance.

Many people mistakenly believe that the marketing audit should be some kind of final attempt to define a company's marketing problems, or, at best, something done by an independent body from time to time to ensure that a company is on the right track. However, many highly successful companies, as well as using normal information and control procedures

Table 3.1 Conducting an audit	
External audit	*Internal audit*
Business and economic environment Economic political, fiscal, legal, social, cultural Technological Intra-company	*Own company* Sales (total, by geographical location, by industrial type, by customer, by product) Market shares Profit margins, costs

The market
Total market, size, growth and trends
(value volume)
Market
    characteristics, developments and trends;
    products, prices, physical distribution,
    channels, customers, consumers,
    communication, industry practices
	Marketing
	    information
	    research
	Marketing mix
	    variables: product management, price,
	    distribution, promotion, operations and
	    resources
	Key strengths and weaknesses

Competition Major competitors Size Market share coverage Market standing and reputation Production capabilities Distribution policies Marketing methods Extent of diversification Personnel issues International links Profitability	

and marketing research throughout the year, start their planning cycle each year with a formal, audit-type process, of everything that has had an important influence on marketing activities. Certainly, in many leading consumer goods companies, the annual self-audit approach is a tried and tested discipline.

Occasionally, it may be justified for outside consultants to carry out the audit in order to check that the company is getting the most out of its resources. However, it seems an unnecessary expense to have this done every year.

Objections to line managers doing their own audits usually centre around the problem of time and objectivity. In practice, a disciplined approach and thorough training will help. But the discipline must be applied from the highest to the lowest levels of management if the tunnel vision that often results from a lack of critical appraisal is to be avoided.

Where relevant, the marketing audit should contain life cycles for major products and for market segments, for which the future shape will be predicted using the audit information. Also, major products and markets should be plotted on some kind of matrix to show their current competitive position.

The next question is: what happens to the results of the audit? Some companies consume valuable resources carrying out audits that produce very little in the way of results. The audit is simply a database, and the task remains of turning it into intelligence, that is, information essential to decision making.

It is often helpful to adopt a regular format for the major findings. One way of doing this is in the form of a SWOT analysis. This is a summary of the audit under the headings of internal strengths and weaknesses as they relate to external opportunities and threats. There will be a number of SWOT analyses for each major product for market to be included in the marketing plan.

The section containing SWOT analyses should, if possible, contain no more than four or five pages of commentary, focusing only on key factors. It should highlight internal strengths and weaknesses measured against the competition's, and key external opportunities and threats. A summary of reasons for good or bad performance should be included. It should be interesting to read, contain concise statements, include only relevant and important data and give greater emphasis to creative analysis.

It is important to remember at this stage that we are merely describing the process of marketing planning as outlined in Figure 3.11. The format of the strategic marketing plan itself (i.e. what should actually appear in the written plan) is given in Table 3.2 (p. 57).

Having completed the marketing audit and SWOT analyses, fundamental assumptions on future conditions have to be made. It would be no good receiving plans from two product managers, one of whom believed the market was going to increase by 10 per cent and the other who believed it was going to decline by 10 per cent.

An example of a written assumption might be: *'With respect to the company's industrial climate, it is assumed that over-capacity will increase from 105 per cent to 115 per cent as new industrial plants come into operation, price competition will force price levels down by 10 per cent across the board; a new product will be introduced by our major competitor before the end of the second quarter.'* Assumptions should be few in number. If a plan is possible irrespective of the assumptions made, then the assumptions are unnecessary.

Setting marketing objectives and strategies

The next step is the writing of marketing objectives and strategies. This is the key to the whole process and undoubtedly the most important and difficult of all stages. If this is not done properly, everything that follows is of little value.

It is an obvious activity to follow on with, since a thorough review, particularly of its markets, should enable the company to determine whether it will be able to meet the long range financial targets with its current range of products. Any projected gap has to be filled by new product development or market extension.

The important point to make is that this is the stage in the planning cycle at which a compromise has to be reached between what is wanted by various departments and what is practicable, given all the constraints upon the company. At this stage, objectives and strategies should be set for three years ahead, or for whatever the planning horizon is.

An objective is what you want to achieve, a strategy is how you plan to achieve it. Thus, there can be objectives and strategies at all levels in marketing, such as for service levels, for advertising, for pricing, and so on.

The important point to remember about marketing objectives is that they are concerned solely with products and markets. Common sense will confirm that it is only by selling something to someone that the company's financial goals can be achieved; pricing and service levels are the means by which the goals are achieved. Thus, pricing, sales promotion and advertising objectives should not be confused with marketing objectives.

The latter are concerned with one or more of the following:

- Existing products in existing markets.
- New products for existing markets.
- Existing products for new markets.
- New products for new markets.

They should be capable of measurement, otherwise they are not worthwhile. Directional terms, such as 'maximize', 'minimize', 'penetrate' and 'increase', are only acceptable if quantitative measurement can be attached to them. Measurement should be in terms of sales volume, value, market share, percentage penetration of outlet and so on.

Marketing strategies, the means by which the objectives will be achieved, are generally concerned with the 'four Ps':

1   *Product*: deletions, modifications, additions, designs, packaging, etc.

2   *Price*: policies to be followed for product groups in market segments.
3   *Place*: distribution channels and customer service levels.
4   *Promotion*: communicating with customers under the relevant headings, i.e. advertising, sales force, sales promotion, public relations, exhibitions, direct mail, etc.

There is some debate about whether or not the four Ps are adequate to describe the marketing mix. Some academics advocate that people, procedures and almost anything else beginning with 'P' should be included. However, we believe that these 'new' factors are already subsumed in the existing four Ps.

Estimate expected results, identify alternative plans and mixes

Having completed this major planning task, it is normal at this stage to employ judgement, experience, field tests and so on to test out the feasibility of the objectives and strategies in terms of market share, sales, costs and profits. It is also at this stage that alternative plans and mixes are normally considered.

General marketing strategies should now be reduced to specific objectives, each supported by more detailed strategy and action statements. A company organized according to functions might have an advertising plan, a sales promotion plan and a pricing plan. A product-based company might have a product plan, with objectives, strategies and tactics for price, place and promotion, as required. A market or geographically based company might have a market plan, with objectives, strategies and tactics for the four Ps, as required. Likewise, a company with a few major customers might have a customer plan. Any combination of the above might be suitable, depending on circumstances.

There is a clear distinction between strategy

and detailed implementation of tactics. Marketing strategy reflects the company's best opinion as to how it can most profitably apply its skills and resources to the marketplace. It is inevitably broad in scope. The plan which stems from it will spell out action and timings and will contain the detailed contribution expected from each department.

There is a similarity between strategy in business and the development of military strategy. One looks at the enemy, the terrain, the resources under command, and then decides whether to attack the whole front, an area of enemy weakness, to feint in one direction while attacking in another, or to attempt an encirclement of the enemy's position. The policy and mix, the type of tactics to be used, and the criteria for judging success, all come under the heading of strategy. The action steps are tactics.

Similarly, in marketing, the same commitment, mix and type of resources as well as tactical guidelines and criteria that must be met, all come under the heading of strategy. For example, the decision to use distributors in all but the three largest market areas, in which company sales people will be used, is a strategic decision. The selection of particular distributors is a tactical decision.

The following list of marketing strategies (in summary form) cover the majority of options open under the headings of the four Ps:

1   Product:
     - Expand the line.
     - Change performance, quality or features.
     - Consolidate the line.
     - Standardize design.
     - Positioning.
     - Change the mix.
     - Branding.
2   Price:
     - Change price, terms or conditions.
     - Skimming policies.
     - Penetration policies.
3   Promotion:
     - Change advertising or promotion.

     - Change selling.
4   Place:
     - Change delivery or distribution.
     - Change service.
     - Change channels.
     - Change the degree of forward integration.

Formulating marketing strategies is one of the most critical and difficult parts of the entire marketing process. It sets the limit of success. Communicated to all management levels, it indicates what strengths are to be developed, what weaknesses are to be remedied, and in what manner. Marketing strategies enable operating decisions to bring the company into the right relationship with the emerging pattern of market opportunities which previous analysis has shown to offer the highest prospect of success.

The budget

This is merely the cost of implementing the strategies over the planning period and will obviously be deducted from the net revenue, giving a marketing contribution. There may be a number of iterations of this stage.

The first year detailed implementation programme

The first year of the strategic marketing plan is now converted into a detailed scheduling and costing out of the specific actions required to achieve the first year's budget.

What should appear in a strategic marketing plan?

A written marketing plan is the back-drop against which operational decisions are taken. Consequently, too much detail should be avoided. Its major function is to determine where the company is, where it wants to go and how it can get there. It lies at the heart of a company's revenue-generating activities, such as the timing of the cash flow and the size and character of the labour force. What should actually appear in a written strategic marketing plan is shown in Table 3.2. This strategic marketing plan should be distributed only to those who need it, but it can only be an aid to effective management. It cannot be a substitute for it.

be for a marketing director to justify all marketing expenditure from a zero base each year against the tasks to be accomplished. If these procedures are followed, a hierarchy of objectives is built in such a way that every item of budgeted expenditure can be related directly back to the initial financial objectives.

For example, if sales promotion is a major means of achieving an objective, when a sales

---

Table 3.2   What should appear in a strategic marketing plan

1.	Start with a mission statement.
2.	Here, include a financial summary which illustrates graphically revenue and profit for the full planning period.
3.	Now do a market overview:
	Has the market declined or grown?
	How does it break down into segments?
	What is your share of each?
	Keep it simple. If you do not have the facts, make estimates. Use life cycles, bar charts and pie charts to make it all crystal clear.
4.	Now identify the key segments and do a SWOT analysis for each one:
	Outline the major external influences and their impact on each segment.
	List the key factors for success. These should be less than five.
	Give an assessment of the company's differential strengths and weaknesses compared with those of its competitors. Score yourself and your competitors out of 10 and then multiply each score by a weighting factor for each critical success factor (e.g. CSF 1 = 60, CSF 2 = 25, CSF 3 = 10, CSF 4 = 5).
5.	Make a brief statement about the key issues that have to be addressed in the planning period.
6.	Summarize the SWOTs using a portfolio matrix in order to illustrate the important relationships between your key products and markets.
7.	List your assumptions.
8.	Set objectives and strategies.
9.	Summarize your resource requirements for the planning period in the form of a budget.

It will be obvious from Table 3.2 that not only does budget setting become much easier and more realistic, but the resulting budgets are more likely to reflect what the whole company wants to achieve, rather than just one department.

The problem of designing a dynamic system for setting budgets is a major challenge to the marketing and financial directors of all companies. The most satisfactory approach would

promotion item appears in the programme, it has a specific purpose which can be related back to a major objective. Thus every item of expenditure is fully accounted for.

Marketing expense can be considered to be all costs that are incurred after the product leaves the 'factory', apart from those involved in physical distribution. When it comes to pricing, any form of discounting that reduces the expected gross income – such as promotional or quantity discounts, overriders, sales commission and unpaid invoices – should be given the most careful attention as marketing expenses. Most obvious marketing expenses will occur, however, under the heading of promotion, in the form of advertising, sales salaries and expenses, sales promotion and direct mail costs.

The important point about the measurable effects of marketing activity is that anticipated levels should result from careful analysis of what is required to take the company towards its goals, while the most careful attention should be paid to gathering all items of expenditure under appropriate headings. The healthiest way of treating these issues is through zero-based budgeting.

We have just described the strategic marketing plan and what it should contain. The tactical marketing plan layout and content should be similar, but the detail is much greater, as it is for one year only.

Marketing planning systems design and implementation

While the actual process of marketing planning is simple in outline, a number of contextual issues have to be considered that make marketing planning one of the most baffling of all management problems. The following are some of those issues:

- When should it be done, how often, by whom, and how?
- Is it different in a large and a small company?
- Is it different in a diversified and an undiversified company?
- What is the role of the chief executive?
- What is the role of the planning department?
- Should marketing planning be top-down or bottom-up?
- What is the relationship between operational (one year) and strategic (longer-term) planning?

Requisite strategic marketing planning

Many companies with financial difficulties have recognized the need for a more structured approach to planning their marketing and have opted for the kind of standardized, formalized procedures written about so much in textbooks. Yet, these rarely bring any benefits and often bring marketing planning itself into disrepute.

It is quite clear that any attempt at the introduction of formalized marketing planning requires a change in a company's approach to managing its business. It is also clear that unless a company recognizes these implications, and plans to seek ways of coping with them, formalized strategic planning will be ineffective.

Research has shown that the implications are principally as follows:

1 Any closed-loop planning system (but especially one that is essentially a forecasting and budgeting system) will lead to dull and ineffective marketing. Therefore, there has to be some mechanism for preventing inertia from setting in through the over-bureaucratization of the system.

2 Planning undertaken at the functional level of marketing, in the absence of a means of integration with other functional areas of the business at general management level, will be largely ineffective.

3 The separation of responsibility for operational and strategic planning will lead to a divergence of the short-term thrust of a business at the operational level from the long-term objectives of the enterprise as a whole. This will encourage preoccupation with short-term results at operational level, which normally makes the firm less effective in the longer term.

4 Unless the chief executive understands and takes an active role in strategic marketing planning, it will never be an effective system.

5   A period of up to three years is necessary (especially in large firms) for the successful introduction of an effective strategic marketing planning system.

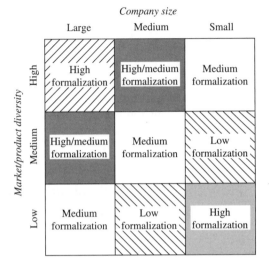

Figure 3.2   Planning formalization

Let us be dogmatic about requisite planning levels. First, in a large diversified group, irrespective of such organizational issues, anything other than a systematic approach approximating to a formalized marketing planning system is unlikely to enable the necessary control to be exercised over the corporate identity. Second, unnecessary planning, or overplanning, could easily result from an inadequate or indiscriminate consideration of the real planning needs at the different levels in the hierarchical chain. Third, as size and diversity grow, so the degree of formalization of the marketing planning process must also increase. This can be simplified in the form of a matrix, Figure 3.2.

It has been found that the degree of formalization increases with the evolving size and diversity of operations (see Figure 3.2). However, while the degree of formalization will change, the need for an effective marketing planning system does not. The problems that companies suffer, then, are a function of either the degree to which they have a requisite

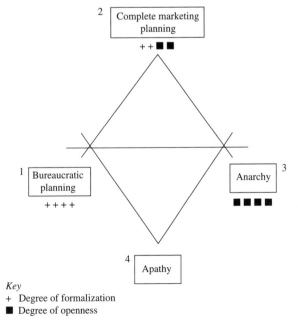

Figure 3.3   Four key outcomes

marketing planning system or the degree to which the formalization of their system grows with the situational complexities attendant upon the size and diversity of operations.

Figure 3.3 shows four key outcomes that marketing planning can evoke. It can be seen that systems 1, 3 and 4 (i.e. where the individual is totally subordinate to a formalized system, or where there is neither system nor creativity), are less successful than system 2, in which the individual is allowed to be entrepreneurial within a total system. System 2, then, will be an effective marketing planning system, but one in which the degree of formalization will be a function of company size and diversity.

One of the most encouraging findings to emerge from research is that the theory of marketing planning is universally applicable. While the planning task is less complicated in small, undiversified companies and there is less need for formalized procedures than in large, diversified companies, the fact is that exactly the same framework should be used in all circumstances, and that this approach brings similar benefits to all.

How far ahead should we plan?

It is clear that one and three year planning periods are by far the most common. Lead time for the initiation of major new product innovations, the length of time necessary to recover capital investment costs, the continuing availability of customers and raw materials and the size and usefulness of existing plant and buildings are the most frequently mentioned reasons for having a three year planning horizon.

Many companies, however, do not give sufficient thought to what represents a sensible planning horizon for their particular circumstances. A five year time span is clearly too long for some companies, particularly those with highly versatile machinery operating in volatile fashion-conscious markets. The effect of this is to rob strategic plans of reality.

The conclusion to be reached is that there is

a natural point of focus into the future beyond which it is pointless to look. This point of focus is a function of the relative size of a company. Small companies, because of their size and the way they are managed, tend to be comparatively flexible in the way in which they can react to environmental turbulence in the short term. Large companies, on the other hand, need a much longer lead time in which to make changes in direction. Consequently, they tend to need to look further into the future and to use formalized systems for this purpose so that managers throughout the organization have a common means of communication.

How the marketing planning process works

As a basic principle, strategic marketing planning should take place as near to the marketplace as possible in the first instance, but such plans should then be reviewed at higher levels within an organization to see what issues may have been overlooked.

It has been suggested that each manager in the organization should complete an audit and SWOT analysis on his or her own area of responsibility. The only way that this can work in practice is by means of a hierarchy of audits. The principle is simply demonstrated in Figure 3.4. This figure illustrates the principle of auditing at different levels within an organization. The marketing audit format will be universally applicable. It is only the detail that varies from level to level and from company to company within the same group.

Figure 3.5 illustrates the total corporate strategic and planning process. This time, however, a time element is added, and the relationship between strategic planning briefings, long-term corporate plans and short-term operational plans is clarified. It is important to note that there are two 'open-loop' points on this last diagram. These are the key times in the planning process when a subordinate's views

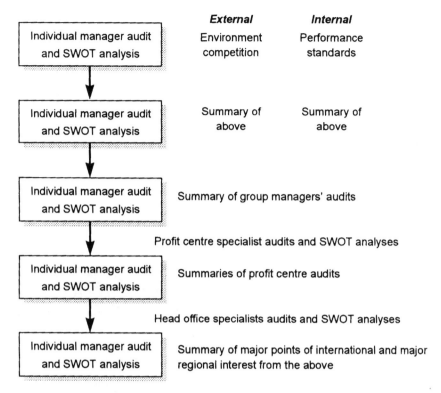

Figure 3.4   Hierarchy of audits

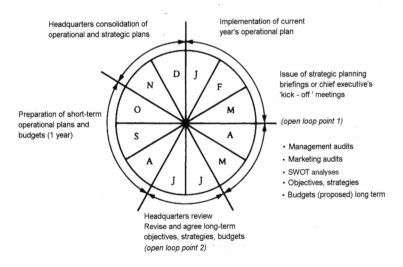

Figure 3.5   Strategic and operational planning

and findings should be subjected to the closest examination by his or her superior. It is by taking these opportunities that marketing planning can be transformed into the critical and creative process it is supposed to be rather than the dull, repetitive ritual it so often turns out to be.

Since in anything but the smallest of undiversified companies it is not possible for top management to set detailed objectives for operating units, it is suggested that at this stage in the planning process strategic guidelines should be issued. One way of doing this is in the form of a strategic planning letter. Another is by means of a personal briefing by the chief executive at 'kick-off' meetings. As in the case of the audit, these guidelines would proceed from the broad to the specific, and would become more detailed as they progressed through the company towards operating units.

These guidelines would be under the headings of financial, manpower and organization, operations and, of course, marketing. Under marketing, for example, at the highest level in a large group, top management may ask for particular attention to be paid to issues such as the technical impact of microprocessors on electromechanical component equipment, leadership and innovation strategies, vulnerability to attack from the flood of Japanese, Korean and Third World products, and so on. At operating company level, it is possible to be more explicit about target markets, product development, and the like.

Part I conclusions

In concluding this section, we must stress that there can be no such thing as an off-the-peg marketing planning system and anyone who offers one must be viewed with great suspicion. In the end, strategic marketing planning success comes from an endless willingness to learn and to adapt the system to the people and the circumstances of the firm. It also comes from a deep understanding about the nature of marketing planning, which is something that, in the final analysis, cannot be taught.

However, strategic marketing planning demands that the organization recognizes the challenges that face it and their effect on its potential for future success. It must learn to focus on customers and their needs at all times and explore every avenue which may provide it with a differential advantage over its competitors.

The next section looks at some guidelines which lead to effective marketing planning.

2 Guidelines for effective marketing planning

Although innovation remains a major ingredient in commercial success, there are nevertheless other challenges which companies must overcome if they wish to become competitive marketers. While their impact may vary from company to company, challenges such as the pace of change, the maturity of markets and the implications of globalization need to be given serious consideration. Some of the more obvious challenges are shown in Table 3.3.

To overcome these challenges the following guidelines are recommended to help the marketer to focus on effective marketing strategies.

Twelve guidelines for effective marketing

1. *Understanding the sources of competitive advantage*

Guideline 1 (p. 64) shows a universally recognized list of sources of competitive advantage. For small firms, they are more likely to be the ones listed on the left. It is clearly possible to focus on highly individual niches with specialized skills and to develop customer-focused relationships to an extent not possible for large

Table 3.3	Change and the challenge to marketing
Nature of change	*Marketing challenges*
Pace of change • Compressed time horizons • Shorter product life cycles • Transient customer preferences	• Ability to exploit markets more rapidly • More effective new product development • Flexibility in approach to markets • Accuracy in demand forecasting • Ability to optimize price-setting
Process thinking • Move to flexible manufacturing and control systems • Materials substitution • Developments in microelectronics and robotization • Quality focus	• Dealing with micro-segmentation • Finding ways to shift from single transaction focus to the forging of long-term relationships • Creating greater customer commitment
Market maturity • Over-capacity • Low margins • Lack of growth • Stronger competition • Trading down • Cost-cutting	• Adding value leading to differentiation • New market creation and stimulation
Customers' expertise and power • More demanding • Higher expectations • More knowledgeable • Concentration of buying power • More sophisticated buyer behaviour	• Finding ways of getting closer to the customer • Managing the complexities of multiple market channels
Internationalization of business • More competitors • Stronger competition • Lower margins • More customer choice • Larger markets • More disparate customer needs	• Restructuring of domestic operations to compete internationally • Becoming customer-focused in larger and more disparate markets

organizations. Flexibility is also a potential source of competitive advantage.

Wherever possible, all organizations should seek to avoid competing with an undifferentiated product or service in too broad a market.

The author frequently has to emphasize to those who seek his advice that without something different to offer (required by the market, of course!), they will continue to struggle and will have to rely on the crumbs that fall from the tables of others. This leads on to the second point.

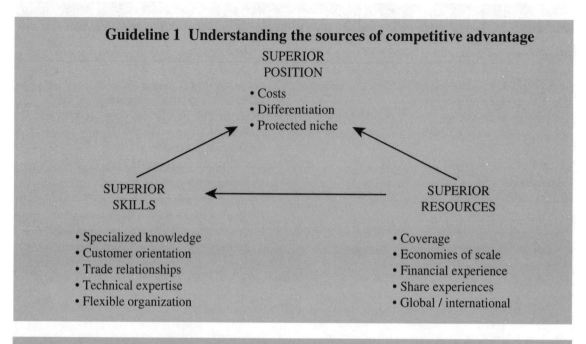

Guideline 1 Understanding the sources of competitive advantage

SUPERIOR
POSITION

- Costs
- Differentiation
- Protected niche

SUPERIOR
SKILLS

- Specialized knowledge
- Customer orientation
- Trade relationships
- Technical expertise
- Flexible organization

SUPERIOR
RESOURCES

- Coverage
- Economies of scale
- Financial experience
- Share experiences
- Global / international

Guideline 2   Understanding differentiation

- Superior product quality
- Innovative product features
- Unique product or service
- Strong brand name
- Superior service (speed, responsiveness, ability to solve problems)
- Wide distribution coverage

Continuously strive to serve customer needs more effectively.

2. *Understanding differentiation*

Guideline 2 takes this point a little further and spells out the main sources of differentiation. One in particular, superior service, has increasingly become a source of competitive advantage. Companies should work relentlessly towards the differential advantage that these will bring. Points 1 and 2 have been confirmed by results from a 1994 survey of over 8000 small and medium sized enterprises (SMEs).

3. *Understanding the environment*

Guideline 3 spells out what is meant by the term environment in the context of companies. There is now an overwhelming body of evidence to show that it is failure to monitor the hostile environmental changes that is the biggest cause of failure in both large and small companies. Had anyone predicted that IBM would lose billions of dollars during the last decade, they would have been derided. Yet it was the failure of IBM to respond sufficiently quickly to the changes taking place around them that caused their recent problems.

Clearly, marketing has a key role to play in the process. For all organizations, this means devoting at least some of the key executives' time and resources to monitoring formally the changes taking

Guideline 3   Understanding the environment
(opportunities and threats)

1   MACRO ENVIRONMENT
  • Political/regulatory
  • Economic
  • Technological
  • Societal

2   MARKET/INDUSTRY ENVIRONMENT
  • Market size and potential
  • Customer behaviour
  • Segmentation
  • Suppliers
  • Channels
  • Industry practices
  • Industry profitability

Carry out a formal marketing audit.

Guideline 4   Understanding competitors

  • Direct competitors
  • Potential competitors
  • Substitute products
  • Forward integration by suppliers
  • Backward integration by customers
  • Competitors' profitability
  • Competitors' strengths and weaknesses

Develop a structured competitor monitoring process. Include the results in the marketing audit.

Guideline 5   Understanding strengths and weaknesses

Carry out a formal position audit of your own product/market position in each segment in which you compete, particularly of your own ability to:

  • Conceive/design
  • Buy
  • Produce
  • Distribute
  • Market
  • Service
  • Finance
  • Manage
  • Look for market opportunities where you can utilize your strengths

Include the results in the marketing audit.

Guideline 6 Understanding market segmentation

- Not all customers in a broadly-defined market have the same needs.
- Positioning is easy. Market segmentation is difficult. Positioning problems stem from poor segmentation.
- Select a segment and serve it. Do not straddle segments and sit between them.

  1 Understand how your market works (market structure)
  2 List what is bought (including where, when, how, applications)
  3 List who buys (demographics, psychographics)
  4 List why they buy (needs, benefits sought)
  5 Search for groups with similar needs.

Guideline 7 Understanding the dynamics of product/market evolution

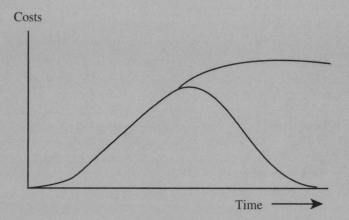

The biological analogy of birth, growth, maturity and decline is apt. Corporate behaviour, particularly in respect of the marketing mix, must evolve with the market.
Share-building in mature markets is difficult and often results in lower prices.
Those with lower costs have an advantage at the stage of maturity.
Life cycles will be different between segments.

place about them. Guidelines 3, 4 and 5 comprise the research necessary to complete a marketing audit. This leads on naturally to the next point.

4. *Understanding competitors*

Guideline 4 is merely an extension of the marketing audit. Suffice it to say that if any organization, big or small, does not know as much about

its close competitors as it knows about itself, it should not be surprised if it fails to stay ahead.

5. *Understanding strengths and weaknesses*

Guideline 5 sets out potential sources of differentiation for an organization. It represents a fairly comprehensive audit of the asset base.

Guideline 8   Understanding a portfolio of products and markets

You cannot be all things to all people. A deep understanding of portfolio analysis will enable you to set appropriate objectives and allocate resources effectively. Portfolio logic arrays competitive position against market attractiveness in a matrix form.

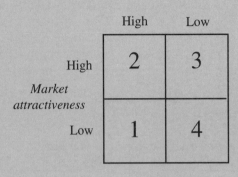

Box 1   Maintain and manage for sustained earnings
Box 2   Invest and build for growth
Box 3   Selectively invest
Box 4   Manage for cash

Together with written summaries of the other two sections of the marketing audit (Guidelines 3 and 4), there should be a written summary of all the conclusions.

If the sources of the company's own competitive advantage cannot be summarised on a couple of sheets of paper, the audit has not been done properly. If this is the case, the chances are that the organization is relying on luck. Alas, luck has a habit of being somewhat fickle!

6. *Understanding marketing segmentation*

Guideline 6 looks somewhat technical and even esoteric, at first sight. None the less, market segmentation is one of the key sources of commercial success and needs to be taken seriously by all organizations, as the days of the easy marketability of products and services have long since disappeared for all but a lucky few.

The ability to recognize groups of customers who share the same, or similar, needs has always come much easier to SMEs than to large organizations. The secret of success, of course, is to change the offer in accordance with changing needs and not to offer exactly the same product or service to everyone – the most frequent product-oriented mistake of large organizations. Closely connected with this is the next point.

7. *Understanding the dynamics of product/market evolution*

Although at first sight Guideline 7 looks as if it applies principally to large companies, few will need reminding of the short-lived nature of many retailing concepts, such as the boutiques of the late 1980s. Those who clung doggedly onto a concept that had had its day lived to regret it.

Few organizations today will need to be reminded of the transitory nature of their business success.

8. *Understanding a portfolio of products and markets*

Guideline 8 suggests plotting either products/services, or markets (or, in some cases, customers) on a vertical axis in descending order of market attractiveness. (The potential of each for the achievement of organizational and commercial

Guideline 9   Setting clear strategic priorities and sticking to them

- Focus your best resources on the best opportunities for achieving continuous growth in sales and profits.
- This means having a written strategic marketing plan for three years containing:
  - A mission statement
  - A financial summary
  - A market overview
  - A SWOT on key segments
  - A portfolio summary
  - Assumptions
  - Marketing objectives and strategies
  - A budget
- This strategic plan can then be converted into a detailed one year plan.
- To do this, an agreed marketing planning process will be necessary.
- Focus on key performance indicators with an unrelenting discipline.

aims and objectives should be used as a criterion as, clearly, they cannot all be equal.) The organization will obviously have a greater or lesser strength in serving each of these 'markets', and this will determine their competitive position. For each location on the graph, a circle, representing the size of current sales, should be drawn.

The graph is divided into a four-box matrix, and each box assessed by management as suggested in the figure. This will give a reasonably accurate 'picture' of the business at a glance and

those benefits outlined in Part 1 of this chapter.

Commercial history has demonstrated that any fool can spell out the financial results they wish to achieve. But it takes intellect to spell out how they are to be achieved. This implies setting clear strategic priorities and sticking to them.

10. *Understanding customer orientation*

Guideline 10 will be familiar to all successful companies. Quality standards, such as ISO 9001

Guideline 10   Understanding customer orientation

- Develop customer orientation in all functions. Ensure that every function understands that they are there to serve the customer, not their own narrow functional interests.
- This must be driven from the board downwards.
- Where possible, organize in cross-functional teams around customer groups and core processes.
- Make customers the arbiter of quality.

will indicate whether or not it is a well-balanced portfolio. Too much business in any one box should be regarded as dangerous.

9. *Setting clear strategic priorities and sticking to them*

Guideline 9 suggests writing down the results in the form of a strategic marketing plan with all

and the like, although useful for those with operations such as production processes, have, in the past, had little to do with real quality, which, of course, can only be seen through the eyes of the customer. (It is obvious that making something perfectly is something of a pointless exercise if no one buys it.)

Guideline 11 Being professional

Particularly in marketing, it is essential to have professional marketing skills, which implies formal training in the underlying concepts, tools and techniques of marketing. In particular, the following are core:

- Market research
- Gap analysis
- Market segmentation/positioning
- Product life cycle analysis
- Portfolio management
- Database management
- The four Ps
  - Product management
  - Pricing
  - Place (customer service, channel management)
  - Promotion (selling, sales force management, advertising, sales promotion)

Guideline 12 Giving leadership

- Do not let doom and gloom pervade your thinking.
- The hostile environment offers many opportunities for companies with toughness and insight.
- Lead your team strongly.
- Do not accept poor performance in the most critical positions.

It is imperative today to monitor customer satisfaction, so this should be done continuously, for it is clearly the only real arbiter of quality.

11. *Being professional*

Guideline 11 sets out some of the marketing skills essential to continuous success. Professional management skills, particularly in marketing, are becoming the hallmark of commercial success in the late 1990s and the early twenty-first century. There are countless professional development skills courses available today. Alas, many directors consider themselves too busy to attend, which is an extremely short-sighted attitude. Entrepreneurial skills, combined with hard-edged management skills, will see any company through the turbulence of today's markets.

12. *Giving leadership*

Guideline 12 sets out the final factor of success in the 1990s – leadership. Charismatic leadership, however, without the eleven other pillars of success, will be to no avail. Few will need reminding of the charisma of Maxwell, Halpern, Saunders and countless others during the past decade. Charisma, without something to sell that the market values, will ultimately be pointless. It is, however, still an important ingredient in success.

Part 2 conclusions

Lest readers should think that these twelve guidelines for success are a figment of the imagination, there is much recent research to suggest otherwise. The four ingredients listed in Figure 3.6 are common to all commercially successful organizations, irrespective of their national origin.

From this it can be seen, first, that the core product or service on offer has to be excellent.

Secondly, operations have to be efficient and, preferably, state-of-the-art.

Thirdly, research stresses the need for

By their own admission 80 per cent of companies in recent research studies did not produce anything approximating to an integrated, co-ordinated and internally consistent plan for their marketing activities.

Marketing's contribution to business success

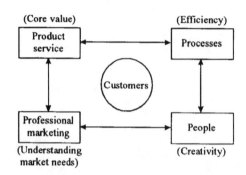

Figure 3.6   Business success

creativity in leadership and personnel, something frequently discouraged by excessive bureaucracy in large organizations.

Finally, excellent companies do professional marketing. This means that the organization continuously monitors the environment, the market, competitors and its own performance against customer-driven standards and produces a strategic marketing plan which sets out the value that everyone in the organization has to deliver.

3 Barriers to marketing planning

As we have seen, the marketing planning process is quite rational and proposes nothing which, on the surface at least, is risky or outrageous. Similarly, the guidelines for marketing competitiveness are built on current good practice and common sense. It is extremely surprising, therefore, that when confronted by an unfriendly economic environment, a majority of business people perpetuate an essentially parochial and short-term strategy as a coping mechanism.

lies in its commitment to detailed analysis of future opportunities to meet customer needs. In other words, identifying what products or services go to which customers. It rewards those managers with a sense of vision who realize that there is no place for 'rear view mirror' planning, i.e. extrapolations from past results. Of course, it is wise to learn from history, but fatal for businesses to attempt to relive it.

It is clear that any attempt to introduce formalized marketing planning systems will have profound implications for the business in terms of its organization and behaviour. Until these implications are recognized and addressed, it is unlikely that strategic marketing planning will be effective. Moreover, the task of designing and implementing sensible planning systems and procedures becomes progressively more complex as the size and diversity of the company grows.

The author's research has identified the items in Table 3.4 as the most frequently encountered barriers to successful marketing planning.

This final section will discuss each of these design and implementation problems.

Table 3.4   Barriers to the integration of strategic marketing planning

1.   Weak support from the chief executive and top management.
2.   Lack of a plan for planning
3.   Lack of line management support due to any of the following, either singly or in combination:
     •   hostility
     •   lack of skills
     •   lack of information
     •   lack of resources
     •   inadequate organizational structure
4.   Confusion over planning terms.
5.   Numbers in lieu of written objectives and strategies.
6.   Too much detail, too far ahead.
7.   Once-a-year ritual.
8.   Separation of operational planning from strategic planning.
9.   Failure to integrate marketing planning into total corporate planning system.
10. Delegation of planning to a planner.

Weak support from chief executive and top management

Since the chief executive and top management are the key influencers in the company, without their active support and participation any formalized marketing planning system is unlikely to work. This fact emerged very clearly from the author's research. Their indifference very quickly destroyed any credibility that the emerging plans might have had, led to the demise of the procedures, and to serious levels of frustration throughout the organization.

There is a depressing preponderance of directors who live by the rule of 'the bottom line' and who apply universal financial criteria indiscriminately to all products and markets, irrespective of the long-term consequences. There is a similar preponderance of engineers who see marketing as an unworthy activity and who think of their products only in terms of their technical features and functional characteristics, in spite of the overwhelming body of evidence that exists that these are only a part of what a customer buys. Not surprisingly, in companies headed by people like this, mar-keting planning is either non-existent, or where it is tried, it fails. This is the most frequently encountered barrier to effective marketing planning.

Lack of a plan for planning

The next most common cause of the failure or partial failure of marketing planning systems is the belief that, once a system is designed, it can be implemented immediately. One company achieved virtually no improvement in the quality of the plans coming into headquarters from the operating companies over a year after the introduction of a very sophisticated system. The evidence indicates that a period of around three years is required in a major company before a complete marketing planning system can be implemented according to its design.

Failure, or partial failure, then, is often the result of not developing a timetable for introducing a new system, to take account of the following:

1   The need to communicate why a marketing planning system is necessary.

2   The need to recruit top management support and participation.

3   The need to test the system out on a limited basis to demonstrate its effectiveness and value.

4   The need for training programmes, or workshops, to train line management in its use.

5   Lack of data and information in some parts of the world.

6   Shortage of resources in some parts of the world.

Above all, a resolute sense of purpose and dedication is required, tempered by patience and a willingness to appreciate the inevitable problems which will be encountered in its implementation.

This problem is closely linked with the third major reason for planning system failure, which is lack of line management support.

Lack of line management support

Hostility, lack of skills, lack of data and information, lack of resources, and an inadequate organizational structure, all add up to a failure to obtain the willing participation of operational managers.

Hostility on the part of line managers is by far the most common reaction to the introduction of new marketing planning systems. The reasons for this are not hard to find, and are related to the system initiators' lack of a plan for planning.

New systems inevitably require considerable explanation of the procedures involved and are usually accompanied by pro formas, flow charts and the like. Often these devices are most conveniently presented in the form of a manual. When such a document arrives on the desk of a busy line manager, unheralded by previous explanation or discussion, the immediate reaction often appears to be fear of their possible inability to understand it and to comply with it, followed by anger, and finally rejection. They begin to picture headquarters as a remote 'ivory tower', totally divorced from the reality of the marketplace.

This is often exacerbated by their absorption in the current operating and reward system, which is geared to the achievement of current results, while the new system is geared to the future. Also, because of the trend in recent years towards the frequent movement of executives around organizations, there is less interest in planning for future business gains from which someone else is likely to benefit.

Allied to this is the fact that many line managers are ignorant of basic marketing principles, have never been used to breaking up their markets into strategically relevant segments, nor of collecting meaningful information about them.

This lack of skill is compounded by the fact that the are many countries in the world which cannot match the wealth of useful information and data available in the USA and Europe. This applies particularly to rapidly-growing economies, where the limited aggregate statistics are not only unreliable and incomplete, but also quickly out of date. The problem of lack of reliable data and information can only be solved by devoting time and money to its solution, and where available resources are scarce, it is unlikely that the information demands of headquarters can be met.

In medium sized and large companies, particularly those that are divisionalized, there is rarely any provision at board level for marketing as a discipline. Sometimes there is a commercial director, with line management responsibility for the operating divisions, but apart from sales managers at divisional level, or a marketing manager at head office level, marketing as a function is not particularly well catered for. Where there is a marketing manager, he tends to be somewhat isolated from the mainstream activities.

The most successful organizations are those with a fully integrated marketing function, whether it is line management responsible for sales, or a staff function, with operating units being a microcosm of the head office organization. Without a suitable organizational structure, any attempt to implement a marketing planning system which requires the collection, analysis and synthesis of market-related information is unlikely to be successful.

Confusion over planning terms

Confusion over planning terms is another reason for the failure of marketing planning systems. The initiators of these systems, often highly qualified, frequently use a form of planning terminology that is perceived by operational managers as meaningless jargon.

Those companies with successful planning systems try to use terminology which will be familiar to operational management, and where terms such as 'objectives' and 'strategies' are used, these are clearly defined, with examples given of their practical use.

Numbers in lieu of written objectives and strategies

Most managers in operating units are accustomed to completing sales forecasts, together with the associated financial implications. They are not accustomed to considering underlying causal factors for past performance or expected results, nor of highlighting opportunities, emphasizing key issues, and so on. Their outlook is essentially parochial, with a marked tendency to extrapolate numbers and to project the current business unchanged into the next fiscal year.

Thus, when a marketing planning system suddenly requires that they should make explicit their understanding of the business, they cannot do it. So, instead of finding words to express the logic of their objectives and strategies, they repeat their past behaviour and fill in the data sheets provided without any narrative.

It is the provision of data sheets, and the emphasis which the system places on the physical counting of things, that encourages the questionnaire-completion mentality and hinders the development of the creative analysis so essential to effective strategic planning.

Those companies with successful marketing planning systems ask only for essential data and place greater emphasis or narrative to explain the underlying thinking behind the objectives and strategies.

Too much detail, too far ahead

Connected with this is the problem of over-planning, usually caused by elaborate systems that demand information and data that headquarters do not need and can never use. Systems that generate vast quantities of paper are generally demotivating for all concerned.

The biggest problem in this connection is undoubtedly the insistence on a detailed and thorough marketing audit. In itself this is not a bad discipline to impose on managers, but to do so without also providing some guidance on how it should be summarized to point up the key issues merely leads to the production of vast quantities of useless information. Its uselessness stems from the fact that it robs the ensuing plans of focus and confuses those who read it by the amount of detail provided.

The trouble is that few managers have the creative or analytical ability to isolate the really key issues, with the result that far more problems and opportunities are identified than the company can ever cope with. Consequently, the truly key strategic issues are buried deep in the detail and do not receive the attention they deserve until it is too late.

Not surprisingly, companies with highly detailed and institutionalized marketing planning systems find it impossible to identify what their major objectives and strategies are. As a result they try to do too many things at once, and extend in too many directions, which makes control over a confusingly heterogeneous portfolio of products and markets extremely difficult.

In companies with successful planning systems, there is system of 'layering'. At each successive level of management throughout the organization, lower-level analyses are synthesized into a form that ensures that only the essential information needed for decision-making and control purpose reaches the next level of management. Thus, there are hierarchies of audits, SWOT analyses, assumptions, objectives, strategies and plans. This means, for example, that at conglomerate headquarters, top management have a clear understanding of the really key macro issues of company-wide significance, while at the lower level of profit responsibility, management also have a clear understanding of the really key macro issues of significance to the unit.

It can be concluded that a good measure of the effectiveness of a company's marketing planning system is the extent to which different managers in the organization can make a clear, lucid and logical statement about the major problems and opportunities they face, how they intend to deal with these, and how what they are doing fits in with some greater overall purpose.

Once-a-year ritual

One of the commonest weaknesses in the marketing planning systems of those companies whose planning systems fail to bring the expected benefits, is the ritualistic nature of the activity. In such cases, operating managers treat the writing of the marketing plan as a thoroughly irksome and unpleasant duty. The pro formas are completed, not always very diligently, and the resulting plans are quickly filed away, never to be referred to again. They are seen as something which is required by headquarters rather than as an essential tool of management. In other words, the production of the marketing plan is seen as a once-a-year ritual, a sort of game of management bluff. It is not surprising that the resulting plans are not used or relegated to a position of secondary importance.

In companies with effective systems, the planning cycle will start in month three or four and run through to month nine or ten, with the total twelve-month period being used to evaluate the ongoing progress of existing plans by means of the company's marketing intelligence system. Thus, by spreading the planning activity over a longer period, and by means of the active participation of all levels of management at the appropriate moment, planning becomes an accepted and integral part of management behaviour rather than an addition to it which calls for unusual behaviour. There is a much better chance that plans resulting from such a system will be formulated in the sort of form that can be converted into things that people are actually going to do.

Separation of operational planning from strategic planning

Most companies make long-term projections. Unfortunately, in the majority of cases these are totally separate from the short-term planning activity that takes place largely in the form of forecasting and budgeting. The view that they should be separate is supported by many of the writers in this field, who describe strategic planning. Indeed, many stress that failure to understand the essential difference between the two leads to confusion and prevents planning from becoming an integrated part of the company's overall management system. Yet it is precisely this separation between short- and long-term plans which the author's research revealed as being the major cause of the problems experienced today by many of the respondents. It is the failure of long-term plans to determine the difficult choices between the emphasis to be placed on current operations and the development of new business that lead to the failure of operating management to consider any alternatives to what they are currently doing.

The almost total separation of operational or short-term planning from strategic or long-term planning is a feature of many companies whose systems are not very effective. More often than not, the long-term strategic plans tend to be straight-line extrapolations of past trends, and because different people are often involved, such as corporate planners, to the exclusion of some levels of operating management, the resulting plans bear virtually no relationship to the more detailed and immediate short-term plans.

This separation positively discourages operational managers from thinking strategically, with the result that detailed operational plans are completed in a vacuum. The so-called strategic plans do not provide the much-needed cohesion and logic, because they are seen as an ivory tower exercise which contains figures in which no one really believes.

The detailed operational plan should be the first year of the long-term plan, and operational managers should be encouraged to complete their long-term projections at the same time as their short-term projections. The advantage is that it encourages managers to think about what decisions have to be made in the current planning year, in order to achieve the long-term projections.

Failure to integrate marketing planning into a total corporate planning system

It is difficult to initiate an effective marketing planning system in the absence of a parallel corporate planning system. This is yet another facet of the separation of operational planning from strategic planning. For unless similar processes and time scales to those being used in the marketing planning system are also being used by other major functions such as distribution, production, finance and personnel, the sort of trade-offs and compromises that have to be made in any company between what is wanted and what is practicable and affordable, will not take place in a rational way. These trade-offs have to be made on the basis of the fullest possible under-

standing of the reality of the company's multi-functional strengths and weaknesses and opportunities and threats.

One of the problems of systems in which there is either a separation of the strategic corporate planning process or in which marketing planning is the only formalized system, is the lack of participation of key functions of the company, such as engineering or production. Where these are key determinants of success, as in capital goods companies, a separate marketing planning system is virtually ineffective.

Where marketing, however, is a major activity, as in fast-moving industrial goods companies, it is possible to initiate a separate marketing planning system. The indications are that when this happens successfully, similar systems for other functional areas of the business quickly follow suit because of the benefits which are observed by the chief executive.

Delegation of planning to a planner

The incidence of this is higher with corporate planning than with marketing planning, although where there is some kind of corporate planning function at headquarters and no organizational function for marketing, whatever strategic marketing planning takes place is done by the corporate planners as part of a system which is divorced from the operational planning mechanism. Not surprisingly, this exacerbates the separation of operational planning from strategic planning and encourages short-term thinking in the operational units.

The literature sees the planner basically as a coordinator of the planning, not as an initiator of goals and strategies. It is clear that without the ability and the willingness of operational management to cooperate, a planner becomes little more than a kind of headquarters administrative assistant. In many large companies, where there is a person at headquarters with the specific title of marketing planning manager, they have usually been appointed as a result of the difficulty of controlling businesses that have grown rapidly in size and diversity, and which present a baffling array of new problems to deal with.

Their tasks are essentially those of system design and coordination of inputs, although they are also expected to formulate overall objectives and strategies for the board. In all cases, it is lack of line management skills and inadequate organizational structures that frustrates the company's marketing efforts, rather than inadequacies on the part of the planner. This puts the onus on planners themselves to do a lot of the planning, which is, not surprisingly, largely ineffective.

Two particularly interesting facts emerged from the author's research. Firstly, the marketing planning manager, as the designer and initiator of systems for marketing planning, is often in an impossibly delicate political position vis-à-vis both their superior line managers and more junior operational managers. It is clear that not too many chief executives understand the role of planning and have unrealistic expectations of the planner, whereas for their part the planner cannot operate effectively without the full understanding, cooperation and participation of top management, and this rarely happens.

This leads on naturally to a second point. For the inevitable consequence of employing a marketing planning manager is that they will need to initiate changes in management behaviour in order to become effective. Usually these are far-reaching in their implications, affecting training, resource allocation, and organizational structures. As the catalyst for such changes, the planner, not surprisingly, comes up against enormous political barriers, the result of which is that they often become frustrated and eventually ineffective. This is without doubt a major issue, particularly in big companies.

The problems which are raised by a marketing planning manager occur directly as a result of the failure of top management to give thought to the formulation of overall strategies. They have not done this in the past because they have not felt the need. However, when market pressures force the emerging problems of diversity

and control to the surface, without a total willingness on their part to participate in far-reaching changes, there really is not much that a planner can do.

This raises the question again of the key role of the chief executive in the whole business of marketing planning.

Part 3 conclusions

Consultants have learned that introducing change does not always mean forcing new ideas into an unreceptive client system. Indeed, such an approach invariably meets resistance for the organization's 'anti-bodies' whose sole purpose is to protect the status quo from the germs of innovation.

A quicker and more effective method is to remove or reduce the effect of the barriers which will stop the proposed improvement from becoming effective. Thus, any attempt to introduce systematic strategic marketing planning must pay due concern to all the barriers listed in this section.

Of course, not all of them will be the same for every organization, but without a doubt the most critical barrier remains the degree of support provided by the chief executive and top management. Unless that support is forthcoming, in an overt and genuine way, marketing planning will never be wholly effective.

Summary

Strategic marketing planning, when sensibly institutionalized and driven by an organization's top management, can make a significant contribution to the creation of sustainable competitive advantage. It is, however, important to distinguish between the *process* of marketing planning and the *output*. Indeed, much of the benefit will accrue from the process of analysis and debate amongst relevant managers and directors rather than from the written document itself.

Twelve guidelines were provided which have been shown to be significant contributors to determining an organization's competitiveness.

Finally, there are many human organizational and cultural barriers which prevent an organization deriving the maximum benefit from strategic marketing planning. Being aware of what these are will go some way to helping organizations overcome them.

References

Burns, P. (1994) Growth in the 1990s: winner and losers, Special Report 12, 3I European Enterprise Centre, Cranfield School of Management, UK.

Buzzell, R. D. and Gale, B. T. (1987) *The PIMS Principles: Linking Strategy to Performance*, The Free Press, New York.

Lubatkin, M. and Pitts, M. (1985) The PIMS and the Policy Perspective: a Rebuttal, *Journal of Business Strategy*, Summer, pp. 85–92.

McDonald, M. (1994) *Marketing – the Challenge of Change*, Chartered Institute of Marketing study.

Porter, M. (1980) *Competitive Strategy: Techniques for Analysing Industries and Competitors*. The Free Press, New York.

Saunders, J. and Wong, V. (1993) Business Orientations and Corporate Success, *Journal of Strategic Marketing*, **1**(1), 20–40.

Further reading

Brown, S. (1996) Art or Science?: Fifty Years of Marketing Debate, *Journal of Marketing Management*, **12**, 243–267. This fascinating and highly readable paper discusses the eternal debate about whether marketing is more art than science. It is recommended here because readers should never lose sight of the need for strategic marketing plans and the process that produces them to be creative as well as diagnostic.

Leppard, J. and McDonald, M. (1987) A Reappraisal of the Role of Marketing Planning, *Journal of Marketing Management*, **3**(2). This paper throws quite a considerable amount of light onto why marketing planning is rarely done. It examines the organization's context in which marketing planning takes place and gives a fascinating insight into how corporate culture and politics often prevent the marketing concept from taking hold.

McDonald, M. (1996) Strategic Marketing Planning: Theory; Practice; and Research Agendas, *Journal of Marketing Management*, **12**(1–3), Jan./Feb./March/April, pp. 5–27. This paper summarizes the whole domain of marketing planning, from its early days to the current debate taking place about its contribution. It also explores forms of marketing planning other than the more rational/scientific one described in this chapter.

McDonald, M. (1999) *Marketing Plans: How to Prepare Them; How to Use Them*, 4th edn, Butterworth–Heinemann, Oxford. This book is the standard text on marketing planning in universities and organizations around the world. It is practical, as well as being based on sound theoretical concepts.

Part Two
The Framework of Marketing

CHAPTER 4

Environmental scanning

DOUGLAS BROWNLIE

Four assumptions are typically made by writers on the subject of environmental scanning. The *first* is that environmental scanning is the key link in a chain of perceptions and actions that permits the organization to adapt to changes in its environment (Dill, 1958; Daft *et al.*, 1988; Dev, 1989; West and Olsen, 1989; Sawyerr, 1993). The *second* is that top managers are responsible for aligning the organization to its environment (Child, 1972; Snow, 1976; Smircich and Stubbart, 1985; Johnson and Scholes, 1993). But, as Aguilar (1967), Kefalas and Schoderbek (1973), Hambrick (1982), Daft *et al.* (1988) and Brownlie (1994a) have all noted, CEOs are not involved in *all* scanning activities, even if they are responsible for bringing together information from various parts of the organization and using it to build a coherent picture.

The *third* assumption flows from the second. It is that top managers have limited time available for environmental scanning and tend to take short cuts in their scanning activities. Rarely do they scan wide *and* deep. The *fourth* assumption concerns how scanning activities should be organized; and this is said to depend on the complexity of the environment. A complex environment calls for sophisticated and systematic (formal) scanning activity that provides access to a variety of media, and can involve many different people and techniques.

Even so, authors argue that top management's scanning activities tend to be conducted irregularly, relying heavily on personal sources, often externally based, which are consulted on an ad hoc basis.

The environment

The starting point for matters of mainstream theory in environmental scanning is typically that of conceptualizing the environment. Definitions of the environment tend to stratify various sectors that exist in two broad layers. The *operating* or *task* environment, or inner layer, is closest to the organization (Thompson, 1967; 1993). It represents that domain in which staff from one organization interact with staff from others in the context of business relationships which provide vehicles for the pursuit of day-to-day activities and goals. The *remote* or *general* environment, or outer layer, refers to those sectors of the environment, often institutional, that indirectly affect the organization's trading operations. It consists of organizations whose influence on a focal organization is mediated by one, two, three or more other organizations. Those inter-organizational links give the environments of organizations their causal texture, so that the effects of a change in any organization in the remote environment may affect the focal organization and others in its operating environment to which it is directly linked

(Emery and Trist, 1965; Bourgeois, 1980). As Daft *et al.* (1988) observe, drawing the boundary between the task and the remote environment depends on how the organization's top managers *choose* to navigate their way over the environmental terrain.

Uncertainty

The next brick in the mainstream theoretical wall concerns that of *uncertainty*. The various sectors in the task and remote environments generate different degrees of uncertainty for the organization's decision makers and therefore come to influence scanning activities in different ways. This uncertainty is perceived by top managers (Bourgeois, 1985; Piercy, 1986; Brownlie, 1998). It refers to the absence of information about organizations, activities and events in the environment. *Perceived uncertainty* is then a function of the *complexity* of the environment and the *rate of change* it is thought to be undergoing. The complexity of the external environment is itself a function of the number and diversity of events and trends in the environment. The rate of change refers to the frequency with which external events and activities shift. And so the greater the complexity of and rate of change in the environment, the greater is the perceived uncertainty (Gioia and Chittipeddi, 1991).

However, as Daft *et al.* (1988) note, uncertainty by itself will not determine environmental scanning behaviour. Unless the external events are perceived as having an *important* impact on organizational goals, managers may have little interest in them and so attention will not be paid to them (Pfeffer and Salancik, 1978; Weick, 1979).

Perceived importance

The next theoretical brick is that of *perceived importance*. It draws its explanatory power from the notion of *resource dependency* (Pfeffer and Salancik, 1978) which refers to the extent to which any sector of the environment provides the organization with resources which can be

employed in pursuit of its goals. Information from important sectors may then be a source of strategic advantage. Daft *et al.* (1988) arrive at the notion of *perceived strategic uncertainty* by combining perceived uncertainty and importance. They theorize that perceived strategic uncertainty generates the need for organizational policy makers to scan events in selected sectors of the environment.

Environmental scanning activity

Various empirical studies have shown that managers scan the environment directly, or learn about it from others, both within and without the organization (Lenz, 1980; Jemison, 1981; Klein and Linneman, 1984; Lenz and Engledow, 1986a). To some extent they can vary the frequency with which they scan the various sectors of the environment and thus the number of times they obtain data about those sectors (Hambrick, 1981). The frequency of scanning in the operating environment tends to be dictated by the frequency with which direct transactions take place between organizations. As Table 4.1 shows, managers can also gain access to various sources or modes of information, typically either personal (human) or impersonal (documentary), both within and without the organization. Table 4.2 comments on the relative importance of those modes. It also suggests that to secure the impact of its work, environmental scanning should seek top management support for and involvement in their activities (Lyles and Lenz, 1982; Lenz and Lyles, 1985; Brownlie, 1994a).

In their study of medium sized manufacturing businesses, Daft *et al.* (1988) found that the frequency of environmental scanning activity was driven by information need and the perceived value of this information for organizational performance. Scanning tended to take place more frequently where the perceived strategic uncertainty was high and the scanning activity itself was focused on specific sectors where this uncertainty, and thus the value of the information, was highest. So, as those authors argue, perceived strategic uncertainty is a

Table 4.1   Sources of information on the business environment

Location	Types	Sources of information on business environment
Inside the company	Written Verbal Combination	Internal reports and memos, planning documents, market research, MIS. Researchers, sales force, marketing, purchasing, advisors, planners, board. Formal and informal meetings, e.g. working parties, advisory committees.
Outside the company	Written	Annual reports, investment reports, trade association publications, institute yearbooks, textbooks, scientific journals, professional journals, technical magazines, unpublished reports, government reports, unpublished papers, abstracts, newspapers, espionage.
	Verbal	Consultants, librarians, government officials, consumers, suppliers, distributors, competitors, academics, market researchers, industry bodies, journalists, spies, bankers, stockbrokers.
	Combination	Formal and informal meetings, membership of government working parties and advisory boards, industry bodies, trade associations.

predictor of the frequency with which sectors of the environment will be scanned.

Two generic approaches to environmental scanning have been posited. The *reactive* approach, or problemistic search for information, is stimulated by a problem the organization has and is directed towards finding a solution to this problem (Cyert and March, 1963). The *proactive* or surveillance approach is exploratory in nature and not directed towards any particular problem (Aguilar, 1967). These polar extremes very often occur together (Etzioni, 1967). As the environment becomes more turbulent and complex, the nature of external events and related organizational problems becomes fuzzier and there tends to be a shift towards *surveillance* so that the gathering of relevant environmental information becomes more unbounded and difficult. This information will then be processed on an irregular

Table 4.2   The relative importance of sources of environmental information

1. Verbal sources of information are much more important than written sources. 75% of information cited by executives was in verbal form.
2. The higher the executive in the organization, the more important verbal sources became.
3. Of the written sources used, the most important were newspapers (two-thirds), then trade publications, then internal company reports.
4. The major sources of verbal information are subordinates, then friends in the industry, and very infrequently superiors.
5. Information received from outside an organization is usually unsolicited.
6. Information received from inside the organization is usually solicited by the executive.
7. Information received from outside tends to have a greater impact on the decision maker than inside information.
8. The outside sources used varied according to the job of the manager. Thus, marketing managers talked more to customers.
9. The larger the company, the greater the reliance on inside sources of verbal information.

or continuous basis depending on the perceived need for information about external events.

Research into the sources, or modes of environmental scanning information, generally shows that personal sources are more important to senior executives than impersonal sources. Indeed, Daft *et al.* (1988) found that as perceived strategic uncertainty increased CEOs tended to rely more heavily on personal sources of information, especially those outside the organization. Personal sources are seen as important because the richness of their content enables subtle signals to be detected and different interpretations of unclear issues to be tested directly (Heil and Robertson, 1991). And often this subtlety is filtered out in written media which tend to communicate tangible data about discrete events. Face-to-face meetings and even telephone calls can provide many different clues and cues. They provide an opportunity to probe various interpretations or 'takes' on a story and to gain rapid feedback on them. This is especially helpful when uncertainty is high and time short. Furthermore, direct contact with authoritative external sources helps to avoid the loss of meaning, or distortion which otherwise occurs when information is passed through intermediaries.

The greater preference for personal sources of information also reflects the inability of managers to acquire hard data about events that are rapidly changing and trends that are unclear. However, it has also been found that managers use multiple sources of information because they often complement each other. A weak signal detected through a discrete personal source may be supplemented or corroborated by data from a written research report (Flax, 1984; Taylor, 1992). So, environmental scanning through one medium may trigger the use of a complementary medium, either within or without the organization. In this way bits and pieces of information from diverse sources can be assembled to provide clues and cues about environmental change (King and Cleland, 1977; Brownlie, 1996).

What environmental scanning can accomplish

Whatever is achieved by environmental scanning will largely depend on the *purpose* an organization has in mind for it; and whatever is possible depends on which visions people believe in and act upon. At the level of detail, felt needs, intentions and realizations vary significantly from organization to organization. Lenz and Engledow (1986a) assert that the demands placed on environmental scanning depend on the role it is expected to play within the broader decision processes of the host organization. Small firms may require to be kept up to date with regulatory and local economic trends likely to have an immediate impact on their day-to-day business prospects in the highly defined context of a served market. Larger firms will share the requirements of the small firm, but will typically expect information broader in scope and of a futures orientation.

Where environmental scanning is tasked to a corporate strategy-making unit it has the responsibility of *monitoring*, *forecasting* and *interpreting* issues, trends and events which go far beyond the customer, market and competitive analyses that many firms perform as a matter of routine. It may be expected to provide a broad but penetrating view of possible future changes in the demographic, social, cultural, political, technological and economic elements of the business environment. Its purpose may then be to arm the firm's strategic decision makers with information, analyses and forecasts – in other words 'intelligence' – relevant to the strategies and plans which govern how the firm is to respond to a changing business environment. It should also provide a basis for questioning the assumptions which underpin the firm's strategic thinking and for generating new assumptions (Brownlie, 1989, 1994b).

On the basis of several empirical studies Jain (1984) argues that environmental scanning's principal accomplishment must be to enable the organization to deal with environmental change. In his view that goal can be achieved through making the following contributions to the firm's strategic management:

- Helping the organization to capitalize on early opportunities, rather than lose these to competitors.
- Providing early signals of impending problems with key business relationships which can be defused if recognized well in advance.
- Sensitizing the organization to the changing demands of its relationships with key suppliers, customers, competitors and other important stakeholders.
- Providing a base of corroborated information about the environment that strategists can utilize.
- Improving the image of the organization with its publics by showing that it is sensitive to the outlooks and interests of its various stakeholders and responsive to their needs.
- Providing a continuing, broad-based educational resource for executives, especially strategic decision-makers.

Those contributions provide a broad context within which to couch the purpose of your own organization's environmental scanning effort. But, be careful to avoid raising unrealistic expectations, especially those that may lead senior managers to expect immediate and tangible improvements to bottom-line results.

In an empirical study of formal environmental scanning in 90 American corporations, Diffenbach (1983) reported that participants found there to be seven types of payoffs from the activity. His findings suggest that although environmental scanning was widely practised and found to be important by many of those who do it (73%), a significant number of respond-ents did not do it (27%), or did it but did not find it very useful (28%). Table 4.3 lists a selection of the comments Diffenbach received from respondents on the subject of the payoffs of organized environmental scanning.

Defining the environment

This is the starting point for matters of theory *and* practice in environmental scanning. Churchman (1968) defines the environment of an organization as 'those factors which not only are outside the system's control, but which determine, in part, how the system performs'. In theory at least the environment is then thought to include all those factors that exert a direct or indirect influence on the firm in any perceptible way (Terreberry, 1968).

Given such an unbounded definition one could argue that the rest of the world then constitutes the organization's environment. Clearly, to take such a broad view has little operational value, since for any single organization, the environment would then contain an infinite number of situations and events, each of which could provide material worthy of environmental scanning. To consider every situation, event, issue and trend, and furthermore, to evaluate the many combinations of relationships between them, is far beyond the capacity of any imaginable method of environmental analysis to deal with the breadth of data (Brownlie, 1994a; Whittington, 1993). Moreover, managers have limited capacity for environmental scanning and organizations have limited resources to devote to it (Lyles and Lenz, 1982). Somehow the potential torrent of environmental data has to be funnelled down into a small stream of highly pertinent data. So, in practice, the task of environmental scanning is made manageable by taking a very selective and carefully considered view of the environment (Brownlie, 1994a). In this way much of the rest of the world will be eliminated from the firm's immediate attention. And, as Pettigrew and Whipp (1991) observe, the choice of environmental definition to drive the scanning process is a creative and political act.

In theory the boundaries of the firm's environment should be defined in such a way that the scanner can identify important from less important constituencies and determine an appropriate time scale for forecasting changes. One

Table 4.3   Payoffs of organized environmental scanning

Increased general awareness by management of environmental changes

- Improved ability to anticipate long-term problems and make adjustments earlier than otherwise.
- Increased responsiveness of operations programmes to environmental concerns.
- Awareness of top-level management of a range of possible futures and how they might affect the company.
- A noticeable tendency for managers to ask themselves if the same approaches used in the past will work in the future.
- Disposition to acting in advance of change.

Better strategic planning and decision making

- Plans and decisions that reflect a greater awareness of political events and economic cycles, and therefore more flexibility and adaptiveness.
- Development of contingency plans.
- More disciplined planning.
- Broadened scope of perspectives, so that one can understand the relevance of external conditions to the business of the company.
- Lengthened planning/decision horizon.
- Gradual and continued incorporation of environmental factors into the corporate decision-making process.
- Improved ability to allocate strategic resources to opportunities createed by environmental change.
- Improved ability to anticipate long-term problems and make adjustments earlier.
- Divisions' product plan awareness of social trends, ecology, shifts in population age profile, geographic migration, and the position of women.
- Wide acceptance of the necessity for a common set of environmental assumptions as a basis for formal planning activities.
- Avoidance of crises.

Greater effectiveness in government matters

- Better government relations and understanding of the role of government.
- Greater success in winning government contracts.
- Ability to take proactive (rather than reactive) positions on government regulatory matters earlier.
- Time to adapt products to noise and pollution regulations.
- Anticipation of government restrictions on medical equipment led to extra effort to develop foreign markets.
- Orderly response to federal legislation and reporting requirements.

Better industry and market analyses

- Higher quality of predictions in market and product forecasts.
- Greater confidence in product forecasts.
- Recognition of possible declining markets and resultant rejection of capital investment for manufacturing facilities to supply those markets.
- Early detection of developing shifts in trends from either excess capacity or insufficient capacity in an industry.
- Stimulus for corporation and groups to assess more variables which affect product lines.
- Identification of changes in buyer criteria due to social changes.
- Reorientation of marketing programme to reflect sun-belt growth.
- Ability to anticipate future needs for new products, e.g. increasing oil and gas exploration creates need for (drilling) systems usable in a wide range of water depths and operating environments.
- Research efforts toward products filling needs created by government and social pressures (e.g. development of diagnostic tests as hedge against malpractice litigation).

Better results in foreign businesses

- Major investment in foreign countries.
- Positive results of overseas investment and market participation.
- Ability to anticipate changes in international markets and ways of doing business in foreign countries.

Improvements in diversifications and resource allocation

- Ability to concentrate our resources in businesses that will be attractive to the corporation in the long term.
- Shifts in production portfolio – away from those products subject to increasing government and social pressures (e.g. 'polluting' processes, 'dangerous' products) toward those less vulnerable to such pressures.
- Guide to acquisitions process.
- Contributed to policy development with

respect to expansion and allocation of capital funds.

- Major diversification which helped company ride out rough time in the aluminium business.

Better energy planning

- Ability to predict economic dislocations resulting from OPEC embargo and to deal flexibly with exchange rates.
- Better energy planning for production facilities.
- Correct anticipation of energy trends in the mid-1960s and consequent development of new energy-efficient glass-forming process.
- Identification of potential impact of energy shortage (about 1971) and the development of marketing programmes and product lines around ability to help customers reduce energy consumption – action led to strengthened market position.
- Development of additional back-up energy sources.

Note: This table lists a selection of the comments on the payoffs of organized environmental scanning obtained by Diffenbach's (1983) survey of US industry practice.

would expect there to be organizations and publics that deserve to be continuously monitored because of their immediate impact on business operations. These would include users, distributors, suppliers, media commentators, competitors for customers and suppliers, workforce, government regulators, trade unions, product and process developers, etc. (see Baker (1992, Chapter 6) and Jain (1985, Chapter 6) for a full discussion of the elements of the business environment). Dill (1958) refers to the origin of such factors as the task environment, which he defines as 'the more specific forces, which are relevant to decision-making and transformation processes of the individual organizations'.

The concept of the task, or operating environment, opens the environmental scanner's 'window on the world' onto the firm's immediate product and supply markets and onto current influences on its position within them. The search for information about this area of the environment should be focused by the needs of

current decision-making and matters of policy having short and long-term effects. The task environment is generally expected to change more rapidly, to be more complex and to be perceived by managers as more immediately important than the remote environment (Daft *et al.*, 1988). Consumer tastes do change, as do the strategies of competitors, suppliers and distributors. But, broad economic conditions or social demographics tend to change more gradually and to exert an indirect influence on the analysis of market operations (Grant, 1991).

A wider view would also cast attention towards those more remote areas of the economy and society where developments might be under way which in the longer term would impinge on the firm's position in its current product and supply markets. For instance, substitute products and processes often originate as spin-offs from technological developments that have been made by organizations outwith the task environment.

Clearly it is important to look further afield than the task environment. Kast and Rosenweig (1974) have suggested a framework by means of which the wider business environment can be divided into areas for investigation and analysis. Table 4.4 reproduces this framework. Given the diversity of any organization's environment, it is unrealistic to treat it as a single entity. The rates of change and complexity of each constituent sector will vary from time to time, suggesting that different approaches may be required in terms of the *frequency* and *scope* of scanning activity. Indeed, Daft *et al.* (1988) found that high-performing organizations tended to tailor their environmental scanning activities according to where the information need was greatest, i.e. where the *perceived strategic uncertainty* was greatest. This involves taking a flexible approach to defining the environment, rather than a fixed monolithic one that is perhaps geared solely to the continuous monitoring of predefined sectors of the environment.

In Daft *et al.*'s study the scanning activity of low-performing organizations tended to be characterized by a lack of flexibility and a reliance on established scanning routines involving the selective monitoring of predefined areas. And unless care is taken the management information systems that are supposed to support environmental scanning activity can restrict this

Table 4.4	Framework for analysis of the wider business environment
Cultural	Including the historical background, ideologies, values and norms of the society. Views on authority relationships, leadership patterns, interpersonal relationships, nationalism, science and technology.
Technological	The level of scientific and technological advancement in society. Including the physical base (plant, equipment, facilities) and the knowledge base of technology. Degree to which the scientific and technological community is able to develop new knowledge and apply it.
Educational	The general literacy level of the population. The degree of sophistication and specialization in the educational system. The proportion of the people with a high level of professional and/or specialized training.
Political	The general political climate of society. The degree of concentration of political power. The nature of political organization (degrees of decentralization, diversity of functions, etc). The political party system.
Legal	Constitutional considerations, nature of legal system, jurisdictions of various governmental units. Specific laws concerning formation, taxation, and control of organizations.
Natural resources	The nature, quantity and availability of natural resources, including climatic and other conditions.
Demographic	The nature of human resources available to the society; their number, distribution, age and sex. Concentration or urbanization of population is a characteristic of industrialized societies.
Sociological	Class structure and mobility. Definition of social roles. Nature of social organization and development of social institutions.
Economic	General economic framework, including the type of economic organization – private versus public ownership; the centralization or decentralization of economic planning; the banking system; and fiscal policies. The level of investment in physical resources and consumption.

Adapted from Kast and Rosenweig (1974).

flexibility, geared as they are to the collection and reporting of a narrow range of highly bounded and organized information on a repetitive basis (Piercy, 1989; Taylor, 1992). So, environmental scanning activity must accommodate changing information needs, rather than being based on hard and fast definitions, habit and stable scanning patterns which were perhaps set in environmental circumstances which no longer apply. It follows then that the frequency of scanning activity and its scope, or focus, will vary from time to time as events and circumstances dictate.

As one of the high priests of orthodox views on environmental scanning, Ansoff (1984) argues, as have others, that the complexity of environmental scanning is determined by two factors: the degree of *environmental uncertainty* as perceived by the organization and measured by the rate of change in the business environment; and the degree of *environmental complexity* also as perceived by the organization and measured by the range of activities in which the firm is currently and likely to be prospectively involved. It is further argued that this complexity can only be reduced to manageable proportions by, first, defining boundaries of the business environment which reflect the firm's core strategy and competencies (Hamel and Prahalad, 1989), or common thread as Ansoff (1968) calls it. However, as Ansoff's later work acknowledges, a process of selective perception and attention operates within the organization by means of which irrelevant 'stimuli and noise' can be screened out. As Hamel and Prahalad (1989) suggest, this process of selective perception and attention, or strategic intent, can itself be an organizational asset.

Given that there are just too many environmental stimuli at any one time for the organization to pay adequate attention to all of them, environmental scanning could be defined as follows:

the process through which environmental stimuli are selected and organized into patterns which are meaningful to the organization in the light of its current and future needs and interests.

In humans, sensation and perception act as two screening stages – what remains thereafter is at best a partial representation of the reality. Ansoff (1984) argues that in the organization the screening process operates by means of three filters, the first of which is controlled by the environmental scanning function, however it is organized, so that it provides a view of the environment which is selective and partial. The techniques used by environmental scanning to collect, synthesize and analyse information on the business environment can be viewed as a filter (the *surveillance* filter) through which information must first pass on its way to the organization's decision makers. The organization and control of environmental scanning is thus of considerable importance to the organization since it determines the width and strength of the overall screening effect (Brownlie, 1994a, 1998).

It is not the purpose of this chapter to acquaint the reader with the details of environmental analysis and forecasting techniques. They can readily be found in a voluminous literature on the subject (see Brownlie and Saren, 1983; Makridakis, 1990; Saunders, Sharp and Witt, 1987; Grant, 1991; Rescher, 1998). Table 4.5 lists a number of the more important techniques and relates them to the environmental condition in which their application seems to be appropriate. Conventional methodologies such as those of marketing research (see Chapter 7), demand forecasting, economic indicators and industry studies are also used (see Chapter 11).

Ansoff (1984, p. 328) argues that the choice of environmental analysis and forecasting technique is too important to be left to the environmental scanning specialist, as he says it is often done in practice. In his view the user of the output of environmental scanning should have an overriding influence on the choice of technique, for as Brownlie (1998) observes, this choice can hold the key to the interpretive territory, or 'spin' to be placed on the data. Consequently, knowledge of the applicability of the technique is more important to the user than knowledge of the details of the technique's execution. Ansoff writes that the filter which is operated by environmental scan-

Table 4.5	Environmental analysis and forecasting techniques			
Techniques	Percentage of companies reporting use of techniques (n = 66)	Applicable environmental turbulence level		
		Low	Medium	High
Expert opinion	86	•	•	•
Trend extrapolation	83	•		
Alternate scenarios	68	•	•	•
Single scenarios	55	•		
Simulation models	55	•		
Brainstorming	45		•	•
Causal models	32		•	•
Delphi projections	29			•
Cross-impact analysis	27			•
Input-output analysis	26	•		
Exponential forecasting	21	•		•
Signal monitoring	12	•	•	
Relevance trees	6		•	
Morphological analysis	5		•	•

Adapted from Ansoff (1984) and Diffenbach (1983).

ning should be sufficiently open to capture a realistic view of the firm's environment. Distortion and oversimplification are thought to occur where a restrictive filter operates.

In Ansoff's view the information provided by environmental scanning passes through two additional filters before it becomes part of the information on which strategic decisions are made. The first of these (the *mentality* filter) operates by virtue of the mental success models, interpretive frameworks, cognitive maps or frames of reference, recipes or assumptions that are utilized by those managers who receive and act on the incoming environmental scanning information (Ansoff, 1984, p. 328; El Sawy and Pauchant, 1988; Spender, 1989; Gioia and Chittipeddi, 1991).

The accumulation of successes and failures that a manager experiences over time is thought to allow him or her to form convictions about things that work and those that do not. By means of this empirically tested 'world model' the experienced manager is then able to cope with the volume and complexity of the information he receives from all sources, including envir-

onmental scanning. As Ansoff (1984, p. 330) notes, 'the [mentality] filter becomes critical whenever the environment moves from one turbulence level to another'. But, as Ansoff (1984) goes on to argue, this model will serve the manager badly when he or she is presented with the novel signals which arise when variables and relationships in the firm's environment are changing, or dynamic. He remarks that under such circumstances 'the manager will filter novel signals which are not relevant to his historical experience, and thus fail to perceive the shape of the new environment; the newly important variables; the new relationships; and the new success factors'. In this way he believes that success will breed failure in a turbulent business environment as managers attempt to cling on to an obsolete model.

Thus, the operation of the mentality filter can seriously impede the firm's ability to react to signals of environmental change even where environment scanning has picked them up. As Pettigrew and Whipp (1991) note in their observations of Jaguar's attempts to change the mental maps of its managers, it is immensely difficult to alter the taken for granted assumptions which staff make of the company's environment and which in turn guide their everyday actions. Jaguar had to forcefully dramatize elements of its environment by bringing them directly into the workplace by means of a black museum that physically and very dramatically made manifest the firm's abysmal record on product quality.

Ansoff (1984) argues that in terms of environmental turbulence a strategic and creative mentality must be cultivated in participating managers in order to suppress the effect of the mentality filter. But, even where this is so, novel information will not necessarily be incorporated into strategic decision making. For this to occur, appropriate managers must also possess the power to convince the dominant coalition of top managers as well as the workforce to pay heed to the information being imparted by environmental scanning.

It is not unusual for a strategic and creative mentality to be received with hostility by peers and indifference or rejection by superiors. As Ansoff (1984, p. 334) notes, 'to assure a firm-wide acceptance of a new mentality it is essential that top management be the leading practitioners of this mentality'. If top management lack the appropriate mentality, they will persist in preventing vital novel signals from affecting strategic decision making. In this way the third filter (the power filter) operates.

By means of Ansoff's three filters, one can easily appreciate why some firms procrastinate and others seem ignorant of the need for a response to environment change. In terms of the more recent parlance of the psychology of personal constructs (El Sawy and Pauchant, 1988), there may be a need to open up and update the cognitive maps, or strategic assumptions of senior staff. Management can then monitor the extent to which key staff in the firm are sensitive to environmental signals as well as their ability to make collective sense of those signals and act upon them (Weick, 1995).

State of the environmental scanning art

Ansoff (1984) links the evolution of management systems to historical developments in the organization's general environment. He characterizes the managerial approach of organizations in the stable environment of the early 1900s as *management by post facto control of performance*. During this period the pace of change was slower than the firm's ability to respond, the nature of this change was familiar and the future visible. By contrast, during the turbulent era of the late 1980s and into the 1990s events have become discontinuous and novel, the pace of change quicker than the firm's ability to respond and the future not at all visible and very surpriseful. Ansoff characterizes the managerial approach of contemporary organizations as *management by flexible and rapid response*. Like Drucker (1969) before him, Ansoff envisages an age of discontinuity wherein previously reliable heuristics about managerial practice and strategic action no longer apply in an organizational environment capable of sudden and wrenching changes.

On the basis of this argument, management systems could be said to have evolved in response to two related trends: the increasing discontinuity, complexity, and novelty of the environmental challenges organizations face; and the decreasing visibility of the future changes in the environment. The growing impact of such trends was largely responsible for the widespread following which the strategic planning credo acquired in the wake of the 1974 and 1979 oil crises. Those events helped to draw attention to environmental scanning as an important element of strategic planning. They also forced environmental scanning procedures to evolve in response to the dual challenges of flexibility and uncertainty confronting the organization and its planning system.

There is a school of thought which disputes the often taken for granted notion of the escalating turbulence and discontinuity of our age. In reviewing some of this work, Lenz and Engledow (1986b) note that because organizational environments are partly comprised of the institutionalized infrastructures of individual industries, it can take some time to develop new structural dependencies for facilitating physical systems and transactions with other organizations. This suggests a more continuous process of change. Damping forces are also said to operate in the general environment by means of the inertia of broad social forces. So there would seem to be processes of adjustment which mitigate against a rapid rate of change.

Diffenbach (1983) traces the early evolution of environmental scanning to the mid-1960s, at which time he says the business environment was generally being studied only for the purpose of making economic forecasts. Only in more recent years does he consider there to have been an appreciation of the need to look beyond short-term market conditions to the wider technological, economic, political, social, cultural and demographic elements of the business environment. He identifies three distinct evolutionary phases, each of which marks a growth in the scope, systematization, futures orientation and top management recognition of environmental scanning activity.

Diffenbach notes that changes first began to occur during what he terms the *appreciation* phase. In his view this was precipitated by an upsurge of academic and professional interest in environmental analysis. A number of publications were spawned advocating the broad view of the business environment – in opposition to the then popularly held view that the organization's environment be bounded by short-term market conditions. The awareness and interest so created led to the second phase – that of *analysis*. It 'involves finding reliable sources of environmental data, compiling and examining the data to discern trends, developments and key relationships. It also includes monitoring environmental developments and anticipating the future.' Interest in environmental analysis and forecasting techniques (see Table 4.5) grew dur-

ing this phase. The third phase is that of *application* which is concerned with integrating the output of environmental scanning into the firm's strategic decision making.

Aguilar (1967) conducted one of the most influential and pioneering investigations of environmental scanning. In this now classic study the broad framework for environmental scanning was originally conceptualized. In his research Aguilar interviewed 137 managers from 41 chemical firms in the USA and Europe. He found a lack of a systematic approach to environmental scanning which was still being reported in the more recent research of Thomas (1980), Fahey *et al.* (1981), Stubbart (1982), Daft *et al.* (1988), West and Olsen (1989), Dev (1989) and Taylor (1992). Aguilar's study revealed that the participants collected sixteen types of information about their business environment: he classified them into the five groupings displayed in Table 4.6.

Aguilar's study concluded that for environmental scanning to make an effective contribution to the formulation of strategy it must be conducted in a systematic fashion. He frequently found environmental scanning effort to be fragmented. It was also inhibited by the failure of participating managers to gather and disseminate information that users considered important; and to make use of accessible information that already resided within the firm. His proposals for overcoming the '*fractionalization*' of environmental scanning effort called for top management involvement in the definition and execution of scanning activities; greater coordination and integration of these activities with strategic planning; and greater support for these activities, not only from top management, but also from line managers.

Despite the considerable body of strategic planning literature which addresses environmental scanning, scepticism still surrounds the extent to which its application is enhancing the quality of strategic decision making (Stubbart, 1982; Lenz and Engledow, 1986b). The purpose of Diffenbach's (1983) study was to make some progress towards answering the doubts of the

Table 4.6 What information do managers need on the business environment?*

Market tidings

Market potential	Supply and demand consideration for market areas of current or potential interest, e.g. capacity, consumption, imports, exports.
Structural change	Mergers, acquisitions and joint ventures involving competitors, new entries into the industry.
Competitors and industry	General information about a competitor, industry policy, concerted actions in the industry, and so forth.
Pricing	Effective and proposed prices for products of current and potential interest.
Sales negotiations	Information relating to a specific current or potential sale or contract for the firm.
Customers	General information about current or near-potential customers, their markets, their problems.

Acquisition leads

Leads for mergers, joint ventures, or acquisitions	Information concerning possibilities for the manager's own company

Technical tidings

New products, processes, and technology	Technical information relatively new and unknown to the company.
Product problems	Problems involving existing products.
Costs	Costs for processing, operations, and so forth for current and potential competitions, suppliers, and customers, and for proposed company activities.
Licensing and patents	Products and processes.

Broad issues

General conditions	Events of a general nature: political, demographic, national, and so forth.
Government actions and policies	Governmental decisions affecting the industry.

Other tidings

Suppliers and raw materials	Purchasing considerations for products of current or potential interest.
Resources available	Persons, land, and other resources possibly available for the company.
Miscellaneous	Items not elsewhere classified.

Source: Aguilar (1967).

* Market tidings (52%) was found by far to be the most popular category of environmental information that participants looked for, followed by technical tidings (17%) and broad issues (12%). Aguilar also identified four approaches, i.e. *undirected viewing, conditioned viewing, informal search and formal search*, to the collection of environmental information and two principal sources of such information (see Tables 4.3 and 4.4).

sceptics. The earlier work of Fahey *et al.* (1981) shared this motivation. As a result of their in-depth study of the environmental scanning practices of 12 large American firms, they proposed a typology of models of scanning, as shown in Table 4.7.

You will observe that the models represent increasing degrees of *systematization, sophistication* and *resource intensity*. *Irregular* systems respond to environmentally generated crises. They are found in firms where the strategic planning culture is not well established. Their emphasis is on finding solutions to short-term problems. Little attention is paid to evaluating future environmental changes. The *periodic* model is more sophisticated, systematic, proactive and resource intensive. It entails a regular review of the task environment and some elements of the wider environment. A forward view is taken. The *continuous* model emphasizes the ongoing monitoring of the business environment, rather than specified issues or events. It draws on the expertise of marketing, sales, purchasing, etc. It operates a clearing-house for

Table 4.7   A typology of environmental scanning systems

	Irregular	Periodic	Continuous
Impetus for scanning	Crisis-initiated.	Problem-solving decision/issue orientated.	Opportunity finding and problem avoidance.
Scope of scanning	Specific events.	Selected events.	Broad range of environmental systems.
Temporal nature	Reactive.	Proactive.	Proactive.
(a) Timeframe for data	Retrospective.	Current and retrospective.	Current and prospective
(b) Timeframe for decision impact	Current and near term future.	Near term.	Long term.
Types of forecasts	Budget-orientated.	Economic and sales orientated.	Marketing, social, legal, regulatory, culture, etc.
Media for scanning and forecasting	Ad hoc studies.	Periodically updated studies.	Structured data collection and processing systems.
Organization structure	Ad hoc teams.	Various staff agencies.	Scanning unit, focus on enhancing uncertainty handling capability.
Resource allocation to activity	Focus on reduction of perceived certainty. Not specific (perhaps periodic as 'fads' arise).	Specific and continuous but relatively low.	Specific, continuous and relatively substantial.
Methodological sophistication	Simplistic data analyses and budgetary projections.	Statistical forecasting oriented.	Many 'futuristic' forecasting methodologies.
'Cultural' orientation	Not integrated into mainstream of activity.	Partially integrated as a 'stepchild'.	Fully integrated as crucial for long-range growth.

Table 4.8   Propositions on environmental analysis and diagnosis

- A firm whose strategy fits the needs of the firm's environment will be more effective.
- The major causes of growth, decline and other large-scale changes in firms are factors in the environment, not internal developments.
- Most top managers gather information about the environment verbally, primarily from subordinates, friends or acquaintances in the industry. Written information, forecasting and management information systems are not significant sources of information for analyses by top managers, but their use may be increasing.
- The more information contacts the strategist seeks, the better environmental analysis. In large organizations, the contacts are primarily internal. In smaller organizations, the contacts are normally external.
- The more sectors and the more factors that are analysed, the more effective is the environmental analysis.
- The more dependent the enterprise is on a sector of its environment (technological, competitor, geographic, supplier, socioeconomic and government) the more it will focus its environmental analysis on the sector.
- The more developed the sector, the more a firm will focus on that sector of the environment.
- The more hostile the sector, the more vital the analysis and diagnosis of that sector of the environment.
- The more volatile and uncertain the sector, the more the diagnosis will focus on that sector.
- The greater the time pressure and cost of search, the less likely it is that in-depth diagnosis will result.
- The greater the complexity of the environment, the more sector managers must focus on.

Adapted from Glueck and Jauch (1984).

environmental information and uses regular information systems for analysis and dissemination. A long-term view of environment change is taken.

Fahey *et al.* (1981) concluded that the models they were proposing did not find widespread application in US corporations. They noted a trend towards greater sophistication, but added that the impact environmental scanning had so far demonstrated did not appear to warrant the major deployment of resources it requires. Of course, the empirical studies of Thomas (1980) and Diffenbach (1983) provide evidence that persuades them, at least, to take the opposite view.

As a result of their work with US industry in the area of strategic management, Glueck and Jauch (1984) offer a number of broadly based propositions concerning the corporate use of

environmental analysis and diagnosis. These are abstracted in Table 4.8.

The paradox of environmental scanning is that by the time sufficient information has been collected to enable a well informed environmental analysis to be made, it may be too late for the firm to respond before the threat strikes, or the opportunity passes (Flax, 1984; Taylor, 1992). Ansoff (1984) offers a weak-signal management approach to strategic management. In his view this overcomes the paradox by enabling the firm to develop a timely response to partially predictable events which emerge as surprises and develop very quickly. At its heart is the continuous monitoring of the firm's external and internal environment for signals of the evolution of strategic issues which the firm considers able to influence its operations. Ansoff's unit of analysis is then the strategic issue rather than the conventional elements of the business environment. Nanus (1982) and Murphy (1989) have also developed issue-driven approaches to environmental scanning.

Ansoff's solution to the paradox is a 'graduated response' based on the amplification of and flexible response to weak signals. As he contends 'instead of waiting for sufficient information to accumulate, the firm should determine what progressive steps in planning and action are feasible as strategic information becomes available in the course of the evolution of a threat or opportunity'. This is a necessarily incomplete discussion of Ansoff's views. Interested readers should refer to Part 5 of his 1984 text for a comprehensive discussion of the subjects of weak-signal management and strategic issue analysis.

Implicit to much of this thinking is the notion that environmental scanning will be conducted by a freestanding specialized unit (Taylor, 1992). Yet, as Lenz and Engledow (1986b) and others observe, there has been limited experimentation and only modest success with such units. Another approach to organizing environmental scanning focuses on establishing more flexible structures which are closely linked to existing decision-making processes. This approach helps to avoid the integration problems which arise through creating a separate unit. Such mechanisms as multidisciplinary task forces and project groups are used as vehicles for organizational learning through involving managers in sense making and sense giving. By virtue of this involvement in interpretation, managers' understandings of the environment can be updated. The Achilles' heel of this approach is that its efficacy depends on the openness of the managers involved. Yet, as Piercy (1985, 1986) and Brownlie (1998) argue, much power in organizations is information-based and managers are noted for using this information in pursuing their own personal agendas. There may be few incentives for maintaining an openness and trust in decision processes supported by ad hoc structures.

In the author's view the state of the art in environmental scanning theory is likely to reside somewhere between Ansoff's (1984) more holistic, if orthodox, views on strategic management, and those informing contemporary developments in the field which originate in the social psychology of organizing (cf. Brunsson, 1990; Weick, 1979, 1995; Piercy, 1986, 1997; Brownlie, 1994a, 1994b, 1998). The current practical state of affairs in industry is more difficult to determine and one still wonders if there has been any widespread evolution in the application of formal environmental scanning post Aguilar (1967). The lack of theoretical development concerning the intra-organizational environment is likely to constrain the development of environmental scanning practice. Lenz and Engledow (1986b) believe that because of this the analytical elements of environmental scanning will remain largely atheoretical and virtually open-ended. Aside from this, there are numerous inter-organization issues that circumscribe environmental scanning practice. They tend to focus on activity, procedure, systems and routine. The following section attempts to outline some of the difficulties that organizations experience with environmental scanning.

Scanning procedures and problems

In recent years two opposing positions have crystallized on the question of how organizations should approach their strategic management (Mintzberg, 1990, 1994). On the one hand, there is the *design school* to which Ansoff's work on strategic planning belongs. It asserts that organizations can and should approach strategy development through a formal planning system; the structures and procedures which constitute this system can be designed in advance in accordance with a set of general planning propositions; and that managers themselves can conceive of goals and strategies prior to taking any action to intervene in situations, i.e. they think rationally, decide and then act.

On the other hand Mintzberg vociferously opposes the views of the planning or design school. On the basis of several in-depth studies of strategy formation, he argues that organizational processes rarely conform to the edicts of the rational planning approach. He asserts that strategies are crafted; that they emerge through a stream of actions and decisions that engage the managers of organizations at any particular point in time. So, organizations learn how to approach the particular problems they face through trial and error; there is no one correct answer, or design that can be worked out in advance. The so-called *learning school* then questions the ability of organizations to be rational and to conceive of goals and strategies that can cope with the unintended consequences of their interventions. Adherents argue that by the time managers conceive of a strategy, they have already intervened in the situation they are trying to understand and control, thus their strategy is already inappropriate as the context has changed.

Those issues are of relevance to environmental scanning. They illuminate some of the organizational choices available with regard to the systems and procedures driving the scanning effort. For instance, should environmental scanning procedures be designed to suit your

organization by means of general principles; or, should the organization learn through trial and error what seems to work in any specific set of circumstances?

It is possible to say that an organization's environmental scanning procedures will evolve over time as its needs change. And it may be unrealistic for the organization that is about to embrace environmental scanning for the first time to expect to put in place a foolproof system from the outset. Several technical and managerial constraints will impede the progress of environmental scanning efforts (see Table 4.10, p. 100). Of course, the organization may shorten the evolutionary period by ensuring top management involvement, not only in the commissioning of the system, but in the various activities and procedures that define its operation.

The provision of top management support throughout the evolutionary period will help to ensure that a viable system emerges from early efforts which are likely to be directed towards the installation of a system that may be modelled on an idealized scanning procedure such as that shown in Table 4.9. There is some doubt surrounding the question as to whether such

---

Table 4.9   A typical sequential model of the ideal scanning procedure

1   *Monitor* broad trends, issues and events occurring in the firm's task environment. This can be complemented by means of identifying a core list of relevant publications and assigning them to volunteers who report important articles to environmental scanning for further study. Selected areas of the remote environment should be reviewed from time to time. External consultants may be employed.

2   *Identify* trends etc. which may have significance for the firm. A scanning team of senior executives should determine and implement the criteria by means of which relevance is established. Weak signals may not be amenable to screening in this way.

3   *Evaluate* the impact of significant trends, etc., on the firm's operations in its current product markets. Those having a significant impact will either be *threats* or *opportunities*. Line managers should participate in the evaluation.

4   *Forecast* the possible future directions of the significant trends, etc., and *examine* the new opportunities and threats they appear likely to generate.

5   *Evaluate* the impact of these threats and opportunities on the firm's long-term strategies. The output of steps 3, 4 and 5 can be summarized by means of an environmental threat and opportunity profile.

off-the-shelf approaches can be effective in specific circumstances. But, an established strategic planning culture should help expedite matters by providing a fairly receptive organizational climate. This cannot be guaranteed. Even strategic planners are apt to react to a threatening newcomer in a way that ensures their territorial boundaries and organizational prerogatives are preserved – particularly if the newcomer is to be funded from the existing strategic planning resource base.

To make an effective contribution to the commissioning of the environmental scanning system, top management should attempt to a establish a procedure by means of which the following parameters can be defined, and redefined from time to time as circumstances dictate:

- The boundaries of both the task and the wider business environment.
- The appropriate time horizon for future studies.
- The allocation of responsibility for environmental scanning.
- The degree of formality circumscribing environmental scanning.
- The links between scanning and the management of key business relationships.

To define the boundaries of the firm's environments in terms of concrete measures is an almost impossible task for all but the smallest of one-product, one-customer firms. Nevertheless, the environmental scanner needs practicable guidelines by means of which he is able to separate relevant from irrelevant environmental information. In theory, the clearer the definition of the environment (i.e. the search domain) the clearer should be the nature of the information to be collected. Search guidelines can be determined in consultation with members of the top management team who can set the context for the information requirements in terms of strategic issues to be confronted. In this sense, large organizations have something to learn from how small firms organize their environmental scanning activities. For small firms even the

thought of a formal, dedicated environmental scanning activity is an overhead too far – a luxury that only large organizations can afford. Yet, if you closely observe the processes of small firms, you will see that they do engage in a form of environmental scanning. It may not be a formalized activity with dedicated staff and resources; rather it takes place within the context of managing key business relationships and is conducted by staff closely involved in the day-to-day ongoing activity of that relationship. For such firms the idea of managing key relationships, those that are already active as well as those that are being nurtured, provides the key organizing principle for activities such as environmental scanning.

However, for large organizations the management problems experienced by environmental scanning tend to increase where its task is to search for information that is poorly defined. The customers of environmental scanning, the strategists, will require intelligence for decision-making and policy formulation. They can exercise pressure on scanning for information that is proportional in some way to the uncertainty they feel and thus to the perceived importance of the information. In many cases those customers will have authority over the scanners, but will also be very dependent on them for essential information. So, in a sense the scanners can exercise some reciprocal counter power. The ability of senior managers to exercise direct authority over environmental scanning may also be curtailed where there is a need for secrecy in search activities. Double-agent anxiety syndrome may emerge because of the arousal of doubt about the loyalty of environmental scanning to the sponsoring top management team.

There are no hard and fast rules for making the distinction between relevance and irrelevance. Both Stubbart (1982) and Diffenbach (1983) found organizations to be continuously frustrated in their efforts to arrive at a workable definition of their business environment. The nub of the problem is one of achieving a balanced view of the scope of the organization's environment. In order to avoid misdirecting effort to peripheral and irrelevant issues it must not be too wide in scope; nor should it be a narrow, data dependent, econometric but relevant, if myopic, view. The nature of this balance will change from time to time and even within and between organization sub-units, especially in diversified firms which will possess several relevant environments (see Table 4.10). The opportunity cost of a constricted view of the organization's environment may greatly exceed the actual cost of scanning areas of the wider environment – particularly where weak signals are to be detected.

In the context of defining information requirements, there is an observed association between relevance and urgency. When information is urgently required, it does tend to become very relevant and significant. There is also a tendency to attribute to it greater reliability than it may deserve, possibly with damaging consequences for the organization. And although environmental scanning may impress the need for caution, an unwillingness to take a position, especially where managers need it urgently, can undermine the position of scanning in the organization. Alternatively, scanning may defer the dissemination of particular items of information until they have enough corroborating data to make a case for prudent interpretation. But, that too may create difficulties for environmental scanning simply because of the delays involved in communicating to senior staff what may end up being seen as important information. So, senior staff must guard against biases in the reporting of environmental scanning. They typically occur through searching only for information of a pleasing sort; through filtering-out information because it is bad news, or may in some way be inconsistent with the scanner's interpretations of senior managers' expectations (Brownlie, 1994a).

Given the difficulty organizations experience in establishing the width of the scan, it is not surprising that they tend to focus on familiar environments – preferring to study remote environments on an ad hoc basis, perhaps with the assistance of futures consultants. A similarly conservative view is often taken of the appropriate time horizon for the future studies to be conducted by environmental scanning. Diffenbach's research (1983) found that divisional management considered such studies to be more useful the shorter the time horizon they took. Corporate management tended to take a longer view.

There do seem to be grounds for linking the time horizon of environmental scanning and the investment/product development cycle of an industry. For example: in the oil industry a scanning term of 25 years ahead is not unusual; in the fashion industry a period of 2 years is more appropriate. If a reasonable forward view is then to be provided, the time horizon of environmental scanning should try to exceed the duration of the organization's strategic plans. If the organization operates a policy of waiting to see what the industry leaders get up to, then environmental scanning activities may be easily resourced, but they may provide a narrow, reactive view which is biased towards the short term. A proactive regime will be more demanding of middle and top management abilities, especially in multiproduct/multimarket firms where a variety of time horizons might apply. The greater the frequency of scanning and the wider the scope, the more the costs of environmental scanning escalate.

The responsibility for environmental scanning can broadly be allocated in three different ways. First, line managers in boundary spanning functions such as purchasing, sales, finance and marketing can be asked to undertake environmental scanning in addition to their other duties. These managers are likely to be able to provide information on some aspects of the business environment and should, therefore, contribute to any environmental scanning system. This approach can suffer disadvantages such as those that follow: line managers may feel a demotivating resentment towards this additional imposition on their time, unless it is seen as an integral part of their job, for which they are given time, as well as training in the analytical, research and

Table 4.10   Deterrents to effective environmental analysis

Interpretation

The problem is that of interpreting the results of environmental analysis into specific impacts on the company's businesses and into specific responses to be made by the businesses. Included is the problem of the results not being in useful or sufficiently precise form.

- Difficulty of structuring studies in a way that results can be seen to be relevant and meaningful to decision makers today.
- Difficulty of reacting because information from environmental analysis is so intangible with regard to timing and impact.
- Difficulty of assessing the implications of general environmental trends for our specific businesses before they exert themselves.
- Difficulty of translating environmental analysis into relevant business terms, e.g. ROI impact.
- Difficulty of quantifying the impact of major threats and developing alternatives to these threats.
- Difficulty of developing the path from assumption to implication to action, e.g. the tendency to relax or stop after stating the assumption, rather than follow through to an action programme.
- Difficulty in seeing the impact of environmental trends on short-range operations, i.e. the gradual, accumulative nature of trends can be deceptive.
- Lack of sufficient involvement by top management for them to not only understand the conclusions of environmental analysis but also to internalize them and change behaviour accordingly.
- Difficulty of translating potential opportunities into action plans, e.g. conversion of traditional furniture ideas into new lifestyle furniture concepts.
- The time and analysis required to apply information to our specific situations, e.g. impact of probable energy shortages or price increases on our market for automotive components.

- Difficulty of institutionalizing environmental planning into the formal planning processes of the company so that division strategies reflect the process
- Difficulty of follow-up planning, e.g. we have pushed ahead on programmes in spite of warning signals that should have alerted us to severe problems.
- Identifying impacts on businesses, particularly when negative.

Inaccuracy/uncertainty

The problem is that either the output of environmental analysis is inaccurate, too uncertain to be taken seriously, or both.

- Uncertainty due to the dynamics of the market place.
- Inaccurate depicting of environmental events.
- So many false predictions.
- Inability to predict the future, e.g. past experience revealed inability of experts to predict the extent of inflationary forces.
- Difficulty of properly characterizing uncertainties in understandable and meaningful terms.
- Difficulty of forecasting the magnitude of the impact of a future trend.
- The moving-target syndrome, e.g. especially regarding governmental activity.
- Difficulty of predicting social aims, e.g. no-growth versus continuing growth, etc.
- Discontinuities in environmental forecasting for which no company can make satisfactory assessments.

Short-term orientation

The problem is that the preoccupation with short-term matters pre-empts attention to environmental analysis.

- Pressure of short-term events, which tend to soak up some of the resources nominally or usefully committed to environmental planning.
- Dislike for spending money today to help solve a speculative problem tomorrow.

- The reluctance to consider more than the short term because that is where the rewards are.
- Competition between short and long term, i.e. most environmental problems emerge slowly and require solutions which only become effective over similarly long periods of time.
- Organization structures and tasks that force managers to focus on the immediate, short-run elements of their jobs, e.g. budgets are for limited periods of time and encourage concern with this year's results, and perhaps next year's.

Lack of acceptance

The problem is that environmental analysis is not accepted within the company.

- Some degree of scepticism as to the possibility of success with environmental analysis – more so at lower levels that at the top.
- Lack of understanding of the usefulness of environmental analysis.
- Difficulty of environmental analysts convincing line managers that the former's output is applicable to the latter's problems.
- The 'we already know our business' attitude on the part of operating management.
- A suspicion in the practical world of business decisions that scenarios and possible occurrences are impractical and somehow dangerous.
- The 'we have been successful without it' attitude.
- A resistance to change in forecasting methods.
- The presumption by too many executives that each of them can be their own expert in

assessing environmental impacts upon the company.
- Lack of commitment and personal involvement of line executives.
- The difficulty of breaking the patterns of thinking in the past.

Diversified businesses

The problem is that diversified businesses mean multiple relevant environments which make environmental analysis too complex.

- Difficulty of applying corporate expertise in environmental analysis at the operating level due to the great diversity of our operations.
- Complexity due to multiple and decentralized organization.
- Need for too large a corporate staff to keep abreast of environments for decentralized, autonomous businesses, and unwillingness of line managers to support a fulltime staff for environmental surveillance at the division level.

Misperceptions

The problem is one of narrow, limited or invalid perceptions of the external environment shared by executives.

- Tendency of managers to think in non-discontinuous terms.
- Unpreparedness of managers, because of education or basic interest, to deal with social, political, and cultural aspects of a rapidly changing environment (many managers are knowledge reductionists rather than holistic).
- Traditional inability to think in world market terms (instead of 'plant countries') when considering trends and factors of a social, political, technological and economic origin.

Source: Diffenbach (1983).

forecasting skills which they are unlikely to possess; the possibly incompatible mentalities of the roles they are asked to play – creative and farsighted thinker on the one hand; hard headed operator on the other (see Table 4.10).

The second approach is for environmental scanning to be made part of the strategic planner's job. The division of the strategic planning labour in this way leads to specialization which may also have some drawbacks. Stubbart

(1982) argues that the tasks of environmental scanning '... cannot be easily abdicated to technical specialists at corporate headquarters. Because these specialists do not have to answer for the results of business unit performance, they often do not understand the technical requirements of the unit's business. And, most importantly, these specialists do not have a system for defining, measuring and interpreting a business unit's environment more accurately than the unit's own management can'.

It may then be desirable for both planners and line managers to be involved in environmental scanning.

The third approach is to establish a separate organizational unit which is responsible for conducting regular and ad hoc scanning at all levels; and for channelling its results to those in the firm for whom they may have some relevance. Until relatively recently, the US firm General Electric was known to operate such a unit and to fund its activities by charging recipients for the environmental information scanning provides.

As this chapter has previously stated, the latter approach seems to represent a theoretical ideal. However, combinations of the first two approaches are most popular with all but the very large diversified firms who can afford to underwrite the operation of a separate unit. Combinations often operate by means of a temporary scanning team. It is likely to be set up on an ad hoc basis to oversee the study of the impact that a controversial environmental trend, issue or event is thought likely to have on various areas of the firm's operations. The team membership may consist of both line and general management. Line managers will scan the product market, whilst top managers scan the wider environment. Line managers may even be temporarily seconded to a staff position for the duration of the study. They will often be closely involved in determining the impact of environmental changes on areas of the firm's operations in which they are experienced. Consultants, either internal or external, may be used where the impact of environmental change is thought likely to threaten the vested interests of line managers in some way (Brownlie, 1989).

There is no clear agreement about the best way to assign responsibilities for environmental scanning. Every organization will experience unique circumstances that merit taking a particular approach which an off-the-shelf environmental scanning system may be incapable of embracing. However, researchers do agree that organizations should involve managers from various functions and of various levels in environmental scanning activities. It could be argued that only by doing so can environmental scanning hope to become an effective and well-integrated contributor to the firm's strategic decision making regime.

Whatever the means by which responsibility for environmental scanning is assigned, the writer argues that an efficient environmental scanning response demands that the bearers should undertake the following tasks:

- To monitor trends, issues and events in the business environment and study their possible impacts on the firm's operations within its key business relationships.
- To develop the forecasts, scenarios and issues analyses that serve as inputs to the firm's strategic decision making.
- To provide a destination to which environmental intelligence can be sent for interpretation, analysis and storage.
- To construct a means of organizing environmental information so that a library or database on environmental developments can be easily accessed, perhaps organized around the key trading relationships of the organization.
- To provide an internal consulting resource on long-term environmental affairs.
- To disseminate information on the business environment by means of newsletters, reports and lectures.
- To work closely with public affairs on the representation of the organization's position on various issues externally.

- To monitor the performance of environmental scanning activities.

It is not only problematic to decide who is to be responsible for environmental scanning activities. The degree of formality that is to circumscribe its activities is also a matter for top management concern. The view that the organization takes will depend on the extent to which top management feels it necessary to be able to exert some control over the day-to-day activities of environmental scanning. Control may be a problem where responsibility for these activities is devolved to line managers whose own day-to-day responsibilities are likely to take precedence over what they may consider to be marginal 'blue sky' and 'ivory tower' exercises. This problem is likely to be exacerbated where no formal system for collecting, analysing and disseminating environmental information has been agreed. The lack of commitment and scepticism that line managers will often express about environment scanning can only be dealt with by means of training and involvement (see Table 4.9).

Yet, some firms are content to take an informal approach to environmental scanning, relying on key executives in sales, marketing, purchasing and finance to keep abreast of changes in the business environment through newspapers, trade literature, customer and supplier feedback, conferences, exhibitions, and personal contacts. Other firms prefer to organize their scanning efforts into a series of structured and pre-planned activities for which specified staff bear responsibility. The difference is really one of degree. Table 4.11 indicates attributes that a formal (informal) approach to environmental scanning is likely to possess to a great (little) extent.

Diffenbach's research found larger US firms to be more likely to take a formal approach to environmental scanning. This is not surprising given that such firms are also more likely to take a broad view of their business environment, competing as they will do in a number of markets with a number of products. But the informal approach is not only the prerogative of the small organization. Diversified firms may prefer to take an informal approach to such scanning activities as long-term forecasting, the generation of alternative scenarios, issues analyses and the management of weak signals. These activities demand a degree of creative thinking that can best be stimulated in an informal environment – even if the output of the process is subjected to a more formal treatment. But, even so, the recent work of Pettigrew and Whipp (1991) found that many large organizations are seriously questioning the assumptions underlying the need for formality and specialization in environmental scanning. They are more concerned about linking the efforts of environmental scanning to the decision-making processes of the organization and to the learning and development of their managers.

Table 4.11   Attributes of a formal approach to environmental scanning

- Environmental trends, events and issues are regularly and systematically reviewed.
- Explicit criteria have been established that can in turn be used to evaluate the impact of environmental trends.
- Scanning activities are guided by written procedures.
- Responsibility for scanning activities has been clearly assigned.
- Scanning reports, updates, forecasts and analyses are documented in a standardized format.
- Such documentation is generated on a regular basis and disseminated to predetermined personnel according to a timetable.
- The application of formal techniques such as delphi studies and multiple scenarios.

Being involved in environmental scanning does give rise to several sources of conflict in the scanner. The first is a consequence of the greater psychological and physical distance that scanners can often feel from other members of the organization. This distance is a function of the boundary spanning role which requires scanners to represent the points of view, values and needs of outsiders, as well as disseminate information that may be perceived by those within the organization as disturbing the equilibrium through its implications for change. Scanners may also spend much of their time outside the organization collecting information and representing the organization's interests in various public platforms.

A second source of conflict arises through scanners having to influence the behaviour and attitudes of members of the organization, typically without possessing any legitimate power over them, or over the outsiders they have to deal with and influence too. And whilst they must exert this influence internally, they too are influenced by the managers whose information needs they service. External information and influences must be transmitted to internal constituencies, as well as internal influences being transmitted externally to outside constituencies. Tensions arise as result of being both the influence and the influenced. So, environmental scanners often find themselves occupying the junction between the organization and its environment where several dynamic sources of conflict converge. There are no easy solutions to the resolution of this conflict and perhaps this is why environmental scanning will continue to be, paradoxically, one of the most important, yet misunderstood of all organization functions.

But, it is possible to end on a positive note by drawing on the ideas of various authors in proposing at least four characteristics that seem to define more effective implementation of environmental scanning:

1   It is carried out by people close to the action as part of their everyday responsibilities (Stubbart, 1982).

2   It is carried out through accessing personal and informal information sources outside the organization (El Sawy and Pauchant, 1988).

3   It communicates information to influential constituencies within and without the organization, and in so doing plays a vital role in managing impressions (Brownlie, 1994b; 1998).

4   The scope is partly bounded, or targeted on key issues affecting the direct concerns of those constituencies (Lenz and Engledow, 1986b).

Conclusion

This chapter has attempted to provide an overview of environmental scanning in organizations and to set out the various theoretical and practical issues that determine its role and function. It argues that environmental scanning is a fundamental element of organization and that anything that can be done to improve the contribution of environmental scanning efforts should be a priority in organizations.

The chapter identifies the various deficiencies of theory and practice in environmental scanning. It suggests that many of them stem from the normative basis of much of the literature and that it is frequently informed by a rather narrowly rational and sterile theoretical view of how people interact and negotiate meaning in organizations. It argues for a more grounded and comprehensive view of inter- and intra-organizational processes. It asserts the important role of non-expert scanners in environmental scanning and draws to attention the role of managers' cognitive frames in interpreting information. It introduces the principle of organizing environmental scanning activities around key business relationships and the various activities which occur within them.

The orthodox methodology of environmental scanning is set out in much of its conventional splendour, and many of its limitations, so that the reader can pick and choose between the many issues that circumscribe its operation in organizations. It cautions that the collection and possession of information about the environment is a small part of a very complex story. Attention is drawn to the constraining and facilitating role of managerial attitudes which are frequently embedded in structures and systems as taken for granted notions, not objective realities. But this is the context within which all organizing activity takes place and the author can think of no reason to believe that environmental scanning is the exception – if the reader can, please write to me as soon as possible.

References

Aguilar, F. (1967) *Scanning the Business Environment*, New York, Macmillan.

Ansoff, I. (1968) *Corporate Strategy*, Penguin, London.

Ansoff, I. (1984) *Implanting Strategic Management*, Prentice-Hall International, Englewood Cliffs, NJ.

Baker, M. (1992) *Marketing Strategy and Management*, 2nd edn, London, Macmillan.

Bourgeois, L. (1980) Strategy and Environment: A Conceptual Integration, *Academy of Management Review*, **5**, 25–39.

Bourgeois, L. (1985) Strategic Goals, Perceived Uncertainty, and Economic Performance in Volatile Environments, *Academy of Management Journal*, **28**, 548–573.

Brownlie, D. (1989) Scanning the Internal Environment: Impossible Precept or Neglected Art?, *Journal of Marketing Management*, **4**(2), 300–329.

Brownlie, D (1994a) Organizing for Environmental Scanning: Orthodoxies and Reformations, *Journal of Marketing Management*, **10**, 703–723.

Brownlie, D. (1994b) Environmental Scanning, Chapter 7, in M. J. Baker (ed.), *The Marketing Book*, 3rd edn, Butterworth-Heinemann, Oxford, pp. 139–192.

Brownlie, D. (1996) The Conduct of Marketing Audits: A Critical Review and Appraisal, *Industrial Marketing Management*, **25**(1), 11–22

Brownlie, D. (1998) High Minds and Low Deeds: on being Blind to Creativity in Strategic Marketing, *Journal of Strategic Marketing*, **6**, 1–14.

Brownlie, D. T. and Saren, M. A. (1983) A Review of Technology Forecasting Techniques and their Applications. *Management Bibliographies and Reviews*, **9**(4).

Brunsson, N. (1990) Deciding for Responsibility and Legitimation: Alternative Interpretation of Organizational Decision-making, *Accounting Organizations and Society*, **15**(1/2), 47–59.

Child, J. (1972) Organization Structure, Environment and Performance: The Role of Strategic Choice, *Sociology*, **6**, 1–22.

Churchman, C. (1968) *The Systems Approach*, Delacorte Press, New York.

Cyert, R. and March, J. (1963) *A Behavioural Theory of the Firm*, Prentice-Hall, Englewood Cliffs, NJ.

Daft, R., Sormunen, J. and Parks, D. (1988) Chief Executive Scanning, Environmental Characteristics, and Company Performance: An Empirical Study, *Strategic Management Journal*, **9**, 123–139.

Dev, C. (1989) Operating Environment and Strategy: The Profitable Connection, *The Cornell Hotel and Restaurant Administration Quarterly*, May, **30**, 19–23.

Diffenbach, J. (1983) Corporate Environmental Analysis in Large US Corporations, *Long Range Planning*, **16**(3), 107–116.

Dill, W. (1958) Environment as an Influence on Managerial Autonomy, *Administrative Science Quarterly*, **2**, 404–443.

Drucker, P. (1969) *The Age of Discontinuity*, Harper and Row, New York.

El Sawy, O. and Pauchant, T. (1988) Triggers, Templates and Twitches in the Tracking of Emerging Strategic Issues, *Strategic Management Journal*, **9**, 455–473.

Emery, F. and Trst, E. (1965) The Causal Texture of Organizational Environments, *Human Relations*, **18**, 21–32.

Etzioni, A. (1967) Mixed Scanning: A Third Approach to Decision-making, *Public Administration Review*, **27**, 385–392.

Fahey, L., King, W. R. and Narayanan, V. K.

(1981) Environmental Scanning and Forecasting in Strategic Planning – The State of the Art, *Long Range Planning*, February, 32–29.

Flax, S. (1984) How To Snoop on Your Competitors, *Fortune*, May 14, 29–33.

Gioia, D. and Chittipeddi, K. (1991) Sensemaking and Sensegiving in Strategic Change Initiation, *Strategic Management Journal*, **12**, 433–448.

Glueck, W. and Jauch, L. (1984) *Business Policy and Strategic Management*, McGraw-Hill, New York.

Grant, R. (1991) *Contemporary Strategy Analysis*, Blackwell, Oxford.

Hambrick, D. (1981) Strategic Awareness Within Top Management Teams, *Strategic Management Journal*, **2**, 263–279.

Hambrick, D. (1982) Environmental Scanning and Organizational Strategy, *Strategic Management Journal*, **3**, 159–174.

Hamel, G. and Prahalad, C. (1989) Strategic Intent, *Harvard Business Review*, May/June, 63–76.

Heil, O. and Robertson, T. (1991) Toward a Theory of Competitive Market Signalling: A Research Agenda, *Strategic Management Journal*, **12**, 403–418.

Jain, S. (1984) Environmental Scanning in US Corporations, *Long Range Planning*, **17**(2), 117–128.

Jain, S. (1985) *Marketing Planning and Strategy*, 2nd edn, South-Western Publishing Company.

Jemison, D. (1981) Organizational versus Environmental Sources of Influence in Strategic Decision Making, *Strategic Management Journal*, **2**(1), 77–89.

Johnson, G. and Scholes, K. (1993) *Exploring Corporate Strategy: Text and Cases*, 3rd edn, Prentice-Hall, Hemel Hempstead.

Kast, F. E. and Rosenweig, J. E. (1974) *Organization and Management: A Systems Approach*, 2nd edn, McGraw-Hill, New York.

Kefalas, A. and Schoderbek, P. (1973) Scanning the Business Environment: Some Empirical Results, *Decision Sciences*, **4**, 63–74.

King, W. and Cleland, D. (1977) Information for More Effective Strategic Planning, *Long Range Planning*, **10**(1), 59–64.

Klein, H. and Linneman, R. (1984) Environmental Assessment: An International Study of Corporate Practice, *Journal of Business Strategy*, 66–75.

Lenz, R. (1980) Environment, Strategy, Organization Structure and Performance: Patterns in One Industry, *Strategic Management Journal*, **1**, 209–226.

Lenz, R. and Engledow, J. (1986a) Environmental Analysis Units and Strategic Decision Making: A Field Study of Selected Leading-edge Corporations, *Strategic Management Journal*, **7**, 69–89.

Lenz, R. and Engledow, J. (1986b) Environmental Analysis: The Applicability of Current Theory, *Strategic Management Journal*, **7**, 329–346.

Lenz, R. and Lyles, M. (1985) Diagnosing and Managing Human Problems in Strategic Planning Systems, *Journal of Business Strategy*, Fall.

Lyles, M. and Lenz, R. (1982) Managing the Planning Process: A Field Study of the Human Side of Planning, *Strategic Management Journal*, **3**(2), 105–118.

Makridakis, S. (1990) *Forecasting, Planning and Strategy for the 21st Century*, Free Press, New York.

Mintzberg, H. (1990) The Design School: Reconsidering the Basic Premises of Strategic Management, *Strategic Management Journal*, **11**, 171–195.

Mintzberg, H. (1994) *The Rise and Fall of Strategic Planning*, Prentice-Hall, Hemel Hempstead.

Murphy, J. (1989) Identifying Strategic Issues, *Long Range Planning*, **22**(2), 101–105.

Nanus, B. (1982) QUEST – Quick Environmental Scanning Technique, *Long Range Planning*, **15**(2), 39–45.

Pettigrew, A. and Whipp, R. (1991) *Managing Change for Competitive Success*, Blackwell, Oxford.

Pfeffer J. and Salancik, G. (1978) *The External Control of Organizations*, Harper and Row, New York.

Piercy, N. (1985) *Marketing Budgeting: A Political*

and Organizational Model, Croom-Helm, London.

Piercy, N. (1986) *Marketing Budgeting: A Political and Organizational Model*, Croom-Helm, London.

Piercy, N. (1989) Information Control and the Power and Politics of Marketing, *Journal of Business Research*, **18**, 229–243.

Piercy, N. (1997) *Market-Led Strategic Change*, 2nd edn, Butterworth-Heinemann, Oxford.

Rescher, N. (1998) *Predicting the Future: An Introduction to the Theory of Forecasting*, State University of New York Press, Albany.

Saunders J., Sharp, J. and Witt, S. (1987) *Practical Business Forecasting*, Gower, Aldershot.

Sawyerr, O. (1993) Environmental Uncertainty and Environmental Scanning Activities of Nigerian Manufacturing Executives: A Comparative Analysis, *Strategic Management Journal*, **14**, pp. 287–299.

Smircich, M. and Stubbart, C. (1985) Strategic Management in an Enacted World, *Academy of Management Review*, **1**(4), 724–736.

Snow, C. (1976) The Role of Managerial Perceptions in Organizational Adaption: An Exploratory Study, *Academy of Management Proceedings*, pp. 249–255.

Spender, J.-C. (1989) *Industry Recipes*, Blackwell, Oxford.

Stubbart, C. (1982) Are Environmental Scanning Units Effective? *Long Range Planning*, **15**(3), 139–145.

Taylor, J. (1992) Competitive Intelligence: A Status Report on US Business Practices, *Journal of Marketing Management*, **8**, 117–125.

Terreberry S. (1968) The Evolution of Organizational Environments, *Administrative Science Quarterly*, **12**, 590–613.

Thomas, P. S. (1980) Environmental Scanning – the State of the Art, *Long Range Planning*, Feb., 20–28.

Thompson, J. (1967) *Organizations in Action*, McGraw-Hill, New York.

Thompson, J. (1993) *Strategic Management: Awareness and Change*, 2nd edn, Chapman and Hall, London.

Weick, K. (1979) *The Social Psychology of Organizing*, Addison-Wesley, Reading, MA.

Weick, K. (1995) *Sensemaking and Organizations*, Sage, London.

West, J. and Olsen, M. (1989) Environmental Scanning, Industry Structure and Strategy Making: Concepts and Research in the Hospitality Industry, *International Journal of Hospitality Management*, **8**(4), 283–298.

Whittington, R. (1993) *What is Strategy and Does It Matter?* Routledge, London.

Further reading

Aguilar, F. J. (1967) *Scanning The Business Environment*, Macmillan. Presents the results of the author's pioneering study of environmental scanning. It is a standard reference text on the subject and has withstood the passage of time.

Brownlie, D. (1994) Organizing for Environmental Scanning: Orthodoxies and Reformations, *Journal of Marketing Management*, **10**(8), 703–724. An analysis of the arguments underpinning various approaches to organizing environmental scanning activities.

Brownlie, D. and Saren, M. (1983) A Review of Technology Forecasting Techniques and Their Application, *Management Bibliographies and Reviews*, **9**(4). A review of the major forecasting methodologies as they find application in the context of technology forecasting.

Daft, R., Sormunen, J. and Parks, D. (1988) Chief Executive Scanning, Environmental Characteristics, and Company Performance: An Empirical Study, *Strategic Management Journal*, **9**, 123–139. The paper reports the results of an empirical study of 50 medium sized US manufacturing firms. Several insights are provided into the procedures and arrangements used in organization for environmental scanning.

Diffenbach, J. (1983) Corporate Environmental Analysis in Large US Corporations, *Long Range Planning*, June, 107–116. Reports the findings of an interesting empirical study. The paper addresses the questions of the usefulness, implementation and payoffs of organized environmental analysis.

El Sawy, O. and Pauchant T. (1988) Triggers, Templates and Twitches in the Tracking of Emerging Strategic Issues, *Strategic Management Journal*, **9**, 455–473. Another interesting empirical study of environmental scanning, this time of the longitudinal sort. It looks at managers' cognitive frames in the scanning process and their influence on strategic issue diagnosis.

Fahey, L., King, W. and Narayanan, V. (1981) Environmental Scanning and Forecasting in Strategic Planning – The State of the Art, *Long Range Planning*, Feb., 32–39. Reports the results of an empirical study which revealed that environmental scanning was not a well established corporate activity and that it faced serious conceptual and organizational difficulties.

Lenz, R. and Engledow, J. (1986) Environmental Analysis: The Applicability of Current Theory, *Strategic Management Journal*, **7**, 329–346. A very incisive piece regarding the theoretical underpinnings of environmental analysis and scanning. It presents five key generic models based upon disciplinary origin and perspective and evaluates each of them along three dimensions.

Nanus, B. (1982) Quest – Quick Environmental Scanning Technique, *Long Range Planning*, **15**(2), 39–45. For those who want a 'quick and dirty', ready-made approach to environmental scanning, this is a paper well worth consulting.

Pettigrew, A., and Whipp, R. (1991) *Managing Change for Competitive Success*, Blackwell, Oxford. A book which is very rich in insights into organizational processes, including environmental scanning. Several case studies are provided of current practice. The reporting approach is in sharp contrast to the mainstream approach in strategic management.

Stubbart, C. (1982) Are Environmental Scanning Units Effective? *Long Range Planning*, June, 139–145. Updates and replicates the work of Fahey *et. al.* Reports some discrepancies which were observed and criticizes the then prevailing normative work.

CHAPTER 5

Consumer decision making: process, involvement and style

GORDON R. FOXALL

Consumer decision making is usually depicted as a cognitive process. Consumers become aware of a need or want and a possible means of satisfying it, typically announced in an advertisement for a new brand. They call mentally on the information they have at hand to evaluate the advertiser's claims and, when that proves inadequate, search for further information – perhaps from other manufacturers and from friends. The ensuing deliberation entails a detailed comparison of the probable attributes of the competing brands and the selection of the brand which comes closest to fulfilling the consumer's goals. When the cognitive models of consumer behaviour were first formulated in the 1960s, it did not seem to matter much whether the consumer was buying a brand in a familiar product class such as medicated shampoo or making a first-time purchase of a new durable. The assumed pattern of decision making, modelled on the information processing of digital computers, was the same.

Real consumers have a habit of disappointing the theoreticians. Empirical research indicates that, far from going through a detailed decision process and becoming loyal to a single brand as the formal models suggest, many consumers (1) show little sign of pre-purchase decision making based on the rational processing of information (Olshavsky and Granbois, 1979); (2) use brand trial – rather than pre-purchase deliberation – in order to obtain information about and evaluate brands (Ehrenberg, 1988); (3) show multibrand purchasing within a small repertoire of brands which share attributes (or characteristics) that are common to all members of their product class (Ehrenberg, 1988); and (4) rely substantially on situational pressures and constraints in making brand decisions (Wilkie and Dickson, 1991).

As a result, the conventional understanding of consumer choice needs to be modified in three ways. First, it must take account of the level of involvement consumers show in the decisions they make, their personal interest and engagement in the process. This refinement of consumer decision models is already under way: issues raised by high and low involvement are quickly becoming standard elements in the consumer behaviour texts, though there remains much room for clarification of the concept and its marketing implications. Second, our models of choice need to take account of the style of decision making preferred by various groups of consumers. Some prefer to work in a detailed, conservative and cautious fashion, buying only after long deliberation and evaluation; others prefer a more impulsive approach, buying many products on trial and possibly discarding them quickly in favour of other novelties. The style of consumer decision making has far-reaching potential implications for consumers' awareness, their openness to marketing information and the ways in which they use it, the purchase decisions they make, and the probability that they will become brand or product loyal. Finally, the situational context in which consumer behaviour occurs needs to receive detailed attention.

The modern message of marketing is that the needs of the consumer are paramount; those of the producer, contingent. So, before we examine the process, involvement and style of consumer behaviour, let us ask why marketers should be interested in all this. Marketing has been defined in a somewhat basic way as whatever comes between production and consumption, the distribution of products and services to those who buy them. Only subsistence economies, where everything is quickly consumed by the family that produces it, can escape making provision for marketing in this fundamental sense. More structured economies, even if they emphasize barter, must tailor production in some degree to the wants of its recipients. They must also make provision for the storage and physical handling of goods and for informing likely consumers about them. The invention of money made economic exchange easier, though more uncertain, for the wants of consumers had to be anticipated before market transactions occurred, perhaps even before production took place. The affluent market economies with which we are familiar today put even greater stress on understanding the consumer, on supplying what he or she will buy rather than what the manufacturer happens to be able to supply or thinks is good for the customer.

A popular view claims, however, that marketing is largely a matter of persuading or even duping customers into parting with their money for products and services they do not want, let alone need. All the paraphernalia of market research, advertising, retail design, and credit provision are seen as manipulating the hapless consumer by removing their discretion and making their decisions for them. Of course, marketing can be a powerful force, communicating ideas and practices to a population that might otherwise remain unaware of them, providing goods that might otherwise be unthought of, 'taking the waiting out of wanting'. No responsible society ought to allow these activities to go unmonitored, nor abuses unchecked, and none does. The network of voluntary and mandatory provisions for the regulation of advertising should be enough to convince us of that.

The influence of marketing is limited in a more fundamental way. Most new consumer products are launched only after the most thorough development process in which they are tested physically, functionally and in terms of their acceptability to consumers. It is true, as the critics allege, that market research, product development and marketing communications are all planned and executed with professional expertise. Yet, even after all the pre-launch testing, test marketing and marketing planning that accompanies most consumer product entries, the majority fail at the stage of customer acceptance. Not because the creation and delivery of these products is poor – we have noted that they are highly sophisticated procedures – but because consumers have choice.

As a result, modern marketing links production and consumption in a particular way, a managerial style known as consumer-orientated management. Unless a firm enjoys a monopoly, its managers have little discretion in the matter of adopting a consumer-orientated approach. Consumer affluence and competition among suppliers give buyers enormous discretion over what they buy, from whom they buy it, and how they pay. They have discretion not only over what they spend their money on but to whom they listen, by whom they are persuaded. And it has long been known that consumers are far more likely to be influenced by the word-of-mouth evaluations of other consumers than by formal marketing communications. This managerial style is forced on to the firm if it is to survive and prosper. The need to understand consumer behaviour is, therefore, premier, if it is to be forecast, anticipated and stimulated by marketing management.

The consumer decision process

This means more than monitoring sales: consumer-orientated marketing needs a far wider definition of consumer behaviour. Engel, Blackwell and Miniard (1993, p. 4) define their subject matter as 'those activities directly involved in obtaining, consuming, and disposing of products and services, including the decision processes that precede and follow these actions'. In addition to making a purchase, therefore, we shall understand consumer behaviour to include any pre-purchase and post-purchase activities that are relevant to marketing management. Pre-purchase activities would include the growing awareness of a want or need, and the search for and evaluation of information about the products and brands that might satisfy it. Post-purchase activities would include the evaluation of the purchased item in use, and any attempt to assuage feelings of anxiety which frequently follow the purchase of an expensive and infrequently-bought item such as a car. Each of these influences whether consumers will repurchase a chosen brand, what they will tell other potential buyers, and how amenable they are to marketing communications and the other elements of the marketing mix.

Consumer behaviour, we have seen, can be modelled as a cognitive process, an intellectual sequence of thinking, evaluating and deciding. These information processing activities are believed to shape the more overt aspects of choice: acquiring information from a salesperson, placing an order, using the product selected, and so on. The inputs to the process are the most basic bits of data available to the consumer, stimuli from the environment in the form of marketing messages and conversations with friends and relatives. The processing itself consists in the mental treatment of these data as the consumer stores them, links them with existing ideas and memories, and evaluates their relevance to his or her personal goals. The outputs are the attitudes the consumer forms towards say an advertised brand, an intention to buy or postpone buying, and – if attitude and intention are positive – the act of purchase. A similar sequence characterizes the use of the purchased item: it is evaluated again in use and a decision is reached about its suitability for repurchase.

Awareness

Figure 5.1, derived from Foxall, Goldsmith and Brown (1998), summarizes the process of consumer decision making. Consumer awareness is not automatic; it is the endpoint of a highly selective procedure. Every day, consumers are bombarded by thousands of messages that seek to persuade them – from advertising, from political organizations, from religious groups, from employers, and from numerous other sources. There is enormous competition for the attention and understanding of the average citizen to the extent that no-one could possibly cope with the cumulative effect on the nervous system of so great a mass of information. Fortunately, most of these social, economic and marketing stimuli in the environment are filtered out by the individual's attentional and perceptual processes and have no effect on the decision process.

Efficiency in decision making requires that attention and perception be selective; a kind of perceptual defence mechanism screens out all but those messages that are familiar, consistent with our current beliefs and prejudices, motives, expectations and wants. Even so-called subliminal messages – an attempt to circumvent this filter by being so weak that they are not recognized by the senses and yet influence our cognitive processes – do not exert an influence on our mental operations. Perception is clearly more than the process in which stimuli impinge on the senses; it is the beginning of information processing, the interpretation of those stimuli to which we pay attention according to our existing mental set-up – attitudes, experience,

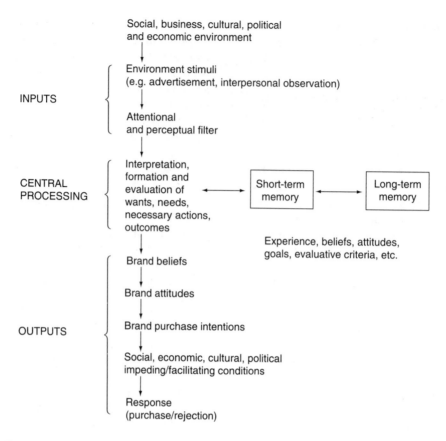

Figure 5.1   Consumer information processing

motivation. Only when an advertising message has got through the filter and had some meaning attached to it in this preliminary processing activity can the consumer be said to be aware of a problem in his or her life (e.g. dandruff), its consequences (possibly for their health and social activity) and the proffered means of overcoming it (the advertised brand of shampoo).

Search and evaluation

Even awareness of a problem does not guarantee that the process of decision making will continue. Only if the problem is important to the consumer and he or she believes that a solution is available will it continue. If a sufficiently high level of involvement or engagement with the problem is present, the consumer is likely to

seek further information to evaluate the claims of the advertiser. Internal search takes place within the consumer's memory system; it is an attempt to locate information in the form of pre-existing knowledge, especially beliefs and attitudes about the problem, the likely solutions, and remedies that are already in use. If the problem or the proffered solution is radically new to the customer, this may prove inadequate and an external search may be necessary. External search may be an active seeking of information from neighbours or colleagues, salespersons or other advertisements, newspapers or magazines, Which? or Consumer Reports.

All of this activity is accompanied by the mental processing of the advertising message in the consumer's short-term and long-term memory stores. We have seen that much information fails to get this far but even that which is stored in short-term memory is there only briefly. If it is not transferred to the long-term store, where it will be effective in this and subsequent decisions, it is lost within about a minute. Three operations may occur in the consumer's memory to ensure that information can be retained and retrieved:

rehearsal – the mental repetition of information which links it to information already stored; encoding – the symbolic representation of information which permits its long-term association with other stored information; and storage – the elaboration of information in which it is organized into structures from which it can be retrieved, i.e. returned from long-term to short-term memory and used in momentary decision making.

The outputs of information processing are the beliefs and attitudes that shape decisions and the intentions that predispose certain actions such as buying, consuming and saving. Beliefs are statements about the product or brand that the consumer assumes to be factual; attitudes are evaluations of the product or brand; and intentions are strong motivations to act in accordance with beliefs and attitudes. Together they form the cognitive (intellectual), affective (evaluative) and conative (action-oriented) components of the consumer's decision activity.

A great disappointment for the information processing approach to consumer decision making was the finding that attitudes, intentions and behaviour often do not correlate well (or at all) with each other (Foxall, 1997). Measuring attitudes and intentions might not, therefore, be a useful way of predicting behaviour; nor might persuasive attempts to change attitudes be the key to prompting changes in consumers' actual brand selections. The work of Fishbein and Ajzen (1975) has done much to resolve this problem. Rather than measure general attitudes towards an object, as previous researchers had tended to do, these researchers chose very specific measures of an attitude towards a

behaviour. By ensuring that the attitude measure corresponded to the measure of behaviour – in terms of the target object, the action or behaviour towards it, the time and the context of the behaviour – they showed that very high correlations could be achieved.

For instance, previous researchers would typically ask how consumers evaluated say chocolate bars (a general or 'global' attitude towards this object) and then expect to forecast accurately whether they would buy a particular brand of chocolate on their next shopping trip (a highly specific behavioural criterion). Fishbein and Ajzen showed that by measuring consumers' attitudes towards a specific act, say buying a stated brand of chocolate on their next supermarket trip, much higher correlations between the evaluation and the act were forthcoming (Ajzen and Fishbein, 1980). The attitude measure used was the sum of a respondent's beliefs about the consequences of the act in question, weighted by their evaluations of those consequences.

By taking another measure of the consumer's subjective norm, Fishbein and Ajzen were able to take into consideration many of the factors other than attitude that determine a consumer's intention to perform a specific behaviour. The subjective norm consists of the respondent's beliefs about the evaluations another person (whom they hold in high regard) would put on the act in question, weighted by their motivation to comply with the other person's evaluations. Attitude and subjective norm correlate with the consumer's behavioural intention, his or her disposition to perform the act in question. And behavioural intentions usually correlate highly with the performance of the behaviour itself.

Fishbein and Ajzen refer to this approach to the prediction of behavioural intentions as the theory of reasoned action. Ajzen (1985) has proposed a second theory, the theory of planned behaviour, which incorporates an additional determinant of intention. This is *perceived behavioural control*, or the individual's beliefs that he succeed in the task in hand. Bagozzi and

Warshaw (1990) have proposed a theory of trying, in which past behaviour is taken into consideration as a means of predicting future choice. A full discussion of these approaches is available in Foxall (1997).

Post-decisional evaluation

Another filtering device determines the extent to which consumers quickly put their intentions into practice, shown in Figure 5.1 as 'impeding and facilitating conditions'. These are the situational variables, such as access to funds or credit, availability of compatible products, social acceptability, that determine whether a particular purchase will take place or not. No amount of strong intention will guarantee purchase in the absence of these and a hundred other facilitating conditions. Purchasing also depends on past behaviour. It would be absurd and naive to suppose that a consumer who had just bought a video recorder based on an obsolete system could simply go through the above decision process and make another, more lasting, purchase a week later.

But the consumer decision process does not end when a purchase has been made. Most important of all from a marketing viewpoint is whether the consumer will buy the selected brand again on a later purchase occasion. The first purchase of a brand – or even the first few purchases – can be considered no more than a trial by the consumer. The clearest indication of whether it is worth buying again comes from its evaluation in use (Ehrenberg, 1988). Something that often needs to be resolved in the case of expensive, infrequently bought items such as consumer durables is the cognitive dissonance or feeling of mental unease that follows their purchase. Cognitive dissonance arises when two contradictory beliefs are held at the same time: 'I have spent so much on this car and my neighbour tells me his gets from 0 to 60 mph a second faster!' People tend to try to reduce dissonance by dropping one or other of the opposing beliefs or by emphasizing one at the expense of the other. The car purchaser might well conclude,

therefore, that his car was more prestigious since it had cost more or had a more auspicious marque. Or that his car was guaranteed for longer, or ran on unleaded fuel, or needed less frequent services. Some advertising is deliberately geared to the needs of the dissonant consumer who has recently purchased; although they are less obvious than they used to be, ads for cars still sometimes stress the performance characteristics of the advertised and competing makes.

Selectivity

We have seen that a frequent assumption in consumer research has been that consumer decision making must be a uniform process for all consumers. Once the stages outlined above had been identified, it was common for researchers and managers to expect all consumers to pass through them in a similar fashion on each purchase occasion. Yet both common sense and our experience as consumers suggests that not all transactions are preceded by this entire process of cognitive learning. Both personal and situational factors often intervene at one or other stage to throw the procedure off course or to circumvent it totally.

A striking characteristic of consumer decision making is the selectivity it entails. Consumers are not exposed to all of the stimuli that might conceivably influence them; their attentional and perceptual processes are highly selective in what they admit and consider; memory processes are similarly limited since the encoding of information and its rehearsal are highly selective, too. Many factors account for the limited consideration sets (the range of brands actively appraised) consumers' decision processes can encompass and the apparently arbitrary processing they receive. Prior experience, personal circumstances, attitudes and expectations, states of deprivation and motivation, and numerous personality dimensions can all give rise to variation in the manner of information processing (Kardes, 1994). The two summary factors which we consider here are involvement and cognitive style.

Consumers are motivated more or less strongly to participate in the full information processing sequence. Sometimes they feel a need to reduce their uncertainty and risk by seeking a broad spectrum of information and evaluating it thoroughly before making a purchase. On other occasions, they will telescope the procedure, apparently muddling through the decision as they call instantly on accumulated knowledge and experience. More recently, substantial attention has been given to one aspect of the decision sequence which may modify its form from situation to situation: the level of involvement which the consumer feels as he or she approaches the decision making process. We discuss that aspect in this section.

Another factor is the style of decision making shown by consumers. Even when two potential buyers go through all of the decision stages outlined above, they may do so in quite distinct ways, considering different information, a varying range of products, and fundamentally different ways of solving their problems. Far less attention has been paid to consumers' decision styles, though research in the last few years shows how crucial cognitive styles are to understanding the entire decision process.

Levels of consumer involvement

Some products such as high performance cars seem inherently involving because of their complexity, risk and cost, while others such as toothpaste seem uninvolving by comparison because of their familiarity, low risk and low cost (Laaksonen, 1994). In fact, while this is true in a general way, involvement is actually a relationship rather than a property of this or that product or service. It reflects not only the degree of uncertainty experienced by a consumer when he or she is faced with consideration of a product but also the personal characteristics of the consumer (some people find everything more involving than others) and on the situation in which purchase and consumption take place. Involvement is commonly defined as the consumer's

personal interest in buying or using an item from a given product field, an approach which nicely summarizes the individual, experiential and situational components of the relationship. This is not the time to go into the concept in detail (though the sources referenced above will be a helpful starting point for those who can) but to note its influence on the decision-making process.

One of the most prominent sources of situational influence on consumer motivation and choice derives from the newness of the product under consideration to the potential buyer (Howard, 1977). Although we speak generally of new products being innovations, such items differ markedly from the radically novel – such as video recorders at the time of their introduction – to the incrementally different – an improved version of an established brand of shampoo. Robertson (1967) categorized innovations in terms of the amount of disruption they caused in existing consumption patterns. Radically new products which had maximal disruptive effect he termed discontinuous innovations. TV aerial dishes, supersonic transatlantic travel and, in its day, television itself all came into this category. Note that the disruption involved is not necessarily a problem to be overcome: in the case of Concorde flights it provided a much improved and superior service for those who both needed it and could afford it. Many new products are not so revolutionary, though they still present additional benefits to the consumer that were not previously available. Electric lawnmowers, for instance, do the same job accomplished by manual versions but more quickly and with less effort. Their 'disruptiveness' consists in the change they effect in consumers' lifestyles. These moderately novel products which do a known job better are called dynamically continuous innovations. Finally, there are the most familiar 'new' products of all, the improved shampoos, slightly faster cars, fourth editions of successful textbooks. These are minimally disruptive of established consumption patterns; they allow life to go on much as before but provide the benefits of the most recent developments in technology and thought. They are continuous innovations.

Genuinely discontinuous innovations are few and far between. When such an item is introduced, it is the first brand in a wholly new product class, right at the beginning of the product life cycle (Howard and Moore, 1982). People are often suspicious of such radical innovations. Most prefer to wait and see what happens to the first adopters before they themselves make a purchase. The consumers who do buy at this stage are usually highly involved in the product field. They are heavy users of whatever preceded the innovation – perhaps radio and movies in the case of television, audio cassettes in the case of VCRs, conventional air travel in the case of Concorde. In terms of personality factors, they have an apparent 'need for newness', wanting to be the first to try novel ideas and thereby to communicate them to other, more cautious consumers who buy later if at all. They are better off than these later adopters, have a higher social status, are upwardly mobile, better educated, and socially integrated with broader horizons.

All of this adds up to a strong personal interest in the product field or what has become known as high involvement. Their decision processes are not necessarily longer or more intensive than those of later adopters; it depends how familiar they are personally with the product field and the new product. In a lot of cases, because of their heavy use of its precedents, they require very little information processing before quickly adopting the discontinuous innovation (cf. Howard, 1989). In other cases, where their personal innovativeness relies more on having the money to spend and seeking the status of being first, they may need to go through most of the stages in the consumer choice process shown in Figure 5.1 before testing the water. What sets both types of early consumer off from later adopters is the degree of involvement they show in the product, their personal interest (in both senses) in possessing and using it and in showing it off.

Their decision process is likely to have been formal: they became aware of the innovation through their more accentuated use of the mass media for such items; their search and evaluation procedures will have been deliberative, even though there is limited information to go on. They may have insisted on trying the product before buying if this is feasible and will have been eager to ascertain its compatibility with their present lifestyle and practices, its advantages relative to what they already use, and maybe its conspicuousness in use (since they are often motivated by the thought of being seen with the radically novel). They are likely to minimize the risks and the complexities involved in owning and operating the innovation, while those who do not adopt at this stage will magnify these 'problems'.

New products that survive the introduction stage of the life cycle attract the attention not only of consumers but of other manufacturers. As the product progresses through the growth stage of the cycle, it is likely to be modified by the original marketer and those who are drawn to enter the field by the expectation of high profits. All of these suppliers introduce changes to the product, tailoring it to the needs of successive market segments and incorporating technological changes as they are created. The new versions they market are often dynamically continuous innovations which attract the initially sceptical consumer who now sees that the early promise of the product has been fulfilled and who is especially attracted by the additional benefits and lower prices offered at this stage. Of course, the first adopters may also be rebuying at this stage and are also pleased to endorse the enhanced brands as they become available. But they are no longer highly involved. Nor are those who now buy for the first time more than moderately involved. This latter group may have had a long decision period prior to buying; since first hearing of the innovation and perhaps dismissing it as some kind of new-fangled gadget that is clearly not for them, they will have become gradually accustomed to its merits. It will have begun to be obvious in the homes or garages of their neighbours, in the soaps on television, in the stores and showrooms in which they browse for and buy other products. All these consumers are likely to be only moderately involved in the product field; after all, its familiarity has removed many of the attractions of being first to own it and it has become more of a necessity than a luxury. Their awareness and evaluation of the product will have come about almost unconsciously as it has slowly been legitimated through the positive experience of others. Their decision process appears to be a curtailed version of that shown in Figure 5.1 because they have gradually formed brand attitudes and intentions without being aware of doing so. The first adopters have done this by using the product and judging its performance; the latest adopters have done so vicariously and informally. Neither group has to form detailed conceptualizations of the product and where it fits into the overall repertoire of products among which they choose. They have gradually formed their ideas of what the product is, what it does and how it relates to other products: at most, they have to compare a new brand in this product field in terms of the dimensions that are important to them (see Howard, 1989).

Finally, as the product field enters its maturity stage, many manufacturers have moved in to the market place, introducing numerous variants of the original innovation. Each of these 'new' versions can be described simply as continuous. The product has become commonplace; its capabilities and limitations are known, its risks are minimal and its price is as low as it is going to get. The least well-off members of the community can afford it and there is no special social kudos attached to owning it (indeed, there may even be ridicule for not owning it). Everybody has one. The very ubiquity of the product means that there is no reason for most consumers to show anything but the lowest level of involvement with it. Those who now buy for the first time have acquired a lot of knowledge about the product field, even if they have not studied it in an involved way. But they hardly have a high or even moderate level of involvement with it. Nor do those earlier adopters who now repurchase the item routinely. The routine buying process that is usual at this stage involves no more than an awareness of the brand's identity, its membership of a known product class and, for repeat buying, a favourable evaluation of how well it has served the consumer. Involvement may be high at the product level as particular situations evoke strong feelings of needing the item: as Otker (1990, p. 31) points out, 'Shampoo can be more important to a teenager on a Saturday evening than anything else in the world'. But the brand – as long as it is an acceptable member of the product class – is far less important.

Consumers' decision styles

Consumers bring distinctive personal approaches to problem awareness, search, evaluation, decision and post-decisional activities. These differences have far-reaching implications for such features of marketing management as market segmentation, new product development and marketing communications.

Psychologists use the term *cognitive style* to refer to the manner in which individuals make decisions and solve problems (Guilford, 1980; McKenna, 1984; Messick, 1984). Cognitive style must be distinguished from cognitive level which is the extent of intelligence, intellectual complexity or capacity shown by a decision maker. When we speak of consumers' cognitive styles, we are not talking about their intelligence or intellectual level. We simply mean the way in which they accomplish decision-making problem solving. No style is inherently superior to any other, though each may come into its own in appropriate circumstances. The theory of adaptive–innovative cognitive styles advanced by Kirton (1994) proposes that everyone can be placed somewhere on a continuum between two extreme styles of decision making. At one extreme, adaptors prefer to make decisions in an orderly and precise manner, and they confine their problem solving endeavours to the frame of reference in which the problem has arisen.

They prefer to seek better ways of accomplishing known tasks, coming up with solutions that can be unobtrusively implemented within their everyday routines. The extreme adaptor is preoccupied with the accuracy of details, prudence, soundness, efficiency, and a degree of conformity. The adaptor is happiest working within a well-established pattern of rules and operating procedures.

By contrast, the extreme innovator prefers to think tangentially, challenges rules and procedures and is uninhibited about breaking with established methods and advocating novel perspectives and solutions. The innovator is easily bored by routine and seeks novelty and stimulating in discontinuous change; he or she tends towards risk-taking, exploration and trial (Kirton 1994). Innovators' solutions generally transcend the context in which the problem has arisen. They tend to produce different ways of behaving which often entail radical change. This dimension of cognitive style is measured by the Kirton adaption–innovation inventory (KAI).[1]

Interest in using this theory and measure in consumer research derives from the fact that the dimensions of personality shown to be weakly characteristic of *market initiators*,[2] the earliest adopters of new brands and products (Figure 5.2), are also characteristic of those high-KAI scorers whom Kirton calls innovators (Kirton, 1994). The early identification of market

initiators during the firm's new product development process is strategically important for four reasons (Goldsmith and Flynn, 1992). First, they represent the immediate source of cash flow to the company eager to start retrieving the expenses of new product development: the fact that initiators are usually heavy users of the product class in question means that they play a disproportionate role in recouping developmental costs. Second, they may provide market leadership and help set up barriers to new competition that prevent other firms making a fast entry into the market. Third, they provide important feedback to the company on further new product development. And, fourth, they communicate the innovation to the less active sections of the market, the bulk of the market who will eventually provide the high levels of sales and profits.

Although personality measures have proved generally poor predictors of consumer behaviour, a considerable body of evidence has identified the personality profile of the earliest adopters of innovations. Market initiators emerge as individuals who have a broader perceptual category width than later adopters, i.e. they perceive novel products as more closely related to those already in use than do the later buyers. Market initiators also show greater tolerance of ambiguity, flexibility, self-esteem and tendency towards sensation seeking than do the later adopters. The evidence in each study is somewhat weak, though positive, but the rationale for expecting market initiators to show an innovative cognitive style stems from the fact that these five cognitive-personality factors also correlate highly and consistently with the KAI, indicating that innovators, as defined by Kirton, are more likely to possess these traits than adaptors.

Studies of consumers' food purchasing

However, the results of an investigation of the cognitive styles of initial adopters of general

---

[1] KAI respondents estimate on 32 five-point ratings how easy or difficult they would find it to sustain particular adaptive and innovative behaviours over long periods of time. The measure is scored in the direction of innovativeness from an adaptive extreme (32) to an innovative extreme (160), and with a theoretical mean suggested by the scale midpoint (96). International general population samples have observed means of 95 +/− 0.05 about which scores are approximately normally distributed within the restricted range of 45–146. The KAI shows high levels of internal reliability and validity and suitability for consumer research (Bagozzi and Foxall, 1996). As would be expected of a measure of style, KAI scores do not correlate with measures of cognitive level such as IQ and intellectual capacity (Kirton, 1994).

[2] This term is used in preference to the more usual 'consumer innovators' to distinguish the first adopters of new products and brands from innovators in the sense defined by Kirton (Foxall, 1995).

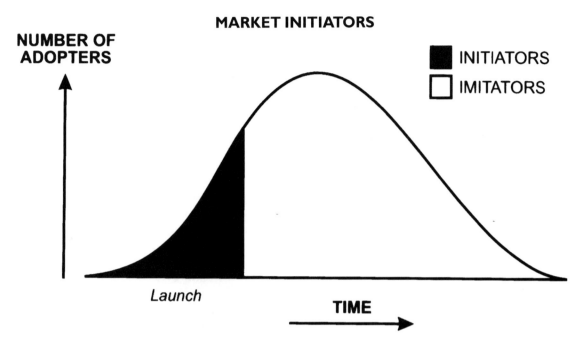

Figure 5.2   Initiators and imitators

new food brands were enigmatic given the expectation that these market initiators would be innovators (Foxall, 1995). KAI scores of respondents did not correlate with the number of new brands purchased and 40 per cent of the sample were adaptors. Most intriguing of all was the finding that the consumers who bought the largest number of new brands were adaptors. A similar pattern of results was apparent from a second study, this time of 'healthy' food products, those promoted on the basis of their alleged contribution to consumers' health and welfare such as wholemeal flour, low sodium salt and low calorie meals. At the time of the study, these products were new to supermarkets; prior to that time they had to be obtained from specialist health food stores. Again the expected correlation did not appear and again 40 per cent of the sample were adaptors. Moreover, purchasers of the very highest level of new products in this class were adaptive (Foxall, 1995).

A possible reason for this unanticipated result emerged from further consideration of adaption-innovation theory. Innovators are likely to purchase novel items impulsively, independently and perhaps haphazardly. By their very nature, they are will probably choose a number of innovative products just to try them out. But, while these sensation-seekers are more likely to try many new products, they are also likely to retain few of them in their repertoires (Mittelstaedt, Grossbart, Curtis and DeVere, 1976). Adaptors, however, will presumably show two patterns of behaviour. Those who are not much interested in the product field will, as we originally thought, be suspicious of new products; in both studies the buyers of fewest brands or products were adaptors. Yet those adaptors who have a high level of personal involvement with a product field will act quite differently. Cognitive style itself does not change much over the lifetime of the individual but its effects can be accentuated by the degree of engagement the individual feels in the activity at hand. The consumer who displays a very high level of commitment to acquiring a healthier lifestyle, for instance, will continue to act consistently with their underlying cognitive style but their behaviour may be quite different from that of a less committed consumer whose cognitive style is similar (Chaffee and Roser, 1986). Those adaptors who are fundamentally 'converted' to the pursuit of a healthier way of life and, thereby, to healthier eating, may well seek out not one or two but as many appropriate items as possible, showing a greater assiduousness in their search and evaluation than other consumers, adaptive or innovative.

This possibility was tested in the third study which was concerned with new brands within 'healthy' food classes (Foxall, 1995). This time, respondents were asked to indicate their level of personal involvement with 'healthy' foods. The instrument used to measure this construct was the Zaichkowsky (1987) personal involvement inventory which measures ego-involvement or the personal interest shown by individuals in a named product field. Once again, no correlation was found between the number of innovations bought and KAI, and well over half the sample were adaptors. More importantly, the results confirmed the hypothesis: the highest level of purchase was shown by more-involved adaptors.

Let us pause a moment to consider the implications of these findings. It appears that the post-launch market for new foods is not a homogeneous collection of innovators whose personalities predispose them to be venturesome, risk-taking, flexible and self-assured – as the textbooks portray initial adopters. Rather, that market consists of three psychographic segments, each with its own personality profile: less-involved adaptors (who buy least), innovators (who buy an intermediate number regardless of their level of involvement), and more-involved adaptors (who buy most). Moreover, each of these segments has its own distinctive style of decision making. Each segment is likely to become aware of new brands/products in a different fashion, to search and evaluate information in its own way, to choose uniquely and to have a distinctive post-decisional

reaction. The launch marketing strategy for a new product needs to accommodate all three.

The conventional wisdom, which assumes a uniform process of consumer decision making, must be modified to include considerations not only of level of involvement but also of consumers' differing cognitive styles. But results for a single product field, even if they are gained from three separate and increasingly sophisticated studies, hardly constitute a court revolution. Replication is required on several dimensions. Foods are often thought of as 'inherently' low-involving items: it would, therefore, be useful to repeat the research using a more 'inherently' involving product. The first three studies have involved the initial stage of the product life cycle: some evidence for or against the presence of differing cognitive styles among consumers of an established product is needed. These three studies have also involved purchasing: what evidence is there of a similar pattern in consumption? And do situational influences, as opposed to cognitive factors, affect the results?

Studies of software consumption

Two further investigations have taken the use of personal computers as their focal interest: the use of a range of software is usually thought to be highly involving, personal computers are well past the introduction stage of their product life cycle, the research involved consumption rather than purchasing, and it allowed situational variables to be examined (Foxall, 1995).

The first of these studies sought a link between KAI and the number of software packages used by home computer owners. Although there was no correlation between the two, a very small group of consumers with high KAI and high PII scores were responsible for the highest level of software applications use. The sample contained both adaptors and innovators once more but, of the two cognitive variables, it was personal involvement with computers and computing that was generally associated with high levels of use-initiation,[3] i.e. a large number of software applications. However, while personal involvement was the major explanatory cognitive factor, both adaptors and innovators were found in substantial proportions among users. In other words, the market contained four segments: first there were groups of less- and more-involved users, each of which could be subdivided into its adaptive and innovative subsegments. Each of these subsegments can be expected to make decisions in its own characteristic style. Finally, this study drew attention to the importance of situational factors in the multiple use of computers. More important than the cognitive variables were the number of years computing experience the respondents had had and the type of computer they owned.

Clearly a more structured study was needed to account in detail for the role of cognitive variables in view of situational factors (Franz and Robey, 1986). The final investigation involved the use of computer software by graduate management students in the Strathclyde Graduate Business School in Glasgow. Students following three programmes took part (Foxall and Bhate, 1999). Those taking the Business Information Technology Studies (BITS) programme were required by their course to make frequent and extensive use of computers; those taking Marketing received instruction in computer use but had discretion over where and when they used the computer as part of their studies; and the students on the Legal Practice programme received minimal instruction in the use of computers and were under little if any pressure to use computing techniques. Both KAI and PII correlated with the number of software applications used, whether or not the course affiliations were taken into consideration.[4] Although situational influences proved stronger than the cognitive factors, two crucial points must be made with respect to the roles of

cognitive style and involvement. Yet again, while involvement played a causative role in the amount of product use undertaken, both adaptive and innovative cognitive styles were represented and could be expected to affect the consumption behaviour of the respondents. The same four segments were apparent as in the study on home computing.

Studies of financial services purchase and consumption

Recent studies have investigated consumer behaviour for financial services. Foxall and Pallister (1998a) investigated four financial products bearing a maturity value or benefit sometime in the future: (i) pensions, (ii) life assurance, (iii) mortgages, and (iv) savings and investment. These products not only contrast with the targets of the earlier research but are of intrinsic interest in view of the extent of strategic change and product development which characterizes the contemporary financial services industry. The opportunity was taken on this occasion to examine the usefulness of an alternative measure of innovativeness, that proposed by Hurt, Joseph and Cook (1977). This scale correlates with the KAI (Kirton, 1994) and so we were confident in assuming that high scorers would possess the characteristics of Kirton's *innovators*, while low scorers would be *adaptive*. Respondents also completed Zaichkowsky's revised PII, revealing their involvement with financial services. The results show a remarkable pattern. Buyers of mortgages were highly-involved adaptors; so were purchasers of pension products. But life assurance purchasers were less-involved adaptors and buyers of savings and investments products were highly involved innovators. Clearly, even within a broadly-defined product category like financial services, consumers vary significantly and each segment requires its own unique marketing approach.

Additional research on financial services has investigated styles of cashless consumption,

---

[3] This term is preferred to the more common 'use-innovativeness', again to avoid confusion (Foxall, 1995).

[4] A study of computer use by managers in an administrative organization has confirmed several of these findings (Foxall and Hackett, 1992).

i.e. consumers' preferred patterns of payment card usage. Szmigin and Foxall (1998, 1999) used the KAI to identify adaptive and innovative consumers whose payment method preferences were investigated using qualitative research methods. Four market segments emerged. For *product enthusiasts,* cards have intrinsic value; these consumers enjoy immediate consumption and find the use of payment cards easy. They delay paying, show little control in their purchasing, and are avid obtainers and users of credit facilities. Their self-indulgence often manifests as impulse buying. These consumers tended to be highly-involved adaptors. *Finessers* pay off their account at the end of each month, incurring as little interest as possible. They also use cheques and debit cards, have many cards and use a wide range of payment methods. They are quick adopters of new payment methods. These consumers were highly-involved innovators. *Controllers* show tight regulation of their financial affairs, prefer credit to debit cards, and pay back what they owe each month. They see little point in store cards and look for tangible benefits from adopting a payment method. In our research, these consumers were predominantly less-involved adaptors. Finally, *money managers* juggle the use of many cards and seek the best advantage from using each (or cash) in each situation they encounter. They are seeking the security of a system of payment that works efficiently and quickly and that is functional. These individuals tended to be less-involved innovators.

Once again, financial services consumers showed several styles of consumption, each linked to a unique pattern of cognitive style and involvement, and requiring a special marketing mix.

Implications for marketing

In order to make sense of these results, let us ask three questions for each of the product classes investigated: (a) do the innovators actually adopt more innovations? (b) what other variables are involved in early adoption? And (c) what are the marketing implications? Table 5.1 summarizes the responses.

In the case of new foods, adaptors buy most; for software applications, innovators are the most likely to adopt most applications; financial services present a more mixed picture. Involvement is a crucial factor in each case and situational variables in some. Overall, the conventional wisdom is sometimes correct but

Table 5.1 Summary of the results

	Food innovations	Home software applications	Organizational software use	Financial services
Do innovators buy or use more?	No - adaptors do	Yes	No. Involved adaptors and innovators	For some products
What other factors influence behaviour?	Involvement	Involvement, situation	Involvement, situation	Involvement, situation
Principal consumer behaviour(s)	Complex Dissonant/ Variety seeking [Habitual]	Dissonant Variety seeking Complex Habitual	Dissonant Complex	Complex
Marketing mix considerations	Dual strategy	Dual strategy	Dual strategy	Tailor to individual product

unsophisticated, and our conclusion is that the marketing strategies must thus be multi-faceted. But how should they be designed and implemented?

One way of trying to make sense of these findings is to assume that the general involvement level engendered by the product is all-important. Foods might be classified as inherently low-involvement items, everyday purchases, continuous innovations. Software, by contrast, would be highly-involving since each application is a discrete, discontinuous use-initiation. And financial services might fall between the two: of medium involvement, representing an infrequent but important purchase, a dynamically continuous innovation. Assael (1996) uses similar dimensions of buying situations to classify the consumer behaviours for different types of product (Bhate, 1992). Hence:

Complex buying behaviour occurs when the consumer is highly involved, the product is expensive and risky and there are perceived differences in the brands available. The consumer in this case goes through a cognitive learning process, i.e. search for information, evaluation of products, etc. Assael (1996) claims that it is typical consumer behaviour for appliances and durables such as 'autos, electronics, photography systems'. Consumers actively search for information to evaluate and consider alternative brands by applying specific criteria such as resolution and portability for a camera and economy, durability and service for a car.

Dissonant buying behaviour occurs when the consumer is highly involved and sees no significant differences among the brands available and buys the product in a hurry but once purchase has been made has second thoughts, and may go out again and collect information to reduce dissonance. Such behaviour is typical of the purchase of adult cereals and snack foods. There is limited problem solving here, because the consumer is not familiar with the brands. A new line of microwaveable snacks might be introduced; unaware of the product class the consumer is attracted to the idea of trial to compare with known snackfoods. Limited information search takes place and limited evaluation of brand alternatives.

Habitual buying occurs when there is no significant difference in brands and the consumer is not highly involved in the purchase, e.g. salt. In such a case, there is no learning process. It is characteristic of athletic shoes and adult cereals. Such choice is repetitive: the consumer learns from past experience and with little or no decision-making buys a brand that is satisfactory. The purchase is important to the consumer because of involvement in sport in the case of athletic shoes and nutritional needs in the case of cereals. Brand loyalty is probable on the basis of satisfaction with a repertoire of known brands. This does not necessarily reflect active brand commitment, just satisficing. Information search and evaluation are limited if they exist at all. Since most brands in established markets are similar however, a consumer may on occasion try a new brand if it appears to provide the characteristics of the product class.

Variety seeking behaviour occurs when there is low involvement and significant brand differences. The consumer chooses something new to relieve boredom. This is typical consumer behaviour for canned vegetables and paper towels. Boredom and a search for variety leads to multi-brand purchasing, when risks are minimal and the consumer has less commitment to a particular brand. The decision is not important enough to make pre-planning worthwhile so the decision is made in the store. There is little to lose by buying a new kind of biscuit on impulse.

The conventional wisdom provides easy prescriptions for managerial action: just focus on market initiators, who can be assumed to be innovators, at each stage of the new product development and marketing process. But the research indicates that there are three problems with that. First, each launch segment has a unique decision-making style. Second, each active segment, therefore, requires its own launch marketing mix, reflecting the decision style and involvement level of its members. Third, post-launch markets – the markets for imitators – are also segmented by decision style and require multi-faceted marketing.

The results show that more than one of these patterns of buying behaviour is characteristic of new product purchasing or use for the same product, at the same time. A more sophisticated analysis is suggested by Figure 5.3 which proposes that complex buying is typical of highly-involved adaptors; dissonant buying, of highly-involved innovators; habitual buying, of low-involved adaptors; and variety-seeking, of low-involved innovators.

Complex consumer behaviour occurs when the consumer is highly involved and perceives the product as discontinuous. The consumer goes through a cognitive learning process, i.e. information search, brand evaluation, detailed post-adoption appraisal, etc. *Such behaviour is typical of highly-involved adaptors.*

Dissonant buying behaviour occurs when the consumer is highly involved but sees no significant differences among the brands available and buys the product in a hurry. Such consumers are likely to continue to seek alternative brands that will fulfil their expectations. *It is typical of highly-involved innovators.*

Habitual buying occurs when there is no sig-nificant difference in brands and the consumer is not highly involved in the purchase, e.g. salt. Extended information processing is unnecessary; experience is the safest guide. *It is typical of low-involved adaptors.*

Variety-seeking behaviour occurs when there is low involvement and brand proliferation. The consumer chooses something new to relieve boredom. *It is typical of low-involved innovators.*

Each active segment has its own decision style and its own level of involvement (see Table 5.2).

For all of the products we have investigated, launch markets are likely to be composed predominantly of involved consumers; the predominant consumer behaviours are therefore complexity and dissonance. However, some less-involved consumers also adopt at this stage: habit and variety-seeking are also likely to be encountered. All four types of consumer behaviour will also be encountered to a different extent in post-launch markets. In fact the market or markets for imitators may be more heterogeneous and require a more dynamic marketing approach.

In general, higher levels of involvement with a product field are considered a sign of

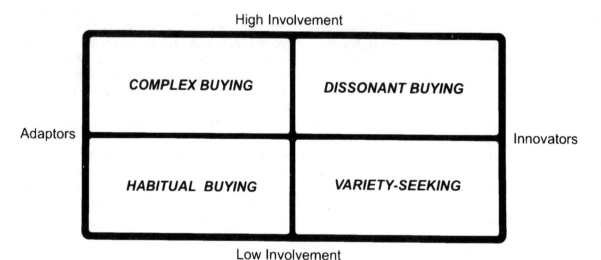

Figure 5.3   Decision styles of market initiators

Table 5.2 Decision styles of market segments				
	Dissonant buying	*Complex buying*	*Variety-seeking*	*Habitual buying*
Problem recognition				
Search and evaluation				
Post-purchase evaluation				

greater problem awareness and pre-purchase search and evaluation, a higher level of purchase, and more detailed and informed post-decisional evaluation. If involvement is, after all, principally a measure of personal interest, it follows that positive behaviours of these kinds will be more probable where such involvement is greater. The appropriate strategies of market segmentation and product positioning have attracted much attention (e.g. Tyebjee, 1979). However, the issue of adaptive–innovative cognitive style complicates the prescriptions offered by this marketing approach. Highly-involved adaptors are far more likely to engage in detailed information processing than innovators, but limited decision making may characterize highly-involved innovators.

The market for new 'healthy' foods contains innovators, more-involved adaptors, and a significant group of less-involved adaptors. That for new software applications contains more-involved adaptors, more-involved innovators, and groups of less active, less involved adaptors and innovators. Because new product marketing relies on the diffusion sequence over time, none of these can be ignored, even at the launch stage. What consumers absorb about an innovation at that stage may colour their impressions for long to come.

Marketing strategies should, therefore, be sensitive to the coexistence of adaptors and innovators in both the initial and established markets for new products. A marketing strategy directed towards, say, the adaptors is likely to alienate the innovators. Perhaps the failure of marketing campaigns which, following the conventional wisdom and textbook prescriptions have been aimed principally at innovators and ignored the fact that initial adopters and use-initiators may be adaptors, have contributed to the high failure rates of new consumer products. But the crucial question now is the likely implications of adaptive–innovative cognitive styles for future marketing campaigns. The following propositions follow from the evidence presented above and a considerable body of research over three decades on consumers' cognitive styles.

Product considerations

We have noted the importance of a consumer's category width – the extent to which he or she perceives an innovation to differ from the norm established by existing products or practices – in determining his or her framework for decision-making. So-called 'broad categorizers' are more willing than 'narrow categorizers' to consider and adopt new brands or products that diverge from the norm. Category width influences the amount of risk the prospective consumer perceives in buying and using an innovation (Venkatesan, 1973). Broad categorizers are also more likely to adopt radical or discontinuous new products, even though they might be dissatisfied with them; and narrow categorizers are more likely to reduce the possibility of making a mistake by confining their attention to incrementally new items. The implication is that adaptors, who are likely to be narrow categorizers, will try to avoid mistakes in their product purchasing even at the cost of losing out on some positive opportunities. They prefer to operate within the structure they have established and are reluctant to change. It seems, therefore, that, in their decision making, adaptors will usually tend to be conservative, and that they are more likely than innovators to be attracted to continuous new products. Innovators, categorizing widely, are less likely to perceive great differences even in discontinuous new products.

Compared with innovators, adaptors are usually more intolerant of change and disruption, unwilling to accept ambiguity, more dogmatic and inflexible. Unless they are highly involved, therefore, they are less likely to embrace new products. When adaptors lack involvement, their lack of experience of new products further reinforces their unwillingness to explore. By being willing to risk making mistakes, innovators are more eager to take advantage of the potential gains from exploration. As a rule, they will try more new products, apparently oblivious of the risk of buying an unsatisfactory item. In the process of decision making, highly involved innovators can be expected to use more of the information available to them than do the less-involved, whether adaptors or innovators. But, since they perceive products as more alike than do adaptors, they have less chance than they of becoming brand loyal.

Marketing communications

Adaptors and innovators are also likely to react in quite different ways to marketing communications, particularly mass advertising, regardless of their level of involvement. Innovators' broader category width, tendency to become rapidly bored with familiar products and behaviours, and capacity to work within several frames of analysis suggests that they would respond more positively than adaptors to two-sided appeals. That is, innovators may prefer messages based on pro and con arguments and become easily bored with repetitive messages that are consistent with their current beliefs. Yet adaptors are more likely to respond favourably to uncomplicated one-sided messages, consistent with their current attitudes and habits. This is not due to their having a lower level of cognitive ability (adaptors and innovators do not differ in terms of intelligence or cognitive complexity) but simply to their preferred style of decision making and problem solving. Adaptors are also more likely to respond positively to credible sources of information which are intended to modify their attitudes and behaviour. In comparison, innovators can presumably cope with more discrepant information even if the source is not well known. They may cope better with cognitive dissonance and perhaps be motivated by it to broaden their search for information. They are more likely than adaptors, who have strong needs for clarity, to remember incomplete messages. Innovators' tolerance of ambiguity might well make them more susceptible to postmodern advertising.

Since adaptors are more cautious and analytical in their judgements, more reflective and tentative in their decision making, they are open to rational, apparently objective appeals based on reasoned arguments. This style of advertising would, however, appear dogmatic and authoritarian to innovators. The more impulsive innovator would presumably be more open to personalized, affective advertising.

All of these differences are important in view of the apparently intransigent nature of cognitive styles. One possibility is that the less involved groups might be the targets for social marketing, the communication of an idea rather than a specific product or product type: 'healthy eating' and 'healthy living' in the first instance; 'getting more out of your computer', in the second. But the problem remains of reaching the more active segments with a message designed to encourage even more extensive purchasing or use that both adaptors and innovators must be reached simultaneously. Even where involvement has emerged as the main explanatory factor in consumer behaviour, the presence of both adaptors and innovators within segments defined by relatively high and relatively low levels of involvement makes a multiple marketing mix strategy inevitable.

Further considerations

In the case of new foods, it is apparent that simultaneous appeals must be made to innovators and highly-involved adaptors. Where the new item is part of a coherent product field such as 'healthy' foods, it may be easier to present it as consistent with the needs and prior behaviour of the involved adaptor (who has already experienced a 'paradigm shift' in embracing healthy eating). The new brand or product can be conceptually positioned by advertising as being close to similar existing means of achieving a healthier lifestyle; its physical positioning in supermarkets can emphasize its continuity with the array of foods the consumer is already enjoying, its incremental contribution to their healthier eating practices. It is this adaptive segment that is likely to form the core of brand/product loyal customers who will ensure its communication to other buyers who form the bulk of the market and its eventual complete diffusion. They are, therefore, to be considered a key primary market.

The innovator segment is far more likely to respond to the more radical presentation of such products as discontinuously new. However, if they were conceptually positioned in this way by advertising, the effect would be to alienate the potentially more important adaptive segment. Perhaps the answer is to use mass advertising as suggested above for the adaptors while restricting appeals to innovators to in-store promotions. The innovators, who are more likely to buy and try on impulse, might acquire some brand awareness from the mass advertising but would receive their greatest motivation to buy from in-store sources of information.

In the case of applications software, the major marketing (as opposed to social marketing) appeals would be to the involved users, both adaptors and innovators. The innovator is more likely to try applications software that is easily available along with other goods, which can be bought on impulse, tried and adopted/rejected with minimal cost in terms of inconvenience, though not necessarily financial cost. The product mix aimed at the innovator segment might, therefore, concentrate on the dissemination of combined software. The accompanying promotional mix might aim to increase users' awareness of the range of possible applications available. More specialized, individualized software for each application could then be offered as experienced innovative users sought more specialized or higher quality applications. It is probable that the adaptor segment would appreciate separate software packages for specific applications, acquired one at a time. These items should be promoted on the basis of their efficiency and reliability. More prestigious outlets, perhaps of a specialized nature, might be appropriate here, and mail order is also likely to appeal. The sales literature should contain detailed specifications and comparisons with other computers which stress the advantages in terms of precision and accuracy, the general acceptability to other users, and the extensively tried and tested application of the advertised brands.

Once again, there may be no need for the campaigns aimed at different segments to be hermetically sealed from one another so long as each is created and presented with sensitivity to the coexistence of alternative cognitive styles among the recipients. Selective perception makes it entirely possible that adaptors will not notice the advertisements aimed at innovators sufficiently to be alienated by them; innovators may receive no more than initial brand or product awareness from the messages directed towards adaptors.

Summary and conclusion

Our understanding of both consumer behaviour and the capacity of marketing activities to influence it rests on knowledge of the ways in which consumers choose. Three aspects of consumer decision making require careful attention: the decision process itself, differences in the level of consumer involvement that surrounds and shapes decision making, and differences in the style of decision making. Most research has been concerned with the first of these. Several models describe in detail the stages consumers may pass through in coming to a decision point and the psychological procedures that accompany them. Questions about the influence of involvement on consumer decision making have been addressed only comparatively recently; yet the issues of intellectual level of information processing and the consumer's level of involvement with the process have far-reaching implications for managerial intervention in the marketplace. Finally, the way in which a consumer characteristically processes information has come on to the agenda of consumer researchers very recently indeed. Again, because consumers do not pass homogeneously through a pre-ordained decision sequence but behave at each stage in accordance with their individual cognitive styles, any attempt by marketing managers to influence the process must take account of the manner as well as the matter of decision processes.

This chapter has taken a consumer-orientated approach to the role of consumer behaviour research. Rather than simply theorize about the likely nature of consumer choice, it has shown how actual consumer behaviour differs from that described by the formal models. It has gone on to show that those deviations in involvement and style that mark consumer behaviour in the real world rather than the textbook, interesting as they are in their own right, have direct implications for marketing management, the design and implementation of marketing mixes that reach consumers.

References

Ajzen, M. (1985) From Intentions to Actions: A Theory of Planned Behavior, in J. Kuhl and J. Beckman, (eds), *Action Control: From Cognition to Behavior*, Springer-Verlag, Berlin, pp. 11–39.

Ajzen, M. and Fishbein, M. (1980) *Understanding Attitudes and Predicting Social Behavior*, Prentice-Hall, Englewood Cliffs, NJ.

Assael, H. (1996) *Consumer Behavior and Marketing Action*, 5th edn, Southwestern, Cincinnati, OH.

Bagozzi, R. P. and Foxall, G. R. (1996) Construct Validation of a Measure of Adaptive–Innovative Cognitive Styles in Consumption, *International Journal of Research in Marketing*, **13**, 201–13.

Bagozzi, R. P. and Warshaw, P. R. (1990) Trying to Consume, *Journal of Consumer Research*, **17**, 127–40.

Bhate, S. (1992) Cognitive Style and Use/Buying Behaviour: A Reappraisal of the Relationship using Involvement as a Mediating Variable. Unpublished PhD thesis, University of Birmingham.

Chaffee, S. H. and Roser, C. (1986) Involvement and the Consistency of Knowledge, Attitudes and Behaviors, *Communication Research*, **13**, 373–399.

Ehrenberg, A. S. C. (1988) *Repeat Buying*, 2nd edn, Griffin, Edinburgh.

Engel, J. F., Blackwell, R. D. and Miniard, P. (1991) *Consumer Behavior*, 7th edn, Dryden, Hindsdale, IL.

Fishbein, M. and Ajzen, I. (1975) *Belief, Attitude, Intention and Behavior: An Introduction to Theory and Research*, Addison-Wesley, Reading, MA.

Foxall, G. R. (1995) Cognitive Styles of Consumer Initiators, *Technovation*, **15**, 269–288.

Foxall, G. R. (1997) *Marketing Psychology: The Paradigm in the Wings*, Macmillan Press, London.

Foxall, G. R. and Bhate, S. (1999) Computer Use-innovativeness: Cognition and Context, *International Journal of Technology Management*, **17**(1–2), 157–172.

Foxall, G. R., Goldsmith, R. E. and Brown, S. (1998) *Consumer Psychology for Marketing*, 2nd edn, International Thomson Business Press, London and New York.

Foxall, G. R. and Hackett, P. (1992) Cognitive Style and Extent of Computer Use in Organizations: Relevance of Sufficiency of Originality, Efficiency and Rule-conformity, *Perceptual and Motor Skills*, **74**, 491–497.

Foxall, G. R. and Pallister, J. (1998a) Measuring Purchase Decision Involvement for Financial Services: Comparison of the Zaichkowsky and Mittal Scales, *International Journal of Bank Marketing*, **16**, 180–194.

Foxall, G. R. and Pallister, J. (1998b) Patterns of

Financial Services Purchasing. Working Paper, Consumer Research Group, Keel University.

Franz, C. R. and Robey, D. (1986) Organizational Context, User Involvement and the Usefulness of Information Systems, *Decision Sciences*, **17**, 329–357.

Goldsmith, R. E. and Flynn, L. R. (1992) Identifying Innovators in Consumer Product Markets, *European Journal of Marketing*, **26**(12), 42–55.

Guilford, J. P. (1980) Cognitive Styles: What Are They? *Educational and Psychological Measurement*, **40**, 715–735.

Howard, J. A. (1977) *Consumer Behavior: Application of Theory*, McGraw-Hill, New York.

Howard, J. A. (1989) *Consumer Behavior for Marketing Strategy*, Prentice-Hall, Englewood Cliffs, NJ.

Howard, J. A. and Moore, W. L. (1982) Changes in Consumer Behavior over the Product Life Cycle, in M. L. Tushman and W. L. Moore (eds), *Readings in the Management of Innovation*, Pitman, Boston, MA, pp. 122–130.

Howard, J. A. and Sheth, J. N. (1969) *The Theory of Buyer Behavior*, Wiley, New York.

Hurt, H. Y., Joseph, K. and Cook, C. D. (1977) Scales for the Measurement of Innovativeness, *Human Communication Research*, **4**, 58–65.

Kardes, F. R. (1994) Consumer Judgment and Decision Processes, in R. S. Wyer and T. K. Srull (eds), *Handbook of Social Cognition*, Vol. 2, Erlbaum, Hillsdale, NJ, pp. 399–466.

Kirton, M. J. (1994) A Theory of Cognitive Style, in M. J. Kirton (ed.), *Adaptors and Innovators: Styles of Creativity and Problem-Solving*, 2nd edn, Routledge, London, pp. 1–36.

Laaksonen, P. (1994) *Consumer Involvement: Concepts and Research*, Routledge, London and New York.

McKenna, F. P. (1984) Measures of Field Dependence: Cognitive Style or Cognitive Ability? *Journal of Personality and Social Psychology*, **11**, 51–55.

Messick, S. (1984) The Nature of Cognitive Styles, *Educational Psychologist*, **19**, 59–74.

Mittelstaedt, R. A., Grossbart, S. L., Curtis,

W. W. and DeVere, S. P. (1976) Optimal Stimulation Level and the Adoption Decision Process, *Journal of Consumer Research*, **3**, 84–94.

Nicosia, J. M. (1966) *Consumer Decision Processes*, Prentice-Hall, Englewood Cliffs, NJ.

Olshavsky, R. W. and Granbois, D. H. (1979) Consumer Decision Making: Fact or Fiction? *Journal of Consumer Research*, **6**, 93–100.

Otker, T. (1990) The Highly-involved Consumer: A Marketing Myth? *Marketing and Research Today*, February, pp. 30–36.

Robertson, T. S. (1967) The Process of Innovation and the Diffusion of Innovation, *Journal of Marketing*, **31**, 14–19.

Szmigin, I. and Foxall, G. R. (1998) Three Forms of Innovation Resistance: The Case of Retail Payment Methods, *Technovation*, **18**, 459–68.

Szmigin, I. and Foxall, G. R. (1999) Styles of Cashless Consumption, International Review of Retail, Distribution and Consumer Research, in press.

Tyebjee, T. (1979) Refinement of the Involvement Concept: An Advertising Planning Point of View, in J. Maloney and B. Silverman (eds), *Attitude Research Plays for High Stakes*, American Marketing Association, 94–111.

Venkatesan, M. (1973) Cognitive Consistency and Novelty-Seeking, in S. Ward and T. S. Robertson (eds), *Consumer Behavior: Theoretical Sources*, Prentice-Hall, Englewood Cliffs, NJ, pp. 354–384.

Wilkie, W. L. and Dickson, P. R. (1991) Shopping for Appliances: Consumers' Strategies and Patterns of Information Search, in H. H. Kassarjian and T. S. Robertson (eds), *Perspectives in Consumer Behavior*, 3rd edn, Prentice-Hall, Englewood Cliffs, NJ, pp. 1–26.

Zaichkowsky, J. L. (1987) The Personal Involvement Inventory: Reduction, Revision and Application to Advertising. Discussion Paper 87–08–08, Simon Fraser University, Faculty of Business Administration.

Further reading

Ehrenberg, A. S. C. (1988) *Repeat Buying*, 2nd edn, Griffin, Edinburgh. A landmark monograph which is fundamental to understanding patterns of buyer behaviour over time on the basis of painstaking empirical observation and analysis. A very necessary antidote to the near-ubiquitous and uncritical presentation of cognitive information processing as the sole approach to understanding consumer choice.

Foxall, G. R. (1997) *Marketing Psychology: The Paradigm in the Wings*, Macmillan, London. *Marketing Psychology* portrays the behaviour of consumers as influenced by its environmental consequences and extends this analysis to marketing management by proposing a novel understanding of the marketing firm. The book undertakes a behaviour analysis of consumer choice, based on a critical extension of radical behaviourism to the interpretation of human economic behaviour. This suggests that consumer behaviour is explained by locating it among the environmental contingencies that shape and maintain it. The analysis of the marketing firm construes marketing management as resting on a behaviouristic understanding of consumer choice and of the role of the firm in the attempted prediction and control of consumer behaviour.

Foxall, G. R., Goldsmith, R. E. and Brown, S. (1998) *Consumer Psychology for Marketing*, 2nd edn, International Thomson Business Press, London and New York. A new edition of this textbook of consumer behaviour which integrates recent thinking and empirical research with the needs of marketing managers to understand their customers and potential customer.

Kardes, F. R. (1994) Consumer Judgment and Decision Processes, in R. S. Wyer and T. K. Srull (eds), *Handbook of Social Cognition*, Vol. 2, Erlbaum, Hillsdale, NJ, pp. 399–466. The entire two-volume handbook is essential reading for consumer psychologists and marketing researchers. Kardes's chapter applies the findings of social cognition research to consumer decision making. It is well informed by the concerns of consumer psychology and marketing management and provides a recent assessment of a fast-growing literature.

Laaksonen, P. (1994) *Consumer Involvement: Concepts and Research*, Routledge, London and New York. A valuable source of recent research and thought on consumer involvement.

Lambkin, M., Foxall, G. R., Van Raaij, F. and Heilbrunn, B. (eds) (1998) *European Perspectives on Consumer Behaviour*, Prentice-Hall, London. The definitive collection of European-authored research on consumer behaviour.

CHAPTER 6

Business-to-business marketing: organizational buying behaviour, relationships and networks

PETER W. TURNBULL

In this chapter an attempt is made to trace the development of research and practice in business-to-business marketing. The term 'business-to-business marketing' is increasingly replacing the more traditional 'industrial marketing' and 'organizational marketing' descriptions and will be used in this chapter to describe those marketing activities of any kind of organization, public or private, which has exchange relationships with other organizations.

The understanding of organizational buyer behaviour can be seen as a process of development over the past forty years within the wider context of industrial or business-to-business marketing theory. Unfortunately, the study of business-to-business marketing has 'been a poor relation within the broad family of attempts to understand the markets and marketing in general' (Ford, 1991, p. 1). Most early theory was based on a rather simplistic transfer of consumer goods based knowledge which

propounded 'effective' marketing largely as a manipulation of the marketing mix. Unfortunately, this approach largely ignored the realities of business-to-business markets. However, a number of researchers have recognized the difference of organizational buyers and their behaviour and a number of paradigms have emerged to better understand and explain the complexity facing researchers and managers working in this field. Perhaps the most important of these more recent conceptualizations is that relating to interaction, relationships and networks originally developed by the IMP (International Marketing and Purchasing) Group (Hakansson, 1982; Turnbull and Cunningham, 1981), which has led to the current interest in relationship marketing.

An understanding of the organizational buying process is fundamental to the development of appropriate business-to-business marketing strategy. The organizational buyer is influenced by a wide variety of factors both from outside and within the organization. Understanding these factors and their interrelationships is critical to the competitive positioning of the business, to the development of appropriate market and product development plans, and to the management of the whole marketing task of the business.

Increasingly, companies are recognizing the significant impact which professional procurement can have on profitability and British manufacturing industry is increasingly buying-in components and subassemblies, rather than manufacturing in-house. For example, some telecommunications equipment manufacturers now buy in items accounting for up to 80 per cent of total cost. Thus, even a 2 per cent procurement saving can have a marked effect on profitability or give the company a significant price advantage in the marketplace. Additionally, professional purchasing also helps secure long-term and improved sources of supply.

This growing importance and recognition of purchasing makes it imperative for business-to-business marketers to also increase their professionalism. A crucial element of such professionalism is, as consumer product marketers have so long recognized, the understanding of buying behaviour. However, in business-to-business markets this is more difficult than in consumer markets and requires an understanding of various academic disciplines which underlie the polyglot area we term organizational buying behaviour. To be effective, marketers must address a number of key questions:

- How is buying behaviour different in business markets?
- Who are the key participants in purchasing?
- What process and procedures are followed in choosing and evaluating competitive offerings?
- What criteria are used in making buying decisions?
- What sources of information and influence are used?
- What organizational rules and policies are important?
- What key relationships exist with other suppliers and buyers?

These and other questions must be considered and answered if the business-to-business marketer is to be truly professional.

This chapter attempts to provide a framework of understanding by which these questions can be addressed. The most important theoretical and research contributions of the last two decades are briefly reviewed to give a comprehensive picture of the current state of the art in the study of organizational buyer behaviour.

Organizations buy a diverse and often highly complex and interrelated range of goods and services as factor inputs to their own product and service portfolio as indicated in the following list:

- raw materials
- buildings, machinery and other capital equipment
- components
- consumable materials
- professional services
- energy
- finance
- labour

Clearly the nature and importance of the type of product/service being purchased will have significant consequences for the purchasing structures, process and criteria.

However, it is important to recognize that no company exists in isolation from other players in the industrial milieu. Success, and failure, depends upon the company's ability to cooperate with its suppliers and customers. The actions of competitors, regulators, governments and many others also have important impacts upon the individual firm.

During the past twenty years a considerable body of knowledge has developed about the structure, dynamics and processes of business relationships and their management. These relationships are at the heart of the reality of business markets and must be understood if we are to manage the complex networks of relationships in which all companies operate.

It will become apparent through the course

of this chapter that organizational buying and marketing is a complex process. Attempts to oversimplify this process ultimately result in a loss of understanding of the dynamics of the process and its constituent elements. However, it is worthwhile to begin with the analysis of the realities of business markets.

The realities of business markets

In trying to understand organizational buying behaviour it is essential to clarify the essential features that characterize the markets and market mechanisms of business markets. For example, we need to recognize that markets are often characterized by customization and dynamism: traditional marketing theory, with its roots in consumer product markets, had typified marketing as a process of manipulation of the marketing mix against predetermined consumer preferences derived from market research. The marketer is seen as the active party whilst customers are essentially passive. This view, however, is not even an adequate representation of what happens in consumer markets: the majority of manufacturers of consumer goods, such as foodstuffs, toiletries and clothing, sell to wholesalers and retailers – not directly to consumers. Thus, they are essentially operating within an organization or business market which displays many of the characteristics of the markets for industrial products such as car components, financial services, etc.

Thus, a reality of marketing per se is that suppliers face concentrated markets where individual customers may be critically important. These customers are not passive but actively search out and interact with selected suppliers, requiring customized products. These markets are characterized by interaction, mutual dependency and trust. Negotiation is common and business success is often determined by the ability of individuals to manage the supplier–customer relationships over considerable periods of time. These interactions may involve many people from different functions and levels in both supplier and customer companies.

Although specific transactions (the focus of much consumer marketing literature) are often important, it is the overall relationship which is critical to success. Thus relationship marketing becomes the 'new' marketing management challenge.

Organizational buying structures

An organization is a group of people pursuing a common aim through coordinated activities. Organizations are characterized by structure, activity and goals. By analysing organizational buying in the light of these three factors it is possible to highlight the essential elements of organizational buying behaviour. A major characteristic of organizational buying is that it is a group activity. It is comparatively rare that a single individual within an organization will have sole responsibility for making all the decisions involved in the purchasing process and commonly we find a number of people from different areas of the business and of varying status involved. This group is usually described as the *decision-making unit* or *buying centre*. Thus, a major challenge facing business marketers and salespeople is the identification of these key individuals who constitute the buying centre, the roles of these individuals and the various factors that may influence its constitution, and the major goals being pursued.

Composition of the buying centre

Much research has focused upon the size and structure of the buying centre, Alexander *et al.* (1961) found that in 75 per cent of the firms they interviewed, three or more people became involved in the buying process. Anyon (1963) suggested that there was an average of six people involved, whilst Hill and Hillier (1977) point out that in situations where certain expensive products are being purchased for the first time, as many as forty people may become involved in the purchase decision. While interesting, generalizations such as these are of little practical help. The business marketer will be more concerned to discover who are the influential people in the different types of organizations they deal with at each stage of the decision-making process and their relative degree of influence.

Shankleman (1970) reporting a study of the purchasing of capital equipment wrote:

The managing director would agree to the equipment budget for the research department expressed solely in terms of money. The research manager would decide which of the various requests for money should have priority and the section head would decide which of the various items should be bought on the basis of a detailed study of the reports made by his team.

Similarly, in an earlier study, Thain (1959) concluded that top management made the fundamental policy decision whether or not to buy but the operational staff decided what to buy.

The structure of the buying centre can also be examined in the light of the different roles of the individuals who constitute it. Webster and Wind (1972a) suggest the major roles found in buying centres to be:

- users
- influencers
- deciders
- gatekeepers

It is apparent that there may be many sources of influence on the buying decision, both formal and informal. By piecing together the suggestions of the various research studies into the composition of the buying centre, it is possible to draw up the following list of roles that may be performed:

1   Policy makers
2   Purchasers
3   Users
4   Technologists
5   Influencers
6   Gatekeepers
7   Deciders

Policy makers

A company may adopt certain general policies in its buying which may affect the purchase behaviour of a single item. For example, it may be company policy to only purchase from British suppliers, or suppliers within a range of fifty kilometres, or for certain items to be multiple sourced.

Purchasers

The purchaser is here defined as the person or persons who have formal authority for ordering the product or service. A considerable amount of research has been completed investigating the importance of the purchasing agent in influencing buying decisions. For example, Weigand (1968) pointed out that the purchasing agent may be no more than a clerical officer and his/her influence on the buying decision may consist of nothing more than filling in the necessary forms to complete the order.

Feldman and Cardozo (1968) and Lister (1967) are among many authors who have pointed out that the purchasing agent's role is dependent upon the management's philosophy towards purchasing. Where this is seen as important the purchasing agent will play an influential part in decision making. In recent years, as the procurement function in business has been given increasing and long overdue importance, buyers have equally become more critical determinants of strategic and operational purchasing decisions.

Nevertheless, it is important to identify the individual who will be primarily responsible for the final ordering of the service. Any assessment of the importance of the purchasing agent must consider the organization's attitude towards the purchasing function, together with the level of risk associated with the purchase. In all instances these considerations are liable to be situation specific and suppliers must, therefore, become aware of the differences between their customers.

Users

These are those people who actually operate the product or service. In certain instances their role will coincide with that of the technologist. It is likely that users will be primarily concerned with product performance and ease of use. Weigand (1968) suggests that users with expert knowledge may exert sufficient influence to override certain commercial considerations such as price or delivery times. It is therefore important that suppliers should establish good relations with all members of a firm who have contact with the service they provide, and ensure that a high level of service is maintained across all their operations.

Technologists

These are the people with the specialist knowledge which enables them to differentiate between the performance of the different products or brands. They are primarily concerned with the technical aspects of the various products or services and these considerations will be of prime importance in their assessment of them. Technologists are likely to be people with professional qualifications and in seeking to influence them suppliers should be aware of the specialized nature of their influence on the buying centre.

An important finding of the International Marketing and Purchasing (IMP) Project Group in studies of purchasing in Western Europe was that purchasing staff and technologists in Germany and Sweden were more highly qualified than their counterparts in Britain. Thus British suppliers operating in these export markets faced more technologically demanding customers. German customers were very critical of the technical competence of British companies and this created a barrier to entry for British exporters (Turnbull and Cunningham, 1981).

Influencers

Webster and Wind (1972b) define this category as:

Those who influence the decision process directly or indirectly by providing information and criteria for evaluating buying actions.

Influencers thus include anybody who has

an influence on the buying process both within and outside the organization. As a category this is too wide to be of any functional use since it can embrace such a wide range of people. However, it does emphasize that there can be substantial inputs from a wide range of different functions into the buying process.

Gatekeepers

The concept of gatekeeper comes from the theory of opinion leadership and communications flow. A gatekeeper is a person who regulates the flow of information and thus plays a major part in determining the attitudes of other members of the buying centre towards a product. It is possible that the role of gatekeeper will be performed by an individual who has another role within the buying centre, for example, the purchasing agent.

Deciders

These are the people who have the formal authority for approving the purchase. It is likely that they occupy senior management positions and therefore, as Shankleman (1970) pointed out, may be concerned only at the policy making level.

These categories are useful indicators of the different areas of interest in the buying centre. A production engineer will view a machine purchase in a different way to a finance director. The transport manager will also take a different view to that of the managing director when the purchase of fleet cars are considered. We should note, however, that these roles can overlap and may vary according to the nature of the purchase and the stage of the buying process.

Having discussed basic purchasing structure, it is important to be aware of the factors that will influence that structure. The next section therefore examines the major variables which determine the composition of the buying centre.

Determinants of the buying centre

It has already been pointed out that the role of the purchasing agent is dependent upon the organization's philosophy towards the purchasing function and is therefore situation specific. While it is possible to suggest certain determining characteristics of the composition of the buying centre, it should be emphasized at the outset that the buying centre's composition will depend upon the specific purchase situation. The importance to suppliers of knowing their customers cannot be over-emphasized. In practical marketing terms such knowledge can only be built up through extensive contact between suppliers and buyers.

Market factors

Wallace (1976) identifies two features relevant to the study of organizational buying. First, those processes which characterize organizations and their members in their purchasing activity and second, those characteristics which differentiate organizational buying markets from consumer markets. It is these characteristics that are referred to here as market factors.

Products and services are often technologically complex and this, combined with bulk purchasing, leads to many industrial purchases being of high value. Also, business-to-business markets are characterized by derived demand and marketing thus requires careful evaluation of the secondary markets which influence demand for the primary product. Furthermore, many business markets are highly concentrated and there tend to be greater differences between buyers. Markets can be either geographically concentrated or concentrated through the size of the firms. As a result, communication channels between industrial buyers and sellers tend to be shorter than in consumer markets.

Finally, many business-to-business markets are characterized by reciprocal trading arrangements between firms which may inhibit buying practice and make it difficult for new suppliers to enter some markets.

Each market will have its own characteristics and the companies that purchase from or within that market will organize their buying departments to meet the particular conditions that prevail. The organization of the buying centre to meet these market characteristics will vary depending upon the size of the company and the service being purchased.

Company factors

Sheth (1973) suggests three major company variables that will influence the composition of the buying centre: company size, degree of specialization and company orientation. It can be expected that as company size increases, the greater the number of buying influences. Additionally, we can generally expect a higher degree of purchasing expertise in large organizations.

A study sponsored by *The Financial Times* (1974) concluded that most companies operating several establishments 'claimed to operate a centralized purchasing policy for the products covered by the survey'. However, the research indicated that companies do in fact vary their practice according to convention or convenience, even within the framework of a centralized policy. Sheth (1973) concludes that the greater the degree of centralization, the less likely the company will tend towards joint decision making.

Organizations with several operating subsidiaries, particularly if these are overseas, will have an overall policy regarding centralization. Even where control is highly centralized, subsidiaries may, nevertheless, be given varying degrees of freedom in choosing suppliers of specified product categories. The degree of centralization may therefore be vital to both the composition of the buying centre for these services, and also relevant to the development of a strategy for international marketing.

Finally, Sheth (1973) suggests that the composition of the buying centre will be dependent upon the company orientation. If a company is technology orientated the buying centre is likely to be dominated by engineering people who will, in essence, make the buying decision.

These various research findings highlight the necessity for a supplier's marketing management to know the policies and buying routines of its customers. By studying both existing and potential customers, suppliers can develop marketing strategies targeted to the important buying influences.

Product factors

The product variable embraces a number of characteristics, including product essentiality, technical complexity, value of the purchase, consequence of failure, novelty of the purchase and frequency of the purchase.

Weigand (1968) defines a product as 'a variety of promises to perform'. Performance will be judged according to the expectations that the individual has of the product and it is important to remember that different people and organizations will have different perceptions and expectations of the product. As Alexander *et al.* (1961) have pointed out:

The broad basic differences between types of goods arises not so much from their variations in their physical characteristics as differences in the ways in which and the purposes for which they are bought.

Where a product is central to an organization's operations it is likely that the purchase will be decided upon jointly by all the parties concerned. This is also likely to be true in instances of high capital expenditure. In both of these instances the consequence of failure may be severe and so where the possibility or the consequence of failure are perceived to be higher it is likely that purchase decisions will be shared.

Bauer (1960) coined the term 'perceived risk' and Cyert and March (1963) applied the concept of risk avoidance as one of their basic concepts explaining the behaviour of the firm. They suggest that, in order to avoid uncertainty and failure, organizations avoid the necessity of having to anticipate events in the future by emphasizing short-term feedback; and impose standard operating procedures to ease the burden of decision making.

Hill and Hillier (1977) use the term 'risky shift' to explain how members of a group take decisions involving a higher degree of risk than they would do as individuals. The 'risky shift'

concept is central to the composition of the buying centre and highlights the point that its composition will vary as a result of the characteristics of the product being purchased and particularly in relation to the perceived risk of the buying situation. More recent work by Greatorex *et al.* (1992) has demonstrated the importance of perceived risk in computer systems purchasing.

Buying situation

Product complexity will be situation specific and should not be regarded per se but rather in the way it is related to the purchaser's technical knowledge and expertise. Knowledge and expertise will arise out of previous experience with the product and consequently lead to a reduction in risk perception. It can therefore be logically concluded that a major determinant of the composition of the buying centre will be the organization's previous experience of the product and the supplier.

Prior experience of the product or supplier will be a determining factor in risk perception. Robinson *et al.* (1967) define three 'buy classes' which are dependent on previous experience: new buy; modified re-buy and straight re-buy. These buy classes influence both the composition of the buying centre and the buying process itself.

New buy: In this situation the organization has no previous experience of the product or supplier. Consequently perceived risk will be high and purchase decisions will be more likely to be made by senior management.

Modified re-buy: The company already has prior experience of the product but the particular purchase situation demands some degree of novelty. This may arise due to different specifications in a product or through change of supplier.

Straight re-buy: This usually entails the routine reordering of products on the basis of decisions that have been made previously. There will be little risk perception in these instances and the purchase decision will be taken by lower management. In such cases there may not be a discrete decision at all but only in relation to the establishment of the order routine. It is usually very difficult to break inertia of routine reordering and a 'new' supplier will have to demonstrate strong reasons to the buying organization to justify the extra risk and effort of changing supplier.

Robinson *et al.* link the buy classes to what they term buy phases or stages in the decision-making process. These stages constitute the last of the variables influencing the composition of the buying centre. The Robinson *et al.* buy classes can be criticized as somewhat simplistic descriptions of the wide variety of buying situations which exist in practice. An alternative analysis of buying situations is proposed by Bunn (1993) who develops a taxonomy of buying situations and patterns. His classification defines six prototypical buying-decisions approaches:

1   Casual purchase
2   Routine low priority
3   Simple modified re-buy
4   Judgemental new task
5   Complex modified re-buy
6   Strategic new task

Bunn (1993) relates these approaches to decision processes such as search behaviour, use of analysis techniques and procedural control and provides a useful review of research in the field.

Stage in the buying process
Organizational buying decisions are not discrete but result from a variety of stages which interact and upon which the final decision depends. As previously noted the composition of the buying centre will vary as a result of the particular activity taking place. Product users may provide the stimulus for a new purchase. In specifying the characteristics of a new product, technologists and finance people may be involved. The purchasing department may

collect information about new products which will then be evaluated by the users and technologists and finance people. In deciding which alternatives should be short-listed the finance department may become involved again, and the final selection may be made at board level where all the company interests will be represented.

Many researchers have attempted to categorize the stages of the buying process. Fisher (1969) categorizes three stages; Cunningham and White (1974) also suggest three stages which lead to the final patronage decision; Dewey (1960) suggests a five-stage framework; Webster and Wind (1972a) classify four basic stages. The similarity of the stages suggest some universal pattern of organizational buying. Nevertheless, all models assume a discrete and ordered process which is unrealistic in practice. Empirical findings have always shown that stages can occur simultaneously or out of sequence etc., depending on the particular buying situation. However, it is useful to review the principal activity steps which usually take place in new buy or modified re-buy purchasing.

Search

Searching for information is a major way of reducing risk and the search for alternative products or suppliers is likely to be most extensive when risk perception is high. Cyert and March (1963) suggested that search, like decision making itself, is problem directed. They made three basic assumptions about organizational search. First that the search is motivated by a problem. Second that the search proceeds on the basis of a simple model of causality, until driven to a more complex one. And third, that the search would be biased by the searcher's perceptions of the environment. The frequency of search is a function of how well present suppliers and products are meeting organizational goals and one reason for frequent search is 'to keep present suppliers honest' by comparing them with alternatives.

The collection of information usually has a cost, either financial or in terms of effort or time expended. Buckner (1967) found that suppliers usually only examine a limited range of suppliers. Limited search can particularly be ascribed to the cost of information gathering. White (1969), however, indicated that a major reason for limiting search was work simplification or avoidance.

The search process may therefore be governed in many instances by satisficing rather than maximizing behaviour, particularly in purchase situations where risk is not felt to be high. Organizational search is a continuous process of data gathering which may relate specifically to products or generally to economic trends or markets. Search relating specifically to purchase situations may occur simultaneously with other stages in the decision process as a continuous activity or else as a series of sequential steps. Webster's research (1965) clearly showed how different sources of information are used at each stage in the adoption process (see Table 6.1). Thus, advertising in trade journals would appear to be the most efficient method of gaining awareness for a product but salespeople are more efficient in generating interest. The research also demonstrated a decreasing reliance on external sources as people become increasingly aware of the product.

Evaluation

Hill and Hillier (1977) suggested that evaluation may consist of two main stages; first, selecting companies to tender and, second, making the final selection of product and supplier. Weigand (1968) also proposed a two-step evaluation process; the identification of an approved list of suppliers from which the purchasing agent is at liberty to select on the basis of price, delivery and a variety of other negotiable factors, followed by the selection decision.

Evaluation must obviously be made against some predetermined criteria, often relating to both product and supplier. Green *et al.* (1968) scaled a number of product and supplier attributes or characteristics and obtained the ranking on a Thurstonian scale shown in Table 6.2.

These findings were borne out by Cunningham and White (1974) who suggested that certain attributes were essential if a supplier was even to be considered but that other factors would decide which supplier was ultimately selected. The former they termed qualifying factors and the latter determining factors. They also found that a favourable reputation for delivery, reliability and service were important prerequisites for increasing the chance of being seriously considered as a potential supplier. The strongest determinant of a buyer's patronage

Table 6.1	Percentage of respondents finding each source important by stage in the buying process				
	Awareness	Interest	Evaluation	Trial	Adoption
Salespeople	84	90	64	70	56
Trade journals	90	38	22	16	8
Buyers in other companies	18	22	28	16	8
Engineers in other companies	26	34	44	20	18
Trade associations	42	24	14	4	8
Trade shows	76	34	16	12	4

Adapted from Webster (1965)

Table 6.2   Importance of different criteria in evaluating products

Performance characteristic (ranked in order of preference)	Scaling value
Quality/price ratio	3.61
Delivery reliability	2.91
Technical ability and knowledge	1.95
Information and market services	1.86
General reputation	1.65
Geographic location	1.63
Technical	1.61
Extent of previous contact	1.44
Importance of client (reciprocity)	0.61
Extent of personal benefits supplied to buyer	—

Source: Green *et al.* (1968)

decision is his/her past experience which itself relates to the buyer's perception of the supplier's reputation.

Particular product or supplier attributes and their relative importance will obviously vary according to the product and the buying situation. Previous research into product and supplier evaluation seems to indicate that evaluation is a two-step process where products and suppliers are measured against some kind of preconceived set of criteria.

This necessarily brief discussion of buying stages underlines several of the models of buying behaviour discussed later in this chapter. Before moving on to this topic, however, it is necessary to consider the last characteristic of organizations – the motivations and objectives of the organizations and their members.

Buying goals

Both Cox (1966) and Campbell (1966) have analysed buying behaviour as a problem solving activity and recognize that the whole purchasing process is designed to meet certain aims or objectives on both the organizational level and the individual level. These objectives, it is suggested, can relate either directly or indirectly to the buying task. However, a variety of factors can intervene between the original purchase objectives and the final buying decision. The

cost of searching for the product or service that exactly fits the purchase specifications may be prohibitive, or, alternatively, such a product or service may not be available. White (1969) indicated that in some instances a major determinant of buying behaviour is the desire for work simplification.

Therefore in many instances both organizations and individuals may be pursuing 'satisficing' rather than maximizing courses of action in their behaviour whereby a compromise will be reached between the attainment of the purchasing objectives and the actual purchase.

Models of organizational buying behaviour

The previous discussion of buying stages is fundamental to an understanding of the various models of organizational buyer behaviour which have been postulated in the past twenty-five years. The purpose of modelling buyer behaviour is to clarify the relationships between various inputs, such as selling, previous experience or competitor activities, and outputs which are the purchase or rejection of a product or service from a particular source.

Many models have been proposed and an excellent summary of the early work in the field is made by Webster and Wind (1972b) in their book, *Organizational Buying Behaviour*. The authors define four main categories of model:

1   Task related
2   Non-task related
3   Complex
4   Multi-dimensional

Task related models

These are based on the view that the desire for rational or optimal outcomes is a fundamental determinant of behaviour. These models focus on concepts such as lowest purchase price; lowest total cost; constrained choice; rational economics; and materials management.

Non-task related models

With non-task related models the perspective shifts from the demands of the task to be accomplished to the personal interests that might be affected by the outcome. Examples of the key concepts used in non-task related models include:

* Individual desire for ego enhancement or personal gain.
* Desire to avoid risk in decision making (Bauer, 1960; Newall, 1977).
* Gratification of buyer and seller through a dyadic relationship (Evans, 1963; Bonoma and Johnston, 1978).
* Lateral relationships between buyer and colleagues (Tosi, 1966).
* Relationships with significant other persons from within the company and their effect on transmission and interpretation of information (Webster, 1965).

Complex models

In the late 1960s several more comprehensive models were postulated, incorporating a large number of variables. For example, the *decision process model* (Wind and Robinson, 1968) depicts decisions as occurring over a considerable period involving segmented stages, i.e. 'problem alternatives' and 'selection'.

The *compact model* (Robinson, Faris and Wind, 1967) attempts to establish general rules that govern the decision process. Three dimensions of influences are proposed: organization structure; elements of the buying process; and the characteristics of individuals. However, in this model no reference is made to the exchanges and negotiation occurring between parties.

We can criticize these models for adopting only a partial approach and even the more complex models fail to cover many of the important points observed by Webster and Wind. Moreover, many are theoretical rather than realistic. They are of limited practical use to the marketing or purchasing practitioner.

In an attempt to be more realistic, Robinson *et al.* (1967) proposed the *buygrid model*. This is based on empirical observations of buyer behaviour in companies. In Table 6.3 we see that decisions are thought to vary on two dimensions. First the stage of the decision (or 'buyphase') and second the nature of the decision itself (the 'buyclass').

The buygrid model offers certain improvements over earlier models. For example it recognizes that buying is often repetitive and has a more normative basis for practising managers. However, Ferguson (1979) found that the buygrid model had only a limited capacity to predict outcomes when he applied it to examples of decision making. In most situations he observed that the proposed systematic decision process was often 'short-circuited'. To overcome these objectives we must turn to the more comprehensive models which incorporate a wider range of variables.

Complex multidisciplinary models

Clearly the models previously described are inadequate both as descriptive representations of reality and as predictive tools. Several models have been developed which attempt to overcome these problems. In an early attempt to integrate various dimensions of consumer buying behaviour Howard and Sheth (1969) developed a behavioural model based on social, psychological, cultural and economic variables.

Table 6.3 The buygrid model

Buyphases	Buyclasses		
	New task	*Modified re-buy*	*Straight re-buy*
Identification of need	X	X	X
Determination of requirement	X	n/a	n/a
Specific description of requirement	X	n/a	n/a
Search for potential sources	X	n/a	n/a
Examination of sources	X	n/a	n/a
Selection of source	X	X	X
Order routine established	X	X	n/a
Evaluation of performance feedback	X	X	X

n/a = not applicable
Source: Robinson et al. (1967)

Subsequently Sheth (1973) proposed a complex model specifically for industrial buyer behaviour, which integrates a large number of variables into one comprehensive model which is briefly described below.

The Sheth model

Sheth's model of organizational buyer behaviour outlined in Figure 6.1 proposes four broad categories of variables:

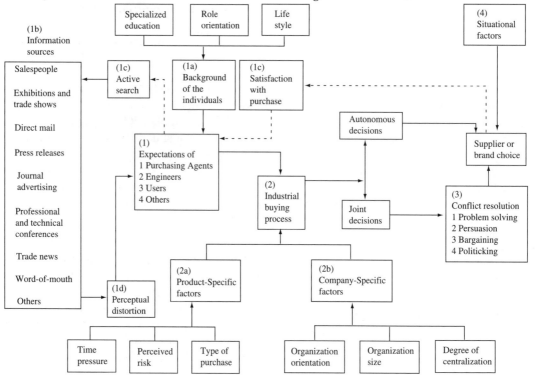

Figure 6.1   Sheth model of organizational buying behaviour (source: Sheth, 1973)

Psychological world of the decision makers
The decision makers' perception of the product's ability to satisfy both implicit and explicit criteria such as quality, delivery time, price, reputation, etc., will vary in accordance with the individual's role, education, life style, past experience and knowledge of the product and supplier. This background, which constitutes a sort of 'black box', leads to individual perceptual distortions which will influence each person's approach to the buying task.

Product and company variables
Product specific factors include perceived risk, type of purchase (new or re-buy situation) and time pressure. Perceived risk and purchase situation have been discussed previously. Time pressure refers to the possibility that decisions may need to be made within a time limit. Sheth (1973) suggests that the shorter this time limit the more likely that the decision will be made autonomously. Company factors include company orientation, company size and centralization, the influence of which has already been discussed.

Structure and methods for problem solving
The decision makers' psychological world and the various product and company variables will lead to the buying task being solved by a particular method. Sheth suggests that these methods can be summed up as either joint or autonomous decision making. Joint decision making often results in conflict between the decision makers and the third stage of Sheth's model concentrates on the reasons for and resolution of this conflict. Conflict may stem from:

(a)   Disagreement on expectations about the suppliers or their products.
(b)   Disagreement about the criteria with which to evaluate suppliers or products.
(c)   Fundamental differences in the buying goals or objectives among the members of the buying centre.
(d)   Disagreement about the style of decision making.

For each of the above bases of conflict the following forms of conflict resolution may apply:

(i)   *Problem solving.* Increased search for information and further deliberation about existing information. This additional information is then presented in such a way that conflict is minimized.
(ii)   *Persuasion.* An attempt is made to show the dissenting members how their criteria are liable to result in corporate objectives not being fulfilled.
(iii) *Bargaining.* The fundamental differences between the parties are conceded and a decision is arrived at on a 'tit for tat' basis. This will either result in a compromise or else allows an individual to make the decision autonomously in return for some favour or promise of reciprocity in future decision making.
(iv)   *Politicking and backstabbing.* These according to Strauss and Sheth are common methods of problem solving in industrial buying.

Situational factors
Sheth argues the organizational buying decisions are often determined by 'ad hoc' situational factors and not by any systematic decision-making process. Thus, specific decisions are a result of certain environmental considerations, such as price controls, the economic environment, strikes, promotional efforts or price changes. These factors can often intervene between the decision-making process and the final decision.

Sheth's model is not intended to be definitive, but offers a framework which draws attention to the dynamics and complexity of organizational buying and presents the relevant factors in a systematic way. The model concentrates on the internal workings of the buying process and does not incorporate external influences and tells us nothing about the relationship between the constituent parts. In discussing the situational factors, Sheth wrote:

What is needed in these cases is a checklist of empirical observations of the ad hoc events which initiate the neat relationship between the theory or the model and a specific buying situation.

We should note here that a universal buying process does not exist and the model's value lies in its application to particular buying situations or organizations. In this manner it can contribute towards a better understanding of the complexities of organizational buying behaviour.

The Webster and Wind model

Webster and Wind's (1972a) model outlined in Figure 6.2 stresses the role of the individual as the real decision maker in the organization. Therefore the individual's motivation, personality, perception, learning and experience are all vital to the actual decision process. This model is truly comprehensive and honours concepts

from the fields of individual, organizational and social psychology, economics, management, sociology and politics.

Webster and Wind recognize the existence of a buying centre and argue that organizational buying is a multi-person process subjected to and influenced by the aggregate behaviour of a number of people, and also by the interaction between them. The activities of both individuals and the collective buying centre are influenced by a variety of factors, some of which are related to the buying task (task variables which include rational and economic motivations) and non-task variables (a variety of emotional or non-rational reasons for purchasing decisions).

Webster and Wind suggest that the final buying decision is dependent on influences exerted from four spheres:

Table 6.4   Key factors affecting organizational buying decisions

Level of influence on behaviour	Source of influence	Types of constraints to behaviour that emerge
1. The firms' environment	Physical, legal, economic, technical, political, cultural, suppliers, customers, governments	Information, products and services, business conditions, values, norms
2. The organization	Business climate, physical climate, technological climate, economic climate, cultural climate, structure of work, personnel, organizational goals	Technology relevant for purchasing organization of the buying centre, buying tasks, members of the buying centre
3. The buying team	Technological constraints, buying group structure, buying group tasks, member characteristics, member goals	Task and non-tasks: – activities – interactions – orientations
4. The individual	Motivation, cognition, personality, learning, roles	Buying decision process, individual DM unit, group DM unit ↓ buying decision

Based on Webster and Wind (1972b)

1   The general environment
2   The organization
3   Interpersonal influences
4   The influence of the individual

It is possible to identify three key elements of the model and their interplay, as shown in Table 6.4.

At the most general level we have the firm's environment. This comprises the wide and

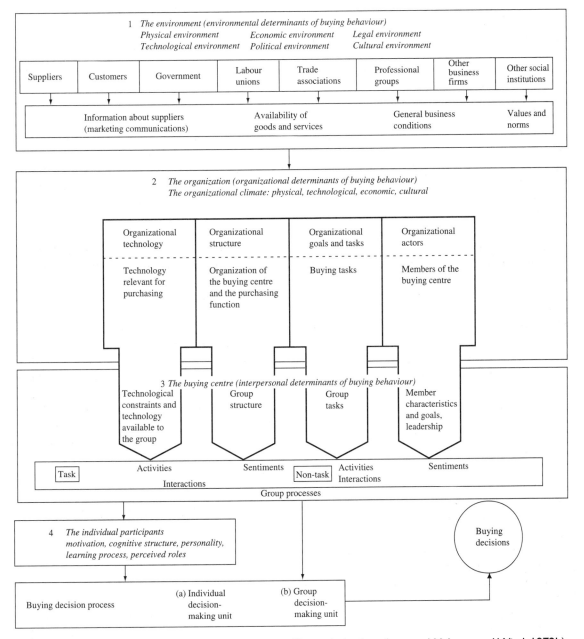

Figure 6.2   Webster and Wind model of organizational buyer behaviour (source: Webster and Wind, 1972b)

complex system of institutions that make up the social and industrial infrastructure. By dictating needs, norms and laws this level of influence affects the practices of the firm and the individual.

Below the firm's environment we encounter the organization's internal environment. Decision making occurs against a background of the firm's technology, the way work is organized, the firm's objectives and goals and the character of individuals themselves.

The third level of influence proposed is that of the decision-making unit. At this level the roles performed by participants in the decision make a major contribution to the eventual outcome. Thus the roles of the 'influencer', 'order placer', 'decider', 'gatekeeper' and 'user' may all be present. Although we might presume the buying centre to have a common set of expectations, the decision itself may be the outcome of several different collective processes, such as bargaining, consensus negotiation and game strategy. Several writers have commented on tactics used by individuals to promote their own interests. For example, Strauss (1962) suggests that purchasers may avoid or enforce company rules or use political or personal persuasion. Walton and McKenzie (1965) stress the importance of distributive and integrative bargaining plus attitudinal structuring in achieving a 'common front'.

The fourth and lowest level of influence – that of the individual – highlights the fact that all behaviour is ultimately conducted at a personal level. Thus motivation, cognition, personality, experience and learning may all affect the outcome of the decision process.

Webster and Wind's model focuses our attention on a number of significant features that are particularly relevant in international marketing. Thus, at the most general level foreign trading partners may well come from very different environments (see Chapter 23). The organizational environments of buying and selling firms may also be different or disjointed. As a result understanding may be poor and communication difficult.

At the second level the model accounts for the fact that firms in different cultures may have very different working climates. In addition the way work is organized could be disparate. At the third level, the model recognizes the possibility of conflicts of interest and the influence of 'significant others'. Perhaps of great interest at the individual level of influence, the model highlights the fact that personal processes and cap-abilities will affect the outcome of decisions. Thus training and experience, cognition, personality and motivation will all affect sales and buying performance. Clearly, important differences in personal factors such as these are more likely in different countries.

In essence, Webster and Wind's model is one of the most comprehensive of its kind and considers a wide range of decision related factors and variables. However, it is still of limited practical help to the marketer because it does not concentrate on the units of analysis that are fundamental to the real life processes that are occurring with prospective and ongoing buyer–seller relationships (i.e. the relationship between individuals and the nature of what is exchanged).

Although it covers a multitude of determinant factors, what is lacking is a focus on the processes that are most important in the long- and short-term aspects of a buying decision. No reference is made to the personal relationships and the atmosphere of the relationship that may evolve between buyer and seller. Seeking to resolve this issue, the International Marketing and Purchasing (IMP) Group developed a model of business-to-business marketing and purchasing as an iterative process based on long-term relationships.

The interaction approach

The *interaction approach* (Turnbull and Cunningham, 1981; Hakansson, 1982) focuses on the most basic elements of the decision process. It stresses the necessity that marketers are perceptive and flexible in the definition and satisfaction of customer needs. This is done by placing greater emphasis on the processes and relationships which occur between and within buying and selling organizations. The interaction approach to business-to-business marketing is now firmly established and recognized in Europe as an important and realistic conceptualization of the realities of marketing and purchasing behaviour in business markets. More recently this has been recognized by scholars throughout the world and Webster (1992), in a discussion of the changing role of marketing, recognizes the limitations of previous models and stresses the need for marketers to understand and manage long-term relationships and networks of organizations. Hakansson (1982) emphasizes the following points to distinguish the IMP Group approach:

- Buyers and sellers are seen as active participants in the transaction. The buyer is thus not limited to a passive role and can seek to influence the nature of the marketing inputs that are offered.
- Buyer–seller relationships are often long term in nature, tend to be based on mutual trust rather than a formal contract and often start months or even years before money and goods are exchanged.

- Complex patterns of interaction evolve between and within the companies and their different departments.
- Because of the complex nature of relationships, marketers and purchasers may be more involved with supporting and maintaining these, than with actually buying and selling.
- The links between buyers and sellers may become institutionalized.

From these observations industrial purchasing decisions may be seen to vary as a function of four main areas of variables. The interrelationships of these four key areas are illustrated in Figure 6.3.

In the brief description of the four areas which follows, we shall emphasize how the interaction model stresses the importance of the individual and the level of his/her interpersonal and intercompany skills.

The interactive process
Relationships between buyers and sellers can be broken into a series of episodes. Each episode contributes to the overall relationship, which will be developed over a greater period of time.

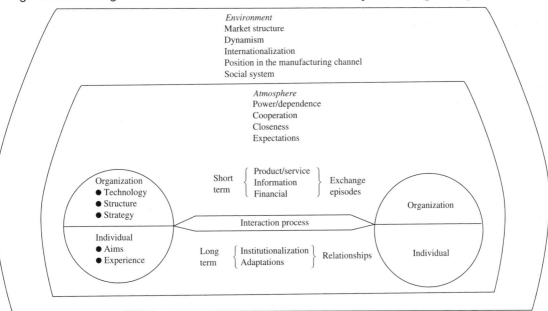

Figure 6.3   Main elements of the interaction model (source: Hakansson, 1982)

These episodes can be considered in terms of elements of exchange. For example, the exchange of the actual product or service, the exchange of information, the exchange of money or social exchanges. The greater the extent of uncertainty concerning these elements, the more likely that increased interaction will take place to resolve these uncertainties and allow the parties to become familiar with each other and develop mutual trust.

The occurrence of episodes over time can lead to the interaction becoming routinized and to preconceptions regarding the role set of both individuals and organizations. Such routine patterns of behaviour may become characteristic of a single relationship or else of a whole industry. Mutual adaptations may occur between buyers and sellers which will result in cost reductions or some other advantage. The existence of such adaptations can serve to bring each party closer together. This can therefore act as a major influence on changing marketing or buying policies.

The participants

Interaction occurs between organizations and individuals and is dependent on the nature of the organization and its members. Relevant factors may be the firm's technology, size, experience and structure or the individual's motives, attitudes and perceptions. These factors have already been discussed at some length in previous sections.

The environment

The interaction process takes place in the general prevailing environmental conditions which will determine certain norms of behaviour and values. Particularly relevant factors may be the market structure, social systems or economic conditions, and the degree of internationalization of the economy and/or the industry.

The atmosphere

The outcome of a relationship is the atmosphere which results from the various exchanges and adaptations. The atmosphere refers specifically

to the degree of closeness between the buyer and seller which will be reflected in the level of conflict or cooperation in their interaction. The nature of the atmosphere can be planned. The development of a close relationship with a 'good atmosphere' may result in advantageous conditions for the buyer and seller. However, in order to avoid power dependence, where one party becomes vulnerable to the power of the other, the 'closeness' of the atmosphere may be regulated and in some circumstances a company may deliberately choose to have a distant, even confrontational style of relationship.

The interaction model focuses on the relationships between individuals both within and between firms. It portrays dynamic and developing relationships, which approximate to the reality of organizational purchasing, in a way that none of the previous models is able to do. In so doing it presents a more complex picture of organizational buying and offers a challenge to the researcher to find a universal pattern of relationships from which to build a comprehensive model.

Metcalf, Frear and Krishnan (1992) have shown how the interaction approach is a valuable paradigm for analysing the relationship development of aircraft engine suppliers and aircraft manufacturing customers whilst Turnbull and Valla (1986a) have developed a strategic planning model based on the interaction approach. Hakansson (1989) also demonstrates the robustness of the approach in applying it to innovation and technology transfer.

Relationships, interdependence and networks

To fully understand the importance of relationships as an input to, and an outcome of, organizational buying and selling we need to examine the investments and bonding processes of the relationship partners and other players in the network. Relationships between companies don't 'just happen'; they are the consequences of efforts made by those companies – without such investments the relationships will not develop and will decline. These investments may be relatively trivial, such as a special delivery schedule, or they may be major changes in product design, for example. Both sellers and buyers make such investments, or adaptations, and these define the nature of the relationships – how the companies 'live together'. Relationship management is the process of planning and controlling these efforts in both companies (Turnbull and Zolkiewski, 1997; Ford, 1998).

It is important to note that all companies have relationships with their customers and their suppliers. It is the nature of the relationships which varies – from close, trusting and productive to arm's-length, conflictional and marginal. The company will have to manage many relationships simultaneously which thus are interconnected. Thus marketing management is very much to do with the managing of an interconnected portfolio of customer relationships.

A company's relationships are one of its major assets – although some relationships might be more of a problem than an asset – and represent considerable investments of technical and managerial resources over time. The concept of relationship investment and bonding has been examined by Turnbull and Wilson (1989) and Wilson and Mummalaneni (1986), who identify the competitive advantage that can derive from strong relationship bonds. The associated concept of relationship portfolios has been examined by Campbell and Cunningham (1983), Fiocca (1982), Rangan, Moriarty and Swartz, (1992) and Turnbull and Zolkiewski (1997). Although all these researchers recognize the major difficulties of definition and measurement of appropriate dimensions of analysis, they agree that, at least conceptually, relationship portfolio analysis, planning and management is an essential part of effective marketing management.

Whilst the interaction approach has been acknowledged as an important development in the process of understanding business markets, it has limitations; the approach was originally based on the analysis of bilateral relationships between pairs of organizations. In reality, of course, no relationship exists in isolation but forms part of a connected and interdependent set of relationships. Thus, the way the parties of a relationship will behave will be affected by their connections to other organizations and the interaction occurring. The study of these sets of relationships has come to be termed *the network approach* and can be seen as a logical development of the earlier research on interaction. However, the analysis of networks is much less well developed although a great deal of work is now emerging (Ford, 1991; Hakansson and Johanson, 1987). At this time, however, it is only possible to conclude that much further research needs to be completed before an adequate understanding of how network positions and dynamics affect the behaviour of buyers and sellers.

We have previously noted in this chapter that the relationship or interaction approach to business markets can give valuable insights into the marketing of consumer products given that the majority of such products are sold to organizational buyers or intermediaries. However, it is interesting to note that relationship management has been relatively recently embraced (very enthusiastically in many cases) by companies dealing directly with consumer markets. This has been most obviously manifested in the numerous loyalty card programmes developed by airlines, retailers, car dealers and many others (see Christopher, Payne and Ballantyne, 1991; Buttle, 1996).

At the heart of this perhaps rather superficial or fashionable management trend is the explicit recognition by those companies involved that strong ties between the supplier and the customer are potentially of huge economic advantage – it is considerably cheaper to keep customers than to gain new ones! It is, of course, critical if these relationship management programmes are to work in the long term, that they offer real benefits to the customer as well as the supplier (see Chapter 26 on relationship management).

We should also note that the challenges of managing an array or portfolio of customers in an FMCG market are conceptually similar to those in, for example, the heavy engineering sector. It is the application of the concept where adaptation and flexibility is the core to success.

Conclusion

In reviewing various models of buyer behaviour an attempt has been made to bring together the various elements of organizational buyer behaviour that were discussed under the headings of organizational structures, activities and goals. No single model adequately explains all the complexities of the organizational buying process and this in itself is a warning against any attempt to construct simplistic models. However, taken together the complex models provide a framework for empirical research into the buying process as each of the relevant areas is treated with different emphasis in each model.

The marketer can no longer presume that the company will be a sole or dominant supplier for ever. Existing relationships must be maintained and strengthened to protect against growing competitive pressures. Equally important, to survive in the increasingly international competitive environment of the next decade, suppliers must aggressively seek to establish new relationships both in domestic and foreign markets.

These twin strategies – defending the existing customer base and proactively seeking new accounts – have a common fundamental requirement, the knowledge and understanding of how organizations buy.

Understanding the dynamics of organizational buying behaviour is essential to all major strategic and tactical planning in business-to-business marketing; the identification of profitable segments and motivating those individuals with product and service offerings appropriate to their needs. Thus every action of the business-to-business marketer is based on the probable response of organizational buyers in relation to adaptations of price, product, distribution, advertising and promotion.

Business-to-business marketing is characterized by complex interaction processes both within the marketing and purchasing companies and between these companies. High technological and financial dependencies are common to business-to-business markets. These dependencies lead to extensive involvement and interchange over long time periods. Thus purchasing is a multiphased and multiobjective process. Due to the complex multidisciplinary and multifaceted nature of the buying process the aim of researchers to develop comprehensive but testable and normative models is still not yet fully achieved.

References

Alexander, M., Cross, T. and Cunningham, S. (1961) *Industrial Marketing*, Richard Irwin, Homewood, IL.

Anyon, G. (1963) *Managing an Integrated Purchasing Process*, Rinehart & Winston, New York.

Bauer, R. A. (1960) Consumer Behaviour as Risk Taking, in R. S. Hancock (ed.) *Dynamic Marketing for a Changing World*, Proceedings of the 43rd Conference, American Marketing Association.

Bonoma, T. V. and Johnston, W. (1978) The Social Psychology of Industrial Buying and Selling, *Industrial Marketing Management*, **7**(4).

Buckner, H. (1967) *How British Industry Buys*, Hutchinson, London.

Bunn, M. D. (1993) Taxonomy of Buying Decision Approaches, *Journal of Marketing*, **57**, Jan., 38–56.

Buttle, F. (ed.) (1996) *Relationship Marketing, Theory and Practice*, Paul Chapman Publishing, London.

Campbell, N. C. and Cunningham, M. T. (1983) Customer Analysis for Strategy Development in Industrial Markets, *Strategic Management Journal*, **4**, 369–380.

Campbell, R. (1966) A Suggested Paradigm of the Adoption Process, *Rural Sociology*, **31**, December.

Christopher, M., Payne, A. and Ballantyne, D. (1991) *Relationship Marketing*, Butterworth-Heinemann, Oxford.

Cox, D. F. (ed.) (1966) *Risk Taking and Information Handling,* Harvard University Press.

Cunningham, M. and White, R. (1974) The Behaviour of Industrial Buyers in their Search for Suppliers of Machine Tools, *Journal of Management Studies,* May.

Cyert, R. and March, J. (1963) *A Behavioral Theory of the Firm,* Prentice-Hall, Englewood Cliffs, NJ.

Dewey, R. (1960) *How We Think,* D. C. Heath and Co., Lexington, MA.

Evans, F. B. (1963) Selling as a Dyadic Relationship, *American Behavioral Science,* **6**, May.

Feldman, W. and Cardozo, R. N. (1968) The Industrial Revolution and Models of Buyer Behaviour, *Journal of Purchasing,* **4**, November.

Ferguson, W. (1979) An Evaluation of the Buygrid Analytical Framework, *Industrial Marketing Management,* **8**(1).

Financial Times (1974) How British Industry Buys, *Financial Times,* November.

Fiocca, R. (1982) Account Portfolio Analysis for Strategy Development, *Industrial Marketing Management,* **11**, 53–62.

Fisher, L. (1969) *Industrial Marketing,* 2nd edn, Business Books, London.

Ford, D. (ed.) (1991) *Understanding Business Markets,* 1st edn, Academic Press, London.

Ford, D. (ed.) (1997) *Understanding Business Markets,* 2nd edn, The Dryden Press, London.

Ford, D. (ed.), Hakansson, H. and Turnbull, P. W. (1998) *Managing Business Relationships,* Wiley, Chichester.

Greatorex, M., Mitchell, V.-W. and Cunliffe, R. (1992) A Risk Analysis of Industrial Buyers: The Case of Mid-Range Computers, *Journal of Marketing Management,* **8**, 315–333.

Green, P., Robinson, P. and Wind, Y. (1968) The Determinant of Vendor Selection. The Evaluation Function Approach, *Journal of Purchasing,* August.

Hakansson, H. (ed.) (1982) *International Marketing and Purchasing of Industrial Goods,* John Wiley, New York.

Hakansson, H. (1989) *Corporate Technological Behaviour: Cooperation and Networks,* Routledge, London.

Hakansson, H. and Johanson, J. (1987) Formal and Informal Cooperation Strategies in International Industrial Networks, in D. Ford (ed.), *Understanding Business Markets,* San Diego, California: Academic Press. Also in Contractor, F. J. and Lorange, P. (1988) *Cooperative Strategies in International Business,* Lexington Books, D. C. Heath & Company, Lexington, Mass.

Hakansson, H., Johanson, J. and Wootz, B. (1977) Influence Tactics in Buyer-Seller Processes, *Industrial Marketing Management,* **5**, 319–332.

Hill, R. and Hillier, F. (1977) *Organizational Buyer Behaviour,* Macmillan, London.

Howard, N. and Sheth, J. (1969) *Consumer Buyer Behaviour,* John Wiley, New York.

James, B. (1966) Emotional Buying in Industrial Markets', *Scientific Business,* Spring.

Kettlewood, K. (1973) Source Loyalty in the Freight Transport Market, Unpublished MSc dissertation, UMIST.

Lister, P. (1967) Identifying and Evaluating the Purchasing Influence, IMRA, August.

Metcalf, L. E., Frear, C. R. and Krishnan, R. (1992) Buyer–Seller Relationships: An Application of the IMP Interaction Model, *European Journal of Marketing,* **26**(2), 22–46.

Newall, J. (1977) Industrial Buyer Behaviour: A Model of the Implications of Risk Handling Behaviour for Communication Policies in Industrial Marketing, *European Journal of Marketing,* **1**.

Rangan, K., Moriarty, R. and Swartz, G. S. (1992) Segmenting Customers in Mature Industrial Markets, *Journal of Marketing,* **56**, 72–82.

Robinson, P., Faris, C. and Wind, Y. (1967) *Industrial Buying and Creative Marketing,* Allyn and Bacon, New York.

Shankleman, E. (1970) Study of Industrial Buying Decisions, *New Scientist,* September.

Sheth, J. (1973) A Model of Industrial Buyer Behaviour, *Journal of Marketing,* **37**(4), October.

Strauss, G. (1962) Tactics of Lateral Relationship – the Purchasing Agent, *Administrative Science Quarterly,* **7**, September.

Thain, D. H. (1959) How Industry Buys – With Conclusion and Recommendations on Marketing to Industry, National Industrial Advertisers Association of Canada.

Tosi, H. L. (1966) The Effects of Expectation Level of Role Consensus on the Buyer–Seller Dyad, *Journal of Business*, October.

Turnbull, P. W. and Cunningham, M. T. (1981) *International Marketing and Purchasing*, Macmillan, London.

Turnbull, P., Ford, D. and Cunningham, M. T. (1996) Interaction, Relationships and Networks in Business Markets: An Evolving Perspective, *Journal of Business and Industrial Marketing Management*, **11**(3/4), 44–62.

Turnbull, P. W. and Valla, J. P. (eds) (1986a) *Strategies for International Industrial Marketing: The Management of Customer Relationships in European Industrial Markets*, Croom-Helm, London.

Turnbull, P. W. and Valla, J. P. (1986b) Strategic Planning in Industrial Markets – An Interaction Approach, *European Journal of Marketing*, **20**(7).

Turnbull, P. W. and Wilson, D. (1989) Developing and Protecting Profitable Customer Relationships, *Industrial Marketing Management*, **18**(1), 1–6.

Turnbull, P. W. and Zolkiewski, J. M. (1997) Profitability in Customer Portfolio Planning, in D. Ford (ed.) *Understanding Business Markets*, 2nd edn, The Dryden Press, London.

Wallace, A. (1976) A Study of the Buying Process for New Products by Intermediate Marketing Organizations in the Channels of Distribution for Grocery Products, unpublished PhD thesis, UMIST.

Walton, R. E. and McKenzie, R. B. (eds) (1965) *A Behavioral Theory of Labour Negotiations*, McGraw-Hill, New York.

Webster, F. C. (1965) Modelling the Industrial Buying Process, *Journal of Marketing Research*, **2**, November.

Webster, F. and Wind, Y. (1972a) A General Model for Understanding Organizational Buyer Behaviour, *Journal of Marketing*, **36**(2), April.

Webster, F. and Wind, Y. (1972b) *Organizational Buyer Behaviour*, Prentice-Hall, Englewood Cliffs, NJ.

Webster, F. E. (1992) The Changing Role of Marketing in the Corporation, *Journal of Marketing*, **56**, Oct., 1–17.

Weigand, R. (1968) Why Studying the Purchasing Agent is not Enough, *Journal of Marketing*, **32**(1), January.

White, J. (1969) Some Aspects of the Marketing of Machine Tools in Great Britain, unpublished PhD thesis, UMIST.

Wilson, D. T. and Mummalaneni, V. (1986) Bonding and Commitment in Buyer–Seller Relationships, a Preliminary Conceptualisation, *Journal of Industrial Marketing and Purchasing*, **1**(3), 44–58.

Wind, Y. and Robinson, P. (1968) Generalized Simulation of the Industrial Buying Process, Marketing Science Institute Working Paper, June.

Further reading

Ames, B. C. and Hlavacek, J. D. (1984) *Managerial Marketing for Industrial Firms*, Random House, New York. Shows how modern marketing management concepts and methods can be applied in the realm of industrial marketing.

Chisnall, P. M. (1985) *Strategic Industrial Marketing*, Prentice-Hall International, Englewood Cliffs, NJ. A clearly written and practical book by a respected British author. It provides a systematic discussion of the principal strategic factors in the marketing of industrial and organizational goods and services.

Ford, D. (ed.), Hakansson, H. and Turnbull, P. W. (1998) *Managing Business Relationships*, Wiley, Chichester. This book should be essential reading for all business-to-business marketing and relationship marketing courses. It provides a synthesis of interaction and network theory, yet written in a practical, managerially-oriented way.

Ford, I. D. (ed.) (1991) *Understanding Business Markets: Interaction, Relationships and Networks*, 2nd edn, Academic Press, London. An edited collection of papers from the IMP Group. Perhaps the most significant contribution to thinking in this field in the last decade.

Hakansson, H. (ed.) (1982) *International Marketing & Purchasing of Industrial Goods: An Interaction Approach*, John Wiley, New York. The theoretical base of the interaction approach to industrial marketing is described in detail and then a series of international case studies are presented which shows the application potential of the theoretical model.

Hutt, M. D. and Speh, T. W. (1985) *Industrial Marketing Management*, 2nd edn, Dryden Press, Trois, MO. Integrates the growing body of literature into an operational treatment of industrial marketing management.

La Placa, P. J. (1984) *Industrial Marketing Management: Cases and Readings*, Random House, New York. An excellent collection of major articles supplemented by a comprehensive selection of case studies. The material is, however, all American based.

Parkinson, S. T. and Baker, M. J. (1986) *Organizational Buying Behaviour*, Macmillan, London. A concise and readable text which uses European case material to develop and enhance the theor- etical material.

Robinson, P. J., Faris, C. W. and Wind, Y. (1967) *Industrial Buying and Creative Marketing*, Allyn & Bacon, New York. Still worth reading as one of the early 'classics' in the field of industrial marketing.

Turnbull, P. W., Ford, I. D. and Cunningham, M. T. (1996) Interaction, Relationships and Networks in Business Markets: An Evolving Perspective, *Journal of Business and Industrial Marketing Management*, **11**(3/4), 44–62. This article provides a comprehensive, critical and well referenced review of the conceptual development of the IMP approach to business-to-business marketing. The evolution of thinking from the initial dyadic approach to relationships to the network concept is explained and the key elements of relationship network management are highlighted. An important review article for both the academic and practitioner audience.

Turnbull, P. W. and Valla, J. P. (eds) (1986) *Strategies for International Industrial Marketing: The Management of Customer Relationships in European Industrial Markets*, Croom Helm, London. From the same group of authors as Hakansson, this book provides interesting and unusual insights into industrial marketing strategies.

Webster, F. E. Jr (1992) The Changing Role of Marketing in the Corporation, *Journal of Marketing*, October, **56**(4). An interesting and important review of how, at last, the Americans have begun to recognize interaction and relationships. Perhaps the article should have been titled 'We get there eventually'!

Webster, F. E. and Wind, Y. (1972) *Organizational Buying Behaviour*, Prentice-Hall, Englewood Cliffs, NJ. One of the milestones in published texts on organizational buying behaviour.

CHAPTER 7

Marketing research

JOHN WEBB

Introduction

Just as marketing had become widely accepted as the business strategy whereby producers of goods and services maintain contact with their customers in the modern world, along comes Brown, Bell and Carson's (1996) *Marketing Apocalypse* which informs us that we are now in a post-modern environment!

Such an environment is characterized, in the above volume, by Michael Thomas, as one where: fragmentation, de-differentiation, hyper-reality, pastiche and anti-foundationalism are the new orders of the day – though their theories would appear to be more relevant to industrialized markets than to the whole world.

Whatever way the marketing environment is characterized, either modern or post-modern, marketing should be seen as an exchange process. In earlier days, when barter was the main system by which goods were swapped for money, or other goods, the close physical proximity of the principles facilitated a valid, meaningful and 'noise-free' process of communication. Both parties were satisfied with the result, otherwise it would not have been concluded; goods were accepted by one side at an agreed price, and the other side received an acceptable level of profit which enabled them to remain in business. Such a direct system of exchange disappeared many years ago. The Industrial Revolution, which began in the late seventeenth century, and its invention of the factory system of mass manufacture, generated a seismic shock, the results which were to accelerate the rate of separation of those that required goods/services and those who sought to supply them. This distance, both 'psychic' and physical, continues to widen to the present day, as Schlegelmilch and Sinkovics (1998) say, 'The nature of change has changed. It is not evolving in comfortable incremental steps, but it is turbulent, erratic and often rather uncomfortable'.

Factors which have had, and continue to have, a catalytic effect on the parties in the exchange process include:

* an acceleration in the globalization of the provision of goods and services
* increasingly rapid rate of technological innovation and implementation
* the fragmentation of markets into smaller and smaller niches
* a population of consumers which is becoming better educated, more discriminating in its purchasing habits, and which has higher expectations of goods and services
* the end of the Cold War, with a resultant increase in the number of independent trading nations
* individual countries becoming ever more multi-cultural with a concomitant rise in the number of specialized goods demanded by each cultural bloc
* the increasing speed, on a global basis, with which information may be transmitted and goods delivered.

All of these facts, plus many others too numerous to mention, have made it more difficult for producing companies, and, to a certain extent the middlemen, to fulfil one condition of marketing philosophy, which it is that it is an exchange process between parties to their mutual satisfaction. Such a principle demands that producers should place the consumer at the focus of their business strategy.

However, if marketing is accepted as an exchange process, and as Bagozzi (1975) writes

in order to satisfy human needs, people and organizations are compelled to engage in social and economic exchange with other people and other organizations . . . they do this by communicating and controlling the media of exchange, which, in turn, comprises the links between one individual and another.

then companies must learn how, not only to communicate with their actual and potential customers, but also to listen to what they are saying. 'Saying' implies the use of language; and the 'language' to be used must be that of the consumer. Organizations must then, in the majority of cases (high technology being something of a case apart), learn consumer-speak, to paraphrase Orwell.

Marketing research is a bundle of techniques which have been developed or annexed from other disciplines that, via the implementation of their new-found linguistic skills, enable companies to generate a stream of valid, timely and apposite information from and about customers concerning their thoughts and ideas about current goods/services and those to which they aspire.

The chapter will be structured as follows: after defining marketing research and detailing the types of research that are available, the process of marketing research will be analysed. The use of secondary data follows, and then the various types of primary quantitative research are described, together with questionnaires and their design. The various forms of qualitative research are discussed, to be succeeded by a description of the way measurement, in theory

and practice, is employed in the research process. The chapter will end with an exposition of the way attitudes are conceptualized and scaled, and how research results should be analysed and presented.

Definitions of the role of marketing research

Marketing research occupies a service function within organizations; its main function is to supply managements with reliable, valid, timely, relevant and current information.

A manager's ability to rely upon their past experience as a guide to the future has been constrained by the factors touched upon in the introduction to this chapter; the amounts of 'danger' in the business environment have increased, and change becomes the only constant. Managers have to take decisions with far-reaching consequences, opportunities must be grasped, threats avoided, markets segmented, target markets selected, control exercised, marketing plans implemented and monitored. But managers do not make decisions in a vacuum – there is an environment, outside their control, of which they must take due note. Marketing research can be viewed as the managerial senses through which managers can view the outside world and then use the inputs from their corporate eyes, ears, etc., to moderate those processes over which they do have control, and thus yoke their internal actions with environmental changes.

Managements should learn to act proactively and not reactively; thus the ability to identify, measure, evaluate and anticipate relevant change is a managerial function which is becoming increasingly critical to the long-term success of organizations. Data should be gathered in such a manner that the end result renders a valid, life-like representation of the situation under investigation and not some cartoon-like image with distorted features.

There are many definitions of marketing research; here is a sample:

Marketing research is the function which links the consumer, customer and public to the marketer through information – information used to identify and define market opportunities and problems; generate, refine and evaluate marketing actions; monitor marketing performance; and improve understanding of marketing as a process.

Marketing research specifies the information required to address these issues, designs the method for collecting information; manages and implements the data collection process; analyses the results; and communicates the findings and their implications. (*The Dictionary of Marketing Terms,* American Marketing Association, 1988)

Marketing research is the systematic and object-ive approach to the development and provision of information for the marketing decision making process. (Kinnear and Taylor, 1996)

Marketing research is the systematic and object-ive identification, collection, analysis and dissemin-ation of information for the purpose of assisting management in decision-making related to the identification and solution of problems and opportunities in marketing. (Malhotra, 1993)

Through these definitions two key words recur – systematic and objective.

- *Systematic:* the research process should be well planned and organized, with rules set in advance of the project being instigated, to govern the types of data to be collected, the way in which it is to be collected, the system of analysis to be employed, etc.
- *Objective:* the research should be conducted in a way that eliminates, as far as possible, bias and the corruption of data by subjectivity/ emotion. Marketing research does not take place in a laboratory but it should, at all times, aim for 'scientific' objectivity.

Types of research

Webb (1992) classifies marketing research into three groups:

1 Exploratory research
2 Conclusive research
3 Performance-monitoring (routine feed-back) research

with each stage in the decision-making process determining the appropriate class of research that should be employed.

- *Exploratory research* – usually employed in the initial stages of the research project, when uncertainty/ignorance are at their highest. It is characterized by flexibility, an absence of formal structure and/or the desire to measure. It may be used to define the parameters of the environment in which the problems/ opportunities exist, and to uncover those salient variables which are relevant to a full understanding of that environment. Exploratory research may alert the researchers to any temporal/seasonal effects which may have an impact upon the results (Radas and Shugan (1998) say 'Virtually every product in every industry in every country is seasonal'); it may identify any dialects/jargon which may be the common currency; and, it may allow an estimation to be made as to how easy/difficult it will be to carry out any subsequent research. Data sources may include secondary sources of data, observation, mini-surveys, and interviews with experts and case histories.
- *Conclusive research* – employed to generate information to evaluate and to select course(s) of action. Conclusive research is formal, objective and systematic; it must include a definition of the objectives of the research, sampling plans, decisions as to what type(s) of survey method to use, possible systems of experimentation, and ways in which the data is to be analysed. The project must always exhibit a valid link between the information that is sought and the possible alternative courses of action under consideration.
- *Performance-monitoring research* – a response to an environmental alteration, an opportunity to grasp or a threat to be avoided, once implemented, cannot be merely ignored; the results of that implementation must be available to management. Monitoring research is the way in which comparisons can be made

between what was planned and what actually happened. Not only should marketing mix variables and the salient variables of the environment be subjected to careful evaluation, but also such measures as sales, market share, profit and ROI.

- *Quantitative and qualitative research methods* are not mutually exclusive but complementary research methods, each having advantages and disadvantages, which may be used to reduce the negative aspects of one system by the use of the other. The choice(s) of what system, or combination of systems to use, should be moderated by the specific factors which are found in each research problem and by the project's research objectives. Many research exercises are made up of elements from qualitative and quantitative research schools.

Flick (1998) says that qualitative research is increasingly used because

'rapid social change and the resulting diversification of life worlds are increasingly confronting social researchers with new social contexts and perspectives. These are so new for them that their traditional deductive methodologies – deriving research questions and hypotheses from theoretical models and testing them against empirical evidence – are failing in the differentiation of objects. Thus research is increasingly forced to make use of inductive strategies.

Table 7.1 compares the two methods

The process of marketing research

The sequence of steps for marketing research is shown below:

1 Set the objectives of the research programme
2 Define the research problem
3 Assess the value of the research
4 Construct the research proposal
5 Specify the data collection method(s)
6 Specify the technique(s) of measurement
7 Select the sample
8 Data collection
9 Analysis of the results
10 Presentation of the final report.

Proctor (1997) says

a systematic approach to problem definition can help to direct marketing research staff in their efforts to obtain relevant information. It is also informative to all those people in the organization who will be affected by the findings and recommendations. Problem definition must take into account the situation of the company and its ability to take sound action. Poorly thought-out marketing decisions can cause major problems; sometimes with disastrous consequences.

He proceeds to quote Rickards' (1974) goal-oriented approach to problem definition which 'employs identifying needs, obstacles and con-

Table 7.1 Comparison of qualitative and quantitative research methods

Qualitative	Quantitative
Open-ended, dynamic, flexible	Statistical and numerical measurement
Depth of understanding	Sub-group sampling or comparisons
Taps consumer creativity	Survey can be repeated in the future and results compared
Database – broader and deeper	Taps individual responses
Penetrates rationalized or superficial responses	Less dependent on research executive skills or orientation
Richer source of ideas for marketing and creative teams	

Source: Gordon and Langmaid (1988)

straints in the search for an adequate definition of the problem:

(1)   Write down a description of the problem, then ask:
        (i)   what do we need to accomplish (needs)?
        (ii) what are the obstacles?
        (iii) what constraints must we accept to solve the problem?
        (iv) redefine the problem, bearing the above in mind.'

Secondary data

Secondary data, which consists of previously published material, should always be consulted before commencing primary research.

Newsom-Smith (1988) says that secondary data can:

1   Provide a background to primary research; if the research has already been conducted by someone else, why repeat it, if the current research objectives are met? Even if it doesn't fulfil exactly what is needed, it may help determine key variables that any subsequent primary research will have to investigate; it may help determine sampling methods/sample sizes; alert researchers to key personnel in the environment, and illustrate active trends.

2   Act as a substitute for field research; primary research can be very costly and secondary data may help save unnecessary expenditure in that published data may fully meet all the current research objectives. Even if not all questions are answered, then the scope of the primary research may be substantially reduced. A cost–benefit analysis should be made to weigh the cost of further costly primary research against the advantages of less detailed, but cheaper, secondary research.

3   Baker (1991) says that some research may only be carried out realistically by the use of

secondary data, i.e. attempting to establish trends in market behaviour. Longitudinal studies are unrealistic propositions for primary research, engendering a reliance on published, historical data. Much of this data concerning market structures and performance come from censuses – a method which may provide superior quality data to that gained by sampling a population – the preferred method used in most field studies. Secondary data may also set the boundaries and establish the state of the environment in which primary research will be undertaken.

4   Acquisition studies; acquisition has been a popular strategy for companies to follow in recent years. Predator companies, who do not wish to alert their 'prey', could hardly mount large primary field studies without drawing attention to themselves. Thus secondary research may be used to gain information on other companies.

But before using secondary data, researchers should ask themselves:

•   Is the secondary data relevant?
•   What is the cost to acquire it?
•   What is its availability?
•   To what extent may the data be biased?
•   How accurate is the data?
•   Is the data sufficient to meet the current project's research objectives?

Sources of secondary data

Luck and Rubin (1987): '. . . a good rule in all research is parsimony; using only meaningful data' – good advice with the plethora of data which is currently available.

The first place to start a search for 'meaningful data' is within the organization itself. With the increasing use of management information systems, functional departments are now much more likely to have collected and stored data in a form readily accessible to research personnel.

Internal sources of data may be divided as follows:

- Accounts; contain information on: customers' names and addresses, types and quan-tities of products purchased, costs of sales, advertising, manufacture, salaries etc., discounts etc.
- Sales records; contain information on: markets, products, distribution systems
- Other reports: contain information on: trade associations and trade fairs, exhibitions, customers' complaint letters, previous marketing research reports, conferences.

If internal sources prove inadequate for the intended task, then external data sources have to be consulted. Where, though, does one start to make sense of the vast amounts of externally published data?

Start with the general and then gradually focus onto the specific. Thus, in an unfamiliar research setting, one should start with those guides, either printed or held on computer, which offer suggestions as to the general direction in which to proceed. From such 'directory of directories' publications, e.g. ABI-Inform, Bookbank and Official Pub-lications of the UK, one may begin with, for example, general industry data, and proceed through specific industry data, via market/category information (as given by Retail Intelligence (Mintel)) down to specific company/product data, as in Mintel Market Intelligence Reports.

Trained librarians offer an excellent way to navigate a course through these huge databases, and are especially useful when first consulting computer databases, which can be very complex – as mistakes in their operation can be costly.

Quantitative primary data

Primary data is that which is collected to fulfil the demands of the current research project, and has to be gathered should secondary sources of data fail to provide the information necessary to meet the research objectives. If individuals hold the data necessary to answer the questions posed by the research objectives, then they may be questioned, observed, or invited to become a member of a continuous research panel.

Survey research

Survey research consists of personal interviews, telephone interviews and mail questionnaires. Each have advantages and disadvantages and the optimum choice, or combination of them, is mostly dependent upon matching individual survey methods with the situation-specific demands of the research objectives. Aaker (1990) says that the following are the main factors to be considered when making this choice: available budget, the nature of the problem, the complexity of the data requirements, the need for accuracy and the constraints of time. No author states only one method may be used for a particular research project; in many situations, several, or all, methods may have to be employed.

Survey methods are good at gathering data on: past and present behaviour; attitudes and opinions; respondent variables; knowledge.

Personal interviews

Personal interviews are classified against their degree of structure and directness: structure is the degree of formality/rigidity of the interview schedule; directness refers to the degree to which the respondent is aware of the purpose of the research.

Unstructured–indirect methods are rarely used in marketing research, unstructured–direct and structured–indirect will be covered in the section on qualitative primary data. Structured–direct is the method most often used in research surveys.

Structured–direct survey methods permit the researcher: to reduce respondent anxiety (increasing rapport and, possibly, the response rates); to guide respondents through complex questionnaires; and, within boundaries, to ask for ambiguous answers to be clarified.

Question wording and order are fixed, with answers being recorded in a standard manner, thus reducing possible interviewer bias – potentially troublesome when multiple interviewers are being used. Standardized formats allow for the use of less skilled interviewers, thus reducing costs. Also, pictures, products, signs etc. may be displayed to refresh respondents' memories or to demonstrate some action

But, personal interviews may be: time consuming, thus the cost per completed interview is high compared with mail questionnaires and telephone interviews; the data gathered may lack depth and richness because of the fixed questionnaire format. Questions are usually closed because of the problems associated with recording the answers to open-ended questions.

Telephone interviews

An administered questionnaire delivered via the telephone. The advantages of this method are: low cost per completed questionnaire; centrally located telephone banks reduce travel times and costs and permit firm administrative control of interviewers, thus reducing the potential for interviewer bias and error. Quicker results may be produced, compared with mail questionnaires and face-to-face interviews; allows for samples to be drawn, easily, from a wide geographical area.

However, there is a problem in establishing rapport with respondents during a call's short duration; this may result in them not being relaxed during the interaction or in allowing them, easily, to terminate the interview. Thus questions must be short and rapidly able to engage the interest of the interviewee. Respondents may confuse a 'research' call with a cold-call telephone sales 'pitch' and terminate the call for fear of being sold something. The sample may not be fully representative of the population, as telephone ownership is not universal (though this reason grows less important as time passes). It is impossible to use visual stimuli to 'jog' respondents' memories or to demonstrate some action.

Mail questionnaires

Mail questionnaires use no interviewer, so that, as a potential source of error, is removed.

Field staff may be reduced to a minimum, resulting in a low cost per completed questionnaire if response rates are high. The relatively anonymous method of data collection may confer on certain respondents sufficient confidence to answer what, to them, are 'embarrassing' questions. They can cover, economically, wide geographical areas. They may gain access to certain areas of the survey's population who refuse to answer personal and telephone interviews. Respondents may fill in the mail questionnaire in their own time, thus reducing some pressure that a few respondents may experience because of the presence of the interviewer; it also allows respondents to consult their files, notes, account records etc.

Its disadvantages are that even though addressed to named individuals, there is no way of knowing who, exactly, filled in the questionnaire. Questions may be read in advance, therefore the ability to control the sequence of their presentation is removed; respondents can see exactly where the questions are leading merely by turning to the end of the document. There is no-one to explain/interpret complicated/ambiguous questions, resulting in the possibility that such questions are either omitted or the answer is guessed. Questionnaires which are long, or which are perceived to be long, may either not be answered at all, or will have large numbers of questions unanswered. High non-response rates will mean that the cost per completed questionnaire can become prohibitively high.

Panel/syndicated research

Data may be gathered from individuals, households, industrial buyers, firms etc. who agree to provide data to research agencies on a regular basis; such data may include information concerning consumer and/or industrial products and store audits. Many panels are computerized; Taylor Nelson AGB uses a sample of 8500 homes who have agreed to provide data on a range of consumer goods. Panellists scan their purchases with a hand-held bar-code reader and the results are sent electronically to the research company for processing and analysis (Crouch and Housden, 1996).

Data sources may be classified into six main groups:

- Consumer data
- Wholesale data
- Advertising evaluation data
- Retail data
- Industrial data
- Media/audience data

Advantages of panel research

Data is generated continuously, so trends such as market share and brand switching etc. may be established, and, as the need to keep generating samples is reduced, the potential effects of sampling error are lessened. Evidence suggests that higher response rates will be enjoyed when compared with rates from ad hoc surveys and the results are likely to be more accurate as panel members become experienced in recording their purchases. Data may be generated for a comparatively smaller outlay, when compared with the costs of mounting an ad hoc survey. Panels/syndicated research can provide data on competitor activities. Because of its continuous nature, this research method is likely to produce results quicker than with an ad hoc survey.

Disadvantages of panel research

The main disadvantages of panel research rest with the sample itself; once the initial sample has been selected, by whatever means (usually probability-based sampling), selected panellists may refuse to join, thus distorting the representativeness of the sample. Of those panellists that do agree to join, some, over time, may drop out, again 'upsetting' the sample's representativeness, and it may be difficult to find new panel members with equivalent characteristics. Some panel members may have to be replaced when they get too old; age itself is not the problem, but the panel organizers have to maintain a panel

that is representative of the general public's demographics. Panel members *may* alter their purchase patterns as a result of being surveyed, but the effect may be reduced by (i) a reasonable turnover of panel members, and/or (ii) disregarding their submissions for the first two to three months of membership.

One form of continuous research which is rapidly gaining popularity is that of the 'loyalty card' system operated by large supermarket chains. Customers register with the company by filling in an application form which asks for details such as name, address, post-code, marital status, number of children etc. The members of the scheme are rewarded with bonus points for a set unit of expenditure; the customers are rewarded with discounts or products redeemed by surrendering a certain number of points, and the company gains access to a huge database.

Observation

All members of a society are observers, though usually only on a casual basis – an insufficiently scientific approach for it to be used as a marketing research technique, as it may be subject to large and unreliable amounts of subjectivity and bias on the part of the observer. Therefore, before observation may be used in research, it must be made more objective and rigorous. Observation may not immediately spring to mind as a marketing research method but there are two situations where it may prove most useful:

1 Where it is the only way of gathering certain types of data, e.g. it might be difficult for respondents to remember their exact journey through a multi-floored department store and the amount of time they spent in each section, but the answer could be obtained by using a trained observer.

2 It may be used to confirm that the results gathered by other methods are valid; though here, it may not be thought of as a technique in its own right, rather as half of a two-pronged investigation.

The following three conditions (Tull and Hawkins, 1993) should be met if observation is to be used successfully:

1 The action must be accessible and overt, thus, the measurement of feelings, motivation, attitude etc. is ruled out.
2 Actions should be frequent, repetitive and predictable.
3 Actions should encompass a reasonably short time span.

Modes of observation are classed according to four main factors: naturalness, openness, structure and directness.

Questionnaires and their design

A questionnaire is an ordered set of questions which may be employed in a variety of research situations. They may vary in structure, i.e. the amount of freedom which is allowed to the respondent in answering the questions. Highly structured questionnaires, with set answer formats, are usually easier to administer, answer and analyse; unstructured questionnaires are, usually, harder to administer, need more thought on the respondent's part and require considerable interpretative skills in their analysis. The situation-specifics of the research context will condition, largely, the type of questionnaire to be employed.

The format of the questions may be dichotomous (a yes/no type answer); multiple-choice, where respondents are invited to select one or a number of responses from a pre-determined list; or open-ended, where the respondents reply using their own words. Though these questions are more difficult to interpret, they go some way in eliminating interviewer bias.

When deciding on the questions, Webb (1992) suggests that the following questions be asked:

(i)   Is the question necessary?
(ii)   Will the respondent comprehend the question?
(iii) Is the question sufficient to elicit the required data?

(iv)   Does the respondent have the necessary data to answer the question?
(v)   Is the respondent willing/able to answer the question?

When phrasing the questions, the questionnaire design should ensure that the vocabulary used is appropriate for the respondent being questioned, and that only the clearest and simplest words are used. Also vague/ambiguous questions should be avoided as should biased words or questions which might 'lead' the respondent. Those questions which contain estimates or which rest on implicit assumptions may be difficult to analyse, and should only be asked if absolutely necessary. All questionnaires should undergo rigorous pre-testing on a sub-sample of potential respondents before their use.

Qualitative primary data

Not all research objectives may be met by the use of a question and answer format. Good though these methods are at gathering data concerning knowledge of facts, incidents of past/present behaviour patterns etc., other areas of human activity do not fall into such convenient and relatively easily accessed categories. Such areas include respondents' attitudes, motivations, opinions, feelings etc., as well as other types of question which might cause respondents to experience heightened levels of anxiety or embarrassment, or where they might feel a difficulty in putting their answers into words.

Qualitative research methods are employed to uncover other ways of gaining access to such types of data; they seek to answer the 'why' and 'how' questions, rather than the 'what happened' or 'how many' types of enquiry.

A comparison between quantitative and qualitative methods has already been given by Gordon and Langmaid (1988) – where they say that qualitative research is used optimally in situations which will increase understanding, expand knowledge, clarify use, generate hypotheses, identify a range of behaviours, explore/explain motivations and attitudes, highlight distinct behavioural groups and provide an input into future research. Qualitative research may also be used for basic exploratory studies, new product development, creative development, diagnostic studies and tactical research projects.

The three main techniques are: group discussions, individual depth interviews and projective techniques.

Group discussions

The driving force of this research tool is the dynamic interaction of the members of the group. Group discussions usually last between one and three hours and employ between six and twelve respondents. Bellenger, Bernhardt and Goldstucker (1976) say that groups may be used to:

1   generate hypotheses subsequently to be tested quantitatively;
2   generate information useful in questionnaire design;
3   provide background information on a product category;
4   gain reactions to new product concepts, for which there is no secondary data;
5   stimulate new ideas concerning the use of older products;
6   generate ideas for new creative concepts;
7   help interpret other qualitative results.

Gordon and Langmaid (1988) report that group discussions may be inappropriate under the following circumstances:

(a)   in intimate/personal situations;
(b)   where there are strong pressures to conform to social norms – peer pressure;
(c)   where detailed case histories are required;
(d)   where the group is likely to be too heterogeneous with respect to the idea/product etc. of interest for a meaningful discussion to be able to take place;

(e)   where 'complex psycho-social issues' are involved;
(f)   where it is difficult to assemble the required sample, e.g. where people are physically widely scattered.

Relaxing, pleasant surroundings are conducive to a free flow of ideas and help to reduce respondents' anxiety. The chair of the discussion (moderator), usually a key member of the research team which has set up the exercise and who will be pivotal in its analysis, should rapidly establish an easygoing but workmanlike rapport with all the respondents.

As group discussions can generate huge amounts of data, which will need lengthy, consequently expensive, analysis, it is vital that they are carefully planned and administered.

Malhotra (1993) gives the following guide for planning and conducting a group discussion:

1   Set the objectives of the research programme and problem definition.
2   Specify the objectives for the qualitative research.
3   State the objectives to be answered by the group discussion.
4   Write a screening questionnaire to exclude group members who do not fulfil the research requirements.
5   Develop a moderator's outline.
6   Conduct group discussion.
7   Analyse the data.
8   Summarize findings and plan follow-up research or action.

Developing the moderator's outline is a very important step and will involve detailed debate between the client, the research team and the moderator. This guide will ensure that all the required areas of interest are covered. It will also go some way to improve the reliability of the research method; a problem which may occur if more than one moderator is going to be involved with the project.

Advantages of group discussions

Cost and speed; since a large number of respondents are being 'processed' simultaneously, data collection and analysis are quicker than for individual interviews.

Many individual decisions are made in a social context – groups provide that context. Society's requirements and perspectives are part of the discussion process and not a mere 'optional extra'.

Group discussions allow for the observation, and analysis, of non-verbal communications: this will enable trained moderators to assess the validity of the respondents' statements.

A group of people, in concert, will generate a far wider range of opinions, insights and information, because of stimulation and/or synergism, than they might have done when examined as individuals. Some respondents may feel 'comforted' by the group and less exposed than they would have done in an individual interview, their anxiety being reduced, the method will enable them to produce more valid responses. The unstructured or semi-structured nature of the discussion allows the moderator to probe behind respondents' answers which are incomplete or ambiguous. As many observers can become involved in the collection of the data, apart from the moderator, a higher level of reliability should result from the analysis.

Disadvantages of group discussions

Only a small number of respondents can become involved; therefore the question of unrepresentativeness arises, and thus the ability to 'project' the results onto a population is curtailed. This, however, does not invalidate the method as a research tool, as the method is usually only used, as in exploratory research, where generalizations concerning a population are not required.

Contrary to the 'comfort' factor already mentioned, some respondents may feel overawed/inhibited by the presence of the other respondents, causing them to act in an atypical manner. Shyer members of the group might be allowed to be 'shouted down', by an ineffective moderator, by those with more dominant personalities; thus an important role of the moderator is to 'bring out' the shyer members of the group and to restrain the enthusiasm of the more extrovert members. If the group reacts, in a negative sense, against the moderator, then the chances of generating valid, useful data are much reduced.

Individual depth interviews

Between the poles of structured–direct interviews (the administered questionnaire) and the unstructured–indirect, lies the topic of this section – the individual depth interview, what Kahan (1990) calls

an unstructured personal interview which uses extensive probing to get a single respondent to talk freely and to express detailed beliefs and feelings on a topic. The purpose of this technique is to get below the respondent's surface reactions and to discover the more fundamental reasons underlying the respondent's attitudes and behaviour.

Group discussions and depth interviews are techniques whose main aim is to seek out, to delve, to try to understand and to explore; therefore, a flexibility of approach is essential – the interviewer must be able to alter and adapt to changing situations which may arise during the interview.

Depth interviews have been found to be most beneficial where:

1 The discussion topic has the potential to be embarrassing, stressful or of a confidential nature.
2 In complex situations, where there is a need to uncover attitudes, motivations, beliefs or feelings.
3 Peer pressure may cause respondents to act in an atypical manner (e.g. when they admit to subscribing to certain societal norms when, in reality, they do not).

4   The interviewer needs to ascertain the chronology or a case history of a certain decision process, e.g. when trying to understand complex buying behaviour patterns.

5   The situation is new and/or complex and exploration of a topic, rather than measurement, is the prime objective.

The nature of the relationship between interviewer and subject in an in-depth interview is of prime importance; it is a one-to-one occasion, with no third party to 'protect' either side. Thus the establishment of a good rapport is an essential interviewer function, and questions aimed at cementing the relationship should come first. Then it is recommended that the general questions gradually give way to the specific, where the heart of the interview lies.

Advantages of individual interviews

Individual interviews provide a great depth/richness of data, with the ability to attach, directly, an opinion to a single individual; something which may not be so easy in a group discussion.

The lack of peer pressure allows for the expression of unconventional, maybe antisocial, opinions, without fear of sanctions, mockery or embarrassment. Interviewers have the opportunity to develop close rapport with the subject – a level of trust which should encourage a freer flow of valid and useful information.

Disadvantages of individual interviews

They are very costly in terms of time/money both to conduct the interview and to analyse the results, and because of this high cost, it is usually possible only to work with small samples, thus limiting the ability of the research team to generalize about the results.

There may be problems in finding interviewers with the requisite skills.

Because of the highly personal nature of the interchange between the interviewer and the respondent and because of the unknowable amounts of subjectivity which may 'colour' the proceedings, it may be difficult to compare the information gathered by one interviewer with that from another.

Projective techniques

Appropriated from psychology/psychiatry, projective techniques rely on the principles that the way people organize and respond to relatively ambiguous stimuli will give trained observers an insight into the respondent's perceptions of the outside world and their reactions to it. Kidder (1981) says that projective techniques are useful in:

... encouraging in respondents a state of freedom and spontaneity of expression where there is reason to believe that respondents cannot easily evaluate or describe their motivations or feelings or where topics on which a respondent may hesitate to express their opinions directly for fear of disapproval by the investigator or when respondents are likely to consider direct questions as an unwarranted invasion of privacy or to find them threatening for some reason.

Projective exercises may be classed as structured–indirect research techniques and they receive their name from the way in which respondents 'project' their feelings, attitudes, beliefs etc. onto a third party or object – emotions which might have remained hidden if the chosen research technique had tried to gain access to their ideas/opinion by means of more direct questioning etc. It is not a technique whereby measurements are made, but more one where those emotions which the majority of the population might have difficulty in articulating are uncovered.

Projective techniques may be used:

(a)   to explore and generate hypotheses, which may then subsequently be tested by more quantitative methods;

(b)   to expose feelings, beliefs, behaviour patterns which would have remained hidden if a more 'direct' research method had been used.

There are a great many techniques used in this method of research, but they may be conveniently grouped under the following headings: completion, association, construction, choice ordering and expressive techniques.

Advantages of projective techniques

Very useful in exploratory studies where emotional guidance, feelings etc. are sought and where inputs to be used in hypotheses generation are required.

They enable researchers to gain access to data which they might have been denied if more direct, interrogative techniques had been employed.

They may be used to 'break the ice', and help in establishing rapport in the initial stages of qualitative studies.

Disadvantages of projective techniques

Expensive; to be of use, highly skilled research workers need to be employed. Also it is only possible to employ small samples using these methods, so the ability to generalize about the results is severely restricted.

It is time consuming, both to administer and to analyse the results.

Some respondents may be too shy to take part in the exercises and refuse to join in – therefore, non-response may be a problem.

There are many opportunities for the results to become 'contaminated' by measurement error; the role of the researcher thus becomes of great importance in the reduction of such error.

The research process and measurement

Having chosen the type, or types, of data collection method to be used to meet the research objectives, market researchers now have to choose the system(s) of measurement to be used. Measurement is part of everyday life; food is bought by weight, petroleum/cooking oil/beer is bought by volume, fabric by length – each product being dispensed by using a characteristic (weight, volume, length etc.) by which certain amounts of the object may be isolated.

In marketing research, measurements are also common; for example, the research objectives might stipulate that the project should ascertain the number of people in a certain age group who buy a certain newspaper, or the number of companies using certain distribution systems over a stipulated time period. Such measurements are relatively easy to make as the characteristics of interest are overt, accessed easily, and of a unitary status, i.e. they only have one dimension – number, length, age grouping etc. However, other marketing research projects are not intended to measure such tangible factors; some measurements are far more complicated because of the ambiguous nature of the answer to the question 'in order to meet the objectives of the research, what is to be measured?'

Torgerson (1958) said of measurement that it is '. . . the assignment of numbers to objects to represent amounts of degrees of a property possessed by all of the objects'. Now while it is a relatively simple process to see how such a definition applies, for example, to age (number of years since birth), weight (number of units of gravitational attraction), height (number of units from some base point), it is not such an unambiguous a process when it is necessary to meas-ure those factors, important in a social research setting, which are far more covert. For example, there is no universally agreed system for 'the assignment of numbers' to a respondent's   attitude towards blood sports, or their motiv-ation in purchasing one brand of motorcar in preference to another.

In measuring such abstract constructs as beliefs, motivations, feelings, attitudes etc., marketing research may have to express them 'in terms of still other concepts whose meaning is assumed to be more familiar to the inquirer' (Green, Tull and Albaum, 1988). To evaluate a research situation, there is a requirement to measure factors/variables, overt and covert, which are relevant; but there is also a need to know *what* to measure. Attitude, for example, can be defined in many ways, some of which have more and some less relevance to a specific situation, because attitude is a multidimensional concept. In making a definition of attitude, some of these components are excluded; thus researchers must note that measurement is never fully able to translate reality into sets of numbers – representation can only ever be incomplete.

Variables are factors relevant to a research situation which vary and in doing so affect the state of that situation. For example, many research studies are concerned with consumer responses to proposed changes in a product's price: thus the dependent variable is consumer response; the independent variables might include packaging, the price of competing brands/products and brand loyalty. The research objectives will have stipulated what the outcome of interest is – the dependent variable (here, consumer response). There may also have been implicit assumptions as to what the independent variables are, but the implicit needs to be made explicit. One way to accomplish this is to construct a model of the research situation. If there is insufficient information to do this, then some other research will be required – exploratory, for example. It may also be possible to determine the significant variables by means of a thorough analysis of the literature – secondary data search.

Southern (1988) writes that there are three important components of the measurement process:

1   Measurement is a process; it is controlled and open, not arbitrary or intuitive.
2   Measurement translates qualities into quantities, the numbers may then be manipulated. However, numbers themselves have no meaning, and those who manipulate them must exercise care if the validity of the relationship between number and characteristic is to be preserved.
3   Measurement has formal rules which may vary depending upon the manipulation, but once set, they must be followed consistently if reliability of data is to be guaranteed.

Green, Tull and Albaum (1988) say that number systems have:

1   Order.
2   Distance – differences between numbers are ordered.
3   Origin – number systems will have a unique origin indicated by zero.

Scales in marketing research

There are four main levels of measurement: nominal, ordinal, interval and ratio, and each makes different assumptions regarding the way in which the numbers reflect the situation under measurement.

Nominal scales assign numbers to objects, variables or people to show that they belong to some stipulated category – categories which are mutually exhaustive and mutually exclusive. In this scale, numbers have no mathematical value, they merely show that the people, objects etc. belong to a nominated group. Thus people who read *The Guardian* might be assigned to the value 7 and those who read *The Times* to the value 456. The only mathematical function which can be undertaken is to count the number of objects inside each category. Bus numbers, bank accounts and football team shirt numbers are all nominal scales.

Ordinal scales rank order objects/people etc. according to the amount of a property which it/they possess. But, respondents in a research programme must be able to discriminate between items of interest with respect to an attribute, i.e. they must have the ability to say, for example, that this coffee tastes better than that coffee. They are saying that this coffee, the preferred one, has more of the attribute 'good taste' than the other does – their second choice. Ordinal scales do not enable researchers to know/infer, by how much one item is preferred over the others in the same category. Thus it is not possible to say if the difference between the first and second and between the second and third is the same, more, or less. Students' examination results, first place, second place, third place etc. are examples of an ordinal scale.

Interval scales possess order and distance, but not a unique origin, i.e. their zero point is arbitrary. Thus meaningful statements about the distance between two objects on a scale may be made. It is permissible with an interval scale to say that the difference between scale points seven and eight is the same as the difference between scale points fifty-seven and fifty-eight. However, interval scales do not allow researchers to make meaningful statements about the value of a scale point being a multiple of another value on the same scale.

Ratio scales possess order, distance and a unique origin indicated by zero. All mathematical operations are allowed here, so it can be said that a reading of eighty on a scale is four times a reading of twenty on the same scale. Three metres is three times larger than one metre and ten kilos is twice as large as five kilos. Measures such as height, weight and volume are examples of ratio scales.

The measurement of attitudes

Marketing research constantly seeks to measure respondents' attitudes towards, for example, a change in packaging, price, a new product, politicians etc. But attitude measurement can sometimes be a rather difficult concept for such a practical subject as marketing research to come to terms with. How have attitudes been defined?

Here are two of the most useful and illuminating definitions.

Allport (1935) says that an attitude is '. . . a mental and neural state of readiness to respond that is organized through experience and exerts a directive and/or dynamic influence on behaviour'.

Fishbein and Ajzen (1975) say that is '. . . a learned predisposition to respond in a consistently favourable or unfavourable manner with respect to a given object'.

There are many other definitions than the above, but there is general agreement that an attitude is a learned mental state of readiness, a

way in which individuals construct their own worlds such that when confronted with a certain stimulus they act in a certain manner.

Attitudes are not held to be the only cause of human behaviour; there are many other factors having an impact upon the individual at the moment at which the behaviour under investigation becomes manifest. Attitudes, though internal to the subject, are conditioned through external experience, but experience is not a random or arbitrary process, but one which is organized through a process known as learning.

Components of attitude

It is widely agreed that attitudes have three components:

1   Cognitive: represents an individual's awareness and knowledge about an object, person etc. They say, 'I have heard about Brand X' or 'I believe that Brand X will carry out this function'.
2   Affective: represents an individual's feelings – good/bad etc. towards an object etc. – and is usually expressed as a preference. They say, 'I do not like Brand C', or 'I like Brand D better than Brand F'.
3   Behavioural: represents an individual's predisposition to action prior to the actual decision being made, or their expectations of possible future actions towards an object etc.

When researching the link between attitude and behaviour, consultants may try to use the information in one or two ways:

1   by measuring the cognitive and affective components to predict future possible behaviour;
2   by altering the cognitive and affective components in order to influence future behaviour.

The measurement of attitudes

Cook and Sellitz (1964) put forward, among other methods, the following way in which measured responses may give an indication as to an individual's attitude. They used techniques which rely on a relatively direct style of question which respondents answer in a way which enables an inference to be made as to the strength and direction of the attitude towards the research's object.

Measurement scales may be divided into two groups: rating scales and attitude scales. Rating scales measure a single component of an attitude, a respondent typically indicating their attitude to an object by means of a placement along a continuum of numerical values or of ordered categories. Scales can be labelled with verbal or numerical descriptors, but in using the former, the researcher should be aware that some respondents may not think that there is the same psychological distance between a 'very' and an 'extremely' as does the constructor of the scale; a pre-test should be made to check on this. By allocating a numerical value to the object, depending on the strength with which they hold a given attribute, measurement scales may be used to measure:

1 a respondent's overall attitude towards an object, product, person etc.;
2 the degree to which something possesses a certain attribute;
3 a respondent's feeling towards a certain attribute;
4 the importance with which a respondent invests a certain attitude.

Non-comparative rating scales – respondents are asked to rate, assign a number, to the object of interest in isolation, there being no standard against which measurements are made. Respondents mark their attitude position on a continuum (a graphic scale) or they may choose a response from a limited number of ordered categories (an itemized scale). For example, the question might be 'How do you like Brand X of chocolate?'

Comparative rating scales – respondents make an assessment of the object of interest against a stated standard. For example, 'How does Brand X of chocolate compare with Brand Y?'

Rank order scales – respondents are asked to rank order a list of objects/items against a stated criterion, e.g. taste, power etc. Rank order scales are ordinal, thus respondents are only able to show the order of their preferences; the research cannot then infer anything about the 'distances' between the items, i.e. it is not possible to say by how much the first item is preferred to the second etc.

Constant sum rating scales – this method overcomes the drawbacks of rank order scales. The respondent is allocated a constant sum (they may be expressed in currency or some other units), usually a round number, 100 units etc., and asked to allocate them between the given items in a way which reflects the object's attributes under investigation. This not only shows the rank order of the items, but also the size of the preference distances.

Attitude scales, which combine many rating scales, are an attempt to overcome the unrepresentativeness that may arise from inferring an individual's overall response to some object etc. by measuring their attitude to only a single aspect of that object etc.; attitude scales try to measure several facets of an individual's attitude to an object, person etc.

The three most popular attitude scales will now be described.

Likert or summated scale

Likert or summated scales require respondents to indicate their degree of agreement or disagreement with a number of statements concerning the attitude being measured. Their responses are given a numerical value and/or sign to reflect the strength and direction of the respondent's reaction to the statement. Thus, statements with which the respondent agrees are given positive or high values, while those with which they disagree are given negative or low marks. Scales may run, for example, from 1 to 5, from 5 to 1 or from + 2, via zero, to –2. Statements should give the respondent the opportunity to express clear, unambiguous statements, rather than neutral, ambiguous ones.

Semantic differential scale

Semantic differential scales are arguably the most widely used of all attitude scales. Respondents show the position of their attitude to the research object on a seven-point itemized scale, thus revealing both the strength and direction of the attitude. The extremities of the continuum are 'anchored' by a pair of polarized adjectives or adjectival statements.

Example: Respondents are asked to record their attitude towards a certain law firm:

```
Unfriendly ........................... Friendly
Modern ........................... Old fashioned
Efficient ........................... Inefficient
Slow ........................... Fast
Pleasant ........................... Unpleasant
```

Osgood, Suci and Tannenbaum (1957), who devised the scale, developed some 50 pairs of bipolar adjectives grouped to measure three fundamental components of attitude:

1   evaluative – negative/positive, good/bad;
2   activity – active/passive, fast/slow;
3   potency – weak/strong.

If phrases, rather than words, are used then the scale will have more meaning for respondents (Dickson and Albaum, 1977). Luck and Rubin (1987) recommend that no side of the scale should be exclusively reserved for either the positive or the negative aspect of the pairs, as this tends to allow respondents to tick only down one side – the 'halo' effect.

Semantic differential scales may be analysed in two main ways.

- Aggregate analysis: where the score is summed for each respondent for all pairs of words/statements, resulting in a numerical value of their attitude. Individual aggregate scores may then be compared with other individuals with respect to the same object, or two or more objects may be compared with respect to the same individual or group of individuals.

- Profile analysis: involves calculating the arithmetic median or mean value for each pair of adjectives for an object for each respondent or respondent group. The profile so derived can then be compared with the profile of the object.

The principal disadvantage of semantic differential scales lies in their construction. For valid results, scales need to be made of truly bipolar pairs of adjectives/phrases; the problem arises when some of the pairs/phrases chosen may not be true opposites in the respondents' minds.

Stapel scale

The Stapel scale is a modified semantic differential scale, and uses a unipolar 10-point verbal rating scale with values from +5 to −5 which measures both the strength and direction of the attitude simultaneously.

For example: respondents are asked to evaluate how well each of the adjectives describes the object under test, e.g. Sheila's apple pie tastes:

+ 5	+ 5	+ 5
+ 4	+ 4	+ 4
+ 3	+ 3	+ 3
+ 2	+ 2	+ 2
+ 1	+ 1	+ 1
Rich	Bitter	Expensive
− 1	− 1	− 1
− 2	− 2	− 2
− 3	− 3	− 3
− 4	− 4	− 4
− 5	− 5	− 5

Stapel scales are easy to administer and require no test that the adjectives are truly in polarity.

Sampling

Without the ability to extract a sample of a population, as opposed to conducting a census, the majority of marketing research projects could not take place. There are four main reasons for this:

- *Cost* – except where the populations of interest are very small, it is usually cheaper to take a sample rather than conduct a census.
- *Time* – a census, compared with a sample for a given population, is always going to be larger (hence it will take longer to collect the results); thus by the time the results have been collected and analysed, the situation under investigation might have changed. Samples may be extracted and analysed much quicker than a census, for a given population.
- *Accuracy* – is defined as the degree of precision with which a measure of a characteristic in a sample compares with the measure of the same characteristic in the population from which the sample was drawn. In sampling, accuracy is affected by (1) sampling error – caused by selecting a probability sample from a population which is not representative of the total population – such error can be reduced by increasing the size of the sample; (2) non-sampling error – all other errors in a marketing research project whose origins are not based in sampling error.
- *The destructive nature of measurement* – one cannot carry out a census on a bottle of whisky (for quality control) and still have any product for sale. Thus sampling is the only alternative if quality assurance is required. Some forms of measurement destroy; for example, one can only measure a population's initial reaction to an advertisement once. But, by extracting non-overlapping samples, such an evaluation may be repeated.

Probability sampling techniques

The units, which constitute a probability sample, are selected randomly, with each unit having a known chance of selection. Thus before a probability sample can be drawn, the project will need to define a sampling 'frame' for the population. Such a frame will need to ensure that each unit is included only once, and that no unit is excluded – thus all units have an equal chance of selection; the frame should cover the entire population and be convenient to use.

A probability sample should attempt to be representative of the entire population – but it can never be an exact replica. However, by applying the rule of probability, generalizations concerning the population may be made and calculations made about the degree of confidence with which the results can be viewed.

Sample error, for probability samples, stems from the variability of the sample and/or the size of that sample.

Simple random sampling

Units are chosen at random from the population. Individual units are assigned a number; a sample of these numbers is then selected either by using a 'lottery' system or by the use of random number tables. The method is simple to use, and it obeys the laws of probability; however, it may produce samples which are highly unrepresentative of the population.

Stratified random sampling

This method accepts the variability of the population and, by stratifying it before the sample is taken, tries to reduce its potential unrepresentativeness. Stratifiers, which may be geographical, demographic etc., are imposed on the population like a grid, dividing it into groups whose members, inside each 'cell', are as alike as possible with respect to the stratifier. Stratified random sampling adopts the position that each group/stratum is a population in its own right and then extracts a sample, by simple random means, from each of them.

In *proportionate stratified sampling*, the size of each sub-sample taken from a particular stratum is proportionate to the size of that stratum in the population. Thus if 25 per cent of the population is aged between 35 and 45, then 25 per cent of the sample should be composed of people in that age group. In *disproportionate stratified sampling*, the proportion of a characteristic, as possessed by the population, is not reflected to the exact extent, in the size of the sub-sample. Such a deliberate 'distortion' of the size of the sub-sample may improve the quality of the data if certain strata have an unusually large influence in the situation under investigation and need to be given a more significant role. Here not every unit has an equal chance of selection, but the chance of selection is still known; thus the laws of probability still rule and appropriate weighting(s) can be used when calculating the results.

The method's major drawback is in finding stratifiers relevant to the research situation.

Cluster sampling

Cluster sampling is similar to stratified sampling in that the total population is divided into strata, but it differs in that instead of sampling from *each* sub-group, a *sample* of the strata is taken, with a simple random sampling then taking place inside each of the selected groups. Thus while in stratified sampling each stratum represents a particular sub-set of the population, in cluster sampling each stratum should be a miniature representation of the full population. It is a method particularly useful in cases where the population is dispersed over wide geographical areas.

A particular form of cluster sampling is called *multistage sampling* and involves more than the single stage of the cluster sampling system. If, after dividing a country into various areas (counties, regions etc.), they are found to have greatly varying sizes of populations, then they are sampled using a system called the probability proportionate to size method. Thus if a county has five times the population of the other counties, then in the sampling process it should be allocated five times the chance of being selected. The first stage thus results in a number of counties etc., drawn from the population of counties. Then the research will select from these areas a number of, for example, cities, and again, they will be selected using the probability proportionate to size method. These stages may be repeated until the research arrives at the desired final sample. The method has the advantage that the process delivers a sample, chosen at random, but concentrated in certain geographical areas; useful when the costs of travel and communication can be high. It also means that probability sampling may be used when, at the macro-level, there is no sampling frame. When the final stage has been completed, and the research has arrived at the micro-level, sampling frames will be available – city maps, electoral rolls etc.

Non-probability sampling techniques

The researcher does not know the chances of a unit's selection if non-probability sampling techniques are employed. Therefore, the ability to generalize about a population, using the laws of probability, is much reduced and it is not possible to calculate the degree of confidence in the results. The sample is chosen at the convenience of the consultant or to fulfil the demands of some predetermined purpose.

Convenience sampling

Here the sample is chosen for the convenience of the research worker. A street interviewer who needs to sample 50 people, for example, might question the first 50 people who walk past the street corner where the interviewer is standing. It is a quick method and carries the minimum cost. It is a method useful in exploratory research.

Judgement sampling

Judgement sampling makes an attempt to ensure a more representative sample than that gathered using convenience techniques. Research consultants use their expertise, or make use of the services of an expert, to evaluate populations and to make recommendations as to which particular units should be sampled. With small populations and accurate assessments and guidance as to a unit's selection, judgement sampling can render samples with less variable error than might result with a sample chosen using a simple random technique, though this cannot be conclusively proved.

Purposive sampling

Purposive sampling does not usually aim for representativeness. Here the choice of the sample is made such that it should meet certain preconditions deemed appropriate to the fulfilment of the objects of the research. Thus a project might stipulate that the top 50 professors of French be interviewed as part of the project; thus there is no true 'sampling', merely the need to contact those units the research has already delineated.

Quota sampling

This attempts to reflect the characteristics of the population in the chosen sample, and in the same proportions. From national statistics, researchers gather the percentages for such 'stratifiers' as age groupings, income levels etc. and use them to construct 'cells'. This results in statements such as '23 per cent of the population is female, aged between 30 and 40 and earning £12 000 to £15 000 per annum'. The sample would then be collected, and 23 per cent of it would have to fulfil those demands. Quota controls must be available, easy to use and current. Quota 'stratifiers' shouldn't be used merely because they are available – they must be relevant to the project. This method may be cheaper to operate than a probability-based method, it is quick to use and relatively simple to administrate – it does not require a sampling frame. However, there is the possibility that the interviewer shows bias in the way the individual units are selected and in the difficulty that may arise in uncovering relevant and available quota controls.

Probability versus non-probability sampling techniques

Tull and Hawkins (1993) provide the following list of factors that are worthy of consideration when choosing a sampling method:

1. Are proportions and/or averages required or are projectable totals needed?
2. Are highly accurate estimations of population values necessary?
3. How large might non-sampling error be? What size of error due to frame choice, non-response, measurement and population specifications is likely?
4. Will the population be homogeneous or heterogeneous with respect to the characteristic of interest?
5. What will be the cost, if the results are above/below the required error tolerance?

They say that '. . . the need for projectable totals, low allowable errors, high population heterogeneity, small non-sampling errors and high expected costs of error favour the use of probability sampling'.

Size of sample

The size of a sample depends, in the main, upon the required degree of accuracy that the research objectives demand. This will depend upon:

1. The degree of variability in the population, the more heterogeneous that population, the larger the sample size required.
2. The presence of population sub-groups; the sample must be large enough to allow for a valid analysis of these.

Sample size estimation depends upon:

- Judgement – rests on the experience of the research consultant. But research workers should beware of making an arbitrary choice, ignoring such factors as cost, value and the required level of accuracy – this is the method of last resort.

- What can be afforded – though commonly used, this method ignores the value of the information to be collected, only looking at the cost. For example, a small sample may be more useful, though of a higher cost per unit, than a larger sample if the collected information is of a high value.
- Required size per cell – used in quota and stratified sampling techniques. It is usual to accept, as a minimum, 30 units per cell, before any statistical analysis can proceed. Thus if there are two age groups and five geographical areas to be sampled, ten cells will result, hence a sample of 300 units is required.
- Statistical methods – sample sizes may be calculated using the formula:

$$\frac{\sigma}{N} = \frac{\text{required level of accuracy}}{\text{level of confidence}}$$

where σ = standard deviation and N = size of sample.

Analysis of the results

The researcher will now be in possession of data from both primary and secondary sources; it must now be processed such that it is possible to draw appropriate conclusions.

In commencing the analysis, two questions need to be answered:

- With reference to the research objectives, what meanings should be obtained?
- What statistical methods should be employed to obtain those meanings given the way in which the data was collected?

Luck and Rubin (1987) define statistical analysis as '... the refinement and manipulation of data that prepares them for the application of logical reference'.

After the statistical analysis stage comes that of interpretation – where data is transformed or refined into a state which will highlight its meaning; inductive and deductive processes are utilized.

Beveridge (1957) says that in inductive reasoning one starts from the position of the observed data and then proceeds to develop a generalization that explains the observed interaction/situation. Deductive reasoning, on the other hand, moves from the general to the specific, by applying a theory to a particular case. Data interpretation should be concluded as objectively as possible. To ensure this, the following points are important:

1. Honest/objective interpretations are aided by not exaggerating or distorting the findings.
2. Interpreters should remember that a small sample will limit the opportunity to generalize about a large population.
3. One should not try to reach a particular conclusion.
4. The validity and reliability of the data must be ensured before interpreting the results and there should be no confusion between facts and opinion.

Thus the steps in the analysis of data are as follows:

1. Put the data in order

Raw data generated by primary and secondary research is not in a suitable state for immediate interpretation; it needs to be transformed.

Editing involves, for example, checking the questionnaire to ensure that all the questions have been answered and that the respondent has given unambiguous answers. If answers are missing or ambiguous, then steps should be taken to either fill them in, or respondents questioned to resolve areas of confusion.

Coding involves the assignation of a number, usually, to each particular response for each question; questionnaires which are pre-coded will save a great deal of time at this stage. Open-ended questions also require coding, and this is usually carried out by expert analysts who review a representative sample of all the questionnaires and devise appropriate categories to which individual answers can be assigned.

Tabulation involves arranging the data such that its significance may be appreciated;

data is placed into appropriate categories which are relevant to the research objectives. Tabulation may be carried out manually, mechanically or electronically. Such tables are very well suited to variables measured by ordinal or nominal scales, because of the limited number of response categories. Cross-tabulation is a more developed form of the one-way tabulation described above and the system allows an investigation into the relationship between two or more key variables by counting the number of responses that occur in each of the categories.

2. Make a survey of the data

Unprocessed data needs to be transformed. The most common way to compress data is to calculate the data's central tendency: mean, median or mode. Other, more complicated measures of central tendency include such measures as dispersion or range, variance and standard deviation, and, if two or more distribution dispersions are being compared, the co-efficient of variation. The results of the analysis do not need to be presented in purely mathematical forms; graphical display is a very useful method of showing, for example, the frequency differences between different categories. Histograms, line and scatter graphs and pie-charts have all been found to be better at communicating results than bald tables of numbers.

3. Select an appropriate method of analysis

If the research objectives cannot be reached by survey and/or cross-tabulation of the data and more sophisticated methods of analysis are required, then consideration should be given as to which particular analytical techniques will provide the appropriate information. However, there is a vast array of available techniques, so some thought needs to be given to the way in which the most appropriate method(s) is/are selected.

Luck and Rubin (1987) offer the following scheme:

1. What is the technique required to show? A common request is to show whether the results are significant, i.e. are there significant differences between various groups or could the results have occurred by chance because only a sample of the population was under investigation, not the entire population.

2. What scale was used to measure variables?
   - Only certain arithmetic manipulations are allowed on certain types of scale – it depends upon what level of measurement was reached.
   - Non-metric scales, where the data was qualitative rather than quantitative, include nominal and ordinal scales.
   Metric scales work in real number systems and include ratio and interval scales.

3. Parametric and non-parametric data.
   - Parametric data is that which is distributed around a mean/central value in a symmetrical manner, as in a normal distribution, has been collected, at least, using an interval scale and may be analysed using probabilistic tests of statistical significance.
   - Non-parametric data has a distribution profile which does not conform to the normal curve of probability, and appropriate tests assume that the variables have been measured using nominal or ordinal scales.

4. Number of variables to be analysed

Univariate analysis: where a single variable is analysed in isolation.

Bivariate analysis: occurs where some form of association is measured between two variables simultaneously.

Multivariate analysis: this investigates the simultaneous relationships between three or more variables.

5. Dependence and independence

Analysis may involve an investigation into the relationship between variables. By relationships is meant that changes in two or more variables are associated with each other. It may be important to be able to calculate by how much the independent variables are responsible for variations in the dependent variable.

6. How many samples are involved?

The choice of an appropriate statistical test depends upon whether the data is being tested to measure (a) the significant differences between one sample and a nominated population, (b) the significant differences between two related or independent samples, (c) the significant differences amongst three related or independent groups, or (d) correlation and their significance tests.

Presentation of the final report

Research reports should say what they are supposed to say and do so in a style appropriate to the intended readership. Those which are intended for a technically educated readership may be written using specialist terms and may discuss, in detail, the complex issues of the research process. Those reports intended for a more general readership should not be used as an opportunity to impress with an overt display of technical language/jargon and subject matter. Readers here are interested in the results, not in the way they were reached, though, of course, the appropriate amount of background to the project will need to be provided.

Conclusion

Marketing research should not be carried out merely for its own sake; it is a business technique to be used as a service, not as a means of providing employment for marketing researchers! But the process does need to be managed by senior management. It may be thought of as the equivalent of a taxi-cab service and its relationship with the passengers. The taxi-driver (marketing researcher) must be able to drive and know how to reach a certain

intended destination. The passenger (client) must know where they wish to go and have the ability to pay the fare. Close co-operation between the parties will result in a mutually beneficial contract; as Zaltman (1998) notes 'Researchers must engage managers and customers more actively in the research undertaking by enabling them to represent fully their thinking'.

References

Aaker, D. A. and Day, G. S. (1990) *Marketing Research*, John Wiley.

Ajzen, I. and Fishbein, M. (1977) Attitude-behaviour Relations: A Theoretical Analysis and Review of Empirical Research, *Psychological Bulletin*, **84**, 888–918.

Allport, G. W. (1935) Attitudes, in C. Murchison (ed.), *Handbook of Social Psychology*, Clary University Press, Worcester, Mass.

American Marketing Association (1988) in P. D. Bennet (ed.), *The Dictionary of Marketing Terms*, American Marketing Association, Chicago, IL.

Bagozzi, R. P. (1975) Marketing as Exchange, *Journal of Marketing*, **39**, 32–39.

Baker, M. J. (1991) *Research for Marketing*, Macmillan, London.

Bellenger, D., Bernhardt, K. L. and Goldstucker, J. L. (1976) *Qualitative Research in Marketing*, Monograph Series No. 3, American Marketing Association, Chicago.

Beveridge, W. I. B. (1957) *The Art of Scientific Investigation*, 3rd edn, William Heinemann, London, pp. 84–85.

Brown, S., Bell, J. and Carson, D. (1996) *Marketing Apocalypse*, Routledge, London.

Chase, D. A. (1973) *The Intensive Group Interviewing in Marketing*, MRA Viewpoints.

Cook, S. W. and Sellitz, C. (1964) A Multiple-indicator Approach to Attitude Measurement, *Psychological Bulletin*, **62**, 36–55.

Crouch, S. and Housden, M. (1996) *Marketing Research for Managers*, The Marketing Series, Butterworth-Heinemann, Oxford.

Dickson, J. and Albaum, G. (1977) A Method for Developing Tailormade Semantic Differentials for Specific Marketing Content Areas, *Journal of Marketing Research*, February, 87–91.

Fishbein, M. and Azjen, I. (1975) *Belief, Intention and Behaviour*, Addison-Wesley, Reading, MA.

Flick, U. (1998) *An Introduction to Qualitative Marketing Research*, Sage, London.

Gordon, W. and Langmaid, R. (1988) *Qualitative Marketing Research*, Gower, London.

Green, P. A., Tull, D. S. and Albaum, G. (1988) *Research for Marketing Decisions*, Prentice-Hall International, London.

Kahan, H. (1990) One to Ones Should Sparkle Like the Gems They Are, *Marketing News*, pp 8–9, September 3.

Kidder, L. H. (1981) *Sellitz, Wrightsman and Cook's Research Methods in Social Relations*, 4th edn, Holt, Rinehart and Winston.

Kinnear, T. C. and Taylor, J. R. (1996) *Marketing Research; An Applied Approach*, 5th edn, McGraw-Hill, International Edition, New York.

Luck, D. J. and Rubin, D. S. (1987) *Marketing Research*, 7th edn, Prentice-Hall International, London.

Malhotra, N. K. (1993) *Marketing Research: An Applied Orientation*, Prentice-Hall International, London.

Marketing Research Society (1979) Qualitative Research – a Summary of the Concepts Involved, Sub-committee of Qualitative Research.

Newsom-Smith, N. (1988) Desk Research, in R. Worcester and J. Downham (eds), *Consumer Market Research Handbook*, 3rd edn, McGraw-Hill, London, pp. 7–27.

Oppenheim, A. N. (1984) *Questionnaire Design and Attitude Measurement*, Heinemann, London.

Osgood, C. E., Suci, G. J. and Tannenbaum, P. H. (1957) *The Measurement of Marketing*, University of Illinois, Urbana.

Parasuraman, A. (1986) *Marketing Research*, Addison-Wesley, Reading, MA.

Proctor, T. (1997) *Essentials of Marketing Research*, Pitman Publishing, London.

Radas, S. and Shugan, S. M. (1998) Seasonal Marketing and Timing in New Product Introduction, *Journal of Marketing Research*, **35**, August, 296–315.

Rickards, T. (1974) *Problem Solving through Creative Analysis*, Gower, Aldershot.

Schlegelmilch, B. B. and Sinkovics, R. (1998) Viewpoint: Marketing in the Information Age – Can We Plan for the Unpredictable? *International Marketing Review*, **15**(2, 3), 162–171.

Sellitz, C., Jahoda, M., Deutsch, M. and Cook, S. W. (1959) *Research Methods in Social Relations*, Methuen, London.

Southern, J. (1988) *Marketing Research*, University of Strathclyde, Distance Learning Unit, M. Com.

Suchman, E. A. (1950) The Scalogram Board Technique, in S. A. Stouffer, L. Guttman, E. A. Suchman, P. F. Laarsfeld, S.A. Starr and J. A. Clausen (eds), *Measurement and Prediction*, Princeton University Press, Princeton, pp. 91–121.

Torgerson, W. S. (1958) *Theory and Methods of Scaling*, John Wiley and Sons, New York.

Tull, D. S. and Hawkins, D. I. (1993*) Marketing Research: Measurement and Method*, 6th edn, Macmillan.

Webb, J. R. (1992) *Understanding and Designing Marketing Research*, The Dryden Press, London.

Weiers, R. M. (1988) *Marketing Research*, 2nd edn, Prentice-Hall International, London.

Zaltman, G. (1998) Rethinking Marketing Research: Putting People Back In, *Journal of Marketing Research*, **34**, November, 424–437.

CHAPTER 8

Quantitative methods in marketing

ARTHUR MEIDAN and LUIZ MOUTINHO

Marketing was one of the last of the major functional areas of management activity to be entered by quantitative methods and techniques in a systematic way, and only in the last four decades or so was any significant progress achieved. This relative lag of quantitative methods progress in marketing was attributed to a number of factors:

1 *The complexity of marketing phenomena.* This is due to the fact that when stimuli are applied to the environment, the responses tend to be non-linear, to exhibit threshold effects (a minimum level of stimulus needs to be applied before response occurs), to have carry-over effects (for example, response to this period of advertising will occur in future) and to decay with time in the absence of further stimulations.

2 *Interaction effects of marketing variables.* This means that the impact of a single controllable marketing variable is difficult to determine due to interactions of the variable with the environment and also with other marketing variables. Indeed, most of the variables in marketing are interdependent and interrelated.

3 *Measurement problems in marketing.* It is often difficult to measure directly the response of consumers to certain stimuli and therefore indirect techniques are often used. An example is the use of recall measures to ascertain the effectiveness of advertisements.

4 *Instability of marketing relationships.* The relationship between marketing responses and marketing decision variables tends to be unstable due to changes in taste, attitude, expectations, and many others. These factors make continuous market measurements and revision of decisions crucial to marketing.

There are several ways in which quantitative methods can be used in marketing. One of these is through the classification of marketing into decision areas which confront the marketing manager and which include product development, pricing, physical distribution, salesforce, advertising and consumer behaviour. However, it is thought to be more appropriate first to classify the techniques which are used in marketing and to fit in the situations where these models are used most frequently. In this way, most of the models and techniques can be analysed. Their validity can be judged from their usage, how accurately they represent the problem environment, their predictive power and the consistency and realism of their assumptions.

In selecting an appropriate method of analysis two major factors should be taken into consideration: first, whether the variables analysed are dependent or interdependent, and second, whether the input data are of a metric or non-metric form. Metric data are measured by interval or ratio scales, while non-metric data are only ordinal scaled. The dependent variables are those which can be explained by other variables, while interdependent variables are those which cannot be explained solely by each other.

Marketing variables are usually interdependent. For example, a firm's objectives are usually interdependent with marketing-mix variables; profits usually depend on sales; market share depends on sales; firms' growth depends on profits and sales and vice versa, etc. Also firms' marketing mix variables such as price, promotion, distribution and product are interdependent

Since marketing research is very often a multivariate analysis involving either dependent or interdependent variables, the major groups of techniques that can be used are as shown in Figure 8.1.

1   *Multivariable methods.* So called because the various techniques attempt to investigate the relationships and patterns of marketing decisions that emerge as a result of the interaction and interdependence among main variables at the same time.

2   *Regression, correlation and forecasting techniques.* **Regression and correlations** are methods that can be employed in inferring the relationships among a set of variables in marketing. **Forecasting methods** are mainly applied in forecasting sales and market demand. Sales forecasting methods are a function of an aggregation of non-controllable environmental variables and marketing effort factors, which have to be taken into consideration.

3   *Simulation methods* are a group of techniques which are appropriate to use when the variables affecting the marketing situation (such

as competition) require complex modelling and are not amenable to analytical solutions. The importance of the simulation technique in marketing is that it offers a form of laboratory experimentation by permitting the researcher to change selected individual variables in turn and holding all the others constant.

4   *Fuzzy sets* could be used for modelling consumer behaviour, marketing planning, new product testing, etc., by determining the rank and size of the possible outcomes.

5   *Artificial intelligence (AI) techniques* are relatively very recent tools for simulating human logic. There are two main models in this set of techniques: expert system – requiring user intervention to accommodate changes within the model – and neural network – less 'rigid' than expert system, facilitating 'retraining' (mainly via addition of new input and output data).

6   *Statistical decision theory or stochastic methods* represent stochastic or random responses of consumers, which allow a multitude of factors that might affect consumer behaviour to be included in the analysis. This means that market responses can be regarded as outcomes of some probabilistic process. Essentially, there are two main uses of these methods: to test structural hypotheses and to make conditional predictions.

7   *Deterministic operational research methods* are OR techniques looking for solutions in cases where there are many interdependent variables and the research is trying to optimize the situation. A classical example of such a situation in marketing is when a company producing various products (or parts) is selling them through two different channels which vary with respect to selling costs, typical order sizes, credit policies, profit margins, etc. Usually in such cases the company's major objective is to maximize total profits by establishing optimal sales target volumes and marketing mixes for the two channels (or customer segments) subject to the existing limiting constraints.

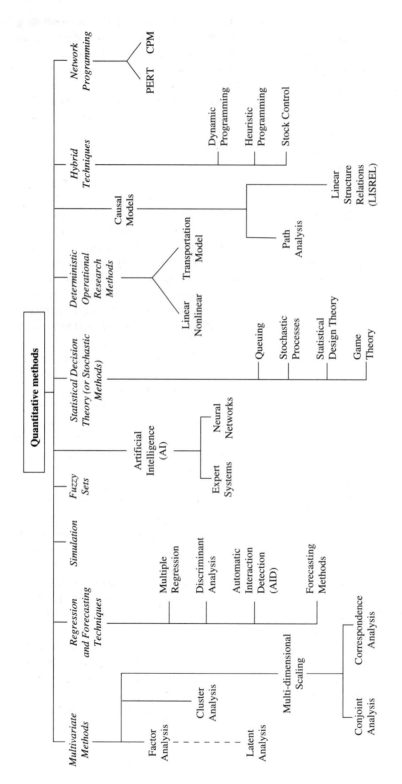

Figure 8.1 The main quantitative methods in marketing – a taxonomy

8 *Causal model* consists of two main analytical models for *testing* causal hypotheses (path analysis and LISREL). **Path analysis** is used on those occasions when some of the variables are unobservable or have modest reliabilities. (This tool should not be confused with the critical path method (CPM) which is one of the networking programming models discussed below.) LISREL is of paramount importance in marketing situations, when we want to investigate both measurement and cause, i.e. structural components, of a system (e.g. in a consumer behaviour study).

9 *Hybrid models* are methods that combine deterministic and probabilistic (stochastic) properties (e.g. dynamic programming, heuristic programming and stock control). These models are particularly useful in handling distribution problems, as explained below.

10 *Networking programming models* are generally used for planning, scheduling and controlling complex projects. There are two fundamental analytical techniques: the critical path method (CPM) and the performance evaluation and review technique (PERT). The differences between the two are first, PERT acknowledges uncertainty in the times to complete the activities while CPM does not. Second, PERT restricts its attention to the time variable while CPM includes time–cost trade-offs. These two together are also called critical path analysis (CPA) techniques.

The ten sets of methods above in no way exhaust the quantitative methods in marketing. The selection of techniques presented in this chapter is based either on their particular current relevance of handling many marketing problems or/and because of their potential in marketing research and analysis.

Multivariate methods

The multivariate methods in marketing are probably the predominant techniques of the last two decades, not only because of the wide variety of flexible techniques available in this category but mainly because they answer the most pressing need of marketing research, which is to obtain the ability to analyse complex, often interrelated and interdependent data. There are six main multivariate sets of methods: factor analysis; latent analysis; cluster analysis; multi-dimensional scaling; conjoint analysis; and correspondence analysis.

Factor analysis

Factor analysis (FA) is primarily a tool to reduce a large number of variables to a few interpretable constructs. The method is used for exploration and detection of patterns in the data with the view to obtaining data reduction, or summarization, which could be more amenable for reaching decisions and taking marketing management actions. The software for FA is readily available and is standard in any SPSS (Statistical Package for Social Science) package. The input data are collected from respondents and the main limitations are how many factors to extract and the labelling of the emerging factors. Factor analysis could be used for analysing consumer behaviour, market segmentation, product/service attributes, company images, etc.

Latent analysis

Latent structure analysis (LA) is a statistical technique somewhat related to factor analysis, which can be used as a framework for investigating causal systems involving both manifest variables and latent factors having discrete components. Latent structure analysis shares the objective of factor analysis, i.e. first, to extract important factors and express relationships of variables with these factors, and second, to classify respondents into typologies.

The latent class model treats the manifest categorical variables as imperfect indicators of underlying traits, which are themselves inherently unobservable. The latent class model treats the observable (manifest) categorical variables as imperfect indicators of underlying traits, which are themselves inherently unobservable (latent). This technique is appropriate for the analysis of data with discrete components.

Essentially, LA attempts to 'explain' the observed association between the manifest variables by introducing one (or more) other variables. Thus, the basic motivation behind latent analysis is the belief that the observed association between two or more manifest categorical variables is due to the mixing of heterogeneous groups. In this sense, latent analysis can be viewed as a data-unmixing procedure. This assumption of conditional independence is directly analogous to the assumption in the factor-analytic model.

The main advantage of latent analysis is that it could be used for investigating causal systems involving latent variables. A very flexible computer program for maximum likelihood latent structure analysis, called MLLSA, is available to marketing researchers. Latent class models have great potential and no doubt will be used more frequently in marketing investigations in the future.

One of the major limitations related to LA concerns the estimation problem, which previously made this class of models largely inaccessible to most marketing researchers. This problem was later solved by formulating latent class models in the same way as in the general framework of log-linear models. Latent structure analysis models have been used in segmentation research, consumer behaviour analysis, advertising research and market structure analysis.

One of the best papers in this field is by Dillon and Mulani (1989). A number of latent structure models have been developed (DeSarbo, 1993) for problems associated with traditional customer response modelling (for example, for more regression, conjoint analysis, structural equation models, multi-dimensional scaling, limited dependent variables, etc.). Such latent structure models simultaneously estimate market segment membership and respective model coefficients by market segment, to optimize a common objective function.

Cluster analysis

Cluster analysis is a generic label applied to a set of techniques in order to identify 'similar' entities from the characteristics possessed by these entities. The clusters should have high homogeneity within clusters and high heterogeneity between clusters, and geometrically the points within a cluster should be close together while different clusters should be far apart.

Cluster analysis is, in a sense, similar to factor analysis and to multi-dimensional scaling in that all three are used for reduced-space analysis. That is, all three methods could facilitate the presentation of the output data in a graphical two-dimensional format that is easier to comprehend and analyse. Cluster analysis is primarily used for segmentation and for decisions on marketing strategies towards different segments and markets (Saunders, 1994) or in situations which involve grouping products, brands, consumers, cities, distributors, etc. The main limitations of this technique are that there are no defensible procedures for testing the statistical significance of the emerging clusters and often various clustering methods yield differing results. There are several types of clustering procedures. In Figure 8.2 a hierarchical clustering of variables associated with a marketing strategy for hotels is presented (Meidan, 1983). The diagram presents the (level of) aggregation (or clusters) or variables that are product (i.e. hotels) characteristics of a strategy, as defined by the suppliers (i.e. hotel managers). Cluster 2 strategy includes variables that indicate that hotels adopting this strategy are more 'aggressive' using, to a larger extent, marketing tools and techniques, while cluster 1 strategy is more 'passive'. Low coefficients of hierarchy (or low dissimilarity) indicate high relationships or high similarity. For example, variables 1 and 2 are highly correlated, that is, they aggregate early, at a coefficient of 0.27. In contrast, variable 12 (use of advertising) is highly dissimilar to

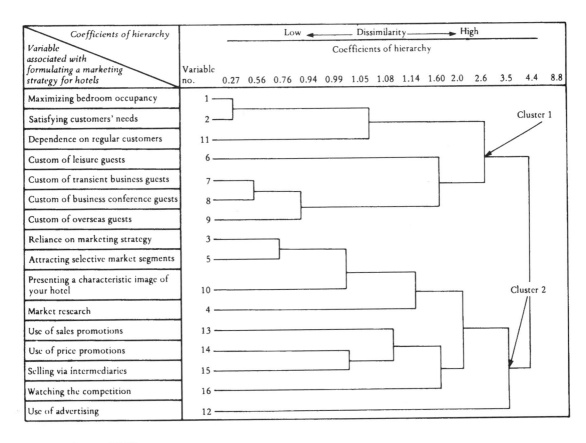

Coefficients of hierarchy Variable associated with formulating a marketing strategy for hotels	Variable no.	0.27	0.56	0.76	0.94	0.99	1.05	1.08	1.14	1.60	2.0	2.6	3.5	4.4	8.8

Low ← Dissimilarity → High
Coefficients of hierarchy

Cluster 1
Cluster 2

Source: Meidan (1983)

Figure 8.2   Hierarchical clustering of variables associated with a marketing strategy for hotels

other variables and associates with the remaining coefficients in cluster 2 only at the 3.5 level. A possible explanation of this could be that hotels adopting the marketing strategy indicated by cluster 2 use an alternative communication mix and/or other marketing tools (e.g. variables 13, 14, 15, 4, 5, 10, etc.).

Multidimensional scaling

Multidimensional scaling (MS) is a measurement technique concerned mainly with the representation of relationship, differences, dissimilarities (or similarities), substitutability, interaction, etc. among behavioural data such as perceptions, preferences and attitudes. The input data on various objects (variables) which are to be analysed are collected from the subjects (respondents) by a number of direct or indirect questions. The questions can be either of Likert type (i.e. a five-point scale questionnaire indicating the level of agreement or disagreement to statements) or, alternatively, asking each of the respondents to rank the variables to be investigated (for example, products, brands, characteristics, etc.). When the number of variables investigated are n, the number of all possible relationships among these variables (along k dimensions) are $n(n-1)/2$. In order to visualize and quantify the overall attitudinal data of these respondents with regard to the n variables investigated along (k) dimensions, the data should be input onto one of the available software packages.

The solution (output) of the MS computer program is of a metric nature, consisting of a geometric configuration, usually in two or three dimensions. The distances between the variables (objects) and/or respondents (subjects) investigated, which are presented as points in the configuration, represent the (dis)similarity, substitutability, relationship, etc. Multi-dimensional scaling is used particularly in its non-metric version, the non-metric multi-dimensional scaling (NMS). The advantage of NMS in relation to, say, factor or cluster analyses is the ability to see the entire structure of variables together and to obtain metric output, from attitudinal (non-metric) input data. In addition, NMS enables easy comprehension of the results since the decision maker can visualize and assess the relationships among the variables.

Multi-dimensional scaling and non-metric multi-dimensional scaling in particular have been successfully applied in investigating various marketing problems (for example, market research, sales and market share, market segmentation, determination of marketing mix, consumer buyer behaviour, brand positioning, branch preference, export marketing, etc.). An introduction to multi-dimensional scaling is presented by Diamantopoulos and Schlegelmilch (1997). Discussion on when to use NMS techniques in marketing research is offered by Coates *et al.* (1994).

Conjoint analysis

This technique is concerned with the joint effects of two or more independent variables on the ordering of a dependent variable. Conjoint analysis, like multi-dimensional scaling, is concerned with the measurement of psychological judgements, such as consumer preferences. Products are essentially bundles of attributes, such as price and colour. For example, conjoint analysis software generates a deck of cards, each of which combines levels of these product attributes. Respondents are asked to sort the cards

generated into an order of preference. Conjoint analysis then assigns a value to each level and produces a 'ready-reckoner' to calculate the preference for each chosen combination. The preference logic of conjoint analysis is as follows. The respondent had to base his or her overall ranking of the versions on an evaluation of the attributes presented. The values that the individual implicitly assigns each attribute associated with the most preferred brand must, in total, sum to a greater value than those associated with the second most-preferred brand. The same relationship must hold for the second and third most-preferred brands, the third and fourth most-preferred brands and so forth. The computation task then is to find a set of values that will meet these requirements.

Potential areas of application for conjoint analysis include product design, new product concept descriptions and testing, price–value relationships, attitude measurement, promotional congruence testing, the study of functional versus symbolic product characteristic, and to rank a hypothetical product against existing competitors already in the market and suggest modifications to existing products which would help to strengthen a product's performance.

The limitations of conjoint analysis are quite clear when, for example, we are using this technique to predict trial rate. These include:

1   Utility measurement rather than actual purchase behaviour is used as the predictor.

2   The configuration of elements used in the concepts may not be complete.

3   In the case of a new product that differs substantially from its principal competitors, the same elements cannot be used for aggregating utilities.

4   The effects of promotion and distribution effort on competitive reaction are not considered.

5   Perceptions from a concept statement and those from the actual product may differ.

6   New products may take several years to reach the market, during which time customer preferences and competitive products may

have undergone substantial changes. Conjoint analysis has been applied widely on consumer research (Vriens, 1994), in advertising evaluation (Stanton and Reese, 1983) and other commercial uses (Cattin and Wittink, 1982).

Correspondence analysis

Correspondence analysis is a visual or graphical technique for representing multi-dimensional tables. It can often be impossible to identify any relationships in a table and very difficult to account for what is happening. Correspondence analysis unravels the table and presents data in an easy-to-understand chart. One approach for generating maps uses cross-classification data (e.g. brands rated as having or not having a set of attributes) as a basis (Hoffman and Franke, 1986). In this approach both brands and attributes are simultaneously portrayed in a single space. This technique is particularly useful to identify market segments, track brand image,

position a product against its competition and determine who non-respondents in a survey most closely resemble. Correspondence analysis shows the relationships between rows and columns of a correspondence or a cross-tabulation table. This method can be used for analysing binary, discrete or/and continuous data. CA belongs to the family of multi-dimensional scaling techniques and could be employed to scale a matrix of non-negative data to represent points (described by rows or columns) in a lower dimensional space. It facilitates both within- and between-set squared distance comparisons (Carroll *et al.*, 1986) and the results could be represented graphically and used as such in marketing investigations.

Figure 8.3 shows the different stages of correspondence analysis. The results of a cross-tabulation is used as raw data in a correspondence analysis. The specific mathematics involved in correspondence analysis can be found in Greenacre (1984).

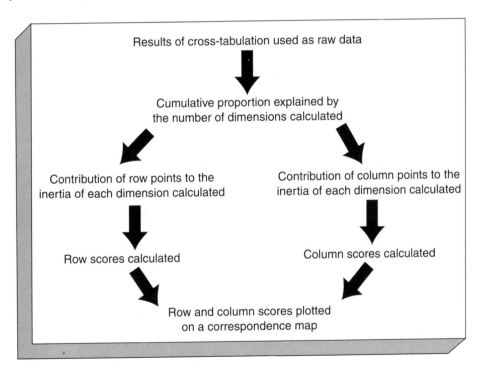

Figure 8.3   Procedural steps for correspondence analysis

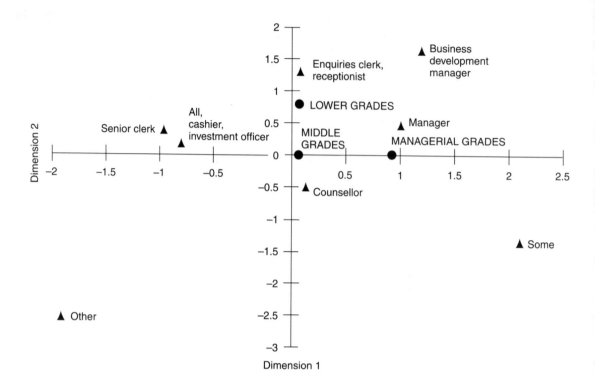

Source: Meidan and Lim (1993)

Figure 8.4   External perceptions of the different grade levels on the issue of identifying customer needs

Figure 8.4 presents the output of a study that maps out how bank branch personnel in various roles see themselves (internal perceptions) and what are their colleagues' (external) perceptions with regard to the 27 selling bank branch functions identified (Meidan and Lim, 1993). The figure represents the output of a study where respondents were asked who they felt were mainly responsible for the selling function of 'Identifying customers' needs' in a bank. The responses of various function holders are indicated by the triangle signs on the map (e.g. counsellor, manager, business development officer, etc.). The respondents themselves were grouped into three categories indicated by the circles (e.g. lower grades (cashier, statements clerk), middle grades (counsellors, officers), managerial grades (branch managers, etc.)).

The interpretation of data output is fairly straightforward although not all dimensions could be labelled. The closer two points are on the map, the closer the relationship. For example:

1   Lower grades tend to believe that the enquiries clerk and receptionist are mainly responsible for identifying customer needs.
2   Middle grades, however, are more inclined to see this as mainly the counsellor's responsibility. Some middle grades also tend to consider it the responsibility of cashiers, investment officers or everyone (all).
3   Managerial grades believe that this function is mainly their own responsibility. These beliefs of various role players within the branch are, of course, of paramount importance as it might lead to under-training for certain function(s) at grade levels where customer contact is higher. Therefore, this kind of

Table 8.1 Main multivariate methods and their marketing applications

Method	Based on	Marketing applications	Main advantages	Main limitations
Factor analysis	Identification of relationships among variables and establishing the 'weight' (factor loadings) for these variables	Determine corporate marketing images, consumer behaviour and attitudes	Data reduction, identification of the main constructs (factors that underlie the data characteristics)	Applicable only to interval-scaled data
Latent analysis	Investigation of both manifest and latent factors by estimating these latent parameters	Segmentation research, market structure analysis (Dillon and Mulani, 1989)	Could be used for investigating causal systems involving latent variables	Difficulties in estimating the latent variables
Cluster analysis	Developing similarity or dissimilarity measures (coefficients), or distance measures, to establish clusters association	Primarily for segmentation studies and strategy (Saunders, 1994)	Enables classification of brands, products, customers distributors, etc.	Different clustering methods could generate different clusters
Multi-dimensional scaling	Calculating the proximity (or alternatively, of dominance) among attributes/ variables and respondents	Market research, market share analysis (Coates et al., 1994), market segmentation, brand positioning, etc.	Presents the entire structure of variables, making it easier to visualize and interpret relationship/similarities among data	Different software packages required for different types of data input
Conjoint analysis	Measurement of psychological judgements by measuring the joint effect of two or more independent variables on the ordering of a dependent variable	Consumer research (Vriens, 1994), advertising evaluations (Stanton and Reese, 1983)	Enables calculation of preferences. Suitable for product design and attitude measurement	Measures first utility rather than behaviour
Correspondence analysis	Graphical technique for representing multi-dimensional tables. For procedure, see Figure 8.3	Selling functions in bank branches (Meidan and Lim, 1993), market segments, track brand images	Can be used for analysing binary, discrete and/or continuous data. Facilitates both within- and between-set squared distance comparison. Fast, easy to interpret	Limited applications in marketing because of lack of suitable software

study could focus the training efforts and needs for specific selling functions and certain grade levels/roles.

The six multivariate methods described above are summarized in Table 8.1

Regression and forecasting techniques

Multiple regression

Regression analysis attempts to investigate the nature (and strength) of relationships, if any, between two or more variables in marketing phenomena. It could be used, for example, to establish the nature and form of association between sales and, say, the number of customers, the nature of competitive activity, the amount of resources spent on advertising, etc. The association between Y (sales) – which is the dependent variable – and the independent variables affecting sales are usually expressed in a mathematical function of the type:

$$Y = f(\chi_1, \chi_2, \chi_3, \cdots \chi_n)$$

The purpose of regression is to make predictions about scores on the dependent variable based upon knowledge of independent variable scores (Speed, 1994).

Regression provides measures of association, not causation; yet regression (and correlation analysis) could assist marketing managers in better understanding the implicit relationships among various independent and dependent variables (for example, age, income, education and amount of credit card usage, or various forms of sales people's incentives and their sales calls/or the number of new orders obtained, etc.).

Discriminant analysis

Like regression analysis, discriminant analysis (DA) uses a linear equation to predict the dependent variable (say, sales). However, while in regression analysis the parameters (coefficients) are used to minimize the sum of squares, in discriminant analysis the parameters are selected in such a way as to maximize the ratio:

$$\frac{\text{Variance between group means}}{\text{Variance within groups}}$$

Discriminant analysis is used in marketing for predicting brand loyalty and buying or attempting to predict consumer behaviour in general; this classification method could be used when the data (the independent variables) are interval scales.

Automatic interaction detection (AID)

The regression analysis mentioned above attempts to identify association between the dependent and the independent variables, one at a time. In addition, the assumption is that the data are measured on interval scales. In many other marketing research situations we need a method able to handle nominal *or* ordinal data and to identify *all* the significant relationships between the dependent and the independent variables. Automatic interaction detection (AID) is a computer-based method for interactively selecting the independent variables in order to be able to predict the dependent variables. It splits the sample of observations into two groups on a sequential routine, trying to keep the sub-groups that emerge as homogenic as possible, relative to the dependent variable. The homogeneity is measured by minimizing the sum-of-square deviations of each subgroup member from its subgroup mean. AID is used in marketing for market segments analysis, analysing the effect of advertising levels on retail sales, predicting consumption/sales and brand loyalty.

The method is not as powerful as regression analysis and since the minimum subgroup size should be no less than 30, the original sample of objects required must be fairly large (1000 or more).

The three regression and forecasting techniques described above are summarized in Table 8.2.

Table 8.2	Regression, automatic interaction detection and discriminant analysis – a comparison			
Method	*Based on*	*Marketing applications*	*Main advantages*	*Main limitations*
Regression analysis	Developing a function expressing the association (or relationship) between dependent and independent variables	For segmentation, consumer behaviour analysis, sales forecasting (Speed, 1994)	Enables predictions about a dependent variable (say, sales figures). Provides measures of association between independent variables and certain important marketing dependent variables	Requires fitting a regression line and determining the parameters. This could be quite complex and lead to certain errors
Automatic interaction detection	A computer-based sequential routine attempting to classify objects into groups as possible, by minimizing the within-group sum of squares	For market segments analysis, assess the effects of advertising on retail sales, predict brand loyalty sales prediction, etc	Suitable for identifying the different variables affecting market segments; determining the importance of each independent variable and the form in which it affects dependent variable	Less powerful than regression. Minimum group size should be no less than 30, and the original sample size should be quite large
Discriminant analysis	Maximize the ratio of variance between group means, not within-group variance	Predicting brand loyalty, consumer innovators, like/dislike of a service (or product), etc	Enables predictions of dependent variables	Identifying the statistical significance of the discriminant function; multiple discriminant analysis requires a computer program.

Forecasting methods

Forecasting methods are mainly applied in forecasting sales and market demand. Chambers *et al.* (1979) classify them into three categories: qualitative techniques, time-series analysis, and causal models. In each category there is a series of models; some are suitable for forecasting initial sales and others for forecasting repeat purchases. Consequently one should make clear the differentiation between diffusion and adoption models, although, unfortunately, the space available here is too short for a detailed presentation.

Probably the most well-known forecasting techniques are the time-series methods. These rely on historical data and, by definition, are of limited application to the forecasting of new product sales.

In order to select a forecasting technique for new products the first principle is to match the methodology with the situation. The degree of newness of the product, for example, is crucial, as are product and market characteristics, the forecaster's ability, the cost, the urgency and the purpose for which the forecast is needed.

The second principle is that at least two methods should be used and one of these should always be the subjective judgement of the forecaster, who must override the formal technique decision when information coming from outside the model clearly shows that the technique's forecast may be at fault. There are powerful arguments for combining forecasts by different techniques. Methods are selective in the information they use so that a combination of methods would incorporate more information and improve accuracy. Doyle and Fenwick (1976) advocate this and produce evidence of improved accuracy.

Simulation methods

The cost, the time involved and other problems associated with field experimentation often preclude a method as a source of information for particular situations. In such instances it is often desirable to construct a model of an operational situation and obtain relevant information through the manipulation of this model. This manipulation, called simulation, describes the act of creating a complex model to resemble a real process or system and experimenting with this model in the hope of learning something about the real system.

Simulations represent a general technique which is useful for studying marketing systems and is one of the most flexible methods in terms of application. Simulation models have been formulated to serve two management functions:

1   Planning
2   Monitoring and controlling operations

Marketing simulations can be conveniently divided into three classes (Doyle and Fenwick, 1976). The first deals with computer models of the behaviour of marketing system components, the second with computer models on the effect of different marketing instruments on demand, and the third with marketing games.

A firm wanting to adopt a simulation model would have to take into account the market characteristics of the environment it operates in and model on this basis.

Fuzzy sets

The fuzzy set theory is a relatively new approach that has been growing steadily since its inception in the mid-1960s. In the fuzzy set theory, an abstract concept such as a sunny day can be considered as a fuzzy set and defined mathematically by assigning to each individual in the universe of discourse, a value representing its grade of membership in the fuzzy set. This grade corresponds to the degree to which that individual is similar or compatible with the concept represented by the fuzzy set. Thus, individuals may belong in the fuzzy set to a greater or lesser degree as indicated by a larger or smaller membership grade. These membership grades are very often represented by real member values ranging in the closed interval between 0 and 1. Thus, a fuzzy set representing our concept of sunniness might assign a degree of membership 1 to a cloud cover of 0 per cent, 0.8 to a cloud cover of 20 per cent, 0.4 to a cloud cover of 30 per cent and 0 to a cloud cover of 75 per cent. These grades signify the degree to which each percentage of cloud cover approximates our subjective concept of sunniness, and the set itself models the semantic flexibility inherent in such a common linguistic term.

Vagueness in describing many consumer behaviour constructs is intrinsic, not the result of a lack of knowledge about the available rating. That is why a great variety of definitions in marketing exist and most of them cannot describe the fuzzy concepts completely. So long as the semantic assessment facets in the construct can be quantified and explicitly defined by corresponding membership functions, the initial steps of the mathematical definition of marketing constructs are achieved.

Recognizing the difficulty of accurate quantification of the semantic assessment facets like product interest, hedonic value and others, some researchers utilize the fuzzy mathematical method (Klir and Yuan, 1995; Zimmerman, 1991) to quantify the assessment facets by membership functions so that the results obtained are more accurate than the traditional statistical methods and more suitable for the semantically modified assessment facets.

The benefits of using fuzzy sets are:

1   The membership function is deliberately designed in fuzzy set theory to treat the vagueness caused by natural language. Therefore, using membership functions to assess the semantically defined measuring facets is more reliable and accurate than using the traditional statistical methods – score points or scatter plot.

2   The membership function standardizes the semantic meaning of assessment facets so that we can compare the degree of the definition of marketing constructs regardless of the differences of timing, situation, consumer and so on.

3   The membership functions are continuous functions which are more accurate in measuring the assessment facets than the traditional discrete methods.

4   The fuzzy mathematical method is easier to perform than the traditional method, once the membership of assessment facets are defined.

Some of the main characteristics, advantages, limitations and applications of simulation and fuzzy sets in marketing are presented in Table 8.3.

Artificial intelligence

Artificial intelligence (AI) models have emerged in the last few years as a follow-up to simulation, attempting to portray, comprehend and analyse the reasoning in a range of situations. Although the two methods of artificial intelligence (expert systems and neural networks) are, in a certain sense, 'simulations', because of the importance and the potential of these methods, we have introduced them under a separate stand-alone heading.

Expert systems

Simply defined, an expert system is a computer program which contains human knowledge or expertise which it can use to generate reasoned

---

Example: Definition – 'consumer involvement'

Consumer involvement can be construed as a fuzzy set. It is a family of pairs $(A_i, \mu_{Ai}(y))$, where for each i in the index set is a fuzzy set ϑ, A_i is a fuzzy set of assessment facet and μ_{Ai} is a membership function from A_i to the unit interval $[0,1]$ which describes the behaviour of the fuzzy set A_i, $\mu_{Ai}(y)$ is the membership function of the assessment facet that takes value on $[0,1]$ for all y in A_i, i.e.

Consumer involvement = $\{(A_i \mu_{Ai}(Y))|\mu A_i;$
$A_i \rightarrow [0,1]_3 \mu_{Ai}(Y)[0,1]yAi\}$

and i, ϑ, A_i is a fuzzy set of assessment facet.

Table 8.3	Simulation and fuzzy sets uses in marketing (the method, advantages, limitations and when recommended to use)			
Method	*Based on*	*Marketing applications*	*Main advantages*	*Main limitations*
Simulation	Conducting experiments using a model to simulate working conditions of the real system	(a) Marketing planning (b) Monitoring and controlling (Kotler and Schultz, 1970), marketing operations (c) Distribution, consumer behaviour, retailing, staffing, advertising (d) Marketing training (Kotler and Schultz, 1970)	(a) A very flexible and simple method easily understood by managers (b) Saves time and resources (c) Simulation has found wide applications in the field of marketing	(a) Tedious arithmetical calculations (b) Rather costly in computer time
Fuzzy sets	The technique is essentially a factual modelling process that attempts to fine tune the expression of knowledge. It does this by using a linguistic scale describing the characteristics under each of the main dimensions of the model to form fuzzy sets; a hierarchical aggregation of information based on fuzzy aggregation operators; and a conceptual hypercube to determine the rank and ranking size of the outcomes. Includes the concept of membership function (between 0 and 1)	Modelling consumer behaviour, marketing planning, new product testing, perceived price testing, marketing communication effects research (Zimmerman, 1991)	Flexibility which accommodates a degree of uncertainty or fuzziness, in diagnosis. This fuzziness is indeed lauded as realistic in expressing human judgement	Difficult measurement scaling and estimation of the bipolar descriptors. Linguistic scale for characteristics description. Description of the values for the parameters of the model

advice or instructions. The knowledge base is usually represented internally in the machine as a set of IF . . . THEN rules and the 'inference engine' of the expert system matches together appropriate combinations of rules in order to generate conclusions.

In determining whether a particular marketing domain is suited for this methodology the following checklist is useful:

- Are the key relationships in the domain logical rather than computational? In practical terms, the answer requires an assessment of whether the decision area is knowledge-intensive (e.g. generating new product areas) or data-intensive (e.g. allocating an advertising budget across media).
- Is the problem domain semi-structured rather than structured or unstructured? If the problem is well structured, a traditional approach using sequential procedures will be more efficient than an expert system approach. This would be true, for example, when the entire problem-solving sequence can be enumerated in advance.
- Is knowledge in the domain incomplete? If the problem is well structured, a traditional approach using sequential procedures will be more efficient than an expert system approach. This would be true, for example, when the entire problem-solving sequence can be enumerated in advance. Moreover, for highly unstructured domains, expert system performance may be disappointing because the available problem-solving strategies may be inadequate.
- Is knowledge in the domain incomplete? In other words, is it difficult to identify all the important variables or to specify fully their interrelationships? Expert systems are particularly applicable in domains with incomplete knowledge.
- Will problem solving in the domain require a direct interface between the manager and the computer system? A direct interface may be necessary in situations calling for on-line decision support. Such situations generally are

characterized by a high level of decision urgency (e.g. buying and selling stocks) or complexity (e.g. retail site selection). Expert systems are particularly useful in these contexts because of their flexible and 'friendly' user-interaction facilities coupled with their ability to explain their reasoning (Rangaswamy *et al.*, 1989). A number of expert systems in marketing have been developed over the years, in particular focusing on the following domains: marketing research, test marketing, pricing, generation of advertising appeals, choice of promotional technique, selection of effective sales techniques, negotiation strategies, site selection, allocation of marketing budget, promotion evaluation, strategic positioning, strategic marketing, assessment of sales territories, brand management, marketing planning, international marketing, bank marketing, tourism marketing and industrial marketing (see Curry and Moutinho, 1991).

The greatest single problem with regard to the effectiveness and applicability of expert system models in the marketing context concerns the construction and validation of the knowledge base.

Neural networks

Neural networks are designed to offer the end-user the capability to bypass the rigidity of expert systems and to develop 'fuzzy logic' decision-making tools. Several authors claim the neural networks provide the user with the ability to design a decision-support tool in less time and with less effort than can be accomplished with other decision-support system tools. Neural networks have been successfully applied in the following marketing areas: consumer behaviour analysis (Curry and Moutinho, 1993), market segmentation, pricing modelling (Ellis *et al.*, 1991), copy strategy and media planning (Kennedy, 1991).

Neural networks use structured input and output data to develop patterns that mimic human decision making. Input data are compared to relative output data for many data points. The relationships between the input data and output data are used to develop a pattern that represents the decision-making style of the user. The development of patterns from data points eliminates the need to build rules that support decision making. Unlike expert systems, which require user intervention to accommodate variable changes within the model, the neural network is capable of retraining, which is accomplished through the addition of new input and output data.

An important strength of this method is its ability to bring together psychometric and econometric analyses so that the best features of both can be exploited. Whereas expert systems are good at organizing masses of information, neural networks may prove capable of duplicating the kind of intuitive, trial-and-error thinking marketing managers typically require. The accuracy of the neural network is not as high as of other methods, yet it has the ability to learn from increased input/output facts and the ability to address data that other decision support systems cannot handle logically.

Table 8.4 presents the main applications, advantages and limitations of expert systems and neural networks.

Table 8.4   Artificial intelligence methods applications in marketing (basic content, advantages, limitations and when recommended to use)

Method	Content	Marketing applications	Advantages	Limitations
Artificial intelligence	A computer program to express the reasoning process by modelling relationships among various variables (see checklist in text)	Marketing research, test marketing, pricing, site selection, tourism marketing and international marketing (Curry and Moutinho, 1991)	Flexible, able to explain reasoning of interactions	Difficulties in construction of the expert system model
Neural networks	Use of structured input and output data to develop patterns that mimic human decision making. Employs a statistically based procedure of iteratively adjusting the weights	Consumer behaviour (Curry and Moutinho, 1993), price modelling (Ellis et al., 1991), media planning (Kennedy, 1991) and market segmentation	Capable of retraining. Able to bring together psychometric and econometric analyses	Low accuracy. More difficult to interpret than the expert systems above

Statistical decision theory or stochastic methods

In this category there are four methods, all of which are useful in solving marketing problems.

Queuing

This method is of importance to large retailing institutions such as supermarkets, petrol stations, airline ticket offices, seaports, airports and other areas where services are available through queuing. A notable problem in retailing institutions is that of making salesforce decisions, the reason being the high cost incurred in hiring sales clerks whose services are almost irreplaceable. Since these sales clerks work in situations which can be systematically regulated and accurately observed, techniques can be used to provide management with information so that the optimal size of the salesforce can be ascertained. A queuing model to determine the optimum number of sales clerks to be assigned to a floor in a department store so as to maximize profitability could be determined. Attention should be focused on five main variables:

1   The number of potential customers arriving and requesting service per unit time.
2   The amount of time required by a sales clerk to wait on a customer.
3   The number of items purchased per customer per transaction.
4   The incremental value to the retail establishment of each item sold (i.e. profits).
5   The amount of time the customer is willing to wait for service.

Most research articles state that the use of queuing theory is mainly concentrated on solving problems in retailing institutions where the model helped management to decide on the size of their salesforce. Perhaps it was the successful application of this technique in this area of marketing that has contributed to its vast improvements and wide applications. There are, however, limitations to this technique, one of which is that queuing systems must be operated over a sufficiently long period to achieve a steady-state solution and it is often difficult to predict the length of time required to achieve this.

Stochastic processes

A stochastic process is a random experiment which occurs over time, the outcome of which is determined by chance. From these random experiments some attributes of interest are observed and numerical values can be given to these attributes according to the probability law. The stochastic process method is commonly used in building brand-choice models of consumers. In all, there are three basic types of stochastic process methods; they are the zero-order, Markovian and learning models, and each has its own set of assumptions.

The zero-order model assumes that past brand choice has no effect on future brand choice. There are studies on the existence of brand or store loyalties using the zero-order model approach which have defined brand loyalty as a proportion of total purchases within a product class that a household devotes to its favourite or most frequently purchased brand.

The Markov model assumes that only the most recent purchases affect the brand-choice decisions. Using the Markovian model, one can measure the expected number of periods before an individual would try a particular brand. Markov models should be used for dynamic market predictions such as equilibrium market shares, average time to trial, which is a measure of the attractive power of the brand, and for evaluating the success of new product introduction. One other area where Markovian analysis has been employed in marketing is in making personal selling decisions were it is used in the modelling of sales-effort allocation to customers.

The third of the stochastic process methods is the learning model, which postulates that brand choice is dependent upon a complete history of past brand purchases as the effect of purchasing a brand is cumulative. Therefore, when applied in the brand-switching complex, this will mean that purchase of a brand will ultimately increase the probability of purchasing the same brand again. This model may be used in monitoring consumer behaviour.

Statistical decision theory

Decision theory is often used to evaluate the alternative outcomes of different decisions and to find the best possible decision. Associated with the statistical decision theory is the decision tree diagram which portrays the various alternative decisions and their consequences. Game theory, discussed below, is commonly regarded as an analytical approach to decision making involving two or more conflicting individuals, each trying to minimize the maximum loss (minimax criterion).

One other application of game theory is for formulating advertising budget decisions. In statistical decision theory, probabilities of each outcome are based upon either past data or subjective estimates. Pricing decisions in advertising is another area where decision theory can be applied. The main disadvantage of this method is the subjective estimation of the probability for each decision.

Decision trees can also be used to decide whether or not to test-market a new product before launching it. Cadbury-Schweppes Ltd used this technique to help in deciding the feasibility of test-marketing a new chocolate product. By carrying out a test-market programme of the new chocolate, the earnings obtained exceeded those of embarking on a national launch without prior test-marketing. This method has been used for making merchandising decisions, such as finding the optimum mix of sizes and widths of fashion shoes to be ordered, especially when the possible alternative choices were numerous and carried high costs.

Game theory

Game theory, when compared with decision theory, has found limited applications in marketing. Nevertheless, it has been applied to retailing institutions in making product decisions. Game theory helps management to decide on its advertising budgets without any prior knowledge of competitors' budgeting decisions.

In pricing advertisements, Higgins (1973) used game theory to provide solutions. The total reward for all the firms included in the pricing decision study was considered fixed, the decision resting on which product price to lower to generate more sales so as to minimize the maximum loss.

A summary of the four major stochastic methods, their possible applications in marketing (with some references), advantages and limitations is presented in Table 8.5.

Deterministic operational research methods

Deterministic techniques are those in which chance plays no part and solutions are determined by sets of exact relationships. Under this heading there are both the linear and non-linear optimization models.

Linear programming

Linear programming (LP) is a mathematical technique for solving specific problems in which an objective function must be maximized or minimized, considering a set of definite restrictions and limited resources. The word 'programming' stands for computing or calculating some unknowns of a set of equations and/or inequalities, under specific conditions, mathematically expressed.

Before the LP technique can be employed in the solution of a marketing problem, five basic requirements must be considered (Meidan, 1981b).

Table 8.5 Statistical decision theory or stochastic methods of applications in marketing (approaches, advantages, limitations and when recommended to use)

Method	Based on	Marketing applications	Advantages	Limitations
Queuing	Probability distribution analysis of data (empirically gathered on how the major factors/ variables will affect the situation-problem under analysis). It is an analysis of queuing systems attempting to determine service levels/ performance	(a) Optimize: sales-force (Paul, 1972), number of checkouts, number of attendants, etc (b) Minimize inventory-carrying costs; suitable and widely used by chain stores, supermarkets, department stores, petrol stations, airline ticket offices, ports, airports, etc	(a) Predicts how different marketing systems will operate (b) Gives explicit expression relating the design of a system to the length and frequency of queues, waiting time, etc	(a) Must be operated a sufficient length of time to achieve a steady-state solution (b) Manager's reluctance to have confidence in this method
Stochastic process	A random experiment which occurs over time and whose outcome is determined by chance. This is an analysis of systems with variable/uncertain components	(a) For building choice, models checking on customers' loyalty (b) Predict buying decisions and future purchasing probabilities	Might predict flow of customers and future purchase probabilities	Suitable for short-run predictions only
Statistical decision theory	This is an analysis of decision-making processes where outcomes are uncertain. Prob-	For decision-making on: budgeting, advertising, pricing test-marketing, new product development,	Simplifies the level of analysis and suggests a number of possible outcomes	Subjective estimation of the probability for each decision might affect the results' validity

Method	Based on	Marketing applications	Advantages	Limitations
	ability of each outcome – based upon past data or subjective estimates – is given adequate weight and is taken into consideration for decision-making	merchandising, optimum mix, etc.		
Game theory	Constant sum game solution, use of a maximum criterion to determine, for example, budget/ resources allocation. Theoretical analysis of competition/collusion between organizations	For decision-making by retailing firms, mainly on: pricing (Higgins, 1973), product stock determination and advertising, budget allocations, also for better decision on negotiation processes	(a) Aids management in decision-making (b) Suggests a useful analytical approach to competitive problems, such as: pricing, advertising outlay and product decisions	Does not have much predictive power compared with other quantitative techniques

1   *Definition of the objective.* A well-defined objective is the target of the solution and the answer to the problem must satisfy the requirements. Objectives such as reduced costs, increased profits, matching of salesforce effort to customer potential or improved media selection can be handled.

2   *Quantitative measurement of problem elements.* A quantitative measurement is needed for each of the elements described in the problem which is an essential condition for applying mathematical models such as hours, pounds (£), etc.

3   *Alternative choice.* It must be possible to make a selection for reaching a solution which satisfied the objective function.

4   *Linearity.* The term 'linearity' describes the problem and its restrictions. Equations and inequalities must describe the problem in a linear form.

5   *Mathematical formulation.* Information must be compiled in such a manner that it is possible to translate the relationships among variables into a mathematical formulation capable of describing the problem and all the relations among variables.

A number of techniques is available for solving a formulated linear programme. A graphical solution is possible when there are three variables only. An example showing the use of LP in determining the best allocation and mix of marketing effort is presented in detail by Meidan (1981b).

One is faced with four kinds of difficulties in using linear programming models:

1   The first difficulty is in describing the problem mathematically. In an industrial situation one must know exactly how much one can use the production resources such as: manpower, raw materials, time, etc.
2   The second problem lies in the interpretation and proper use of the objectively obtained optimum solution. One may need to analyse additional business considerations, over and above the ones used in describing and formulating the problem.
3   Even if the problem had been correctly stated and formulated, technical limitations may exist such as the amount of data a computer can handle or that no solution exists (for example, the number of constraints and/or variables may be too large).
4   A further limitation lies in the reliability of the proposed solution. This could arise when a linear assumption is taken for a real non-linear behaviour of the component.

Physical distribution

Designing an optimal physical distribution system is dependent on choosing those levels of services that minimize the total cost of physical distribution, whose objective function might read: $C = T + F + I + L$, where C = total distribution cost, T = total freight cost, F = total fixed warehouse cost, I = total inventory cost and L = total cost of lost sales.

Given the objective function, one seeks to find the number of warehouses, inventory levels and modes of transportation that will minimize it, subject to at least three constraints:

1   Customer demand must be satisfied
2   Factory capacity limits must not be exceeded
3   Warehouse capacity cannot be exceeded.

The linear programming model has been used in solving distribution problems particularly in the transportation of finished goods to warehouses. The aims were to minimize transport costs subject to certain constraints, such as warehouse costs (Kotler, 1972). Other uses of LP models in marketing include site location, physical distributions and blending products.

Warehouse location

Chentnick (1975) discusses the various methods of locating warehousing systems which are of interest as their usefulness is indicated, thus suggesting the advantage of linear programming in comparison to other methods. Broadly, the function of a warehouse can be broken down into five areas:

1   Storage
2   Assembling of customer orders
3   Service of customers
4   Economies of scale by bulk buying and delivery
5   Processing and final packaging.

There are two definable sets which characterize the two methods of solution to the warehouse location problem (Meidan, 1978):

1   The infinite set assumes that the warehouse can be positioned anywhere on the map: obvious slight adjustments can be made later to allow for rivers, mountains, etc. A main assumption is that transport costs are directly proportional to distance (as the crow flies) and this is questionable in many situations.
2   The feasible set assumes a finite number of possible locations and both costs of buildings and haulage can be calculated with a high degree of precision.

Media selection

One area in marketing where linear programming models have been extensively used is in advertising decisions, especially in media-mix decisions in a market segment. Higgins (1973), for example, proposed the use of this model for deciding on the optimum paging schedule for colour supplements of newspapers.

Marketing-mix decisions and budget allocations

The marketing mix refers to the amounts and kinds of marketing variables the firm is using at a particular time and includes price, advertising costs and distribution expenditures, each of which could be subdivided into further variables.

Product mix and the multi-product marketing strategy problem

The problem of product mix, i.e. variety and quantity of products produced, is commonly encountered by almost all multi-product firms during the planning period. Here the objective is to maximize current profits subject to the various constraints such as its capacity, demand levels and quality. Such problems necessitate the use of linear programming.

Other marketing management applications for LP

Wilson (1975) cites a number of potential applications of LP including new product decisions, resolving conflict in market segmentation and the choice of a new market from a set of possible alternatives, and gives an example of its use in allocating a salesforce to new products. Goal programming, on the other hand, may be used when a minimum knowledge of the situation and realistic objectives are available. Here the subjective constraints placed on the model give direction to an objective and hence an area of solutions, i.e. constraints become goals.

The transportation model

The transportation model is a specialized class of linear programming model. Like the linear programming models, its aim is to optimize the use of resources with the exception that it requires separate computational techniques not normally used in other models.

The transportation model seems to have limited application and the area of marketing where it has been used is in making distribution decisions. This limited usage is the result of the way in which the model is formulated. The major deterministic operational research techniques and their marketing applications, limitations and advantages are summarized in Table 8.6.

Causal models

Under this heading we have two main techniques: path analysis and linear structure relations (LISREL). Both these methods are relatively new to marketing. Of the two, LISREL is more widely applied because of its versatility.

Path analysis

Path analysis (PA) is a method for studying patterns of causation among a set of variables, which was popularized in the sociological literature (Hise, 1975). Though path diagrams are not essential for numerical analysis, they are useful for displaying graphically the pattern of causal relationships among sets of observable and unobservable variables. Path analysis provides means for studying the direct and indirect effects of variables. PA is intended not to accomplish the impossible task of deducing causal relations from the values of the correlation coefficients but to combine the quantitative information given by the correlations with such qualitative information as may be at hand on causal relations, to give quantitative information.

Path analytic models assume that the relationships among the variables are linear and additive. Path coefficients are equivalent to regression weights. Direct effects are indicated by path coefficients. Indirect effects refer to the situation where an independent variable affects a dependent variable through a third variable, which itself directly or indirectly affects the dependent variables. The indirect effect is given by the product of the respective path coefficients.

In a recent example, developed for a tourism marketing study (McDonagh *et al.*, 1992), PA was used to measure the effects of three major environmental factors (exogenous variables): preservation of local landscape; preservation of architectural values; and

Table 8.6 Some major deterministic operational research techniques applicable in marketing (the method, advantages, limitations and when recommended to use)

Method	Based on	Marketing applications	Main advantages	Major limitations
Linear programming	Objective and constraint linear functions	(a) Advertising (Higgins, 1973), space optimal media mix allocations (b) Distribution problems, site location (Kotler, 1972) (c) Budget allocation, new product decision (Wilson, 1975) (d) Blending product mixes (e) Marketing mix decisions	(a) Maximizes profitability of allocations, subject to constraints (b) Minimizes costs (c) Aids management in decision making	(a) Difficult to obtain and formulate the various functions (b) Constraints must be altered as soon as external and/or internal factors change
Transportation model	Transportation/ allocation matrix ascertaining the minimum costs, routes, quantities supplied etc.	To allocate resources, supply etc. by reducing transportation costs. Suitable particularly for department stores, truck rental firms, transport companies	Very suitable for managerial decision making	Inaccurate in the longer run as a result of changes in costs
Non-linear programming	Non-linear objective functions and non-linear constraint relationships	To find the maximum return to a new product search, subject to budget constraint	(a) When the relationships are non-linear (b) When the objective function is non-linear while the constraints are non-linear	Difficult to establish non-linear relationships

overcrowding, as a direct causal impact on two critical endogenous variables: (1) concern towards a policy of global conservation and (2) preservation of cultural values.

LISREL

LISREL (linear structural relations) is a method of structural equation modelling that allows the researcher to decompose relations among variables and to test causal models that involve both observable (manifest) and unobservable (latent) variables. Path analysis and LISREL models are two important analytical approaches for testing causal hypotheses. Essentially, the analyst wants the reproduced correlations to be close to the original correlations. The LISREL model allows the researcher simultaneously to evaluate both the measurement and causal (i.e. structural) components of a system.

LISREL allows for a holistic, more realistic conception of social and behavioural phenomena. It recognizes that measures are imperfect, errors of measurement may be correlated, residuals may be correlated and that reciprocal causation is a possibility. *A priori* theory is absolutely necessary for covariance structure analysis. An important strength of structural equation modelling is its ability to bring together psychometric and econometric analyses.

Many applications of LISREL modelling can be seen in such areas as consumer behaviour, personal selling, new product adoption, marketing strategy, organizational decision-making, distribution channels, advertising research and international marketing. For a detailed example of application of LISREL, see Moutinho and Meidan (1989). Table 8.7 summarizes the two causal models applications in marketing.

Hybrid models

Under this category there are three different types of methods used in solving marketing problems: dynamic programming; heuristic programming; and stock control models.

Dynamic programming

As stated by Budnick *et al.* (1977), dynamic programming is a recursive approach to optimization problems which works on a step-by-step basis utilizing information from the preceding steps. The model has been used to aid decision-making in areas such as distribution (i.e. the minimization of transportation costs), the distribution of salespeople to various territories (in such a way that maximum profits will be obtained) and determining the best combination of advertising media and frequency under a budgetary constraint.

Heuristic programming

Heuristics is commonly defined as the use of rule of thumb for solving problems. Therefore, heuristic programming techniques are based on an orderly search procedure guided by these rules of thumb and are mainly applied to problems when mathematical programming techniques are either too expensive or complicated. However, they do not guarantee optimal solutions. In the past, heuristic programming has been applied fairly extensively in certain areas of marketing.

Taylor (1963) devised a graphical heuristic procedure to derive solutions to the problems of media scheduling that suggested the optimal number of advertisements to be placed in each medium and the size of each insertion. The number of insertions was determined by graphical methods which attempted to find the point where the marginal returns to the last insertion equalled the marginal cost of the advertisements for each medium.

A summary of the main characteristics, advantages, limitations and applications of dynamic and heuristic models in marketing is presented in Table 8.8.

Table 8.7	Causal models applications in marketing (the techniques, advantages, limitations and when recommended to use)			
Model	*Content*	*Marketing applications*	*Advantages*	*Limitations*
Path analysis	Provides the means for studying the direct and in-direct effects of variables, by offering quanti-tative informa-tion on the basis of qualita-tive data on causal relations	Tourism market-ing (McDonagh *et al.*, 1992), other applica-tions (Wasser-man, 1989)	Displays graph-ically the pat-tern of causal relationships	Assumes relation-ships among variables are linear
LISREL (linear structural relations)	A structural equa-tion modelling, that enables one to decom-pose relations among variables and test causal models that involve both observable and unobservable variables	Consumer behav-iour, personal selling, market-ing strategy, international marketing (Moutinho and Meidan, 1989)	Provides an inte-gral approach to data analysis *and* theory con-struction. The method easily handles errors in measure-ment. Ability to bring together psychometric and econo-metric analyses	Requires an *a priori* theory for structure analysis

Stock control models

The distribution side of marketing has been suc-cessfully modelled using quantitative methods for a number of years. The objective of the distri-bution system is to get the right goods to the right places at the right time for the least cost, and involves decisions on such problems as the number, location and size of warehouses, trans-portation policies and inventories. In this sec-tion the inventory decision will be discussed but it must be realized that inventory represents only one part of the local distribution network, a complete analysis of which is outside the scope of this chapter. The inventory decision has two parts to it: when to order (order point), and how much to order (order quantity). These are not independent and can be deduced from a stock control model. The ordering of goods involves costs, such as transportation and handling, which increase the number of orders placed.

On the other hand, the storage of goods also involves costs such as storage space charges, insurance costs, capital costs and depreciation costs. The first two decrease and the last two types of costs increase with the order quantity.

Table 8.8   Dynamic, heuristic and network programming applications in marketing (the methods, advantages, limitations and when recommended to use)

Model	Based on	Marketing applications	Advantages	Limitations
Dynamic programming	Recursive optimization procedure; optimizing on a step-by-step basis	Solving media selection problems; distribution (minimization of transportation costs; distribution of salespeople to various sales territories)	(a) Maximizes the objective over the planning period (b) Introduces new factors, e.g. 'forgetting time', 'accumulation or intersections' (c) Wide potential application in industry	The programming procedure is rather complex; computational difficulties
Heuristic programming	Orderly search procedure guided by the use of rule of thumb. Based on 'marginal approach' or trial and error	Media selection and scheduling; warehouse location; salesforce allocation; decision on the number of items in a product line; suitable for making product promotion decisions	(a) Good, flexible, simple and inexpensive method (b) Combines the analysis into the style of decision making and the reasoning used by managers	Does not guarantee optimal solution
Network programming (PERT and CPM)	Presents the wide range of critical activities that must be carried out and co-ordinated. PERT acknowledges uncertainty in the times required to complete	Planning, scheduling and controlling complex marketing projects (Bird *et al.*, 1973), e.g. building new stores, new product development (Robertson,	(a) Sequences and times of activities are considered, responsibilities allocated and co-ordinated in large/complex marketing projects (b) Project time	(a) Difficulties in estimating costs and times accurately particularly for new projects (b) Of use only when functions and

Model	Based on	Marketing applications	Advantages	Limitations
	activities while CPM does not. PERT deals only with the time factor. CPM refers to the time-costs trade-offs as well	1970), product commercializa-tion, advertising-sales relationships (Johansson and Redinger, 1979), distribu-tion planning (LaLonde and Headon, 1973)	can be forecast and completion time may be shortened	activities can, in fact, be separated

The simplest model assumes that demand is constant, shortages are not allowed (no stockouts), immediate replacements of stocks and a regular order cycle. If C = cost of holding of one unit of stock/unit time, C_o = cost of placing an order, d = demand rate (units/unit time), q = order quantity in units and t = order cycle time (order point), mathematical analysis shows that the total costs (ordering plus stockholdings) are minimized when the following order quantity is used:

$$q^* = dt^* = \sqrt{\frac{C_o d}{C}}$$

q^* = is often referred to as the economic order quantity (EOQ). The simplest model can be improved by relaxing some of the assumptions.

Network programming models

Network programming models are the methods usually used for planning and controlling complex marketing management projects. There are two basic methods: critical path method (CPM) and PERT (performance evaluation and review technique).

Critical path analysis

Critical path analysis, in its various forms, is one of the techniques developed in recent years to cope with the increased need for planning, scheduling and controlling in all functions of management. For a number of reasons, this technique is particularly applicable for use in marketing management. First, marketing management, by definition, involves the co-ordination of many other functions and activities: advertising; distribution; selling; market research; product research and development. Second, much of the work in marketing can be of a project nature (for example, new product launch, organization of a sales promotion, setting up of a new distribution system).

CPA is based on the assumption that some of the activities of a marketing project are in a concurrent relationship and take place simultaneously. The advantages to be gained from CPA in marketing are similar to those obtained in other functions, except that the centrality of the marketing function, particularly in some consumer goods firms, increases its desirability.

There are a large number of possible applications of PERT and CPM methods; for new product launch (Robertson, 1970); distribution; planning (LaLonde and Headon, 1973); sales negotiations; and purchasing (Bird *et al.*, 1973); launching a marketing company/project/department; sales promotions; conference organization; advertising campaigns; new stores opening; realigning sales territories, etc.

Budnick *et al.* (1977) proposed using network planning for product development, while others suggest the use of CPM to co-ordinate and plan the hundreds of activities which must be carried out prior to commercialization of a new product. Johansson and Redinger (1979) used path analysis to formulate an advertising–sales relationship of a hair-spray product.

Conclusion

The marketing research literature does not specify which quantitative method is most 'popular'. One can only conclude that the multivariate methods, as well as the stochastic and hybrid techniques and models, are widely used. Correspondence analysis is a method with much potential in marketing, as it displays all the benefits of multi-dimensional scaling and could be used with a variety of data inputs. The flexibility of both simulation and heuristic programming models mean that they can be applied to almost any situation where other models fail to give satisfactory results. In the last few years, causal models – in particular, LISREL – and artificial intelligence techniques have been widely used. Fuzzy sets is a new method that has been only very recently applied in marketing. Expert systems is a method which is currently systematically applied in many marketing problem areas. Queuing theory, network planning and transportation models are more restricted in their applications in marketing as they are formulated to solve problems in specific areas. Regarding deterministic techniques, these are suitable for finding optimum solutions to problems, particularly when set relationships exist between the variables. In summary, the usage of different types of models depends largely on the problem under investigation as well as on the type of data available and their level of interrelationships.

This chapter has attempted to present the application of the main quantitative methods in marketing. A taxonomic structure was adopted and all the techniques were broadly classified under nine headings: multivariate methods;

regression and forecasting techniques; simulation and fuzzy sets methods; operational research techniques; causal models; hybrid techniques; and network programming models. Advantages and limitations in the usage of each of these methods were discussed. However, the use of different types of methods depends largely on the marketing management situation of the problem under consideration.

References

Bird, M. M., Clayton, E. R. and Moore, L. J. (1973) Sales negotiation cost planning for corporate level sales, *Journal of Marketing*, **37**(2), April, 7–11.

Budnick, I., Mojena, R. and Vollman, M. (1977) *Principles of OR for Management*, Irwin, Homewood, IL, p. 135.

Carroll, J., Green, E. and Schaffer, M. (1986) Interpoint distance comparisons in correspond-ence analysis, *Journal of Marketing Research*, **23**, August, 271–290.

Cattin, P. and Wittink, D. R. (1982) Commercial use of conjoint analysis: a survey, *Journal of Marketing*, Summer, 44–53.

Chambers, J. D., Mullick, S. K. and Smith, D. D. (1979) How to choose the right forecasting technique, *Harvard Business Review*, July–August, 45–74.

Chentnick, C. G. (1975) Fixed facility location technique, *International Journal of Physical Distribution*, **4**(5), 263–275.

Coates, D., Doherty, N. and French, A. (1994) The new multivariate jungle, in *Quantitative Methods in Marketing* (Ed. Hooley G. J. and Hussey, M. K.), Academic Press Ltd, pp. 20–220.

Curry, B. and Moutinho, L. (1991) Expert systems and marketing strategy: an application to site location decisions, *Journal of Marketing Channels*, **1**(1), 23–27.

Curry, B. and Moutinho, L. (1993) Neural networks in marketing: modelling consumer responses to advertising stimuli, *European Journal of Marketing*, **27**(7), 5–20.

DeSarbo, W. S. (1993) A lesson in customer response modeling, *Marketing News*, **27**(12), June, H24–H25.

Diamantopoulos, A. and Schlegelmilch, B. B. (1997) *Taking the Fear out of Data Analysis*, The Dryden Press, pp. 209–18.

Dillon, W. R. and Mulani, N. (1989) LADI: a latent discriminant model for analysing marketing research data, *Journal of Marketing*, **26**, February, 15–29.

Doyle, P. and Fenwick, I. (1976) Sales forecasting using a combination of approaches, *Long Range Planning*, June, 61–64.

Ellis, R., LeMay, S. and Arnold, D. (1991) A transportation backhaul pricing model: an application of neural network technology, in Johnson, C., Krakay, F. and Laric, M. (eds), *Proceedings of the AMA Microcomputers in the Marketing Education Conference*, San Diego, California, August, pp. 15–17, 1–11.

Finerty, J. J. (1971) Product pricing and investment analysis, *Management Accounting*, December, 21–37.

Greenacre, M. J., *Theory and Applications of Correspondence Analysis*, Academic Press, New York, 1984.

Higgins, J. C. (1973) Some applications of operational research in advertising, *European Journal of Marketing*, **7**(3), 166–175.

Hise, D. R. (1975) *Causal Analysis*, Wiley, New York.

Hoffman, L. and Franke, R. (1986) Correspondence analysis: graphical representation of categorical data in marketing research, *Journal of Marketing Research*, **23**, August, 213–227.

Johansson, J. K. and Redinger, R. (1979) Evaluating advertising by path analysis, *Journal of Advertising Research*, 29–35.

Kennedy, M. S. (1991) Artificial intelligence in media planning: an exploration of neural networks, in Gilly, M. C. *et al.* (eds), *Enhancing Knowledge Development in Marketing*, AMA Educators' Summer Conference Proceedings, Volume 2, San Diego, California, pp. 390–397.

Klir, J. G. and Yuan, B. (1995) *Fuzzy Sets and Fuzzy Logic: Theory and Application*, Prentice-Hall.

Kotler, P. (1972) *Marketing Management, Analysis Planning and Control*, Prentice-Hall, Englewood Cliffs, NJ, p. 364.

Kotler, P. and Schultz, R. L. (1970) Marketing simulations: review and prospects, *Journal of Marketing*, July, 237–295.

LaLonde, B. and Headon, R. (1973) Strategic planning for distribution, *Long Range Planning*, December, 23–29.

Mazanec, J. A. (1994) *A priori* and *a posteriori* segmentation: heading for unification with neural network modelling, in Chias, J. and Sureda, J. (eds), *Marketing for the New Europe: Dealing with Complexity*, 22nd European Marketing Academy Conference Proceedings, Volume I, Barcelona, Spain, 25–28 May, pp. 889–917.

McDonagh, P., Moutinho, E., Evans, M. and Titterington, A. (1992) The effects of environmentalism on the English, Scottish, Welsh and Irish hotel industries, *Journal of Euromarketing*, **1**(3), 51–74.

Meidan, A. (1978) The use of quantitative techniques in warehouse location, *International Journal of Physical Distribution and Materials Management*, **8**(6), 347–358.

Meidan, A. (1981a) Optimising the number of salesmen, in Baker, M. J. (ed.), *New Directions in Marketing and Research*, University of Strathclyde, Glasgow, pp. 173–197.

Meidan, A. (1981b) *Marketing Applications of Operational Research Techniques*, MCB University Press, p. 86.

Meidan, A. (1983) Marketing strategies for hotels – a cluster analysis approach, *Journal of Travel Research*, **21**(4), Spring, 17–22.

Meidan, A. and Lim, I. (1993) The role of bank branch personnel in the sales process – an investigation of internal and external perceptions within the branch, *Proceedings of the 1993 MEG Conference: Emerging Issues in Marketing*, Loughborough Business School, Volume 2, July, pp. 660–670.

Moutinho, L. and Curry, B. (1994) Consumer perceptions of ATMs: an application of neural networks, *Journal of Marketing Management*, **10**(1), 191–206.

Moutinho, L. and Meidan, A. (1989) Bank customers' perceptions, innovations and new technology, *International Journal of Bank Marketing*, **7**(2), 22–27.

Paul, R. J. (1972) Retail store as a waiting line model, *Journal of Retailing*, **48**, 3–15.

Rangaswamy, A., Eliahberg, J. B., Raymond, R. and Wind, J. (1989) Developing marketing expert systems: an application to international negotiations, *Journal of Marketing*, **53**, 24–39, October.

Robertson, A. (1970) Looking out for pitfalls in product innovation, *Business Administration*, June, 39–46.

Saunders, J. (1994) Cluster analysis, in G. J. Hooley and M. K. Hussey (eds) *Quantitative Methods in Marketing*, Academic Press, London, pp. 13–28.

Speed, R. (1994) Regression type techniques and small samples, in G. J. Hooley and M. K. Hussey (eds) *Quantitative Methods in Marketing*, Academic Press, London, pp. 89–104.

Stanton, W. W. and Reese, R. M. (1983) Three conjoint segmentation approaches to the evaluation of advertising theme creation, *Journal of Business Research*, June, 201–216.

Taylor, C. J. (1963) Some developments in the theory and applications of media scheduling method, *Operational Research Quarterly*, 291–305.

Vriens, M. (1994) Solving marketing problems with conjoint analysis, in G. J. Hooley and M. K. Hussey (eds), *Quantitative Methods in Marketing*, Academic Press, London, pp. 37–56.

Walters, D. (1975) Applying the Monte Carlo simulation, *Retail and Distribution Management*, February, 50–54.

Wasserman, D. (1989) *Neural Computing: Theory and Practice*, Van Nostrand Reinhold, New York.

Wilson, J. M. (1975) The handling of goals in marketing problems, *Management Decision*, **3**(3), 16–23.

Zimmerman, H. J. (1991) *Fuzzy Set Theory and its Applications*, 2nd edn, Kluwer Academic Publishers Press.

Further reading

Diamantopoulos, A. and Schlegelmilch, B. B. (1997) *Taking the Fear Out of Data Analysis*, The Dryden Press, London. This is an excellent text, easy-to-read, refreshing and amusing, yet introducing a very robust content.

Hooley, G. J. and Hussey, M. K. (1994) *Quantitative Methods in Marketing*, Academic Press, London. This is a good book, introducing a collection of different quantitative research methods ranging from LISREL to neural networks. A new edition is coming out in 1999.

Kinnear, T. C. and Taylor, J. R. (1996) *Marketing Research: An Applied Approach*, 5th edn. McGraw-Hill, New York. An excellent textbook for introductory marketing research.

Lillien, G. L. and Rangaswamy, A. (1998) *Marketing Engineering – Computer-Assisted Marketing Analysis and Planning*, Addison-Wesley, Harlow, UK. Excellent new text on quantitative and computer modelling techniques with CD-ROM included. Techniques range from cluster analysis and conjoint analysis to AHP and neural networks.

Moutinho, L., Goode, M. H. and Fiona Davies, F. (1998) *Quantitative Analysis in Marketing Management*, Wiley, Chichester. This is a very recent text which includes chapters on statistical analysis, forecasting, decision theory and new quantitative methods, among others.

Sharma, S. (1996) *Applied Multivariate techniques*, Wiley, Chichester. Very good book on the topic. Issues covered range from factor analysis, cluster analysis and discriminant analysis to logistic regression, MANOVA and covariance structure models.

Zimmerman. H. J. (1991) *Fuzzy Set Theory and its Applications*, 2nd edn, Kluwer Academic Publishers Press. This is probably the best and most up-to-date text on fuzzy sets theory and applications.

Market segmentation

MARTIN EVANS

1   To show that whereas the tradition of grouping individuals together as far as possible within relatively homogeneous segments has been one of the major cornerstones of marketing, this paradigm has changed to more personalized targeting as markets fragment.
2   To examine relevant dimensions of segmenting and targeting, such as demographics, psychographics and geodemographics.
3   To explore the fusion of personalized data from a variety of sources, such as those in (2) and from transactional data, which lead to the new *biographical segmentation*.
4   To review aspects of the management of the segmentation process.

Introduction

Marketing is concerned with satisfying customer needs and wants as a means to achieving the goals of the organization. However, although the human condition means we all have a similar need structure, the same needs will not be salient to every person at the same point in time. The notion of varying salient needs (or other buying factors) in different individuals (or in organizations) provides the rationale for market segmentation. Those with similar salient needs and values may be grouped together to form a market segment if their buying behaviour is seen to be sufficiently homogeneous and at the same time different from those of other groups. Marketing then has the task of deciding which segments to target with distinct marketing mixes.

A useful illustration of segmentation is the toothpaste market in terms of the benefits shown in Table 9.1. What is shown is that even in such an apparently non-differentiated market, there are different consumer segments that buy in different ways for a variety of reasons and on this basis can be targeted with different marketing mixes. This is a fundamental rationale for market segmentation.

This chapter firstly looks at the progression from mass production through product differentiation to market segmentation. Next, an especially relevant segmentation theme for marketers is analysed and illustrated, namely the trend toward increasingly personalized targeting. This is based on the relative decline of demographic segmentation variables, partly due to their lack of explanatory depth and their relatively broad targeting capabilities. The rise of psychographics and geodemographics will be shown to have added to demographics' decline because of their potential abilities to understand target customers in great detail – even individually. This theme is further developed by behavioural transactional data which allows marketers to identify who is buying what, when, how frequently and in what quantities – and the fusion of these approaches has led to the development of *biographics*. The essence, for the marketer, is to identify segments in ever more focused ways and for them to target markets not only in terms of niches but increasingly as *individual* customers and potential customers. Finally, the chapter provides a short review of some of the planning issues surrounding market segmentation.

Product differentiation to market segmentation

The toothpaste example given in Table 9.1 demonstrates an application of targeting different customer groups with different marketing mixes. However, it has not always been like this. The famous saying in the car industry by Henry Ford, concerning the model T, that customers could have any colour as long as it was black, was a reflection of the mass marketing of the time. Great economies of scale were achieved through the long production runs of mass producing standardized products for an apparently homogeneous market. In a classic paper by Wendell Smith, who was one of the originators of segmentation thinking, the development of segmentation is explored (Smith, 1956). As mass

production and consumption continued, many organizations attempted to gain some competitive advantage and developed the strategy of product differentiation. As Smith stated: 'Product differentiation is concerned with the bending of demand to the will of supply.' In this way, a variety was offered to buyers.

This is the key to product differentiation because, although the result might in some cases look very similar to segmentation, differences in product, image, distribution and/or promotion are offered to the market. Perhaps such differences do indeed appeal to different groups within the overall market, but if they do it is mainly due to coincidence. True segmentation starts with identifying the requirements and behaviour of segments and varying marketing mixes accordingly in order to more deliberately match marketing offerings with customer behaviour.

Product differentiation clearly represents a product orientated approach in that it is an 'inside out' management attitude to marketing planning. Market orientation starts with understanding of the market and identification of market needs and behaviour. In this sense it is an 'outside in' planning approach. This is the segmentation approach and declares that marketing offerings cannot generally hope to be all

Table 9.1	Toothpaste consumer benefit segments			
	Sensory segment	*Sociable segment*	*Worrier segment*	*Independent segment*
Main benefit	Flavour, appearance	Bright teeth	Decay prevention	Price
Demographic factors	Children/ young people	Teens	Large families	Men
Lifestyle factors	Hedonistic	Active	Conservative	Concerned with value
Brands label	Colgate, Stripe	Ultra-Brite, Macleans	Crest	Cheapest own brands on sale

Adapted from Haley (1968)

things to all people and that differences between groups and similarities within groups may be analysed for marketing planning purposes.

Although the manifestation of market segmentation appears to reflect a division of the market into smaller groups, it is more helpful and appropriate to consider segmentation as an aggregating rather than divisive process. In this way customers are grouped together as far as it is meaningful for them to be targeted with distinct marketing mixes.

Having said this, there is always a danger of segmenting 'too far'. Market 'fragmentation' or 'oversegmenting' may create too small and unprofitable segments and becomes thus less efficient – the baffling array of shampoos is, perhaps, an example, as might be the plethora of different rail tickets depending on day, time, advance booking, type of rail card and so on. However, individualized (custom) segmentation or mass customization is the legitimate polar opposite and is the direction in which marketing is certainly taking the segmentation issue.

Segmentation criteria

Segmentation involves identifying homogeneous buying behaviour within a segment (and heterogeneous buying between segments) such that each segment can be considered as a target for a distinct marketing mix. To help with this process, potential segments should satisfy a number of criteria (Frank *et al.*, 1972). These are related to typifying the segments, homogeneity, usefulness, and strategic use in marketing management. The four main criteria and nine subcriteria are (van Raaij and Verhallen, 1994):

1 Typifying the segments
   * Identification: Differentiation of segment from other segments.
   * Measurability: Identification of segments in terms of differences in individual and household characteristics or other 'measurable' characteristics should be possible.

2 Homogeneity
   * Variation: Heterogeneity between segments in terms of behavioural response (Engel *et al.*, 1972).
   * Stability: The segments should be relatively stable over time. Also, switching of consumers from one segment to another should not be frequent. There should be stability at the individual level.
   * Congruity: Homogeneity within segments in terms of behavioural responses.

3 Usefulness
   * Accessibility: Segments should be accessible in terms of the use of media and distribution outlets. Segments are being reached in a 'communicative and distributive' manner. Segments should react consistently to communicative, promotional, distributional and product-related stimuli. This means that it must be possible to reach the segment, for example selecting appropriate advertising media that match the segment's media profile or selecting appropriate distribution channels, again through a matching of market profile with the profile of those most likely to frequent different types of retail outlets. These factors have traditionally been in demographic terms, but increasingly since around the start of the 1980s other more sophisticated market profiling and targeting dimensions have been explored and used.
   * Substantiality: Segments should be of sufficient size to enable specific marketing actions. This does not mean that segments need to be especially large, but profitable enough to have distinct marketing mixes aimed at them.

4 Strategic criteria
   * Potential: The segments should have enough potential for marketing objectives, e.g. profitability.
   * Attractiveness: Segments should be structurally attractive to the producer, e.g. create a competitive advantage for the company (Porter, 1979).

The above criteria are also of great significance in researching potential segments. The measurability criterion gives research direction in identifying primary or active segmentation variables. The substantiality criterion indicates market size, potential and share as dimensions to research. Accessibility suggests the importance of secondary or passive characteristics. Note the distinction between active and passive variable; active variables are the variables that are used in forming the segments, whereas passive variables are used afterwards to characterize the formed segments more completely.

Another practical point is that research methods may determine segmentation. If some variables of market behaviour are difficult, time consuming, or costly to research, sometimes the market will be segmented according to those dimensions that are more conveniently analysed, such as age, gender and socio-economic variables – not an approach to advocate, but one which is often manifested in reality.

It is not always the case that for each segment a different product must be developed. This might be the case, but equally there might be different prices charged in different segments for the same product or service, e.g. gas, electricity and train travel, or for different segments based on levels of repeat purchase and loyalty. Similarly, there could be differences in promotion – Levi's, for example, advertise on television for a fairly wide market but the same product lines are also promoted with quite different images and themes in the 'style' press (e.g. *The Face*), targeted at the 15–19-year-old fashion opinion leaders (Edmonson, 1993). There again, there are examples of where distribution might be the main mix difference between segments. A women's clothing manufacturer might produce a range of dresses but have alternate batches go into department stores and more down-market multiple retailers. There would probably be branding and price differences here as well but the primary difference would be based on retail outlet and hence segment targeted.

Bases for segmentation

Segmentation bases may be objective or subjective. An objective base may be measured unambiguously, e.g. age and gender, or may be taken from registrations of transactions, e.g. checkout scanning data. Subjective bases need to be measured with the respondents themselves and are often 'mental constructs' such as attitudes and intentions.

We can also analyse segmentation bases in terms of three levels. At the general level, segmentation is based on more or less permanent consumer characteristics such as gender, age, income, social class, occupation, family composition, and lifestyle. These characteristics are the same for different products, services and usage situations.

For domain-specific segmentation, there are different product classes and consumption domains, such as breakfast, washing clothes, or commuting. When these are taken into account, the segmentation is domain-specific. The toothpaste benefit segmentation is an example of the domain-specific approach. We will briefly return to benefit segmentation towards the end this chapter to discuss how the 'use' based approach has been extended to more of a 'situation' (or occasion of use) base.

For specific level segmentation, customers are segmented into, for example, heavy and light users of specific brands. Segmentation of present customers is also at the specific level.

Combining the three levels of segmentation and the distinction of objective and subjective variables is shown in Table 9.2. All segmenting bases can be categories within this framework.

This section now continues with a discussion of bases for segmenting markets but at the same time traces the trend of increased focusing of segmentation and targeting from general demographic groups through better understood psychographic and domain-specific segments to more specific individualized targeting via marketing databases and *biographic segmentation*.

Table 9.2 Classification of segmentation variables		
	Objective	*Subjective*
General level (consumption)	Income, age, education level, geographic area	Lifestyle, general values, personality
Domain-specific level (product class)	Usage frequency, substitution, complementarity	Perception, attitude, preference, interests, opinions,
Specific level (brand)	Brand loyalty (behaviour), usage frequency	Brand loyalty (attitude), brand preference, purchase intention

It is not too long since the main market profiling on which organizations relied was, in general, in demographic terms – and some still rely on little more, even today. It became the norm for markets to be profiled as in terms of age, gender and social grade. However, there have been criticisms of social grade, in particular, and marketing has sought – and now found – alternative, more sophisticated segmenting bases.

Before moving on to the alternatives, it is worth exploring basic demographics further. Indeed it is no surprise that demographic variables have been favoured for so long. First, they are generally easy to study. A market research interviewer needs only to ask respondents to point to their appropriate age category on a showcard, to note gender of the respondent and to ask the respondent to give the occupation of the chief income earner in their household. Such simple research, together with the geographic area in which the research is conducted or in which the respondent resides, will provide the basic profile with which marketers are so familiar.

Demographics

Age

Age is still a valid base for many markets. 'Young adult' and 'teenage' segments have become important spenders, for example, demanding their own products and searching for their own identity. Their numbers have of course declined through what was called in the UK, the 'demographic timebomb' of the mid to late 1980s. The phrase was coined because it reflected a dramatic change in the number of people in this age group and the fact that the change held all sorts of implications for marketers and social planners alike. Although the 18–24s of the mid 1980s have moved on in age terms themselves, they are still important as the now older group because they are still, of course, a very sizeable group. As for the 18–24s of today, there may not be so many of them but it is important to target them, either in their own right or as opinion leaders, especially in fashion markets (Evans, 1989).

A complicating factor is that this group has been found to be especially individualistic and sceptical of marketing activity. This doesn't make them difficult to reach, but it is proving harder to influence them. They have been labelled as 'generation X' and Coupland (1991) and Ritchie (1995) have analysed their behaviour and attitudes. It is possible that marketing can provide some of what generation X might be looking for – greater interactivity and participation in marketing communications. The issue of individualism is discussed further under psychographics, later in this chapter.

At the other end of the age spectrum, it is noticeable that the size of older age segments have been increasing as society ages. The over 50s are clearly different from the group on which marketers have traditionally concentrated their targeting. For a start, they are physically different – age catches up and is manifested in wrinkles, thinning hair, sagging everything! From a marketing perspective these physical characteristics can produce market segments worth targeting with anti-wrinkle cream, hair restorer, health products and even plastic surgery. But the over 50s are now much more interesting to direct marketers than these more obvious factors suggest.

One explanation for this is that the generation called the 'baby boomers' – those born in the years following the Second World War – became a very important target for marketers. They were involved in a massive social revolution which changed music, fashions, political thought and social attitudes forever. They were the generation to grow up in the 1960s when the term 'teenager' hadn't been used previously. They were not 'small adults' who, in previous generations, had worn similar clothes to their parents. The new generation, however, wanted their own culture, their own fashions, music, and their own social attitudes which rejected the values of their parents – often violently in street demonstrations; remember Paris, 1967, Kent State University, 1968, Trafalgar Square, London, 1969. None of this had happened to previous generations of teenagers/20 somethings. Indeed a popular phrase in the 1960s was 'never trust anyone over 30'!

Coupled with this desire for ownership of their thoughts and lives, the baby boomer generation was the most affluent (generally) of any 'youth market' until their era, so they were able to engage in the consumer market and marketers responded with a fashion and music explosion of which we had previously never seen the like.

It is now this generation which is turning 50, because they began to be born after the Second World War which ended in August 1945, so the first of the generation turned 50 in 1996 and millions will do this through the first couple of decades of the new millennium. It is also a large market, not least because of their reason for being conceived – the end of the war, with the return of the armed forces to their loved

ones – and the release of pent-up tension due to the awful nature of war itself.

Such a consumerism-literate market should be extremely attractive. Indeed in the USA a baby boomer will turn 50 every 6.8 seconds in 2001! Not all the over 50s are baby boomers, of course; those in their 60s and 70s and indeed the over 70s are from other generations with lifestyles and attitudes of their own. Overall, the over 50s have been termed the 'third age'. They represent about a third of the population (in the late 1990s) and are some 18 million strong in the UK. By 2020 they will represent about a half of the UK population.

There are other sub-markets here. One factor to consider is whether they are in work or 'retired' in all its various forms. One of the greatest social/economic changes since around 1980 has been the incidence of early retirement as organizations downsize/rationalize their workforce. This has meant that in many organizations as soon as one reaches 50 there is a fair chance of being targeted for early retirement. Such a change in lifestyle can be profound, so it isn't enough to talk of becoming 50 or 65, but rather of employment status as well.

Many of these early-retireds will find new employment – perhaps several small jobs, perhaps in totally new careers, perhaps for some it is the opportunity to do 'what they always wanted to do'. For others it can mean the scrap heap at 50, with a severely restricted income and little hope for the future.

In general terms, however, the ageing baby boomer generation is the most wealthy, in terms of inheritance from their parents. That previous generation was 'blessed' with low house prices when they bought and a lifestyle which was much less materialistic. As a result their estates have often (but clearly not always) been of significant proportions and this wealth is cascading down to the new over-50 market.

Research amongst the over 50s has revealed several characteristics. The over 50s don't like to be portrayed as 'old' but at the same time would see through attempts to portray them as 'young', so caution is needed. There has certainly been a move to using old*er* models and stereotypes in marketing to these older segments – such as with Joanna Lumley – and these are generally welcomed.

Often, the over 50s have learnt what they like and dislike. They more easily reject irrelevant marketing offerings than perhaps their younger and slightly more expansive counterparts might. Not surprisingly many are becoming concerned about their health and mortality and so the market for health and anti-ageing products and services is an obvious one. Many are responsive to discounts and special offers – for example, B&Q's have discount periods for the older customer (coupled, it should be noted, with a policy of employing the over 50s as staff).

There are differences between those in their 50s, 60s and above. Those in their 60s generally prefer to use cash and are rather cautious consumers. Those over 70 are perhaps even further along this continuum. There has certainly been an explosion of magazine titles aimed at various over-50 groups, demonstrating that the market is not homogeneous and that the various groups can be reached. The profiling in this sector is not merely on the basis of age, however; social grade and geodemographics are also being used and there is a trend toward overlaying this with attitudinal research. An example of this comes from the analysis of the Target Group Index in 1993 (Cummins, 1994) which found, based on shopping attitudes and behaviour, that there are 'astute cosmopolitans', constituting about 19% of the 50–75s and who are discerning consumers. There are also the 'temperate xenophobes' (20% of 50–75s) who are less likely to go abroad or eat 'foreign food'. The 'thrifty traditionalists' make up 20% and a further 19% are 'outgoing funlovers'! The largest group is the 'apathetic spender' (21%) who use credit cards to extend their purchasing power beyond what they can really afford (Cummins, 1994).

So it is important not to generalize when targeting the over 50s and to take into account the very real differences between the subgroups. These are issues which marketers should clearly bear in mind when designing the tactics of marketing campaigns.

Gender

Gender too has been a long-established segmentation variable. Not only in the sense of there being products for men and for women, but rather that traditionally most consumer goods were bought by women. Women would be the purchasers for the household; they may not have been the deciders or the final users of everything they bought, but at least they did most of the buying. As a consequence, much marketing activity was directed towards women, with a few changes of approach over the years. Female stereotyping has been the focus of much criticism over the last couple of decades. In the mid-1970s there was a general reliance on either the 'mother' or 'mistress' images of women in advertising. Towards the end of that decade criticisms centred on these approaches becoming less and less realistic (Scott, 1978). During the 1980s we had the emerging 'career woman' stereotype, but even this was limited and not always appropriately implemented.

Gender is still relevant in segmentation terms. One important trend for the 1990s is the continued change in respect of the 'feminal consumer' (Henley Centre, 1992). Increases in the divorce rate and the 'singles' market have added to the more general changes in sex roles, with women becoming more individualistic through their own careers rather than being housewives per se. Marketing to women, however, may still be in need of updating. There are new female roles such as the independent assertive woman, independent passive woman and independent sexual woman. Some of these clearly relate to what in popular culture has been termed 'girl power'.

The concept of the 'new man' emerged towards the end of the 1980s and we saw the manifestation of this in the advertising of cars for example. Audi's 'caring-sharing' man who holds the baby was quite different from the aggressive and selfish boy racers of earlier periods. Whether the 1990s really saw a significant shift towards the caring and sharing new man is debatable. What is clear is that, as female roles change, so inevitably do male roles. The increase in the divorce rate affects both sexes and produces sizeable singles markets, some male, some female, but all requiring greater independence in buying terms. Recent male images include the family man, the yob lad, modelling man, househusband man, as well as gay images.

In marketing terms, there is an increasing amount of evidence to suggest that targeting needs to be either male or female in tone, style, wording and design. Work by Pidgeon (1997) for example shows how direct mailings of different styles, appeal in differing ways to men and women. If direct marketing practices what it preaches, then it needs to target individually, not merely according to name and address drawn from lists but also in terms of the content and tone of voice. One interesting finding in research which extended Pidgeon's (1997) is that men appear to be less concerned with practical details in direct mailing material relating to cars than are women. Indeed the male respondents in this research were more interested in 'long red bonnets' (Nairn and Evans, 1998)!

Social grade

Marketers have, especially in the past, adhered to the basic principle of social stratification but have long avoided researching possible segments on the basis of social class in any true sociological sense. This would involve rather complicated assessment of income, wealth,

power and skill. So instead in the UK and many other European countries social grade is used. In the UK the occupation of the 'chief income earner' in the household is the determinant and a six-fold classification results: A, B, C1, C2, D, E (Table 9.3). Many commercial market research programmes have found significant differences in buying behaviour between respondents in the various social grades.

The traditional justification for the continued use of social grade is basically twofold. It is simple to research. All that is required is for data to be analysed according to the occupation of the 'chief income earner in the household' (MRS, 1981). Second, social grade appears to have been a reasonably good discriminator of buying behaviour, and, as Table 9.4 suggests, it is reasonably stable for political preferences.

However, during the 1980s in particular, a number of significant criticisms of social grade were made. There are inevitable anomalies in its use. For example, nearly a third of those earning over £21 000 are C2DE and half those earning £15 000–£21 000 are C2DE. Thus, the traditional strong correlations between social grade and income have been destroyed. Some in C2, such as highly skilled manual workers, will be earning more than some middle managers in group B.

It was also shown that of 400 respondents to earlier surveys who were re-interviewed to

Table 9.3 Social grade in the UK

Social grade	Social status	Head of household's occupation	Percentage
A	Upper middle class	High managerial, administrative or professional	2.7
B	Middle class	Intermediate managerial, administrative or professional	15.2
C1	Lower middle class	Supervisory, clerical, junior managerial or administrative	4.1
C2	Skilled working class	Skilled manual workers	27.1
D	Working class	Semi- and unskilled manual workers	17.8
E	Lowest levels of subsistence	State pensioners, widows, casual lowest-grade workers	13.0

Table 9.4   Social grade reliability over time

	Conservatives				Labour				Liberal/Democrats			
Social grade	1983	1987	1992	1997	1983	1987	1992	1997	1983	1987	1992	1997
A,B	60	57	56	41	10	14	20	31	28	26	22	22
C1	51	51	52	37	20	21	25	37	26	22	17	16
C2	40	40	38	27	32	36	41	50	26	22	17	16
D,E	33	30	30	21	41	48	50	59	24	20	15	13

UK electorate 1983–1997

Source: Sunday Times/MORI (1992) and http://www.mori.com/ge_1997.htm

confirm their social grade, 41 per cent had been allocated to the wrong group and this is an indication of instability of the system (O'Brien and Ford, 1988).

However, if we integrate the above demographic variables and perhaps discover that those most interested in our product or service are predominantly, say, 'AB male, 45–54', we have a combination of some of the most used segmentation variables of recent decades. Inferring activities, interests and opinions – and indeed buying behaviour – of segments like this, or of others such as 'C1 female 18–24' or 'C2 male 25–34', is quite simple. If you try this you will find it probably can be done easily in a couple of minutes, showing the power of stereotypes – but also revealing the probable inaccuracies of inference alone.

Family lifecycle

However, one framework that to some extent combines age and gender variables is based on the family lifecycle concept and shows how the family unit's interests and buying behaviour is changing over time due to the progression from the single bachelor stage, to newly married, married with children, married with children who no longer live in the parental home ('empty nest'), and finally to the solitary survivor stage. Buying needs, values and behaviour clearly differ for the various stages. An updated lifecycle model for the UK is shown in Table 9.5 (Lawson, 1988).

A recent promotional campaign by Barclays Bank depicted the life stages through which their customers go, by picturing a young single man, then a couple with a family and an older couple whose children had left home, and suggesting that the bank has financial service products to suit not just each stage 'now' but each individual as they progress through these stages of the lifecycle. The Prudential even used a caterpillar to reflect how we metamorphose through life stages – promising equally evolutionary financial products to match each lifestage.

It has been found that some product categories, like life assurance, are predominantly chosen by the husband, while other categories, like food and children's clothing, are 'wife dominated', and yet others, such as choice of holiday and housing, are based on joint decision making, including the children to some extent (Davis and Rigaux, 1974).

Considering the influence of children, all one needs to do is to observe what happens as they go around the store with their parents – children will pick up various items, sometimes asking nicely for them, sometimes screaming if they don't get them and sometimes surreptitiously putting them in the basket – perhaps especially at the supermarket checkout! The 'pester power' (Carter, 1994) is highly observable.

What some marketers do is to target their advertising at a slightly older age group so that

Table 9.5 A UK modernized family lifecycle	
Lifecycle stage	*Percentages of households*
Bachelor	1.7
Newly married couples	3.8
Full nest 1 (with pre-school children)	14.6
Full nest 1 (lone parent)	1.5
Middle age, no children (aged 35–44)	1.5
Full nest 2 (school-aged children)	2.1
Full nest 2 (lone parent)	2.4
Launching families (with non-dependent children)	7.8
Empty nest 1 (childless aged 45–60)	11.6
Empty nest 2 (retired)	11.7
Solitary survivor (under 65)	3.3
Solitary survivor (retired)	17.4

the 'trickle down' theory operates – younger children see the product being used by their elders and want to follow their lead. By the time it has trickled down to them, the older ones have been enticed to the next craze.

The concept of a 'brand' is probably just beginning to be understood by children when they reach 5 or 6. Parents are targeted with a 'sensible' message and children with a more persuasive one. This can be related to Freudian psychology – the balance between the id and the superego, the kids' appeal being more id but tempered by a superego appeal to the parents ('naughty but nice'!). The ego can then more easily rationalize the purchase as being logical.

With children of about 7 or 8, parental influence is less constraining and the children themselves develop a repertoire of acceptable brands, TV advertising and observation of older children being the main influences. Parents might be motivated to buy their children those products which help their development but often they are persuaded to buy things which add to their children's street credibility – the 'right' brand.

When children are of primary school age it is often school friends who become more important product influencers than parents. Observa-

tion and word of mouth are then very important in developing children's preferences.

Many marketers have really taken this on board and have started to get into schools with various sponsorship and 'educational' ventures. Schools need the help to ease financial hardship associated with their budgets but some teachers are uncomfortable with this way of getting to the children's market.

Any viewing of TV at 'children's' times will confirm saturation by commercials aimed at children. Younger children may merely watch these as entertainment but as they grow, the brand and image become important and salient in children's minds as a result of associative learning processes and vicarious learning (seeing others using the product). Personalities and cartoon characters are also heavily used to target children.

As well as child-related consumption, we are also concerned here with the role of children in determining more adult purchases. That is, which car the parents will buy and where to go on holiday and so on.

The family is a decision making unit and there are different roles for each member. There will be deciders, influencers, buyers, users and gatekeepers (holders of information), and different members can play each of these roles at different times – including children. Children are increasingly influencing choice of housing, durables, clothes, TV, video, cars, holidays as well as in the more conventional areas such as sweets.

Parents have succumbed to a youth culture and look to their children for what is 'hip' to buy! In one survey (BBC2, 1997) it was found that 72 per cent of parents admitted to £20 of their weekly spending being influenced by their children, 22 per cent of parents thought that up to £50 of weekly spending was a result of pester power and even 4 per cent thought that up to £100 of their weekly spending was based on this! This would amount to £5bn per year if averaged across the UK.

Clearly there are ethical issues here. Children have not fully matured, by definition, yet they are being heavily targeted, sometimes in subtle ways by marketers who want them to develop brand preferences. Some retailers even have loyalty schemes for babies! The Royal Bank of Scotland obtained details of children from subscriptions to the Disney Book Club and sent them offers for a credit card. Children as young as 5 received the mailing offering a 9.9 per cent APR (Anon, 1997)!

Consider, also, the effect in the US of the heavy branding policies targeted at children – there are stories of 10-year-olds mugging and even killing for the 'right' brand of trainers when pester power fails with their parents. Most UK marketing trade bodies outlaw practices which exploit minors.

The concept of a decision-making unit at household level raises some issues for the direct marketer – the extent to which targeting is individualized, possibly even preventing the roles of influencer, decider, buyer and user to interact – or whether targeting should be at household level.

The concepts here have been extended and applied within practical market analysis programmes such as SAGACITY, given in Table 9.6. SAGACITY combines an abbreviated family lifecycle with income and occupation. The result is a series of twelve categories based on life stage, whether both partners are working or not, and on 'blue collar' or 'white collar' occupations (Research Services Ltd, 1981).

It is perhaps a significant indicator of the end of marketing's love affair with social grade that from 1988 Granada TV replaced social grade as one of the profiling characteristics in its audience research with family lifecycle – they call it 'life stage' (O'Brien and Ford, 1988).

Current marketers often consider segmentation by life stage. An example is the Tesco Clubcard which results in transaction analysis based initially on life stage, then overlaid by other characteristics such as vegetarianism, diabetes, etc. In February 1996 Tesco, via their data analysts DunnHumby, identified 12 different segments and targeted each with a different version of their club magazine. By November 1996 the figure had risen to 5000! Their aim was to be literally one-to-one within two years of that date (Hay, 1996). One of the main restrictions on this at the time was printing capability. The obstacle of data overload had apparently been solved and the advent of digital printing means that one-to-one mailings are now practicable.

	Table 9.6 Twelve SAGACITY categories		
1	Dependent	1.1 White collar	1.2 Blue collar
2	Pre-family	2.1 White collar	2.2 Blue collar
3	Family	3.1 Better off	3.11 White collar 3.12 Blue collar
		3.2 Worse off	3.21 White collar 3.22 Blue collar
4	Empty nest	4.1 Better off	4.11 White collar 4.12 Blue collar
		4.2 Worse off	4.21 White collar 4.22 Blue collar

Ethnicity

Another demographic base that marketing has not been especially strong in using is ethnicity (Piper, 1977). Ethnic segments are being targeted but there is perhaps still a long way to go. Ethnic segments have their culture, language, religion and distinct requirements. It is not always appropriate for them to be targeted with products and services by merely changing the promotion to them. Different coloured skin, for example, has different moisture content and the formulation of cosmetics should be different, not merely suggesting how people of different colours can select from existing ranges to arrive at appropriate colour combinations.

There are, now, market research agencies that offer specialized services to research ethnic segments, so the argument of a decade or so ago that they are difficult to research is not as strong as it once was. Also, with the developing ethnic media it is equally possible to reach ethnic segments with marketing messages, in addition to direct targeting via lists.

A sensitive issue is whether targeting at ethnic segments is in some way racist. The argument is that if ethnic segments differ in their needs and values, they should be treated differently. This does not mean that they are discriminated against, but many marketers are still fearful.

Geographics

There is much debate about 'global marketing' or at least pan-European marketing due to the EU single market and technological facilitators such as satellite broadcasting and international direct mailing operations. However there is evidence to suggest that for many products and services geographic market segments will stay and even become more heterogeneous at regional and even local level (Henley Centre, 1992). Table 9.7 reflects some attitudinal differences between nations according to an international Gallup survey (1982). Again it is partly this pluralism in the marketplace that is fuelling a trend toward greater targeting and focusing of marketing activity toward smaller niche markets.

Any marketing campaign that travels across borders must be cognisant of such differences. In Spain, for example, many young people remain at their parental home until they

### Table 9.7	International attitudinal differences

Percentages agreeing with:	US	GB	WG	F	I	JP
Freedom being more important than equality	72	69	37	54	43	37
Equality being more important than freedom	20	23	39	32	45	32
Very proud to be (American, French, etc.)	80	55	21	33	41	30
Confidence in major institutions:						
Press	49	29	33	31	46	52
Education	65	60	43	55	56	51
Civil service	55	48	35	50	28	31
Having 'great' pride in the work you do	84	79	15	13	29	37
'Thou shalt' still applying today:						
Not steal	93	87	81	69	93	66
Not kill	93	90	88	80	96	65
Not commit adultery	87	78	64	48	62	47

Key:	US United States, GB Great Britain, WG West Germany, F France, I Italy, J Japan are well into their 20s and 30s. Some don't pay rent and as a result are able to afford more expensive cars and other products than their parents!

In discussing international contexts, a mention of the Internet is relevant. Berthon *et al.* (1996) state that a presence on the medium is 'international by definition' and 'compared to other media, the Web provides a more or less level playing field for all players, regardless of size'. The Internet, then, provides for marketing internationally, but the sensitivities and culture of different nations must be taken on board because it is all too easy to offend – and indeed to break national laws.

Some examples (Sampson, 1998) will demonstrate. Virgin Atlantic Airways maintained a Web site and placed details of its trans-Atlantic airfares. The Web site described a return airfare of under $500. A prospective passenger wishing to buy one of these tickets was told that this special price was no longer available and the alternative was a ticket costing over $500. Under US law the airline was obliged to keep the information up to date, and, as it had inadvertently failed to do so, it ended up paying the US Department of Transport $14 000. Clearly UK companies which do business with customers in other countries need to be aware of the laws applicable there when promoting their goods and services via the Internet. Perhaps the most problematic area will be in the financial services industry, as this sector is closely regulated in most countries. Still on the theme of international conflicts, the Italian company Tattilo Editrice SpA made erotic pictures available over the Internet. The milder pictures were made available to all visitors to the Web site, whether or not they had a subscription. More explicit pictures were available to those who wished to subscribe to a special service. Tattilo is an Italian company, based in Italy, and both services were made available from computer equipment located in Italy. The domain name (that is the Internet address) of the Web site was *playmen.it.* Playboy Enterprises Inc (the publisher of *Playboy* magazine) had failed to obtain protection for its Playboy trade mark in Italy in a previous case brought against Tattilo. However, Playboy brought proceedings against Tattilo in the New York courts claiming that Tattilo had infringed Playboy's US registration of the Playboy trade mark by, amongst other things, its use of the *playmen.it* address because the service was available to US citizens. The court agreed and ordered Tattilo to either refuse subscriptions from US customers or shut down its Internet site, even though that site was in Italy. Tattilo was also ordered to pay to Playboy the gross profits it had earned from subscriptions to the service by US customers and all gross profits earned from the sale of goods and services advertised on the Playmen site. Interestingly, the court stated that '*Cyberspace is not a safe haven*'.

Psychographics

Although not new in concept, or even in practice, a variety of 'psychographic' approaches have emerged during the 1980s and 1990s.

Lifestyle

Lifestyle is based typically on the presentation to respondents of a series of statements (Likert scales). Table 9.8 reproduces a short selection of the (246) lifestyle statements used in the Target Group Index annual research programme (BMRB, 1988).

All items are graded using a five-point Likert scale: definitely agree/tend to agree/

Table 9.8 Examples of lifestyle statements

I buy clothes for comfort, not for style
Once I find a brand I like, I tend to stick to it
I always buy British whenever I can
I dress to please myself
My family rarely sits down to a meal together at home
I enjoy eating foreign food
I like to do a lot when I am on holiday

neither agree nor disagree/tend to disagree/ definitely disagree, with an additional 'not applicable' category. An example will demonstrate the approach. In the 1980s Levi Strauss in the USA went through a new product development programme concerning a range of up-market men's suits. The market research programme revolved around an attempt to discover 'lifestyles'. This is concerned with investigating activities, interests and opinions, sometimes referred to as AIO analysis. Such lifestyle data is then cluster analysed to produce groupings of respondents which are relatively homogeneous and at the same time hetero-geneous *between* clusters in terms of their activities, interests and opinions. Each cluster would then be allocated a somewhat glib title. In the lifestyle research programme, Levi Strauss coined the following: 'classic independent', the 'mainstream traditionalist', the 'price shopper', the 'trendy casual' and so on (BBC, 1984). This sort of profile will help determine appropriate product/service features, and will help to arrive at an advertising message which is congruent with the segment's lifestyle.

A UK lifestyle typology was named Taylor Nelson's Applied Futures (McNulty and McNulty, 1987) and identified the following segments including 'the belonger, the survivor, the experimentalist, the conspicuous consumer, the social resistor, the self-explorer and the aimless'. The self-explorer group was the fastest growing and further reinforces one of the

propositions of this chapter, namely that some markets have become more orientated to self-expression and individualism. Note that the Levi example above also identified the 'classic independent' segment.

This traditional form of lifestyle (AIO) segmentation provides useful insight into what makes people 'tick'. It is based upon trad-itional market research; administering Likert scaled statements concerned with activities, interests and opinions to a sample of consumers. The data is anonymized and the resulting profiles are very useful for determining the style and mood of promotional messages, for example.

A more recent development in lifestyle research and segmentation is the 'lifestyle survey' which is based on a somewhat different basis. These surveys are designed by companies such as NDL and CMT and these essentially ask respondents to 'tick' those responses that apply. Table 9.9 demonstrates some typical questions, some of which will be sponsored by specific companies.

Table 9.9 reflects just a portion of typical current lifestyle surveys. Many more questions are included, covering claimed buying behav-iour across many different product and service categories. Some questions will be sponsored by specific companies – for example a car insurance company might sponsor a question asking for the month in which the car insurance is renewed. Because these surveys are not anonymized, the

---

Table 9.9   Contemporary 'lifestyle' research

Please indicate your marital status
(single, married, divorced/separated, widowed)
What is your name and address?
What is your partner's full name?

Holidays:
How much are you likely to spend per person on your next main holiday
up to £500 ☐   £501–£999 ☐   £1000–1499 ☐   £1500–£2000 ☐   £2000 + ☐
In which country are you likely to take your next main holiday?
In which month are you likely to take your main holiday?

data will be filed in a database by name and address of respondent, it is likely that in the month prior to that respondent's renewal date, he or she will receive direct mailings soliciting defection to the sponsoring company.

Although the industry has claimed there is now a lifestyle census, the reality is somewhat different. Admittedly a large number of individuals (around 20 million in the UK) have responded, but the survey is by definition a self-selected sample and it is known that some respondents do not tell the whole truth in completing the questionnaire (Evans *et al.*, 1997). The difference between the more traditional form of lifestyle segmentation and the current approach is that the former builds psychographic profiles of segments from relatively small data sets and expands these to generalize patterns within the larger population. The latter, however, has the ability to list names and addresses of those who claim to be interested in specific products, brands and services and it is this, of course, that direct marketers value. It provides data on what respondents claim they buy but doesn't in itself reveal the same type of *affective* data on opinions and 'outlook on life' that can be derived from traditional AIO analysis.

Personality variables

A superficially attractive variable for segmenting markets is personality. The logic would be that we buy products and services that in some way reflect or extend our personality traits. A classic study in the US revealed Ford owners to be more independent and go-getting than their Chevrolet counterparts (Evans, 1959). Unfortunately, personality has had a mixed reception in research programmes. Even replications of this study produced conflicting results, so personality appears to be a less reliable segmentation variable than other variables.

However some personality variables do offer the marketer much scope for segmentation and these are: innovativeness, self-monitoring, and inner versus outer directedness. Self-monitoring is the degree to which persons adapt

themselves to their social environment. Persons high in self-monitoring behave chameleon-like and are always trying to make good impressions on others. It is important for them to be accepted by others. They tend to buy products and brands that contribute to making favourable impressions on their reference group. Persons low in self-monitoring behave more according their own beliefs and attitudes and are less influenced by the perceived or actual approval of their social environment.

Inner and outer directedness looks similar to self-monitoring, but is somewhat different. Inner directed people are concerned with their own thoughts and problems. Outer directed people are more social and looking for contacts with other people.

Perhaps one of the problems with personality as a segmentation variable is that an objective personality test might reveal our true personality but we might not know that this is how we are or we may not agree with it. We might want to disguise our true personality and therefore buy brands that in some way extend those traits we want to portray – and perhaps different traits at different times in different social circumstances. This leads us to a consideration of how we might *want to be* and *how we think we are*, rather than how we *actually* are, according to some externally determined tests and criteria. This is self-concept theory.

Self-concept

This variation on the personality theme in psychographic segmentation is based not on what sort of personality traits consumers possess, as identified through administering standardized personality inventory tests, but on how consumers perceive themselves.

Self-concept is indeed an alternative, worthy of consideration. It is based on the premise that we buy those brands which extend the personality characteristics that we think we possess, or that we would like to possess or that we want others to think we have. The self-concept approach is usually based on semantic

differential scales showing series of bipolar
adjectives (Table 9.10) for which respondents
may be asked to position how they see various
brands, and/or themselves and/or their ideal
self-concept. The brand preferred would then be
the one closest to (greatest degree of congruence
with) the segment's self-image or ideal self-
image. With distance scores this degree of congruence is calculated and this helps to identify
appropriate brand images to create and project.
The smaller the distance score, the greater the
degree of congruence between brand- and self-
images. Brand preferences can perhaps even be
predicted on the basis of such congruence.

The variants of 'self' are based on the actual
self and the more aspirational ideal self and also
on whether consumption is private or more conspicuous (having social connotations) (Table
9.11). Perhaps the most appropriate variants of

'self' for the respective buying contexts are the
actual self in the private context and the ideal
self in the social context.

More support for this approach comes from
a change in social attitudes. There has been a
trend toward individualism and self-expression
which could be manifested in the purchasing of
products and services which more closely
match brand image and self-image. Indeed the
manifestation is clear – there is greater pluralism
in the market today and this was predicted more
than twenty years ago (Henley Centre, 1978;
Shay, 1978).

More recently, research reported by Pub-
licis (Block, 1992) suggests that from 1973 to
1989 there had been a shift in 'motivators' from
functional and rational factors (40 to 27 per cent
of the population) and 'outer directedness' (static at 35 per cent) to more 'inner directedness' (25
to 38 per cent of the population). A specific example revolves around some group discussions
conducted for Levi Strauss in the mid 1980s and
which revealed general praise for Levi's advertising in which rock music soundtracks were
used. Many in the groups, however, expressed
their own personal music tastes to be orientated
towards different specific music styles of the
time. The result was a poster campaign that
showed twelve head shots of different young
people who clearly had different fashion tastes,
many of them music based. The copy headline
of 'we cut our jeans the way you cut your hair:
blue jeans cut twelve ways' was the result. The
manifestation of such pluralism in society can
easily be seen in shopping centres where there is
greater diversity in styling than was the case
fifteen years ago.

Could it therefore be the case that marketing might turn to self-concept research as a natural explanatory and predictive variable based
on demand side 'individualism' and supply
side 'individual targeting'?

The concept of postmodernism also
includes a greater individualism, pluralism, and
even fragmentation (van Raaij, 1993). Perhaps a
current trend which develops this theme is for
individualism to be partially replaced with

Table 9.10 Self-concept distance scores (seven-point scale)

Sophisticated   Plain

A	B	S	–	–	–	–
1	2	3	4	5	6	7

Appealing   Reserved

S	B	–	–	–	A	–
1	2	3	4	5	6	7

Daring   Cautious

–	S	B	–	–	A	–
1	2	3	4	5	6	7

Sensitive   Insensitive

A	B	–	S	–	–	–
1	2	3	4	5	6	7

S = self-image
A = brand image of A
DA = distance between S and A
B = brand image of B
DB = distance between S and B

$$DA = \sqrt{(3-1)^2 + (6-1)^2 + (6-2)^2 + (4-1)^2} = 7.3$$
$$DB = \sqrt{(3-2)^2 + (2-1)^2 + (3-2)^2 + (4-2)^2} = 2.6$$

Table 9.11 Actual and ideal self in a private and social context		
	Actual self	*Ideal self*
Private context	How I see myself now*	How I would like to see myself
Social context	How I think others see me	How I would like others to see me*

* Perhaps the most appropriate variant of 'self' for the respective buying contexts are the actual self in the private context and the ideal self in the social context.

tribalism (Patterson, 1998) which overcomes the problem of being 'isolated' through individualism but also allows individualistic behaviour amongst kindred spirits – and different forms of such affiliation in different social circumstances. Thus we still see a fragmentation of the market, in which the same individual can have multiple roles.

Geodemographics

In the UK in 1979 Richard Webber moved out of the Centre for Environmental Studies where he found that in order to understand 'catchment' areas in detail he could analyse the local census data. The study of catchment areas was useful in determining where and how to target community and social facilities. On a grander scale, he was a prime mover in the development of a system of analysing the national census data for commercial purposes. This he achieved by joining CACI (an American based marketing agency) and developing ACORN (A Classification of Residential Neighbourhoods). From the 1981 UK Census, some forty variables were cluster analysed and the emerging clusters of households led to the creation of 39 neighbourhood types.

The significance of this is that the research is based on the census, not on sample surveys. Marketers now have information on all households. Admittedly, names and addresses cannot be revealed from the census, but the statistics for enumeration districts can be. These are groupings of around 170 households. Such data can be linked with the postal code database (there is one

post code for approximately 15 households) and with the electoral register (another database) and ultimately it is possible to identify individual households within each neighbourhood cluster.

There are 'me-toos' of the original ACORN system. Richard Webber himself set up one of the newer competitors after he left CACI to join another similar agency, CCN (Consumer Credit Nottingham, but now called Experian, following the link with the American company of that name) and developed MOSAIC which analyses the census data together with credit company records and even a database on county court bad debt cases. These come under the heading of one of the more recent types of market analysis and segmentation: geodemographics. Such systems are also being used to analyse catchment areas, analogous to Webber's original local government task. The basic proposition is that 'birds of a feather flock together', making neighbourhoods relatively homogeneous. An easy criticism in riposte is that 'I am not like my neighbour'. However, geodemographics have proved to be reasonably robust overall.

Because there has been a full geodemographic analysis of the Target Group Index (this is an annual report in 34 volumes of buyer profiles in most product-markets and based on samples of over 20 000) it is easy to determine each geodemographic category's interest in the product concerned. In fact the TGI sample design is now based on geodemographic categories. In addition, the National Readership Survey is similarly analysed by geodemographics and this can provide readership profiles for media selection purposes.

In addition to geodemographics we now have something of a merger taking place, between geodemographic and psychographic databases. 'ACORN Lifestyle' includes psychographic data. In other European countries similar systems exist, for example, under the names Geo Market profile and Omnidata. Several geodemographic companies, such as MOSAIC, now operate throughout many European countries.

The 1991 Census provided updated versions of ACORN, with 54 neighbourhood types (see Table 9.12). With the expansion of databases in marketing and the linking of these, the biggest growth sector in marketing in the 1990s is in this area.

The census in 2001 may have some additional questions relevant to the direct marketer. The following is a selection being tested prior to that census (Rees, 1997):

'Are you in receipt of unpaid personal help?'
'Do you provide substantial unpaid personal help for a friend or relative with any long term illness, health problems or disability?'
'Does your household's accommodation have a garden or yard?'
'Do you consider you belong to a religious group?' (list of categories provided)
'What is your total gross income from all sources?'

These questions could provide some additional data for geodemographics/lifestyle databases; for example, income is a useful measure of potential disposable income, the possession of a garden would be of interest to garden products direct marketers, levels of personal help might be of interest to service providers and the questions about religion could be used to target individuals by church organizations – which are increasingly turning to marketing. The 1991 census included a controversial question about ethnic origin; will the questions above prove equally controversial?

It can be argued that geodemographics

Table 9.12 Updated ACORN profiles based on 1991 Census

Categories	Percent of pop.	Groups	Percent of pop.
A Thriving	19.7	1 Wealthy Achievers, Suburban Areas	15.0
		2 Affluent Greys, Rural Communities	2.3
		3 Prosperous Pensioners, Retirement Areas	2.4
B Expanding	11.6	4 Affluent Executives, Family Areas	3.8
		5 Well-Off Workers, Family Areas	7.8
C Rising	7.5	6 Affluent Urbanites, Town and City Areas	2.3
		7 Prosperous Professionals, Metropolitan Areas	2.1
		8 Better-off Executives, Inner City Areas	3.4
D Settling	24.1	9 Comfortable Middle Agers, Mature Home Owning Areas	13.4
		10 Skilled Workers, Home Owning Areas	
E Aspiring	13.7	11 New Home Owners, Mature Communities	9.7
		12 White Collar Workers, Better Off Multi-Ethnic Areas	4.0
F Striving	22.7	13 Older People, Less Prosperous Areas	3.6
		14 Council Estate Residents, High Unemployment	11.5
		16 Council Estate Residents, Greatest Hardship	2.8
		17 People in Multi-Ethnic, Low-Income Areas	2.1
Unclassified	0.5		0.5

opened the flood gates as far as more individualized targeting is concerned. Before their appearance marketers relied on demographics with perhaps the odd flirtation with psychographics, often based on sample surveys of about 1000. Geodemographics then came along with their census basis, with millions of records, and the ability to analyse such volumes of data was provided through advances in computer technology and databases.

The point being made here, though, is that markets are being analysed in ever more sophisticated and detailed ways and this is leading to the identification and targeting of smaller but better defined segments. Markets themselves are fragmenting, not least because of a trend toward individualism which in turn provides support for smaller but more individualistic or tribal segments. Technology is facilitating this segmentation through more sophisticated, but easier, analysis of marketing databases and it is also facilitating targeting, via mailings, telemarketing, cable and interactive TV and the Internet. Already traditional television advertising is losing ground to techniques that can focus attention on those who are more likely to be interested in specific products or services. It might fight back, though, because it is now possible to target an individualized TV message, analogous to personalized mailing, to a unique address via fibre optic cable (Channel 4, 1990). The move toward using transactional data and overlaying it with a variety of profiling data is moving us to another segmentation category, *biographics*. This might lead to the ultimate form of segmentation – the individual!

The ACORN profiles in Table 9.12 are not restricted to the UK; they are found around the world, so such databases are becoming much more pervasive and international in character.

Biographics

However, geodemographics are, like demographics, basically profiling characteristics – more sophisticated, but profiles nevertheless. What we have seen during the 1990s is a progression from profile data to *transactional data*. Profiling, as has been discussed, has moved through demographics, geodemographics and various forms of psychographics to the most recent version of lifestyle data, which is now being fused with geodemographics by CACI and Experian.

With reference to *transactional data*, an inspection of a resulting retail loyalty scheme database revealed, for a certain Mrs 'Brown', her address and a variety of behavioural information including: she shops once per week, usually on a Friday, has a baby (because she buys nappies), spends £90 per week on average and usually buys two bottles of gin every week (Mitchell, 1996). By knowing what individual consumers buy, the retailer might be able to target them with relevant offers whilst the consumer saves money in the process. If a 'relationship' develops, the retailer is moving from the more expensive 'acquisition' to the much cheaper 'retention' of consumers – and several writers advocate this in times of low industry growth (Rossenberg and Czepiel, 1989).

Bar codes on products can be matched with customers via credit and debit (Switch) cards. The next phase of these developments is the use of 'smart' cards on which can be stored a vast amount of information on the owner, from age and date of birth to previous purchases and even medical records. Retail checkouts will be able to read some of this information and match special offers with individual customers. For example, special offers relevant to a shopper's child's birthday can be made at the right time and the shopper's new purchases can be added to the bank of information on their previous purchases and hence the amount and quality of information grows – and so does the 'relationship' with individual customers (Foenander, 1992) and demonstrates the trend toward CUSTOM market segmentation.

Now that transactional data is at the heart of many databases, overlaid with this multitude of profile data, we are perhaps moving into the era of *biographics* (Figure 9.1) – the fusion of

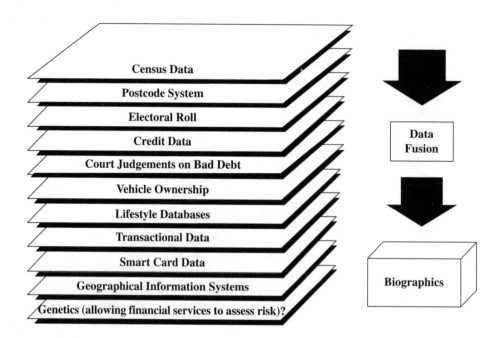

Census Data
Postcode System
Electoral Roll
Credit Data
Court Judgements on Bad Debt
Vehicle Ownership
Lifestyle Databases
Transactional Data
Smart Card Data
Geographical Information Systems
Genetics (allowing financial services to assess risk)?

Data Fusion

Biographics

Source: Evans, 1998

Figure 9.1   Layers of database marketing

profile and transaction data. Indeed, 'data matching is the key because it bridges sources' (di Talamo, 1995); the ability to match names, addresses, purchasing behaviour, and lifestyles all together onto one record allows companies to build a picture of someone's life. Database linking occurs on two levels. First, on an industry level – census data, geodemographics, and lifestyle data build up a broad picture of the population – ideal for segmentation purposes. Second, at the individual company level, matching this data to credit history, actual purchasing behaviour, media response, and the recency, frequency, and monetary (RFM) value of purchases can potentially describe one's life, hence the analogy with a *biography*.

Custom marketing

This is applied when a market is so diverse that the company attempts to satisfy each customer's unique set of needs with a separate

marketing mix. The marketing response to the increasing individualism is extreme market segmentation (or even market fragmentation as is a clear theme of this chapter), and the coverage of *biographics* is a further reflection of the trend.

Domain-specific and specific segmentation

At the beginning of this chapter a three-level distinction was made between segmentation at the general, domain-specific and specific level. We now turn to more examples of segmentation at the domain-specific and specific levels. At the domain-specific level, benefit segmentation, situation-based segmentation, problem segmentation, and person–situation segmentation are described. At the specific level, segmentation based on buying intensity and brand loyalty are discussed.

Occasions of use or for purchase

Earlier an analysis of the toothpaste market in benefit terms was provided (Table 9.1). This approach is a good example of domain-specific segmentation and is essentially user-based. A variant of this is situation-based segmentation. It has not gained much ground, mainly because of lack of empirical data or case histories on its use and effectiveness, and for confidentiality reasons (Stout *et al.*, 1977).

The development of situation-based segmentation goes back to Coca-Cola's discovery in 1973 that consumers were seeking different benefits based on different consumption occasions during the day.

Problem segmentation

Problem segmentation may be especially used in financial markets (Martin, 1988). With respect to banking, segments are identified as 'the harmonious', having no area of frustration about banks, 'the access deprived', who are annoyed by the difficulty of having their transactions processed easily and quickly, 'the personally inconvenienced', who are frustrated by the behaviour of bank staff, 'the exploited', who see banks only as using them to make as much money as possible, and 'the pragmatists', who are annoyed by the two factors that directly affect their net return from a relationship with a bank: loss of time or difficulty in accessing the bank, and financial net return. 'Problem segmentation gives a market segmentation basis which is determinant, appropriate for managerial application and is associated with adverse consumer behaviour' (Martin, 1988). These problems may be connected to specific persons, as shown by the segments above, or to specific occasions, e.g. financial problems and mortgages that are connected to buying a house.

Person–situation segmentation

Person–situation segmentation is based on the interaction of consumer characteristics, product benefits and occasions of use (Dickson, 1982). Persons with specific characteristics may want to use products with specific benefits in specific situations. Table 9.13 provides an example with respect to the suntan lotion market with four situations and four target groups. Note that person and situation benefits are critical in product differentiation in this market. In principle, four times four products may be designed. Taking skin colour and skin factors into account, even more different product formulas may be marketed.

Buying intensity – volume segments

Buying intensity is based on consumers' levels of buying activity. Often markets may be divided into heavy, medium and light users of a product or a brand. If it is about beer drinking in general, it is an example of domain-specific segmentation. If it is about a specific brand of beer, it is an example of segmentation at the specific (brand) level. For instance, the 20 per cent who are heavy beer drinkers may be buying 80 per cent of the beer of a particular brand. This is the 20/80 rule (Pareto principle) of many markets (Twedt, 1964). It is important for direct marketers to know the characteristics of the heavy and medium buyers and increasingly, through transactional data, their names and addresses are also known. They usually have been found to contribute the greatest profitability and are the segments that direct marketers want to target most.

The corollary to this – in an extreme form – is the 'sacking' of those customers who don't contribute enough! They are de-listed or effectively excluded by such techniques as requiring a certain level of their opening bank deposit if we are concerned with a banking product, for example.

Brand usage and loyalty

With regard to brand usage and loyalty, a number of segments may be distinguished: brand-loyal users, brand switchers, new users, and non-users (Floor and van Raaij, 1993).

1 Brand-loyal users

Some consumers use only one brand – this is called undivided brand loyalty. The main

Table 9.13 Person–situation segmentation

Situations	Young children	Teenagers	Adult women	Adult men	Situation benefits
Beach/boat sunbathing	Combined insect repellent		Summer perfume		Windburn protection Product can stand heat Container floats
Home-poolside sunbathing			Combined moisturiser		Large pump dispenser Won't stain wood, etc.
Sunlamp bathing			Combined moisturiser and massage oil		Designed for type of lamp Artificial tanning
Snow skiing			Winter perfume		Protection from rays Anti-freeze formula
Person benefits					
	Special protection Non-poisonous		Female perfume	Male perfume	
		Fits in jean pocket Used by opinion leaders			

Source: Dickson (1982)

marketing effort for this segment is to keep these customers loyal. This is called 'shepherd' or retention marketing.

Loyalty is more than regular purchasing. Dick and Basu (1994) in their conceptualization of the loyalty phenomenon argue that 'relative attitudes' are also important. That is, loyalty depends not only on positive attitudes toward the store or brand, but on differentiated attitudes toward the alternatives (Figure 9.2). In other words if a consumer is positive toward store A, and not very positive towards B and C, then the consumer might indeed develop loyalty toward A. On the other hand if there are fairly similar positive attitudes toward A, B and C then there is unlikely to be real loyalty. In this case the consumer might patronize a particular store regularly but due to factors such as convenience and familiarity.

This analysis is useful because it is an explanation of why apparent loyalty (at least regular patronage) might not be true loyalty.

Conversely it contributes to our understanding of why some consumers exhibit aspects of real loyalty without holding particularly strong positive attitudes toward that store. In this latter case the argument would be that a positive but weak attitude toward A might be accentuated by even weaker positive attitudes towards B and C.

Dick and Basu (1994) describe a situation in which relative attitude is low (little to choose between the alternatives) but which is also characterized by high store patronage and they describe this as 'spurious loyalty'. Where, alternatively, there is low patronage but strongly differentiated and positive attitudes toward A, this is 'latent loyalty'. Otherwise expected high patronage in this case might be inhibited by co-shoppers' preferences, for example (Figure 9.2).

When it comes to real loyalty itself, it is clear by now that they see this as where there is both high patronage and a positive attitude toward the store which is not matched by similarly positive attitudes toward alternative stores.

Repeat Patronage

		High	Low
High	Relative Attitude	Loyalty	Latent Loyalty
Low		Spurious Loyalty	No Loyalty

Source: Dick and Basu (1994)

Figure 9.2   Loyalty segments

These are potential market segments which marketers would want to progress toward the upper left quadrant.

2 Brand switchers

Some consumers may use two or more brands, depending on the situation, the price ('price-buyers') or consumers who are searching and have not yet found their preferred brand. These switches may be occasional, after which, they return to the original brand. It may also reflect divided brand loyalty, using two or more brands almost with the same frequency. Marketing efforts are directed to convert these 'partially loyal' customers to undivided loyal customers. Why these customers do not prefer the brand all the time is an area for study. It is easier to convert brand switchers to one brand than to convert consumers who are loyal to another brand.

Several reasons may exist for brand-switching behaviour. Some consumers may not yet have found their preferred brand and switch brands to try several brands before becoming loyal to one brand. Other consumers are price-buyers and buy brands that are 'on sale' (sales promotion). Still other consumers buy different brands for different occasions, e.g. one brand of beer for their own use and another brand for parties.

3 New users

Consumers who are entering the market, for instance young people starting to live on their own, or people immigrating into the country. This is an attractive target group for marketing

because these consumers might become loyal to the brand for a long period. In some countries, 'congratulation services' give free samples of different brands of products (coffee, tea, news-paper, magazine, etc.) and discounts to local stores to newly married or people who have moved to another home. These 'life transitions' of people are often accompanied with changes in brand and store loyalty.

4 Non-users

Non-users are consumers who decided not to use the product at all, for instance non-meat eaters, non-smokers or non-drinkers. These are unattractive target groups for marketers, because these people are strongly convinced not to use the product or the brand. It is even uneth-ical to try to persuade an adolescent non-smoker to start smoking.

Forward and backward segmentation

Forward segmentation may be contrasted with backward segmentation (Wind, 1978; van Raaij and Verhallen, 1994). An example of forward segmentation would be where it has been decided to segment according to the level of usage (active variable) and then to conduct research to determine the (say) demographic characteristics (passive variables) of the heavy users, light users, and so on.

Backward segmentation, however, is where segments are for instance formed on lifestyle variables or on the basis of similar attitudes, interests and opinions (active variables). Then the formed segments are described in terms of their buying behaviour (passive variable).

There may be good reasons at marketing strategy level for deciding to target medium and light users. The forward approach, although it does not sound as market orientated as backward segmentation, can be legitimized. Backward segmentation on the other hand probably, in practice, requires some predetermined hypotheses as to which base to research, so there may not be much pure backward segmentation in the real world. The risk of backward segmentation is that the segments prove not to be relevant or different in their buying behaviour after all.

In Figure 9.3, forward and backward segmentation are compared. In forward segmentation, segments are formed based on their buying behaviour. These segments are afterwards described with person variables such as attitudes, perceptions, and lifestyle. In backward segmentation the segments are formed based on person variables. Afterwards the buying behaviour of these segments is investigated.

Business-to-business market segmentation

Although the principles apply to all markets, business markets are sometimes segmented in ways somewhat peculiar to the organizational context. Business markets can be segmented with many of the same variables used in consumer research and geographical bases and several behavioural variables are often used.

Organizational characteristics are similar to consumer demographics, except that the population is composed of organizations not individuals. The marketer must identify the industry affiliation, the size of the organization, and its geographic location. For example, many organizations divide their markets geographically because their customers are often concentrated geographically.

A company sometimes segments a market on the basis of the types of organizations in the market. Different types of organizations often require different product features, distribution systems, price structures, and after-sales services. Because of these variations, a company either may concentrate on a single segment with one marketing mix or may focus on several groups with multiple mixes.

Buying procedures in various kinds of organizations may be sufficiently different that they require special marketing efforts. Marketers who sell to governments, for example, must know how to prepare proposals, bids/tenders and contracts.

Volume segmentation is also a well used segmentation base for organizational markets. The size of an organization can be an important determinant of purchasing activity. Some of the size-related variables are annual sales volume, number of employees, and number of locations. An organization's size may affect purchasing procedures and the types and quantities of products or services desired. Size can thus be an effective variable for segmenting an organizational market.

In consumer marketing, a market segment is defined as a group of consumers with homogeneous needs. In specialized industrial markets, however, this definition is often not managerially useful: situation specific variables are usually much more relevant than general customer characteristics. In industrial marketing, benefits sought depend less on the

Segmentation	Active variables	Passive variables
Forward	Buying behaviour	Person variables
Backward	Person variables	Buying behaviour

Figure 9.3   Forward and backward segmentation

internal psychology or socio-economic characteristics of the buyer and more on the external end use of the product.

Perhaps the most common way of segmenting an industrial market is, therefore, by end use. How a company uses products affects the types and amounts of the products purchased as well as the method of making the purchase. For example, computers are used for engineering purposes, for performing basic scientific research, and for business operations such as telephone service and airline reservations. A computer producer may segment the computer market by types of use because needs for computer hardware and software depend on the purpose for which the products are purchased.

Other bases used less frequently to segment markets include the personal characteristics of the decision-making units, such as the function of the buying unit, and the DMU's degree of source loyalty. For instance the organizational market can also be segmented by characteristics of the buying centre. Three characteristics of the buying centre to consider when segmenting the market are: (1) stage in the buying decision process, (2) uncertainty perceived in the buying centre, and (3) degree of buying responsibility decentralization.

The Robinson, Faris and Wind (1967) 'Buy-Grid' model of industrial buying behaviour could provide yet another segmentation framework. This is based on its two main dimensions of level of buying decision (new task, modified re-buy, straight re-buy) and stage in the buying process (identifying a buying need, evaluating suppliers, placing the order and so on) and in some ways is a model that combines dimensions already explored with respect to consumer marketing, namely, the level of buying intensity and state of readiness through other pre- and post-purchase sequential models of buying.

Planning segmentation

The market segmentation planning process can be divided into five stages:

1. The identification of active variables that might be used for segmenting markets.
2. The development of market segment profiles.
3. The organization needs to forecast the total market potential (buying behaviour) for each segment. Within this stage, an analysis of competitive forces operating within each segment should be carried out as well as the definition of the marketing mix designed to serve each market segment.
4. The application of forecasting procedures in order to calculate the company's market share for each segment. During this stage, the company should also estimate the trade-off between allocated costs and delivered benefits for each market segment.
5. The assessment of delivered benefits from each segment in relation to corporate goals, which will provide the rationale and justification for further development of each market segment. This market segmentation decision process cycle is completed when the company decides on the selection of market target segments.

The company has to decide on how many segments to cover and how to identify the best segments. There are four alternatives to cover a market:

1. Undifferentiated targeting, where the organization decides to ignore market segment differences and targets the whole market with one market offering. It focuses on what is common in the needs of consumers rather than on what is different and relies on mass distribution and mass advertising.
2. Differentiated targeting, where several segments are identified and targeted.
3. Concentrated targeting, where one segment is targeted exclusively.
4. Custom targeting, where the market is so pluralistic that each customer is targeted with a different mix and the trend toward this has been one of the main themes of this chapter.

Piercy and Morgan (1993) extend the discussion of segmentation planning by considering the more practical aspects of implementing segmentation strategies, not so much in the market place but more in an organizational context.

They reinforce the view that there isn't a single correct way of segmenting a market and extend this by proposing that choice depends heavily on what the organization is trying to achieve and on such factors as its access to – and interest in – various techniques and resources to research and implement what conventional segmentation might recommend. They point in addition to a kind of gap between the findings of segmentation research in markets and the management and implementation of segmentation strategies. With respect to applying segmentation criteria, they suggest that at an operational level the 'measurable, accessible, substantial' approach might be adopted. However, at a strategic level it might be more important to evaluate on the basis of the extent to which a segmentation approach can create and/or sustain competitive advantage, or its congruence with corporate values and culture.

Conclusions

To conclude this chapter, aspects of the planning segmentation have been discussed as have methods of segmenting consumer and business markets. The synergy between the trends towards smaller segments, individualization and custom marketing have been explored. Marketers have personal and purchase characteristics of customers in their database and are using this information for personalized propositions.

Rather than relying exclusively on generalized characteristics such as age, social grade and gender, from which buying behaviour is often inferred, the trend is away from profiling and toward using transactional data for targeting. The resulting segmentation data leads to targeting those who are known to buy in that product category on the basis of fusion between behavioural, attitudinal and profiling *biographics*.

References

Anon (1997) Taking Advantage of Children, *Sunday Times,* 28th September.

Barlow, R. (1992) Relationship Marketing – The Ultimate in Customer Services, *Retail Control,* March, 29–37.

BBC (1984) Not By Jeans Alone, Commercial Breaks.

BBC 2 (1997) The Money Programme, October.

Berthon, P., Pitt, L. and Watson, R. (1996) The World Wide Web as an Advertising Medium: Towards Understanding of Conversion Efficiency, *Journal of Advertising Research,* Jan/Feb 43–54.

Block, R. (1992) Sales talk, BBC Radio 4, January.

British Market Research Bureau (BMRB) (1988) The Target Group Index.

Carter, M. (1994) Kids Take Control of the Trolleys, *Marketing Week,* 4 November, pp. 21–22.

Channel 4 (1990) Direct Marketing, Equinox Series.

Coupland, D. (1991) *Generation X: Tales for an Accelerated Culture,* Abacus.

Cummins, B. (1994) Time Pundits, *Marketing Week,* 8 April, pp. 29–31.

Davis, H. and Rigaux, B. (1974) Perception of Marital Roles in Decision Processes, *Journal of Consumer Research,* **1,** 51–61.

di Talamo cited by Reed (1995) p. 41.

Dick, A. S. and Basu, K. (1994) Customer Loyalty: Toward an Integrated Framework, *Journal of the Academy of Marketing Science,* **22**(2), 99–113.

Dickson, P. R. (1982) Person–Situation: Segmentation's Missing Link. *Journal of Marketing,* **46**(4), 56–64.

Donovan, J. (1996) The True Price of Loyalty, *Marketing Week Customer Loyalty,* February 8th, xi–xiii.

Edmonson, R. (1993) Levi Zips into Youth Market with Hip Ads. *Marketing,* 17 June.

Engel, J. F., Fiorillo, H. F. and Cayley, M. A. (1972) *Market Segmentation: Concepts and Applications,* Holt, Rinehart & Winston, New York.

Evans, F. B. (1959) Psychological and Objective Factors in the Prediction of Brand Choice: Ford versus Chevrolet, *Journal of Business*, **32** (Oct), 340–369.

Evans, M. (1994) Domesday Marketing? *Journal of Marketing Management*, **10**(5), 409–431.

Evans, M. J. (1989) Consumer Behaviour Toward Fashion, *European Journal of Marketing*, **23**(7), 7–16.

Evans, M. J. (1998) From 1086 and 1984: Direct Marketing into the Millennium, in Special Issue of *Marketing Intelligence and Planning* on Direct Marketing, **16**(1), 56–67.

Evans, M. J., O'Malley, L., Mitchell, S. and Patterson, M. (1997) Consumer Reactions to Data-Based Supermarket Loyalty Schemes, *Journal of Database Marketing*, **4**(4), 307–320.

Floor, J. M. G. and van Raaij, W. F. (1993) Marketing–Communicatie Strategie [Marketing–Communication Strategy], Stenfert Kroese, Houten, The Netherlands.

Foenander, J. (1992) The Use of Smart Card Technology for Target Marketing in the Retail Sector, *Journal of Targeting, Measurement and Analysis for Marketing*, **1**(1), 55–60.

Forster, S. (1997) Direct Marketing in the Travel and Tourism Sector, IDM lecture, UWE, Bristol, May.

Frank, R. E., Massy, W. F. and Wind, Y. (1972) *Market Segmentation*, Prentice-Hall, Englewood Cliffs, NJ.

Gallup (1982) A Comparison Between American, European and Japanese Values. World Association for Public Opinion Research Annual Meeting, 21 May, Maryland, USA.

Haley, R. I. (1968) Benefit Segmentation: A Decision Oriented Research Tool, *Journal of Marketing*, July, 30–35.

Hamilton, R., Haworth, B. and Sadar, N. (1982) Adman and Eve. Department of Marketing, Lancaster University.

Hay, S. (1996) IDM lecture, November, UWE, Bristol.

Henley Centre for Forecasting (1978) Planning Consumer Markets and Leisure Futures.

Henley Centre for Forecasting (1992) Presentation to Market Research Society, 5th March, Bristol.

Lawson, R. W. (1988) The Family Life Cycle: A Demographic Analysis, *Journal of Marketing Management*, **4**(1), 13–32.

Market Research Society (1981) Working party report on social grade, MRS, London.

Martin, J. (1988) Problem Segmentation, *International Journal of Bank Marketing*, **4**(2), 35–57.

McNulty, C. and McNulty, R. of Taylor Nelson (1987) Applied Futures, Social Value Groups.

Mitchell, A. (1996) Interview transcribed from BBC Radio 4 'You and Yours', January.

Nairn, A. and Evans, M. J. (1998) Direct Mailshots: The Gender Effect, Academy of Marketing Conference, July, Sheffield.

O'Brien, S. and Ford, R. (1988) Can We At Last Say Goodbye to Social Class? *Journal of the Market Research Society*, **30**, 289–332.

Patterson, M. (1998) Direct Marketing in Postmodernity: Neo-Tribes and Direct Communications, *Marketing Intelligence and Planning*, **16**(1), 68–74.

Pidgeon, S. (1997) The Success and Future of Gender-Specific Fund-raising Propositions, *Journal of Not for Profit Marketing*, **2**(1), 22–34.

Piercy, N. and Morgan, N. (1993) Strategic and Operational Market Segmentation: A Managerial Analysis, *Journal of Strategic Marketing*, 123–140.

Piper, J. (1977) Britain's Ethnic Markets, *Marketing*, January, 18–21.

Porter, M. E. (1979) How Competitive Forces Shape Strategy, *Harvard Business Review*, **57**(2), 137–45.

Reed, D. (1995) Jumping on the Bandwagon, *Marketing Week*, 24 March, pp. 25–26.

Rees, P. (1997) ESRC/JISC Questionnaire to Users of Census data: Views about the 2001 Census of Population, Summer.

Research Services Ltd (1981) SAGACITY.

Ritchie, K. (1995) *Marketing to Generation X*, Lexington Books, New York.

Robinson, P., Faris, C. and Wind, Y. (1967) *Industrial Buying and Creative Marketing*, Allyn and Bacon, New York.

Rossenberg, L. J. and Czepiel (1989) A Marketing Approach for Customer Retention, *Journal of Consumer Marketing*, **1**, 45–51.

Sampson, P. (1998) Direct Marketing and the Law, in L. O'Malley, M. Patterson and M. J. Evans (eds), *Exploring Direct Marketing*, Thomson Press.

Scott, R. (1978) The Female Consumer, Associated Business Programmes, London.

Shay, P. A. (1978) Consumer Revolution is Coming, *Marketing*, September, p. 12.

Smith, W. R. (1956) Product Differentiation and Market Segmentation as Alternative Marketing Strategies. *Journal of Marketing*, **21**, July, 3–8.

Stout, R., Guk, R., Greenberg, M. and Dublow, J. (1977) Usage Incidents as a Basis for Segmentation, in Y. Wind and M. Greenberg (eds), *Moving Ahead with Attitude Research*, American Marketing Association.

Sunday Times/MORI (1992) Portrait of the Electorate, 12 April.

The Polls' http://www.mori.com/ge_1997.htrr

Twedt, D. W. (1964) How Important to Marketing Strategy is the Heavy User? *Journal of Marketing*, **28**(1), 71–2.

van Raaij, W. F. (1993) Postmodern Consumption, *Journal of Economic Psychology*, **14**, 541–563.

van Raaij, W. F. and Verhallen, T. M. M. (1994) Domain–Specific Market Segmentation, *European Journal of Marketing*, **28**(10), 49–66.

Wind, Y. (1978) Issues and Advances in Segmentation Research. *Journal of Marketing*, **42**(3), 317–337.

Women in Media (1981) Women in Advertising, WIM Video, London.

Further reading

Evans, M. J. (1994) Domesday Marketing, *Journal of Marketing Management*, **10**(5), July, 409–431. This paper discusses the trend towards identifying smaller and smaller segments and targeting consumers increasingly as individuals, based on a knowledge of individual buying and other behaviour. An analogy is made with the *Domesday Book* in that details down to household level are increasingly known and used.

Evans, M. J. (1998) From 1086 and 1984: Direct Marketing into the Millennium, *Marketing Intelligence and Planning* (Special Issue on Direct Marketing), **16**(1), 56–67. This might be subtitled 'Domesday 2' because it explores more recent developments in the synergy of segmentation data sources and extends the discussion of implications for marketing and markets of such trends.

Frank, R. E., Massey, W. F. and Wind, Y. (1972) *Market Segmentation*, Prentice-Hall, Englewood Cliffs, New Jersey. A thorough analysis of the benefits, procedures and methods of segmenting markets.

Haley, R. I. (1968) Benefit Segmentation: A Decision Oriented Research Tool, *Journal of Marketing*, July, 30–35. This is the classic paper in which benefit segmentation is clearly expounded together with useful examples of the application of the approach.

Smith, W. R. (1956) Product Differentiation and Market Segmentation as Alternative Marketing Strategies, *Journal of Marketing*, July, 3–8. Explains in simple but detailed terms how product differentiation and market segmentation differ and their relative values. The basis of segmentation thought is contained here.

Tynan, A. C. and Drayton, J. (1987) Market Segmentation, *Journal of Marketing Management*, **2**(3), 301–335. A thorough review of market segmentation. The paper also includes a comprehensive list of useful references.

Wells, W. D. (1975) Psychographics: A Critical Review, *Journal of Marketing Research*, May, 196–213. A very readable paper explaining psychographics using straightforward examples to illustrate how psychographics can be applied.

Wind, Y. (1978) Issues and Advances in Segmentation Research, *Journal of Marketing Research*, August, 317–337. Extremely useful paper on segmentation, especially in terms of the research and planning processes involved in segmentation decisions.

CHAPTER 10

The evolution and use of communication and information technology in marketing

KEITH FLETCHER

Introduction

In the 1980s a major interest of both academic writers and practitioners was the way in which information technology could be used by a firm to gain competitive advantage. A number of writers gave anecdotal evidence of major successes in this area and others suggested conceptual frameworks to help in the analysis and identification of IT opportunities. By the end of the decade it had become clear that IT was not the panacea for all ills, and that its implementation brought with it a new set of problems. While many firms have gained benefits from adopting IT, a number of writers have warned about the dangers of IT as a competitive burden if it is adopted for the wrong reasons or implemented poorly. In the 1990s concern has continued to focus on the problems involved in successfully implementing such strategies and systems, and the changing role of marketing in such IT driven companies. One feature of this changing role has been the increased focus on the communication abilities of IT, and hence the expansion of the term IT to CIT, communication and information technologies.

This chapter explains the nature of CIT and why it is of such importance. It then looks at the way the use of CIT in marketing has been evolving over the years and the new strategic dimension that the use of CIT in marketing has developed. Using a three-level analysis of industry, firm and strategy, the way in which CIT is changing exchange relationships, the nature of competition is explained, and strategic responses outlined. The nature of CIT in marketing is studied including database marketing, which is requiring a fundamental rethink of the firm's relationships with its customers, and the nature of loyalty, as firms attempt to employ relationship marketing approaches.

CIT and marketing

Communication and information technology has three main strands – computing, microelectronics and telecommunications – which are combined together to provide a wide variety of products and services. This has led to some confusion in people's minds as to exactly what information technology is. The UK Department of Industry definition is that IT is the 'acquisition, processing, storage and dissemination of vocal, pictorial, textual and numeric information by a micro-electronics based combination of computing and telecommunications'.

The recent increased emphasis on the latter element, telecommunication innovations and the growth of the World Wide Web (WWW), has led to the use of the term CIT by many commentators, to highlight this change of focus.

Information technology in the 1990s has now reached such a level of sophistication that many of the previous problems relating to the nature of marketing and the information needs of the marketing manager no longer exist. However, due to the developments in CIT it is no longer meaningful to speak of information processing and communications as independent activities. The roles of computing and communications are so entwined that their business value depends on the total system (Hammer and Mangurian, 1987). CIT thus includes computers, information networks, videotex, on-line databases and software, as well as fax machines, mobile telephones, cable television and other forms of personal and mass communication.

It has been suggested that by the end of the 1990s a corporation without a computerized database will be as anachronistic as a corporation in 1992 without computerized accounts. A marketing database will be vital to sustain a competitive advantage, and loyalty marketing and relationship marketing will be standard practices of successful companies.

Marketing has, in many ways, been the last bastion holding out against the use of CIT in its activities. While an increasing number of managers are becoming computer-literate it has become increasingly important that marketing managers are fully aware of the potential of CIT to achieve marketing objectives.

Marketing is concerned with customer relationships and CIT is having a major impact in this area by changing both the nature of the relationship and the balance of power. Porter and Millar (1985) pointed out that linkages not only connect individuals' activities inside a company, as with marketing and production, but also create interdependencies between its value chain and those of its suppliers. Increasingly, companies are forging closer links with customers and suppliers. A manufacturing company cannot move to just-in-time production without working closely with its suppliers. Electronic data interchange can facilitate these links but is driven by the core business need to integrate more closely with customers and suppliers. It has become accepted that relationships are a prerequisite to survival in today's business world, and through CIT linkages and the creation of relationships, significant competitive advantage can be created. Examples would be the growth of loyalty cards in retailing, although it is not clear whether the competitive advantage gained is sustainable, or whether the retailers involved are using the customer information strategically.

Competitive advantage can be defined as anything that favourably distinguishes your firm or its product from those of competitors in the eyes of customers or end users. These distinguishing factors can be enhanced with CIT, such as reduced cost, better service through speed of response or information provision, or simply a feeling by customers that the manufacturer understands their needs and values them, because of its flexibility and responsiveness. While the importance of getting close to customers and integrating the total marketing system has long been appreciated by marketing managers, it has only been in recent years that information technology has provided them with the means to achieve this objective. CIT allows the relationships within the marketing system to be managed to the mutual advantage of all parties.

Hammer and Mangurian (1987) suggest an impact/value framework for understanding the way in which the technology can create business opportunities. The potential impact of CIT is classified into three areas: compression of time, overcoming the restrictions of geography and the restructuring of relationships. Time compression takes place through clear communication links between sites or organizational units or between parts of the business process. Telecommunication networks allow limitations imposed by geography to be overcome as well as the organizational relationships both within the firm and between the firm and other entities. The potential business value of CIT comes not only from increased productivity through greater efficiency, but also in greater effectiveness (better management). By providing relevant information through a decision-support system then better decision making is possible.

Finally, CIT can bring about an innovation or enhancement of the quality of products and services, thereby improving the company's competitive position. The grid characterizes the business value of CIT in terms of increased operating efficiency, improved business effectiveness or a basic transformation of a firm's business functions. This is shown in Figure 10.1.

Marketing is concerned with satisfying customers' needs by providing products and services which give benefits the customers value, and CIT allows new benefits and enhanced value to be incorporated into products and services. More effective selling means capturing suppliers, agents and customers in an information net, on which they come to depend. The very goods themselves become so

intimately connected to conditions, instructions and guarantees that it is becoming hard to tell whether customers buy the product or the information layer that surrounds it.

Finally, marketing is concerned with communicating to the market through advertising media and direct marketing, and CIT is changing channels and methods available to do this. The total marketing system is thus fundamentally changing, requiring marketing managers to understand the changes that are taking place.

CIT's challenge to marketing

Marketing is facing many challenges as it enters the new millennium. Marketing's position at the interface between a firm and its markets and the changes in these markets is creating many opportunities and threats. It is an essential aspect of the marketing manager's job to monitor the environment, normally as part of the situation analysis when designing marketing strategy. Based on an understanding of these changes, many of which will have been created by CIT, a strategic position will be adopted and marketing plans modified. Increasingly this

| | Impact/value framework value | | |
	Efficiency	Effectiveness	Innovation
Time	Accelerate business process	Reduce information float	Create service excellence
Geography	Recapture scale	Ensure global management control	Penetrate new markets
Relationships	Bypass intermediaries	Replicate scarce knowledge	Build umbilical cords

Figure 10.1   Impact/value framework.

strategic position will be based on the exploitation of information and associated technology.

This challenge is not new. As early as 1984 Schultz and Dewar spoke of technologies' challenge to marketing management. First they argued that IT had created obsolescence in the traditional sales and marketing practices of firms, and that IT would fundamentally change the marketplace by changing the nature of products, the structure of markets, the nature of competition and the buying process, while also forcing a restructuring of traditional marketing and sales methods and control systems. They argued that a re-evaluation of the organization must take place, such as the power balance of departments, with manufacturing becoming of increasing importance, and the power balance with retailers and distributors (because of the linkages and bar-coding which allows retailers to track inventory via product codes and have reliable information facilitating their demands on manufacturers to an extent previously unthinkable). A reprioritization of marketing functions and lines of responsibility would therefore be necessary, leading to better integration and restructuring of activities around customers rather than products.

Second, they argue that the marketing mix must be improved by practices such as emphasizing the concept of service and the increased use of non-personal selling methods to contact each prospect individually. Schultz and Dewar conclude by saying that the solution for marketing management is clear, they must adapt and change or disappear. Traditional marketing management methods of the 1980s would be obsolete in the 1990s. Some of Schultz and Dewar's predictions can be seen to be happening, such as the growth in the use of direct marketing at the expense of traditional above-the-line activities, the increased use of electronic markets in both the business and consumer spheres, the increased attention to customer service, and the changing power balance between retailers and manufacturers, to name but a few.

Blattberg, Glazer and Little (1994) reiterate the point that the information revolution is likely to transform both the firm and the marketing function. They note the evolutionary nature of marketing and the 'age of addressability' (Blattberg and Deighton, 1991) which arrives when marketing moves from mass marketing approaches using broadcast media to reach the target audience, to a new interactive approach:

> Broadcasting targets an audience much as a battleship shells a distant island into submission: addressable media initiates conversations. The new marketing does not deal with consumers as a mass or segment, but creates individual relationships, managing markets of one addressing each in terms of its state of development. (Blattberg and Deighton, 1991, p. 5)

Similar comments have been made by other authors (Rapp and Collins, 1990; Gummesson, 1987). Gummesson claims:

> The present marketing concept, as it appears in research, textbooks and seminars, is unrealistic and needs to be replaced. One reason is its inability to absorb new developments in marketing and its rigid attachment to traditional consumer goods marketing.

This approach believes marketing should be viewed as relationship management, using interactive media, integrated into strategic planning. Such an approach, which requires a customer information file and a knowledge of database marketing techniques, should place marketing in a pivotal role. However a survey by Coopers and Lybrand (1993) identified that while marketing as a discipline was as vital as ever, marketing as a department was increasingly failing to live up to expectations. The report argues that marketing is at a crossroads and while marketing is fundamental to a firm's success, marketing departments are not carrying out their role effectively, efficiently or completely. The findings cast doubt on marketing departments' ability to meet the pressures placed on them by the information revolution. Unfortunately, if marketing departments do not evolve to manage the new 'Age of Addressability', then other functions will take over.

Evolution of CIT in marketing

The initial focus of information systems and computers was on improving the efficiency of information usage, but Ackoff (1967) spoke of misinformation systems, which provided data not information and were unrelated to decision needs. The system was designed around the technology rather than the users and the information typically had an accounting bias. Management thus had an overabundance of information, but of the wrong sort, arriving too late or buried among a mass of irrelevant data. While CIT and information systems should have been a boon to marketing managers, research evidence suggests that this was not the case (Jobber, 1977; Fletcher, 1983).

The evolution of computing and communications has led to a matching evolution in the applications to which the technology is being put. The consulting firm Price Waterhouse has noted the changing nature of benefits which users are expecting from CIT. In the mid-1980s the majority of firms were using CIT to gain cost savings and to allow them to cope with increased data. However, by the 1990s the focus had changed to using CIT in front-office applications to gain competitive advantage (Price Waterhouse, 1990). Back-office applications had been mainly involved with administration, i.e. software for high-volume routine transaction processing such as order processing, accounts, inventory control, management of information systems, etc. Front-office applications were to do with defending business position by tying in existing customers and suppliers or business improvement and the expansion of business through CIT enabled strategy product improvements, etc. (e.g. supplying parts information or ordering facilities to direct representatives, agents and customers).

It is predicted that this trend towards using CIT in a much more proactive market-orientated way will continue. It should be noted, however, that the front-office applications are usually based on long experience with back-office ones. As existing business practices have been computerized and firms have become used to the skills and processes required to run such systems they are in a position to become pro-active in their use of CIT.

It has been suggested that there are distinct stages in the growth of CIT each with its own distinctive applications and managerial problems. Gibson and Nolan (1974) initially suggested four stages of EDP growth. This was later extended to six stages by Nolan, as follows:

Stage one   –   Initiation
Stage two   –   Contagion
Stage three –   Control
Stage four   –   Integration
Stage five   –   Data administration
Stage six   –   Maturity

Nolan gave a number of criteria, which he called benchmarks, by which a firm could judge at which stage it was presently in. These related to the applications portfolio (the use to which the system was being put), the organization of the data-processing staff, the nature of planning and control activities for data processing and the level of user awareness or involvement. In the initiation phase the main objective is to establish whether computing is feasible in the organization's particular business and often these applications which are obviously candidates for automation are developed. In the contagion phase computing expands into other application areas as the organization begins to build confidence. There is a proliferation of databases and hardware. In the next phase top management is concerned about the rising expenditures on computing and growth slows as the organization formalizes planning and control. At this point a change takes place over the nature of the CIT applications. Initially, the technology was being used for tactical purposes – typically automation of existing processes or back-office applications. At about stage three a transition point is met and the orientation of management shifts from management of the computer to management of the data resources. The value of the information is recognized for strategic purposes and front-office applications are frequently developed.

The movement through these stages is one of organizational learning and thus Nolan argues that a firm must understand the implications of the different stages on its own internal organization and the applications to which it wishes to put CIT. It has been suggested that each different technology may have its own evolutionary growth curve and thus office automation would probably, for most UK firms, be at a high level whereas marketing systems for most firms will be at a low one. It is also important to understand that a large company may have divisions simultaneously at different stages. Nolan suggests how a firm can assess its present level of CIT sophistication and thus identify the necessary actions to move it to the next stage of growth. A similar audit must be done of the sophistication of the marketing and management of the firm such that CIT strategy and marketing strategy do not get out of touch. Increasingly, in recent years attention has been on how strategic information systems planning (SISP) can incorporate both business strategy and CIT strategy while recognizing the part that organizational infrastructures and processes and IS infrastructure and processes must play in supporting this overall strategic alignment process.

Each stage depicts a set of formal planning and organizational and control practices which match the abilities and experience of senior management; the awareness of users, the coverage of applications and the demands of the technology. It has been suggested that each stage lasts three to five years, but that an organization can find itself stuck in one stage, often the third stage, for seven or more years. If organizational learning underpins the curve and this learning is achieved mainly through experience, it would appear that stages cannot be missed out. The management challenge therefore is to anticipate the next stage and avoid either an excessive crisis or an undue delay in the evolution. While

the initial stage model was born of the DP area it has been shown to apply to office automation, telecommunications and end-using computing (Earl, 1989).

It has been suggested that similar phases can be applied to marketing (Shaw and Stone, 1988). In phase one the marketing databases are basic sales databases, often organized around the product. A customer might appear many times under different product categories and the databases have normally grown from accounting systems and are inadequate for marketing purposes. The marketing orientation of companies at this stage is also likely to be low and a sales or production orientation may dominate.

In phase two, sales and marketing databases are well organized but proliferate with different marketing channels using different databases. A customer focus is possible and the firm can identify the nature of the relationship with a particular customer across different products. The database can thus be analysed to help develop strategy. However, there is frequently a lack of integration of campaigns and the focus is frequently still tactical. Even at phase two, firms are learning which kind of data are important, the interrelationships of data, conflicts and stresses which must be resolved and how database marketing can be used professionally.

In phase three, one database drives all customer communication and management and thus campaigns are much more coordinated. This leads to problems of integration, and campaign management systems are required. In phase four, many functions are automated with enclosed loops, but they need each other's information for every part of their plan, execute, monitor and report cycle. Marketing strategy now combines the lifetime management of customers with the management of campaigns of particular products and services. Limited research exists in this area but there is some empirical evidence that the model can be applied equally well to marketing systems as to other functional areas (Fletcher, 1992), although there are problems in operationalizing some of the measures.

One conclusion from the evolutionary stage models is that the technology itself is of only limited importance to the firm but that the applications and the organizational structures supporting these applications are critical (Fletcher and Wright, 1995, 1997). The same technology can be used for tactical or back-office applications or for strategic and front-office applications. The competitive advantage comes not from the technology but what is done with the technology. It is not possible for an organization lacking in marketing skills to gain them from the purchase of technology. If a firm does not know how to use a business information library to conduct an environmental analysis, then providing the information on-line will not bring any advantages. If a firm does not have a customer orientation then its customer database will be little more than a mailing list. If a firm has no understanding of the strategic process and the strategic options then CIT will not be successfully used strategically. A continual process of organizational learning is therefore required as firms learn by doing. As firms become more proficient in strategic planning both of business activities and of the nature of CIT investments then an integrated approach can be taken to the use of CIT in business strategy.

Often CIT opportunities are not exploited due to non-supportive corporate environments, particularly when the benefits are qualitative or diffused through the organization as with decision-support systems. The high initial investment in hardware, software and training is beyond the reach of many companies, especially when the technology is at the leading edge and unproved.

The design of an information system for marketing managers therefore requires an analysis of the uses for which it is to be put, and the benefits that the firm hopes to acquire. To make full use of the marketing opportunities which come from the application of CIT then the focus should not simply be on the cost benefits available from greater efficiency, but on ways in which CIT can be used to give a long-term sustainable competitive advantage. This requires the marketing manager to consider the strategic role of CIT.

CIT and marketing strategy

Many firms, particularly in the USA, have realized that the investment in CIT should be seen not simply as a corporate overhead to be absorbed as part of the cost of doing business but as a competitive weapon in its own right. This requires senior managers to view CIT not as a part of the infrastructure servicing the rest of the organization to be left to computer specialists, but as a strategic resource.

A framework for studying the potential impact of CIT on a firm's business has been provided by Parsons (1983). He suggests that senior management must understand how CIT may impact upon the competitive environment and strategy of the business if they are to allocate sufficient resources to CIT. The three areas he focuses on are industry level, firm level and strategy (Table 10.1).

Industry-level impact of CIT

At the industry level, CIT changes the nature of the industry itself, shortening industry life cycles, changing the nature of the product and services, opening up new markets by erasing geographical limitations, and, with new products and services such as home banking, meeting innovative needs. By changing the economics of production, as with the newspaper industry, or the nature and efficiency of distribution, many traditional and fundamental assumptions within the industry must change. This macro-environmental view is a major part of strategic planning and in some industries such as banking is likely to highlight substantial opportunities or threats created by CIT. In some firms this has forced them to re-evaluate their mission statement or definition of their business.

Table 10.1 Parsons' IT framework	
Industry level	
IT changes on industry	Products and services
	Markets
	Production economics
Firm level	
IT affects key competitive forces	Buyers
	Suppliers
	Substitution
	New entrants
	Rivalry
Strategy level	
IT affects a firm's strategy	Low-cost leadership
	Product differentiation
	Concentration on market
	or product niche

What business are we in?

One of the essential elements of the strategic process is the answer to the question 'What business are we in?' This definition should then be used to guide the activities of the firm while making strategic choices. One of the consequences of CIT is that it encourages, and in some cases forces, a redefinition of the firm's business. As CIT allows institutions to offer new services, their traditional view of their business becomes increasingly restrictive. American Express reportedly views itself as being not in the financial services business but the information business.

American Airlines is an example of a business that has gained a major competitive advantage by selling not airline seats but information. In 1975 United Airlines offered to link travel agents directly into its Apollo booking system. American Airlines followed with SABRE, which had the added attraction of listing over 400 competitors' flights as well. As virtually all America's travel agents book through computerized reservation systems and travel agents provide the majority of the airline business, any system which attracted them would potentially benefit the operating airline. In SABRE's case the attrac-

tion for travel agents was that there was not a need to shop around for information as American Airline provided it through its alphabetical listing of airlines. The fact that American Airlines, listed as AA, came first in the list and was thus most likely to be accessed for details of seat availability was a fortunate coincidence. As competitors offered their own system the American government was forced to step in and regulate the area, banning some of the more obvious bias. In a bid to attract the travel agents the airlines improved their systems by including more information, this time on hotel reservations and car rental. The cost of these systems became a major barrier to entry as no airline could exist without access to one. Some decided it was cheaper to use SABRE than build their own, and with a charge for each booking American Airlines recognized that what has started as an aid to efficiency could become a profit centre and marketing tool in its own right. The reservation system allows airlines to recognize frequent fliers, identify traffic trends, and in minutes identify underbooked flights, allowing immediate marketing responses. The effectiveness of marketing tactics used to attract identified target segments can also be easily monitored, all at a fraction of the time and cost possible without the system.

The trend seems to be for consortia to form to develop even more advanced reservation systems, and this has increased the pressure for an international code of conduct. What is clear is that to define a business in terms of the product or basic service being sold is an error, as it restricts corporate vision.

It has been suggested (Abell, 1980) that to specify what business a firm is in, a firm must look at three important areas. First, what customer *groups* are being satisfied? Second, what customer *needs* are being satisfied? Third, what technology is being employed to satisfy the customer?

The definition of customer groups tends to be a 'what is at present' rather than a 'what might be' question. Unless the customers have unique characteristics, in terms of geography, size or other features which add to switching costs, then poaching by other firms is extremely likely.

Similarly, with customer needs, competitive advantage can be gained by identifying an unmet need or by satisfying it to a greater degree than competitors, as did American Airlines; however, these gains are often transient. In the past it has frequently been the third criterion, the differing technological base and experience of suppliers, which has allowed firms to identify their competitors and thus position themselves. The ubiquitous nature of CIT has meant that previously unrelated industries are being brought together by a common technology, making even this criterion redundant. The boundary lines between the technology of information handling and transmission, telephone, newspapers, printing, photocopying, broadcasting, are decaying as CIT develops. Facsimile machines now photocopy and transmit, telephones can be used to communicate between computers, electronic newspapers and video magazines are available, and cable networks link television sets and computers. The demarcations between the technology are therefore blurring. Information is frequently a common denominator of many industrial practices and exchanges, such that telecommunications and computers link them all. A definition of a business must therefore be based not on what the supplier thinks is being sold but on what the customer thinks is being bought.

Computer-mediated environments

Earlier sections have detailed the move from the traditional mass marketing model of passive one-to-many communication to an interactive model in computer mediated environments, receiving response and feedback, allowing one-to-one communication. A further refinement of the model has been suggested by Hoffman and Novak (1996).

The traditional mass media model (Figure 10.2(a)) is the basis for most marketing approaches where the firm is seen as transmitting content through a medium to many unrelated consumers. No interaction is assumed in this model. In the next model (Figure 10.2(b)) feedback is allowed as a form of interactivity, as with two consumers talking to each other, although Hoffman and Novak point out that the model can easily be extended to include many-to-many personal communication as with teleconferencing or on-line chat rooms. The third model (Figure 10.2(c)) changes the view of the medium as a conduit to one where consumer-to-consumer interactivity is replaced by machine-to-machine interactivity utilizing global networks. Thus many-to-many interactivity is possible. In this situation 'the primary relationship is not between the sender and the receiver, but rather with the mediated environment with which they interact' (Hoffman and Novak, 1996).

The concept of interactivity

The concept of interactivity has been seen as a key distinguishing feature of the new communications media (Peters, 1998). The ability of computer networks to enable communication from anywhere in the globe at any time removes the constraints of time and space associated with traditional marketplace exchanges. Second, the

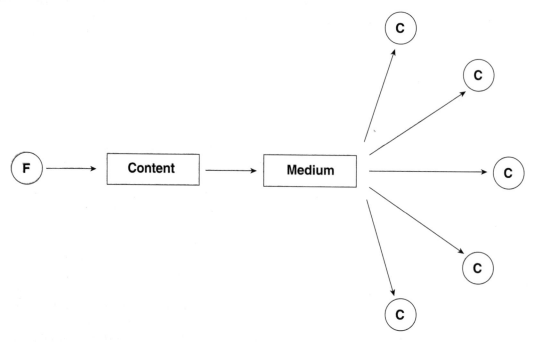

Source: Hoffman and Novak (1996)
Figure 10.2(a)   Traditional one-to-many mass marketing communication model (F = firm; C = consumer).

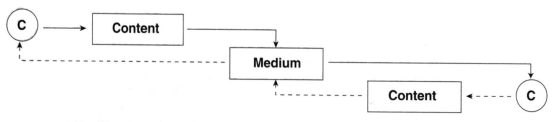

Source: Hoffman and Novak (1996)
Figure 10.2(b)   Model of interpersonal and computer-mediated communication (C = consumer).

shift from one-to-many communication models to many-to-many where communication can come from both directions results in all parties now playing a role in generating information outputs. This raises the possibility of consumer controlled, or even initiated, product design customization and information search. Consumers thus target advertisers as opposed to advertisers targeting consumers. The decision as to what content will be seen and when, and the opportunities for the manipulation of the content, are in the hands of the consumers themselves (Peters, 1998).

Characteristics of the new interactive media

Four key areas differentiating interactive media from traditional mass media are suggested by Peters: communication style, social presence, control of communication contact and control of communication content.

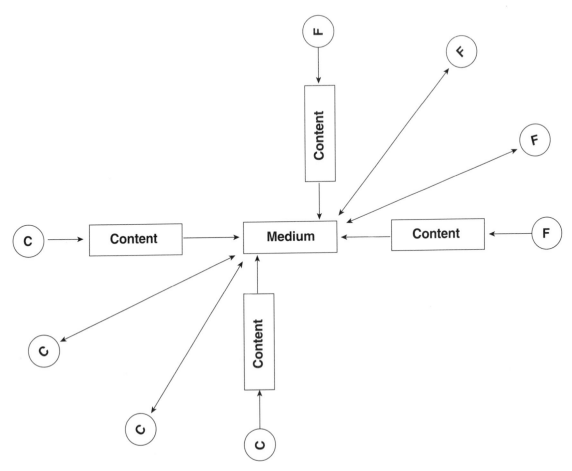

Source: Hoffman and Novak (1996)

Figure 10.2(c)   A model of marketing communications in a hypermedia CME (F = firm; C = consumer).

Communication style

Communication style refers to the temporal (or time) dimension of communications. Synchronous communication involves immediate giving, receiving or responding to information, such as in face-to-face conversation or telephone conversations. This can be compared to asynchronous communication style where a time lag operates, as with written mail, e-mail or even direct response advertising.

Social presence

Social presence is the feeling that communication exchanges are sociable, warm, personal, sensitive and active (Peters, 1998). This is affected by channel attributes which influence the perception of how 'rich' the medium is in giving immediate feedback, multiple cues, natural language and personal focus. These concepts of style and social presence can be applied to marketing media, as in Figure 10.3.

Consumer control of contact and content

The ability to control the pace and presentation of product information is a major influence on individuals' willingness to engage in computer-mediated marketing activity, and hence the user-friendly computer interface is an essential

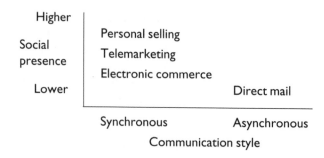

Figure 10.3   Communication media and social presence.

ingredient of computer-mediated communications. The ability of all parties to customize message content is a key element of interactivity, as compared to the traditional model where the senders alone are in control of this element. This flexibility rivals even the most responsive of the more traditional media, personal selling. These aspects of control of content and contact place differing marketing communications in different interactivity relationships, as in Figure 10.4.

One of the key features of the new electronic communication methods is the ability to control these two dimensions and it is interesting to note that direct mail, one of the cornerstones of 'one-to-one' marketing media, is at the opposite end of the spectrum to the newer electronic commerce media, such as the Web.

An important aspect of consumer experience in utilizing computer-mediated environments is the concept of flow (Hoffman and Novak, 1996). Flow can be defined as those optimal and enjoyable experiences in which we feel a sense of exhilaration, and a deep sense of enjoyment. The concept of flow is applicable to use of computer-mediated environments because of the presence of machine interactivity – the experience of interfacing with the computer environment itself. As consumers vary in their ability to achieve flow, the propensity to repeat a computer-mediated experience will vary with the degree of satisfaction with the experience. Computer-mediated environments, such as the Web, must therefore design interfaces with both functional and psychological benefits and consequences in mind, particularly in situations where repeat interactions are required, such as in electronic markets.

	Consumer control of **content**	
	Greater	Lesser
Greater *Consumer control of* **contact**	Electronic commerce	Personal selling
Lesser	Telemarketing	Direct mail

Figure 10.4   Consumer control of content and contact of different marketing communications.

Electronic markets

The potential benefits of CIT include enhanced communication, increased efficiency in decision making and better information flows. This allows the extension of markets across geographical and industrial boundaries, and improved relationships between elements of the supply chain. This can be seen in the creation of electronic markets where computer-to-computer buying and selling takes place. For computer-to-computer trading a common communications standard needs to exist, either as an industry standard or by the vendor providing the suitable software and equipment. The creation of an electronic market reduces inefficiencies and improves buyers' access to sellers, while disseminating full, accurate and immediate information. Electronic trading is now new but the most recent development is the network of computer terminals allowing large numbers of people access to remote centralized markets.

Perhaps one of the most well-known electronic markets is the buying and selling of stocks and shares. The 1987 stock market crash focused attention on the dangers of 'program trading', where individual traders program their systems to buy or sell shares automatically when prices reach predetermined levels. It was suggested that this automatic selling contributed to the crash when computers themselves created a drop in prices, by their prior decisions, resulting in further automatic sell-off. During this period of extreme volume and volatility, nine of the twelve computer systems of the New York Stock Exchange broke down at some point, adding to the panic and confusion.

CIT makes it so much easier to exchange information that it encourages the growth of geographically dispersed markets, as did its predecessors, the telegraph and telephone. For each exchange to take place a cost is incurred and the more exchanges that take place, the greater the potential for cost savings. The customer benefit comes from making more advantageous matches between buyers and sellers. CIT can help both buyer and seller to link their needs more closely. By the constant exchange of information, stocks can be reduced and delivery improved, giving benefits to both parties and improving the general efficiency of the market. Commerce based around Internet protocols is really no different from doing business by any other form. It involves showing your product to your intended customer base, receiving orders, processing them, shipping a product or service of some sort and providing some element of customer feedback in the process. Some web sites can be static if the product range does not change very much whereas others, such as Dell's Web store which generates £1.25 million of business every day, are much more complex allowing customization and tracking of orders.

Firm-level impact of CIT

The second level of Parsons' three-level impact of CIT focuses on the firm itself. Porter (1985) describes five basic competitive forces which determine a firm's profitability and the nature of competition:

1   The threat of new entrants.
2   The threat of substitute products or services.
3   The bargaining power of suppliers.
4   The bargaining power of buyers.
5   Rivalry among existing firms.

Munro and Huff (1985) have shown how CIT has the power to change these competitive forces, as in Table 10.2. This can affect relative bargaining power in negotiations over price, product and other decisions during the exchange process.

Many of the potential changes brought about by CIT require the cooperation of suppliers, buyers or the intermediaries supporting the firm's interaction with buyers, and these change the complex relationship between the participants.

Table 10.2   Porter's five forces

Force	IT potential
Buyers	Reduce buyer power by increasing switching costs to buyers, e.g. link technology systems with home banking, computer-to-computer ordering, locking-in buyers.
Suppliers	Supply chain management by retailers, and JIT manufacturing systems demand much more from suppliers and transfer costs. Suppliers of information, as with EPOS systems controlled by retailers, gain power.
Substitutes	IT creates substitutes for many products and services, as with electronic mail and hardcopy letters and communications. IT can be used to shorten NPD processes to duplicate or replace products, and by adding benefits can create unique packages.
New entrants	Existing entry barriers are often negated, new ones created, by the requirements for investment in computer and telecommunication networks.
Rivals	IT changes rivalry as in IT-based consortia (e.g. Unichem) using shared databases and ordering facilities. New rivals are created.

CIT and buyer/supplier power

The ability to identify and switch between suppliers can do much to reduce a manufacturer's costs. A few suppliers, of labour, energy, components or whatever, can force concessions from a buyer if no choice is available. Conversely, strong buyer groups can force concessions from suppliers if they are the dominant or only users of the producer's products.

There has been considerable interest shown in the changing power balance between suppliers, manufactures and retailers. Power reflects the degree to which one firm can influence the actions and decisions of another, and has been classified into reward, coercive, expert, referent and legitimate power. Its application by relationship between manufacturers, retailers and buyers has been shown by Guiltiman and Paul (1982) (see Table 10.3).

From the seller's point of view the three most important kinds of power are reward, referent and expertise. The use of coercion to force the other party to accept the exchange, as when the buyer takes the majority of a supplier's production and threatens to change supplier, is unlikely to achieve commitment or satisfaction. CIT has allowed greater rewards, or benefits, to be bundled into an offering thereby increasing

reward power. It allows access to databases and expert knowledge through information systems, thus increasing expert power. Similarly, by allowing retailers to conduct direct product profitability analysis of individual items, by the analysis of EPOS scanning data, they now have more information than manufacturers, allowing them to use coercive power in refusing shelf space, leveraging one supplier's goods against another, and insisting on just-in-time delivery and flow-through distribution.

The installation of up-to-date scanning equipment has also helped stores to improve their image of efficiency and reliability, in the same way that robotics and on-line ordering can improve the image and status of manufacturing firms. Legitimate power only plays a part when the participants of an exchange agree to a long-term relationship to justify the cost of investment.

The parties that take part in an exchange are each attempting to maximize their own utility. If a long-term orientation to the firm's activities is taken, and if future exchanges are valued, then the well-being of both parties is an essential aspect of the exchange. This mutual dependence is an essential aspect of such CIT linkages as just-in-time (JIT) manufacturing and supply chain management. JIT requires the supplier to

Table 10.3 Power bases

Power base	To a manufacturer	To a buyer or distributor
Reward	Ability to offer product with low prices, quantity discounts, or extra benefits	Ability to offer large buying volume
Coercive	Ability to withdraw product (with the loss of sales) when no comparable alternative is available to buyer	Ability to reject offer (with little or no loss of sales) when no equivalent distribution or buyers are available to sellers
Expert	Ability to offer superior or needed technical assistance	Ability to provide unique distribution support
Referent	Ability to offer prestige brand name	Ability to offer image of quality retail outlet or serve as prestige example of satisfied buyer
Legitimate	Contractual provision that requires distributor to carry full line	Contractual provision that requires seller to provide warranty repair and exclusive distribution

produce and deliver to the original equipment manufacturer (OEM) the necessary units in the correct quantities at the correct time, within agreed performance specifications every time (Hayes, 1981). Supply-chain management looks at the total supply chain, usually from the retailer's viewpoint, and integrates it using modern electronic data processing and telecommunication tools to support systems integration, functional integration and optimization of inventory and capacity utilization (Houlihan, 1982).

It has been suggested that JIT exchange relationships have the greatest degree of dependency and risk with a tangled web of relations and the need for high communication of both a formal and an informal nature (Frazier *et al.*, 1988). While JIT has received considerable attention in the purchasing, materials and logistics literature, marketing academics do not seem to have recognized the importance of JIT to them.

The introduction of JIT requires reliability from suppliers in delivering quantity and quality and this changes the mix of suppliers who can or who want to meet the standards.

Similarly, the use of single sourcing makes a manufacturer vulnerable if commitment is required, considering the added costs and skills necessary for the supplier to integrate with the manufacturer systems.

The benefits from this cooperation and commitment can be substantial, with examples being given (Stevens, 1988) of one firm achieving a reduction of inventory from 2.8 months to 1.3 months and a labour reduction of 30 per cent. Space was reduced by 5 per cent, work in progress from 21 days to 1 day and production increased by 200 per cent. Stevens gives examples of other UK firms making similar savings.

If links are made with inter-organizational information systems then other major improvements in efficiency can be made. General Motors tied its CAD/CAM and order entry systems to its suppliers' production systems. The suppliers' computers communicate directly with General Motors' robot-based assembly line in an integrated flexible manufacturing system (Cash and Konsynski, 1985). Another example is of a large retailer who has linked its materials-ordering system with the primary supplier's computer, and continually monitors the supplier's finished goods inventory, factory scheduling and commitments to ensure that sufficient inventory will be available to meet unexpected demand from the retailer (McFarlan, 1984).

Houston and Gassenheimer (1987) remind us that good marketing management emphasizes the building of long-term relationships, which results in a well-established set of expectations about the nature and outcomes of exchange. This requires a balance of the various, often conflicting, functional objectives a participating firm will have. Relationships are likely to evolve as each party to the exchange develops a dependence, and discrete transactions are transformed into more durable associations supported by shared goals, planning and commitment to the relationship (Dwyer *et al.*, 1987).

JIT and supply-chain management could not exist without improved information flow between the participants and IT has provided the technology and software to make this possible. In 1988 agreement was reached on EDIFACT (electronic data interchange for administration, commerce and transport). This created an internationally agreed common language necessary for communication. Previously a domestic common language had been agreed called TRADACOM (Trading Data Communications). This standard had been promoted by the Article Numbering Association (ANA) to improve data exchange between companies, allowing direct computer-to-computer communications between otherwise incompatible systems. It is estimated that 80 per cent of all electronic data interchange (EDI) transactions passing between British companies in 1988 were based on TRADACOM.

Competition

The remaining three competitive forces identified by Porter relate to competition and are the threat of new entrants, the threat of substitute products or services, and rivalry among existing firms. New entrants are a constant threat to existing firms as they reduce market share and, by increasing competition, often reduce profitability as they attempt to gain a foothold. In growing industries demand may increase sufficiently to accommodate the new entrants, but in a mature industry reduced market shares and sales can well result in the departure of one or more of the less efficient founder firms. Entry barriers, such as the high cost of manufacturing plant, the investment required to build distribution networks, the building of reputation or low-cost structures based on experience, all deter new entrants. CIT is changing the cost of entry, particularly manufacturing costs.

Mass production with undifferentiated products is no longer necessary to gain economies of scale. Increasing use of computer-controlled manufacturing processes means that greater production variability can be achieved with little or no sacrifice of scale economies. A standard 'core' product can be created with the customization of end products, even if they are configured from identical components. CIT has made diversity as cheap as uniformity. Similarly, a new entrant can invest in new technology, learning from the experiences of existing producers, and leapfrog them in terms of cost reduction and productivity. By the time the other firms have caught up, the new entrant may be firmly established in the market and may dominate certain key segments.

CIT also creates substitutes for many products and services. Electronic databases allow quick searching by key words and are replacing library research and consulting firms, electronic newspapers (such as the experiment by the *Birmingham Mail and Post*). Electronic journals and magazines already exist, although they have met with limited market success. CIT has mainly been used as a component of a larger product, such as with speedometers in cars and control mechanisms in washing machines, their incorporation bringing cost reductions and improved performance. In some products, such as quartz watches, the cost and performance improvements have been much more drastic, making previous products and most of the

Swiss watch industry redundant. CIT often enables a simplicity of design or construction which allows the cost savings to support aggressive pricing strategies. Alternatively, added functions or benefits can be incorporated into the product, increasing its value over competitors in the eye of the consumer.

While rivalry is an essential aspect of competition, most managers have, consciously or unconsciously, learnt acceptable and unacceptable rules of competition to ensure that profitability levels are kept adequate for all. These cosy arrangements may lead to the formation of cartels and cooperative agreements to keep out new entrants. The danger of new entrants is they may disrupt the agreements, or disturb the passive state of mind of existing firms. This negative, reactive approach ensures that potentially disruptive marketing strategies are not attempted.

CIT, by changing the market environment and creating new opportunities and threats, tends to disrupt relationships between market participants. CIT allows greater coordination and control of activities, regardless of location. The restructuring of operations is frequently possible to allow better matching of competitive strategy and market needs. As discussed earlier, suppliers, manufacturers, intermediaries and customers may find that it is worth entering into mutually beneficial agreements. Some competitors may similarly find that they can use each other's facilities, as with American Airlines' reservation system and the sharing of ATMs by banks, in a way which improves efficiency while maintaining competition. The balance between cooperation and competition can be a difficult one for firms to achieve and can encourage vertical or horizontal integration and take-overs.

Strategy-level impact of CIT

The third level suggested by Parsons relates to the effect of CIT on a firm's strategy and how it attempts to satisfy the market. Marketing emphasizes that the product bought by the consumer is not simply the tangible physical object but the totality of benefits and values which are perceived as flowing from ownership and use of the product. Thus the value of a product is derived from all aspects of the firm's operations which synthesize into the aspects visible to the consumer, summarized in the marketing mix.

Value has been defined as that amount buyers are willing to pay for a product or service, and a business is profitable when the value it creates exceeds the cost involved in performing all the firm's operations necessary to bring the product into being. Porter (1985) has popularized the idea of the value chain to illustrate how a firm creates value. He classifies the activities of a firm into the primary activities involved in the physical creation of the product (such as manufacturing, delivery, sales) and the support activities that service the primary activities and allow them to take place (general management, accounting, personnel). All these independent activities are linked in various ways and contribute to the end product as purchased by the consumer. The efficiency with which they are performed determines the cost and value created. The firm's activities are also part of a wider set of activities which together form the marketing or value system. Suppliers, intermediaries and end users have their own value chains which link together to form a channel transporting and transforming raw materials to final product and end user.

The firm, to gain competitive advantage, must look for ways of improving its own activities, or the linkages between activities, or the linkages between elements of the wider value system. Porter gives examples of how CIT is permeating the value chain at every point and transforming both the way in which value-adding activities are performed and the nature of linkages among them.

Management is being improved through information systems and various computer models which improve decision making. Computer-aided design, computerized accounting and costing procedures, electronic mail, on-line search procedures and electronic data interchange all improve the information-processing components of the support activities. The primary activities have similarly been affected by automated warehousing, automatic identification techniques, computer-aided manufacturing, automatic order processing, database and telemarketing, portable computers for sales people, computerized fault identification for after-sales service, etc.

The introduction of CIT is frequently cost-led rather than market-led, resulting in long-term strategic advantage often being lost. Wiseman and MacMillan (1984) have suggested that a 'strategic target' should be chosen on which to focus the advantage gained by CIT. Focusing on the value system, they suggest suppliers, customers or competitors. Suppliers include those who provide raw material, capital, labour and services. Customers comprise users, retailers, wholesalers and distributors. Competitors include existing rivals, potential new entrants, substitute products or any firm that the linkages in the value system mean that changes in one area will impact upon another, allowing multiple targets.

Once a target has been chosen, the strategic 'thrust' or approach must be chosen. Two major generic approaches frequently cited are differentiation and cost. CIT can reduce costs in any part of the value chain by reducing waste, improving productivity, identifying marginal customers, etc., and this is frequently the spur to CIT adoption. In following a differentiation strategy CIT is used to add unique features or benefits, or to contribute to existing aspects of the mix in a way which will set it apart from competitors. Parsons (1983) argues that firms pursuing a differentiation strategy are most successful when they establish uniqueness in several categories and gives examples of cost and differentiation strategies.

The enhanced value given to a product or service which differentiates it from competition can help to 'lock-in' customers, particularly if the 'switching-cost' is high. Once a relationship has been built up, and time, money and effort have been invested in the relationship, then the 'emotional' as well as the financial cost of change can be high. The reduction in cost in any part of the value chain may also be used 'offensively' if it allows flexibility on process structures. An example is an airline seat reservation system, where day-to-day price changes are possible as demand changes. The choice of a low-cost strategy against a differentiation strategy should be based on how well the application matches the strategic needs of the company and competitive conditions.

Wiseman (1988) points out that while a strategic thrust may initially be very successful, it often has the effect of destabilizing the entire industry. The creation of competitive advantage by the use of CIT signals a new era of megacompetition, in which competitors counterattack by adopting the technology themselves and offer similar or better benefits. Wiseman puts forward the axiom that successful strategic use of CIT spurs strategic responses. It therefore becomes important to capitalize on being first, despite the risks of so doing. In deciding on whether to launch a pre-emptive strike the response lag of competitors must be considered to determine the duration, vulnerability and value of competitive advantage derived from the thrust.

Other strategies include the firm concentrating on a market niche, distinguishing itself by unusual cost or product features. Porter calls this a focused strategy, while marketers will recognize it as a concentrated, rather than differentiated, segmentation strategy. As with the differentiated strategy, the firm must ensure that its competitive advantage is sufficiently entrenched, or the entry barriers and switching costs are sufficiently high, to ensure that other, larger, firms will not be attracted into the segment. Substitution will always be a threat to a firm following this strategy, particularly if competitors are allowed to close the competitive gap by their own investment in CIT and marketing strategies.

Innovative offerings, which better satisfy the customer, and increased cooperation between suppliers and customers, can improve efficiency and hence customer service. A focus strategy therefore uses both low cost and differentiation to satisfy a particular niche in a novel way.

Business process redesign and marketing

The 1980s saw a number of government bodies supporting and promoting the use of CIT in business, while, at the same time, academics were stressing benefits that could be gained from the use of IT, and various examples were given to highlight the advantages that some firms had gained. By the second half of the 1980s a few warning voices had been raised. Warner (1987) gives examples of the use of IT in manufacturing where IT has been used inappropriately to give competitive advantage. Warner argues that the proper role of IT in a system cannot be correctly assessed until the system has been restructured for maximum efficiency using conventional means. Information technologies should be considered only after conventional improvements and system reorganization have been exhausted, if an expensive white elephant is to be avoided. Similarly, it has been suggested that the concept of gaining competitive advantage by linking organizations with information technology has taken on an overtone of dogma in many business circles in recent years (Benjamin *et al.*, 1990).

Benjamin *et al.* argue that the reality of developing and maintaining electronic linkages between companies is not as easy or as profitable as the optimistic preaching of CIT apostles led people to believe. What was suggested as a way of gaining competitive advantage has increasingly become a necessary way of doing business. They conclude that the majority of firms are finding that EDI applications are a competitive necessity where the system had to be developed as a defensive measure to stay even with the competition, and cost savings must be derived to cover the investment. While many firms enjoy the competitive advantage from EDI, this is frequently short-lived and

where the competitive advantage is maintained this is not from the technology but by the organizational mindset that focuses on customer value and then supports a process that continually innovates and adds features valuable to the customer.

A similar point is made by Wiseman (1988). He argues that successful use of CIT for strategic purposes spurs strategic responses. The emergence of strategic CIT induced competitive advantage by one company signals a new phase in the accelerating race to exploit information technology in an industry. Wiseman states that pre-emptive strikes which attempt to capitalize on first-mover advantage can lead to great rewards but also carry great risks. Strategists need to consider both the response lag question (how long it will take rivals to respond to the strike) and the response barrier question (what factors are likely to slow or delay the response). Answers to these questions bear directly on the duration, vulnerability and value of any competitive advantage derived from the thrust.

It has also been suggested that the massive investment in computers in the USA has not brought about any overall improvement in productivity. Bowman (1986) reports on a 1986 survey in the UK which confirmed that for many manufacturing plants the perceived payoff to date from new technology seemed 'to have been low or even non-existent'. He reports that 50 per cent of the £1 billion a year spent by British firms on software is wasted because of the poor quality of the product and that 20 per cent of firms' total CIT spend was going down the drain because of such elementary failings as allocation of resources, disregarding customer service, and over-engineering or over-spending. He argues that the well-organized firm using conventional technology will have nothing to fear from the ill-organized firm which has put all its faith in super-modern technology. Ernst (1989) also states that simply automating is not enough. While adding automation to an existing business environment typically results in a marginal saving of 10–20 per cent, when improvements are made to existing business processes a company can see savings of over 70 per cent.

Business process redesign

The conclusion reached in the 1990s is that a sweeping reorganization of work itself is required to gain advantage from CIT. This is frequently called business process redesign. *Business Week* (1993) argues that it has taken companies a generation or more to truly master the new technology, having now reached the stage where they have fully incorporated information technology into various aspects of the organization. They are now ready for the real breakthrough, which is not in the technology but in the sweeping changes in management and organizational structure that are redefining how work gets done.

This process of re-engineering, a process that questions traditional assumptions and procedures, means breaking down the old functional barriers, in marketing, engineering, manufacturing and finance for instance, and redeploying workers in new multi-disciplinary ways. Once the work has been redefined the 'new' information technology then plays a key role. User-friendly software, distributed information systems, hand-held terminals all give people on the front line the knowledge they need to act quickly and effectively.

Davenport and Short (1990) also argue that business process redesign and information technology are natural partners but that the relationship has not yet been fully exploited. They define business processes as a set of logically related tasks performed to achieve a defined business outcome. The recipients of the outcomes from the business system are the customers who are either internal or external to the firm. The processes also cross organizational boundaries. Watkins (1992) has argued that business process redesign is the third stage of development of IT, the first stage being when IT was used for tactical reactive reasons similar to Stages 1–3 in the Nolan evolutionary stage.

Stage 2 he sees as IT being used for strategic purposes and IT and business strategy being integrated. The majority of companies in the UK financial services market, Watkins says, are moving slowly but surely to this stage of market-led integrated IT. While these Stage 2 developments will have a major impact on the organizations, the next stage of IT development, business process redesign, will revolutionize it.

Instead of CIT replicating and improving manual systems to make them more efficient or to deal with more complex products, business process redesign companies rethink how they can redesign their business processes using the latest technology and then decide on the best organizational structures. Since Stage 3 technology involves radical change, relatively few companies are prepared to go down this route unless they are already in crisis and require drastic restructuring. The level of integration and co-ordination required for successful business process redesign is such that unless collaborative structures and working practices are established between marketing finance, HR and CIT specialists, at least at the start of the integrated CIT phase, then business processes redesign is doomed from the outset.

It is to be expected, then, that the use of CIT in marketing and sales will follow similar patterns. Initially, one would expect simple stand-alone IT applications to proliferate such as portable computers to salespeople, software packages to help sales planning or advertising expenditure. Other software packages would be to help the strategic planning process such as basic expert systems shells or spreadsheet-based market planning aids. Such use of IT can be made with existing organizational structures and practices and can be adopted on an *ad hoc* basis. Such applications of IT will have little impact upon the basic nature of marketing or the basic functions of a marketing manager. As a firm becomes more sophisticated in its use of CIT in marketing and sales it is likely to move into the area of database marketing as suggested by Moriarty and Swartz (1989).

Moriarty and Swartz state that marketing

and sales costs average 15–35 per cent of total corporate costs and that by automating the sales and marketing functions companies can significantly increase productivity and sales. They show how systems similar to these used in office automation can be applied to what they call marketing and sales productivity systems to help the marketing and sales personnel to operate more efficiently. Also, by automating the collection and analysis of marketing information the timeliness and quality of marketing and sales executive decision making can be improved. They argue that the networks created make direct sales and direct marketing more efficient by automating highly repetitive support tasks and by reducing the time salespeople spend on non-selling tasks.

It is clear from the examples given by Moriarty and Swartz that they are speaking of a low-level database marketing system but they recognize that in successful implementations both the organization and the system itself have gone through an interactive process of change, altering the technology to fit the marketing/sales environment, then altering the environment to fit the technology. Thus database marketing can be seen simply as a way of conducting existing practices more efficiently or of redesigning the whole marketing operation using CIT as the lever.

Database marketing

The introduction of computers into selling is not a new development. Many of the problems of sales management appear well suited to quantitative and hence computer solutions. The determination of optimum size and structure of territories and sales quotas have all had computer models created. Other packages have been written to aid the selling process by developing customer targets and call norms, allocating time between customers, pre-call planning and qualifying leads. As selling has increased in sophistication it has become increasingly more marketing orientated, taking a longer-term view of profits by considering the long-term

satisfaction of customers, rather than immediate sales targets. This aim is to build long-term sales relationships, with CIT being used to develop and move the customer from lower to higher stages of the loyalty ladder (Figure 10.5).

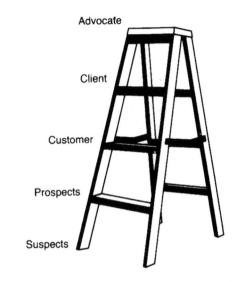

Figure 10.5   The loyalty ladder.

Different contact strategies can then be designed suitable for each stage of the ladder, which are treated as marketing objectives. Computer-generated mail-shots or direct response advertising aimed at obtaining literature requests will help to generate leads, avoiding the need for cold calling on potential prospects. A personalized follow-up letter or brochure to the prospect will help to stimulate interest and a telemarketer call can help to prepare the ground for actual contact by the more expensive salesforce. At the presentation, portable videos and other audio-visual equipment are increasingly being used, as are portable computers, which allow the salesforce to give instantaneous quotes or details on product availability.

The heart of database marketing (DBM) is that customer information file and developments in computer technology have made it possible to store an increasing amount of information on existing or potential customers. Whereas in the past the customer information file was simply a list of names and addresses, increased information on past purchasing behaviour as well as on other activities, interests and opinions allows firms to profile customers and score them in a way previously not possible or affordable.

For some firms database marketing is an evolution rather than revolution in techniques, but in marketing terms a fundamental change is taking place. Companies are centring their business around their customers rather than their products, and the customer database allows companies to communicate directly with clearly defined target segments in an interactive cost-effective manner. Database marketing is thus a new approach to marketing, being a new way of doing business and requiring a redefinition of the relationship between a company and its customers.

Confusion sometimes exists regarding database marketing as the terms 'database marketing' and 'direct marketing' are often used interchangeably by some direct marketers, yet there is an obvious difference – the database. This contains details of customers and prospects allowing accurate segmentation, profiling and scoring, perhaps along with a list of suspects (individuals in the marketplace who may later become prospects and customers). This customer database becomes the corporate resource which will drive all marketing programmes, and with sophisticated systems will integrate with the company's strategic or management information system.

The aim of such integration around the customer is to unlock the infamous 'islands of information' that exist within a company (McFarlan and McKenney, 1983), gaining competitive advantage through so doing. The customer list is thus at the heart of database marketing. Any list which is composed from an identifiable market segment has considerable sales value, but for individual companies the most effective list is that of current and recent customers (it has been shown that a past customer will be four times more likely to make a repeat purchase than a similar prospect).

Lists can be created by the company from past records or by various promotional devices, such as exhibitions, competitions, coupons or direct-response advertising. They can be also rented or bought from specialized agencies. The list is used to stimulate marketing activities and the response from these activities is fed back to improve and update the list. Database marketing is a circular activity where every reiteration improves the total value of the database. The main features of database marketing are that:

1   The results are measurable, and therefore effectiveness can be tested.
2   It is flexible in both timing and objectives and therefore controllable.
3   It is complementary to other elements of the promotional mix.
4   It is selective, assuming that a suitable list or database is available.
5   It is interactive, requiring a response from the prospect or customer.

The shift in database marketing from a broadcast or shotgun approach to directly addressing customers is a quite radical change in its consequences for marketing practice (Blattberg and Deighton, 1991). While broadcast media send communications, the addressable media used by DBM sends and receives. The aim of DBM is not to batter its distant customer into submission but to initiate a conversation with the aim of building a relationship. Database marketing does not deal with customers as a mass or as segments, but creates individual relationships, managing markets of one, addressing each customer in terms of his or her own stage of development. Blattberg and Deighton argue that the DBM will result in customers shaping the firms that serve them by their requests and Von Hippel (1982) and others have noted this trend towards the customer-active paradigm as compared to the manufacturer-active paradigm. Marketing will also be more accountable. Instead of manufacturers feeling they had to spend money on advertising but not knowing which parts of it were most effective, calculation of lifetime values of customers will mean that marketing efficiency can be measured accurately. It is also argued that the distributors' steady erosion of manufacturers' power will slow and may even reverse as manufacturers take back functions from channel members and use electronic data systems to administer them. Segmentation will also no longer become a threat to manufacturers who have been afraid of fragmentation of markets but will become an opportunity as improved marketing efficiency and innovative channels will allow segments and niches to be reached cost-effectively.

Rapp and Collins argued in the mid-1980s that a great wave of change was taking place in marketing and that much of the traditional mass-marketing approach was losing its efficiency and would be forced to give way to the new way of relating to customers as made possible by database marketing. In 1990 they continued their argument that profound changes in the marketplace are forcing the development of a whole new way of thinking about the very nature of the marketing concept. They argue (Rapp and Collins, 1990) that there has been a steady progression from mass marketing, to segmented marketing, to niche marketing, to the next step, which is being promoted by database marketing, i.e. individualized marketing. By having a database of the individual identities and marketing profiles of the customers, individual needs and interests can be served and the computer can be used to target, contact, persuade, sell and build a profitable relationship with individual prospects and customers known to the marketer. Database marketing constantly redefines the market in terms of current consumer behaviour and selects only those individuals best suited to receive the product or service message leading to the sale.

This trend towards individualized marketing is not an isolated commercial phenomenon but is part of a broad societal shift in our time. The traditional distinctions of above- and below-the-line advertising have become irrelevant and the boundaries and barriers between different functional areas of advertising, sales promotions, exhibitions and direct marketing are now redundant.

There is still a great deal of resistance to the idea of database marketing, partly through ignorance and partly through the desire of the traditional marketers to maintain their existing ways of doing things. In the same way that other functional areas resisted change and resisted the integration of technology into their function, marketing managers are showing a marked reluctance in some areas to adopt the new approach. As with other CIT-based initiatives, those firms who fully adopt the new technology are likely to achieve first-mover advantage. But equally, as with other areas of CIT, there are numerous examples of firms who have invested a great deal of money in new database marketing systems only to find that they have failed or did not bring the benefits expected. By learning from the mistakes of other CIT interventions, marketers should be able to avoid the obvious pitfalls and ensure that CIT in marketing and sales is used for sustained advantage.

Another call to replace the old marketing concept with a new approach has been made by Gummesson (1987). He argues that marketing should be seen as relationship management: creating, developing and maintaining a network in which the firm thrives, with this relationship being interactive and long term. A firm's position in the market can thus be judged by the number of customer relationships it has built. Marketing is not primarily concerned with the manipulation of the four Ps but with reaching a critical mass of relations with customers, distributors, suppliers, individuals, etc. He argues that the customer can be seen as coproducer. The interactive relationships are not only marketing interactions but are also interactions during which the service is produced. Moreover, the customer starts to consume the service during the marketing and production process. As added value is increasingly added to the product, the difference between the tangible product and the service provided, in the eyes of the customer, is likely to reduce significantly.

Another point Gummesson makes is the inter-functional dependency of different parts of the company. Marketing cannot live an isolated life, it is intertwined with all other functions of the firm. One of the pillars of the network inter-action theory is marketing's dependency on technology in R&D, purchasing and manufac-turing. As a result, the marketing function is spread throughout the firm – the marketing department sometimes becoming insignificant or even non-existent. (Porter's concept of the value chain encourages such a view, where mar-keting is simply the end product of the exchange process.) Gummesson concludes that the boundaries of marketing responsibility are devolved and are no longer identical with the marketing department. Everyone becomes what he calls a part-time marketer. A prerequis-ite for successful external marketing is the cus-tomer/supplier relationship that links everyone together inside the company with internal marketing directed towards a company's own personnel.

Business process redesign frequently takes a similar view that traditional organizational structures and barriers are irrelevant to the free flow of information and thus a new corporate ethic is required to gain maximum value from the investment. Increasingly, the view seems to be, as with TQM, that a customer must be the overriding focus which integrates all the vari-ous aspects of the firm's activities, rather than some artificial technological or organizational constraint.

Conclusion: marketing's role in the future

The new role for information systems and CIT within the organization will stimulate major changes in both formal and informal structures. There is lack of agreement as to the exact changes CIT will bring, with Gerdon (1983) arguing that many of the assumptions about the computer are wrong, particularly our percep-tions about how the computer affects the top manager's job. He suggests that although a top manager may find a personal computer interest-ing it will not alter the way he or she does the job.

Drucker (1988), on the other hand, says that the typical large business 20 years hence will have fewer than half the levels of its counterpart today and no more than a third of the managers. He argues that the typical business will be knowledge based, an organization composed largely of specialists who direct and discipline their own performance through organized feed-back from colleagues, customers and headquar-ters. The organization will thus no longer resemble the typical manufacturing company but instead will be far more likely to resemble organizations such as hospitals, universities or a symphony orchestra. Drucker blames this change on the information technology which will transform business enterprises when the organization becomes information based in the fullest sense, the organization of knowledge specialists.

Rockart and Short (1989) also point to the lack of consensus on the organizational struc-ture needed to cope with CIT but argue that the nature of competitive forces are driving the need to manage interdependence of organiza-tional subunits. The technology's major impact on the organization, they say, will lead to major changes in managerial structure, roles and process, the importance of a team of specialists as identified by Drucker, and a corporate disin-tegration with much less hierarchically based organizations. This business integration will be supported by systems and data integration, the interdependence they point out being due to the value chain approach, where every part of the organization contributes to the final customer satisfaction.

A clear conclusion from all the various writers from the different specialisms is that a new phase of business is being entered. As organ-izations reach mature stages of CIT growth then they must move into a strategic dimension. To obtain sustainable competitive advantage from their strategies they must change the way they are doing things, as in business process redesign.

Total organizational ethos is required to ensure that the interconnected parts of the organization support each other. The elimination of functional barriers brought about by the new work practices will mean that no department or section can feel separate from the market or customer. Total organizational commitment is necessary from all individuals. As the entire organization becomes aware of the contribution they make to customer satisfaction so it is likely that the marketing department itself will simply be relegated to managing the marketing mix. The more substantial elements of marketing and marketing orientation will have been adopted throughout the organization and thus incorporated into general corporate strategy. The adoption of database marketing by a firm will be necessary as the value of customers is fully appreciated. Traditional marketing practices and organization will be as redundant as the mass-selling approaches of many production-orientated firms to date.

Marketing has always claimed a unique position in the organization in that it had a boundary-spanning role. It thus claims that it is in the best position to identify changing trends in the marketplace environment and to adapt the firm to these opportunities or threats through the strategic marketing process. The boundary-spanning role also allows it to integrate the total business operation around customer needs. For many firms this role is a vain hope rather than actuality, but if marketing managers do believe that this is their function then they should plan for the integration, recognizing the redefinition of their own role and activities that this will entail.

One problem is integration, not of the technology which is a problem for the IS manager, but the integration of CIT and DBM into marketing strategy itself. Firms frequently look at CIT in a tactical sense and thus do not gain the full advantage possible. This is sometimes because the firm does not have a sufficiently well-thought-out strategy to plan for the integration of CIT or DBM. If the firm reacts on a day-to-day basis to the problems it faces in the marketplace

then it will not be able to justify or even recognize the long-term strategic advantage possible from the use of CIT. The firm must therefore be sophisticated enough in its own activities to move onto the highest scale as identified by Nolan and others.

Another of the problems for both the CIT and marketing manager is trying to work out the type, cost and frequency of information required. Unless care is taken, marketing managers will request a surfeit of information, which will take them years to consider and/or use. The ability of the new technologies to capture information creates the danger that the marketing manager will be as overwhelmed with misinformation as his or her predecessors in other functional areas. A clear marketing strategy is needed to allow the firm to recognize the relevance of the information to gaining stated objectives. The information should be stored on the database on a need-to-know basis rather than a nice-to-know one. At the same time, it should be recognized that the data must be constantly updated if they are to be of use.

The volatile and dynamic nature of the change discussed will therefore impact upon marketing in both positive and negative ways. As the nature of the competitive environment changes, and business relationships become formalized through IT links, then marketing as a function within the business system must also change. Whether this results in a diminution of marketing to managing mix elements or a new integrated role will depend very much on the reactions of marketing practitioners and academics to the challenges discussed in this chapter.

References

Abell, D. (1980) *Defining the Business: The Starting Point of Strategic Planning,* Prentice-Hall, Englewood Cliffs, NJ.

Ackoff, R. (1967) Management misinformation systems, *Management Science,* **14**(4), 147–156.

American Marketing Association (1989) *Marketing News,* **23**(9).

Benjamin, R., Delong, D. and Scott Morton, M. (1990) Electronic data interchange: how much competitive advantage? *Long Range Planning,* **23**(1), 29–40.

Blattberg, R. and Deighton, J. (1991) Interactive marketing: exploiting the age of addressibility, *Sloan Management Review,* **33**, Fall, 5–15.

Blattberg, R. C., Glazer, R. and Little, J. (1994) *The Marketing Information Revolution,* Harvard Business School Press, Boston, MA.

Bowman, W. (1986) The puny payoff from office computers, *Fortune,* 26 May, 20–24.

Brancheau, J. and Wetherbe, J. (1987) Key issues in information systems management, *MIS Quarterly,* March, 27.

Business Week (1993) The technology payoff, special report, 14 June.

Cash, J. and Konsynski, B. (1985) I.S. redraws competitive boundaries, *Harvard Business Review,* March/April, 134–142.

Caulkin, S. (1989) Crippled by computers, *Management Today,* July, 85–89.

Coopers and Lybrand (1993) *Marketing at the Cross Roads: A Survey of the Role of Marketing,* Coopers and Lybrand.

Davenport, T. and Short, J. (1990) The new industrial engineering: information technology and business process redesign, *Sloan Management Review,* **11**, Summer, 11–27.

Drucker, P. (1988) The coming of the new organization, *Harvard Business Review,* January/February, 45–53.

Dwyer, F., Schurr, P. and Oh, S. (1987) Developing buyer seller relationships, *Journal of Marketing,* **51**, April, 11–27.

Earl, M. (1989) *Management Strategies for Information Technology,* Prentice-Hall, Englewood Cliffs, NJ, pp. 29–30.

Ernst, R. (1989) Why automating isn't enough, *Journal of Business Strategy,* May/June, 38–42.

Fletcher, K. (1983) Information systems in British industry, *Management Decision,* **21**(2), 23–36.

Fletcher, K. (1992) Database marketing in the UK automotive industry: some empirical evidence, in K. Grunert and D. Fugledge

(eds), *Marketing for Europe – Marketing for the Future,* 21st Annual Conference of the European Marketing Academy, Aarhus, 26–29 May, pp. 389–408.

Fletcher, K., Buttery, A. and Deans, K. (1988) The structure and content of the marketing information system: a guide for management, *Marketing Intelligence and Planning,* **6**(4), 27–35.

Fletcher, K. and Wright, G. (1995) Organizational, strategic and technical barriers to successful implementation of database marketing, *International Journal of Information Management,* **15**(2), 115–126.

Fletcher, K. and Wright, G. (1997) The challenge of database marketing, *Journal of Database Marketing,* **5**(1), 42–52.

Frazier, G., Spekman, B. and O'Neal, C. (1988) JIT relationships in industrial markets, *Journal of Marketing,* **52**(4), 52–68.

Gerdon, J. (1983) Will the computer change the job of top management? *Sloan Management Review,* **25**(1), 57–60.

Gibson, C. and Nolan, R. (1974) Managing the four stages of the EDP growth, *Harvard Business Review,* January/February, 76–88.

Guiltiman, J. and Paul, G. (1982) *Marketing Management: Strategies and Programs,* McGraw-Hill, New York.

Gummesson, E. (1987) The new marketing – developing long-term interactive relationships, *Long Range Planning,* **20**(4), 10–20.

Hammer, M. and Mangurian, G. (1987) The changing value of communications technology, *Sloan Management Review,* **28**(2), 65–71.

Hayes, R. (1981) Why Japanese factories work, *Harvard Business Review,* **59**, July/August, 57–66.

HMSO (1988) *Vanguard: Opportunities for Education and Training to Accelerate the Update of Value-Added and Data Services in the UK,* HMSO, London.

Hoffman, D. and Novak, T. (1996) Marketing in a hypermedia computer-mediated environments, conceptual foundations, *Journal of Marketing,* **60**(3), 50–68.

Houlihan, J. (1982) Supply chain management: the modern approach of logistics, *Focus: The Journal of the Institute of Physical Distribution Management,* **1**(3), 12–16.

Houston, F. and Gassenheimer, J. (1987) Marketing and exchange, *Journal of Marketing,* **51**, October, 3–18.

Jobber, D. (1977) Marketing information systems in United States and British industry, *Management Decision,* **15**(2), 297–304.

Kemerer, C. and Sosa, G. (1988) Barriers to successful strategic information systems, *Planning Review,* **16**, September/October, 20–23.

Loeffler, L. (1988) *Marketing News,* 14 March, 8–9.

McFarlan, F. W. (1984) Information technology changes the way you compete, *Harvard Business Review,* May/June, 98–103.

McFarlan, F. and McKenney, J. (1983) *Corporate Information Systems Management: The Issues Facing Senior Executives,* Irwin.

Moriarty, R. and Swartz, G. (1989) Automation to boost sales and marketing, *Harvard Business Review,* January/February, 100–109.

Munro, M. and Huff, S. (1985) Information technology and corporate strategy, *Business Quarterly,* **50**, Summer, 18–24.

Nolan, R. (1979) Managing the crisis in data processing, *Harvard Business Review,* March/April, 115.

Oasis (1989) *A Report on the Management of Marketing Information,* Oasis and Institute of Marketing.

Parsons, G. (1983) Information technology: a new competitive weapon, *Sloan Management Review,* **25**, Fall, 3–14.

Peters, L. (1998) The new interactive media: one-to-one but who to whom? *Marketing Intelligence and Planning,* **16**(1), 22–30.

Porter, M. (1985) *Competitive Advantage,* Free Press, New York.

Porter, M. and Millar, V. (1985) How information technology gives you competitive advantage, *Harvard Business Review,* July/August, 149–160.

Price Waterhouse (1990) *Information Technology Review,* B. Martin (ed.), Price Waterhouse, London.

Rapp, S. and Collins, T. (1987) *Maxi Marketing,* McGraw-Hill, New York.

Rapp, S. and Collins, T. (1990) *The Great Marketing Turn-around,* Prentice-Hall.

Rockart, J. and Short, J. (1989) IT in the 1990s: managing organizational independence interdependence, *Sloan Management Review,* **30**, Winter, 7–17.

Schultz, D. E. and Dewar, R. D. (1984) Technological challenge to marketing management, *Business Marketing USA,* March, 30–41.

Shaw, R. and Stone, M. (1988) *Database Marketing,* Gower, Aldershot.

Spraque, R. and Watson, H. (1979) Bit by bit to decision support systems, *California Management Review,* **22**(1), 61–68.

Stevens, G. (1988) Can JIT work in the UK? *Logistics Today,* **7**(1), 6–9.

Von Hippel, E. (1982) Get new products from customers, *Harvard Business Review,* **60**, March/April, 117–122.

Warner, T. (1987) Information technology as a competitive burden, *Sloan Management Review,* Fall, 55–60.

Watkins, J. (1992) Information systems: the UK retail financial services sector in information systems for strategic advantage, in K. Fletcher (ed.), *Marketing Intelligence and Planning,* **10**(6), 13–17, MCB Publications.

Wiseman, C. (1988) Attack and counter attack: a new gain in information technology, *Planning Review,* September/October, 7–12.

Wiseman, C. and MacMillan, I. (1984) Information systems as competitive weapons, *Journal of Business Strategy,* **5**(2), 42–49.

CHAPTER 11

Developing marketing information capabilities

NIGEL F. PIERCY and MARTIN EVANS

Introduction

To readers progressing through the preceding chapters it will be clear that processes of developing and generating marketing plans and strategies are built on a foundation provided by various forms of marketing information and intelligence. Earlier chapters have illustrated much of the diversity in the sources of marketing information which confront the marketing manager and planner. For instance, the scenarios built through environmental analysis, predictions from models of buyer behaviour, outcomes suggested by management science models and computerized expert systems are a growing burden on the marketing executive, striving to make sense of a complex marketplace and to make sound decisions.

Indeed, the recent studies of market orientation as an operational measurement and management tool rest firmly on the central importance of market information – the collection and sharing of intelligence for the market to influence behaviour and decision making across the company (Kohli and Jaworski, 1990; Jaworski and Kohli, 1993). In this sense, marketing information is a critical tool in shaping the culture of an organization, developing learning capabilities (Narver and Slater, 1990;

Slater and Narver, 1995), and building real customer focus (Piercy, 1997). However, these studies underline an important point: the issue is understanding not information as such.

The critical issue addressed in this chapter is how to build a framework which provides marketing executives with a mechanism for effectively exploiting the volume and diversity of marketing information available, i.e. a framework for actively *managing* the marketing information function as a key resource to support marketing decision making. Perhaps most important, however, we will argue that while competencies in the management of marketing information are important, the most important issue is developing and sustaining an important capability – to understand and respond to fast-changing customer needs and market realities. We will introduce the tool of 'market sensing' to explain this point.

The structure of this chapter involves expanding on the issue of information management in marketing in several important ways involving the concept of information as a 'marketing asset' or resource, and one which can provide a key source of competitive and strategic advantage. With the strategic nature of the marketing information function as our point of departure, we examine the process of information systems design for marketing, together with the problems inherent in applying this process. Further insights come from examining the massive impact of new information technology on the marketing function, particularly in the development of direct marketing strategies and what these mean to customer relationships.

The underlying goal we are pursuing here is reflected aptly in a statement by Paul Allaire, then chairman of the Xerox Corporation: 'to do things differently, we must see things differently' (Adams, 1993). This is a very different and more fundamental issue than simply learning techniques of data collection and analysis. For this reason, the chapter concludes with an agenda for management use in evaluating the marketing information issue for their organizations and for developing a marketing information strategy.

Marketing as an information function

Christopher *et al.* (1980) suggested that: 'Good information is a facilitator of successful marketing and indeed, seen in this light marketing management becomes first and foremost an information processing activity.' The argument that information processing should be seen as the fifth 'P' in the marketing mix (Piercy, 1983a) is based on a view of marketing as a 'boundary-spanning' activity, i.e. acting as the interface between the core of the organization and the marketing environment (Jemison, 1984). Indeed, it has been argued that it is largely through carrying out this boundary-spanning role, i.e. absorbing environmental uncertainty and interpreting the market environment for the rest of the organization, that marketing gains influence in strategic decision making (Piercy, 1985; Lysonski, 1985). This involves, in essence, creating from the pool of information that the marketing environment represents a picture of the world which enables others in the organization to forecast, plan and make decisions. At its simplest, if the marketing department (or, it should be noted, some other subunit in the organization) does not convert the uncertainty of the marketing environment into a sales forecast, there is no basis for planning production,

personnel requirements or the financing of operations.

In this sense, the management of critical types of marketing information is at the very centre of the status of marketing management and the implementation of the marketing concept in an organization (see Chapter 21 for more coverage of the link between marketing information and the implementation of marketing strategies).

In these terms, the challenge to marketing executives is not simply to adopt the latest information technology but to actively manage the process of 'environmental enactment' (Piercy, 1992) in their organizations, in the way summarized in Figure 11.1. The practical side of this argument is that marketing information is concerned with creating a picture of the marketplace for people in the organization which they will use in making the decisions. This picture is likely to be highly imperfect, but it provides a frame of reference for decision making. In this sense there are few imperatives more urgent for marketing executives, when for most organizations so much depends on their ability to understand and respond to demands for service, quality and responsiveness to the market. We will use 'market sensing' as a route to making this theory operational.

From competence to capabilities in marketing information systems

Traditionally the information issue in marketing has been one of technique – data collection and analysis in surveys, tests and intelligence gathering. To some extent this emphasis is continued in the new technology of database management and data mining. As suggested in Figure 11.2, we see competencies in the techniques of marketing research, marketing intelligence and data mining are only a means to an end. The important end is to achieve superior market sensing, because this creates new and important marketing capabilities.

Our argument is that information in

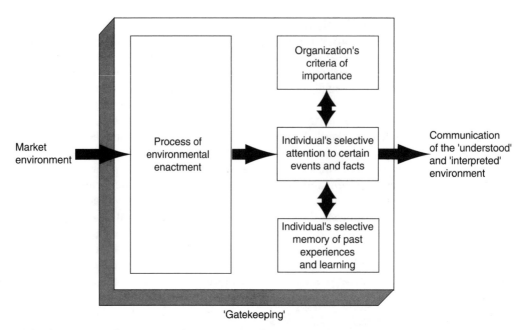

Figure 11.1   Marketing information and environmental enactment

marketing is important only when it builds such new capabilities for marketing action. Techniques of data management on their own are not the only key. The critical issue is how people in a company *understand* their customers, their competitors, and the opportunities for innovation, and how that understanding changes the way marketing is put into practice. This is the reason for emphasizing market sensing linked to capabilities, instead of simply traditional competencies in information collection and reporting.

Market sensing

Our understanding of the information issue in marketing has evolved quite dramatically in the recent past – driven in part by the new technologies and databases being created and their impact on direct marketing and relationship marketing strategies (see pp. 274). The information issue in marketing has become the area making the greatest and most significant difference to market strategies, marketing

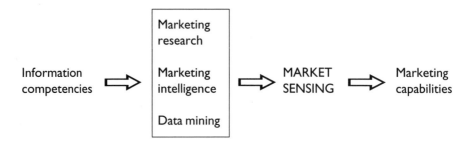

Figure 11.2   From competencies to capabilities

programmes and customer satisfaction. Information offers this leverage because it is not simply about surveys and collecting facts and figures, or building computerized databases. Marketing information is about how we understand, think about and deal with the environment, i.e. the customer, the partner and the competitor. This is why information gives leverage – if you can influence how decision makers and operational staff *think* about the marketplace, then you have a good chance of influencing what they *do*.

For this reason we start our consideration of capabilities created by marketing information by discussing *market sensing* – how those inside the company understand and react to the marketplace. To illustrate our reasoning, consider the following cases:

- *Encyclopaedia Britannica* was first published in Edinburgh more than 200 years ago. However, during the early 1990s CD-ROM technology gained acceptance in the consumer market for encyclopaedias, especially in the key US market. The management of *Encyclopaedia Britannica* did not respond to this threat, because they simply did not believe that CD-ROM technology could undermine their traditional market. By 1998, both the US and UK direct sales forces had closed, the company was an 'also-ran' in the CD-ROM encyclopaedia market, which is dominated by Microsoft's Encarta. An extreme example of faulty market sensing.

- Waterford Wedgwood plc, the Irish manufacturer of crystal and china, entered the 1990s with declining sales and growing competition from low-cost crystal makers in Eastern Europe. Against conventional advice, Waterford's management believed there was an opportunity in the market for cheaper crystal products. This was not just a 'hunch' – management's belief in the existence of price-conscious buyers who would be willing to pay a high but 'sensible' price for crystal products was tested and confirmed by focus groups conducted in three countries and 30 hours of

taped interview with consumers. Waterford designed the Marquis brand products to be different enough from traditional Waterford (in price and design) to avoid weakening the equity of the main brand, but to still gain from the Waterford brand identity. By 1994 Waterford's sales were up by around 30 per cent and share of the US premium crystal segment was up by 7 per cent to 34 per cent, based on inspired market sensing.

These examples reinforce the importance of market sensing, or market understanding by managers, as being more than merely sophisticated marketing research or technology-driven marketing information systems. An interesting observation is that *Encyclopaedia Britannica* could probably have commissioned market research in the 1980s to 'prove' that CD-ROM was a fad that would not affect the published encyclopaedia business and Waterford could have run surveys to demonstrate that a lower-priced brand would destroy the premium crystal market in the USA.

Conventional marketing research is often very limited in what it can really do. It is also badly abused in many situations, and at the heart of the problem is that we have been brought up in traditional marketing to expect far too much from marketing research:

- Companies want to know things so we ask people questions and call it market research. Why do we believe that people know, or will tell us the things we want to know? Sophisticated techniques were used to test the taste of Coca-Cola's 'new Coke' on 190 000 people prior to launch. The taste test results were positive. The product failed miserably. People do not buy the product for its taste – new Coke just was not 'cool'. Bob Worcester of the MORI research agency says: 'Ten per cent of people believe ICI makes bicycles. You show them a list of products like paints and fertilisers, throw in bicycles as a dummy, and one in ten will tick it'. Fifty years ago, a US academic surveyed Americans' attitudes towards the Metallic Metals Act – 38 per cent said it should be passed. There was no such thing as the Metallic Metals Act.

- How often is it true that market research gives us the answers we want because it studies the segment of the market that gives the 'right result'? Of course most existing customers say they are satisfied – why should they own up to being stupid and buying the wrong product: what about the customers who left or never tried us? Marketing data-bases, like those created from the retailer loyalty schemes, are powerful tools – but what about consumers who do not join the scheme, or only visit the store infrequently? Are they of no interest, because profiling them by recency, frequency and monetary value will tell you they do not matter?
- When Disney transferred its Disneyland format to Europe – EuroDisney near Paris – the company lost $921 million in the first year. The decision to enter the European market was well supported by research: figures showed the growing number of European visitors to the US theme parks. In the conventional Disney way, the location was based on modelling population figures – 17 million people live within a two-hour drive of the Paris site, and 109 million within a six-hour drive, which are much better figures than the US parks show. The figures were encouraging, but the launch of EuroDisney was an expensive lesson in the importance of market understanding, not market research. The company ignored the failure of amusement parks in France, it dismissed anti-Disney demonstrations as insignificant, and it ignored the fact the European holiday patterns are completely different from those in the USA – people in Europe have longer holidays and spend less on each. Excellent research that ignores the things that really matter (because no-one asks the right questions) reinforces company myopia and costs a lot of money to put right.
- Research can provide the perfect justification for ignoring new market opportunities. Initial

evaluations of tofu, organic tomatoes and alfalfa sprouts as food suggested they were for 'weirdos' only. Organic food is one of the fastest growing categories in the fresh food sector. Often the future is not well predicted by opinion polls – evidence the poor predictions made by most of the pollsters over the UK General Election in 1992 (MRS, 1994).

Testing information priorities

At the individual company level, when you look at the things that are studied by market analysts and researchers, published by research agencies and reported in marketing information systems, important questions are whether they are really the things that *matter* to managers in understanding the market, or the things that are always measured because they are easiest to measure.

Figure 11.3 suggests that information differs in two respects: *importance* and *urgency*. Different types of research question are then:

- *Priorities* – important and urgent questions that need speedy answers to support management decision making. Issues like quality performance and brand performance would probably fall here – they are core issues for most companies and if things go wrong they need to react.
- *Time wasters* – questions that do not really matter, they may be 'nice to know', but that is all. These are trivia.
- *Short-term dilemmas* – urgent but unimportant questions that should be resolved by a judgement call, not extensive study. Dwight Reskey of Pepsi-Co calls these 'the curse of the brand manager' – issues such as the colour of the package, the typeface for the logo, Reskey describes these as the 'tyranny of the in-box. People busy themselves with lots of tiny, immediate projects, winning momentary job satisfaction while avoiding bigger issues that are important to their business'.

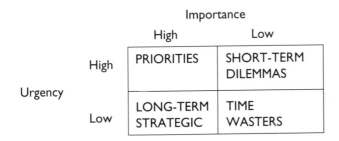

Source: Piercy (1997)

Figure 11.3   Marketing information priorities

- *Long-term strategic* – questions that may not be important to the day-to-day running of the business, but are critical to long-term direction. This might include questions like: 'Are there limits to our growth potential in this market, and what are they?'

The challenge is simply this – look at what happens in a company and see where the efforts and resources go. How much of the information collected and disseminated is truly strategic (i.e. vital to the long-term direction of the business) and how much goes on short-term dilemmas and time wasters?

Many managers will challenge these arguments – they have been trained to believe that precise information and immaculate information systems are the hallmark of professional marketing. The difference is actually very real. It is the difference between what we know and understand and what can be measured scientifically and presented to us in research reports. This leads to three points of comment about traditional marketing research and conventional information systems:

- If something is true and you know it to be true, having someone measure it and write you a report about it does not make it any more or less true – it simply stops you doing something about it, while you wait for the research to be done.
- Most conventional marketing is crude and arbitrary in the assumptions it makes – this reflects technology and budgets, not

competence – and measuring the wrong things badly is not an effective basis for making important decisions.

- The real challenge is not making marketing research and information systems more sophisticated, it is trying to ensure that the things that managers 'know' and 'understand' are the right things and they are well understood. As we will see shortly, this is actually something we can work on. It also leads to identifying the important information needs and the role that marketing research and the new technology of databases can usefully play.

Managing the market sensing process

We have said that the difference between market sensing and conventional market research or information systems is that our focus is on managers' *understanding* of the market (Piercy and Lane, 1996). Understanding is not the same as information. It is about developing new ways of looking at the outside world, to improve the way in which we develop our market strategies and deliver our marketing programmes. This is a process which we can *manage* for greater effectiveness in most companies. This is not something to be taken lightly. What we are building is a challenge to the organization's culture. The underlying problem is that marketing researchers and planners *telling* people what their problems are has proved to be an ineffective approach to winning people's commitment and achieving effective strategy implementation.

Changing the way we see things

This suggests the need for an approach to improving the understanding that managers and specialists have of their markets, which uncovers the problems to be solved and identifies the new challenges to be met, but which involves 'finding out' what matters, not just being told. In this situation the role of the marketing planner or analyst becomes one of managing the *process* of market sensing, not simply the provision of information and conclusions.

A structure for market sensing

The goal is simply to provide a structure for executives and planners to articulate what they know about changes outside the company, and to identify the most critical gaps in that knowledge (Piercy and Lane, 1996). There are two stages. First, the framework in Figure 11.4 provides a mechanism for capturing information.

The task is to brainstorm the events in the chosen part of the company's environment which might take place or which are currently developing. The most important events are listed on the form. However, the framework also requires that we identify specific effects on the company if this event takes place.

Second, the events are entered on the model in Figure 11.5 – positioned by the scores we have placed on the probability of each event occurring and the effect of the event if it does occur. The broad categories of event are categorized into:

*   *Utopia* – events with a very good effect which are very likely to occur;

Environment	Time-frame
Dimension	Market

Events	Specific impacts	Probability
		Effect
1.		
Code:		
2.		
Code:		
3.		
Code:		
4.		
Code:		
5.		
Code:		
6.		
Code:		

Source: Piercy (1997)

Figure 11.4   A framework for market sensing

- *Field of dreams* – events which are highly desirable but seem unlikely to happen the way things are at the moment;
- *Danger* – events which are very threatening to the company and which are very likely to happen;
- *Future risks* – undesirable events which seem unlikely to happen but which we may want to monitor in case they become more likely; and
- *Things to watch* – where we do not see the probability as very high and the impact is relatively neutral but where monitoring is needed in case either of these changes.

What we now have is a model of the outside world, which we can use for testing the robustness of proposed market strategies, identifying information gaps and evaluating market attractiveness. However, making this truly effective is far more about how the process of market sensing is *managed*, rather than just filling in forms and building models.

Managing market sensing

The methodology described above is very simple to implement. It is accessible and provides a structure for the information and intelligence in the company, and captures a picture of the outside world as it is currently understood in the company. This is, however,

only a starting point in achieving our goal of building and sharing real market understanding so that it impacts on strategic decisions and implementation. There are a number of key issues to be addressed in managing this process, which are summarized as a checklist in Figure 11.6. These key issues include:

- Choosing the appropriate environment to evaluate.
- Sub-dividing the environment to focus attention.
- Identifying the specific impact of environmental changes.
- Interpreting the model of the environment for strategy building.

Interpreting the model

Probably the most important issue is how we interpret the model of the environment which has been built. Here there are several questions that demand attention. Given that the model is a picture of the things happening outside which we regard as most important to the survival and prosperity of the company, then we should demand responses to the following questions:

- We have identified the changes in this market which are potentially very advantageous for our performance in this market, and which

PROBABILITY OF THE EVENT OCCURRING

	High	Medium	Low
Ideal	UTOPIA		FIELD OF DREAMS
EFFECT OF THE EVENT		THINGS TO WATCH	
Disaster	DANGER		FUTURE RISKS

Source: Piercy (1997)

Figure 11.5   A model for market sensing

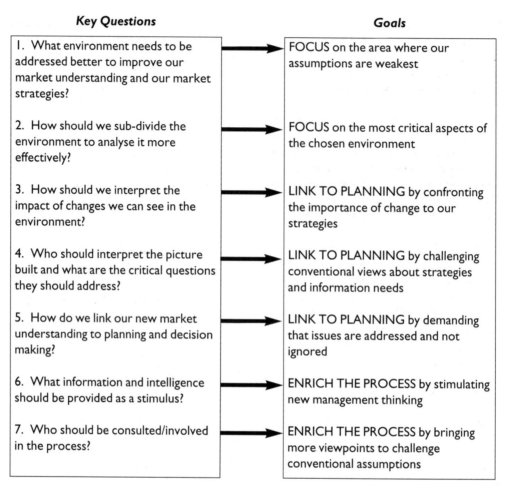

Key Questions   **Goals**

1. What environment needs to be addressed better to improve our market understanding and our market strategies? → FOCUS on the area where our assumptions are weakest

2. How should we sub-divide the environment to analyse it more effectively? → FOCUS on the most critical aspects of the chosen environment

3. How should we interpret the impact of changes we can see in the environment? → LINK TO PLANNING by confronting the importance of change to our strategies

4. Who should interpret the picture built and what are the critical questions they should address? → LINK TO PLANNING by challenging conventional views about strategies and information needs

5. How do we link our new market understanding to planning and decision making? → LINK TO PLANNING by demanding that issues are addressed and not ignored

6. What information and intelligence should be provided as a stimulus? → ENRICH THE PROCESS by stimulating new management thinking

7. Who should be consulted/involved in the process? → ENRICH THE PROCESS by bringing more viewpoints to challenge conventional assumptions

Source: Piercy (1997)

Figure 11.6   Checklist for managing market sensing

are likely to happen (Utopia in the model) – the question is: *where, explicitly and realistically, are we exploiting those factors in our market strategies?*

- We have also identified the changes in this market which are potentially major threats, and which are also likely to happen (Danger in the model) – the question is: *where, explicitly and realistically, are we defending against these changes in our market strategies?*
- If it has been done properly, the model we have produced shows the things that are most important to our position in this market – the

question is: *are we monitoring and evaluating these factors in our marketing information system?*

- Are there things we can do to *reduce the uncertainties* about important issues to improve the power of the model?
- Are there things we can do to *change* the position of important events in the model?

The approach described is accessible and easily applied, though it may achieve these characteristics at the expense of sophistication and rigour – the professional analysts and researchers can probably produce a more thorough and certainly a more sophisticated picture of the world – but then we are back where we started and it remains *their* picture of the world, not the manager's. This approach underlines the role of marketing information and intelligence as the driver of market sensing and the quest for new and superior marketing competencies.

Information as a marketing panacea?

However, before continuing to consider the actual structure of the marketing information systems and its development process, there are certain reservations to be expressed. These points are important to avoid 'overselling' the marketing information system to the manager and to maintain some practical reality in what follows.

First, it is possible to enumerate certain 'myths of marketing information' and to challenge management to remove these from their thinking about the information issue in marketing (Piercy, 1997):

- *Myth 1 – We need more information –* Why, what will it be used for, and how will this improve the effectiveness of our marketing?
- *Myth 2 – We need marketing information faster –* Why, how will this improve things?
- *Myth 3 – If we try hard enough, we can know everything –* This is always an illusion; the most important things are usually the ones we cannot know for certain.
- *Myth 4 – We know what marketing information we want –* The evidence suggests otherwise.
- *Myth 5 – We know why we want the information –* Generally, our understanding of how managers use information is very limited.
- *Myth 6 – We know what we don't need to know –* Not until we have a good handle on what we do need to know; return to Myth 4.
- *Myth 7 – We measure what matters –* Usually well worth testing very thoroughly.
- *Myth 8 – We know what we know –* How often is information collected wastefully because we did not audit what we already had?

- *Myth 9 – We know who decides what we know –* Are we sure (see below)?

These points may seem cynical, but each 'myth' is associated with a serious problem we face in managing the information issue in marketing if we are to get beyond the most superficial levels.

Second, it must be noted that information management requires resources – financial, physical, managerial and human. Without adequate resourcing and the commitment of appropriate managerial effort, no development process is likely to succeed – token efforts will produce token results. In short, there is a cost involved which may be substantial, although it should clearly be balanced against the value of what it is hoped to achieve. It is hoped that what follows will provide a basis for realistically assessing that value.

Third, for reasons which will be expanded shortly, there is typically no clear and obvious relationship between the development of the marketing information function and commercial success – a point which has been reiterated by many writers over the years (e.g. Jeuck, 1953; Davidson, 1975; May, 1981). To look for immediate 'bottom-line' impact is to take a simplistic view of how marketing information is used, and to assume that an activity like market research *makes* decisions rather than simply supports the decision-making process.

This leads to a fourth, but related, point: that the impact of information on decision making is complex and frequently covert. In fact, our understanding of managerial decision making remains limited, although it is apparent in reality (rather than the simple 'go/no-go' model assumed by the management scientist) that marketing information is sought for reasons other than making simple choices between known options using explicit criteria. It has been suggested, for instance, that in reality:

- Managers seek information to justify what has already been decided (Cyert *et al.*, 1956).
- Marketing information may be used as a

weapon to make salespeople 'properly optimistic' (Hardin, 1969).

• Managers may use information as a way of delaying decisions rather than making them (Samuels, 1973).

• Marketing information may serve an 'organizational' function, for example providing common ground or a shared frame of reference, acting as a collective memory, functioning as a stabilizing factor, or even just providing reassurance.

Indeed, one writer suggests:

There are many uses of research which are often dismissed as purely irrational without further thought. They can, however, be seen to stem from the needs of organizations as such, and the really rational approach would align them as legitimate functions which need not be ignored or swept under the carpet. (Channon, 1968)

Not unrelated to this complexity and covertness in the organizational role of marketing information is a fifth point: that information systems development has led on occasion to 'management suspicion and disappointment' (Holtgrefe, 1986). Indeed, one symptom of the information systems that embodies unrealistic management expectations is that it is simply not used by managers themselves.

In fact, a sixth point should be made: if handled badly, developing a marketing information system may actually damage the existing decision-making processes. One paper attempts to identify these adverse 'hidden side-effects' (Haskins and Nanni, 1986). This suggests that:

1   The information system is a constrained set of data, with the result that managers may build a false picture of the world if they use only that constrained data set, so decisions are made with unnecessarily limited information – which is probably the same information set used in earlier decisions.

2   The information in the system is likely to represent the systems designer's view and

understanding of the world rather than the manager's.

3   While the data in the system may be frequently changed, the structure or frame of reference of the system is more likely to remain static, neglecting the fact that as the world changes so should the configuration of data represented by the information system (Haskins and Nanni, 1986).

Relationship marketing and the information revolution in marketing

It can be argued that technological developments in the collection and use of marketing information have led to a change in the marketing paradigm itself away from transactional marketing and toward relationship marketing (Evans, 1998). This is concerned with all activities directed towards attracting, developing and retaining customer relationships.

Gronroos (1990) indicates that there are a number of strategies open to marketers, along what he calls the 'marketing strategy continuum'. At its extreme, *transactional* exchange involves single, short-term exchange events encompassing a distinct beginning and ending. Consumer goods firms with mass markets and little contact with their ultimate customers are most likely to place themselves at this end of the continuum. On the other hand, *relational* exchange involves transactions linked together over an extended time frame. These exchanges trace back to previous interactions and reflect an ongoing process. Gronroos suggests that most consumer goods companies are more likely to be on the transaction end. Despite this, there have been many attempts to apply relationship marketing concepts to consumer markets. The main elements come from research in industrial marketing which indicate that relationships are complex, long term in nature, and mutually beneficial. The new methods of obtaining and using market information in the 1990s have been a major catalyst in encouraging organizations to move toward this paradigm and have made many of our traditional beliefs about marketing information systems obsolete.

It is the *marketing database* which is at the heart of this and whereas it can merely be used as a list from which to target customers via direct marketing activity, it can, alternatively, potentially provide a wealth of information on the market and on customers within it. In this context, the database provides information for both planning and analysis purposes: the database can be analysed for the most attractive segments, for campaign planning and predicting campaign response. Strategically, the database can be used for (Fletcher *et al.*, 1990):

- changing the basis of competition,
- strengthening customer relationships,
- overcoming supplier problems,
- building barriers against new entrants,
- generating new products.

Shaw and Stone (1988) take this further by proposing a four-stage process of development of the marketing database. In *phase one* they suggest the database is merely a sales database originating from accounting systems and focusing more on product sales rather than customers. The *second phase* is where there are often multiple databases for different sales territories or retailers and although they can be well used within the sector they cover, there can often be overlapping effort due to lack of communication and coordination – customers might receive direct mailings from the same company, but different and even conflicting ones from different parts of that company! This is a real problem of lack of integration as well as no strategic use of the database and we submit that this is actually quite widespread – organizational structures often mean that direct mar- keting is a separate function from sales, PR and so on and that each tries to maintain its own integrity by keeping vital information (even customer lists) to themselves.

Phase three sees more of a customer focus and one database coordinates all communication with customers. Analysis is according to

profiles, transactions and other relevant factors in order to determine how to target segments and individuals. In *phase four*, there is true integration, when different organizational functions, not just marketing, are linked with the marketing database.

In parallel with this analysis, Parkinson (1994) identifies three levels of IT application within marketing. The first is concerned with the management of transactions, the second is concerned with profiling, targeting and developing effective direct marketing and the third level is concerned with marketing productivity analysis, modelling (discussed later) and their link with strategic planning.

If the organization is not truly customer orientated (a theme of this chapter) then there will only be a tactical role for the marketing database, but if used strategically, then it has a central role to play – as DeTienne and Thompson (1996) imply in their definition of database marketing:

Database marketing is the process of systematically collecting, in electronic or optical form, data about past, current and/or potential customers, maintaining the integrity of the data by continually monitoring customer purchases and/or by inquiring about changing status and using the data to formulate marketing strategy and foster personalized relationships with customers.

We discuss the trend toward relationship marketing shortly.

On the other hand, if used merely tactically, the nature of the marketing database does not need to refer greatly to corporate strategy or organizational structure (Cook, 1994). Under such circumstances it is more concerned with 'the next event' than with a longer term view of customers. Bigg (1994) and Cook (1994) suggest that it is actually more usual for organizations to employ the database at the tactical rather than at the strategic level.

The 'customer database is an opportunity for organizations to mechanize the process of learning about customers' and this needs to be iterative because 'the database transcends the status of a record keeping device and becomes an implement of ever-increasing organization knowledge' (DeTienne and Thompson, 1996). In this sense the marketing database can focus on a whole range of different categories – for example, new prospects, best prospects, loyals and so on – and essentially, these can be boiled down into acquisition or retention strategies.

Retailers, for example, are capturing transactional data at point of sale via loyalty card schemes – for example, Tesco, Safeway and Sainsbury. By mid 1998 Tesco had analysed their customer database and identified 60 000 different segments – each of which was targeted differently (Anon., 1998). The aim is one-to-one targeting. The company analysing the Tesco data is DunnHumby, and Clive Humby (1996) describes the interrogation of data and states that it is not worth including 'everything'. There is always the danger of 'paralysis by analysis'! Humby goes on to suggest that 'it is not the detailed transaction data that is of interest, but patterns in transactions, such as an increasing balance over time of the range of products pur-

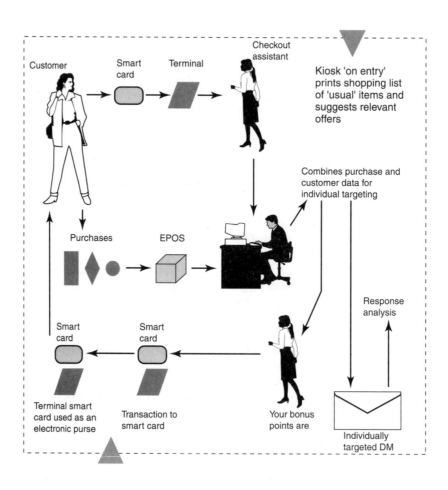

Figure 11.7 Barcodes, scanners and databases

chased' (Humby, 1996). Figure 11.7 shows how transactional data can be captured and used. It is even possible for customers to be given personalized shopping lists (based on their purchasing history) and relevant 'offers' from kiosks as they enter the store!

One point we would make, however, is that the attraction of the database, with its transactional data overlaid with demographic, psychographic and geodemographic data (leading to the creation of the new biographics), might sometimes be seen to negate the need for more traditional market research. Database data clearly can provide valuable information on who is buying what, when, how and where, but it is market research that can get beneath the surface even further and discover reasons 'why' behaviour is as it is – given, that is, the reservations made earlier about traditional market research! This is expanded upon in the later section on 'market research'.

A related issue is raised by Fletcher and Peters (1996) with respect to the use of market research data to populate databases for personalized selling. The main problem is one of using marketing research data for selling purposes (selling under the guise of research: 'sugging'). Direct marketing needs to be able to identify individuals and even if they do not use the personal details for immediate selling, they are keen to develop databases of personal information – 'dugging' (data under the guise of research). The Market Research Society has long outlawed this practice but has now compromised over the issue by having dual codes of conduct for the two 'reasons' for data collection. These issues are well explored by Fletcher and Peters (1996) and their research revealed practitioners to be reasonably comfortable with the situation. Researchers and sellers were keen to make it clear to their informants of the purpose to which personal details might be put. However Fletcher and Peters show that privacy issues are highly relevant here and have not been resolved.

As it stands at present, however, the MRS Code (1997) overcomes the conflict with the phrase:

members shall only use the term *confidential survey research* to describe projects which are based upon respondent anonymity and do not involve the divulgence of names or personal details of informants to others except for research purposes.

The new code excludes, from its 'confidential research' principles, the collecting of personal data for sales or promotional approaches to the informant and for the compilation of databases which will be used for canvassing and fund-raising. In such circumstances the data collector should not claim to be involved in a confidential survey and should make this clear to the informant.

In a variety of empirical research studies (Evans, 1996; O'Malley 1996; Patterson *et al.*, 1997) consumers have expressed concerns over the lack of privacy of their personal details – '1984' it may not be, but the privacy issue arising from the collection and use of ever more personalized information clearly needs constant vigilance and this will be an issue for the future as well as for the present.

A development process for the marketing information system

The goal of superior market understanding and enhanced marketing capabilities, in the context of a profound information revolution, provides a new foundation for understanding the information issue in marketing. However, it is also valuable to examine conventional models of information systems, to provide a structure for managing the information assets inside a company that stimulate our market sensing.

Framing the marketing information system

Views of what the marketing information system should be are highly varied, although the structure in Figure 11.8 provides a conventional view of the components of a marketing information system. This model allows us to enumerate the characteristics which have been associated with the marketing information system:

- It stores and integrates information on marketing issues from many sources.
- It provides for the dissemination of such information to decision makers and other users.
- It supports marketing decision making in both planning and control.
- It is likely to be computerized and to use electronic communication channels.
- It is not just a new name for market research!

This model has been used widely to study company practices and it identifies four components of a marketing information system, mainly in terms of the source and type of information concerned.

Marketing productivity analysis is concerned with using the information already available in the financial and administrative systems, such as cost and sales data. This is the first stage at which it may be possible to evaluate the relationship between marketing inputs (sales time,

management effort, promotion and advertising expenditure, etc.) and the outputs generated (orders received, sales revenue, etc.). Until relatively recently the comparison of inputs and outputs on this basis was unnecessarily crude, but it was frequently highly seductive and full of useful insights if used carefully. The techniques available included: expense and effort to sales ratios (Wilson, 1981); creative sales analysis (e.g. business gains as compared to business losses to diagnose marginal sales trends; Piercy, 1978); and the development of marketing cost accounting reporting, which links costs and returns to given marketing entities (Barrett, 1986). Indeed, one analyst (Simmonds, 1986) has attempted to provide a framework for using accounting tools to measure competitive position. This framework takes basic accounting indicators such as sales, cash flow, and so on, and derives a series of indicators of competitive position which can be interpreted to evaluate the impact of marketing strategies on relative market position in financial terms. These data sources and the analyses they are capable of producing are available in even the most rudimentary marketing information system.

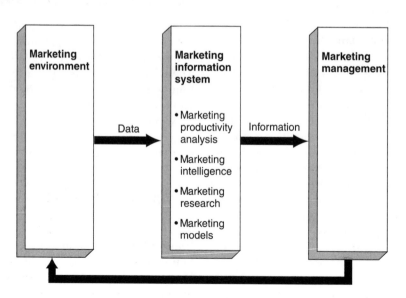

Figure 11.8   Structure of the marketing information system

Now, however, the trend toward marketing 'direct' enables greater use of *productivity analysis* because response rates can be more easily identified and attributed. Much of this has come about due to the impact of IT on marketing, notably the database. Examples include customer records, results from sales promotion campaigns (coupons, competitions, etc.) and from *transactional* data – the latter being one of the major growth areas for contemporary marketing.

Such data can also be used to 'score' customers – another emerging measure of *marketing productivity*. Most items of data are scorable – for example, we might know from previous campaigns that we have had a greater success rate when marketing to those with the 'Mr' title rather than Mrs or Ms, in which case we can give a quantitative weight to 'title'. Postcode is especially revealing because we can profile geo-demographically from this and again compare with previous success/failure rates to score the geodemographic cluster and the postcode itself, at different levels – for example, do we have more success in Cardiff (CF) or Bristol (BS)? This is an example of scoring from two of the most basic elements of data. By adding lifestyle and transactional data and scoring all those in the database on a weighted index which incorporates all of these variables, very useful league tables for targeting purposes can be produced and these provide detailed measures of *marketing productivity*.

Marketing database 'data' becomes 'information' when we identify the 'recency, frequency and monetary value' (RFM) of customer orders:

- *Recency* – just knowing they have purchased from us in the past is important but not sufficient; we are probably less interested in those who bought from us in 1984 but not since.
- *Frequency* – a one-off purchase may also make a customer less attractive (depending, of course, on the product-market in which we operate). So knowing how often they buy from us is an important measure.
- *Monetary value* – small orders are usually less attractive than larger ones, so this is yet another measure of significance.

Indeed marketers are increasingly concentrating on their 'better' customers – those who have the highest monetary value (and frequency) of purchase and are segmenting on the basis of 'volume' because in this way they are more cost effective, because they concentrate on those who bring greater returns. Vilfredo Pareto's theory of income distribution has been transferred and borrowed by direct marketers to support the proposition that 80 per cent of sales come from just 20 per cent of customers – in many markets the ratio can be even more polarized (95 : 5 is not uncommon). The Pareto principle is often quoted by direct marketers and is certainly relevant to this discussion of RFM analysis. RFM analysis clearly, by the nature of the variables involved, means that transactional data must be tracked by the database – actual purchase history is needed.

In addition to leading to the identification of volume segments and best prospects, the RFM information also contributes to the calculation of 'lifetime value' – another of the new cornerstone productivity measures. 'Lifetime' is perhaps a little of an overstatement – it doesn't mean the lifetime of the customer, but rather a designated period of time during which they are a customer of your organization. Sometimes we might only use a 'lifetime' period of three years. It would probably be better to refer to *longtime* value analysis but whatever period is relevant, however, the concept of what that customer is worth to the organization in sales and profit terms over a period of time is a critical marketing productivity analysis concept.

This brief overview of some of the emerging measures of internal market information shows how sophisticated database marketing, in particular, is moving us from the days of 'not knowing which half of one's advertising is effective', to having the capability to measure more precisely marketing inputs and outputs within this area of marketing productivity analysis.

Marketing intelligence involves a variety of types of data, broadly concerned with 'environmental scanning' (Aguilar, 1967). The question of environmental appraisal was studied in Chapter 4, so relatively little comment is made here. Certainly, it has long been known that managers come to know the world through a relatively disorganized type of environmental scanning or viewing. In some ways the context here is the least tangible of the marketing information system, since environmental scanning of the marketing environment is less focused and constrained than marketing research. Indeed, what is studied may sometimes be less than obviously relevant to decision making, but may be a highly significant stimulus to market sensing.

Attempts have certainly been made by some companies to formalize the marketing intelligence function, in the way illustrated in Table 11.1, which describes some of the work done at Levi Strauss. Others have noted the advantages in formalizing the intelligence function (Evans, 1988; Evans *et al.*, 1996; Moutinho and Evans, 1992; Piercy, 1978, 1992; Vasconcellos, 1985) and provide actionable frameworks for management attention to assist managers in focusing on the longer term.

In terms of the organizational issues involved in environmental scanning, three scanning modes were identified by Jain (1990). These modes suggested that scanning be conducted by: line managers, planners, or a specific environmental scanning department. Cravens *et al.* (1980) suggested that the main commitment should be by line managers, although Jain (1990) questions the abilities of line managers to free their thinking from their own specialist areas to achieve the needed breadth of perspective. On the other hand, line manager involvement

Table 11.1   Environmental scanning at Levi Strauss

Environmental factors	Scanning	Interpretation
Social, for example population changes, leisure time and recreation, fashion trends, preferences for natural fabrics.	For example, changing age distribution in USA market – monitoring trends in birth rate and population discovers that teenager market segment in the USA is shrinking.	Shrinking market potential in largest market segment.
Economic, for example economic growth and inflation, imports to the USA, clothing spending, retail changes.	For example, imports of jeans to the USA – monitoring growth in Far East production and quota agreements suggests import growth in USA.	Imports will probably gain higher share of USA market for Levi Strauss products.
Governmental, for example import barriers, retail price maintenance, metrication, flame-proofing standards in clothes.	For example, monitoring USA government consumer protection bodies finds reduced budgets and less attention to flammability research, suggesting less chance of new standards for general clothing.	Slowed rate of this environmental force.

Source: Piercy and Evans (1983)

brings 'ownership' and may achieve greater impact on the firm, but at the expense of some sophistication (Piercy, 1997). Indeed, Aguilar (1967) suggested that it is a problem in environmental scanning if those collecting intelligence are not the decision makers, because it is then difficult to collect the right kind of information. Similarly, Fahey and Narayanan (1986) note: 'Perhaps the most significant problem in many organizations is inadequate linkage between environmental analysis and strategy analysis'.

In spite of such moves towards making intelligence gathering more systematic, there remains the basic problem that much intelligence is composed of 'soft' or qualitative data, which are often difficult to integrate into an information system, and which are difficult to evaluate in terms of their validity or reliability. However, this is an information source easy to underestimate, and it should be incorporated into our model (see Gilad, 1989, for further guidance on the role of organized competitive intelligence in strategy development).

Marketing research involves the process of generating information around given problems or areas of interest, using either secondary or published data sources, or the undertaking of primary research to generate new flows of data from the marketplace. This is not the place to attempt a detailed technical study of marketing research techniques (see the sources suggested in Further reading), although there is much to recommend the discipline and structure of a process-based approach to marketing research, of the type illustrated in Table 11.2. The value of this model is that it provides a vehicle for planning research projects as well as for evaluating and controlling research done internally or externally.

Our present interest lies not in the techniques of doing marketing research but in terms of managing the process shown in Table 11.2, i.e. the problems of definition and communication in the research process. In information management terms, the critical tests for evaluating marketing research projects lie, first, in the ability to specify precise objectives, which lead to a list of

---

Table 11.2 A processual approach to marketing research

Stage 1 Defining and clarifying the marketing problem
- Setting the objectives for research.
- Producing a data list, i.e. the specific pieces of data required.

Stage 2 Determining the sources of information
- Can the research objectives be met from secondary published sources – can they be trusted?
- Do the objectives require primary research – if so, who or what are the relevant sources?

Stage 3 Designing a data-collection strategy
- What measurement method is to be used – observation, personal interviewing, postal questionnaire?
- What type of questionnaire is needed?
- What sampling is appropriate?

Stage 4 Data collection
- Implementing the data collection strategy – interviewing, etc.

Stage 5 Data processing
- Editing, coding and tabulating the data, testing the results.

Stage 6 Communicating results
- Designing reports and presentations which match the research objectives specified in stage 1.

pieces of information needed for a particular purpose; and, second, in the degree to which useful results are communicated to the users or sponsors of the research. In developing the marketing information system it is necessary to accept that primary marketing research may be the only way to produce the information needed (although arguably it is the last resort, not the first), but that we face important and challenging problems in:

1   Managing the process of research and the interface between research users and research providers.
2   Validating the research process.
3   Integrating the results of the research process into the corporate database or 'memory'.

An example of integration is between marketing databases and market research data. Consumer panels, for instance, are linked with geodemographic or lifestyle databases to produce T-groups. The 'T' means that 'horizontally' database data provides tremendous breadth of data over millions of consumers but the 'vertical', from market research, provides greater depth of information over a period of time (because panels are 'continuous' data sources). Figure 11.9 summarizes the characteristics of the T-group (Cowling, 1996).

However, in the information systems context, Barnard (1992) suggests that technological developments in marketing research techniques – scanning data, database marketing, and so on – can lead to 'information anxiety' due to data overload. He suggests that more sophisticated computing may be the way of making sense of the huge volumes of data now being created – in particular, he cites expert systems as a development in this area. Indeed, computer forecasting and modelling techniques have already facilitated a shift from descriptive to predictive research in marketing, especially in new product, pricing, positioning and advertising studies.

Management science in marketing is concerned essentially with the application of simulation and model-building techniques for marketing planning and control. A previous

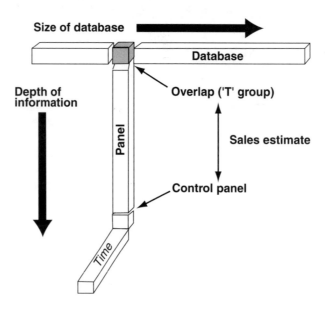

Figure 11.9   T-groups

section discussed transactional data as being at the heart of many of the new marketing databases. Overlaid with a multitude of profile data, we are moving into the era of *biographics* – the fusion of profile and transaction data. Indeed, the ability to match names, addresses, purchasing behaviour and lifestyles all together onto one record allows companies to build a *model* of someone's life – that is, the state of the art with respect to *market modelling* is not so much '*market*' modelling as modelling '*individual*' buying behaviour. Database linking occurs on two levels. First, on an industry level – census data, geodemographics and lifestyle data build up a broad picture of the population – ideal for segmentation purposes. Second, at the individual company level matching this data to credit history, actual purchasing behaviour, media response, and the recency, frequency and monetary value of purchases can potentially describe one's life.

Other dimensions of modelling from database data revolve around data mining, which we mentioned earlier. *Data mining* is a 'process of extracting hidden or previously unknown, comprehensible and actionable information from large databases'. From this there are two approaches that data mining can adopt. The first is *verification driven*, 'extracting information to validate an hypothesis postulated by a user'. The second approach refers to the digging around in databases in a relatively unstructured way with the aim of discovering links between customer behaviour and almost any variable that might potentially be useful. This second approach is *discovery driven*, 'identifying and extracting hidden, previously unknown information . . . [to] scour the data for patterns which do not come naturally to the analysts' set of views or ideas'. There is a parallel with market research versus environmental scanning, because the former focuses on specific problems and the latter has a wider ranging brief to identify anything in the marketing environment which might have a relevant impact upon the marketing operation.

Marketers are investigating a variety of marketing modelling approaches based on their database data. For example some have examined consumers' individual biorhythms and star signs as predictors of their purchasing patterns (Mitchell and Haggett, 1997; Murry, 1998).

A number of dedicated tools are available for analysing databases. One such 'product' is VIPER software developed by Brann Software. This tool allows very fast linking and analysis of different databases. Figure 11.10 demonstrates a print-out from VIPER-processed queries on a lifestyle database (NDL), linked with a geo-demographic (ACORN) database and a geographical information (MAPINFO) system. The questions asked might have been: select those (name and address) who claim to play badminton, drink above average quantities of wine and live in Aberdeen.

The graphical print-out of the model combines data from all of the databases interrogated and shows in both topographical form, where these people live, and also in tabular form, the actual names and addresses of the individuals concerned. VIPER is not the only database interrogator on the market but it does reflect the sort of capability that is now available for market modelling. The speed with which the analysis is completed is indeed impressive – and on what is now a relatively standard desktop PC.

Another recent approach to model building is also based on computer technology – expert systems. Although in its infancy in terms of practical application, this development is being researched by a number of marketing analysts and planners (e.g. Wright and Rowe, 1992; Curry and Moutinho, 1993; McDonald, 1989). The underlying concept is that high-level computer programs can provide decision makers with suggestions and recommendations based on a set of rules which have been constructed to analyse and interpret data. There are many barriers to the application of expert systems in marketing – particularly the loose and frequently complex relationships between customers, suppliers and competitors in a rapidly changing marketing environment. For example, one study by Mingers and Adlan (1989) found that

1000 papers on expert systems had been published between 1984 and 1988, but only 10 of the expert systems discussed in those papers were in regular use.

A further and linked development here may be the application of neural networks to processing and making sense of 'fuzzy' information from the marketing environment (Curry and Moutinho, 1993).

The techniques in this area have been considered in earlier chapters, and our focus here, as with marketing research, is not the techniques of applying these methods but on the problems of managing and exploiting the information they generate. By reviewing the components of the marketing information system in this way it is possible to claim some consensus about what the system should be and contain. What we have yet to confront are the problems of *integrating* these various components.

In a study into the use of public relations in the motor industry Evans and Fill (1998) found that there was often little sharing of what could have been synergistically useful information from the databases of direct marketing departments, PR departments and from those of the

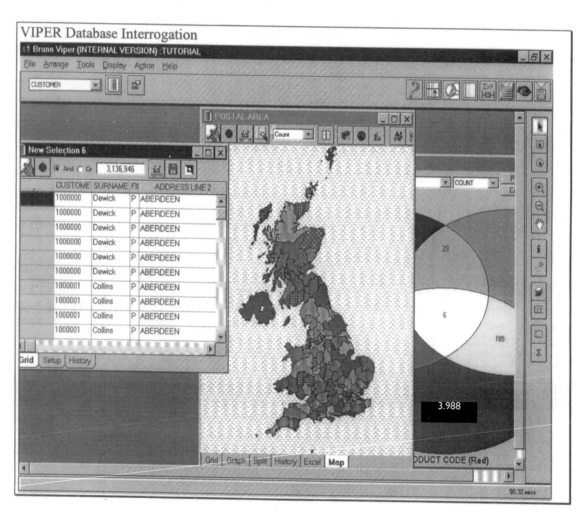

Figure 11.10 Interrogating marketing databases

salesforce. 'Integration' continues to be a problem within marketing and the information area parallels that of marketing communications, as Goften (1996) observes:

there's nothing more sad than the spectacle of an ad agency deploying one concept and a PR agency pursuing another. It's not only a crime against the economic use of resources but no service at all to either client or consumer.

The need for integration can be easily demonstrated. In even quite simple cases it is possible to obtain directly conflicting views about what is happening in the real outside world, depending on which corporate information sources we use and when we stop looking further. There are no easy answers to the integration problem, although it has long been analysed as one of the critical issues facing us in designing marketing information systems (Westwood *et al.*, 1975). The problem is largely one of designing an holistic model, such as Kotler's (1971) Marketing Information and Analysis Centre, to function as the 'marketing nerve centre for the company'.

Developing the marketing information system

Table 11.3 shows a simple model for systems development in marketing, which follows a logic of reviewing the present information systems, assessing information needs and remedying shortfalls. Such a model provides a reasonable basis on which to proceed, but its application is unlikely to be free from complications.

Measurement of current information flows

The problems of measuring current information flows and data uses are primarily, but not wholly, logistical. In anything but the smallest company, actually finding out what information is generated and what happens to it is likely to be a lengthy process of interviewing and questionnaire surveys, leading to flow-charting to describe information practices which have built up – possibly over a substantial period of time, with all the idiosyncrasies and historical oddities that this may involve. However, even this apparently innocuous part of the process has been associated with real practical difficulties: market research reports found to have been suppressed; misleading and incomplete responses from executives about information they have; defensiveness and protectiveness about current information practices; and so on (Piercy, 1979).

Developing a marketing information system must be seen in many cases as an innovation for the company – with all that this implies about the potential for resistance to change. Over and above this resistance, even at this preliminary stage, it is important to recognize that information is not a neutral commodity in organizations – it is a source of power, of political influence, or organizational status. Actions which may be, or may be perceived to be,

---

Table 11.3 A simple model of systems development
Stage 1   Measure present information flows and uses.
Stage 2   Identify marketing management information needs.
Stage 3   Design new information flows to close the gap between stages 1 and 2.
Stage 4   Reconcile these with the overall information system.
Stage 5   Implement
Stage 6   Revision

threatening are likely to be resisted and manipulated.

In fact, the whole marketing information system development process is likely to have a political dimension, to which we will give attention as an aspect of systems implementation. However, throughout the process it is important to be aware of the need to identify the entrenched interests inside and outside the marketing department (for example, sales managers whose 'private files' are their power base in the company; product managers whose main goal is to suppress any information undermining the position of the brands they champion; the finance department using its 'confidential' cost information to maintain a political 'vet' over marketing department activities; and so on). Might similar politics have been behind the lack of integration of the sales, PR and direct marketing databases, to which we referred earlier? Allowances will have to be made for such barriers.

Identifying marketing management information needs

The very core of the marketing information system development process is the identification of the management information needs the system is to address, and it is likely that this is the area where the most intractable and difficult problems will be faced. A number of points which have been found to emerge as critical issues are discussed below.

Context

A first point relating to context is to note that any idea of a universal or standard set of marketing management information needs is likely to be highly misleading (notwithstanding the views put forward in the promotional literature of suppliers of decision-support software products). Research has shown that marketing departments take many forms, and can be distinguished by size and type of responsibilities (Piercy, 1986c, 1993). Such variations suggest

most emphatically that defining marketing management information needs requires detailed situational study, not universal prescriptions for all companies.

A second point of context related to the existence of 'myths' surrounding the use of information in organizations is the danger of creating 'misinformation systems' (Tricker, 1971; Ackoff, 1967). In particular, there are significant dangers in the assumptions that 'more' and 'faster' are necessarily advantages when we are designing information availability and flows.

Practical limitations

In addition to recognizing such issues of context, it is important to note that there are a number of limitations inherent in what we are trying to measure here. Often managers appear not to know themselves what their information needs are. It is this which provides one of the most fundamental limitations. Quite simply, asking managers to tell us their information needs may not work.

It has been noted that when asked such questions, managers tend to respond: that they do now know; that they need what they currently receive; or they need everything they can be given. In the end, information needs should reflect the tasks carried out by the manager, and in this sense they can be specified only when the decision-making process has been modelled. From this, however, arises a second practical limitation, in the sense that many management information needs may not be 'knowable' or at least not easily predictable.

In practical terms, it is relatively straightforward to model operating decisions in marketing – stock re-order levels, routine price discounts, and so on – and to define information needs in this way. It may even be relatively simple to model the marketing planning process to isolate routine information needs – market research, competitive changes, results against plan, etc. What remains largely intractable is predicting the information needs of strategic decision makers in marketing, on the grounds that:

Top executives' activities are dynamic, ever-changing, and therefore one cannot predetermine exactly what information will be needed to deal with changing events at any point in time. These executives are, and must be, dependent on future-oriented, rapidly assembled, and most-often subjective, informal information. (Rockart, 1978)

Similarly, it has been noted by Mintzberg (1985) that:

It is necessary to look at the content of managers' information, and at what they do with it. The evidence is that a great deal of managers' inputs are soft and speculative . . . Furthermore, very analytical inputs – reports, document, and hard data in general – seem to be of relatively little importance to managers.

It is perhaps for reasons such as this that Feldman and March (1981) put forward the following conclusions after an extensive review of how senior managers in many different types of organizations use information. They make six observations about the gathering and use of information in organizations:

1   Much of the information that is gathered and communicated by individuals in organizations has little relevance to the decisions that must be made.
2   Much of the information used to justify decisions is collected after those decisions have already been made.
3   Much of the information gathered in response to requests for information is not considered in the making of the decisions for which it was requested.
4   Regardless of the information available at the time a decision is first considered, it is likely that more information will be requested.
5   Managerial complaints that the organization does not have enough information to make the decision occur while available information is ignored.
6   The relevance of the information provided in the decision-making process to the decision

being made is less obvious than is the insistence on the need for the information.

This suggests that:

It is possible, on considering these phenomena, to conclude that organizations are systematically stupid . . . Perhaps the stories of information perversity tell us less about the weaknesses of organizations than about the limitations of our ideas about information. (Feldman and March, 1981)

In short, at the operational level and in short-term planning it may be possible to predict many routine information needs and to meet these. However, as we move from operations to strategy, the ability to predict and programme decisions and our understanding of how managers use information is far less. This means that our abilities to predict and fill information needs are correspondingly less. Indeed, it may be that the best we can aim to provide at this level is an accessible database that will respond to such requests as 'give me everything we know about . . . ', and some approach to highlighting or flagging significant factors for management attention – as with the 'critical success factors' approach discussed below.

A third limitation also arises from the points made above. This is that managers at all levels differ substantially in their problem-solving styles and hence information needs. For example, we may observe that managers appear to search unsystematically for information and to pay attention to some sources and not others, and find such phenomena as the 'private' or 'secret' personal filing systems that individuals build. It may be noted that idiosyncrasy in information use may be inconvenient to the systems designer, but may also be central to the manager's personal effectiveness as a decision maker.

Thus far, our concerns in approaching the task of identifying marketing management information needs has been heavily grounded in the context of making the measurements and the practical limitations which exist. We can now turn to the methods available to help in solving the problems we have identified.

Table 11.4   Measuring marketing information flows

1   Contact established with key interviewees, who can identify key decision and personnel.
2   Unstructured interviews with decision-making participants to identify roles played.
3   Interview data converted to flow charts.
4   Flow charts from interviews are amalgamated.
5   Validity of flow charts tested with original interviewees and others in the company, and modified.

Source: Hulbert *et al.* (1972)

Models for analysis

In terms of measurement techniques, one tested procedure is shown in Table 11.4, involving the use of interviews, questionnaires and flow charts to build a picture of the existing marketing information systems. However, moving from what is to what should be requires more than this. Two approaches are worth noting: Munro's (1978) data analysis/decision analysis and Rockart's (1978) 'critical success factors' model.

Munro's approach offers two complementary methods of analysing managers' information needs. Data analysis involves the study of information flows compared to perceived information needs, while decision analysis involves modelling the major decisions made and identifying information needs from these models. The stages in each approach are summarised in Table 11.5. Munro's suggestion is that:

Where the decision is 'programmed' . . . it is advisable to use data analysis. On the other hand, for decision situations which are poorly understood, data analysis offers no help . . . the experience of attempting to construct a decision model for poorly understood decision situations frequently results in a greatly improved understanding of both the decision process and the information required.

A further attack on the problem of senior managers' strategic information needs is provided by the 'critical success factors' approach (Rockart, 1978), which focuses on the limited number of areas in which results, if they are satisfactory, will ensure successful competitive performance for the organization. There are the few key areas where 'things must go right for the business to flourish' (Rockart, 1978). An

example of the use of this approach is given in Table 11.6.

A more recent development of a similar type is 'benchmarking'. This involves the measurement and evaluation of our operations and performance compared to the best-performing companies in our industry. This may be broad (e.g. competitive positioning, advertising strategy, and so on) or relatively narrow (salesforce compensation, distribution coverage in the market, and the like). The benchmarking approach has four stages:

1   Select the most relevant and useful benchmark issues.
2   Identify the 'best' in our industry or market.
3   Collect the internal and external data on each benchmark.
4   Analyse and report to top management.

Similarly, benchmarking aims to focus our attention on the things that matter most in the marketplace, and to collect the information that tells us how well we are doing on these things.

While none of these approaches give complete answers, they do provide a starting point in taking seriously the issue of identifying and classifying different types of information need in marketing.

Designing the marketing information system

To the extent that it proves possible to identify marketing management information needs in the context described above, then much of what remains is relatively straightforward 'gap-filling'

	Table 11.5 Data analysis and decision analysis	
	Data analysis	*Decision analysis*
Methodology	1 Examine all reports, files, and other sources of information used by the manager. 2 Determine with the manager the use made of each source of information examined. 3 Identify redundant information sources/flows to be eliminated. 4 Identify with the manager unsatisfied information needs.	1 Identify with the manager major decision responsibilities. 2 Identify the policies and organizational objectives relevant to the decision responsibilities. 3 Examine the steps and processes involved in making each major decision. 4 Develop a flow chart of each decision. 5 Use the flow chart to determine information required at each step in the decision. 6 Identify redundant information and unsatisfied information needs.
Advantages	Incorporates managers' views of information requirements. Effective with structured decisions. Flexibility. Speed.	Links information needs to decisions and objectives. Effective with unstructured decisions. Information can be matched to personal decision-making style. May improve the decision process as well as information flows.
Disadvantages	Managers are relied upon to identify and describe accurately their information needs. Information needs are not linked to decisions and objectives. No established procedures or standards.	Information requirements may change if the manager is replaced. Specifying decision processes is difficult. More time-consuming.

Source: Piercy and Evans (1983)

using the model of marketing information types discussed earlier. What is apparent in many practical situations, however, is the need for a design strategy for the marketing information system. One approach (Howard *et al.*, 1975) distinguishes three different information systems design strategies, appropriate in different circumstances:

1 *Supplemental strategy* – to automate and facilitate information flow and storage, orientated towards data input and output. In situations of high uncertainty and complex problem solving this approach may be the most useful.

2 *Modification strategy* – of making information more widely available and oriented towards changing the communication structure. This may be appropriate under conditions of moderate uncertainty and relatively unstructured objectives.

3 *Replacement strategy* – of replacing information processing and decision rules with new rules and systems. This is appropriate where the environment is stable, and objectives are well structured because decision processes are likely to be highly routinized.

Table 11.6   Analysing critical success factors

An example: Microwave Associates

Critical success factors	Measurements
Image in the stock market	Price/earnings ratio
Technical reputation with customers	Orders/quotations ratio
	Field interviews by salespeople
	Changes in the percentage of each major customer's business being obtained
Market success	Market share changes by customer
	Market growth rates
Risk in major bids and contracts	Experience with similar products
	Experience with the customer
	Prior customer relationships
Profit margin on projects	The profit margin on the bid compared to other projects
Morale	Staff turnover, absenteeism, etc.
	Informal feedback
Performance against budget on key jobs	Time against plan
	Cost against budget
	Profile across major jobs

Source: Piercy and Evans (1983)

The underlying point is that the strategy of marketing information systems design should be seen as contingent on surrounding conditions and the particular company's situation. This contingency view relates to: the sophistication which it is appropriate to attempt; the scope of developments which are to be planned; and the expenditure of resources on the information systems project. At the very least, this provides a basis for setting realistic expectations for what is to be attempted, to avoid some of the disappointment and frustrations which are associated with this type of development.

Implementation and review

Up to this point our concern has been mainly with analysis and planning. Clearly, major attention also needs to be devoted to putting information systems development plans into effect. At this point, two issues are selected for attention: the responsibility for marketing information systems development; and the need for a strategy of change.

Marketing information systems responsibility

There are evident attractions in the clear allocation of responsibility for marketing information systems development to individuals or groups. We have argued elsewhere the case for a marketing information analyst, whose role is to study marketing management information needs, and the ways in which these needs can be met, using the type of methodology discussed in this chapter. However, when thinking of problems of implementation there are two other points to be borne in mind. First, it has been noted by Buzzell *et al.* (1969) that:

Management must decide how to organize MIS development activities. This is a much more complex problem than might be assumed. Sophisticated MIS requires the co-ordinated efforts of a great many departments and individuals.

The implication is that successful implementation may require the involvement of a team, in the form of a committee, working party, project team, and so on. It should also be noted that others have made a substantial case for active user participation in the whole information systems development process – suggesting that this 'ownership' may be the key to success.

Second, as well as the number of people involved, there is some suggestion that the organizational level of the key players may also be critical. If we believe marketing information systems design to be important, then this should be reflected in senior management involvement. Indeed, Keen (1980) goes as far as to see a senior 'fixer' as the key to coping with the organizational problems inherent in information systems change.

Strategic marketing information system development

Throughout this consideration of marketing information systems development, stress has been placed on the need to take a strategic view. By this it is meant that the whole information function should be tied to the strategic future of the firm. The alternative is a series of *ad hoc* responses to short-term problems, and missing many of the potential gains from information management, as they have been identified here.

For example, a study by Kench and Evans (1991) explored the strategic versus tactical nature of information systems in marketing in companies of varying size. These researchers concluded that tactical and operational information needs were readily understood in companies, but that at the strategic level there was a

vacuum. Information systems, they found, were assessed in terms of the sophistication of the hardware used, and were perceived as something run and owned by the IT people. This suggests that in many companies there is still much to be done to unleash the real potential of information technology and information systems in supporting marketing decision makers.

In particular, where marketing information systems change is involved, it has been suggested that we should write a scenario, in the way suggested in Table 11.7, to provide a broad view of the goals and the obstacles faced, before becoming involved in purely tactical development actions.

Conclusions and a new management agenda

The view we have taken here is that competencies in marketing information functions have the potential to unleash new types of marketing capabilities. In this way, we may start by developing competencies in traditional areas of marketing research and intelligence-gathering, and the newer area of data mining, but the critical issue becomes management understanding of the marketplace and the customer. We examined 'market sensing' as a route to managing this process of understanding, and exploiting the organization's information competencies to produce new marketing capabilities.

The importance of market sensing is underlined by the context for marketing information – the massive and continuing change in information technology. This is providing the potential for moves toward a relationship approach, because it is facilitating the collection of individualized information which in turn can be used to treat individual customers as individuals – and on this basis to develop relationships with them. However, the market sensing approach means *more* than gathering and using personal information – it also requires marketers to convert the

Table 11.7	Scenario writing for information systems development
Objectives	What are we trying to do?
	What resources are needed?
	Who controls these resource, directly or indirectly?
Problems	What elements are critical?
	Are any of these elements 'owned' by monopoly interests?
	Will their 'owners' cooperate – what is the effect of the MIS on the distribution of 'ownership'?
	Can uncooperative 'owners' be avoided or bought off?
	Will they respond with delays or token support?
	Will they provide massive resistance?
Games	How are people likely to (a) divert resources, (b) deflect goals, (c) dissipate energies?
	How can this be countered?
Delay	How much delay should be expected?
	What negotiations are necessary?
	What resources are available for negotiation?
	Would project management structures help?
Fixing the game	What management is needed?
	What resources do they have to help?
	What incentives are there for them to play the 'fixer' role?
	Can a coalition be built to fix the game?

Source: Piercy and Evans (1983)

increasing mountain of data that is being collected into real *understanding* of customers and markets and using this knowledge to create more meaningful and sustainable competitive advantage.

From this strategic vantage point we then return to the more conventional tools of marketing information systems components and development processes. We believe that the marketing information system of the future will be almost unrecognizable compared to our history in this field. Nevertheless, these conventional tools provide an initial structure for articulating and operationalizing our marketing information assets.

We suggest that the management agenda that is emerging should address issues of this kind:

- How well does the company focus its efforts on understanding the useful and important issues on which performance depends (see Figure 11.3)?

- Are we succeeding in not simply developing competencies in information collection and dissemination, but in market sensing to develop and enhance marketing capabilities (see Figure 11.2)?

- Are we actively managing the process of market sensing to build and share market understanding and responsiveness throughout the company (see Figures 11.4–11.6)?

- Are we tracking the impact of information technology in our market and developing appropriate responses? For example, are we integrating data from traditional market research sources with the new biographic sources? Are we clear about the attitudinal and behavioural impact on individuals of the collection and use of their personal details? Are we using such data in strategic or merely tactical ways? Also, are we really using the biographic fusion of data to improve targeting and efficiency (Evans, 1998)?

* Do we have a clear view of how we are developing our informational resources and developing them as support and challenge to our process of market sensing?
* Are we developing an information strategy that will enhance our capabilities and performance for the future?
* Are we using the availability of more individual-specific information coupled with technological facilitators to really create a paradigm shift in marketing itself in our own organization?

References

Ackoff, R. L. (1967) Management misinformation systems, *Management Science*, **14**(14), 147–156.

Adams, M. (1993) *Seeing Differently: Improving the Ability of Organizations to Anticipate and Respond to the Constantly Changing Needs of Customers and Markets*, Marketing Science Institute Report, 93–103.

Aguilar, F. J. (1967) *Scanning the Business Environment*, Macmillan, London.

Anon. (1998) Tesco revels in redemption, *Precision Marketing*, 28 September, p. 1.

Antoniou, T. (1997) Drilling or mining? Handling and analysis of data between now and the year 2000, *Marketing and Research Today*, May, 115–120.

Barnard, P. (1992) New directions in world research, *ADMAP*, October, 22–31.

Barrett, T. F. (1986) Issues in the design of marketing accounting systems, in N. Piercy, (ed.), *Management Information Systems: The Technology Challenge*, Croom Helm, London.

Biel, A. L. (1967) Management goals and marketing research: the dilemma of organization, *Proceedings*: ESOMAR/Wapor Congress.

Bigg, A. (1994) Techno Tactic, *Campaign*, 8 July.

Brown, D. C. (1985) The anatomy of a decision support system, *Business Marketing*, June, 80–86.

Buzzell, R. D., Cox, D. F. and Brown, R. V. (1969)

Marketing Research and Information Systems: Text and Cases, McGraw-Hill, New York.

Cash, J. I. and Konsynski, B. R. (1985) IS redraws competitive boundaries, *Harvard Business Review*, March/April, 142–143.

Channon, C. (1968) The role of advertising research in management decision making, *Proceedings*: Market Research Society Conference.

Christopher, M., McDonald, M. and Wills, G. (1980) *Introducing Marketing*, Pan, London.

Christopher, M., Payne, A. and Ballantyne, D. (1991) *Relationship Marketing*, Butterworth-Heinemann, Oxford.

Cook, S. (1994) Database marketing: strategy or technical tool? *Marketing Intelligence and Planning*, **12**(6), 4–7.

Cowling, A. B. (1996) Big issues for the next five years: data fusion, reach the parts others don't, *IDM Symposium*, May.

Cravens, D. W., Hills, G. E. and Woodruff, R. B. (1980) *Marketing Decision Making: Concepts and Strategy*, Irwin, Homewood, IL.

Cross, R. (1992) The five degrees of customer bonding, *Direct Marketing*, November, 33–58.

Cyert, R. M., Simon, H. A. and Trow, D. B. (1956) Observation of a business decision, *Journal of Business*, **29**, 237–248.

Curry, B. and Moutinho, L. (1993) Neural networks in marketing, *Proceedings*: Marketing Education Group Conference, 188–199.

Davidson, J. H. (1975) *Offensive Marketing*, Penguin, London.

DeTienne, K. B. and Thompson, J. A. (1996) Database marketing and organizational learning theory: toward a research agenda, *Journal of Consumer Marketing*, **13**(5), 12–34.

Earl, M. (1983) Emerging trends in managing new information technologies, in N. Piercy (ed.), *The Management Implications of New Information Technology*, Croom Helm, London.

England, L. R. (1980) Is research a waste of time? *Marketing*, 16 April, 56–57.

Evans, M. (1988) Marketing intelligence: scanning the marketing environment, *Marketing Intelligence and Planning*, Summer.

Evans, M. (1996) Direct mail and consumer response: an empirical study of consumer experiences of direct mail, *Journal of Database Marketing*, 3(3), 250–261.

Evans, M. (1998) From 1086 and 1984: direct marketing into the millennium, *Marketing Intelligence and Planning*, 16(1), 56–67.

Evans, M. and Fill, C. (1998) Public relations and multi step flows of communications within motor markets, International Conference of Marketing Communications, University of Strathclyde, April.

Evans, M., Moutinho, L. and van Raaij, F. (1996) *Applied Consumer Behaviour*, Addison Wesley Longman, Harlow.

Evans, M., O'Malley, L. and Patterson, M. (1996) Direct mail and consumer response: an empirical study of consumer experiences of direct mail, *Journal of Database Marketing*, 3(3), 250–261.

Fahey, L. and Narayanan, V. K. (1986) *Macroenvironmental Analysis for Strategic Management*, West, St Paul, MN.

Feldman, M. S. and March, J. G. (1981) Information in organizations as signal and symbol, *Administrative Science Quarterly*, 26, 171–186.

Fletcher, K. (1982) Marketing information systems: a lost opportunity, *Proceedings Marketing Education Group Conference*, Lancaster.

Fletcher, K. and Peters, L. (1996) Issues in consumer information management, *Journal of the Market Research Society*, 38(2), 145–160.

Fletcher, K., Wheeler, C. and Wright, G. (1990) The role and status of UK database marketing, *Quarterly Review of Marketing*, Autumn, 7–14.

Gilad, B. (1989) The role of organized competitive intelligence in corporate strategy, *Columbia Journal of World Business*, 24(4), 29–35.

Goften, K. (1996) Integrating the delivery, *Marketing*, October 31, viii–iix.

Graf, F. (1979) Information systems for marketing, *Marketing Trends*, 2, 1–3.

Greenley, G. E. (1986) *The Strategic and Operational Planning of Marketing*, McGraw-Hill, New York.

Gronroos, C. (1990) Relationship approach to marketing in service contexts: the marketing and organizational behaviour interface, *Journal of Business Research*, 20 (January), 3–11.

Hardin, D. K. (1969) Marketing research – is it used or abused? *Journal of Marketing Research*, 6, 239.

Haskins, M. E. and Nanni, A. J. (1986) *MIS Influences on Managers: Hidden Side Effects*, University of Virginia.

Herring, J. (1992) The role of intelligence in formulating strategy, *Journal of Business Strategy*, September, 54–61.

Holtgrefe, G. (1986) *DSS for Strategic Planning Purposes: A Further Source of Management Suspicion and Disappointment?* Vrije University.

Howard, J. A., Hulbert, J. and Farley, J. U. (1975) Organizational analysis and information systems design: a decision-process perspective, *Journal of Business Research*, 3(2), 133–148.

Hulbert, J., Farley, J. U. and Howard, J. A. (1972) Information processing and decision making in marketing organizations, *Journal of Marketing Research*, 9(2), 75–77.

Humby, C. (1996) Digging for information, *Marketing*, 41–42, 21 November.

Jain, S. C. (1990) *Marketing Planning and Strategy*, 3rd edn, South-Western, Cincinnati, OH.

Jaworski, B. J. and Kohli, A. K. (1993) Market orientation: antecedents and consequences, *Journal of Marketing*, 57 (July), 53–70.

Jemison, D. B. (1984) The influence of boundary spanning roles in strategic decision making, *Journal of Management Studies*, 21(2), 131–152.

Jeuck, J. E. (1953) Marketing research: milestone or millstone? *Journal of Marketing*, 17, 381–387.

Jobber, D. (1977) Marketing information systems in United States and British industry, *Management Decision*, 15(2), 297–304.

Johnson, G. and Scholes, K. (1993) *Exploring Corporate Strategy*, 3rd edn, Prentice-Hall, Englewood Cliffs, NJ.

Johnston, S. and Woodward, S. (1988) Marketing management information systems – a review of current practice, *Marketing Intelligence and Planning*, 6(2), 27–29.

Keen, P. G. W. (1980) *Information Systems*

and Organizational Change, Massachusetts Institute of Technology, Boston, MA.

Kench, R. and Evans M. J. (1991) IT: the information-technology dichotomy, *Marketing Intelligence and Planning*, **9**(5), 16–22.

Kohli, A. K. and Jaworski, B. J. (1990) Market orientation: the construct, research propositions and managerial implications, *Journal of Marketing*, **54**(2), 15–22.

Kotler, P. (1971) *Marketing Decision Making: A Model Building Approach*, Holt, Rinehart and Winston, New York.

Leech, M. (1980) Research's future imperative, *Marketing*, 16 July, 33–34.

Lyonski, S. (1985) A boundary theory investigation of the product manager's role, *Journal of Marketing*, **49**, Winter, 26–40.

McDonald, M. (1989) Marketing planning and expert systems, *Marketing Intelligence and Planning*, **7**(8), 16–23.

Market Research Society (1994) The opinion polls and the 1992 General Election, Market Research Society, London, July.

Market Research Society (1997) Code of Conduct, Market Research Society, London.

Martell, D. (1986) Marketing information and new technology, in N. Piercy (ed.), *Management Information Systems: The Technology Challenge*, Croom Helm, London.

Mason, R. and Mitroff, I. (1973) A program of research on management information systems, *Management Science*, **19**, 475–478.

May, J. P. (1981) Marketing research: illuminating neglected areas, *Journal of the Market Research Society*, **23**(3), 127–136.

Mingers, J. and Adlan, J. (1989) Where are the 'real' expert systems? *OR Insights*, **2**, 6–9.

Mintzberg, H. (1985) Planning on the left side and managing on the right, *Harvard Business Review*, **54**(4).

Mitchell, V. W. and S. Haggett (1997) Sun-sign astrology in market segmentation: an empirical investigation, *Journal of Consumer Marketing*, **14**(2), 113–131.

Moutinho, L. and Evans, M. (1992) *Applied Marketing Research*, Addison Wesley, Wokingham, UK.

Munro, M. C. (1978) Determining the manager's information needs, *Journal of Systems Management*, **29**(6), 34–39.

Murry, J. (of National Westminster Bank) (1998) as reported by *'You and Yours'*, BBC Radio 4, 26th June.

Narver, J. C. and Slater, S. F. (1990) The effect of a market orientation on business profitability, *Journal of Marketing*, **54**(4), 20–35.

O'Malley, L., Patterson, M. and Evans, M. (1996) Intimacy or intrusion? The privacy dilemma for relationship marketing in consumer markets, *Journal of Marketing Management*, **13**, 541–559.

Parkinson, S. (1994) Computers in marketing, in M. Baker (ed.), *The Marketing Book*, 3rd edn, Butterworth-Heinemann, Oxford.

Patterson, M., O'Malley, L. and Evans, M. (1997) Database marketing: investigating privacy Concerns, *Journal of Marketing Communications*, **3**(3), September.

Piercy, N. (1978) *Low Cost Marketing Analysis*, MCB University Press, Bradford.

Piercy, N. (1979) Behavioural constraints on marketing information systems, *European Journal of Marketing*, **13**(8), 261–270.

Piercy, N. (1981) Marketing information – bridging the quicksand between technology and decision making, *Quarterly Review of Marketing*, **7**(1), 1–15.

Piercy, N. (1983a) Information processing – the newest mix element, in Christopher, M., McDonald, M. and Rushton, A. (eds), *Back to Basics: the 4Ps Revisited*, Marketing Education Group Conference Proceedings.

Piercy, N. (1983b) Retailer information power: the channel marketing information system, *Marketing Intelligence and Planning*, **1**(1), 40–55.

Piercy, N. (1983c) Marketing and new technology, in N. Piercy (ed.), *The Management Implications of New Information Technology*, Croom Helm, London.

Piercy, N. (1985) *Marketing Organization: An Analysis of Information Processing, Power and Politics*, Allen and Unwin, London.

Piercy, N. (1986a) *Marketing Budgeting – A Political and Organizational Model*, Croom Helm, London.

Piercy, N. (ed.) (1986b) *Marketing Asset Accounting*, MCB University Press, Bradford.

Piercy, N. (1986c) The role and function of the chief marketing executive and the marketing department, *Journal of Marketing Management*, **1**(3), 265–290.

Piercy, N. (1997) *Market-Led Strategic Change: Transforming the Process of Going To Market*, Butterworth-Heinemann, Oxford.

Piercy, N. and Evans, M. (1983) *Managing Marketing Information*, Croom Helm, London.

Piercy, N. F. and Lane, N. (1996) Marketing implementation: building and sustaining a real market understanding, *Journal of Marketing Practice: Applied Marketing Science*, **2**(3), 15–28.

Proctor, R. (1992) Marketing information systems, *Marketing Intelligence and Planning*, **29**(4), 55–60.

Rackoff, N., Wiseman, C. and Ullrich, W. A. (1985) Information systems for competitive advantage: implementation of a planning process, *Management Information Systems Quarterly*, December, 285–294.

Reddy, N. M. and Marvin, M. P. (1986) Developing a manufacturer-distributor information partnership, *Industrial Marketing Management*, **15**, 157–163.

Rockart, J. F. (1978) *A New Approach to Defining the Chief Executive's Information Needs*, Centre for Information Systems Research, Massachusetts Institute of Technology.

Rubin, R. S. (1986) Save your information system from the experts, *Harvard Business Review*, July–August, 22–24.

Samuels, J. A. (1973) Research to help plan the future of a seaside resort, *Proceedings*: 12th Marketing Theory Seminar, Lancaster University.

Schlackmann, W. (1979) The participation concept as a key factor in integrating professional services within the modern corporation, *ADMAP*, **15**(6), 292–297.

Seger, E. (1977) 'How to use environmental analysis in strategy', *Management Review*, March.

Shaw, R. and Stone, M. (1988) Competitive superiority through database marketing, *Long Range Planning*, **21**(5), 24–40.

Shrivastava, P. and Etgar, M. (1984) A decision support system for strategic marketing decisions, *Systems, Objectives, Solutions*, **4**, 131–139.

Simmonds, K. (1986) The accounting assessment of competitive position, in Piercy, N. (ed.), *Marketing Asset Accounting*, MCB University Press, Bradford.

Skyrme, D. J. (1989) The planning and marketing of the market intelligence function, *Marketing Intelligence and Planning*, **7** (1/2), 5–10.

Slater, S. F. and Narver, J. C. (1995) Marketing orientation and the learning organization', *Journal of Marketing*, **59** (July), 63–74.

Thorpe, R. M. (1985) *The External Environment of Organizations*, MCB University Press, Bradford.

Tricker, R. I. (1971) Ten myths of management information, *Management Accounting*, **49**(8), 231–233.

Uhl, K. P. (1974) Marketing information systems, in R. Ferber (ed.), *Handbook of Marketing Research*, McGraw-Hill, New York.

Vasconcellos, P. (1985) Environmental analysis for strategic planning, *Management Planning*, January–February, 23–30.

Walker, J. (1996) SMART Move but will it deliver the goods? *Precision Marketing*, 6 May, 18–21.

Weick, K. (1969) *The Social Psychology of Organizing*, Addison-Wesley, Reading, MA.

Westwood, R. A., Palmer, J. B., Zeithin, D. M., Levine, D. M., Thio, K. and Charley, R. (1975) Integrated information systems, *Journal of the Market Research Society*, **17**(3), 127–182.

Wilson, R. M. S. (1981) *Financial Dimensions of Marketing*, Macmillan, London.

Wiseman, C. and Macmillan, I. C. (1984) Creating competitive weapons from information systems, *Journal of Business Strategy*, Autumn, 42–49.

Wright, G. and Rowe, G. (1992) Expert systems in marketing, *Marketing Intelligence and Planning*, **10**(6), 24–30.

Further reading

Market sensing

Piercy, N. F. (1997) *Market-Led Strategic Change: Transforming the Process of Going To Market*, Butterworth-Heinemann, Oxford.

Piercy, N. F. and Lane, N. (1996) Marketing implementation: building and sustaining a real market understanding, *Journal of Marketing Practice: Applied Marketing Science*, **2**(3), 15–28.

Information systems and competitive advantage

Fletcher, K. (ed.) (1992) Information systems for strategic advantage, *Marketing Intelligence and Planning*, **10**(6), Special Edition. This Special Issue of *Marketing Intelligence and Planning* contains a useful and interesting collection of papers on marketing information systems, covering issues which range from organizational matters and the role and stage of development of IT, to the application of marketing information systems in specific sectors such as financial services. There are also papers on database marketing and expert systems in marketing.

King, W. R. (1986) Developing strategic business advantages from informational technology, in N. Piercy (ed.), *Management Information Systems: The Technology Challenge*, Croom Helm, London.

Porter, M. E. (1985) How information gives you competitive advantage, *Harvard Business Review*, July–August, 149–160.

These two readings provide some lasting insights into how developing information systems is about changing competitive stance, not simply internal systems.

The marketing information system

Fletcher, K. (1991) *Information Technology and Marketing Management*, Prentice-Hall, Englewood Cliffs, NJ. This book stands almost on its own as an attempt to evaluate how new information technology has affected marketing management and the marketing information systems, and provides some guidance on how to cope with this type of change.

Marshall, K. P. and LaMotte, S. W. (1992) Marketing information systems: a marriage of system analysis and marketing management, *Journal of Applied Business Research*, **8**, 61–73, Summer. This provides a synthesis of literature from marketing, management and information systems to develop a useful multidisciplinary process of marketing information systems development.

Moutinho, L. and Evans, M. (1992) *Applied Marketing Research*, Addison-Wesley, Reading, MA. This up-to-date text includes detailed coverage of marketing research and its application to marketing management, and also more general reviews of marketing information systems and environmental scanning in marketing.

Piercy, N. and Evans, M. (1983) *Managing Marketing Information*, Croom Helm, London. This is a treatment of the development process involved in developing a marketing information system in more detail than is provided in this chapter.

Information and organizational development

Piercy, N. (1985) *Marketing Organization: An Analysis of Information Processing, Power and Politics*, Allen & Unwin, London. This book provides a more theoretical foundation for the links between informational, organizational and processual issues in marketing, by focusing on information and organization strategies in marketing.

Piercy, N. (1997) *Market-Led Strategic Change: Transforming the Process of Going to Market*, Butterworth-Heinemann, Oxford. Although this is a more general study of strategic change in marketing, Chapter 6 examines the role of information in managing the process of strategic change in organizations, and offers some managerial tools and diagnostics for working on the marketing information function.

IT and database development

Evans, M. (1998) From 1086 and 1984: direct marketing into the millennium, in *Marketing Intelligence and Planning*, **16**(1), 56–67. Special Issue on Direct Marketing.

Fletcher, K. (1996) *Information Technology and Marketing Management*, Prentice-Hall, Englewood Cliffs, NJ.

O'Connor, J. and Galvin, E. (1997) *Marketing and Information Technology*, Pitman, London.

O'Malley, L., Patterson, M. and Evans, M. (1998) *Exploring Direct Marketing*, Thomson International, London.

Part Three
Managing the Marketing Function

CHAPTER 12

Managing the marketing mix

PETER DOYLE

Introduction

Introduction

This chapter evaluates the concept of the marketing mix and its main constituent elements and addresses the problems inherent in uniting these into unique and distinctive combinations. Subsequent chapters will then examine the key considerations associated with each of the main mix elements: product development and management; pricing; selling; advertising and promotion; and distribution and service.

In most firms marketing-mix decisions are led by the marketing department, but inevitably other functional areas play a key role. Engineering and R&D management are significantly involved in product policy; finance, production and other departments influence pricing and distribution decisions. Hence management of the marketing mix is unlikely to be effective without a marketing orientation forming a common culture throughout the business. In many firms, able marketing decision makers are frustrated by a production-orientated approach and lack of understanding of the marketing concept among other functional areas. These issues are discussed by Baker in Chapter 1.

Marketing-mix decisions usually centre around a particular product or service, or closely related group of products and services. However, as Wensley shows in Chapter 2, the decisions are normally circumscribed by strategic considerations. Some products may have been singled out by top management as 'stars' and as such will be more abundantly financed to achieve longer-term goals. Other products at the end of their life cycle might be 'milked' – advertising and support cut back and prices pushed up to generate cash flow. The types of portfolio planning techniques discussed in Part One are now a common influence in marketing-mix decisions.

In the following pages the essential background to marketing-mix management is discussed: target marketing; the differential advantage and the key analyses for developing the marketing mix.

There are two key decisions which are central to marketing management: the selection of target markets which determine where the firm will compete and the design of the marketing mix (product, price, promotion and distribution method) which will determine its success in these markets.

Selection of target markets

A market is defined as the set of actual and potential buyers of a product. In today's rapidly changing environment products and markets have a limited life expectancy. A firm which does not update and change its products and markets is unlikely to be successful for long. A major job of management is to determine which markets offer the business opportunities for profit and growth in the future. Market research is the tool used to generate the information for reaching such decisions. Three areas for research are particularly important. First, the firm will want to estimate the size and growth potential of alternative markets since in general it will prefer to operate in growth rather than mature or declining markets. Second, it will wish to judge the strength of competition in candidate markets. How tough is the competition? Will it be possible to carve out a niche without strong reaction from existing competitors? Third, choice of target market will be influenced by the fit of the market requirements with the firm's own core capabilities. A heavy engineering company, for example,

is unlikely to be effective in switching to fast-moving consumer goods where it lacks technological or marketing expertise. In general, a company will seek product and market opportunities in areas where it has the core capabilities to form the basis for a competitive edge.

After a broad market is identified comes the key task of *market segmentation. Undifferentiated marketing* (Figure 12.1), a single marketing mix offered to the entire market, is rarely successful because markets are not homogeneous but made up of different types of buyers with diverse wants regarding product benefits, price, channels of distribution and service. A market segment is a group of buyers with similar purchasing characteristics. For example, the car

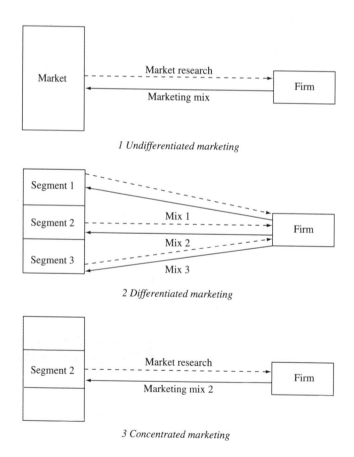

1 Undifferentiated marketing

2 Differentiated marketing

3 Concentrated marketing

Figure 12.1   Marketing segmentation and alternative marketing strategies

market might be divided into an economy segment (buyers looking for a cheap form of car transportation), a status segment, a sporting-orientated segment, etc. In developing a marketing plan, the marketers usually have to design appropriate offers for each segment if they are to compete. *Differentiated marketing* is the policy of attacking the market by tailoring separate product and marketing programmes for each segment. *Concentrated marketing* is often the best strategy for the smaller firm. This entails selecting to compete in one segment and developing the most effective marketing mix for this

submarket. Ford, for example, now pursue a policy of differentiated marketing whereas Volkswagen has traditionally concentrated on the smaller car market.

Developing the marketing mix

The marketing mix is the set of choices which defines the firm's offer to its target market. McCarthy (1996) has popularized the four Ps definition of the marketing mix – product, place, promotion and price (Table 12.1). Buyers in the

Table 12.1 Components of the marketing mix

Product	Price	Promotion	Place
Quality	List price	Advertising	Distributors
Features	Discounts	Personal selling	Retailers
Name	Allowances	Sales promotion	Locations
Packaging	Credit	Public relations	Inventory
Services			Transport
Guarantees			

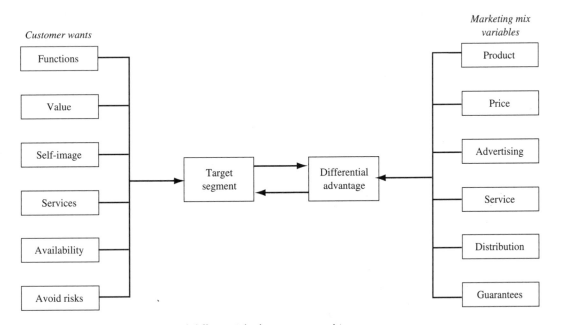

Figure 12.2 The marketing mix and differential advantage: matching customer wants

target segment have a set of wants and by research and successful adaption marketers will develop an offer to match them (Figure 12.2). 'Product' includes a number of decision elements as do the other Ps shown in Table 12.1. As emphasized earlier, the marketing mix for one segment may need to be quite different from that of another. In tailoring its mix a firm will seek to offer one which target customers will see as superior to that offered by competition. This goal of offering a marketing mix superior to competition is termed the *differential advantage*.

Four key marketing principles

In analysing marketing problems and developing marketing plans four concepts play a central role: marketing segmentation, the differential advantage, positioning strategy and relationship management.

Market segmentation

Pigou (1932) and Chamberlin (1938) developed the basic theory of market segmentation, showing that where different segments exist with separate demand functions, the monopolist would maximize profits by charging different prices to each of the segments. There are many practical examples of this type of price discrimination, for example a public utility charging different rates for business and domestic consumers. The concept of segmentation in marketing, however, is much more general. The marketer recognizes that consumers differ not only in the price they will pay but also in a wide range of benefits they expect from the 'product' and its method of delivery. The firm can discriminate not only in price but potentially in any of the four Ps. For example, the market for electronic calculators is made up of a number of segments including a segment of 'scientific users', an 'office' segment and a 'general public' segment. Each segment is likely to have a different price elasticity but, in addition, each desires different 'products': the scientific segment requir-

ing more sophisticated features and offices wanting greater robustness, for example. The channels utilized will also vary: scientists will be best sold to via personal selling or specialist journals, offices via specific distributors and the general public through the major retail chains. Similarly, the advertising and promotional strategies will differ in media and message between each segment.

Segmentation is central to marketing because different customer groups imply different marketing-mix strategies. The technique of segmenting a market also reveals profit opportunities and 'strategic windows' (Abell, 1978) for new competitors to challenge established market leaders. As a market develops, new segments open up and older ones decline. Within most markets is a mix of fierce and relatively weak competitive segments, slow and high growth segments (for example, the segment of people wanting large, luxury cars has declined relative to the economy segment). The marketing strategist will be seeking to identify those dynamic segments offering the best growth and profit possibilities.

Differential advantage

Target market segmentation is, however, insufficient for strategic planning since, in general, other companies will also be competing for any segment chosen. To be successful, marketers must also develop a differential advantage which will distinguish their offer from competitors in the segment. Only by creating such a differential advantage can the firm ordinarily obtain high profits. In a market where no firm has a differential advantage consumers choose on the basis of price, and price or 'perfect' competition ensures that profits are pushed towards zero. The task of the modern business is to seek what may be termed a 'quasi-monopoly – to make itself unique to consumers so that they will not switch to competitors for minor price advantages. High-profit firms such as Glaxo, Marks & Spencer, Avon Cosmetics, Ikea, Yamaha and Procter & Gamble are generally those which have succeeded in creating such consumer preferences. These differential advantages may be obtained potentially via any element of the marketing mix – creating a superior product to competition, more attractive designs, better service, more effective distribution, better advertising or selling, and so on. The keys are understanding that an 'advantage' is based upon research into what customers really value and that a 'differential' is derived from an evaluation of competitive strategies and offers.

Positioning strategy

Positioning is the amalgam of these two earlier principles. Positioning strategy refers to the choice of target market segment which describes the customers the business will seek to serve, and the choice of differential advantage which defines how it will compete with rivals in the segment. Thus Porsche is positioned in the prestige segment of the car market with a differential advantage based on technical performance. The Mothercare store is positioned to serve mothers with young children with a differential advantage based on breadth of merchandise assortment for that target segment. The appropriateness and effectiveness of the positioning strategy is the major determinant of a business's growth and profit performance.

Relationship management

Early descriptions of the marketing mix suggested that marketing amounted to one-off transactional relationships between the seller and the buyer. But today the focus is on developing long-run relationships with customers. It is dangerous to exploit buyers for short-run gain; the marketing mix should be formulated to create long-run, mutually beneficial relationships. Satisfied customers are assets with years of income-generating potential. Invariably, they are easiest to interest in new products and line extensions which offer the company additional opportunities for growth and profits. Marketers need to look for a marketing mix which will incentivize customers to buy into a long-term

relationship. (For a review of this new emphasis in marketing see Webster, 1992.)

Key analyses for developing marketing strategy

In formulating its choice of target market segment, marketing mix and differential advantage the firm will focus its research in six major areas.

Market analysis

As described earlier, before committing itself further the company should assess the growth and profit opportunities likely to be open to it in the candidate market.

Customer analysis

The firm will need to research how the market is segmented, which of these segments are the most attractive and what are the benefits desired by customers within each of these segments. Knowledge of such factors will be central to designing its product and offer. In addition, to develop its promotional and distribution strategy it will need to determine who are the key people affecting product choice in the buying group (the household or buying organization) and what type of buying process occurs before a decision is reached (for example, how information is sought, how alternatives are compared).

Competitive analysis

Developing a differential advantage means making target buyers an offer superior to competition. Clearly, therefore, this strategy requires identifying who the competitors are now and whether new ones may emerge in the future. The marketer needs to judge what their strategic objectives are, how their offer is perceived by buyers and how it may change in the future. Finally, it is crucial to estimate how competitors are likely to react to any strategic initiative on your part. If you introduce a new product or cut prices in an effort to gain market share, is this initiative likely to be nullified by speedy retaliation from competition? (For a thorough discussion of competitive analysis see Porter, 1980.)

Trade analysis

Most companies do not sell all their goods directly to the final consumer but use trade intermediaries – wholesalers, distributors, agents and retailers – to do this for them. Such an arrangement offers the company economies in marketing and distribution and the opportunity to sell to wider markets. On the other hand, these intermediaries are normally independent and their commercial goals will not be identical to those of the individual manufacturers they buy from. Thus the company will need to consider how to motivate the trade to give its product preferential treatment in their presentations to the public.

Trade analysis should be focused around the following questions:

1   What role does the product play in the trade's merchandise mix (for example, traffic generation or margin generation)?
2   How does the trade merchandise the product (for example, self-service versus personal selling)?
3   How satisfied is the trade with the marketing and trade strategies of competitors?
4   What differential advantage might be obtained through actions such as generous trade terms, extensive advertising, improved delivery, etc.?

Environmental analysis

Strategy formulation needs also to consider the changing environment of the business. Success will be affected by broad changes in the economic, demographic, sociopolitical and technological environment. In the more immediate marketing environment, management must study the problems and opportunities being cre-

ated by new consumer tastes, changing patterns of distribution (for example, from independent shops to multiple grocery-type shops) and emerging products. Such forces curtail the product life cycle of existing products and necessitate continual strategic innovation and repositioning if the firm is to maintain its viability.

Economic and stakeholder analysis

In assessing a strategy the firm will want to assess the financial implications and its impact on stakeholder groups of importance to the firm. For a business the strategy will need to generate an adequate level of profit to satisfy shareholders and provide for the firm's continuing investment requirements. Since investment generally anticipates profit return, the cash requirements will also have to be considered – can the business finance the marketing strategy? Other stakeholder or interest groups that may constrain the policy include consumer organizations, the local community, government regulatory bodies, unions and suppliers. The well-designed strategy will have considered the impacts on all relevant parties.

Marketing-mix decisions

Market research and business appraisal to complete these six analyses, together with judgements about how the company is to position itself against potential target market segments and to develop a differential advantage, are implemented by management decisions on the marketing mix. Important normative rules for optimizing the marketing mix have been developed by economists. These rules stem from the classical model of the firm in which output and price are the only decision variables and where sales are optimized at the point at which marginal revenue equals marginal cost. Dorfman and Steiner (1954) extended this to include other 'marketing-mix' variables, namely advertising and product quality. The Dorfman–Steiner theorem showed that short-run profits are maximized where the company balances lower prices, increased advertising expenditure and higher-quality products in such a way as to equate:

$$\xi q \frac{P}{C} = \xi = \mu$$

where the first expression is the elasticity of demand with respect to quality improvement multiplied by price over average unit cost, the second is the price elasticity of demand and the third is the marginal revenue product of advertising.

The Dorfman–Steiner theorem provides an important insight for designing the marketing mix and several studies have tried to estimate and apply their rule (for example, Lambin, 1969; Corstjens and Doyle, 1981). In practice, however, its use is limited for a number of important reasons. In particular, it is extremely difficult to estimate these marginal effects, especially in oligopolistic markets where competitive reaction is a major dilemma and where many variables (advertising, intensity of distribution and price) interact with one another. Also, the firm is generally not seeking to maximize profits solely, but may have a range of strategic goals (growth, risk avoidance, supporting complementary products in the firm's range, etc.). Some of these issues become clearer when the elements of the marketing mix are considered.

Product policy

Economic theory has little to say about product policy because the theory of consumer behaviour treats the products themselves rather than the benefits or characteristics they possess as the direct objects of utility. Under such an assumption little can be said about the key questions of how one product competes with another or how one can develop a superior product. Recently economists have tried to fill this gap by developing a new theory of consumer behaviour which defines a product as a bundle of characteristics

which are the ultimate goal of the buyer. As Lancaster (1966) has shown, this opens the possibility of a much more fruitful set of insights into consumer behaviour.

Paradoxically, this notion that consumers are interested in the benefits provided by a marketer's offer rather than the product itself has always been central to marketing theory. The 'new economics' mirrors an approach which has been long applied in marketing to the study of brand preferences. To a marketing manager a product is the constellation of benefits generated by the physical product, its design, features, packaging, style and service support, which together provide satisfaction to the consumer. It is often said that much of IBM's original success was based on its recognition that the cost and complexity of computers would make them unattractive to industry executives. At the same time, IBM knew that these executives increasingly needed more effective systems for efficiently and rapidly handling and manipulating information. IBM's offer was not a computer but a 'management information system' made up not only of the hardware but software, attractive input/output and related periph-erals, technical support, training, installation, operational back-up and easy financial arrangements. The founder of Revlon Cosmetics, one of the most successful consumer goods com-panies, put the distinction between products and benefits more colourfully when he said 'in the factory we make cosmetics, in the store we sell hope!'

For marketing it is crucial to see how the product's benefits are perceived by consumers rather than how they are defined by production experts. *Product positioning* is a market research technique which seeks to elicit from buyers a description or 'map' of how alternative brands are perceived. Figure 12.3 shows a positioning study by Johnson (1971) of the US beer market. The dimensions (characteristics) buyers appear to use when judging beers are lightness and mildness. The circles show the preference of buyers. Since, of course, different segments have differing tastes, these are spread and the

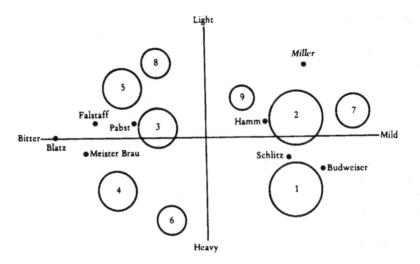

Figure 12.3 A product positioning study of the US beer market

radius of the circle indicates the estimated size of each consumer segment. Positioning studies have obvious uses in product planning: they show the strengths and weaknesses of the manufacturers' brands along the dimensions which are important to consumers, they show how closely competitive brands are seen and they indicate where different segment preferences are. Such insights have obvious implications for repositioning the product by quality changes, design, packaging or advertising modifications and also for new product development.

Product positioning models suggest seven alternative strategies marketers can pursue by modifying their product or persuasive communications (Boyd *et al.*, 1972):

1   Developing a new brand.
2   Modifying the existing brand.
3   Altering beliefs about the company's brand.
4   Altering beliefs about the competitors' brands.
5   Altering the importance attached to the individual characteristics.
6   Calling attention to neglected characteristics.
7   Shifting consumer preferences.

Pricing policy

The economic theory of price shows that profits are maximized when prices are set to equate marginal revenue and marginal cost. An obvious practical problem is that other variables usually affect demand both independently and interactively with price. For example, some studies have shown that advertising increases price elasticity. In principle, modern econometrics provides methods of estimation in such circumstances and there have been a number of successful empirical applications published (see Hanssens *et al.*, 1990).

In general, however, few firms explicitly follow the economic model in developing pricing policy. Most find estimating the parameters of the demand function too difficult time-consuming and expensive. In addition, with such a rapidly changing marketing environment, few would expect such parameters to be stable. In practice, management price on the basis of more intuitive judgements about the nature of cost, demand and competition. Pricing is also significantly affected by the firm's objectives. Where the firm has, for example, a long-run strategic goal of winning a dominant market share then its price is likely to be significantly lower than for a firm aiming to maximize current profits.

In setting prices the manufacturer has to consider not only its own profitability and the reaction of buyers, but other parties too. The company's distributors must be given an adequate profit margin to ensure that they have sufficient incentive to push the product. The decision maker will also have to consider the likely reaction of competitors to a switch in pricing policy. Not only are existing competitors affected by pricing policy but the level of profit margin is likely to influence the entry rate of new competitors. From time to time, government agencies also affect pricing policy for anti-inflation or anti-monopoly reasons.

Studies show that in practice almost all companies price on the basis of cost-plus. Price is determined by adding some fixed percentage to total unit cost. Unfortunately, such findings do not really tell us much without a theory of how the mark-up percentage is determined. The major determinant of the potential mark-up is the product's differential advantage. The greater the perceived value it has over competitive products, the more the consumer will pay. The most sophisticated marketing companies like Hewlett-Packard and 3M Corporation calculate this perceived value to the consumer in considerable detail before making a pricing decision (Leszinski and Marn, 1997). The McKinsey management consulting firm advocates calculating this value by comparing the product's total costs and benefits with those of a 'reference product': for example, the market leader.

Consider a company seeking to price a new industrial product X in a market where the brand leader is product Y. Users of Y pay £3000 for the product, another £2000 to set up the product (for example, transportation, engineering, installation) and over the life of the product spend another £5000 in maintenance and operating costs, making a total life-cycle cost of £10 000. Suppose the new product X has features which lower start-up and post-purchase costs to £4000 (compared with £7000 for product Y), yielding a £3000 life-cycle saving. Then the economic value to the buyer of product X is £6000. That is, the consumer should be willing to pay up to £6000 for the new product. At £6000 there would be no incentive to switch from the brand leader. Hence, the supplier might decide to price it at £4000 to produce a £2000 'customer savings incentive'.

The most common types of pricing policies firms pursue in practice are the following.

Market-penetration pricing

Here the firm prices low, sacrificing short-term profits, to aim at a dominant market share. Circumstances favouring this policy are:

1. Where the market is highly price elastic,
2. Where total unit costs will decline substantially with production experience,
3. Where a low price will discourage new competitors entering the market.

Market-skimming pricing

This entails setting high initial prices which yield high profit margins over a relatively small volume and generally for a short period of time. It is a viable option where:

1. A segment of significant size exists which will buy at the high initial price,
2. The firm has limited production capacity or resources with which to expand,
3. The high initial price will not attract an immediate competitive takeover of the market,
4. The high price creates an image of a superior product.

Cost-orientated pricing

Most firms, as noted, set prices largely on the basis of product costs. *Mark-up pricing* and cost-plus pricing set price by adding some fixed percentage to the unit cost. *Target pricing* is another cost-orientated pricing approach that sets prices to achieve a certain target return on investment.

Perceived-value pricing

Unlike the cost-orientated policies, this approach, as described earlier, bases price on demand considerations – on how the buyers perceive the value of the product relative to competition. To be effective this approach requires market research to obtain an accurate picture of the market's perceptions.

Price discrimination

This is another common form of demand pricing whereby the firm seeks to charge different types of customer with different prices for the same or similar product. Where segments exist with different price elasticities this type of discrimination allows the firm to achieve higher profits. To be successful, customers in the higher-price segment must not be allowed to buy from the lower-price segment. In addition, the practice should not lead to serious customer resentment.

Companies change their prices and strategies over time. The most common stimuli to price increases are rising costs of increased demand for the firm's product. Price cutting can be initiated from excess capacity in the industry, the loss of market share or because the company decides to strengthen its position in the market.

Promotional policy

After a company has designed a product and offer to match the wants of its target market segment, it needs to communicate this offer to buyers and persuade them to try it. There are four main tools which may be used to achieve these goals: advertising; personal selling; sales promotion and public relations. In general, before purchasing a product buyers have to be brought through various stages of the communications process. First, they have to be made *aware* of the product's existence. Second, they have to *comprehend* the benefits the product offers. Third, they need to become *convinced* that it will meet their wants. Finally, they have to be brought to the point of making a positive *purchase* decision (Aaker and Myers, 1996).

The different communications tools are frequently used to achieve specific communications goals. Advertising is particularly good at making the market aware of a new product, but it is usually far less effective than personal selling at closing the sale. Personal selling is usually a very costly means of creating awareness and comprehension, but more efficient at stimulating conviction and purchase. There are also differences between consumer and industrial goods. Sales promotion and publicity tend to be used for both types of marketing but because of the larger number of buyers which characterize consumer marketing, mass media advertising is more important there, whereas personal selling is usually the major selling medium in industrial marketing.

Here we shall note the key decision areas in advertising. In planning advertising, marketers, usually in conjunction with their advertising agency, will need to make five decisions. First, they will need a clear definition of the target market segment to which the advertising is to be directed. They will then need to determine the most effective media (newspapers, journals, TV, radio, posters, etc.) for getting their message to these people. Increasingly, agencies use a computer program to seek an optimum combination of media which will deliver the desired number of exposures to the target audience. Linear programming, heuristic programming and simulation models have all been used as aids to help planners determine the media mix which maximizes effective exposure subject to budget and other company constraints. The third area for decision is on the form and content of the message or copy to be expressed in the advertising. In general, the advertising agency will try to create a message which will express the differential advantage of the product in a manner which makes it believable, desirable and exclusive. The other two decision areas concern determining how much should be spent on advertising and how the investment should be subsequently evaluated and controlled.

Econometric studies have been widely used to estimate the pay-off of advertising and determine the optimum advertising budget. For example, in a study for a major alcoholic drink product, Corstjens and Doyle (1981) used time-series data to estimate the demand function of the brand as:

$$q_t = 4.27 - 0.004B_t + 0.245A_t - 1.20P_t + 0.672q_{t-1}$$

where q_t = sales of the brands at time t in units, B_t = industry sales of the product class, A_t = brand advertising expenditure (in logs) and P_t = price (in logs) of the brand at time t.

This equation explained 85 per cent of the variation in sales of the brand. From this it was possible to calculate the short- and long-term advertising elasticities for the brand as 0.14 and 0.43 respectively. Then using the Dorfman–Steiner theorem (which shows that at the optimal level of advertising, the marginal revenue product of advertising equals the price elasticity of demand), it was shown that the optimal long-term advertising ratio was 13 per cent of sales for this brand.

Distribution policy

Distribution management is concerned with decisions on moving goods from the producer to the target consumers. Decisions about distribution channels are very important because they intimately affect all other marketing mix choices and because, once made, they are not easily changed. In principle, a manufacturer can choose between selling the goods directly to the consumer and using a variety of distributors and retailers.

The marketing distribution channel undertakes a number of tasks besides the physical transportation and storing of goods. Intermediaries may also undertake market research for the manufacturer, promotion, pricing and negotiation with the customer, and financing the sale and purchase of the goods. Manufacturers use intermediaries to perform some or all of these functions as this often leads to superior efficiency in marketing the goods to the customers. Intermediaries, through their experience,

specialization and contacts can often offer the manufacturer more than it can achieve by going direct.

In developing a distribution strategy the manufacturer will make choices about the types of intermediary to use (agencies, distributors, retailers, etc.), the number to use, the specific tasks they are to undertake (storage, advertising, pricing, transport, etc.) under which the intermediary will undertake these tasks. Central to the problem of channel management is the recognition that distributors are independent businesses with goals that are at least partially conflicting with those of the manufacturer. Whether the manufacturer can design the channel to meet its own goals depends upon the power it has and the ability to motivate the intermediaries to cooperate. Knowledge of these marketing issues has been enriched by a considerable number of research studies by behavioural scientists (for example, Stern and El-Ansary, 1996). One of the remarkable changes in the last two decades has been the growth in power of the major retail chains at the expense of grocery manufacturers. Increasing concentration in grocery retailing has meant that manufacturers depend on the major chains to give them effective distribution and the retailers have not been slow to utilize this power in demanding higher margins and better terms from their suppliers in exchange for cooperation.

In choosing distribution channels the manufacturer will seek intermediaries which meet four criteria. First, intermediaries should be orientated to serving its target market. A manufacturer of fashionwear for upper-income women will need to get its product into retail outlets effectively serving such a clientele. Second, the firm will want distributors which help it to exploit its differential advantage. If the product's competitive edge is in sophisticated technology features offering cost savings to buyers, then the manufacturer will need dealers capable of explaining these benefits to prospects. Third, working with a particular channel must be economically rational for the manufacturer. Direct selling with a company salesforce is a powerful channel but it is too expensive for companies without a significant market share. Finally, the manufacturer will be influenced by the control and motivation of prospective intermediaries. A distributor selling a wide range of successful competitive products might give insufficient attention to a newcomer's product.

Distribution channels once established are not easy to change. Yet as the manufacturer's circumstances or the market evolves it often becomes necessary to adapt or even radically revise existing distribution channels. When starting out, a manufacturer may choose distributors to market its product because this will reduce overhead costs. But if the company grows it is likely to become increasingly financially attractive to switch from distributors to direct selling because the higher overheads can now be spread over a larger volume. In addition, channels, like products, are subject to life cycles and highly successful forms of distribution give way to new forms more effectively geared to today's markets. Variety stores and small supermarkets have lost ground to superstores, catalogue showrooms and discount stores (see Davidson *et al.*, 1983). Such forces mean that the firm must be continually monitoring the performance and prospects of its distribution arrangements and be prepared to adapt them when conditions change.

Conclusion

In today's rapidly changing and highly competitive international environment a business can be successful only if its offer matches the wants of buyers at least as effectively as its best competitors. Marketing management is the task of planning this match. It is based upon the analysis of customers, competitors and distributors, the selection of target market segments and the design of marketing mixes which will provide the firm with a differential advantage. An organization's success in creating a differential advantage determines its international competitiveness and profit performance.

The changing environment – changing wants, new competitors and technologies, different stakeholder pressures on the firm – means that a differential advantage is never secure. Change requires the firm continually to reposition itself by shifting from declining to emerging market segments and renewing its differential advantage by such measures as improving its product features, adapting new technologies or higher levels of service. Businesses which fail to develop such repositioning strategies gradually lose contact with buyers and give way to firms which are more successfully marketing orientated.

References

Aaker, D. A., and Myers, J. C. (1996) *Advertising Management*, 4th edn. Prentice-Hall, Englewood Cliffs, NJ.

Abell, D. F. (1978) 'Strategic windows', *Journal of Marketing*, **42**, No. 2, April, 21–26.

Boyd, H. W., Ray, M. L. and Strong, E. C. (1972) 'An attitudinal framework for advertising strategy', *Journal of Marketing*, **36**, No. 2, April, 27–33.

Chamberlin, E. H. (1938) *The Theory of Monopolistic Competition*, Harvard University Press, Cambridge, MA.

Corstjens, M. and Doyle, P. (1981) 'Evaluating the profitability of advertising for heavily advertised brands', *European Journal of Operational Research*, **8**, No. 3, November, 249–255.

Davidson, W. R., Sweeney, D. J. and Stampfl, R. W. (1983) *Retailing Management*, 6th edn, Wiley, New York.

Dorfman, R. and Steiner, P. O. (1954) 'Optimal advertising and optimal quality', *American Economic Review*, **59**, June, 817–831.

Hanssens, D. M., Parsons, L. J. and Schultz, R. L. (1990) *Market Response Models: Econometric and Time Series Analysis*, Kluwer, Boston.

Johnson, R. M. (1971) 'Market segmentation: a strategic management tool', *Journal of Marketing Research*, **8**, No. 1, February, 15–23.

Lambin, J. J. (1969) 'Measuring the profitability of advertising: an empirical study', *Journal of Industrial Economics*, **17**, No. 2, April, 86–103.

Lancaster, K. J. (1966) 'A new approach to consumer theory', *Journal of Political Economy*, **74**(2), April, 132–157.

Leszinski, R. and Marn, M. V. (1997) 'Setting value, not price', *McKinsey Quarterly*, No. 1, 98–115.

McCarthy, E. J. (1996) *Basic Marketing*, 12th edn, Irwin, Homewood, IL.

Pigou, A. C. (1932) *The Economics of Welfare*, Macmillan, London.

Porter, M. E. (1980) *Competitive strategy*, Macmillan, New York.

Shapiro, B. P. and Jackson, B. B. (1978) 'Industrial pricing to meet consumer needs', *Harvard Business Review*, **56**, No. 6, November, 119–127.

Stern, L. W., and El-Ansary, A. I. (1996) *Marketing Channels*, 5th edn, Prentice Hall, Englewood Cliffs, NJ.

Webster, F. E. (1992) 'The changing role of marketing in the corporation', *Journal of Marketing*, October, 1–17.

Further reading

Doyle, P. (1998) *Marketing Management and Strategy*, 2nd edn, Prentice-Hall International, Hemel Hempstead, UK. Geared more to the European market. Less academic than Kotler and focusing on how to approach the key marketing mix in practice.

Hooley, C. J. and Saunders, J. (1997) *Competitive Positioning*, 2nd edn, Prentice-Hall International, Hemel Hempstead, UK. As the chapter emphasized, segmentation and positioning are at the heart of marketing. These topics are very well covered in this text by two well-known British academics.

Kotler, P. (1997) *Marketing Management: Analysis, Planning, Implementation and Control*, 9th edn, Prentice-Hall, Englewood Cliffs, NJ. Still by far the most comprehensive and up to date of the American MBA textbooks. Not the most stimulating read but an essential encyclopaedia for any marketing professional or student.

CHAPTER 13

New product development

SUSAN HART

Introduction

Underlying themes of previous chapters – particularly those dealing with the nature of marketing, competitiveness and strategies for success – deal with the dynamics of consumers, competitors and technologies, all of which require companies to review and reconstitute the products and services they offer to the market. This, in turn, requires the development of new products and services to replace current ones, a notion inherent in the discussion of Levitt's (1960) *Marketing Myopia*. This chapter is concerned with the set of activities required to bring new products and services to market, known as the new product development (NPD) process.

NPD is a thriving activity. In 1996 in the US, marketers launched almost 26 000 new products in food and beverages, health and beauty and household and pet products. This was an increase of 23 per cent on the previous year (*Grocer*, January 18, 1997, p. 15). But a success rate of less than 10 per cent must mean a lot of effort goes to waste. In this chapter, the activities required to develop new products are discussed in the light of an extensive body of research into what distinguishes successful from unsuccessful new products. For a fuller discussion of that research see Craig and Hart (1992) and Montoya-Weiss and Calantone (1994).

The process of developing new products

Considering successful innovations of the past 20 years, one might be tempted to think that they are all good ideas: the Walkman, laser printers, automatic teller machines. And so they are, but does that mean that they could not have failed? What were the basic ideas? The Walkman: portable, personal audio entertainment. The laser printer: fast, accurate, flexible, high quality reproduction. Automatic teller machines: 24-hour cash availability from machines. As ideas, these might have been transformed into products in numerous ways, perhaps less successfully than the products we now find so familiar and convenient.

Imagine the alternative forms for personal audio entertainment: a bulkier headset which contains the tape-playing mechanism and earphones; a small hand-held player, complete with carrying handle, attached to earphones via a cord; a 'backpack' style player with earphones. All of these ideas would have delivered to the idea of 'portable, personal audio entertainment', but which if any of these would have enjoyed the same success as the Walkman? And the automatic teller machines? These might have been developed as stand-alone units, much like bottle banks, requiring the identification of ideal locations, planning permission and consumer confidence to enter them. Would they have been as widespread as the hole-in-the-wall?

Think of another 'good idea' – the light-weight, low-pollution, low-cost, easily-parked town car. Now imagine one realization of the idea: three-wheeled, battery-run (with 80 km worth of charge only), and, for the British weather, an *optional* roof. This realization is, of course, the widely-quoted failure, the C5. Yet the *idea* remains a good one. The issue at stake here is that good ideas do not automatically translate into workable, appealing products. The idea has to be given a physical reality which performs the function of the idea, which potential customers find an attractive alternative for which they are prepared to pay the asking price. This task requires new product development to be managed actively, which is the subject of this chapter.

The activities carried out during the process of developing new products are well summarised in various new product development (NPD) models. These are templates or maps which can be used to describe and guide those activities required to bring a new product from an idea or opportunity, through to a successful market launch. NPD models take numerous forms.

One of the most recognized NPD models is that developed by the American consultants, Booz Allen Hamilton (BAH) (1982). This model is shown in Figure 13.1.

Each of the stages is described below in turn.

The stages of the new product development process

New product strategy

A specific new product strategy explicitly places NPD at the heart of an organization's priorities, sets out the competitive requirements of the company's new products and is effectively the first 'stage' of the development process. It comprises an explicit view of where a new programme of development sits in relation to the technologies that are employed by the company and the markets which these technologies will serve. In addition, this view must be communicated throughout the organization and the extent to which this happens is very much the responsibility of top management. In fact, much research attention has focused on the role of top management in the eventual success of NPD. While Maidique and Zirger (1984) found new product successes to be characterized by a high level of top management support, Cooper and Kleinschmidt (1987) found less proof of top management influence, discovering that many new product failures do often have as much top management support. More recently, Dougherty and Hardy (1996) found that although lip-service was given to the importance of innovation, it often takes a backseat compared to other initiatives such as cost-cutting and down-sizing, especially where there is less of a history of success in developing new products. And yet, one of the most important roles which top management have to fill is that

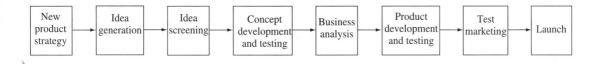

Figure 13.1   The Booz Allen Hamilton model of new product development

of incorporating NPD as a meaningful component of an organization's strategy and culture.
In some cases it is necessary for the firm to
change its philosophy on NPD, in turn causing a
change in the whole culture. Nike's NPD
process has changed dramatically over the last
10 years. Previously they believed that every
new product started in the lab and the product
was the most important thing. Now they believe
it is the consumer who leads innovation and the
specific reason for innovation comes from
the marketplace. The reason for this change is
the fierce competition that has developed in recent
years within the athletic shoe industry so that
product innovation no longer led to sustained
competitive advantage and so manufacturers
could no longer presume that if Mike Jordan
chooses a certain shoe everyone else in America
will follow. More emphasis was then put on
marketing research and targeting smaller
groups of individual customers, with the
emphasis changing from push to pull NPD.
The distinction between technology-push and
market-pull is covered a little later in this chapter.

While NPD is central to long-term success
for companies, it is both expensive and risky,
and a majority of 'new' products and services
are not entirely 'new'. The new product strategy
specifies how innovative the firm intends to be
in its NPD and how many new product projects
should be resourced at any one time. The seminal work of Booz, Allen and Hamilton in 1968
and in 1980 revealed the importance of this
specification. In their 1968 study, an average of
58 new product ideas were required to produce
one successful new product. By 1982, a new
study showed this ratio had been reduced to
seven to one. The reason forwarded for this
change was the addition of a preliminary stage:
the development of an explicit, new product
strategy that identified the strategic business
requirements new products should satisfy.
Effective benchmarks were set up so that ideas
and concepts were generated to meet strategic
objectives. Seventy-seven per cent of the companies studied had initiated this procedure with
remarkable success.

When ideas were generated in line with
strategic objectives an extremely effective 'elimination' of ideas which in the past cluttered and
protracted the NPD process occurred. Although
written in the early 1980s, the lessons to be
learned from the work of BAH are still relevant.
For example, consultant with PRTM, Mike
Anthony, describes a company staffing 22 projects, when it had capacity for only nine, and
typically would only turn out three new products which would make money. Clearly an
agenda – strategy – for cutting down on the
effort going into 22 projects would give rise to
the opportunity to increase the resources channelled into the remaining projects (*Industry
Week*, December 16, 1996, p. 45). Setting a clear
strategy for new product development also sets
up the key criteria against which all projects can
be managed through to the market launch. New
Product Strategy, which has also been called the
Product Innovation Charter and New Product
Protocol (Crawford, 1984; Cooper, 1993) has
been shown to enhance the success rates of the
eventual market launch (Hultink, Griffin, Hart
and Robben, 1997).

While it is often argued that new product
development should be guided by a new product strategy, it is important that the strategy is
not so prescriptive as to restrict, or stifle, the creativity necessary for NPD. In addition to stating
the level of newness, a new product strategy
should encompass the balance between technology and marketing, the level and nature of new
product advantage, and the desired levels of
synergy and risk acceptance. Each of these is discussed below:

1 *Technology and marketing*: One of the most
   prevalent themes running throughout the contributions on strategic orientations is the merging
   of the technical and marketing strategic thrusts.
   This is also seen as a dichotomy between allowing
   the market to 'pull' new products from companies
   and companies 'pushing' new technologies onto
   markets. The advantage of the former is that
   new products, being derived from customers,
   are more likely to meet their need, while the

advantage of the latter is that the new technology will meet needs more effectively than its incumbent and will be harder for competitors to emulate, leading to greater sales, profit and competitive advantage for longer periods of time. Each, however, has disadvantages. With new products developed through market pull, there is a greater tendency for the new products to be only marginally better than existing products on the market, leading to product proliferation, possible cannibalization of brands and an 'advantage' over competitors that is short lived as it is based on technologies with which most of the market players are familiar. With technology-push new products, there is the risk that the new technology is not, in fact, relevant for customers and is rejected by them. As ever, the emphasis should be on achieving a balance between the two: there should be a fusion between technology-led and market-led innovations at the strategic level (Johne and Snelson, 1988; Dougherty, 1992). Both Sony and Canon employ 'strategic training' for their engineering and R&D staff, which includes professional training in marketing Harryson (1997).

2 *Product advantage*: The literature refers to new product strategies which emphasize the search for a differential advantage, through the product itself (Cooper, 1984). Product advantage is of course a subjective and multi-faceted term, but may be seen as comprising the following elements: technical superiority, product quality, product uniqueness and novelty (Cooper, 1979), product attractiveness (Link, 1987) and high performance-to-cost ratio (Maidique and Zirger, 1984). The 'war' between Lever Brothers' Persil Power and Ariel Future shows how these companies were competing, strategically, on a platform of technologically-based product advantage. In the battle for cleaning power, Lever Brothers' technological advantage was systematically discredited by the competitors and shown to damage clothes, thereby destroying any potential advantages to customers.

3 *Synergy*: A further strategic consideration discussed here is the relationship between the NPD and existing activities, known as the synergy with existing activities. High levels of synergy are typically less risky, because a company will have more experience and expertise, although perhaps this contradicts the notion of pursuing product differentiation.

4 *Risk acceptance*: Finally, the creation of an internal orientation or climate which accepts risk is highlighted as a major role for the new product strategy. Although synergy might help avoid risk associated with lack of knowledge, the pursuit of product advantage must entail acceptance that some projects will fail. An atmosphere that refuses to recognize this tends to stifle activity and the willingness to pursue something new.

Once the general direction for NPD has been set, the process of developing new ideas, discussed below, can become more focused.

Idea generation

This is a misleading term, because, in many companies, ideas do not have to be 'generated'. They do, however, need to be managed. This involves identifying sources of ideas and developing means by which these sources can be activated to bring new ideas for products and services to the fore. The aim of this stage in the process is to develop a bank of ideas that fall within the parameters set by 'new product strategy'. Sources of new product ideas exist both within and outside the firm. Inside the company are technical departments such as research and development, design and engineering work on developing applications and technologies which will be translated into new product ideas. Equally, commercial functions such as sales and marketing will be exposed to ideas from customers and competitors. Otherwise, many company employees may have useful ideas: service mechanics, customer relations, manufacturing and warehouse employees are continually exposed to 'product problems' which can be translated into new product ideas. Outside the company, competitors, customers, distributors, inventors and universities are fertile repositories of information from which new product ideas come. Both sources, however, may have to be organized in such a way as to extract ideas. In short, the sources have to be *activated*. A myriad of techniques may be used to activate sources of new ideas, including brainstorming, morphological analysis, perceptual mapping and scenario planning.

Once a bank of ideas has been built, work can begin on selecting those that are most promising for further development.

Screening

The next stage in the product development process involves an initial assessment of the extent of demand for the ideas generated and of the capability the company has to make the product. At this, the first of several evaluative stages, only a rough assessment can be made of an idea, which will not yet be expressed in terms of design, materials, features or price. Internal company opinion will be canvassed from R&D, sales, marketing, finance, production, to assess whether the idea has potential, is practical, would fit a market demand, could be produced by existing plant, and to estimate the payback period. The net result of this stage is a body of ideas which are acceptable for further development. Checklists and forms have been devised to facilitate this process requiring managers to make 'guestimates' regarding potential market size, probable competition and likely product costs, prices and revenues. However, as at this stage of the process managers are still dealing with ideas, it is unrealistic to imagine that these 'guestimates' can be accurate. The 'newer' the new product, the more guesswork there will be in these screening checks. It is not until the idea is developed into a concept (see below) that more accurate data on market potential and makeability can be assembled.

Concept development and testing

Once screened, an idea is turned into a more clearly specified concept and testing this concept begins for its fit with company capability and its fulfilment of customer expectations. Developing the concept from the idea requires that a decision be made on the content and form of the idea. For example, a food company which has generated the idea of a low-calorie spread as a sandwich filler will decide on the *type* of spread; a low-calorie peanut butter, fish or meat paté or a mayonnaise-based concoction. All these concept variations may be specified and then subject to concept tests. Internally, the development team needs to know which varieties are most compatible with current production plant, which require plant acquisition, which require new supplies, and this needs to be matched externally, in relation to which versions are more attractive to customers. The latter involves direct customer research to identify the appeal of the product concept, or alternative concepts to the customer. Concept testing is worth spending time and effort on, collecting sufficient data to provide adequate information upon which the full business analysis will be made.

Business analysis

At this stage, the major 'go/no-go' decision will be made. The company needs to be sure that the venture is potentially worthwhile, as expenditure will increase dramatically after this stage. The analysis is based on the fullest information available to the company thus far. It encompasses:

1   A market analysis detailing potential total market, estimated market share within specific time horizon, competing products, likely price, break-even volume, identification of early adopters and specific market segments
2   Explicit statement of technical aspects, costs, production implications, supplier management and further R&D.
3   Explanation of how the project fits with corporate objectives.

The sources of information for this stage are both internal and external, incorporating any market or technical research carried out thus far.

The output of this stage will be a development plan with budget and an initial marketing plan.

Product development and testing

This is the stage where prototypes are physically made. Several tasks are related to this development. First, the finished product will be assessed regarding its level of functional performance. This is sometimes known as 'alpha testing'. Until now, the product has only existed in theoretical form or mock-up. It is only when component parts are brought together in a functional form that the validity of the theoretical product can be definitively established. Second, it is the first physical step in the manufacturing chain. It is not until the prototype is developed that alterations to the specification or to manufacturing configurations can be designed and put into place. Third, the product has to be tested with potential customers to assess the overall impression of the test product.

Some categories of product are more amenable to customer testing than others. Capital equipment, for example, is difficult to have assessed by potential customers in the same way as a chocolate bar can be taste-tested, or a dishwasher evaluated by an in-house trial. One evolving technique in industrial marketing, however, is called 'beta-testing', practised informally by many industrial product developers.

Test marketing

The penultimate phase in the development cycle, test marketing consists of small-scale tests with customers. Until now, the idea, the concept and the product have been 'tested' or 'evaluated' in a somewhat artificial context. Although several of these evaluations may well have compared the new product to competitive offering, other elements of the marketing mix have not been tested, nor the likely marketing reaction by competitors. At this stage the appeal of the product is tested amidst the mix of activities comprising the market launch: salesmanship, advertising, sales promotion, distributor incentives and public relations.

Test marketing is not always feasible, or desirable. Management must decide whether the industrial costs of test marketing can be justified by the additional information that will be gathered. Further, not all products are suitable for a small-scale test launch: passenger cars, for example, have market testing complete before the launch, while other products, once launched on a small scale, cannot be withdrawn, as with personal insurance. Finally, the delay involved in getting a new product to market may be advantageous to the competition, who can use the opportunity to be 'first-to-market'. Competitors may also wait until a company's test market results are known and use the information to help their own launch, or can distort the test results using their own tactics. Problems such as these have encouraged the development and use of computer-based market simulation models, which use basic models of consumer buying as inputs. Information on consumer awareness, trial and repeat purchases, collected via limited surveys or store data, are used to predict adoption of the new product.

Commercialisation or launch

This the final stage of the initial development process and is very costly. Decisions such as when to launch the product, where to launch it, how to launch it and to whom will be based on information collected throughout the development process. Table 13.1 summarizes the decisions required to complete the launch of a new product.

Location will, for some companies, entail the number of countries into which the product will be launched, whether national launches will be simultaneous, or roll out from one country to another (Chryssochoidis and Wong, 1998).

Launch strategy also includes any advertising and trade promotions necessary. Space must be booked, copy and visual material prepared, both for the launch proper, and the pre-sales into the distribution pipeline. The salesforce

Table 13.1 Launch strategy decisions	
Variables	*Previous study*
STRATEGIC LAUNCH VARIABLES	
Firm strategy	
Innovation strategy	2,3,4,5,8,9,11,12,17,19
Degree of forward & backward integration	1,4,7
Size of production scale entry	1,4
Product strategy	
Product innovativeness	1,10
Relative product newness	1,10,19
Quality	1,4
Market strategy	
Breadth of segments served	1,4
Stage of the product on its PLC	1,12,19
Target market growth	13,19
Number of competitors	12,19
TACTICAL LAUNCH VARIABLES	
Product	
Breadth of the product line	1,4
Direct manufacturing costs	4
Services	1,4
Price	
Pricing strategy: skim or penetrate?	1,4,12,14,16,17,18
Promotion	
Advertising	14,15,16,17,18
Promotion	14,15,16,17
Distribution	
Distribution intensity	1,4,12,15,16,17,18
Sales force effort	14,15,17

1	Biggadike (1979)	12	Choffray and Lilien (1984)
2	Glazer (1985)	13	Cooper (1984)
3	Green and Ryans (1990)	14	Cooper (1993)
4	Lambkin (1988)	15	Crawford (1984)
5.	Lieberman and Montgomery (1988)	16	Little (1975)
6	MacMillan and Day (1987)	17	Urban and Hauser (1991)
7	Roberts and Berry (1985)	18	Wind (1982)
8	Robinson and Fornell (1985)	19	Yoon and Lilien (1985)
9	Ryans (1988)		
10	Schmalensee (1982)		
11	Urban et al. (1986)		

Source: Hultink, Griffin, Hart and Robben (1997).

may require extra training in order to sell the new product effectively.

The final target segments should not, at this stage, be a major decision for companies who have developed a product with the market in mind and who have executed the various testing stages. This should have been identified through the various concept and product testing phases of the development. Attention should be more focused on identifying the likely early adopters of the product and focusing communications on them. In industrial markets, early adopters tend to be innovators in their own markets. The major concern of the launch should be the development of a strong, unified message to promote to the market, which reinforces the nature of the new product, its benefits over competitive products and its availability to customers. Recent research by Hultink, Griffin, Hart and Robben (1997) has shown the importance of having the tactics of the launch consistent with the level of innovativeness in the new product. In other words, the commercialization of the new product cannot successfully make claims for it that are dubious. The most successful launches they studied were innovations aimed at carefully selected niche markets, supported by exclusive distribution and pricing.

This explanation of the new product development process has used the model forwarded by Booz Allen Hamilton as an example; there are numerous other models, which are similar in their representation of a series of activities necessary to bring new products to market. The next section of the chapter considers the usefulness of these models.

Usefulness of models

The usefulness of the process models, such as that by BAH, lies in the way in which they provide an indication of the 'total' number of tasks that might be required in order to develop and launch a new product. The whole procedure has been described as one of information processing (de Meyer, 1985; Allen, 1985), so it is of value if

those executing the task of developing new products are given guidance regarding what information is required, where it might reside and to what use it might be put. A recent article by Ottum and Moore (1997) showed that, in particular, the processing of market information (defined as market size and customer needs and wants) is associated with superior new product performance. Table 13.2 shows the decisions required at each stage of the NPD process, together with an indication of the information needed to take that decision and its likely source.

The models of new product development processes as described above tend to be idealized and for this reason may be quite far removed from a specific, real instance of NPD. A number of authors have researched to what extent the prescriptive activities of the NPD process are undertaken by companies. In 1986, Cooper and Kleinschmidt used a 'skeleton' of the process taken from a variety of normative and empirically based prescriptive processes developed by other authors and found that there is a greater probability of commercial success if all of the process activities are completed. This finding is confirmed in another study which replicates the investigation in Australian companies (Dwyer and Mellor, 1991). Research by Page (1993) showed that a majority of American companies' studies do carry out these main activity stages. A more recent study of NPD practices in the UK and The Netherlands has shown that companies do carry out the activities prescribed by the BAH model but that the emphasis of every stage is on ascertaining the extent to which the product under development is acceptable to the market (Hart, Tzokas, Hultink and Commandeur, 1998). This is not surprising since the process of developing a new product is inherently risky, plagued as it is by uncertainty at every stage. Over the process, the uncertainty is reduced – be it regarding technology, makeability or potential customer response.

While it may be desirable to have a complete process of NPD, each additional activity

Table 13.2   Analysis of the NPD process based on Booz Allen Hamilton (1982)

Stage of development	Decision to be taken	Information needed for stage; nature of information	Sources of information
1. Explicit statement of new product strategy, budget allocation	Identification of *market* (NB not product) opportunities to be exploited by new products	Preliminary market and technical analysis; company objectives	Generated as part of continuous MIS and corporate planning
2. Idea generation (or gathering)	Body of initially acceptable ideas	Customer needs and technical developments in *previously* identified markets	Inside company: salesmen, technical functions Outside company: customers, competitors, inventors, etc.
3. Screening ideas: finding those with most potential	Ideas which are acceptable for further development	Assessment of whether there is a *market* for this type of product, and whether the company can make it. Assessment of financial implications: market potential and costs. Knowledge of company goals and assessment of fit	Main internal functions: – R&D – Sales – Marketing – Finance – Production
4. Concept development: turning an idea into a recognizable product concept, with attributed and market position identified	Identification of: key attributes that need to be incorporated in the product, major technical costs, target markets and potential	*Explicit* assessment of customer needs to appraise market potential *Explicit* assessment of technical requirements	Initial research with customer(s). Input from marketing and technical functions
5. Business analysis: full analysis of the proposal in terms of its business potential	Major go/no go decision: company needs to be sure the venture is worthwhile as expenditure dramatically increases after this stage Initial marketing plan Development plan and budget specification	Fullest information thus far: – detailed market analysis – explicit technical feasibility and costs – production implications – corporate objective	Main internal functions Customers
6. Product development: crystallizing the product into semi-finalised shape	Explicit marketing plan	Customer research with product. Production information to check 'makeability'	Customers Production
7. Test marketing: small-scale tests with customers	Final go/no go for launch	Profile of new product performance in light of competition, promotion and marketing mix variables	Market research; production, sales, marketing, technical people
8. Commercialization	Incremental changes to test launch Full-scale launch	Test market results and report	As for test market

extends the overall development time and may lead to late market introduction. There can be a price to pay for late market introduction. For example, Evans (1990) has quantified the consequence of extending the development time: delaying launch by six months can equal a loss of 33 per cent in profits over five years. Therefore a trade-off has to be made between completing all the suggested activities in the NPD process and the time which these activities take. Means of effecting this trade-off are discussed later in the chapter, but there is compelling evidence to suggest the importance of marketing activities in achieving NPD success.

As the result of their research findings Johne and Snelson (1988) advise companies to be novel in the market research approaches as well as to seek emerging new product opportunities and to offer more applications advice to customers so that they can create different ways of using products. Wind and Mahajan (1987) present a conceptual argument in which they identify a key role for marketing in what they call 'marketing hype'. 'Marketing hype' is a prelaunch activity encompassing concept testing, product testing and new product forecasting models. The importance of the market research activities in the NPD process is again highlighted by Cooper and Kleinschmidt (1986; 1987; 1990). Much of the extensive research of the Design Innovation Group has concentrated on the importance of good market research.

An opposing view cites the well-known example of the Sony Walkman product development in which the company entrepreneurs doggedly ignored the limiting factor of current demand patterns (Morita, Reingold and Shimomura, 1987). In the case of true innovations the role of traditional marketing and market research may be less useful. This does not, however, remove the importance of marketing's role in NPD. Despite these well-known examples, many others confirm the importance given to market research by practising product developers. Land Rover spends £1 million per annum on market research, compared to £20 000 five years previously (Gabb, 1991). Phileas Fogg, in

launching new size bags of its Tortilla Chips, based the decision on market research (*Marketing*, 1994). Even where formal market research is not used, companies such as Boeing, Hewlett Packard, and Motorola all involve customers directly in their innovation programmes (Nauman and Shannon, 1992).

In summary, the models can provide a useful framework on which to build a complete picture of the development, particularly with regard to the potential advantage of the product viewed from the customers' perspectives.

Criticisms of models

Despite its apparent usefulness, the BAH model, and, by implication, its derivatives have been criticized on a number of counts.

Idiosyncrasy

The NPD process is idiosyncratic to each individual firm and to the new product project in question. Its shape and sequence depends on the type of new product being developed and its relationship with the firm's current activities (Cooper, 1988; Johne and Snelson, 1988). In addition to the need to adapt the process to individual instances, in real situations there is no clear beginning, middle and end to the NPD process. For example, from one idea, several product concept variants may be developed, each of which might be pursued. Also, as an idea crystallizes, the developers may assess the nature of the market need more easily and the technical and production costs become more readily identified and evaluated.

Iteration

The iterative nature of the NPD process results from the fact that each stage or phase of development can produce numerous outputs which implicate both previous development work and future development progress. Using the model provided by Booz Allen Hamilton, if a new product concept fails the concept test, then there is no guidance as to what might happen next. In reality, a number of outcomes may result from a failed concept test, and these are described below.

- *A new idea:* It is possible that although the original concept is faulty, a better one is found through the concept tests; it would then re-enter the development process at the screening stage.
- *A new customer:* Alternatively, a new customer may be identified through the concept testing stage, since the objective of concept testing is to be alert to customer needs when formulating a new product. Any new customers would then feed into the idea generation and screening process. Figure 13.2 shows these and other possibilities and illustrates how, viewed as linear or sequential, the BAH model is inadequate, particularly regarding up-front activities.
- *Related strands of development:* A further point in relation to the sequencing of product development tasks is the existence of related strands of development. These related strands of development refer to marketing, technical (design) and production tasks or decisions that occur as the process unwinds. Each strand of development gives rise to problems and opportunities within the other two. For example, if, at the product development stage, production people have a problem which pushes production costs up, this could affect market potential. The marketing and technical assumptions need to be reworked in the light of this new information. A new design may be considered, or a new approach to the marketplace may be attempted. Whatever the nature of the final solution, it has to be based on the interplay of technical, marketing and manufacturing development issues, meaning that product development activity is iterative, not only between stages, but also within stages. Indeed, since many of the linear models do not adequately communicate the horizontal dimensions of the NPD process, several 'new generation' models have been developed These include the stage-gate model by Robert Cooper

(1993) and the 'fifth generation innovation process' by Rothwell (1994) and the 'blocked' model by Saren (1994). This new generation of process models build on the idea of 'parallel processing', which acknowledges the iterations between and within stages, categorizing them along functional configurations. The idea of parallel processing is prescriptive: it advises that major functions should be involved from the early stages of the NPD process to its conclusion. This, it is claimed, allows problems to be detected and solved much earlier than in the classic task-by-task, function-by function models. In turn, the entire process is much speedier, which is now recognized to be an important element in new product success. Hence, these are presented as solutions to the dilemma raised earlier, that the execution of the activities is required but not at the expense of speed in the process. Other related techniques which allow firms to accelerate their NPD include Quality Function Deployment (QFD), increasing rewards for R&D performance, relying on external sources of technology and improving the interface among the relevant functional areas (Calantone *et al.*, 1997). So important is the last of these methods that we revisit the substantial amount of research it has attracted towards the end of this chapter.

The inclusion of third parties in the process

Another criticism of the 'traditional' process model forwarded by BAH and others is that it fails to show the importance of parties external to the firm who can have a decided impact on the success of new product development. Research by Littler, Leverick and Bruce (1995) showed that 'collaborative' product development, which may include suppliers, customers and even in some instances, competitors, were common in industries such as telecommunications. Eisenhardt and Tabrizi (1994) studying the computing industry revealed that developments which involved suppliers could help accelerate development time. In the development of the Land Rover Discovery, 'outside' parties such as suppliers were brought in at an early stage. Similarly, Intel's development of the Pentium departed from its traditional models of development and involved both major customers and software suppliers in the design of the new product (Wheatley, 1994).

that of suppliers, where changes to supply may be required or advantageous.

The Stanford Innovation Project (Maidique and Zirger, 1984) identified functional co-ordination as a critical factor contributing to the development of *successful* new products. Support for the importance of functional co-

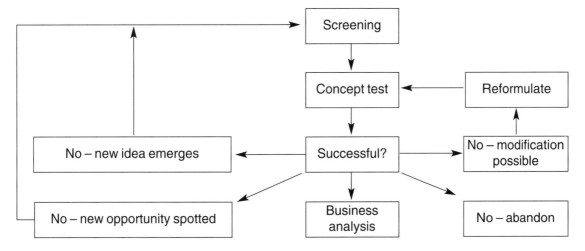

Figure 13.2   Iteration in the NPD process

These shortcomings emphasize that the management of the NPD process is more than simply the number and sequencing of its activities. The extent to which the activities can or cannot be effectively carried out demands attention to the *people* or *functions* within the process. It is to these issues that we now turn our attention.

People involved in the NPD process and the way in which these people are organized are critical factors in the outcome of new product developments. In order to combine technical and marketing expertise, a number of company functions have to be involved: R&D, manufacturing, engineering, marketing and sales. As the development of a new product may be the only purpose for which these people meet professionally, it is important that the NPD process adopted ensures that they work well and effectively together. Linked to this is also the need for the voice of the customer to be heard, as well as

ordination is to be found in numerous studies, including Pinto and Pinto (1990), who found that the higher the level of cross-functional cooperation, the more successful the outcome of new product development. The benefits of   a close relationship between functional co-ordination and an integrated set of NPD activities have already been highlighted, including the reduction of the development cycle time, cost savings and closer communication so that potential problems are detected very early on in the process (Larson, 1988). Although integration of all the relevant functional specialisms into the NPD process is necessary, one particular interface has been given more attention in research – the R&D/marketing interface, due to the impact of this interface on the success with which a technological development can be made to match customer need.

Although a host of issues pertain to the integration of the R&D and marketing

Table 13.3 The role of market information in achieving critical success factors

Success factor	Studies citing importance	Operationalization of success factors	Expected market information elements
		STRATEGIC SUCCESS FACTORS	
Product advantage	Cooper 1990; Cooper and Kleinschmidt 1987; 1990.	Excellent relative product quality in comparison to competitive offerings; good value for money (perceived by the customer); excellence in meeting customer needs; inclusion of benefits perceived by the customer as useful; benefits which are obvious to the customer; superior price/performance characteristics; unique attributes	Customer perceptions of competitive offerings; technological dimensions of competitive offerings; customer perceptions of new product's attributes & benefits; Feedback from customers after trial; feedback on customer understanding of the message; perceptual maps - based on customer data; technical specifications, product design information; attributes and features specifications
Well-specified protocol	As above; Rothwell 1972; Rothwell et al. 1974; Rubenstein et al. 1976.	Firm's knowledge and understanding, prior to development, of: the target market; customer needs, wants, preferences. The product concept; product specifications and requirements	Research information detailing market demographics/ psychographics; customer needs, wants and preferences; technical specifications, product design information, attributes and features specifications (prior to development)
Market attractiveness	Maidique and Zirger 1984; de Brentani 1991.	High growth rates, high market need for product type; stability of demand; relative price insensitivity; high trial of new products	Economic market data; economic trends; level of employment; income levels; inflation rates.
Top management support	Ramanujam and Mensch; McDonough 1986.	Levels of risk aversion; aspects of corporate culture	Risk involved; identification of product champions; power and influence distribution among managers.
Synergy/familiarity	Maidique and Zirger 1984; Rothwell et al. 1972; 1974.	Knowledge of technology; relevance to other projects; access to scientific institutes and laboratories.	Extent of new knowledge involved; technology centres where knowledge resides; key scientists; technological networks of firms.
		DEVELOPMENT PROCESS ISSUES	
Proficiency of pre-development activities	Cooper & Cooper and Kleinschmidt as above, Rubenstein et al. 1976; Voss 1985.	Proficiency of concept screening; preliminary market and technical assessment; preliminary business analysis; preliminary technical assessment	Research on customer perceptions, gap analysis, needs analysis, concept tests; market size potential, market segments; technical feasibility, preliminary costs; market size, likely price, profit, break-even etc.
Proficiency of marketing activities	Roberts and Burke 1974; Rothwell et al. 1972, 1974; Cooper 1979, 1980; Maidique and Zirger 1984; Link 1987	Proficiency of concept, product and market tests, service, advertising, distribution and elements of market launch	Market information for the acceptance of alternative product concepts or designs, customer preference data; market profile information, information concerning the distribution channels of interest
Proficiency of technological activities	Rothwell et al. 1972, 1974; Maidique and Zirger 1984.	Proficiency in physical product development; in-house and in-use test iterations; trial production runs; technology acquisition	Technical solutions to functional and marketing problems; technical information on test performance; Information on production costs and problems; information on suppliers' developments and adjacent technologies
Integration of R&D and marketing	Maidique and Zirger 1984; Takeuchi and Nonaka 1986; Rubenstein et al. 1976; Gupta and Wilemon 1990; Rochford and Rudelius 1992.	Amount of information shared; agreement on decision-making authority; functional involvement at each stage	Relevance, novelty, credibility, comprehensibility of information Timeliness of information provision
Speed in development	Takeuchi and Nonaka 1986; Dumaine 1992; Cooper and Kleinschmidt 1994.	Time-to-market; product launched on schedule; no. of competitors on market at time of launch.	Timeliness of information exchange; competitive information.

functions, one of the most powerful is that of how information is handled throughout the NPD process.

Information

The role which information can play in facilitating an efficient NPD *process* and achieving *functional coordination* is implicit in the literature on success in NPD. The notion of reducing uncertainty as the main objective of the project development activities is reiterated throughout the literature: project activities *'can be considered as discrete information processing activities aimed at reducing uncertainty . . . '* (Moneart and Souder, 1990, p.92). These activities include gathering and disseminating information and making decisions based upon this information, which must include evaluations of *both the market and technical aspects* of the development project. Indeed, it is ultimately this information which is evaluated during the NPD process review through the 'gates'.

In order to reduce uncertainty, it is not sufficient that information be processed, it also has to be transferred between different functions (Moneart and Souder, 1990). In this way the uncertainty perceived by particular functions can be reduced. At the same time the efficient transfer of quality information between different functions encourages their coordination (Moneart and Souder, 1990).

As well as reducing uncertainty, the transfer of information between the two functions is perceived by both sides to be a key area for establishing *credibility* as a necessary input to the integration described in the previous section. The research by Workman (1993) showed, for example, that in Zytech, lack of credibility between functions inhibited integration.

Information, therefore, is a base currency of the NPD process; evaluative information is crucial and must be efficiently disseminated to facilitate communication. It is even possible to analyse the various factors which have been shown to correlate with NPD success in such a way as to reveal the information needs of the process for greater success. An example of the information elements implied by the numerous studies into success and failure is given in Table 13.3.

The foregoing discussion of the usefulness of existing models shows that while it is useful to have a checklist of the crucial tasks needed to ensure that new products meet customer needs, any useful framework must allow for numerous inputs from a variety of functions both within and outside the company and must allow for both vertical and horizontal flows of market and technical information across these functions throughout the NPD project. Below an alternative framework for NPD is discussed, called the multiple convergent approach.

The multiple convergent approach

In suggesting a way forward in NPD research which builds on process models but which also takes account of the lessons to be learned from studies of success and failure in NPD, the multiple convergent process attempts to break down research-discipline boundaries, which has direct and explicit consequences for people. This model is conceptually derived from the idea of parallel processing, and is shown in Figure 13.3.

Although models based on parallel processing were an improvement on earlier versions, there was an inherent problem in their parallelism. Definitions of 'parallel' refer to 'separated by an equal distance at every point' or 'never touching or intersecting', and while there are references to simultaneity, it is a somewhat troublesome notion that suggests functional separation, when all the performance indicators in NPD point to the need for functional integration. On the other hand, 'to converge' is defined as 'to move or cause to move towards the same point' or to 'tend towards a common conclusion or result', and is therefore, a more precise indicator of what is required of NPD management.

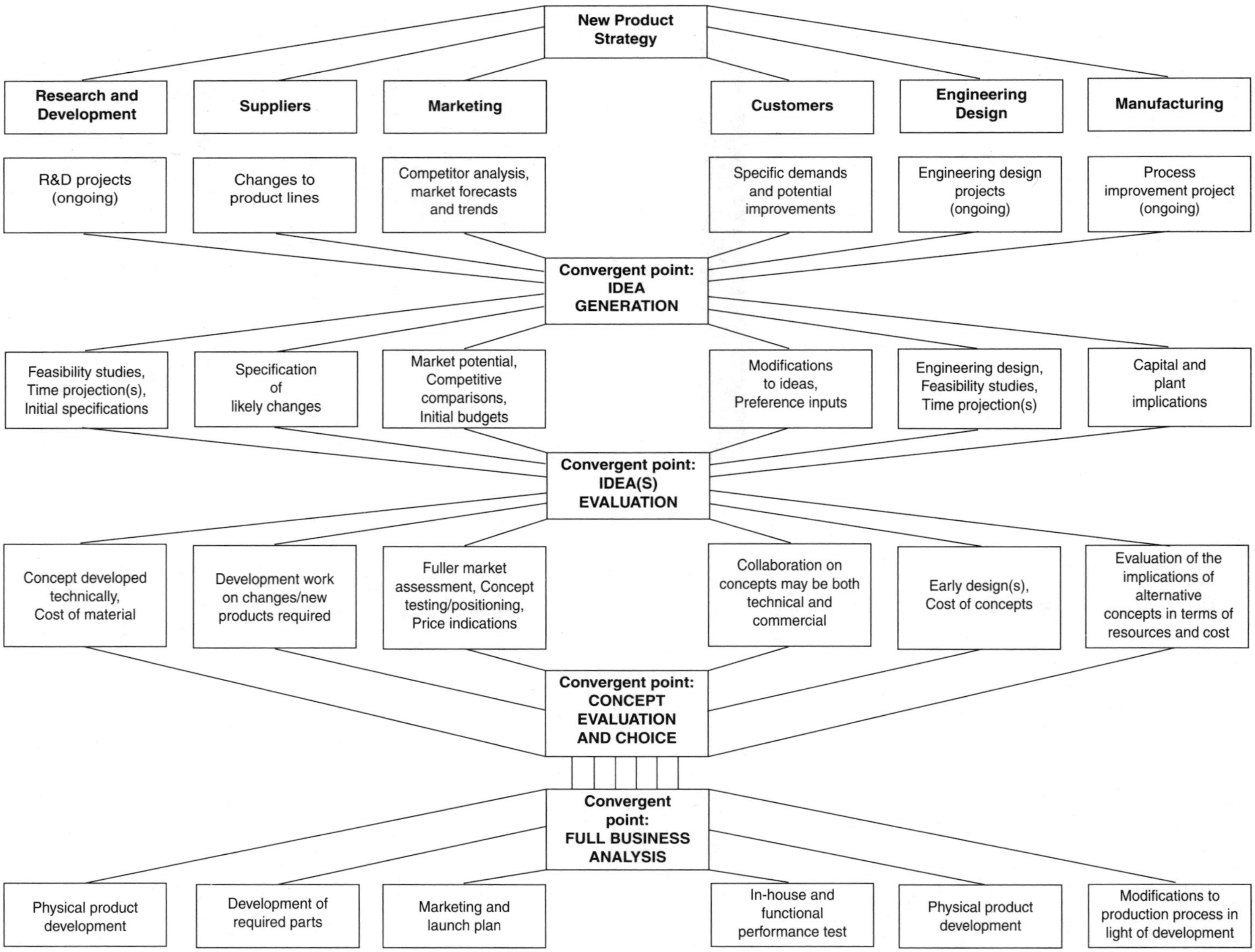

Figure 13.3 The multiple convergent approach

Realizing, however, that there are still functionally-distinct tasks which must be carried out at specific points throughout the NPD process, it is clear that the tasks will be carried out simultaneously at some juncture and that the results must *converge*. Due to the iterations in the process, this convergence is likely to happen several times, culminating at the time of product launch. As previously mentioned, the process is a series of information gathering and evaluating activities, and as the new product develops from idea to concept to prototype and so on, the information gathered becomes more precise and reliable and the decisions are made with greater certainty. Therefore as the development project progresses, there are a number of natural points of evaluation and a number of types of evaluation (market, functional) which need to be carried out in an integrated fashion. These convergent points can be set around decision outputs required to further the process.

The advantages of viewing the process this way are as follows:

1   Iterations among participants within stages are allowed for.
2   The framework can easily accommodate third parties.
3   Mechanisms for integration throughout the process among different functions are set in the convergent points.
4   The model can fit into the most appropriate NPD structures for the company.

Iterations within stages

As the relevant functions are viewed in terms of their contribution to each stage in the process by their specialist contribution, the cross-functional linkages between stages are incorporated. The extent of involvement of different bodies or outside parties will be determined by the specific needs of each development in each firm. Thus, within stage iteration can benefit from both task specialization which will increase the quality of inputs and integration of functions via information sharing and decision making.

Accommodation of third parties

Several studies have shown the importance of involving users in the NPD process to increase success rates (Von Hippel, 1978; Biemans, 1992). Equally, there is growing interest in the need for supplier involvement, in order to benefit from the advantages of supplier innovation and JIT (just-in-time) (Ragatz, Handfield and Scannell, 1997).

Mechanisms for integration

Although the need for cross-functional integration has been widely claimed, there is some evidence to suggest that, in practice, this is not easy to achieve. In Biemans' study, most of the companies showed an understanding of the need to integrate R&D and marketing activities, although the desirability of this is not considered to be automatic, based on the evidence of the companies surveyed. As outlined earlier in the chapter, the key element in integration is the amount of information sharing, and the multiple convergent process offers the opportunity for information sharing which is neglected by other models. Clearly, a host of other factors are likely to influence the amount of cross-functional information sharing, including organizational climate and structure. This said, the multiple convergent model carries within it the impetus for information sharing through the convergent points that can be located liberally throughout the process.

However, studies stress that the appropriate level of integration must be decided upon, and that this level is dependent upon organizational strategies, environmental uncertainty, organizational factors and individual factors. This requires attention, not only to the process of developing new products, but also to the mechanisms used to manage the people responsible for bringing new products and services to the market.

Managing the people in NPD

The process of developing successful new products needs to match technological competence with market relevance. Based on our discussions thus far, numerous inputs are required to achieve these twin goals. Much research has

integration and coordination, at the same time as preserving the efficiencies and expertise within functional speciality. Olsen, Walker and Ruekert (1995) identified seven types of new product structure, or coordination mechanisms, which they describe in terms of four structural attributes: complexity, distribution of authority, formalization and unit autonomy. These are

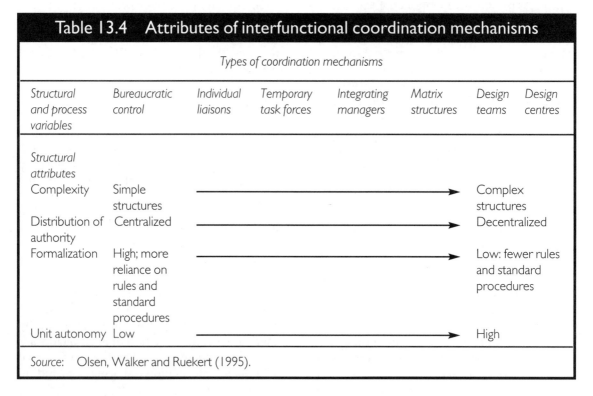

Table 13.4   Attributes of interfunctional coordination mechanisms

	Types of coordination mechanisms						
Structural and process variables	Bureaucratic control	Individual liaisons	Temporary task forces	Integrating managers	Matrix structures	Design teams	Design centres
Structural attributes							
Complexity	Simple structures						Complex structures
Distribution of authority	Centralized						Decentralized
Formalization	High; more reliance on rules and standard procedures						Low: fewer rules and standard procedures
Unit autonomy	Low						High

Source: Olsen, Walker and Ruekert (1995).

been carried out into various aspects of 'coordination' and 'integration' of the perspectives of different disciplines in new product development. This research is confusing, however, not only because of the sheer number of aspects of functional coordination which have been investigated, but also because of the variety of terms used to refer to what this article calls 'functional coordination'. Pinto and Pinto (p. 203) make an informative summary of the different terms which have been used. Whatever the precise definition, it is important for companies to institute NPD processes and design structures which promote

shown in Table 13.4 and discussed below, briefly.

Bureaucratic control

This is the most formalized and centralized and the least participative mechanism, where a high level general manager coordinates activities across functions and is the arbiter of conflicts among functions. Each functional development operates with relative autonomy within the constraints imposed by hierarchical directives and, therefore, most information flows vertically within each department. In such a mechanism, the different functional activities work sequentially on the developing product.

Individual liaisons

Individuals within one functional department have to communicate directly with their counterparts in other departments. Therefore they supplement the vertical communication found in bureaucracies.

Integrating managers

In this coordination structure, an additional manager is added to the functional structure, responsible for coordinating the efforts of the different functional departments, but without the authority to impose decisions on those departments. Thus, such integrating managers have to rely on persuasion and on their ability to encourage group decision making and compromise to achieve successful results.

Matrix structures

Whereas all the previous mechanisms maintain the primacy of the functional departmental structure, a matrix organization structures activities not only according to product or market focus, but also by function. Thus, individuals are responsible to both a functional manager and a new product manager.

According to this research, two newer structural forms have appeared in order to improve the timeliness and the effectiveness of the product development efforts within rapidly changing environments. These forms are:

Design teams

Like the matrix structure, design teams are composed of a set of functional specialists who work together on a specific NPD product. The difference is that such teams tend to be more self-governing and have greater authority to choose their own internal leader(s) who have more autonomy to establish their own operating procedures and to resolve internal conflicts.

Design centres

These centres have many of the same characteristics as a design team. However, such a centre is a permanent addition to an organization's structure, and members of the centre are involved in multiple development projects over time.

As one moves from bureaucratic control toward more organic and participative structures, the structural complexity of the mechanisms increases. Authority becomes more decentralized, rules and procedures less formalized and less rigidly enforced, and the individual units tend to have more autonomy. Consequently, members of relatively organic structures are more likely to share information across functional boundaries and to undertake

Table 13.5 Managing the new product design and development process

Function	Percentage of companies (N = 369)*
Technical dept	40
Chief engineer	10
New product manager	17
New venture team	7
New product team (ft)	42
New product team (pt)	18
New product dept	10
Marketing dept	49

* Most companies used more than one system.

interdependent tasks concurrently rather than sequentially.

In other words, as we move from left to right, structures become less 'mechanistic' and more 'organic' (Burns and Stalker, 1961). Relatively organic mechanisms such as design teams have some important potential advantages for coordinating product development. Indeed, the participative decision making, consensual conflict resolution and open communication processes of such a structure can help reduce barriers between individuals and functional groups. Such participative structures can also create an atmosphere where innovative ideas are proposed, criticized and refined with a minimum of financial and social risk. Besides, by facilitating the open exchange of creative ideas across multiple functions, the likelihood of producing innovative products that successfully address the market desires as well as technical and operational requirements is increased.

Finally, reduced functional barriers help ensure that unanticipated problems that appear during the development process can be tackled directly by the people concerned. This reduces the possibility that vital information may be delayed, lost or altered.

On the other hand, more participative structures have also some potential disadvantages, especially in terms of costs and temporal efficiency. Creating and supporting several development teams can lead to overabundance in personnel and facilities. The main reason for this is that employees have less relevant experience when developing innovative product concepts and then depend more heavily on other functional specialists for the expertise, information and other resources needed to achieve a creative and successful product. And these flows of information and resources are facilitated by less formal participative coordination structures. Thus, there is potential for stagnation in the process if the focus of control is unclear.

In the light of this discussion, let us now look at what kinds of structures are used for NPD.

Structures used by industry

Many studies of innovation and product development give evidence of the 'structures' used to organize the process. Hart and Service (1989) found a number of mechanisms used in their UK survey of new product design and development, shown in Table 13.5.

Their findings are similar to those of Mahajan and Wind (1992). The most recent survey of 'Best Practices' among US product developers reported by Griffin (1997) found that the most common mechanism was to locate NPD responsibility with a function, mostly marketing, R&D or engineering.

These studies and others tend to show that multiple structures are used for organizing the NPD effort within a firm, depending upon the factors driving the innovation (i.e. its strategy) and the level of innovativeness of the development. For example, Page's (1993) research shows that the most common mechanism used for NPD is that of a 'multi-disciplinary team', but this was used in combination with other mechanisms, such as product manager, new product manager and new product departments.

Structures used by companies may exist either within or outside what might be termed 'existing line functions', (such as marketing, R&D or engineering) although this is rarely made explicit. A brief explanation of the main mechanisms used by companies is given below. Those which exist outside existing line structures are venture teams and NPD departments.

Venture teams tend to be a permanent 'maverick' group, with high status, separate budgets and report to the MD. Their respon-sibilities can vary, but include opportunity identification and feasibility studies, through to management of the new product development.

The advantages are that, freed from the 'humdrum' of current business, creativity can be encouraged, and the development has high level support. On the other side, they can turn into acquisition hunters, may be prone to get into unrelated areas and can be seen as a waste of time if they acquire such information from inside the company, which might occur if they get involved with the development of existing products. Guinness has set up a dedicated new business unit to develop products in 'non-traditional areas'. The unit is named 'Guinness Ventures' and will focus at a global level, outside the usual boundaries of the company's R&D activity (*Marketing*, October 13, 1994).

New product departments or divisions

These have the same status as functional divisions and are essentially outside the 'mainstream' of business. They are usually staffed by a combination of functions. They may be used in different ways: as idea hunters, where ideas are passed to the 'mainstream' for development, or as developers, who manage the new product from idea through to the market launch. In the latter instance, the 'handover' of the product will take place at the launch, which may engender feelings of 'not invented here'. However, the rationale for the complete segregation of new product activity is to encourage new ideas for products not contaminated by the vested interests of those managing the amount business. If, however, new product activity does need to draw on experience of current technologies in current markets, then some linkage with those managing the current business is clearly beneficial.

Multi-disciplinary teams, new products' committees, new product teams, product managers and new product managers are all linked – some more directly than others – to the existing line structures. Indeed Page's (1993) study showed that the line functions most involved in new product development were marketing, R&D and engineering. The various teams, committees or individuals may be given 'part-time' responsibility for NPD.

There is an inevitable tension between the need for integration and existing authority and responsibility lines. Due to this tension, many firms will locate responsibility for NPD in one function, and bring others in as and when required. This, of course, raises problems in that development work may be in conflict with the management of current business. This would be

manifested in time pressures, whereby development work is squeezed by existing product management, stifled creativity, due to procedures in place for existing products and, finally, fresh business perspectives may be lacking in people who are expert in managing the current business.

Alternatively, a post of new product manager may be created in marketing or technical departments. The part time option can suffer from time pressures and conflict of roles as besets much matrix structures and, worse, NPD can become something of a secondary goal. In addition, the individual new product manager tends not to be interdisciplinary which forces negotiation with other departments, as opposed to collaboration. As a result, there tends to be a 'pass-the-parcel' approach to the development project, which gets shunted around from one department to the next. Finally, this mechanism tends to be low level with little leverage for important resource decisions, leading to an incremental approach to NPD and a new product committee. This is made up of senior managers from salient functions, and has the purpose of encouraging cross-functional co-operation at the appropriate senior level. However, these mechanisms may suffer from a remote perspective, as the line managers are not really carrying out the task.

Location of new product activity inside or outside existing functions requires a trade-off. Since autonomous structures are designed to allow the unfettered development of new ideas, product with greater levels of advantage, without much reliance on the existing business, it follows, logically that this type of development is precisely what they should carry out.

Once these autonomous units become involved with what Johne and Snelson call 'old product development' their inevitable reliance on those within the line function may cause a conflict. In any case, perhaps the efficiency of an autonomous unit to redevelop current lines is questionable. Indeed, the research by Olson, Walker and Ruekert (1995) showed that 'organic, decentralized participative co-ordination mechanisms *are* associated with better development performance . . . *but only* when used on projects involving innovative or new to the world concepts with which the company has little experience on which to draw' (p. 61).

A number of companies' recent stories highlight this finding in practice. Guinness' new business unit and the development of Chrysler's Neon, a 'sub-compact' car, used what they call 'platform teams', which are autonomous groups consisting of all the professionals required to design and produce a new car, or 'platform' (*Fortune*, January 1994).

This section has introduced some of the complexities involved in designing mechanisms which provide the appropriate balance between creativity and innovation on the one hand, and building on the expertise accumulated with regard to technologies and markets on the other. Although much research points to the need for cross-functional teams, the extent to which these should be autonomous will depend, among other things, on the type of new product development being pursued. In addition it is noteworthy that in Griffin's latest study, 'structure does not contribute materially to differentiating the Best from the Rest' (p. 443). It seems, then, that research is still some way from explaining how companies can best organize their NPD efforts in order to achieve the cross-functional integration and information sharing that does seem so central to successful NPD.

Conclusion

This chapter has focused exclusively on how new products are developed. Starting with the proposition that it takes more than a good idea to make a successful new product, it has described the main activities needed to bring a new product to market successfully. In so doing, the main critical success factors for NPD which have been revealed through research have been woven into the discussion of the process models commonly exhorted as the blueprints for

success. This discussion has, in turn, highlighted the importance of market information to the successful completion new product development projects but it has also shown that blind adherence to a model for NPD cannot be productive as the whole business needs to be characterized by flexibility and open to creativity from various sources within and outside companies. The argument has presented information as a central thread of successful NPD. The NPD process is one of uncertainty reduction which requires information, constant evaluation of options, which requires information and integration of various functional perspectives, also requiring the sharing of information.

References

Allen, T. J. (1985) *Managing the Flow of Technology*, MIT Press, Cambridge, MA.

Biemans, W. (1992) *Managing Innovations Within Networks*, Routledge, London.

Booz, Allen and Hamilton (1968) *Management of New Products*, Booz Allen Hamilton, Chicago.

Booz, Allen and Hamilton (1982) *New Products Management for the 1980s*, Booz Allen Hamilton, New York.

Bruce, M. (1992) *The Black Box of Design Management*, Marketing Working Paper Series, UMIST.

Burns, T. and Stalker, G. M. (1961) *The Management of Innovation*, Tavistock, London.

Calantone, R. J., Schmidt, J. B. and di Benedetto, A. (1997) New product activities and performance: The moderating role of environmental hostility, *Journal of Product Innovation Management*, **14**(3), May, 179–189.

Chryssochoidis, G. M. and Wong, V. (1998) Rolling out new products across country markets: An empirical study of the causes of delays, *Journal of Product Innovation Management*, **15**(1), 16–41.

Cooper, R. G. (1979) The dimensions of new industrial product success and failure, *Journal of Marketing*, **43**(1), 93–103.

Cooper, R. G. (1984) How new product

strategies impact on performance, *Journal of Product Innovation Management*, **1**, 5–18.

Cooper, R. G. (1993) *Winning at New Products; Accelerating the Process from Idea to Launch*, Addison-Wesley, Reading, MA.

Cooper, R. G. (1988) The new product process: a decision guide for management, *Journal of Marketing Management*, **3**(3), 238–255.

Cooper, R. G. and Kleinschmidt, E. J. (1986) An investigation into the new product process; Steps, deficiencies and impact, *Journal of Product Innovation Management*, **3**, 71–85.

Cooper, R. G. and Kleinschmidt, E. J. (1987) New products; What separates winners from losers?, *Journal of Product Innovation Management*, **4**, 169–184.

Cooper, R. G. and Kleinschmidt, E. J. (1990) New product success factors; A comparison of 'kills' versus successes and failures, *R&D Management*, **20**(1), 169–184.

Craig, A. and Hart, S. (1992) Where to now in new product development research?, *European Journal of Marketing*, **26**, 1–49.

Crawford, C. M. (1984) Protocol: New tool for product innovation, *Journal of Product Innovation Management*, **2**, 85–91.

de Meyer, A. (1985) The flow of technological innovation in an R&D department, *Research Policy*, **14**, 315–328.

Dougherty, D. (1992) A practice-centred model of organizational renewal through product innovation, *Strategic Management Journal*, **13**, 77–92.

Dougherty, D. and Hardy, C. (1996) Sustained product innovation in large, mature organizations: overcoming innovation-to-organization problems. *Academy of Management Journal*, **39**(5), 1120–1153.

Dwyer, L. M. and Mellor, R. (1991) Organization environment, new product process activities and project outcomes, *Journal of Product Innovation Management*, **8**(1), 39–48, March.

Eisenhardt, K. M. and Tabrizi, B. N. (1994) Accelerating adaptive processes: product innovation in the global computer industry, *Administrative Science Quarterly*, **40**(1), March, 84–110.

Evans, S. (1990) Implementation framework for integrated design teams, *Journal of Engineering Design*, **1**(4), 355–363.

Gabb, A. (1991) How the Discovery took off, *Management Today*, October, 64–68.

Griffin, A. (1997) PDMA research on new product development practices: updating trends in benchmarking best practice, *Journal of Product Innovation Management*, **14**(6), 429–458.

Gupta, A. K., Raj, S. P. and Wilemon, D. (1985) The marketing – R&D interface in high-tech firms, *Journal of Product Innovation Management*, **2**, 12–24.

Gupta, A. K. and Wilemon, D. (1988) The credibility – co-operation connection at the R&D marketing interface, *Journal of Product Innovation Management*, **5**, 20–31

Harryson, S. J. (1997) How Canon and Sony drive product innovation through networking and application-focused R&D, *Journal of Product Innovation Management*, **14**(3), 288–295.

Hart, S. J. and Baker, M. J. (1994) Learning from success: Multiple convergent processing in new product development, *International Marketing Review*, **11**(1), 77–92.

Hart, S. J. and Service, L. M. (1988) The effects of managerial attitudes to design on company performance, *Journal of Marketing Management*, **4**(2), 217–229.

Hart, Tzokas, Hultink and Commandeur (1998) How companies steer the new product development process, *Proceedings of the Annual Conference of the Product Development Management Association*, Atlanta, Georgia.

Hill, P. (1988) The market research contribution to new product failure and success, *Journal of Marketing Management*, **3**(3), 269–277.

Hultink, E. J., Griffin, A., Hart, S. and Robben, H. S. J. (1997) Industrial new product launch strategies and product development performance, *Journal of Product Innovation Management*, **14**, 246.

Industry Week (1996) New Improved American Dream, *Industry Week*, December 16, 45.

Johne, A. F. and Snelson, P. (1988) Marketing's role in new product development, *Journal of Marketing Management*, **3**, 256–268.

Larson, C. (1988) Team tactics can cut development costs, *Journal of Business Strategy*, **9**(5), September/October, 22–25.

Levitt, T. (1960) Marketing myopia, *Harvard Business Review*, July-August, 45–56.

Link, P. L. (1987) Keys to new product success and failure, *Industrial Marketing Management*, **16**, 109–118.

Littler, D., Leverick, F. and Bruce, M. (1995) Factors affecting the process of collaborative product development: A study of UK manufacturers of information and communications technology products, *Journal of Product Innovation Management*, **12** (1), 16–23

Mahajan, V. and Wind, J. (1992) New product models: Practice, shortcomings and desired improvements, *Journal of Product Innovation Management*, **9**, 128–139

Maidique, M. A. and Zirger, B. J. (1984) A study of success and failure in product innovation: The case of the US electronics industry, *IEEE Transactions on Engineering Management*, **31**, 192–203.

Moneart, R. K. and Souder, W. E. (1990) An information transfer model for integrating marketing and R&D personnel in NPD projects, *Journal of Product Innovation Management*, **7**(2), 91–107.

Montoya-Weiss, M. M. and Calantone, R. (1994) Determinants of new product performance: a review and meta-analysis, *Journal of Product Innovation Management*, **11**(5), 397–417.

Morita, A., Reingold, M. and Shimomura, I. (1987) *Made in Japan*, Penguin, London.

Nauman, E. and Shannon, P. (1992) What is customer-driven marketing? *Business Horizons*, Nov-Dec, 44–52.

Olsen, Walker and Ruekert (1995) Organizing for effective new product development: The moderating influence of product innovativeness, *Journal of Marketing*, **59**, 48–62

Ottum, B. D. and Moore, W. L. (1997) Information processing and new product success, *Journal of Product Innovation Management*, **14**, 258–273.

Page, A. L. (1993) Assessing new product development practices and performance: Establishing crucial norms, *Journal of Product Innovation Management*, **10**, 273–290, September.

Pinto, M. B. and Pinto, J. K. (1990) Project team communication and cross-functional co-operation in new product development, *Journal of Product Innovation Management*, **7**(3), 200–212, September.

Ragatz, G. L., Handfield, R. B. and Scannell, T. V. (1997) Success factors for integrating suppliers into new product development, *Journal of Product Innovation Management*, **14**(3), 190–202.

Rothwell, R. (1994) Towards the Fifth Generation Innovation Process, *International Marketing Review*, **11**(1), 7–31.

Saren, M. S. (1994) Reframing the process of new product development: From staged models to blocks, *Journal of Marketing Management*, **10**(7), 633–644.

Shocker, A. D. and Hall, W. A. (1986) Pre-market models: A critical evaluation, *Journal of Product Innovation Management*, **3**(2), pp. 86–107.

The Grocer (1997) Size is everything, *The Grocer*, January 15, p. 15.

Von Hippel, E. (1978) Successful industrial products from customer ideas – presentation of a new customer-active paradigm with evidence and implications, *Journal of Marketing*, January, 39–49.

Wheatley, M. (1994) Orchestrating the big project, *Management Today*, May, 50–54.

Wind, J. and Mahajan, V. (1987) Marketing hype: A new perspective for new product research and introduction, *Journal of Product Innovation Management*, **4**, 43–49.

Workman, J. P. Jr (1993) Marketing's limited role in NPD in one computer systems firm, *Journal of Marketing Research*, **30**, 405–421.

CHAPTER 14

Pricing

ADAMANTIOS DIAMANTOPOULOS

For what is a man if he is not a thief who openly charges as much as he can for the goods he sells?

Mahatma Gandhi

Introduction

Pricing is an issue about which academics and practitioners have been at each others' throats for a very long time. While nobody knows exactly when the 'war' was started – or by whom for that matter – Dean's (1947, p. 4) description of company pricing policies as 'the last stronghold of medievalism in modern management' was probably one of the earliest attacks in the literature about the way companies think about and go about making pricing decisions. Over the next forty years or so, several academics followed in Dean's footsteps by criticizing practitioner approaches to pricing as lacking in rationality and professionalism; failing to understand the proper role of costs; and bypassing profit opportunities as a result of applying routinized pricing formulae (e.g. Backman, 1953; Staudt and Taylor, 1965; Nimer, 1971; Marshall, 1979; Nagle, 1987). The following quote encapsulates the essence of the criticism: 'many managers do not understand how to price, and are insecure about the adequacy of their current pricing methods. As a result, they rely on oversimplistic rules of thumb and place an exaggerated emphasis on costs' (Morris and Morris, 1990, pp. xvii–xviii).

On their part, practitioners have responded by largely *ignoring* what academia has to say about pricing. While an enormous literature on pricing has developed over the past half century (for comprehensive reviews see Diamantopoulos, 1991, 1995; Diamantopoulos and Mathews, 1995), there have been no radical changes in the actual pricing practices of firms; indeed, 'the pricing literature has produced few insights or approaches that would stimulate most businessmen to change their methods of setting prices' (Monroe, 1979, p. 93). For example, a comparison of the adoption of cost-plus pricing methods over a fifty-year period concludes that 'in spite of the fact that the intervening years have seen countless references to the fact that cost-plus pricing pays insufficient attention to environmental dynamics, it remains the predominant price-setting methodology' (Seymour, 1989, p. 4). Practitioners have also been quick to criticize academics as being unable to *really* understand what pricing is all about. In the words of one executive, 'company pricing policy is an area where the academic world has long since retreated in despair of ascribing consistency of principles or rationality of practice' (Alfred, 1972, p. 1).

Thus the field of pricing is characterized by a paradox. On the one hand, 'price theory is one of the most highly developed fields in economics and marketing science' (Simon, 1979, p. ix). On the other hand, 'there is hardly another business subject area that has had so little reverberation in practice as has price theory' (Diller, 1991, p. 17). Several reasons seem to underlie this paradox.

First, a lot of academic work on pricing has been focusing on pricing *models* of various sorts (for relevant reviews, see Monroe and Della Bitta, 1978; Monroe and Mazudmar, 1988; Nagle, 1984; Rao, 1984, 1993). While these models are characterized by a high degree of rigour and enable the derivation of 'optimal' prices, pricing strategies, discount structures, etc., they 'do not provide *operational* rules for management to follow' (Monroe and Della Bitta, 1978, p. 426, emphasis added). Moreover, such models are typically very 'heavy' mathematically and thus not particularly appetizing for most business executives. Last – but certainly not least – a lot of price modelling has been concerned with 'mathematical elegance, often at the expense of realism' (Diamantopoulos and Mathews, 1995, p. 18) and has ignored the fact that 'pricing in reality follows a much more complex pattern which does not lend itself so readily to mathematical generalization and diagrammatical simplification' (Liebermann, 1969, p. 20). Taken together, these shortcomings go a long way towards explaining 'the minimal contributions of models in the pricing area' (Jeuland and Dolan, 1982, p. 1).

Second, the priorities of managers and the research interests of academics in the pricing field have not always (or even mostly) coincided. As Bonoma *et al.* (1988, p. 359) observe 'it is not that academics cannot solve managerial pricing problems or that they have no interest in solving them. Rather, it seems that academic researchers have not known, or do not focus on, the key pricing concerns of managers in order to conduct rigorous pricing research'. To the extent that the issues deemed important by managers have not been adequately addressed by researchers, it is not surprising that 'pricing theory and pricing research have won little recognition in practice' (Simon, 1982, p. 23). On the positive side, the gap may be closing, as indicated by the increasingly managerial orientation of several pricing texts published in the last ten years (e.g. Montgomery, 1988; Seymour, 1989; Morris and Morris, 1990; Monroe, 1990; Nagle and Holden, 1995; Dolan and Simon, 1996).

Third, pricing has always been a 'difficult' area to study empirically, not least because of confidentiality reasons. As Bain (1949, p. 149) observed half a century ago, 'the reluctance of businessmen to confide to economists their methods of price calculation and the character of their associations with rival firms . . . has been a serious barrier to close investigation of price policy as seen by the price maker'. In this context, the participation rates of firms in empirical pricing surveys have often been disappointing (cf. Diamantopoulos, 1991), lending credibility to the view that 'it has not been the tradition of management to be "friendly" to the needs of academic researchers in the area of pricing' (Monroe and Mazudmar, 1988, p. 387). While the adoption of process-oriented methodologies which rely on close co-operation with managers (e.g. Howard and Morgenroth, 1968; Capon *et al.*, 1975; Farley *et al.*, 1980; Bonoma *et al.*, 1988; Woodside, 1992; Diamantopoulos and Mathews, 1995) may overcome the shortcomings of survey-based approaches, gaining *initial* access to firms is likely to remain a key obstacle in the empirical study of pricing practices.

Fourth, in the past, a lot of the recommendations arising from academic research on pricing have been difficult to implement by firms because of information processing capability limitations. It is all very nice to suggest that comprehensive price analyses should be undertaken involving estimation of price response functions, assessment of competitive reactions, and calculations of marginal costs (to name but a few) before prices are set. It is quite another thing to actually *do* this effectively if you do not have access to the relevant information and/or lack the capability to analyse whatever information you might be able to get hold of. In fact, there is evidence suggesting that firms *knowingly* operate sub-optimal pricing systems simply because they are convenient and inexpensive (Seymour, 1989). Recent developments in information technology in terms of better and cheaper applications software, decision support systems, and web-based platforms, should enhance the capability of firms to engage in more sophisticated analyses of pricing parameters. Even such basic applications as spreadsheets can make the life of a price decision maker *much* easier (see, for example, Laric, 1989); indeed, 'the development and acceptance of the personal computer offers the pricing manager immediate electronic data procession capabilities' (Morris and Morris, 1990, p. 164). The point is that pricing approaches/systems formerly seen as being 'esoteric', 'slow' or 'expensive' (or all three) are increasingly becoming much more manageable and within the reach of most firms.

Against this background, the rest of this chapter focuses on some key issues relating to the pricing decision that have direct implications for practitioners. Specifically, insights gained from the theoretical and empirical pricing literature are used to develop a better *understanding* of the price variable, focusing in particular on the role of the *customer* (i.e. the 'demand' side). The intention is *not* to provide an 'off the shelf' recipe for better pricing because 'no known body of doctrine or proven procedures would lead an executive to the best price for his offering' (Oxenfeldt, 1975, p. viii). Rather the aim of this chapter is to help the reader develop his/her *own* perspective about customer-oriented pricing and, hopefully, apply the insights gained to the specific pricing situation he/she may be facing. Accordingly, no attempt is made to focus the discussion on a particular industry, type of product, or set of competitive conditions.

In the next section, the critical importance of price as a decision variable is highlighted and the need to manage it effectively emphasized. This is followed by an examination of the linkages between price, volume, cost and profit distinguishing between accounting relationships and causal relationships. Finally, specific attention is drawn to the most important 'pillar' of price: customer demand. Due to space restrictions, the other two pillars of price – competition

and costs – are only considered to the extent necessary to put demand considerations in context. The reader is urged to follow up on the issues raised here (and many more) by consulting the pricing texts included in the reference list at the end of the chapter.[1]

Is price really that important?

The most common – and obvious – rationale given for the importance of price is that price is the only element in the marketing mix that generates revenue; all other elements are associated with costs. Such costs are necessarily incurred in *creating* value via product development, promotion and distribution. In contrast, pricing can be seen as a value *extraction* activity (Dolan and Simon, 1996) since it is through pricing that the 'level of reward is set for all the planning, financing designing, productive efficiency, skill, and quality that have gone into the product' (Marshall, 1979, p. 1). However, the unique role of price as a revenue-generating marketing mix element is by no means the *only* characteristic that makes price so important. Consider the following:

- Price has a very strong impact on sales volume and market share; empirical studies (reviewed in Tellis, 1988 and Sethuraman and Tellis, 1991) have shown that, for most products, price elasticity is substantially higher than advertising elasticity – up to twenty times higher!
- Not only does price have a strong influence on demand but such influence is manifested much faster than for other marketing mix instruments (e.g. advertising) for which considerable time lags may be involved (e.g. Ehrenberg and England, 1990).
- Compared to the rest of the marketing mix elements, price can be modified relatively quickly; the downside is, of course, that this

---

[1] The works of Monroe (1990), Nagle and Holden (1995) and Dolan and Simon (1996) are highly recommended in this respect.

applies equally to the competition as well! Making/responding to price changes can take place within a short time period, whereas initiation of or reactions to changes in product formulation, advertising, etc., can take much longer due to the nature of the preparations involved (e.g. Simon, 1992).

- Competitive reactions to price variations both in terms of speed and in terms of intensity tend to be much more severe than competitive reactions to changes in other marketing mix variables; for example, it has been estimated that reaction elasticities to price variations are almost twice as high as reaction elasticities to advertising changes (e.g. Lambin, 1976).
- Irrespective of situation, the manipulation of price is not associated with an initially negative cash flow (e.g. Simon, 1989); in contrast, the manipulation of other marketing mix elements (e.g. promotion, personal selling) typically results in expenses that are only recovered at a later time (as in the case of a new product where initial investments have to be set against future income streams).
- The 'leverage' effect of price on profit (discussed in detail in the next section) is much greater than that of other profit drivers; for example, it has been argued that 'improvements in price typically have three to four times the effect on profitability as proportionate increases in volume' (Marn and Rosiello, 1992, p. 84).
- Price often fulfils two functions simultaneously: it reflects the 'sacrifice' that the buyer must make in order to acquire the product/service involved and it also acts as a signal of the quality of the product (Monroe, 1990); no other element of the marketing mix serves such a dual function.
- Pricing has also been identified as a key factor governing new product success or failure (e.g. Cooper, 1979); a crucial criterion affecting supplier choice in business-to-business markets (e.g. Shipley, 1985); and the most likely aspect of a firm's activity to draw government attention and/or be subjected to regulation (e.g. Reekie, 1981).

In the light of the above, it is perhaps not surprising that price has been described as a 'dangerously explosive variable' (Oxenfeldt, 1973, p. 48) which, if not properly managed, 'can cripple a business, no matter how otherwise efficient it may be' (Marshall, 1979, p. 1). The first step towards effective price management is *understanding*: understanding how price interacts with volume and costs to produce a profit (or loss) and understanding how the 'demand side' works. It is to these issues that we now turn.

The drivers of profit: price, volume and cost

Figure 14.1 shows the familiar decomposition of profit into revenue and cost elements. The revenue side is a function of the price level and the sales volume (in units) sold at that price, while the cost side is made up of the fixed costs – which are incurred regardless of the volume of sales attained – and the variable costs (which are dependent upon the volume produced and sold). Thus there are four distinct forces that 'drive' profit: price, volume, variable unit cost, and fixed cost (note that sales volume is the only profit driver which operates both on the revenue *and* the cost side; this has important implications as will become clear shortly).

Given the four drivers of profit, an important question concerns their *relative* importance. In other words, assuming that all other factors remain constant, what is the effect on profit of 'improving' each driver by a certain amount? Clearly, the notion of 'improvement' is different for the revenue and cost sides, i.e. an improvement in price and sales volume refers to an *increase* from existing levels, while an improvement in variable and/or fixed cost refers to a *reduction* from current levels.

Table 14.1 shows the differential impact on profit of a 10 per cent improvement in each profit driver; it is clear that, by far, the greatest 'leverage' effect on profit comes from improving price. This is not an accident reflecting either the

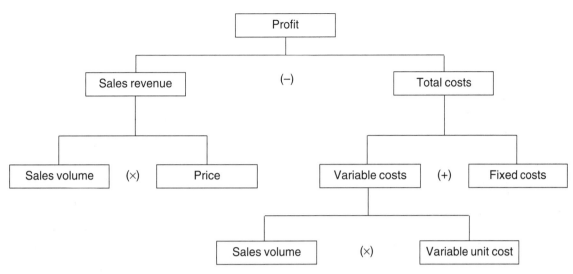

Figure 14.1 The determinants of profit.

specific improvement considered (i.e. 10 per cent) or the particular starting values in Table 14.1; experimentation with different figures will not fail to demonstrate that 'price drives profit like no other factor' (Dolan and Simon, 1996, p. 24).

At this stage, the reader may be getting a bit uncomfortable – and rightly so – with the sim- plifying assumption that 'all other factors remain constant' when the profit impact of a particular profit driver is considered.[2] After all, if one 'improves' price by raising it by 10 per cent, surely there will be some reduction in sales volume? And if volume is reduced, there could also be a 'knock on' effect on variable cost – say, if any scale economies can no longer be realized.

Table 14.1   Effects on profit of a 10 per cent improvement

	Before	After	Profit (£) Before	After	Profit improvement
Price (£)	100	110	30 000	40 000	33.3%
Sales volume	1 000	1 100	30 000	35 000	16.7%
Variable unit cost (£)	50	45	30 000	35 000	16.7%
Fixed cost (£)	20 000	18 000	30 000	32 000	6.7%

[2] Note, however, that in many instances the assumption of all other factors remaining constant is not as far-fetched as it might first seem. For example, empirical research has revealed that companies often face a situation in which manipulation of price *within certain limits* is not accom- panied by volume fluctuations (see, for example, Skinner, 1970; Hankinson, 1985; Wied-Nebbeling, 1975, 1985; Diamantopoulos and Mathews, 1993, 1995). Such situations arise because of buyer switching costs (Buckner, 1967), loyalty considerations (Albach, 1979) and/or 'lazy' competitors (Wied-Nebbeling, 1975). Under such con- ditions there is a clear opportunity to increase profitability by means of (moderate) price increases *without* sacrificing volume; given the leveraging effect of price on profit (see Table 14.1), the resulting gains can be very substantial indeed.

Such concerns are well justified and serve to highlight the *definitional* nature of the relationships in Figure 14.1. The decomposition of profit into the four profit drivers highlights what are essentially *accounting* links rather than *causal* relationships; the latter are shown in Figure 14.1 which explicitly considers the indirect effects of prices on costs (via sales volume) and also introduces competitive considerations as an additional – albeit indirect – influence on profit.

So does Figure 14.2 render Figure 14.1 obsolete? Not at all. The definitional relationships in Figure 14.1 can be used to build scenarios of the following sort: if we were to increase price by X per cent, what would be the acceptable decrease

ity. For example, if a 10 per cent price decrease requires a 25 per cent increase in sales volume to result in the same overall profit level (this would be the case in the example in Table 14.1, where variable costs are 50 per cent of the original price), to what extent is this rise in sales volume realistic? Will existing customers really buy that much more of our product and/or sufficient numbers of new customers attracted to bring about the needed extra volume? And will our competitors sit back and do nothing when we lower our prices by 10 per cent or will they retaliate by matching or even exceeding our price cut? And is there any possibility that the whole thing may backfire if customers *perceive* that the

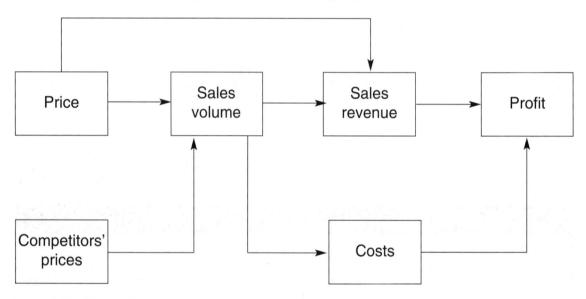

Figure 14.2   The road to profit.

in sales volume to return the *same* profit? Or, if we were to decrease price by Y per cent what would be the necessary increase in sales volume to maintain the current profit? Or, if we managed to reduce our variable unit costs by Z per cent, what sort of price reduction could we afford without hurting our profitability? Having computed the answers to these questions by reference to Figure 14.1, one can then use Figure 14.2 as a framework for evaluating whether the expected effects are likely to materialize in real-

price reduction also reflects a quality reduction and end up buying *less* rather than more? Questions of this nature go a long way towards making the implications of any pricing moves transparent and identifying potential sticky points.

As can be seen in Figure 14.2, sales volume plays a crucial role in the system of relationships between price, cost and profit. As a *dependent* variable, sales volume (q) reflects customer demand and is a function of both the firm's own price (p) and that of competitors (p_j); the specific nature of the relationship between volume and price is captured by the price response function, $q = f(p, p_j)$.[3] As an *independent* variable, sales volume (q) is a determinant of the firm's costs (c), a relationship which is captured by the cost function, $c = g(q)$. Thus, ultimately, cost is a function of price and *not vice versa*[4] or, what amounts to the same thing, any pricing system that uses costs as the *basis* of price determination is illogical and bound to result in suboptimal decisions;[5] as Backman (1953, p. 148) aptly put it a long time ago, 'the graveyard of business is filled with the skeletons of companies that attempted to price their products solely on the basis of costs'.

The above should not be interpreted as implying that costs have no place in pricing decisions. Costs *are* important but only as *constraints* on the viability or relative attractiveness of different pricing alternatives;[6] they are not important, or even relevant, as *guides* to setting prices, not least because 'the customer does not care about the firm's costs . . . only about the *value* he/she is getting' (Diamantopoulos, 1995, p. 187, emphasis in the original). In fact, the most fundamental lesson in pricing is that '*price is a statement of value not a statement of cost*' (Morris and Morris, 1990, p. 2, emphasis in the original); the next section shows why is this the case.

Price from the customer's perspective

The very definition of price as 'the amount of money we must sacrifice to acquire something we desire' (Monroe, 1990, p. 5) provides clear cues as to the way in which customer consider-

ations impact on pricing. Several points are important here.

First, the notion of price as a 'sacrifice' implies that the buyer must give something up. In this context, 'what must be given up includes not only the monetary price, but also the time and effort that the buyer must invest' (Morris and Morris, 1990, p. 3). Thus the *purchase* price alone may *not* fully capture the buyer's total sacrifice; things like start-up costs (e.g. transportation and installation) and post-purchase costs (e.g. maintenance and risk of failure) may also be important and should be borne in mind by the price decision maker. Failure to consider the buyer's associated *life-cycle* costs is a common pricing mistake and – particularly in industrial markets – can result in lost opportunities for gaining/keeping customers (see, for example, Forbis and Mehta, 1978; Shapiro and Jackson, 1978; Christopher, 1982).

Second, in incurring a 'sacrifice', the buyer must be *able* to do so. The *ability to pay* is a function of the particular customer's economic circumstances (e.g. disposable income) and can be viewed as a constraining factor on the type and amount of purchases a particular customer can make over a particular period; thus the ability to pay reflects the 'budget constraint' often mentioned in conventional microeconomic theory. In practice, obstacles relating to the ability to pay may be overcome by changing the time of payment (e.g. providing a period of interest-free credit), the method of payment (e.g. offering an instalment plan) or the form of payment (e.g. providing a trade-in facility).

Third, not only must a potential buyer be able to pay the price, he/she must also be *willing*

[3] It is assumed here that competitive actions directly impact upon the firm's own demand, i.e. there is interdependence among suppliers (oligopolistic market structure). In the case of a single supplier (monopoly) or many suppliers with differentiated products (monopolistic competition), the price response function reduces to $q = f(p)$.

[4] Since $q = f(p, p_j)$, and $c = g(q)$, it follows that $c = h(p, p_j)$; this demonstrates the irrationality of cost-based approaches according to which 'price is considered a function of cost,

whereas the true causal relationship is just the reverse' (Simon, 1989, p. 48).

[5] There are some very special (read: extremely rare) circumstances under which a cost-based approach can lead to optimal (i.e. profit maximizing) prices; for more details, see Simon (1989 or 1992).

[6] For example, variable costs or marginal costs act as short-term price floors (assuming no capacity constraints), while total costs act as long-term price floors; for comprehensive analyses, see Riebel (1972) and Reichmann (1973).

to do so. *Willingness to pay* is a complex function of a particular buyer's perceived evaluation of the product/service involved, the actual price, competitive offerings, and his/her *reference* price. The latter represents the amount that the customer regards as fair/appropriate/acceptable for the particular purchase and acts as a standard for evaluating other prices. Reference prices are influenced by such factors as the last price paid, an 'average' price based on historical experience of purchases, the prices of competing products, and expectations about future prices. Note that it is not necessarily the *actual* prices of previous purchases and/or competing offerings that combine to form a reference price but prices as *recalled/perceived* by the buyer. Indeed, the price decision maker should appreciate that

buyers do not have perfect information regarding available products and their prices. Even if such information were available, people are not perfect information processors . . . As a result, buyers are not always very price aware (Morris and Morris, 1990, p. 60).

Obstacles related to the willingness to pay are much more difficult to identify and overcome than obstacles relating to the ability to pay. Not only must the potential buyer be convinced that he/she can *afford* to buy the product but also that he/she will be making the *right choice*. Thus, non-price instruments (such as advertising and promotion) must be employed to convince the buyer that the product offers superior *value* (see below) and/or to influence the reference price used by the buyer (e.g. as when a 'regular' price is advertised alongside with the 'special deal' price at which the product is actually offered).

Fourth, the extent to which a buyer will *decide* to incur the sacrifice implied by the price depends on how he/she will *judge* what he/she will get *in return*. This is the essence of the notion of *value*: a trade-off between the bundle of benefits to be received (as reflected in the product) and what has to be given up (as reflected in the price). In seeking particular benefits, the buyer focuses on a desired set of attributes (which typically differ in their relative importance) and

subjectively evaluates different products on these attributes. The outcome of this evaluation is then compared to the price of the product and the 'best value' is the one that offers the most benefit (in terms of the customer's desired set of attributes) for the least price. Put simply, 'the customers' goal is to obtain the most value for their money . . . Their concern is to get their money's worth' (Nagle, 1987, p. 2).

Fifth, and related to the previous point, to provide value from a *buyer's perspective*, it is necessary that

the benefits delivered by the products or services match the benefits wanted by the customers or users . . . a product or service is purchased because of its ability to perform a certain function, solve a particular problem, or provide specific pleasures. It is what the product or service does and how well it does it that provides value (Monroe, 1990, pp. 91–92).

This is, of course, a central tenet of marketing; however, its price-specific implications – as reflected in buyer deliberations regarding value – are often forgotten (if ever realized in the first place).

Sixth, given that 'if the customer can select between different competitive products, he will most likely prefer the one which offers the highest net value' (Simon, 1989, p. 1), the aim of the price decision maker *must* be to offer *superior value*. Creating and sustaining superior value lies at the heart of developing (and maintaining) competitive advantage and there only two ways to it: 'either offering customers lower prices than competitors for equivalent benefits or providing unique product benefits that more than compensate customers for paying a higher price' (Morris and Morris, 1990, p. 3). In following the first route, the control of *costs* becomes crucial as offering a lower price than competitors *while maintaining adequate profit levels*, requires 'aggressive construction of efficient-scale facilities, vigorous pursuit of cost reductions from experience, tight cost and overhead control, avoidance of marginal customer accounts, and cost minimization in areas like R&D, service, sales force, advertising, and so on' (Porter, 1980,

p. 35). In following the second route, the firm strives for *uniqueness* in some respect, which usually involves 'a trade-off with cost position if the activities required in creating it are inherently costly, such as extensive research, product design, high quality materials, or intensive customer support' (Porter, 1980, p. 38). Note that costs are still important, as any 'premium prices will be nullified by a markedly inferior cost position' (Porter, 1985, p. 14).

Finally, it is important to realize that buyers often have *absolute limits* on what they are prepared to pay for a particular product. The upper limit (known as the *reservation price*) reflects the *maximum* price that a customer is willing to pay and represents the *marginal* value of the product to the buyer over other consumption alternatives. If the actual price exceeds the reservation price, then no purchase will take place. The lower limit reflects a *minimum* price below which 'quality is regarded as unacceptable' (Simon, 1989, p. 185); if the actual price falls below that limit then – in the absence of any other information – the customer will also not make a purchase. Lower limits are particularly important when price is used – at least partly – as an indicator of quality(see also next section).[7]

From the above, it can be seen that understanding the role of customer considerations in pricing is much more complex than might be initially thought. Of particular importance, in this context, is the fact that customers are likely to be very *heterogeneous* in terms of their knowledge, perceptions of, and reactions to, price. Differences in the nature, number, and relative importance attached to different product attributes; differences in the nature, level and stability of reference prices used; and differences in the magnitude of reservation prices, all combine to produce different value perceptions of a particular offer by different buyers (and hence different likelihoods to buy). Thus one challenge for price

management is to capitalize on such differences by *customizing* prices; in this context,

different customers have different levels of willingness and ability to pay. A common failing in pricing practice is not to adapt prices to these realities, thereby foregoing significant profit opportunities (Dolan and Simon, 1996, p. 116).

Price customization can take place according to customer characteristics, geographic location, transaction size, timing of the purchase, and distribution channel (to name but a few).[8] However, irrespective of whether price customization or a 'one price policy' is to be pursued by the firm, the decision maker requires knowledge regarding how customers are likely to respond to prices of different magnitudes; this is the issue of *price sensitivity* and is discussed in the next section.

Understanding price sensitivity

The conventional analysis of price sensitivity stems from economic theory and its analysis of *price elasticity* (ε). This shows the percentage change in quantity demanded (i.e. sales volume) as a result of a percentage change in price:

$$\varepsilon = \% \text{ change in sales volume} \div \% \text{ change in price.}$$

Thus, a price elasticity of –2.0 implies that a 10 per cent *increase* in price would result in a volume *decrease* of 20 per cent (–2.0 · 10 per cent). If $\varepsilon = 0$, then demand is said to be *perfectly inelastic* as sales volume is completely unresponsive to price changes. If $\varepsilon = -\infty$, demand is said to be *perfectly elastic* as sales volume goes up from zero to infinity as a result of a price change (a very rare case). If $\varepsilon = -1$, then demand is said to have *unitary elasticity*, i.e. a given percentage

---

[7] For a review of the conditions that are likely to encourage such a function of price and the relevant empirical evidence, see Rao and Monroe (1989) and Zeithaml (1988).

[8] Good discussions of price customization can be found in Simon (1992), Nagle and Holden (1995) and Dolan and Simon (1996).

change in price is accompanied by exactly the same percentage change in sales volume. If $-1 < \varepsilon < 0$ then demand is said to be *inelastic* as the proportionate change in sales volume is smaller than the change in price. Finally, if $-\infty < \varepsilon < -1$, then demand is said to be *elastic* as the proportionate change in sales volume is greater than the change in price. Table 14.2 shows the implications of different elasticity values in terms of their effects on sales revenue.

- The formula is based on a ceteris paribus (i.e. 'all other things being equal') assumption, which implies that the only variable that affects changes in sales volume is the change in price; prices of competitors, incomes, preferences, etc. are assumed to be constant. This assumption is obviously questionable, particularly in the case of oligopolistic markets where interdependence among suppliers is likely to lead to reactions when prices are changed

Table 14.2 Impact of price elasticity on sales revenue

Demand is	Price increase	Price decrease
Perfectly inelastic	Revenue increases	Revenue decreases
Perfectly elastic	Revenue decreases	Revenue increases
Unitary elasticity	Revenue does not change	Revenue does not change
Inelastic	Revenue increases	Revenue decreases
Elastic	Revenue decreases	Revenue increases

While the concept of price elasticity is very useful for thinking about the likely effects of price changes on sales volume, a great deal of caution is necessary when applying it. For example, in the light of Table 14.2, one may be tempted to rush into recommendations of the sort 'if a price elasticity of less than 1 is found, a price increase can be immediately recommended, since this means that the percentage of decrease in sales volume is smaller than the percentage of increase in price' (Dolan and Simon, 1996, p. 30). However, this assumes that (a) the firm is willing to sacrifice *some* sales volume, and (b) the revenue gains are going to be translated into *profit* gains. Neither of these assumptions may be warranted because 'the goal may be to maintain a presence in the market, take customers from competitors, or use the product to help sell other products in the line, even at a revenue loss ... [or] costs would rise reflecting less efficient use of resources or less economical raw material purchases' (Morris and Morris, 1990, p. 45 and p. 101).

In general, the following caveats apply when using the formula for price elasticity:

(e.g. price wars in the case of price reductions).

- A distinction needs to be made between market (or primary) price elasticity, i.e. that relating to the market demand, and brand price elasticity, i.e. that relating to the particular brand under consideration. For example, while the demand for an overall product category may be inelastic, demand for particular brands within this category may be elastic. Moreover, price elasticity can vary substantially across different product brands within a particular class. For example, 'the sales of small market share brands tend to be more price sensitive than those of brands with larger market shares' (Nagle, 1987, p. 79), while 'price cuts by higher quality tiers are more powerful in pulling customers up from lower tiers, than lower tier price cuts are in pulling customers down from upper tiers; i.e. customers "trade up" more readily than they "trade down" ' (Dolan and Simon, 1996, p. 87). What these considerations also imply is that depending on how broadly one defines the market, different elasticity estimates may result.

- From the price elasticity formula, it is not immediately apparent that the value of ε is not the same at all prices; for example, an elasticity estimated around a price of, say, £2.00 will not be the same as an elasticity estimated around a price of, say, £10. A constant elasticity at all prices within a given range is very much the exception rather than the rule.[9]

- While also not obvious from the elasticity formula, 'because customers differ in the amount of value they attach to a product or service and in their ability to pay for an item, their elasticities also differ. One customer may respond very little to fairly large changes in price while another reacts strongly to a relatively minor price change for the same product' (Morris and Morris, 1990, p. 46). Indeed, differences in price elasticity are a major basis for segmenting a market with a view of customising prices (see, for example, Simon, 1989).

- Since individuals tend to be more sensitive to the prospect of a loss than to the prospect of a gain (Kahneman and Tversky, 1979), computations of price elasticity based on price increases of a certain magnitude may produce different results than those based on price decreases of the same magnitude.

- Price elasticity does not remain constant over time, since 'the percentage change in a product's sales is usually not the same in the long run as in the short run' (Nagle, 1987, p. 77). Factors such as inventory building, substitute awareness, 'lock-in' contracts, new product introductions, and price expectations all combine to introduce differences in the magnitudes off short- versus long-term price elasticities.[10]

- The conventional analysis of elasticity and the associated revenue implications shown in Table 14.2 are based on the assumption of an inverse price–volume relationship (i.e. price and volume move in opposite directions); however, 'if buyers infer quality to the product or service on the basis of price and thereby perceive a higher priced item as more attractive, a positive price–quantity relationship ensues' (Monroe, 1990, pp. 37–38).

- The price elasticity formula provides no clue as to why demand may be elastic or inelastic, i.e. the conditions under which buyers are likely to be more or less price sensitive. This is perhaps the greatest shortcoming of the economic analysis of price sensitivity since it fails to provide the price decision maker with a framework within which the various factors that may influence the degree of price sensitivity can be considered.

Bearing the above in mind, what are the key factors that contribute to customers' price sensitivity (or lack of)? Several – often interrelated – factors have been identified in the literature as summarized below.[11]

- **Availability of acceptable substitutes** – this is probably the most obvious factor that affects price sensitivity and has long been pointed out as such by economic theory. The fewer the substitutes from which a customer can choose, the lower the price sensitivity for any particular alternative. Conversely, even if market (i.e. primary) demand is inelastic, brand elasticity may still be high because of the availability of alternative products and/or sources of supply.

- **Awareness of available substitutes** – while the existence of many substitutes is a necessary condition for high price sensitivity, it is not a sufficient condition. Customers must be aware that such substitutes do in fact

---

[9] Indeed, a typical mistake that decision makers make is to assume that the price elasticity of demand is equal to the slope of the demand curve (i.e. the price response function); this is *not* the case even when a linear demand function (i.e. of the form $q = a - b \cdot p$, where $a, b > 0$) is involved. For more details – as well as a description – of the properties of the *iso-elastic* (i.e. constant elasticity) price response function, see Simon (1992).

[10] For a discussion of the dynamics of price elasticity for different types of products, see Simon (1979), Shoemaker (1986), Kucher (1987), Lillien and Yoon (1988) and Parker (1992).

[11] For more details and illustrative examples, see Morris and Morris (1990), Simon (1992), and Nagle and Holden (1995).

exist and it cannot be taken for granted that customers will be well informed about substitute availability (or even that they will always try to become informed). As Nagle (1987, p. 60) points out, 'the existence of less expensive alternatives of which buyers are unaware cannot affect their purchase behavior'.

- **Transparency of prices** – this is a factor contributing to substitute awareness. If price features frequently in advertisements, brochures, etc., of the product in question, then buyers are likely to be more price aware. Moreover, if price comparisons are easy to undertake as a result of similar pricing conventions by different suppliers (e.g. petrol prices), the buyers will be able to determine the true price differences involved. Both these factors are likely to impact positively on the degree of price sensitivity.

- **Purchase frequency** – this is a factor affecting the amount of information possessed by buyers. For products that are frequently purchased, buyers are more likely to develop a good appreciation of the various product alternatives and range of prices available and, thus, become more price sensitive than for infrequent purchases.

- **Product uniqueness** – this is an extremely important factor affecting price sensitivity and one that is largely under the firm's control. If the product contains important features that are highly valued by buyers and differentiate the offering from those of competitors, price sensitivity is likely to be low. Not only may customers be willing to pay a price premium to obtain the unique attributes embedded in the product but they may also view competitive products as less than acceptable substitutes. Note that 'unique attributes' do not refer to physical characteristics only; intangible elements (e.g. a solid reputation for excellent service) may be just as important in creating a 'unique value effect' (Nagle and Holden, 1995) as tangible elements.

- **Ease of product comparison** – this is a factor that is particularly important for industrial purchases and refers to the extent to which the buyer finds it easy to undertake comparisons between alternative products and/or suppliers. When products are difficult to evaluate before the purchase and the cost of failure is high (e.g. mainframe computers), buyers may only consider offers from 'known' or 'approved' suppliers and thus be willing to pay a premium for this 'peace of mind'. In a consumer goods setting (e.g. with food items), while comparison of alternative offers is normally less risky than in industrial contexts, it has to be borne in mind that 'a buyer can compare a new brand with one he regularly buys only if he is willing to risk the cost of an unknown purchase only once' (Nagle, 1987, p. 61).

- **Importance of purchase** – this refers to both the absolute amount of what the price of the item represents and the relative importance of the purchase as a proportion of the buyer's income. As the importance of the purchase increases so does the degree of price sensitivity. The more, in absolute terms, a buyer spends on a product, the greater the gain from even small reductions in price and, therefore, the greater the incentive to shop around (e.g. compare the purchase of a washing machine with that of a new car). Moreover, the greater the significance of the purchase in relation to the buyer's income, the greater the benefit from finding cheaper sources of supply (e.g. wealthy families may spend more on food and be less price sensitive than lower-income families, since the latter's overall spending on food represents a greater proportion of their income).

- **Shared cost** – this refers to the proportion of the total price actually paid by the buyer. In many cases, the buyer does not incur the entire cost associated with a purchase as part (or even all) of the cost is paid by someone else; obvious examples here are insurance payments, tax deductions (credits) and compensation for business travel. The smaller the proportion of the total price that the buyer must pay himself/herself, the lower the price sensitivity for the purchase under consideration.

- **Switching costs** – this relates to costs that a buyer must incur beyond the purchase price when switching from one product/brand/supplier to another. Sometimes, a product (e.g. a software program) is used with assets bought previously (e.g. a mainframe computer) and which can only be replaced in the long run. In other instances, there are 'sunk' investments in developing relationships with suppliers, learning to use a particular product, and establishing routines to handle transactions efficiently. Under such conditions, the buyer becomes 'locked in' to a particular product and/or supplier and price sensitivity tends to be low due to the high switching costs involved (at least in the short run).

- **Proportion of product price on total cost** – this factor is particularly important in industrial markets where products are purchased as a direct result of demand for other (final) products. This derived demand situation implies that 'the more price sensitive the demand for a company's own product, the more price sensitive that company will be when purchasing supplies' (Nagle, 1987, p. 63). Further, the extent of price sensitivity will depend on the proportion of the final product's cost that is accounted for by the price of the raw material or part involved; the greater this proportion, the greater the price sensitivity. In a consumer setting, a similar effect can be observed; for example, when purchasing a new car, the buyer is likely to be less sensitive to the price of, say, a CD-player as an add-on extra than would be the case if a separate purchase (i.e. divorced from the car purchase) was contemplated.

- **Inventory considerations** – this influence on price sensitivity applies primarily in the short term and its impact tends to be transitory. If buyers can stock current purchases for future use (e.g. if the product is not perishable) and if they expect that future prices are likely to be higher than current prices, then short-run price sensitivity will be higher. Conversely, buyers may run down their inventories if they feel that current prices are likely to be reduced in the future. In assessing the likely impact of inventories on price sensitivity, it is essential to appreciate that it 'depends critically on buyer expectations about future prices . . . a price must be judged high or low relative to the prices buyers expect in the future rather those prices that prevailed in the recent past' (Nagle, 1987, p. 71).

- **Price as indicator of quality** – this refers to the extent to which price acts not only as a measure of sacrifice for acquiring the product but also as a signal about the product's quality. This function of price is typically associated with image products, prestige/exclusive products, and products for which the 'objective' evaluation of their quality is difficult. The more buyers use/rely on price as a criterion for evaluating quality, the less price sensitive they are likely to be; in fact, 'customers may actually expect the price to be somewhat steep' (Morris and Morris, 1990, p. 44).

A careful analysis of the above factors will go a long way towards providing price decision makers with a clear picture of the way current and potential buyers are likely to respond to price and of the existence of any market segments with differential price sensitivities. Ideally, such an analysis ought to be followed by more formal research to develop *quantitative* estimates of customers' reactions to price because, ultimately, 'only if we know, in quantitative terms, how customers respond to our own price and to competitive prices can we make a rational price decision' (Dolan and Simon, 1996, p. 45). Unfortunately, despite the existence of a wide variety of different pricing research methodologies,[12]

'companies do not approach demand elasticity in a systematic, strategic fashion ... Qualitative approaches are relied upon more heavily in demand

---

[12] These range from pricing experiments and customer surveys to conjoint analysis applications and econometric analyses of historic market data; non-technical overviews of the available methodologies can be found in Gabor (1988), Simon (1989), Seymour (1989), Monroe (1990), Nagle and Holden (1995) and Dolan and Simon (1996).

measurement than are quantitative approaches. Firms typically do not maintain detailed price data bases, nor do most regularly make efforts to estimate demand sensitivity' (Morris and Morris, 1990, p. 53; see also Morris and Joyce, 1988).

This contrasts sharply with companies' practices on the cost side, where sophisticated costing systems are very much the rule rather than the exception; however, as already argued, it is not cost that determines price: it is the customer and his/her perception of value. A costing system however refined and sophisticated can tell us *nothing* about the customer – a demand measurement system, on the other hand, can tell us *a lot*.

Conclusion

Price is probably the most important but least well-managed element of the marketing mix. A key reason for this deficiency appears to be a lack of understanding of how customer considerations impact upon pricing, i.e. how the demand side 'works'. This chapter aimed to show how price features in buyers' purchasing decisions and how price sensitivity develops as a result of different influences. The intention was to highlight the key principles of a customer-oriented approach to pricing and provide the reader with sufficient building blocks to enable the construction of his/her own perspective within the particular pricing situation he/she might be facing. It seems appropriate to conclude the chapter with a simple thought: 'anything that reduces the buyers' cost of evaluating an alternative . . . will increase buyers' sensitivity to low-price offers' (Nagle, 1987, p. 62). Isn't everybody getting connected to the Internet nowadays . . . ?

References

Albach, H. (1979) Market organization and pricing behaviour in oligopolistic firms in the ethical drugs industry: An essay in the measurement of effective competition, *Kyklos*, **32**(3), 523–40.

Alfred, A. M. (1972) *Pricing Decisions*, Scott, Foresman & Co., Glenview, Illinois.

Backman, J. (1953) *Price Practices and Price Policies*, The Ronald Press, New York.

Bain, J. S. (1949) Price and production policies, in H. S. Ellis (ed.), *A Survey of Contemporary Economics*, Blackiston Company, Berkeley, California.

Bonoma, T. V., Crittenden, V. L. and Dolan, R. J. (1988) Can we have rigor and relevance in pricing research?, in T.M. Devinney (ed.), *Issues in Pricing – Theory and Research*, Lexington Books, Lexington, MA.

Buckner, H. (1967) *How British Industry Buys*, Industrial Market Research Ltd, London.

Capon, N., Farley, J. U. and Hulbert, J. (1975) Pricing and forecasting in an oligopoly firm, *Journal of Management Studies*, **12**, 133–56.

Christopher, M. (1982) Value-in-use-pricing, *European Journal of Marketing*, **16**(5), 35–47.

Cooper, R. G. (1979) The dimensions of new product failure, *Journal of Marketing*, **43**, 93–103.

Dean, J. (1947) Research approach to pricing, in *Planning the Price Structure*, Marketing Series No. 67, American Management Association, New York.

Diamantopoulos, A. (1991) Pricing: theory and evidence – a literature review, in M. J. Baker (ed.), *Perspectives on Marketing Management*, **1**, Wiley, London.

Diamantopoulos, A. (1995) Pricing, in M. J. Baker (ed.), *Marketing Theory and Practice*, 3rd edn, Macmillan, London.

Diamantopoulos, A. and Mathews, B. P. (1993) Managerial perceptions of the demand curve: Evidence from a multi-product firm, *European Journal of Marketing*, **27**(9), 3–16.

Diamantopoulos, A. and Mathews, B. P. (1995) *Making Pricing Decisions: A Study of Managerial Practice*, Chapman & Hall.

Diller, H. (1991) *Preispolitik*, Kohlhammer, Stuttgart.

Dolan, R. J. and Simon, H. (1996) *Power Pricing: How Managing Price Transforms the Bottom Line*, The Free Press, New York.

Ehrenberg, A. S. C. and England, L. R. (1990) Generalizing a price effect, _Journal of Industrial Economics_, **39**, 47–68.

Farley, J. U., Hulbert, J. M. and Weinstein, D. (1980) Price setting and volume planning by two European industrial companies: A study and comparison of decision processes, _Journal of Marketing_, **44**, 46–54.

Forbis, J. L. and Mehta, N. T. (1978) Value-based strategies for industrial products, _Business Horizons_, **21**, October, 25–31.

Hankinson, A. (1985) Pricing decisions in small engineering firms, _Management Accounting (UK)_, **63**, 36–7.

Howard, J. A. and Morgenroth, W. M. (1968) Information processing model of executive decision, _Management Science_, **14**, March, 416–28.

Jeuland, A. and Dolan, R. (1982) An aspect of new product planning: Dynamic pricing, in A. Zoltners (ed.), _TIMS Studies in the Management Sciences_, Special Issue on Marketing Models, North-Holland, Amsterdam.

Kahneman, D. and Tversky, A. (1979) Prospect theory: An analysis of decision under risk, _Econometrica_, **47**, March, 263–91.

Kucher, E. (1987) Absatzdynamik nach preisaenderung, _Marketing ZFP_, **3**, August, 177–86.

Lambin, J. J. (1976) _Advertising Competition and Market Conduct in Oligopoly Over Time_, North-Holland, Amsterdam.

Laric, M. V. (1989) Pricing analysis using spreadsheets, in D. T. Seymour (ed.), _The Pricing Decision_, Probus, Chicago, IL.

Liebermann, S. (1969) Has the marginalist anti-marginalist controversy regarding the theory of the firm been settled?, _Schweizerische Zeitschrift fuer Volkswirtschaft_, **105**(4), 535–49.

Lillien, G. L. and Yoon, E. (1988) An exploratory analysis of the dynamic behavior of price elasticity over the product life cycle: An empirical analysis of industrial chemical products, in T. M. Devinney (ed.), _Issues in Pricing – Theory and Research_, Lexington Books, Lexington, MA.

Marn, M. and Rosiello, R. (1992) Managing price, gaining profit, _Harvard Business Review_, September–October, 84–94.

Marshall, A. (1979) _More Profitable Pricing_, McGraw-Hill, London.

Monroe, K. B. (1979) _Pricing: Making Profitable Decisions_, McGraw-Hill, New York.

Monroe, K. B. (1990) _Pricing: Making Profitable Decisions_, 3rd edn, McGraw-Hill, New York.

Monroe, K. B. and Della Bitta, A. J. (1978) Models for pricing decisions, _Journal of Marketing Research_, **15**, August, 413–28.

Monroe, K. B. and Mazudmar, T. (1988) Pricing-decision models: Recent developments and research opportunities, in T. M. Devinney (ed.), _Issues in Pricing – Theory and Research_, Lexington Books, Lexington, MA.

Montgomery. S. L. (1988) _Profitable Pricing Strategies_, McGraw-Hill, New York.

Morris, M. H. and Joyce, M. L. (1988) How marketers evaluate price sensitivity, _Industrial Marketing Management_, **17**, 169–76.

Morris, M. H. and Morris, G. (1990) _Market-Oriented Pricing – Strategies for Management_, Quorum, New York.

Nagle, T. (1984) Economic foundations for pricing, _Journal of Business_, **57**, January, 3–26.

Nagle, T. (1987) _The Strategy and Tactics of Pricing_, Prentice-Hall, Englewood Cliffs, NJ.

Nagle, T. and Holden, R. K. (1995) _The Strategy and Tactics of Pricing_, Prentice-Hall, Englewood Cliffs, NJ.

Nimer, D. A. (1971) There's more to pricing than most companies think, _Innovations_, August. Reprinted in I. R. Vernon and C. W. Lamb (eds) _The Pricing Function_, (1976), Lexington Books, D. C. Heath & Co, Lexington, MA.

Oxenfeldt, A. R. (1973) A decision making structure for price decisions, _Journal of Marketing_, **37**, 48–53.

Oxenfeldt, A. R. (1975) _Pricing Strategies_, American Management Association, New York.

Parker, P. M. (1992) Price elasticity dynamics over the adoption life cycle, _Journal of Marketing Research_, **29**, August, 358–67.

Porter, M. E. (1980) _Competitive Strategy_, Free Press, New York.

Porter, R. H. (1985) On the incidence and duration of price wars, *Journal of Industrial Economics*, **33**, June, 415–26.

Rao, V. R. (1984) Pricing research in marketing: The state of the art, *Journal of Business*, **57**, 39–60.

Rao, V. R. (1993) Pricing models in marketing, in J. Eliahsberg and G. L. Lilien (eds), *Handbooks in OR & MS,*. Vol. 5, Elsevier, Amsterdam.

Rao, V. R. and Monroe, K. B. (1989) The effect of price, brand name, and store name on buyer's perceptions of product quality: An integrative review, *Journal of Marketing Research*, **26**, August, 351–7.

Reekie, W. D. (1981) Innovation and pricing in the Dutch drug industry, *Managerial and Decision Economics*, **2**(1), 49–56.

Reichmann, T. (1973) *Kosten und Preisgrenzen. Die Bestimmung von Preisuntergrenzen und Preisobergrenzen im Industriebetrieb,* Gabler, Wiesbaden.

Riebel, P. (1972) *Kosten und Preise*, 2nd edn, Opladen, Westdeutscher Verlag.

Sethuraman, A. and Tellis, G. J. (1991) An analysis of the tradeoff between advertising and price discounting, *Journal of Marketing Research*, **28**, May, 160–74.

Seymour, D. T. (ed.) (1989) *The Pricing Decision – A Strategic Planner for Marketing Professionals,* Probus, Chicago.

Shapiro, B. P. and Jackson, B. B. (1978) Industrial pricing to meet consumer needs, *Harvard Business Review*, **56**, November/December, 119–28.

Shipley, D. D. (1985) Resellers' supplier selection criteria for different consumer products, *European Journal of Marketing*, **19**(7), 26–36.

Shoemaker, R. W. (1986) Comment on dynamics of price elasticity and brand life cycles: An

empirical study, *Journal of Marketing Research*, **23**, February, 778–82.

Simon, H. (1979) Dynamics of price elasticity and brand life cycles: An empirical study, *Journal of Marketing Research*, 16 November, 439–52.

Simon, H. (1982) *Preismanagement,* Gabler, Wiesbaden.

Simon, H. (1989) *Price Management*, North-Holland Publishing Company, Amsterdam.

Simon, H. (1992) Pricing opportunities – and how to exploit them, *Sloan Management Review*, Winter, 55–65.

Skinner, R. (1970) The determination of selling prices, *Journal of Industrial Economics*, **18**, 201–17.

Staudt, T. A. and Taylor, D. A (1965) *A Managerial Introduction to Marketing,* Prentice-Hall, Englewood Cliffs, NJ.

Tellis, G. J. (1988) The price elasticity of selective demand: A meta-analysis of econometric models of sales, *Journal of Marketing Research*, **25**, November, 331–41.

Wied-Nebbeling, S. (1975) *Industrielle Preissetzung,* Mohr Siebeck Verlag, Tuebingen.

Wied-Nebbeling, S. (1985) *Das Preisverhalten in der Industrie,* Mohr Siebeck Verlag, Tuebingen.

Woodside, A. G. (1992) Ecological research on pricing decisions in manufacturer-distributor channels, *Proceedings of the American Marketing Association Conference*, Summer, 474–80.

Zeithaml, V. A. (1988) Consumer perceptions of price, quality and value: A means-end model and synthesis of evidence, *Journal of Marketing*, **52**, July, 2–22.

CHAPTER 15

Selling and sales management

BILL DONALDSON

Introduction

The role of selling is continuing to change and evolve in response to dramatic moves in the way buyers and sellers interact. Individual knowledge, skills and abilities are still required, perhaps more than ever, but teamwork and technology are also vital ingredients in an effective organizational response to the needs and demands of customers. The salesforce have always been ambassadors for their firm but in a turbulent business environment the information and persuasion role of salespeople is being absorbed into their relationship role. Salespeople must take responsibility for creating, developing and maintaining profitable relationships with their customers. This being so, the need is paramount to focus on how to win, develop and retain customers to achieve the marketing and sales objectives of the firm. This puts the spotlight once again on the role of selling in the marketing mix and on the management of sales operations. Sales operations are the revenue generation engine of the organization and thus have a direct impact on the success of the firm.

In this chapter we consider how selling is changing and evolving. We examine the new role of salespeople and re-define the sales encounter in different exchange situations. We then address some of the key issues in managing the salesforce as they relate to marketing.

The changing role of salespeople

Consider the following statistics. In 1970, 80 per cent of grocery products were sold to 1656 buying points, the remaining 20 per cent to thousands of smaller units. By 1980, 80 per cent of grocery products were purchased from only 656 buying points. Today 80 per cent is bought from only six major buying points (Keynote, 1997). Less dramatic but similar trends can be found across industries and the effects on salespeople and on the efficiency of sales operations has been radical. These changes imply a new perspective for integrating sales and other forms of communication with the operational side of the business. Driven by an urgency arising from more complex supply chains, fewer and larger purchase points, the availability and use of IT in customer contact operations, relative increased costs of labour, and the continuing internationalization of business, sales operations are now different. These factors contribute positively to the need for more efficient exchange and communication systems between firms and their customers, predicated by increases in the costs of acquiring new customers, and the need to retain the existing customer base and stimulate the purchasing power of those customers already on the books.

Personal selling can be defined as the personal contact with one or more purchasers for the purpose of making a sale. To be effective, marketing management need to integrate personal selling with other promotional elements, with other organizational functions such as distribution and production and with the customer and competitive structures prevailing in the market. The importance of personal selling is such that expenditure on the salesforce usually exceeds the budget for all other marketing communications activities added together, with the possible exception of advertising in large, fast-moving consumer goods companies or direct marketing organizations.

Personal selling has several interrelated roles within the communications mix. The information role is part of a two-way process whereby information about the company's product or offer needs to be communicated to existing and potential customers and, in the reverse direction, customers' needs are correctly interpreted and understood by management. Salespeople impart knowledge about products or services which provide benefits to customers and also a range of information on promotional support, finance, technical advice, service and other elements which contribute to customer satisfaction. Salespeople are also the face-to-face contact between purchasers and the company and for good reason are referred to as 'the eyes and ears of the organization' since senior management's customer contact may be limited.

A second role salespeople must fulfil is persuasion. The importance of correctly identifying customers' needs and market opportunities cannot be overstated. Nevertheless, in competitive markets, prospective customers are usually faced with an abundance of choice. As a result adoption of the marketing concept can be no guarantee of competitive advantage. Purchasers will have to be convinced that the company has correctly identified their needs and that the offer provides benefits over any other firm. Salespeople are part of this process through persuasion and service.

A third role is relationship building and salespeople must initiate, build and develop relationships between the firm and its cus-

tomers. Owing to their boundary-spanning role, the salesforce of a company has traditionally been a vital link between the firm and its customers (Cravens *et al.*, 1992) and a prime platform for communicating the firm's marketing message to its customers and the voice of the customer to the firm. In the high-tech, nano-second '90s it is easy to overlook the importance of personal relationships and how the interaction with customers has changed, if at all. Sales practices need to be re-engineered to maximize the salesforce potential in this new environment.

The nature of the personal selling task is continuing to change in that selling to customers has been replaced by cooperating with customers. The goals and objectives for the salesperson have also changed from achieving or exceeding target, selling X products in Y period and maximizing earnings, to that of building repeat business with the firm's existing and potential customer base. The emphasis has shifted from 'closing' the singular sale to creating the necessary conditions for a long-term relationship between the firm and its customers that breed successful sales encounters in the long run. This shift renders obsolete many of the currently available sales management practices and the sales philosophy and culture that has driven the development of the sales management field for decades. It also questions sales performance measures based on individual criteria and sales management practices which reflect recruitment, training and rewards based on sales volumes rather than relationship performance. The role of the salesperson seems to have moved away from traditional aggressive and persuasive selling, to a new role of 'relationship manager' (Crosby *et al.*, 1990). Also, in practice, we are witnessing a tendency to change the sales lexicon from salesforce to sales counsellors, professional representatives or sales consultants (Manning and Reece, 1992; DeCormier, and Jobber, 1993). Perhaps the change in the title is designed to facilitate the transition of the salesforce's tasks from selling to advising and counselling, from talking to listening and from pushing to helping, as suggested by Pettijohn *et al.* (1995). This transition is not only a matter of title. The new reality of relationship marketing directs salespeople and sales managers to develop long-lasting relationships with their customers based on mutual trust and commitment (Morgan and Hunt, 1994).

The costs of personal selling

According to a 1997 survey, the average cost of an outside salesperson is £49 699 per annum (Reward Group/CIM, 1997). Yet the time actually spent face to face with customers is typically around 20–30 per cent of working hours. This raises the question of what form of communication is both effective and efficient in today's marketplace. The most significant difference between selling and other elements in the marketing communications mix is the personal contact but this comes with a relatively high price tag. The need for this personal contact will vary depending on such factors as the scale of risk, size of investment, type of customer, frequency of purchase, newness of product and many other factors. In some situations the information or persuasion role can be achieved by imper-

sonal means of communication, particularly advertising.

Advertising is impersonal, indirect and aimed at a mass audience, whereas selling is individual, direct and much more adaptable. With advertising the message is more limited, cheaper per contact but unidirectional, relying on a pull approach rather than personal selling which is two-way, but employs a push strategy and is relatively expensive per contact. Today, yet another dimension needs to be considered. This is the role and position of direct marketing as a form of communications. In Table 15.1 we compare advertising, direct marketing and personal selling.

Therefore, a primary task of management is to be clear on the role of personal selling and what exactly it is we want salespeople to do. Information technology (IT) is the set of technologies related to the processing and communication of information including computer and electronic databases, advanced telecommunications, CD-ROMs and the Internet. These technologies have led to new and powerful ways to reach customers and are changing the way firms interact.

The use of marketing databases, telemarketing and the Internet are having a significant

Table 15.1 Choice of communication: comparing advertising, direct marketing and personal selling

Personal selling	Direct marketing	Advertising
Individual directionality	Individual directionality	Mass audience directionality
Personal, direct contact	Personal, indirect contact	Impersonal, indirect contact
Highly adaptable	Adaptable but relatively fixed format	Fixed format
Working in-depth	Working on one-to-one	Working in breadth
Two-way	Two-way	One-way
Direct feedback	Indirect feedback	Organized feedback (MIS, market research)
Expensive per contact	Inexpensive per contact	Relatively inexpensive (cost per 1000 criteria)
Push effect	Pull effect	Pull effect

impact on how sales operations are managed and will continue to do so. For example, the Internet is a powerful tool for providing information and will be an important means of buyer–seller communication. Many traditional intermediaries, particularly those who do not stock a physical product, will find that consumers empower themselves to collect information and make the purchase decision. This changes the information role of salespeople, and travel agencies, car dealerships and financial intermediaries are likely to be most affected by such a process. The demand for secondary sources of information is passing from a number of individual and independent sources to software programs which can browse the Internet and report the findings directly to users (Autonomy and Melting Pot are examples of this kind of service). Information itself is the market opportunity and the facilitation between source and consumer the new challenge.

The incredible success of the Internet in terms of access and users has not yet been matched by sales effectiveness. If anything telephone, e-mail and fax are more essential and powerful at present. In terms of information provision, the Internet is unrivalled. It can reach an audience cheaply with the message you want to convey and allows full interaction – the ultimate in communication. However, unless the web-site is properly designed and maintained it may prove damaging. To create a web-site, identify the information you want to communicate and which the users will need, ensure that it is effectively linked to other databases and that as a communication vehicle it conveys the image as well as the content you wish to get across.

Just as telemetry (automatic reordering) and electronic data interchange (bar coding, etc.) have removed many mundane order processing tasks such as stock checking, inventory management and order filling and processing, so the Internet is likely to remove much of the more mundane information role that salespeople perform. The result will be a changing role for salespeople to a more highly skilled,

more well informed, computer literate person operating as customer account manager and coordinating the difficult interface between customer and company.

What we expect salespeople to do – the sales process

Despite what has been said, the correct approach and technique in selling is still, and always has been, vitally important. While cautioning against the idea of the one best or universal way to sell, nevertheless there are some appropriate guidelines that can be recommended in sales encounters.

Stage 1 Generating leads and identifying prospects

Most salespeople create sales with existing customers and relationship maintenance is a key role. Nevertheless the job also entails gaining new customers. The first step in achieving this is to identify suitable prospects. Many companies provide leads for salespeople from formal sources (Glenigan is one example from the building industry) or perhaps from response enquiries as a result of trade shows, direct mailing, telemarketing or advertising. Salespeople will also generate their own leads from lists/directories, through personal contacts, newspapers or by telephone prospecting. However, a lead is a suspect that has to be qualified to become a prospect. To qualify a lead, it is important to ensure that the potential customer needs the product or service in question or has a problem to be solved and that they have the resources and authority to influence or decide on the purchase. Further, that the potential account will be profitable.

Stage 2 Pre-call planning

An old rule of thumb suggests that a good sales process is 40 per cent preparation, 20 per cent presentation and 40 per cent follow-up. Regardless of the accuracy of these percentages, there is no doubt that success can be linked to preparation. All sales calls should have an objective, preferably with a specific outcome or action on the part of the prospect. Pre-call planning involves setting objectives, gathering information about the buyer and their company, deciding what questions to ask and what you intend to say. Remember that situation questions are important in the sales process but you do not want to ask questions you can and should have known from other sources. Information such as the size of the firm, their products and services, their competitors, names of people in important executive positions, current and previous sales history should be part of pre-call preparation. Further information, such as the customer's buying processes, their current suppliers and their future plans can be identified in the initial stages of the sales interview. Ways to establish credibility and trust for the salesperson and their company with the buyer should be part of the pre-call preparation.

Stage 3 The approach

Getting an audience with a prospect can often be difficult and indeed harrowing for the inexperienced salesperson. Although the role of selling should not be technique driven there is a skill in getting to see the right people so that your message can be communicated and understood. Ultimately, it will be on what you do and how you do it that builds long-term customer relationships but getting there in the first place can be difficult. Experienced salespeople will recommend the importance of getting past the gatekeeper (receptionist, secretary or personal assistant) and building a relationship not only with the buyer but their gatekeepers and other influencers in the buying process. Making appointments is, in most cases, essential to establishing a professional approach but letters of introduction and using third party references can also be crucial. Establishing rapport, whether on the basis of similarity or expertise, is necessary before exchange takes place. For larger sales and new products, where the risk for the buyer is greater, establishing credibility is vital. The well known company has a distinct advantage in this stage and the salesperson from a less well known company has to work doubly hard to reassure the buyer (Levitt, 1967).

Stage 4 The presentation

As Rackham's work has shown, the ability to ask questions and the right type of question differentiates successful and less successful salespeople (Rackham, 1995). Nevertheless, too often salespeople over-emphasize the oral presentation and ignore the written sales proposal, the quotation or the subsequent follow-up, which technically can also be considered part of the presentation. It is vital to ensure that the buyer's needs have been correctly identified, that the solution offered is as expected and, if possible, that the customer's expectations are exceeded rather than merely satisfied. Further, in the right circumstances the use of visuals can reassure the buyer and instil confidence in the salesperson, their product and their company. Most experienced salespeople rate canned and stylized presentations much less important than the well-organized and individually tailored presentations (Hite and Bellizzi, 1986). Research in manufacturing has also shown that there is a need to segment customers and target your demonstration depending on the type of product. Many demonstrations were too long for the product and customer, in other words overselling (Heiman and Muller, 1996). Industrial buyers are looking for credibility, reliability, responsiveness and the ability to provide answers from salespeople, rather than aggressiveness or persuasiveness (Hayes and Hartley, 1989).

Stage 5 Overcoming objections

It is human nature that a buyer may stall and raise objections to a sales presentation. Again, experienced salespeople will claim that objections are to be welcomed since they confirm the buyer's interest in the product or service although the idea of questions is to reveal real needs so that surprises are kept to a minimum. Good salespeople differentiate between types of objections. Some objections are no more than clarifying questions and should be welcomed. However, there are also objections that express real concerns. The advice here is to listen carefully to the problem, clarify that both parties understand the real issue and agree how it can be solved. Listening enhances trust in the salesperson and leads to anticipation of future interaction (Ramsey and Sohi, 1997). Traditionally, salespeople have put too much emphasis on the ability to overcome resistance by technique instead of by sound solutions that meet the buyers' real needs and provide clear benefits. In other words salespeople have been overly concerned with a performance orientation rather than a learning orientation but those who learn, and learn how to adapt, will increase their performance (Sujan, Weitz and Kumar, 1994). Effective communication is helping the customer learn (Wernerfelt, 1996).

Stage 6 Closing

Since most selling is repeat business to existing and known customers, closing is a bad idea. Nevertheless, the salesperson has set an objective and achievement of this objective is necessary to progress the relationship. Very often salespeople just simply forget to ask for the order. They are so busy with their presentation that asking for commitment is neglected or forgotten. In some cases, adding on extra features and advantages that the buyer may not be interested in, loses the sale by not asking for a decision at the right time. Effective closing means agreeing on the objectives that both parties are trying to meet and which take the relationship forward to further integrated activities.

Stage 7 Follow-up

Vital to the customer driven business is what happens after the sale. Most buyers object when

promises are not delivered and the salesperson doesn't do what was expected. In the modern business this is fatal – where building relationships and the ability to deliver as promised, go the extra mile and delight the customer are at the heart of what a business should be about. The most important question a salesperson can ask is 'What do I need to do, Mr or Mrs Customer, to get more of your business?'.

Sales management issues

Sales management must also adapt to changes in market conditions. The need for closer, more demanding relationships with selected customers brings new problems and opportunities in the organization and deployment of salespeople. Traditional approaches to determining salesforce size, territory deployment and call patterns can be brought into question. As a result, salesforce size may need to be assessed on an estimate of the future revenue stream expected from a customer and the service that customer will require. Call rates, travel patterns and frequency of visits may change. In some cases companies may have permanent staff on their customers' premises. Marketing orientation would suggest such customer-based sales solutions to be appropriate, but the cost effectiveness of sales operations may need to be even more carefully assessed than in the past.

Similarly, traditional means of setting sales targets on sales volume and revenue may need to be replaced by measures which reflect the new customer relationship job to be done. More appropriate targets are likely to be the retention rate of customers, the contribution these customers make and the satisfaction level they have in doing business with the firm. This is in keeping with a customer-focused, quality-based strategy that leading-edge firms pursue. This has implications is the kind of people to be recruited, who need to be relationship orientated, financial aware, marketing trained, computer literate and skilled negotiators. Individual ability and technique will still be important but this must be coupled with sound management, particularly in the areas of recruitment, training, leadership, remuneration and control. These issues are considered in the following sections.

Recruitment and selection

Recruiting and selecting suitable applicants is one of the most important and difficult jobs the sales manager can undertake. Formally addressing the recruitment process will help in defining the job, attracting the most suitable applicants and avoiding unnecessary problems and costs. The time and expense in recruiting is not insignificant, including advertising, selection procedures, and first and second interviews. Add to this other costs, including induction training, the potential cost of lost sales, the costs of dismissal if the wrong applicant is selected and the cost of repeating the process. Recruitment costs can be a major headache for sales managers as well as for the recruits themselves.

To overcome some of these difficulties recruitment should be seen as part of a process which includes job analysis, manpower planning, job description, job specification, recruitment, screening and selection. This process should be systematic and thorough and a planned approach will increase the success rate in selection, build a reputation as a desirable, progressive employer and sharpen the firm's competitive edge thus improving effectiveness and efficiency in sales operations. The starting point in recruitment is job analysis. Job analysis specifies the tasks involved in a particular job and the factors which affect job performance, including the reporting relationship, the role and tasks necessary to perform effectively, the environment in which the job operates including policies on sales, distribution and competitors and company rules and regulations. Sales managers should be careful not to be too intuitive in their job analysis. Of course the job should reflect corporate ethos, marketing strategy and the specific reporting relationships but job analysis also requires assessment of what existing salespeople do.

The second stage is manpower planning, which has both qualitative and quantitative dimensions. Initially, an assessment should be made as to how adequate and effective the current salesforce is in meeting sales objectives. What characteristics are considered necessary to do the particular selling job? These are the knowledge, skills and abilities an individual should possess. The second factor is the turnover in personnel. That is, people may be recruited to *add* to the salesforce, while others will be recruited to *replace* those who are promoted, leave, retire or are dismissed. A measure of turnover is the number of people who leave per annum divided by the total number in the salesforce.

The next stage is to write a job description for an individual in a sales position, including the integration of the job into a team or organizational unit. The job analysis is the cornerstone on which the job description for the salesperson is based. Therefore the job description should begin with repeating the main duties, tasks and responsibilities of the job. The key areas can vary but a job title, the main purpose of the job, key and secondary activities and performance measures should be included. It is preferable to be specific in the job description about job functions and duties. For example, indications can be given on time allocated to prospecting, travelling, merchandising, servicing, reporting as well as selling time. The approach should cover the most important aspects of the job, essential and preferable criteria, the necessary education, qualifications, experience and other attributes and an assessment of the validity and reliability of previous methods.

A variety of potential sources can be used to recruit new salespeople. These sources can vary as to their adequacy and consistency in obtaining the best possible candidates for sales positions. Good recruitment policies will take a planned approach to this problem. For example, turnover rates will indicate how many and how often replacements are likely to be required. Further, analysis of previous recruits can indicate more and less productive sources. This analysis can be extended to discriminate between high, average and low performers. One study (Avlonitis, Manolis and Boyle, 1985) suggested that sources of recruits could be linked to selling styles. For example, recruitment for missionary selling jobs favours employment agencies. For trade selling, sources are primarily from advertisements and educational institutions, while for technical selling, recruiters rely more on personal contacts. The use of different sources is, and should be, related to job- and company-specific criteria, as well as the matching characteristics between buyer and seller.

When the number and type of salespeople has been determined and the various sources have been selected to obtain the necessary applicants, it is then essential to evaluate these in order to recruit the best, that is, those most suitable to the job and the firm. One possible cause of high turnover in sales personnel is that badly suited applicants are recruited in the first place. Turnover rates (that is, number who leave per annum over number in salesforce) which are above industry averages or seem to be increasing over previous periods, indicate a problem and an unnecessary cost. These turnover rates do vary, being higher in salesforces where the average age is younger, higher in consumer goods than industrial goods companies and significantly higher in the first three years of service. For example, higher turnover rates are found in new, young, consumer goods salespeople. In financial services, 80 per cent of life insurance salespeople leave within two years of joining their company and only 8 per cent had been with their company more than four years (LIMRA, 1992).

Related to the turnover level are the costs of recruiting, selecting, training and supervising new recruits who are poor performers. In addition to these costs, a salesperson leaving the company may well have a negative effect on sales in their territory and, if joining a competitor, business may be lost. The average lost sales multiplied by the number who leave will represent the total cost of lost business.

Commensurate with cost is the time factor. From a decision to recruit or replace through sourcing, interviewing, screening, second or third interviews, checking references, medical, to placing and accepting an offer may take several months.

Training

In addition to recruiting the most appropriate people for the job based on the job specification, every sales manager must try and improve their subordinates' individual effectiveness by appropriate training. Much training is wasted because it covers areas that the person already knows about. For this reason, it is important to separate induction training for new recruits from that suggested for existing staff. Again, planning is important so the first stage, prior to training, is to conduct some audit of training requirements.

This is stage one in the process, determining needs; stage two is designing the programme; stage three is conducting the training and finally evaluating the results. The vice president of the US pharmaceutical giant Merck, with a salesforce of 3000, on receiving an award as the sales company of the year in 1993 declared that 'training is the key'. To reinforce this a 1993 study suggested that it is not the amount of money spent on training that counts but how the money is spent. Higher performers do not outspend lower performers, but they allocate the funds in different ways. High performers have longer induction training, three to nine months, whereas lower performers spend less than three months with new recruits. High performers do less classroom and role playing but more on-the-job training. Training also has an important role in establishing the values and beliefs that an organization represents in establishing corporate culture within the salesforce.

Leadership and supervision

The ability to get the best from subordinates is a valued characteristic and is referred to as leadership quality. However, leadership is best explained in the context in which it is exercised and sales managers should assess their leadership style and its appropriateness to the people and circumstances in which it is applied.

In today's organization where rationalizing, downsizing and restructuring are being implemented, sales managers must encourage their people to adapt and be flexible. Such movers and shakers have been called transformational leaders who can get their salespeople to perform beyond typical expectations. However, in most situations, sales managers who have not proved themselves by having previously been a successful salesperson will find it hard, if not impossible, to be convincing in this role. Qualities thought to be important in sales managers vary and often extend to a variety of characteristics, usually ending with an ability to walk on water and other superhuman powers.

Perhaps more revealing are studies that reflect how salespeople feel about their boss. The major complaints usually focus on the following:

- Managers do not spend enough time with their salespeople.
- They do not listen to salespeople's concerns.
- They do not take these concerns seriously.
- They do not follow up to resolve problems.

Again the difficulty may be that many sales managers have not been trained in management or prepared for the new skills and tasks that they are now asked to perform.

Remuneration

Arguably, the most influential factor in the motivational mix is remuneration, which can incorporate basic financial rewards and special incentives. Financial incentives are a popular means used to motivate sales personnel. Sales managers can remunerate salespeople using salary, commission, bonus or a combination of these. Most sales managers, based on their experience, seem to feel that a balance of types of remuneration is most appropriate. A recent study found that most UK companies offer combination remuneration comprising salary and commission or salary and some form of bonus, especially performance related pay (Donaldson, 1998). This research also found that a number of salespeople consider job security of higher value than the level of remuneration. Other studies into the effects of pay on the motivation of salespeople have found, for example, that older salespeople with larger families valued financial rewards more whereas younger better educated sales staff who had no family valued the so-called higher order rewards such as recognition, liking and respect and sense of accomplishment (Churchill and Pecotich, 1982). The variety of payment plans in operation, even within similar industry and sales situations, suggests that management do not fully understand the effect of payment on their employees' motivation. If a company's main objectives were on relationship building and long-term customers, a higher salary and lower incentive component would be recommended. The difficulty with such rules is that within any one salesforce there is no one remuneration package that suits everyone and we have to settle for one that best meets the needs of most of our salesforce.

Evaluation and control

Setting targets and quotas for salespeople has a direct effect on their motivation. Targets not only direct sales effort and provide evidence for performance evaluation but they can also act as an incentive and motivator. It is not only the target and system of control that is important but the way the target is determined, communicated and applied. For this reason a system of management by objectives based on the participation and involvement of salespeople themselves, is an appropriate option (Donaldson, 1998).

A problem already identified is that sales tasks and sales effort often can have an indirect rather than a direct effect on sales performance.

Missionary or specification selling, such as pharmaceuticals, is particularly prone to this difficulty. For others, organizational complexity or dual effort with intermediaries may confuse the sales process and its effect on performance. Nevertheless, accurate and timely feedback for salespeople has a positive effect on job performance and job satisfaction (Doyle and Shapiro, 1980). At one level evaluation of salespeople is easy – they either make target or they don't! The problem with the link between sales effort and sales response is that it is neither simple nor direct. Most companies do conduct some form of evaluation but few do this in a formal way that evaluates causes as well as outcomes. Part of the problem with evaluation is that to do it properly, far from being easy, it is time-consuming, costly and downright difficult. At the individual salesperson level evaluation, it is necessary to identify above and below average performers, to identify possible candidates for promotion or dismissal, and to identify areas of weakness in salespeople in carrying out their tasks in meeting sales objectives. For management, evaluation is necessary to assess the efficacy of sales management practices such as territory deployment, recruitment, training, remuneration and so on. Again, our starting point is an audit of current performance.

Conclusion

Personal selling and sales operations are still key to the effective implementation of marketing plans. The role of personal selling is changing as new and different ways such as the telephone, electronic interchange and the Internet can be found to inform and persuade customers. The salesperson must adapt and there is evidence that marketing and sales roles are becoming not only interdependent but also interchangeable. Positions such as business development manager, customer account manager and category manager reflect that salespeople must be better trained and qualified, able to work in teams and be capable of coordinating

within their firm and at the boundary between the firm and their customer. The traditional sales process still applies in many exchange situations but the key role for salespeople is to build, maintain and promote long-term profitable relationships with customers. This puts an additional burden on management to recruit, train, lead, reward and monitor effective sales performers since this role is crucial to the prosperity of their business.

References

Avlonitis, C. J., Manolis, C. K. and Boyle, K. (1985) Sales management practices in the UK manufacturing industry, *Journal of Sales Management*, **2**(2), 6–16.

Churchill, G. A. and Pecotich, A. (1982) A structural equation investigation of the pay satisfaction–valence relationship among salespeople, *Journal of Marketing*, **46** (Fall), 114–124.

Cravens, D., Grant, K., Ingram, T., LaForge, R. and Young C. (1992) In search of excellent sales organizations, *European Journal of Marketing*, **26**(1), 6–23.

Crosby, L. A., Evens, R. K. and Cowles, D. (1990) Relationship quality in service selling: an interpersonal influence perspective, *Journal of Marketing*, **54** (July), 68–81.

Decormier, R. A. and Jobber, D. (1993) The counsellor selling method: concepts and constructs, *Journal of Personal Selling and Sales Management*, **23**(4), 39–59.

Donaldson, B. (1998) The importance of financial incentives in motivating industrial salespeople. *Journal of Selling and Major Account Management*, **1**(1), July, 4–16.

Doyle, S. X. and Shapiro, B. P. (1980) What counts most in motivating your salesforce? *Harvard Business Review*, May–June, 134–139.

Hayes, H. M. and Hartley, S. W. (1989) How buyers view industrial salespeople, *Industrial Marketing Management*, **18**, 73–80.

Heiman, A. and Muller, E. (1996) Using demonstration to increase new product acceptance: controlling demonstration time, *Journal of Marketing Research,* **XXXIII** (November), 422–430.

Hite, R. E. and Bellizzi, J. A. (1986) A preferred style of sales management, *Industrial Marketing Management,* **15**(3), 215–223.

Keynote Ltd (1997) *Retailing in the UK,* Keynote Publications, London.

Levitt, T. (1967) Communications and industrial selling, *Journal of Marketing,* **31** (April), 15–21.

LIMRA (1992) *Report on UK Life Insurance.* Life Insurance Marketing and Research Association, London.

Manning, G. L. and Reece, B. L. (1992) *Selling Today: An Extension of the Marketing Concept,* 5th edn, Allyn and Bacon, Boston.

Morgan, R. M. and Hunt, S. D. (1994) The commitment–trust theory of relationship marketing, *Journal of Marketing,* **58** (July), 20–38.

Pettijohn, C., Pettijohn, L. and Taylor, A. (1995) The relationship between effective counselling and effective behaviors. *Journal of Consumer Marketing,* **12**(1), 5–15.

Rackham, N. (1995) *Spin Selling,* Gower, Aldershot.

Ramsey, R. P. and Sohi, R. S. (1997) Listening to your customers: the impact of perceived salesperson listening behavior on relationship outcomes, *Journal of the Academy of Marketing Science,* **25**(2), 127–137.

Reward Group (1997) *Sales and Marketing Rewards 1997,* Rewards Group/CIM, Stone, Staffordshire, UK.

Sujan, H., Weitz, B. A. and Kumar, N. (1994) Learning orientation, working smart, and effective selling, *Journal of Marketing,* **58** (July), 39–52.

Wernerfelt, B. (1996) Efficient marketing communication: helping the customer learn, *Journal of Marketing Research,* **XXXIII** (May), 239–246.

Further reading

Carlisle, J. A. and Parker, R. C. (1989) *Beyond Negotiation,* Wiley, Chichester.

Cooper, S. (1997) *Selling Principle, Practice and Management,* Pitman, London.

Donaldson, B. (1998) *Sales Management: Theory and Practice,* 2nd edn, Macmillan, Basingstoke.

Hartley, B. and Starkey, M. W. (1996) *The Management of Sales and Customer Relations,* Thomson Business Press, London.

Jobber, D. (ed.) (1997) *The CIM Handbook of Selling and Sales Strategy,* Butterworth-Heinemann, Oxford.

Rackham, N. (1995) *Spin Selling,* Gower, Aldershot.

Steward, K. (1993) *Marketing Led, Sales Driven,* Butterworth–Heinemann, Oxford.

CHAPTER 16

Branding

PETER DOYLE

Introduction

The role and valuation of brands has recently become a controversial issue. Not only is the importance of successful brands emphasized by marketing managers, but some financial executives have developed a new enthusiasm for brands, having seen that their inclusion in the balance sheet enhances shareholder funds, reduces company gearing, and so facilitates further growth by acquisition. This chapter explores five key questions about brands:

1   What is a successful brand?
2   What is the value of a brand?
3   How are successful brands built?
4   What are the comparative advantages of buying brands versus building and developing them internally?
5   What are the logic and economics behind brand extension strategies?

The successful brand

Before defining a brand, it is first necessary to define a *product*. The concept of a product is not straightforward. First, products and brands are mistakenly often associated only with fast-moving consumer goods. But today, the most rapidly growing and profitable products are in services: financial; retail; and management.

Also, besides products and services, people, places and ideas can be thought of as 'products'. Politicians, filmstars and privatization schemes are now marketed in much the same way as Coca-Cola or Crest toothpaste.

Second, products mean different things to people *inside* the business from what they do to people *outside*. Inside, to the firm's managers and accountants, a product is something produced in the factory or the office. It is about materials, components, labour costs, quality and output specifications. But outside, to the consumer, a product is something different – it is a means of meeting his or her needs or solving their problems. These needs and problems are as likely to be emotional and psychological as functional and economic. It is a product's ability to meet these needs and aspirations which creates its value. The value of a product is not what the producer puts in, but what the consumer gets out. As the chief executive of Black & Decker put it, 'Our job is not to make 1/4-inch drills, but to make 1/4-inch holes'. Or the chairman of Revlon Cosmetics, 'In the factory we make cosmetics, but in the store we sell hope'. Similarly, IBM has always maintained it 'doesn't sell products. It sells solutions to customers' problems' (Rodgers, 1986).

A product, then, is *anything which meets the needs of customers*. When several companies are offering rival products, they will want to identify and distinguish their particular offering.

This is called 'branding', so there is a Black & Decker brand, a Revlon brand and an IBM brand. But the focus here is not on brands *per se*, but on successful brands. Because people are aware of a specific brand does not mean that it is successful. People recognized brands like the Sinclair C5, the Ford Edsel, the Co-op, or Wimpy restaurants, but they did not develop preferences for them. The Landor survey (1991) found, for example, that British Telecom was in the UK's top ten brands for awareness, but in terms of esteem it was rated number 300. BT has been referred to as a strong *negative* brand. It was known for all the wrong reasons.

A positive or successful brand can be defined as follows: *A successful brand is a name, symbol, design, or some combination, which identifies the 'product' of a particular organization as having a sustainable differential advantage.* 'Differential advantage' means simply that customers have a reason for preferring that brand to competitors' brands. 'Sustainable' means an advantage that is not easily copied by competitors. That is, the business creates barriers to entry, for example by developing an outstanding reputation or image for quality, service or reliability (for a useful study of the issues surrounding the concept of a differential advantage see Day and Wensley, 1988). Brands like IBM, Coca-Cola, Sony and Marks & Spencer are successful brands because they have such sustainable differential advantages, which, as shown below, invariably result in superior profit and market performance. Successful brands are *always* brand leaders in their segments.

Two implications of this definition can be noted. First, brands are only assets if they have sustainable differential advantages. If they are negative or neutral brands like BT, Woolworth, or the Austin Maestro, they should not appear on the balance sheet, however much is spent on advertising. Any profit these brands achieve is through their property or distribution investments rather than through the brand's differential advantage.

Similarly, if the differential advantage is not sustainable, it should not appear on the balance sheet. In some markets such as games or children's toys, a successful brand often has a life expectancy of only six months and thereafter has no value.

Second, like most other assets, brands depreciate without further investment. If management fails to re-invest in enhancing quality, service and brand image then the brand will decline. Hoover, Singer, Fridgidaire, and MG are examples of brands which were once so successful as to be almost generic names for the product, but which have since declined or disappeared due to lack of investment.

This is often underestimated. Most models suggest that brands tend to decay logarithmically (e.g. Hanssens *et al.*, 1990). This means that in the short term, managers can increase profits without damaging the brand's market share, by cutting back brand support. However, the mistake is thinking that brand disinvestment can be continued. Without adequate support, typically after around a year or two, the brand enters a period of spiralling decline.

How brands work

Brands work by facilitating and making more effective the consumer's choice process. Every day an individual makes hundreds of decisions. He or she is besieged by countless products and messages competing for attention. To make life bearable and to simplify this decision-making process, the individual looks for short-cuts. The most important of these short-cuts is to rely on *habit* – buy brands that have proved satisfactory in the past. This is particularly the case for low-involvement purchases, which make up most of the things people buy. This does not mean that people are totally brand-loyal, of course, since most of them know that many brands will satisfy their needs. Most people ask for Coca-Cola but they are not too disappointed when they are offered Pepsi.

But this habit rule is not just based upon

experience of use, it can also be based upon longstanding *perceptions*. People can have quite strong brand preferences even though they have never bought the products. This is especially true for aspirational products. My son has long had a preference for a Porsche, even though he has still to wait another five years before he is old enough for a driving licence. Such preferences or brand images are based upon cultural, social and personality factors, as well as commercial stimuli like advertising, public relations and prominence of distribution.

Even with non-routine, supposedly highly rational purchasing situations in the industrial sector, where decisions are taken by technical personnel, it is remarkable how important brand image is in the choice process. Even industrial buyers tend to rely on experience and long-held attitudes about the brand, rather than undertake a zero-based approach to the wide range of alternative options (Levitt, 1983). As the cynical IBM salesperson is supposed to have said to a purchasing manager, 'Nobody's ever been fired for buying IBM'.

ive (e.g. quality, value for money), or abstract and emotional (e.g. status, youthfulness). The personality of the brand is a function of its rational characteristics but this has to be augmented and communicated to consumers through advertising, design, packaging and effective distribution and display. These position the brand's personality in the consumer's mind, generate confidence, and create the purchasing environment. A more complete description of consumer behaviour and its implications for brands can be found in a number of excellent texts including Schiffman and Kanuk (1997); Engel *et al.* (1994).

The value of a successful brand

Successful brands are valuable because they can create a stream of future earnings. It is useful to dissect the mechanisms by which brands generate these income streams.

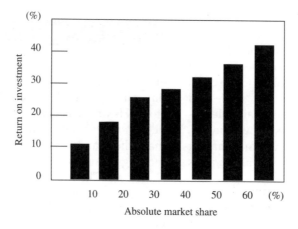

Source: Buzzell and Gale, 1987

Figure 16.1   The relationship between market share and profitability

Successful brands are those which create this image or 'personality'. They do it by encouraging customers to perceive the attributes they aspire to as being strongly associated with the brand. These attributes may be real and object-

Brands, market share and profits

A successful brand is one which customers want to buy and retailers want to stock – it achieves a high market share. Brands with a high market

Table 16.1 Market share rank and average net margins for UK grocery brands

Rank	Net margin (%)
1	17.9
2	2.8
3	−0.9
4	−5.9

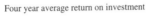

Four year average return on investment

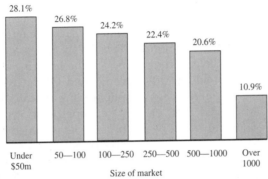

Source: Clifford and Cavanagh, 1985

Figure 16.2 Size of market and business performance

share are much more profitable. The well-known PIMS findings (Buzzell and Gale, 1987), based on detailed studies of 2600 businesses, showed that, on average, products with a market share of 40 per cent generate three times the return on investment of those with a market share of only 10 per cent (Figure 16.1). Weak brands mean weak profits. A UK study shows that for grocery brands the relationship is even stronger. The number-one brand generates over six times the return on sales of the number two brand, while the number three and four brands are totally unprofitable (Table 16.1). The pattern is similar in the USA, where a recent survey of American consumer goods showed that the number-one brand earned 20 per cent return, the number two around 5 per cent and the rest lost money (*The Economist*, 1988).

The value of niche brands

The above findings do not mean that the brand has to be large in absolute terms. It is normally much more profitable to be number one in a small niche market than to be number three in a huge market. It is market share which is the key to performance, not absolute sales. In fact, Clifford and Cavanagh (1985) provide convincing evidence that a strong brand in a niche market earns a higher percentage return than a strong brand in a big market (Figure 16.2). In large markets, competitive threats and retailer pressure can hold back profits even for the top brand.

Brand values and prices

Because successful brands have differential advantages, they are normally able to obtain

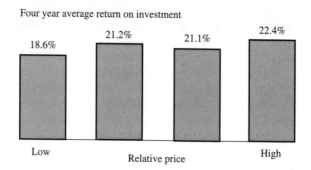

Four year average return on investment

Source: Clifford and Cavanagh, 1985

Figure 16.3 Relative price of products and business performance

higher prices than less successful brands. Sometimes this occurs at the customer level but more frequently it is earned at the retailer level. Strong brands can resist pressure from the trade for discounts. This, in turn, generates superior earnings. Clifford and Cavanagh (1985) found that, on average, premium price products earned 20 per cent more than discount brands (Figure 16.3).

Brand loyalty and beliefs

Successful brands achieve higher customer loyalty. Unsuccessful brands or new brands have to attract customers. This affects the net margin because it is much more expensive in advertising, promotion and selling to win new customers than to hold existing satisfied ones. One study suggested that it cost six times as much to win new customers as to retain current users (Reichheld, 1996).

Strong brands can also override the occasional hitches and even disasters which can destroy weaker brands. After terrorists poisoned samples of the leading analgesic, Tylenol, in 1987, US retailers had to remove entirely the brand from their shelves for several months. Once the scare was over, however, customers went back to the brand they trusted, leading to a remarkably complete recovery for Tylenol. Tom Peters tells a revealing story about Federal Express (FEX), which has a superb reputation for service. He telephoned FEX twenty-seven

times over a six-month period to request service. Twenty-six times a FEX employee answered before the first ring of the telephone had been completed. On the twenty-seventh time the telephone rang repeatedly without any response. After repeated rings, he put the phone down because he assumed that *he* had made the mistake of calling the wrong number! Of course, if this had been a neutral or negative brand it would have simply reinforced one's current image of the brand.

Common products, unique brands

Today, competition can quickly emulate advances in technology or product formulation. Competitors can quickly copy a cigarette, a soft-drink formula or PC specification. But what cannot be copied is the Marlboro, Coca-Cola or Sony brand personalities. Studies show overwhelmingly that the best feasible strategy is to focus on brand differentiation (Figure 16.4), rather than cost and price, as a way of building profitability and growth. While the best strategy in theory is both low cost and high differentiation, in practice it is worth paying some cost penalty to achieve strong differentiation.

The brand growth direction matrix

The product life cycle is a well-known phenomenon. The product peaks and eventually dies as

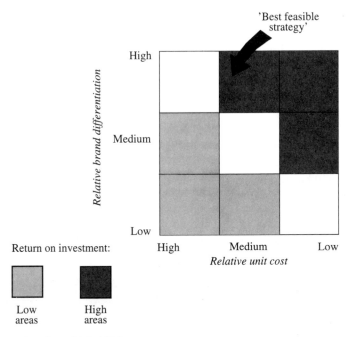

Adapted by author from Hall, 1980

Figure 16.4   Brand differentiation, unit cost and business performance

its markets mature and new technologies replace it. But this life cycle refers to products, not to brands. There is no reason why a brand cannot adapt to new technologies and move from mature into new growth markets. The brand growth direction matrix (Figure 16.5) indicates the main growth opportunities available. Initially brand share is the strategic focus. But most of the successful brands which have lasted the decades have shifted to incorporate *new* technology, ingredients and packaging developments to circumvent the product life-cycle. Similarly, Johnson and Johnson's Baby Shampoo is only one of the many examples of brands which have moved into *new market segments* to continue growth. The fourth growth direction is towards *global branding*, which appears to offer increasing opportunities to

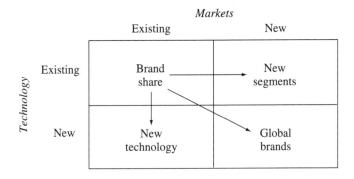

Figure 16.5   Brand growth direction matrix

today's multinationals. Growth based upon continuously developing successful brands appears to provide a more secure foundation than that based upon unrelated acquisitions or new untried products where failure rates are as high as 95 per cent.

Competitive depositioning

The brand leader is in an enormously strong position to fend off attacks. First, it has financial strength – almost invariably it will have the highest market share and the higher profit margins. This should enable it to outgun competitors in terms of aggressive promotion and innovation. Second, the trade is always reluctant to add new brands if the existing brand leader satisfies the customers and themselves. Third, the brand leader can exploit its superiority, as Coca-Cola does with its 'real thing' advertising. Without a major strategic window only a

substantial underinvestment in quality and brand support is likely to dethrone a successful brand.

Motivates stakeholders

Companies with strong brands find recruitment easier. People want to work with companies that exhibit success. Strong brands also widen share ownership by increasing awareness and understanding of the company. Finally, successful brands elicit local authority and governmental support. Western countries, for example, compete with inducements to attract the better-known Japanese companies to build their brands with them.

The creation of successful brands

Brands are rarely created by advertising. This is often misunderstood because the advertising is

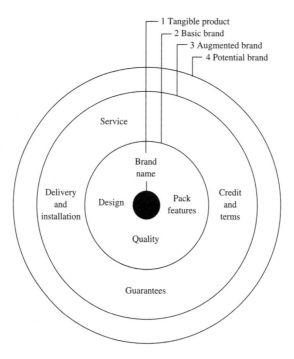

Adapted by author from Levitt, 1983

Figure 16.6   What is a brand?

Table 16.2 Britain's top ten brands	
1 Marks & Spencer	6 Boots
2 Cadbury	7 Nescafé
3 Kellogg	8 BBC
4 Heinz	9 Rowntree
5 Rolls-Royce	10 Sainsbury

Source: Landor Imagepower Survey (1991).

generally much more visible than the factor which creates the differential advantage. For example, Singapore Airlines is a strong brand and does some attractive advertising. But the advertising is not the basis of the brand – rather, the advertising communicates and positions it. The basis of the brand is the superior customer service provided by the cabin staff. This, in turn, is largely achieved by Singapore Airlines putting in more cabin staff per plane than other airlines. Equally striking is the fact that Britain's strongest brand – Marks & Spencer – has historically done little or no advertising at all. There is little correlation between the amount spent on advertising and the strength of the brand.

The other common mistake is to think that brand loyalty is irrational. A survey on branding by *The Economist* (1988) reflected this view:

People all over the world form irrational attachments to different products. Humans like to take sides ... By most 'tangible' measures, BMW cars and IBM computers are not significantly better than rivals, but customers will pay significantly more for them.

Levitt (1983) provides a framework for understanding how successful brands are created and why customers are not 'irrational' to choose them (Figure 16.6).

At the core of every brand there is a *tangible* product – the commodity which meets the basic customer need. For the thirsty customer, there is water. For the production manager with a data-storage problem, there is the computer. This tangible product is what economists believe rational consumers should base their choices on.

But to generate sales in a competitive environment, this tangible core has to be put in the form of a *basic* brand. It has to be packaged conveniently, the customer needs to know the features of the product and its quality. It should be designed to facilitate ease of use. But there are further ways to *augment* the brand to enhance its value by guaranteeing its performance, providing credit, delivery, and effective after-sales service. Finally, there is the *potential* brand, which consists of anything that conceivably could be done to build customer preference and loyalty. Which of these dimensions appear to be most important in practice?

1   *Quality is number one.* Overwhelmingly the most important determinant of brand strength is its perceived quality. Britain's top ten brands (Table 16.2) are all quality brands. The PIMS analysis showed that brands with high perceived quality earned double the return on investment and return and sales of low-quality brands (Figure 16.7).

Quality generates higher margins in either or both of two ways. First, quality boosts market share, which results in lower unit costs through economies of scale. Second, by creating a differential advantage, quality permits higher relative price.

2   *Build superior service.* Service is perhaps the most sustainable differential advantage. While products are easily copied by competitors, service, because it depends on the culture of the organization and the training and attitudes of its employees, is much more difficult. McDonald's, IBM, Singapore Airlines and Federal Express are all brands built on service.

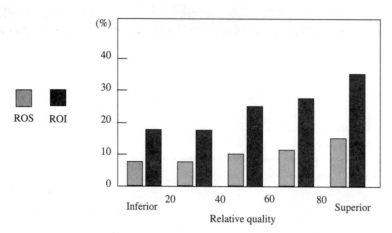

Source: Buzzell and Gale, 1987

Figure 16.7   Quality and profitability

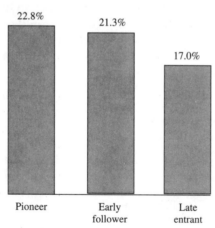

Source: Clifford and Cavanagh, 1985

Figure 16.8   Timing of market entry and business performance

A study by Albrecht and Zenke (1985) showed the importance of service: In their sample survey, 67 per cent of customers changed brands because of poor service. Of these customers who did feel unhappy with the service provided by the bank, hotel or supplier, only 4 per cent bothered to complain – they just did not expect any satisfaction. Of those that did complain, 91 per cent dropped the brand permanently. But interestingly, suppliers which dealt with com-

plaints fast and generously held on to the vast majority of dissatisfied customers. In fact, there was some evidence that really effective responses to complaints actually increased brand loyalty.

3   *Get there first.* Perhaps the most common means of building an outstanding brand is being first into a market. This does not mean being technologically first, but rather being first into the mind of the consumer. IBM, Kleenex, Casio and McDonald's did not

invent their respective products, but they were first to build major brands out of them and bring them into the mass market. It is much easier to build a strong brand in the customer's mind and in the market when the brand has no established competitors. This is why Clifford and Cavanagh (1985) found that pioneering brands earned on average more than one-third higher returns on investment than late entrants (Figure 16.8)

There are five ways of 'getting there first':

(a) Exploiting new technology (e.g. Microsoft, Intel);

(b) New positioning concepts (Body Shop, Virgin);

(c) New distribution channels (e.g. First Direct);

(d) New market segments (e.g. Dell);

(e) Exploiting gaps created by sudden environmental changes (e.g. beef substitutes).

4 *Look for differentiation.* In building brands the principle is to invest in markets which are highly differentiated or where such differentiation can be created, as for example Virgin or Levi jeans have done in recent years. Where markets are strongly differentiated, i.e. different segments are looking for different bundles of attributes, then both niche brands and big power brands can potentially earn very high returns on investment. Power brands like Sony, Marks & Spencer and Coca-Cola can earn high returns because they are perceived as high-quality brands in most of the segments. Niche brands like Gucchi or Irn Bru can earn high profits by being preferred in one segment even though their overall rating in the broad market is not great. In markets which are undifferentiated, however, i.e. where customers do not see much difference between the brands, none typically earns exceptional returns.

To summarize, building successful brands is about quality, service, innovation and differentiation. What, then, is the role of advertising? Advertising has two functions in building successful brands. First, successful advertising accelerates the communications process. Marks & Spencer built a great brand without advertising. They relied primarily on their high street presence, customer experience with the brand, and word of mouth. But it took them 30 years to build the strong brand of today. Now, one cannot wait that long – competition would preempt the brand before it had positioned itself in the customer's mind. Advertising speeds up the process of generating awareness and interest in the brand. The second function of advertising is to position the brand's values in a manner which appeals to the target customers and increases confidence in the choice process. The creative messages of the Levi or the Nescafé advertisements, for example, present the brand as having a set of values which match the aspirations of target customers.

Buying brands versus building brands

Today there are two routes a company can follow to obtain brands: it can build and develop them; or it can acquire them, or, rather, acquire companies which possess them. The former is obviously a high-risk, slow and expensive route. Studies have shown clearly that a very high proportion of new brands tested and introduced into the market fail. It takes time and investment to build a brand and position it in the minds of consumers. In contrast, acquisitions are a deceptively quick route to obtaining a brand portfolio and it is a route which is increasingly followed today, especially by British companies. It also appears a cheap alternative, especially if the acquirer is exchanging high-valued shares in buying a company operating on a lower price–earnings ratio. Unfortunately, there is comprehensive evidence that most such acquisitions fail to generate long-term value for the acquiror's shareholders or build lasting brand portfolios (e.g. Porter, 1987). How can this dilemma be explained and resolved?

Previous studies (Doyle, 1987, Doyle *et al.*, 1986) suggest that the approach companies adopt depends upon what their primary objectives are. Some companies have objectives which are primarily about marketing and market share. Others are primarily orientated to return

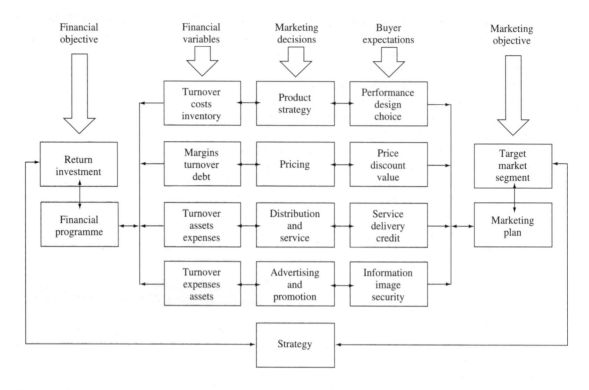

Figure 16.9   Marketing and financial objectives of the business

on investment and financial objectives (Figure 16.9). Generally, companies which have objectives that are mainly marketing ones ('right-hand companies'), choose to build brands. Companies whose objectives are primarily financial, ('left-hand companies'), are orientated towards buying brands or companies with brands.

Japanese companies, for example, tend to be overwhelmingly right-hand orientated. The objective is market share. They believe that the most appropriate way to achieve market share is the development of strong brands which offer customers differential advantages. So they adopt a classical marketing approach – understand the expectations of customers in the target market segments and seek to match them. They seek to build brands that provide the customers with value and which beat the competition. Japanese companies rarely acquire because they believe that they have the skills to do it better. It

is not surprising that most of the great new global brands in the last decade have been Japanese – Sony, Toyota, National Panasonic, Honda, Canon, Casio, etc.

British companies, on the other hand, have been more left-hand or financially orientated. Stock market pressures have made return on investment the primary goal and financial budgets rather than marketing plans the main planning mechanisms. In these companies, products, pricing and promotional decisions are dictated mainly by financial constraints rather than marketing requirements. One result is that while there have been very few major global brands developed by British companies in the last ten years, they have led the world in acquisitions.

During the past twelve months, for example, British companies have acquired four times the amount of all Japanese companies, five times American companies and twenty times as much as German businesses.

	Build	Buy
Table 16.3 Building versus buying brands		
Market attractiveness		
Market growth	High	Low
Strength of competitors	Weak	Strong
Retailer power	Weak	Strong
Relative cost of acquisitions		
Industry attractiveness	High	Low
Valuation of company	Full	Undervalued
Restructuring potential	Low	High
Brand's potential	Realized	Unrealized
Acquisitions potential synergy		
Cost reduction potential	Low	High
Marketing competence	Unchanged	Increased
Complementarity	Low	High
Relevant management expertise	Low	Transfers
Brand's strategic opportunity		
Product performance	Breakthrough	Me-too
Positioning concept	New	Mature
Market opportunity	High	Low
Corporate situation		
Growth potential	High	Low
Cash situation	Average	Abundant
Marketing/R&D capability	Strong	Weak

The recent debate about brands in the balance sheet in Britain is essentially about acquisition strategy rather than about building customer value. Acquisition-orientated managers have observed that if brands are put in the balance sheet, then balance sheet gearing can be reduced, retained earning enhanced and so further acquisitions are facilitated. Paradoxically, companies that put brands in the balance sheet are likely to put *less* emphasis on brand building and brand development than those that do not follow this practice.

Of course, acquiring brands sometimes makes sense. The problems with acquisitions are, first; that in the long run the evidence suggests they rarely work. Second, they do not create coherent brand strategies, especially at the international level. In general, the company ends up with a rag-bag of brands with different brand names in different countries, different positioning strategies and no synergy with the existing business. Table 16.3 suggests a checklist which appraises those conditions when acquiring companies with brands makes sense.

If it is a low-growth unattractive market, building a brand costs too much. It is generally cheaper to buy competition and competitors' retail space than to beat out well-entrenched brands. This is why companies like Hanson and BTR have focused their acquisition strategies on these dull mature markets. The other advantage of these types of markets is that the relative cost of acquisitions may be low. Often the stock market undervalues these apparently dull companies and there is substantial restructuring potential in selling off parts after the acquisition.

Acquisitions work when there is real potential synergy – when the acquiror can reduce the joint costs or improve marketing competence by coming together. Finally, the strategic opportunities offered by the acquiror's existing brand portfolio and its corporate cash situation, play a major role. If the company's current products are me-too, if it has limited skills but abundant cash spun off from its portfolio of mature products, then acquisitions appear attractive. By contrast, it is generally better to develop and build on the company's own brands if these are operating in growth markets, if the company possesses potentially strong brands and if inside the company there are strong marketing and development skills. These five sets of factors are the key criteria in making judgements about the balance between building and purchasing brands.

Brand-extension strategies

Brand-extension strategies are another controversial area in branding. Brand extension means transferring the name of a successful brand to additional products possessed by the company. The advantages of such extensions may be three:

1   It encourages customer confidence in a new product.

2   It may create scale economies in advertising and promotion.

3   It opens distribution and retail channels.

The dangers are that it confuses the brand identity and can degrade the reputation of a successful brand.

What are the principles in striking a balance? The right approach depends on the similarity of the position strategies of the brands. Four brand extension options can be identified (Table 16.4).

1   If the brands appeal to the same target segment and have the same differential advantage, then they can safely share the same company name or range. Here, there is consistency in the positioning strategies – examples of this type of extension would include IBM, Timotei (from Unilever), Dunhill and Sony – the same name applied to different products.

2   If the differential advantage is the same but the target market differs, then the company name can be extended because the benefit is similar. However, it is important to identify the 'grade'. For example, both the Mercedes-Benz 200 and 500 series offer differential advantages based upon quality, but the more expensive 500 series appeals to a much more

Table 16.4   Brand-extension strategies

Brand positioning grid		
	Differential advantage	
	Similar	Different
Similar	Company or range name (IBM, Timotei)	Company plus brands (Kellogg's Cornflakes, Kellogg's Rice Krispies)
Target market segment		
Different	Company plus grade ID (Mercedes 200 Mercedes 500)	Unique brand names (P&D: Tide, Bold, Dreft, Ariel . . .)

prestige segment of the market. The supplemental number acts to preserve the prestige positioning of the latter mark.

3   If a company has different differential advantages, then it should use separate brand names. It can find some synergy if the brands are appealing to the same target market, by using the same company name with separate brand names. For example, different brands of Kellogg's may well be selected within the same family unit.

4   But if both the target customers and the differential advantages are different then using unique brand names is logically the most appropriate strategy. So Procter & Gamble believe that it is worth losing out on the advantages of a common corporate name in order to separately position the brands in the market – to give each brand a distinct positioning appeal to a separate benefit segment. Similarly, Honda separately positioned its Acura brand because it wished to position it uniquely away from its existing models.

Conclusion

Successful brands are built upon the principle of seeking to build sustainable differential advantages for the customer. The levers for developing such brands are four: quality; service; innovation; and differentiation. Strategies based upon acquiring brands generally fail to work because they are more usually geared to satisfying the interest of the stock market rather than the long-term interests of customers. The danger of the 'brand in the balance sheet' argument is that it leads to weaker rather than stronger branding strategies. Finally, on brand extension strategies, there are real advantages in brands sharing a corporate logo, but care is required in not eroding a successful brand's unique positioning.

References

Albrecht, K. and Zenke, R. (1985) *Service America*, IEE/Dow Jones, Homewood, IL.

Buzzell, R. D. and Gale, B. T. (1987) *The PIMS Principles: linking strategy to performance*, Collier Macmillan, New York.

Clifford, D. K. and Cavanagh, R. E. (1985) *The Winning Performance: How America's high growth midsize companies succeed*, Sidgwick and Jackson, London.

Day, G. S. and Wensley, R. (1988) Assessing advantage: a framework for diagnosing competitive superiority, *Journal of Marketing*, **52**(1), April, 1–20.

Doyle, P. (1987) Marketing and the British chief executive, *Journal of Marketing Management*, **3**(2), Winter, 121–132.

Doyle, P., Saunders, J. and Wong, V. (1986) A comparative study of Japanese marketing strategies in the British market, *Journal of International Business Studies*, **17**(1), Spring, 27–46.

The Economist (1988) The year of the brand, 24 December.

Engel, J. F., Blackwell, R. D. and Minniard, P. W. (1994) *Consumer Behavior*, Dryden, Furt Worlt.

Hall, W. K. (1980) Survival strategies in a hostile environment, *Harvard Business Review*, **58**(5), September, 60–72.

Hanssens, D. M., Parsons, L. J. and Schultz, R. L. (1990) *Market Response Models: Econometric and Time Series Analysis*, Kluwer, Boston.

Landor Associates (1991) *The World's Leading Brands*, Landor Associates, London.

Levitt, T. (1983) *The Marketing Imagination*, Collier Macmillan, New York.

Porter, M. E. (1987) From competitive advantage to corporate strategy, *Harvard Business Review*, **65**(3), May, 43–59.

Reichheld, F. F. (1996) *The Loyalty Effect*, Harvard Business School Press, Boston.

Rodgers, B. (1986) *The IBM Way*, Harper and Row, New York.

Schiffman, L. E. and L. L. Kaunk, *Consumer Behaviour*, 6th ed., Practice-Hall, Englewood Cliffs, 1997.

Further reading

Aaker, D. A., *Managing Brand Equity Capitalizing on the Value of a Brand Name*, Free Press, New York, 1991. Currently the most comprehensive and practical review of the role of brands and how to build them. Many good examples, although overwhelmingly an American orientation.

De Chernatony, L. and McDonald, M., *Creating Powerful Brands*, Butterworth-Heinemann, Oxford, 1992. An insightful work on creating, developing and managing brands strategically. Some good examples from European companies.

Journal of Brand Management, Henry Stewart Publications, London. This new journal carries a range of practitioner-oriented studies on the topic of building successful brands.

CHAPTER 17

Promotion

KEITH CROSIER

In this chapter we turn to the question of *promoting* a product or service that has already been developed (Chapter 13) and priced (Chapter 14), and will concurrently be sold (Chapter 15) and distributed (Chapter 19). What exactly is involved in the management of this particular element of the marketing mix?

Defining the promotional mix

As Figure 17.1 shows, using McCarthy's useful *'four Ps'* terminology, we are here concerned with deploying and controlling a mix within a mix. Let us agree to call it the *promotional mix*, but take note that many recent textbooks prefer a different description of the activities it embraces: for instance, *Marketing Communications: Principles and Practice* (Kitchen, 1998) and *Marketing Communications: An Integrated Approach* (Smith, 1993) versus *Below-the-Line*

Promotion (Wilmshurst, 1993). This variation may well supplant our more logical usage during the life of this edition, thanks to the rapidly developing fashion for a holistic approach to treatment of the promotional mix which its advocates call 'integrated marketing communications'.

It is not possible to discuss the management of all nine ingredients separately within the confines of a single chapter. Instead, the following working definitions are proposed, demonstrating the close family similarities among them while emphasizing fundamentally important points of difference.

- **Advertising** is promotion via an advertisement in a chosen advertising medium or the Internet, guaranteeing exposure to a general or specific target audience, in return for an advertising rate charged by the media owner, web site owner or Internet service provider, plus the cost of producing the advertisement or 'hypertext' material.
- **Publicity** is promotion via a news release to chosen news media, delivering exposure to a known target audience if newsworthiness earns an editorial mention, in return for the cost of producing and distributing the release.
- **Direct marketing** is promotion via a direct mail, e-mail or telemarketing initiative, guaranteeing exposure to identifiable individuals in a

chosen target audience in return for the price of postage, computer time or telephone calls plus the cost of producing the mail shot, e-mail message or telesales operator's script.

- Sponsorship is promotion via association with an entity, event or activity, typically delivering exposure to a primary target audience by means of the sponsor's logo and to a sec-

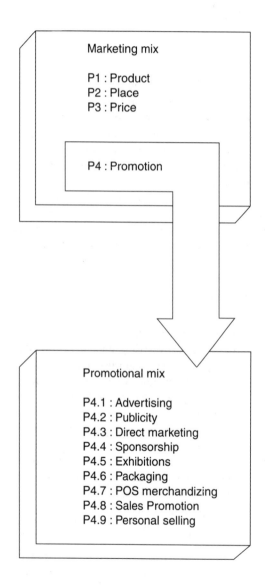

Figure 17.1   The promotional mix

ondary one by means of reference to the sponsor in associated media coverage, in return for the price of a negotiated sponsorship contract plus the cost of producing visual identification material.

- Exhibitions are promotion via display and the presence of sales representatives on an exhibition stand, delivering exposure to visiting potential customers, in return for the rate charged for the space by the exhibition promoter plus the cost of building, installing and stocking the stand.
- Packaging is promotion via display, guaranteeing exposure to customers at the point of sale, in return for the cost of designing and producing the package.
- Point-of-sale (or 'POS') merchandising is promotion via various forms of display, acting as a reminder to customers of previously noticed promotional messages, in return for the cost of producing the material used.
- Sales promotion is promotion via a diverse range of initiatives not so far defined, delivering exposure to a general target market and in some cases offering an incentive for individuals to respond actively, in return for the cost of producing and distributing the material used.
- Personal selling is promotion via a sales pitch made by a sales representative to a 'prospect' or by a retail sales assistant to a customer, guaranteeing exposure to self-selected members of a target market, in return for the cost of remunerating and training the sales personnel delivering the pitch.

Inclusions and exclusions

Two ingredients of the promotional mix proposed here are sufficiently distinct from the rest to merit chapters in their own right. *Sales promotion* (Chapter 18) encompasses a large range of diverse initiatives, typically combining the straightforward communication that characterizes the other seven ingredients of the mix with price-related incentives for the customer to respond actively, thereby overlapping with another of the four Ps. *Personal selling* (Chapter

15) is the only promotional technique to involve face-to-face communication between seller and buyer, and is normally the focus of an organizational division quite separate from that with responsibility for the rest of the mix. Consequently, the rest of this chapter will restrict itself to the other seven ingredients.

Some authors accord individual status within the mix to promotional literature, such as product leaflets, sales brochures, corporate prospectuses or annual reports. Others subsume those devices into the catch-all sales promotion category. Where they are located is less important than the fact that they are certainly another means of promoting the product or service. These printed promotional devices are being joined at an increasing rate by electronic equivalents: the various kinds of web sites and web pages to be found on the Internet.

Readers of the marketing literature will sooner or later encounter the implication that *public relations* is an ingredient of the promotional mix. However, the Institute of Public Relations defines its purpose as 'to establish and maintain goodwill and mutual understanding between an organization and its publics'. Clearly, this activity has a broad and strategic focus, in contrast to the specific tactical aims of ingredients of the promotional marketing mix. To use an alternative terminology, it is corporate communication rather than marketing communications. One must suspect that colloquial usage is confusing public relations with *publicity*, presumably because of the seductive semantic similarity and the fact that news releases and press conferences are the main tools of the trade. In fact, PR campaigns often also involve corporate advertising and sponsorship, not to mention a range of other initiatives beyond the boundaries of the promotional mix. To take account of all this, academic authors have recently begun to distinguish marketing public relations from corporate public relations, or MPR from CPR. That is a well intentioned development, but it would be enough to use existing terminology correctly.

Accounts of *direct marketing* campaigns often include references to *direct response advertising* and *mail order* advertising. These are not distinct forms, but only variations on the main theme. They aim to 'sell off the page' by giving the audience the facility to respond via clip-out coupons, Freepost, Freefone or e-mail.

In practice, marketing managers often add advertising to *direct mail* or *point of sale*, whereas our working definitions make it clear that these two are not a form of advertising at all, since the channel of delivery and the structure of the costs are quite distinct. Moreover, the appropriate mode of communication will normally be radically different in each case. They are also likely to describe an individual *sales promotion* initiative as simply a promotion, inviting confusion with the broader meaning of the term.

Publicity versus advertising

The careful distinction our working definitions draw between *advertising* and *publicity* is by no means universally observed in practice, a tendency compounded by the fact that three major world languages render advertising as publicité, publicidad and publicidade. Conversely, English-speakers routinely describe publicity as 'free' advertising, which they contrast with 'paid' advertising. The danger in this usage is that it conceals a fundamental strategic difference: users of publicity spend relatively little in the hope that a third party will relay a version of their message without adding a counterproductive editorial spin, whereas the user of advertising is paying relatively heavily for the certainty that it will appear where, when and how they intended. Cost and control are thus traded off against one another.

It is often assumed that favourable publicity can be bought by taking advertising space in a newspaper or magazine, but professional etiquette in fact keeps such subterfuges to a minimum. For example, *Cosmopolitan* magazine responded firmly to one such allegation in 1994 by issuing a statement that 'the marketing manager quoted was incorrect in his/her assumption that spending a significant amount on advertising gives the right to demand editorial coverage . . . [which is] judged purely on its relevance and interest to our magazine's 2.3 million readers'. There is one exception to this rule, the advertisement features, or *advertorials*, which are a familiar feature of many newspapers and magazines. However, the code of practice governing press advertising in the UK requires that

features, announcements or promotions that are disseminated in exchange for a payment or other reciprocal arrangement . . . should also be clearly identified and distinguished from editorial. (Advertising Standards Authority, 1995: clause 23.2).

The equivalent codes regulating broadcast advertising explicitly forbid influence on the content or scheduling of a radio or television programme by advertisers or sponsors (Independent Television Commission, 1997: Standard 5 and Radio Authority, 1997: Rule 1).

New media

Academic colleagues and students are apt to object that conventional descriptions of the promotional mix do not yet include the new media or interactive media, by which they mean communication between sellers and buyers via the Internet. In fact, its use for marketing purposes can be easily accommodated within descriptions of existing practices, as our working definitions show. In the same way that mail shots and telesales calls are no more than different manifestations of direct marketing, a banner advertisement at a web site is a new version of a poster site on a roadside hoarding.

Furthermore, the experience of their own free access to the World Wide Web and e-mail, a consequence of its origin in scientific research and proliferation in universities, seems to have led them to overestimate the extent of adoption by mainstream customers for commercial products and services. The Internet Service Providers Association estimates that 1.5 million people in the UK had access to the Net at home and 3 million at work, at the beginning of 1998. They

predicted that those figures would have risen to 4.2 and 4.7 million respectively by the year 2000. However, given that there is bound to be a significant overlap between those two categories, the total target audience is probably no more than half the 12-million strong readership of the *News of the World*. Moreover, its profile is highly unrepresentative of the general population: industry surveys suggest that fully 95 per cent are male and two-thirds under thirty-five. Though these early adopters of the technology will soon be joined by an early majority, it will take much longer for technophobes to become a minority.

Access to the Internet is by no means the same thing as exposure to the promotional messages it carries. Internet-linked computers are often used as nothing more than word processors or record keepers, and the exchange of personal or business e-mail messages accounts for well over half all Internet traffic. Users have to elect to browse the Net before they become part of an advertiser's audience. If they do so, and pursue hyperlinks within and between sites, they will accidentally encounter a variety of banner advertisements in the same way as they pass poster sites in the streets outside. However, the literature of conventional advertising makes the point strongly that such potential exposure is by no means the same thing as noticing the identity of the advertiser or pausing to take in the message.

To find and read a marketer's web site requires a positive search, among a great deal of competing non-commercial material. Some marketers are beginning to reduce the random aspect of exposure by including WWW addresses in their media advertising. Potential customers with PCs can thereby obtain promotional information anonymously, rather than by requesting literature or being subjected to a sales pitch at the point of sale. However, other advertisers create over-designed web sites which take so long to download on the average PC that 'visitors' depart elsewhere, unless they are already sales prospects and determined to have the information. The design of sites and banners is routinely delegated to information technology specialists with no background in marketing, with predictable communication consequences, while advertising agencies are staffed by Luddites, if a fairly recent field survey is indicative (Crosier and Abbott, 1996). Meanwhile, the initially low price of space on the Internet is escalating. In 1997, *Playboy* magazine was charging £50 000 per quarter for an advertisement within its web site, on the grounds of 800 000 recorded hits per day.

The conclusion must be, for the time being, that the new media are passing through the early stages of an awareness explosion but have not yet reached the point at which real understanding of their commercial application is widespread among marketing practitioners.

Above, below and through the line

Traditionally, marketing practitioners have distinguished promotional methods as being either 'above the line' or 'below the line'. For reasons which will be explained in full later, advertising lies above and everything else below – except personal selling, which is not normally assigned to either category.

Industry folklore has it that this hypothetical boundary was first delineated in the 1950s by Procter & Gamble.

Given the semantic loading of the adjectives above and below in everyday speech, it is all too easy to assume that one ingredient of the promotional mix is somehow superior and the others collectively inferior. Indeed, there is ample anecdotal and observable evidence that this lazy assumption is often made in practice, resulting in the marked imbalance in the allocation of total promotional funds shown in Table 17.1. The originators of the 'line' remain to this day massive spenders on media advertising, apparently in preference over other means to the same end. Yet the definitions and discussion in the previous session make it clear that advertising is not in fact superior to the rest in any general, systematic way.

A trend which may eventually banish this promotional apartheid has been gaining momentum in recent years. Throughout the twentieth century until the present decade, marketers seeking assistance with the formulation and execution of promotional strategy had either enlisted the services of experts in the separate disciplines individually or turned to an advertising agency for a multi-disciplinary solution. The former 'à la carte' approach has always been much less usual than the latter, and full service advertising agencies dominate the list of service providers in the promotional busi-

Table 17.1 Shares of total UK promotional expenditure, 1997		
	£ million	%
Advertising	11 599	51.6
Sales promotion	7500	33.4
Direct mail	1540	6.8
Exhibitions	849	3.8
Point-of-sale	600	2.7
Sponsorship	380	1.7
Total	22 468	100

Source: Advertising Association (1998); Institute of Sales Promotion (direct, 1999), Point of Purchase Advertising Institute (direct, 1999).

Notes: The Advertising Association's *Marketing Pocket Book* gives no estimate of expenditure on publicity or packaging. The figure for advertising does not include the amount spent to buy World Wide Web sites. Since 1995, direct mail has been the only form of direct marketing for which expenditure figures have been published.

ness. The best of these agencies can in fact deliver in-house expertise in sales promotion, direct marketing and the rest, but most will simply sub-contract that aspect of promotional campaign development to a third party. The client thereby unintentionally delegates responsibility twice over, and loses control of strategy commensurately. Furthermore, they remain *advertising* agencies, staffed by *advertising* people, despite the full-service capability. It would be surprising if they did not exhibit a tendency, putting it no more strongly, to approach promotional strategy from the advertising standpoint and treat the rest of the promotional mix as a selection of possible back-up options. That tendency is reinforced by the fact, to be explained in detail later, that their main source of income is commission on the purchase of advertising media on their clients' behalf. In short, the very existence of so many advertising agencies had until recently predicated a bias towards above-the-line campaign strategy.

In 1988, an agency appeared on the scene in Scotland which was dedicated to abandoning conventional demarcations and offering a 'full-service multi-disciplinary' service. Five years later, what was then the world's largest advertising agency, Saatchi & Saatchi, dropped the word 'advertising' from its title and proclaimed itself a 'through-the-line communications agency'. The founding partners of the Scottish originator, now called DMS Menzies, had ex-perienced the conditioned reflex in favour of an advertising-led strategy while working as a team at the full-service advertising agency responsible for promotion of the national Garden Festival. Hindsight leaves no room for doubt that the nature of the event demanded a multi-disciplinary strategy, but the agency had in fact recommended spending most of limited promotional funds on press and television advertising. The partners were later reported in the business press to have said they were 'frankly, not absolutely convinced that we were right' at the time, but the eventual campaign did earn the agency a healthy amount of media commission.

In an industry always quick to coin neolo-

gisms, their new venture was dubbed a through-the-line agency, but the managing director was quoted as preferring to think of the line in question as a stultifying irrelevance:

We operate with a total disregard for the line. We are neither above-the-line specialists, nor [do we] concentrate on below-the-line activity. Basically, we ignore the line.

In other words, like any full-service advertising agency, it offers clients expertise above and below the line. The difference is that its amalgamation of experts from the various disciplines carries no historical baggage and reflects no rigid below- or above-the-line philosophy, so that planning teams should be free to formulate wholly unconditioned promotional strategies. Furthermore, clients devolve responsibility for campaign development at only one level, instead of tacitly giving an above-the-line agency permission to sub-contract below-the-line planning to yet another tier of expert outsiders.

These statements and actions are evidence of a crystallizing belief that promotional mix deployment decisions in practice must derive from a methodical and thorough situational analysis undertaken without prejudice. Let us consider a case in point. Suppose that you have been briefed by the manufacturer of a material for dental fillings which is white and costs less than either gold or silver amalgam. What key ingredients of such an analysis might form the basis of decisions to allocate promotional effort among the available elements of the mix?

Your answer may perhaps include such factors as: the explicability of the product; its newsworthiness; potential controversy; the accessibility of at least two key audiences; questions of image; budget; controllability of feasible options. Sufficiently detailed explanation of the product to dentists might be thought to demand an *advertisement* in a professional magazine, provided they can be depended on not to ignore it altogether, or a carefully constructed *direct mail* shot, if they have not been made resistant to such initiatives by the sheer volume they receive.

Generating the complementary demand-pull among dental patients would seem to require a much less complex but far more emotionally loaded message directed at family decision-making gatekeepers, the delivery of which could perhaps be best accomplished by means of *publicity* targeted at women's magazines. On the other hand, it might be thought desirable to maintain a vaguely mysterious high-technology aura around the product. The product's newsworthiness is self-evident, but the details could contain the germ of a controversy, placing particular emphasis on the issue of control over publicity initiatives. It could be reasoned that consumer *sales promotions* are a feasible option only once the patients have been brought to the point-of-sale by other forces, but dentist incentives could be a fruitful if high-risk ploy.

Whatever the outcome of your personal analysis, a dominantly above-the-line strategy would be hard to justify even if you did happen to be employed by an advertising agency. Likewise one based largely on sales promotion or concentrating heavily on packaging, even if those were your home disciplines. For this particular product, a through-the-line solution seems inescapable.

During the 1990s, line-shunning total communications agencies have proliferated, though without any noticeable diminution in the number of existing full-service advertising agencies or specialists in individual below-the-line disciplines. Simultaneously, textbooks have been advocating what they prefer to call 'integrated marketing communications': for example, Belch and Belch (1998) in the USA and Kitchen (1998) in the UK. It remains to be seen what lasting effect this momentum will have on approaches to promotional strategy development in practice.

The promotional budget

Decisions about the allocation of effort above and below the line cannot be made, of course, until it has been established how much money is available to be spent on media buying, the distribution of news releases, telemarketing costs, sponsorship deals, the designing and production of packaging, point-of-sale and sales promotion materials, and so on. This amount is formally defined as the promotional *appropriation*, reflecting the fact that it is *appropriated* from the total funds allocated to the marketing effort. In Britain, but less so in America, it is more likely to be called the 'promotional budget'.

In fact, a budget is not an *amount* of money, as in colloquial usage, but a *plan* for spending it, as in the Chancellor's annual Budget speech. It describes sources and uses of funds over a given future period, normally a year. By demanding forward planning, providing an integrated framework for operational decisions, and establishing quantifiable standards of cost-effective performance, it formalizes *control* over expenditure. If a statement of the promotional appropriation is not accompanied by such a plan for spending it, there is far too much scope for profligate waste of scarce funds in a business that is notoriously image-conscious and fashion-led. As a noted author from within the business remarks in a book significantly titled *Accountable Advertising*,

It is no longer enough for the marketing director to determine how much it is right to spend on advertising . . . [he or she] still has to make this decision but must now do more – justify it. (Broadbent, 1997, p. xv).

The most crucial control mechanism in a promotional budget will be the *cost-effectiveness* criteria it specifies. The tedious but straightforward process of recording all the many costs attributable to a campaign presents no practical difficulties. However, reliable measures of the effectiveness of a campaign are rarely encountered in practice beyond the direct marketing and advertising disciplines. Even in those two cases, criteria are severely limited. The success or failure of a direct marketing initiative is normally reported in terms of coupon returns, enquiries or off-the-page orders; its communicative efficacy is seldom tested in any way. Advertising effectiveness is typically measured by criteria such as awareness, recall, attitude change and sales movements. Yet there has never been convincing proof that the first three actually increase the probability that the audience will subsequently take appropriate action, while the fourth makes dubious assumptions about short-term cause and effect. Those arguments will be taken up later in this chapter. Meanwhile, we have to conclude that promotional expenditure may be scrutinized and contained, but is not controlled in any meaningful sense of the word. Readers interested in pursuing the issue of *budgeting* further should consult Broadbent's excellent 'handbook for managers', mentally converting from advertising to the rest of the promotional mix as necessary. The rest of this section will concern itself with *appropriation setting*.

The term 'appropriation' is a salutary reminder that managers charged with responsibility for promotional strategy and planning do not enjoy the luxury of deciding the funds available to them. Until the 1960s, relatively powerful advertising managers did have considerable influence on the amount of money they were held accountable for spending wisely. A decade later, Rees (1977) in Britain and Dhalla (1977) in America independently found that the executive with responsibility for advertising, by then as likely to be a marketing manager or brand manager, typically made an initial bid in competition with other claimants on total funds set aside for marketing, but that the decision process was notably hierarchical. Thereafter, heads of each major function within the marketing division negotiated for their slice of the pie, and the outcome of that competition was scrutinized at board level, where vested interests might result in further bargaining. Almost invariably, the chief executive retained sole authority for approval of the advertising appropriation, and the decision was duly transmitted down the organization to those who would be answerable for using it productively. The generally political nature of the process was confirmed a decade later in Britain by Piercy (1987), and there is no reason to suspect any significant change since then. Nevertheless, textbooks conventionally imply that the appropriation is indeed set by those responsible for spending it. The reality that it is not has an important but unremarked impact on strategic planning: a ceiling is imposed on spending which may bear little relationship to promotional objectives or the firm's situation relative to the competition.

Whoever actually decides the amount to be spent on advertising is likely to use one or more of a set of well known standard methods. Non-standard nomenclature disguises the fact that they can be grouped into the four categories in Table 17.2. The thumbnail sketches which follow are substantially expanded in Chapter 5 of

Table 17.2 Methods for determining the promotional appropriation

Executive judgement	Internal ratios	External ratios	Modelling and experimentation
AYCA = all you can afford	A/S ratio = advertising-to-sales ratio	Competitive parity	Adstock
Affordable approach	Case rate	Dynamic difference	AMTES = area marketing test evaluation systems
Arbitrary method	Historical parity	Market share method	Econometrics
Notional sum	Inertia method	Share of voice	Prescriptive models
	Marginal costing approach		Simulation
	Per-unit allowance		What-if models
	Same as last year		

Broadbent (1989), the more specific predecessor to his handbook of budgeting cited above.

The application of *executive judgement* may seem an unacceptably vague and risky approach to such an important decision. However, we shall see that the other methods available to decision makers are themselves illogical, inflexible, based on large assumptions, or all three. Therefore, though the everyday descriptions of this approach to the task hardly inspire confidence, the accumulated wisdom and intuition of experienced practitioners should not be undervalued.

The best known *internal ratio* is advertising-to-sales, which sets the appropriation at a given percentage of either the previous year's figure or the forecast for the coming year. It has the respectability of being an arithmetic formula, but suffers the serious logical flaw that the ratio itself must be decided before the method can be used. In practice, that is normally done by the application of executive judgement or by reference to industry norms, which may not be appropriate to the particular circumstances. Furthermore, it is potentially disastrous to apply this method when sales have been falling. If the purpose of advertising is to help generate sales, then spending a constant ratio of a decreasing amount is a curious way to go about rectifying the situation.

The most familiar *external ratio* is competitive parity, which matches the appropriation to the estimated expenditure of a significant competitor or to the prevailing norm, with the aim of buying a fair share of voice in the general advertising hubbub. The more everyone follows everyone else, the less logical it is to believe that competitors are behaving rationally or the collective wisdom is correct. Furthermore, the method takes no account of the need for a new entrant to a market to take the risk of disproportionately heavy expenditure to gain a foothold.

The reliability of the many proprietary *modelling and experimentation* procedures depends upon the assumptions made and formulae used, and the average practitioner lacks the mathematical sophistication to evaluate those. Using them is in that case rather like buying a pig in poke from a magician. For a dispassionate review of what is available, see Chapter 8 of Broadbent (1997).

The *objective-and-task* is widely treated as the best option on the grounds that it is more 'logical': starting with objectives and calculating the cost of the tasks required to achieve them, instead of starting with a sum of money and then deciding what to do with it. However, it does not follow that the means of achieving the objectives will be obvious and the costs unequivocal. Practical guides are apt to conclude with the exhortation to 'estimate the required expenditures', a nasty sting in the tail. Nevertheless, this procedure does force decision makers to be more rigorous in their approach to an absolutely crucial task.

A collective weakness of all five methods is their tendency to focus on short-run profit maximization at the expense of long-term goals. Indeed, the very convention of annual budgeting can in practice encourage strategically questionable revision of existing promotional campaigns. The highly effective thematic continuity of BMW and British Airways advertising, for example, is the exception rather than the rule.

The practical usefulness of this worryingly vague technology can be improved by treating the content of Table 17.2 as an à la carte menu, rather than table d'hôte. Any and all feasible options can be chosen from it, a variety of 'answers' obtained, and executive judgement applied to the task of deriving the best solution from them. Survey evidence suggests that, on average, two options are combined to arrive at the amount to be spent on advertising. It appears that no equivalent studies relating to other ingredients of the promotional mix have so far been published.

Three of the available appropriation-setting methods have dominated practice over the years. Data from a number of surveys in Britain and America between 1973 and 1985 show *executive judgement* narrowly ahead of the *A/S ratio*, with *objective-and-task* in third place and the next most popular far behind (Broadbent, 1989). Since 1986, surveys in the USA, Canada, Britain and a number of other European countries have identified the same three favourites, with the order of popularity exactly reversed (e.g. Synodinos *et al.*, 1989). This finding might be taken as an improvement, but for the comments made earlier about the pitfalls of applying the objective-and-task method in practice.

It is lastly far from reassuring to report that, in Britain, neither the second edition of a handbook on how to plan advertising (Cooper, 1997) nor a guide to best practice from the Institute of Practitioners in Advertising (Butterfield, 1997) makes any mention at all of appropriation setting procedures, admirable though both of them otherwise are.

Deploying the promotional mix

Practising managers faced by the choice of eight broad means to achieve promotional objectives within the budget need a formal framework for deciding which to use and which not, in a particular strategic situation, and how much weight to give to each one chosen. An overall constraint on choice will of course be imposed by the funds appropriated for the purpose, the subject of the previous section, and an influence inevitably exerted by the industry-wide trends reported in the one before. Decision-makers will furthermore monitor the tactics of their competitors, debating the relative merits of head-to-head assaults versus outflanking manoeuvres. Taking those factors as given,

Table 17.3 proposes seven other variables, in the form of a checklist for cost-effective deployment of the promotional mix. To illustrate how this template might be used in practice to include or exclude available options, consider its application to the case of *advertising* a new cinema complex via 48-sheet posters (20 feet by 10, unmetricated).

Posters are seen by anybody and everybody: pedestrians, motorists, users of public transport. The proposed campaign therefore could reach the required *target* audience of 18–35-year-old couples, but with a great deal of wastage in the process unless particular sites could be identified on the basis of audience profiles provided by an industry-wide programme of continuous research, and bought individually. The *message* a poster can deliver is self-evidently limited to what can be encapsulated in a short statement in large letters, or conveyed non-verbally. In this case, that is not a disadvantage, for the fact that a brand new, purpose-built, conveniently located multiplex has opened will be enough to encourage trial among potential visitors. Poster campaigns are normally bought as package deals, at *prices* which are middling in advertising terms but high by comparison with most other ingredients of the promotional mix. For instance, the rate for 700 48-sheet sites around the UK was about £350 000 per month in 1997. Buying local sites individually, which this advertiser needs to do, is significantly more expensive than the pro-rata fraction: up to £800 per site per month in Scotland, for example. The *cost* of producing such a

Table 17.3   A promotional mix checklist

Target:	Can this option reach the right audience?
Message:	Can it deliver this kind of message?
Price:	What will we be charged to use it?
Cost:	What will it cost us produce the material?
Receptivity:	Will the audience accept the message?
Modulation:	Will the vehicle affect their 'reading' of it?
Measurability:	Can we reliably assess effectiveness?

large item of high-quality full-colour print work, in sufficient quantity to allow for periodic renewal at each site as the weather took its toll, would also be high. The *receptivity* of typical audiences is much less of a problem than critics of advertising would have us believe. The most recent in a series of surveys of public attitudes in the UK found that only 9 per cent of a 522-strong sample of the general population said they 'disliked' or 'did not really like' the posters they encountered in their daily lives; 52 per cent had no opinion, one way or the other (Advertising Association, 1996).

Because posters are seen as a rather brash medium, audiences may add subjective interpretations to the objective content of the message. This *modulation* is not as strong as that due to the 'tone of voice' of most newspapers, for example, and could in any case suit the brand image of a cinema complex. *Measurability* is a complicated matter (taken up at the general level later in this chapter). The industry-wide research mentioned earlier can produce likelihood-to-see values for 73 000 poster sites around the country, but that is only a start. There is no easy way to find out how many members of a target audience did see a given site, notice the poster on it, take in the message, or act accordingly. The choice of this option would thus be something of an act of faith. Other promotional options are significantly more measurable, but the assessment of effectiveness is a general problem, taken up later in this chapter.

On balance, poster advertising seems an expensive but potentially effective option for reaching the target audience with the required message. Two shorter, non-specific examples will show how different the outcome of applying the checklist can be in other cases.

Direct marketing by mail can *target* highly specific audiences. The mode of *message* delivery permits much more detail than a poster, though it is limited by the recipient's interest and patience. The *price* consists only of postal charges, potentially reduced by volume discounts. However, considerable *cost* is likely to

be incurred in producing the kind of mail shot that actually engages the favourable attention of prospective customers. Furthermore, the intrusive reputation of direct mail results in generally low *receptivity*, so the price and cost per converted call can be substantial. Because the verbal message is typically reinforced by visual devices, often in considerable quantity and variety, *modulation* is unavoidable and far from uniform. *Measurability* is self-evidently straightforward.

Publicity can deliver a simple or detailed *message* to a general or specific *audience*. There is no *price* at all, and the *cost* is very low. Audiences do not generally stop to think whether reportage and editorial comment are spontaneous or the result of a press release, so *receptivity* is a negligible consideration. On the other hand, the potential for *modulation* is highest among all ingredients of the promotional mix, because a third party has been invited to act as interpreter between the originator and the audience. Someone else's agenda can thus determine the form and content of the eventual message. As for *measurability*, the volume of coverage resulting from the initiative can easily be monitored, quantified, and classified as productive, neutral or damaging. However, the effect on the target audience will be a matter of pure speculation.

An underlying dimension in all these hypothetical cases is the issue of *controllability*. It is worth reminding ourselves that the marketing mix and its sub-mixes are normally defined as the 'controllable variables' in the marketing equation. The degree of control which can in fact be exerted over the outcome of a promotional initiative is therefore a crucial strategic issue. The three examples above include the two ends of a broad spectrum: advertising is highly controllable, but at a price; publicity is virtually uncontrollable, but cheap. The third may at first seem to occupy a position towards the low end, for authors and commentators generally emphasize the assumed high resistance to its output: mail shots, mail drops, telesales calls, and unsolicited promotional messages received by fax or e-mail. On the other hand, prolific use by such sophisticated marketers as BT or the Consumers' Association suggests that it can yield cost-effective results when applied efficiently.

Among the other techniques in the promotional mix, sponsorship is a relatively new phenomenon, which has been growing rapidly in recent years. Marketers in the UK spent roughly £350 million on commercial support for the arts and sport in 1996 (Advertising Association, 1997), in return for direct exposure and secondary publicity, plus an unknown further amount on sponsorship of television and radio programmes. This strategy poses special controllability problems. For instance, sportswear manufacturers have established formal associations with performers or teams who later generated nothing but negative publicity, an outcome which must have reflected to some extent and in some way on the sponsor. Similarly, event organizers who struck lucrative deals with tobacco companies a decade ago have since inherited a public relations liability, thanks to a sea-change in official and public attitudes to smoking. Yet no one has so far proposed any systematic way to measure the positive or negative results of a sponsorship campaign. Meanwhile actual and potential beneficiaries are learning their true value as promotional vehicles, and raising the initially rather modest stakes. It is therefore very likely that the issue of *controllability* will assume much greater significance in future.

As for the rest of the promotional mix, it might be an interesting intellectual exercise to make a personal judgement about the location of each ingredient in the spectrum, all other things being equal.

Developing the promotional message

Originators of promotional messages normally delegate the task of converting abstract strategy into the concrete words and images (see 'Working relationships', p. 398). The recipient of that responsibility will be either a specialist intermediary with expertise in the particular promotional technique concerned, or a *full-service advertising agency* (see 'Above, below and through the line', p. 383). It is likely to describe itself as an 'agency', the originator as 'the client' and the process as 'creative planning'.

Creative planning starts with a *client brief*, from which the agency distils an internal *creative brief*. Specialists in turn convert that into the *creative executions* which in due course become finished messages in the form of advertisements, mail shots, promotional packs, or whatever. An authoritative explanation of the processes which produce these transformations is surprisingly elusive. Textbooks and professional monographs focus instead on the executional techniques and outcomes. The framework presented in Figure 17.2 reflects a personal view, drawing upon industry seminars and conversations with practitioners. The sequence of events is by no means invariable, and the process may be altogether less methodical in practice.

Creative planning is a team operation at the agency. It involves *account managers* (see 'Working relationships'), who keep the client involved throughout the process, *account planners*, who bring a research-based understanding of the target audience to the task, *copywriters*, who produce the words to convey the message, and *art directors*, who devise the images to reinforce it. Their collective aim is to meet the objectives in the client brief, and outflank the opposition in doing so.

The process begins with the isolation of specifically creative objectives from guidelines in the brief, including a clear statement of the key messages and target audiences. The next stage is likely to be a think-tank session, at which the remit is to 'apply lateral, disruptive thinking to the problem', in the words of a prominent creative director. It was inspiration by such means that redefined Lucozade as an energy drink for teenagers and the Automobile Association as 'the fourth emergency service'. Raw ideas of that kind are next subjected to the discipline of scrutiny against research-based analysis of probable audience responses, and the survivors refined into more precise communication con-

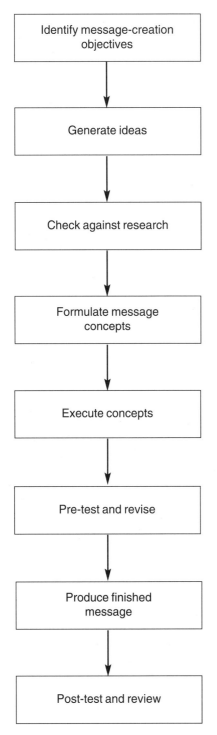

Figure 17.2   The message development process

cepts. For example, *The Times* emerged from this stage of creative planning as the newspaper for 'changing times', and travelling by Virgin Atlantic Airways as a way to 'get a life'.

Concepts must next be converted into creative executions. Evans (1988) provides an expert description of the craft which produces *copy* and *visuals*, then melds them into a finished creative solution, and of the skills which in turn convert that into advertisements, mailers, shelf displays and the like. Beware, however, that time has overtaken most of the technical detail. In particular, the process by which roughs hand drawn by visualizers were transformed into finished artwork which a paste-up artist married with the results of photo typesetting to produce the masters required by a printer has been outmoded by Apple Mac software and ISDN data-transmission technology. Next comes a vital precaution against wayward creativity: pre-testing the outcome on a sample of the target audience and reviewing the strategy in the light of the findings. In practice, agencies and clients will sometimes place their faith in the creative development process and back their own judgement. Once the campaign has run, however, it would be extremely unusual not to conduct a post-test of effectiveness. Findings relevant to creative strategy can be compared with the objectives set at the start of the process, and the conclusions held as an input to the next creative planning cycle.

In contrast to the dearth of published material on creative planning, there is an abundance of literature on its results, which can yield insights into the planning behind them. The most accessible current source is a series of collections of winning submissions for Britain's biennial Creative Planning Awards competition (Account Planning Group, 1993, 1995, 1997).

Delivering the promotional message

The promotional mix offers a very diverse set of message-delivery channels. For example, the gap between originator and audience might be

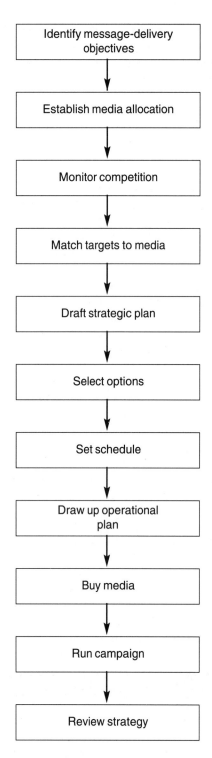

Figure 17.3 The message delivery process

bridged by a team chosen for a sports sponsorship linkage, by telemarketing operators, by the ambience in which packages are displayed or, most obviously, by the media in which publicity and advertising appear. Little has been written formally on the process of selecting specific options within the first four general choices, but a whole sub-industry is devoted to the last. This section will therefore restrict itself to advertisers, and their approach to *media planning*.

The complex task of allocating available funds appropriately among proliferating *media options* is almost invariably delegated to an *advertising agency* or *media independent* (see 'Working relationships'). This section will use 'agency' to stand for both. Developing the plan for de- livering the message is a team operation, involving *account managers* (see 'Working relationships'), who keep the client involved throughout the process, *media planners*, information technologists with access to a vast array of media research, and *media buyers*, who bargain with the *media owners*. Their collective aim is to find the right targets, outflank the competition, and do so cost-effectively.

Planning the correct strategy for delivery of the message starts with the *client brief*, from which an internal *media brief* is distilled. Specialists apply that to the twin tasks of *media selection*, choosing the vehicles to deliver the creative strategy to the target audience, and *media scheduling*, fixing the timing of individual *exposures* over the duration of the campaign. The classic British textbook is Broadbent and Jacobs (1984), to which no equally detailed successor has yet appeared. Beware, however, that the media landscape has changed radically since it was published; the general principles are all that remain valid. The framework presented in Figure 17.3 reflects a personal view, based on their work and observation of practitioners in action.

The process begins with the isolation of objectives in the client brief relevant to such media-related factors as the 'mood' or 'tone of voice' of the advertising and the description of the target audience. The latter must include a clear psychographic profile, for the sophisticated and comprehensive databases built up by industry-wide *media research* over many years can tell planners a great deal about associated media-consumption habits. An essential second step is to establish the *media allocation* within the advertising appropriation, for it places a limit on what is practically possible. The team will next monitor competitors' media usage, in order to find unoccupied ground in the communication landscape. For example, the agency which launched the Häagen-Dazs brand in Britain deliberately avoided the orthodox medium for ice cream advertising, television, and caught Unilever off guard with a poster campaign that cost less than £500 000.

These preliminaries completed, media planners can construct a broad-brush *strategic plan*, by matching the objectives in the media brief to the audience-delivery capabilities and message-modulation propensities of the five so-called 'major media' comprising the UK *media mix*: press, television, radio, cinema and outdoor. This traditional, simplistic categorization is rapidly becoming outmoded in the face of the well chronicled information explosion, but remains the standard for the time being. The confines of a single chapter do not permit a review of their key characteristics, but thumbnail sketches can be found in an encyclopaedic dictionary of marketing and advertising terms (Baker, 1998), under the five relevant headwords plus 'major media' and 'media share'. No single textbook can be recommended as providing a more comprehensive review that is reasonably up to date.

Once the strategic plan has been debated, refined and agreed, the emphasis shifts to the tactical level. Making choices among the *media options* within each class is in essence a matter of evaluating them with respect to nine key variables. Nine have already been identified in the broader context of choices among the ingredients of the promotional mix, and are listed in Figure 17.1. In addition, media planners need to

take into account the *creative scope* offered by an option under consideration: will it place constraints on the execution of the creative strategy being developed simultaneously? They will also be influenced by its *user-friendliness*: the degree of effort required to book and control a campaign. Media buying has become generally easier during the past decade, but there can still be considerable variation from one case to the next.

With the choices of media made, the planners turn their attention to the building of a *media schedule* which delivers the message to the required audience in the right way at the right times. Given that personal viewing, listening and reading habits vary considerably within any audience, frequency and volume of exposure to any schedule can never be uniform. Conceptually difficult discussions in journals and at seminars of threshold pressure, decay rates, wearout, saturation and supersaturation bear witness to the fact that scheduling is an extremely complex undertaking.

In practice, a first step towards selection and scheduling decisions will be to feed performance requirements into on-line media selection programs or desktop software packages, the price of both having fallen in recent years to the point that any agency which regularly buys media for its clients must regard computer assistance as an affordable resource. The systems cannot make decisions by themselves, however; this highly numerate and technologically sophisticated discipline still depends significantly on the collective experience and wisdom of its practitioners.

By such processes, the strategic plan is in due course transformed into a costed *operational plan*, which is in turn translated into a campaign schedule by *media buyers*. These specialists have the disposition needed to haggle successfully with the hard-nosed representatives of the media sales houses and advertising departments. Bargaining skills are especially important in buying television advertising time, which is effectively auctioned. The complexities of media buying are well explained in Chapter 8 of

Brierley (1995). Because the cost of a schedule reflects deals struck with suppliers, it may vary significantly from the forecast in the operational plan, which is consequently reviewed and if necessary revised at intervals. At the end of the campaign, the planning team will assess the cost-effectiveness of their media strategy, and retain the findings in mind as part of the history influencing each future iteration of the planning cycle.

Examples of media planning in practice can be found in the relevant passages of the winning submissions for the biennial IPA Advertising Effectiveness Awards (Institute of Practitioners in Advertising, 1981–97). If esoteric vocabulary acts as a barrier to understanding the finer points of a particular media strategy, definitions of key terms can be found in Baker (1998). The vital sources of media research are described in detail in Chapter 9 of Brierley (1995).

The medium and the message

Independent observers encountering the twin disciplines of developing and delivering the promotional message inevitably begin to wonder which comes first. In principle, neither should; in practice, it will depend on circumstances. After the *client brief* has been brought to the agency by the *account manager*, the creative and media teams will at first plan independently but in parallel. Once they reach the stages, respectively, of defining key communication concepts and deciding a broad media strategy, each must cross-check the developing plan with the other and, via the account manager, with the client. There is no point in devising a creative strategy which cannot be executed in the media vehicles capable of reaching the target audience, or buying a media vehicle which delivers the right audience at a favourable cost if it cannot offer the required creative scope. Furthermore, we have already seen, in 'Deploying the promotional mix', that the audience's reading of a message can be modulated by their perception of the channel or vehicle which delivers it. This

vehicle effect or rub-off value can apply to the team chosen for a sports sponsorship linkage, the regional accents of telemarketing oper-ators, the ambience in which packages are displayed or, most obviously, the media in which publicity and advertising appear.

Nevertheless, popular accounts of the advertising do generally stress the creative aspect. That bias prompted a prominent speaker at an industry seminar to 'explode the myth that media is an add-on service which lies dormant whilst the brand team are developing creative work, and is then called upon to write a plan which delivers the messages to the target audience'. On the contrary, 'a good media brief is as important as a good creative brief. It should excite the planning team into exploring new opportunities to deliver the brand message with impact . . . to be surprised'. In short, the only intellectually proper response to the chicken-and-egg question is neither, however equivocal that may sound.

Interactions within the marketing mix

The fact that one of the four Ps, promotion, is explicitly associated with communication conceals another of crucial strategic significance: that the other three also have the potential to convey a message. A hypothetical case example will illustrate.

This time, it is necessary to take on the role of a complete outsider, unencumbered by the prejudices learnt through observation and consumption: a visitor from the Martian Business School, let us say, on a fieldwork project to find out more about the rather special relationship between earth beings and their personal transportation vehicles. Two such visitors land in a mixed suburban location with which you are familiar and set about trying to deduce by direct scrutiny which of the visible marques will prove to enjoy the highest general esteem. Having formed their objective opinion, they embark upon some limited consumer research. In response to a very direct line of questioning, they are surprised to find that a particular

Bavarian brand seems a strong contender and determine to find out why.

They are first offered 'German engineering quality' as a self-evident explanation. Leaving aside the difficult question of earthly attitudes to nationality and foreign competition, and passing over the doubtful proposition that their informants have personally assessed this criterion by lifting bonnets and slamming doors at random, they seek to find the rationale in verifiable facts. Which engines have won the contest on the proving ground of the Grand Prix racing track? Renault and Honda. Which marque has consistently been found by consumer testing organizations to be most reliable in use? Toyota. Which ones have the best record of resistance to corrosion? Japanese. Which are most likely to treat as added-cost extras the interior equipment offered as standard in general? German. A dispassionate Martian can only conclude that the positioning suggested by the realities of the *product* is at odds with the consumer perception.

Attention is therefore turned to the *price*. The visitors are assured that this is high, a fact which, in the local socio-economic context, confers both prestige and desirability on publicly consumed durable goods. Resigned to the quaint cause-and-effect equation, they nevertheless find the purported fact hard to accept, having already seen a full-page advertisement in a national newspaper emphasizing that the newest sports saloon from this manufacturer is its most accessible, mentioning a price prefixed by the adjective 'just', and having heard a series of national radio commercials explaining that contract hire terms competed directly with those for archetypal company-car workhorses from Ford and Vauxhall. The price is evidently not especially high. As for the hint of exclusivity, objective Martian research has already established that about 50 000 of the marque are sold in Britain every year and that its market share there is almost twice that held by Honda and only just behind Citroen's. A second of the four Ps is conveying an objective message at odds with the subjective positioning.

The visitors turn their attention to *place* in the quest for a rational ingredient in an apparently irrational recipe. They soon find a main dealership dressed in a high-technology corporate identity, rigorously controlled from Munich, which gives out the first signals consistent with the marque's evident mystique. The reception area within resembles a private hospital: carpets on the floor, clean upholstery on the seats and suits on the personnel. They notice that customers are not accused of having deviously maltreated their own vehicles. From the reception area, they can see nothing more of the workshop than a rank of radiantly healthy post-operative patients waiting under cover for their caring owners to take them home. This is the kind of treatment that certainly confers prestige on its recipients. The catch is, however, that only users will normally be aware of the fact.

So the visitors' scrutiny is lastly turned on *promotion*, specifically the ubiquitous advertising. They note that the messages give prospective buyers very few objective reasons for choosing the marque, but plenty of visual imagery, and that the choice of media guarantees exposure to tens of thousands who will never be customers. The detached Martian intelligence detects, however, that the real target audience is non-users. By consistent and single-mindedly high-style delivery of subtle, soft cues, the advertising has built the image of a discerning motorist in the minds of those who have limited experience of the actual product even as a passenger and therefore have no reason to counter-argue. Drivers of the marque can thus see themselves as others see them: they are, as it were, driving the advertisements. The fourth of the four Ps is conveying the expected message.

To leave our visitors and sum up, the key issue is that an admired brand leader is pursuing a promotional strategy which comes dangerously close to placing all its communicative eggs in one basket: the P that is explicitly associated with communication. In so doing, it risks the consequences of ignoring the potential for *synergy* among the elements of the marketing mix – or, more damagingly, *counter-synergy*.

It is arguable that the first two of the four Ps have the potential to convey implicit messages which contradict those explicitly delivered by the fourth, and that the third can only redress the imbalance if something else brings potential customers to the point of sale. This is a knife-edge strategic situation for the future of a brand that has become contradictorily commonplace for something held to be exclusive (it is, of course, BMW). If the promotional initiative is lost for any reason, counter-synergy could threaten to reverse in the next decade the marketing success that has been achieved only during the last.

The moral of this fable is that marketing managers are practising yet another form of Levitt's celebrated myopia if, simply by default, they ignore the interacting communicative potential of the marketing mix elements as a system and focus their attention instead on the one labelled promotion.

The promotional plan

The kind of strategic and tactical decisions discussed so far in this chapter will require eventually to be formalized into a *promotional plan*, to be disseminated to those charged with the responsibility for translating them into action. Given the obvious importance of such a document, it is surprising that most textbooks and guidebooks for practitioners fall short of the ideal when they focus within the total marketing plan on the sub-plan relating to promotion or communication. An honourable exception is the very detailed treatment in Stapleton and Thomas (1998). For present purposes, Table 17.4 aims to provide a usable template for the construction of a workable plan. It signals its intended use as an action plan by posing questions to be answered. Those are hopefully reasonably self-explanatory, but further comments on particular headings are called for here.

Within 1.1, it will be vital to specify as part of the product or service profile the *benefits* that can be delivered to potential customers in the target audience. In practice, promotional plans are apt to concentrate on the technical specifica-

tion of the offering, in a production-oriented manner that should be anathema to anyone who has studied marketing. Similarly, the audience profile needs to go beyond mundane geo-demographic data if the information is to realize its potential as a key factor in the development of message and delivery strategies. *Acorn Lifestyles* is probably the best known of many target-market classification systems available in Britain, all capable of providing the necessary psychographic and sociographic descriptions: for example, 'LW75: Homesharers in very affluent areas', which is elaborated in a 'neighbourhood overview' and thumbnail personal sketch in the user guide. This is a massive improvement over the typical descriptions in statements of advertising objectives in practice, such as 'ABC1 18–34-year-olds in major conurbations'.

Item 2.1 of the plan recalls the issue of interaction within the marketing mix, raised in the preceding section of this chapter. Item 2.2 draws attention to the important fact that the execution of promotional strategies may in practice be constrained by precedents set in previous campaigns and by non-negotiable requirements set at a high level in the organizational hierarchy. The power of precedent is illustrated by a pair of real-life advertising campaign objectives: to employ very modern imagery and yet to preserve 'the St Ivel heritage'. The product was a modern yellow-fat spread, but the maker has a long history in the dairy produce business and evidently wished to continue the established precedent of emphasizing that heritage even while addressing a modern audience about a modern product in a modern way. The result was a television campaign that combined fashionable video techniques and audio effects with such traditional symbols as a five-barred gate, milk churns and the rising sun. The power of the so-called mandatory is well illustrated by a manual of textbook dimensions, *Lo Stile Olivetti* (*The Olivetti Style*), issued to managers with marketing communications responsibilities by a company with very firm views about the projection of its identity in all contexts and all countries. Though such precedents and manda-

Table 17.4 Structure and content of the promotional plan

1   RAW MATERIALS

    What and whom is this plan about?

1.1 Product or service profile
    Specification: what can it do?
    Benefits: what can it offer?

1.2 Company or organization profile
    Specification: what do we do?
    Identity: how do we present ourselves?
    Image: how are we seen?

1.3 Audience profile
    Socio-demographics: who are they, and where?
    Psychographics: what do they want?

1.4 Market profile
    Structure: what does it look like?
    Competition: who is there with us?
    Dynamics: what is in the future?

2   CONSTRAINTS

    What externalities need to be taken
    into account?

2.1 Marketing mix
    Product policy: what effect on promotion strategy?
    Pricing policy: what effect on promotion strategy?
    Place policy: what effect on promotion strategy?

2.2 Givens
    Precedents: what is traditional?
    Mandatories: what is compulsory?
    Appropriation: what funds are available?
    Allocations: how and where are they to be spent?
    Control: how will cost-effectiveness be monitored?

3   OBJECTIVES

    What is this plan meant to achieve?

3.1 Goals: what are our overall, long-term aims?
3.2 Targets: what are the intermediate aims of this plan?
3.3 Criteria: how will communication effectiveness be measured?

4   STRATEGY

    How will this plan meet its objectives?

4.1 Message: what do we want to tell the audience?
4.2 Creative: how do we want to tell them?
4.3 Delivery: what means will we use to do so?

5   TIMETABLE

    How will the strategies become a campaign?

5.1 Timescale: how soon must the objectives be met?
5.2 Schedule: what needs to happen when?

6   IMPLEMENTATION

    How will the campaign be managed?

6.1 Authority: who can say yes or no?
6.2 Responsibility: who will co-ordinate it?
6.3 Delegation: what will be sub-contracted?
6.4 Procedures: how will we keep track of progress?
6.5 Evaluation: how will we measure results?

tories may be a procedural irritant for those who have to observe them, companies have a perfect right to establish them and the writers of promotional plans an obligation to make them explicit to all concerned.

Item 2.3 reminds us that the whole plan is somewhat hypothetical if there are no clear answers to the three questions posed. An earlier section in this chapter, 'The promotional budget', emphasizes the vital difference between the act of setting a budget and the process of budgetary control. It also contains the reason for the first question not being 'how much shall we spend?': that amount is very seldom decided by the person who is held accountable for the way it is spent. Item 3.3 is perhaps the most crucial one in the plan. It will be re-encountered in the section 'Assessing campaign effectiveness' (p 409).

The content of Part 4 will vary considerably according to the particular pattern of deployment of the promotional mix. The amount of detail and the precise content will furthermore depend upon decisions made about subcontracting the execution of promotional strategy or retaining responsibility in-house, made explicit at item 6.3. Many of the factors governing such choices can be inferred from the explanations and discussions in the next two sections of this chapter. The completed promotional plan may in turn become the template for construction of a *client brief*. We have already seen, in 'Delivering the promotional message', that most marketers elect to delegate the task of translating promotional strategy into promotional campaigns to a range of professional intermediaries expert in the individual disciplines of the marketing mix. The starting point of this process should obviously be a coherent statement of what these collaborators are expected to achieve on their client's behalf. This brief will in practice be an appropriate synopsis of the promotional plan. Its purpose is to provide the necessary guidance, not to give instructions to collaborators who have been employed for their collective experience and expertise. It is a moot point how much detail is needed to discharge that task

effectively and efficiently. The only possible answer is the one traditionally given about the length piece of string. As the Incorporated Society of British Advertisers puts it in a practical guide: 'A good brief will be as short as possible but as long as is necessary.' This perhaps implies that brevity should be the overriding aim. The recipient can always ask follow-up questions.

Working relationships

The *originators* of promotional campaigns typically involve expert *intermediaries* in the process of transmitting the required messages to their chosen target *audiences* via the most appropriate communication *vehicles*. The result in practice is a variety of working relationships, which can occur in a number of combinations according to circumstances. The most straightforward pattern of all is seen in a form of promotion which happens to be excluded from our version of the promotional mix. In the case of personal selling, an employee of the originator communicates with an individual in the target audience and there is no intervening vehicle to modulate the message (see 'Delivering the promotional message', p. 391). By contrast, advertisers typically enlist the aid of advertising agencies in addressing whole target audiences via advertising media, while simultaneously using other ingredients of the promotional mix and employing other intermediaries. Figure 17.4 attempts a consolidation of all possible variations in a single system diagram.

Arrow 1 symbolizes the kind of message delivery system in which no intermediary is involved. The most obvious case in point is a sales representative delivering a pitch to a prospect, but personal selling is excluded from our version of the promotional mix. The nearest admissible equivalent would be a direct mail shot created, executed and distributed by in-house specialists. Such an uncomplicated arrangement offers two key benefits, the first of which is strong *control* over the over the content, construction and tone of the message. There is

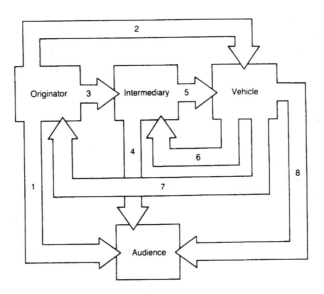

Figure 17.4 The four parties to the advertising transaction

no scope for expert outsiders to argue successfully for alternative modes of execution, which may not necessarily achieve any improvement in communication. The second benefit is the lack of scope for *modulation* of the message. Although the two parties are not quite face-to-face and the mail is strictly speaking an intervening vehicle, this system of communication is so much a part of everyday life that perceptions of the transmission medium will have virtually no effect upon interpretation of the message. There may be resistance to the very fact that the initiative is an unsolicited mail shot, but that is a broader issue. Though this option thus offers a very low level of risk, the success of the outcome depends crucially on the originator's own communication *expertise*.

Arrows 2 and 8 together depict a situation in which the promotional message reaches the audience via a transmission vehicle. For example, a press release might be delivered to the trade press by a machine-tool manufacturer's in-house publicity department. Only if the writer of the release is very practised in the craft will the text survive the process more or less intact. If editors do not ignore it altogether, they will treat it as the raw material for their own

news item or story, to be given a spin that matches the style of their publication and the interests of their readers, and decide when the outcome should appear. The originator thereby loses *control* over the outcome, to a largely unpredictable extent. Thereafter, the modified message becomes susceptible to *modulation*, as readers interpret it according to their perception of the publication in question. There is thus a significantly higher risk of ineffective communication than in the situation summed up by *arrow 1*.

Arrow 3 symbolizes the decision to subcontract the job of converting strategies into tactics, rather than carrying out all the necessary tasks in-house. The quid pro quo of any such delegation is that the originator must allow the intermediary to argue for its own expert view of the most effective means to the end: the client provides the brief, and the agency produces the solution. A degree of *control* is thereby sacrificed as *expertise* is acquired. *Arrow 4* represents the situation in which the intermediary subsequently transmits the message directly to the audience, for example by running a direct marketing campaign. *Arrow 5* applies when a transmission vehicle enters into the equation, the communication route being completed by *arrow 8*. That is how about four in every five advertising campaigns are managed in practice. It is a less common choice for publicity initiatives, but equally possible. The introduction of a vehicle into the process compounds the loss of control in the case of 'free' publicity, as we have just seen, but not in the case of 'paid-for' advertising. In exchange for the price of space or time, the media owner undertakes that advertisements will appear in the booked position at the booked time and in the form in which they are submitted. This option is thus a matter of trading acquired expertise and (potentially) lower cost against reduced control.

Arrows 6 and 7 refer specifically to professional conventions affecting the working relationship among advertisers, agencies and media owners. Though it is logical to think of advertisers as the sellers in the transaction, because they use advertising to promote their offering to the audience, they are also buyers – of a commodity from media owners and a service from agencies. However, by long established standard practice explained in 'Remuneration' (p. 404), an agency buys the advertising space and time required for a client's campaign from the media owners at one price and claims reimbursement in due course at another. Because typical agencies depend on the difference between the two for roughly two-thirds of their total income, an unwritten code of professional conduct dictates that media owners do not sell direct to advertisers (*arrow 7*) – but make their sales pitch to the advertisers' agencies (*arrow 6*). In practice, they naturally present the case for their medium to both parties – demand-pull to reinforce supply-push – but are careful to observe the correct priority.

The role of the media owners in the system is actually slightly more complex than this, for they have two functions. The first, their editorial function, is to deliver news and entertainment to readers, viewers and listeners; their second function, *advertisement sales*, is to deliver a certain portion of their total space or time to advertisers, who subsidize the price of news and

entertainment by paying for the opportunity to address those readers, viewers and listeners.

Thus, as *arrow 8* symbolizes, advertisements come to audiences from media owners, strictly speaking. But advertisers expect the audience to perceive them as the source of the message, which they presumably will except in very unusual situations, which brings us back to the starting point of this elaboration of Figure 17.4, *arrow 1*.

The truism that all service industries are people businesses can in this case be a useful reminder that the working arrangements just described in the abstract as elements of a system exist in practice as a series of relationships between people. The effectiveness of the system depends on their ability to collaborate constructively. From that point of view, the interface between originator and intermediary is critical.

The executive charged with responsibility for managing the originator's marketing mix will normally be a *brand manager* or *marketing manager*, though the title may sometimes be as specific as advertising manager or marketing communications coordinator. This is the person who delivers the client brief to the intermediary. The recipient, responsible for interpreting it to the expert specialists within the intermediary's organization, is generically described as an *account handler*, though individual titles range from account executive through account supervisor and account manager to account director. The description originated in the advertising business, where 'account' defines a single piece of business awarded to an advertising agency. It has since been adopted by equivalent specialists in direct marketing and sales promotion, and by the generalist integrated marketing communications agencies described in 'Above, below and through the line' (p. 383). The more self-explanatory description 'client service' is often applied to the function, but seldom to the person.

It would be logical to assume that the duties are shared more or less equally in such a working partnership, but the fact is that the onus for maintaining a good working relationship rests mainly on the intermediary.

As in any other kind of service organization, the quality of after-sales customer-service is a critical factor in the winning of repeat business, and it is the account executive's job to deliver it. In particular, his or her role is to minimize the potential for *culture clash* between agency and client. This is crucial because the atmosphere and ethos of typical examples of the former and latter could hardly be more different. Agency creative types do not sit opposite client R&D people at briefing meetings: instead, brand managers report client priorities to account executives, and account executives propose agency solutions to brand managers.

It follows that two skills in particular are essential attributes of effective account executives: *negotiation* and *coordination*. The latter is vital because one person is dealing on behalf of a whole organization. Without it, advertising campaigns will resemble horses designed by committees, deadlines will be missed, opportunities lost and much more besides.

Negotiation is not simply a matter of standing between the two parties keeping their respective specialists apart. An essential aspect of the job is to be advocate for the point of view of each side when with the other: somewhat akin to the role of industrial relations negotiators. Although clearly employed by the agency, account executives have to live in no-man's-land between agency and client. Certainly, if the relationship is to endure, they must be as conscientious in explaining the client's needs and attitudes to the agency people as they are in advocating the agency's solutions and attitudes to the client – however irritating and petty a client's tinkering with creative treatments or media plans may seem. As one account executive vividly explained in a presentation to a class of university students: 'Whenever I'm at the client's office, I must be the agency's man; back at the agency, I must be the client's man.' Divided loyalty is part of the *modus operandi* – and a positive one, given that the job remit is after-sales service.

Not all exponents of account handling are conscientious diplomats, negotiators, facilitators, coordinators and organizers, however. As a former board director of a large London agency, now better known as an émigré to Provence, puts it: 'The best account executives are shrewd business operators and perceptive judges of advertising and human nature. The worst are glorified bag carriers, ferrying messages back and forth between agency and client with all the interpretational skills of a yo-yo' (Mayle, 1990). However effectively or ineffectively client service is delivered in practice, this particular working relationship tends to be shorter lived than the norm in other professions. There is evidence that more than three-quarters last less than ten years (Briggs, 1993).

Given the obvious potential for breakdown inherent in a delicately balanced interpersonal relationship that demands so much of one party, it would be useful to have a reliable picture of the state of relations in practice. Unfortunately, the most recent survey data found are more than ten years old, restricted to Scotland, and relate only to the clients of advertising agencies. They suggest that hardly anyone on the client side of the relationship saw any reason for pessimism: a third of respondents professed themselves 'completely satisfied' and almost 60 per cent were 'fairly satisfied'. Earlier surveys had found between two-thirds and three-quarters of brand managers and chief executives throughout Britain to be enjoying 'happy' relations with their agencies.

If such optimism was justified in the 1970s and 1980s, there is ample non-survey evidence that it no longer is in the 1990s. Increasingly frequent trade-press reports of newsworthy rifts led *Marketing* to comment editorially in November 1993 that 'in private, there isn't a single agency in town that won't own up to a story of bitter relations with clients . . . not just in client/advertising agency relationships, but also in those with other marketing services companies'. The reason was thought to be a downward spiral of cause and effect.

Industry analysts reported that average profit margin among advertising agencies had fallen to a quarter of previous levels over four years. The predictable round of redundancies and recruitment freezes resulted in seriously reduced levels of client service without in itself producing the necessary reductions in total operating costs. Other efforts to remedy the situation included cutting corners in other areas, such as production, and charging fees for services previously subsidized from earnings. The inevitable consequence was that clients complained about poor service, falling quality standards and excessive fees. This trend also affected agencies specializing in other ingredients of the promotional mix, to a greater or lesser extent, but one particularly damaging cause-and-effect equation was peculiar to advertising. (Interested but non-expert readers may need to refer to 'Remuneration' for clarification of some terms in the explanation which follows.) Because media commission accounted at the time for almost three-quarters of a typical advertising agency's income, an alternative to cutting costs in sensitive areas was to recommend media schedules featuring expensive media and heavy exposure. This risky tactic duly backfired by generating widespread pressure on the client side for rebating agreements, which could only further erode profit margins already pared to the bone.

These are much more specific causes than the bland reasons offered in a *Marketing* survey a decade earlier by 100 respondents who had recently parted company with their advertising agencies, equally applicable to degenerating relations in other promotional-mix disciplines: 'in a rut', 'results fell short of expectations', 'did not understand our problems' and 'could not develop the right chemistry'.

It is thus clear that not only does the very fact of delegation to an intermediary mean a loss of control over strategy, but also that there is an inherent tendency to instability in such working relationships. In that case, one might justifiably wonder why marketers do not in fact execute their promotional campaigns in-house. There are three key reasons. First, they often cannot afford to pay the salaries needed to recruit their own experts in the particular disciplines. It was in the early 1980s that the salaries of top copywriters in London, for example, passed into the six-figure range. Second, because promotional campaigns normally consist of discrete initiatives rather than continuously evolving programmes, originators cannot keep such specialists fully occupied throughout the year. They find themselves paying for substantial periods of downtime, to borrow an engineering concept. Lastly, few marketing departments if any can offer the degree of stimulation and motivation that agency specialists derive from working for a considerable variety of clients over the course of a typical career. Recruitment would thus be a problem even if the price could be afforded. Therefore, it has become normal practice to buy a share in the collective skills of established service providers, rather than to try developing them in-house. The loss of *control* is offset by the acquisition of affordable *expertise*.

Choosing a working partner

An obvious way to reduce the probability of a premature rift in the somewhat precarious originator–intermediary working relationships is to take as much care as possible over the selection process that initiates it. Analogies with courtship and marriage characterize the relatively few discussions of this subject in the literature: see, for instance, the otherwise dependable White (1993: Chapter 4). That is perhaps only echoing the language used by respondents to the *Marketing* survey mentioned earlier, but is unhelpful. Apart from trivializing an important decision, it offers as a template a procedure that is normally far more emotional than rational, and an institution by no means always effective or durable.

Therefore, this section proposes an appropriately systematic approach to the task, based on an excellent pamphlet published by the Incorporated Society of British Advertisers (ISBA), plus the often bitter fruits of personal experience at first and second hand. It assumes that an originator, henceforth 'the client', is set-

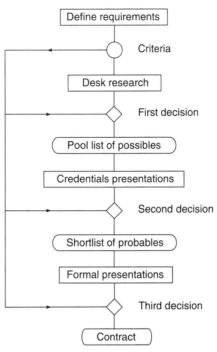

Figure 17.5   Choosing a working partner

ting out to find a suitable intermediary as a working partner, henceforth 'the agency', though the process does occasionally operate in reverse. Figure 17.5 summarizes it as a step-by-step guide.

Step 1, formally defining what will be required of the agency, often falls victim in practice to the false doctrine: 'cut the cackle and get down to business.' To avoid the necessary intellectual effort would prejudice the outcome at the very outset, for this crucial step is the source of decision criteria needed three times during the process, and avoids the need to reinvent the wheel each time. The requirements should be discussed and agreed by all who have a legitimate interest in the outcome, and then recorded formally.

Step 2 is in effect window shopping. Sources of this preliminary information include the trade press, a range of directories, the World Wide Web, and the informal grapevine within the business. Trade associations such as the Institute of Practitioners in Advertising (IPA),

the Institute of Sales Promotion and the Direct Marketing Association will provide a list of suitable agencies, in exchange for a statement of requirements and a company profile. If the prospective client is seeking an advertising agency, video presentations prepared to a standard specification can be viewed anonymously at the premises of the Advertising Agency Register. At this stage, no agencies need know that a search is in progress. If any clue is given, unsolicited sales pitches will inevitably ensue, muddying the waters and making an eventual objective decision much more difficult.

Step 3 is to draw up a pool list of agencies who seem capable of meeting the criteria defined at Step 1. How many it contains should reflect a pragmatic judgement about the decision makers' span of attention at the next stage. In a recent actual case, it comprised two incumbents and five others.

At *Step 4*, the client goes public for the first time by inviting credentials presentations from the agencies on the list. Approaches from others can be expected, as the grapevine goes into action and the trade press probably reports the move. The professional convention is that the presenting agencies do not respond to this invitation, provided it is specific, with speculative campaign plans and a full-blown pitch for the business. Instead, they typically provide a philosophy statement, staff profiles, a client list and case histories plus, depending on the promotional discipline involved, showreels of television and cinema commercials, radio reels, dossiers of print work, and other samples of their work. It is a moot question whether these presentations should take place at the contenders' premises or on home ground. In the first case, valuable impressions can be gained from non-verbal signals but control over the process is sacrificed; in the second, there is less risk of being overwhelmed by a practised presentation team but no chance to form an opinion about the agency as an organization. Wherever the presentations do happen, they should be seen by a panel, not an individual. *Step 5* can then be the result of informed debate, structured by the criteria defined in Step 1.

Step 6 is to invite survivors on the resulting shortlist to make a formal presentation, which they are likely to describe more graphically as their pitch for the business. It is the client's responsibility to set the ground rules. Each contender should be given the same brief, including an unequivocal figure for the first year's promotional budget. Ideally, some way should be found to ensure that they all spend the same amount on their presentations, so that like is compared with like. It is important to beware of the specialist pitching team, who will not be the people eventually working on the business if the pitch is successful. The client must take the opportunity to establish who will be, and to raise any key issues that the presentation does not itself address. A leaflet on best practice in the management of the pitching process, issued jointly by the IPA and ISBA, is adamant about the number of contenders that should be invited to pitch: 'Decide on a list of three agencies – four

if the incumbent is involved ... Don't be seduced into lengthening the list.'

At *Step 7*, the choice criteria are consulted for the last time, and the decision made. If requirements were never defined in the first place, and formal criteria are therefore unavailable, ISBA can provide a thirteen-item checklist and a ranking matrix of ten attributes to be scored on six-point scales. Although the emphasis is on objective comparison of competing pitches, intuition does have a part to play in making a decision about long-term working relationship. As ISBA puts it, 'a clinical and relatively simplistic approach should not be followed too slavishly'. Prudent clients will give themselves time to think after all presentations have been seen, perhaps asking to meet the team that will be allocated to their account, and possibly researching the comparative merits of the competing promotional strategies. However, the ISBA/IPA guide says: 'As soon as possible after all the presentations, normally not more than one week, decide on the winning agency ... Ensure that all pitching agencies learn on the same day . . . After the pitch, give the losing agencies the courtesy of a full lost-order meeting.'

Until quite recently, *Step 8* was likely to consist of no more than a handshake, imitating the gentlemen's agreements common in the true professions. The transformation of successful agencies from small partnerships into large listed companies has fortunately brought with it more businesslike practices. Advertisers and agencies entering a working relationship today can reduce the likelihood of damaging arguments later by adopting *Some Suggested Provisions for Use in Agency/Client Agreements*, published by the IPA.

And that is it, a properly systematic procedure for arriving at an especially crucial decision.

Remuneration

The intermediary in a working relationship is paid for its services by the combination of fees and expenses which is the norm in the professions, unless it happens to be an advertising agency. In that case, fees paid by its client make the smallest contribution to total income. The rest is provided by a paradoxical and complicated system of remuneration (American usage prefers 'compensation'), which has its roots in the history of the advertising business. Outsiders have no reason to understand it, insiders often half-understand it, and commentators usually misunderstand it. A thorough explanation is indicated.

As early as the beginning of the nineteenth century, the proliferation of newspapers, magazines and poster sites was making it very difficult for British advertisers to keep track of the options available, deal efficiently with the profusion of media owners, monitor that their advertisements appeared as booked, and check that they were charged at the correct rates. This situation provided an obvious opportunity for entrepreneurial intermediaries. One such group, calling themselves *advertising agents*, charged advertisers for expert advice and assistance. A second wave, which history has dubbed *space brokers*, bought advertising space speculatively and re-sold it to advertisers at a *mark-up*, accompanied by 'free' advice on campaign planning. By mid-century, the sellers of advertising space had recognized that these intermediaries were in fact the primary customers for their commodity, and were allowing them a routine discount on the price. They were thus transformed into *commission* earning sales agents for the media owners, whereas the other group remained *fee* earning agents to their clients, the advertisers.

During the second half of the same century, in America, one space broker negotiated a fixed-percentage commission discount, and another published a directory of every media owner's pre-discount list prices for space. The whole system thereby became transparent. Brokers took to charging advertisers the list price; advertisers could check that brokers were charging exactly what they would have had to pay if they had booked the space direct. The latter were pleased

to have the work taken off their hands at no charge; the former were content to let their commission subsidize any further service rendered. The advertising agents took a back seat.

In due course, English law established that the firms which were by now calling themselves advertising agencies were neither brokers nor agents. The case of *Tranter v. Astor*, tried in 1917, found that they were *principals*, making the contract with the media owners in their own right, not as agents for advertisers. That ruling was re-affirmed by *Emmett v. DeWitt* in 1957. The result is that present-day advertising agencies must pay for all space and time ordered, even if their client is unwilling or unable to reimburse them. Many have suffered *bad debts* as a consequence over the years, usually because a client goes into receivership. They have a claim on the wound-up business, of course, but are normally far down the list of creditors.

For this *media commission system of advertising agency remuneration* to work properly, media owners must deny the commission discount to advertisers acting as principals: that is, placing orders direct. Outsiders typically find it hard to believe that a media owner could in practice resist a demand for commission from an advertiser with the buying muscle of BT, for example, who spent £9 short of £114 million on advertising in 1996. But advertisers of that type and size invariably use advertising agencies anyway, so they might as well buy media by that route and benefit from the associated subsidized services. That fact, plus the twin forces of historical precedent and professional etiquette, have so far maintained this feature of the system intact.

It is obviously also important that only bona fide agencies receive commission by right. For a long period in the history of the system, the media trade bodies awarded 'recognition' to agencies that met certain criteria. For complex reasons, precipitated by the appearance of media independents in the 1970s, in effect a re-incarnation of the original space brokers, the universal and exclusive recognition agreement was eventually abandoned. Brierley (1995, pp. 65–68) provides a thorough account of the details. Nevertheless, media owners' sales contracts still require agencies to meet their own criteria of eligibility for commission.

The following example will illustrate remuneration-by-commission in operation.

Example 1
Advertiser ABC approves a media schedule proposed by agency XYZ, which includes a three-month package of 125 48-sheet poster sites costing £225 000. XYZ makes the booking and sets about preparing the posters to occupy the sites. The campaign in due course begins, and the media owner invoices XYZ £225 000 minus commission at 15 per cent = £191 250. This is the standard discount for all media in Britain except small-circulation newspapers and magazines.

XYZ pays by the due date in the media sales contract, and bills ABC for £225 000, the price of the package verifiable in *British Rate & Data*. When ABC pays, XYZ makes a profit of £33 750.

If agencies do not in fact pay by the due date, which can be as little as two weeks after the first advertisement appears, the terms of the contract entitle the media owner to reduce the commission rate progressively. It is therefore in their best interest to bill clients immediately and settle media invoices promptly. However, normal business practice does not require a client to pay up in turn before thirty days after the invoice is rendered, and most will take anything up to three months to do so. Agencies, reluctant to press for payment too strongly for fear of losing an account, must therefore keep a very close eye on *cash flow* at all times.

So much for the basic modus operandi. The first of many complications now arises. It does not take special knowledge to guess that £33 750 would not reimburse XYZ for the cost of designing and producing 125 posters measuring 20×10 ft, plus enough spares to allow for routine maintenance over six months, let alone subsidizing the creative and media planning behind the work. When the commission system evolved, high production costs were not an issue. Today, in addition to large posters printed on vinyl-coated paper, advertisers specify high-quality four-colour double-page advertisements in glossy magazines, sixty-second mini-epics on television and cinema screens, and much more besides. Over the intervening years, agencies had to meet escalating production costs out of commission that increased only in line with media price inflation. The media owners could not subsidize the agencies by raising prices further, or they would kill demand for their commodity. The agencies dare not propose unrealistically heavy media schedules, to gain the economies of scale, for fear of losing the business altogether. Meanwhile, creative people were demanding ever higher rewards for their increasingly specialized skills. It soon became clear that no-one could expect agencies with ambitious clients to survive any longer on media commission alone.

A new convention duly emerged that some consequential costs could be charged direct to the client as top-up *fees*. It is typical of this outwardly dynamic but inwardly conservative business that there is no official, definitive list of what can be included and what not. The IPA's guidelines for agency–client agreements are both vague and ambiguous, while a report on remuneration practices throughout Europe says 'The range of services provided at no charge will depend on each individual relationship. Where non-commissionable agency services are charged (work done within the agency), this is normally done on the basis of a prior estimate' (European Association of Advertising Agencies, 1994: p. 21).

The increasing sophistication of media production processes has also resulted in agencies sub-contracting increasing amounts of work. They could hardly be expected to invest in a printing plant capable of handling the work required for ABC's poster campaign, for instance, or a television studio. Furthermore, we have already seen that full-service advertising agencies routinely carry out non-advertising assignments for their clients, such as sales promotion campaigns or market research surveys, normally commissioning them from third parties. In all such situations, the convention is that a *mark-up* is added to the agency's buying price in order to arrive at the client's buying price. The IPA's guidelines recommends a clause in an agency's contract that the client will pay 'the net cost of all these materials and services bought for you, plus X per cent of such net cost'. The key point about this percentage is that it is in fact standard: a figure which makes the agency's reward for commissioning and coordinating the sub-contract the same as it would be if the supplier's bill had been discounted by 15 per cent. In other words, it derives absolutely directly from the media commission convention.

The following example will illustrate the mark-up arithmetic:

Example 2
Client ABC instructs agency XYZ to supply promotional calendars. The agency finds a capable supplier at a competitive price, and places the order. The supplier duly delivers the goods and charges XYZ £1912.50. The agency invoices ABC, adding enough to their buying price to earn themselves the same margin as if they had been given a 15 per cent discount by the supplier.

We know from the previous example, by moving the decimal point, that the required mark-up is £337.50, which our calculator tells us is 17.65 per cent of £1912.50. We also know that XYZ needs to charge ABC £2250. To double-check the equation: 1912.50 + (0.1765 × 1912.50) = 2250.06, which is quite close enough.

So XYZ renders an invoice to ABC for £2250, which reimburses the price paid on ABC's behalf and compensates XYZ for the work it did in arranging and delivering this full-service extra.

Thus the X per cent referred to in the IPA's guidelines will be 17.65 per cent. This remarkably precise figure is confirmed by the European Association of Advertising Agencies (1994, p. 21): 'In addition to the agency retaining 15 per cent on the gross media billings, it is normal for practice for all . . . outside purchases which are billable to be charged at cost plus 17.65 per cent.'

To summarize the story so far, the normal pattern of remuneration for a conventional advertising agency is a combination of a *commission* discount allowed by media owners on the price of

advertising space and time bought on behalf of its clients, plus top-up *fees* and *mark-up* on sub-contracted services, paid by the clients themselves. The first of these has always dominated, in Britain, America and elsewhere. Various industry estimates suggest that it accounts for somewhere between two-thirds and three-quarters of a typical advertising agency's total remuneration.

Whereas an agency could negotiate the level of a service fee, its earnings in commission and mark-up are limited to a fixed proportion of the amount a client is willing to spend on advertising media and ancillary services. The findings just reported therefore mean that, effectively, agencies can compete for business only on such non-price dimensions as experience and reputation. In practice, however, some will offer *commission rebating* deals as a ploy to win new business or retain a client threatening to move the account elsewhere. Indeed, the impetus may come from a high-spending client expecting to benefit from the economies of scale.

Commentators routinely describe rebating in terms that imply an entirely impossible mechanism. The trade press may report that an agency has agreed to cut commission to less than 15 per cent or hand back some of it to the client. An otherwise reliable American textbook cited elsewhere in this chapter (Belch and Belch, 1998) suggests that few advertisers there 'still pay a 15 per cent commission' and that, consequently, 'the agency's fee is less than 15 per cent'. Advertisers cannot cut a discount awarded automatically by media owners, and there would in any case be no benefit to the client if they could. Nor can they hand back a sum of money that exists only as a discount, let alone to a third party who did not give it in the first place. They do not pay the commission, of course, and their fee is something quite separate from their commission. Such mistakes are not simply careless, but downright misleading. Let us return to the first example, and work in a rebate:

Example 3
Agency XYZ agrees to give a 2 per cent commission rebate to client ABC, and subsequently books a

three-month package of 125 48-sheet poster sites at a rate card cost of £225 000. The media owner in due course charges XYZ that amount minus 15 per cent, which is £191 250. They in turn invoice ABC for the rate card cost, verifiable in *British Rate & Data*, minus 2 per cent:

225 000 − (0.03 × 225 000) = 220 500.

When ABC pays, XYZ makes a profit of £220 500 less £191 250 instead of £225 000 less £191 250: £29 250, not £33 750. Their margin has thus been cut by £4500.

What has actually happened is a second discount in the transaction, which leaves the agency's commission intact but *has the same effect as* reducing it. 'Commission rebating' is thus an entirely inaccurate description, unfortunately entrenched in the vocabulary of the business.

On the face of it, a 2 per cent discount is hardly generous. Shoppers would not see it as a bargain at the sales, and traders will regularly deduct 5 per cent for cash in hand. However, £4500 is 13.3 per cent of £33 750. XYZ's apparently minor concession to ABC has thus reduced its profit on the transaction by just over 13 per cent, or substantially more than an eighth. Given that advertising agencies' net profit margins are typically around 2 per cent, according to conventional wisdom in the industry, many who practise rebating land themselves in a serious financial predicament. On the other hand, the trade press periodically reports that others have lost multi-million pound accounts by refusing to do so.

Those who do succumb have to make up for lost revenue in some way, such as by: cutting corners on creative work for the client; recommending unnecessarily expensive media schedules; proposing extra add-on services; claiming more top-up fees; cutting back on the account-handling service; or cross-subsidizing from other clients. Clients who demand rebates thus commit themselves to a game of swings and roundabouts. If too many agencies join in, the outcome is bound to be long-term damage to the business as a whole. That said, XYZ was the only party to suffer in the case example; the media owner's

revenue is unchanged, and ABC is £4500 better off. It is therefore hardly surprising that powerful clients continue to press for rebates.

Clear as the dangers of rebating are, there is a case to be made for it. The crux of the argument is the size of the advertiser's budget. There can be no doubt that a £2 250 000 national television campaign would not require XYZ to expend ten times the creative and administrative costs it did on the £225 000 poster campaign, let alone a hundred times more than it would have devoted to £22 500-worth of press advertising. On that basis, it is not unreasonable to expect agencies to be satisfied with remuneration that diminishes prorata as spending increases. If one of them takes the initiative by charging a client less than the actual price of media bought, the argument goes, it has done nothing more than reduce its service charge to an amount that matches the work done.

The debate is likely to continue. Meanwhile, a pan-European research study (European Association of Advertising Agencies, 1994: pp. 5–7) found that 16 per cent of responding agencies had rebated in 1989, and 17 per cent in 1992.

Journalists and other commentators regularly assert that payment by *fee*, the amount being preferable linked to results, is replacing the anachronistic and perennially controversial media commission system. Like their statements about rebating, this claim requires closer inspection. In fact, the same survey of practice in Europe reported that only 19 per cent of the agencies in the sample had charged their clients fees in 1989, and 23 per cent in 1992. A survey of British agencies by a London stockbroker in the late 1980s had found the proportion to be exactly 30 per cent. If there is any trend away from commission, it is both weak and slow.

A fee system does have the obvious appeal of reflecting pragmatic reality instead of historical precedent and legal convention, but agencies seeking to implement it have to surmount several practical obstacles. First, they will continue to receive the media commission discount. It does not have to be claimed, and media owners would be unwilling to make special billing arrangements for a few agencies. The discount accumulated therefore has to be calculated for each client periodically, and a credit issued against the fee. A new internal data-handling system will probably be needed to accomplish this. Deciding the amount of the fee poses a second set of problems. Like setting a price, the process demands identification and isolation of the costs to be offset and decisions about the margin required. The calculation will have to be based on past costings, or on forecasts. In either event, the process is notoriously like trying to steer a car by looking in the rear-view mirror. When each fee is re-negotiated at the end of a budget period, the client is likely to exert strong downward pressure. That will produce the same consequences as the notorious rebating, if the agency gives in. Moreover, other fee-charging agencies are free to start price wars. Lastly, if the fee is to be pegged to results, the agency will face the considerable difficulties involved in measuring them and isolating those attributable to the advertising campaign: see the section on 'Assessing campaign effectiveness'.

Furthermore, advertisers and media owners both have a vested interest in retention of the commission system. The former have reason to suspect that a fee set on the basis of overheads, salaries, production costs and a reasonable profit margin would be a larger amount than 15 per cent of media bills plus 17.65 per cent mark-up on non-media work plus chargeable costs. The latter value the control that progressive reduction of the commission percentage gives them over their own cash flow, and would much rather deal with a small number of advertising agencies than a large number of advertisers.

Despite being declared an anti-competitive business practice by the Sherman Anti-Trust Act in the USA in 1955, The Restrictive Trade Practices Act in Britain in 1976, and a ruling by the Office of Fair Trading in 1978, the *media commission system of advertising agency remuneration* remains the norm in both countries, in Japan and across most of Europe. Its robust state of

health is attributable to considerable practical appeal, for it

- has a long historical pedigree
- is generally familiar in the business
- is easily put into practice
- requires very little computation
- involves almost no negotiation
- suits two of the three parties involved very well.

Assessing campaign effectiveness

In an ideal world, measuring the effectiveness of a promotional initiative would be a simple matter of using a measuring *instrument* to compare actual *performance* with explicit *criteria* derived from predetermined *objectives*. An automotive engineer, for instance, might wish to bench-test an engine for acceptably silent running. That general objective could be translated into a criterion specifying decibel level at a given distance from an engine operating at a given number of revolutions per minute under given laboratory conditions. That criterion would in turn determine the measuring instrument: an audiometer. The readings taken at the instrument would establish that the engine could or could not meet the criterion and that its design therefore was or was not *effective* in that respect. Unfortunately, this straightforward procedure typically fails at the very first stage in the context of assessing promotional effectiveness. The fact is that practitioners typically experience substantial difficulty in articulating objectives that are either achievable or measurable.

Some advertising examples will illustrate the problem. All the quoted statements have appeared in trade publications. Only the brand names have been removed, to protect the guilty. First, consider this aim for the promotion of boxed chocolates: 'to position Brand A as the ultimate.'

This clearly demonstrates two common tendencies: to mistake aspirations, often grandiose, for realistically achievable objectives; to charge promotion with the attainment of objectives it could hardly achieve in isolation from other elements of the marketing mix.

Next, for Brand B, an ice-cream gateau: 'to very quickly establish awareness of a product known to be very interesting to the customer and thereby maximize consumer trial.' Here, we clearly see another common failing: lack of precision and quantification. Awareness of *what* about the product? Among *which* target audience? *How much* awareness, and by *when*? *What* constitutes maximized trial and by *when* is it to be achieved? Precisely *who* are customers?

If criteria are thus unspecified, the tendency is for ready-made tests to substitute for purpose-designed measures. It certainly happens when, as is common, no objectives have ever been stated. This is not semantic quibbling. Consider the normal British driving test, for instance. It is a legitimate test of something, to be sure, but not a specific measure of driving performance in any rigorous sense. Its objective is to identify potentially dangerous drivers (counter-productive promotional campaigns) rather than to measure degree of ability at the wheel.

Two case histories published formally by famous advertising agencies illustrate this point. One concludes with the bold assertion that an advertising campaign for a breakfast cereal was 'performing consistently with the defined objectives', which were: 'to provide advertising that is interesting/amusing [sic] to children; to communicate to children that Brand C are the most exciting/best tasting [sic] breakfast cereal; to reassure mothers that Brand C are a nourishing breakfast cereal for their children.' The implied criteria are thus interest, entertainment, communication and reassurance. Effectiveness was in fact measured in terms of a quite unrelated yardstick: 'sales started to increase . . . the findings would suggest that advertising has made a significant contribution to the brand's volume growth.' Disregarding the weasel-wording, we can accept that an improvement in sales volume does satisfy an implicit general objective of any advertising campaign, though

we would have to reserve judgement on the difficult issue of causation. But there is no evidence whatever that entertainment, communication or reassurance were achieved.

The second case history sets out objectives equally explicitly by saying 'the advertising had to achieve three things: be quite clear about what Brand D really is; confirm very modern user imagery; confirm the Brand D heritage'. The second two criteria are admittedly harder to define in this example, but measurement would certainly be expected to relate to communication, imagery and attitudes with respect to the newly launched yellow-fat spread. In fact, the claimed proof of effectiveness again moved the goalposts: 'within days, sales started to move up . . . within a month, ex-factory shipments were more than 60% above previous levels . . . housewives do understand more clearly what Brand D is . . . and they use it for the whole family, not just slimmers.' The first two achievements are so short-run as to be meaningless in the context of a launch and could obviously be attributable to many variables other than advertising. The third does demonstrate achievement of one implied criterion but is significantly qualified. The last one introduces a completely new criterion, presumably relating to competitive comparisons.

In short, *surrogate* tests are being substituted in practice. Investigation of further case histories would soon lead to the conclusion that they are typically based on a common explanation of how advertising is thought to work, which could equally easily be applied to any other ingredient of the promotional mix. It is unlikely that practitioners themselves are consciously aware that this is happening. As a guide to best practice from the Institute of Practitioners in Advertising puts it, they 'may follow very varied mental models but they too seldom articulate them' (Broadbent, 1995, p. 17).

This particular model is the 'hierarchy of effects', which first appeared in the literature more than seventy years ago. A textbook by a famous American market researcher of the day included a conceptual framework for testing the effectiveness of advertisements, which argued that 'to be effective, an advertisement must be . . . seen, read, believed, remembered, and acted upon' (Starch, 1923). That initiative was closely followed by another for the effective delivery of a sales pitch, which should gain attention, generate interest, create desire and precipitate action (Strong, 1925). Under an acronym derived from the initials of those four required responses, AIDA, it was soon transferred to the formulation of advertising strategy, and has remained popular ever since.

After a considerable interval, the generic description 'hierarchy of effects' was coined by Lavidge and Steiner (1961) to describe a six-step 'model for predictive measurement of advertising effectiveness'. In the same year, a five-step framework for 'defining advertising goals for measured advertising results' was proposed by the Association of National Advertisers in New York (Colley, 1962). It too became known by an acronym, this time derived from the description rather than the steps: 'Dagmar'. The only further progress in the subsequent three decades has been a relatively little noticed article with the telling subtitle 'keeping the hierarchy concept alive' (Preston and Thorson, 1984).

Table 17.5 proposes a consolidation of these five paradigms, and could accommodate other family members not reported here. The left-hand column uses terms from the originals to define the response required from the audience for the initiative to be effective. The right-hand column relates each response to the generic cognitive-affective-conative (C-A-C) pattern of response to stimuli other than advertisements. Since cognitive responses are the outcome of thinking about what is happening, affective responses result from an emotional reaction to the stimulus, and conative responses involve consequent actions, this model is popularly summed up as think-feel-do.

The hierarchy-of-effects hypothesis provides an intuitively reasonable *description* of what is happening, but offers no *explanation* of how or why. It has furthermore been subjected to continuous theoretical criticism over the past thirty years, beginning with a widely reported evaluation of Lavidge and Steiner's model by Palda (1966), who doubted that the accomplishment of one step necessarily increased the probability of the next and called into question their very sequence. Others subsequently demonstrated the existence of do-feel-think, think-do-feel and do-think-feel variations. The role of promotion would obviously be rather different in each case, and therefore the criteria of effectiveness.

One might expect that these theoretical shortcomings would by now have invalidated the hierarchy of effects as a framework for the measurement of effectiveness, but all the evidence is that they have not. Therefore, we have to recognize that AIDA and its kin will remain the implicit conceptual underpinning of present-day practice until marketing academics are able to produce a better model which practitioners can understand and are willing to use. Evidence that this state of affairs is no closer than it ever has been is to be found in two authoritative reviews commissioned by the Advertising Association (McDonald, 1992; Frantzen, 1994). If progress towards that better model is in fact made within the shelf life of this edition of *The Marketing Book*, the impetus is likely to have originated in the 'planning' discipline within advertising agencies.

The context of promotional practice

Practitioners of any discipline should want to understand the economic, social and cultural context within which they operate. Those with responsibility for deployment of the promotional mix *need* to, for theirs is an overtly persuasive and very public activity. Therefore, we conclude this chapter by examining the relevant attitudes of policy formers and opinion leaders in Britain, reporting British public opinion and outlining the domestic regulatory system. Inevitably, the focus will be on advertising rather than the less high-profile elements of the promotional mix.

To place these external views in a proper

Table 17.5 The hierarchy-of-effects model of promotion	
Effectiveness criterion:	*C-A-C equivalent:*
Action	Do
Conviction	Feel
Sympathy	Feel
Comprehension	Think
Interest	Think
Attention	Think

context, it will help to bear in mind these relevant characteristics of the social and economic environment in which contemporary advertising takes place:

- A highly developed consumer economy, in which advertising bridges the gap between producers and consumers.
- Well-educated and fairly sophisticated consumers.
- Articulate consumer pressure-groups.
- A highly sophisticated promotional business.
- Consumer-protection legislation.
- Formal statutory control over broadcast advertising.
- Self-regulatory codes of practice relating to non-broadcast advertising, sales promotion and direct marketing.

Academics, politicians and media commentators feature prominently in the ranks of those who hold generally negative views about the ingredients of the marketing mix. Since many studied economics in the course of their higher education, that is typically the basis of their arguments. As an occasional paper from the Advertising Association comments:

The normal progression is for someone to suggest the use of advertising exercises an unhealthy influence on some desirable economic function, whereupon defenders cast doubt upon the logic and/or the evidence of the original argument. This usually develops into an increasingly esoteric debate, whose details can be understood by hardly anybody (Lind, 1998: p. 18).

An interested outsider can detect three dominant pairs of argument and counter-argument, as follows:

Proposition 1:	A *cost* that drives up prices.
Counter 1:	Stimulates *demand*, holds prices in check.
Proposition 2:	Sets up *barriers to entry* and thereby reduces consumer choice.
Counter 2:	Facilitates *competition* and thereby creates choice.
Proposition 3:	Appeals to *emotion not reason*.
Counter 3:	Delivers welcome *added values*.

With respect to propositions 1 and 2, it is highly arbitrary to single out advertising as the culprit. As White (1980) put it: 'When economists say that customers are paying for the advertising when they buy the product, they are guilty of a false analysis – unless they also say that the customer is paying for the sales forces, the delivery vans, the warehouses and the order clerks.'

Likewise, it is not typically promotion that monopolists use to erect barriers against competitors but rather price wars and saturation of distribution channels. Furthermore, effective advertising is not a matter of simply quantity: quality counts heavily when consumers are sophisticated and know how to play the game.

White puts it well again: 'In fact, the possibility open to new challengers of using media advertising, with its rapid coverage of mass audiences, tends to make monopolies more rather than less vulnerable to attack'. The Cola wars of the 1980s bear this out. PepsiCo used heavy advertising to attack Coke's market dominance and succeeded in increasing its share by 20 per cent. Coca-Cola retaliated not by counter-advertising but by starting a price war.

Proposition 3 presupposes that consumers should want reasons and hard facts, not emotional involvement or intangible satisfactions. It is a reflection of the long-standing economic model of 'rational man'. Yet it was an economist who remarked more than 40 years ago: 'There is tremendous spiritual satisfaction in buying a trusted brand of cocoa – not a shovelful of brown powder of uncertain origin.' Note the word 'trusted': it expresses the concept of an intangible added value. The danger of the economists' line of argument is that it denies legitimate subjective satisfactions. Shoppers do not need to buy the best if the second- or third-best pleases them more. Nor must they always buy the most economical if they trust the promoted brand more. That is why supermarket shoppers often buy Cadbury's drinking chocolate instead of Safeway's own brand, of course. Readers keen to pursue the economic case for and against advertising will find an excellent review in Lind (1998: pp. 10–33).

Not only economists have strong views about promotion; it is regularly subject to cultural and ethical criticism. Such commentators are generally journalists, politicians, consumerists and academics. Three main strands are discernible in their objections:

Proposition 1: Can control consumption behaviour.
Proposition 2: Can debase cultural values.
Proposition 3: Can control the media.

The first of these rests on the implicit belief that relatively powerful advertisers can manipulate relatively powerless audiences, which in turn hinges on the 'mad scientist' view of advertising people. Those who take this view normally cite the immensely influential book, *The Hidden Persuaders*, first published in 1957 and re-issued with an added introduction and epilogue

in 1981 (Packard, 1991). They do not always mention that the author was a crusading journalist who wrote a series of trenchant critiques of American business, or that the cases he reports all took place over forty years ago, when times were distinctly different.

If advertising people do have special powers, whether based on psychological principles as Packard suggests or derived from whatever else, these remain the most closely guarded of secrets. Even those who work in the business cannot explain what they are.

It is, furthermore, an uncomfortably contradictory fact that, on average, four in every five new products fail in the marketplace despite introductory advertising. Either the hidden persuaders are very bad at making use of their special powers or modern audiences are better than the critics think at resisting the promotional hype.

Proposition 2 has been regularly heard from academics and media commentators over the years. An author then at Bristol University, for example, asserted that 'Advertising is a main voice in our culture, and what it says is largely malignant' (Inglis, 1972). Equally uncompromising statements are to be found in a seminal textbook by an academic turned television producer (Williamson, 1978), still regularly quoted twenty years on.

Politicians hostile to advertising are normally of the left. This is a fact of political life, not a value judgement, and there is little sense in shying away from the issue when advertising practitioners need to be vitally interested in it. In the early 1970s, an opposition Green Paper propounded the ideological thesis that 'advertising tends to encourage gross materialism and dissatisfaction' (Labour Party, 1972). By the end of the decade, the Secretary of State for Prices and Consumer Protection had entered the lion's den at an Advertising Association annual conference to announce the Labour government's plans for strongly increased formal regulation of advertising. In March 1986, the Party's consumer charter confirmed the aim of a future government to introduce a statutory code of advertising practice. From the practitioners' point of view, this is alarming sabre-rattling.

Such critics seem to detect an organized conspiracy to corrupt society, masterminded on Madison Avenue or in Covent Garden. Supporters of advertising respond that advertisements in fact hold a mirror up to our culture, rather than shaping it, and that the audiences concerned are fully capable of decoding them in their own way and forming their own value judgements. They argue that the critics' view of popular culture, including contemporary advertising, is condescending to the populace.

The third proposition, potential control of the media, is, of course, based on the fact that the press, ITV and independent local radio are all subsidized to a greater or lesser extent by advertising revenue. It is therefore presumed that they will be unwilling to bite the hand that feeds them if it deserves to be bitten in the public interest. There is no evidence that any British advertiser has ever managed to exert such influence; indeed, news has occasionally been made by failed attempts. Nevertheless, observers were concerned that the introduction of programme sponsorship might provide companies with sufficient power to influence editorial comment. In response, the statutory bodies which control commercial broadcasting in Britain have both amended their codes of practice relating to advertising (Independent Television Commission, 1997; Radio Authority, 1997).

Media owners themselves counter-argue that advertising revenue guarantees editorial freedom. Without it, they would need either to charge prices for the product that would guarantee its demise or to ask for a government subsidy. The second solution raises, they point out, the equally dangerous possibility of political control, a familiar obstacle to reporting matters of public concern in too many other countries.

What is not clear about the non-economic criticisms of advertising described is why the critics should assume the worst possible case. There is a strong hint of the polemic in their approach to the issues, which seems unneces-sary in the face of a typically British middle-of-the-road approach to the business of producing advertisements. This not to deny that promotion of all kinds is sometimes misleading, vulgar, full of innuendo or aesthetically disastrous. However, any practitioner consciously setting out to inflict such material on the audience must first deliberately ignore such well established regulations as the British Codes of Advertising and Sales Promotion, the ITC Code of Advertising Standards and Practice, The Radio Authority Advertising and Sponsorship Code, or the Direct Marketing Association Code of Practice, and secondly face up to the consequences. For further details of these and other forms of control against malpractice, see Baker (1998) under 'advertising control', 'direct mail' and 'sales promotion'. As for manipulation: if the average Western consumer is not in fact sophisticated enough to cope with advertising, then the right counter-measure is *consumer education* rather than more constraints. If we believe people can be taught to recognize and resist political indoctrination, there is no reason to suppose education cannot do the same where promotional initiatives are concerned.

Readers interested in pursuing socio-cultural arguments for and against advertising will find an excellent review in Lind (1998: pp. 34–65) and an absorbing textbook-length treatment in Fowles (1996).

Having considered the views of professional observers, we turn now to the attitudes of the ordinary citizens at whom most promotional initiatives are directed. The Advertising Association has commissioned nine large-scale replicated surveys of public opinion since 1961. In the most recent of these, only 5 per cent of the sample chose advertising from a list of a dozen general social topics as one they 'talked most about with their friends'; 3 per cent said they 'felt strongly' about it, and the same proportion felt something should actually be done about it.

All respondents were nevertheless asked to express an opinion about the abstract concept, advertising, by means of a five-point scale: approve a lot or a little, disapprove a lot or a little, or don't know. Fewer than one in six (16 per cent) took the opportunity to pass negative judgement. They were then invited to express their feelings about the concrete manifestations of the abstract concept, advertisements, on a five-point scale offering the option to like or quite like, dislike or not really like, or be indifferent. Less than a fifth of the sample (18 per cent) answered negatively about television commercials, roughly one in six (12 per cent) about posters and one in ten about press advertisements. The survey report concludes that ordinary people in Britain overwhelmingly accept the existence of an advertising industry and enjoy its output. Nevertheless, advertisers 'should never become complacent about public attitudes . . . advertising is far too much in the public eye (and in its ears) for the industry to let its standards fall' (Advertising Association, 1996: p. 2).

Though disapprovers are a minority, it would be interesting to know their reasons. Surprisingly, the Advertising Association has not asked that question since 1976, at which time the answer was broadly that advertising drives up prices, is misleading, and creates false needs. Another obvious reason for negative opinion is that there is simply too much of it. In 1983, *Which?* magazine surveyed 1300 subscribers, presumably more likely than average to have critical views of advertising, and found that: 53 per cent thought the volume of advertising they noticed was 'about right'; 36 felt there 'should be less'; 11 per cent believed there should be none at all. There has been no increase in the 'minutage' permitted on television or in the number of poster sites around the country since then, so it could be expected that contemporary opinion will be little different.

It is plain that, although advertising affects almost everybody's daily life, it is not something that most find at all salient. Some would argue that they should. Furthermore, the overwhelming majority give it a vote of approval when their attention is directed to the subject, and confess willingly to liking the advertisements they encounter in all media. Fewer than half think

they are subjected to too much advertising. We may suspect that the answers would be less favourable if the questioning were about sales promotion or direct marketing, but corresponding figures are hard to find.

Thus, the environment within which British practitioners ply their trade today is undoubtedly benevolent, whatever the critics may say. One can only repeat the Advertising Association's warning not to relax the high standards of quality and self-discipline which have allowed such a positive atmosphere to be maintained for more than thirty years.

References

Account Planning Group (1993, 1995, 1997) *Creative Planning > Outstanding Advertising*, volumes 1 to 3, The Account Planning Group, London.

Advertising Association (1996) *Public Attitudes to Advertising 1996*, The Advertising Association, December, London.

Advertising Association (1997) *Marketing Pocket Book*, NTC Publications, Henley-on-Thames.

Advertising Association (1998) *Marketing Pocket Book 1999*, NTC Publications, Henley-on-Thames.

Advertising Association (1998) *Making Sense of Advertising*, The Economics Committee of The Advertising Association, April, London.

Advertising Standards Authority (1997) *The British Codes of Advertising and Sales Promotion*, The Advertising Standards Authority, February, London.

Baker, M. J. (ed.) (1998) *Macmillan Dictionary of Marketing and Advertising*, 3rd edn, Macmillan, London.

Belch, G. and Belch, M. (1998) *Advertising and Promotion: an Integrated Marketing Communications Perspective*, McGraw-Hill, New York.

Brierley, S. (1995) *The Advertising Handbook*, Routledge, London.

Briggs, M. (1993) Why Ad Agencies Must Change, *Admap*, January, p. 22.

Broadbent, S. (1989) *The Advertising Budget*, NTC

Publications and Institute of Practitioners in Advertising, London.

Broadbent, S. (1995) *Best Practice in Campaign Evaluation*, Institute of Practitioners in Advertising, London.

Broadbent, S. (1997) *Accountable Advertising*, Admap Publications, Henley-on-Thames.

Broadbent, S. and Jacobs, B. (1984) *Spending Advertising Money*, 4th edn, Business Books, London.

Butterfield, L. (ed.) (1997) *Excellence in Advertising: The IPA Guide to Best Practice*, Butterworth–Heinemann, Oxford.

Colley, R. H. (1962) Squeezing the Waste out of Advertising, *Harvard Business Review*, **40**, September/October, 76–88.

Cooper, A. (ed.) (1997) *How to Plan Advertising*, 2nd edn, Cassell in association with The Account Planning Group, London.

Crosier, K. and Abbott, J. (1996) Net Benefits: Sizing up a Marketing Communications Vehicle for the Twenty-First Century, *Proceedings of the First International Conference on Corporate and Marketing Communications*, Keele University, April.

Dhalla, N. K. (1997) How to Set Advertising Budgets, *Journal of Advertising Research*, **17**, October, p. 11.

European Association of Advertising Agencies (1994) *Client/Advertising Agency Partnerships in the New Europe*, NTC Publications, Henley-on-Thames.

Evans, R. (1988) *Production and Creativity in Advertising*, Pitman, London.

Fowles, J. (1996) *Advertising and Popular Culture*, Sage Publications, Thousand Oaks, California.

Frantzen, G. (1994) *Advertising Effectiveness: Findings from Empirical Research*, NTC Publications, Henley-on-Thames.

Independent Television Commission (1996/7) *The ITC Code of Advertising Standards and Practice*, and *The ITC Code of Programme Sponsorship*, The Independent Television Commission, London, Summer 1997 and Spring 1997 respectively.

Inglis, F. (1972) *The Imagery of Power*, Heinemann, London.

Institute of Practitioners in Advertising (1981–97) *Advertising Works*, volumes 1 to 9, NTC Publications, Henley-on-Thames.

Kitchen, P. J. (ed.) (1998) *Marketing Communications: Principles and Practice*, International Thompson Business Press, London.

Labour Party (1972) *Opposition Green Paper: Advertising*, Labour Party, London.

Lavidge, R. C. and Steiner, G. A. (1961) A Model for Predictive Measurements of Advertising Effectiveness, *Journal of Marketing*, **25**, October, 59–62.

Lind, H. (ed.) (1998) *Making Sense of Advertising*, Economics Committee of the Advertising Association, London.

McDonald, C. (1992) *How Advertising Works: A Review of Current Thinking*, NTC Publications, Henley-on-Thames.

Mayle, P. (1990) *Up the Agency*, Pan, London.

Packard, V. (1991) *The Hidden Persuaders*, Penguin, London.

Palda, K. S. (1966) The Hypothesis of a Hierarchy of Effects: A Partial Evaluation, *Journal of Marketing Research*, **3**, February, 13–24.

Piercy, N. (1987) Advertising Budgeting: Process and Structure as Explanatory Variables, *Journal of Advertising*, **16**(2), 59–65,

Preston, I. L. and Thorson, E. (1984) The Expanded Association Model: Keeping the Hierarchy Concept Alive, *Journal of Advertising Research*, **24**(1), February/March, 59–65.

Radio Authority (1997) *The Radio Authority Advertising and Sponsorship Code*, The Radio Authority, March, London.

Rees, R. D. (1977) *Advertising Budgeting and Appraisal in Practice: Research Study No. 11*, The Advertising Association, London.

Smith, P. R. (1993) *Marketing Communications: An Integrated Approach*, Kogan Page, London.

Stapleton, J. and Thomas, M. J. (1998) *How to Prepare a Marketing Plan: A Guide to Reaching the Consumer Market*, 5th edn, Gower, Aldershot, Chapter 9.

Starch, D. (1923) *Principles of Marketing*, A. W. Shaw, Chicago.

Strong, E. K. (1925) *The Psychology of Selling*, McGraw-Hill, New York.

Synodinos, N. E., Keown, C. F. and Jacobs, L. W. (1989) Transnational Advertising Practice: A Survey of Leading Brand Advertisers in Fifteen Countries, *Journal of Advertising Research,* **29**(2), April/May, 43–50.

White, R. (1993) *Advertising: What It Is and How to Do It,* 3rd edn, McGraw-Hill, New York.

Wilmshurst, J. (1993) *Below-the-Line Promotion,* Butterworth–Heinemann, Oxford.

Williamson, J. (1978) *Decoding Advertisements: Ideology and Meaning in Advertising,* Marion Boyars.

CHAPTER 18

Sales promotion

SUE and KEN PEATTIE

Introduction

In 1697 Jonathon Holder, a London haberdasher, decided to offer customers spending over a guinea in his shop a free stock and price list. His pioneering decision to offer his customers 'something extra' was not universally welcomed. The newspapers of the day condemned this sales promotion as *'a dangerous innovation'* and one which, *'would be destructive to trade, if shopkeepers lavished so much of their capital on printing useless bills'*. Over three hundred years later trade still flourishes, and so do sales promotions, which now account for more 'capital' than any element of marketing communications except selling. Despite sales promotions' growing importance, something of the scepticism that Mr Holder encountered lives on. In the study and practice of marketing, sales promotion has always been overshadowed by the more glamorous world of advertising. This situation is now changing, with sales promotion beginning to attract the academic study and practitioner scrutiny that its cost and increasingly strategic role surely demands. Between 1965 and 1983 only about 40 academic studies of sales promotion were published (Blattberg and Neslin, 1990), compared to over 200 published between the mid-1980s and mid-1990s (Chandon, 1995).

Sales promotion defined

Sales promotion is frequently defined as marketing communications which is not advertising, selling or public relations (see Chapter 12). Unfortunately, many definitions explaining what this includes are flawed, by failing to embrace all of the marketing tools regarded as sales promotions in practice. We can define sales promotions as 'marketing activities usually specific to a time period, place or customer group, which encourage a direct response from consumers or marketing intermediaries, through the offer of additional benefits.'

The three key elements of this definition are that sales promotions are:

1   **Non-standard.** Promotions are usually temporary, and may be limited to certain customer groups (such as airline frequent flyer schemes) or specific to a particular distribution channel (as in 'tailor-made' promotions involving a producer and a single retailer).

2   **Response orientated.** Promotions seek a direct response from customers, or those who deal with customers on the producer's behalf (see Figure 18.1). The direct response sought is not necessarily a sale. Promotions may encourage consumers to send for a brochure, visit a dealer or consume a sample. The ultimate aim is always sales, but this is true of all marketing activity.

3   **Benefit orientated.** Promotions offer their targets additional benefits, beyond the 'standard' marketing mix. The enhanced mix could include extra product, a reduced price or an added item, service or opportunity.

The everyday vocabulary of marketing promotions is full of inconsistencies. For simplicity and brevity, the word 'promotion' will be used in this chapter to refer to a sales promotion, rather than its broader context of marketing promotion.

Understanding sales promotion – a tale of price and prejudice

Sales promotion is a catch-all term covering a multiplicity of marketing activities. In the past, our understanding of promotions has been hampered by a tendency to bundle all the different types together for study and discussion (Peattie and Peattie, 1993). Coupons and discounts are among the most widely used promotions, and research evidence and practical experience from such price-base promotions dominates the literature. This has encouraged:

•   A limited view of what promotions can achieve.
•   An overly rational–economic view of their effects on consumers.

•   A tactical and short-term view of promotion, since economic incentives are only effective while they are on offer.
•   A negative perception about the impact that promotions may have on brands and brand positioning.

All of these negative perceptions of sales promotion, and more, were encapsulated in Jones' (1990) *Harvard Business Review* article 'The Double Jeopardy of Sales Promotion'. He concluded that companies, faced with saturated markets, have been misguidedly channelling money away from above-the-line advertising and 'fighting with fury for market share; using promotions (generally a high cost activity) as the main tactical weapon.'

Such indictments, published in leading journals, have helped to prejudice many management academics and some practitioners against promotions. However it is worth remembering that many of the most outspoken critics (Jones included) are former top advertising practitioners. It is also worth noting that much of the criticism, including that by Jones, is based on an assumption that 'in most circumstances, promotions mean price reductions'.

The reality is that sales promotions need to be understood for what they are – a diverse and versatile marketing toolkit, in which many of the tools

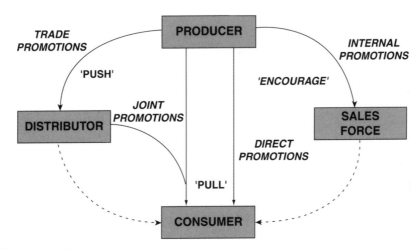

Figure 18.1   Sales promotion targets

emphasize creativity over simple economics. The different promotional tools vary in terms of:

1   **Their targets** (see Figure 18.1). 'Push' promotions target marketing intermediaries, supporting the selling effort to get products onto retailers' shelves; while 'pull' promotions target consumers and complement advertising in persuading them to pick products off the shelves again.

2   **Type of benefits offered.** One fundamental distinction is between value increasing and value adding promotions. Value increasing promotions alter the product/price equation by increasing the product quantity or quality, or decreasing its price. Value adding promotions leave the basic product and price intact, and offer something different in terms of premiums (free or self-liquidating), information or opportunities. The benefits can be instant (scratch-and-win competitions), delayed (postal premiums) or cumulative (loyalty programmes).

3   **Product/market suitability.** While canned beers favour '13% extra free' offers, or on-pack competitions and coupons, unpackaged draft beers require special price evenings,

gamecard competitions and promotional merchandise catalogues. Internationally, promotions vary in their popularity and suitability. Average annual coupon redemptions per household run at 81 in the USA, 16 in the UK, 1.5 in Spain (source: NCH Promotional Surveys) and zero in Germany where they are illegal. In Japan redeeming coupons at point-of-sale is considered embarrassing, and so competitions are the most popular promotional tool.

4   **Consumer appeal.** Consumers like extra benefits. A 1986 Harris/Marketing Week poll revealed that over 60 per cent of Britons had responded to a promotion during the previous month. However, different types of promotion appeal to different people. Research by Gallup and numerous sales promotions agencies suggests that our age, sex, nationality, outlook, socio-economic grouping and ethnic origin can all influence which promotions we prefer.

5   **Marketing capabilities.** Free samples are obviously useful for encouraging product trial, while a prize draw can provide a mailing list for future promotions.

6   **Implementation priorities.** While printing

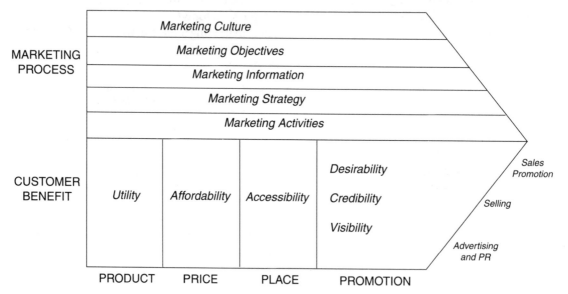

Figure 18.2   Satisfaction chain

security is important for gamecards, accurate redemption forecasting is vital for coupons and giveaways, and anticipating competitor reaction is important in price promotions.

Space constraints prevent a detailed discussion of each technique, but Table 18.1. provides examples of, and notes on, some of the most popular forms of consumer promotions.

Sales promotion is perhaps the most widely misunderstood element of the marketing mix. One frequently overlooked point about promotions, particularly value increasing ones, is that they are not so much a distinct element of the marketing mix, as a customization of another mix element. Each mix element offers different benefits to customers (see Figure 18.2). To increase the desirability of the total product offering, sales promotions can:

- Enhance the product offering's utility by enhancing quality, or adding extra tangible benefits.
- Improve affordability by increasing the quantity offered, decreasing the price or easing the payment terms.
- Improve accessibility by gaining access to distribution channels and through extras such as free delivery.
- Support the advertising, sales and PR effort to boost the product's visibility and credibility through eye-catching and newsworthy promotional materials, and by creating subjects for advertising campaigns or discussions with customers.

The sales promotions planning process

Figure 18.3 illustrates a somewhat idealized view of the steps involved in an effectively planned promotion. Amidst the competitive cut and thrust of marketing reality, the practical execution will frequently involve a less orderly decision-making process. However, the model's underlying message of the importance of

consistency between any promotion and the overall marketing and marketing communications effort holds good however tactical a particular promotion might be (for further details on the management of trade and consumer promotions see Shimp, 1997). This planning process has many similarities to advertising campaigns, including:

- External agencies that frequently play an important role in planning and implementation.
- A choice of media; promotions can be delivered on-pack or in-store, via direct mail, or in printed media including newspapers and magazines, catalogues and other promotional literature.
- A peculiar jargon, which can be decoded using the Macmillan Dictionary of Marketing and Advertising (Baker, 1998).
- Codes of practice, regulatory bodies and complex legal requirements which influence their development. Promotions are bound by the same laws as advertising, and also by more specific legislation such as the Lotteries and Amusements Act 1976, or the Price Marking (Bargain Offers) Order 1979 (for full details see Circus, 1989).

The major differences in planning for advertising and promotions occur during campaign objective setting and evaluation. In terms of objective setting, promotions present a more complex set of possible alternatives than advertising. In addition to encouraging sales or product trial, they can pursue a wide range of other strategic and tactical objectives including:

- Creating awareness or interest.
- Assisting in the launch of a new brand or the reinvigoration of a mature one.
- Overshadowing a competitor's promotional or other activities.
- Deflecting attention away from price competition.
- Reinforcing advertising themes.

Table 18.1 Major forms of consumer promotions

Promotion	Key user sectors	Notes	Examples
Discount Pricing & Sales	FMCG firms, Retailers	Additional volume must compensate for lost revenue. Can spark price wars. Generally a defensive move.	January sales. Retailer campaigns, e.g. Tesco's "Checkout" & "Asda Price".
Money-off Coupons	FMCG, Grocery retailers	Redemption rates determine costs. Requires earlier cooperation. Allows some differential pricing	Mattel Inc's 1988 toy marketing campaign involved 582 million coupons.
Refunds	FMCG, Mortgages, Consumer durables	Avoids problems of reference price changes. Non-redemptions reduce costs compared to discounts	The "More Money With Sony" direct mail cashback offer. Trade in allowances. "Cash-back" mortgage offers.
Samples	Foods, Toiletries, Computer software	Expensive. Encourages trial. Effectiveness hard to measure. Can generate market research	Agree shampoo became No.1 in the US market in 6 months by using 31 million samples.
Payment Terms	Consumer durables, Retailers	Reduces real cost rather than price. Useful for seasonal demand smoothing.	PC vendors offering 6 to 12 months interest-free credit on new PC purchases.
Multipacks & Multibuys	Packaged goods, Retailers	Best for small, high purchase frequency items.	Boots "3 for the price of 2" campaign. Safeway's "Multisave".
Special Features	Consumer durables	Often packaged as a "special" or "limited" edition.	Audi's giveaway of a free catalytic converter.
Quantity Increases	Packaged foods, canned and bottled drinks	Relies on ability to customise packaging processes.	Canned beers feature regular 500 ml for the price of 400 ml offers.
In-pack Premiums	Packaged goods	Items placed in foodstuffs needs care regarding food safety	Ovaltine's "Treasure Hunt" coin-in-every-tin promotion. Tetley Tea Folk collectable figurines boosted 1996 market share by 2%.
In-mail Premiums	Packaged goods	Usually relies on handling houses for redemption	Merchandise such as the Kodak Gold Collection or Pepsi "Stuff".
Piggy-back Premiums	Packaged goods	Usually joint promotions. Can generate complementary sales and encourage product trial	"Free Gillette GII with Kleenex For Men" gained Gillette 100,000 trials & KFM 13% extra sales.

Competitions	Packaged goods, Retailers	Good for creating interest and reinforcing ad campaigns. Needs care with legalities	McDonalds $ 40 M Treasure Hunt. Heinz's "Win a Car a Day for 100 Days" campaign.
Information	Industrial firms, Consumer durables Services	Important for reducing perceived risk. Provides consumer benefits of convenience and saved time.	Product catalogues. Holiday brochures. Investment prospectuses. CD-Rom catalogues.
Valued Packaging	Retailers, FMCG Firms.	Packaging can be useful in itself, or can provide a game, activity, recipe or other information	Persil's EcoBox offer. Sony's tape ten pack in a free cassette case offer. 1995-1996 Savoy Brands International distributed over 700 million collectable milkcaps in 9 Latin American countries.
Loyalty Cards	Retailers	Card applications and usage can be linked to EPOS information for database marketing and targeted promotion opportunities. Some concerns about level of loyalty achieved.	Tesco's Club Card, Safeway's ABC Card, Boots Advantage Card.
Gift Coupons	Petrol retailers, Draft beers	Useful for non-packaged goods. Helps encourage repeat purchases.	Gift collections from BP, Esso, Shell and Texaco. Air miles.
Product trial	Consumer durables	Often twinned with a competition. Needs close sales support.	200 000 Apple Macs were "home tested", 40% led to sales.
Guarantees	Consumer durables, Retailers	"Pricebeat" promises often back up sales to reduce perceived risk.	Safeway's " Refund & Replace" offer.
Buyback offers	Consumer durables	Costs depend upon redemption rates. Overedemption can be insured against.	Sanyo's 1988 ten year buyback pledge boosted TV sales by 62%.
Clubs	Airlines & hotels, Children's products	Useful for generating customer loyalty.	Marriott Hotels' "Honoured Guest" scheme. The Halifax's "Little Xtra" children's club.

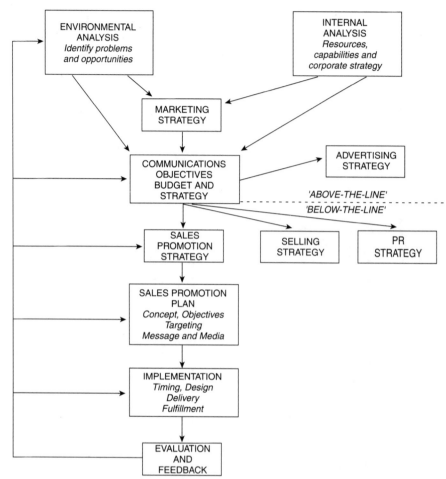

Figure 18.3   The sales promotion planning process

- Developing a relationship with customers.
- Gathering consumer information.

Trade promotions can aim to:

- Encourage or reward sales efforts from inter-mediaries.
- Increase or maintain floor or shelf space for products.
- Encourage stocking up by intermediaries.
- Gain support for special displays or other pro-motional activities.
- Gain access to new sales outlets.
- Insulate intermediaries from temporary sales downturns or pressure on margins.

- Reinforce communication to, or education of, intermediaries.

In terms of measurability the direct nature of the consumer response makes their short-term effects easier to measure accurately than those for advertising, particularly with the advent of information from electronic point of sale (EPOS) systems. In recent years Heinz have run competitions offering prizes worth six fig-ures. These were backed up by a sophisticated monitoring system using feedback-scratch cards, to analyse the effects on behaviour and buying patterns among participants. With 60 per cent of 30 000 surveyed participants to three competitions returning cards, Heinz have built up an accurate picture of the effect that such promotions can have, and their effectiveness when used through different grocery chains. One drawback of the measurability that direct responses allow, is that the less measurable indirect responses relating to brand awareness or image tend to be overlooked.

This chapter aims to emphasize the differences between promotions and advertising, which are perhaps best summed up by Hugh Davidson (1975) as follows:

In general the purpose of advertising is to improve attitudes towards a brand, while the object of promotion is to translate favourable attitudes into actual purchase. Advertising cannot close a sale because its impact is too far from the point of purchase, but promotion can and does.

The comparative ability of promotions to close sales reflects three key differences to advertising, each of which form a theme for the rest of this chapter:

- Communication capabilities.
- Relationship building capabilities.
- Flexibility and manageability.

Sales promotion and advertising – the line and the pendulum

Communications budgets are often spoken of as being invested 'above-the-line' and 'below-the-line'. This 'line' originally denoted whether or not communications efforts were channelled through advertising agencies (see Figure 18.3). With sales and PR often classified as separate functions, 'below-the-line' has become synonymous with sales promotions. The existence of this conceptual divide casts advertising and sales promotion in the role of rivals for the biggest share of a company's marketing communications budget.

During the 1980s there was a gradual shift in marketing communications emphasis and expenditure away from traditional 'brand sell' advertising and towards sales promotion. This shift of emphasis reflects growing doubts about the cost effectiveness of advertising in the face of rising prices and increased advertising 'clutter'. Between 1983 and 1987 the revenue produced by a given level of advertising dropped by almost 20 per cent (source: *Financial World*, 3/11/87). Increasing consumer hostility towards advertising has fuelled these doubts. A 1993 survey of 1000 UK adults by *Marketing Week* and *The Human Factor* indicated that nearly half of the population claim (perhaps rather optimistically) to be 'advertising immune' and over one third felt that advertising was 'a bad influence on society'. The advent of videos and remote controls which allow adverts to be 'zapped' has also eroded television advertisers' confidence in their ability to reach their target audience.

Over time, the emphasis placed on advertising and promotions within markets and firms often resembles a pendulum swinging backwards and forwards across that imaginary line. Each time a blue chip company changes its marketing communication emphasis towards one side of the line, it is interpreted as the beginning of the end for the other. At the start of the 1990s the swing towards promotion was exemplified by Heinz, who in 1992 cut their US advertising budget and transferred $100 million into (mostly trade) promotions. The result was an immediate 7.3 per cent market share gain for Heinz ketchup alone, reversing a six month sales decline. By 1992 American packaged goods manufacturers were spending three times as much on consumer and trade promotions as on media advertising (Shimp, 1997). However, this proliferation of promotions led to concern about 'overkill', and the mid 1990s saw a swing back towards advertising in many markets. In 1996 Procter & Gamble signalled its desire to reduce its dependence on promotions by withdrawing couponing as an 'experiment' in three US cities. It was then forced to abandon the experiment four months early in the face of opposition from retailers and customers.

Nineteen-ninety-seven proved to be a difficult year for the advertising industry, in which it came under attack from the key brands that sustain it. Dominic Cadbury, Chairman of Cadbury

Table 18.2 Recent trends and expenditure in US sales promotions

Promotion type	1996 expenditure ($ billions)	Comments
Premium incentives	20.5	Split between business-to-business incentives ($7.5 bn), consumer premiums ($5.5 bn), travel ($6 bn) and gifts ($1 bn). Recent growth has been concentrated in travel and also in promotional phone cards which in only four years have become worth $500 m.
Point of purchase	12.6	Experienced 5% growth 1995/6. The largest user (tobacco products) faces a legislative ban. Key growth sector is sporting goods.
Ad specialities	9.5	Ad specialities refers to promotional items (logoed hats, T-shirts, pens, mousepads). Increased by 18%; key users are healthcare, financial services, computer firms. Trend towards upmarket suppliers, e.g. Fruit of the Loom T-shirts and Waterford crystal.
Couponing	6.4	Despite unfashionable image, 300 billion coupons reached 55 million US households. Trends towards shorter duration (3 months in 1996 compared to 10 months in 1980) and better targeting. Steady growth in machine distributed and 'paperless' coupons.
Speciality printing	5.6	Some major promotions (e.g. McDonald's Monopoly and Taco Bell's Star Wars game) led to strong growth in printing and distribution of game promotion pieces.
Sponsorships	5.4	Saw a 15% increase with ten sponsors paying $40 million each to sponsor both the Lillehammer and Atlanta games.
Promotional licensing	5.0	Continued steady growth with films like Batman & Robin, Hercules and Jurassic Park: The Lost World being linked into fast food, soft drinks, toys.
Product sampling	0.86	Not the most popular technique due to cost and logistical complexity. Still showed 11% growth and there is increasing diversity in methods and locations used to deliver samples to customers.
Interactive	0.82	Web sites now have banners offering games, coupon order forms, sample or catalogue requests. Cowles/Simba Information reported 147% growth in web based promotions in 1996.

Source: 1997 Annual Report of the US Promotion Industry

Schweppes, publicly rebuked marketers for their obsession with the 'froth' of advertising. Niall Fitzgerald, Chairman of Unilever stated that 'I do not find today's advertising agencies being much of a match for tomorrow's marketing opportunities.' Paul Polman, Vice President and General Manager of Procter & Gamble, the world's biggest advertiser, attacked the 47 per cent rise in TV advertising costs between 1992 and 1997 as 'unacceptable'. It was perhaps indicative that Saatchi and Saatchi, a brand synonymous with above-the-line activity, chose in 1997 to drop the word 'advertising' from its title as too limiting.

Debates about which side of the line is the wisest destination for marketing funds tend to be inconclusive. Advertising and sales promotion are both effective techniques, which work best as complementary components of a strategically planned and integrated communications campaign. The trend towards such integration and the blurring of that imaginary line, has led to:

- The proliferation of 'integrated communications' (or 'through the line') agencies handling campaigns on both sides of the line.
- An increase in 'spadspend', advertising expenditure to reinforce promotions. This accounts for an estimated 20 per cent of all advertising, with around $20 billion spent in 1996 on advertising about sales promotions in the USA (source: 1997 Annual Report of the Sales Promotion Industry). An example is the 'Good food costs less at Sainsbury', campaign highlighting promotional price offers.
- More themed promotions aiming to reinforce brand values and advertising messages. Heinz use of prizes in groups of 57 for their competitions is a simple example of brand theming.
- Some very novel approaches to managing the promotional effort. Sega invited the winners of a promotional competition to form a 'think tank' with brand managers and advertising agency account managers to help plan their future campaigns.

The growing importance of sales promotion

Measuring total sales promotion expenditure accurately is virtually impossible due to its fragmented nature and the diversity of definitions of what it should include. While some estimates include all direct mail costs, others exclude them. Yet direct mail is actually a medium for sales promotion (and advertising), with approximately 80 per cent of mailshots containing some form of promotion. Although we can only estimate the overall growth in promotions, evidence of it confronts us every time we enter a supermarket. Some of the components of total promotions expenditure can also be measured accurately, even if we cannot agree what constitutes the whole. For example, we know that in 1996 the UK saw just over 4 billion coupons distributed, with over 210 million redeemed (Source: NCH Promotional Services). Table 18.2 shows the figures for different elements of promotional expenditure for 1996 for the USA, the market that leads the world in the use of sales promotion.

There are seven key factors driving the growth in promotions:

1   **Increasing 'respectability',** partly through greater use by market leaders. The three largest distributors of coupons in the UK in 1996 were Heinz, Procter & Gamble and Unilever, and other major promoters include brands such as McDonald's, Coca-Cola, Pepsi, British Airways and Cadbury's. Credibility has also been boosted by increasing professionalism among sales promotion agencies.

2   **Increased impulse purchasing.** Point of Purchase Institute research data indicates that the majority of all purchase decisions are finalized in-store, and can therefore be influenced by in-store promotions.

3   **Shortening time horizons,** reflecting increasing market volatility and rivalry, and accelerating product life cycles (Shultz,

1987). These make the fast sales boost that promotions can offer attractive.

4 **Micro-marketing approaches,** in response to fragmenting markets, where promotions can provide more tailored and targeted communication than mass media.

5 **Declining brand loyalty** (see Chapter 5). Caused by widening choice, narrowing perceived differences between brands, and (in fast moving consumer goods, or FMCG, markets) retailer own brands becoming increasingly credible.

6 **A 'snowball' effect.** In some markets companies increasingly feel obliged to match rivals' sales promotion activity, or risk losing market share and competitive position (Lal, 1990).

7 **Affordability.** National mass media has become prohibitively expensive for many companies, particularly during recessionary squeezes on marketing budgets. Promotions allow national coverage at a lower cost, cost sharing with co-promoters, and can even be self-funding.

The recent rush to offer the consumer extra value has some potential drawbacks. Some critics suggest that overuse is training customers to buy products only on promotion, while others claim that promotional overkill is desensitizing consumers to their benefits. There is also the concern that emphasizing promotions leads marketers to focus on short term tactical issues instead of longer term strategy (Strang, 1976).

Consumers and sales promotion

There is general agreement that the marketing mix should be managed as an integrated whole. However, in practice the approach to managing the mix frequently follows the product, price, place, promotion sequence reflecting the perceived importance of each element in winning customers (see Figure 18.4). Once the product is specified, part of the total available market will be lost because the product features (such as

colour, size, flavour or facilities) are unsuitable for some potential customers. Further customers will be screened out who desire, but cannot quite afford the product, others will find the channels used inconvenient, and still more will remain untouched by the brand's advertising. The specification of the standard marketing mix therefore creates a customer group for whom the basic product offer is not ideal. These marginal consumers represent a prime target for promotions which, by offering additional benefits, may overcome their reservations about the brand to stimulate a purchase.

The targeting of such marginal consumers is standard practice in political marketing, but has often been neglected by commercial marketers. Cummins (1989) suggests that such non-core, low-loyalty consumers 'tend to be regarded by many companies with the distaste felt for the morally promiscuous'. In fact, the promotional battle to capture and convert marginal consumers can be an important part of marketing strategy because:

1 They are very lucrative. Extra sales from marginal consumers, minus variable costs, equals pure profit.

2 Those who like the brand may become loyal consumers.

3 Each marginal consumer won over deprives a competitor of a potentially lucrative sale.

The good news for marketers needing to win over additional consumers, is that promotions are a very effective persuader. In their research into coffee purchasing (a process one might expect to involve a high degree of personal taste and brand loyalty), Fraser and Hite (1990) concluded that

The vast majority of consumers are promotion responsive . . . Promotional incentives are effective in capturing brand choices, encouraging purchase acceleration and stimulating category demand. Many customers use and expect deals, and many more are induced to alter purchase behaviours by deal offers.

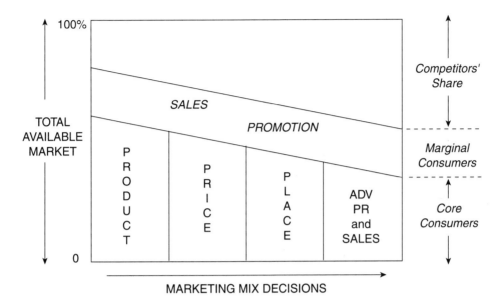

Figure 18.4   Promotions and the marketing mix: a sequential model

There are four main dimensions of consumer behaviour which determine people's response to promotions:

1   **Value consciousness.** Promotions enhance the value of the product offering. Price and product based promotions are most directly targeted at consumers' desire for value.
2   **Susceptibility to promotions.** Beyond simple economic rationality, people vary in their responsiveness to promotions (Lichtenstein et al., 1990). Many people enjoy the sense of being a 'smart shopper' which judicious use of promotions can provide. Susceptibility can vary in relation to the nature of the product being purchased (Bawa and Shoemaker, 1987) and also to the nature of the shopping trip and retail environment (Chandon, 1995).
3   **Brand loyalty.** Promotions can overcome consumer loyalty to a competitor's brand to encourage brand switching, or they can capitalize on core customer loyalty and encourage increased usage.
4   **Attitude to risk.** By reducing price, allowing product trial, providing information or improving warranty or payment terms

promotions can overcome consumers' innate conservatism and reduce the perceived risk they associate with purchase.

A promotion does more than provide an opportunity to stimulate a simple response from a consumer. It provides opportunities to change the consumer's whole relationship with a given brand (see Figure 18.5) in three ways.

1   **Conversion.** Chapter 5 stressed the importance of encouraging product trial to convert potential users into customers. Promotions are effective as trial incentives, because they reduce perceived risk and can attract non-users through additional benefits rather than relying on the attraction of an unfamiliar product. Consumers who are satisfied with a promoted brand have an increased probability of repeat purchases in future. This is particularly true of previous non-users (Rothschild and Gaidis, 1981). Neilsen Promotion Services found that 55 per cent of consumers who enter competitions will select a brand because of a competition, and that 95 per cent of those will repurchase in future.

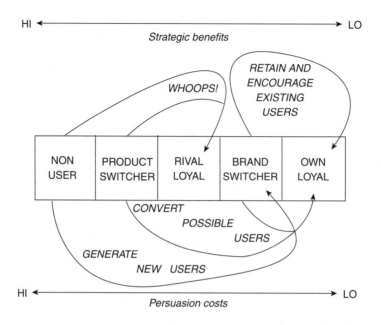

Figure 18.5   The roles of promotion in converting consumers

2   **Retention.** Providing delayed or cumulative benefits can help to encourage repeat purchases. 'Collect and save' schemes or 'money off next purchase' coupons can help to retain promotion-sensitive brand switchers.

3   **Acceleration.** McDonald's reached a point where awareness levels were becoming difficult to improve through advertising, resulting in declining business potential from new customers. They have therefore switched an increasing proportion of a billion-dollar communications budget into promotions aimed at getting more business from existing customers. The 'Happy Meal' promotions provide sets of novelties for children to collect, changed at regular intervals to accelerate visit frequency.

Communicating through sales promotions

Like advertising, promotions seek to connect with the customer to generate awareness, inform, entertain, and generally persuade the customer to change their attitudes and behaviour in the brand's favour. Communicating effectively requires the marketer to develop the right message, select an appropriate medium, and accurately target the campaign. When it comes to targeting, promotions are more flexible than advertising, which essentially presents one message at a time to the entire audience (a 'shotgun' approach). Promotions can communicate different messages to different customer groups. Ulay products were having problems reaching their target market, 'women aged 18 to 65 and older', with a universal advertising theme. This prompted their 'Woman of the World' competition, offering various holiday prizes ranging from an art tour of London to trekking in the Far East, designed to appeal to the full range of age groups.

Advertising's approach to communication is rooted in the early physical systems based approaches to human communication developed in the 1940s and 1950s by the likes of Lasswell and Schramm (Buttle, 1990). The message is seen as a 'magic bullet' transferring encoded information from a sender (the advertiser) to be absorbed and decoded, relatively passively, by a receiver (the target audience). Promotions reflect more contemporary theories of human communication, which stress its social context and processes of sharing, response and interaction. Promotions communicate with the aim of encouraging interaction between the producer and the consumer, through a sale, the clipping of a coupon or the testing of a product sample.

In terms of persuasion, promotions' direct response orientation has focused attention on the 'action' phase of the AIDA model (see Chapter 17) when discussing their communications capabilities. In fact, promotions work effectively during each phase of this communication process:

1 **Attention.** Promotions are undoubtedly attention grabbing. Words such as 'Extra', 'Free', 'Win' and 'Special' all help promoted products to stand out on the shelves of today's supermarkets which can contain over 35 000 different products jostling for the consumer's attention. Spillers' 1996 'Purrfect Taste' promotion was an excellent 'attention getter'. When shoppers passed the Spillers' display in Somerfield's stores, a 'voicebox' was triggered by laser so that a voice then challenged them to try new Spillers' Purrfect. The end consumer's attention was also attracted by an innovative mailing containing an aroma burst strip to appeal to cats, which was sent to a mailing list of known cat food buyers.

2 **Interest.** Promotions can inject novelty and even fun into the most familiar or mundane of products. Financial services companies have found that promotional competitions create considerable interest among customers and staff, which can be important in a price competitive market with an intangible product (Peattie and Peattie 1994). Barclays Bank's 1998 Nest Egg competition encouraged customers to discuss their savings needs with a 'Personal Banker' with the lure of £100 000 in prizes and a free Cadbury's Creme Egg for everyone.

3 **Desire.** Encouraged by the offer of additional benefits. Research by Millward Brown and ASL into the 1996 Cadbury's Coronation Street interactive on-pack promotion showed that 26 per cent of adults were aware of the promotion and that the lure of the 8 million prizes made 13 per cent feel encouraged to buy more Cadbury's bars.

4 **Action.** Promotions differ from advertising (with the exception of direct response advertising, see Chapter 17) in seeking a direct response. The responses which a promotion might try to generate include encouraging consumers to:

- Accelerate their purchase timing of a brand.
- Select a brand for their initial purchase.
- Stay loyal to a brand.
- Switch brands.
- Replace a consumer durable.
- Overcome their previous objections to a brand and sample it.
- Gather information about a brand.

Promotions can also go beyond prompting action to create interaction and consumer involvement with a brand, by requiring them to analyse and rank its attributes, create a recipe around it, test drive it or sum up its virtues in ten words or less. While advertising is a one-way communication process, promotions can create a dialogue. Competitions, direct mail promotions and sampling programmes are increasingly being used to gather information from consumers, as well as to send messages to them. Guinness used questions on a competition leaflet to help pinpoint more accurately their key competitors in the canned beer market. Beamish Stout capitalized on their sponsorship of Inspector Morse by sending out a squad of 'policewomen'. They persuaded drinkers to 'help with their enquiries', and combined an effective sampling promotion with a major market research exercise.

Building relationships through promotions

Because promotions go beyond the 'magic bullet' approach to communication, they create opportunities to build relationships between the promoter and the target. Three areas in which relationship building is central are in trade promotions aimed at retailers and distributors, in supporting and encouraging sales activity, and in developing marketing partnerships with other companies.

Trade promotions are less varied than the consumer promotions in Table 18.1, but operate from similar principles. Intermediaries are offered special discounts or payment terms, gifts, contests, sales information or extra product to gain their enthusiasm and shelf space. For example, in Spring 1996 UK computer dealers were sent a ceramic musical money box modelled on the Microsoft Mouse 2.0 in a cheese wedge shape box along with a brochure and some cheese wedge sales aids. The number of dealers making Mouse 2.0 sales between May and July then increased by 55 per cent.

At the dark end of the spectrum, bribery could qualify as a form of promotion, and in offering intermediaries extra benefits, a producer must always be sensitive to their targets' policies towards the acceptance of promotional gifts. This issue made the headlines during 1997 when the UK Government announced action to control the offering of promotional incentives for doctors by drug companies. An example of a relatively sophisticated relationship building promotion is JVC's Pro-S club for top performing video dealers. The club provides dealers with high levels of marketing support in return for specific commitments on how JVC products will be presented and supported.

During the last decade, retailer mergers, increasingly centralized buying and the provision of marketing information from EPOS systems have all shifted power away from producers towards retailers (Shultz, 1987).

Many products now rely heavily on retailer support, and increasing trade promotions reflects their importance in maintaining good channel relationships. Intermediaries have begun to strongly influence the extent and nature of producer promotions, as evidenced by the retailer resistance encountered by Procter and Gamble when it attempted to reduce its reliance on promotions.

Promotions also play an important part in supporting the sales efforts of industrial marketers. The negotiation of special deals for key customers, participation at trade fairs, product samples and the provision of product information all play a vital part in reducing the buyers' perception of risk and helping to win contracts. Promotional gifts as humble as calendars, pens and mugs all play a part in communicating, and in keeping the promoter's name at the potential purchaser's fingertips.

Salesforce contests are another form of promotion used by around three quarters of all companies. Their effectiveness is often undermined in practice by overemphasizing financial incentives and by allowing them to become an expected part of salesforce remuneration. A more creative approach to internal contests is demonstrated by Swissair's Swingo competition, which was open to all staff and was based around air traffic movements. It met its key aims of testing and improving product knowledge, aiding training and enhancing customer service. It also appealed to employees to the extent that their personalized game cards became regarded as status symbols.

Promotions allow producers to join forces to take advantage of synergies between their products or similarities between their target markets. This can create some unlikely alliances, unthinkable in terms of joint brand-sell advertising. Barclays Bank teamed up with Kellogg's to offer on-pack bank deposit coupons aimed at getting children to eat more cereals and open a bank account. The award for the least likely combination, but one with an interesting slant on reinforcing brand values, comes from the 1998 promotion from the Clorets breath

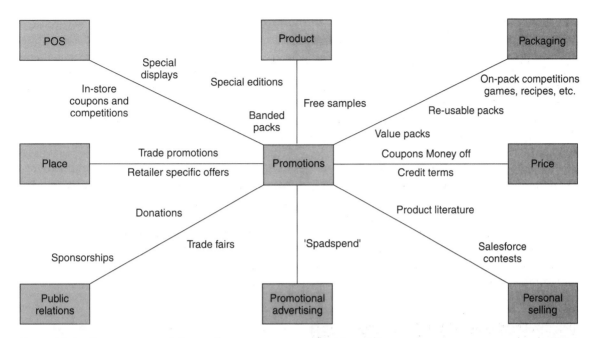

Figure 18.6 Promotions and the marketing mix: an integrated model

fresheners brand offering a free curry from The Curry Club. In America General Motors (GM) teamed up with Procter & Gamble to give away 750 1998 Cadillacs at a cost of $9 million. This was both companies' biggest ever promotion. For P&G, Cadillacs as prizes attracted consumers while reinforcing P&G's quality image, while the seven key P&G brands involved gave GM a direct communication channel into 98 per cent of American homes. The link between entertainment and refreshments has also led to a wide range of co-promotions, with different fast food and soft drink brands locked in a fierce bidding war for the right to develop promotions based on the latest movie blockbusters.

Sales promotion's role in the marketing mix

The relationship building capabilities of promotions is just one of several factors causing a re-evaluation of what promotions can achieve for marketers. Relationship building requires a much longer-term approach to promotions

management than the 'quick fix' campaign stereotype. The highly successful Lever and British Rail 'two for the price of one' train ticket offer required two and a half years of planning and negotiation.

The growing awareness of the potential strategic importance of promotions is leading to a more integrated approach to their management and their role within the marketing mix. The intertwining of promotion with the rest of the mix is demonstrated by Figure 18.6. The model's 'nine Ps' are less memorable than the classic four, but they demonstrate the difficulties of isolating promotions within the mix (and it is worth emphasizing that the interactions mentioned are only an illustrative selection). To take one example, there are now more than 200 promotional magazines published and distributed by companies in the UK and around 20 have a circulation of over a million readers. Many would classify this as public relations activity rather than a sales promotion, and the issue is complicated further by the likes of the Sainsbury's magazine which is unusual in being sold rather than distributed free.

The entangling of promotions with the rest of the mix accounts for the problems that occur when people attempt to define or measure sales promotion activity. Quelch (1989) also suggests that in practice it is the failure to integrate promotions effectively into the mix that leads to problems and to much of the criticism of promotions. On the positive side, this lack of clear boundaries can be viewed as providing an unrivalled opportunity for marketing managers to find innovative and creative ways of reaching customers. Robinson and Shultz (1982) suggest that the internal boundary spanning nature of promotions make them an ideal 'bridge', providing opportunities to integrate the communications efforts of advertising, selling and PR which may each be the responsibility of different managers.

Sales promotions – the most manageable P?

Sales promotions appeal to marketing managers because they are flexible and fast acting. They are also more directly controllable than other elements of the marketing mix, because generally speaking:

- Developing new products is a slow process which often relies on technical specialists.
- Permanent price changes depend on financial management's cooperation internally and customer acceptance or rivals' reactions externally.
- Channel changes involve lengthy negotiations with third parties.
- Advertising campaigns are planned slowly and carefully to nurture the image of the brand.

For the marketer looking to make a mark in a new job, under pressure to respond to competitors or struggling to meet tough sales targets, promotions can offer a speedy solution. Promotions' origins as tactical weapons make them very responsive and manoeuvrable, and well suited to just-in-time approaches to the

management of inventories and businesses. This has been taken to extremes by companies such as Mrs Fields' Cookies with outlets being linked directly to the central information system. This allows sales patterns to be analysed, and any necessary point-of-sale promotional offers suggested, in 'real time' (Haeckel and Nolan, 1993).

There is a wealth of common sense advice available to marketers on how to successfully and strategically manage promotions, mostly covering points such as:

- Look to add value rather than cut prices wherever possible.
- Link the promotion closely to the brand values.
- Theme promotions to reinforce advertising themes.
- Develop synergies with sales and PR campaigns.
- Search out cross-promotional opportunities.
- Reward loyal users and encourage repeat purchases.
- Ensure that the promotion is carefully targeted with quantified objectives, and overseen by a sufficiently senior executive.
- Constantly monitor and re-evaluate progress.

Sales promotions mismanagement

Sales promotions can achieve many marketing objectives, but they have definite limitations. They will not compensate for fundamental weaknesses in the rest of the marketing mix, they will not revive the fortunes of an outdated brand, and overuse can be counterproductive. Despite their manageability, promotions frequently run into problems. Advertising, with its fixed up-front costs, is often considered to be more risky than sales promotions, whose costs are generally more spread out and related to sales volume. However, while misconceived advertising dents credibility and wastes communications budgets, a bungled promotion can also incur significant public relations and other 'clean-up' costs. This was graphically illustrated by the Hoover 'Free Flights' fiasco where a drastic underestimate in the redemption rate of a flights giveaway led to losses initially estimated at £20 million, and a great deal of adverse publicity.

The ways in which promotions can go wrong are many and varied, from Pepsi's virtually vowel free 'Spell Your Surname and Win' contest, won by an unexpectedly large number of people called Ng, to lightning wiping out Bayard Sales' sole copy of its promotional database. There are eight major dangers associated with promotions:

1 **Promotional price wars.** These erode margins instead of boosting sales (see Chapter 14). A variation of these are 'coupon wars' which have recently occurred within the UK grocery market. Tesco's pledge to redeem anyone's coupons drew an angry response from its rivals and prompted Asda to distribute 50 per cent discount coupons in areas without Asda stores.

2 **Misredemption of coupons.** This presents a major hazard, with one US gang defrauding manufacturers of a staggering $186 million (Shimp, 1997). Marketers frequently budget for around 20 per cent misredemptions, but the problem may recede with technical advances such as coupon barcode scanning.

3 **Reference price changes.** A promotional price attracts customers by undercutting the expected 'normal' price. Too long or too frequent price promotions lower customers' 'reference' price, so that they see a return to the original price as an increase (Lattin and Bucklin, 1989).

4 **Printing errors.** Gamecard promotions require careful attention to printing accuracy and security. Esso's Noughts and Crosses game had to be withdrawn after its first two weeks after twenty £100 000 first prize winning tickets emerged when only two should have existed for the entire promotion.

5 **Overredemption.** Coupons, giveaways and buyback schemes are all based around esti-

mates of the response. A promotion which is unexpectedly successful in attracting customers (as happened to Hoover) can result in disastrous losses. Misjudging the extent or timing of consumer response can also lead to stock-outs and subsequent customer dissatisfaction. Allied Signal Plastics promised customers 48-hour delivery of any quantity of its most popular resins. However, within days of starting the promotion, the company had to abandon it because it could not meet the expectations that were generated.

6 **Quality dissonance.** Reducing prices, or offering low quality free gifts or competition prizes, risks devaluing an otherwise strong brand in consumers' minds.

7 **Tax.** Several major promoters including McDonald's, Boots and Sony have found themselves in high profile legal clashes with the Customs and Excise Service over VAT payments on sales promotions.

8 **Fulfilment problems.** Every year, between 200 and 300 promotions result in complaints to the Advertising Standards Authority. Around 90 per cent of these are upheld for breaching the Institute of Sales Promotion (ISP) Code of Practice. About 20 per cent of all such problems are not related to the sponsor, but lie with the handling houses which oversee the logistics of fulfilment.

Promotions encounter such problems because they usually do not enjoy the rigorous planning and control afforded to advertising campaigns. Time pressure and a tendency for the implementation and evaluation of promotions to be delegated too far down the organization contribute to this situation, which was summed up by a classic article by Roger Strang (1976) entitled 'Sales Promotions: Fast Growth, Faulty Management'. Most promotional pitfalls can be avoided by:

- Greater attention to the promotional planning process detailed in Figure 18.3.
- Addressing the type of common sense questions contained in the COMPETE USING

Table 18.3   The COMPETE USING PROMOTIONS checklist

Concept	Do we need a promotion? If so, why? Is the promotional effort best aimed at the consumer, the trade or both? Will the promotion be shared with another producer or a retailer? If so, how will costs and responsibilities be divided?
Objectives	What are the marketing communications objectives? What message will it send to consumers and what effect should it produce? Is it only short-term sales uplifts, or are there more long-term objectives such as generating new users or raising product awareness? Should the promotion target all markets and consumers or be more selective?
Mechanics	What types of promotion are feasible, which best suit the product, and which are most likely to meet our objectives? How will it reach consumers? Can a tried and trusted technique be given an innovative and creative edge? What could go wrong logistically and how could it be prevented?
Practical issues	Who will handle the planning and design, in-house or agency? Who will manage the campaign internally? What actions must take place, when, and by whom, to implement the promotion? Will fulfilment be handled internally or by a handling house? Will enough stock be available?
Expenditure	How much of the marketing budget and the time of marketing management should the promotion consume? Should it be supported by 'spadspend'? What level of uptake is expected? How likely and costly could an excessively high level of uptake be? Is sales promotion insurance needed?
Timing	Should the promotion be used to counteract seasonal lows, reinforce seasonal highs or 'spoil' rivals' promotions? Should the duration be long to maximize sales, or short to prevent loss of consumer interest? How long should special packs, coupons or leaflets etc. be available for? Should the benefits be instantly available, delayed or cumulative? What redemption deadline should be set?
Evaluation	How will the effectiveness of the promotion be measured in terms of achieving its objectives? Who should be responsible for evaluation, when and using what measures?

PROMOTIONS checklist (Table 18.3) while planning the promotion campaign.
* Adhering to the ISP Code of Practice.

There are some indications that sales promotions are becoming more effectively managed as the industry matures. In 1996 American companies spent around $1 billion on research related to promotions according to US promotion industry figures.

The future of sales promotion

One golden rule of promotions management is that overuse of any technique will blunt its effectiveness. Innovation and creativity are key success factors, and recent advances in packaging and information technology have provided many exciting new ways to offer customers extra benefits.

1   **High-tech coupons:** may make coupon clipping a thing of the past. Vision Value Network video terminals, adopted by over 800 US grocery stores, offer consumers in-store paper and 'paperless' coupons, automated bank debit payments and a frequent shopper club. Sinfonia Marketing Systems in France has introduced the Promocarte, a smart card which can hold and automatically redeem

coupon information based on previous pur-chases.

2   **EPOS systems:** which allow the banding of products in a logical rather than a physical sense. Safeway's 'Linksave' and 'Multisave' promotions involve the EPOS system identi-fying and refunding the price of the third instance of a 'buy two, get one free' product, or automatically refunding a 'piggyback' pur-chase. This removes much of the repackaging and logistical costs associated with product based promotions.

3   **Packaging innovations:** allow increasingly versatile and novel sample packs, or encapsu-lations for use in letterbox drops or as attachments to products and magazine covers. Jacob's 'Fridge 'em to Win' competition used thermochromic ink (which only showed the win/lose message when chilled) on the wrapper of each Club biscuit to encourage users to buy and refrigerate them during the traditionally slow summer period. Initial results showed a 48 per cent increase in sales volume.

4   **Customer database systems**: Marks & Spencer were pioneers in establishing a cen-tral marketing database through which all sales promotion campaigns could be man-aged. This allows the generation of effectively targeted direct mail campaigns, and the accurate measurement of each campaign's results. The US Fairmont Hotel chain's computer network analyses the habits of regular busi-ness travellers. This ensures that wherever travellers stay, their tastes in everything from drinks and newspapers to wake-up times can be anticipated.

5   **Customer information systems:** IBM's Ultimedia Touch Activity Centre (a kiosk dis-playing touch-screen driven product informa-tion) allows customers to view products, product information, prices and availability, and place credit card orders. During in-store tests this proved popular with older con-sumers, who liked the convenience, detail of information available and the sense of control provided. In industrial markets companies

including Universal Office Supplies, RS Com-ponents and SKF are replacing traditional product catalogues with on-disk catalogues which include automatic order processing software and in-built key customer discounts.

Summary – the changing concept of sales promotion

For many years a widespread view of promo-tions was as short term, tactical tools, often added into the marketing mix of struggling FMCG brands to boost sales. This attitude was summed up in the assertion by Ken Roman of Ogilvy & Mather, that promotions *rent* cus-tomers while product benefits (and by implica-tion their communication through advertising) *own* customers.

Much of the early academic research into promotions produced very critical appraisals of their effectiveness (e.g. Dodson *et al.*, 1978; Doob *et al.*, 1969). However, such research was flawed by a concentration on price based promotions, by ignoring the indirect effects of promotions, and by taking a very narrow view of consumer response. More recent research into promotions demonstrates that:

- They can boost a brand's sales, awareness levels and image (Aaker, 1991; Davies and Saunders, 1992).

- They are effective in encouraging switching between brands, product categories and retailers (Walters, 1991).

- They can overcome significant levels of brand loyalty to 'poach' consumers (McAllister and Totten, 1985).

- They are most effective when backed up by advertising (Bemmaor and Mouchoux, 1991).

- Trade promotions help to secure intermedi-aries' enthusiasm and support, and can help to build or reduce trade inventories (Hardy, 1986).

Recently the prejudices against promotions have begun to lessen. A new wisdom is emerging which views them not as a 'bolt-on extra', but as an essential and integral part of the marketing mix, and vital to the process of building and managing successful brands. This new wisdom involves a belief that:

1   **Top brands promote.** Looking at the UK Sales Promotion Consultants' Association's industry award winners for 1996, the client list reads like a selection from the 'Who's Who' of brands and includes Microsoft, Cadbury, St. Ivel, Budweiser, Southern Comfort, Britvic, Golden Wonder, Robinsons squashes, Dairy Crest, Conoco, Rothmans, PepsiCo, Jacob's, Trebor Bassets, Spillers, BAA, and The Daily Telegraph.

2   **Promotions aren't necessarily temporary.** Nor are they of purely short-term value. Airline frequent flyer schemes were originally conceived as temporary, but have gone on to represent an industry fixture generating at least $6 billion annually in additional revenues (plus sales from hotel tie-ins and other travel-related products). The Miss Pears Competition ran for 65 years. The effects of a promotion can also linger far beyond its duration. A promotion communicates to all those consumers who encounter it, not just those who take advantage of it, and can therefore play an important part in brand awareness building. Goodyear's German 'Looking for Winners' promotion increased turnover in participating outlets by 25 per cent and boosted general brand awareness from 12.5 to 30.5 per cent (Toop, 1992).

3   **Promotions have a strategic role.** This complements their more traditional tactical capabilities (Peattie and Peattie, 1997). One symptom of this is the emergence of very large 'mega-promotions' supported by advertising and public relations campaigns. British Airways' World's Greatest Offer involved free flight giveaways and other promotions with a combined cost of around £50 million in a very high profile campaign. Another symptom is the emergence of internationally coordinated sales promotion campaigns (Toop, 1992), developed by companies including Kodak, Mars, Distillers, Ford and American Express.

4   **Promotions suit a wide range of markets.** The stronghold of sales promotion reflects its FMCG origins, and packaged goods in particular, but their use has spread throughout a wide range of markets. Promotions can be found encouraging people to open bank accounts (especially students), donate to charity, test drive cars, purchase shares or submit papers to academic conferences.

5   **Promotions can reinforce brand loyalty.** Promotions, particularly price cutting, have been blamed for the general erosion of brand loyalty. Whether increasing promotion is a symptom or a cause of eroding brand loyalty is open to debate. What is often overlooked, is that promotions also build brand loyalty, by providing extra benefits for existing customers and by encouraging repeat purchases through devices such as 'money off next purchase' coupons, 'one entry per proof-of-purchase' competitions, or cumulative customer loyalty programmes.

6   **Promotions can strengthen brand positioning.** A 1985 study by Frankel & Co. and Perception Research Services found that, following exposure to adverts featuring promotions for a brand, consumers' opinion of the brand (on issues like quality, value and caring about customers) improved by over 8 percentage points, compared to those exposed to only 'brand sell' adverts.

McKenna (1990) predicted a renaissance of business based on a marriage of the 'soft skills' and creativity of marketing with the power of new technology. Many might relate to this in terms of advertising, where technology allows us to view spectacular computer-created images which go beyond anything reality has to offer. However, it is in sales promotions that many of the most exciting marriages of technology and creativity are occuring (Peattie and Peters,

1997). An example comes from Hiram Walker who spent $10 million on the *Cutty Sark Virtual Voyage*, a two and a half minute virtual reality experience allowing participants to act as the legendary smuggler William McCoy, fighting high seas, pirates and hostile stowaways to bring the bottles of *Cutty Sark* ashore. Surviving a virtual life-or-death experience to rescue a brand is an experience which is almost bound to cement the participants' relationship with that brand. Another example comes from Hewlett-Packard's MOPy fish, a virtual pet which can be downloaded from the Internet and can act as a computer screensaver. The HP web site will also provide items of 'tank' furniture including a plant, rock, bubbles and a thermometer. These can only be downloaded in exchange for MOPy points, and the chief way of accumulating these, is to use your HP printer to make 'Multiple Original Printouts'. In exchange for 3200 points you can acquire some aphrodisiac fish food which makes MOPy, who was developed using over one million photographs of a real parrot fish, become so affectionate that it will plant a kiss on the inside of the monitor. Quite what Mr Holder would make of MOPy's antics is hard to imagine, but the general principle of getting extra custom out of people by offering them additional benefits is one that he would recognize and approve of.

It is a pity that marketing academics continue to be so pre-occupied with issues of promotional price reduction, coupon redemption and their effect on consumer behaviour and reference pricing, when marketing practice is injecting so much creativity and diversity into the growth in sales promotion. The variety of benefits that customers, and companies, can enjoy from sales promotions is well illustrated by the retailing formula of the UK's largest hi-fi retailer, Richer Sounds. The company's strategy is based on being fiercely price competitive. Regular sale items and a 'price beat' pledge to undercut competitors means that customers are never short of rational economic benefits from Richer's promotions. The communications benefits of promotions is reflected in their cata-logue/magazine which has an annual circulation figure of over 5 million. Customers get information related benefits from free hi-fi guides and a free technical helpline. Nervous first time buyers are welcomed in with a special free gift and a promise of additional help, while more mature customers are offered additional benefits through the 'Life Begins at 40 Club'. Customers gain security benefits from product demonstrations, an extended warranty scheme, a 50 per cent buy-back option, and (on some products) trial facilities. Free in-store refreshments, coupons for free tapes, impromptu contests and free lollipops for children also help to enhance the customer's shopping experience. Perhaps the most distinctive element of the company's promotions is the element of 'fun'. This is reflected in an invitation to bring your pets to listen to your prospective purchase, an offer of a free umbrella if you make a purchase when its raining, and the offer of a free box of Johnson's cotton buds to open up the ears of any customer who fails to hear the difference between Richer's systems and similarly priced 'midi' systems. Although it would be easy to dismiss elements of their promotions as 'gimmicks', they are a crucial part of a marketing strategy which has enabled the company (for the last six years) to record the highest value of sales per square foot of any retailer in the world.

In Chapter 16 Peter Doyle illustrated how brand strength can overcome adversity, by using the example of Tylenol's recovery following poisoning incidents by terrorists and the brand's subsequent withdrawal. Another aspect of this story is the role that promotions can play in the achievement of strategic objectives such as a brand's rehabilitation following disaster. The recovery of Tylenol was a remarkable testament to the brand's robustness, but it was also considerably aided by the 40 million $2.50 coupons issued to reactivate former users.

The implications for marketing management of the boom in promotions is becoming increasingly clear; what sales promotion lacks in glamour compared to advertising, it more than makes up for in flexibility and effectiveness. In today's competitive marketplace, the professional management of sales promotion has become a matter of life and death for an ever growing number of brands.

References

Aaker, D. A. (1991) *Managing Brand Equity*, The Free Press.

Baker, M. J. (1998) *Macmillan Dictionary of Marketing and Advertising*, 3rd edn, Macmillan.

Bawa, K. and Shoemaker, R. W. (1987) The Coupon-Prone Consumer: Some Findings Based on Purchase Behaviour Across Product Classes, *Journal of Marketing*, **51**(4), 99–100.

Bemmaor, A. C. and Mouchoux, D. (1991) Measuring the Short-Term Effect of In-Store Promotion and Retail Advertising on Brand Sales: A Factorial Experiment, *Journal of Marketing Research*, **28**(2), 202–214.

Blattberg, R. C. and Neslin, S. A. (1990) *Sales Promotion: Concepts, Methods and Strategies*, Prentice-Hall, Englewood Cliffs, NJ.

Buttle, F. A. (1990) Marketing Communication Theory: Review and Critique, in A. Pendlebury and T. Watkins (eds), *Recent Developments in Marketing: Marketing Educators Group 1990 Conference Proceedings*, Oxford.

Chandon, P. (1995) Consumer Research on Sales Promotion: A State-of-the-Art Literature Review, *Journal of Marketing Management*, **11**, 419–441.

Circus, P. J. (1989) *Sales Promotion Law: A Practical Guide*, Butterworth Legal Publications.

Cummins, J. (1989) *Sales Promotion: How to Create and Implement Campaigns that Really Work*, Kogan Page, London.

Davidson, J. H. (1975) *Offensive Marketing*, Pelican, London.

Davies, M. and Saunders, J. (1992) The Double Delight of Sales Promotion, in Whitelock *et al.* (eds), *The New Europe and Beyond, Proceedings of the 1992 Marketing Educators Group Conference*, Salford, pp. 371–381.

Dodson, J. A., Tybout, A. M. and Sternthal, B. (1978) Impact of Deals and Deal Retractions on Brand Switching, *Journal of Marketing Research*, **15**(1), 72–81.

Doob, A. N., Carlsmith, J. M., Freedman, J. L., Landauer, T. K. and Solong, T. (1969) Effect of Initial Selling Price on Subsequent Sales, *Journal of Personality and Social Psychology*, **2**(4), 345–350.

Fraser, C. and Hite, R. (1990) Varied Consumer Responses to Promotions: A Case for Response Based Decision Making, *Journal of the Market Research Society*, **32**(3), 349–375.

Haeckel, S. H. and Nolan, R. L. (1993) Managing By Wire, *Harvard Business Review*, **71**(5), Sept/Oct, 122–32.

Hardy, K. G. (1986) Key Success Factors for Manufacturers' Sales Promotions in Packaged Goods, *Journal of Marketing*, **50**(3), 13–23.

Jones, J. P. (1990) The Double Jeopardy of Sales Promotion, *Harvard Business Review*, **68**(5), 145–152.

Lal, R. (1990) Manufacturer Trade Deals and Retail Price Promotions, *Journal of Marketing Research*, **27**(6), 428–44.

Lattin, J. M. and Bucklin, R. E. (1989) Reference Effects of Price and Promotion on Brand Choice Behaviour, *Journal of Marketing Research*, **26**(4), 299–310.

Lichtenstein, D. R., Netemeyer, R. G. and Burton, S. (1990) Distinguishing Coupon Proneness From Value Consciousness: An Acquisition-Transaction Utility Theory Perspective, *Journal of Marketing*, **54**(3), 54–67.

McAllister, L. and Totten, J. (1985) Decomposing the Promotional Bump: Switching, Stockpiling and Consumption Increase, paper presented at ORSA/TIMS 1985 Joint Meeting.

McKenna, R. (1990) Marketing is Everything, *Harvard Business Review*, **68**(1), 65–79.

Peattie, K. and Peattie, S. (1993) Sales Promotions: Playing to Win? *Journal of Marketing Management*, **9**(3), 255–70.

Peattie S. and Peattie, K. (1994) Promoting Financial Services with Glittering Prizes, *International Journal of Bank Marketing*, **12**(6), 19–29.

Peattie, K., Peattie, S. and Emafo, E. B. (1997) Promotional Competitions as a Strategic

Marketing Weapon, *Journal of Marketing Management*, **13**(8), 777–89.

Peattie, K. and Peters, L. (1997) The Marketing Mix in the Third Age of Computing, *Marketing Intelligence and Planning*, **15**(3), 142–50.

Quelch, J. A. (1989) *Sales Promotion Management*, Prentice-Hall, Englewood Cliffs, NJ.

Robinson, W. A and Shultz, D. E. (1982) *Sales Promotion Management*, Crain Books, Chicago.

Rothschild, M. L. and Gaidis, W. C. (1981) Behavioural Learning Theory: Its Relevance to Marketing and Promotions, *Journal of Marketing*, **45**(2), 70–78.

Shimp, T. A. (1997) *Advertising, Promotion and Supplemental Aspects of Integrated Marketing Communications*, Dryden Press.

Shultz, D. E. (1987) Above or Below the Line? Growth of Sales Promotion in the United States, *International Journal of Advertising*, **6**, 17–27.

Strang, R. A. (1976) Sales Promotion: Fast Growth, Faulty Management, *Harvard Business Review*, **54**(1), 115–124.

Toop, A. (1992) *European Sales Promotion: Great Campaigns in Action*, Kogan Page.

Walters, R. G. (1991) Assessing the Impact of Retail Price promotions on Product Substitution, Complementary Purchase, and Inter-store Sales Displacement, *Journal of Marketing*, **55**(2), 17–28.

Further reading

Cummins, J. (1989) *Sales Promotion: How to Create and Implement Campaigns that Really Work*, Kogan Page, London. A concise and practical guide to choosing and using sales promotions techniques, with a useful summary of the legalities involved and some helpful contact addresses. Ideal quick starter text.

Chandon, P. (1995) Consumer Research on Sales Promotion: A State-of-the-Art Literature Review, *Journal of Marketing Management*, **11**, 419–441. A superbly thorough and interesting review of the evolution of research into how and why promotions can influence consumers. It reflects the weakness of the discipline in the over emphasis on short-term, rational–economic price effects, but provides some useful criticism of the different research traditions and highlights areas for future research.

Davies, M. and Saunders, J. (1992) The Double Delight of Sales Promotion, in Whitelock *et al.* (eds), *Marketing in The New Europe and Beyond, Proceedings of the 1992 MEG Conference*, Salford, pp. 371–381. A neat encapsulation of the reasons why sales promotions can and do play a role in building brand equity as well as boosting sales.

Engel, J. F., Warshaw, M. R. and Kinnear, T. C. (1994) Promotional Strategy: *Managing the Marketing Communications Process*, 8th edn, Irwin, Homewood, Illinois. Provides an excellent and detailed analysis of the total marketing communications process and its place within marketing strategy and the organization. Takes a very strategic and integrated approach to the relationship between promotions and the other elements of marketing communications.

Peattie, K. and Peattie, S. (1993) Sales Promotion: Playing To Win? *Journal of Marketing Management*, **9(3)**. Using promotional competitions as a focus explores the often neglected possibilities that value adding promotions present for marketers in terms of influencing consumer behaviour and meeting a range of marketing objectives.

Quelch, J. A. (1989) *Sales Promotion Management*, Prentice-Hall, Englewood Cliffs, NJ. Uses some very detailed and interesting cases to illustrate perspectives on sales promotion theory covering different types of markets and targets. Includes a rarity, a vigorous defence of price promotions.

Robinson, W. A. and Schultz, D. E. (1982) *Sales Promotion Management*, Crain Books, Chicago. Although now looking a little dated, this provides an excellent insight into the management and execution of sales promotion. Inclines towards a tactical view of promotions, but shows their ability to solve (and sometimes cause) a variety of marketing problems.

Shimp, T. A. (1997) *Advertising, Promotion and Supplemental Aspects of Integrated Marketing Communications*, 4th edn, The Dryden Press, Fort Worth. Although sales promotion is still overshadowed by advertising within this text, it provides good coverage of many of the important crossover points between sales promotion and the marketing mix, such as direct mail and point-of-purchase promotion. The coverage of consumer behaviour in relation to promotions and promotions planning is excellent. The variety of interesting cases and references provided makes this a particularly helpful book for academics.

Toop, A. (1992) *European Sales Promotion: Great Campaigns in Action*, Kogan Page, London. Demonstrates the growing strategic importance of promotions within the marketing mix of leading multinational companies through a series of well dissected case studies. Helps to capture the creative excitement and fun involved in top-notch promotions, and charts the emergence of the concept of pan-European sales promotions.

CHAPTER 19

Customer service and logistics strategy

MARTIN CHRISTOPHER

Introduction

Traditionally, the routes to competitive advantage have typically been based upon strong brands, corporate images, effective advertising and, in some cases, price. These are the classic components of conventional marketing strategies. More recently however there have been a number of signs that suggest that the power of the brand – in both consumer and industrial markets – is in decline (Brady and Davis, 1993). For whatever reason the customer seeks more than 'brand value', as it is sometimes called, and is looking increasingly for *value* in a much wider sense.

In the new paradigm of marketing the emphasis changes from brand value to customer value. Essentially this means that the supplying organization must focus its efforts upon developing an 'offer' or 'package' that will impact customers' perception of the value they derive through ownership of that offer. This value might either be derived through the delivery of benefits in performance terms and/or in the form of a reduction in the customer's costs. The argument that is increasingly being heard is that a critical component of such customer value is *service*.

Service is a concept that we all understand yet find difficult to articulate. It is multifaceted having many dimensions and it can be seen as that part of the marketing mix which has the capacity to customize or individualize the offer. Customer service may also be thought of as the summation of all those activities that enable customer satisfaction actually to be delivered.

The decline of the brand

There is strong evidence from many markets that brand loyalty amongst customers is not what it was. Perhaps because of growing buyer sophistication, or because of a growing similarity in the composition and functionality of competing products, or because of the emphasis on price competition and frequent discounting activity, the power of the brand seems to be in decline (Brady and Davis, 1993). This phenomenon seems to be widespread – from computers to cigarettes.

It is important to distinguish between brand *loyalty* and brand *preference*. Many customers have a preference for a brand or a supplier and will typically express that preference through their purchasing behaviour. However, when the preferred brand is not available those same customers will quite readily chose an acceptable substitute. This is equally true in industrial markets or consumer markets, for example the choice of suppliers to a just-in-time manufacturer is very much influenced by delivery reliability. Similarly a retailer in making shelf space allocation decisions will look very carefully at vendors' logistics performance.

The traditional means through which marketers have differentiated their offer from those of competitors, such as advertising and claimed product superiority, need to be augmented by a greater emphasis upon building customer relationships through service. Today's customer is far more sensitive to service than was previously the case. Survey after survey suggest that perceived quality and service outstrip price as the determining factor in choice of supplier in many markets.

The revised model of marketing effectiveness that is increasingly being recognized is shown as Figure 19.1, which emphasizes that relationships with customers are of equal importance as the relationships we have with consumers and that both of these need to be underpinned by superior supply chain management.

What is being suggested is that it is no longer sufficient to have a strong franchise with the *consumer* – meaning that because of superior brand values or corporate image the supplier can expect continuing market success. Strong consumer franchises need to be augmented by equally strong relationships with channel intermediaries – the *customer* franchise. Supporting both of these franchises is a cost-effective supply chain.

Much has been written elsewhere about the marketing actions necessary to create enduring consumer franchises (Aaker, 1991) and there is no need to retrace that ground here. However rather less attention has been paid to the issue of building customer franchises and achieving superior supply chain performance, at least in the marketing literature.

Developing a customer franchise

In many industries there has long been a tradition of adversarial relationships between suppliers and their customers – whether those

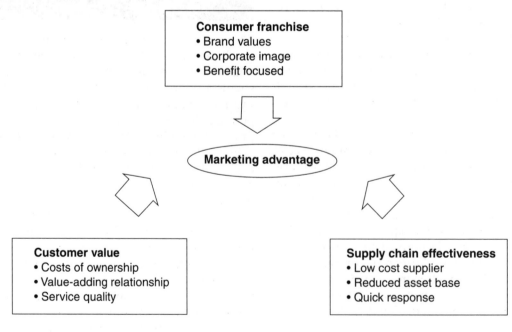

Figure 19.1   Marketing and logistics converge

(a) Traditional Buyer / Supplier Interface

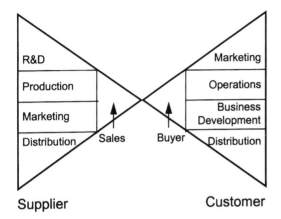

(b) Building Stronger Partnerships Through Multiple Linkages

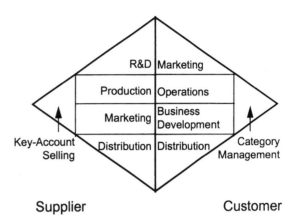

Figure 19.2   The move towards trade marketing

customers be distributors or manufacturing intermediaries. This hostility has been mutual and there has been little attempt to cooperate and to seek win–win solutions. Now however there are growing signs in many industries that this is changing. There is a recognition by suppliers that intermediaries and distributors often hold the key to the marketplace. Similarly customers are realizing that closer relations with suppliers can lead to quality improvements, innovation sharing and cost reduction.

The trend is increasingly towards 'single sourcing', meaning placing all of the purchase requirements for an item with just one supplier. This is the reverse of the conventional notion that purchases should be spread between competing suppliers to avoid placing 'all of the eggs in one basket'. Companies like Rover Group in the automobile industry a few years ago had over 2000 suppliers; it is now down to nearer 500. Nissan in the UK by contrast, starting their operations with a 'clean sheet of paper', have only 200 suppliers. The advantage of developing closer relations with a limited number of suppliers is that opportunities for mutual benefit through a partnership approach become a reality. Instead of win–lose it is possible to move to win–win. Many companies have adopted

just-in-time (JIT) manufacturing strategies but have done so by pushing the responsibility for inventory holding upstream to their suppliers. In such cases there will probably have been no overall cost reduction in the distribution channel, only a transfer of costs. Indeed sometimes the total costs may increase because of the need for the supplier to make more frequent deliveries of small quantities to the JIT customer. In contrast, companies working in partnership seek to identify opportunities to reduce or eliminate costs, not to simply play an industrial version of 'pass the parcel'.

In retailing, as in other forms of distribution, there is also now a growing recognition that cooperation, rather than conflict, in the marketing channel can build competitive advantage. Major suppliers to the retail trade such as Unilever and Nestlé are putting as much effort into 'trade marketing', as it is called, as they expend on traditional brand marketing. There is a strong desire by such companies to broaden the relationship with their customers away from the fairly limited connection shown as Figure 19.2(a) in which the main point of contact was between a key account executive from the supplier and a buyer from the retailer. Figure 19.2(b) depicts the alternative approach where multiple contacts are established, e.g. the supplier's R&D team with the customer's marketing team, the supplier's logistics team with the customer's operations team and so on.

Such a relationship should prove to be more enduring because it is built upon the search for mutual advantage – not just narrow self-interest. In this scheme of things the role of the key account manager is to manage a team-based approach to relationship building with the customer. Whilst this approach has been adopted with success by an increasing number of suppliers to the retail trade, it is equally powerful in any type of business-to-business marketing.

The impact of superior supply chain performance

As customer service comes to be recognized as a highly effective way to differentiate the offer – even in a commodity type market – then the challenge becomes one of how to structure and manage logistics systems capable of meeting customer requirements consistently and efficiently.

Effective logistics systems can both enable a supplier to achieve lower costs and at the same time enhance the impact it has upon the customer's performance. A prime objective of any business should be constantly to seek out ways of reducing the customer's *total costs of ownership* whilst lowering their own costs.

The concept of total costs of ownership is quite simple. Essentially any transaction will involve the customer in a number of costs – not just the price that is charged. These costs might include inventory carrying costs, warehousing and handling costs, ordering costs, quality inspection costs and even stock-out costs, for example. Anything that the supplier can do to reduce or eliminate these costs will enhance its attractiveness to the supplier. On occasion, because total costs of ownership are lowered through superior supplier logistics, it may even be possible to justify a higher price (see Figure 19.3).

One way in which customer ownership costs can be lowered is by the establishment of 'quick response' logistics systems. In quick response logistics the aim is to capture information on product usage as far down the supply chain as possible and to translate that information rapidly into physical replenishment. The

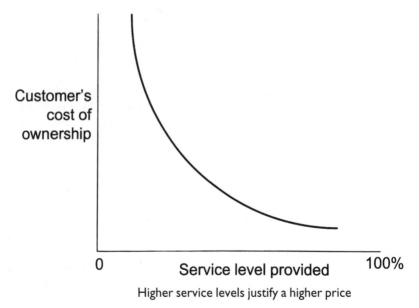

Figure 19.3   Costs of ownership

key to making quick response work is shared information. One chemical company for example has installed remote monitoring equipment in the storage tanks of its major customers for bulk liquid chemicals. It can monitor, through telemetry, the actual level of product in the tanks and with that information it can schedule production optimally and consolidate deliveries with other customers to achieve transport economies. The benefit to the customer is that they no longer need to manage their own inventory and issue purchase orders, but only pay for what they use and their inventory carrying costs are eliminated, yet they never go out of stock! To the supplier, the benefit is that they can now manage their materials flow optimally and not be taken by surprise by 'rush' emergency orders.

In North America, major retailers such as Wal-Mart have linked the laser scanners at their check-out counters direct to suppliers such as Procter and Gamble. In real-time Procter and Gamble can monitor off-take of their products store by store and, on the basis of that information, plan production and delivery to optimize their own costs as well as reducing the amount of stock that Wal-Mart needs to carry. The change that this type of logistics development has brought about in buyer–supplier relationships is radical. The idea is now one of 'vendor managed inventory', where the supplier becomes responsible for managing the customer's inventory to the benefit of both parties. For example at Wal-Mart there are fewer stock-outs and higher stock-turns, which has encouraged them to devote more shelf-space to those products. In the first year of this partnership relationship between Wal-Mart and Procter and Gamble it was reported that Procter and Gamble's business with Wal-Mart grew by $200m, or 40 per cent.

The integration of logistics and the related information flows both upstream and downstream in the marketing channel has come to be known as 'supply chain management'. It reflects an understanding that managing the interfaces between organizations is just as important as managing processes within the organizations themselves. It is at the interfaces that inventories are created, delays occur and service failures are most typically encountered. In many markets there is an observable correlation between successful companies and the extent to which they seek to manage the supply chain as an 'end-to-end' system. These companies understand that supply chains compete – not individual companies.

Broadening the concept of customer service

Much of the recent focus on customer service has been towards what might be termed 'the people dimension'. It is often not difficult for competitors to imitate technologies, product features, emotional appeals and conventional marketing strategies. What they cannot imitate is the inherent corporate culture and shared values which distinguish the customer service-oriented business. Thus a crucial element of the new paradigm of marketing is the focus upon developing attitudes and beliefs within the company that create a 'climate' in which customer satisfaction is the *raison d'être* of the organization. However, whilst it is clearly paramount that every business has motivated employees who share common values about the importance of customer satisfaction, it is also essential to have in place the systems that can ensure the consistent reliable 'delivery' of the service package. These systems must themselves be capable of providing the flexible response that individual customers require. Service has to be tailored to the needs of specific customers if it is to be a true source of differentiation. The idea is to create enduring relationships with customers not just through superior products but also through superior service. This twin focus on total quality and service as a source of customer satisfaction has come to be called 'relationship marketing' (Christopher, Payne and Ballantyne, 1991).

The impact of customer service and total quality improvement can be enduring, leading

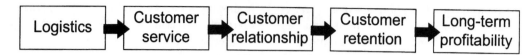

Figure 19.4   Logistics and profitability – the linkages

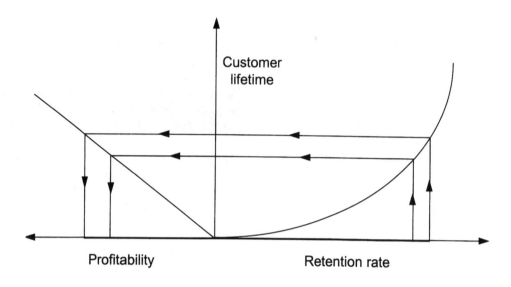

Figure 19.5   Better customer retention impacts long-term profitability

to longer-term relationships with customers, improved retention rates and, hence, greater profitability. The connection between logistics performance and profitability is summarized in Figure 19.4.

The proposition, and it is supported by a growing body of evidence, is that superior service helps build relationships with customers which then leads to improved rates of customer retention. The work of Reichheld and Sasser (1990) and others has highlighted the impact that customer retention has on profitability. The first critical finding emerging from these studies is that the longer customers stay with us, the more profitable they become. When this relationship is linked to the customer retention rate a powerful profit multiplier emerges. The logic is quite simple:

- Customer retention relates directly to the average 'life' of a customer, e.g. a 90 per cent

retention rate means that we lose 10 per cent of our customer base each year; thus on average we turn our customer base over every 10 years. With a 95 per cent retention rate the lifetime doubles to 20 years.

- The longer a customer stays with us the more they are likely to see us as a preferred supplier, even single sourcing on us. The evidence also suggests that the costs to service these customers reduce as we establish closer relationships and linkages in the supply chain; similarly the cost of selling to these loyal customers diminishes.

- The combined effect of a high retention rate and the enhanced profitability of loyal customers can lead not only to higher profit but to a better 'quality of earnings' as the customer base is less volatile. A company with lower market share but high customer retention can often be more profitable than a company with the reverse characteristics.

Figure 19.5 models the relationship between retention rates, customer lifetime and profitability.

Customer satisfaction at a profit is the goal of any business organization and the role of the logistics system is to achieve defined service goals in the most cost-effective way. The establishment of these service goals is a prerequisite for the development of appropriate logistics strategies and structures. There is now widespread acceptance that customer service requirements can only be accurately determined through research and competitive benchmarking. Research amongst customers may also reveal the presence of significant differences in service preferences between customers, thus pointing towards alternative bases for market segmentation based upon service needs. Knowing more about customers' service requirements and how they differ can provide a powerful basis for the development of strategies geared specifically towards improving customer retention.

Time-based competition

Organizations that are responsive to customer needs also tend to focus on 'time' as a source of competitive advantage (Stalk and Hout, 1990). There are a number of key time-related dimensions in marketing, e.g. time-to-market, time-to-manufacture, time-to-replenish and so on. Clearly the faster we can complete processes then the more quickly we can respond to customer requirements and to market changes. However the importance of time extends beyond this; simply put, the shorter the time it takes to do things, the more flexible we can be in our response.

One of the main reasons why companies rely on forecasting and hence on inventory is because they have long lead-times to source, manufacture and deliver. The longer the response time the greater the reliance upon the forecast, hence the more inventory that is required. Conversely the shorter the response time the less the reliance on the forecast and the less the need to cover uncertainty with inventory. At the same time, shorter lead-times mean we can offer greater variety. If in one factory it takes several hours to change from making one product to another (set-up time) but a competitor's factory can make the same change in seconds, then very clearly the competitor can offer greater variety to customers.

When we talk about lead-times we mean not only the time it takes to make something, but also the time it takes to gather material from suppliers, to process customer orders and to deliver the product to the customer. By focusing upon lead-time reduction the firm can achieve a substantial improvement in customer service.

Benetton, the Italian fashion manufacturer, has achieved its strong position world-wide not just through its innovative styles and its strong brand, but through the speed with which it can respond to changes in the market. Even though trends in styles and colours will differ from one corner of the globe to another and even though fashion life cycles are short and fickle, Benetton can usually match the market requirement through its advanced logistics systems. By capturing information at the point of sale and swiftly transferring details of what is selling back to the point of production, whole weeks are taken out of the total response time.

Combined with the flexibility in manufacturing for which Benetton are renowned and with state-of-the-art, computerized, global distribution systems, this gives Benetton the ability to get a product into the retail store within weeks of the order being placed. Traditionally, in that industry, it will take months to meet a replenishment order, if indeed it can be achieved at all.

Focusing on time reductions in the logistics pipeline also has the benefit of making the company less reliant upon forecasts. If the lead-time for response to customer requirements is, say, ten weeks, then clearly we have to forecast ten weeks ahead and carry ten weeks of inventory.

If that lead-time can be reduced to five weeks, then the forecast horizon is halved, reducing the forecast error and the need for inventory is also substantially reduced. The closer lead-times of response get towards zero, then the greater the ability of the organization to meet customer requirements at less cost, yet paradoxically, with the ability to be much more flexible in meeting the demands of the marketplace.

Competing through capabilities

As the power of the brand declines, organizations are having to reappraise their traditional definitions of strengths and weaknesses. The view now gathering ground is that the real opportunities for differential advantage come from capabilities or the things we excel at, our 'distinctive competencies'.

Thus in a market characterized by shortening life cycles, for example, the ability to get new products to market in ever-shorter time frames becomes a source of competitive advantage. Likewise information systems that can capture demand as it happens and production systems than can respond rapidly are a major strength in a volatile market. Similar advantages accrue to organizations with order fulfilment and logistics systems that enable superior levels of customer service to be achieved.

None of this is to deny the importance of strong brands supported by motivated employees, but they are no longer enough by themselves. Conversely strong brands and motivated employees supported by best-in-class capabilities will be difficult for competitors to attack. Indeed wherever enduring leadership in any market is encountered it tends to support this contention – names such as McDonald's, Marks & Spencer, Disney and, more recently, British Airways, come to mind.

The more that organizations come to recognize the importance of competing through capabilities the more they will be forced to accept the need to switch the focus in the business away from managing functions to managing the processes that create those capabilities. All businesses are based upon a limited number of core processes. These include:

*   New product development
*   Demand generation
*   Order fulfilment
*   Supplier management process
*   Customer management process

These are supported by other processes such as information systems, strategic planning and performance measurement processes.

A major feature of processes is that by

(a) Vertical organizational focus

Traditional, functional organization

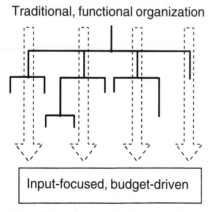

Input-focused, budget-driven

(b) Horizontal organizational focus

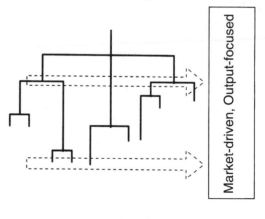

Market-driven, Output-focused

Figure 19.6   The shift from functions to processes

definition they are cross-functional and hence they must be managed cross-functionally. This has led to the notion of the 'horizontal organization' (Ostroff and Smith, 1992) which is market-facing and market-driven – as distinct from the conventional business which is 'vertical', focused around functions and is inward looking and budget-driven.

Companies as diverse as Xerox and Unilever are now transforming their organizations to become market-driven and to shift the locus of power from functions to core processes; in effect turning the organization chart through 90°. Figure 19.6 highlights the fundamental change in orientation that such a strategy requires.

The achievement of this transformation must begin with the recognition that logistics is essentially a planning orientation; in other words the logistics management process entails the linking of production plans with materials requirements plans in one direction and distribution requirements plans in the other. The aim of any organization should be to ensure that production produces only what the market requires whilst purchasing supplies production with what it needs to meet its immediate requirements.

How can this fairly obvious idea be converted into reality?

The key lies in the recognition that the order and its associated information flows should be at the heart of the business. It may be a truism but the only rationale for any commercial organization is to generate orders and to fulfil those orders. Everything the company does should be directly linked to facilitating this process and the process must itself be reflected in the organizational design and in its planning and control systems. All of this leads to the conclusion that the order fulfilment process should be designed as an integrated activity of the company with the conventional functions of the business supporting that process.

Developing a market-driven logistics strategy

It is a fundamental tenet of market-oriented companies that they seek to focus all their actions towards the goal of customer satisfaction. To support this goal it is imperative that the logistics strategy of the organization be designed to support its marketing strategy.

The successful creation of a market-driven logistics strategy must inevitably begin with a clear understanding of the service needs of the market. To be more precise it requires a definition of the value preferences that discriminate one market segment from another. A logistics system is a value delivery system; thus the aim should be to tailor as closely as possible a logistics strategy capable of delivering appropriate value package to the different value segments.

The starting point, as always, is market knowledge. Research into customers' service and value preferences is an essential foundation for developing innovative and competitive logistics strategies. Because customer needs and value preferences differ, there is a requirement to engineer flexibility into the organizations logistics processes.

To highlight this principle the case of Dell Computers is worth studying. For a company that only began life in 1984, Dell has achieved amazing success, to the point where is it one of the most profitable companies in the personal computer (PC) market. Its success is not so much due to its products – they embody the same technology as their competitors – but rather the way in which they have developed a supply chain to support an innovative channel management and customer service strategy.

To quote Michael Dell, the founder:

Our net income grew faster than sales as we continue to improve costs and to capture economies of scale. They stem from a decade of developing and implementing strategies designed to maximize the inherent strengths of the Dell direct business model. We believe our business model will remain the engine of our growth because it provides us with a number of competitive advantages:

- First, we bypass computer dealers and avoid related price mark-ups. This became a dramatic advantage as competition in the indirect channel drove up the cost of dealer incentives.
- Second, we build each system to a specific customer order, which eliminates inventories of finished goods to resellers and enables us to move new technologies and lower cost components into our product lines faster.
- Third, our direct contacts with thousands of customers every day enable us to tailor our support offerings to target markets and to control the consistency of customer service around the world.
- Fourth, we leverage our relationships with key technology partners and with our customers to incorporate the most relevant new technologies into our products rapidly.
- Finally, our low inventory and low fixed-asset model gives us one of the highest returns on invested capital in our industry. (Dell Annual Report, 1998).

By following a strategy of direct distribu-

tion, Dell is able to achieve a higher level of customization than many of its competitors whilst operating a low-cost supply chain. The results have been impressive. In just fifteen years of existence, the company had overtaken IBM to become the world's number two manufacturer of PCs and the most profitable.

Dell has recognized that it can gain a significant competitive advantage through its exploitation of a non-traditional distribution channel. Dell also makes great use of its direct customer contact to research needs and to gain feedback. Its pioneering use of the Internet has further strengthened its ability to provide tailored solutions to individual customers' specific needs through a sophisticated software-driven supply chain management process.

In many respects the way in which Dell has combined a direct distribution strategy with the technology of the Internet presents a possible model for the future. The trend towards direct distribution can only be accelerated by the widespread use of the Internet and electronic commerce generally. The role of the traditional intermediary in the distribution channel is under threat. Unless such intermediaries can find new ways to add value for customers then their future may be limited.

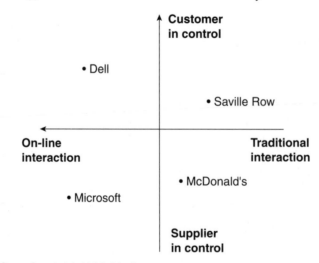

Source: Adapted from Steve Bowbrick, Web Media

Figure 19.7   Customers take control in an on-line world

The challenge increasingly will be to seek out new ways in which customer demand can be captured and satisfied more cost-effectively. At the same time customers in every market are seeking tailored solutions to their buying needs, calling for radically different channel strategies and operations capabilities. As we enter the era of 'mass customization' (Pine, 1993) the focus on supply chain management will inevitably increase.

Figure 19.7 highlights the fundamental change that is taking place in the marketplace as technology and supply chain capabilities enable radically different channel strategies to be implemented and supported. Being in the top left-hand quadrant of the model shown in Figure 19.7 can bring many advantages both in terms of customer focus as well as cost reduction. The challenge to those organizations who find themselves stuck with traditional distribution channels is to find new ways to create value for their customers by making better use of their trad-itional distribution channels. Distributors will increasingly need to take on additional value-creating roles if they are to survive in the future. Innovative approaches to channel strategy, combined with appropriate use of information technology and supply chain capability will increasingly be fundamental to marketplace success.

Changing the marketing focus

A central theme of this chapter has been the need for a change in the traditional focus of marketing which, in the past at least, has been primarily on winning customers and building market share. The new focus, it is suggested, should be as much upon the retention of existing customers as it is upon the gaining of new ones. The challenge now becomes one of how to develop marketing strategies that will do both these things. Relationship marketing is emerging as a new paradigm that recognizes the need to build long-term relationships with customers built upon service and quality.

It is for this reason that logistics management is now seen by many companies as a critical component of their marketing strategy. Logistics focuses upon the physical satisfaction of demand and it provides the key to meeting the ever-growing demand for quick and reliable response.

It is becoming evident that to compete and survive in today's volatile marketplace requires processes that are capable of providing high levels of product availability and variety yet which are low cost and reliable. Whilst these goals might appear incompatible, an increasing number of companies are proving otherwise. By asking fundamental questions about the way they do things and with a willingness to reengineer their business processes, these companies are emerging as the leaders in their markets.

References

Aaker, D. A. (1991) *Managing Brand Equity*, The Free Press, New York.

Brady, J. and Davis, I. (1993) Marketing's Mid-Life Crisis, *McKinsey Quarterly*, No. 2, 17–28.

Christopher, M., Payne, A. and Ballantyne, D. (1991) *Relationship Marketing*, Butterworth-Heinemann, Oxford.

Ostroff, F. and Smith, D. (1992) The Horizontal Organization, *McKinsey Quarterly*, No. 1, 148–168.

Pine, J. (1993) *Mass Customisation*, Harvard Business School Press.

Reichheld, F. and Sasser, E. (1990) Zero Defections: Quality Comes to Services, *Harvard Business Review*, September–October, 105–116.

Stalk, G. and Hout, T. (1990) *Competing Against Time*, The Free Press, New York.

Further reading

Albrecht, K. and Bradford, L. (1990) *The Service Advantage*, Richard D. Irwin. To remain competitive in a changing marketplace requires a clear understanding of customers' needs and attitudes. This practical guide takes the reader through a customer research programme. Whilst aimed specifically at companies in the service industries, the guidance it provides has wider applicability.

Christopher, M. (1992) *The Customer Service Planner*, Butterworth-Heinemann, Oxford. This book emphasizes distribution and logistics as the main drivers of service performance. The key to success in customer service management is to strive to develop 'delivery systems' which are superior in the sense that they improve our customers' competitiveness and hence our own.

Christopher, M. (1998) *Logistics and Supply Chain Management*, 2nd edn, Pitman Publishing. The goal of supply chain management is to link the marketplace, the distribution network, the manufacturing process and the procurement strategy in such a way that customers are serviced at higher levels yet at lower total cost. This book highlights the role of logistics in achieving these goals.

Christopher, M., Payne, A. and Ballantyne, D. (1991) *Relationship Marketing*, Butterworth-Heinemann, Oxford. The strategic emphasis of relationship marketing is as much on keeping customers as it is on getting them in the first place. The aim is to provide unique value in chosen markets, sustainable over time, which brings customers back for more. This book emphasizes both quality and customer service as the critical foundations for long-term customer relationships.

Schonberger, R. (1990) *Building a Chain of Customers*, The Free Press, New York. This book provides a practical framework for linking the final marketplace with the operations and supply processes of the business. Every organization has internal and external customers and the challenge is to link them together in such a way through seamless and responsive processes that are superior to those of competitors, both in terms of costs and service.

CHAPTER 20

Controlling marketing

KEITH WARD

Overview

Controlling both the 'effectiveness and efficiency' of marketing requires an integrated partnership between finance and marketing managers. Financial control can only be exercised in advance of financial commitment and this necessitates a rigorous financial evaluation of *proposed* marketing expenditure, as well as the application of effective financial controls as the expenditure actually takes place.

Marketing activities are normally absolutely critical to the most common long-term financial objective of commercially oriented organizations, which is creating shareholder value. The best way to create shareholder value in the long term is to develop and then exploit a sustainable competitive advantage. This enables the business to generate a rate of return substantially in excess of that required by its investors, i.e. a super profit.

However developing a sustainable competitive advantage normally involves significant up-front expenditures by the business. These expenditures are high-risk, long-term investments and should be rigorously evaluated and controlled, even though any resulting competitive advantage may be intangible (such as a brand). The best financial evaluation techniques for such long-term investments use discounted cash flows to take account of the timing differences between the expenditures and the resulting cash inflows.

If these long-term marketing investments are successful then the business has created a marketing asset, which may continue to produce high returns for many years to come. This will only be true if the marketing asset is properly maintained after it has been successfully developed. A sensible approach to controlling marketing, therefore, is to distinguish between development marketing expenditure and maintenance marketing expenditure as their objectives are significantly different.

The objective of *development marketing expenditure* is to create a valuable long-term asset and hence the returns from this type of investment will be received over the economic life of the asset. Conversely *maintenance marketing expenditure* is designed to keep the existing marketing assets in their present valuable condition, and the returns are much more short term. Indeed it can be argued that the failure to spend adequately on maintenance is often reflected very rapidly in declining sales revenues and profit streams.

These different objectives and time-scales mean that different financial evaluation and control techniques should be applied to development and maintenance activities. The control process must be tailored to the needs of the business.

This tailoring process is particularly important in designing the appropriate financial planning and control system for the organization. There are widely differing competitive strategies which can be implemented, even in the same industry at the same time, and these differing strategies require suitably tailored control processes and performance measures. There is a need for a hierarchy of both economic and managerial performance measures for all businesses, but it is critical that some of these performance measures incorporate indications of how well the business is doing in terms of its long-term objectives.

It is particularly important that the performance measures are tailored to the key strategic thrusts of the business; if these change, the financial control process may need to be changed as well. One common strategic marketing thrust is to develop strong brands as a source of sustainable competitive advantage. A brand-led strategy requires a good brand evaluation process if the high brand expenditures are to be properly financially evaluated and controlled. Brands can be based on either products or customers, but other types of marketing strategy can also be customer led or product based.

In a customer-led strategy, the long-term customer relationship should be regarded as a critical asset of the business; thus development expenditure is invested to win the customer and maintenance expenditure is needed to retain the relationship for its full potential economic life. Life cycle customer account profitability analysis is therefore important in such a relationship-marketing oriented business.

Similar issues occur with product-based strategies and a suitably tailored response is required. Product life cycle costing is quite a well developed technique in some industries. It uses the concept of the experience curve to establish the long-term decline in real per-unit costs over time as cumulative volume increases. This declining cost analysis can be used to develop a marketing strategy where current pricing is based on anticipated long-run costs rather than the current much higher short-term costs. Resulting short-term losses can be regarded as an investment in developing a sustainable competitive advantage based on the faster progress down the experience curve

which could lead to a sustainably lower cost position in the long term.

The need for closely integrated involvement of finance and marketing managers creates the opportunity for a marketing finance manager to work in the marketing area. Such a role can help immensely with the important financial evaluation of marketing expenditures and their subsequent control. It can also act as the focus for coordinating the important strategic competitor analyses which require inputs from many parts of the business.

Introduction

In many businesses, the marketing function and the finance function can often find themselves in apparent direct conflict, due to the lack of the kind of close working relationship which finance has developed with other areas of the business, such as operations or production. Indeed it can be the case, in some companies, that marketing managers feel that their finance colleagues' main interest in marketing is to try to stop them spending money. Conversely, it can appear to these same finance managers that the principal objective of their marketing colleagues is to spend as much money as possible on increasingly esoteric advertisements, very expensive trade and consumer promotions, higher customer discounts, etc.

Clearly, if the business is to achieve its long-term objectives, it is essential that its marketing expenditures are well directed and effectively controlled. Such effective control can only be exercised if the marketing and finance areas work together in an integrated partnership. A significant challenge facing the finance function in many businesses, therefore, involves changing their perceived involvement in marketing activities from that of a cost adding constraint to that of a value adding, enabling, participative role. The organizational structure implications of this change are considered towards the end of this chapter, but 'controlling marketing' requires involvement in two closely related but distinct aspects of marketing activities.

Prior to the actual *commitment* by the organization to spend money, a rigorous financial evaluation should be carried out. This is because true financial control can only be exercised in advance of any legally binding, financial commitment; once committed, the business will incur cancellation charges, or even still have to pay the full cost, if it changes its mind. This financial evaluation compares the proposed expenditure against the potential benefits, taking into account the risks involved in the particular activity. This evaluation should include any other potential ways of achieving the same benefits.

The financial evaluation process should also indicate how the success/failure of the expenditure can be assessed and how quickly this assessment can be made. It may also be possible to improve the overall probability of success before committing the majority of the expenditure; this may be achieved by market research activity. This risk-reducing type of marketing expenditure should itself be evaluated financially and any early warning indicators of success/failure should be identified. Any marketing activities where such early indicators can be identified are significantly lower risk than those where 'success' can only be assessed after all the expenditure has been incurred. If the initial expenditure has clearly failed then the business can avoid incurring the rest of the expenditure if early and effective financial controls have been identified.

'Controlling marketing' can, therefore, be regarded as two interrelated processes of financial evaluation and financial control. As discussed in depth during this chapter, much of the challenge relates to putting financial values to marketing activities and objectives. Within the marketing area many specific control measures have been developed to evaluate and control a wide range of marketing activities. Indeed, as discussed in other areas of the book, different marketing objectives are achieved by very specifically aimed marketing techniques. Unfortunately far too often these very different marketing approaches are financially controlled using a single financial measure, which is consequently often inappropriate. This is exacerbated because the most common financial control measures consider the efficiency with which the activity has been carried out, rather than the effectiveness with which it has achieved its predetermined objectives.

An example using advertising expenditure may make this clearer. The 'efficiency' of purchasing media advertising (whether TV air-time or newspaper space, etc.) can be measured in terms of the cost per thousand customers reached by the campaign. However such an efficiency based measure says very little about how 'effective' the advertising expenditure was in terms of achieving its predetermined objectives. These marketing objectives could range from creating brand awareness, through changing the attitudes of potential customers or stimulating trial by new customers, to increasing the rate of usage by existing customers – each of which would probably use a different style of advertisement.

In marketing terms the achievement of these objectives should be measurable, e.g. any increase in brand awareness can be measured by testing what brand awareness there was before the advertising campaign and re-testing afterwards. Thus marketing can normally 'prove' whether they have achieved their marketing objective, but the key financial *evaluation* question is whether achieving this objective was financially worthwhile. The company may plan to spend £5 million on a national advertising campaign which is designed to increase brand awareness from 30 per cent to 40 per cent within the target market group of consumers. The brand awareness both before and after the campaign could be tested in order to see if the marketing objective was achieved and the efficiency with which the £5 million expenditure was spent could be monitored. However, the money has not necessarily been effectively spent, unless the benefit of increasing awareness by 10 per cent has been financially evaluated as being significantly greater than the £5 million cost which is to be incurred. Clearly, to be of any value as a financial control, this financial evaluation must be undertaken prior to the expenditure being committed, i.e. the advertising being booked. Even more clearly, such an evaluation, which relies on estimates of the increased future sales revenues which are expected to result ultimately from increased brand awareness, cannot be conducted by the finance function in isolation. It requires an integrated approach from both marketing and finance, as does the ongoing control as the expenditure is committed. This is necessary as it may be possible to reduce the related risk by phasing the advertising expenditure in order to check that it is generating the increased awareness required (e.g. by doing a regional test first).

Against this backdrop of an integrated, coordinated approach to trying to control marketing effectiveness rather than just efficiency, this chapter considers a range of marketing strategies and the consequences for the required financial control system.

A market-focused mission

The most common financial objective of commercially oriented organizations is to create shareholder value. Consequently the differentiating elements within mission statements and long-term corporate objectives relate to the ways in which (i.e. the 'hows') this shareholder value is to be created on a sustainable basis.

Shareholder value is only created when shareholders achieve a total return (which can only be generated by dividend yield and/or an increase in the value of their investment) which is greater than the return which they require from that investment. This definition emphasizes that shareholder value is not automatically created when a company makes a profit. The level of this profit must be placed in the context of the rate of return required by the shareholders, and this required rate of return is determined by the level of risk perceived by the shareholders with regard to this investment.

As shown in Figure 20.1, shareholders naturally dislike risk in that they demand increasing rates of return for increasing risk perceptions. However what is often forgotten, even by finance professionals, is that the upward sloping 'risk adjusted required rate of return line' in Figure 20.1 is, in reality, the shareholders' indifference line. In other words, moving from one point on the line to any other point on the line merely compensates the investor for

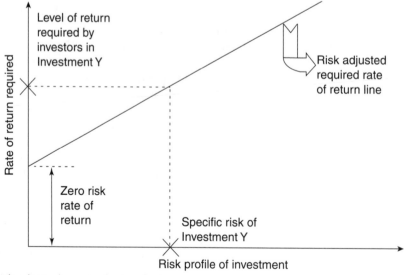

Figure 20.1   Risk-adjusted required rate of return

a change in their risk perception; it does not create shareholder value.

Shareholder value is only created when total returns are greater than required returns and this relationship should be used by the company to assess any investment proposal. Investment decisions will only create real shareholder

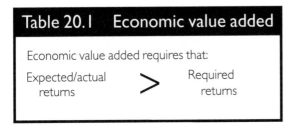

value when the expected return from the investment is greater than the shareholders' required rate of return; i.e. the investment is expected to create 'economic value added'. This is encapsulated in Table 20.1 and should be applied to all

marketing investments, as is discussed in the next sections of this chapter.

This relationship can also be explained by reference to our risk/return graph as is done in Figure 20.2. As previously stated, moving along the shareholders' risk/return line neither creates nor destroys shareholder value. Shareholder value is only created by implementing a strategy which enables the business to move 'above the line', as shown in Figure 20.2.

As can be seen from the diagram, the company can move in one of three possible 'value adding' directions. It can decide to try to increase return, even though it accepts that such a strategy will increase its risk profile as well; the economic value added comes from increasing the expected return proportionately more than the risk perception increases. Many marketing-led growth strategies could fall into this category; including launching existing products into new markets, developing new products for

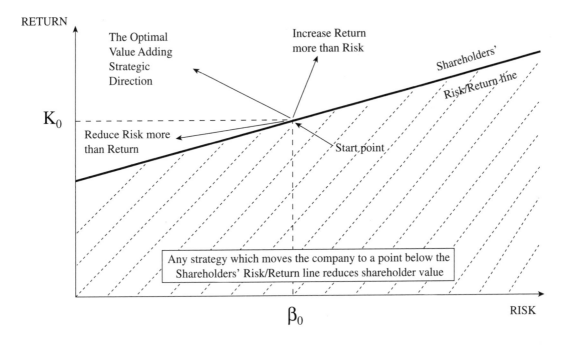

Figure 20.2 Economic value adding strategies – utilizing a strong sustainable competitive advantage

existing customers and, particularly, trying to increase market share in a mature, non-growing, highly competitive, existing market. It is vitally important that the financial evaluation, which is carried out prior to these marketing initiatives, considers not only the projected increased future returns but also the increases in the risk profile of the business. (These issues are considered in detail later in the chapter.)

A second value creating option is deliberately to reduce the expected rate of return in the future but to do so in a way which will reduce the associated risk to an even greater extent. This more than proportionate reduction in risk perception makes the slightly lower expected return more valuable to the shareholders than the previous higher, but more risky, rate of return. There are several marketing strategies which seek to create economic value added through this route and these include long-term discount arrangements designed to create customer loyalty. These more loyal customers should generate more consistent, less volatile rates of return in the future and volatility in the level of financial return is a key indicator of risk.

However the most attractive value adding, strategic direction is obviously to increase the expected rate of return while, at the same time, reducing the risk perception. This reducing risk perception can result in a reduction in the required rate of return, so that the economic value added gap between expected and required rates of return can be substantial. Not surprisingly, because it is the attractive strategic direction to take it is also the most difficult to achieve. In order to generate increased future rates of return with reduced levels of risk, the business must have developed a strong 'sustainable competitive advantage', which is, of course, the main objective of modern corporate and competitive strategies. A strong sustainable competitive advantage should enable a company to increase its future rates of return to levels well above both its required rate of return and the rates of return of its competitors.

However its sustainable competitive advantage could also mean that, even in the event of a down-turn in the market, its rates of return are less volatile in the future than those of its competitors. If this is the case, the company's risk profile will be lower than its competition, which could result in a lower required rate of return.

This introduces the key concept, which will be utilized through the chapter, of *a 'super profit'*, which is the excess return achieved by a business due to the development and maintenance of a *sustainable* competitive advantage. The 'excess' return represents the surplus expected or actual return over the rate of return required by investors.

A sustainable competitive advantage

A key aspect of a competitive advantage in terms of its ability to create shareholder value is its sustainability. If competitors can match the competitive advantage immediately, or even relatively quickly, the company will be unable to exploit it to achieve a super profit. This actually highlights an important but simple way of considering any sustainable competitive advantage; it should act as an effective *entry barrier* which stops competitors from coming into the attractive market created by the business. This is shown diagrammatically in Figure 20.3. When any company is achieving a super profit in a particular market, the market is financially attractive to lots of other companies. If these other companies were all able to enter this market, they would rapidly drive down the rate of return for *all* companies in the market to the required rate, thus removing the super profit of the original company and ending the creation of shareholder value. This is what would happen under the economic definition of perfect competition; thus, another way of thinking about *sustainable* competitive advantages is that they can only exist under conditions of imperfect competition.

The possible entry barriers shown in Figure 20.3 are not meant to be totally comprehensive

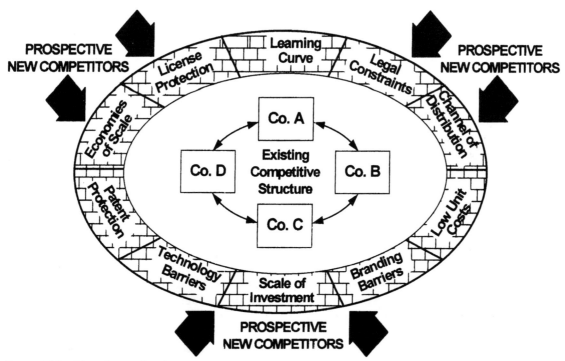

Figure 20.3   Use of entry barriers

but they illustrate a number of important issues relating to sustainable competitive advantages and their financial control. It is clear that some potential entry barriers are the direct result of marketing activities, e.g. branding and control of the channel of distribution, but several more can only be fully exploited through the implementation of the appropriate marketing strategy (such as low unit costs, technology barriers, etc.). However all these entry barriers are normally only developed by substantial investment (i.e. up-front) expenditures and this investment must be regarded as very high risk. If the entry barrier does not work, e.g. if competitors can find a way around it or through it, the company will be unable to generate a return on its expenditure designed to develop the competitive advantage.

It should also be clear from the illustrations of entry barriers that they have a finite life cycle (the best example of this is a patent which expires at the end of 20 years). The company may be able to extend the economic life of some

entry barriers by carefully managing the sustainable competitive advantage (e.g. as has been done by certain brands, such as Coca-Cola and Marlboro), but this will normally require additional expenditure on maintaining the entry barrier. Alternatively the business may decide to reinvest part of its initial super profits in developing a replacement sustainable competitive advantage for when the initial advantage ceases to be effective. Examples of this are pharmaceutical companies which often invest heavily in branding their patented drugs during the patent period. This actually reduces the level of super profit during this period as they are then effectively a monopoly supplier, but it can create strong customer loyalty, which can work as a very effective competitive advantage once the patent has expired.

These development, maintenance and reinvestment activities must be subjected to the rigorous financial evaluation already discussed and this is considered in detail below. However, these entry barriers are the really important sources of shareholder value creation and should therefore be managed as the key *assets* of the business. Unfortunately, apparently because many of them are intangible and somewhat nebulous to most finance managers, many companies still regard their fixed assets (factories, offices, plant and machinery, etc.) as the only real assets of the business. Without any intangible marketing assets to exploit, these tangible assets would probably generate, at most, the shareholders' required rate of return.

All of these sustainable competitive advantages are, by definition, really relative statements in that they refer to things which the business does better, cheaper, faster, etc., than anyone else. They also need to be considered in the context of the customers who are willing to continue to pay a price for the good or service which enables the supplier to generate a super profit. In other words, the customers must still perceive themselves as getting good value for money, sometimes despite the absence of direct, effective viable competition. This means that the financial evaluation and control process must also have an external focus in that it must include an analysis of competitors and customers. This competitor analysis must not be limited only to obvious existing competitors, as new potential competitors may be attracted to any industry or sector which is generating significant super profits. Indeed existing customers and even suppliers may be tempted to become competitors through vertical integration if the potential returns are high enough. It is essential that the company's current position is protected as far as possible by investing in creating strong entry barriers to deter all the identified potential competitors. Once again, finance managers are most unlikely to identify, on their own, all the potential novel marketing strategies which competitors may initiate to try to break through an existing entry barrier. Competitor analysis therefore needs to be done as a coordinated effort, utilizing all the knowledge and skills available within the business.

Investing in developing a sustainable competitive advantage

As stated above, many marketing activities should be evaluated and controlled as strategic investment decisions, irrespective of how they are treated for financial accounting purposes. Any financial investment involves spending money now in the expectation that, in the future, returns will be generated to more than recover the initial expenditure. Where the period over which these expected returns will be received is likely to be much longer than the current financial year, it is important that a proper financial evaluation is carried out. This is particularly vital where these investment expenditures are regarded as high risk, due to the volatility associated with the potential outcomes. If the success of these investments is also critical to the achievement of the organization's long-term objectives and overall mission, the need for a sound financial evaluation and control process is absolutely paramount.

In very many businesses, these factors are most obviously present in the key marketing investments which are being made in developing brands, entering new markets, launching new products, developing new potential channels of distribution such as the Internet, etc. Thus it is vital that these high-risk, long-term investments are financially evaluated using the most sophisticated techniques available. Many companies would automatically calculate a full discounted cash flow for even the simplest, relatively small investment on labour saving machinery in their factory or their operations areas. Yet these same companies often do not carry out such a long-term financial evaluation of even much larger expenditures in the marketing area. Indeed it is still not uncommon to find almost no *financial* justification supporting many significant marketing initiatives; the rationale for the decision is based on the fact that the initiative is 'strategically important' or that 'it has to be done'.

There appear to be many reasons for the lack of sound financial controls in this area. Almost all marketing expenditure is charged (i.e. written off) to the profit and loss account in the year in which it is spent, irrespective of the time-frame over which the returns may be generated. This is in accordance with the 'prudent' view underlying financial accounting, because the returns from these marketing expenditures cannot be guaranteed. However there is no way that any new brand launch, new market entry, or major new product development, is financially justifiable by considering only the returns generated in the first year. All investment decisions must be financially evaluated by comparing the expenditures needed against the future expected returns. Where these returns are only expected well in the future, they should be included as their present value equivalent so that the comparison is validly based (the details of this technique, which is the discounted cash flow referred to above, are outside the scope of this chapter but are covered in any good finance text). The actual accounting treatment is irrelevant to this decision evaluation process, as economic business decisions should be based on the future differential cash flows arising from the decision.

Another apparent justification for not applying financial rigour to major marketing investment decisions is that it is very difficult to estimate accurately the future cash flows which may arise quite some time into the future from such expenditures. This is, of course, true but it is also true of many major investments in more tangible assets, where these same companies still try to prepare full financial evaluations. Indeed most of these companies would find it unacceptable to consider any major tangible asset investment which was not supported by a full cash flow projection into the future.

It can be, and it often is, argued that the cash flows from many marketing investments are even more difficult to project as they can be dramatically affected by competitor responses or unexpected shifts in the market. This merely indicates the high risk nature of many marketing investments. A major focus of the financial evaluation should therefore be on highlighting the key risks, how they can be quantified and, wherever possible, how they can be removed or minimized. This is the very essence of good financial control and may indicate a need for extensive market research or more thorough competitor analysis before committing the majority of the expenditure.

Marketing investments cannot be left out of the financial evaluation and control process as they are, for most businesses, the major source of long-term shareholder value. As indicated in Figure 20.3, there are several entry barriers that do not directly depend on marketing but most of these are short-lived advantages due to competitor responses. Product innovations are a good example of this unless they are protected by a patent or other restriction on competitive copying. Once the innovation is launched, competitors will attempt to copy the new product, or even improve on it. In many industries the time lag before these competitors can launch their own versions is now very short; e.g. in retail financial services this time lag can normally be measured in weeks not years. Thus the product innovation does not, of itself, create a long-term sustainable competitive advantage but, if allied to the appropriate marketing strategy, the business may be able to exploit it to create considerable shareholder value. Each individual innovation could be exploited very rapidly as long as marketing creates very strong immediate awareness and instant access to the product (e.g. in retail financial services, mass advertising linked with a telephone sales system). This strategy increases the associated risk because all the marketing expenditure is required up-front; doing extensive market research could easily give away to competitors the product innovation and hence enable them to launch their versions nationally at exactly the same time.

An alternative strategy could be to build a brand around the innovations developed by the company, so that it develops a reputation as the leading innovator in the industry. This branded reputation may attract a substantial loyal group of customers and this could create the ability to earn a super profit; each new product innovation therefore reinforces the brand attributes rather than having to earn a super profit itself.

Marketing assets: development and maintenance expenditures

It has already been argued that the most valuable real assets possessed by most businesses are in the marketing area. The proper definition of an asset is anything which will generate future net cash inflows into the business; this clearly includes brands, trademarks, customers, channels of distribution, products, etc. Thus assets are by no means limited to the normal tangible items which appear on the balance sheet of the company. This more general attitude to marketing assets has important implications for the control of marketing.

Many businesses still persist with the classification of marketing expenditures between 'above-the-line' (meaning mainly media advertising) and 'below-the-line' (meaning promotions for both trade and customers, etc.). This distinction literally refers to where the expenditures tend to be shown in the profit and loss account but, in today's marketing environment, they have almost no relevance at all. The increasing power of many channels of distribution (such as supermarket retailers) and even consumers, let alone industrial customers, together with an increasing fragmentation in mass advertising mediums (e.g. TV channels), has led to a significant increase in the proportion of many marketing budgets which is spent 'below-the-line', i.e. directly to channels and end customers. If this is a more effective means of achieving the marketing objectives of the business, it is extremely sensible to do this; the change in classification is irrelevant.

A much more important way of analysing marketing expenditure has unfortunately been ignored by many companies. Creating any valuable long-term asset requires the investment of

substantial funds, as has already been discussed. This is also true of marketing assets, which require significant expenditure during their developing periods. This development expenditure creates the attributes of the asset (e.g. brand awareness, distribution access, customer loyalty), which will generate the super profit returns of the future.

Once the marketing asset has been developed to its full potential, as with any asset, it must be properly maintained or it will decline in value very rapidly. A feature of many marketing assets (such as brands) is that some of their attributes can decline very quickly (such as brand awareness) if they are not properly maintained. Thus another component of the marketing budget is maintenance expenditure. Development expenditure is designed to increase the long-term value of the marketing asset by improving specific attributes of the asset, while maintenance expenditure aims to keep these attributes at their existing levels.

It has already been stated that really valuable assets (i.e. those that represent a sustainable competitive advantage) have a finite economic life and this is equally true for marketing assets. Thus the mix of development and maintenance marketing expenditure will change over the life cycle. During the initial launch period all the marketing expenditure will be development activity as it is aimed at building the value of the asset; also, there are no attributes to be maintained. Once the asset starts to be established, the existing attributes need some level of maintenance expenditure but the majority of marketing effort still goes to developing the asset to its optimum level. Once this is reached there is no longer a financial justification for more development expenditure, and all the current marketing activity (which may be considerably lower than during the development phase) should be targeted at maintaining the asset's current position and strengths.

Eventually the marketing asset will approach the end of its economic life and, at this time, the business may reduce the marketing expenditure below the full level required properly to maintain the asset. In other words, the decline stage is managed so as to maximize the cash flows received by the business. Indeed this is the critical financial performance measure for any marketing asset; the objective is to maximize the super profits earned over the economic life of the asset. Due to the long life cycle of many of these assets, this has to be expressed in terms of the net present values of the cash flows expected to be generated over this economic life.

Also because the economic life can, in certain cases, be extended, some marketing expenditure may be targeted at extending the economic life of the asset. An alternative strategy may be to transfer the existing strong asset attributes (such as from a brand) from a declining product to a new growing product. Even though doing so will accelerate the decline of the current product, it may extend the economic life of the 'brand' asset by associating it with another appropriate product.

This distinction between development and maintenance expenditure is very important because the timing of the returns from each type is very different. Development expenditure represents a long-term investment and the returns may not be received until several years later. Thus the expenditure is incurred now but the financial benefit is not felt this year. The impact of maintenance expenditure is likely to be much quicker because, as the attributes decline, there is likely to be a corresponding fall off in sales revenues and profits. This timing difference means that different financial evaluation and control processes must be used for each type of expenditure.

In many companies, the marketing budget represents a very significant proportion of total expenditure. When the company comes under short-term profit pressure it is, therefore, very common for the financial director to look to marketing to make a substantial contribution to any required reduction. Under the traditional classification system, it is easy to predict where most of these cuts in marketing expenditure are likely to fall: on the long-term development expenditures. This is because reducing these develop-

ment activities will have no negative impacts on sales revenues in the short term, whereas cutting maintenance activities would probably reduce sales this year.

Unfortunately the impact of reducing development marketing expenditure will be felt in the future because the asset will not be as fully developed. At least by segmenting marketing expenditure the consequences of this short-term action will be more clearly highlighted and the future expectations for the business can be appropriately modified. However the best way of really focusing on these issues is through a well designed financial planning and control process.

Financial planning and control process

The main objectives of any financial planning and control process are to enable the organization to develop, implement and control a strategy which seeks to achieve its long-term objectives and overall mission. A good control process would indicate when modifications were needed in the overall strategy through short-term feedback loops and appropriate performance measures. Thus, as indicated in Figure 20.4, the long-term objectives must be consistent with the short-term budgets actually used by the company on a regular basis.

It is an obvious but important statement that this year's budget must be the first year of the long-term plan but, in many companies, this does not stay the reality as the year unfolds. No plan is ever implemented without significant modifications, not least because there are always unforeseen changes in the external environment. Hence, during the year, the tactics and even the strategy may need to be changed. It is important that these required changes are, as far as possible, still consistent with the long-term objectives of the business. At least these long-term objectives should be taken into account as the possible modifications to the strategy are being considered. Unfortunately, in many cases,

Figure 20.4   Very simple business model

changes are made during the year which enable the short-term budget to be achieved *at the expense* of these long-term objectives.

This can happen because the performance measures in use within most businesses focus almost exclusively on the short-term budget period (i.e. this year). This would not necessarily matter as long as these performance measures include clear indicators of how the business was doing in terms of its long-term objectives. In most cases these longer-term performance indicators are missing. Hence, as discussed in the previous section, it is quite common for the main performance measures to focus on sales revenues and profits this year, even though the long-term strategy may be based on the business developing new sustainable competitive advantages. This concentration on short-term performance increases the pressure on managers to compromise on longer-term investments in order to deliver the required performance now. Marketing expenditure is the major target area for this due to the expensing, in accounting terms writing off all expenditure in the current year, including long-term development activities; few people would consider it completely sensible to stop half-way through building a new factory in order to try to boost profits this

year, yet companies often curtail marketing development spending on brands, etc. to achieve the same thing.

It is, therefore, very important that businesses develop an appropriate set of performance measurements, which are both closely integrated with their long-term objectives and provide early indications when things are going wrong. A business actually needs performance measures at three different levels if it is really to stay in control of its long-term performance.

The highest level of performance measure relates to the overall economic performance of the company, as this is of fundamental interest to its shareholders. In other words, is the business operating in attractive markets and industries where shareholder value can be created? If not, the long-term strategy should be either to change the competitive environment in order to make it more attractive (e.g. rationalize the industry or develop a new form of sustainable competitive environment) or to exit from this industry in order to invest in more attractive areas.

This top level of performance measure says very little about the relative performance of the business and its managers. In certain very financially attractive industries the relatively few companies involved may all earn super profits and hence create shareholder value. Equally in an extremely over-supplied, very unattractive industry, the best management team in the world should lose less money than all the others but they will find it impossible to create shareholder value. Thus the second tier of performance measure is needed to put the absolute level of economic performance into an appropriate relative context; a 40 per cent p.a. return on assets looks less impressive if all competitors are achieving over 60 per cent!

This introduces a key issue for performance measures. Some performance measures are designed to reflect the economic performance of the total business or of a particular part, while others focus on the managerial performance of the people running the business or parts of it. Few performance measures work successfully in both areas because, while economic performance measures must take into account all the factors affecting the business, managerial performance measures should only include elements where the manager can exert a degree of control. It is unfair, and extremely demotivating, to hold managers accountable for something over which they can exercise no control.

At the very top of an organization (e.g. the main board of directors in a publicly quoted group of companies) there may be very little need to distinguish between economic and managerial performance measures. If the current areas of activity become unattractive, the board can reorganize the group to focus on more attractive areas and even could exit from the now unattractive businesses. At lower levels within the business, managers have increasingly less freedom of action or managerial discretion. Hence different managerial performance measures must be used for different levels. The challenge is to ensure that each level of performance measure is consistent with the overall objectives of the total business. This concept, which is generally known as goal congruence, is based on the simple maxim of 'what you measure is what you get'; i.e. people tend to try

to achieve the objectives they are set. If, by achieving their objectives, they move the business away from its long-term objectives and strategy, it is the fault of the people setting the objectives, not the people doing the achieving!

Salesforce performance measures can provide two examples of these problems. Any sales manager with responsibility for a normal field salesforce has, in reality, relatively little discretion in terms of the cost of that salesforce. Salesforce total costs are made up of a large number of different items, as is illustrated in Table 20.2. At first sight, therefore, it appears that the responsible manager can influence the total salesforce costs of £10 million in a number of ways. However, on closer examination it becomes clear that there is only one real cost driver for the field salesforce.

If salaries per employee are reduced to levels below those prevailing in the industry, this is likely to lead to the loss of the best salespeople. Similarly, attempting to reduce petrol or car expenses per head or accommodation and subsistence per salesperson will reduce the effectiveness of the salesforce, if these relationships have been properly established in the past. The separate cost items per salesperson can be defined fairly tightly for most industries, so that the only real controllable variable is actually the number of salespeople employed by the company. The financial evaluation and control process should consequently focus on justifying the number of salespeople by considering the relative financial contributions from different sized salesforces, and on validating the engineered cost relationship being used by the salesforce (this relationship is itself slightly dynamic as the costs per employee will change if the size of the salesforce changes significantly).

The other performance measure issue for this field salesforce is how the performance of an individual salesperson should be assessed. In many companies this is done by setting sales revenue targets or sales volume targets against which each salesperson is measured. The problem is that an exclusive focus on short-term sales

Table 20.2   Field salesforce cost structure

Salaries	×
Other employment costs	×
Commission	×
Recruitment	×
Car expenses	×
Telephones	×
Petrol	×
Accommodation	×
Subsistence	×
Entertaining	×
Samples	×
Consumables	×
Training	×
Support costs	×
	£10 million

At present, 100 sales people are employed by the company

revenues or volumes may be counter-productive to the long-term strategy of the business. For example, many branded fast-moving consumer goods companies consider improving the quality of the product received by the consumer as being very important to their long-term success. For many of these companies, the freshness of the product is a significant factor in its overall quality, while they incentivize their salesforce to sell as many goods as possible. The potential problem is that the salesforce do not sell direct to the consumer but to the channel of distribution (e.g. the retailer) which supplies to the consumer. More sales into the channel pipeline do not automatically lead to more purchases out of the channel by these consumers; if this does not occur there is a risk of more retail stocks and consequently less fresh, poorer quality ultimate purchases by the consumers. However no blame should be allocated to the salesforce, they merely achieved their objective of higher sales! What is needed are performance measures which are completely in line with the long-term objectives of the business.

Thus the third level of performance measures are very specific to the particular business and its long-term objectives. They must be appropriately tailored to the business and the level within the business at which they are being applied. It has already been established that there is a vast range of potentially successful competitive strategies, which are based on a specific mix of sustainable competitive advantage. Several of these different strategies may be being implemented in various segments of the same industry at the same time. The performance measures used should be appropriate to the specific requirements of the competitive strategy, which clearly means that different companies in the same industry may be using very different performance measures. Indeed the focus of their financial planning and control system should probably have far more in common with a company in a completely different industry but which is implementing a very similar strategy, than with a company in its own industry which is implementing a completely different strategy.

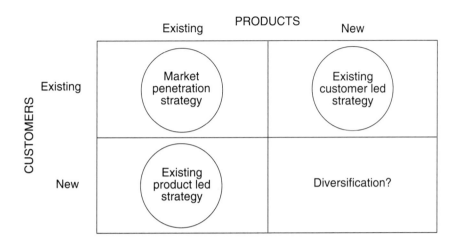

Figure 20.5   Potential strategic thrusts of businesses (based on the Ansoff matrix)

A key issue for a really good financial planning and control system is that it is tailored to the needs of the business. This means that, if the needs of the business change because the strategy has changed, the control system and the resulting tailored performance measures should also change. Unfortunately many companies are struggling to control their marketing activities because they are still using control systems designed for previous competitive strategies.

One way of illustrating this problem uses a development of the Ansoff matrix to highlight the different strategic thrusts which a business can have. The Ansoff matrix has been used for many years as a marketing planning tool as it indicates the way in which a business can try to fill the gap between the simple extrapolation of its current level of performance and the performance required to achieve its long-term objectives. The beauty of the matrix is that it describes these strategic options in very clear terms; i.e. increase the share of existing markets with existing products, sell new products to existing customers, sell existing products to new customers, or sell new products to new customers.

The Ansoff matrix illustrated in Figure 20.5 has only been modified in terms of descriptions applied to the boxes for selling new products to existing customers and selling existing products to new customers. Before considering these, the other two possibilities will be briefly examined from a financial control perspective.

The implications of growing the business by selling more existing products to existing customers has been researched extensively over many years with some very unsurprising results. Strategies to increase market share have been shown to create shareholder value most clearly when the market is growing strongly. This is because, if the market is static or declining, any increase in volume by the company has to be generated at the direct expense of competitors. They are likely to respond aggressively, possibly via a price war which could reduce the total profitability of the industry and all the players in it. Thus the strategy may be successful in gaining market share but it will not necessarily generate super profits. If the total industry is growing strongly, there is less chance of such aggressive competitive reaction as their own sales volumes and revenues may still be increasing despite them losing market share.

Selling new products to new customers has also been quite well researched and the shareholder value creation is also disappointing. Many companies seem to adopt this strategy as a risk-reducing strategy but a 'new, new'

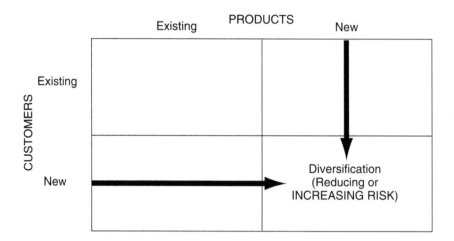

Figure 20.6   Diversification using the Ansoff matrix

strategic thrust is really an increase in risk, because it is not normally built on any existing competitive advantage, as shown in Figure 20.6.

This introduces the modification to the Ansoff matrix shown in Figure 20.5 because the key strategic thrust relates to the existing source of competitive advantage on which the growth strategy is based. In the case of selling new products to existing customers, this should be the loyal base of existing customers for whom new products are to be developed or acquired. Correspondingly the strategy of finding new customer groups, markets or segments in which to sell existing products should be built on an existing successful product which is capable of generating a super profit in its existing market.

These strategic thrusts are examined in more detail in the following sections which deal respectively with brand-led, customer-led and product-led strategies.

Brand-led strategies

Brands can be based either around products (e.g. Coca-Cola, Marlboro, Microsoft, Intel) or around customers (e.g. Marks & Spencer, Tesco, Virgin). They are, therefore, considered before either customer-led strategies or product-led

strategies, as a number of common issues can be more simply dealt with.

The nature of brands has been separately dealt with in Chapter 16 and so this section focuses on the financial control issues in a brand-led strategy. If a competitive strategy which is based on brands is to be successful, the brand must enable the business to earn a super profit on its more tangible assets, i.e. the brand becomes an intangible asset of the business. However brand assets can achieve this super profit in different ways and these different ways require appropriately tailored control processes and performance measures.

A strong brand may enable the branded 'product' to be sold at a higher price than its unbranded equivalent. Alternatively an equally strong brand could be sold at the same price as other products, but command a significantly greater share of the market on a consistent basis. A third branding positioning would be to combine a slightly higher price together with a higher market share. It is important that the control process understands and focuses on the specific brand strategy.

There are a number of stages involved in developing, and then maintaining, a brand as an asset. Some success, although not necessarily uniform success, must be achieved at each stage

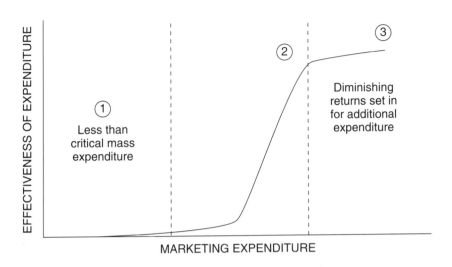

Figure 20.7   Relationship of marketing expenditure and effectiveness

if the brand is to have a sustainable super profit earning capability. As discussed earlier and elsewhere in the book, marketing has developed specific effectiveness measures for each element in the brand building process (e.g. awareness creation, propensity to purchase, ability to purchase such as distribution, trial rates, repeat purchase incidence, and levels of regular usage).

The financial control challenge is to develop a financial model which can incorporate these non-financial effectiveness measures into a comprehensive brand evaluation process. Several companies are now using such overall brand evaluation models as key elements in evaluating and controlling their brand marketing expenditures. These models are based on the discounted cash flows which are predicted to be generated by the brand and an assessment of the strength of brand, which is used to determine the discount rate applied to the cash flows (the stronger the brand, the lower the discount rate applied). It is clear that many judgements must be used to arrive at the brand value but this is not the point. This is a broad evaluation process and, therefore, it is the movements and trend in the brand attributes (the true brand strength indicators) and hence in the value which is

important, rather than the absolute value at any point in time.

This type of model can be used to evaluate proposed incremental development expenditure on the brand and to ascertain the required level of maintenance expenditure (that level which should keep the brand strength score at its current level). However these evaluations are still not simple because the relationship between marketing expenditure and its effectiveness is by no means linear. As can be seen from Figure 20.7, there is a level of marketing expenditure which produces very effective returns but, if the company spends significantly more or less than this amount, the financial return can be dramatically reduced.

If too little marketing support is provided (area 1 in Figure 20.7), this low level of marketing expenditure is likely to be wasted. The effectiveness may be very low due to the relatively higher level of competitive expenditure or other general marketing activity which drowns out the company's specific marketing message (sometimes referred to as 'noise' in the system). Thus, this adds a further complication in that the effectiveness of one company's marketing expenditure is affected by the marketing activities of its competitors. Consequently marketing

Table 20.3		Share of voice (SOV) compared to share of market (SOM)		
$\dfrac{SOV}{SOM}$	$>$	1	⇨	A development/investment strategy
$\dfrac{SOV}{SOM}$	$=$	1	⇨	A maintenance/holding strategy
$\dfrac{SOV}{SOM}$	$<$	1	⇨	Normally a cash/profit extracting strategy

expenditure planning must be done against assumptions and expectations regarding the expenditures of competitors, as is discussed below.

At the other end of Figure 20.7, marketing expenditure is also likely to be unproductive, but this time it is because the law of diminishing returns has set in. If the level of marketing expenditure was reduced slightly, the overall effectiveness would be largely unaffected but the financial return could be improved significantly.

As already mentioned, the required level of marketing expenditure must be assessed by reference to competitive levels of activity. One quite simple and increasingly common relationship can give assistance here, although it does not provide a complete solution to what is a complex area. The relationship is between the proportionate share of the total marketing expenditure spent by the company's brand (i.e. its share of voice) compared with the relative share of market achieved by the brand (i.e. its value market share). As shown in Table 20.3, the ratio of SOV/SOM can be greater than 1, equal to 1, or less than 1.

If a brand is proportionately outspending its share of market (i.e. SOV/SOM above 1) then the company is investing in developing the attributes of the brand. This investment should have been rigorously financially evaluated before commitment and should be controlled by monitoring changes in the brand attributes. Once the brand has been fully developed, the marketing support should be designed to maintain the brand at its current position. The required level of maintenance marketing expenditure should still be assessed by reference to competitive levels of expenditure; the objective may well be to achieve a SOV/SOM ratio of 1. However this required expenditure must still be financially justified by evaluating the sustainable level of cash inflows which can be generated by maintaining the brand.

There is potentially one brand in any market which may be able to sustain its current market share while spending proportionately less on marketing support than its share of market (i.e. having a SOV/SOM ratio below 1). This is the brand with the dominant market share, because such a brand often achieves economies of scale in its marketing expenditure which are not available to its smaller competitors. Thus, due to its dominant market share, it can still significantly outspend, in absolute terms, all of its competitors, while spending proportionately below its market share. If it actually spent at its proportionate rate it would find itself in area 3 of Figure 20.7, i.e. in the area of rapidly diminishing returns.

Notwithstanding this powerful sustainable competitive advantage, in most cases, an SOV/SOM ratio below 1 indicates that the brand is not being properly maintained and will, in the long term, decline in strength. This may be the appropriate strategy if the brand and/or the market are coming to the end of their life cycles. However one particular strength of brands is that it is often possible to transfer the brand attributes to another product before the decline of the original product has irretrievably damaged the brand attributes. If the brand is successfully transferred to another product, the economic life of the brand has clearly been extended. This transfer of brand attributes should be financially compared with the alternative strategy of developing a new brand specifically designed for the new product. Similar financial justifications should be done for all brand umbrella and brand extension strategies as they involve significant risks, which must be taken into account, as well as reducing the brand investment needed for developing a new independent brand.

Customer-led strategies

As stated above, brands can be built around products or customers but a customer-based brand is designed to encourage existing loyal customers to try new products which are launched under the same brand (e.g. retailer brands such as St Michael, Tesco and Sainsbury) Figure 20.8.

Thus any customer-led strategy is, by definition, built around the existing customers of the business. A critical question for evaluating such a growth strategy is, therefore, 'which customers should form the basis for future growth?'. If the organization has an overall objective of creating economic value added, the obvious answer is to base the strategy around those customer groups from which the company can generate sustainable super profits.

This requires a strategically oriented, long-term customer account profitability (CAP) analysis to be carried out. This CAP analysis should indicate the relative profitability of different groups of customers, but it should not be used as an attempt to apportion the net profit of the business among the different customers. Indeed apportioning (or 'spreading') costs among customers can destroy the main benefits from the CAP analysis. The analysis should support important strategic decisions regarding which customer segments should be invested in, etc. Thus the resulting information must be relevant to these decisions and this is not achieved if a large proportion of indirect costs are apportioned to these customers.

The key phrase is direct attributable costing, where the real cost drivers for each major customer related cost are identified. These cost drivers are what causes the cost to be incurred

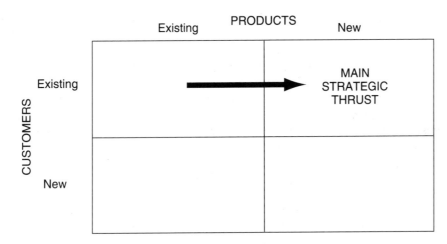

Figure 20.8   Customer-led strategies: maximizing the value of existing customers

	£
Gross Sales by Customer	x
Less Sales Discounts & Allowances	x
Net Sales by Customer	x
Less Direct Cost of Sales	x
Gross Customer Contribution	x

Less Customer Specific Marketing Expenses	x	
Direct Sales Support Costs	x	x
		x

Less Customer Specific Direct Transaction Costs		
Order Processing	x	
W/Housing & Distribution	x	
Invoice Processing	x	
Inventory Financing	x	
A/Cs Receivable Processing & Financing	x	
Specific Sales Support	x	x
		x
Less Customer Attributable Overheads		x
Net Customer Contribution		x

Figure 20.9   Customer account profitability analyses: illustrative example for an FMCG company selling through retailers

by the business and what makes the level of the cost change. If they are identified, this will indicate how customers should be grouped together. The idea is to group together customers who are treated very similarly and to separate groups where there are significant differences in the costs incurred; and, hence, potentially in the rates of financial return achieved. The sort of CAP resulting analysis is illustrated in Figure 20.9, and this shows that only customer specific elements should be included.

As the customer segmentation becomes greater (i.e. the customer groups get smaller and smaller, with the greatest segmentation being to individual customers), it is clear that less and less costs are directly attributable to each group of customers. Hence, for different levels of resource allocation decision, different levels of segmentation will be needed, and the CAP analysis system must be able to cope with this requirement for hierarchical segmentations.

Many companies now operate quite sophisticated CAP systems of this sort but, if the strategy is to be based around customers, the analysis needs to be done on a long-term basis. Such long-term CAP analyses are less common. The idea is to evaluate which types of customer are worth investing in because, over their economic life cycle, the business expects to be able to generate a positive net present value from the investment. This type of marketing strategy is commonly referred to as relationship marketing (and this is considered in detail in Chapter 2) because the business tries to develop (i.e. invests in) a long-term relationship with the customer. If this type of marketing strategy is in use, the business needs to tailor its management accounting system to treat these customer relationships as a long-term asset of the business. Thus development and maintenance expenditures are as relevant here as in the earlier discussion on brands.

If the main strategic thrust of the business is based on customers, it is also important that these customers form an important element in the performance measures used for the various areas within the business. If this is not done, many of the business support areas will focus on achieving their own performance measures, often to the detriment of the long-term development of these critical customer-based assets.

This CAP analysis is complicated even further when the business sells through an indirect channel of distribution to the ultimate user of the product; e.g. as is done by many consumer goods businesses which sell directly to wholesalers, distributors or retailers, which then sell on to the consumers. Increasingly this type of business wants to have sound financial analysis on both its direct customers and its ultimate but indirect consumers. Thus many fast-moving consumer goods companies, particularly in the USA, have invested very large sums of money in developing very extensive *consumer* databases. This enables them to know much more about who eventually uses their product, even though they bought it indirectly. Clearly, if the strategy is to develop new products (which will appeal to these same consumers), this knowledge is critical. However it also illustrates a significant potential competitive advantage for the indirect channel of distribution (e.g. the retailer), because they can gain even more detailed customer information much more cost effectively. This is being used very proactively by major retailers with their significant investments in both customer loyalty programmes (such as store cards, etc.) and retailer branding, which enable them to develop appropriately designed and tailored new products.

Product-based strategies

An alternative, but possibly equally attractive, strategic thrust is to base future growth around existing products (Figure 20.10). These products may also be strongly branded but the critical element in the strategy is that the growth opportunities are based on finding new markets, new segments, or new customer groups to which to sell these products.

Not surprisingly, this strategic thrust should be built on those products which can achieve a sustainable level of super profit in their existing markets. Hence a key financial analysis for such strategies is a soundly based, decision-focused, long-term direct product profitability (DPP) analysis. As with the customer profitability analysis, the objective of DPP is to indicate the relative profit contributions from the different product groups. Therefore apportioning indirect costs in an attempt to arrive at a 'net profit' for each product can destroy the validity of the analysis and lead to disastrous decisions being taken.

As shown in Figure 20.11, the allocation of product specific costs to appropriately grouped products can highlight significant differences in the relative profit contributions from these differing products. Once again, if this analysis is to be used to support long-term strategic decisions (such as to identify those products which should be launched internationally), the analysis must consider the long-term sustainable profitability of the products.

In some industries this can be done by using product life cycle costing techniques which have been developed over many years. It is now well established that the costs of producing many products (both goods and services) decline, in real terms, over time due to a number of factors. These include learning by employees which makes them more efficient, the introduction of new technologies and economies of scale and scope. These are combined together in the 'experience curve' concept which enables businesses to predict the rate of decline of their real production costs per unit as cumulative volume increases.

This predictive knowledge can be used in the marketing strategy because the business could set its prices today based on its long-term costs rather than its current costs; this is diagrammatically illustrated in Figure 20.12.

This pricing strategy would probably result in the business making a loss on its current sales;

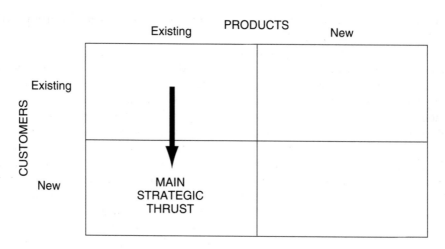

Figure 20.10   Product-led strategies: maximizing value of existing products

		£
Gross Sales by Product		x
Less Product Specific Discounts & Rebates		x̲
Net Sales by Product		x
Less Direct Costs of Product		x̲
Gross Product Contribution		x
Less Product Based Marketing Expenses	x	
Product Specific Direct Sales Support Costs	x̲̲	x̲
		x
Less product Specific Direct Transaction Costs		
Sourcing Costs	x	
Operations Support	x	
Fixed Assets Financing	x	
Warehousing & Distribution	x	
Inventory Financing	x	
Order, Invoice & Collection Processing	x̲̲	x̲
		x
Less Product Attributable Overheads		x̲
Direct Profit Profitability		x̲̲

Figure 20.11   Direct product profitability analyses: illustrative example of a manufacturing company's DPP analysis

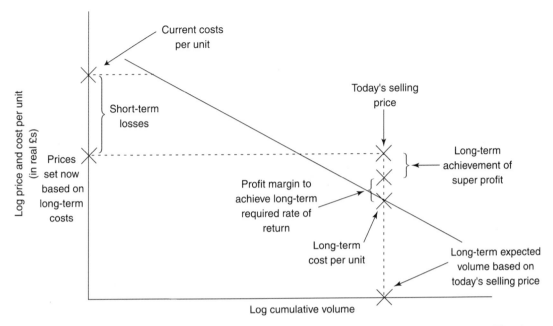

Figure 20.12 Life cycle costing techniques: strategic use of experience curves in setting prices. The short-term loss per unit, if successful, is really an investment in developing a long-term sustainable cost advantage

but these sales should increase rapidly, as the low prices stimulated demand. These increasing sales volumes should propel the business rapidly down its experience curve – towards its long-term cost level, at which it should achieve a super profit. If it can gain a sustainable long-term cost advantage over its competitors by this strategy, it should regard the initial losses as an investment in creating a sustainable competitive advantage.

The idea of having a sustainable cost advantage also indicates another important aspect of product-based strategies. The management accounting needs of a low-cost-based strategy are fundamentally different to those of product-based strategies built on differentiated or value added products. As was discussed early in the chapter, any sustainable competitive advantage is a relative concept which must be evaluated and controlled by reference to an appropriate set of competitors.

Thus the required competitor analysis focuses on the source of relative competitive advantage or disadvantage. Where the main basis of competition is on price, because there is no customer perceived difference among competing products, the relevant competitor analysis should concentrate on cost benchmarking. In this commodity-based, price-conscious environment, the lowest-cost supplier will normally win and relatively small cost differences can be critical.

However, if the basis of competition is differentiation rather than price, an excessive emphasis on external cost comparisons or even internal cost reductions can be very counterproductive. A cost difference no longer necessarily indicates a competitive advantage or disadvantage because it may be the source of the customer-perceived differentiation, which in reality creates the economic value added. For these businesses, the focus needs to be on the value added elements rather than on the costs. This forces finance managers to become involved in the assessment of 'perceived use values' (where the perception is by the customers) of the differences between competing products. The perceived added value is then compared to the incremental cost incurred in achieving the difference, with any resulting positive value gap being evaluated for sustainability.

This type of involvement raises several issues for the way marketing and finance need to work together.

Organizational structures: marketing finance managers

If the integrated and tailored approach to controlling marketing which has been set out in this chapter is to be achieved, marketing and finance managers need to work very closely together at all stages of the marketing process. The rigorous financial evaluation of strategic marketing decisions requires a close involvement of finance managers at the earliest stage possible. Yet this close involvement must continue during the implementation of the strategy if proper control is to be exercised and the necessary amendments to the strategy are to be made in a timely manner.

This continuous close involvement can only really be achieved if finance has a substantive presence within the marketing area. Increasingly this is being achieved by the creation of the roles of marketing finance managers, who are physically located in the marketing area and are seen as part of the marketing management team. As such they are automatically involved in the development of the marketing strategy, its implementation, modification and control. Indeed in some businesses they now share some managerial performance measures with their marketing colleagues, yet they have a clear financial responsibility to remain objective in their financial evaluations.

The marketing finance manager can also act as a coordinator and facilitator for the many inputs which are needed for the strategic competitor analysis which has been advocated during the chapter. In some companies this analysis has been supplemented by customer profitabil-

ity analyses and even supplier profitability analyses; where well done, these enable a complete picture of the industry value chain to be developed. This can aid the strategy development process immensely as it can indicate future opportunities and threats at different levels in the total supply chain.

Conclusion

Controlling marketing involves far more than recording and analysing the accounting transactions which result from marketing activities. It should be regarded as a two-stage process involving the pre-commitment financial evaluation of proposed marketing expenditures as well as the ongoing control over these expenditures as they take place.

The objectives of these different marketing activities are very diverse but marketing has, itself, developed appropriately tailored evaluation processes and non-financial effective measures. The challenge for finance is to find equally tailored and value-added ways of controlling marketing expenditures, which link these activities to the overall objectives of the organization.

This requires a high degree of integration between marketing and finance, and a substantial level of tailoring in the marketing accounting system and resulting performance measures. Ideally, if the marketing strategy changes significantly, this should lead to a corresponding change in the tailored marketing accounting system. If such a change is not made, it is quite likely that the business will be using inappropriate performance measures, which may motivate marketing managers to act against the long-term best interests of the overall business. Another potential risk is that the management information system does not provide adequate timely decision support information for the new, key strategic decisions which the business faces as a result of the change in strategy. Many businesses are taking critical marketing decisions with very little strategic financial evaluation, because they do not have suitably tailored marketing accounting systems. In such businesses there is no real 'strategic control over marketing'.

This chapter has tried to indicate how such strategic control over marketing can be achieved. Many of the areas considered in the chapter require complete books to deal with them in depth. Obviously restrictions of space have necessitated a very brief overview of these areas; however there are recommendations for further reading which should enable those interested to examine particular areas in significantly greater depth.

Further reading

Sustainable competitive advantage and competitive strategy

Bowman, C. and Faulkner, D. (1997) *Competitive and Corporate Strategy*, Irwin.

Hamel, G. and Prahalad, C. K. (1994) *Competing for the Future*, HBS Press.

Porter, M. E. (1980) *Competitive Strategy*, Free Press, New York.

Porter, M. E. (1985) *Competitive Advantage*, Free Press, New York.

Financial planning and control processes

Goold, M. and Campbell, A. (1987) *Strategies and Styles*, Blackwell, Oxford.

Kaplan, R. S. and Norton, D. P. (1996) *The Balanced Scorecard*, HBS Press.

McDonald, M. H. B. (1995) *Marketing Plans*, Butterworth–Heinemann, Oxford.

Mintzberg, H. (1994) *The Rise and Fall of Strategic Planning*, Prentice-Hall, Englewood Cliffs, NJ.

Ward, K. R. (1992) *Strategic Management Accounting*, Butterworth–Heinemann, Oxford.

Brand-led strategies

Crainer, S. (1995) *The Real Power of Brands*, FT Pitman, London.

Kapferer, J. N. (1992) *Strategic Brand Management*, Kogan Page.

Murphy, J. (ed.) (1989) *Brand Valuation*, Hutchinson, London.

Customer-led strategies

Burneff, K. (1992) *Strategic Customer Alliances*, FT Pitman, London.

Christopher, M., Payne, A. and Ballantyne, D. (1993) *Relationship Marketing*, Butterworth–Heinemann, Oxford.

Hallberg, G. (1995) *All Consumers Are Not Created Equal*, Wiley.

Product-based strategies

Day, G. S. (1986) *Analysis for Strategic Market Decisions*, West.

Johnson, H. T. (1992) *Relevance Regained*, Free Press, New York.

Johnson, H. T. and Kaplan, R. S. (1987) *Relevance Lost: The Rise and Fall of Management Accounting*, Free Press New York.

Shank, J. K. and Govindarajan, V. (1993) *Strategic Cost Management*, Free Press, New York.

CHAPTER 21

Marketing implementation, organizational change and internal marketing strategy

NIGEL F. PIERCY

Introduction

The most central point to be made in this chapter is that one of the most significant frontiers for marketing is implementation but also, by implication, the organizational changes that are required to achieve the effective implementation of marketing strategies and programmes. The central issue here is the manager's pragmatic question: 'We know what marketing *is*, but how do we do it?' One analyst summarized this problem in the following way:

Marketing for a number of years has been long on advice about *what to do* in a given competitive or market situation and short on useful recommendations for *how to do it* within company, competitor and customer constraints ... experiences with both managers and students argue strongly that these parties and customer constraints often strategy-sophisticated and implementation-bound (Bonoma, 1985).

An internal market perspective

One approach to understanding the significance of organizational change and development to marketing strategy implementation is by adopting an internal market perspective (Piercy, 1995, 1998a). The importance of this internal market perspective to developing coherent marketing implementation strategies may be underlined as follows:

- Much contemporary thinking and practice in strategic marketing is concerned with managing relationships: with the customer, and with partners in strategic alliances. However, a further aspect of relationship management and relationship marketing is the relationship with the employees and managers, upon whose skills, commitment and performance the success of a marketing strategy unavoidably relies. This is the internal market inside the company. The logic being followed by an increasing number of companies is that building effective relationships with customers and alliance partners will depend in part (and possibly in large part), on the strengths and types of relationships built with employees and managers inside the organization.

- Many companies emphasize the centrality of competitive differentiation to build market position. Yet truly exploiting a company's potential competitiveness and its capabilities in reality is often in the hands of what Evert Gummesson (1991) has called the 'part-time marketers', i.e. the people who run the business and provide the real scope for competitive differentiation. Indeed, in some situations, the employees of a company may be the most important resource that provides differentiation – Avis achieves high customer satisfaction and customer retention through its superior employee skills and attitudes, not because the cars it rents out are any different from those of its competitors (Piercy, 1997).

* In a similar way, the growing emphasis on competing through superior service quality relies ultimately on the behaviour and effectiveness of the people who deliver the service, rather than the people who design the strategy.
* Indeed, increasingly it is recognized that one of the greatest barriers to effectiveness in strategic marketing lies not in a company's ability to conceive and design innovative marketing strategies or to produce sophisticated marketing plans, but in its ability to gain the effective and enduring implementation of those strategies. One route to planning and operationalizing implementation in strategic marketing is 'strategic internal marketing.

This chapter will examine the implementation question in marketing and then introduce strategic internal marketing as a managerial approach to dealing with the organizational problems uncovered by our analysis.

A fundamental problem: the strategy formulation – implementation dichotomy

However, many difficulties arise in dealing with the implementation issue, not simply because implementation itself is problematic, but because conventional approaches to marketing planning and the generation of marketing strategies have generally adopted the view that strategy formulation and implementation are distinct and sequential activities – a characteristic styled the 'formulation–implementation dichotomy' by Cespedes and Piercy (1996). Where it exists this 'dichotomy' is fraught with dangers:

* It ignores, or underestimates, the potential synergy between the process of marketing strategy formulation and a company's implementation capabilities (Bonoma, 1985).
* It reduces the ability of an organization to establish competitive advantage which draws on its unique distinguishing characteristics, i.e. what it is good at or best at in the marketplace (Hamel and Prahalad, 1989).
* It risks divorcing the strategies and plans produced from the realities of the organization (Hutt et al., 1988).
* It takes no account of the need for marketing to span not merely the external market boundaries recognized in conventional models of marketing but also the internal boundaries with other functional and organizational interest groups (Aldrich and Herker, 1977; Spekman, 1979; Ruekert and Walker, 1987).
* It underestimates the significance of the political and negotiating infrastructure of the organization, as it impacts on the support of key managers for strategies, and on the process of gaining the commitment of organizational members at all levels (Pfeffer, 1981; Piercy, 1985).

Given the high priority for developing new ways of more effectively handling the implementation problem in marketing, and the dangers of not doing so, the goal of this chapter is to approach the marketing implementation issue by asking four important questions:

1 Can we relate our marketing plans and strategies to the real organizational context for marketing in a particular company, by evaluating the degree of 'organizational stretch' for which we are asking?

2 Can we identify the most important sources

of implementation problems in an organization by evaluating the existence of strategic gaps?

3 Can we then look at the problems faced in having these strategic gaps addressed, and the barriers to this process of change in the organization?

4 Can we use internal marketing techniques to develop implementation strategies (or at least to provide better guidance as to which marketing strategies not to pursue, because the hidden implementation barriers and costs are too great)?

The underlying rationale for this approach is that it is organizational context that links strategy formulation and implementation in marketing, and thus it is working on this context that provides us with a way to overcome the dichotomy discussed above (Walker and Ruekert, 1987; Piercy, 1990, 1997). However, this link is potentially complex, since the strategy formulation or planning process is itself inextricably part of the organizational context in which managers work. Understanding the gap between the generation of marketing strategies and their implementation may be improved by: examining the formal organizational positioning and structuring of marketing, including the information and intelligence systems, and the operation of key decision making processes like budgeting and planning – and using that understanding to build an explicit implementation framework of internal marketing to provide a parallel to the more conventional external marketing strategy.

Organizational stretch and implementation capabilities

Implementation capabilities

The greatest single danger in underestimating the marketing implementation issue is that we assume it away – we believe that any company can implement any strategy, if we simply 'man-

age' properly. Traditional approaches to implementation are particularly susceptible to this trap. In conventional approaches if we think about implementation at all, then we see it as the logistics of getting things 'organized':

- We focus on developing the organizational arrangements needed for the new strategy – allocating responsibilities across departments and units, and possibly creating new organizational structures where necessary.
- We allocate resources in the form of budgets and headcount to support the activities underpinning the strategy to the appropriate part of the organization.
- We produce 'action lists' and 'action plans' and do presentations to tell people the way things are going to be done.
- We develop control systems to monitor outcome performance in sales, market share, profit, and so on, to evaluate the success of the strategy, and to take remedial action if things are not turning out how we wanted them.

There are very substantial problems in approaching implementation in this way. First, it is illogical to plan strategies that are not firmly rooted in the organization's capabilities, and yet we seem to set up planning systems to do precisely this. Second, organizational arrangements and resource allocation are important, but on their own they are very weak, and usually very slow, approaches to the organizational change inherent in many new strategies. Third, outcomes likes sales, market share and profit, are what we want to achieve, but the driver of these outcomes is likely to be the behaviour of people in the organization who impact on what the customer receives in service and quality, which suggests we should manage the behaviour not just the outcomes.

It is all too easy to underestimate how serious the consequences may be of designing robust and well-researched innovative market strategies that are a poor fit with our capabilities, systems and policies. We have described in some detail elsewhere the failure of a market segmentation strategy in a commercial bank (Piercy and Morgan, 1993). This failure was because an innovative, new segmentation scheme based on customer benefits was incompatible with the organizational structure, information systems, and culture of the company. Reading through this case example may provide some new insights into our own problems with new market strategies.

In fact, a starting point in taking organizational and behavioural realities seriously may be to recognize that implementation capabilities are a corporate resource of some importance – but one which is not generally well-understood. In fact, a company's implementation capabilities may be:

- time specific, in the sense that a company may gain or lose the competencies on which a strategy relies for execution, so implementation capabilities change;
- culture specific, where components of a strategy assume understanding and abilities that do not exist in other cultures, perhaps exemplified best by the belief that different countries have equal access to employees able and willing to deliver high levels of customer service;
- partial, since a company may be well equipped, for example, to launch a product and provide technical service but be unable to provide other components of the strategy like customer service;
- latent, in the sense that a company may actually possess the technical and human resources required by a marketing strategy but lack the ability to deploy those resources through lack of learning or management experience;
- internally inconsistent, since some parts of a company may be better suited to execute a strategy than others;
- strategy specific, because there may be specific skills and competencies highly suited to a particular strategy but not the flexibility to change to meet new strategic imperatives; and even

- person specific, in the sense that implementation capabilities may rely on a specific manager, who exerts the abilities and influence needed to achieve effective implementation (Piercy, 1998b).

Such characteristics pose severe difficulties in conceptualizing and evaluating implementation capabilities as part of marketing strategy models, and more immediately for practitioners in managing the execution of strategy.

Organizational stretch

A simple diagnostic may assist in addressing the question of marketing strategy implementation capabilities with a company, using the model of organizational stretch shown in Figure 21.1.

In this approach, *conventional strategies* are a continuation of the past – the company continues an old strategy that it is good at implementing, while the *obsolete strategy* is one where previous execution capacity no longer exists (e.g. key personnel have left, resources become unavailable). Perhaps the most important distinction, however, is the difference between *synergistic strategy* (a marketing strategy that we assume the company will be good at executing) and the *stretch strategy* (a new strategy requiring substantial new capabilities in execution). The challenge to executives is to adopt a process and organizational perspective to better distinguish between synergy and stretch characteristics of new marketing strategies.

For example, the major grocery retailers Tesco and Sainsbury successfully pursued growth by moving into petrol retailing, which closely matched their skills and capabilities and in which they have become market leaders. Most recently, the same retail companies have started to operate retail banks. They are finding the processing and service requirements for banking somewhat different to those needed in grocery retail, and more important, customer expectations of a bank appear greatly more demanding than those placed on a grocery chain. What appears in rational/analytic terms

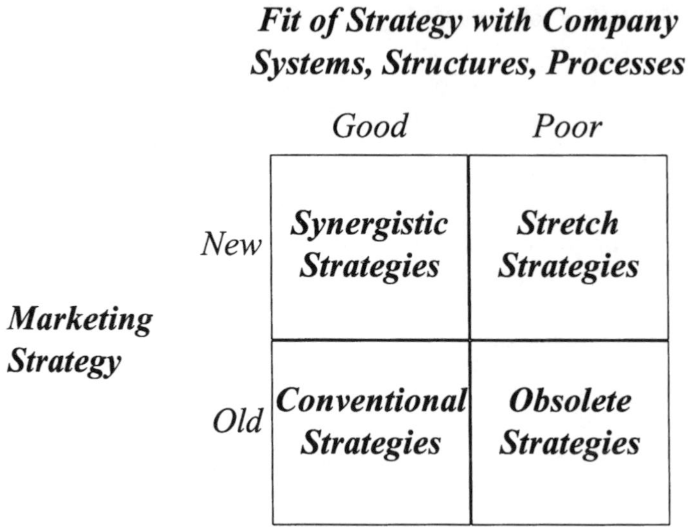

Fit of Strategy with Company
Systems, Structures, Processes

		Good	Poor
Marketing Strategy	*New*	*Synergistic Strategies*	*Stretch Strategies*
	Old	*Conventional Strategies*	*Obsolete Strategies*

Figure 21.1   Organizational stretch and implementation capabilities

to be a synergistic strategy may in reality be a stretch strategy. This model can be used to assist executives in confronting the underlying implementation realities in new marketing strategies. For example, it has been suggested that it is easy to underestimate the degree and type of organizational stretch that is needed to implement relationship marketing strategy effectively – a 'paradigm shift' in marketing strategy suggests the need for a parallel and equal shift in important organizational characteristics (Piercy, 1998a). Certainly we need to understand that implementation capabilities may be closely related to the organizational positioning of marketing, and the way that positioning is changing in many major organizations.

The organizational positioning of marketing

Recognizing the importance of implementation capabilities as a resource makes it clearer also that effective strategy implementation relies on more covert aspects of the marketing organization than is commonly recognized. Effective strategy implementation rests not simply on techniques of action planning, budgeting, and resource allocation, as well as administrative systems design; it rests on the underlying beliefs and attitudes of organizational participants, and over and above this on the dominating management interests and culture in the organization.

The importance of this possibly self-evident statement is that what can be observed in many international organizations is the loss of the formal organizational position of the marketing function, and even more significantly the weakening of management belief in marketing as a strategic force. The combination of such forces amounts to the weakening of the marketing paradigm which is becoming a major influence on the marketing strategy implementation capabilities of organizations (Piercy, 1998b).

Marketing organization

Conventionally, marketing organization has been concerned with the formation and internal structuring of marketing departments. In fact, the strategic significance of organizational issues in marketing and strategy implementation in particular is gaining new attention:

Had we been contemplating the future of marketing a decade ago, organizational issues would have been at the periphery ... As we approach the millennium, organizational issues are rising to the top of the agenda on the future of marketing. (Day, 1997)

However, predictions of the future for the marketing organization suggest radical, unfamiliar, and revolutionary change to effectively implement the strategies organizations will have to pursue to survive and prosper. Webster (1997) describes this new organizational reality for the future in the following terms:

- Successful organizations will be customer focused not product or technology focused, supported by a market information competence that links the voice of the customer to all the firm's value-delivery processes.
- Customer relationships will be seen as the critical strategic assets of the business, which will be reflected in organizational arrangements with key customers and reseller partners to integrate marketing competencies around customers and markets.
- Strategies and organizational arrangements will be linked by customer-driven value-delivery processes that are flexible and evolve in response to market change.
- The most serious competitive threats will be from competitors who fundamentally redesign their marketing organizations and systems for going to market, not just their products, because customers will increasingly buy the firm's value-delivery system not just products.
- Successful marketing organizations will have the skills necessary to manage multiple strategic marketing processes, many of which have not traditionally been seen as in the domain of marketing (e.g. súpply chain management, customer linking, product offering development).

To this add the growing evidence that many companies will go to market through networks held together by a variety of contracts, alliances, partnerships, joint ventures and other links – i.e. as virtual or hollow organizations

(e.g. see Cravens *et al.*, 1996). It is the unsurprising that commentators point to the 'reinvented organization' needed to compete on capabilities, offer superior customer value, and implement complex relationship strategies (Cravens *et al.*, 1997).

However, what remains hidden within these new organizational forms and networks is the question of how organizations can establish, maintain and sustain strategy implementation capabilities. For example, in the airline industry as companies move towards hollow structures (the airline as brand and booking system employing only core service and operational staff), it is already becoming apparent that in devolved network organizations, partners may not be committed to the service quality and excellence needed to sustain the airline's brand. This suggests that new organizational forms will bring a whole new agenda of problems associated with implementation capabilities.

Turning from this scenario of future revolution to the present status quo of the marketing organization also indicates more immediate issues of implementation capabilities.

It is more than a decade since it was suggested that the formal organizational positioning and structuring of the marketing function appeared to be subject to an underlying life cycle (Piercy, 1985). Since then, it has been shown, for example, that the organization of marketing in British companies has frequently fallen very short of the integrated models familiar in the prescriptive literature (Piercy, 1986). We found, for example, stereotypical marketing organizations in British manufacturing firms to include limited/staff role forms, responsible for limited areas like market research and some sales promotion: strategy/services forms, with planning responsibilities and little line responsibility; and selling-oriented forms, involved almost wholly in field sales operations (see Figure 21.2). The significance of these observations lies primarily in the symbolism of structure rather than the administrative substance. Tokenism in formal organizational arrangements for marketing was taken as indicative of a lack of resource control

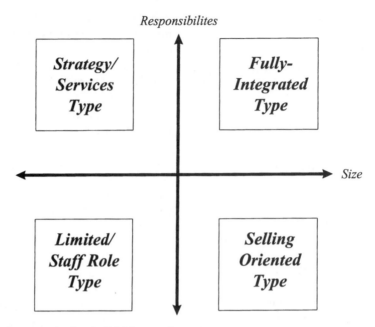

Figure 21.2   Marketing organization in British manufacturing companies

and strategic influence for marketing in British companies (Piercy, 1986).

More recently, the organization of marketing in Britain has been characterized by the downsizing and closure of conventional marketing departments, reinforced by the impact of category management and trade marketing strategies, and the resurgence of the power of sales departments in managing customer relationships in business-to-business markets (Piercy, 1997).

Correspondingly, many popular approaches address marketing as an issue of process not

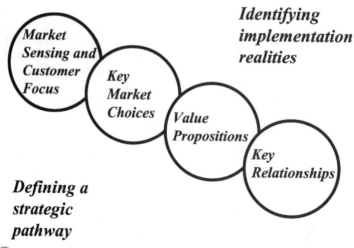

Source: Piercy (1997)

Figure 21.3   The process of going to market

function – for example, as the 'process of going to market', which cuts across traditional functional and organizational boundaries (see Figure 21.3). The implications of such marketing process models for the redundancy of traditional functional structures may be extreme, with the unintended side effect of further weakening the marketing paradigm in organizations.

Attacks on marketing

Underpinning these signs of a weakening marketing paradigm in organizational terms, there have been many more general attacks on the role of marketing in companies from diverse sources. At one level, business commentators and consultants point to the attractiveness of reengineering around business processes to avoid the need for marketing (e.g. Mitchell, 1996), and the growing cynicism of customers about some aspects of marketing. At another level, analysts point to 'marketing's failure as strategy' (Webster, 1997). For example, Doyle (1997) has suggested that very few British companies have moved beyond the 'marketing' trappings of advertising and promotion, to implement robust marketing strategies, delivering long-term customer and shareholder value.

Illustrative of the outcome of such factors is the emerging relationship between marketing and operations in companies. While this interface has been studied in a variety of ways, perhaps the most topical approach is to evaluate the emerging impact of 'lean thinking' and supply chain management on the role of marketing. A new management approach that may have the effect of undermining the influence of marketing in modern corporations is the 'lean enterprise' model developing out of the automotive sector (Piercy and Morgan, 1997). This is no more than a single example of one of the emerging management philosophies that may conflict with conventional marketing approaches and undermine the marketing implementation capabilities of organizations. This case may be framed by considering how marketing has largely failed to respond effectively to the wide-

spread moves to corporate downsizing and delayering, to integrated logistics systems and new approaches to supply change management, and perhaps most especially to the management movements associated with total quality management (TQM) and business process reengineering (BPR) (Morgan and Piercy, 1996).

This lack of response may be described in terms of an important loss of intellectual leadership for marketing scholars vis-à-vis corporate practice, and a loss of influence for marketing executives in many major corporations as their role in managing marketplace contingencies has been displaced by other disciplines (Day, 1992, 1994). The implications for weakened strategy implementation capabilities are serious.

The impact of process models on marketing

As noted above, part of this new organizational context is shown by the trend to organize around process instead of function, and the development of new organizational forms like hollow or network organizations.

For example, one view of the new marketing organization is shown in the model of value processes in Figure 21.4. A process perspective appears useful, although as yet largely undeveloped, in building insight into issues like implementation in an organizational context. However, there are various ways of conceptualizing process for these purposes. Most commonly, process is understood in terms of its substantive *content* – the new product development process, the planning process, for example. In addition, processes may be conceived in terms of their *purposes* – value-defining, value-developing, and value-delivering processes, for instance (Webster, 1997).

Understanding a process perspective may be critical to identifying and managing strategy implementation capabilities in new organizational forms. For example, a number of studies of key marketing decision-making processes have proposed that such processes should be

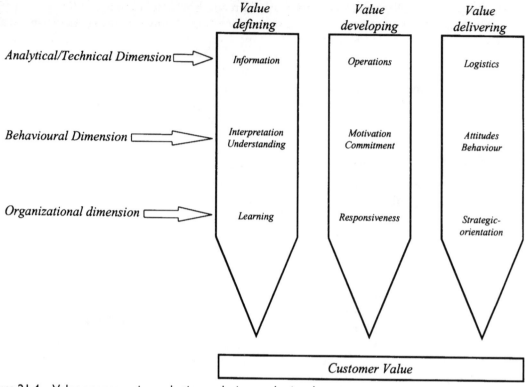

Figure 21.4   Value processes in marketing replacing marketing departments

analysed in terms of their organizational dimensions. Studies of marketing budgeting and resource allocation (Piercy, 1987), marketing planning (Piercy and Morgan, 1994), and marketing control (Piercy and Morgan, 1996) have shared a model that suggests that many decision-making processes can usefully be analysed in terms of an analytic/technical dimensions. We might, for example, consider value processes in the way shown in Figure 21.4. This suggests that to understand the capability of value processes to deliver value, or to implement a value-based marketing strategy, it is useful to examine not simply the analytic/technical aspects of the process (the information gathered, the operations systems, and the logistics for value delivery) but also the behavioural aspects of the process (in terms of the abilities of individuals to interpret information and develop market understanding, and their motivation, commitment, and behaviour in

developing and delivering value to customers) and the organizational or contextual aspects of the process (the learning capabilities and responsiveness of the organization, and its management's strategic orientation). An important issue is the consistency between the analytic, behavioural, and organizational dimensions of process, although this is frequently covert. Consistency between the dimensions of a process is likely to have a substantial impact on implementation capabilities.

For example, while value defining may be driven by the abilities of the organization to collect and disseminate information, 'market sensing' that leads to effective implementation of value-based strategy is likely also to be a function of the interpretative abilities and inclinations of individuals and the organization's learning capabilities.

While value developing relies on operations capabilities, it is also shaped by the organ-

Table 21.1 Customer relationship management at IBM

- Most of IBM's marketing activities are now embedded in a global initiative called customer relationship management (CRM).
- CRM works through core processes:
  - Market management – to identify and select key market segments
  - Relationship management – handles interaction between IBM and the customer with established customers
  - Opportunity management – as soon as a sales opportunity is identified, the opportunity manager has the role of finding the right 'opportunity owner' who can offer the right type of expertise and the right level of interaction (e.g. mass customization versus one-of-a-kind), drawing on the next processes
  - Offering information – keeping track of every product or solution developed by the company or its business partners, so no-one in IBM has to waste time re-inventing the wheel
  - Skills management – a worldwide database of IBM personnel's skills, graded on scales from levels 1 to 5
  - Solution, design and delivery – each offer and bid is tracked to check the result
  - Customer satisfaction management – handling customer feedback and complaints
  - Message management – handling communications
- The goal is co-ordination of customer relationships through managing business processes that cut across boundaries to achieve maximum effectiveness.

Source: Piercy, (1997)

ization's responsiveness to market-based change and the motivation and commitment of individuals to implementing change. Value delivering involves supply chain capabilities and logistics, but also the attitudes and behaviours of service personnel, salespeople, distributors, and other participants, as well as the priorities communicated by the strategic orientation of management. The danger lies in equating capabilities in the analytic/technical dimension of process, with corresponding capabilities in the behavioural and organizational dimensions. The challenge is to evaluate and manage for consistency in the process, even if this means adapting and reshaping marketing strategy to fit better with the organization's implementation capabilities.

While this model is no more than illustrative, it serves to underline the point that if implementation is viewed in process terms, then implementation capabilities are a function of the individual behaviours and motivation of individuals in the organization, and the underlying organizational context in which the process operates. If implementation is viewed in these terms, the question of the strength of the marketing paradigm becomes critical to evaluating true implementation capabilities. At its simplest, if the people in an organization do not believe in marketing and customer imperatives, and management priorities are focused elsewhere than the customer marketplace, the marketing strategy implementation capabilities are likely to be low.

How seriously major firms are taking the management of marketing processes in these new structures is well illustrated by the customer relationship management initiative at IBM. The main characteristics of this programme are summarized in Table 21.1.

The impact of network organizations on marketing

As we saw earlier, one of the most important responses by companies to new competitive and market conditions has been the emergence of strategies of collaboration and partnership with other organizations as a key element of the process of going to market – these have variously been termed marketing partnership, strategic alliances and marketing networks (Piercy and Cravens, 1995). These new collaborative organizations are distinctive and different. They are:

characterized by flexibility, specialization, and an emphasis on relationship management instead of market transactions . . . to respond quickly and flexibly to accelerating change in technology, competition and customer preferences. (Webster, 1992)

The emergence of networks of collaborating organizations linked by various forms of alliance and partnership has already become a dominant strategic development in many industries. For example:

- At Corning Inc almost 50 per cent of revenue comes through alliances and joint ventures;
- At the leading computer company Compaq, the strategy is to pursue the information superhighway through twenty strategic alliances with telecommunications and software companies.
- The international airlines business is dominated by a small number of groupings of airlines operating as competing alliances across the world.
- Outsourcing and networking has become a major strategy at marketing research agencies like A. C. Nielsen (Piercy and Cravens, 1995).

For these reasons, it is important that our thinking about the implementation of our own strategies, and also our understanding of the emerging forms of competition we face in the market, should embrace the strategic alliance and the resulting growth of networks of organizations linked to various forms of collaborative relationship.

However, when we think about implementation capabilities in these new types of networked organizations major questions remain unresolved. The role of marketing in network organizations is unclear. In some models, like the 'marketing exchange company', the hub of the network is the marketing facility (Achrol, 1991). Others suggest that the critical role for marketing in the alliance-based network is applying relationship marketing skills to managing the links between partners in the network (Webster, 1992). Certainly, there is a compelling argument that the concepts and processes of relationship marketing are pivotal to the management of value through mutual co-operation and interdependence (Sheth, 1994), and we have seen that co-operation and interdependence are central features of network organizations. It is too early to reach conclusions about the role that marketing can and will take generally in these new organizational forms, although it is highly likely that there will be some redefinition of its role which may be radical and which will directly influence strategy implementation capabilities.

Identifying implementation problems in marketing

This more complex organizational setting and its impact on strategy implementation capabilities underlines the importance of adopting practical approaches to the implementation issue. A first step in confronting the marketing implementation issue is to build a picture of the ways in which a company's marketing plans and strategies fail to reach the marketplace. One method for achieving this is the analysis of strategic gaps: the gaps between strategic intent and strategic reality.

Marketing intentions and marketing realities

The analysis of strategic gaps involves evaluating the differences which exist between the marketing strategies which planners have formulated inside the organization, and the delivery of these promises in the customer marketplace. This has

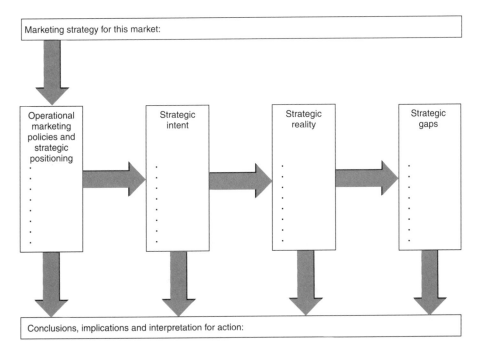

Figure 21.5   Strategic intent versus strategic reality

been stylized elsewhere as the contrast between 'intended' and 'realized' strategies (Mintzberg, 1988). For present purposes this can be reduced to something very simple:

- Intended strategy or strategic intent – what management and planners inside the organization think the business is about in the marketplace; and
- Perceived strategy or strategic reality – what the business is actually about in the marketplace, as it is seen and understood by salespeople, distributors and customers.

The approach illustrated in Figure 21.5 leads to some of the most significant practical questions to be confronted in dealing with the implementation issue.

The technique is straightforward and easily applied, but can be exceptionally productive in isolating the existence and underlying reasons for implementation problems in marketing. The procedure is as follows:

1   *Identify the market in question and the marketing strategy* which is being (or will be) pursued. This is frequently where we encounter the first difficulties – when executives struggle to aptly describe their market, or to encapsulate in a few words the strategy for that market, then we may have found the first source of implementation barriers. If we truly understand our marketing strategy, we should be able to articulate it in a few key points. If we cannot do this, it raises the question of whether we really have a strategy for this market.

2   *Translate the marketing strategy into the practicalities of operational marketing policies*, and what this is intended to achieve in strategic position in the market in question. This should be done in each area of the marketing programme. The question to address is: For our marketing strategy to be effectively implemented in this market what do we have to achieve with:

  - Our products and services, in terms of

such issues as quality compared to our competitors, fullness of range, image and brand identity compared to alternatives, design attributes, functional features and 'extras', reliability of service, and so on;

• Our pricing and value, in terms of the real position in price level against the competitors and alternatives, and how we are seen in 'value for money' compared to others in the market;

• Our marketing communications, in terms of the quality and role of our selling efforts and coverage of the market, the image and awareness created by advertising, the effectiveness of our sales promotions, and so on, all as compared to the competition;

• Our distribution, in terms of the availability of the product in the marketplace, the quality of the service provided in customer waiting time, service provision, maintenance, and so on; and

• Our strategic positioning, in terms of the stage of the product life cycle reached, the strength of our market position, our success in achieving differentiation in the customers' eyes and what we have achieved in customer satisfaction levels compared to the competition.

This analysis defines the *strategic intent* – what our marketing strategy has to achieve in practical terms to become a reality in the marketplace. The goal is to reduce this intent to a few major points under each heading.

3   *Evaluate the strategic reality* – address each of above questions again, but now in terms of what we have actually achieved on each issue of marketing programme and strategic position. This is normally quite a lot different from the strategic intent. The richness and insight produced here is also greatly enhanced by asking a new and different group of people for their perceptions. If the strategic intent is defined by the marketing planners or marketing and general management, then the strategic reality may be best identi-

fied by the salesforce, by the distributors or even by customers themselves.

4   *Identify the strategic gaps* – at this stage we are simply comparing the strategic intent and the strategic reality, and noting or summarizing the differences as strategic gaps.

5   *Interpreting the strategic gaps* – the most important stage of this technique is where we stand back from the analysis of intent and reality and the differences between them, and see what insights we have gained into the real problems of marketing implementation in the situation we are studying. To see what conclusions we can draw, we may address the following types of questions:

• How serious are the gaps we have found between the marketing strategy and the real marketplace situation (and how confident are we that we have genuinely uncovered that reality)?

• Why do the strategic gaps exist – what could be done to move the reality closer to the intent, but would this be possible, and would it be economical?

• Are some of the strategic gaps actually impossible to close on any sensible basis, for example is the marketing strategy hopelessly out of line with the resources and capabilities of this company at this time?

• Where (if anywhere) have management and the marketing planners confronted the strategic reality in this marketplace, as it is described to us by the salesforce, the distributors and the customers?

• Is the problem one of reformulating the strategy (i.e. moving the intent closer to the reality) or an issue for managerial action (i.e. attempting to bring the reality closer to the intent)?

Figure 21.6 shows an example of how this approach was adopted with one organization – a computer manufacturer – in which top management had difficulty in understanding why their marketing strategy for recovering market share in a critical market was floundering. In this example the information is laid out in a

Company:	Market:
XYZ Computers Ltd	Financial departmental systems

Strategy: Regain lost market share (get back to 20% from present 10%) by positioning as a specialist, high-quality systems supplier marketing total business solutions

Operational marketing policies	Strategic intent	Strategic reality	Strategic gaps
Products and services	• Technical superiority • Maximum service content • Specialist supplier	• The product is difficult to use • We are seen as a computer specialist	• Systems/solutions versus computers
Pricing and value	• High price but high value • Flexibility	• Expensive and over-priced • Intractable	• Value/quality perception problem • Real flexibility?
Communications: • Selling • Advertising • Promotion	• Advertising to reinforce positioning • Regular sales coverage of all accounts • Industry/sector based promotion and training events	• Our advertising is computers, not customer 'business solutions' • We have less sales coverage than the competition • We are seen as computer trainers not hardware suppliers	• Positioning problem? • Market coverage
Distribution: • Channels • Logistics • Service	• Use direct channels • Offer rapid installation • Provides 7-day servicing • Provide technical consultancy • Emphasize personal relationships	• Customers go to traders, not direct • We ignore advisers and recommenders • We talk to users not decision makers • Customers do not trust us	• Understanding of the customer decision-making units? • The real service needs? • Demand for hardware versus demand for services
Strategic positioning • Product/market life cycle • Strategic position • Competitive differentiation • Customer satisfaction	• Rapid market growth for next 5 years • We take a dominant position through technological superiority • Focus on customer visits, social events, etc.	• The market is already mature • We can take a tenable position at best • Our position is likely to weaken • Everyone visits and entertains – mostly better than we do	• Market assumptions? • Customer perceptions? • Real competitive strengths?

Conclusions, implications, actions
  • The major product/value issue is 'technical' (our company) versus 'customer-oriented' (the competitors)
  • We urgently need to reassess the market in terms of the important customer decision-making units and priorities/needs to different players
  • We need to investigate further our real position in the market
  • We need to study the growth prospects here (if any)

Figure 21.6 Analysing strategic gaps

worksheet format as discussed elsewhere (Piercy, 1997), but the important point of the case is the great contrast between the strategic intent as defined by senior managers and the perception of the real marketplace situation, or strategic reality, held by key members of the salesforce. This disparity was true in each area of the marketing programme, as well as in the resulting strategic position in this market. The barriers to implementation of the marketing strategy were fundamental, representing very real gaps: in understanding the customer's view of the product and the value of the company's total offering to the market; in attacking the real drivers in the critical customer decision-making units; in the company's real strength in communications and distribution coverage; and in the real future for the company in this market. As can be seen, this analysis provided a very different agenda to be addressed in implementing the marketing strategy in question and, it should be noted, not the agenda that management was expecting to identify. Their view had moved from blaming the salesforce for under-performing to reconsidering the assumptions they had made in building their marketing strategy, and questioning the attractiveness of this market as a continuing target.

The point of this example is that it can produce useful insights into the marketing implementation problem in a company in two ways. First, it can uncover how well the company translates its marketing strategies into the practicalities of integrated operational marketing programmes and plans of action. Second, this analysis forces management to look at the business from the point of view of operational personnel and paying customers, which can be very revealing in its own right, and frequently uncovers yet more of the underlying reasons why marketing strategies do not reach the marketplace level of the business.

Generally, this type of analysis is likely to uncover Strategic Gaps which may be explained for the following types of reasons:

• Strategic gaps may exist because there are too many internal barriers and obstacles, reflecting both open issues like resource and skills shortages, but also more covert questions like political resistance to change.
• Strategic gaps may exist because line management simply does not accept the validity of the strategic intent, i.e. they have no commitment of 'buy-in' to the marketing strategy.
• Strategic gaps may exist because the strategic intent is out of line with real corporate capabilities, i.e. what the organization is really capable of doing, as opposed to top management's idealized view of how things should be in their company.

• Strategic gaps may exist because when marketing plans and strategies have been constructed, the implementation issue has not been addressed in an explicit and detailed way – simply expecting things to happen because a plan has been written is often ineffective.
• Strategic gaps may exist because line managers do not understand or take seriously the Strategic intent represented by the marketing plans and strategy.

Each of these possible conclusions may lead us to different aspects of the implementation issue in marketing. This is recommended as a starting point which leads us quickly towards specific issues, rather than just the general question of implementation. Attention now turns to how we may be able to address the strategic gaps we have identified and their underlying causes, and the possible barriers to this process of change.

Implementation barriers in marketing

One point which should be borne in mind is that frequently it is not enough simply to locate and identify implementation problems in a company. To cope with those problems is likely to require rather more effort. Indeed, there is an underlying danger that marketing executives tend to underestimate the degree and type of change that is required in their organizations, if their marketing strategies are to be successfully implemented. In many ways it is understanding this issue that is the key to the paradox that while marketing implementation problems may often come down to very simple and obvious factors, actually solving such implementation problems may be extremely difficult. These hidden dimensions of the marketing implementation problem may reduce to such issues as:

• The separation of planning from management, leading to an absence of management involvement and commitment.

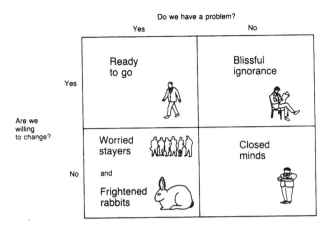

Figure 21.7   Is there an implementation problem?

- Unrealistic optimism about markets, competition and a company's capabilities because planners are separated from the problems of actually running the business.
- The implementation issue is recognized too late in the process, so managers are left trying to gain implementation through coercion, and ignore the underlying costs of organizational change (see below).
- The existence of implementation problems is simply denied by management who cannot believe that their decisions will not be put into effect.

Do we have an implementation problem in marketing?

Perhaps the most basic reason the marketing implementation issue is ignored when marketing plans and strategies are formulated is that executives do not believe that they have a marketing problem or that they need to change anything to get their strategies implemented. One observation (Piercy, 1997) is that companies, and in fact different units within the same organization, differ significantly in two important respects:

1   The perception that there is a marketing problem in the organization, which should be taken seriously; and

2   The willingness to try something new to solve the problem.

This suggests the model in Figure 21.7. A first step in working with a company to get to grips with the marketing implementation issue may be to ask where this business unit or department falls on the model in Figure 21.7. Which of the following best describes the situation we face in implementing our marketing strategy?

- Closed minds – people do not believe there is any significant marketing problem, and therefore see no reason to change the way they do things.
- Worried stayers and frightened rabbits – where people know that they have major marketing problems, but are either unwilling to change the way things are done in their company or simply do not know how to change.
- Blissful ignorance – situations where people believe they are always open to new ideas and change, but they do not really need to do anything differently, because they do not really believe that they have any problems.
- Ready to go – the only situation where we can reasonably expect new marketing solutions to be implemented is where people are willing to change and adopt new ways of doing things, and they accept that there are important marketing problems to be solved.

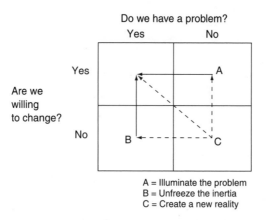

Figure 21.8   Implementation strategies

The chances are that it is only with the 'Ready to go' case that we can expect implementation of new marketing strategies to happen, and it is also likely that in many cases this is not the situation we will find. The conclusion is that we may need to think of different implementation strategies depending on the type of barrier we face: pressure to maintain the status quo, lack of perception or understanding of marketing problems to be solved, or both of these.

It is often suggested that while resistance to change is a well-known organizational phenomenon (e.g. Darling and Taylor, 1989), it is surprising that we should suggest that executives do not see or recognize that there are marketing problems. Bonoma and Clark (1990) offer some insight into this issue with their 'marketing performance assessment' framework. Their underlying arguments are that:

- Management satisfaction with marketing performance (and thus whether management think there are marketing problems or not) depends in large degree on what management expected to achieve in the first place. In short, the argument is that regardless of the real potentials in the market, satisfaction or dissatisfaction will be predicted by management's high or low expectations.
- How much marketing effort we have to make to get a given result depends on our skills, competencies and structures. We may get good

results with small effort, or bad results after massive expenditures of effort, depending on the match between our capabilities and market characteristics. This enormously complicates the problem of seeing whether we have a marketing problem or if one is on the way.
- Results depend not least on the environment – market trends and changes, competitive actions, and so on. Our results may look good or bad because of factors totally outside our control or ability to predict. We may do well because we are in the right place at the right time, and this may further obscure the need for marketing changes for the future and make it difficult to isolate marketing implementation problems.

The underlying point is the need to think of *implementation strategies* which address both issues of inertia and understanding of the real marketing problems, as suggested in Figure 21.8.

However, we have argued elsewhere (Piercy, 1997) that building such approaches to marketing implementation may involve us in operating on the underlying decision-making processes of the organization and its 'inner workings', rather than in just writing implementation strategies. For example, to illuminate the marketing problem may involve having executives and key players in the organization work on environmental scanning or participate in marketing planning itself, so they discover and address the real issues, rather than being told

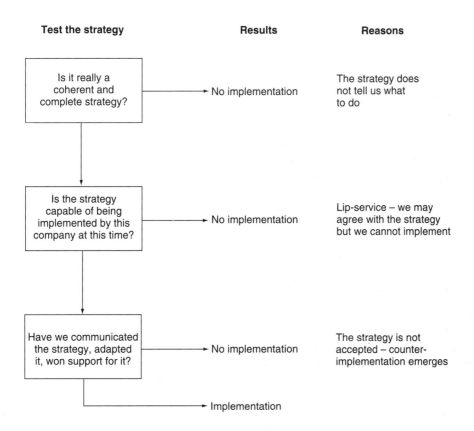

Adapted from Piercy, 1992

Figure 21.9   Testing marketing strategies

what they are. Similarly, overcoming a reluctance to change may be addressed through our internal marketing techniques (see below), but we need to seek a genuine understanding of *why* people in an organization cling to the familiar and established way of doing things. Argyris (1985), for instance, speaks of the 'defensive routines' that people build to protect themselves from the discomfort and disruption of having to change – the 'designed error' in implementation processes, such that we know things are going wrong but choose to do nothing about it.

Testing the strategy

However, as a start, the framework in Figure 21.9 suggests a number of critical questions that should be asked of the marketing strategy or plan,

before we assume that marketing failures are due to a company's low execution or implementation skills. These questions involve challenging:

1   The completeness and coherence of the strategy – if it is vague and missing important details, then how can we expect it to be implemented?
2   If the strategy is innovative and brilliant, but beyond the company's capabilities, then the most we can expect is lip-service. Bonoma (1985) outlines some of the common problems created here as: (a) management by assumption – we assume 'someone' will get the detailed work done, so in practice, no-one does it; (b) structural contradictions – we create marketing strategies that conflict

with our systems and structures and just expect people to cope; (c) empty promises marketing – we build marketing strategies and plans that rely on abilities and resources that we have not got and cannot get; or (d) bunny marketing – we have no clear marketing strategy, so we create a profusion of plans instead (Bonoma's analogy is the man with lots of rabbits who needed an ox, but no matter how much he bred the rabbits, he never seemed to end up with an ox).

3   If we have not made the effort to communicate and to win support for the plans and strategies with key players inside the organization, then it is likely that non-acceptance and counter-implementation will follow, rather than the 'ownership' and commitment that is needed to gain implementation.

However, while the first stage in our thinking about implementation problems should be to ask such questions about the strategy itself, the fact remains that there may also be problems that genuinely do reflect a company's capabilities and resistance to unwelcome change.

If our analysis of strategic gaps (Figure 21.5), internal perception of marketing problems and willingness to change (Figures 21.7 And 21.8), sources of marketing and the robustness of our marketing strategy (Figure 21.9) leads us to the conclusion that there are significant marketing implementation problems, then we may need a framework for planning and building a marketing-implementation strategy. Although it is far from the perfect answer, one approach to this is to use internal marketing as the structure for our implementation strategy, and the direct counterpart to our conventional external marketing strategy.

Marketing implementation and internal marketing strategy

If we reach the stage where we wish to build an explicit implementation strategy for our marketing plans, then the conventional literature offers little other than action plans and schedules. One method which has proved useful in coping with the implementation issue is to use strategic internal marketing.

Internal marketing can encompass many different issues relevant to strategy implementation. In different circumstances, the internal marketing process might include the following types of activity and programme:

- Gaining the support of key decision-makers for our plans – but also all that those plans imply in terms of the need to acquire personnel and financial resources, possibly in conflict with established company 'policies', and to get what is needed from other functions like operations and finance departments to implement a marketing strategy effectively;
- Changing some of the attitudes and behaviour of employees and managers, who are working at the key interfaces with customers and distributors, to those required to make plans work effectively (but also reinforcing effective attitudes and behaviour as well);
- Winning commitment to making the plan work and 'ownership' of the key problem-solving tasks from those units and individuals in the firm whose working support is needed;
- Ultimately, managing incremental changes in the culture from 'the way we always do things' to 'the way we need to do things to be successful' and to make the marketing strategy work; and
- Building key internal alliances, for example with Human Resource Management to influence employee skills and behaviour, or with the sales organization to link marketing imperatives to salesperson behaviour.

In fact, it follows from the emergence of the internal marketing paradigm from diverse conceptual sources that the practice of internal marketing and its potential contribution to marketing strategy are similarly varied. It is possible to consider the following 'types' of internal marketing, although they are probably not equal in importance:

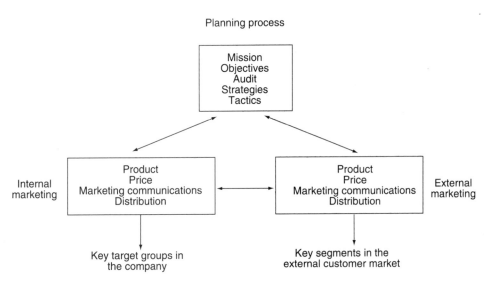

Figure 21.10　Internal and external marketing strategy

- internal marketing that focuses on the development and delivery of high standards of service quality and customer satisfaction;
- internal marketing that is concerned primarily with development of internal communications programmes to provide employees with information and to win their support;
- internal marketing which is used as a systematic approach to managing the adoption of innovations within an organization;
- internal marketing concerned with providing products and services to users inside the organization; and
- internal marketing as the implementation strategy for our marketing plans.

Here we are concerned mainly with the last of these.

The purpose of this approach is to capture our ideas about what has to be done to close the strategic gaps we have found, or to gain the effective implementation of our external marketing plans and strategies. The attraction of the framework is that it utilizes the same structure and analytical tools as external marketing planning, and directly parallels this familiar process throughout. The specific goals of the internal marketing strategy are taken directly from the requirements of the external marketing strategy.

One way of presenting this to a company is shown in Figure 21.10. This model suggests that internal marketing sits alongside external marketing and can be put into exactly the same structure (see below for examples). Internal marketing is taken as the output from the conventional external marketing programme – it simply asks for each element of the external marketing strategy and programme: what will be required inside the company; who will have to change what they do, learn new ways of doing things, give up existing practices, free resources and time, and so on. However, internal marketing analysis is also an *input* to the conventional planning process, in identifying both the constraints and barriers in the internal marketplace as well as important capabilities, which should be considered in building external marketing strategies (this is one way of coping with the strategy formulation/implementation dichotomy we considered earlier).

The structure of the internal marketing programme can be put into exactly the same terms as the conventional external marketing programme:

- *The market* – these are the individuals and groups inside the organization who are our internal customers, because without their acceptance and commitment to the external marketing strategy, it will not work.
- *The product* – at its simplest level the 'product' is the external marketing plan and strategy. However, at a deeper level the product for the internal market is all the changes and innovations that are needed to make the external strategy work, including changes in peoples' attitudes and behaviour.
- *The price* – this is not our costs, but what we are asking our internal customers to give up in order for our external strategy to be effectively implemented. The price may be the opportunity cost of other projects given up, or the costs to people of adjusting to change.
- *The marketing communications* – the most tangible aspect of internal marketing is the communications media and messages used to inform and persuade the internal customers. This may start with written communications and presentations, but may end up as being more about listening to the problems people perceive with the new strategy, and as necessary. Ultimately communication is a two-way process – we know this in our external marketing, and should not forget it in our internal marketing.
- *Distribution* – is concerned with all the ways we have to deliver the 'product' and the 'message' to the internal customer. It may start with meetings, workshops, committees, internal communications vehicles and the like, but may end up as far more concerned with the internal processes of the organization. For example, Ulrich (1989) has described the practices of major US organizations like General Electric, Marriott, DEC, the Ford Motor Company, Honeywell and others in working for the real customer commitment they need from their employees if their service-based external marketing strategies are to work. Their practices involve giving external customers a significant role in such internal

processes as: staff recruitment and selection decisions; staff promotion and development choices; staff appraisal, right from setting the standards to measuring the performance; operating staff reward systems both financial and non-financial; organizational design strategies; and internal communications programmes. This suggests that the most potent distribution channel for internal marketing may also be more to do with process and culture than simply holding meetings or sending out written communications.

- *Market research* – as with external marketing, we need to remember the role of research and analysis techniques in identifying the internal market characteristics and changes which are significant to the implementation of our external strategies.

It will be apparent from the way the internal marketing structure has been described above that we are concerned with far more than simply producing 'glossies' to persuade people in the organization to support our marketing strategy (although this may be one of the things that we have to do in some situations). We may end up more concerned with the underlying process and culture of the organization, and thus its real capabilities to implement a marketing strategy. This again directly parallels the way we look at the external customer – at different levels.

For example, Tables 21.2 and 21.3 summarize two company cases where the internal marketing framework is used at different levels to understand the real implementation problems and to develop appropriate responses, i.e. effective implementation responses. To make the levels clearer, the tabulated cases suggest that we look at internal marketing first at a *formal* level, where the concern is with open and rational presentation issues, second at an *informal* level, where the issues are about the 'inner workings' of the company, and third at a *processual* level, where we confront the underlying processes of change in the organization and the cultural barriers we may face.

Table 21.2 Internal marketing in a financial services organization

Internal marketing	Formal	Informal	Processual
		Internal marketing levels	
Product	Integration of selling efforts around key customers, as a key marketing strategy	Head-office group-based planning and resource allocation with greater central control	Change in the individual manager's role from independent branch 'entrepreneur' to group-based collaborator
Price	Branch profit/ commission from independent selling to smaller customers, to be sacrificed to build long-term relationships with key accounts	Loss of freedom/independence of action in the market-place. Potential loss of commission-earning power	Time, effort and psychological 'pain' of collaborating with former 'competitors' with different ethnic/educational/professional backgrounds – the 'banker versus the hire-purchase salesman'. Fear that the other side would damage existing customer relationships.
Distribution	Written strategic marketing plans. Sales conferences	Written communications. Informal discussion of chief executive's 'attitude'. Redesign of commission and incentives systems in both companies	Joint planning/problem-solving teams for each region – built around central definition of target market segments. Combining/integrating management information systems, and changing its structure to reflect new segments
Communications	Formal presentation by chief executive at conferences. Written support from chief executive. Redesign market information systems to be more up to date	Sponsorship by chief executive – 'the train is now leaving, the station you are either on it or . . .' (written memo sent to all branches)	Social events. Joint training courses. Redefinition of markets and target segments
Internal market targets		(1) Branch managers of retail banks and finance company offices (2) Divisional chief executives for the banks and the finance company	

Source: adapted from Piercy and Morgan (1991)

Table 21.3 Internal marketing in a computer company

| | Internal marketing levels | | |
Internal marketing	Formal	Informal	Processual
Product	Marketing plan to attack at small industry as a special vertical market, rather than grouping it with many other industries as at present, with specialized products and advertising	Separation of resources and control of this market from the existing business unit	Change from technology-oriented management to recognition of differences in buyer needs in different industries – the clash between technology and customer-orientation
Price	Costs of developing specialized 'badged' or branded products for this industry	Loss of control for existing business unit	Fear of 'fragmentation' of markets leading to internal structural and status changes
Distribution	Written plan. Presentations to key groups	Support for key plan by key board members gained by pre-presentation 'softening-up' by planners	Action planning team formed, including original planners, but also key players from business unit and product group – rediscovering the wheel to gain 'ownership' / Advertising the new strategy in trade press read by company technologists and managers
Communications	Business unit board meeting. Product group board meeting.	Informal meetings	Joint seminars in applying IT to this industry, involving business unit managers and key customers / Joint charity events for the industry's benevolent fund
Internal market targets	Main board meeting Salesforce conference	(1) Business unit management (2) Product group management (3) Salesforce	

Source: Adapted from Piercy (1997)

The case summarized in Table 21.2 describes the problems faced in a financial services organization in implementing a strategy of key customer focus, developed by a central team of planners, but relying on branch management co-operation and commitment – as well as requiring the collaboration of two traditionally separate and competing field divisions – for effective implementation. The desirability of this strategy was well known in the company, and it had frequently been included in group marketing plans, but with little or no success in implementation. The analysis in Table 21.2 suggests that while there were practical barriers to implementing the strategy at tactical level – threats to commission earnings, the need for better market information, and so on – there were far more substantial, but covert, blockages to implementation hidden in the culture of the organization. As a result, it can be seen that simply issuing written plans and instructions achieved little, and neither did 'sabre-rattling' by the chief executive. In fact, although attractive in attacking the external market, it was also true that the new strategy would have a considerable and unwelcome impact on the power and freedom of decentralized managers, compared to the planners at the centre, and would substantially change their evaluation and earnings prospects. More intractable still were the political barriers represented by the costs to the managers concerned with collaborating with counterparts in another division, who had historically been perceived at best as competitors – a cultural divide made worse by ethnic and educational background differences between the divisions. Implementation of the strategy was only achieved after operating on the process and culture of the company by building joint planning and problem-solving teams from the two divisions on a regional basis. This was exceptionally expensive, and some would argue that if the company had been able to see these hidden costs of organizational change at the outset they would have been well advised to abandon the apparently 'attractive' marketing strategy. However, while the process of change is

continuing in this organization, managers do now speak of the 'cultural change' in the organization and there are tangible operating changes in how the two division work together. This suggests that the process of internal marketing and organizational change described above may have had the effect of creating new implementation capabilities for the future in this company, and this may be the primary long-term benefit created.

While the financial services example above is primarily 'top-down', the case in Table 21.3 concerns a computer company where the marketing strategy was to adopt a vertical marketing approach to a small industry, where market share had been lost. This case is primarily concerned with the 'bottom-up' pressure by a group of managers in a large organization to pioneer and introduce a market-focused strategic plan for a particular customer's industry. This was seen as part of a more general need to move the whole of the organization from a technology-orientation where the prime purpose was to sell 'boxes' (i.e. computers) to a customer-orientation with a main purpose of producing customer business problem 'solutions'. Again the internal marketing starts with formal presentations but continues to informal communications and ways of dealing with the hostile reaction of the established business units to the weakening of their control over resources. Ultimately, implementation of the external vertical marketing strategy relied on building teams to take 'ownership' of the new strategy and to collaborate with key customers in a cultural transition from technology-orientation to customer-orientation (which is what the vertical marketing strategy was really about). One critical element of this was a programme of customer events, where a major objective was simply to expose senior company managers to customers and their views! Again, the strategy was put in place with some limited degree of success, but at some substantial costs. It is still relatively early days with this strategy, but there has been some success – some market share has been regained at a difficult time for the industry;

the industry-specific marketing activities have succeeded. However, far less has been achieved in the related issue of industry-specific products.

This suggests that in our present study of the marketing implementation issue, strategic internal marketing offers us three possible advantages:

1   It provides an operational framework for analysing the internal changes necessary to put the external marketing strategy into effect and for building an internal programme to achieve this.

2   As a framework it directly parallels conventional external marketing – in analysing the customers and building a marketing strategy and programme around them – and can be used at both an overt and relatively superficial level, but can also go deeper into the issues of process and culture in the organization, if this is necessary to get to the real implementation barriers and obstacles.

3   The strategic internal marketing framework offers us a way of evaluating the costs of implementation and organizational change early enough that we can decide whether or not to pursue the external strategy in question.

Conclusions

There can be little doubt that one of the major challenges facing marketing analysts in an era of market turbulence and reinvented organizations is the construction and development of better approaches to the implementation of marketing plans and strategies. We saw initially that this area is not simply problematic in its own right, but that it is further complicated by the tendency of planners and analysts to separate the implementation issue from the process of generating exciting and innovative marketing strategies. It is this dichotomy between strategy formulation and implementation issues which lies at the heart of many of the implementation failures that marketing executives describe. The simple fact is that implementation *is* strategy, and no marketing plan or strategy which does not explicitly, realistically and in detail address the implementation issue can possibly be regarded as satisfactorily completed. However, it is equally important that the way we address implementation issues should go beyond the simple issuing of instructions and building of detailed actions plans (although that may follow). What we are seeking is the development of convincing and operational implementation strategies in marketing.

We introduced the notions of implementation capabilities and 'organizational stretch' to describe the issues that managers must confront in building strategy implementation approaches. These issues highlight the importance of understanding the organizational context in which marketing must be implemented. We saw that the organizational positioning of marketing may be currently weak (probably leading to weak strategy implementation capabilities). However, the future of the marketing organization in the process-based organization and the hollow or network organization is even more uncertain. We argued that these radical organizational changes will place even higher priorities on understanding and sustaining implementation capabilities.

The price of ignoring the implementation issue, or treating it as simply tactical, may be considerable in terms of the costs of failed plans and strategies, missed opportunities to exploit competitive advantages, and the damage caused by ignoring the real workings of the infrastructure of the organization which we hope will put our marketing strategies into effect. These are not easy issues to resolve, but we described several ways in which progress may be made:

•   By recognizing the degree of organizational stretch that a new strategy represents.

•   By putting implementation into the context of the organizational realities of a weaker marketing paradigm, process-based management and new types of structure.

- By focusing attention on the issues with highest priority through the evaluation of strategic gaps.
- By examining the reasons for those strategic gaps in terms of implementation barriers and the match between our strategies and the characteristics of the company.
- By using the strategic internal marketing framework as an operational method for dealing with these issues realistically.

The evaluation of strategic gaps asked us to identify the marketing strategy we are pursuing (or wish to pursue) in a given market, and to identify what we have to achieve in marketing programme elements and strategic position for that strategy to become real. this strategic intent is then contrasted with strategic reality (i.e. what we have actually achieved in practical marketing and positioning) to identify strategic gaps The most revealing part of the exercise is in attempting to identify the reasons for the strategic gaps we have identified – the strategy, its translation into practical operational marketing terms, or the ability of the organization to successfully deliver that strategic intent into the real marketplace.

Pursuing that latter questioning into the underlying reasons for implementation barriers raises further issues, such as:

- The acceptance by key people of the existence of marketing problems that need to be solved, compared to their willingness to change and learn new ways of doing business, suggesting the need for different implementation approaches.
- Comparing the marketing strategy and the company's execution skills as relative contributors to implementation problems – and testing the key attributes of the strategy.

None of these are complete or universal approaches to the implementation issue, but all are capable of generating insights and a better understanding of what is necessary for marketing strategies to be effectively implemented.

This leads finally to the consideration of internal marketing strategy as a framework for building and applying a marketing implementation strategy. The attraction of this framework is that it mirrors and parallels the conventional external marketing strategy, and allows us to use the same terms and analytical methods with the critical internal customers that we are accustomed to use with the conventional external customers. However, we noted that the source of the internal marketing model is in the services field, where internal marketing is largely concerned with improving the performance of operational employees at the point of sale. In this present context, internal marketing is a different and strategic issue, which is concerned with identifying and acting on those things and people which have to change inside the company for the external strategy to be effectively implemented. We examined some cases of internal marketing strategy in companies to make the further point that there are different organizational levels at which internal marketing may operate. While it may be easiest to see internal marketing operating at the formal level – where the product is the plan or strategy, the price is that costs of change and communication and distribution are about formal communications – it is perhaps even more important to see internal marketing operating at the deeper level of the decision-making processes and cultural attributes of the organization. It is only in this way that we can get beyond the production of simple action plans and directives, and confront the underlying pressures towards maintaining the status quo, organizational inertia and 'defensive routines' to avoid change – i.e. the real implementation issues in our organizations.

There are no simple and easy-to-apply methods to deal with the implementation issue in marketing. It is hoped that the approaches suggested here may be useful at the operational level. Nonetheless, the implementation issue remains one of the greatest practical and theoretical challenges for the marketing analyst, consultant, teacher and practitioner in the future.

References

Achrol, R. S. (1991) Evolution of the marketing organization: New forms for turbulent environments, *Journal of Marketing*, **55**(4), 77–94.

Aldrich, H. and Herker, D. (1977) Boundary spanning roles and organizational structure, *Academy of Management Review*, **2**, April, 217–30.

Argyris, C. (1985) *Strategy, Change and Defensive Routines*, Harper and Row, New York.

Bonoma, T. V. (1985) *The Marketing Edge: Making Strategies Work*, Free Press, New York.

Bonoma, T. V. and Clark, B. (1990) Assessing marketing performance, in T. V. Bonoma and T. J. Kosnik (eds), *Marketing Management: Text and Cases*, Irwin, Homewood, IL.

Cespedes, F. V. and Piercy, N. F. (1996) Implementing marketing strategy, *Journal of Marketing Management*, **12**, 135–160.

Cravens, D. W., Greenley, G., Piercy, N. F. and Slater, S. (1997) Integrating contemporary strategic management perspectives, *Long Range Planning*, **30**, 493–506.

Cravens, D. W., Piercy, N. F. and Shipp, S. H. (1996) New organizational forms for competing in highly dynamic environments: the network paradigm, *British Journal of Management*, **7**, 203–218.

Darling, J. R. and Taylor, R. E. (1989) A model for reducing internal resistance to change in a firm's international marketing strategy, *European Journal of Marketing*, **23**(7), 34–41.

Day, G. S. (1992) Marketing's contribution to the strategy debate, *Journal of the Academy of Marketing Science*, **20**(4), 323–329.

Day, G. S. (1994) The capabilities of market-driven organizations, *Journal of Marketing*, **58** (October), 37–53.

Day, G. S. (1997) Aligning the organization to the market, in D. R. Lehman and K. E. Jocz (eds), *Reflections on the Futures of Marketing*, Marketing Science Institute, Cambridge, Mass., pp. 67–98.

Doyle, P. (1997) Go for robust growth, *Marketing Business*, April, 53.

Gummesson, E. (1991) Marketing-orientation revisited: the crucial role of the part-time marketer, *European Journal of Marketing*, **25**(2), 60–75.

Hamel, G. and Prahalad, C. K. (1989) Strategic intent, *Harvard Business Review*, May/June, 63–76.

Hutt, M. D., Reingen, P. H. and Ronchetto, J. R. (1988) Tracing emergent processes in marketing strategy formation, *Journal of Marketing*, **52**(1), 4–19.

Mintzberg, H. (1988) Opening up the definition of strategy, in J. B. Quinn, H. Mintzberg and R. M. James (eds), *The Strategy Process*, Prentice-Hall International, London.

Mitchell, A. (1996) Stemming the sea change, *Marketing Business*, November, 24–27.

Morgan, N. and Piercy, N. F. (1996) Competitive advantage, quality strategy and the role of marketing, *British Journal of Management*, **7**, 231–245.

Pfeffer, J. (1981) *Power in Organizations*, Pitman, Marshfield, MA.

Piercy, N. F. (1985) *Marketing Organisation: An Analysis of Information Processing, Power and Politics*, Allen & Unwin, London.

Piercy, N. F. (1986) The role and function of the chief marketing executive and the marketing department, *Journal of Marketing Management*, **1**(3), 265–289.

Piercy, N. F. (1987) The marketing budgeting process, *Journal of Marketing*, **51** (January), 45–59.

Piercy, N. F. (1990) Marketing concepts and actions: implementing marketing-led strategic change, *European Journal of Marketing*, **24**(2), 24–42.

Piercy, N. F. (1992) *Market-Led Strategic Change*, Butterworth-Heinemann, Oxford.

Piercy, N. F. (1995) Customer satisfaction and the internal market: marketing our customers to our employees, *Journal of Marketing Practice: Applied Marketing Science*, **1**(1), 22–44.

Piercy, N. F. (1997) *Market-Led Strategic Change: Transforming the Process of Going To Market*, Butterworth-Heinemann, Oxford.

Piercy, N. F. (1998a) Barriers to implementing relationship marketing: analyzing the internal marketplace, *Journal of Strategic Marketing*, **6**, 209–222.

Piercy, N. F. (1998b) Marketing implementation: The implications of marketing paradigm weakness for the strategy execution process, *Journal of the Academy of Marketing Science*, **26**(3), 222–236.

Piercy, N. F. and Cravens, D. W. (1995) The network paradigm and the marketing organization, *European Journal of Marketing*, **29**(3), 7–34.

Piercy, N. and Morgan, N. (1990) Internal marketing strategy: leverage for managing marketing-led strategic change, *Irish Marketing Review*, **4**(3), 11–28.

Piercy, N. and Morgan, N. (1991) Internal marketing – the missing half of the marketing programme, *Long Range Planning*, **24**(2), 82–93.

Piercy, N. F. and Morgan, N. (1993) Strategic and operational market segmentation – A managerial analysis, *Journal of Strategic Marketing*, **1**, 123–140.

Piercy, N. F. and Morgan, N. (1994) The marketing planning process: Behavioral problems compared to analytical techniques in explaining marketing plan credibility, *Journal of Business Research*, **29**, 167–178.

Piercy, N. F. and Morgan, N. (1996) Customer satisfaction measurement and management: A processual analysis, *Journal of Marketing Management*, **11**, 817–834.

Piercy, N. F. and Morgan, N. (1997) The impact of lean thinking and the lean enterprise on marketing; Threat or synergy? *Journal of Marketing Management*, **13**, 679–694.

Ruekert, R. W. and Walker, O. (1987) Marketing's interaction with other function units: a conceptual framework and empirical evidence, *Journal of Marketing*, **51**(1), 1–19.

Sheth, J. N. (1994) Relationship Marketing: A Customer Perspective, Relationship Marketing Conference, Emory University, Atlanta, June.

Spekman, R. E. (1979) Influence and information: an exploratory investigation of the boundary person's basis of power, *Academy of Management Journal*, **22**(1), 104–117.

Ulrich, D. (1989) Tie the corporate knot: gaining complete customer commitment, *Sloan Management Review*, Summer, 19–27.

Walker, O. C. and Ruekert, R. W. (1987) Marketing's role in the implementation of business strategies: a critical review and conceptual framework, *Journal of Marketing*, **51**, July, 15-33.

Webster, F. E. (1992) The changing role of marketing in the corporation, *Journal of Marketing*, **56** (October), 1–17.

Webster, F. E. (1997) The future role of marketing in the organization, in D. R. Lehman and K. E. Jocz (eds.), *Reflections on the Futures of Marketing*, Marketing Science Institute, Cambridge, Mass., pp. 39–66.

Further reading

Bonoma, T. V. (1985) *The Marketing Edge: Making Strategies Work*, Free Press, New York. This is now almost the classic treatise on the marketing implementation issue. Based on executive company case and interview research, it contains many insights and frameworks for analysing the implementation issue in marketing.

Cespedes, F. V. (1991) *Organizing and Implementing the Marketing Effort*, Addison-Wesley, Reading, MA. This is an excellent attempt to relate organizational context to the problems of making marketing effective, with a wealth of case material in support. It also provides some valuable literature reviews on a broad base, concerned with marketing implementation and organizational change.

Cespedes, F. V. and Piercy, N. F. (1996) Implementing marketing strategy, *Journal of Marketing Management*, **12**, 135–160. A theoretical review of the underlying organizational problems in implementation, going deeper into certain of these issues.

Cespedes, F. V. and Piercy, N. F. (1996) Implementation of Strategy, in M. Warner (ed.), *International Encyclopaedia of Business and Management*, Routledge, London. A more detailed and broader review of strategy implementation which has many implications for marketing in the context of strategic management.

Cravens, D. W., Greenley, G., Piercy, N. F. and Slater, S. (1997) Integrating contemporary strategic management perspectives, *Long Range Planning*, **30**, 493–506. This article reviews the sources of market-based strategic management and the reinvented organizations emerging in diverse markets.

Cravens, D. W., Piercy, N. F. and Shipp, S. H. (1996) New organizational forms for competing in highly dynamic environments: the network paradigm, *British Journal of Management*, 7, 203–218. This article discusses the emergence of new alliance and network-based organizational forms to cope with new marketing environments, and reflects on the implications for strategy implementation.

Giles, W. D. (1991) Making strategy work, *Long Range Planning*, **24**(5), 75–91. This is an excellent summary of the conclusions reached by Giles as a result of many years' practical experience as a marketing manager and consultant, and confronts the underlying implementation issue through re-examining the characteristics of marketing planning as a process.

Piercy, N. (1994) Marketing implementation: analysing structure, information and process, in Saunders, J. (ed.), *The Marketing Initiative*, Prentice-Hall, Hemel Hempstead. This is an attempt to integrate the theoretical and empirical sources of the author's approach to the implementation question, examining research works on the organization of marketing in the UK, information and intelligence systems characteristics, and the operation of budgeting and planning processes in marketing, leading to central questions about achieving the implementation of marketing strategies and the potential role of internal marketing.

Piercy, N. (1997) *Market-Led Strategic Change: Transforming the Process of Going to Market*, Butterworth-Heinemann, Oxford. This book, in its second edition, represents an attempt to put marketing into this context of the process of going to market, rather than a marketing department. This places the issue of strategy implementation and strategic change in marketing with the new context of cross-functional and intra-organizational value-creating processes, which underpin the achievement of customer focus and developing superior customer value. The book describes a strategic pathway comprising: market sensing and customer focus, key market choices, the development of a value proposition, and the management of a network of key relationships (with customers, collaborators, competitors and co-workers). The book provides worksheets and diagnosis for managers to use in confronting the implementation and change problems that the companies face. The material is supported by an Instructor's Manual.

Piercy, N. (1998) Marketing implementation: The implications of marketing paradigm weakness for the strategy execution process, *Journal of the Academy of Marketing Science*, **26**(3), 222–236. A study of the implementation issue as it is developing in modern organizations, where the marketing concept competes for management attention with other conflicting paradigms like the lean enterprise, from an increasingly weak organizational position. Concludes that marketing in the future must focus on organizational stretch and acquire a new vocabulary to enumerate and defend marketing capabilities.

Walker, O. C. and Ruekert, R. W. (1987) Marketing's role in the implementation of business strategies: a critical review and conceptual framework, *Journal of Marketing*, **51**, July, 15–33. An important, if somewhat theoretical, treatment of the implementation issue in marketing, which emphasizes different perspectives on the problem and develops propositions about the organizational structures and processes best suited for implementing different types of strategy.

Part Four
The Application of
Marketing

CHAPTER 22

Organizational marketing

DALE LITTLER

Introduction

Organizational marketing is in essence concerned with the exchange of goods and services between organizations which then resell them or employ them in the production of other goods and services. The term has largely replaced 'industrial marketing' which was initially used to embrace marketing between companies engaged in the production of commodities or in manufacturing (in mainly what are referred to as the 'smokestack' industries). It is considered more contemporary than 'business-to-business' marketing which may be seen as excluding marketing in non-profit making (and therefore strictly non-business) environments, such as charities, political parties and local authorities.

Organizational markets account for a large proportion of a country's GDP. The output of all consumer goods is preceded generally by a chain of organizational marketing activities that in themselves account for significant economic activity. Many of these organizational markets are substantial in themselves. For example, the expenditure on defence equipment was almost £9bn in 1994/95, the sales of industrial gases amounted to £458m in 1995, and steel tubes £1284m (Office for National Statistics, 1997). Some major consumer markets such as ice cream and household textiles accounted for sales of £528m and £889m respectively in 1995, yet each of these consumer markets would have involved significant exchanges of organizational goods and services (for example, fats, milk and cream, sugar, plant and equipment, detergents etc., in the case of ice cream) (Office for National Statistics, 1997).

Many companies buy in a significant and even in some cases a major proportion of their components and services. Car manufacturers for example are large purchasers of parts and sub-assemblies amounting to several hundreds of millions of pounds. Companies such as British Airways are increasingly looking towards outsourcing of many of their business activities (such as distribution, information systems management, maintenance) because they want to focus on those elements of the process of developing offerings where they can add the most value, preferring to enter into contracts with suppliers which can provide generally, but not necessarily, supporting activities more efficiently. Companies such as Hays plc provide *inter alia* distribution services, mail room management and personnel services. The purchasing of goods and services by organizations is likely to increase as more and more companies off load activities traditionally regarded as part of their core activities but now viewed as peripheral. The decision to buy externally rather than produce in itself raises issues of single as against multiple sourcing; the nature of the relationship with suppliers (transaction versus relationship approach); and the planning, control and ethics of the exchange between supplier and purchaser. The increasing popularity of collaboration in all markets and the enhanced role of IT are also affecting the structure and form of organizational relationships.

Although the importance of marketing in organizational markets has been widely recognized, it may have been more extensively and effectively implemented in consumer rather than organizational goods companies (Ames, 1970), although even in consumer goods companies there may have been more emphasis on the mechanics (market research surveys, use of branding, mass advertising) than the essence – striving to obtain a deeper understanding over time of customer requirements and the dynamics shaping them. In all organizations, there is the possibility that history and experience has resulted in an engineering, sales or R&D dominated culture. However, the need for a greater market orientation will be critical because of intensifying competition as a result of rapid technological change, the lowering of tariff barriers, the trend for companies to internationalize, deregulation and the breakdown, because of *inter alia* privatization, of comfortable supplier–customer relationships which often dominated public sector markets. In general, customers have a greater opportunity to exercise discretion.

A failure to embrace marketing throughout the organization is likely to have a significant impact on organizational performance and indeed many studies have emphasized the role of marketing in overall organizational competitiveness (e.g. Central Advisory Council for Science and Technology, 1968; NEDO, 1981). Other research suggests that sustainable international competitiveness might be more effectively secured through the blending of marketing with an innovative technological capability (Wong and Saunders, 1993). Certainly organizations are likely to enjoy greater commercial success if they are able to innovate successfully (Pavitt, 1980; Freeman, 1982) and this will be based on a deep understanding of the preferred specifica-

tions of customers (Littler and Sweeting, 1985); effective inter-functional co-operation within the organization (Bruce and Cooper, 1997) with marketing have a leading role; and the expeditious use of pricing, communications and distribution and the other elements which come under the traditional umbrella of marketing.

In this chapter, the different types of organizational products and services (with organizational goods being used henceforward to embrace both products and services) are considered. The major features of organizational markets and of the demand for organizational goods are described; the procurement process is outlined; and finally the implications for marketing management are drawn.

Organizational products and services

Although there are many goods, such as capital plant and equipment, which are clearly identifiable as 'organizational goods', there are others, such as telephones, computers and even carpets which are sold to both consumers and organizations. The major feature differentiating consumer from organizational goods is the purpose for which they are sold. In organizational markets, goods are purchased for resale or for their use in the production of other goods.

There are a variety of types of organizational goods and the manner in which they are bought and sold, and therefore the manner in which they are marketed can differ markedly.

Various means of classifying organizational goods have been proposed, ranging from the extent to which they have been processed in a hierarchy from basic raw materials, to semi-processed products to completed equipment (IMRA, 1969) through to the extent to which they are involved in the product (Kotler, 1988). In general, the broad categories of organizational goods shown in Table 22.1 can be identified.

Table 22.1 Broad categories of organizational goods

Raw materials	Basic natural commodities, such as agricultural produce, e.g. hops, vegetables; and natural materials, e.g. coal, unprocessed oil, aluminium ore.
Processed materials	These have undergone some processing and although incorporated in the product are not identifiable, e.g. cement, steel, ethylene.
Components	Manufactured parts, e.g. transistors, compressors, tyres, light fittings. They can be standardized or customized.
Accommodation	The space on which and within which the production occurs, e.g. land, buildings, etc.
Fixed plant	Includes capital plant such as packaging equipment, generators.
Movable equipment	This is used in the production process but is not integrated in the final product, e.g. fork lift trucks, hand-power tools, computers.
Maintenance, repair and operating supplies	Used to facilitate the continued operation of the organization, e.g. paint, adhesives, electricity, lubricating oils.
General services	Office cleaning, equipment maintenance.
Specialist services	Logistics management, management of IT services.
Professional services	Marketing research, auditing, consultancy.

Organizational markets

There are at least four types of organizational markets:

1   *Producer markets:* goods are purchased by organizations that employ them to produce other goods, either for sale to consumers or to other organizations. Examples of these types of goods include machine tools, computer business systems, specialist chemicals such as surfactants.

2   *Reseller markets:* These involve the purchase of goods and services by those involved in distribution such as wholesalers and retailers. Many goods are not sold directly by their producers to the final users or consumers, but involve an intermediary of some sort. In some sectors of the consumer market, such as grocery purchases, a major proportion of the market is accounted for by four retailers, which consequently have acquired considerable purchasing power. In these large organizations, buying is often undertaken centrally, and suppliers will generally make a senior executive responsible for liaising with such key accounts. In some sectors, technological developments are having profound implications for distributors and the structure of distribution channels. For example, some manufacturers have developed and adopted processes such as just-in-time to reduce inventory and space requirements by providing delivery from suppliers of materials and components only when they are needed in the production process. This obviously necessitates detailed interaction with suppliers and the use of computer systems enabling the automatic transmission of the requisite information. Similarly, retailers are adopting computerized electronic point-of-sale systems which relay data from the checkout, thereby permitting *inter alia* automatic reordering directly from producers. The introduction of 'loyalty cards' enables retailers to monitor consumer purchasing patterns, ascertain the contributions of products and discern emerging purchasing trends. This intelligence naturally augments the power of the retailers which demand *inter alia* the requisite flexibility from suppliers to enable the reseller to respond quickly, appropriately and optimally to changes in demand.

3   *Government markets:* These involve the purchase of goods by central and local

government. Total UK government expenditure is substantial although an increasing proportion is allocated to decision making bodies such as Government agencies or 'trusts' which have significant autonomy and are, therefore, more accurately categorized as 'institutional markets'. Government, however, will still affect the level of expenditure and often provide policy guidelines. Moreover, government maintains direct responsibility for many major decisions, which will tend to be made centrally, such as armaments procurement and the construction of new motorways, as well as for expenditure on its own administration. However, increasing emphasis on the use of market mechanisms by some governments means that a significant proportion of public purchasing is becoming more closely aligned to that in the private sector.

4   *Institutional markets:* These embrace those areas outside of producer, reseller and government markets which are concerned with providing some form of social or other service. They may be either in the public (financed by central government or local authorities) or private sector. In the case of the former, as noted above, institutions may have a degree of discretion over their own purchases, even though in some cases technical criteria may be established by government. Examples of institutions include schools, prisons, hospitals, universities and charities.

Features of organizational markets

There are several distinctive features of organizational markets. First, the purchasing process can often be lengthy and intricate, involving detailed negotiations about specifications which may require the use of external consultants, the identification of suppliers which satisfy technical and other pre-requisites, the development of appropriate evaluation criteria, and invitations to bid or the solicitation of quotations. The process may entail the participation of several individuals who collectively comprise the decision making unit (or DMU) (Brand, 1972). Thus,

the decision to invest in a major piece of production equipment could involve production engineers, accountants and the purchasing department as well as external consultant engineers. Webster and Wind (1972) have identified several roles within the DMU: users, influencers, buyers, deciders and gatekeepers. This means that buying influence may be diffused through the firm, and the successful completion of a transaction may involve convincing several and in some instances a considerable number of personnel in the purchasing organization. Transactions may therefore be prolonged because of the involvement of and consultations between several parties. The decision-making procedures of some organizations may involve several committees and layers of authority, and can thereby further lengthen the purchasing process. Protracted negotiations are also likely to be a feature of purchasing decisions that involve substantial investments or customized products where there will be a need to agree on specifications. These and other aspects of organizational purchasing behaviour are however discussed in more detail in Chapter 6.

Second, it is often argued that purchasers in organizational markets are more 'rational' than those in consumer markets because they are likely to have greater technical knowledge, have a relatively detailed understanding of the functions and features they require, aim to identify competing alternatives, and devise appropriate criteria for evaluating them. For example, many firms may establish a firm set of criteria (such as product performance, quality control procedures, financial soundness) for evaluating new vendors, while existing vendors' performance may be assessed periodically and systematically, using such factors as the quality of information provided, delivery, product quality, innovative capability.

However, as Marrian (1965) wrote some years ago:

A characteristic which has enjoyed considerable vogue in marketing regarding the industrial and ultimate consumer markets is that of the former consisting of buyers who are rational, expert and possessing complete knowledge of values and substitute products . . . it cannot be ignored that the designated organizational buyer, while he is constrained by organization policy, is subject also to personal goals and aspirations in executing his organizational role.

It may be that in the majority of purchasing decisions there is no conflict between the aspirations and values of the individual decision maker and the requirements of the business. However, it can be expected that purchasing decisions will be directed and shaped by the experiences, pre-dispositions and motives of those making them, whilst the 'personal chemistry' between those involved can itself affect the supplier–customer relationship. Even those who appear to strive to be concerned to be objective and optimize economically may have personal agendas (such as the minimization of effort in making the purchase) or preferences that unduly affect the decision, while often the search for information and the process of assessment may be little more than formalities to justify a decision that may at least implicitly have already been made. In addition, the political context within which purchasing decisions are made needs to be fully appreciated. For example, Pettigrew (1975) found that 'gatekeepers' can structure the outcome of a buying process by affecting the flow of information to suit their objectives. The search for scapegoats for past inadequate organizational performance, the urge to be dissociated from discredited former executives and the desire to be seen to exercise power and authority are among the influences which can affect purchasing behaviour. In some cases, alterations in suppliers may be made because, for example, new executives want to signify that their presence symbolizes change, or because they have developed preferences in previous organizations for particular suppliers. Moreover, the buying procedures may not be as comprehensive as may often be assumed. For example, there is evidence that experience rather than the application of a consciously devised set of evaluation criteria was an important influence on the patronage decision which was often made without obtaining competitive quotations (Cunningham and White, 1974).

There may also be strong inclination to continue with existing suppliers unless there are major reasons for change. Even where unsatisfactory performance has been experienced, the emphasis may well be on resolving difficulties to avoid changing the source of supply. There may also be considerable switching costs because any change in supplier may require adaptations to existing processes and procedures, new learning, reformulations, or even the purchase of different machinery. The comfortability that flows from existing and well tried relationships, the significant costs that can attend the disruption from altering suppliers and often the high value attached to the social relationships which have evolved between those on both sides will tend to result in significant inertia in inter-organizational relationships. Much effort will often be expended on making these work effectively, although changes in relevant personnel, significant downturns in customer performance or major changes in strategy can herald a reappraisal of purchasing policy.

Third, organizational markets tend to be concentrated. Often, only a small percentage of buyers will account for a major proportion of total purchases (the Pareto 20/80 rule often applying, see Figure 22.1). Markets may also be geographically concentrated, with major purchasers, for historical, economic or other reasons, being clustered in particular regions.

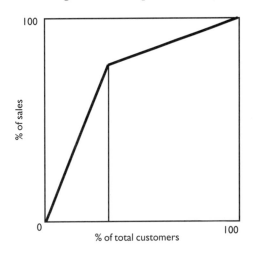

Figure 22.1 Percentage of sales versus percentage of total customers

This concentration of organizational markets suggests that it is possible to identify and possibly develop a clear profile of major purchasing organizations. These form 'primary' accounts for which suppliers often make senior executives responsible. Such 'key account managers' may have responsibility for, *inter alia*, keeping customers advised of technological advances made by the supplier, facilitating dialogue about future technological developments, and ensuring that product development is informed by the existing and future requirements of customers. The contemporary emphasis is on collaboration between suppliers and customers with the aim of improving efficiency, quality, effective product development and, in turn, profitability of all the parties in the supply chain. 'Partnership' is the focus of managerial effort.

Fourth, systems development and marketing is an important aspect of many organizational markets. For example, for expensive capital projects, such as power stations or missile defence systems, one organization, called the 'turnkey' contractor, may be responsible for the design, development and management of the project, involving the co-ordination of often a large number of consultants and subcontractors. In other cases, suppliers may be expected to develop, adapt, deliver and install equipment and ensure its effective operation in situ. There is also a trend for organizations to seek external contractors for parts of their operations, such as distribution and management of such facilities as computers. In this way, they can focus on what they term their core business activities and thereby concentrate on developing the key competencies which are the basis of their competitive advantage.

Increasingly, customer organizations may seek systems solutions, rather than, say, just particular hardware. Thus, an organization may require the development and implementation of an information system which demands not only the computer equipment but also the supply of a range of software, the effective implementation of the system, including the training of the oper-

ators, its maintenance and its continued updating in the light of future technological developments. By adding value in this way to what they offer, organizations may secure a marketing edge as well as enhanced profitability.

Fifth, competitive tendering is often used, particularly for public sector, technically complex and costly projects, and this may be conducted on a secret or 'sealed bid' basis, with bidders putting forward tenders unaware of the costs of the bids of their rivals. Selection will tend to be made on the basis of the lowest cost bid, provided all other criteria are satisfied. In addition, large scale, technically novel and generally complicated projects may often be accompanied by contracts which detail the agreed terms, establish performance and other targets, and specify penalties for non-compliance.

Demand for organizational products and services

The demand for organizational goods is derived from that for the goods which they help to produce, and ultimately, from demand in the final consumer market. The further down the production chain, away from consumer demand, the less likely the demand for the organizational good will be affected by changes in consumer demand.

There are many factors over which the organizational market has little control that affect consumer demand and it might be expected that the demand for many organizational goods would be relatively price inelastic because the lower price of a particular machine tool will not lead to a manifest decrease in the price of the final consumer good. However, reliability and running costs will have a marked effect.

In some cases, organizations have, with mixed success, attempted to stimulate consumer demand through, for instance, advertising. Du Pont, for example, has advertised its synthetic fibres and its synthetic shoe-upper material, Corfam, with a view to creating a favourable consumer disposition to products in which they are used.

The demand for certain classes of goods, particularly capital equipment, is unlikely to be very responsive to changes in consumer demand. Capital goods can service a range of output and significant increases in demand will be needed to prompt decisions to expand capacity. Growth in demand can, for example, often be met by utilizing under-employed capacity, increasing the number of shifts or through other changes in efficiency; whereas there will have to be significant declines in consumer demand over the longer term for there to be any marked impact since plant can be taken out of service ('mothballed') and the replacement of plant postponed. Decisions on whether or not to replace or augment capital goods are made irregularly and in expectations of a favourable market outlook for their products, although plant which operates at significantly higher levels of efficiency may be purchased even if the end market is stable or contracting. Again, some organizational services, such as accountancy, will not demonstrate a high price elasticity of demand since they have considerable economies of scale, while where an organizational good has a variety of applications, its overall demand may only be marginally affected by changes in demand in one of the end use markets. However, although overall price elasticity of demand may be low, the price elasticity of demand for the output of specific organizations may well be high. A supplier's market share may be significantly affected by its price relative to its competitors *ceteris paribus*, although price may not be regarded as important where the organizational good accounts for only a small proportion of the total cost. In some cases, such as components bought in large volumes, significant savings may be realized from only small changes in cost, and it is likely that intensified competition compels purchasers to pay increasing attention to price.

Customers may not always respond in the way and to the extent expected to alterations in an organization's prices. For instance, they may view price decreases as heralding further declines and therefore postpone purchase; although in some cases, price increases may be viewed as the beginning of a long-term trend and there may be an exaggerated response as customers bring forward purchases in anticipation of further price increases. However, there is substantial evidence that a range of factors, in addition to price, are employed to discriminate between individual suppliers.

Non-price factors affecting demand

It is accepted that effective marketing involves the development and selling of offerings consisting of a set of customer perceived values. These can include reliability, additional functionality, greater service support, higher performance on critical criteria. In many cases, price may be only one of several variables affecting the decision to purchase and, indeed, in some cases, where for example lower operating costs or higher overall quality of output are essential, it may not be a major influence. Thus, in a study of the reasons why UK companies purchased foreign built textile machinery, Rothwell (1977) found that price was specifically mentioned only in a minority of cases. It was features such as service and technical performance that were apparently of greater concern. Other studies also suggest that price may be only one of a range of factors affecting the decision to purchase. For instance, Rothwell (1981) examined the reasons for the agricultural machinery purchases of a sample of UK farmers. He identified price and non-price factors affecting the decision, and found that there was a marked dominance of non-price over sales price. Criteria such as speed and production rates; reliability, flexibility and adaptability in use; performance; and ease of use and maintenance, were considered relatively more important. In the case of purchases of steel castings by UK and Canadian manufacturers of pumps and valves, delivery and reliability emerged as key influences (Cunningham and Roberts, 1974; Banting, 1976).

Other factors identified as important included: the provision of technical support; speed of response in quoting; and replacement guarantee. Research has also highlighted the importance of the technical features of the good (Pavitt, 1980) as these affect the quality of the output, reliability and overall performance. It is also clear that customers will be concerned about the longer-term viability of their suppliers where, for example, there may be the need for future upgrading as a result of technological change.

In any case, the initial purchase price is generally only one component of the total costs associated with an organizational good. Purchasers will also take account of depreciation, maintenance and operating costs and disposal costs. They are also likely to be concerned with dependability of delivery, or of reliability in operation, especially in the case of continuous production processes where 'downtime' can be costly. It is the total value to the customer/user in terms of the cost savings, convenience and quality improvements that is likely to be of importance and it is the realized benefits to the customer of the use of the good over its lifetime that the marketer should emphasize (Anderson et al., 1993).

Other aspects of demand

Demand for an organizational good can generally be disaggregated into relatively coherent clusters according to one or more dimensions such as: end-uses, size of customer organization, location, technology, importance to the supplier organization, level of service required and so on. There may be some intra-segment variation in requirements, but this general approach may be a convenient way of structuring the market and organizing the marketing effort. Where an organizational good has different end uses, it is necessary, when assessing total demand, to estimate the total and change in demand in each and the consequential implications for the overall demand for the good. Where there are a wide variety of end uses and

distribution intermediaries are used, the information on the range of applications and the quantities employed in each may not be easily available, while distributors may be reluctant to reveal to suppliers any information they have on end uses in order to exercise some power over the distribution channel. For instance, some retailers are acquiring considerable, detailed customer information through the use of Electronic Point of Sale (EPOS) which enables *inter alia* the pattern of demand for specific products to be monitored; and customer 'loyalty cards' and store credit cards which enable demographic and other consumer data to be correlated with goods purchased. Such data can be employed to enhance the power of the retailer *vis-à-vis* the supplier; alternatively they can be shared with suppliers, perhaps on a proprietary basis, in order to enhance the efficiency and effectiveness of the process of producing, distributing and marketing goods.

Procurement

Procurement is usually depicted as a process consisting of several stages, with the number and/or relevance of the states varying according to whether or not the purchase is a 'new phase task', a 'modified re-buy' or a 'straight re-buy' (Robinson *et al.*, 1967); for more detail see Chapter 6. Robinson *et al.* (1967) developed a buy grid model in which they correlated these buy classes with the eight stages of the procurement model. Wilson (1997) extended the number of stages to twelve. The process will not necessarily consist of distinct stages; it is clear that there will often be iterations between one or more of them. In summary, the various stages can be seen to include:

1   The identification of the requirement: there is an awareness of the need to purchase the good.
2   The definition of the requirement: often, but not inevitably, as a result of consultations within the organization, the type, quantity, pricing range, distribution, etc. of the good is specified.

3   The decision on whether or not to make or buy the product: the decision may be based on, *inter alia*, relative costs of manufacturing in house or outsourcing and the availability of suppliers which meet the purchaser's criteria.

4   The establishment of criteria for evaluating and selecting suppliers.

5   The search for possible suppliers (which may overlap with (3) above).

6   The invitation to potential suppliers to submit proposals.

7   The evaluation of potential suppliers: this may include assessment of the offerings, financial soundness, technical competencies, etc.

8   Negotiation with short-listed suppliers to obtain the optimum financial and other terms.

9   The selection of one or more suppliers: this may involve a complex of iterations between the purchaser and one or more short-listed suppliers and the involvement of several people within the purchasing organization until the most acceptable terms and conditions are agreed.

10   Feedback and assessment of the procurement process.

11   Reassessment of the requirement in the light of technical and other changes.

It would appear that procurement has become increasingly professional, attended by a concentration of procurement responsibility: in many organizations there is identified responsibility, often in centralized purchasing departments, staffed by experienced and trained executives. They generally negotiate purchases of all goods and services on behalf of the organization and come to arrangements on prices and other conditions of supply. The centralization of purchasing can facilitate the development of detailed knowledge of customers and markets and the procurement function may be structured according to, for example, the markets in which the organization is engaged.

Traditionally, procurement may have been reactive, a purchase being the response to requests from within the organization. It is often depicted as being traditionally transactional and adversarial, each purchase being geared to getting the maximum terms for the purchaser. In some cases, this perspective may well be accurate; in others, there is no doubt that significant relationships are built up between generally, individual representatives of purchasers and suppliers, as described earlier (see also Chapter 6).

Contemporary thinking emphasizes the strategic role of procurement (Ford *et al.*, 1998) in assisting the purchasing organization to gain a competitive advantage through working in partnership with its suppliers in developing new specifications and technologies. More generally, there is greater emphasis on cooperation between the two parties to optimize quality and other relevant factors and to lower costs for the value chain as a whole.

An increasing trend is for organizations faced with intense international competition to seek the lowest-cost sources of supply and the most appropriate technology. This may require extensive international search and the establishment of international and even global supply networks which raises particular issues of management and control to ensure quality and the attainment of delivery and ethical criteria.

Management implications

Marketing management is generally regarded as involving the manipulation of the marketing mix (McCarthy, 1960). This dominant approach to marketing management is often represented as the mechanistic application of a set of rules or guidelines by a distinct marketing function acting independently (Kotler, 1988). This approach has been increasingly criticized (see Kent, 1986) especially so in the case of organizational markets where there is more likely to be mutual recognition between buyers and sellers, protracted interaction for many types of purchases and, in some cases, long-term social relationships (Hakansson, 1982).

It may be more appropriate to regard organizational marketing as relationship management (Gronroos, 1991) rather than the development and implementation by suppliers of a set marketing recipe as is recognized even by some of the protagonists of the traditional approaches to marketing (Kotler, 1990). The marketing manager can be regarded as part of a team, which might include, *inter alia*, finance, R&D, production as well as other functional areas since all in some way have a bearing on the provision of the final offering (Gummesson, 1987; Gronroos, 1989). Many of those outside the marketing function may have a role to play in developing satisfactory solutions to customers' problems or requirements, whether it be in formulating a financing package, adapting products to customer specifications, providing appropriate levels of supporting service or devising desired delivery schedules.

It is also clear that organizational marketing requires a subtle appreciation of customers' decision processes and the influences impacting on them. Within organizations, these may vary for types of purchases – new task, straight re-buy and modified re-buy (Robinson *et al.*, 1967) – as well as for class of product (e.g. operating supplies versus capital goods). The decision may be relatively straightforward, whereas, as has been noted, in other cases it may involve a complex of influences and procedures (Dawes *et al.*, 1992). Obviously, the amount of effort invested in understanding such internal processes will depend on the perceived importance of the customer. The emphasis on co-operative as opposed to adversarial inter-organizational relationships has led to the notion of partnerships (Batchelor, 1993) between suppliers and their customers with the development of mutually compatible procedures, assistance between the two parties to meet organizational objectives such as certain profit levels and so on. Collaboration between customers and suppliers is particularly significant in the area of product development (Littler *et al.*, 1993) where it is recognized (von Hippel, 1997) that customers may be an invaluable source of ideas for new products as well as acting to evaluate the evolving new product. They may also in some cases provide some develop-

ment capital. Some might argue that, given scarce resources, collaboration and the consequential emphasis on relationship management are only appropriate for 'primary' accounts, those which have strategic or financial importance, and for complex and expensive purchases, whereas the less important 'secondary' accounts may be treated more impersonally, possibly through intermediaries. However, information and communication technologies permit continued cost-effective interaction with customers. The introduction of electronic data interchange (EDI) is an important step forward in relationship management, although there is the attendant danger that technology replaces personal interaction which, as research indicates (Wilson and Littler, 1992) is a crucial element in effective supplier–customer interaction.

That much of organizational marketing either involves collaboration in various guises or can be viewed as increasingly centred on the management of relationships does not imply that many of the traditional instruments of marketing are redundant. There may, however, be differences in emphasis. It is obvious, for example, that there will be greater attention on personal approaches to marketing as a means of selling, facilitating collaboration, assessing customer satisfaction, ensuring speedy resolution of complaints, and in collecting detailed information to be employed, *inter alia*, in market analysis and product development. Nevertheless, conventional forms of mass communication can have a significant role in creating and maintaining awareness, of advising of new development, etc. Research indicates that opinion leaders within organizations tend to be relatively heavy consumers of media messages (Martilla, 1971; Moriarty and Spekman, 1984) which are often regarded as credible and valuable sources of information. In addition, exhibitions can have a particular relevance for the organizational marketer. Attendance is a means of continuing social interactions with customers (who might in many cases be suspicious of absentees), of obtaining market intelligence informally and of generally reassuring existing and potential customers by reinforcing a position as a credible supplier.

The perspective of organizational marketing presented here is one where certainly with 'primary' accounts, future plans and developments are shared at an early stage within the limits of appropriate commercial confidentiality; market analysis is undertaken with customers; prices are negotiated often with a view to the longer-term viability of customers and suppliers; there is continued monitoring of customers' changing attitudes towards and demand for service (Coppett, 1988; Powers, 1988), this being an increasingly important means of adding value; and where there is a recognition that many employees not traditionally regarded as marketers can affect the interaction with customers. Overall there is openness to forging durable links with customers based on a willingness to provide additional services and a 'problem solving' capability that enhances customers' competitiveness and, thereby, the supplier's marketing advantage.

References

Ames, B. C. (1970) Trappings vs Substance in Industrial Marketing, *Harvard Business Review*, 93–102.

Anderson, J. C., Jain, D. C. and Chintagunta, P. K. (1993) Customer Value Assessment in Business Markets, *Journal of Business-to-Business Marketing*, **1**(1), 3–29.

Banting, P. M. (1976) Customer Service in Industrial Marketing: A Comparative Study, *European Journal of Marketing*, **10**(3), 136–145.

Batchelor, C. (1993) Planning Your Future Together, *Financial Times*, 3 August, p. 8.

Brand, G. T. (1972) *The Industrial Buying Decision*, Cassell/Associated Business Programmes, London.

Bruce, M. and Cooper, R. (1997) *Marketing and Design Management*, International Thomson Business Press, London.

Central Advisory Council for Science and Technology (1968) *Technological Innovation in Britain*, July, HMSO, London.

Coppett, J. I. (1988) Auditing Your Customer Service Activities, *Industrial Marketing Management*, November, 277–284.

Cunningham, M. T. and Roberts, D. A. (1974) The Role of Customer Service in Industrial Marketing, *European Journal of Marketing*, Spring, 15–28.

Cunningham, M. T. and White, J. G. (1974) The Determinants of Choice of Supplier, *European Journal of Marketing*, **7**(3), 189–202.

Dawes, P. L., Dowling, G. R. and Patterson, P. G. (1992) Factors Affecting the Structure of Buying Centres for the Purchase of Professional Business Advisory Services, *International Journal of Research in Marketing*, **9**, 269–279.

Ford, D. *et al.* (1998) *Managing Business Relationships*, John Wiley and Sons, Chichester.

Freeman, C. (1982) *The Economics of Industrial Innovation*, 2nd edn, Penguin, Harmondsworth, Middlesex.

Gummesson, E. (1987) The New Marketing – Developing Long-term Interactive Relationships, *Long Range Planning*, **4**, 10–20.

Gronroos, C. (1989) Defining Marketing: A Market Oriented Approach, *European Journal of Marketing*, **21**, 52–60.

Gronroos, C. (1991) The Marketing Strategy Continuums: A Marketing Concept for the 1990s, *Management Decision*, **1**, 7–13.

Hakansson, M. (ed.) (1982) *International Marketing and Purchasing of Industrial Goods: An Interaction Approach*, John Wiley.

IMRA (1969) *Regulations*, Industrial Marketing Research Association, Lichfield.

Kent, R. A. (1986) Faith in the Four Ps: An Alternative, *Journal of Marketing Management*, **2**.

Kotler, P. (1988) *Marketing Management: Analysis Planning and Implementation and Control*, 6th edn, Prentice Hall, Englewood Cliffs, NJ.

Kotler, P. (1990) Speech at the Trustee Meeting of the Marketing Science Institute in November 1990 in Boston referred to in *Marketing Science Institute Review*, Spring, 1991.

Littler, D. A., Bruce, M., Leverick, F. L. and Wilson, D. F. (1993) *Collaboration in Product Development*, mimeo, Manchester School of Management, UMIST.

Littler, D. A. and Sweeting, R. C. (1985) Radical Innovation in the Mature Company, *European Journal of Marketing*, **19**(4), 33–34.

McCarthy, E. J. (1960) *Basic Marketing*, Irwin, Homewood, IL.

Marrian, J. (1965) Characteristics of Industrial Goods and Markets, in A. Wilson (ed.), *The Marketing of Industrial Products*, Hutchison, London, p. 14.

Martilla, J. A. (1971) Word of Mouth Communication in the Industrial Adoption Process, *Journal of Marketing Research*, VIII, 173–178.

Moriarty, R. T. and Spekman, R. E. (1984) An Empirical Investigation of the Information Sources Used During the Industrial Buying Process, *Journal of Marketing Research*, XXI, May, 137–147.

NEDO (1981) *Industrial Performance: Trade Performance and Marketing*, HMSO, London.

Office for National Statistics (1997) *Annual Abstract of Statistics*, The Stationery Office, London.

Pavitt, K. (1980) Introduction, Chapter 1 in Pavitt, K. (ed.), *Technical Innovation and British Economic Performance*, Macmillan, London.

Pettigrew, A. W. (1975) Industrial Purchasing as a Political Process, *European Journal of Marketing*, **9**(1).

Powers, T. L. (1988) Identify and Fulfil Customer Service Expectations, *Industrial Marketing Management*, November, 273–276.

Robinson, P. J., Farris, C. W. and Wind, Y. (1967) *Industrial Buying and Creative Marketing*, Allyn and Bacon, Boston, MA.

Rothwell, R. (1977) Users and Producers Perceptions of the Relative Importance of Various Textile Machinery Characteristics, *Textile Institute and Industry*, July.

Rothwell, R. (1981) Non-price Factors in the Export Competitiveness of Agricultural Engineering Goods, *Research Policy*, **10**, 260–288.

Von Hippel, E. (1997) Transferring Process Equipment Innovation from User-Innovators to Equipment Manufacturing Firms, *R&D Management*, **8**(1), 13–22.

Webster, F. E. and Wind, Y. (1972) *Organizational Buying Behavior*, Prentice-Hall, Englewood Cliffs, NJ.

Wilson, D. F. and Littler, D. A. (1992) International Collaboration, in R. Sally, R. Spencer and J.-P. Valla (eds), *Business Networks in an International Context: Recent Research Developments*, Proceedings of the 8th IMP Conference, Lyon, France.

Wilson, D. F. (1997) Purchasing Process, in B. R. Lewis and D. Littler (eds), *Encyclopedic Dictionary of Marketing*, Blackwell, Oxford.

Wong, V. and Saunders, J. (1993) Business Orientations and Corporate Success, *Journal of Strategic Marketing*, **1**(1), March, 20–40.

Further reading

Campbell, N. C. O. and Cunningham, M. T. (1983) Customer analysis for strategy development in industrial markets, *Strategic Management Journal*, **4**, 369–380. Presents a methodology for analysing the customer portfolio to guide in the strategic allocation of marketing resources.

Chisnall, P. M. (1995) *Strategic Business Marketing*, 3rd edn, Prentice-Hall. Provides an effective overview of organizational marketing.

Gronroos, C. (1989) Defining marketing: a market-oriented approach, *European Journal of Marketing*, **1**. Points to the importance of the relationships building between buyers and sellers.

Gross, A. C., Banting, P. M., Meredith, L. N. and Ford, I. D. (1993) *Business Marketing*, Houghton Mifflin, Boston, MA. For those who want to have a comprehensive overview of the subject with both North American and European examples.

Gummesson, E. (1987) The new marketing – developing long-term interactive relationships, *Long Range Planning*, **4**. Highlights the fact that in organizational markets there are many employees outside of marketing which affect sales. He terms these 'part-time' marketers.

Von Hippel, E. A. (1978) Customer-active paradigm for industrial product idea generation, *Research Policy*, **7**, 249–266. Highlights the importance of the user in the new product development process and points to some important implications for organizational marketing.

CHAPTER 23

International marketing – the issues

STANLEY J. PALIWODA

Overview

This chapter presents a distillation of thought and practice in an area of activity that was once seen only as constituting a different application of marketing but today has come of age. Consolidation is evidenced by the creation of the special interest groups or SIGs now existing for the study and dissemination of international marketing thought and practice amongst marketing educators and researchers within both the American Marketing Association and the Academy of Marketing. Given the way in which this literature has expanded in a number of different lines of enquiry, what is provided here is more of a roadmap with references to specific sources for further information.

The starting point of inquiry: 'Why go abroad?' is perhaps the most basic of questions. There follows a discussion of global trends, of change agents, differences between domestic and international marketing, the effects of culture, psychic distance and international marketing segmentation. Next, environmental or situational analysis and the SLEPT framework are discussed together with ways in which to classify and minimize risk. Operationalization of international marketing comes in at the end, reviewing experiential exporter profiles and for-

eign market entry strategies. Continuing and future challenges in international marketing are reviewed as well as ways in which to maintain a sustainable advantage in a highly competitive dynamic market. Conclusions are offered together with some further reading and some useful web sites.

Why market abroad?

The exchange process which forms the basis of international marketing is different from that found in the domestic market and extends beyond simple exporting. To export means simply to send or carry abroad, especially for trade or sale. International marketing goes beyond that in introducing the concept of the end user, as a focal point, moving the orientation away from finding sales for a company's existing products to actually analysing the market and assessing whether the company is able to produce a product or service for which there is either current or potential demand given that other factors can be controlled such as price, promotion and distribution. International marketing can be very profitable as it commands a premium price for customized yet standardized offerings but it is a serious business, which requires the long-term commitment of resources. It will mean the outlay of a substantial investment in a foreign market, often with a long projected payback. This issue of an acceptable time horizon is quite crucial. It is important then to differentiate between a short-term sales-oriented approach and a longer-term entry strategy of three to four years, which is aimed at market building.

Global trends and strategic responses

World-wide, important trends can be detected: economic integration and industrial concentration continues apace but especially in Europe, and the following visible signs are beginning to come into focus:

> Trend to fewer larger groupings is evident in food, cars and media.
> Retailers are showing distinct signs of both internationalization and concentration.
> A three-tiered Europe is emerging with Germany, France, Belgium, Luxembourg, and Holland at the core, Britain and Denmark on the outside looking in, because of their domestic policies, and others such as Italy, Spain, Portugal, and Ireland, Greece still suffering from weak currencies.
> European middle-sized companies still anchored in national markets are at risk since they could be squeezed since they do not have the advantage of size or of flexibility.
> A weak Asia with key economies such as Japan and South Korea in recession will have significant effects upon the world economy. The loss of markets in that region will force companies to seek markets elsewhere, hence we can expect a displacement effect and can expect to witness even keener competition in the West as a result.

Change agents

Markets are changing demographically, politically and economically and the techniques of bringing goods to market and arranging financing, as well as the means of financing themselves, are changing. Increasingly, the world over, economies are being subjected to the same social, economic and political forces which shape our own markets. Ohmae (1990) put it rather succinctly in identifying three global trends which he felt could not be ignored:

> Increasing market fragmentation. Today there are specialist competitors with tailored offerings.
> Traditional market boundaries are blurring with substitutes from new technologies.
> The transformation of previously self-contained national markets into linked global markets.

Ohmae combined these three trends then with the four I's which he identified with the 'boundaryless' economy, namely: industry, investment, individuals, and information. All of these are highly mobile resources and so emphasize the dynamism of the international marketplace. While the environment has changed, so too have consumers; Ohmae sees the world as changing and that change being driven by the realization that across developed markets, consumers have similar needs and desires.

Developed markets have affluent, knowledgeable consumers who share similar tastes and needs, hence this growing phenomenon of an international marketplace for goods and services which knows no frontiers. The term 'triad' was first coined by Kenichi Ohmae and refers to the increasing product standardization found across markets and the consequent supposed homogenization of consumers in the developed market economies of Europe, North America and Japan. Ohmae drew two important conclusions from this phenomenon:

> That this therefore reaches beyond taste to worldview, mindset and thought processes in a mental programming as first described by Hofstede.
> Teenagers around the world have in common that they have been subjected to a multimedia-rich, instant response, electronic environment.

Michael Porter, the Harvard economist, has views quite different from those of Ohmae. Porter saw successful internationalization arising from a successful national competitive advantage. It was necessary to be successful in the home market first. Porter has more or less substituted 'competitive advantage' for what used to be called 'comparative advantage'. Porter's work does not help to explain the more recent phenomenon of the small highly competitive niche company which is 'born global', requiring internationalization to fully exploit its technological niche. Ohmae focused on the need to be an insider within the developed market economies of the triad comprising Europe, North America and Japan, a total of more than 640 million educated consumers with broadly similar spending patterns, tastes and desires, leading then into his thesis of the Californiaization of consumers (Ohmae, 1994). Porter shares some similarities but is different, however, and sees the macro environment as being shaped by what he terms currents and cross-currents, as below:

1   *Currents* which drive international competition, as evidenced by:
   - Growing similarity of countries with universal features, large retail chains, and TV advertising and credit cards.
   - Falling tariff barriers.
   - Technological revolutions which reshape industry and create shifts in leadership.
   - Integrating role of technology. Improved communication dismantles geographical barriers to trade and improves information in a world where buyers are increasingly aware of world markets.
   - New global competitors. The Pacific Basin countries have become fully-fledged competitors to well-established Western rivals.

2   *Cross-currents* which make the pattern of international competition different from earlier decades, evidenced in:
   - Slowing rates of economic growth.
   - Changes in the basis of competitive advantage. Labour cost, natural resources and

technology access is less important than before.
   - New forms of protectionism, e.g. requirements for local content and local ownership.
   - New types of government inducement, working between governments to attract foreign direct investment.
   - Joint ventures, proliferating coalitions among firms from different countries. Broader, deeper collaboration than the marketing joint venture and production licences of the past.
   - Growing ability to tailor to local conditions. New technologies support globalization but allow customized tailored product offerings. The need to standardize products world-wide is diminishing.

Add to this the diverse arguments now being propounded for relationship marketing to build upon existing networks, and the overall rationale for international marketing becomes clearer. More than one type of international strategy can be viable in a given industry. Johanson and Mattson (1986) put forward the argument that the internationalization of the firm is affected by the internationalization of its markets. The marketing mix may still contain the same 4Ps of product, price, promotion and place of sale but each P introduces new variables now that it has been transposed from a purely domestic setting to an international marketing environment. The environment is seen now as dynamic not static and markets have been re-interpreted here as networks of relationships between firms.

Figure 23.1 has four cells, each of which depicts a company and its environment at different developmental stages of internationalization.

The early starter is the company which has few rather unimportant relationships abroad but is no different in this respect from its competitors, so this kind of situation is a developmental one which, for example, faced Europe at the start of this century.

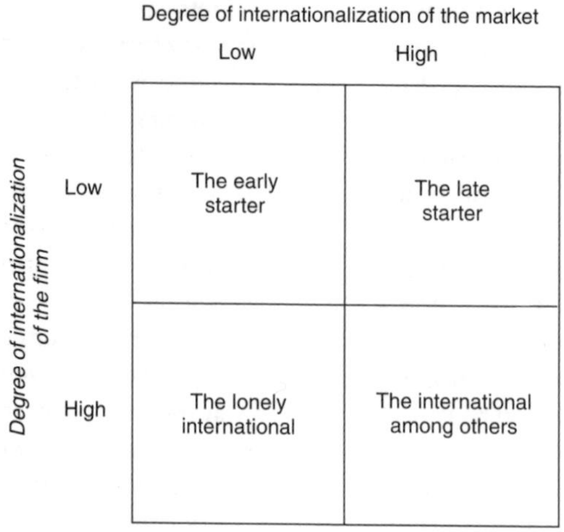

Degree of internationalization of the market

Low   High

Source: Johanson and Mattson, 1986

Figure 23.1   Market internationalization

The lonely international. The firm is highly internationalized while its market environment is not.

The late starter. Indirectly involved with foreign markets. This is a specialized company, which has to decide whether to adapt or to get customers to adapt.

The international among others. Both the firm and its environment are highly internationalized.

Aside from the fact that Johanson and Mattson blow away the traditionally-held concept of passive markets where sellers have only the four variables – product, place, promotion and price – to play with, they also introduce explanations for internationalization that are more industry and company specific. Raw material extraction may have forced some firms to become multinational at the turn of the century so as to assure themselves of reliable sourcing. This is the case of the 'early starter', whereas the 'late starter' is one who has realized belatedly that the growth opportunities are all abroad but so, too, are the competition. The 'lonely international' is not only more adventurous but has resource, know-

ledge and skills to redeploy. It is driving the competition, not being driven by it. The last cell, the 'international among others', is a company that is competent internationally but does not enjoy any sustainable competitive advantage over its competitors in this regard. Conditions describe a high degree of internationalization of the market and the degree of internationalization of the firm is already high, so here is a company that must hunt with the rest of the pack.

International marketing: the quintessential differences

Essentially, markets are unlike because the forces that drive them are different or function to a lesser or greater degree compared to home. Most commonly, per capita income is sought as a guide to personal disposable income available for product purchases. This is simply naïve in that a company requires a market to have size, measurability, plus the ability and willingness to buy before it has a market. What is required therefore is knowledge, for with knowledge it is possible to plan for products, which build upon similarities across countries and therefore maximize the opportunities for segmentation, standardization and economies of scale. However, it also has to be said that there may also be mandatory requirements for product modification as well as some compelling reasons for product modification in view of lower disposable incomes, poor infrastructure, traditional shopping habits, etc. Frozen foods will only sell if consumers have domestic freezers and will only sell in bulk if consumers have both large chest freezers and the means of transportation to carry these goods home. Entering a market first may well bring 'first mover' advantage but the cost may well include investing in the infrastructure so as to make your product distribution concept workable.

Enduring differences between domestic and international marketing

If we have only 4Ps to worry about, we exclude much from our consideration. The 4Ps are in fact a gross oversimplification of the vast number of variables to be managed within the marketing function, especially in the international arena where the marketing manager's own knowledge of the foreign market is limited and so the number of variables on which we need information thereby increases dramatically. It overlooks many of the individual variables in return for making a simple point and providing a mnemonic for marketing students and managers. Paliwoda (1995) identified a ten-point checklist for approaching international marketing, consisting of:

> People – should be our main focus: all stakeholders, internal and external to the firm, employees and customers.
> *Process* – which is unique to the corporate culture.
> Positioning – differentiation from rivals.
> *Power* – market power transferability from home country to host country.

Product/service – delivering value added through the channel to the foreign consumer. Promotion and publicity – what is available, what is allowable, what is free.
Pricing – an overplayed dimension and the weakest factor with which to lead.
Place of sale/distribution – delivery. From arrival portside to the final consumer through channels as diverse as the Internet.
Planning and control – with flexibility. Monitoring is one aspect but another is the ability to plan ahead with room to manoeuvre so as not to forestall strategic alternatives.
Precedents learned from market scanning. Through environmental scanning at home and abroad, it is possible to earn strategies that nay be borrowed from other companies in other industries in other countries and applied to your own situation.

The benefits of international marketing are many; for instance, it dissipates risk and provides a sort of insurance of a foreign market alongside the domestic market. There are advantages not only in sales volume but also in a price premium of the foreign market over even the domestic market. Access to sought-after commodities or inputs to the production process provide a further rationale, particularly where costs are lower. Over time, different arguments have been made and some have lost their relevance as our economies modernize and integrate, particularly with other European partners. Michael Thomas (1996) pointed to the following as concepts, which remain not proven:

> Product life cycle
> Wheel of retailing
> Hierarchy of advertising effects
> The Boston box (BCG matrix)
> Information processing paradigms of consumer behaviour
> Stages in internationalization process models.

Not all of these will be explored in this chapter but what emerges is that as individuals we are seeking laws, regularity and predictability.

Effects of culture

Language is important to conduct business successfully and here there is a net advantage for the English speaking countries. Overall, English with 427 million speakers is second to Mandarin Chinese (726 million speakers) in terms of the number of people who speak the language. However, in many countries, English is a second language and the first or second language for business. Foreign investors such as the Japanese and South Koreans have established themselves in Britain because they feel comfortable with the language. A further advantage is that foreign students wishing to learn English bring £500 million each year into the British economy. In most countries and within most multinational corporations, irrespective of ownership or where they may be registered, the business language is English, and not just internally; English language will be prominent on all products, services and communications as well. This has an important value that must not be overlooked. Telecommunications have developed in English speaking countries. This was the case with the telegraph, radio, telephone and now Internet. Countries such as France – and the province of Quebec in Canada – have actively resisted this English invasion and sought to place curbs on the use of certain words so as to outlaw 'franglais' but now, even in Russia, the same cry is being heard of the widespread use of English language on billboards and general advertising. An inability to speak English means today an inability to be heard. English will continue to be prominent as it is being learned by the wealthy and well educated in all parts of the world. The question also must arise as to whether, with different levels of fluency and regional variations, not just in dialect but in word usage and meaning, do people actually mean what they say and do they understand what we mean to say?

International marketing and the interface with local culture

To understand culture, we have to realize that it is behavioural attitudes which we as members of a society learn and pass on to others. Whereas exporting is about sending products and services blindly into foreign markets for others to distribute, promote and sell to final customers, the intelligent international marketer recognizes the importance of maintaining control over branded products at the point of sale. Culture for the international marketer is seen to operate at three levels:

> *Habits and conventions.* On this level we may be able to most effectively change behaviour by influencing potential users, possibly by demonstration of a better, more modern, more intelligent way of doing a certain frequently repeated daily task or chore. With habits which rely on automatic responses, if we are able to demonstrate a better way of doing something and that product concept does not ask us to challenge our own value system, then we can usually rely on that idea being successfully adopted. For example, electronic calculators have been successfully taken up everywhere. No disquiet has been voiced over the demise of the abacus or slide rule.
>
> *Mores* is a Latin word for 'morals' or 'customs' and is taken often to mean the established religion of a particular society and the norms which it observes. Attempts to challenge the established religion within a country will not meet with success. With regard to international advertising, scantily clad women must not appear in advertising destined for Muslim countries or Muslim regions. Sometimes it is not the fundamentalists or adherents who may raise the problem but those who do not practise the religion in question but nevertheless feel a certain unease over issues such as shops being open on a Sunday or extensions to the licensed drinking hours for bars and hotels.

Laws. There is very little international law, and so with the exception of cases such as the Law of the Sea and areas where international treaties are seen to prevail, usually it is then only domestic law which may have extra-territorial reach. This is primarily the case with US law, which affects the operations not only of US multinationals but other Western companies represented in the USA as well. The lack of international law means there is a gap to be filled in the case of international trading disputes. In effect, the various industrial arbitration councils whose establishment is not formally recognized but whose judgements have always been accepted in subsequent actions in civil courts of law often undertake this. Where existing law prohibits the sale of a product, the only strategy may be to try to have that law rescinded. This means lobbying for a change in legislation or even new legislation to enable this new and proposed product or service to be offered to the buying public. This could range from a variation being required in planning permission to allow out-of-hours shopping centres. Sunday opening of shops or settling the ethical questions raised by medical science such as in-vitro fertilization and human embryo experimentation and storage. As laws reflect a society's attitude towards a certain issue at a given moment in time, and society changes, there is always scope and argument for legal revision. In the USA and Japan, the EU is seen as being an effective legislative agency in its own right, lobbying is becoming more intense while in a corresponding, separate movement, markets slowly become more similar. New services, such as satellite television, are not national but international in character and require special legal attention for their effective regulation.

Psychic, or psychological, distance

Psychic, or psychological, distance (also socio-cultural distance) affects both supplier and buyer. For a supplier, knowledge of a market takes away the fear and lessens risks, both actual and perceived. For marketers, unlike sociologists or social anthropologists, the aim is to identify that which unites people as a common characteristic or feature, which is to be found with the same degree of frequency across national boundaries. The more we know of a target market and the degree that it approximates to our own, the better placed we are to design an acceptable offering.

In numerous studies, newcomers to exporting have been found to export first to those markets which are more like extended domestic markets because of similarities of language, customs and institutions. British exporters were long able to find the psychological distance between themselves and Australian, Canadian, Nigerian or Ghanaian buyers much less than that existing with French or another very closely neighbouring European country. Language, history, institutions, currency and familiar standards of size, weight or volume influence greatly the perceived degree of foreignness. The European Union is proceeding apace with harmonization and common measures including a common currency.

Segmentation

Having identified a sufficient number of people who could be prospective customers, it is necessary to find out more about their market characteristics in terms of personal disposable income and the degree to which this target segment is either dispersed throughout the length and breadth of the country, or found to be concentrated in the main urban centres.

Before proceeding further with considerations of product distribution, we have to establish that the product is legal in the country in which it is to be sold and that the resources exist to target the chosen target segment effectively. Some companies seek to promote their highly standardized product to essentially the same segment across national frontiers, i.e. a buying public with very similar profiles as in the case of the major credit cards such as Visa Gold or the travel and entertainment cards of Diners Club and American Express. Essentially this is an international segment who share many commonalities, including travel.

It may also be possible to sell the same products to different segments in foreign markets. However, to do this successfully may require product or communication strategy modifications. Small companies with a niche product may be able to do this as successfully as their multinational counterparts.

What, then, are the reasons for marketing abroad?

Product life cycle effects are often cited but seldom proved. Where a product on the home market enters a mature phase, theory argues that the company concerned may then be able to find new export markets abroad where product markets have not reached the same stage of development. This argument, however, becomes increasingly less relevant with the passage of time as a result of two trends. First, competition today, being international rather than domestic for all goods and services, has reduced the time lag between product research, development and production, leading to the simultaneous appearance of a standardized product in all major world markets, as with Microsoft and the launch of their Windows 95 operating system. Second, it is not production in the highly labour-intensive industries that is moving to the low-labour-cost countries with freeport advantages, such as Taiwan, but the capital-intensive industries, such as electronics, creating the anomalous situation of basing production for high-value, high-technology, goods, in the countries least able to afford but best able to produce and export them. Competition in a chosen target market may be less intense than at home or there may be the promise of tariff barriers to exclude potential competitors in return for a substantial foreign investment in plant machinery and know-how.

Excess capacity utilization. When the domestic market experiences a downturn or reaches saturation, companies may turn to export markets to make good the shortfall. For companies in industries requiring long production runs to ensure commercial viability, foreign orders may make the crucial difference between profit and loss. However, there is no commitment to exporting or to foreign markets at this stage.

Another feature, which may also appear, is that low prices are often quoted to ensure sales success in order to secure long production runs or to sell of high inventory levels. It is indeed possible for a company which has a mature product line to regard its original investment in product research and development to have been long since recouped and therefore to price on the basis of actual production costs plus overheads. This is profitable exporting, but means that a company will be charging a different price in foreign markets from that which it charges in its own domestic market. This invites charges of 'dumping' which in the case of the USA and also the EU are assessed on two criteria: the basis of injury to local industry and whether the price being charged is lower than the price charged in the producer's own domestic market. This strategy may succeed in the short term, solving the need for near-capacity production runs. Finding foreign customers on whom to offload production means also that the company does not have to resort to discounting for established customers, thereby protecting its price structure and avoiding the setting of precedents for future price negotiations.

Geographical diversification arises where companies find it preferable to remain with the product line which they know and are successful with rather than diversifying into new product lines or product technologies. This is a strategy of finding new markets for existing products.

Market potential as assessed by the population and their purchasing power. There are few untapped markets left. Cuba is certainly one, but various economic and political US sanctions are in place to discourage foreign companies considering moving there although some countries are now doing so, most notably Canada. China is the most populous of the developing countries but it is not untapped. Your competition is aware of what China has to offer. The capacity to consume or to absorb the product has to be matched with the capacity to pay for it. High levels of indebtedness in the Third World have created financial innovations in the variants of countertrade now available, much to the displeasure of the World Bank and IMF. Strategic advantage may also be interpreted as market 'spoiling'. The purpose here is less actively to pursue a market than to register a presence with a competitor, particularly where this also concerns market entry into a rival's domestic market. Timing is on the side of the existing market player who draws revenue from sales while his competitors plan their response. In world markets, it is the case that multinationals view market segments for the presence of their multinational rivals. Narrowly defined segments in which there is little competition add to their total corporate power structure. A small but significant base in one part of the world may enable a multinational to access other markets in the same region and, at the same time, discourage competitors. Market entry can be viewed also as an offensive strategy, showing that by entering a rival's home market, the company is capable of taking occasional retaliatory action. Entry can then be seen as a warning against a multinational rival of its presence in the rival's home market, and its ability therefore to undercut the rival's home base and therefore the market for its main product.

Situational analysis

Complexity and uncertainty predominate in the international arena but the risks and the attendant expectations of return are what in turn make it so appealing. It is unwise to skimp on research because it costs too much, or is not relevant to what is considered the mainstream domestic market business, or is not as accurate as domestic market or because it is felt (but not proved) that the company already knows how to sell. Environmental scanning is wider in scope than traditional market research. There is a need for a comprehensive background report alongside studies of market potential as these factors could affect market access and the ongoing internal operations of foreign companies in the host country. A simple but useful mnemonic is SLEPT:

> social
> legal
> economic
> political
> technological.

This framework using a series of questions can help orient the company towards the most efficient use of its resources.

Where are you now?

Chapter 10 by Keith Fletcher is useful in its discussion of the evolution and use of IT to even answer some questions such as 'What business are we in?' However, here are some checklists, to help with positioning:

> Is there a new company or subsidiary following a merger, take-over, joint venture or strategic alliance?
> Are new products compatible with existing lines?
> Could you rethink marketing strategy to bring a closer fit between product and prospect?
> Is there a mismatch now between your product and the target segment?
> Has the target segment profile changed?
> Has the distribution channel changed due to either new entrants or new and improved competitive offerings?

Is this a new product in terms of concept and brand that you are trying to introduce to international markets?

Are you looking abroad because of competition at home or because your domestic competitors are looking abroad also?

Have you compared growth potential at home with that abroad?

What flexibility do you have to market your product at home versus abroad?

How would you describe the current market situation for this product in your home market?

Does it differ when we look at foreign markets?

Are there certain economic constraints regarding production runs or anything else which would affect either the quality that needs to be manufactured or the quantity that needs to be delivered to any one customer?

Are there any other problems confronting you now or likely to confront you in the near future which you can foresee?

Have you undertaken any regular monitoring either of the home market or your target foreign market to foretell the unforeseen?

Lastly, monitoring performance relative to the marketplace should be an ongoing activity that never ends, although the excuses certainly should.

Where do you want to be?

There are differences between companies as to whether they perceive foreign market entry as:

A strategic or tactical option, i.e. whether they see entry into the target market as being of potential value in the medium to long term or whether it is a spoiling tactic undertaken by multinationals as they pursue their global quest for global market share.

Whether in terms of motivation and behaviour it is opportunity seeking or problem solving behaviour that is being reflected. For-

eign market entry may be motivated by a desire to reduce current excess capacity. Alternatively, there may be a genuine desire to continue to service the target market in question. The underlying motivation is an important factor as it determines the company's degree of commitment to foreign markets as well.

What do you need to get you there?

It has often been said that knowledge is power. Well, no more so than in international markets where your company is at the disadvantage of competing with local companies which presumably know the market conditions better. Knowing market conditions allows a company to fine-tune a technological advantage and turn it into a marketing advantage. Panasonic became the best known brand in Poland shortly after the country became a market economy in 1990 for the simple reason that Panasonic had studied the Polish market situation and saw that voltage surges were common. A high voltage surge would knock out most equipment but what Panasonic did was brilliant and yet so basic. They simply incorporated resistors into television sets for Poland and became known as a manufacturer that made television sets especially for the Polish market. The Polish television market had belonged to the Russians and there were many foreign competitors now but Panasonic's action saw off the competition. Knowledge of market conditions can be vitally important in formulating marketing strategy.

Today, licensing is seldom found without the sale also of know-how, which may simply be the transferral of production experience and so training or updating to a new licensee of the most modern production methods. However, it is with franchising that we see the sale of marketing know-how embodied in a successful branded product or service and encapsulated in a livery, logo or design so as to make it universally recognizable. In brand recognition there is market power.

Requirements for success in foreign markets

This can be summarized in terms of three main elements, each comprising a number of variables:

marketing policy elements: market selection, pricing, packaging;

firm-specific factors: technology, planning, control;

external factors: diplomatic relations; subsidies, market accessibility; market potential.

You therefore need to know:

the effects of culture on your company offering and intended service levels;

market research of markets abroad, as indicated;

that psychic or psychological distance brings distant countries nearer and distances neighbouring countries on the basis of cultural similarities (also known as socio-cultural distance);

the segmentation possibilities, as indicated;

the modes of market entry, of which more later.

In sum, there are more than four simple Ps to worry about!

Success in foreign markets is evidenced by the following:

a match between competencies of the firm with the opportunities and threats of the marketplace;

a competitive advantage that is sustainable in the light of probable competitive moves;

a corporate commitment of time and of resources;

acculturation meaning that a knowledge of the culture is as important as a knowledge of the language. In that way, social rituals such as the differences between the French and the British over observance of the lunch break, may be better understood and accommodated.

Market research comprises hard and soft facts

The purpose, process and limitations of market research are discussed in Chapter 7. However, in reviewing environmental scanning, Douglas Brownlie commented in Chapter 4 on the lack of empiricism and hard science, a point, which has to be echoed here, especially with regard to:

Culture, e.g. language, dress.

Traditions that are important within the society and have their own rationale.

Social customs, e.g. forms of communication, addressing hierarchies, perhaps even the need to have a drinking partner on the negotiating team. In some countries it was the case that you could not do business unless you had been out with the client and got drunk with them. That achieved an important social breakthrough and after that point, it would be possible to converse on a friendlier basis as you had shared something together. Some companies have actually employed individuals for foreign business and particularly negotiating teams because the most important asset that they could offer was a cast iron liver! The requirement to imbibe in volume in certain cultures remains, and it is not just impolite to refuse; to decline means simply that you lose all prospect of doing business there.

As an activity, international market research attracts only a small percentage of a company's total market research budget. Many companies do not spend money on foreign market research or else entrust an on-the-spot foreign market appraisal to one of the most junior members of the firm often entering into a particular target market for the first time, without any proper briefing or linguistic skills. What often results is a 'go/no go' decision based on a poor understanding of the specific market characteristics. Market entry decisions should be approached as part of the company's ongoing strategic planning and development. A decision to enter a market should only be taken with a proper understanding and appreciation of what is currently happening in the target market and what is likely to happen.

Market research is possible but obviously less reliable in those markets where market research data are scarce or the data available are not directly comparable due to the different statistical bases being used. Source credibility and comparability of results are the major headaches experienced. The more volatile the market, the greater the likelihood that there will be a scarcity of the type of data required.

To research country markets effectively, governmental sources should be used where they exist. Where these are deficient, there are a number of agencies, including the US Central Intelligence Agency and many specialist companies such as Business International S.A. and others, which offer best estimates as to probable production and consumption figures. A company that thinks it knows its market should then assess its state of preparation against the Industrial Marketer's Checklist provided free by the Department of Trade and Industry. Identification of national personal disposable income levels on its own, is not very meaningful as it is an average and does not necessarily reflect the ability to purchase within that particular market in the domestic currency. Domestic purchasing power is often greater than indicated by a translation of local currency into US dollars. One should seek to identify important affluent target segments within a national market with data on lifestyles, educational background, location and spending patterns, all of which are useful indicators for any company seriously considering market entry.

What is important to remember is that GNP per capita as a measure of national wealth is an arithmetic mean, which gives a value for national wealth when calculated on a per capita basis. It does not equate with disposable income actually available to citizens to spend, nor their willingness to spend it. This statistic on its own is fairly meaningless, as it offers no guidance as to the dispersion of wealth across the population or the possible identification of important affluent segments across a nation. Segmentation remains the key marketing tool with the identification of feasible cross segments as the means to international access and profitability, because little product modification will then be required.

Classifying and minimizing risk

International marketing differs from domestic marketing in that when the company is dealing with its own domestic market, key variables can be taken as known, such as:

> political risk
> economic/financial risk
> commercial risk
> taxes and legislation relating to company incorporation.

To a marketer in his or her own country, these are background factors which influence the business climate, but in the international context they become unknown factors which could assume important proportions particularly when combined with historical, cultural and linguistic differences.

Political risk

To illustrate this, the Middle East may perhaps be popularly perceived as an area of political uncertainty, yet many British companies can claim punctual payment for supplies and that expropriation has not taken place in recent years. Instead, the various oil states who were previously only oil producers have engaged in forward vertical integration to control refining, shipping and to some degree, retail distribution within Europe. On the other hand, a quite different form of political risk emerged in calm, politically stable France, when a socialist government under Mitterand started to create widespread uncertainty when it embarked on a nationalization policy. The greatest risks need not arise from within the most politically unstable economies. Country membership of the EU is also another factor minimizing political risk as perceived by trading partners. This is beginning to spread now to the Central and East European adherents presently waiting in line for EU membership possibly within the next six years.

International trade sanctions and embargoes may be found in place against specific countries. Important also to consider are the Voluntary Export Restraints (VERs) whereby exporting nations, most notably Japan, agree to curb exports to importing nations beyond a certain amount on pain of unspecified sanctions. Another quite different form of government intervention is through a countervailing duty. By introducing a countervailing duty, a government increases the selling price of the cheapest imported good to the level of the cheapest domestic competitor by means of a specific tax. In this way, governments may discriminate against cheap imports and effectively price them out of the market by instantly removing their price competitiveness.

The World Trade Organization (WTO) has now taken over the role of arbiter of free trade from GATT, the General Agreement on Tariffs and Trade that was created to facilitate free trade in the aftermath of World War II. GATT had been created in different times when sovereign nations existed. Today, the move is towards the formation of economic trading blocs and so a new organization had to be created. China is the one major trading country that is not yet a member but the nation will have to meet some rather stringent demands relating to freeing controls on its foreign trade before being able to join this organization.

Economic/financial risk

Similarly, there are economic risks where there are difficulties in repatriating capital due to host government exchange controls, high taxation or a rapidly devaluing currency. However, this may be surmounted by resorting to devices such as management fees, royalties, and repayments on loans and/or interest, leasing, or intra-corporate transfers, known also as 'transfer pricing'. As it is entirely the responsibility of the individual company to price final goods, intermediate goods, such as assemblies and components that are transferred within the company also provide an opportunity to move money out of one country into another where levels of taxation may also be lower.

Transfer pricing then may become a political issue when foreign subsidiaries are seen to be exporting but are recording losses. The price at which goods are to be transferred remains at all times a company issue over which the national customs services have no control.

Given a situation where multinational corporations control more than two thirds of world trade, transfer pricing is viewed by politicians as an ever-constant threat to the nation state. To counter this, many large companies such as Exxon take the trouble to produce a code of ethics in which they publish the basis on which they transfer goods between company subsidiaries. Most commonly, this is found to be 'arms' length' pricing, which means setting a market price as though to an outsider. However, the basis of this pricing has never been fully defined to the satisfaction of all.

Other possibilities include 'cost plus' pricing which means including a percentage such as 10 per cent for overheads, including administration. Transfer pricing could therefore provide a means for a company to close down a plant abroad by showing how unprofitable it was by simply sending imports with a high transfer price. Alternatively, a plant in a low labour cost country with a very favourable tax regime could be seen as even more profitable if benefiting from low transfer prices from the parent company organization. Taxation and politics are important factors in this highly sensitive area of operations.

Commercial risk

The uncertainty of the ultimate acceptability of the goods to the final consumer. However, even small companies are aware today of prevailing international industrial standards for technical equipment as there are few national markets left. In the pursuit of critical mass and the need for economies of scale in production, domestic markets are rarely large enough to satisfy customers. Consequently, producers have sought every opportunity to standardize their products and make them available to an ever-larger number of markets. The British Standards Institution scheme THE (Technical Help for Exporters) was created to provide British manufacturers with information on national product standards world-wide. However, even if manufactured to acceptable national standards, there is still the risk that the goods may yet be found to be unacceptable to consumers in the target market, perhaps because of price, design, lack of state-of-the-art technology, inappropriate brand name or inability to provide the package of benefits, including service, which customers, particularly in Western developed markets, have come to expect.

The risks of transportation, transhipment, pilferage, damage and loss are risks against which the supplier may obtain insurance, but increasingly this is only available at a high price and against demands that the exporter gives the insurance company all its export business and not just the risky part of the export portfolio, or, alternatively, accept perhaps only 30 per cent cover. Insurers are providing less of a service nowadays and are dictating terms, pointing to the bad debt provisions of the major clearing banks and state export insurance agencies. To some degree, improved export packing and product packaging have reduced some of this risk but certain regions of the world are more risky in this sense than others.

The ability of the buyer to pay for the goods ordered. Again there has been a mistaken assumption that it is less important to have insurance cover for an importer in North America as opposed to South America. This confuses the solvency of the nation with the solvency of an industrial buyer, to say nothing about actual intent to pay. Financial status reports on a buyer should always be obtained whenever there is a shadow of doubt. Insurance is available to an exporter, but the cost increases with the exposure to risk and so the exporter should decide whether to proceed knowing fully the risk and whether he or the buyer is to accept the costs of insurance cover.

Control and ownership are further points to consider given that in the most common form of going international, the use of an agent, the question of control usually concerns the conflict of interest where an agent is sharing his time over a portfolio of products for which he receives differential rates of commission. Control for the supplier must mean direction of the use of the company's name, product, representation and customer service offered.

Ownership may imply but does not mean control in practice. It usually means only that large-scale investment in a sales subsidiary and/or manufacturing plant has taken place and that there will be a payback period before this investment is able to achieve a significant return. More effective control may be achieved by other means that do not involve equity or ownership but may be a form of leverage over the foreign partner exercised via the flow of funds, components, technology, and know-how by the Western partner. In longer-term agreements, the search for a continuing form of leveraged control over a foreign partner is difficult.

You need to identify good markets with sustainable potential:

> Companies differ from academics, they want sure-fire winners not theories!
> What measures are used for analysis? The traditional per capita GNP or PPP (purchasing power parity)? These are just two measures of personal disposable income, but both are flawed. See any current issue of the Economist for a discussion of PPP and international comparisons on this measure or Paliwoda and Thomas (1998) for a detailed discussion of both GNP and PPP. (Further explanation of per capita GNP is found below).
> The effects of EU harmonization are leading

to the number of psychologically close countries increasing for West Europeans, with pending EU membership applications taking the potential size of the EU to 25 countries! Computerization has created open access to information and made it a global commodity. There is little excuse today for being ill informed about anything.

Now back to the simplistic 4Ps

Price

This always has a strategic role in terms of positioning the brand. Winkler's chapter in the previous edition of this book is useful in that it takes pricing out of this narrow box and emphasizes instead how marketing can create price inelasticity. Pricing is strategically important from export contract pricing to final sale to the ultimate consumer. Garda (1995) discusses how tactical pricing can protect the company's pricing structure by tracking competitive bids made by rivals; timing price increases rather than following competitors can shift customer perceptions. Further confusion can be caused amongst competitors by making price information confidential to each customer thereby making it difficult for competitors to follow. Customer price sensitivity and switching costs are further keys to tactical pricing.

The 'Euro' currency introduced by the European Union in 1999 will usher in a new era where there will be the closest situation we have ever experienced to date of global pricing amongst the fifteen markets. Pricing will become transparent and easily comparable across the fifteen states of the EU. The strategic implications are far reaching. Marginal pricing is tantamount to 'dumping' which can take three forms: sporadic, predatory or persistent. Each implies a different competitive threat from an aggressive foreign supplier.
Countertrade (CT) is a relatively new generic term for barter, which today has many possible variants, allowing the overseas buyer to pay partly in cash and partly in goods. The merchantability of the countertrade goods determines whether or not a countertrade specialist is required to offload those goods and realize a cash value for them. The costs of countertrade transactions can escalate dramatically depending upon the goods offered, and even where specialist equipment of high quality is offered, it can have serious supplier displacement effects at home. However, while the total trade in countertrade has declined from 1989 estimates of around 30 per cent of world trade, in the aerospace and computer industries particularly, it would be virtually impossible to conduct business without recourse to such contract alternatives. Paliwoda and Thomas (1998) discuss the countertrade variants at length with examples.
Transfer pricing, as referred to earlier. Price harmonization between country markets is impossible to achieve except within fixed bands, but when this gap widens, it opens up. The real challenge is the advent of the Euro currency, which was introduced from 1999. It will be the first time that direct comparisons can be made for the same branded product across markets and in exactly the same currency.

Product

Market research answers the question as to what sort of product or brand is required in terms of:

Branding and the degree of local protection.
Patent and trademark issues, and again the degree of protection for those intellectual and industrial property rights.
Conflicting pressures to standardize or modify for local markets.
Packaging for various export markets.
Certification of origin, which allows imports right of access.

Place of sale (or channels of distribution to be employed)

If proof were required that the concept of the 4Ps described only passive markets then this is a good example. More is required than simply to make a product or service available and much is required of the producer by intermediaries within the channel to measure commercial success. Christopher (Chapter 19 in this manual), writes not of distribution but of customer service and logistics strategy.

Length of distribution channel may be less a function of economic activity than of history, e.g. the Japanese have the longest distribution channels in the world, from producer to consumer. Long channels mean added costs and loss of control over product and intermediary.

Black markets, which illegally distribute illicit or rationed goods at high prices.

Grey markets where the incidence of parallel exports/imports referred to above is ever increasing, and threatening manufacturers, but still is being championed by the EU in the name of free trade. This is increasing in pharmaceuticals because of the high value added involved.

Freeports account now for more than 9 per cent of world trade. Those freeports of the Pacific Basin which encourage manufacture, assembly and transhipment of goods for export are particularly important and are now actively competing with each other. The costs however, of building port cargo handling facilities such as those found in Singapore are very high but Malaysia is or was actively doing so until the advent of the 'Asian 'flu' which curtailed many of the more ambitious infrastructure projects. Freeports are located mainly within the NICs or the Third World and it is difficult to compete with these freeports on price as their governments have in many cases exempted the freeports not only from taxes and duties which would otherwise be payable, but also from minimum wage controls and health and safety at work legislation which might apply outside the freeport area. This creates a cost advantage but creates also a legislative anomaly within a jurisdiction. Freeports now exist in all parts of the world but their operating regulations vary widely. To be successful, they need to have a location as well as cost advantage.

Promotion

There are a number of questions here, starting with the degree of similarity with the domestic market and the availability and regulation of suitable advertising media: personal selling, sales promotion, direct mail, trade shows and exhibitions, sampling, contest and competitions, merchandizing displays and public relations or publicity. Chapter 17 of this manual discusses these aspects. Where similar market conditions and media are found then the question arises as to whether a successful domestic advertising campaign can be transferred abroad, thus eliminating origination costs. Further possibilities arise with the use of collaborative joint advertising with distributors, wholesalers or major retailers.

Essentially, markets are unlike because the forces that drive them are different or function to a lesser or greater degree compared to home. Most commonly, per capita income is sought as a guide to personal disposable income available for product purchases. This is simply naïve in that a company requires a market to have size, measurability, plus the ability and willingness to buy before it has a market. What is required therefore is knowledge for with knowledge it is possible to plan for products, which build upon similarities across countries and therefore maximize the opportunities for standardization and economies of scale. However, it also has to be said that there may also be mandatory requirements for product modification as well as some compelling reasons for product modification in view of lower disposable incomes, poor infrastructure, traditional shopping habits, etc.

Operationalization of international marketing

Experiential research on exporters

Experiential research on exporters has identified several phases:

From work initially conducted in Sweden by Johanson and Weidersheim-Paul (1975) and replicated later in the USA by Bilkey and Tesar (1977) and by Cavusgil (1980), we know of the following behavioural phases of exporters:

> The company is totally uninterested.
> The company will fulfil unsolicited orders but no more.
> The company will undertake market research of that market.
> The company begins to export to a psychologically close country.
> The company is now experienced and ready to export to any market.

Of these stages, the most important was the finding relating to psychological closeness. Psychological closeness or as it will be referred to later, psychological distance or socio-cultural distance, is a key to understanding exporter behaviour.

Selection of a foreign market entry mode

When selecting a foreign market entry mode, consider:

> There is no single 'best' strategy, so adopt a contingency approach.
> Have you considered the needs and desires of the local market?
> Has anyone asked the local natives about their expectations?
> Can you reconcile their expectations with your demands of a new market?
> Note that as socio-cultural distance

increases, firms are more likely to choose contractual rather than investment modes.

Three basic choices

The issue of mode of market entry choice ties in with the degree of commitment which the company has to export business generally as well as to corporate policy which may rule out certain types of overseas association, e.g. joint equity venture or trading with a certain country or political or economic bloc on the basis of human rights record or political repression. There is no single 'best' strategy which may be adopted for market entry. There is no correct answer only to say that this must be examined within an exclusive situational context. For each market, this may throw up new and exciting but untried alternatives, leading an experienced inter-national marketing firm to be able then to boast of a portfolio of different market entry modes currently in operation internationally. Situation 'fit' is the answer. While the choice of entry mode is wide, the costs of making a mistake are heavy. Selection is best made against a number of criteria such as the company's estimation of the perceived value of this particular market and their total commitment to it, whether short or long term.

> export, and, taking it further
> contractual modes, and
> investment modes.

Four underlying dimensions

Choice of mode of market entry may be dependent upon the firm's needs with regard to the following (Driscoll and Paliwoda, 1997):

> Control dissemination risk, i.e. authority over operational and strategic decision making.
> Dissemination risk or the extent to which a firm perceives that its firm specific advantages will be expropriated by a contractual partner.
> Resource commitment, that is, the financial,

physical and human resources that firms
commit to enter foreign markets.
Flexibility or the ability of a firm to change
entry modes quickly and with minimal costs
in the face of evolving circumstances. This is
inversely related to resource commitment.

Seven situational influences

From in-depth interviews conducted by Driscoll
and Paliwoda (1997), a number of situational
variables emerge which have been classified
into two broad groupings of firm specific (or
ownership) advantages and location advantages.

> product differentiation;
> tacit know-how;
> international experience;
> governmental intervention;
> market attractiveness;
> socio-cultural distance;
> country risk.

However, only one variable – socio-cultural
distance – was found to have a statistically significant influence on mode choice. Increasing
socio-cultural distance between a firm's home
country and its host country makes it more
likely that the firm will choose contractual
modes of entry over investment modes. One
other variable, tacit know-how, approaches significance suggesting that as know-how becomes
more tacit in nature, firms prefer the use of
investment entry modes to contractual modes.
These findings confirm mode choice as comprising a number of decision dimensions, each of
which is influenced by different situational factors. Examining the ability of various mode
choice dimensions to differentiate among distinct mode options, it has been shown that
resource commitment, control and dissemination risk are the most important aspects of
mode choice. Of the three, resource commitment
appears to be the most prominent consideration.
The results confirm that socio-cultural distance
and tacit know-how play an important role in

mode choice. This research had indicated that in
making mode choices, international marketers
frequently have preferred modes of entry that
they may use over and over again irrespective of
the entry situation. The dangers of this strategy
are two-fold. First, a firm may forfeit a promising market because its institutionally accepted
mode is incapable of penetrating the foreign
market. Second, although, the firm may be able
to penetrate the market, its mode of entry may
prevent it from fully capitalizing on market
opportunities. Being aware of and avoiding the
pitfalls inherent in institutionalizing entry
modes might lead to more long-term success in
international markets.

Continuing and future challenges

Paliwoda and Ryans (1995) set out eight new
directions in international marketing:

> Impact of economic integration within the
> European Union. The international scramble
> for membership of economic blocs. The
> potential for an organization such as APEC
> (Asia Pacific Economic Cooperation) with
> nineteen country membership.
> Strategic alliances increasing in all industries
> across all nations.
> Standardization strategy, which is increasing,
> means segmentation and pre-testing are
> necessary.
> Time to market and product differentiation
> (physical and psychological) is important.
> Need for awareness, image and preference
> data has led to new types of market
> research.
> Regulation important in a world trade order
> dominated not by trading nations but by eco-
> nomic blocs such as the EU which accounts
> for about 40 per cent of world trade. The
> rise therefore of a new organization in the
> World Trade Organization (WTO).
> Major changes in distribution channels, e.g.
> concentration in retailing, and rise of inter-
> national retailing. Problem of finding
> exclusive agents and representatives.

World-wide, consumers are becoming more price sensitive, so private labels are a response by retailers to ensure margins and customer loyalty.

Maintaining a sustainable advantage

Both Doyle (Chapters 12 and 16) and Wensley (Chapter 2) provide excellent reviews in this manual of general marketing strategy. Comments here focus on international marketing strategy.

Traditional marketing theory dictates that by adjusting the 4Ps for the correct marketing mix, companies are able to communicate effectively with their buying public. The marketing mix, reduced to only 4Ps, assumes passive markets while the interaction approach accepts that there are dynamic relationships between buyers and sellers involving product and process adjustments, logistical coordination, knowledge about the counterpart, personal confidence and liking, special credit agreements and long-term contracts. Getting established in a new market involves creating a network new to the firm. It has to build relationships new to itself and its counterparts. This may lead to the breaking of old existing relationships, sometimes adding a new relationship to an existing one. Either the buyer or the seller may take initiatives. Markets then are seen only as networks of relationships between firms. This environment is not static but dynamic. The opportunities exist then for grey markets, for parallel exports and parallel imports whereby domestic wholesalers effectively disrupt a manufacturer's official channels of distribution in a foreign market with exports designated for the home market. The aim is to take advantage of a higher profit margin in the price differential between home and overseas markets. This trade is not illegal and is encouraged by the EU in the interest of free trade. It may have been brought about by a particularly favourable foreign rate of exchange, but, given the volatility of exchange rates, this can change suddenly in the opposite direction. For the manufacturer concerned, who

is facing hostile distributors abroad, the option is to take the product off the market at home, increase the price on the home market or do nothing and wait for exchange rates to move against the domestic wholesalers who are doing this exporting.

Levels of personal disposable income vary across markets. There are differences in inflation rates, access to personal credit, product prices, specifications and sizes. All this serves to create confusion and to make direct comparisons very difficult. In such circumstances, grey marketers can flourish.

> Will this strategy ward off known threats, exploit opportunities, enhance current advantages and provide new sources of advantages?
> Can this strategy adapt to different foreseeable environments?
> Can competitors match, offset or leapfrog the expected advantages?

Conclusions

International marketing is not to be seen as an esoteric interest or as a standby when the domestic market undergoes an economic downturn. It is increasingly becoming a vital commercial activity for companies of all sizes and commitment. With greater moves towards political and commercial harmonization worldwide, the potential market that a company can reach correspondingly increases. Small companies in high technology sectors of industry have increasingly to turn not to the domestic market but to international or even the global market for their specialized products and services.

International marketing is different from marketing simply within one's own domestic economy. Variables, which can be assessed in the domestic context (for example, political change, rate of inflation, pending political legislation and likely political responses), are known in the domestic context but unknown when one starts to consider the international marketing arena. There are just too many variables to consider and to amass all that knowledge would require resources instil. For large companies it is not a problem but for the smaller companies it is a minefield although the range and quality of information is rapidly improving through access to new information tools such as the Internet where banks, Dun & Bradstreet and others may be easily contacted for their valued opinion, which may come at no cost.

Again, markets are not passive but active, even if your company happens to treat the domestic market as passive. Do not assume that your standard marketing mix will work even if successful at home – the examples of truly global brands are few. Coca-Cola and Pepsi-Cola are seen as archetypal global brands but remember that they are also fast moving consumer goods and that they both satisfy a very basic need, i.e. thirst. IBM as a brand has been less successful in maintaining the stranglehold over personal computers that Microsoft has achieved world-wide but again, there is a world-wide need for information technology being satisfied by an industry that is internationally concentrated. On the other hand, Gucci has been very success-ful in opening shops in China where the per capita disposable income is amongst the lowest in the world, proving the point that there is always a market segment to be found that is willing to pay a premium for prestige, status and quality.

Markets are constantly changing. Demograph-ically, Western Europe's population is becom-ing older while economically it remains affluent. The challenge arrives early in the new millennium around 2006–2111 when the bulk of the population enters retirement or early retirement. Those in employment will have to shoulder the responsibility for all those in retirement. It creates many new mar-keting opportunities for creative segmenta-tion as the newly retired and affluent still have the health and the wealth to enjoy them-selves. Many new leisure and tourism oppor-tunities are likely to arise.

Lifestyle changes have arisen over the years

as a result of lobbying regarding green issues or eating a healthier, lower-fat diet or using less packaging or avoiding certain products entirely. Consequently, we have fewer one-product companies. Both Coca-Cola and Pepsi-Cola have responded to the consumer demand for new diet products that are low fat, low calorie, sugar free. Elsewhere affluent consumers have to live with themselves for using disposable nappies, which are not degradable over less than 500 years. A demand is there to be met for there is as yet no such supply.

Money will never go out of fashion but every-where plastic cards are replacing cash trans-actions. Elsewhere financial creativity is required when dealing with markets where there is a willingness to buy but not the means with which to pay. Credit and leasing terms and countertrade have stepped into this vacuum.

Internationalization of minimum threshold product and service standards as embodied in the ISO 9000 and 1400 series of standards, creates a new dynamic for international sup-plier comparison and partly compensates also for smaller unknown companies, giving them the ability to compete internationally with confidence, almost as a brand.

Competitive conditions are going to become tougher. Market dynamics create constant change. Asian 'flu has affected what has been the powerhouse of international trade. How-ever, Central and Eastern Europe is now a focus of much economic activity and continu-ing productivity gains through harmonization within the EU is making Europe a good place in which to invest once again.

Internationalization is the only means by which companies can exist in the future. Be proactive rather than reactive.

Success requires constant market monitoring and performance evaluation but before the reader starts to wonder whether he or she can fit in with this new world trade order, take heed of the advice of Tom Peters for the managers of tomorrow:

Over the years, we have developed a style of doing business that is detached, calculating, dispassionate, analytical, methodological, dull and hard. My own hypothesis about tomorrow's survivors is that they will be fast, intuitive, opportunistic, hustling, caring, and trusting. Empathizing, cheer leading, emotional, mistake making and action taking.

We make the mistake often of assuming that there is an explanation for everything but as Michael Baker has often stated, marketing is part art and part science. When we are dealing with the buying public, we are dealing with people and so an irrational human element is ever present. They, as consumers, are the ones who will control our future.

References

Bilkey, W. J. and Tesar, G. (1977) The export behaviour of smaller Wisconsin manufacturing firms, *Journal of International Business Studies*, **10**(1), 93–8.

Cavusgil, T. S. (1980) On the internationalization process of firms, *European Research*, November, 273–281.

Driscoll, A. M. and Paliwoda, S. J. (1997) Dimensionalising the international market entry mode, Special Issue on Internationalization, *Journal of Marketing Management*, **13**(1–3), 57–88.

Drucker, P., Ohmae, K., Porter, M. and Peters, T. (1990) *Management Briefings*, Special Report No 1202, Economist Intelligence Unit, London, April.

Garda, R. A. (1995) Tactical pricing, in S. J. Paliwoda and J. K. Ryans Jr (eds), *International Marketing Reader*, Routledge, London.

Johanson, J. and Mattson, L. G. (1986) International marketing and internationalization processes – a network approach, in P. W. Turnbull and S.J. Paliwoda (eds), *Research In International Marketing*, Croom-Helm, London.

Johanson, J. and Weidersheim-Paul, F. (1975) The internationalization process of the firm: four Swedish case studies, *Journal of Management Studies*, October, 305–322.

Ohmae, K. (1990) *The Borderless World: Power and Strategy in the Interlinked Economy*, Harper Business, New York.

Ohmae, K. (1994) The Nintendo kids' brave new borderless world, *The Japan Times*, 16 November, p.19.

Paliwoda, S. J. (1995) *The Essence of International Marketing*, Prentice-Hall, Hemel Hempstead. (Also available in Spanish.)

Paliwoda, S. J. and Ryans, J. K. Jr (1995) *International Marketing Reader*, Routledge, London.

Paliwoda, S. J. and Thomas, M. J. (1998) *International Marketing*, 3rd edn, Buttwerworth-Heinemann, Oxford.

Russow, L. C. and Okoroafo, S. C. (1996) On the way towards developing a Global Screening Model, *International Marketing Review*, **13**(1), 46–64.

Thomas, M. J. (1996) Post Modernism for Dummies, Occasional Paper, Department of Marketing, University of Strathclyde, Glasgow.

Further reading

Albers-Miller, N. D. (1996) Designing cross-cultural advertising research: a closer look at paired comparisons, *International Marketing Review*, **13**(5) 59–74.

Alex Lawrie (1996) Export Business Briefing, in association with the Institute of Export, London.

Coviello, N. and Munro, H. (1997) Network relationships and the internationalization process of small software firms, *International Business Review*, **6**(4), 361–386.

Diamantopoulos, A. and Horncastle, S. (1997) Use of export marketing research by industrial firms, *International Business Review*, **6**(3), 245–270.

Douglas, S. P. and Craig, C. S. (1992) Advances in international marketing, *International Journal of Research in Marketing*, **9**, 291–318.

Douglas, S. P. and Craig, C. S. (1993) *International Market Research*, Prentice-Hall, Englewood Cliffs, NJ.

Easton, G. and Hakansson, H. (1996) Markets as networks, *International Journal of Research in Marketing*, Special Issue, **13**(5).

Egan, C. and Shipley, D. (1996) Strategic orientations towards countertrade opportunities in emerging markets, *International Marketing Review*, **13**(4), 102–120.

Hobsons Publishing in association with the Institute of Export and Department of Trade and Industry (1991) *Finding out_ About International Trade*.

Keng, K. A. and Jiuan, T. S. (1989) Differences between small and medium sized exporting and non-exporting firms: nature or nurture, *International Marketing Review*, **6**(4), 27–40.

Leeflang, P. S. H. and van Raaij, W. F. (guest editors) (1995) *International Journal of Research in Marketing*, Special Issue: The Changing Consumer in the European Union, **12**(5).

Millington, A. I. and Bayliss, B. T. (1997) Instability of market penetration joint ventures: A study of UK joint ventures in the European Union, *International Business Review*, **6**(1), 1–18.

Morgan, R. E. and Katsikeas, C. S. (1997) Export stimuli: Export intention compared with export activity, *International Business Review*, **6**(5), 477–500.

OECD (1997) *Globalisation and Small and Medium Enterprises*, 2 vols. Paris.

Paliwoda, S. J. and Thomas, M. J. (1998) *International Marketing*, 3rd edition, Buttwerworth-Heinemann, Oxford.

Quester, P. G. and Conduit, J. (1996) Standardisation, centralisation and marketing in multinational companies, *International Business Review*, **5**(4), 395–422.

Roos, J., von Krogh, G. and Yip, G. (1994) An epistemology of globalizing firms, *International Business Review*, **3**(4), 395–410.

Sharman, G. H. (1978) *Thinking Managerially about Exports*, 2nd edn, The Institute of Export, London.

Shipley, D., Egan, C. and Wong, K. S. (1993) Dimensions of trade show exhibiting management, *Journal of Marketing Management*, **9**(1), January, 55–64.

Tanzi, V. and Davoodi, H. (1998) Roads to nowhere: How corruption in public investment hurts growth, *Economic Issues*, No. 12,

International Monetary Fund, Washington, DC.

Twells, H. (1995) *Exporter's Checklist*, 2nd edn, Lloyds of London Press in association with the Institute of Export, London.

Wood, V. R. and Robertson, K. R. (1997) Strategic orientation and export success: an empirical study, *International Marketing Review*, **14**(6), 424–444.

Useful international marketing web sites

AC Nielsen – market research, information and analysis in over 90 countries: www.nielsen.com

Airlines of the Web: www.itn.net/airlines

American Demographics: www.marketingtools.com/Publications/AD /Index.HTM

APEC (Asia Pacific Economic Cooperation): www.apecsec.org.sg/apecpnewg.html and www.iijnet.or.jp/vj/p-asia/g-info/ S1-J.html

APEC (home page of the Asia Pacific Economic Cooperation Secretariat): www.apecsec.org.sg/apecnet.html

Arab.Net: www.arab.net/

ASEAN and Pacific Studies: merlion.iseas.ac.sg/asean.html

Asia Business Connection: http://asiabiz.com/news.html

Asia Business Daily: http://infomanage.com/~icr/abd

ASM Group's Asian Sources Online: www.asiansources.com

Canada Up Close: http://strategis.ic.gc.ca

CIA World Factbook: www.odci.gov/cia/ publications/nsolo//wfb-help/index.htm

Currency Exchange: www.fx4business.com

ExportNet: www.exporttoday.com

International Business Forum: www.ibf.com

Mellinger Global Trade Center:
www.tradezone.com/tz

Price Waterhouse:
www.i-trade.com/infsrc/pw

Statistical Agencies on the Internet:
www.science.gmu.edu/csi779/drope/
govstats.html

Statistics UK: www.emap.com\cso

Statistics USA: www.stat-usa.gov

Statistics Canada – reputedly the best governmental statistical reporting service:
www.statcan.ca

TradePort – extensive information on international business: www.tradeport.org

Trade Statistics: www.census.gov/ftp/pub/
foreign-trade/www/

TradeWave Galaxy – public and commercial
information and services:
www.einet.net/galaxy.html

Trading Standards Net – consumer legislation
and full list of product recalls:
www.xodesign.co.uk/tsnet

Transition Brief – Newsletter of CCET
(Centre for Cooperation with Economies in
Transition), OECD:
www.oecd.org/sge/ccet/

Translations Service:
www.globalink.com/home.html

UK Based Servers: http://src.doc.ic.ac.uk/
all-uk.html

UNDP – UN Development Program Human
Development Report 1997 discusses world
poverty and a six-point strategy for poverty
reduction:
www.undp.org/undp/hdro/index.htm

US Dept. of Commerce: www.doc.gov/
CommerceHomePage.html

US – Fedworld: www.fedworld.gov

US House of Representatives:
http://www.house.gov/

US International Trade Commission (ITC) –
weekly updates of new trade dispute filings
and press releases: www.usitc.gov

US News and World Report Online:
www.usnews.com

US on EU: Country Report on Economic Policy
and Trade Practices, gopher:
UMSLVMA.UMSL.EDU:70/00/library/
gophers/CRPT0023

US Trademark Library: www.micropat.com

US WEST features 50 000 suppliers from
USA, Mexico, Canada:
http://export.uswest.com

US WEST Export Yellow Pages:
http://yp.uswest.com

USA – Economic Bulletin Board, gopher:
//una.hh.lib.umich.edu/11/ebb

US National Trade Databank: www.stat-
usa.gov/BEN/Services/nidbhome.html

UT-LANIC (University of Texas Latin American Network Information Center):
http://lanic.utexas.edu/la/region.html

UT-MENIC (University of Texas Middle East
Studies): http://menic.utexas.edu/mes.html

Virtual Reference Desk:
http://thorplus.lib.purdue.edu/reference/
index.html

Wall Street Journal Interactive Edition:
www.update.wsj.com/

Wall Street Net: www.netresource.com/wsn/

Web Page for Global Business:
www.seattleu.edu/~parker/
homepage.html

Web sites for international information:

http://www.ustr.gov/

http://www.i-trade.com/

http://www.stat-usa.gov
/BEN/subject/trade.html

http://www.itaiep.doc.gov/

Western European geography software:
http://ourworld.compuserve.com/
homepages/torpedo

White House (Welcome to the White House):
www.whitehouse.gov

World Bank: www.worldbank.gov/

World Health Organisation, gopher:
gopher.gsfc.nasa.gov

World History Chart: www.hyperhistory.com

World Population Clock:
www.census.gov/cgi-bin/ipc/popclockw

World Wide Web Virtual Library:
http://W3.org

World Trade Analyzer – Trade Compass:
ww.tradecompass.com/trade_analyzer

WTCA On-Line – World Trade Centers Association On-Line: www.wtca.org/etindex.html

WTO (World Trade Organization): Agreement Establishing the WTO:
www.soton.ac.uk/~nukop/data/
fullrecs/1660.htm

WTO: www.unicc.org//wto/Welcome.html

WWW Yellow Pages: www.cba.uh.edu/
ylowpges/ylowpges.html

CHAPTER 24

Marketing for non-profit organizations

KEITH BLOIS

Introduction

There are a great many activities within a society which have as their focus issues and activities upon which no value can be easily placed. For example the National Trust is concerned with conserving the beauty of outstanding landscapes and buildings; Greenpeace attempts to make individuals, organizations and nations more environmentally aware; etc.

The majority of the organizations which have been created to support these types of activities hold some form of non-profit status. The issue which this chapter seeks to address is how far and in what form is marketing applicable to such organizations? Inevitably such a question impacts upon value judgements about the way society is organized. This cannot be avoided. All that can be hoped is that the issues are presented in a balanced way.

What is a non-profit organization?

Within the UK there is no agreed definition of what 'a non-profit organization' is. The term, together with others such as 'voluntary organization', 'charity', etc. which are often associated with it, is perhaps only defined by considering what has been described as 'a residual concep-

tion' (Paton, 1991) that is what is left of the economy if business and government are excluded. Paton proposes that the continental term 'the social economy' should be applied to it. However, as he says, such a residual conception is an 'ill-defined and disputed sector' and with regard to the charity sub-sector it has been stated that it 'can hardly be called a coherent sector at all' (Prochaska, 1997).

However, there is an expectation amongst the public that certain types of activities will be undertaken by non-profit organizations, charities or voluntary organizations. Furthermore the general public seems to have some expectations about the behaviour of such organizations which includes: maintaining the highest ethical standards; not paying competitive salaries (though some do; Parris, 1997); not being too 'commercial' – whatever that means (though many do use the latest commercial practices; Goodman and Plouff, 1997); etc. A further difficulty is that the missions of such organizations, which range from those concerned with human needs (e.g. AIDS research) through to those dealing with inanimate matters (e.g. The National Trust), evoke strong emotional responses amongst some groups in society. These responses can be positive or negative. A final difficulty is that, increasingly non-profit organizations are finding themselves in competition with for-profit businesses and also government bodies.

With so many terms not subject to agreed definitions the following discussion will necessarily lack precision, but hopefully not clarity. An additional problem is that the term 'non-loss organization' initially appears more appropriate for most organizations which are found in the social economy. After all, if for more than a short while their expenditure exceeds their income, then inevitably problems arise. Indeed the Charities Act 1992 stated that where charities allow their organizations to continue to trade when 'a prudent man of business' would not, then the trustees can be prosecuted. However, the term 'non-loss organization' does not take account of the fact that many organizations, commonly considered as being 'non-profit', do maintain activities designed to make profits to be used in pursuit of their mission and to contribute to their running costs.

The term 'not for profit organization' recognizes that profits may be needed though only as a means to an end. It also captures the non-loss aspect and recognition of this perhaps indicates a way to move towards defining the term 'non-profit organization' (rather than trying to introduce the term 'not for profit').

The term 'non-profit' can be applied to those organizations:

1   whose prime goal is not the creation of profits; but,
2   which may pursue profit-making activities although only in support of their prime goal.

The definition of a non-profit organization which will be used in this chapter will therefore be:

A non-profit organization is an organization whose attainment of its prime goal is not assessed by economic measures. However, in pursuit of that goal it may undertake activities intended to create profit.

Thus an organization may have as its prime goal the alleviation of poverty through the distribution of funds amongst specified groups in the population. To be able to achieve this goal it will need money both to cover its running costs and to distribute to its target group. It might obtain these funds in a variety of ways, including seeking donations. It might also undertake some commercial activities such as running a shop, organizing jumble sales, etc. with the intention that these activities will make profits which will only be used to meet the organization's need for funds.

The definition of a non-profit organization, set out above, makes no reference to its legal status and an organization falling within this definition might take any one of several legal forms. Indeed, it is possible, though unusual, for a public limited company to be considered to be a non-profit organization within the terms of this definition. (It is, of course, important to differentiate between those public limited companies which fail to make profits and those which are non-profits by this definition.) Although the definition does not mention the organization's legal status this does not mean that it is unimportant. In fact the most effective way for a non-profit organization to achieve its goal may not be to take the status of limited company. It might for example be better to seek charitable status and there can be substantial benefits for an organization which follows this course although having charitable status also imposes limits on an organization's activities, mode of operation and development. For example a charity usually cannot make a gift of an asset to anybody – even another charity.

This issue of legal status has become increasingly complex especially since more companies are now operating in those areas, such as the provision of homes for the elderly, which have traditionally been dominated by charities. Also charities by developing their profit-making activities are impinging more and more on traditional for-profit organizations' activities – for example greetings cards, shops selling foods, etc. Companies whose main business is in such fields understandably feel that charitable status gives non-profit organizations unfair advantages by enabling them to avoid certain costs. The debate about, for example, whether or not charities should be granted certain tax exemptions (e.g. exemptions from corporation tax and relief on business rates) not available to a company is part of an on-going discussion of the advantages that 'charities' have over companies with whom they compete (Parris, 1997).

Managerial implications of being a non-profit organization

Before trying to determine what role marketing might play in the operations of non-profit organizations it is necessary to consider their organizational characteristics. Given the wide variety of organizations which come within the definition set out above, it is not surprising that it is difficult to describe their organizational characteristics. However, it is suggested (Hasenfeld and English, 1974; Hofstede, 1981) that there are a number of characteristics which can be observed in such organizations. Yet given the wide variety of organizations which can be described as non-profit it will not be surprising to find that there are some non-profit organizations to which not all (or even none) of these apply and some 'for profit' organizations to which some (or even all) apply.

Ambiguous goals

Voluntary, charitable and professional bodies are often the scene of conflict over their specific goals. Such conflicts can arise amongst the employees (including the management team) but particularly between the governing body (the trustees or the directors) and the employees. Many employees of non-profits have strong commitments to the organization's mission and indeed often work in poor conditions and for low wages simply because of their commitment to that mission. Indeed many would not accept such salaries and working conditions in a for-profit organization. The governing body is often primarily made up of people who are not

employees and not infrequently they are people who fulfil this role out of a sense of public duty. This is not say they have no commitment to the organization's mission – they more often than not have taken great care when choosing which organization to help. However, they are not committing their career to the organization. More importantly their role imposes legal responsibilities on them which may make them, with regard to a wide range of issues, more cautious than the employees might wish them to be. For example as far as charities are concerned, the 1992 Charities Act created 13 criminal offences – mostly associated with financial impropriety – with which Trustees can charged!

There can also be clashes of views between employees and any voluntary workers about an organization's mission. Understandably career objectives, the desire for job security, etc. may lead full-time employees to seek to change an organization's goal. This was observed by Perrow (1970) when after the conquering of polio the full-time employees of the American Foundation for Infantile Paralysis, in an attempt to ensure their continued employment, sought to find new goals for the Foundation.

It is therefore quite easy for governing bodies and for employees to adopt different attitudes to a particular issue – especially those issues which have financial implications for the organization. The setting of goals can therefore be quite contentious, time consuming and subject to frequent reappraisal.

Lack of agreement on means-ends relationships

Even where an organization has clear and agreed goals, there may be disagreement as to how best to achieve these goals. This may be because of lack of knowledge as to how to achieve the goal, lack of agreement as to which method most effectively leads to the goal's attainment or the refusal of some members of the organization to accept some methods of operation (for example the use of 'commercial practices') which others believe will lead to the achievement of the goals.

This lack of agreement makes budgeting very difficult. Furthermore in many non-profit organizations' labour costs are a major item of expenditure and estimating such costs can be complicated because it may sometimes be possible to substitute volunteers for full-time employees. However, the availability of volunteers is usually unpredictable.

Environmental turbulence

Non-profit organizations' missions and goals are usually more constrained (if ambiguous) than for-profit organizations; any turbulence in their environment may thus cause considerable difficulties. Depending upon their exact legal form most non-profit organizations are quite limited in the fields of activity in which they can be involved. As a result, changes in legislation, technology, the structure of society, etc. seem to impact on many non-profit organizations more than for-profit organizations. The process of working out the best responses to such changes can be time consuming as can be the process of obtaining commitment to agreed responses. For example, the decision of the Marriage Guidance Council to change its name to Relate, partially in response to the acceptance of the fact that for some years many of the couples with which it had been dealing were not married, followed a considerable debate about its role and who it aims to serve.

Where the mission of the organization requires stability then it can be very difficult for it to manage turbulence effectively. Thus an organization seeking to manage a nature reserve will try to maintain a stable physical environment over a number of years perhaps even decades. Growth in public mobility with the potential of a rapidly increasing number of visitors may well create major problems for the management as it attempts to fulfil this mission. It is also likely to result in debates as to whether or not the mission should be changed to place greater or even less emphasis on public access. On one hand greater access, perhaps leading to greater public support both financially and politically, but simultaneously risking damaging the very environment that it seeks to protect.

Unmeasurable outputs

Even where a non-profit organization's goals are clearly specified and agreed upon, it may be impossible to measure their level of achievement with any reasonable degree of accuracy. It is not, for example, obvious how the output of the Samaritans should be measured. An additional problem for some organizations is that the nature of their clients and their needs makes it very difficult to measure their success. Many drug addicts will only approach an organization for help if guaranteed anonymity. Others do not have fixed addresses. It follows that keeping track of such clients is extremely difficult if not impossible and therefore measuring an organization's level of output and success is difficult.

Where output cannot be measured directly proxy measures will often be sought. However measures such as the average time spent with each patient, the number of patients seen, etc., which might be used in the case of a clinic, are potentially misleading as measures of goal achievement and can be mischievous in their effect upon employees' attitudes and behaviour. There is also a danger, where measures of output are not available, that, as an alternative, measures of inputs will be used to assess the organization's efficiency – this in the limited sense of measuring whether or not inputs are rising or falling over time.

A further problem of unmeasurable outputs is that much management time may have to be spent on resource allocation and on seeking to devise ways of monitoring (frequently in response to the demands of their funding body) outputs to support claims for more resources. Given the nature of many organizations' outputs this often seems like chasing the will o' the wisp.

The effects of management intervention are unknown

In many non-profit organizations the link between management actions and results are not well understood. This problem arises in part from the difficulty in measuring outputs discussed above. Yet, even where outputs can be measured or an acceptable proxy is found, difficulties still exist. Very often this is because the prime goals of both the organization and its employees and volunteers are not susceptible to monetary evaluation. This makes the assessment of the effects of a management decision much more difficult because the use of monetary value as a uniform unit of measurement is inappropriate.

Who are the non-profit organizations' customers?

For many non-profit organizations this appears to be a trivial question. However, for some organizations, while the answer is obvious, the implications of the answer do not always appear to be fully comprehended or thought through – especially by the general public. Consider an organization like a privately funded hospice. Who is the customer here? Instinctively many people will say the terminally ill patient is 'the customer' but is this really so as, except in a minority of cases, most of the patients do not or cannot pay for the hospice's services? Surely the customers are those who in various ways fund the hospice.

Wensley (1990) has pointed out there are limits to the marketing analogy and has suggested a supplier/user taxonomy which creates four categories of user namely: customer; 'consumer'; patient; and, 'client'. This is helpful as it demonstrates, in particular, that the conflation of the terms 'customer' and 'consumer' enables many commentators to finesse crucial issues and certainly for many commentators the terms 'customer' and 'consumer' are used as if they are interchangeable. Even if this was not the case, it

is questionable whether or not a user of professional services should become a customer in the sense that this is a category of provider which both specifies the product that the user needs and actively helps in the choice between alternative suppliers. After all the role of a provider of professional services is to advise the user of the service as to what their needs are.

Various arguments are used to assert that those who are served by non-profit organizations are very close to being customers. For example, it has been stated that 'The rhetorical significance of the customer (viz., in public services) was recognized in the launch of the Citizen's Charter.' (Richards, 1992). The standards set by these charter(s) are also frequently imposed upon those non-profit organizations which are funded by Government bodies. Richards claims that they reinforce the customers' voice in a situation where no alternative supplier exists. What seems to be ignored in this claim is that these charters were formulated by politicians and bureaucrats and not on the basis of customer surveys.

For many non-profits the users are not their customers. Their customers are those who in a variety of ways provide the resources required to keep the organization running. This fact can lead to a situation where, if they accept McKitterick's (1957) dictum, it is possible that they may be led away from their mission! Indeed it will be argued below that where the user is not the customer 'that "simple" marketing remedies or language have little value' (Wensley, 1990).

Marketing activities of non-profit organizations

Typically most non-profits have to interact with several constituencies but this is not a distinctive feature of non-profit organizations. Indeed organizations which do not face this problem are the exception rather than the rule. However starting with the concept of 'exchange', which is usually taken to be central to the concept of marketing, it becomes apparent that non-profit organizations undertake at least five different types of marketing activity which are directed at different constituencies. These are:

- commercial marketing;
- social marketing;
- marketing to donors;
- marketing to funders; and,
- cause-related marketing.

Commercial marketing

Many non-profits effectively run businesses for the reason set out above which is to create a source of income. Members of the public are aware that many non-profit organizations include amongst their activities such functions as running shops (the total number of UK charity shops in 1997 was estimated to be 5000), selling products by mail-order, etc. which the general public would understand to be 'marketing activities'. Indeed this is one reason why many charities are either set up or own 'non-profit companies limited by guarantee'. The application of a marketing orientation to such activities is no different than the marketing of such activities by for-profit organizations. However, some people involved with non-profit organizations do question the appropriateness of such activities for their organizations. There are two quite different reasons why this is the case – both of which relate to the problems considered above that non-profits face with regard to ambiguous gaols and lack of agreement on means–ends relationships.

First some people question the appropriateness of their organization using marketing techniques and orientations because of its perceived connotations and associations. This attitude may be based upon a number of views ranging from the feeling that 'being commercial is not nice' (Landry *et al.*, 1985) through to a belief that capitalism is exploitative and that marketing is inextricably associated with capitalism. Although it is possible to argue with people holding such views it is unlikely that they will change their position based, as it tends to be, on a belief about the way society should be organ-

ized. The second reason is the risk that the fund-raising will become dominant in a critical and perhaps contradictory way. For example, 'What are the implications for radical environmental groups of their trading activities?' (Batsleer and Randall, 1991).

Social marketing

The prime objective of some non-profits is the dissemination of ideas and information. For others, while this is not a prime objective, it is an important part of their activity and so, for example, some organizations concerned with heart disease have placed advertisements encouraging healthy eating habits. Others believe that only by changing the public's attitudes can they achieve their long-term goals. Thus Chiswick Family Rescue (now called 'Refuge') has a threefold aim: to help women and their children find a sanctuary from domestic violence; to obtain a coordinated policy within the criminal justice system of arrest and prosecution of all offenders; and, to provide relevant education and training in the work place and schools.

Many marketing writers would argue that social marketing activities might be appropriate for an organization such as Refuge as a form of support for its latter two aims. However, the debate about whether social marketing is different from public relations and/or education has been long and inconclusive. Furthermore the confusion has been added to by some writers apparently mixing up social marketing and societal marketing.

Social marketing may also assist a non-profit organization in the marketing of any goods it sells as a way of generating funds for its support. Why else do customers so often pay more than 'the going price' for an item purchased from a non-profit organization? Presumably because they recognize and approve of the cause supported by the funds generated by the sale. It is through social marketing that organizations such as Traidcraft may be able to increase the numbers in the population prepared to purchase their products.

Marketing to donors

The third area is those activities concerned with the generation of funds other than through the marketing of products. There are three separate types of donor each of which requires quite different approaches. The first are the individual donors. The second are organizational donors such as charitable bodies and other organizations. The third is 'official' sources (discussed below under 'Marketing to funders') such as central and local government and their agencies. Although various estimates have been made as to the sums coming from these different groups it seems generally accepted that individual donations are a small and diminishing proportion of the total and that 'official' sources are by far the largest source.

Exchange 'is the act of obtaining a desired product from someone by offering something in return' (Kotler, 1991) and 'exchange' is the core concept which defines marketing's field of study. One side of the exchange for non-profit organizations is clearly the donor's gift but unless the donor gets something in return there is no exchange and therefore the relationship is arguably not a marketing issue. Clearly marketing techniques might be used to identify the potential donors and to build up donor segments (Sargeant, 1995) but it is possible for an organization to use marketing techniques without it being committed to a marketing orientation.

It has been argued (Blau, 1964) that donations are made so that donors may earn the approval of their peers. The exchange here is indirect because the donation to the organization is exchanged for approval gained, not from the organization but from the social group from which the donor seeks approval. However, this view ignores the fact that many individual donors choose to remain anonymous. In such circumstances what exchange is there other than, presumably, some sense of inner satisfaction on the donor's part?

There is little agreement amongst academics or practitioners in the field of non-profit organizations as to what individual donors seek (Hibbert, 1995; Mathur, 1996) and consequently how they should be approached. So much depends upon the individual donor's values. For example, while advertisements designed to prick consciences such as one stating: '£15 can intoxicate you for the night or inoculate this child for life' are increasingly used and are seen as successful, at least as evaluated by measures of recall (Snowden, 1995), many fund raisers feel that to 'sell' social approval is ethically questionable and that some donors do not like being associated with causes which use such approaches. Given that, as will be discussed below, the value to commercial organizations of association with charities in particular 'is precisely the high ethical standards underlying charities that can make them attractive to marketers' (Reed, 1995) then it is in the non-profit's direct interests to strike a careful balance on these matters.

Marketing by those non-profit organizations which deal with the poor or those with physical or mental disabilities needs to be handled with great sensitivity. In fact often those approaches which are likely to make the greatest impact on actual and potential donors must be rejected because of their effect on those who the organization seek to serve (Levy, 1990). Thus many of those who have to live in residential homes bitterly resent donors being invited to visit their homes 'to see the good that is being done'. Such visits even by the most sensitive of people can be humiliating for the residents but ideas of applying relationship marketing to fund-raising (Humphries, 1993) can result in managers being pressurized to agree to such activities. Indeed there has been criticism from authoritative independent bodies, such as the King's Fund, that disabled people are too often represented in advertisements without their prior agreement.

An additional issue is that the achievement of social approval may only be tenuously related to the nature of the non-profit organization's activities. The social approval arises from the act of giving itself rather than the purpose for which the donation will be used. It is not uncommon for donors (including those who make very considerable commitments in terms of time and effort – such as sponsored marathon runners) to be quite ignorant and almost unconcerned as to the use to which their gifts will be put, any concern as to the precise use often only being expressed in a negative manner such as 'as long as it's not going to . . .'.

If social approval is important to a significant number of donors then how can this be managed? The problem for non-profit organizations in dealing with such donors would seem to be to create some mechanisms for helping them to obtain the social approval which they seem to seek/like/appreciate/accept. There may be other words which could be added to this list but it is long enough to indicate the range and complexity of the motivations of donors. The dangers of not offering a donor a chance of obtaining significant social approval when they want it and vice versa are considerable. Thus some charities have found that a number of those who make substantial donations expect to be made trustees – it looks good in books like *Who's Who* – but that they then seldom attend the trustees' meetings. Finally some donors may dissociate themselves from non-profit organizations which appear to court donations by offering visible social recognition.

Whether or not they are seeking social approval, donors will expect that the resources transferred to the organization will be used effectively. Often, however, the recipient of the service is unknown to the donor so that the actual use to which their gift is made cannot be observed. The organization's legal form may then be seen by the donor as a partial safeguard. Certainly the legal forms which most non-profit organizations take ensure that 'profits' cannot be distributed and that trustees and management committees cannot take actions which will benefit them personally.

Predominately donors give money but of course many donors also give other resources and especially their time. For example, a company might offer, free of charge, the use of spare facilities such as a warehouse for storage or empty seats on a plane for an overseas aid charity's employees. Individuals give their time by sitting on committees and helping to run the organization in variety of ways. They sometimes do this in their 'spare' time but employers will sometimes give them time off, with pay, or encourage them to undertake pro bono work. Solicitors, accountants, surveyors and architects, for instance, have traditionally provided many services to charities at no charge or at a much below the market rate. (The difference between pro bono and voluntary work is that pro bono work makes use of the status of the organization rather than just the individual's skills, i.e. they write letters on the organization's notepaper. Given that outsiders and sometimes even people within the non-profit organization benefiting from this generosity do not know that this is pro bono and not full-fee work, there is little benefit even in PR terms for the firm involved. In the main it is simply 'old fashioned' generosity.)

Many marketing writers believe that effective use of social marketing techniques might be seen as a way of increasing donations through raising donors' awareness of the organization and its role. Therefore planning activity directed at donors should be carefully co-ordinated with any social marketing which is undertaken.

Marketing to funders

Many non-profit organizations find that, either directly or through a third party, a considerable part of their income comes from government (central and/or local). There are a variety of reasons why governments choose to fund organizations to carry out activities for which they are responsible rather than perform them themselves. It can be that it is felt that there is a benefit in a non-government body offering a service to the community: the employees do not have to meet Civil Service standards in terms of behaviour; clients who might be shy of involvement with officialdom may be prepared to deal with a third party; etc.

There are also other primarily economic reasons and many non-profit organizations believe that the use of third parties has increased in popularity with governments because it is a cheaper way of providing such services. By sub-contracting certain activities the government can create competition with all the benefits that this is supposed to bring such as tight cost control, new product development, etc. In addition non-profit organizations' salary and other costs are frequently much lower than any official body would have to meet because the staff's commitment often means that, rather than see a cause collapse, they will work for salaries and with employment conditions that would not be acceptable to central or local government employees. In addition there is the possibility that a non-profit organization will make use of volunteers rather than incur the costs of employing part-time or full-time staff.

At a superficial level the problems for a non-profit organization seeking funding from government are no different than those faced by many for-profit organizations. Where a non-profit organization seeks funds from an official body the so-called 'contract culture' means that the non-profit organization finds itself in a position where it is negotiating in exactly the same way as a for-profit organization would with one of its customers. Indeed under this approach it is now not unusual for non-profit organizations to find themselves in competition with for-profit organizations. The potential funder regards itself as acting as a customer to whom the non-profit organization is seeking to sell its products. (This reflected in the terminology now being used in the NHS where the customer is not the patient (who is a 'user') but the purchaser – for example a Regional Health Authority!)

The marketing problem in these circumstances at first seems no more or less difficult than that faced by other organizations competing with others to gain the 'business' of an organizational buyer. Admittedly, the non-profit organization frequently faces a customer who is a monopsonist but this too is not such an uncommon situation in the for-profit field. Further-more, although only rarely is a physical product involved, professional service marketing is now a well developed subject. However, as will be discussed below, seeking support from such funders does present a fundamental problem for non-profits regarding their responsibilities towards those they seek to serve.

Cause-related marketing

Giving donations is still the most common form of commercial organizations' involvement with non-profit organizations but an increasing number are using cause-related marketing campaigns. This is an approach where a firm establishes a marketing programme, with which a non-profit organization agrees to be associated, that results in the commercial organization making a donation to the non-profit. The donation is typically related (though a maximum sum may be specified) in some way with the level of sales in a specified period of a product or group of products marketed by the commercial organization. The range of activities has included a building society donating £1 to the NSPCC for every account opened by teenagers; a donation to the National Children's Homes from a FMCG manufacturer for every tin of a particular range of product purchased; advertising space being made available on a firm's product for which the non-profit receives a fee; etc. The latter example makes clear how valuable some commercial organizations see association with an appropriate non-profit to be. For they are not only prepared to give the non-profit advertising space but they then pay the non-profit for agreeing to its name being inserted in that space!

Strikingly most of the literature about cause-related marketing clearly approaches the issue from the commercial organization's point of view (e.g. Varadarjan and Menon, 1988). However, with the increasing sophistication of many non-profits' approaches to marketing (linked in part with their recruitment of people with commercial marketing experience) the non-profits are becoming very aware that they have something which is tradable. Indeed the following comment 'We are selling a valuable concept. An association with a well-known brand and an organization which is a superb deliverer of services' was not made by a FMCG marketing manager but by a representative of UNICEF (Fletcher, 1995)! It is also now not uncommon for a company to invite a number of non-profit organizations, with which it would like to be associated in a cause-related marketing campaign, to make competitive bids for the association. In other words this selection process is similar to that used when choosing, say, an advertising agency!

Non-profits are therefore thinking carefully about whether they should agree to have their name associated with commercial organizations and, if they decide to proceed, which ones and at what price? Thus they have, whether approaching or being approached by a company for a relationship, to think very carefully about the risks involved. It might be harmless for a sports organization to be associated with the makers of certain brands of running shoes, but, given the bad publicity some of these companies are currently receiving, it would be very risky for a children's charity to become involved with them (*The Independent*, 1997). However this is easy to decide at the end of 1997 when the bad publicity is common knowledge but there is always the risk that what appears to be a respectable company might either be less respectable than thought or run into some unfair adverse comment about their use of child labour – as one of Britain's most respected retail chains did recently. Furthermore the non-profits when exploring a cause-related marketing opportunity have to use a different approach than when they are seeking a donation. The reason for this is that typically companies treat cause-related campaigns as marketing costs while donations come under the PR budget and therefore quite different justification of these activities is required.

However attractive cause-related marketing appears to be for non-profits it is clear that, in addition to being very cautious as to which commercial organizations they become associated, they have to continuously monitor all aspects of the relationship very carefully. It is therefore very far from being an inexpensive activity for the non-profit organization. Furthermore there are two groups of non-profits for whom cause-related marketing is unlikely to be appropriate. The first is those, like many environmental and overseas aid groups, which believe that they need to be free to criticize any commercial organization. Certainly some overseas aid groups would have been in difficulties if they had entered into cause-related marketing programmes with some instant coffee producers. The second group is those which have what has coyly been called 'hard' tasks such as caring for the adult mentally ill and mentally handicapped. It is difficult to conceive of a commercial organization which would find such charities to be 'a good fit' with their marketing campaigns. Cause-related marketing can offer opportunities to the 'children's and animals' charities but this is unlikely to be the case for many other non-profit organizations.

Non-profit organizations as barriers or facilitators?

Does this then mean that essentially the issue of marketing for non-profit organizations is not a distinctive one? There is in fact in this context a substantial problem with which many non-profit organizations struggle. It is a serious one and its discussion inevitably goes far beyond the normal range of marketing discussions. Essentially what many non-profit organizations are doing when negotiating with actual and potential donors is one of two things. They may be acting as a barrier to the imposition of a price on activities on which society has not placed a valuation and, some would argue, cannot and should not place a valuation. Alternatively they may be acting as a facilitator of a process which is intent upon placing a market valuation upon activities which have never previously had a price formally attached to them.

In discussing this issue it is of course very difficult to remain objective. This becomes evident when it is recognized that the type of example which excites one reader may be a matter of indifference to another and vice versa. Thus, if the following discussion had considered a non-profit organization concerned with running a music society or with animal welfare rather than the mentally ill, the response of some readers would be quite different. The difficulty is of course that many non-profit organizations' missions are concerned with matters which are to some sections of the population extremely emotive issues.

Consider an organization concerned with rehabilitating, through care in the community, those who have had mental problems which are so severe that they have received in-patient treatment but have now been discharged from hospital.

The 'barrier' approach

For an organization acting as a 'barrier', its negotiations with its customer(s) would revolve around the cost of providing the supervisors, facilities, etc. necessary to rehabilitate such people. Some figure of the average cost per patient per week might be estimated and negotiations would revolve around the reasonableness of that figure. There would however be no argument linking the cost of providing the therapy required and the value of the rebuilt lives. The calculation would simply be based upon the cost of providing the level of support that experience and/or expert advice indicated as necessary.

This approach attempts to obtain the funding necessary to create a therapeutic capacity whose effectiveness might be measurable but not, by definition, its efficiency. It is an approach which encapsulates the original concept of a charity which is that it is an organization for the help of those who are unable to help themselves (*Oxford English Dictionary*). The role of the non-profit organization is thus seen to be a barrier between the helpless and the 'discipline' of the market.

In such circumstances social marketing may be seen to assume a very important role. In theory governments allocate funds to those purposes which the electorate indicate are important to them. (It is necessary to say 'in theory' as even political scientists seem uncertain as to the actual process by which this works.) However, it is clear that governments seldom allocate substantial funds to those activities in which the electorate has indicated it has no sympathy and/or interest. It is therefore critical that non-profit organizations pursue activities which raise the electorate's interest and support for their organization's mission. Only if this is achieved is it likely that the government will be sympathetic to an organization's appeals for funding. Equally commercial donors will only commit themselves to support non-profit organizations which evoke public interest for there appears to be a growing view that firms want both their donations and their cause-related activities 'to be tangibly correlated' (Mullen, 1997).

However, concerns have been expressed that using social marketing in this way could lead to its development into a form of propaganda with power invested in the marketers and those with access to the most funds (Laczniak *et al.*, 1979). Indeed the distinctions between social marketing, education and propaganda would here seem to be very subtle.

The 'facilitator' approach

The facilitator approach entails attempting to place a monetary value upon the therapy provided. For example, a high proportion of those whose mental illness has been so severe that they have been in hospital become, when discharged, long-term unemployed and a number also end up in prison. There are ways of estimating the cost of such people to society through the costs of their unemployment benefits, social security support, etc. If the cost of providing successful therapy is estimated to be less than the cost to society of the patient remaining unemployed then a non-profit organization concerned with such people can argue that the therapy it offers is 'a good investment'.

Essentially this approach considers the person being helped as a unit of resource to be processed for a fee. Viewed in this way the patients 'have become valuable to service providers in both the public and private sector by virtue of the money that can be obtained from third parties for their care. After all, the essence of a commodity in the market place is that it can be used to generate money as it is processed, improved or simply stored'. (Lewis *et al.*, 1989)

The marketing activity with regard to the potential funder is quite simply a matter of guaranteeing a specified level of service for that fee. It is really no different than the marketing activity of any for-profit professional service organization.

The facilitator approach will make many people uncomfortable and tries to answer the question 'how much are "users" worth?' (Hawker and Ritchie, 1990) but the problem is that there are large numbers of people in society who, even on the most optimistic assumptions, can never be anything but a cost. Indeed Dahrendorf (1988), talking about the poor and unemployed, was wrong when he said 'In a very serious sense, society does not need them. Many in the majority class wish that they would simply go away; and if they did their absence would barely be noticed'. In fact society would notice if they did 'go away' for it would have to bear considerably fewer costs.

The facilitator approach accepts that an economic value can be placed on an organization's activities. It is a route down which it is difficult to resist moving for, when funding is tight, the funders are able to dictate the terms of the negotiation. Thus a non-profit organization can feel compelled to argue in terms of economic value if this is the approach which a potential donor is determined to use. After all often the alternative is a reduction in the organization's level of activity or even its closure. However, once down the facilitator line of argument it may be difficult for a non-profit organization to get back to the 'barrier' role.

Oscar Wilde said that the cynic knows the price of everything but the value of nothing. Many people in society do not expect non-profit organizations to justify the value of what they do in economic terms but believe that they should be evaluated in terms of their contribution to creating a particular type of society. Yet official funding bodies are mandated by democratically elected governments to obtain value for money – a procedure which is simple enough when constructing a new building or putting out a contract for a new road. How such an evaluation is made when a choice has to be made between supporting, say, an Asian community centre in a racially sensitive area; a local amateur theatre group; or, a charity concerned with a rare health condition is much less clear.

The problem is that society has yet to come to terms with the moral dilemma of how to manage the supply of services for those who cannot afford them. As *The Independent* (12 March, 1993) stated, when commenting upon survey results which showed that over 50 per cent of the respondents thought that there should be no limit at all on health spending: 'That cannot be: since demand would be infinite, the costs would continue to rise until there were no longer enough healthy earners to keep alive the growing army of elderly patients.' Indeed the whole issue of the allocation of resources is a matter for on-going political debate and it is for this reason that the range of activities which are considered the responsibility of either non-profit organizations or commercial organizations as distinct from the state varies widely between societies.

Is a marketing perspective of any other value in non-profit organizations?

McKitterick (1957) stated that:

The principal task of the marketing function in a management concept is not so much to be skilful in making the customer do what suits the interests of the business, as to be skilful in conceiving and then making the business do what suits the interest of the customer.

In this context the difficulty with McKitterick's thiry year old statement centres upon the question: 'Who is the customer?' If the customer is the official funder then many non-profit organizations believe that doing what suits the interests of the customer would result in them failing their users. This could be the case where a non-profit organization finds that the official funders expect it to adopt a facilitator approach while its members believe that by doing so they will find it impossible serve the needs of some of their users.

The same may be true with regard to other sources of funds. For example it is not unknown for non-profit organizations to find it best to avoid being too explicit about the work they do. A charity which cares for the needy child might find it quite difficult to interest a commercial organization in a cause-related marketing campaign if its definition of 'needy' children is seen to encompass children who are drug addicts and have criminal records. It has also been suggested that the World Wildlife Fund found that funds were easier to raise when it did not stress its policies regarding conservation (Bonner, 1993).

However, if members of non-profit organizations could learn to apply McKitterick's dictum to their users then some benefit may be achieved. Such people are often involved with a non-profit organization because its mission is congruent with their beliefs or convictions. Their commitment to the mission is based upon a genuine desire to serve the public but for some their pre-occupation with their mission (and its importance to them) can blinker them to the developing needs of their users. In consequence they may fail to see how their organization can develop its offerings to its clients and thus increase their satisfaction. Indeed recognizing what is really in the interest of the users can be a disturbing question for some charity workers. For example, accepting that the mentally ill should be allowed and will benefit from helping to organize and run the organization which cares for them may be very difficult for some supervisors (both employees and volunteers) to accept. The 'Does he take sugar?' syndrome is not unknown even amongst devoted charity workers.

Perhaps the marketing metaphor has a useful role if it can persuade the members of such organizations not only to think of their users as 'customers' but to encourage them to act like customers and then apply McKitterick's statement to them – customers being of course people who have the right to exercise choices and express opinions about the products on offer. This is already happening, and, for example, in the case of those with physical or mental disabilities they are being encouraged to recognize that they are not 'patients (citizens)' but 'citizens (patients)'. In a democracy a citizen's rights would encompass those of a customer.

Regarding the user as a customer will not help non-profit organizations to raise more money from their funders. It should though increase their users' satisfaction and this might be monitored by their funders. It should also ensure that whatever funds are raised will be used in ways which are most appropriate as judged by the users rather than the organization's workers.

Conclusions

It has been suggested that marketing can help non-profit organizations in a number of quite straightforward ways. Raising funds by commercial activities, social marketing and marketing to funders are all activities to which non-profit organizations can apply conventional marketing activities.

The recognition that the user is frequently not the customer is important as certain uncomfortable consequences may arise from this fact. However, treating their clients 'as if' they were customers may help to ensure that the organization recognizes the need to monitor and, if necessary, adapt its mission towards those it claims to serve.

Obviously marketers as a profession cannot seek to dictate to society or government how society should be organized. However, it would be irresponsible for marketers to fail to discuss and point out the limits of the marketing analogy. Is there a danger, if marketing is applied to all of the non-profit sector's activities, that society, as we know it, will be metamorphosed into one which knows the price of everything and consequently fails to see the value of some things?

References

Batsleer, J. and Randall, S. (1991) Creating common cause: Issues in the management of inter-agency relationships for voluntary organizations, in J. Batsleer, C. Cornforth and R. Paton, (eds), *Issues in Voluntary and Non-profit Management*, Addison-Wesley Publishing Company, Wokingham.

Blau, P. M. (1964) *Exchange and Power in Social Life*, John Wiley and Sons, Inc., New York.

Bonner, R. (1993) The hype is as high as an elephant's eye, *The Independent*, 10 April p. 27.

Dahrendorf, R. (1988) *The Modern Social Conflict*, Weidenfeld & Nicholson, London.

Fletcher, K. (1995) Good cause and effect, *Marketing*, July 20, p. 31.

Goodman, S. and Plouff, G. (1997) Artificial intelligence marketing hits the non-profit world, *Fund Raising Management*, **28**(4), 16–17.

Hasenfeld, T. and English, R. A. (1974) Human Service Organizations, University of Michigan Press, Ann Arbor.

Hawker, C. and Ritchie, P. (1990) Contracting for Community Care: Strategies for progress, King's Fund Project Paper 84.

Hibbert, S. A. (1995) The market positioning of British medical charities, *European Journal of Marketing*, **29**(10), 6–26.

Hofstede, G. (1981) Management control of public and not-for-profit activities, *Accounting, Organizations and Society*, **6**(3), 193–211.

Humphries, D. (1993) Fundraising's fine but are you making friends as well? *Charity*, March.

Kotler, P. (1991) *Marketing Management: Analysis, Planning, Implementation and Control*, Prentice-Hall, Englewood Cliffs, NJ.

Laczniak, G. R., Flusch, R. and Murphy, P. E.

(1979) Social marketing: Its ethical dimensions, *Journal of Marketing*, **43**(2), Spring, 29–36.

Landry, C. *et al.* (1985) *What a Way to Run a Railroad*, Comedia Publishing Group, London.

Levy, L. (1990) A positive image: Bitter sweet charity, *Marketing*, 15 March, 34–35.

Lewis, D., Shadish, W. and Lurigio, A. (1989) Policies of inclusion and the mentally ill: Long-term care in a new environment, *Journal of Social Issues*, **45**, 173–186.

McKitterick, J. B. (1957) What is the Marketing Management Concept? in F. M. Bass, (ed.), *The Frontiers of Marketing Thought and Science*, American Marketing Association, pp. 71–81.

Mathur, A. (1996) Older adults' motivations for gift giving to charitable organizations: an exchange theory perspective, *Psychology and Marketing*, **13**(1), 107–123.

Mullen, J. (1997) Performance-based corporate philanthropy: How 'giving smart' can further corporate goals, *Public Relations Quarterly*, **42**(2), 42–48.

Parris, M. (1997) Uncharitable thoughts – opinion, *The Times*, 12 December, p. 22.

Paton, R. (1991) The social economy, in J. Batsleer, C. Cornforth and R. Paton (eds), *Issues in Voluntary and Non-profit Management*, Addison-Wesley, Wokingham.

Perrow, C. (1970) *Organizational Analysis*, Tavistock Publications, London.

Prochaska, F. (1997) Let charity begin with charities, *The Times*, 18 December, p. 20.

Reed, D, (1995) Alms nous, *Marketing Week*, **18**(11), 51–54.

Richards, S. (1992) Who defines the Public Good? Public Management Foundation, Working Paper, November.

Sargeant, A. (1995) Do UK charities have a lot to learn? *Fund Raising Management*, **26**(5), 14–16.

Snowden, R. (1995) Charity tactics arouse interest, *Marketing*, 23 February, p. 15.

Vallely, P. (1995) Ever heard the Algerian national anthem? Why Nike wanted you to, and how the stunt failed, *The Independent*, 6 December, p. 19.

Varadarjan, R. and Menon, A. (1988) Cause related marketing: a coalignment of marketing strategy and corporate philanthropy, *Journal of Marketing*, **52**, 58–74.

Wensley, R., (1990) The voice of the consumer?: Speculations on the limits to the 'marketing analogy', *European Journal of Marketing*, **24**(7), 49–60.

Further reading

Andreasen, A. R. (1996) Profits for nonprofits: Find a corporate partner, *Harvard Business Review*, **74**(6), 47–59.

Batsleer, J. and Randall, S. (1991) Creating common cause: Issues in the management of inter-agency relationships for voluntary organizations, in J. Batsleer, C. Cornforth and R. Paton (eds), *Issues in Voluntary and Non-profit Management*, Addison-Wesley, Wokingham.

Bruce, I. (1995) Do not-for-profits value their customers and their needs? *International Marketing Management*, **12**(4), 77–84.

Sargeant, A. (1995) Do UK charities have a lot to learn? *Fund Raising Management*, **26**(5), 14–16.

CHAPTER 25

Social marketing

LYNN MacFADYEN, MARTINE STEAD and GERARD HASTINGS

Introduction

The term social marketing was first coined by Kotler and Zaltman back in 1971 to refer to the application of marketing to the solution of social and health problems. Marketing has been remarkably successful in encouraging people to buy products such as Coca-Cola and Nike trainers, so, the argument runs, it can also encourage people to adopt behaviours that will enhance their own – and their fellow citizens' – lives. In essence social marketers argue that it is possible, at least to some extent, to sell brotherhood like soap.

This chapter will examine these ideas. It begins by explaining why social marketing is needed and how it has developed. It then examines current definitions of social marketing, before identifying ways in which it differs from its commercial counterpart. The chapter then looks at how these differences impact on the practice of social marketing, focusing on segmentation and the marketing mix.

Why do social marketing?

Efforts to influence and improve the quality of our lives can be traced back through history. Chartists, parliamentary reformers, Luddites, suffragettes, feminists and many others have tried to change the social circumstances of particular groups, as well as society as a whole, with varying degrees of success. Today, health promoters, government agencies and other non-profit organizations use marketing expertise to achieve similar goals. Social marketing is a social change management technology which offers a framework with which to change the unhealthful or unsocial behaviour of others (Kotler and Roberto, 1989)

Many social and health problems have behavioural causes: the spread of AIDS, traffic accidents and unwanted pregnancies are all the result of everyday, voluntary human activity. The most dramatic example of this is tobacco use, which kills one in two smokers (Peto, 1994) – an estimated 6 million people in the UK alone since the health consequences were first established in the early 1950s. Social marketing provides a mechanism for tackling these problems by encouraging people to adopt healthier lifestyles.

However, there are many instances where the individual finds it hard to change his or her behaviour: protecting oneself from HIV is challenging if condoms are difficult to obtain; traffic accidents may result from poor roads as well as bad driving; and the addicted smoker struggles to quit. Health problems have a social, as well as an individual, dimension. This phenomenon is most clearly demonstrated by the epidemiological data which show that poverty is one of the most consistent and basic predictors of ill-health in the UK (Smith, R., 1997; Jarvis, 1994; Marsh and MacKay, 1994), Europe (Whitehead and Diderichsen, 1997), the USA (McCord and Freeman, 1990; Pappas *et al.*, 1993) and the southern hemisphere (WHO, 1995) The lack of opportunity, choice and empowerment it generates prevents people from adopting healthy lifestyles.

Social marketing also has a great deal to offer here by influencing the behaviour, not just of the individual citizen, but also of policy makers and influential interest groups. Social marketers might target school governers to get condoms distributed through schools, or local councils and motoring organizations to get roads improved. For example, Case 2, which is discussed later in the chapter, explains how social marketing was used to advance water fluoridation, a measure that greatly improves dental health without any behaviour change at all on the part of the individual citizen.

Social marketing is now widely practised in both the developing (Manoff, 1985; Brieger *et al.*, 1986/7) and the developed world (e.g. Hastings and Elliot, 1993; Fishbein *et al.*, 1997; Hastings and Haywood, 1991).

Social marketing, like generic marketing, is not a theory in itself. Rather, it is a framework or structure that draws from many other bodies of knowledge such as psychology, sociology, anthropology and communications theory to understand how to influence people's behaviour (Kotler and Zaltman, 1971). Like generic marketing, social marketing offers a logical planning process involving consumer oriented research, marketing analysis, market segmentation, objective setting and the identification of strategies and tactics. It is based on the voluntary exchange of costs and benefits between two or more parties (Kotler and Zaltman, 1971). However, social marketing is more difficult than generic marketing. It involves changing intractable behaviours, in complex economic, social and political climates with often very limited resources (Lefebvre and Flora, 1988). Furthermore, while, for generic marketing the ultimate goal is to meet shareholder objectives, for the social marketer the bottom line is to meet society's desire to improve its citizens'

quality of life. This is a much more ambitious – and more blurred – bottom line.

The development of social marketing

Social marketing evolved in parallel with commercial marketing. During the late 1950s and early 1960s, marketing academics considered the potential and limitations of applying marketing to new arenas such as the political or social. For example, in 1951, Wiebe asked the question, 'Can brotherhood be sold like soap?' Having evaluated four different social change campaigns, he concluded that the more a social change campaign mimicked that of a commercial marketing campaign, the greater the likelihood of its success. To many however, the idea of expanding the application of marketing to social causes was abhorrent. Luck (1974) objected on the grounds that replacing a tangible product with an idea or bundle of values threatened the economic exchange concept. Others feared the power of the marketing, misconceiving its potential for social control and propaganda (Laczniack *et al.*, 1979). Despite these concerns, the marketing concept was redefined to include the marketing of ideas and the consideration of its ethical implications.

The expansion of the marketing concept combined with a shift in public health policy towards disease prevention began to pave the way for the development of social marketing. During the 1960s, commercial marketing technologies began to be applied to health education campaigns in developing countries (Ling *et al.*, 1992; Manoff, 1985). In 1971, Kotler and Zaltman published their seminal article in the *Journal of Marketing*, 'Social marketing: an approach to planned social change'. This was the first time the term 'social marketing' had been used and is often heralded as its birth. They defined social marketing as

the design, implementation and control of programs calculated to influence the acceptability of social ideas and involving considerations of product planning, pricing, communication, distribution and marketing research (p. 5)

In practice, social marketing was being explored by a number of people at the same time, including Paul Bloom, Karen Fox, Dick Manoff, and Bill Novelli. Early examples of social marketing emerged during the 1960s as part of international development efforts in Third World and developing countries (Manoff, 1985; Walsh *et al.*, 1993). For example, family planning programs in Sri Lanka moved away from clinical approaches and examined the distribution of contraceptives through pharmacists and small shops (Population Services International, 1977). They began to experiment with marketing techniques such as audience segmentation and mass communication. Similarly, oral rehydration projects in Africa began to take a more consumer oriented approach to programme development. Important initiatives in the developed world included the Stanford Heart Disease Prevention Program, the National High Blood Pressure Prevention Program, and the Pawtucket Heart Health Program (Farquhar *et al.*, 1985; National Heart, Lung and Blood Institute 1973; Lefebvre *et al.*, 1987). While many of these early programmes were primarily exercises in social communications, they were important for the inception of social marketing.

By the 1980s, academics were no longer asking if marketing should be applied to social issues, but rather how should this be done? During this period, practitioners shared their experiences and made suggestions for the development of social marketing theory and practice (Ling *et al.*, 1992). Fox and Kotler (1980) described the evolution of social advertising into social communications. Bloom (1980) explored the evaluation of social marketing projects and found that many studies were poorly designed and conducted. In 1981, Bloom and Novelli reviewed the first ten years of social marketing and advocated more research to dispel criticism that social marketing lacked rigour or theory. They identified a need for research to examine audience segmentation, choosing media channels and designing appeals, implementing long-term positioning strategies, and organizational and management issues (Bloom and Novelli, 1981).

Lefebvre and Flora (1988) and Hastings and Haywood (1991, 1994) then gave social marketing widespread exposure in the public health field, generating lively debates about its applicability and contribution. While social marketing was being practised in many countries by this time, the publication of these papers was followed by a widespread growth in its popularity (Lefebvre, 1996). Centres of expertise began to emerge, most notably at the College of Public Health at the University of South Florida, the Centre for Social Marketing at Strathclyde University in Scotland, and at Carleton University in Ottawa, Canada.

A number of books have been published on the subject, illustrating the historical evolution of social marketing's definition. Seymour Fine's *Marketing of Ideas and Social Issues* (1981) viewed social marketing as the marketing of ideas to solve consumer problems. Kotler and Roberto's (1989) *Social Marketing: Strategies for Changing Public Behaviour* characterized social marketing as a social change management technology. Andreasen's (1995) book *Marketing Social Change* makes further refinements, arguing that social marketing should focus on changing behaviour, rather than ideas, and introduces the transtheoretical model to the discipline (see p. 23).

Today, social marketing specialists are relatively clear on its definition, but outwith the discipline, especially in public health and health promotion, confusion is still apparent, with social marketing often being equated with social advertising. Correcting these misapprehensions is a key challenge for the new millennium, and the instigation of two annual conferences, one targeting academics and the other practitioners, and the founding of a peer reviewed journal – *Social Marketing Quarterly* – will help meet it.

Defining social marketing

Kotler and Zaltman's (1971) early definition of social marketing emphasized the marketing mix and the marketing planning process. The authors observed the tendency for 'campaigners' to focus solely on the role of advertising and the mass media. They argued that the role of the mass media had been over-estimated, and that more attention should be given to developing the social product, price and distribution, as well as to the role of market research. The authors' emphasis on the 'design, implementation and control of programs' (p. 7) illustrated their belief that social marketing should take the form of long-term programmes rather than short term campaigns, and that strategic planning was required to manage this.

As social marketing developed, this early conceptualization was criticized for its imprecision (Andreasen, 1994). In particular Rangun and Karim (1991) note the potential for the operationalization of this definition to confuse social marketing with societal marketing and socially responsible marketing. *Societal marketing* is concerned with the ethical or societal implications of commercial activity. So, the 'societal marketing concept' encourages firms to 'market goods and services that will satisfy consumers under circumstances that are fair to consumers and that enable them to make intelligent purchase decisions, and counsels firms to avoid marketing practices which have dubious consequences for society' (Schwartz, 1971, p. 32). In short societal marketing is concerned with ensuring that commercial marketers go about their business properly, without prejudicing either their customers or society as a whole.

Socially responsible marketing harnesses desirable social causes, such as the environment and consumerism, to advance the interests of a commercial organization (Kotler *et al.*, 1996). Public concern about the environment or the social implications of commercial activity can lead to bad publicity for the organization. Some organizations have chosen to act proactively and position themselves as socially responsible or ethical organizations – the Body Shop or ice cream producers Ben and Jerry's are typical examples. However, this does not constitute social marketing, because as with other for-profit organizations, the success of the Body Shop or Ben and Jerry's is measured by shareholder value and profitability and not, for example, by improvements to the environment.

Similarly, commercial organizations which market ethically sound products, such as condoms, are not engaged in social marketing because their success is measured in terms of commercial goals rather than reductions in the prevalence of sexually transmitted diseases.

To confuse things further, however, it is possible for commercial marketers to do social marketing. Procter and Gamble, for example, have contributed to a major social marketing drugs prevention initiative in the North East of England (Home Office, 1998). Nonetheless, such activities will always remain marginal compared with the company's main concern of commercial success. Engaging in it does not make them social marketers any more than corporate donations to good causes would make them a charity.

Social marketing should also be differentiated from *non-profit marketing* (Fox and Kotler, 1980), of which it is sometimes considered a subset (Blois, 1994; see also Chapter 24 Marketing and non-profit organizations and Chapter 26 Green marketing). Non-profit marketers are concerned with the marketing management of institutions or organizations in the non-profit arena: hospitals, cancer charities or educational institutions. As with socially responsible marketing, the difference lies in the objectives of the two activities: non-profit marketers are ultimately concerned with the success and survival of their organization; social marketers with changes in their target population. Again, however, there is a confusing degree of overlap. There are some bodies whose primary business is social marketing, such as the Health Education Authority in England or the Centers for Disease Control in the USA, who may also use non-profit marketing to manage their own organization. On the other hand, there are non-profit organizations like the Cancer Research Campaign, whose primary function is to raise money for cancer research, who may sometimes get involved in social marketing activities.

To help clarify matters, a special edition of the *Social Marketing Quarterly* invited key figures in the field to define social marketing, which was then 25 years old (Albrecht, 1996):

Definitions of Social Marketing:

"*Social marketing is the simultaneous adoption of marketing philosophy and adaptation of marketing technologies to further causes leading to changes in individual behaviours which ultimately, in the view of the campaign's originator, will result in socially beneficial outcomes.*" (Michael Basil)

"*Social marketing is the application of marketing concepts and techniques to exchanges that result in the achievement of socially desirable aims; that is, objectives that benefit society as a whole.*" (Susan Dann)

"*Social marketing is an attempt to influence consumers for the greater good, and as such, always has an ethical aspect; specifically social marketing seeks to induce consumer change that is deemed to be inherently good, as opposed to change that is good merely because it increases profits or non-profit earnings.*" (Rob Donovan)

"*Social marketing is the application of appropriate marketing tools and the systematic analysis, development, implementation, evaluation and integration of a set of comprehensive, scientifically based, ethically formulated and user-relevant program components designed to ultimately influence behaviour change that benefits society.*" (Brian Gibbs)

"*Social marketing is a program planning process which promotes voluntary behaviour change based on building beneficial exchange relationships with a target audience for the benefit of society.*" (Susan Kirby)

"*a large scale program planning process designed to influence the voluntary behaviour of a specific audience segment to achieve a social rather than a financial objective, and based upon offering benefits the audience wants, reducing barriers the audience faces and/or using persuasion to influence the segment's intention to act favourably.*" (Beverly Schwartz)

A number of key, common elements arise from these different definitions of social marketing. The first is the focus on voluntary behaviour change. The second is that social marketers try to induce voluntary behaviour change by applying the principle of exchange – the recognition that there must be a clear benefit for the customer if change is to occur. Third, marketing techniques such as consumer oriented market research, segmentation and the marketing mix should be used.

Andreasen's (1995) definition of social marketing encapsulates these points:

social marketing is the application of commercial marketing technologies to the analysis, planning, execution and evaluation of programs designed to influence the voluntary behaviour of target audiences in order to improve their personal welfare and that of society (p. 7)

More recent definitions have begun to discuss the key role of long-term relationships in social marketing (e.g. Hastings *et al.*, 1998b).

Pulling these threads together, for a social change campaign or programme to be defined as social marketing it must contain the following elements: a consumer orientation (Lefebvre and Flora, 1988; Lefebvre, 1992; Andreasen, 1995), an exchange (Lefebvre and Flora, 1988; Lefebvre, 1996; Leathar and Hastings, 1987; Smith, W. A. 1997) and a long-term planning outlook (Andreasen, 1995). Social marketing is often perceived to be concerned only with individual behaviour, but as noted earlier it can also be used to change the behaviour of groups and organizations, and to target broader environmental influences on behaviour (Lefebvre, 1996; Goldberg, 1995). Each of these essential elements of social marketing is now discussed in turn.

(i) A consumer orientation

Consumer orientation is probably the key element of all forms of marketing, distinguishing it from selling, product- and other expert-driven approaches (Kotler *et al.*, 1996). In social marketing, the consumer is assumed to be an active participant in the change process. The social marketer seeks to build a relationship with

---

Case I: A consumer-driven approach to safer sex

Leading AIDS charity London Lighthouse wanted to produce a consumer-driven guide on safer sex for people with HIV/AIDS, but research with the target audience revealed that they had no need for sex education. After all, most of the respondents had acquired HIV through unsafe sex and were perfectly capable of learning from their own mistakes.

However, at a more subtle level the prospect of a leaflet was welcomed for three reasons. First, it could provide reassurance that people with HIV/AIDS were not alone, that other people were struggling with the same problems. Second, it would bring formal recognition and legitimacy: if you have a leaflet written for you, you at least exist; you are a significant sub-group of society. Third, it would acknowledge that it is acceptable for HIV positive people to think about having sex – a particularly important point, given that most other AIDS messages imply that acquiring HIV is the end of the world.

These perceptions fundamentally changed how Lighthouse viewed the leaflet, and in this way the target audience influenced its context, purpose and very existence (Hastings, 1994).

---

target consumers over time and their input is sought at all stages in the development of a programme through formative, process and evaluative research. Case 1 illustrates how the consumer influenced the purpose, context and very existence of a safer sex initiative.

In short, the consumer centred approach of social marketing asks not 'What is wrong with these people, why won't they understand?' but, 'What is wrong with us? What don't we understand about our target audience?'

(ii) An exchange

Social marketing not only shares generic marketing's underlying philosophy of consumer orientation, but it also its key mechanism, exchange (Kotler and Zaltman, 1971). While marketing principles can be applied to a new and diverse range of issues – services, education, high technology, political parties, social change – each with their own definitions and theories, the basic principle of exchange is at the core of each (Bagozzi, 1975). Kotler and Zaltman (1971) argue that:

'marketing does not occur unless there are two or more parties, each with something to exchange, and both able to carry out communications and distribution' (p. 4).

Exchange is defined as an exchange of resources or values between two or more parties with the expectation of some benefits. The motivation to become involved in an exchange is to satisfy needs (Houston and Gassenheimer, 1987). Exchange is easily understood as the exchange of goods for money, but can also be conceived in a variety of other ways: further education in return for fees; a vote in return for lower taxes; or immunization in return for the peace of mind that one's child is protected from rubella.

Exchange in social marketing puts a key emphasis on voluntary behaviour. To facilitate voluntary exchanges social marketers have to offer people something that they really want. For example, suppose that during the development of a programme to reduce teenage prevalence of sexually transmitted diseases (STDs) by encouraging condom use, research with the target finds that they are more concerned with pregnancy than STDs. The social marketer should consider highlighting the contraceptive benefits of condoms, rather than, or at least as well as, the disease prevention ones. In this way consumer research can identify the benefits which are associated with a particular behaviour change, thereby facilitating the voluntary exchange process.

(iii) Long-term planning approach
Like generic marketing, social marketing should
have a long-term outlook based on continuing

programmes rather than one-off campaigns. It
should be strategic rather than tactical. This is
why the marketing planning function has been a

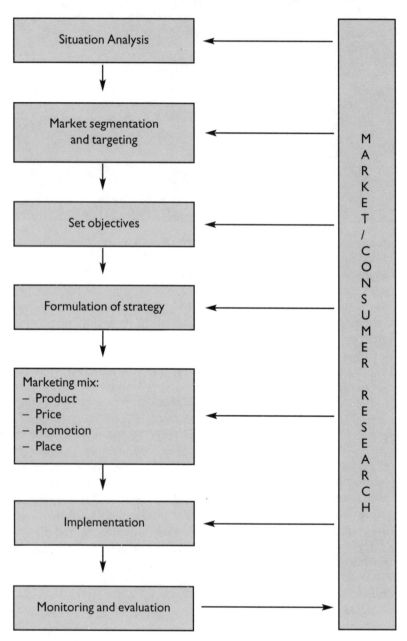

Source: Hastings and Elliot (1993)

Figure 25.1   A social marketing plan for road safety

consistent theme in social marketing definitions, from Kotler in 1971 to Andreasen in 1996.

The social marketing planning process is the same as in generic marketing. It starts and finishes with research, and research is conducted throughout to inform the development of the strategy. A situational analysis of the internal and external environment and of the consumer is conducted first. This assists in the segmentation of the market and the targeting strategy. Further research is needed to define the problem, to set objectives for the programme and to inform the formulation of the marketing strategy. The elements of the social marketing mix are then developed and pre-tested, before being implemented. Finally, the relative success of the plan is monitored and the outcome evaluated.

Figure 25.1 shows a social marketing plan produced for a road safety initiative. With minimal changes it could just as easily be applied to baked beans.

(iv) Moving beyond the individual consumer
Social marketing seeks to influence the behaviour not only of individuals but also of groups, organizations and societies (e.g. Hastings *et al.*, 1994c; Lawther and Lowry, 1995; Lawther *et al.*,

1997; Murray and Douglas, 1988). Levy and Zaltman (1975) suggest a sixfold classification of the types of change sought in social marketing, incorporating two dimensions of time (short term and long term) and three dimensions of level in society (micro, group, macro). In this way social marketing can influence not just individual consumers, but also the environment in which they operate (see Table 25.1).

Group and macro level change are important because they also impact on health and lifestyle decisions. For example, people's choices about taking up exercise may be limited by their income, local service provision or social mores. Macro-level factors can also have a more direct impact on health: for example, the presence of fluoride in the water (whether natural or artificial) can improve dental health, especially among children. This example demonstrates that there are many measures that can be taken to improve people's health without the individual citizen having to do anything at all. Better roads, reduced industrial pollution and improved safety standards on cars are similar examples.

Case 2 shows how marketing was used to facilitate water fluoridation.

Table 25.1 Types of social change, by time and level of society

	Micro level (individual consumer)	Group level (group or organization)	Macro level (society)
Short-term change	**Behaviour change**	**Change in norms Administrative change**	**Policy change**
Example:	Attendance at stop-smoking clinic	Removal of tobacco advertising from outside a school	Banning of all forms of tobacco marketing
Long-term change	**Lifestyle change**	**Organizational change**	**'Socio-cultural evolution'**
Example:	Smoking cessation	Deter retailers from selling cigarettes to minors	Eradication of all tobacco-related disease

Adapted from Levy and Zaltman, 1975

Case 2:   Water Fluoridation

Water fluoridation involves adjusting the natural level of fluoride in the public water supply so as to produce substantial improvements in the dental health of the population – especially among children and those living in deprived communities. Water fluoridation is a classic example of health promotion – safe, simple, effective – but, in the UK at least, not happening. No new water fluoridation schemes have gone ahead since the necessary legislation was passed in 1985.

Introducing water fluoridation in the UK is a complex process. Local health authorities request (but do not tell) water companies to start adding fluoride to the water once they have formally consulted the public and the relevant local government authorities. Research with the general public found that they were largely supportive of fluoridation and wanted to be kept informed of developments, but confirmed that they had little role to play in actively progressing the initiative. Furthermore they were quite happy with the state of affairs, seeing it as a job for the health professionals, to whom they were prepared to defer.

Thus fluoridation is an example of a valuable public health measure which will not be progressed by any behavioural change in the general population. Nonetheless, social marketing has a key role to play: its concepts of consumer orientation, voluntary involvement and mutually beneficial exchange are still very useful. In this case the key consumers are local authorities and water companies, whose co-operation can be encouraged by emphasizing the benefits to them of fluoridation. Market research showed these to differ for the two groups.

The local government authorities were not interested in public health, at least for its own sake, and being, Labour-dominated, had no love for health authorities or their (Conservative) government-inspired policies. Their main concern was to represent and meet the needs of their constituents. If they were going to 'buy' fluoridation, their interest in and ownership of it would need to be stimulated by emphasizing the benefits that fluoridation would bring to their voters and by reminding them that the first UK fluoridation schemes, back in the 1960s, had been introduced by local authorities, not health authorities. In short, if they were going to buy it, fluoridation had to meet their political needs.

Similarly, the private water companies were not interested in public health. They wanted to provide their customers with clean, wholesome water, and their shareholders with a reasonable return. However, they were interested in helping the government carry out its policies, retaining good relationships with public health professionals in their area and positive public relations. At a more practical level, they also needed a fluoridation product that met their technical requirements: that would suit their existing plant and have an acceptable safety standard, for example. They needed more than the basic 'benefit to the public' product that would satisfy the local authorities.

Finally segmentation and targeting ensured that the correct fluoridation product was marketed to the two customer groups.

Adapted from: Hastings *et al.* (1998a)

Behavioural influence theories confirm that environmental factors, as well as individual characteristics, determine behaviour. For example, social cognitive theory (Maibach and Cotton, 1995), posits that health behaviour change occurs as a consequence of a number of personal factors (knowledge, skills, self-efficacy, outcome expectations and personal goals) and environmental factors (social, institutional and physical). Marketing theory also distinguishes between the immediate environment and the wider social context (Hastings and Haywood, 1994).

Similarly, when Wallack talks about 'upstream' activity (Wallack *et al.*, 1993) he is arguing that in some situations it is more effective for social marketers to deal with the upstream determinants of the behaviour they want to change, than with the downstream manifestations of that behaviour. To stop young people from smoking the social marketer should direct attention not at the young people but at the tobacco industry which encourages them to smoke and at the retailers who sell them cigarettes. In short, Wallack argues that we should be seeking to address flaws, not in the 'loose thread of the individual', but in the 'fabric of society' (Wallack *et al.*,1993, p. 69). Wallack overstates his case. Good social marketers should do both. Figure 25.2 shows how this might operate for adolescent smoking.

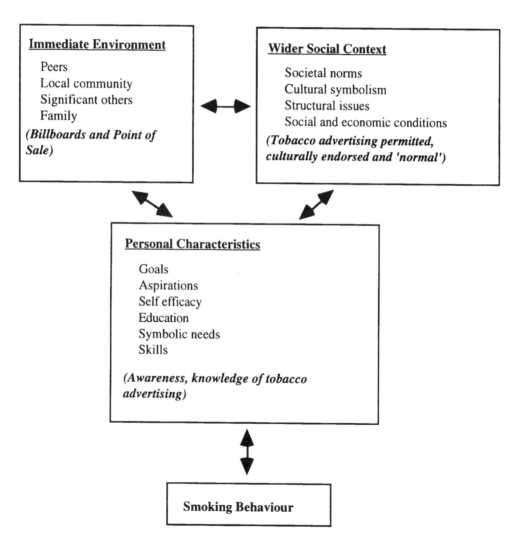

Source: MacFadyen *et al.* (1998)

Figure 25.2   How tobacco advertising may influence children's smoking

Departures from commercial marketing

The last section highlighted the common features of social and commercial marketing, and showed that these lead to broadly similar strategic processes. However there are also important differences between the two approaches. Specifically, in social marketing:

- The products tend to be more complex.
- Demand is more varied.
- Target groups are more challenging to reach.
- Consumer involvement is more intense.
- The competition is more subtle and varied.

These differences have an important impact on the ways in which social marketing plans are implemented. The remainder of this section will look at the differences between social and commercial marketing in more detail. The subsequent sections will then examine the influence they have on the use of the two key marketing tools: segmentation and the marketing mix.

(i) The products are more complex
The marketing product has traditionally been conceived of as something tangible – a physical good which can be exchanged with the target market for a price and which can be manipulated in terms of characteristics such as packaging, name, physical attributes, positioning and so on. As marketing has extended its scope beyond physical goods, marketers have had to grapple with formulating product strategy for less tangible entities such as services (see Chapter 29 in this volume for a discussion of the characteristics of services; Woodruffe, 1995). In social marketing, the product is extended even further from the tangible to encompass ideas, and behaviour change. Figure 25.3 illustrates the different types of social marketing product.

Under behaviour, Kotler and Roberto (1989) distinguish between adoption of a single act (having a cholesterol check) and adoption of a sustained practice (changing one's diet). A further distinction could be made between adoption of a new behaviour (taking up jogging), desistence from a current behaviour (giving up drinking), and non-adoption of a future behaviour (not taking drugs). In practice, the behavioural objective may be some combination of these. So, for example, a driving safety initiative may seek both to prevent drivers from drink-driving (desistence) and to encourage them to use a designated-driver system (adoption).

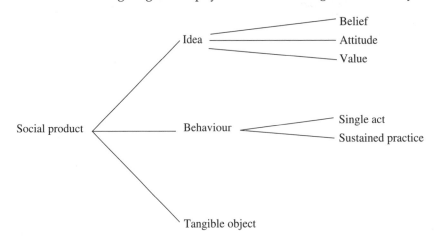

(Adapted from: Kotler and Roberto 1989)

Figure 25.3   The social marketing product

Even where the behaviour change being sought by the social marketer involves a tangible object (the third category) such as condoms, Kotler and Roberto point out that the social marketer is not in the business of selling condoms per se, but of selling a change in attitudes (more favourable beliefs about condom use) or behaviour (correct use of condoms) in order to bring about the social or health benefit which condom use can confer – improved reproductive and sexual health and more satisfying relationships. Kotler and Roberto (1989) caution that family planning social marketers 'who say their product is a condom misunderstand their market' (p. 140).

As a partial solution to this difficulty, some commentators suggest conceptualizing a 'core product' such as 'safer driving' (Kotler and Zaltman, 1971, p. 7), which may be accompanied by a range of 'buyable' products and services such as road safety campaigns, driver training and transport policies which contribute to the objective. Fine (1981) suggests a similar conceptualization, in which a 'class of products' – e.g. 'education' – might comprise various product 'forms', such as adult education classes, literacy training and so on.

This complexity makes social marketing products difficult to conceptualize. As a consequence, social marketers have a bigger task in defining exactly what their product is and the benefits associated with its use. This is discussed further in the section on the marketing mix, below.

(ii) Varied demand

Marketing cannot create needs but commercial marketers do manage to harness needs previously unknown for new product categories such as CDs, catalytic converters and 'new' washing powders. Social marketers must not only uncover new demand, but in addition must frequently deal with negative demand when the target group is apathetic about or strongly resistant to a proposed behaviour change. Young recreational drug users, for instance, may see no problems with their current behaviour

(Andreasen, 1997). In these situations, social marketers must challenge entrenched attitudes and beliefs. De-marketing approaches may help here (Lawther *et al.*, 1997; Hastings *et al.*, 1994a).

Rangun *et al.* (1996) suggest a typology of the benefits associated with a behaviour change. The benefits may be: tangible, intangible, relevant to the individual or relevant to society. Demand is easier to generate where the benefits are both tangible and personally relevant. In those situations where the product benefits are intangible and relevant to society rather than the individual (as with CFCs in aerosols), social marketers must work much harder to generate a need for the product. This, they argue, is the hardest type of behaviour change, as the benefits are difficult to personalize and quantify.

(iii) Challenging target groups

Social marketers must often target groups whom commercial marketers tend to ignore: the least accessible, hardest to reach and least likely to change their behaviour. For example, health agencies charged with improving population health status must, if they are to avoid widening health inequalities further in the general population (Whitehead, 1992; Smith, R., 1997), target their efforts at those groups with the poorest health and the most needs (Hastings *et al.*, 1998b). Far from being the most profitable market segments, these groups often constitute the least attractive ones: hardest to reach, most resistant to changing health behaviour, most lacking in the psychological, social and practical resources necessary to make the change, most unresponsive to interventions to influence their behaviour and so on. This poses considerable challenges for segmentation and targeting, as discussed later in the chapter. Case 3 illustrates the problem vividly.

(iv) Greater consumer involvement

Marketing traditionally divides products into high and low involvement categories, with the former comprising purchases for items such as cars or mortgages which are 'expensive, bought

---

Case 3:   Cervical screening: barriers to segmentation in social marketing

A public health department wishes to encourage women within a certain age range in the health authority area to attend for cervical screening. There are a number of possible ways in which this population can be segmented, including:

- socio-demographic (social class, education, income, employment);
- psychographic (beliefs re. preventive health, fatalism, attitudes towards health services);
- health behaviour (smokers/non-smokers etc.);
- previous usage behaviour (attendance for screening); and so on.

From available secondary research into the characteristics of attenders and non-attenders for cervical and other screening (e.g. Thorogood et al., 1993; Austoker et al., 1997; Sugg Skinner et al., 1994), the public health department could make certain assumptions about the women most likely to respond positively to the programme: ABC1, well-educated, in work, positive beliefs about ability to protect oneself from cancer, favourable attitudes towards health service and so on. If the screening programme were to be run as a profit-making service, this would be the segment to target. The screening agency could develop messages consonant with these women's beliefs, deliver them through workplaces at which the women are most likely to be employed, utilize media most likely to be consumed by them, and so forth. However, the health authority's objective is not to run the most profitable screening service possible but to make the biggest possible impact on public health by reducing incidence of cervical cancer. To do this, the screening programme needs to reach those groups with the highest risk of cancer – the groups who, the same research shows, are the least likely to attend for screening.

---

infrequently, risky and highly self-expressive' (Kotler, 1994) and the latter comprising items such as confectionery or cigarettes which are much more habitual. High involvement products typically command careful consideration by the consumer ('central processing') and demand detailed factual information from the marketer. Low involvement products are consumed much more passively, with very limited (or no) search and evaluation ('peripheral processing'), and simple advertising emphasizing 'visual symbols and imagery' (Kotler, 1994) is called for.

Or, as Petty *et al.* (1988) expressed it, for high involvement products consumers are attracted by the tangible attributes of the products, the 'steak', but for low involvement purchases, consumers are more attracted by the intangible qualities or the 'sizzle'.

Both the categorization scheme – high and low – and its marketing implications need to be extended in social marketing. Social marketing frequently deals with products with which the consumer is very highly involved (complex lifestyle changes such as changing one's diet fall into this category). While high involvement can result in a motivated and attentive consumer, higher involvement may be associated with feelings of anxiety, guilt and denial which inhibit attempts to change. At the other extreme, social marketers might seek to stimulate change where there is very low or no involvement – for example, persuading Scots to save water. Thus taking the example of smoking, involvement can be divided into at least four levels:

- *Very high, or hyper involvement:* the smoker who can't quit despite deep concern about the consequences of continuing, and is typically in a state of defensive denial.
- *High involvement:* the smoker who is motivated and struggling with some success to quit.

- *Low involvement*: the smoker who knows of the consequences of smoking but does not care enough about them to make the decision to quit.
- *Very low involvement*: the smoker who is unaware of the health risks and has never considered quitting.

In addition, there may be an additional category of *negative involvement* amongst those who see the health risks and forbidden nature of tobacco as part of its attraction.

The type of campaign that will address these categories cannot be determined by simply applying marketing's rubric that 'the greater involvement, the greater the need for factual information'. For example, very low involvement may well respond well to factual information and hyper involvement to emotional messages offering reassurance and empowerment.

(v) More varied competition

Social marketers, like their commercial counterparts, must be aware of their competition (Andreasen, 1995). The most obvious source of competition in social marketing is the consumer's tendency to continue in his or her current behavioural patterns, especially when addiction is involved. Inertia is a very powerful competitor.

Other sources of competition involve alternative behaviours. For example, time spent donating blood is time which the consumer could spend doing other more enjoyable, more convenient and more personally beneficial activities.

Competitive organizations include other health promoters, educators or government organizations trying to use similar methods to reach their target audiences. For example, the typical doctor's surgery in the UK displays such a plethora of leaflets and posters that any one message or idea stands little chance of being noticed. Social marketers must then be innovative and careful not to overwhelm their target audience.

Finally, one of the most serious forms of competition comes from commercial marketing itself where this markets unhealthful or unsocial behaviours. The most obvious examples are the tobacco and alcohol industries.

In summary, therefore, social marketing differs in a number of ways from commercial marketing. These differences have a big impact on implementation and the next two sections look specifically at how this is manifested in segmentation and the use of the marketing mix.

Segmentation in social marketing

The particular characteristics of social marketing create a number of barriers to segmentation and a need for specialized segmentation criteria (see also Chapter 9). These phenomena are discussed in turn.

(i) Barriers to segmentation in social marketing

Despite the importance of segmentation, many social marketing programmes employ 'undifferentiated target marketing' (Andreasen, 1995, p. 174), treating the target group as a relatively homogeneous mass for whom a single strategy is developed, or adopting relatively basic segmentation approaches based on simple demographic variables such as age or gender (see Chapter 9). This limited application of segmentation is attributable to a number of factors:

- *Ambitious objectives*: Social marketing is typically concerned with ambitious objectives (e.g. reduce incidence of dental caries) which involve targeting very large populations (e.g. all parents of children under five).
- *The operating environment*: Social marketing organizations are much more subject to political and policy demands than commercial organizations. A national body may be required by statute to deliver a programme to the whole population, or it may be local public health policy to target an initiative at a whole population sub-group (for example, in the UK mammography screening programmes are

required to target all women over 50). In this environment, it is difficult for a social marketing organization to concentrate resources on specific market segments even where this would increase the likelihood of effectiveness.

- *Culture*: There may be cultural and philosophical resistance to the idea of segmentation (Bloom and Novelli, 1981); for example, it may be seen as unethical for a health professional, in offering a product to one particular market segment, to withhold it by implication from another. Alternatively, segmentation on the basis of need can lead to accusations of discrimination and stigmatization.
- *Resources*: Finally, social marketing organizations may lack an understanding of the potential of more sophisticated segmentation approaches, the information on which to base such approaches, or the skills and resources to implement them (Andreasen, 1995; Currence, 1997).

Some of these barriers are surmountable, particularly those in the fourth category. Social marketers can acquire better understanding of the potential and uses of segmentation, and as social marketing evolves, lessons learnt will disseminate through the field, as in commercial marketing. Useful segmentation case studies such as the '5-a-Day' initiative to promote fruit and vegetable consumption (see Case 4) and the American Cancer Society's campaign to promote mammography screening, which utilized sophisticated database information (Currence, 1997), are already contributing to this.

In addition, social marketers may have access to other valuable – and free – databases themselves. For example, in the UK, health promoters may be able to use the National Health Service patient register, either on its own or combined with additional information of the sort outlined in Case 4.

However, the other barriers to segmentation are more fundamental. For example, as already discussed, because of the nature of their objectives, social marketers have less freedom than commercial marketers to choose target segments.

Ethical considerations may also prevent a social marketer from targeting a particular segment even where this segment is identifiable,

---

Case 4:   '5 A Day for Better Health' – segmentation in a social marketing programme

This programme in the USA aiming to increase fruit and vegetable consumption was one of the first large applications of marketing database technology to a health promotion initiative (Lefebvre *et al.*, 1995). Quantitative and qualitative research was conducted before programme planning to quantify the nature of the problem, to explore possible messages, and to begin to identify potential segments. This information was then augmented by data collected annually from the Market Research Corporation of America's survey of 2000 representative US households' food consumption, attitudes, interests, lifestyle and media habits. Data from the survey were analysed to profile two population segments, those eating five fruit and vegetables a day and those eating around three a day, in the contemplation stage (i.e. reportedly trying to eat more) (Prochaska and DiClemente, 1983). This latter was the target group.

To refine this profile further, the intervention planners added a question on previous day's fruit and vegetable consumption to an omnibus survey, the DDB Needham Lifestyle Survey of 4000 individuals. From these two information sources, people in the target group could be identified as impulse buyers who led hectic lives with little spare time. Their media habits were also described. As a result of this profiling, the intervention planners could not only build up a clear 'visual representation of the target' (Lefebvre *et al.*, 1995, p. 233), but could also develop a 'personality' or 'tonality' for the campaign (p. 224), and choose appropriate communication materials and channels.

<table>
<tr><td colspan="2">

Case 5: **Ethical problems in social marketing segmentation**

A government social marketing initiative in the north-east of England is seeking to reduce adolescent drug use and associated harm through a social cognitive schools and media programme (Home Office, 1998). Drugs prevention literature indicates that current drug use status is an important variable which should be addressed in designing such programmes: the most effective interventions are those which, among other things, target users and non-users separately with product offerings tailored to their current experiences and attitudes regarding drugs (Bandy and President, 1983; Makkai *et al.*, 1991; Werch and DiClemente, 1994). However, had the programme developed a range of intervention components for young people already using drugs – who could in principle have been identified from extensive baseline data gathered on the target population before the programme began – it would never have secured the necessary cooperation of the schools, communities and parents who understandably would not have wanted their young people to be labelled as drug users (Stead *et al.*, 1997a). Building and managing the relationship with these key gatekeepers and stakeholders was critical to the programme's existence. The only option was to adopt a non-stigmatizing undifferentiated targeting strategy – offering the programme to all young people in all schools in the area.

</td></tr>
</table>

accessible, and the most in need. Case 5 illustrates how a government drugs prevention initiative using social marketing principles was unable overtly to target young drug users for fear of stigmatization. In this instance, a partial solution was found by combining blanket targeting with self-selection, whereby young people with particular interests and needs could 'opt in' to certain components, such as peer-led workshops (Home Office, 1998). The assumption is that small groups with similar interests and experiences regarding drugs will naturally gravitate towards suitably tailored offerings.

(ii) Segmentation criteria in social marketing
Commercial marketers typically segment according to three broad criteria: personal characteristics, behavioural characteristics and benefits sought by consumers (Wilkie, 1994), all of which are relevant to social marketers. They are illustrated in Table 25.2, along with some additional attributes which are of particular relevance to social marketing.

Table 25.2 Major segmentation approaches

Characteristics		Attributes	Social marketing
	Demographic	Age, Gender, Social class, Ethnicity, Family profile, Income, Employment	+ Health status
Personal	Psychographic	Lifestyle, Personality	+ Health beliefs, motivation, locus of control
	Geodemographic	Geographical area, Neighbourhood type	+ Residence in disadvantaged area
Behavioural		Usage, Loyalty, Response, Attitudes	+ Health behaviour, Stage of Change
Benefits		Benefits sought	+Barriers

1 Personal characteristics The relevance of *demographic* segmentation to social marketing is widely accepted. As noted at the beginning of the chapter, for many health and social problems, the main predictors of mortality, morbidity, health behaviour and health risk continue to be demographic. The role of poverty has already been highlighted, but ethnicity (Kochanek *et al.*, 1994), gender (for types of cancer and for coronary heart disease), and age (for the prevention of substance and tobacco use) are also very significant. Existing health status may be an additional characteristic addressed in this classification; for example, health promotion programmes may be directed at people with asthma or diabetes (so called secondary prevention).

Moving beyond basic demographic characteristics, the application of *psychographic* segmentation in social marketing is less well-established. However, its relevance is clear. Many of the major causes of mortality and morbidity in the developed world are lifestyle-related, and health promoters have in the last twenty years or so re-oriented their efforts from a focus on specific disease prevention to a focus on the lifestyle risk factors which impact on a wide range of disease – exercise, nutrition, smoking, drinking, safer sex. Knowing that middle aged C2DE men are at most risk of coronary heart disease is not sufficient: the social marketer needs to understand why some men in this group are motivated to engage in lifestyle behaviours which are protective of their health and why others are not, and to develop product offerings accordingly. Social marketers need to adopt segmentation approaches that acknowledge the complex psycho-social determinants of health behaviour (Slater, 1995).

Information which enables the social marketer to distinguish between targets on the basis of their values, beliefs and norms is also important. Various behaviour change theories, such as the theory of reasoned action (Fishbein and Ajzen, 1975), social learning theory (Bandura, 1977, 1986) and social cognitive theory (Maibach and Cotton, 1995) have posited that traits such

as attitudes and norms influence adoption of health and risk behaviours (e.g. Manstead, 1991; Fishbein *et al.*, 1997). Increasingly these theories are being adopted as the theoretical basis for segmented social marketing interventions (e.g. Fishbein *et al.*, 1997).

2 Geodemographics Geodemographics is the classification of people on the basis of where they live (Sleight, 1995). The geographical distribution of much ill-health (e.g. Whitehead, 1992; Smith, R., 1997) and the clustering of health and social problems in certain areas, particularly urban areas of deprivation (e.g. Glasgow City Council 1998), suggest that this approach can contribute usefully to social marketing. Obvious applications of geodemographics to social marketing are in selecting channels for health advertising, identifying locations for health services, and direct mail.

A number of syndicated geodemographic information systems have been developed in the commercial marketing context (Sleight, 1995). While these are already proving to be useful to social marketers, public health is very often most concerned with geodemographic segments who are of least interest to many commercial marketers – the very poor. Classification systems such as ACORN and MOSAIC provide socio-economic indicators of small areas, and these can be combined with classification systems such as the Carstairs index for Scotland (McLoone, 1991) which provide a measure of affluence or deprivation within postcode sectors. Measures of deprivation such as housing tenure, telephone and car ownership and financial status can also be incorporated to provide accurate targeting data for social marketers.

3 Behavioural characteristics In commercial marketing, behavioural characteristics may include volume of product usage – heavy, medium, light users – transactional history (previous usage), readiness to use, responsiveness, and attitudes towards usage (Wilkie, 1994).

Again, these categories are of relevance to social marketing. Social marketers planning an initiative to encourage participation in a health promotion clinic could segment on the basis of current health behaviour, previous usage of health clinics, frequency of GP consultation and so on. Health service records held by GP practices and health authorities provide valuable information on patients' previous transactions with health services as well as on their current health behaviours (e.g. smoking, drinking, use of medicines).

A particularly important behavioural characteristic in social marketing is the concept of readiness to change. The transtheoretical model of behaviour change (Prochaska and DiClemente, 1983) posits that behaviour change is not a discrete event, but a process that occurs through several stages: precontemplation, contemplation, preparation, action and maintenance. The model was initially developed to explain smoking cessation behaviour, but has since been applied to smoking, alcohol and drug addiction, weight control and eating disorders, safer sex behaviour, exercise participation, mammography screening, sunscreen use and other health behaviours (Prochaska *et al.*, 1994). During precontemplation, individuals either do not want to change their behaviour or are unaware of its consequences for themselves or others. During contemplation, they begin to think about the costs and benefits of changing their behaviour. In preparation, the individual is motivated to change and makes initial mental and practical preparations. During the action stage the individual is in the process of changing, following which he or she may either proceed to maintenance or relapse to an earlier state.

The model is helpful in two ways. First, it emphasizes that behaviour change is complex and multi-staged, and that relapse may occur a number of times. Second, it provides a framework for designing appropriate messages and support interventions. By understanding the target audience's readiness to change, the social marketer can develop strategies appropriate to the group's needs and wants (Werch and DiClemente, 1994). For example, Andreasen (1995) proposes a series of marketing tasks for each stage of change. During precontemplation, the marketer must create awareness and interest

in the behaviour and it may be necessary to try to shift value and belief systems. During contemplation the marketer must persuade and motivate to enhance the benefits of the behaviour (e.g. mobilize social influence) and reduce the costs associated with change (time, effort or money). Andreasen deals with preparation and action stages simultaneously, and proposes that marketers must focus on creating action by, for example, focusing on skills training exercises or confidence building. Finally, to maintain change, social marketers should consider reducing cognitive dissonance through reinforcement.

4 Benefit characteristics Classification by benefit sought is specific to the particular product being marketed; for example, the market for cigarettes could be segmented on the basis of those who seek status (e.g. smokers of exclusive brands of cigarettes and cigars), those who need a cost effective nicotine fix (e.g. established smokers), and those who seek reassuringly mainstream smokes (e.g. adolescents).

This type of segmentation analysis seems at first glance to have less relevance in social marketing than the preceding three types. Social marketing targets very often do not welcome efforts to ameliorate their health and social circumstances (Levy and Zaltman, 1975), and if they are fundamentally resistant to changing behaviour may see no benefits in the messages and support being offered to them to facilitate this process. However, social marketers still need to think in terms of consumers and the benefits they seek rather than products. For example, Case 6 shows how benefit segmentation enhanced an attempt to influence oral health in Scotland. The target (retailers) was segmented on the basis of function (marketing staff, space planners and buyers) and different product benefits identified for each. This case also illustrates how important segmentation is when targeting not only the final consumer, but also those decision makers who can influence their operating environment.

Another example is exercise. A comparative study into younger and older people's perceptions of exercise (Stead *et al.*, 1997b) found

Case 6:   The immediate environment – a case of candy

A recent attempt to redress the appalling oral health record of five-year-old children in west, central Scotland examined one immediate environmental influence on confectionery consumption – the availability of candy at supermarket checkouts.

Scotland is renowned for its sweet tooth and Scottish children consume 28 per cent more confectionery than their counterparts in the rest of the UK. Candy is frequently used to reward or pacify children who come to associate comfort or praise with these sweet and familiar foodstuffs, thereby reinforcing their liking for them. Children often successfully 'pester' their parents for candy in supermarkets and shops. The strategic positioning of candy at the till-points greatly exacerbates this problem.

Research was conducted to inform a policy which would address the problem of confectionery at till-points. An audit of store policy and in-depth interviews with policy makers was conducted. This work identified the group of decision makers within each organization and the criteria for making space allocation decisions.

It was found that space planning decisions were rigorous and predictable: confectionery was placed at the point of sale to maximize profits from the available space. Three broad groups with an interest in confectionery policy were identified – marketers, space planners and buyers – and the barriers to adopting a confectionery policy reflected each party's needs. The research concluded that any initiative must demonstrate customer loyalty (to satisfy marketers), be profitable (to satisfy space planners) and offer long-term profitability for the products and alternative merchandising arrangements (to satisfy buyers). As a result, possible initiatives to remove confectionery from the immediate environment are being explored including: endorsement schemes, community partnerships and public opinion surveys.

	Marketing staff	*Space planners*	*Buyers*
Exchange	Customer loyalty	Profitability	Supply relationships
Intervention	Endorsement schemes	Economic Benefits	Long-term profitability
	Public opinion surveys	Competitive advantage	Alternative merchandising strategies

that different sub-groups perceived different benefits in the product 'physical activity': some, typically younger men, wanted to compete against an opponent while others aimed to better their own personal targets – to run faster or swim further for example. A third group was most concerned with body image and a fourth enjoyed the prospect of meeting new people, maintaining friendships, and just 'getting out'.

These benefit segments formed the basis of a targeted strategy to encourage physical activity.

The same research also examined perceived and actual barriers to participation in exercise. Again, it was possible to differentiate between segments whose lifestyle, health, health beliefs, personal circumstances and awareness prevented their involvement in exercise, to develop appropriate communication and support strategies for each segment. Given the type of 'negative demand' social marketers often face (see 'Departures from commercial marketing' above), barrier segmentation is perhaps of particular value to social marketers.

It also suggests that social marketers should go one step further, and, despite the potential philosophical problems noted above, segment their markets in terms of need. As well as bringing the standard segmentation benefits, this will ensure that limited resources are used most efficiently. Need can be classified in a number of ways. Andreasen (1995) suggests that three factors should be considered: problem incidence (rates of need or problem per segment), problem severity (severity of need or problem per segment), and 'population defencelessness', ability per segment to cope with the problem or need (p. 177).

The social marketing mix

The marketing mix (see Chapter 12) also has to be adapted for use in social marketing. This section examines the relevance and application of each element of the mix (see Table 25.3).

(i) Product

As described above, social marketing products are frequently intangible and complex behaviours. This makes it difficult to formulate simple, meaningful product concepts (Bloom and Novelli, 1981). To take an example, 'reducing one's fat intake' is a complex behaviour in a number of ways: it involves a change in food choice, menu design, shopping behaviour, food preparation, personal habits, family routines, wider social norms and so on. Further, it is a behaviour which needs to be practised not just

Table 25.3   The social marketing mix

Tool		Types
Product	The offer made to target adopters	Adoption of idea (belief, attitude, value) Adoption of behaviour (one-off, sustained) Desistence from current behaviour Non-adoption of future behaviour
Price	The costs that target adopters have to bear	Psychological, emotional, cultural, social, behavioural, temporal, practical, physical, financial
Place	The channels by which the change is promoted and places in which the change is supported and encouraged	Media channels Distribution channels Interpersonal channels Physical places Non-physical places (e.g. social and cultural climate)
Promotion	The means by which the change is promoted to the target	Advertising Public relations Media advocacy Direct mail Interpersonal

Adapted from Kotler and Roberto, 1989 p. 44

once but repeated and sustained over a long period of time (Kotler and Roberto, 1989). As a first step towards formulating product concepts, social marketers need to identify and clarify their product attributes. In commercial marketing, product attributes range on a continuum from the tangible (colour, taste, shape, size, packaging, performance) to the intangible (brand, image, status). Social marketing product attributes are largely situated at the intangible end of this continuum. Some potential classifications of product attributes are suggested below:

- *Trialability*: Can the behaviour be tried out beforehand before permanent or full adoption (e.g. wearing a cycling helmet)?
- *Ease*: How easy or difficult is it to adopt the behaviour (wearing a seat belt versus giving up smoking)?
- *Risks*: What are the risks of adopting the behaviour?
- *Image*: Is the behaviour attractive or unattractive?
- *Acceptability*: Is the behaviour socially acceptable?
- *Duration*: Is the behaviour to be practised once or repeatedly? Is it to be sustained over a short or long term?
- *Cost*: Does the behaviour have a financial cost or not (eating a healthier diet may involve more expense, drinking less alcohol does not)?

Analysing product attributes in this way helps social marketers to formulate meaningful and communicable product concepts. For example, in addressing teen smoking, research may suggest that image is a key issue, rather than the avoidance of health risks. The social marketer can then put particular emphasis on producing non-smoking options that are cool and trendy – such as freedom of choice – rather than ones that major on the health benefits of quitting.

A second major potential problem with the product for social marketers is flexibility. It is commonly argued that social marketers have less flexibility than commercial marketers in

shaping their product offerings (Bloom and Novelli, 1981), for a number of reasons. First, the resources, technology and skills to develop alternative products may not be as readily available to the social marketer as they are in commercial marketing, so the range of product innovation options is smaller. Fox and Kotler (1980) note that the anti-smoking social marketer seeking to develop the most attractive substitute product really should invent a safe cigarette, but is constrained by technological, financial and political factors. Second, product offerings may be constrained by political factors outwith the social marketer's control. Government policy or local public health strategy may dictate that only one behaviour or way of practising the behaviour should be endorsed. For example, harm minimization, as opposed to abstention, solutions to the problem of drug abuse may be unacceptable in certain political climates.

Thirdly, social marketing's offerings often appear to be 'absolutes' in that the social or health benefit pertains only if the behaviour is adopted wholesale (so partial or temporary adoption is not possible) or is adopted in one particular form (so different forms of the behaviour cannot be marketed to different adopter groups). An example of such an absolute is smoking, where only total abstinence produces meaningful health benefits, as opposed to drinking, where different moderation messages can be promoted. Immunization and fluoridation of the public water supply are also examples of absolutes.

However, many other social marketing offerings are 'relative', in that a health or social benefit accrues even if the behaviour is adopted only in a moderate way. Exercise by elderly people is one example (Stead *et al.*, 1997b). Nutrition is another instance where social marketers can develop a wide range of product offerings for different target segments: the fruit and vegetable consumption programme outlined in Case 4 above is one such example.

Furthermore, even in the case of absolute products, although social marketers may have limited control over the fundamental aspects of their offerings, they do, like commercial marketers, have potential control over how their products are perceived and positioned. For example, in Case 2 above, different water fluoridation products were offered to local councils and water companies.

(ii) Price

Only a few of social marketing's products have a monetary price (condoms are an obvious example: see Harvey (1997) and Dahl *et al.*, (1997) for discussion of pricing strategy in contraceptive social marketing). However, there are almost always costs associated with behaviour change which act as obstacles to marketing social change; these may be financial, time, embarrassment, effort, inertia, pain, perceived social exclusion (e.g. Marteau, 1990). However, there should be benefits also. These may be tangible and personal benefits such as a longer life or intangible, societal benefits such as a better environment. Rangun *et al.*, (1996) argue that there are four broad types of social marketing initiatives according to this cost–benefit analysis:

(i) *Low cost and tangible, personal benefits*, e.g. cervical screening for women. In this case the target perceives clear, direct benefits to themselves. As change is easy, relative to the three other types of initiative, communication and information are key elements of the social marketing strategy.

(ii) *Low cost and intangible, societal benefits*, e.g. recycling programmes. Here the behavioural change is relatively easy to adopt, but the benefits are not perceived to be as relevant to the individual. The authors argue that convenience is the key to this type of programme and the ultimate benefit to the target and to society should be stressed.

(iii) *High cost and tangible, personal benefits*, e.g. smoking cessation programmes. In this case there is a very clear personal benefit to adopting the suggested behaviour, but the costs associated with doing so are high. It is suggested that the social marketer adopts a strong 'push marketing' approach supported by communications campaigns and community level initiatives.

(iv) *High cost and intangible, societal benefits*, e.g. CFCs in aerosols. This is clearly the hardest type of behaviour change to induce as the costs are high and the benefits are hard to personalize and quantify. In this case, it may be necessary to adopt de-marketing approaches, use moral persuasion or social influence.

(iii) Place

Kotler and Zaltman (1971) suggest that place should be defined in social marketing as encompassing distribution and response channels, and 'clear action outlets for those motivated to acquire the product' (p. 9). Where there is a communications element to a social marketing initiative – for example, television advertising, outdoor advertising, direct mail, health education leaflets – place applies to the media channels through which messages are to be delivered. Place can also apply to distribution channels where a social marketing programme has a tangible product base (e.g. condoms, needle exchanges). In these two instances and in social marketing programmes where a specific service is being offered – for example, an antenatal class or workplace smoking cessation group – place variables such as channel, coverage, cost, timing (Kotler and Roberto, 1989), location, transport (Woodruffe, 1995) and accessibility (Cowell, 1994) are all relevant. For example, an initiative to increase uptake of cervical screening could reduce the costs of attending by manipulating the place variables of distance, time, and convenience (offering screening at flexible times and in different locations).

In addition, many social marketing initiatives depend on intermediaries such as health professionals, pharmacists, teachers, and community workers to act as distribution channels for media materials or as retailers for a particular behaviour change product – for example, GPs are often given responsibility for changing smoking and drinking behaviour (Kotler and Roberto, 1989). Where intermediaries are to act primarily as distribution agents for media products, key variables such as accessibility and appropriateness should be considered. When these intermediaries have a more complex role (e.g. youth workers and teachers delivering a sex education curriculum), place variables such as source visibility, credibility, attractiveness and power (Percy, 1983; Hastings and Stead, in press) should guide the selection of appropriate agents and inform the sort of support and training which is offered to them. For example, the drugs prevention literature has examined the relative merits of teachers, youth workers, police and peers as delivery channels for drugs prevention messages (e.g. Bandy and President, 1983; Shiner and Newburn, 1996).

Social marketers are often dependent on the goodwill and co-operation of intermediaries for access to their end targets. This is particularly the case when dealing with sensitive health issues or with vulnerable groups such as young people, where there is usually a need to communicate not only with young people themselves but also with key groups such as parents, teachers and politicians. These groups may act as 'gatekeepers', controlling or influencing the distribution of a message to a target group, or as 'stakeholders', taking an interest in and scrutinizing the activities of the prevention agency (McGrath, 1995). If an initiative is to be effective, it needs to satisfy the information and other needs of these two groups and to maintain their support. Communicating with gatekeepers and stakeholders is therefore just as important as communicating with the direct target group, and it should be approached in the same way in order to be effective (Hastings and Stead, in press).

In Table 25.1, one category of social marketing objectives is concerned with influencing policy and social norms. Here, 'place' becomes the centres of influence on public opinion and policy. In this context media advocacy is likely to become particularly important (see below).

(iv) Promotion

Of the four marketing mix tools, promotion has received the most attention in social marketing.

Indeed, the prominence of social advertising in social marketing practice and literature has contributed to a tendency among non-marketers to perceive the two as synonymous (Stead and Hastings, 1997; Sutton, 1991; Andreasen, 1994). In turn, this perception has given rise to criticisms of social marketing as ineffective because media interventions alone are deemed to be insufficient to change behaviour (Tones, 1994), expensive and difficult to do well (Bloom and Novelli, 1981; Stead and Hastings, 1997) and lacking new insights (Tones, 1994).

Three decades of mass media social advertising campaigns on smoking prevention, smoking cessation, exercise, nutrition, drug use, safer sex and other health issues have refined theoretical and practical understanding of how communication campaigns should be developed, designed, targeted, implemented and evaluated in order to have the best impact on public awareness, opinions and behaviour (e.g. Atkin and Freimuth, 1989; Backer *et al.*, 1992; Flay, 1987; Hastings and Haywood, 1991; Leathar, 1988; Maibach and Cotton, 1995; Reid, 1996; Slater, 1995; Solomon, 1989; Worden *et al.*, 1996). The conclusions are broadly in accord with mainstream marketing communication theory, so require no repetition here (see Chapter 17).

However two aspects of social marketing communication do warrant further examination: branding and media advocacy. The first because it is underdeveloped in the social sector and would benefit from further thought by mainstream marketers, and the second because it is well advanced in social marketing and therefore may provide some useful insights.

Branding

In commercial marketing, branding (see Chapter 16) provides a crucial means of enhancing the product. Brands are deliberately designed to hone the emotional benefits of the product, thereby adding value and encouraging consumption and loyalty.

Similar thinking can be applied in social marketing. For example, Lefebvre (1996) argues that all health communications have an emotional dimension – a 'personality' or 'tonality' – whether the health promoter intends it or not. The message, channel and execution all contribute to this. He cautions that health communicators – just like their commercial counterparts – must use research, design and careful targeting to ensure that the tonality matches the needs of their target audience.

Leathar (1981) and Monahan (1995) endorse the notion that health communicators should actively promote positive images about health. For example Monahan concludes her paper:

Positive affect can be used to stress the benefits of healthy behaviour, to give individuals a sense of control, and to reduce anxiety or fear. All of these tactics are likely to enhance the success of a communication campaign.

On a more specific level, qualitative research conducted with pregnant women (Bolling and Owen, 1997) also emphasizes the importance of emotional communication, concluding that messages have to be sympathetic, supportive and non-judgmental. The primary need, the research suggested, is to establish a sense of trust.

Taking things a step further, social marketers have also adopted the idea of branding. Case 7 describes an attempt to brand positive health in Scotland during the 1980s. The brand was called 'Be All You Can Be'.

Media advocacy

Another channel by which social marketers seek to influence public opinion and policy makers is via unpaid publicity in the mass media. This involves negotiating with and satisfying media gatekeepers: newspaper editors and journalists, television and radio producers, advertising regulation authorities. Health promoters often see the mass media and themselves as having conflicting priorities (e.g. Atkin and Arkin, 1990). However, generating effective unpaid publicity relies not only on producing the 'right' message or story but on tailoring the message or

---

Case 7: Branding in social marketing.

During the 1980s, SHEG, the government body responsible for health education in Scotland, were facing three problems with their use of the media. Their campaigns tended to be fragmented, topic based rather than whole person oriented and authoritarian rather than empathetic. Material seemed to be telling people how to run their lives, rather than enabling and encouraging them to make their own informed health decisions.

These problems could not be solved within individual campaigns, however carefully pretested or creatively developed. It was therefore decided to develop an overview or 'umbrella' campaign that could communicate a general lifestyle message of empowerment. In addition the campaign needed to link the positive imagery to clear solutions to real health problems – that is, provide branded health products. The result was 'Be All You Can Be', a communication campaign which ran in broadcast and print media, promoting a theme of empowerment and positive health. An extensive communication and awareness monitor showed that it became familiar to, and was strongly endorsed by, the Scottish population.

However, there were problems with the campaign. First, the general Be All You Can Be messages left people uncertain as to what they should do next. People needed specific guidance to work out a response. Second, the campaign was restricted to the media, with few links to other delivery modes, again making it appear insubstantial. In essence, the campaign was succeeding in promoting a corporate identity for health, but not offering the branded products that enabled people to buy into it.

Sources: Hastings and Leathar (1987), Leathar (1988)

story so that it meets the priorities and needs of the newspaper, radio or television station for topical, newsworthy, human interest material (e.g. Meyer, 1990).

In other words, the media are a target audience in their own right, with their own needs, expectations and opinions. They can be segmented just as the end target audience of young people or the community can: for example, different press releases may be needed for tabloid and broad sheet newspapers. Building up good personal relationships with the media helps the process, as does making available well-trained media spokespeople. Research can also play a crucial role in generating controversy (e.g. Wallack, 1990; Hastings *et al.*, 1994a). Again, effectiveness depends on understanding the media gatekeepers' needs and agenda.

Conclusion

Over the last thirty years social marketing has established itself as a coherent and valuable discipline, taking the principles of commercial marketing and applying them to the resolution of important social problems. Its overlaps with commercial marketing create strong strategic links between them, but its unique characteristics mean that the resulting strategies are frequently implemented in different ways. This has set up a symbiotic relationship of mutual respect and learning – it is no accident that Philip Kotler is a key figure in the evolution of both fields of endeavour. The inclusion of this chapter in a core marketing text also underlines this connection.

Social marketing faces three main challenges over the next decade. First, it must continue to develop its theoretical base using rigorous research combined with marketing's magpie like capacity to steal ideas from every other social science discipline. Second, it must establish its credentials more firmly outwith the marketing domain, by successfully tackling real social problems. Until now, the vast majority of our effort has focused on health problems, and these are likely to remain central to the discip-

line. However, other arenas, such as crime prevention, Third World development and the alleviation of poverty, could also benefit from social marketing. There is need to produce and publish reliable case studies in these areas.

Finally we need to provide more educational opportunities in social marketing. Only when well trained social marketers, who can live and breath the discipline, join the major agencies of social change will its full potential be realized.

References

Albrecht, T. L. (1996) Defining social marketing: 25 years later, *Social Marketing Quarterly*, Special issue: 21–23.

Andreasen, A. R. (1994) Social marketing: its definition and domain, *Journal of Public Policy and Marketing*, **13**(1), 108–114.

Andreasen, A. R. (1995) *Marketing Social Change: Changing Behaviour to Promote Health, Social, Development, and the Environment*, Jossey-Bass Publications, San Francisco.

Andreasen, A. (1997) Challenges for the science and practice of social marketing, Chapter 1 in M. E. Goldberg, M. Fishbein and S. E. Middlestadt (eds), *Social Marketing: Theoretical and Practical Perspectives*, Lawrence Erlbaum Associates, Mahwah, NJ.

Atkin, C. and Arkin E. B. (1990) Issues and initiatives in communicating health information to the public, Chapter 1 in C. K. Atkin. and L. Wallack (eds), *Mass Communication and Public Health: Complexities and Conflicts*, Sage, Newbury Park, CA.

Atkin, C. K. and Freimuth, V. (1989) Formative evaluation research in campaign design, Chapter 6 in R. E. Rice and C. K. Atkin (eds), *Public Communication Campaigns*, 2nd edn, Sage, Newbury Park, CA.

Atkin, C. K. and Wallack, L. (eds) (1990) *Mass Communication and Public Health: Complexities and Conflicts*, Sage, Newbury Park, CA.

Austoker, J., Davey, C. and Jansen, C. (1997) *Improving the Quality of the Written Information Sent to Women About Cervical Screening. NHS*

Cervical Screening Programme Publication No 6, NHSCSP Publications, London.

Backer, T. E., Rogers, E. M. and Sopory, P. (1992) *Designing Health Communication Campaigns: What Works?* Sage, Newbury Park, CA.

Bagozzi, R. (1975) Marketing and exchange, *Journal of Marketing,* **39**, October, 32–39.

Bandura, A. (1977) *Social Learning Theory,* Prentice Hall, Englewood Cliffs, NJ.

Bandura, A. (1986) *Social Foundations of Thought and Action: A Social Cognitive Approach,* Prentice Hall, Englewood Cliffs, NJ.

Bandy, P. and President, P. A. (1983) Recent literature on drug abuse prevention and mass media: focusing on youth, parents and the elderly, *Journal of Drug Education,* **13**(3), 255–271.

Blois, K. (1994) Non-profit marketing, Chapter 30, in M. J. Baker (ed.), *The Marketing Book,* 3rd edn, Butterworth–Heinemann, Oxford.

Bloom, P. N. (1980) Evaluating social marketing programs: problems and prospects, the 1980 Educators Conference Proceedings, American Marketing Association, Chicago.

Bloom, P. N. and Novelli, W. D. (1981) Problems and challenges in social marketing, *Journal of Marketing,* **45**, 79–88.

Bolling, K. and Owen, L. (1997) *Smoking and Pregnancy: A Survey of Knowledge, Attitudes and Behaviour,* Health Education Authroity, London.

Brieger, W. R., Ramakrishna, J. and Adeniyi, J. D. (1986/7) Community involvement in social marketing: Guineaworm control, *International Quarterly of Community Health Education,* **7**(1), 19–31.

Cowell, D. W. (1994) Marketing of services, Chapter 29, in M. Baker (ed.) *The Marketing Book,* 3rd edn, Butterworth–Heinemann, Oxford.

Currence, C. (1997) Demographic and lifestyle data: a practical application to stimulating compliance with mammography guidelines among poor women, Chapter 8 in M.E. Goldberg, M. Fishbein and S.E. Middlestadt (eds), *Social Marketing: Theoretical and Practical Perspectives,* Lawrence Erlbaum Associates, Mahwah, NJ.

Dahl, D. W., Gorn, G. J. and Weinberg, C. B. (1997) Marketing, safer sex and condom acquisition, Chapter 11 in M.E. Goldberg, M. Fishbein and S.E. Middlestadt (eds), *Social Marketing: Theoretical and Practical Perspectives,* Lawrence Erlbaum Associates, Mahwah, NJ.

Farquhar, J. W., Fortmann, S. P., Maccoby, W., Haskell, W. L., Williams, P. J., Flora, J. P., Taylor, C. B., Brown, B. W., Jr, Solomon, D. S. and Hulley, S. B. (1985) The Stanford Five City Project: design and methods, *American Journal of Epidemiology,* **122**, 323–334.

Fine, S. (1981) *The Marketing of Ideas and Social Issues,* Praeger, New York.

Fishbein, M. and Ajzen, I. (1975) *Belief, Attitude, Intention and Behaviour: An Introduction to Theory and Research,* Addison-Wesley, Reading, Mass.

Fishbein, M., Guenther-Grey, C., Johnson, W., Wolitski, R. J., McAlister, A., Rietmeijer, C. A., O'Reilly, K. and others (1997) Using a theory-based intervention to reduce AIDS risk behaviours: the CDC's AIDS Community Demonstration Projects, Chapter 9 in M. E. Goldberg, M. Fishbein and S. E. Middlestadt (eds), *Social Marketing: Theoretical and Practical Perspectives,* Lawrence Erlbaum Associates, Mahwah, NJ.

Flay, B. R. (1987) Mass media and smoking cessation: A critical review, *American Journal of Public Health,* **77**, 153–160.

Fox, K. F. A. and Kotler, P. (1980) The marketing of social causes: The first ten years, *Journal of Marketing,* **44**, 24–33.

Glasgow City Council (1998) *Glasgow Figures No. 2: Poverty and Deprivation in Glasgow.* Glasgow City Council, Glasgow.

Goldberg, M. E. (1995) Social marketing: are we fiddling while Rome burns? *Journal of Consumer Psychology,* **4**(4), 347–370.

Harvey, P. D. (1997) Advertising affordable contraceptives: the social marketing experience, Chapter 10 in M. E. Goldberg, M. Fishbein and S. E. Middlestadt (eds), *Social Marketing: Theoretical and Practical Perspectives,* Lawrence Erlbaum Associates, Mahwah, NJ.

Hastings, G. B. (1994) Sex, AIDS and research, *Social Marketing Quarterly*, **3**, p.1.

Hastings, G. B. and Elliot, B. (1993) Social marketing in practice in traffic safety, Chapter III in *Marketing of Traffic Safety*, OECD, Paris, pp. 35–53.

Hastings, G. B. and Haywood, A. J. (1991) Social marketing and communication in health promotion, *Health Promotion International*, **6**(2), 135–145.

Hastings, G. B. and Haywood, A. J. (1994) Social marketing: a critical response, *Health Promotion International*, **9**(1), 59–63.

Hastings, G. B., Hughes, K., Lawther, S. and Lowry, R. J. (1998a) The role of the public in water fluoridation: Public health champions or anti-fluoridation freedom fighters? *British Dental Journal*, **184**, 39–41.

Hastings, G. B. and Leathar, D. S. (1987) The creative potential of research, *International Journal of Advertising*, **6**, 159–168.

Hastings, G. B., Lawther, S., Eadie, D. R., Haywood, A. J., Lowry, R. J. and Evans, D. (1994a) General anaesthesia: Who decides and why? *British Dental Journal*, **177**, 332–336.

Hastings, G. B., Ryan, H., Teer, P. and MacKintosh, A. M. (1994b) Cigarette advertising and children's smoking: why Reg was withdrawn, *British Medical Journal*, **309**, 933–937.

Hastings, G. B., Smith, C. S. and Lowry, R. J. (1994c) Fluoridation – a time for hope, a time for action, *British Dental Journal*, May, 273–274.

Hastings, G. and Stead, M. (in press) Using the media in drugs prevention. Drugs Prevention Initiative paper, Home Office, Central Drugs Prevention Unit, London.

Hastings, G. B., Stead, M., Whitehead, M., Lowry R., MacFadyen, L., McVey, D., Owen, L. and Tones, K. (1998b) Using the media to tackle the health divide: Future directions, *Social Marketing Quarterly*, **IV**(3), 42–67.

Home Office (1998) Managing a drugs prevention programme: the experience of ne choices 1996–1998. Newcastle: Northumbria Drugs Prevention Team, Home Office.

Houston, F. S. and Gassenheimer, J. B. (1987) Marketing and exchange, *Journal of Marketing*, **51**(October), 3–18.

Jarvis, M. J. (1994) A profile of tobacco smoking, *Addiction*, **89**, 1371–1376.

Kochanek, K. D., Maurer, J. D. and Rosenberg, H. M. (1994) Why did black life expectancy decline from 1984 through 1989 in the United States? *American Journal of Public Health*, **84**, 938–944.

Kotler, P. (1994) Reconceptualizing marketing: an interview with Philip Kotler, *European Management Journal*, **12**(4), 353–361.

Kotler, P., Armstrong, G., Saunders, J. and Wong, V. (1996) *Principles of Marketing*, (European edition), London, Prentice-Hall.

Kotler, P. and Roberto, E. L. (1989) *Social Marketing: Strategies for Changing Public Behaviour*, The Free Press, New York.

Kotler, P. and Zaltman, G. (1971) Social marketing: an approach to planned social change, *Journal of Marketing*, **35**, 3–12.

Laczniak, G. R., Lusch, R. F. and Murphy, P. E. (1979) Social marketing: its ethical dimensions, *Journal of Marketing*, **43**, Spring, 29–30.

Lawther, S., Hastings, G. B. and Lowry, R. (1997) De-marketing: Putting Kotler and Levy's ideas into practice, *Journal of Marketing Management*, **13**(4), 315–325.

Lawther, S. and Lowry, R. (1995) Social marketing and behaviour change among professionals, *Social Marketing Quarterly*, **II**(1), 10–11.

Leathar, D. S. (1981) Defence inducing advertising, in Taking Stock: what have we learned and where are we going? Proceedings of 33rd ESOMAR Congress, Monte-Carlo, September 1980, 153–173, Reprinted in *Journal of the Institute of Health Education*, **19**(2), 42–55.

Leathar, D. S. (1988) The development and assessment of mass media campaigns: the work of the Advertising Research Unit. Be All You Can Be Case Study – Part 2, *Journal of the Institute of Health Education*, **26**(2), 85–93.

Leathar, D. S. and Hastings, G. B. (1987) Social marketing and health education, *Journal of Services Marketing*, **1**(2), Fall, p 49–52.

Lefebvre, R. C. (1992) The social marketing imbroglio in health promotion, *Health Promotion International*, **7**(1), 61–64.

Lefebvre, R. C. (1996) 25 years of social marketing: looking back to the future, *Social Marketing Quarterly*, Special Issue, 51–58.

Lefebvre, R. C., Doner, L., Johnston, C., Loughrey, K., Balch, G. I. and Sutton, S. M. (1995) Use of database marketing and consumer-based health communication in message design: An example from the office of cancer communications' '5 A Day for Better Health' program, Chapter 12 in E. Maibach and R. L. Parrott (eds), *Designing Health Messages. Approaches From Communication Theory and Public Health Practice*, Sage, Newbury Park, CA.

Lefebvre, R. C. and Flora, J. A. (1988) Social marketing and public health intervention, *Health Education Quarterly*, **15**(3), 299–315.

Lefebvre, R. C., Lancaster, T. M., Carleton, R. A. and Peterson, G. (1987) Theory and delivery of Health Programming the the Community: the Pawtucket Heart Health Program, *Preventative Medicine*, **16**, 80–95.

Levy, S. J. and Zaltman, G. (1975) *Marketing, society and conflict*, Prentice Hall, Englewood Cliffs, New Jersey.

Ling, J. C., Franklin, B. A. K., Lindsteadt, J. F. and Gearion, S. A. N. (1992) Social marketing: its place in public health, *Annual Review of Public Health*, **13**, 341–362.

Luck, D. J. (1974) Social marketing: confusion compounded, *Journal of Marketing*, **38** (October), 70–72.

MacFadyen, L., Hastings, G. B., MacKintosh, A. M. and Lowry, R. (1998) Tobacco advertising and children's smoking: moving the debate beyond advertising and sponsorship. Proceedings of the 27th Emac Conference, Stockholm, Track 3: *Marketing Strategy and Organization*, 431–456.

Maibach, E. W. and Cotton, D. (1995) Moving people to behaviour change: A staged social cognitive approach to message design, Chapter 3 in E. Maibach and R. L. Parrott (eds), *Designing Health Messages. Approaches From Communication Theory and Public Health Practice*, Sage, Newbury Park, CA, pp. 41–64.

Makkai, T., Moore, R. and McAllister, I. (1991) Health education campaigns and drug use: the 'drug offensive' in Australia, *Health Education Research Theory and Practice*, **61**, 65–76.

Manoff, R. K. (1985) *Social marketing: new imperative for public health*, Praeger, New York.

Manstead, A. S. R. (1991) Social psychological aspects of driver behaviour, in *New Aspects of Driver Behaviour*: Proceedings of a conference organized by the Parliamentary Advisory Council for Transport Safety (PACTS), PACTS, London.

Marsh, A. and MacKay, S. (1994) *Poor Smokers*, Policy Studies Institute, London.

Marteau, T. M. (1990) Reducing the psychological costs, *British Medical Journal*, **301**, 26-28.

McCord, C. and Freeman, H. P. (1990) Excess mortality in Harlem, *New England Journal of Medicine*, **322**, 173–177.

McGrath, J. (1995) The gatekeeping process: The right combinations to unlock the gates, Chapter 11 in E. Maibach and R. C. Parrott (eds), *Designing Health Messages. Approaches From Communication Theory and Public Health Practice*. Sage, Newbury Park, CA.

McLoone, P. (1991) Carstairs scores for Scottish postcode sectors from the 1991 census, Public Health Research Unit, University of Glasgow, Glasgow.

Meyer, P. (1990) News media responsiveness to public health, Chapter 3 in C. K. Atkin and L. Wallack, (eds), *Mass Communication and Public Health: Complexities and Conflicts*, Sage, Newbury Park, CA.

Monahan, J. L. (1995) Thinking positively: using positive affect when designing health messages, Chapter 5 in E. Maibach and R. L. Parrott (eds), *Designing Health Messages. Approaches From Communication Theory and Public Health Practice*, Sage, Newbury Park, CA.

Murray, G. G. and Douglas, R. R. (1988) Social marketing in the alcohol policy arena, *British Journal of Addiction*, **83**, 505–511.

National Heart, Lung and Blood Institute (1973) The Public and High Blood Pressure: A Survey – DHED Publication No. 73.736, National Heart, Lung and Blood Institute, Bethesda, Md.

Pappas, G., Queen, S., Hadden W. and Fisher, G. (1993) The increasing disparity in mortality between socio-economic groups in the United States, 1960 and 1986, *New England Journal of Medicine*, **329**, 103–109.

Percy, L. (1983) A review of the effect of specific advertising elements upon overall communication response, in *Current Issues and Research in Advertising*, University of Michigan.

Peto, D. (1994) Smoking and death: The past 40 years and the next 40, *British Medical Journal*, **309**, 937–8.

Petty, R. E., Cacioppo, J. T., Sedikides, C. and Strathman, A. I. (1988) Affect and persuasion: a contemporary perspective, *American Behavioural Scientist*, **32**, 355–371.

Population Services International (1977) Preetni Project. Transferred to Sri-Lanka FPA, *PSI Newsletter* (November/December) 4.

Prochaska, J. O. and DiClemente, C. C. (1983) Stages and processes of self-change of smoking: toward an integrative model of change, *Journal of Consulting and Clinical Psychology*, **51**, 390–395.

Prochaska, J. O., Vlicer, W. F., Rossi, J. S., Goldstein, M. G., Marcus, B. H., Rakowksi, W., Fiore, C., Harlow, L. L., Redding, C. A., Rosenbloom, D. and Rossi, S. R. (1994) Stages of change and decisional balance for 12 problem behaviours, *Health Psychology*, **13**(1), 39–46.

Rangun, V. K. and Karim S. (1991) *Teaching Note: Focusing the concept of Social Marketing*, Harvard Business School, Cambridge, MA.

Rangun, V. K., Karim, S. and Sandberg, S. K. (1966) Do better at doing good, *Harvard Business Review*, May–June, 4–11.

Reid, D. (1996) How effective is health education via mass communications? *Health Education Journal*, **55**, 332–344.

Schwartz, G. (1971) Marketing: The societal marketing concept, *University of Washington Business Review*, **31**, 31–38.

Shiner, M. and Newburn, T. (1996) Young people, drugs and peer education: an evaluation of the youth awareness programme (YAP), DPI, Home Office, London.

Slater, M. D. (1995) Choosing audience segmentation strategies and methods for health communication. Chapter 10 in E. Maibach and R. L. Parrott (eds), *Designing Health Messages. Approaches From Communication Theory and Public Health Practice*, Sage, Newbury Park, CA.

Sleight, P. (1995) Explaining geodemographics, *Admap*, January, 27–29.

Smith, R. (1997) Gap between death rates of rich and poor widens, *British Medical Journal*, **314**, 9.

Smith, W. A. (1997) Social marketing: moving beyond the nostalgia, Chapter 2 in M. E. Goldberg, M. Fishbein and S. E. Middlestadt (eds), *Social Marketing: Theoretical and Practical Perspectives*, Lawrence Erlbaum Associates, Mahwah, New Jersey.

Solomon, D. S. (1989) A social marketing perspective on communication campaigns, Chapter 4 in R. E. Rice and Atkin, C. K. (eds), *Public Communication Campaigns*, 2nd edn, Sage, Newbury Park, CA.

Stead, M. and Hastings, G. (1997) Advertising in the social marketing mix: Getting the balance right. Chapter 3 in M. E. Goldberg, M. Fishbein and S. E. Middlestadt (eds), *Social Marketing: Theoretical and Practical Perspectives*, Lawrence Erlbaum Associates, Mahwah, NJ.

Stead, M., MacKintosh, A. M., Hastings, G., Eadie, D, Young, F. and Regan, T. (1997a) Preventing adolescent drug use: design, implementation and evaluation design of 'ne choices'. Paper presented at Home Office, DPI Research Conference, Liverpool, Dec. 3–5.

Stead, M., Wimbush, E., Eadie, D. and Teer, P. (1997b) A qualitative study of older people's perceptions of ageing and exercise: the implications for health promotion, *Health Education Journal*, **56**, 3–16.

Sugg Skinner, C., Strecher, V. J. and Hospers, H. (1994) Physicians' recommendations for mammography: do tailored messages make a difference? *American Journal of Public Health*, **84**(1), 43–49.

Sutton, S. M.(1991) In AED, Social marketing: views from inside the government. 30th Anniversary Seminar Series. Academy for Educational Development.

Thorogood, M., Coulter, A., Jones, L., Yudkin, P., Muir, J. and Mant, D. (1993) Factors affecting response to an invitation to attend for a health check, *Journal of Epidemiology and Community Health*, **47**, 224–228.

Tones, K. (1994) Marketing and the mass media: theory and myth. Reflections on social marketing theory, *Health Education Research Theory and Practice*, **9**(2), 165–169.

Wallack, L. (1990) Improving health promotion: Media advocacy and social marketing approaches, Chapter 11 in C. Atkin and L. Wallack (eds), *Mass Communication and Public Health: Complexities and Conflicts*, Sage, Newbury Park, CA, pp. 147–163.

Wallack, L., Dorfman, L., Jernigan, D. and Themba, D. (1993) *Media Advocacy and Public Health*, Sage, Newbury Park, CA.

Walsh, D. C., Rudd, R. E., Moeykens, B. A. and Moloney, T. W. (1993) Social marketing for public health, *Health Affairs*, Summer, 104–119.

Werch, C. E. and DiClemente, C. C. (1994) A multi-component stage model for matching drug prevention strategies and messages to youth stage of use, *Health Education Research, Theory and Practice*, **9**(1), 37–46.

Whitehead, M. (1992) The health divide, in P. Townsend, M. Whitehead and N. Davidson (eds), *Inequalities in Health: The Black Report and the Health Divide*, 2nd edn, Penguin, London.

Whitehead, M. and Diderichsen, F. (1997) International evidence on social inequalities in health, in F. Drever and M. Whitehead (eds), *Health Inequalities: Decennial Supplement*, Office for National Statistics Series DS, No 15, The Stationery Office, London.

Wiebe, G. D. (1951/52) Merchandising commodities and citizenship in television, *Public Opinion Quarterly*, **15** (Winter), 679–91.

Wilkie, W. L. (1994) *Consumer Behavior*, 3rd edn, Wiley, New York.

Woodruff, K. (1996) Alcohol advertising and violence against women: a media advocacy case study, *Health Education Quarterly*, **23**(3), 330–345.

Woodruffe, H. (1995) *Services Marketing*, M&E Pitman, London.

Worden, J. K., Flynn, B. S., Solomon, L. J., Secker-Walker, R. H., Badger, G. J. and Carpenter, J. H. (1996) Using mass media to prevent cigarette smoking among adolescent girls, *Health Education Quarterly*, **23**(4), 453–468.

World Health Organization (1995) *Bridging the Gaps, World Health Report for 1995*, World Health Organization, Geneva.

Further reading

Andreasen, A. R. (1995) *Marketing Social Change: Changing Behaviour to Promote Health, Social, Development, and the Environment*, Jossey-Bass Publications, San Francisco.

Goldberg, M. E., Fishbein, M. and Middlestadt, S. E. (eds) (1997) *Social Marketing: Theoretical and Practical Perspectives*, Lawrence Erlbaum Associates, New Jersey.

Hastings, G. B. and Haywood, A. J. (1991) Social marketing and communication in health promotion, *Health Promotion International*, **6**(2), 135–145.

Hastings, G. B. and Haywood, A. J. (1994) Social marketing: a critical response, *Health Promotion International*, **9**(1), 59–63.

Kotler, P. and Roberto, E. L. (1989) *Social Marketing: Strategies for Changing Public Behaviour*, The Free Press, New York.

Kotler, P. and Zaltman, G. (1971) Social marketing: an approach to planned social change, *Journal of Marketing*, **35**, 3–12.

Maibach, E. and Parrott, R. L. (eds) (1995) *Designing Health Messages: Approaches from Communication Theory and Public Health Practice*, Sage, Newbury Park, CA.

Web sites

The Centre for Social Marketing, University of Strathclyde, Scotland:
http://www.strath.ac.uk/Departments/Marketing/Research/CSM.html

The Health Education Board for Scotland:
http://www.hebs.scot.nhs.uk
The Social Marketing Network, Canada:
http://www.hc-hc.gc.ca/socialmarketing

CHAPTER 26

Green marketing

KEN PEATTIE and MARTIN CHARTER

Introduction

As we enter a new millennium, making mankind's economic and social development more environmentally sustainable is the greatest challenge facing governments, businesses, managers and management disciplines. Sustainability was once a vision of the future shared by an environmentally-orientated few. The publication of the Brundtland Report 'Our Common Future' in 1987 brought the issue into the mainstream. Following the 1992 Rio Earth Summit, the majority of the world's governments adopted sustainability as a goal, and over 1000 of the world's largest companies soon followed by signing up to the International Chamber of Commerce's Charter for Sustainable Development. The real challenge lies in turning these good intentions into meaningful progress towards sustainability in the face of powerful vested interests, a deeply entrenched and environmentally-hostile management paradigm, and a global economy with tremendous momentum on a growth-maximizing trajectory.

For marketing, this provides a number of challenges. In the short-term, ecologically-related forces have become significant external influences on companies and the markets within which they operate. In the longer term, the pursuit of sustainability will demand fundamental changes to the management paradigm which underpins marketing and the other business functions (Shrivastava, 1994). This chapter aims

to illustrate how the 'green challenge' is exerting an influence on current marketing practice, and how its implications will require a more profound shift in the marketing paradigm to allow marketers to continuing delivering customer satisfaction at a profit, well into the next millennium.

Green marketing in context

Management theory in general is firmly rooted in an economic and technical systems perspective which concentrates on exchanges, products, production and profits. Over time it has evolved to become more 'human' with the emergence of disciplines like organizational behaviour, human resource management, business ethics and societal marketing. The fact that businesses are physical systems which exist within a finite and vulnerable physical environment has, until recently, largely been ignored as a management and marketing issue. Green marketing furthers the evolution of marketing beyond societal marketing, to embrace society's increasing concern about the natural environment (Prothero, 1990). We can define it as:

The holistic management process responsible for identifying, anticipating and satisfying the needs of customers and society, in a profitable and sustainable way.

The difference between the green marketing concept and societal marketing lie in:

- An emphasis on the physical sustainability of the marketing process, as well as its social acceptability.
- A more holistic and interdependent view of the relationship between the economy, society and the environment.
- An open-ended rather than a short-term perspective.
- A treatment of the environment as something with intrinsic value over and above its usefulness to society.
- A focus on global concerns, rather than those of particular societies.

The greening of marketing is being driven forward by what can broadly be termed the 'Green Movement'. It has evolved from the environmentalism which became prominent during the early 1970s and which spawned the 'ecological marketing' concept (Hennison and Kinnear, 1976). This ancestry often causes green marketing to be treated with a sense of 'deja vu'

by marketing academics and practitioners. However, there are some important differences between the 1970s and the 1990s which are summarized in Table 26.1.

Combining environmental concern (which traditionally involves encouraging conservation), with the discipline of marketing, (which aims to stimulate and facilitate consumption) can appear somewhat paradoxical. Sustainability is the keystone of the green marketing philosophy, which resolves this apparent paradox. A sustainable approach to consumption and production involves enjoying a material standard of living today, which is not at the expense of the standard of living of future generations. Although sustainability is often talked about in environmental terms, it is also concerned with the relationship between society and the environment and therefore combines social, environmental and ethical concerns. At its heart are two deceptively simple sounding elements:

Table 26.1   The evolution of environmental concern

Factor	1970s environmentalism	1990s Green
Emphasis	On 'environmental' problems	On the underlying problems with our social, economic, technical or legal systems
Geographic focus	On local problems (e.g. pollution)	On global issues (e.g. global warming)
Identity	Closely linked to other anti-establishment causes	A separate movement embraced by many elements of 'the establishment'
Source of support	An intellectual elite, and those at the fringes of society	A broad base
Basis of campaigns	Used forecasts of exponential growth to predict future environmental problems (e.g. Limits to Growth)	Uses evidence of current environmental degradation (e.g. the hole in the ozone layer)
Attitude to businesses	Business is the problem. Generally adversarial	Businesses seen as part of the solution. More partnerships formed
Attitude to growth	Desire for zero growth	Desire for sustainable growth
View of environment/ business interaction	Focused on negative effects of business activity on the environment	Focuses on the dynamic inter-relationship between business, society and the environment

1   Using natural resources at a rate at which environmental systems or human activity can replenish them (or in the case of non-renewable resources, at a rate at which renewable alternatives can be substituted in).

2   Producing pollution and waste at a rate which can be absorbed by environmental systems without impairing their viability.

Green marketing's key concepts of sustainability and holism are both apparently simple, but can be extremely difficult to translate into action. This is largely because conventional management wisdom emphasizes reductionalism and specialism, and is founded on economic theories which mistakenly treat environmental resources as limitless, free (beyond the cost of extraction) or, for market-less commodities like stratospheric ozone, worthless. Green marketing attempts to relocate marketing theory and practice away from the economic hyperspace in which it has evolved, and bring it back down to earth and reality.

Reconceptualizing the marketing environment

Companies benefit from a marketing orientation in many ways, and one of the most important is

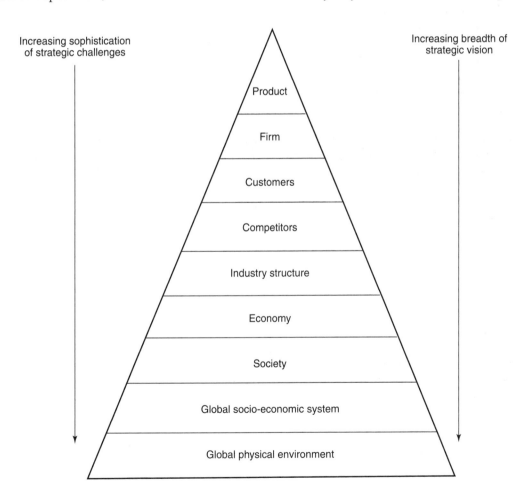

Figure 26.1   The physical environment as the foundation of the marketing environment

that it makes them externally focused on the marketing environment. However, marketing theory has followed the tradition of mechanistic economic models, which dismiss the ecological contexts in which economic activity occurs (Capra, 1983). So entire books discussing the marketing environment dedicate chapters to the social, cultural, technological, economic and political environments, without discussing the physical environment which underpins them, and on which they all depend. At best, the response to increased environmental concern has been to try to accommodate it within existing models of the environment (of the PEST type) by discussing it as a political pressure, an influence on the economics of business, a social trend or a technological challenge. Figure 26.1 visualizes the marketing environment as composed of layers of issues and interactions, with the physical environment as the foundation on which societies and economies are based. The most immediate issues for marketing managers are typically internal ones relating to the product and the company itself, and externally to customers. Beyond this, the analysis of the environment broadens out externally through different, but interwoven, levels of environment. Each level has important implications for marketing, but dealing with the deeper levels of the environment is perhaps a more difficult strategic challenge, due to their increasing breadth and complexity, and their decreasing proximity to the company itself. The physical global biosphere may seem distant to many companies' day-to-day activities, but ultimately all business activity depends upon it, and its continuing stability and viability.

Problems in the underlying global physical environment will impact firms, and their products and strategies, through interactions with each layer of the model.

Global physical environment

Scientific evidence continues to mount recording deterioration in many different aspects of the biosphere, creating a scientific and political consensus that action is needed to better safeguard it, and its future viability, from human activity and exploitation. At the simplest level the environment affects businesses because it represents the physical space within which they and their customers exist, and it provides the resources upon which they depend. For some companies there is a very direct relationship between the health of the environment and their business prospects. The fishing industry's agenda is dominated by the need to protect stocks from over-fishing. The tourism industry is at the forefront of efforts to translate sustainability into practice, because of the ruinous impact that attracting unsustainable numbers of tourists to a resort will eventually have, and because of the potential disruption that changes to weather patterns could have.

Although global issues such as climate change and ozone depletion dominate the headlines, the green agenda contains a vast array of issues, each of which creates marketing opportunities and threats for different businesses. So, while concern over the thinning ozone layer has posed a major threat to CFC producers, the ensuing warnings about the increased risk of skin cancer has provided a somewhat grim opportunity for the manufacturers of skin care products. Global warming is seen as a threat to the car and power generation industries and agriculture, while creating opportunities in markets for insulation and other energy-saving products. The loss of biodiversity is a threat for the pharmaceuticals industry which depends on rainforest plants in particular as a source of new compounds, but has created ecotourism opportunities based around unique habitats and rare species. Some issues, such as over-fishing, are industry specific, while others like global warming have a much wider impact.

Global socio-economic system

The biosphere is global in nature, since it knows no geo-political boundaries. Recent decades have also seen a more global perspective with the emergence of global companies, markets, technologies and socio-cultural trends. The green challenge is being reflected through increasing international environmental legislation (such as the Montreal Protocol to reduce CFC use, or the world-wide ban on commercial whaling), and intergovernmental conferences. Although issues of social concern vary over time and between countries, survey data reveals that concern about the state of the environment is spread across the planet, and (contrary to many people's expectations) is shared by the populations (if not always the governments) of the less-industrializsed as well as the industrialized nations. However, the 1997 Kyoto Intergovernmental Conference on Climate Change demonstrated the difficulties of gaining international agreement to tackle common environmental problems.

Society

Within societies, concern about the environment is generally increasing (e.g. Leeflang and van Raaij, 1995) and is being reflected in a number of ways including:

- *Changing values.* Social attitudes towards the environment have changed, so that it is perceived as vulnerable, valuable and in need of protection. This has been reflected in changes in the values associated with products and their features. Kodak's disposable camera therefore was transformed into a recyclable camera; detergents that once washed 'whiter-than-white' now give a 'natural snowy white' wash; and Germany has witnessed something of a cultural backlash which has taken some of the 'prestige' out of owning large-engined cars.
- *Pressure group activity.* The 1980s saw a considerable increase in the size, budgets and sophistication of environmentally related pressure groups. Companies that have found themselves the targets of high-profile campaigns include Shell, Mitsubishi Electric and McDonald's. The 1990s has been characterized by companies such as McDonald's adopting a partnership, rather than adversarial, relationship with environmental groups.

- *Media interest.* An increasing amount of media output is devoted to nature and environmentally related messages, and examples of poor eco-performance are a favourite target for investigative journalism. As Mulhall (1992) notes 'The massive impact of instant media in accelerating the message of gross environmental incompetence by our leaders can be summarized in three letters – CNN. It means that a company's reputation can be destroyed globally in one day'.
- *Political and legal interest.* The environmental agenda of green political parties has been increasingly absorbed by mainstream political parties, and this has led to an increase in the volume and rigour of the environmental legislation that companies must respond to. Companies that rely on mere compliance risk being left behind by the upward 'ratcheting' of legislation. In the USA, the trend towards forcing the CEOs of polluters to make personal court appearances, and in some cases jailing them, has helped to focus corporate minds.
- *Public opinion.* EU surveys tracking public attitudes to the environment for more than 15 years have revealed that a majority of people are increasingly concerned about the state of the global and national environment (in both the short and the long term) and also consider that 'protecting the environment and preserving natural resources are essential to economic development'.

On particularly sensitive issues all of these dimensions of increased societal concern can combine to present any companies involved with a considerable strategic, marketing and public relations challenge, as Shell discovered when trying to decommission the Brent Spar oil rig.

The economy

Conventional wisdom saw environmental protection as a trade-off with economic growth. Recognition is growing that the two are interlinked in many complex ways, and that long-term economic growth may be dependent on better environmental protection. For example, World Resources Institute figures show that in 1990 eleven nations had water supplies below the bare minimum necessary to allow economic growth. Key areas where the environment is influencing economic issues include:

*   *Production economics.* Environmental considerations are radically altering the production economics of some front-line industries such as cars, chemicals and power generation. Rising landfill costs and tougher regulations on emissions mean that production costs are increasingly influenced not by what goes into a product, but by what is thrown away when making it. Many chemicals such as acetone are now more expensive to dispose of legally than to manufacture. The BSE crisis within the UK beef industry has also demonstrated the economic damage that poor eco-performance can have on an entire industry.
*   *Investor pressure.* Research by Touche Ross in 1990 revealed that only 9 per cent of UK firms felt under shareholder pressure to improve eco-performance, compared to 20 per cent in The Netherlands and 70 per cent in Denmark. In the UK there are over 60 ethical and environmental investment funds, managing over £1.47 billion of funds, and enjoying an average growth rate of 34 per cent between 1989 and 1997 (source: Ethical Investment Research Service).
*   *Green taxes.* These already operate in many Scandinavian countries, and were introduced into the UK with the landfill tax in 1996. Although industries have tended to recoil from the idea of green taxation, research by Cambridge Econometrics has shown that a shift in UK taxation away from payrolls, and towards pollution and resource use, would reduce the net costs of those companies who account for 70 per cent of UK exports. Proposals for 'energy taxes' to help combat global warming would ensure that the entire business community directly felt the consequences of environmental degradation.
*   *Access to capital.* In the USA, the introduction

of retrospective clean-up costs for environmental damage has increased the financial risks of companies in 'dirty' industries to the extent that bank lending and insurance coverage are increasingly dependent on an ability of firms to demonstrate good environmental performance.

Industry structure

Industry structures have conventionally been visualized as composed of linear exchanges. The green challenge is one of many forces encouraging a more relationship-based view of industry structures, particularly through an emphasis on recycling and supply loops. These feature relationships in which the customer returns products or packaging to the manufacturer, and in the process becomes another form of supplier. Xerox, for example, in 1990 recovered $400 million worth of parts from customers through its 'closed loop' supply chain management (Stenross and Sweet, 1992). The changes that greening is bringing to industry structures include:

*   *The threat of substitutes.* In some markets, greener alternatives for customers are emerging from products which use radically different technologies or which utilise traditional 'low-tech' solutions. Heinz, for example, were surprised by an unaccountable jump in the US sales of their gallon containers of spirit vinegar. This was traced to a trend among consumers to return to traditional cleaning materials such as vinegar and bicarbonate of soda in the face of concerns about the toxicity of more modern cleaning agents (Scerbinsky, 1991).
*   *Supplier relationships.* Greening is forcing many companies to reconsider supplier relationships, since their total environmental impact will be strongly influenced earlier in the supply chain. Environmental supplier audits are being used by companies such as IBM, BT and McDonald's to monitor and often to improve their suppliers' eco-performance,

and if necessary to de-list the 'greyest'. Boots for example are collaborating with suppliers to reduce the number scoring poorly on their Environmental Management Index. A key feature of the greening of industries has been the need for partnership approaches between companies and their suppliers (Morton, 1996).

* *Market entry barriers.* Some countries, such as Germany, have particularly strict environmental legislation (e.g. their 'Green Dot' packaging ordinances), which can act as an entry barrier for foreign firms. For some companies, good environmental performance can act as a key to gain entry into a new market. Varta batteries had failed in several attempts to translate their European market strength into penetration of the UK market, but this was achieved very rapidly in 1988 with the introduction of their innovative mercury-free battery range.

Competitors

Much has been made of the potential of good eco-performance to generate competitive advantage (e.g. Elkington, 1994, Azzone and Bertele, 1994). In a wide range of markets, including detergents, retailing, batteries, white goods, cars, toilet paper and banks, companies have used eco-performance as a basis on which to compete. Global competition and continuous improvement philosophies have narrowed the differences between products to the extent that 'softer' issues such as perceived environmental impact can act as a 'tie-breaker' for the consumer trying to choose brands (Christensen, 1995). However, experience also shows that environmental disasters such as the *Exxon-Valdez* or *Braer* oil spills, or spills at major chemicals plants will put all players in an industry under increased stakeholder pressure. This suggests that as the green challenge deepens, it may reduce the intensity of competitive rivalry, instead of acting as a new arena for it to be played out in. Many key environmental problems confront entire industries and require industry-wide responses. Alliances are emerging between rivals to address common environmental challenges and to develop greener technologies. In the USA, Ford, Chrysler and GM have collaborated in an effort to develop low-emission vehicles, and also to pool millions of dollars to lobby against stricter greenhouse gas restrictions. The Industrial Coalition for Ozone Layer Protection is a consortium of major US and Japanese electronics companies, collaborating to replace CFCs as electrical solvents.

Customers

The world-wide boycott of CFC driven aerosols in the late 1980s demonstrated the potential of consumers to unite behind an environmental issue that they understood and could relate to, in a way that enforced rapid change to an entire industry. Following this, there was considerable effort put into identifying and understanding the 'Green Consumer'. Mintel's 1991 UK Green Consumer Survey, and a 1992 McCann Erickson/Harris survey of European consumers both showed that over half of all consumers desired greener products, were willing to pay extra for them, and were willing to accept some limited trade-off between their functional quality and their eco-performance. In the UK the attitudes revealed by Mintel were translated into a change in consumer behaviour, which saw 46 per cent of women and 31 per cent of men actively seeking green alternatives while shopping. In the USA the situation is even more pronounced, a 1990 survey of 1000 consumers by J. Walter Thompson revealing that 82 per cent were willing to pay a 5 per cent premium for greener products, with 64 per cent willing to boycott products from a 'dirty' company.

The identity, characteristics and sincerity of these 'green consumers' has been the dominant theme in discussions about green marketing, but this emphasis may be misplaced. Partly this is because the conventional concept of the green consumer may be both an oxymoron and poorly conceived. Secondly, the most important impacts that environmental concern are having are often in business-to-business marketing, not in supplying the ultimate consumer (Morton, 1996).

Firms

Concern about the environment is being reflected in many aspects of companies. This can include environmental management appointments; the introduction of green auditing and reporting systems; and changes to company policies and facilities to reduce waste and pollution. Corporate strategies and cultures are increasingly being orientated towards the environment, often to reflect external stakeholder pressure, and also to reflect the concerns of employees and investors. *Purchasing Magazine*'s 1993 survey of US corporate buyers found that green purchases were more often a response to internal suggestions than the communications efforts of the suppliers.

Marketing strategy conventionally follows, and is interwoven with, corporate strategy. For many marketers the need to improve the eco-performance of the products they manage reflects the need to contribute to the pursuit of a corporate goal. In a McKinsey survey of top management within Fortune 500 companies, 92 per cent of respondents placed the environment as one of the top three management priorities for the forthcoming decade (Walley and Whitehead, 1994). A company's environmental commitment can be communicated through an environmental policy, strategy or statement. By 1991 over half of all European companies surveyed by Touche Ross had developed an environmental policy. A survey of the UK's top 150 companies revealed that over two thirds had amended their mission statements to reflect increased environmental concern (Peattie and Ringler, 1994).

Products

Environmental concern is creating demands for new products (such as pollution control equipment) and is causing existing products to be reconsidered and in many cases redesigned, re-formulated or produced differently. The impact on products will vary across markets. In some, such as cars, cleaning products or paper products, changes in response to the green challenge are widespread. In others, such as food, financial services or computers, examples of change are more sporadic. In America, there were estimates that by 1990 10 per cent of all products launched claimed some form of green credentials (Davis, 1991); and within Europe, a survey of multinationals by Vandermerwe and Oliff (1990) found that in response to the green challenge:

- 92 per cent had significantly changed their product offerings.
- 85 per cent had changed their production systems.
- 78 per cent had changed the focus of their marketing communications.

Environmental concern can also lead to the repositioning of products. In response to concern about exposure to ultra-violet radiation and the risk of skin cancer, sun tan lotions have changed from an emphasis on sun exposure and beauty to an emphasis on skin protection.

The greening of marketing strategy

The evolution of the green challenge has brought about a change in the relationship between marketing and the physical environment (for details see Menon and Menon, 1997). The environmental concern of the 1970s inspired a raft of environmental legislation, and a relatively reactive response among companies. The emphasis was on compliance, and bolting on 'end-of-pipe' technologies to alleviate pollution. Environmental response was viewed as an additional cost burden and as an operational issue, which concerned a relatively small number of 'front line' industries such as oil, chemicals and cars. During the 1980s and 1990s a more proactive style of corporate response has emerged, and the front line has broadened to include a much wider range of industries. This was demonstrated by a 1992 survey of Fortune 500 companies conducted by Abt Associates which revealed a shift away from a technical, compliance-orientated approach towards a more proactive green strategy orientation (Hochman *et al.*, 1993). Companies have begun to recognize that environmental responsiveness is something which customers, investors and other stakeholders take an interest in, and which can provide opportunities for innovation and competitive advantage. The precise nature of the pressures on companies to improve environmental performance and the opportunities that greening will present, will vary considerably between different types of industries according to the nature of their products, technologies and customers.

Competitive advantage and the environment

During the 1990s the argument that greening can act as a source of competitive advantage has emerged, and been supported by authors such as Elkington (1994) and Porter and van der Linde (1995). Obvious examples come from companies such as The Body Shop who compete on the basis of strong eco-performance and by tapping into customer demand for greener products. Porter and van der Linde's argument is that the search for environmentally superior solutions leads to innovation and the creation of more efficient and effective technologies. Their logic is that tough environmental legislation (often vigorously opposed by companies) actually increases innovation and competitive performance. This is what Varadajan (1992) termed 'enviropreneurial marketing'. Certainly, countries like Germany with relatively tough environmental legislation have developed strong clean technology sectors, and their companies have been able to penetrate emerging export markets. German companies hold an estimated 37 per cent of the European market for pollution control and clean-up technology, and 70 per cent of the US air pollution control market.

Others have argued that it is difficult in practice to achieve and sustain competitive advantage from good eco-performance (e.g. Walley and Whitehead, 1994). The issues have often proved complex and costly to address; customers have often proved difficult to convince; greener product offerings have sometimes struggled to compete on technical merits against conventional products, and the media has often proved more critical of those attempting to improve their eco-performance and capitalize on it, than of the most polluting and wasteful companies. Despite this, it is clear that poor eco-performance can put a company at a massive competitive disadvantage. Exxon's combined bill for clean up costs, fines and legal costs was estimated at over $3 bn in the immediate aftermath of the *Exxon-Valdez* disaster, which also left 41 per cent of Americans describing themselves as 'angry enough to boycott Exxon products' (Kirkpatrick, 1990).

For the marketing strategist it is vital to understand the potential impact of the green agenda on the business and its customers, and also the strengths and weaknesses of the company's eco-performance. Good eco-performance is important in many markets because it provides:

* *New market opportunities*, through access to growing green markets. Estimates for the expenditure on environmental technologies and services between 1991 and 2000 are £140 bn for the UK, £860 bn for the EC and £1060 bn for the USA (source: The Centre for Exploitation of Science and Technology, 1991).
* *Differentiation opportunities*. AEG increased their 1989 UK sales by 30 per cent within an otherwise static white goods market, following an advertising campaign stressing the relative energy and water efficiency of their products.
* *Opportunities for cost advantages*. Although conventional wisdom associates good eco-performance with investment and increased costs, this is partly a reflection of the 'end-of-pipe' methods used (since adding a catalytic

converter onto a car can only increase its costs). Investments using a more radical, clean technology approach are being shown to be capable of reducing material and energy inputs, and cutting inefficient pollution and waste. 3M's famous Pollution Prevention Pays campaign saved the company in excess of half a billion dollars in its first fifteen years.

- *Niche opportunities.* In the short term, greener products such as organic food and cruelty-free cosmetics frequently succeed within market niches comprised of the most environmentally aware consumers and marketed at premium prices. However, when such products catch the imagination of the mass market, the niche can rapidly expand to encompass the bulk of the market.

The green consumer

For companies in industrial markets, or those serving government bodies, improved environmental performance may be enforced through changes to purchasing specifications. For companies in consumer markets, the signalling of the need to go green from the market can be far less clear. It seems logical for marketers, when faced with a population professing increased environmental concern, to respond by trying to identify 'green consumers' and finding out what motivates purchases of environmentally marketed products. If this can be done, and appropriate market offerings created, then the competitive advantage opportunities outlined by Porter and others can be achieved.

Academic researchers and market research agencies have put a great deal of effort into attempting to define and understand the relationship between peoples' environmental concern and their purchasing behaviour. Many factors have been proposed as influences on green consumer behaviour such as changing consumer values, demographic factors, knowledge of environmental problems and alternative products, perceived personal relevance and the ability of the individual to make an effective contribution (for a model which integrates the

majority of these, see Dembkowski and Hanmer-Lloyd, 1994). There has been a good deal of contradictory evidence in attempts to link factors such as gender, age or level of environmental knowledge to green consumption (Miller, 1993; Peattie, 1995). The difficulties in isolating green consumer behaviour reflect several factors:

- It overlooks the point made by Kardash (1974) that all consumers (barring a few who enjoy contrariness for its own sake) are 'green consumers' in that, faced with a choice between two products that are identical in all respects except that one is superior in terms of its eco-performance, they would differentiate in terms of the environmentally superior product.
- By attempting to relate a consumer's environmental concern to purchases, marketing researchers may be looking in the wrong place. Many of the most significant contributions that consumers can make towards environmental quality come in product use, maintenance and disposal, or in delaying or avoiding a purchase through a 'make do and mend' mentality.
- Environmental improvements in products are often entangled with economic or technical benefits. Therefore drivers may choose lead-free fuel for environmental or economic reasons, or they may choose organic food for reasons of environmental concern, personal health concern or simply for the taste benefits.
- Different answers are achieved depending on what is defined as constituting green consumer behaviour, and whether environmental concern is defined in general or specific terms. General environmental concern is often measured by researchers, but it is less easily related to products than specific environmental concerns (such as concern for dolphins translating into the purchase of rod-and-line caught tuna fish).

Perhaps the solution to understanding green purchasing behaviour, is to try and understand the purchase rather than the purchaser. If we accept Kardash's proposal that, all other things being equal, most customers would differentiate in favour of greener products, then understanding environmental purchasing behaviour (and often the lack of it), is assisted by looking at the extent to which other things are not 'equal'. Many green purchases involve some form of compromise over conventional purchases. The compromise can take a variety of forms including:

- paying a green premium. This can be imposed by economic necessity where improving eco-performance increases production costs. Alternatively it can be created by marketing strategies in which greener products aimed at green market niches are given a premium price irrespective of production costs;
- accepting a lower level of technical performance in exchange for improved eco-performance (e.g. green detergents);
- travelling to non-standard distribution outlets (e.g. specialist green retailers).

Where there is a compromise involved in making a greener purchase, a key factor which will determine whether or not customers will pay more, or accept reduced technical performance, is the confidence they have in the environmental benefits involved. Customers will need to be confident that:

- the environmental issue(s) involved are real problems;
- the company's market offering has improved eco-performance compared to competitor or previous offerings;
- purchasing the product will make some sort of material difference.

This approach can help to explain some of the inconsistencies in the research findings into green consumer behaviour. The majority of consumers profess concern for the environment, a desire to buy greener products and a willingness to pay for them or accept technical performance reductions. The numbers of consumers measurably changing their purchasing behaviour to buy green is much less, and this has generally been interpreted as a failure to back up intentions with purchase and a tendency to over-report social and environmental concerns (Wilson and Rathje, 1990). This undoubtedly explains part of the discrepancy, but the missing element is the confidence that customers have in companies' green marketing offerings. A BRMB/Mintel survey found that 71 per cent of UK consumers thought that companies were using green issues as an excuse to charge higher prices.

Attempts to relate environmental knowledge to green consumption have produced inconsistent results, but researchers have assumed that increasing environmental knowledge will lead to an increased desire to purchase green products. The reverse may be true, in that increasing environmental knowledge may sometimes reduce the consumers' confidence in the effectiveness of market-based solutions for environmental challenges, and it may make them more aware of the short-comings of products seeking to market themselves on a green platform.

Eco-performance

For proactive companies seeking to gain competitive advantage, and for the more reactive companies seeking to avoid the costs and potential for competitive disadvantage associated with environmental damage, the key issue is their 'eco-performance'. This represents the impact that products and businesses have on the human and natural environment within which they exist, but it is not a straightforward concept. A question like 'What constitutes a green product?' has no simple answer. Is it one that has achieved sustainability? One that is better than its competitors? One that is less harmful than the product it replaces? Or one produced by a company with an accredited environmental management system?

The eco-performance of businesses and products, like the demand of consumers, comprises many different shades of green. Trying to identify a company as either green or 'dirty' is rather misleading, in the same way as trying to classify a company as marketing orientated or not. Such polarized distinctions are inappropriate for a performance continuum, and the relativity of eco-performance is reflected in Charter's (1992a) concept of 'greener' rather than 'green' marketing.

The pursuit of sustainability is the underlying principle of green marketing, and a company can justifiably claim green credentials if it is demonstrably and consistently moving towards sustainability. Achieving sustainability is not a pre-requisite for a valid claim to be green, just as 100 per cent customer satisfaction is not a prerequisite to claim a marketing orientation. In many markets, economic and technical considerations preclude sustainability as a short-term objective for green companies, even though sustainability can be their ultimate goal.

Measuring and managing the eco-performance of products is made difficult by the variety of factors which can contribute to a good or bad customer perception of eco-performance. Some companies have run into problems by claiming their products as 'green' by focusing simply on the product itself, while ignoring the environmental performance of the means of production or the company as a whole. For example, the £8 million advertising campaign launching Ariel Ultra as a green detergent was somewhat negated by front page news coverage highlighting that it had been tested on animals. Companies whose green strategy is product-orientated or one-dimensional, instead of holistic, are prone to exposure by green interest groups, to charges of hypocrisy and green hype, and to a loss of consumer confidence in their green message. Developing a more holistic green strategy requires an appreciation of the product itself, what goes into it, and what goes into, and out of, the environment as a result of its production and use. This process is analogous to Porter's value chain approach, as shown in Figure 26.2.

For those companies that are serious about green marketing, the success factors can be summarized as the seven Cs, creating a strategy that is:

1   *Customer-orientated:* in addressing environmental issues that concern customers and creating product offerings that balance improved eco-performance with customer needs for functionality, value and convenience.
2   *Commercially viable:* in ensuring that any technical and economic barriers can be overcome to produce a product offering that will both meet customer needs and make a profit.
3   *Credible:* to customers, senior managers and other stakeholders.
4   *Consistent:* with corporate objectives, strategies and capabilities.
5   *Clear:* it shouldn't be shrouded in environmental or technical jargon.
6   *Coordinated:* with the operational strategies and plans of the other business functions.
7   *Communicated:* effectively internally and externally. Internal marketing does just not mean launching environmental policies to staff; it also means keeping the momentum going as the environment becomes assimilated as one of many 'key business issues'.

Going green – the philosophical challenge

Adopting green marketing as a response to the needs of customers and other stakeholders requires the development of new products, processes, and philosophies which reflect the organization's environmental commitment. In its underlying quest to satisfy consumers, and in the marketing activities involved, green marketing resembles conventional marketing. The difference between the two lies in a philosophy which tries to balance the techno-economic market perspective with a broader socio-

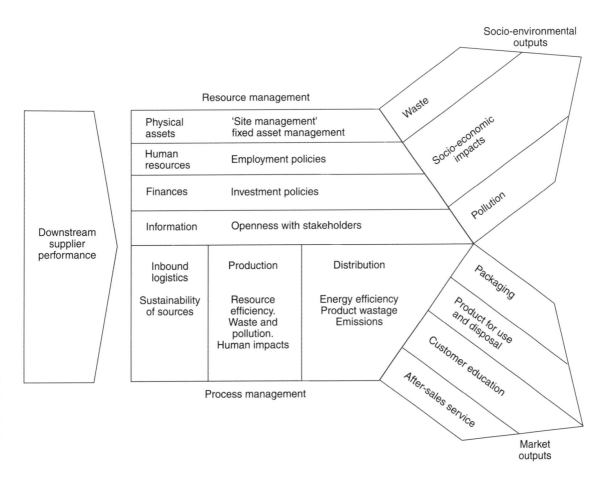

Figure 26.2   Components of environmental performance

environmental approach. This requires a re-evaluation of some fundamental marketing concepts including:

- Marketing's legitimacy. Marketing's role in driving forward economic growth by stimulating demand, and its role in satisfying customer wants have always legitimized marketing, to the extent that the benefits of ever increasing consumer choice and economic growth have gone unquestioned. The green challenge has changed this. Mulhern (1992) proposes the need to focus on customer welfare rather than purely on customer wants. Issues such as passive smoking and car safety (which usually equates to driver safety) have highlighted the

failure of marketing to address the needs and welfare of non-consumers. Durning (1992) points out that only one fifth of the world's population have sufficient disposable wealth to make consumption choices and belong to the 'consumer class'. He also questions the morality of that richest fifth continuing to enjoy a standard of living that the planet cannot sustain, and which the remaining four fifths can aspire to (encouraged by the images from marketing communication) but are unlikely to attain. The need for sustainability also requires us to question the validity of striving to satisfy all current consumer wants, if they are at the expense of future generations of consumers.

- Consumers. Henri Fayol once quipped about sending out for workers, but human beings turning up instead. Similarly, green marketers need to reconsider their approach to consumers. The word 'consumer' epitomizes a view of customers, not as people, but as a means of consumption. Marketing theory tends to deal with a very limited number of customer wants or needs at a time. However, peoples' needs and wants are many, varied and often potentially incompatible. One may yearn to live in an area free from the pollution, congestion and danger posed by cars, and yet be unwilling to give up the benefits of personal mobility that car ownership provides. Just as a product is more accurately analysed as a 'bundle of benefits', a customer should be considered as possessing a 'bundle of wants and needs'. In the face of conflicting desires to consume and conserve, customers may increasingly seek satisfaction through non-purchase decisions (such as repairs). By contributing to reduced environmental degradation, green consumer behaviour addresses an inherent human need for a viable environment, which may sometimes be at the expense of more explicit material wants. Recent years have witnessed an increasing range of conservation-orientated behaviour among consumers, from the recycling of cans and bottles to the boom in returning consumer durables to the supply chain through small ads or car boot fairs.
- Customer satisfaction. In the past, customer satisfaction has been judged in terms of the performance of the product at the moment (or during the period) of consumption. A green consumer may reject a product because they become aware of the environmental harm that the product causes in production or disposal. They may also avoid a product because they disapprove of the activities of the producer, its suppliers or investors.
- The product concept. If green consumer satisfaction depends upon the production process and on all the activities of the producer, we are approaching the situation where the company itself is becoming the product consumed (Peattie, 1995). Drucker's (1973) famous concept that 'Marketing is the whole business seen from its final result, that is from the customers' point of view', seems set to become an enforced reality for many businesses, because the green movement means that customers (or those who influence them) are now actively looking at all aspects of their company. As Bernstein (1992) comments 'The consumer wants to know about the company. Companies won't be able to hide behind their brands. Who makes it will be as important as what goes into it since the former may reassure the customer about the latter.' To solve intractable eco-conundrums, it will be essential to re-focus on customer orientated needs as opposed to product orientated solutions. This may mean re-focusing a business towards a 'purer' marketing orientation, for example, away from car manufacturing towards the provision of transportation and mobility. Electrolux in Belgium have instigated a programme of installing centralized 'textile care centres' of leased washing machines in apartment buildings, on the basis that people have no innate desire to own a washing machine, but instead simply require clean clothes.
- Criteria for success. Traditional marketing theory implies that if the four Ps are right, then success will follow in the form of a fifth P, 'profits'. Green marketing success involves ensuring that the marketing mix and the company meet four 'S' criteria (Peattie, 1990):

  1 Satisfaction of customer needs.
  2 Safety of products and production for consumers, workers, society and the environment.
  3 Social acceptability of the products, their production and the other activities of the company.
  4 Sustainability of the products, their production and the other activities of the company.

- De-marketing. One unavoidable conclusion of green marketing logic is that where a product is being consumed and produced in an unsustainable way, it may have to be de-marketed (either voluntarily or forcibly) to reduce consumption. This may sound unlikely, but within tourism, destinations such as Cyprus have developed a successful policy of attracting fewer but wealthier tourists in an effort to conserve the quality of the destination itself (Clements, 1989).

Companies seeking to pursue improved eco-performance will find it difficult without addressing these philosophical aspects. This is analogous to total quality management, where the difficulties that many western com-panies have experienced in implementing it, reflects their focus on attempting to apply the management tools and techniques, without embracing the underlying philosophy as their Japanese competitors have done. An example of an explicit green business philosophy, comes from The Body Shop:

Our products reflect our philosophy. They are formulated with care and respect. Respect for other cultures, the past, the natural world, and our customers. It's a partnership of profits with principles. (Anita Roddick, from The Body Shop promotional literature 1990)

Going green – the management challenge

For companies seeking eco-performance improvement as a component of their corporate strategy and/or philosophy, marketing has a vital part to play, and yet a part which in the past has often been unfulfilled. Lent and Wells (1992) found that 77 per cent of top managers in Fortune 500 companies saw the environment as strategically important, and 63 per cent of production managers were getting involved in environmental management initiatives. Only 28 per cent of their marketing colleagues were matching their involvement. Similarly it is common to find eco-design initiatives within companies being driven by environmental managers rather than their marketing colleagues. It is perhaps the

lack of a marketing orientation that has led to the common experience among companies in the early stages of greening, of hitting what Robert Shelton of Arthur D. Little describes as a 'Green Wall' (Shelton, 1994). This is often caused by the failure to integrate environmental management initiatives effectively with business strategies and values, and a failure to market the initiatives effectively internally. Coddington (1993) recommends that firms engaged in a greening process should set up an environmental task force in which marketers play a leading role. He identifies two sets of strengths that marketers can contribute to the greening process, the marketing perspective and the marketing skillset. The greening challenge requires creativity, the ability to work effectively across internal organizational boundaries and excellent communication skills. Coddington identifies marketing managers as being often 'superbly qualified' for the task because:

- Marketers are able to identify and analyse the marketing implications of corporate environmental exposures and initiatives.
- Marketers can help to identify new business product and service opportunities that arise out of those same environmental exposures and initiatives (Anheuser Busch's waste initiatives for example led to their establishment as one of the world's largest aluminium recyclers).
- Marketers can work to ensure that when corporate environmental policies are developed, the marketing implications are given due consideration.
- As a matter of course, marketers must co-ordinate their activities across multiple departments (R&D, manufacturing, packaging, sales, public relations).
- Marketers are professional communicators. This skill is enormously useful in virtually every aspect of environmental management – on the task force itself, and in such areas as environmental management training, emergency response training, community relations and other domains which put a premium on communications.

B&Q have produced a detailed environmental policy statement which defines the responsibilities of different functions including marketing, finance, personnel, logistics and systems. It also demonstrates the leadership role that marketing should play in the greening process:

The marketing director is the main board director responsible for environmental issues and is therefore ultimately responsible for researching the issues, writing the policy and auditing progress. As marketing director he also has responsibility to ensure that the environmental policies and targets of marketing are implemented.

In market development B&Q shall monitor through market research, customers' concerns and perceptions on environmental issues and customers' understanding and appreciation of B&Q's response to them. Market development will also incorporate environmental considerations into the strategic planning in the company and refer to strategic environmental issues in the five year plan.

Marketing services is responsible for most of the purchasing decisions handled by marketing. They shall ensure that 'point of sale' material, carrier bags and all their other purchases consider environmental specifications. These include use of recycled post consumer waste, recyclability, and waste minimization. Marketing services will ensure that no misleading environmental statements or claims are made on any POS material or other communications such as press enquiries. Marketing recognizes that some of the products it sells have distinct environmental attributes, for energy efficiency equipment and home composting. We also recognize a need to inform our customers more about our environmental policies and the environmental performance of all products.

(*Source:* 'How green is my hammer', B&Q's Environmental Review, 1993).

The main practical differences between green marketing and conventional marketing concern the holistic nature of the green marketing challenge, the novel challenges it presents in terms of information and the marketing audit, and finally in terms of the shifts it requires in timescales for planning and decision making.

Towards holism – broadening the scope of marketing in practice

Although the marketing philosophy embraces the entire business, the sphere of influence of marketing and marketers in practice is often more limited. Carson's (1968) observation that, for many companies, marketing is 'the integration, just below senior management level, of those activities related primarily towards customers', unfortunately still holds true in many of today's firms. A range of organizational forces tend to restrict the influence of marketing, or split it into operational marketing tasks handled by marketers, and strategic marketing decisions handled by top management (Peattie and Notley, 1989).

As green issues have increasingly come to influence customers and competitiveness, green marketing and the management of eco-performance need to escape their functional boundaries to become pan-organizational management concerns, in much the same way that quality slipped its functional bonds to become total quality management. Within the USA there is now a trend towards the merging of quality with green marketing management to create the philosophy of total quality environmental management (TQEM) (Hochman *et al.*, 1993). Green marketing requires marketers to have an appreciation of, and influence over, all aspects of a business, its products and its production system. How energy efficient is our production process? Where are raw materials sourced from? Where is spare capital being invested? Such questions were once not the concern of marketers, but they have become relevant because the answers could now influence stakeholder perceptions and consumer behaviour.

A 'stakeholder approach' is vital for the development of appropriate and holistic green philosophies, strategies and policies. Internally and externally organizations face an increasing depth of interest in their eco-performance and an ever increasing range of interested parties. Table 26.2 demonstrates the perceived

Table 26.2 Perceived importance of stakeholder influence on environmental policy development (%)

Customers	75
Employees	70
Suppliers	55
Government	48
Media	46
Pressure groups	30
Trade unions	18

Source: Charter (1990).

importance of a selection of key stakeholders, in terms of the proportion of surveyed companies that cited their influence.

A green firm needs to take a holistic view of its various stakeholders and their relationships with the firm and each other, with each being viewed as a customer. They also need to relate to customers and other stakeholders beyond just providing products for them, but by taking some responsibility for their products and the impacts they have on society and the environment. The concept of companies taking greater responsibility for their customers and products has been reflected in the idea of 'brand managers' being replaced by 'brand stewards'. In agro-chemicals markets where difficulties with correct product use often occur in countries with low literacy rates among farmers, some companies are using the concept of brand stewardship to ensure that products are used correctly. Dow Corning, for example, demands that its sales staff:

1   inform customers about known hazards relating to the products;
2   advise customers to use products in accordance with label recommendations;
3   insist that distributors pass on handling, use and disposal information to their customers;
4   report and respond vigorously against cases of misuse;
5   co-ordinate visits by company staff to customer sites, to ensure safe use and disposal of products.

New marketing information challenges

Green marketing requires marketers to obtain and provide a variety of information which may be new to them concerning the environmental impact of products, suppliers and production processes. Stakeholders increasingly demand information about eco-performance which companies have traditionally been reluctant to provide. A 1991 sample of 670 UK companies' annual reports analysed by *Company Reporting* revealed only 3 per cent highlighting environmental information, most of which was meaningless. Satisfying the green customer (and the terms of the EC directive 90/313, Freedom of Access to Information on the Environment) requires a new openness which will force marketers away from a view of the production process as a 'black box' into which the customer is not encouraged to peer. This is particularly the case in industrial markets where it is becoming the norm among leading companies to insist upon environmental auditing and reporting by all suppliers.

Meeting the needs for environmentally related information, both as an input into the development of marketing and corporate strategy, and as an output for stakeholders, involves:

*   Environmental scoping reviews and audits for existing facilities.
*   Environmental impact assessments (EIAs) conducted as part of the development process for new products or facilities.
*   Environmental information systems (EISs) to support management decision making.
*   Risk analysis to determine the likelihood and potential impact of environmental incidents and the costs of prevention and contingency measures.
*   An action-orientation to ensure that the gath-

ering of information is translated into positive action. Conducting environmental audits will not make a company green, just as conducting financial audits will not make it profitable.

It is essential for a company to focus on the environmental outcomes of decision-making, as well as the 'hard' eco-performance of products and process. This involves answering such questions as:

- What are the environmental impacts of our marketing decisions?
- What information is needed to improve the quality of those decisions?
- Where do we get that information?
- What information do we have in-house?
- What do we need to acquire from outside?

Changing the marketing time frame

Green marketing focuses on the performance of products before purchase and after use, which requires a new time perspective for marketers. A 'cradle-to-grave' view of products may mean that their performance must be considered over a period of years instead of months. For consumer durables, the question of actual durability assumes a new importance. Evidence suggests that many products currently exist only as semi-durables; a survey examining the life cycles of domestic appliances found that a high percentage of appliances discarded on rubbish dumps had little wrong with them and required only simple and cheap repairs (source: *New Scientist*, 24/12/88). Creating more durable products can form an important part of a green strategy. Agfa Gevaert switched from a policy of selling photocopiers, to leasing them on a full service basis. This led to a product re-design brief based around durability, and the upgrading of the copy drums from a lifespan of under 3 million to over 100 million copies.

The need to examine the impact of products from cradle to grave, is leading towards the concept of re-marketing or even closed-loop (waste free) marketing. Various tools are being developed to aid the green marketer to assess the full environmental impact of products, the best known being lifecycle analysis and eco-balance analysis. The greatest difficulty for the marketer is to know how far forward or back, and down how many of the branches of the supply chain, such an analysis should go. An example of a cradle-to-grave life cycle is provided in Figure 26.3.

The practical challenge – greening the marketing mix

Green product management

In the new climate of environmental concern, eco-performance is an important product dimension, which needs to be understood and managed, whether or not the company is pursuing a green strategy. Analysing the eco-performance of a product needs to be multi-dimensional, since it is influenced by many factors, and it also should be done with reference to competitors' offerings. A green performance matrix, like the one shown in Figure 26.4, can aid this process.

Green product attributes fall into two general categories. First there are those relating to the tangible product (or service encounter) itself. Second there are those that relate to the processes by which the product is developed and the attributes of the producer itself. Combining these creates a new 'total product concept' (Peattie 1995).

The challenge in developing a total green product is to improve eco-performance while producing acceptably comparable levels of functionality and service, at a competitive price. This is not an easy task, but one which has been accomplished by some pioneering green companies such as Ecover within the highly competitive green detergent market. Their approach involves adopting cleaner technologies that design out waste in the manufacturing processes, rather than using 'end-of-pipe' solutions which inevitably represent an added cost.

In October 1992 in Belgium, Ecover launched the world's first ecological factory. Their approach was to ensure that all processes, products and philosophies are sufficiently green to meet increasingly close stakeholder scrutiny. Innovations range from the use of factory bricks derived from coal slag, to monetary incentives given to employees for the use of company bicycles. Ecover are also championing the concept of a zero-impact business park which produces no, or minimal, environmental pollution and has energy efficiency and recycling 'built-in' (Develter, 1992).

Greening creates a new emphasis on a prod-ucts performance at the end of its useful life. Improving the post-use eco-performance of products requires the integration of opportunities for some or all of the 'five Rs' into the product concept:

1   *Repair.* A modular design approach and good after sales service provision can make repairing products cost effective and extend their useful life.
2   *Reconditioning.* In the automotive market a wide range of reconditioned parts, from tyres to engines, can be purchased.
3   *Re-use.* The average dairy milk bottle is used twelve times.

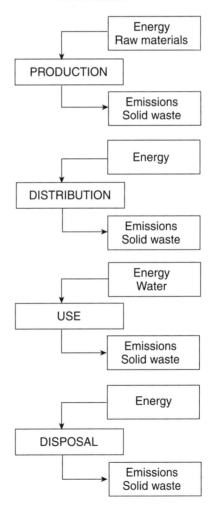

- Design
- Choice of material
- Extraction of raw materials
- Material manufacture
- Use of recycled materials
- Transport of materials and components
- Manufacture of components
- Washing machine manufacture

- Packaging
- Transport

- Operation
- Durability
- Reliability
- Detergent use
- Water use

- Collection, transport
- Recycling
- Landfill, incineration

Figure 26.3   A washing machine's life cycle

4   *Recycling.* Products ranging from beer cans to BMWs are now designed to be recyclable.
5   *Re-manufacture.* To create new from old, such as the re-manufacture of used laser printer cartridges performed by Onyx Associates.

Green packaging

Packaging has been an obvious starting point for many companies' green marketing efforts, since packaging can often be safely reduced without expensive changes to core products or production processes and without a risk of disaffecting customers. So where shampoos like Head and Shoulders once came in a stout plastic bottle housed within a cardboard box, they now come just in a bottle. This provides both environmental and direct cost benefits. The Packaging Audit System developed by Boots led to

initiatives in the use of display trays and reusable transit containers which have proved to be 'a critical success factor and a source of competitive advantage' (Ashton, 1996).

Reducing and recycling packaging is also a key feature of government policy within Europe. The UK government has a target to recycle 25 per cent of household waste by the year 2000, while the controversial German Waste Packaging Ordinance forces producers and retailers to accept all waste packaging returned by consumers and includes mandatory deposits on many containers to encourage returns.

In addition to the removal of unnecessary layers and provision for recycling, there are a range of ways in which the design of packaging can be made greener which can be identified using the checklist given on page 613 (Chick, 1992):

Product attribute	Comparative green performance				
	Best possible	Among the best	Above average	Better than some	Poor
Raw materials					
Energy efficiency					
Waste					
Pollution					
Packaging					
Lifespan					
Re-usability					
Recyclability					
Effect on customer behaviour					
Green associations and linkages					
Socio-economic impact					

Figure 26.4   The green performance matrix

Checklist for choosing or designing a greener pack

- Does the production of the packaging material have an adverse effect on the environment? e.g.
  - Does the material come from a scarce or seriously declining source?
  - Is production of the material energy-intensive?
- Design or choose packaging where the materials can be easily re-used or recycled. Does the combination of materials create difficulty for recycling?
- Avoid *coloured* polyethylene terephthalate (PET).
- Ensure the chemicals used in a pack do not cause environmental damage (e.g. CFCs), or choose a chemical-free alternative pack (e.g. pump-action sprays).
- Do environmental protection laws in any proposed market either constrain the use of chosen materials or increase their production or disposal costs?
- Can concentrated products that fit into smaller packages be developed?
- Avoid excess packaging: only use what is necessary.
- Use reclaimed (secondary) materials wherever possible, which encourages the development of the recycling industry.
- Support resource-efficient reclamation schemes; consider whether material identification would help. It is vital that any collection system coincides with the development of markets and that companies start to 'sell' the re-usability or recyclability of their product.
- Give proper consideration to pollution that may be caused during manufacture or as post-consumer waste, e.g. pigments formulated with cadmium, lead or chromium.
- Ensure the pack, the information and the overall appearance encourages the efficient use, re-use and disposal of the contents and the pack.
- Consumer education material and advertising should be considered as an accompanying option to the pack.

- Establish a system for checking and collating information about the environmental implications of different materials, processes, etc.
- Ensure appropriate training has been given to designers, marketers, advertisers, packaging engineers, etc.

Green communication

Many companies have sought to promote themselves and their products through explicit or implicit association with the environment and good eco-performance. There has been considerable concern over whether or not much of the green promotion (particularly advertising) being used is misleading (e.g. Carlson *et al.*, 1993). However, given the complexities of the issues involved, messages that are both straightforward enough for consumers, yet sufficiently comprehensive and qualified to satisfy regulators and activists, can be hard to create. Environmental issues is an area where there are important opportunities in combining with corporate communications efforts (as for example with Norsk Hydro's highly successful Environmental Report), and where a communications approach based on openness and education more than promotion will often pay dividends.

There are a range of issues in managing the green communications mix:

- *Advertising:* do our products lend themselves to convincing and distinctive green images?
- *Direct mail:* how can we avoid being labelled 'junk mailers'?
- *Sales promotion:* can consumers be offered incentives to change their purchasing and product use decisions in favour of green products and the environment? For example Lever's offer of the Persil EcoBox to encourage the use of Persil refills.
- *Personal selling:* have the salesforce been made aware of the environmental implications of the company and its products and processes?

- *Public relations:* has an environmental audit been undertaken? Are results accessible?
- *Sponsorship:* is there an environmental project that fits our communications objectives?

Green issues provide good opportunities for both informative and emotive marketing communications. Fort Sterling's green brand Nouvelle captured 3 per cent of the £500 million toilet tissue market in its first year with a modestly funded advertising campaign which used such hard-hitting copy as 'It feels a little uncomfortable using toilet tissue that wipes out forests'. The key is to understand the concerns of stakeholder audiences and then to communicate effectively and efficiently.

Green pricing

Going green may affect the cost structures of a business with a knock-on effect on prices, particularly if pricing is on a 'cost plus' basis. Developing new sustainable raw material sources, complying with legislation, writing off old, 'dirty' technology, capital expenditure on clean technology and the overheads associated with greening the organization can impose a heavy cost burden. (These extra costs are often spoken of as a green premium, although in reality they represent the removal of a subsidy provided to products by the environment and the failure to address environmental costs.) However, this can be counterbalanced by the savings made by reducing raw materials and energy inputs, by reducing packaging, by finding markets for by-products and by switching to lead-free distribution. If costs are looked at holistically and managed on a portfolio basis, then wider eco-efficiency process benefits, when added to premium demand benefits, can counterbalance the costs of greening to make a positive contribution to profitability.

Consumer demand for green products can also allow for the addition of a green price premiums, as applies to free-range eggs and dolphin friendly (rod-and-line caught) tuna. However, marketers should exercise caution in taking advantage of such opportunities, as any

suggestions of profiteering may undermine the development of a credible green image.

Green logistics

A great deal of the environmental impact of products relates to the fuels consumed and materials used and wasted in transporting products to customers. One of the predictions about the transformation towards a sustainable global economy is a return to an emphasis on more localized production and distribution. International distribution systems are often only viable because their socio-environmental costs are not met.

An example of logistics forming a key component of a greening strategy comes from B&Q, whose logistics function has been rewarded with several major awards for environmental excellence. Their 1993 Environmental Review included:

1   The development of 'centralized distribution' at B&Q, bringing environmental benefits such as reduced vehicle movements and a reduction in transit packaging.
2   The establishment of a policy and targets aimed at reducing vehicle emission impacts.
3   The reduction of transit packaging in conjunction with suppliers, aiming for a 30 per cent reduction in the total corrugated board used by UK suppliers within the first year.
4   A cost and benefit analysis undertaken into the practicalities of store-based collection and recycling systems for packaging materials.
5   Insistence that logistics sub-contractors operate an environmental policy consistent with B&Q's and commission their own comprehensive environmental audit.
6   The promotion of environmental awareness both within the B&Q's logistics department and its subcontractors.

The future of green marketing

A key question for marketers is 'How will the green challenge evolve?' Environmental concern has always moved up and down society's agenda according to the perceived state of the environment and the current importance of other issues. However, a 'ratchet effect' operates, ensuring that short-term fluctuations in green interest translate into a long-term deepening of concern. In comparison to the power of the global economy, environmental concern can appear a rather insubstantial force. Looking at the size, power, momentum and sheer technological sophistication of the global economy, it can appear, much as the *Titanic* did, completely unsinkable. The *Titanic's* progress was interrupted by an iceberg, which although largely hidden and undetected, proved nonetheless fatal. It would be comforting to believe that global economic progress will not be hindered by environmental intervention but, technological miracles notwithstanding, this seems unlikely. The hope of environmentalists is that a new course can be plotted, and the ship turned around, before the catastrophe becomes too close to avoid. The difficulty is that moving marketing towards a more environmental paradigm will mean abandoning some of the simple ideas and assumptions that help marketing academics and practitioners to cope with its complexities. It means abandoning a view of products in simple terms as solutions to consumption problems, and accepting that both consumption and products can cause problems. It means confronting the socio-environmental damage caused by products and production systems instead of dismissing their impacts as 'externalities', and assuming that someone else will find and fund solutions to them. It means confronting the needs of those who don't consume as well as those that do, and considering the needs of future customers instead of only those of the present. Otherwise the global economy will continue environmentally 'overtrading' in a way that can only impoverish future generations.

For anyone who thinks that the environment will somehow go out of fashion as an issue for marketers, there are two important points to be aware of. The first is Ehrlich and Ehrlich's

(1990) IPAT model which expresses the overall impact of economic activity on the physical environment as:

$$\text{Impact} = \text{Population} \times \text{Affluence} \times \text{Technology}$$

According to UN forecasts, the world's population could reach 8 billion as early as 2015, a 60 per cent increase from 1985 levels. This would mean that just to restrict the rate of environmental damage to current levels, there would have to be a drastic adjustment either in the standard of living that we enjoy, or in the environmental impact of the technologies used to satisfy our demand for goods and services. If mankind were to continue current rates of population growth, consumption and methods of production, then by 2030 critical natural resources would last less than a decade more, and humankind would generate 400 billion tons of solid waste each year, enough to bury Los Angeles 100 metres deep (Frosch and Gallopoulos, 1989).

The second factor is the arrival of a new generation of more environmentally literate consumers, employees and investors. This results from the integration of the environment into education, and the 'Blue Peter effect' of practical environmentalism becoming integrated into popular children's entertainment. The Henley Centre's 'Young Eyes: Children's Vision of the Future Environment' studying 10–14 year-olds revealed high levels of environmental concern, a belief that environmental problems are urgent and likely to affect society directly in their lifetime, and a tendency towards realistic and pragmatic values rather than woolly idealism. Among undergraduates there have also been measurable increases in environmental concern and an increasing tendency to consider eco-performance when considering potential employers (Charter, 1992c).

Green demand and green marketing is likely to evolve in three phases:

1   *Substitution.* Characterized by green consumers differentiating between products on

the basis of perceived eco-performance, much confusion over concepts and terminology, and with a great deal of sales and public relations activity dressed up as green marketing. The result has been increasing consumer cynicism about green claims, as demonstrated by Gerstman & Meyers' Third Annual Environment Survey finding that 91 per cent of US consumers rated marketers as 'the least concerned about the environment'. There has also been a great deal of 'spotlighting', the singling out of particular industries, companies and products for praise or condemnation, sometimes with little relation to the actualities of eco-performance. Environmental improvements are often limited to end-of-pipe changes to production systems, the substitution of damaging ingredients such as CFCs and the elimination of excess packaging.

2 *Systemization.* The establishment of BS 7750 and ISO 14001 standards for Environmental Management Systems and the EC Ecolabel Scheme should move the entire 'game' onto a new plane of recognized (if flawed) performance criteria and evaluation. Businesses will move towards the redesign of products and production systems, and the implementation of environmental reporting and management systems. Better information for consumers will allow more informed and consistent green purchasing. Provision of environmental information and provision for the recycling of products will become standard practice, and governed by increasingly stringent legislation.

3 *Societal change.* The deepening environmental crisis will eventually lead to a more radical shift in consumer behaviour challenging the very basis of demand and consumption. This will be part of a wider social, political and economic upheaval to develop a more sustainable society. Consumers will increasingly become conservers and will seek opportunities to recycle or recondition products, and to achieve satisfaction through non-purchasing based activities.

When any given market will reach the first, or the second phase of green consumption is anyone's guess. However, the longer the delay before reaching phase 3, the greater the upheaval involved will be. Marketers are faced with a very simple choice, to pursue improved environmental performance or not. The consequences of that choice will depend upon the evolution of the green agenda in relation to their industry, as demonstrated by Figure 26.5.

Some environmentalists have criticized green marketing on the basis that 'Changing our shopping habits will not save the world.' This is true, but if it creates improvement in the eco-performance of businesses, it will buy much needed time in which to understand how to make the more important changes to our economic, technical and political systems, in order to manage our environment in a sustainable way.

Currently green marketing is viewed as one of many options for generating competitive advantage. This rather ignores one important factor – the customer. People want greener products from greener companies. If a company is not improving its eco-performance as fast as constraints of cost, technology and consumer understanding allow, it is questionable as to whether they are practising marketing at all.

Green marketing's early progress has concentrated on the greening of the tangible marketing mix, along with the production system that underpins it. What many companies have yet to recognize, is that greening represents a massive internal marketing challenge. Marketers have a duty to voice the consumer's demands for improved environmental performance within all aspects of the business, and to take a lead in making it happen. A tall order for marketers? Perhaps, but this is what the marketing philosophy is all about – getting the entire business behind the effort to satisfy the customer. It is a familiar rallying cry for marketers, but this time the stakes are a little higher, and winning the battle just might help to save the world!

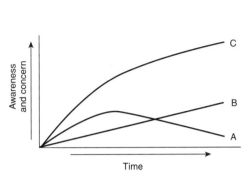

Scenarios Greener marketing	Without	With
A	No change	No change
B	Gradually forced to adopt greener strategy – may lose market share	Possible market gains available – strong future likely
C	Loss of market share likely and long-term survival unlikely	Secure market share – secure future likely

Figure 26.5 Potential scenarios for environmental awareness and concern

References

Ashton, C. (1996) Behind the Store Facade: Environmental Issues in Mainstream Retailing, *Environmental Excellence*, IFS International Ltd, March, pp. 12–15.

Azzone, G. and Bertele, U. (1994) Exploiting Green Strategies for Competitive Advantage, *Long Range Planning*, **27**(6), 69–81.

Bernstein, D. (1992) *In The Company of Green: Corporate Communication for the New Environment*, ISBA, London.

Capra, F. (1983) *The Turning Point*, Bantam.

Carlson, L., Grove, S. J. and Kangun, N. (1993) A Content Analysis of Environmental Advertising Claims: A Matrix Method Approach, *Journal of Advertising*, **22**(3), 27–39.

Carson, D. (1968) Marketing Organization in British Manufacturing Firms, *Journal of Marketing*, **32**, 268–325.

Charter, M. (1990) *The Greener Employee*, KPH Marketing, Alton.

Charter, M. (1992a) Emerging Concepts in a Greener World, in Charter, M. (ed.), *Greener Marketing*, Greenleaf, Sheffield.

Charter, M. (1992b) Greener Marketing Strategy, in Charter, M. (ed.), *Greener Marketing*, Greenleaf, Sheffield.

Charter, M. (1992c) Greener People, in Charter, M. (ed.), *Greener Marketing*, Greenleaf, Sheffield.

Chick, A. (1992) Greener Packaging, in Charter, M. (ed.) *Greener Marketing*, Greenleaf, Sheffield.

Christensen, P. D. (1995) The Environment: It's Not Time to Relax, *McKinsey Quarterly*, **4**, 146–154.

Clements, M. A. (1989) Selecting Tourist Traffic by Demarketing, *Tourism Management*, June, 89–95.

Coddington, W. (1993) *Environmental Marketing*, McGraw-Hill.

Davis, J. J. (1991) A Blueprint for Green Marketing, *Journal of Business Strategy*, **12**(4), 14–17.

Dembkowski, S. and Hanmer-Lloyd, S. (1994) The Environmental-Value-Attitude-System Model: A Framework to Guide the Understanding of Environmentally Conscious Consumer Behaviour, *Journal of Marketing Management*, **10**(7), 593–603.

Develter, D. (1992) *Ecover – The Ecological Factory Manual*, Ecover Publications, Oostemalle, Belgium.

Drucker, P. F. (1973) *Top Management*, Heinemann, London.

Durning, A. T. (1992) *How Much is Enough?* Earthscan, London.

Ehrlich, P. R. and Ehrlich, A. H. (1990) *The Population Explosion*, Simon & Schuster, New York.

Elkington, J. (1994) Toward the Sustainable Corporation: Win-Win-Win Business Strategies for Sustainable Development, *California Management Review*, **36**(2), 90–100.

Frosch, R. A. and Gallopoulos, N. E. (1989) Strategies for Manufacturing, *Scientific American*, September, pp. 144–152.

Hennison, K. and Kinnear, T. (1976) *Ecological Marketing*, Prentice-Hall, NJ.

Hochman, D., Wells, R. P., O'Connell, P. A. and Hochman, M. N. (1993) Total Quality Management: A Tool to Move from Compliance to Strategy, *Greener Management International*, **1**(1), 59–70.

Kardash, W. J. (1974) Corporate Responsibility and the Quality of Life: Developing the Ecologically Concerned Consumer, in K. E. Henion, and Kinner (eds), *Ecological Marketing*, American Marketing Association.

Kirkpatrick, D. (1990) Environmentalism: The New Crusade, *Fortune*, February 12, pp. 44–52.

Leeflang, P. S. H. and van Raaij, W. F. (1995) The Changing Consumer in the European Union: A Meta Analysis, *International Journal of Research in Marketing*, **12**, 373–387.

Lent, T. and Wells, R. P. (1992) Corporate Environmental Study Shows Shift from Compliance to Strategy, *Total Quality Environmental Management*, Summer, 379–94.

Menon, A. and Menon, A. (1997) Enviropreneurial Marketing Strategy: The Emergence of Corporate Environmentalism as Market Strategy, *Journal of Marketing*, **61**(1), 51–67.

Miller, C. (1993) Conflicting Studies Still Have Execs Wondering What Data to Believe, *Marketing News*, **27**(12), 1.

Morton, B. (1996) The Role of Purchasing and Supply Management in Environmental Improvement, in *Proceedings of the 1996 Business Strategy and the Environment Conference*, Leeds, ERP Environment, pp. 136–141.

Mulhall, D. (1992) Environmental Management: The Relationship Between Pressure Groups and Industry – a Radical Redesign, in D. Koechlin and K. Muller (eds), *Green Business Opportunities*, Pitman Publishing, London.

Mulhern, F. J. (1992) Consumer Wants and Consumer Welfare, in T. C. Allen *et al.* (eds), *Marketing Theory and Applications*, Proceedings of the 1992 AMA Winter Educators' Conference, pp. 407–412.

Peattie, K. J. and Notley, D. S. (1989) The Marketing and Strategic Planning Interface, *Journal of Marketing Management*, **4**(3), 330–347.

Peattie, K. J. (1990) Painting Marketing Education Green: Or How to Recycle Old Ideas, *Journal of Marketing Management*, **6**(2), 105–127.

Peattie, K. J. and Ringler, A. (1994) Management and the Environment: A Comparison Between the UK and Germany, *European Management Journal*, **12**(2), 216–225

Peattie, K. (1995) *Environmental Marketing Management: Meeting the Green Challenge*, Pitman, London.

Porter, M. E. (1991) America's Green Strategy, *Scientific American*, April, 168.

Porter, M. E. and van der Linde, C. (1995) Green and Competitive: Ending the Stalemate, *Harvard Business Review*, Sept–Oct, 120–133.

Prothero, A. (1990) Green Consumerism and the Societal Marketing Concept – Marketing Strategies for the 1990s, *Journal of Marketing Management*, **6**(2) 87–104.

Pujari, D. and Wright, G. (1996) Developing Environmentally-Conscious Product Strategy: A Qualitative Study of Selected Companies in Britain and Germany, *Marketing Intelligence and Planning*, **14**(1), 19–28.

Roberts, J. A. (1996) Green Consumers in the 1990s: Profile and Implications for Advertising, *Journal of Business Research*, **36**, 217–231.

Scerbinsky, J. (1991) Consumers and the Environment: A Focus on Five Products, *The Journal of Business Strategy*, **13**(4).

Shelton, R. D. (1994) Hitting the Green Wall: Why Corporate Programs Get Stalled, *Corporate Environmental Strategy*, **2**(2), 5–11.

Shrivastava, P. (1994) CASTRATED Environment: GREENING Organizational Studies, *Organization Studies*, **15**(5), 705–726.

Stenross, M. and Sweet, G. (1992) Implementing an Integrated Supply Chain: The Xerox Example, in Christopher, M. (ed.) *Logistics and*

Supply Chain Management, Pitman Publishing, London.

Vandermerwe, S. and Oliff, M. (1990) Customers Drive Corporations Green, *Long Range Planning*, **23**(6), 10–16.

Varadajan, P. R. (1992) Marketing's Contribution to Strategy: The View From a Different Looking Glass, *Journal of the Academy of Marketing Science*, **20**, 323–343.

Walley, N. and Whitehead, B. (1994) It's Not Easy Being Green, *Harvard Business Review*, **72**(3), 46–52.

Wilson, D. C. and Rathje, W. L. (1990) Modern Middens, *Natural History*, May, pp. 54–58.

Further reading

Charter, M. (1999) *Greener Marketing*, 2nd edn, Greenleaf, Sheffield. An edited collection which provides detailed coverage of the strategic implications of the greening of marketing, and follows through the practicalities in terms of the extended marketing mix. The themes of the text are reinforced through a collection of detailed case studies covering a wide range of organizations.

Coddington, W. (1993) *Environmental Marketing*, McGraw-Hill, New York. Takes a very practical approach to developing competitive advantage from improved environmental performance, mostly from the perspective of American consumer goods companies. Provides useful coverage of the problems of developing a greener organization as a foundation for the greening process.

Develter, D. (1992) *Ecover Manual*, 2nd edn, Ecover Publications, Oostemalle, Belgium. A comprehensive manual covering Ecover's experience in developing the world's first ecological factory. Demonstrates the wealth of detail that must be dealt with to ensure that the means of production, as well as the product itself, is environmentally sound.

Durning, A. T. (1992) *How Much is Enough?* Earthscan, London. A scathing and thought-provoking indictment of over-consumption.

Provides a stimulating challenge to many of the fundamental assumptions about marketing, its legitimacy, and the way it is practised.

McDonagh, P. and Prothero, A. (1997) *Green Management: A Reader*, Dryden Press, London. An excellent edited collection of papers combining the deeply philosophical with the highly practical. The practical papers have a strong marketing bias, and the entire collection is invaluable for putting marketing and the environment clearly in its organizational, social and global context.

Menon, A. and Menon, A. (1997) Enviropreneurial Marketing Strategy: The Emergence of Corporate Environmentalism as Market Strategy, *Journal of Marketing*, **61**(1), 51–67. Analyses the evolution of the relationship between marketing and the environment and in particular at the emerging of 'enviropreneurial marketing'. Provides a useful discussion of the driving forces behind the greening of marketing, the opportunities that it provides, and the relationship with corporate strategy.

Peattie, K. (1995) *Environmental Marketing Management: Meeting the Green Challenge*, Pitman, London. A book which attempts to pull together much of what was written about marketing and the environment in the late 1980s and early 1990s to develop a comprehensive picture of what the green challenge means for marketing. Discusses the environment as a philosophical, strategic and practical challenge for marketing management, and illustrates the issues with short case studies at the end of most chapters.

Shrivastava, P. (1994) CASTRATED Environment: GREENING Organizational Studies, *Organization Studies*, **15**(5), 705–726. An astonishing article which deconstructs the existing management paradigm to detail exactly how and why it is inherently incompatible with the physical environment within which it exists. Outlines a new environmental management paradigm and points the way forward towards a more sustainable way of managing businesses.

Wehrmeyer, W. (1993) *Environmental References in Business*, Greenleaf, Sheffield. An invaluable stepping stone to 'everything you ever wanted to know about green marketing but were afraid to ask', with over 2700 classic and 'cutting edge' articles indexed and referenced.

CHAPTER 27

Marketing for small-to-medium enterprises

DAVID CARSON

Introduction

What is 'marketing for SMEs' and why should it be treated as a separate topic? There are two strong reasons why it is important to view marketing as being different in this context. One is the recognition that SMEs (small to medium sized enterprises), are not simply little big business. By a definition of size they are certainly small to medium sized in relation to large corporations; however, as a consequence of its size an SME has unique characteristics which make it distinctly different, not only to large corporations but also to many or all other enterprises. A significant second factor is the relative number of SME enterprises to large corporations; in any market or region the vast majority of enterprises will be SMEs with only a few large corporations. A consequence of this is that most people who work in marketing are likely to work in SMEs. Of course, many high profile marketing jobs will belong in large organizations but most marketing and related jobs are to be found in SMEs. Further support for this argument can be found by recognizing the growing size of the service sector of any economy and acknowledging that most service firms are inherently marketing orientated and also SMEs.

There are a number of implications arising from the above which this chapter attempts to address. Consideration is given to the unique characteristics of SMEs and how these characteristics impact upon the activities of SMEs. Recognition is also given to the influence of the entrepreneur/owner/manager and his/her strengths and weaknesses. A significant realization arising out of this is the incompatibility of SME capabilities and activities and much of marketing theory. This is illustrated in this chapter by comparing textbook marketing theory and SME marketing in practice. Following this an examination is made of the nature of SME marketing which allows a framework to be devised for effective SME marketing based upon the inherent strengths of such enterprises. This framework is presented as a model of SME marketing.

At the conclusion of this chapter the reader can expect to have gleaned an understanding of SMEs' marketing practices and a realization that this marketing is different to conventional descriptions and practices as preached in the textbook literature. The reader is not required to decide whether one or the other is better, but it is hoped that s/he will have an appreciation that there is some sort of difference which needs to be acknowledged. The reader can expect to know how an SME entrepreneur can improve his/her marketing activity within the resource constraints inherent in such enterprises.

The origins of this chapter lie in many years of involvement with SMEs from a variety of perspectives, as owner and partner in several enterprises and as consultant, trainer, educator and researcher of SMEs. In all of these activities, there is the firm belief that every SME is unique and as a consequence, the marketing activity is also uniquely different. Of course, it is possible to generalize but in doing so it is also important to remember the unique individuality of SMEs.

Characteristics of SMEs

There is purposefully no attempt in this chapter to define the term SME. There are many definitions incorporating some or all of aspects covering number of employees, revenue and turnover, size and range of products and markets, and so on. Suffice to acknowledge here, the term SME as definition in itself, that is, 'small-to-medium-size-enterprise'. SMEs are just this, they are small to medium sized relative to large corporations. A significant differentiator between SMEs and large corporations is that of resources. All enterprises have limitations as to what they can or wish to do. Any managerial activity will be inhibited by lack of finance, people and expertise. However, the larger an organization, the more scope it has to generate funding for projects, moving people around according to where they're needed most and if necessary, buying in expertise where and when it is needed. In the case of SMEs few if any of these options are available.

A distinctive characteristic of SMEs is a lack of finance. True some SMEs may begin life as cash rich and perhaps some will grow into cash rich enterprises, but for the vast majority of SMEs lack of cash and financial resources impose severe limitations upon activities. The reasons for this may be many. For example, when an enterprise is established it invariably soaks up all available capital resources in structuring the business and seeding initial market development. Thus, at the start-up stage most enterprises will experience financial limitations. Most enterprises after start up are reliant upon

income generation to fund the initial investment and gain a surplus. Such surpluses will fund future growth which in turn requires further returns. Since just about every SME needs to grow in order to sustain and strengthen the business base, then just about every SME experiences financial limitations throughout the growing years. Until certain thresholds are reached, financial constraints tend to dominate decision making. Indeed, as an enterprise expands so does the complexity of its financial requirements and commitments.

Partly as a consequence of financial limitations, SMEs also have human resource limitations. Most people employed in SMEs work in a logistical process/delivery capacity. An SME tends to have few management decision makers, indeed, much of the meaningful decision making is undertaken by the owner/manager or the entrepreneur. SMEs tend not to have specialist experts whose job is to do one task only. Instead, managers in an SME are 'generalists' who carry out a wide variety of tasks and decision making. As a consequence, decision makers' attention is often distracted away from a specific function which can often be to the detrimental inefficiency of a given functions performance.

Both of the limitations of lack of finance and lack of specialist expertise serve as severe constraints upon marketing ability and activity (Carson *et al.*, 1995). Small firms will often have very limited funds available for marketing purposes and what is more, limited marketing expertise in carrying out marketing decisions and activities. Therefore, that marketing which is performed may be undermined by simply not having enough money to spend with the added danger that even this limited spend may be used incorrectly or inefficiently. Even if marketing money is spent wisely, the nature of an SME, in that it is 'small' relative to its market place and position within that market, means that its marketing will invariably have a limited impact upon the market. The old metaphors of 'small fish in a large pond' and 'a drop in the ocean' serve to illustrate this significant limitation. Of course, the consequence of such limited impact upon the market is that SMEs must adapt and focus any marketing practice to suit the individual and unique characteristics of the enterprise.

Characteristics of entrepreneurs/owners/managers

One of the major influences upon an SME's marketing practice is that of the lead entrepreneur/owner/manager. Indeed, it is probably this individual's influence which most characterizes the style and nature of marketing performed by an SME. There is a large literature which is devoted to defining the characteristics of entrepreneurs (Timmons, 1978; Meredith *et al.*, 1982; Hofer and Bygrave, 1992). Typically they are perceived to be risk takers and in being so, to be opportunistic and visionary; innovative and creative; adaptive and change oriented. Perhaps two further characteristics are the most influential with regards to marketing, the perception that entrepreneurs are individualistic and highly focused upon the enterprise's well being.

Individualistic can of course mean a variety of things, however in the case of entrepreneurial behaviour it is often manifest as the nature of an individual's personality and how this impacts upon his/her decision making. The issue is not whether an individual is aggressive, persuasive, assertive, placid, or some other personality trait, it is in terms of how the 'individualistic' characteristic impacts upon marketing decision making. Bearing in mind the SME limitations discussed above and in consideration of how these can impact upon 'individualistic' decision making, such decision making will invariably be simplistic because of the limited expertise with regards to marketing. It will be haphazard and unstructured because it is reactive to events and intuitively individualistic. All of these characteristics can lead to apparently irrational decision making which has a predominately short-term focus.

The highly focused nature of entrepreneurial decision making is centred around the enterprise's well being. The entrepreneur is continuously concerned with ensuring the survival and safety of the enterprise. While it can be argued that SMEs are highly customer oriented, the dominating preoccupation of the entrepreneur is to maintain positive revenue and cash flows towards profit. This assertion would suggest that the lack of finance limitation is dominant within the entrepreneur's thought process. Whatever, the highly focused nature of entrepreneurs can sometimes manifest itself as being obsessively self-centred about the enterprise and its well being.

Acknowledging that the influence of the entrepreneur has a huge significance upon the character and style of SME decision making, it is not to say that such influence is detrimental to decision making effectiveness or business success. Established entrepreneurial SMEs benefit hugely from the influence of the lead entrepreneur. Whilst the limitations of SMEs may represent inherent weaknesses, the entrepreneur will counteract these weaknesses by bringing inherent strengths to the SME. These strengths are centred around the entrepreneurial network and his/her competencies for doing business. Both these phenomena are described and discussed later in this chapter.

In summary, we can say that most enterprises can be categorized as SME and that these enterprises have distinctive characteristics which differentiate them, not only from large corporations but also from most other enterprises. It is recognized that SMEs have several severe limitations represented by lack of finance, lack of expertise and lack of market impact. Within this limiting framework the influence of the entrepreneur/owner/manager is acknowledged, particularly in relation to the distinctive style and focus of decision making. In compensating for much of the limitations it is recognized that entrepreneurs will possess or develop counteractive capabilities for decision making specifically refined to exploit the opportunities best suited for an SME.

Incompatibility of marketing theory to SMEs

It is clear from the previous section that the inherent characteristics and style and influence of entrepreneurs will impact substantially, perhaps even completely upon the type and nature of marketing in SMEs. An interesting question is to ask, 'What is the type and nature of marketing in SMEs'? Simply by asking such a question suggests that somehow SME marketing may be different to marketing elsewhere. In which case how and in what way might it be different? Perhaps more fundamentally, do SMEs perform marketing according to textbook frameworks and if so, then what are the differences? Alternatively, if SMEs do not do marketing according to textbook frameworks then why not and what is the type and nature of such marketing if it does not conform to textbook frameworks?

In considering some of these issues it is perhaps useful to examine the inherent characteristics of some textbook marketing approaches. The rest of this section considers these characteristics in relation to marketing planning and market research and also by way of example, textbook issues of segmentation and niche marketing, market share and pricing.

Marketing planning

This is a much vaunted tool of good professional marketing which has many clear and precise descriptions in the textbook literature. There is no doubt that it has substantial benefits when used comprehensively. The literature is in general agreement that it is a valued tool of marketing. Consider for a moment, the inherent characteristics of marketing planning. It is fundamentally sequential in that it follows a careful and logical process from appraisal through to evaluation and analysis before devising carefully considered and alternative courses of action for implementation. It is also formal and

structured in its frameworks. By its very nature it carries comprehensive time scales covering short-, medium-and long-term dimensions.

The prior debate on entrepreneurial characteristics contended that decision making is inherently simplistic and haphazard, undisciplined and spontaneous, unstructured and irrational and invariably short-term in time scales. In comparison to the inherent characteristics of marketing planning outlined above, there is a clear incompatibility between this textbook technique and the way entrepreneurial decision making is naturally performed. Indeed, it would be very unnatural, if not impossible, for an SME entrepreneur/owner/manager to plan marketing according to textbook frameworks. SMEs, because of their relative smallness and therefore their lack of market or industry dominance, must be very flexible and reactive to changes in market circumstances; a formal marketing planning procedure would inhibit such flexibility and reactivensss.

Market research

Textbook market research frameworks can be traced back to the rigour and validity requirements of social science research. Again such rigour requires formality, sequentiality, validity and correct application of one best method for research. As with the incompatibility of marketing planning, SMEs' inherent limitations make it virtually impossible for such enterprises to carry out market research according to textbook principles. Lack of money and expertise combined with short time scales would make it unlikely that SMEs entrepreneurs/owner/managers would do textbook market research. Instead, the inherent characteristics of the entrepreneur mean that a much more casual and natural approach to market research is done. In fact, it is unlikely even to be recognized as market research; instead it is more about 'gathering information' which may occur by any method or means. Correctness and rigour are not considerations. Intuitive judgement is the basis of evaluation.

Segmentation, niche marketing and market share

These are well recognized marketing strategy tools in the textbook literature, indeed, much of the support literature for SME development advocates that such enterprises follow these strategies. However, in practice, whilst many SMEs may in fact attempt to implement such strategies, the relative smallness of SMEs and their vulnerability to market forces means that they will often 'fall-into' market niches which previously had not been considered. Equally, whilst a market segmentation strategy may be advocated, the opportunistic nature of the entrepreneur will often take an SME outside such segments to an extent they become meaningless.

Market share is of little consequence to SMEs. The resources needed to measure market share would far outweigh any benefits, especially when the outcome is likely to be a percentage figure which is so small as to be meaningless. Even if market share is known, it is unlikely an SME can do much to increase it since it has neither the resources nor the ability to make significant impact upon the market. For most SMEs, the strive for increased revenues and the subsequent positive effect on the enterprise's well being are much more important than knowing whether or not market share has grown.

Pricing strategies

The textbook literature advocates elaborate alternatives on pricing strategies which have an implied aspect of control over the consumer's decision making perception. However, because of SMEs' relative smallness, such control is almost impossible without substantial differentiation which most firms do not enjoy. An option advocated by the textbook literature is to use price discounting as a sales stimulation, however, given the limitation of finance and the implications for adverse cash flow and the innate survival and enterprise protection instinct of the entrepreneur, this is neither an attractive or natural option.

These are just a few examples of the incompatibility of marketing theory in the context of SMEs. Of course, there are those who will argue that any marketing theory can be applied in any context, and taken in the most general sense this would be a fair argument. However, SMEs do not function at a 'general' level, they operate at the 'situation specific' level – a circumstance which is uniquely individualistic. In applying general marketing principles to a 'situation specific' SME, another well known analogy comes to mind – 'putting round pegs into square holes' with enough forced manipulation they can be made to fit, but not perfectly.

So, if marketing theory is incompatible with SME marketing characteristics, what is the alternative? A useful start point is to consider which aspects of marketing that fit closest to SME characteristics and which can be performed by entrepreneurs/owners/managers as *they* 'do business'. Thus, let us consider the nature of SME marketing.

Nature of SME marketing

In the general sense, the basic principles and concepts of marketing are as relevant to SMEs as to any other domain. However, as illustrated by the examples in the previous section, some theories, tools and techniques of marketing are not as relevant or useful to SMEs. The nature of SME marketing is that of a concept which is dominated by the inherent characteristics of the entrepreneur/owner/manager and the SME itself. Thus, the inherent limitations of SMEs and the resultant characteristics that they create, coupled with the way entrepreneurs/owners/managers take decisions will determine, indeed dictate, the nature of SME marketing. These underlying factors are taken into account later in this chapter; at this point let us consider some other aspects of influence and consequence in relation to the nature of SME marketing.

The life cycle stage of SMEs

SMEs will perform marketing differently according to their stage of life. A start-up SME's marketing will likely be characterized, indeed dominated, by reactive marketing practices, in terms of reacting to customer enquiries and market changes. As the business develops, much of the marketing will be characterized by experimenting or tinkering with a variety of marketing techniques, for example, the creation of a brochure or a visit to an exhibition. As the enterprise becomes established over a number of years it will have developed its own marketing style and practice which it has learned and shaped along the way. The enterprise will know what works for it and what does not. It is unlikely to accommodate wider or new marketing perspectives until it encounters a significant change of some kind, for example, a new market venture. In moving through the various life cycle phases, an SME will progress from what is sometimes an uncontrollable marketing circumstance to one in which it feels that every aspect of marketing it performs is controlled. Again because of the inherent characteristics, this 'controlled' marketing is likely to be quite conservative and restricted to the tried and trusted methods refined over the years. Thus, whilst marketing activity is established, comfortable, affordable and apparently working, it is also potentially complacent, dull, unimaginative and perhaps inefficient. However, it feels safe, after the traumas probably experienced at various times in the tinkering period, nothing too radical or different is tried; caution and conformity prevail.

Conformity with industry norms

Generally, SMEs must 'conform' to established norms in order to do business, primarily because they are small and cannot hope to 'buck' established practices. What are the established norms? Any industry or market will exist within certain customs and practices outside of which it is difficult to find acceptance. Examine any industry and these 'norms' can de identified. For example, in the way products are presented, where and to whom, the way and when they are distributed, the degree of service that is expected and provided, the price parameters, margins

and mark-up that exist, the hiarachical infrastructures, the traditions and histories, the precedents and rules that exist and which must be adhered to. These established norms are so strong in most markets/industries that they create their own distinctive characteristics which determine how business is done. The most striking illustration of these established norms comes sharply into focus in two areas. When an enterprise enters a new export market, an emphasis is placed upon understanding the culture of a region in general and the culture of doing business in particular. Of course this cultural understanding involves much more than just sociological issues, it also involves understanding of a variety of expectations and practices. A depth of understanding is required before a business can expect to successfully exploit opportunities previously identified. Another, less common area is where someone launches a new business in a market area in which they have no prior experience. Most of the initial period is taken up with finding out how to do things, who to contact and rely upon, what will please and offend, what is expected as a minimum, what levels of service, price, delivery, quality are expected and how these all interrelate.

Such industry norms will require an SME to use established and existing distribution channels, to price within certain known and expected parameters, to provide certain expected levels of quality and service, and so on. To step too far away from any of these norms will require the SME to have some significant differentiation in some aspect of its business. Such circumstances are rare in the extreme. Most SMEs can only hope to attain some marginal differentiation to exploit and because of this must conform to the industry customs and practices in presenting this differentiation. Take a few examples by way of illustration, if normal distribution channels rely on intermediaries such as trade distributors, an SME which by-passes these will meet with a variety of resistance unless it achieves differentiation. Retailers or end users will be wary of doing business for fear of upsetting the wider industry supply channels. Consider also, price/profit mark-up and margins. An SME failing to offer prices that fall within expected parameters, either positive or negative variance, will meet with query and resistance. Too low a price margin/mark-up and interest is spurned, too high margin/mark-up and suspicion and credibility doubts arise.

There are only a few circumstances where industry norms may not apply. One is were a large dominant player within a close knit market community decides to 'break-the-mould' by some act of marketing variance, others will be forced to follow. Such an option is not open to an SME unless it possesses a huge differentiation in relation to product or technological innovation,

a rare circumstance in normal everyday trading, although history will record many examples. Another circumstance is where a market enters a period of dynamic change, such as technological developments or consumer attitudinal shifts. In such circumstances opportunities will exist to break and create new industry/market practices. Such dynamic change occurs only occasionally but when it does occur it is significant. For example, in the tourist industry when the advent of cheap air travel created a huge new market expansion and many new entrants, and currently in the financial services industry where de-regulations and greater consumer awareness and spending power allow many new ways of doing business, such as 'service

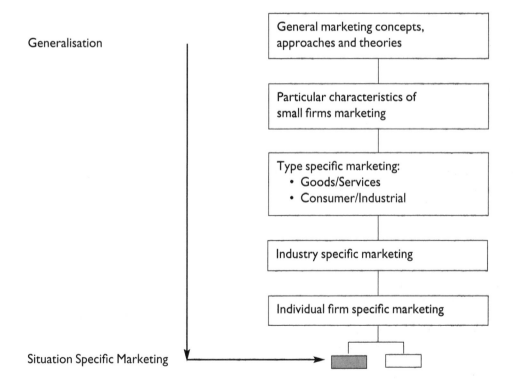

Figure 27.1   Situation specific marketing

Adapted from K. J. Blois (1974) 'The Marketing of Services: An Approach', *European Journal of Marketing*, **8**, 137–149.

direct' concepts. In both of these circumstances SMEs can actually be more dynamic and effective than large established organizations who can sometimes find it difficult to break away from their long established and traditional practices.

In summarizing the nature of SME marketing, we have acknowledged the inherent influence of SME characteristics and the entrepreneur/owner/manager. In addition we have highlighted two other factors of significance, the SME stage of life cycle and the industry/market norms by which most SMEs must conform, except in an few exceptional circumstances. A model of 'situation specific' marketing serves to illustrate and integrate this discussion (see Figure 27.1).

Marketing principles, concepts and theories at the most general level can apply to SMEs as much as in any other domain. However, to actually perform marketing certain factors must be taken into account, perhaps to 'filter' and 'refine' marketing towards the unique and individualistic character of an individual SME. Some marketing theories can contribute to this process, for example, the theories and principles behind goods/services marketing or industrial/consumer marketing. Taking account of the inherent characteristics of any of these contexts will automatically guide marketing frameworks. Obvious illustrations are provided by services marketing being characterized by aspects of intangibility and industrial marketing being characterized by aspects of relationship.

In a similar way, (discussed earlier), any firm's marketing will be influenced and characterized by the nature of the industry or market it exists within. Although service firms or industrial firms may have inherent characteristics of influence dictated by the characteristics of services and industrial marketing, they will also be characterized by the nature of their industry or market. So, for example, service firms in a particular food sector will all behave in a similar fashion which is dictated by the industry/market customs and practices. Any variation or

innovation will most probably occur within the normal expected parameters of doing business which have evolved and become established over time.

The variation and innovations are of course what makes any enterprise unique. For example, two service firms situated side by side, as is often the case with two SME restaurants, will still have differentiations which make them unique. Their names will be different and these names will conjure a difference of perception. Their interior design and atmosphere will create further differentiation. The attitude and appearance of staff will create further difference, the variety and quality of the menu clearly will also have an influence. A whole host of influences will create a specific situation which is unique to the individual firm. It is the collective combination of all these factors which forms the basis of an enterprise's marketing activity and message. Thus, while both such enterprises are influenced by the same inherent characteristics of both their marketing domain and their industry/market, the decisions of the entrepreneur/owner/manager will create a differentiation which is unique.

This issue of the influence of the entrepreneur/owner/manager upon the decision making of an SME is worthy of further consideration, in terms of how an entrepreneur can not only create differentiation but also how s/he can improve the impact and efficiency of marketing decisions and activities of the SME. Such impact and efficiency will undoubtedly build upon inherent and learned strengths that best reflect the constraints and resources of an SME.

SME marketing based on strengths

A number of approaches are described here, which both reflect and contribute to SME marketing based upon strengths. In this section the following are considered:

•   adaptation of standard textbook marketing
     frameworks

- marketing in 'context' (situation specific marketing)
- 'alternative' SME marketing
- competency marketing
- network marketing
- scope of 'innovative' marketing

It needs to be recognized that while each of these approaches are about marketing, in practice none of these are likely to be performed as marketing. Instead, they will be performed as part of 'doing business' and taking decisions. As an illustration of this notion, consider the marketing activity of *pricing*. Decisions on pricing will probably be driven by considerations with regards to cost or cash flow, as much as any specific pricing policy. Of course, such decisions will impact upon pricing and an entrepreneur will be intuitively aware of this in the same way s/he will be aware of a price change because of competitive pressure and how this will impact upon bottom line costs and cash flows within the business. Thus, although the following descriptions focus upon marketing aspects, they must be considered in the wider context of overall business decision making as much as marketing decision making.

Adaptation of standard textbook marketing frameworks

In most SMEs marketing will be performed in some form or other. Marketing is inherently and intuitively performed in SMEs. Since most SMEs will have a *product* or *service* which they will offer at a *price* and they will *promote* this through some kind of medium that reaches their market *place*, it can be easily determined that SMEs marketing can be described under the frameworks of the 'four Ps'. Again, at the general level, this is undoubtedly true, however, in just about every circumstance an entrepreneur will 'adapt' this concept to suit the situation specific of his/her firm. Since this situation specific will be structured around the functions and activities of the firm itself, the marketing activity

will be closely allied to this. Therefore, if image and personal service are important features of an enterprise's standing, these will be an integral part of its marketing mix. Often the product *is* the firm, so this too will be an integral part of its mix. Such an SME's marketing mix therefore, may be nothing more than this. Of course, many of the 4P aspects will be inherent in the SMEs activities, for example, communication and delivery will be inherent aspects of image and personal service. Clearly, the concept of the '4Ps' will be adapted to suit the SME. An entrepreneur may find it sufficient to describe a marketing mix as product, image and personal service.

For an SME practitioner to accept a concept such as the '4P's' it must have relevance, therefore, if a simple '4Ps' description is not relevant to an entrepreneur it will not be used. There is a significant point here, that is, marketing activities in SMEs will always by pragmatic, practical and relevant to the individual SME; anything which does not meet these conditions is academically theoretical and of little value.

An illustration of 'pragmatic, practical and relevant' adaptation is provided by the marketing planning process. This was highlighted earlier as being of little relevance to SMEs because of its logical foundations which are incompatible with the inherent characteristics of SMEs and entrepreneurial decision making practices. However, some aspects of the marketing planning process may be performed in a pragmatic, practical and relevant sense. Take as a point in example, the notion of market feasibility analysis incorporating external and internal analysis over a wide range of issues. The textbook descriptions of this aspect of the process will outline a comprehensive list of aspects for consideration in a 'complete' market analysis, thus external issues may be outlined as covering market environment; marketing information; market knowledge; market segmentation; market opportunities; competition, and so on. Similarly, internal issues may be outlined as covering internal environment; marketing variables; marketing organization; marketing systems; marketing strategies and plans, and so on. The entrepreneurial adaptation of this is simply an intuitive consideration of those issues concerned with all/any aspect outside of the firm's influence and control (external) and those issues that are within the firm's control (internal). This is the market feasibility analysis process in practice, but it will bear no relationship, either conceptually or descriptively, with any textbook description.

Thus, SMEs will pragmatically adapt any marketing theory to make it relevant to the way they do business. Whether this looks like or meets the criteria of good textbook marketing has no consideration with an entrepreneur, it is the intuitive performance in practice which is the prime consideration.

Marketing in 'context'

It has been argued above that in practice any marketing in SMEs is intuitively performed and that this marketing practice will be set in the situation specific of the firm (Figure 27.1). Some

indication of how this marketing is determined is given in relation to incorporating a number of factors of influence which must be taken into account when determining what or how to do marketing in SMEs. Some mention was made to the 'context' of marketing and how certain marketing characteristics will impact upon the type and style of marketing that will be carried out by an SME. Taking this logic a little further it is possible to construct a 'marketing in context picture' for any SME by taking account of a number of factors of significance.

While marketing activity and environment can be and are complex, it is still possible to identify the essential key factors which determine and dictate the type and style of marketing that can and should be performed. Firstly, consider the key marketing characteristics that stem from the relevant domains of marketing. There may be many but they are easily clustered within a common grouping, for example, services marketing will generate its own list of services characteristics which belong in some form or other to any services context. Similar lists of

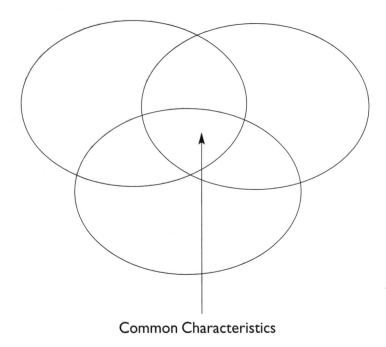

Common Characteristics

Figure 27.2   Marketing in context – common characteristics

characteristics can be generated for any domain of marketing. Any student or practitioner of marketing will be able to generate such lists of characteristics simply by thinking of the definitional context of the groupings. So as for services, consumer marketing has distinctive characteristics; similarly industrial marketing; and so on. Of course, since we are concerned with SME marketing, then the inherent characteristics of SMEs can be generated. In most marketing in context situations there will be two or three key groupings of characteristics which impact upon the marketing activity performed. Not all characteristics will impact upon the marketing in the same way or with the same degree of influence. Neither should the groupings be considered in isolation, in fact it is how

they interact together that determines the significance of influence. By visually overlapping the identified groupings it is possible to determine with some degree of accuracy the *commmon* characteristics and their linkages between groupings and to evaluate the *most significant*; these therefore, represent the inherent *features* and *factors* of influence. Figure 27.2 offers a simple illustration of this process. Each circle may represent known characteristics belonging to a given domain of marketing. By considering a number of these domains of marketing together, rather than in isolation, it is possible to arrive at those characteristics which are common and which therefore, are most significant in a given marketing in context.

This process will allow an assessment of

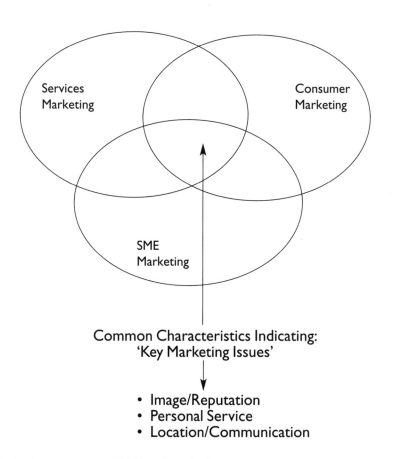

Figure 27.3 Marketing in context – SME hotel marketing

'key marketing issues' which belong to any firm in a given context. These key marketing issues are those aspects of marketing which any firm in a given context will simply have to perform; it cannot ignore these if it is to do business. How well it performs these key marketing issues will determine how successful it is.

This process is applied to an example of an SME hotel in tourism marketing. The inherent characteristics of tourism marketing are that it is a service and that it has a predominately consumer-based marketing orientation. Issues of domestic or international may or may not have significance. Of greater significance is the SME dimension. Thus an illustration of marketing in this context would be something like Figure 27.3.

Common characteristics are easy to identify. Service marketing characteristics of intangibility and service delivery are closely related to SME characteristics of personal/unique service and lack of resources for any tangible and impersonal service. Similarly, consumer marketing characteristics of retail location and communication are uniquely influenced by SME characteristics and limitations. Thus, the key marketing issues which arise out of these and other common characteristics are image/reputation; personal service; and location/communication. The intuitive logic for these three key marketing issues are as follows:

- *Image/reputation*—That any SME hotel will seek to emphasize its smallness as differentiation from large corporate chains. It will build competitive advantage by establishing a reputation for 'homeliness', 'family orientation', 'friendliness', 'intimacy', etc. The reputation will serve to 'promote' the SME by word of mouth communication and publicity.
- *Personal service*—Further enhancement of the image and reputation will come from attention to providing a personal service which is focused upon individual customers needs. Strong emphasis will be given to developing 'regular' customers who are known by name.
- *Location/communication*—This is emphasized

because an SME hotel will need to draw on the marketing aspects of its local environment and infrastructure and it will use appropriate literature to communicate this. It cannot hope to promote this message itself to a wider market, instead it will rely upon the local tourist industry to do this.

Of course, there will undoubtedly be other aspects of marketing that an SME hotel may wish to engage, however, it simply cannot ignore these key marketing issues. These key marketing issues are almost imposed upon the context because of the underlying inherent characteristics. An SME hotel may want to do mass media communication to reflect mass consumer marketing, but it simply cannot hope to do such even if the outcomes were desirable or controllable. It will of course employ a variety of industry marketing activities as part of its ongoing revenue generation. For example, functions and events built around themes of interest to its local community as well as the transient market.

Thus, the message from 'marketing in context' is that because of certain inherent characteristics which will impact upon an SME in its given context, it cannot ignore these and indeed, they will determine and perhaps dictate the type and style of marketing that an SME can perform.

Competency marketing

Competency marketing is a term which means using inherent and learned skills (competencies) to do marketing. To do marketing means anything which impacts upon, or which influences marketing, as well as actually performing marketing activity. This is in recognition that marketing decisions are often inseparable from any other decisions in an SME. Many entrepreneurs/owners/managers will perceive themselves to have limited marketing ability, primarily because their prior interests and background mean that they are unlikely to bring meaningful marketing experience and skills to a business. Many will bring a 'technical' competency to the enterprise. Many will learn new competencies as the business develops. Primary amongst these learned competencies is that of 'doing business', which is the manifestation of a range of competencies coming together as contributors to decision making. Again, much has been written about management and decision making competencies; as many as several hundred have been identified (Mintzberg, 1973; Boyatzis, 1982; Koontz *et al.*, 1984; Kotter, 1990; Tichy and Charan, 1991).

Obviously, since marketing is derived from management, many of the known management competencies could be relevant to marketing in some way. Consideration of what the marketing job entails will group marketing into two categories, those competencies which are analytical and those which are creative. However, in once again taking account of the hugely strong influential characteristics of SMEs and entrepreneurs/owner/managers, such competency groupings need to be adapted and refined to suit these inherent characteristics. Taking account also of the interactive relatedness of SME decision making it is important that competency marketing in SMEs is compatible with this dimension.

Most entrepreneurs will learn their marketing skills by experience and practice. However, it is not uncommon to hear entrepreneurs describe marketing as 'just common sense', or 'I don't know anything about marketing' whilst demonstrably performing marketing activity. Indeed, entrepreneurial characteristics/competencies/skills can be closely aligned to marketing characteristics, for example, both have characteristics of *vision* and *creativity*; *communication* is inherent to both; *adaptability* and *flexibility* also; *opportunism* is another common competency factor. On this latter factor entrepreneurs will often perceive themselves to be opportunistic to the point of enthusiasm; recently for example, an entrepreneur, in responding to the notion of problems experienced stated, 'I don't see problems, I see opportunities'.

Taking cognisance of the above dimensions and focusing upon the one most significant core competency concept for SMEs it is that of *experiential knowledge*. This contains four significant marketing competencies which are entirely compatible with the entrepreneurial way of doing business. One competency component is knowledge itself; such knowledge will cover a range of aspects, particularly about how to do business and what is needed to do it successfully. Knowledge is a significant competency, in a variety of ways; it can relate to technical expertise, business acumen, including knowledge of the market environment, etc. A second competency component is experience derived from accumulated knowledge of doing business and which is evolved and developed by accumulation of experience over time, learning from successes and failures. It is obvious how these two competency components are integral to experiential knowledge; however, there are two further competency components which contribute significantly to experiential knowledge, one is communication competency which reflects both the marketing and entrepreneurial focus of SME decision making. Communication competency is a reflection of an ability to communicate to and with all interactive parties. It is a competency which can be improved through the development of knowledge and experience competencies. A final competency, the level of which is clearly derived from the accumulation of the others, is that of judgement ability which clearly impacts upon the quality and timing of decision making.

From a marketing in SME perspective, these four competencies can be considered together, because of their clear interaction and inter-connection. Thus, we can describe marketing competency in SMEs to be that of experiential knowledge, that is, knowledge acquired through experience and developed as an accumulation of knowledge and experience built upon and from communication and judgement. Such experiential knowledge represents a powerful SME marketing tool that can significantly compensate for the inherent SME limitations, particularly with regards to marketing activity.

Experiential knowledge is something which every entrepreneur/owner/manager will acquire over time. It will develop intuitively as the enterprise becomes established and customs and practices emerge and evolve. The point here is that it will develop naturally, the question though is whether the level and quality of experiential knowledge is of the best possible or whether it is just mediocre. For an entrepreneur/owner/manager who can utilize experiential knowledge proactively and in an accelerated way, by concentrating on developing experiential knowledge and therefore competency marketing, this will substantially strengthen his/hers and the SME's marketing effectiveness.

Network marketing

Networks and networking have been debated for sometime in the literature (Aldrich and Zimmer, 1986; Johannisson, 1986; Andersson and Soderlund, 1988; Dubini and Aldrich, 1991; Anderson *et al.*, 1994; Hansen, 1995). Much of the discussion has been focused on identifying specific types of networks and how they are used and why they exist. Fundamental definitions of networks include personal contact networks (PCNs); social networks; trade and business networks. Such networks can exist in isolation or more often they will be interactive and overlapping. The type of network or variety of networks is not a concern here. Neither is it important to precisely define the concept of networks other than a description which acknowledges that 'a network is a collection of individuals who may be known or not known to each other and who, in some way contribute something to the entrepreneur/owner/manager, either passively, reactively or proactively, whether specifically elicited or not'.

What is the value of networks and networking to SMEs? Networking is both a natural and an acquired skill or competency of the entrepreneur. Entrepreneurs may not be aware that they have a 'network' as such, since the way they perform networking is a process which is haphaz-

ard, disjointed, spontaneous and opportunistic, and consists of one-to-one interactions with a few or a variety of individuals. Sometimes entrepreneurs will consciously seek out information from certain individuals believed to have a contribution to make, on other occasions information will be gleaned sub-consciously as part of naturally doing business or as part of an informal conversation. Networking can be both proactive and passive depending upon the issue at hand. Indeed, on the same issue it can be proactive with some individuals in the network and passive with others. Similarly, it can be both overt and covert depending on the closeness or otherwise of individuals to the entrepreneur. Timescales within networking can vary enormously, some individuals may be networked continuously and frequently, whilst others may only be contacted infrequently and occasionally. Sometimes, the entrepreneur will have a clear issue in mind and will raise this issue with individuals in a way which is deemed to be appropriate for that individual to respond with meaningful feedback. On other occasions, knowledge or information will be acquired as part of other apparently unrelated conversation or observation. Some individuals may receive a flurry of contact at a particular time and then find that no contact is made for some time before contact is re-established. It is unlikely that any one aspect of networking will lead to decisive decision making by the SME entrepreneur, instead networking will represent an array of assessments which all contribute towards a final decision. The point here is that normally, entrepreneurial networking has no fixed or standard mechanism in operation, there is seldom an agenda or objective because there is no demonstrative 'process' in operation. Networking can be likened to a cloud; when observed it can be seen but it is difficult to make tangible contact with all its dimensions. It will appear to be in constant flux but at the same time it is always recognizable.

Similar to the importance of competency development for SMEs, networks and networking are hugely important to SMEs. Indeed, it might be argued that SMEs would find it extremely difficult to become established without networking and that networking is an integral part of the continued existence and survival. It is safe to say that entrepreneurs/owners/managers in SMEs intuitively build a network of contacts around themselves that serve a multiplicity of purposes. Indeed, one might go further and argue that networking is an inherent and significant characteristic of entrepreneurship. The fact is that where there are entrepreneurs there are networks.

Networking is very useful to SME entrepreneurs/owners/managers, mainly because it is integral to doing business, it does not have to be constructed and contrived, it is not a task to be completed, it is simply part of everyday business activity and therefore happens anyway. All entrepreneurs do networking in some form or other; indeed, like in any aspect of life, some will be better at networking than others. Whatever, because networking is such an intuitively natural dimension of entrepreneurial SME activity, it represents a significant strength for marketing purposes. Since SMEs are invariably 'close' to their customers, aspects of marketing such as relationship and communication are important. Networking is precisely the mechanism by which SMEs can meaningfully achieve such aspects of marketing and in a way that is compatible with their resource constraints.

Accepting that networking happens intuitively and naturally, is it possible to 'improve' networking competency? Here lies a key, networking is indeed a competency skill and therefore it can certainly be developed and improved. Similar to the notion of accumulation of experiential knowledge through a conscious accelerated development, networking competency can be accelerated by a consciously proactive approach. Such an approach simply requires an entrepreneur to address an issue or problem of marketing around a two-part construct. First, loosely define the issue or problem, then make a list of people who might offer an opinion on the issue. These people are likely to be regular contacts of the entrepreneur, although with a little

concentration some lesser contacts may emerge. The entrepreneur is now in a position to trawl his/her newly defined network. Nothing much has changed except that the trawling process may accelerate because it has been consciously defined and the trawl is now proactive and not simply naturally occurring. The entrepreneur will intuitively know what information is good, through the dimension of experiential knowledge, and will be able to make a judgemental assessment of the issue and a decision on how to address it.

Indeed, the two dimensions of networking and competencies together can represent the core essence of SME marketing which impacts upon the nature, type and style of SME marketing activity. These dimensions represent significant strengths which can be utilized effectively for successful SME marketing.

The importance of these strengths can be seen when the SME business environment is considered. The vast majority of SMEs operate in two main sectors in any economy. Many operate in a 'business-to-business' environment whereby they deal with other business, both large and small. The essence of such business relates closely to the SME strengths discussed above, in that it allows SMEs to utilize networking amongst a relatively close-knit and familiar environment and to exploit experiential knowledge of an industry or market. A second major area for SMEs is that of services, both consumer and industrial services. This area allows SMEs to exploit the well recognized 'closeness' to the customer and consequent customer orientation of SMEs. Of course, taken in the broadest sense, these two areas or sectors can represent all sectors of enterprise and since most sectors are populated by a majority of SMEs in terms of numbers of businesses, then this can be deemed to be true.

Clearly, the dimension of network marketing is inexplicably linked with competency marketing and both will be set within the domain of marketing in context and all of this will result in some form of adaptation of marketing tools and techniques to suit the unique characteristics of

SMEs. One further piece of the 'jigsaw' of SME marketing remains to be set in place.

Innovative marketing

Like much of the emphasis in textbook marketing literature, which is essentially inappropriate for SMEs because they are concerned with 'how to do' more than 'how to construct', the literature on innovation is often inappropriate or of marginal value. A large portion of entrepreneurial and SME literature is devoted to innovation in recognition that a distinctive characteristic of SMEs is creativity and innovation. The problem is that the vast majority of literature on innovation is focused on 'product innovation' on the assumption that this is where most SMEs are innovative. It may be true to say that SMEs display a high degree of product innovation since many new SME enterprises will be founded upon a new and innovative product or service, and such innovations are easily identified as fact. However, in most cases, the vast majority of SMEs develop products which are

only marginally differentiated from others and much of the product innovation is in response or reaction to customer demand. Fair enough, SMEs' entrepreneurial flexibility will meet the demands of customers and the outcomes can be construed as product innovation.

Whether the above reasoning is accepted or not, it is contented here that innovative marketing in SMEs is much wider than simple product innovation, indeed, much research in the area recognizes this wider spectrum (UIC/AMA Marketing/Entrepreneurship Interface Symposium Proceedings, 1987–1997). Of course, many writers have already acknowledged this but much of their insight has been lost behind the higher profile of product innovation in SMEs. Innovative marketing covers the full spectrum of marketing related activity in an SME. The concepts addressed above, networking, adaptation, etc., are clear demonstrations of innovative marketing. It is useful to reflect on why these concepts and indeed innovative marketing exists within SMEs. It can be deemed to stem from the immensely strong and influential

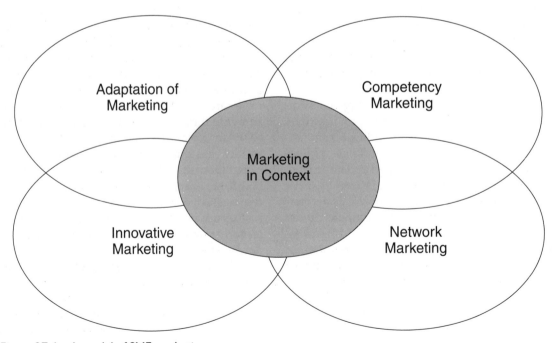

Figure 27.4   A model of SME marketing

inherent characteristics of SMEs and entrepreneurs/owners/managers. It is also useful to acknowledge that as a result of this influence, the focus of perception or need is to '*do things*' that achieve results which serve the survival and development objectives of an enterprise. Therefore innovative marketing is profoundly pragmatic in achieving objectives. Some manifestations of innovative marketing are:

- aspects of added value which are designed to enhance the product or service;
- personal selling which is built around an intuitive assessment of the personality of the customer/buyer, including adapting to the mood of the buyer;
- distribution, delivery and customer service, which are largely reactive to requirements.

The point to emphasize here is that innovative marketing is not simply focused on product innovation, instead it covers the whole spectrum of marketing activity within an SME; consequently, there is likely to be more innovation in other aspects of marketing activity than there will be around the product or service.

Conclusion: a model of SME marketing

This chapter has been framed around a pragmatic model of SME marketing. This model is illustrated in Figure 27.4. It incorporates the dimensions of adaptation of marketing techniques, competency marketing, networking marketing, and innovative marketing. These approaches are centred around the notion that all SME marketing is done in a unique context and that cognisance of this context must be carefully taken into account.

The unique context of SME marketing is built upon recognition of the huge influence of the inherent characteristics of SMEs, particularly the limitations of resources, and the inherent characteristics of the entrepreneur/ owner/ manager upon marketing and related decision making.

This model is not intended as an alternative theory of marketing which inherently rejects other established theories trusted and recognized by the marketing establishment. Instead, it should be viewed as a model of marketing 'application' in SMEs. The model requires students of marketing to adopt an 'experienced', 'real-world' perspective of marketing. It represents 'how-to-do-marketing' rather than 'what-marketing-is', and as such is highly compatible with SME entrepreneurs/owners/managers' way of thinking, indeed, way of 'doing business'.

Acknowledgements

Acknowledgement is made for the valued support and contributions to the conceptual frameworks contained in this chapter by research colleagues, Senior Lecturer in Marketing, Dr Audrey Gilmore, and research assistants, Darryl Cummins and Aodheen O'Donnell, the SME Marketing Research Unit, University of Ulster.

References

Aldrich, H. and Zimmer, C. (1986) Entrepreneurship Through Social Networks, in D. Sexton and R. W. Smilor (eds) *Art and Science of Entrepreneurship*, Ballinger Publishing Company, pp. 3–23.

Anderson, J. C., Hakansson, H. and Johanson, J. (1994) Dyadic Business Relationships Within a Business Network Context, *Journal of Marketing*, **58** (4), 1–15.

Andersson, P. and Soderlund, M. (1988) The Network Approach to Marketing, *Irish Marketing Review*, **3**, 63–68.

Blois, K. J. (1974) The Marketing of Services: An Approach, *European Journal of Marketing*, **8**, 137–49.

Boyatzis, R. E. (1982) *The Competent Manager: A Model for Effective Performance*, John Wiley & Sons, New York, NY.

Carson, D., Cromie, S., McGowan, P. and Hill, J. (1995) *Marketing and Entrepreneurship in SMEs: An Innovative Approach*, Prentice-Hall, UK.

Dubini, P. and Aldrich, H. (1991) Personal and Extended Networks are Central to the Entrepreneurial Process, *Journal of Business Venturing*, **6**, 305–313.

Hansen, E. L. (1995) Entrepreneurial Networks and New Organization Growth, *Entrepreneurial Theory and Practice*, **19**(4), 7–20.

Hofer, C. W. and Bygrave, W. D. (1992) Researching Entrepreneurship, *Entrepreneurial Theory and Practice*, Spring, 91–100.

Johannisson, B. (1986) Network Strategies: Management Technology for Entrepreneurship and Change, *International Small Business Journal*, **5**, 19–30.

Koontz, H., O'Donnell, C. and Weinrich, H. (1984) *Management*, McGraw-Hill, New York, NY.

Kotter, J. P. (1990) What Leaders Really Do? *Harvard Business Review*, May/June.

Meredith, G. G., Nelson, R. E. and Neck, P. A. (1982) *The Practice of Entrepreneurship*, International Labour Office, Geneva.

Mintzberg, H. (1973) *The Nature of Managerial Work*, Harper and Row, New York, NY.

Tichy, N. and Charan, R. (1991) Speed, Simplicity and Self-confidence: An Interview with Jack Welsh, *Harvard Business Review Classic from Managers as Leaders*, Harvard Business School Press, Boston.

Timmons, J. A. (1978) Characteristics and Role Demands of Entrepreneurship, *American Journal of Small Business*, **3**, 5–17.

UIC/AMA Marketing/Entrepreneurship Interface Symposium Proceedings 1987–1997, available from University of Illinois at Chicago, Department of Entrepreneurship Studies.

Further reading

The following is useful further reading which covers the broad basis of the issues discussed in this chapter.

Carson, D., Cromie, S. McGowan, P. and Hill, J. (1995) *Marketing and Entrepreneurship in SMEs: An Innovative Approach*, Prentice-Hall, UK.

Hisrich, R. D. and Peters, M. P. (1995) *Entrepreneurship: Starting, Developing and Managing a New Enterprise*, 3rd edn, Irwin, Holmewood, Ill.

Levinson, J. C. (1984) *Guerrilla Marketing: Secrets for Making Big Profits from your Small Business*, Houghton Mifflin, Boston.

Prushan, V. H. (1997) *No-Nonsense Markeing: 101 Practical Ways to Win and Keep Customers*, Wiley and Sons, USA.

Smith, J. (1996) *Guide to Integrated Marketing*, Entrepreneur Magazine Series, Wiley and Sons, USA.

UIC/AMA Marketing/Entrepreneurship Interface Symposium Proceedings 1987–1997, available from the University of Illinois at Chicago, Department of Entrepreneurship Studies.

CHAPTER 28

Retailing

PETER J. McGOLDRICK

Introduction

Originally defined as 'the sale of goods in small quantities', a better working definition of retailing is:

the sale of goods and services to consumers for their own use.

This distinguishes retailing from the supply of goods, in quantities large or small, to industrial buyers. It also recognizes the adoption of retailing terms and concepts by a wide range of services providers. For example, banks and other financial services providers use the term 'retail' to differentiate their consumer and their corporate activities (McGoldrick and Greenland, 1994). As the marketing of services is considered elsewhere, the focus of this chapter is upon the sale of goods to consumers.

There is nothing very new about the basic principles of retailing. It is still all about the identification and satisfaction of consumer needs and wants, at a profit. What has developed quite dramatically in recent years is the way in which retailers pursue these basic principles. Progressively, the folklore and rules of thumb that guided many decisions have been replaced by rigorous analysis and scientific modelling. While creativity and flair still have their place, it is fair to say that the science of retailing has now been born.

In part, this new sophistication in retailing can be ascribed to the growth in size and power of major retailers, discussed in earlier chapters. Much of the 'received wisdom' on marketing, imported from the United States, still tends to relegate the role of the retailer to that of a channel of distribution for manufacturers' goods. This is a dangerously myopic view, in a world in which it is equally appropriate to view manufacturers as channels of supply for powerful retailers. As retailers extend this power across national frontiers, they are joining the ranks of oil companies, car makers and computer manufacturers as the world's largest companies.

With this size comes the ability to invest in the best equipment, the latest techniques and, most importantly, the most able management. This is reflected by the increased interest in retailing courses and careers amongst our best undergraduate and graduate students. Retailing has indeed come of age as a worthwhile area of study and as a rewarding and highly professional area of management.

This brief tour of retailing considers first how retailing has evolved, and some of the theories that attempt to explain retail change. Attention then turns to the structure of retailing, examining first the different types of retail organization, then the various types of outlet. Retail strategy is then considered briefly, stressing the importance of customer focus. The specific functions of retailing are then examined, representing an extended 'retail marketing mix'. Given the emphasis in recent years upon retail internationalization, particular attention is given to that element of retail strategy. The chapter concludes by looking at non-store retailing, notably the emerging forms of electronic retailing.

Evolution of retailing

The growth of power

Retailing has always been a major component of economic activity. In Great Britain alone, there are 196,653 retail businesses, with a total turnover of £148 743 million, employing 2.3 million people (NatWest Markets, 1998). On a wider scale, there were 3.3 million retail enterprises in the EU employing 14 million people (Eurostat, 1997; European Retail Digest, 1997). Within Western Europe as a whole, there were over 4 million retail outlets, capturing 39.5 per cent of consumer expenditure, compared with 61.5 per cent in Eastern Europe and 31.3 per cent in North America (Euromonitor, 1995). Such expressions of scale cannot alone capture the major changes that have taken place, as retailing has switched from a more passive to a highly proactive role within the overall marketing process.

Many of the revered concepts of marketing, including the marketing mix, originated in a period when the manufacturer was truly 'king'. Post-war product shortages focused attention upon production, which gave way to an emphasis upon branding as shortages diminished. Inevitably, retailing tended to be depicted as just part of the marketing channels, largely controlled by manufacturers. The last two

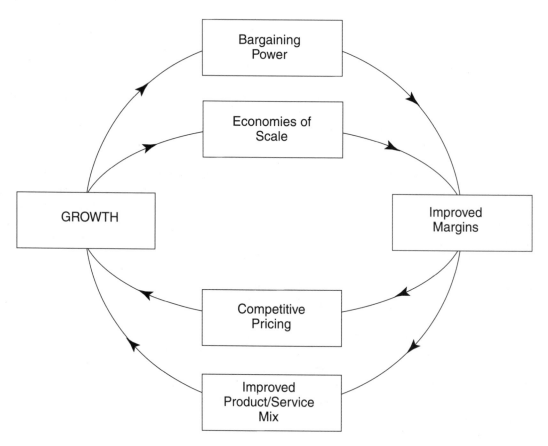

Figure 28.1   The retail growth cycle

decades have seen retailers grow in size and sophistication, often exceeding that of their largest suppliers.

Figure 28.1 depicts in outline the growth cycle of powerful retailers. Growth enhances bargaining power and helps in the achievement of other economies of scale. The improved margins thus gained may be used to achieve further growth, through competitive pricing and/or a product-service mix which offers superior value to customers. As the growth cycle continues, major retailers have invested in better management and superior information systems. Their power has been increased further by the development of retailer brands, extensive advertising and sophisticated trading environments.

Many large retailers have subsumed the roles traditionally ascribed to wholesalers, increasing further their dominance of the marketing channel. It is now equally appropriate to present a view of consumer goods marketing that is retailer driven (McGoldrick, 1990). Within this alternative view, manufacturers may be depicted as part of the 'channels of supply', with only limited power to influence the marketing strategies of major retailers. Large scale retailers have truly evolved from shop-keeping to strategic marketing.

Theories of retail change

Given the dynamic nature of retailing, several theories have developed to explain aspects of evolution and change. Two of the most influential are the 'wheel of retailing' and the 'retail life cycle'. These and other theories of retail change are discussed in detail by Brown (1987).

The wheel of retailing suggests that new types of retailers tend to enter as low-price, low-margin, low-status operators. Over time, they acquire more elaborate facilities, incur higher operating costs and cease to be as price competitive. Eventually, they mature as higher-cost, higher-price retailers, vulnerable to newer types who enter at the first phase of 'the wheel'. Many examples can be found of retail types and indi-

vidual companies that have evolved in this way, including department stores and supermarkets. The process has been ascribed to various influences, including a shift away from the aggressive management style of the founders, the attraction of the up-market segments, a preference amongst leading retailers for non-price forms of competition, and possible 'misguidance' by suppliers of elaborate equipment and fitments. It is also possible that the boom–recession cycles within most advanced economies contribute to the process, encouraging trading-up during the boom years and encouraging new forms of price competition during recessions.

The retail life cycle concept derives from the better known product life cycle. Retail institutions and formats appear to be moving from innovation to maturity with increasing speed. Davidson *et al.* (1976) estimated that the city centre department store took some eighty years to mature, whereas the home improvement centre in the USA took only fifteen years. Figure 28.2 shows the four main phases of the retail life cycle, illustrating that the life cycle phase for any given retail format may differ greatly between the countries of Europe.

Types of retail organization

The growth of retailer power and influence has stemmed largely from the concentration of trade into the hand of fewer, larger enterprises. This section looks first at this process of concentration, involving the shift of trade from independent to multiple retailers. Consideration is then given to symbol retailing, franchises and co-operatives.

Independents and multiples

The term 'multiple' signifies more than one outlet but different data sources use different definitions, e.g. at least two, five or ten outlets. In Great Britain, nearly 70 per cent of retail trade is accounted for by multiples with 10 or more outlets. The concentration of trade is especially marked in the grocery sector and, as Table 28.1 illustrates, it is still growing rapidly. The top seven multiples ran just 8 per cent of all grocery outlets in 1997, yet took nearly 70 per cent of grocery turnover. Concentration levels are also growing in other retail sectors. Multiples account for 69 per cent of mens' wear trade, 74.2 per cent of womens' wear, 76.9 per cent of elec-

trical appliances and 70.4 per cent of DIY (NatWest Markets, 1998).

Retail structures contrast markedly across different countries, and different continents. In Western Europe as a whole, there were 135 inhabitants per outlet, similar to the ratios in Asia (130) and Oceania (134), but contrasting with North America (324) (Euromonitor, 1995).

Table 28.1	Concentration in the grocery trade			
	Percentage of outlets		*Percentage of turnover*	
	1995	*1997*	*1995*	*1997*
Top seven multiples	7.5	8.0	65.6	69.2
Other multiples	6.9	9.2	16.1	16.4
Co-operatives	6.0	6.1	8.6	7.0
Independents	79.6	76.7	9.7	7.4

Source: Derived from: Neilsen (1998)

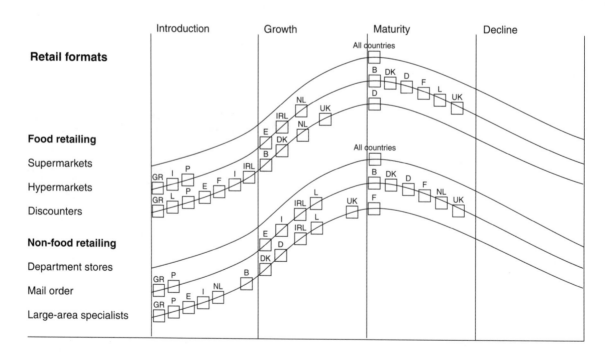

Source: Eurostat, 1993, p. 20

Figure 28.2   Retail life cycles in EU countries: B, Belgium; D, Germany; DK, Denmark; E, Spain; F, France; GR, Greece; I, Italy; IRL, Ireland; P, Portugal; L, Luxembourg; NL, Netherlands; UK, United Kingdom

	Table 28.2	Contrasting retail structures	
Country	*No. of outlets*	*outlets per 1000 inhabitants*	*No. of persons employed per outlet*
Greece	175 000	17.40	1.90
Italy	888 330	15.65	2.69
Portugal	132 094	13.36	2.76
Spain	511 927	13.08	3.00
Belgium	121 912	12.07	1.94
Denmark	47 597	9.19	4.17
Norway	38 401	8.91	3.21
Luxembourg	3 587	8.95	5.45
Ireland	29 337	8.29	4.48
France	451 800	7.84	4.48
Netherlands	102 900	6.69	6.19
Sweden	54 549	6.23	5.29
Switzerland	41 935	6.13	7.65
United Kingdom	330 491	5.76	6.66
Finland	28 309	5.57	4.66
Germany	435 471	5.37	6.58
Austria	40 040	4.99	7.24

Source: Eurostat (1997)

Table 28.2 expresses two measures of 'retail density'. By Western European standards, Austria, the UK, Germany, Finland and Switzerland show high levels of outlet concentration, whereas Greece, Portugal, Spain and Italy still have more outlets, relative to population levels. Employees per outlet provide another comparison of structure, ranging from 7.24 in the UK to 1.90 in Greece.

Not all small stores are independently owned; the convenience store or 'c-store' format has been developed by multiples, voluntary groups and franchisers. For example, Alldays operates over 500 such outlets, an increasing proportion of their stores being franchises (see below). Definitions of the convenience store vary somewhat but Nielsen (1998) suggest the following criteria:

- self service;
- 1000–3000 sq.ft selling area;
- parking facilities;
- open seven days a week for long hours;
- wide range but limited brand choice, including groceries, toiletries, some medicines, alcohol and stationery; some also offer video hire, take-away foods and petrol.

It was estimated in 1998 that there were 6500 c-stores in the UK, including those developed on petrol forecourts.

Voluntary groups

One response of independent retailers and wholesalers to the growth of the multiples has been the formation of 'voluntary', 'symbol' or 'affiliation' groups. Within this form of contractual chain, a group name is utilized and the retailers are normally required to buy a given proportion of their merchandise through the group. The organization typically provides buying and other marketing services, including special promotions, advertising and frequently

Table 28.3 Examples of voluntary groups		
Sector	*Group*	*UK outlets*
Grocery	Spar	2700
	Happy Shopper	2000
Chemists	Vantage	2500
	Numark	1030
Department stores	Associated Independent Stores	540
Hardware	Fair & Square	485

Source: Derived from: Nielsen (1998)

own brands. The group is therefore able to achieve some of the buying power and economies of scale characteristic of major multiples.

Table 28.3 gives examples of voluntary groups in four sectors. In that restrictions apply to the opening of pharmacies in the UK, in order to protect the network of outlets, this sector has been protected somewhat from the full effects of multiple completion. The voluntary groups hold over 50 per cent of this sector, Vantage and Numark being the major groups. In the grocery sector, the leading player is Spar, which also operates in 17 of the 19 European countries within Nielsen's analysis (Nielsen, 1998). This international presence gives Spar a European grocery share of 2.2 per cent, close to the shares of Aldi and Carrefour.

Euromonitor estimates for 1995 showed a great diversity in percentage penetration within the total retail trade of other European markets:

Belgium   13
Denmark   36
Finland   42
Netherlands 30
Norway   20
Spain   4
Sweden   39
Germany   35

This type of affiliation appears well suited to areas of low population densities but the volun-

tary groups are under pressure from the multiples in most countries.

Franchises

Franchising, in various forms, has a long history both in Europe and in the USA. Its fastest growth as an element of retail structure occurred through the 1980s. From 2600 franchised units in the UK in 1980, the number grew to 21 500 by 1996, of which 4500 could truly be classified as retail outlets (Key Note, 1997). Franchising can take many different forms, notably the following.

1   The manufacturer–retailer franchise: common in the sale of cars and petrol.
2   The manufacturer–wholesaler, franchise: e.g., franchises to bottle Coca-Cola or Pepsi-Cola.
3   The wholesaler–retailer franchise: includes some voluntary groups, discussed above.
4   The business format franchise: typical in fast food or car hire.

The benefits of franchising can flow from achieving the best of both worlds in business, combining the power, sophistication and reputation of a large organization with the energy, motivation and commitment of the independent owner-manager. For well conceived and well managed business formats, franchising has proved to be a powerful vehicle for expansion, as in the cases of Body Shop, Benetton and Seven-Eleven Japan (Sparks, in McGoldrick, 1994).

Co-operative societies

There is essentially one co-operative movement in the UK but its retail activities have been fragmented into a large number of relatively autonomous societies. This fragmentation has been a major reason for the decline in the share of retail trade held by the co-operatives, in spite of the potential for buying power and economies of scale within the movement as a whole. The Co-op share of UK retail sales fell from 5.6 per cent in 1982 to 4.2 per cent in 1992. Table 28.1 illustrated that their grocery share declined from 8.6 to 7.0 per cent between 1995 and 1997.

Whereas 231 individual societies existed in 1977, this had fallen to 52 by 1997; significant mergers have occurred since then. Rationalization of outlets has continued and the societies have developed strength in discounting and neighbourhood retailing.

In some countries of Europe, the co-operatives hold a far higher share of retail sales. In Switzerland, the two major co-operatives, Migros and Co-op Schweiz, held 27 per cent of all retail sales, 38 per cent of the food trade. The co-operatives also held over 20 per cent of the food trade in the Scandinavian countries. If the co-operative societies had combined both nationally and internationally, they could well have been Europe's largest retail organization.

Major retail formats

The type of organization that owns or manages a store is not always obvious to the consumer. Other, more striking characteristics of shops serve to differentiate one format from another in the minds of shoppers. A retail format can be defined along a number of different dimensions, including:

single store	group of stores
in-town	out-of-town
large	small
innovative	mature
food	non-food
specialized	generalized
niche	commodity
high added value	discounter

This section examines briefly shopping centres, retail parks, superstores, hypermarkets, department stores, variety stores and a number of formats that use the term 'discounter'.

Shopping centres and retail parks

The term 'shopping centre' is normally applied to a coherent, planned and controlled group of retail establishments, as distinct from the more random grouping of a 'shopping district'. In Europe, the most typical location for shopping centres is still within existing town centres; the out-of-town centre is a relatively recent phenomenon. Whereas out-of-town centres developed from the 1920s in the USA, some fifty years elapsed before they started to make an impact in Europe.

The differences between the USA and European development patterns can be ascribed in part to differences of economics, geography and demography. Most of all, the more restrictive planning regulations within most European countries have served to restrict developments out-of-town. The planning debates revolve around a range of economic, environmental and social issues, summarized in McGoldrick and Thompson (1992).

The move out of town has been described as three 'waves' of development (Schiller, in McGoldrick and Thompson, 1992). The first comprised the superstores, selling mostly food and limited ranges of non-food items. The second wave of decentralization involved bulky goods, such as DIY, carpets, furniture, large electrical items and garden centres. The third wave involved clothing and other comparison shopping, representing the most direct threat to

Table 28.4 Shopping centres in five countries			
Country	*Centres* *(no.)*	*Retail space* *(million sq. ft)*	*Sq. ft* *per person*
United Kingdom	768	142.1	280
France	611	134.6	258
Netherlands	139	20.5	137
Spain	262	39.8	87
Germany	102	45.2	27

Note: Many UK sources measure space in square feet: one square metre is equal to 10.76 sq. ft.

Source: derived from NatWest Markets (1998)

existing town centres. The decision by Marks & Spencer to develop out of town, both within major new centres and in freestanding schemes with food superstore partners, was a major element of this third wave. The late 1980s and early 1990s saw the opening of four especially large out-of-town centres in the UK, each in excess of one million square feet. Situated in Tyneside, South Yorkshire, West Midlands and Essex, each represented a full alternative to the traditional town centre.

Table 28.4 illustrates a further contrast between the form of retailing in different European countries. Both the UK and France have a relatively high level of shopping centre provision, compared with that of Germany. However, changes in planning regulations and trading restrictions are already serving to reduce these differences.

Retail parks are more utilitarian groupings of 'retail sheds' and are also termed 'retail warehouse parks'. They offer convenient access and car parking arrangements but lack the indoor malls and many of the other comforts of the new, out-of-town shopping centres. The first such scheme opened in the UK in 1982; by 1997, there were 474 in operation (NatWest Markets, 1998). They involve far lower development costs than the major, full service shopping centres, which typically include extensive leisure and catering facilities. The trading format of the retail park has proved fairly resilient to adverse economic conditions and their development has

continued, shifting the balance away from traditional town centres.

Factory outlet centres made their appearance in the UK in 1992. By 2000, some 23 such centres will be trading. They comprise groupings of mainly designer outlets, selling below the normal price for these brands. One of the largest, Cheshire Oaks, includes 300 000 sq. ft of retail area and 120 factory outlets (NatWest Markets, 1998).

Department and variety stores

In most new shopping centres, developers seek to ensure that they attract key 'anchor tenants' in the form of major department and variety stores. Ironically, the market shares of both these retail formats have tended towards decline in most European countries.

According to the International Association of Department Stores, a department store must have at least 2500 sq. metres of space (26 900 sq. ft). Furthermore, it must offer a product range that is both wide and deep in several product categories. The Association estimates that there were around 960 such stores in the EU in 1990, a slight decline from 1112 in 1980. Table 28.5 summarizes the changes in market share, showing decline in France, Germany and the UK. Spain is one of the few countries within which this format is growing, the leading operator being El Corte Inglés. In the UK, the leading department store retailers are John Lewis and Debenhams, each with around 20 per cent of the sector share. John Lewis is the more productive in terms of space utilization, achieving £453 per year per sq. ft, compared with £200 at Debenhams (Retail Review, 1998).

Table 28.5 Department store shares		
Percentage share of retail trade held by department stores		
1970	*1980*	*1990*
France	3.4	2.9	1.9
Germany	11.0	7.2	5.6
U.K.	5.5	4.7	4.0
Source: Tordjman (1993).		

Many European variety stores were founded in the 1930s by department store operators, in order to offer a lower priced, lower service and lower assortment format. Examples include Prisunic by Printemps and Priminime by Bon Marche. In the UK, there are few such links between the department and variety store sectors and variety stores hold a relatively strong 6.2 per cent of retail trade, compared with 2.1 per cent in France and 1.1 per cent in Germany.

Marks & Spencer, the leading variety store in the UK, holds a 15.1 per cent share of the clothing market and 3.3% share in food retailing (Retail Review, 1998). Many variety stores have traded up and diversified; on the other hand, department stores have tended to withdraw from some product ranges in the face of specialist, lower priced competition. Accordingly, the distinction between the department and variety formats has become blurred.

Superstores and hypermarkets

Whereas the supermarket format has reached maturity in most countries (Figure 28.2), the superstore and hypermarket formats have been claiming increased share in most countries. Being situated mostly outside traditional shopping centres, they tend to enjoy greater accessibility by car, greater economies of scale and the benefits of being purpose built. Superstores form the 'anchor stores' of retail warehouse parks and of many partnership schemes, such as the Marks & Spencer–Tesco partnership at Handforth, Cheshire.

In Britain, a superstore is defined as having at least 25 000 sq.ft of selling space while a hypermarket has at least 50 000 sq. ft. Some sources use the near equivalent metric measures of 2500 m^2 and 5000 m^2 respectively. Comparisons between countries encounter great difficulties as these thresholds vary considerably. In some cases, the terms imply large stores selling primarily groceries; in others, the terms are used with more flexibility to describe any large scale, specialist format, offering a strong depth of assortment, trading on one level and providing ample car parking. Having noted these caveats, Table 28.6 offers an indication of growth within five countries of Europe. There are however new regulations upon large store and centre developments, introduced by the governments of France, Germany, Italy, the Netherlands and Spain (NatWest Securities, 1997).

Table 28.6 Hypermarkets and superstores of 2500 m^2 and over		
	1990/91 (no.)	*1995/96* (no.)
France	914	1,089
Netherlands	31	40
Spain	151	221
United Kingdom	733	1,053
Sweden	63	77
Source: derived from Institute of Grocery Distribution (1997)		

Discounters

Like so many of the descriptive terms in retailing, 'discounter' is regrettably imprecise. As the wheel of retailing concept suggests, many new concepts have entered by offering prices at levels below existing competition, i.e., by discounting. Accordingly, the term 'hard discounter' has been adopted in some countries to distinguish between new, deep discount formats and other, more mild manifestations of price competition.

In the context of food retailing, Tordjman (1993) distinguished between the key financial and operational characteristics of discounters and hypermarkets, as shown in Table 28.7. This demonstrates the ability of the format to produce reasonable net margins through the strict control of operating costs. As Figure 28.2 depicted, the discount food format is in growth within most countries but has reached maturity in Germany. Table 28.8 summarizes the shares held by food discounters in 14 European countries, showing also the expected growth in outlet numbers.

The concept of the warehouse club represented an addition to hard discounting in Europe in the 1990s. These clubs started to develop from 1982 in the USA; the first such unit opened in the UK in 1993, after strong opposition from major supermarket chains. Warehouse clubs charge a membership fee to customers, which ensures selectivity and generally greater loyalty. A wide range of mostly packaged foods and non-foods is offered, usually in large or multiple packs, in sparce surroundings of 100 000 sq. ft or over.

Retailing strategy

Each element of the value chain can serve to increase value, real or perceived. Most elements incur costs but can contribute to the process of differentiation. For comprehensive discussions of strategic planning in retailing, see Johnson (1987). Strategies for change and renewal in retailing are suggested in the *McKinsey Quarterly* (Burns *et al.*, 1997).

Understanding needs and wants

Fundamental to the formulation of retail marketing strategy is a clear understanding of customer needs, motives and patronage decision processes. Without this, there is a tendency for strategy formulation to dwell upon the range of

---

Table 28.7 Discounters and hypermarkets compared

Typical key indices	Discount supermarket	Hypermarket
Store size (m²)	600	6,000
Number of lines	1000	35,000
Stockturns per year	40	22
Gross margin % of sales	14.5	16.0
As % of sales:		
Labour	5	7
Distribution	2	3
Property	1	2
Other costs	3	2
Net margin as % of sales	3.5	2.0
Asset turnover (times)	7	9
Return on investment (%)	24.5	18.0

Source: derived from Tordjman (1993).

	Table 28.8 Food discounters in Europe		
Country	*Number of stores*		*Percentage share of turnover 1996*
	1996	*2000 (f)*	
Austria	395	414	17
Belgium	628	634	25
Denmark	648	654	20
Finland	782	793	12
France	1656	2080	7
Germany	8910	8930	30
Italy	745	1195	10
The Netherlands	584	615	13
Norway	890	895	37
Portugal	135	350	9
Spain	1275	1435	9
Sweden	238	240	11
Switzerland	615	625	8
United Kingdom	1832	2122	11

Source: derived from: Nielsen (1998); Institute of Grocery Distribution (1997).

existing solutions, rather than developing formats to satisfy specific sets of consumer requirements.

The constant and widespread interface between retailers and their customers can easily lead to an illusion of empathy. In some large organizations however, the key decision makers have become remote and largely isolated from their customers. It then becomes all too easy to impose their own value and preferences, in the sincere belief that these reflect those of the customers: this is somewhat improbable. Sophisticated retail marketers have had to develop new ways of hearing and understanding their customers, and their non-customers.

The research industry has responded with a range of information services, including tracking studies of customer attitudes/opinions and large panels of shoppers, whose purchase and patronage decisions are monitored in considerable detail. These data are however in the public domain, albeit to the exclusive club of competitors that can afford to purchase. In-house focus groups can also help to keep decision makers

attuned to customer needs; however busy the diary or crowded the in-tray, some marketing managers insist on taking time out to attend these discussions, or simply to talk to shoppers using their stores.

Complaints/suggestions should also be welcomed positively, rather than seen as a nuisance to be handled. There are few more cost effective approaches to diagnosing dissatisfaction, often before it becomes fatal, or of identifying new ways of satisfying customers. In the words of Jeremy Mitchell (1978):

When the complaints stop coming . . . it will mean the business is dying. The consumers will have made the ultimate protest. They will have gone elsewhere.

Image and brand equity

The accumulation of customer perceptions relating to an organization comprise that seemingly nebulous commodity: image. Having been convinced of the strong relationship between good image and good financial performance,

retailers and researchers have invested extensively in the techniques to measure, compare
and track images.

The study of images has been given further

impetus through the development of the concept of brand equity (Aaker, 1991). This forges a
clear link between the psychological domain of
perceptions and images, and the financial

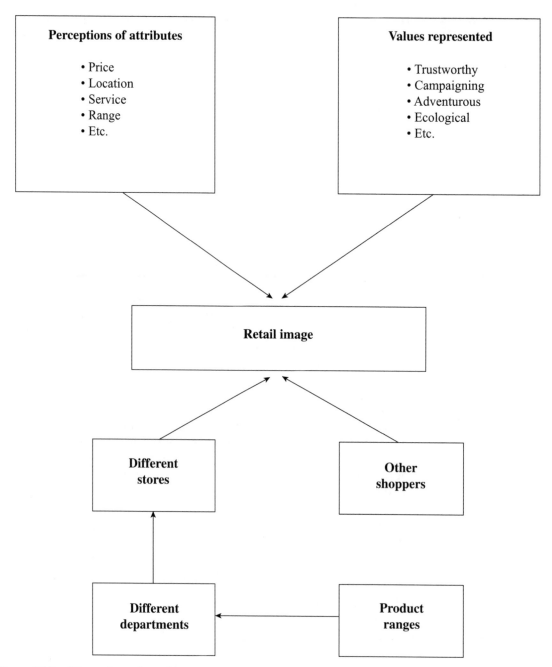

Figure 28.3   Dimensions of retail image

domain of assets and equity. Image is taken out of the nebulous role of 'soft data' and moved centre stage as a key measure of company performance, where it matters most, in the mind of the consumer.

Early work on image monitoring tended to dwell upon the more tangible attributes, such as perceptions of locations, prices, etc. Although these attributes are of no less importance today, the battle for effective differentiation has extended the concept of image towards the values that the 'retail brand' represents for consumers. For example, shopping in a discount store such as Aldi reinforces for some the need to be seen by friends and family as thrifty, or the need to beat the marketing embellishments of the superstores. If the growth of discounters in Europe were ascribed simply to economic motives, limited insight would be yielded into the best ways of harnessing, or of combating, the format.

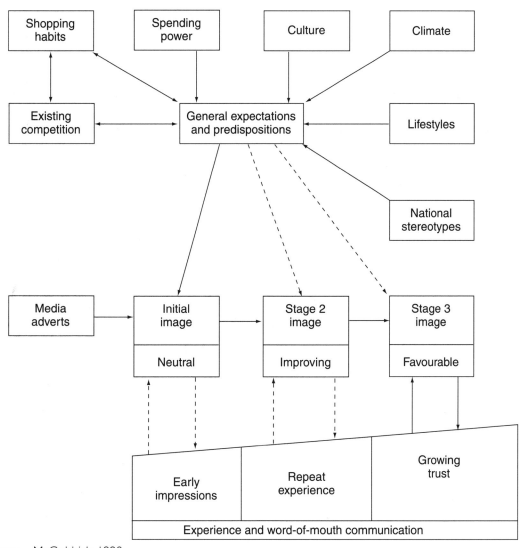

Source: McGoldrick, 1998

Figure 28.4   Determinants of international image

The intricacy and multidimensionality of retail images is summarized in Figure 28.3. Retail image comprises a bundle of perceptions of attribute strengths/weaknesses, plus beliefs about the inner and outer directed values to which the retailer contributes. The bases of these beliefs, however, are also multifaceted. Perceptions are based upon individual stores, departments and product ranges, which can of course vary within a chain. The importance of measuring perceptions of clienteles has also been recognized: a major reason why stores are excluded from a shopper's list of alternatives is because other shoppers are too affluent/poor, trendy/conservative, etc.

The critical role of image in the formulation and evaluation of retail strategy has also been realized in the international setting. A strong image in the home market may have little or no brand equity in the new market, unless that market comprises many tourists or expatriates from the home market. In most cases, the image has to be created, providing an opportunity to monitor the birth and development of an image.

Based upon studies of Marks & Spencer's images in a number of international markets, Figure 28.4 summarizes the development of image. Initial images are heavily influenced by advertising and by general pre-dispositions, including national stereotypes. Initial experience or word-of-mouth communication tends to lead fairly quickly to images of such attributes as prices and fashion. It takes longer for beliefs to develop as to some of the values which are part of the core proposition within the home market, such as beliefs about trust and the integrity of the retailer.

Positioning and the value proposition

As the attributes, values and dimensions of image monitoring become ever more intricate, the opportunities to differentiate through positioning abound. Until relatively recently, positioning was typically defined in highly tangible terms, such as price levels and the age range of the target shoppers. Thus, using a simple, two-dimensional chart, a shoe retailer could identify gaps in the market, for example, for more expensive shoes for shoppers under 30, or for budget shoppers in their 40s.

These early approaches to positioning were appealing in that they focused upon easily defined market segments. However, they tended to lead to mob positioning, with most retailers chasing the (seemingly) most profitable target markets. They also offered little scope for more creative approaches to identifying viable and profitable targets. There are numerous examples of retailers with similar price levels, similar product ranges, similar age targets, yet most dissimilar levels of customer appeal. While these stores may be close on the retailers' positioning maps, they are clearly differentiated in the customers' mental maps. Yet another reason emerges to use the best available techniques to explore perceptions, beliefs and values represented by retailers.

Another development in retail marketing has been the emergence of store positions not previously considered attractive, or even viable. For example, the combination of wide assortments and low prices was not considered to be an attractive financial proposition, however attractive it may be for the consumer. The advent of the 'category killer', sometimes ascribed the alternative title 'power retailer', has changed the rules (Rogers, 1996). For many people, Toys'R'Us symbolizes this format, with a combination of wide choice, reasonable prices, efficient systems and easy access (Tordjman, 1994).

The category killer format has proved attractive for relatively infrequent, comparison purchases, where a large/vast choice adds significant value for the consumer. DIY would appear vulnerable/attractive to this format: why drive between several, modest sized DIY stores to compare similar, restricted ranges, when a single, longer drive reaches a genuinely expanded range? Thus, the development of the B&Q warehouse format, trying to head off the US competition, and offering a learning experience in developing systems to handle greatly expanded assortments. IKEA and Olympus Sportsworld are other examples of the format.

Positioning is therefore a multidimensional exploration of mindspace, to identify gaps in consumer preference maps. However, the identification of gaps does not alone ensure their attractiveness. A sophisticated blend of financial and psychological modelling is required to predict the viability of the new market position. Neither is simple but the prediction of consumer preferences is undoubtedly the greater chal-

lenge. It requires an understanding of the complex systems of trade-offs that consumers make when choosing a store.

Figure 28.5 offers a simple but useful summary of this difficult area of analysis. At the core of retail marketing strategy there must be a focus upon values, as perceived by the target customer. In general, they seek more of the positive attributes, less of the negative attributes, such as cost, risk, time effort and stress. The better understanding of the response patterns and trade-offs within the 'value equation' is,

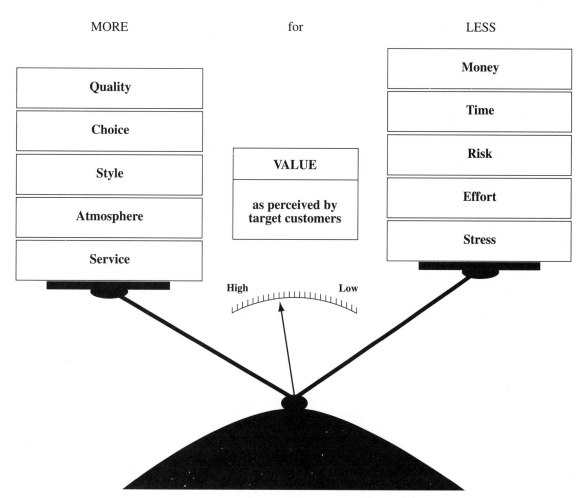

Figure 28.5 The value equation (developed from *Chain Store Age Executive*, 1994)

without doubt, a worthwhile area of development in the new science of retailing.

Loyalty: schemes or strategies?

It is appropriate to conclude this section with comments on one of the biggest preoccupations of retail strategy in recent years: loyalty schemes. In the centuries to come, retail historians may well be puzzled as they content analyse thousands of pages of trade journals. Why was all the emphasis in 1997 on loyalty schemes, in 1993 on discounters, in 1990 on customer service(s), in 1987 on design, etc., etc.? Surely, if everyone was doing the same thing, no-one would stand out from the crowd? It is hard to deny that there have been distinct waves of emphasis in retail strategy over the last 20 years, as illustrated by Figure 28.6. We can all argue exactly when each phase started and ended; more difficult to argue is the fact that

these emphases, for a short period of time, become obsessions, if not fixations. This leads us to sad conclusion: *most retail strategies have been formed in someone else's head office!*

One beneficial difference between this 'wave' and previous ones is that it focuses upon the consumer, rather than upon a specific aspect of the mix. Loyalty schemes are driven by the philosophy that it is cheaper to retain a customer than it is to attract a new one, or to recover a lost one. They come in many different shapes and forms: a succinct review of these is provided by Sopanen (1996). Some schemes have proved prohibitively expensive, necessitating their reduction or withdrawal. Other have produced loyalty to the loyalty scheme, rather than to retailers, giving them a status similar to trading stamps, largely abandoned in the 1970s.

In theory, a loyalty scheme which is well thought out, rather than hastily bought in, can yield considerable information benefits. To that

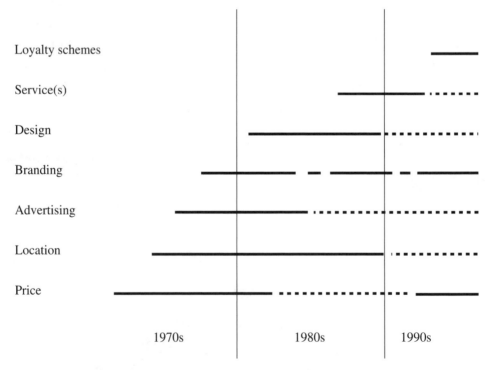

Source: McGoldrick and Andre, 1997

Figure 28.6 Waves of emphasis in retail strategy

mass of EPoS data can be added information about the income, family, age, etc., of the purchaser. For the first time since the corner shop, where most customers were known by name, retailers have the potential to practice elements of one-to-one, micromaketing.

However, as most retailers are still grappling to harness the full information benefits of EPoS data, they can only scratch the surface of this potential. While the concept of a 'segment of one' makes obvious sense in business-to-business marketing, retail marketing involves a vast number of (relatively) small accounts. Computers can be programmed to tailor incentives, offers and communications to (assumed) customer types but mistakes will inevitably occur. At best these will be amusing, at worst they will be totally alienating. As loyalty schemes lose their distinctiveness, becoming imitated and institutionalized, a major challenge for retail marketing will be to demonstrate that they add sufficient value for the consumer, the retailer and shareholder.

Retail functions

Given the enormous breadth of activities that comprise retailing, it is possible here to provide only a glimpse of its major functions. A more comprehensive treatment is provided in the chapters of McGoldrick (1990) and the case studies of McGoldrick (1994). The emphasis here is to:

1   Indicate the role of each function within the overall process of marketing consumer goods.
2   Outline the significance of each function within the strategic mix and within the value chain of retailers.

Location

Store location decisions are probably the single most crucial elements of retail marketing strategy. They represent long-term investment decisions which, if incorrect, are very difficult to change. While good locations cannot alone compensate for a weak overall strategy, a poor location is a very difficult deficit to overcome. Bad location decisions also undermine the asset value of the retail organization; such stores are difficult to sell.

The retail location decisions must address macro and micro issues; they are often depicted in three stages (Brown, 1992).

1   Search—identifying geographical areas that may have market potential.
2   Viability—evaluating the turnover potential of the best available sites.
3   Micro—examining the detailed features of the short-listed sites.

Clearly, not all location decisions pass through this sequence, and a great deal of intuition and executive judgement is still applied. A number of more systematic techniques are available to assist decision makers.

1   *Checklists*—very detailed lists of factors relevant to location evaluations have been evolved and are widely used. The factors include many aspects of the population within the catchment area, competition (existing and potential), accessibility by car and by foot, and the specific costs of developing a store on that site.
2   *Geographic information systems* (GIS)—can provide detailed analysis of many checklist factors, such as income, employment and expenditure profiles within specified localities.
3   *Analogue methods*—extrapolate the performance of a site under consideration, based upon analogous sites already in operation.
4   *Regression models*—help to forecast turnover by modelling the influence of location factors which contribute to, or detract from, the turnover of existing stores.

Although no self-respecting retailer would set aside the checklist, or the need to experience the 'look-feel' of a potential site, GIS offers immediate answers to many 'what if?' questions. These questions are not restricted to new sites but can be extended to the evaluation of branch performance, set against an objective model of potential. The knowledge of neighbourhood characteristics provided by GIS can also guide decisions about product ranges, price levels and promotion at the branch level.

Product selection and buying

The buying function represents the main interface between retailers and other members of the supply chain. Accordingly, many suppliers create specialist sales teams to serve key retail accounts, developing a close knowledge of the organization and the individuals involved. In some retail organizations, individual buyers have extensive autonomy within their specific product category; in others, the buying team is the norm, which typically includes selectors, merchandisers, technologists and quality controllers.

Numerous criteria must be considered by retail buyers, not least of which are the projections of sales and profitability. Product selection is also a key element of differentiation and buyers are becoming increasingly proactive in sourcing items that will help to provide a competitive edge. Buyers must also consider the capabilities of the supplier, in terms of volume, flexibility and reliability.

Nowhere is the shift of power from manufacturers to retailers more directly manifest than in the buying offices of major retailers. The 'table banging' style of buying, characteristic of the early days of retailer power, has indeed given way to more sophisticated and, sometimes, longer-term forms of retailer–manufacturer relationship. Talk of 'relationship marketing' can however obscure the considerable power of the retail buyers within that relationship. To their economic buying power, retailers have now added more focus, expertise and information, increasing further their overall power. Major retailers have established team buying, typically involving a merchandiser, a technolo-gist and a buyer/negotiator. This gives the product category expertise of a team, while avoiding the inflexibility of a large buying committee.

Another development in retail buying has been the increased interest in sourcing directly from other countries (Liu and McGoldrick, 1996). To an extent, some manufacturers have brought this upon themselves, having out-sourced increasing proportions of their production to areas with lower labour costs. In doing so, they have in effect relegated their roll to that of intermediaries: major retailers have little time for dispensable intermediaries. Retailers in some categories have found international sourcing be the only way of maintaining a choice of viable sources, and of differentiating through new and different products. Some retailers have developed extensive sourcing networks themselves, some have appointed agents, others have developed international buying alliances.

The old adage that information is power is well illustrated in retail buying. Models of direct product profitability (DPP) continue to develop, helping to pinpoint item and category profitability. The data from point of sale scanners, plus similar records of goods received, provide daily information on stocks and sales. There can be some benefits in judicious sharing of some of this information with suppliers, if this helps to achieve zero inventories, just-in-time deliveries, etc. To an extent, this may push stockholding costs back up the supply chain but it does provide better product availability and space utilization for the retailer. Most retailers however see much work still ahead in creating fully integrated information systems. As this goal is approached, it brings more power to the retailers, their buying teams in particular.

In the USA, the Robinson Patman Act limits the scope of major retail buyers to obtain better terms, purely on account of their buying power. Such legislation has been considered but not implemented in the UK. Accordingly, large retailers can demand a wide range of additional benefits, analysed by the Office of Fair Trading (1985).

Retail brands

A significant manifestation of retailer power has been the ability of major retailers to develop their own brand product ranges. These are defined as products sold under a retail organization's house brand name, which are sold exclusively through that retail organization's outlets. The name may be that of the retailer, for example Tesco, or a name closely linked with the company, such as Marks & Spencer's St Michael brand. From time to time, grocery retailers have also launched ranges of 'generics', a low priced, plain label variant upon the own brand concept.

Retailer brands have been especially important within grocery retailing. The three leading grocers in the UK, Tesco, J. Sainsbury and Safeway, derived 45, 56 and 45 per cent of their turnover respectively from their own brands in 1997 (Retail Review, 1998). Table 28.9 summarizes own brands across Europe. Such brands are not restricted to grocery sectors; with 100 per cent own brands, Marks & Spencer has been described as 'a manufacturer without factories'. This company is totally involved in the specification, design and quality control processes.

The primary driver of own-brand development has been to produce better margins, often around 10 per cent better, while simultaneously increasing pressure upon manufacturers. More recently, as retailers have become more accomplished and confident in their brand building, other motives have played an increasing role. The potential contribution of own brands to store image and maintaining store loyalty has been recognized, as own brands have evolved from 'copy-cat' to differentiation status. Indeed, retailers such as Marks & Spencer and the Body Shop can claim impressive records of product innovation, to the extent that own brands can trade in a premium position.

To cater for differing retail objectives and market conditions, a range of own brand positions have evolved, from the most basic 'generic' products, through to the top quality, premium own brands. Although retailer brands are strongly associated with the grocery industry, they also have a formidable presence in clothing retailing. Here, the ability to co-ordinate aspects of product and store design is a significant additional motive.

Table 28.9 Retailer brand shares in Europe

Country	Percentage of grocery trade	
	1991	1993
Switzerland	40	41
United Kingdom	30	31
Germany	23	24
Belgium	19	20
France	18	19
Denmark	18	19
Netherlands	16	17
Austria	11	12
Spain	5	8
Italy	5	7
Portugal	1	3

Source: Derived from Samways (1996)

The implications for manufacturers have been serious indeed, with retailers able to switch sources of own brands, if prices or specifications cannot be agreed. Some manufacturers have learnt to coexist as largely anonymous suppliers of major retailers, freed of most marketing expenditures but with extreme dependence upon the retailer(s). Others, such as Kellogg's, have maintained a vigorous stance: 'if our name is not on the box, then it was not made by Kellogg's'. A similar stance was taken by Heinz, although this changed, with the company now adopting a 'mixed branding' policy. This has the advantages of maximizing plant utilization and maintaining influence, if not control, over product differentiation. The old adage 'if you can't beat them, join them' also holds true.

The evolution of own brands has demanded the development of skills in design and product testing, previously in the domain of the manufacturer. Leading grocers now employ large teams of food scientists to help develop, specify and test product characteristics. Consumer tests area also of critical importance, to ensure that the effect on image is the right direction. Retailers must also monitor possible consumer resistance to own brands, if their predominance in displays is creating the impression of a restriction of choice.

Retail pricing

One of the most complex area of retail decision making is that of pricing. Whereas a manufacturer may have 50–100 items to price, a superstore or department store retailer may be responsible for a thousand times more SKUs (stock-keeping units). Added to this complexity is the fact that chain store retailers operate in many different geographical markets.

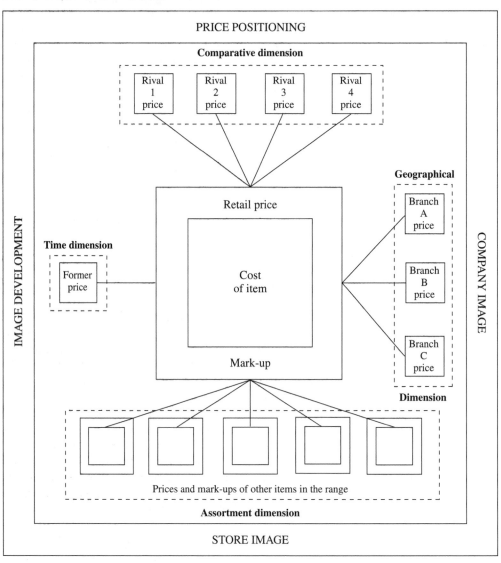

Source: McGoldrick, 1990

Figure 28.7 A multi-dimensional framework for retail pricing

Figure 28.7 summarizes the main dimensions of retail prices: developments within each are considered briefly.

The 'comparative dimension' represents the many differences in price between those of the retailer and those of direct and indirect, local and national competitors. This comprises a vast number of price comparisons, far more than can be collected to inform each pricing decision. The information industry has responded with a range of pricing data, some comprising a pooling of retailers' own scanner data, others deriving information from the purchase records of large panels of consumers. In some sectors, such as clothing retailing, much comparative data on prices and markdowns are still obtained by auditors visiting a sample of stores at regular intervals. The complexity of price comparison extends still further when international markets are involved (McGoldrick *et al.*, 1996).

The 'geographical dimension' reflects the fact that all retailing is local retailing, for chain stores and independents alike. Many chains that initially charged uniform prices in all their locations have shifted progressively towards greater local adaptation, reflecting better the local market conditions. Some use relatively crude stratifications of locations, others now try to tailor more precisely their product/price mix to each locality. Again, the external information from GIS, combined with internal EPoS data at store level, provide the basis for cost-effective local pricing.

The 'assortment' dimension of retail pricing concerns the thousands of decisions between prices of categories and items within the range. Decisions based upon crude mark-up rules are giving way to more intricate approaches, information again being the catalyst. EPoS provides great scope to experiment with price, controlling the inputs (prices) and monitoring the outputs (sales) precisely. Assortment pricing decisions should also be informed by research into consumers' awareness of items prices. Through this type of research, the 'leader line' pricing technique was evolved. Within this approach, the prices of (say) 250 grocery prices

on high awareness items are held at very low levels, creating a beneficial image of prices across the whole assortment.

Time is also a critical dimension of retail pricing, and an area of great concern in recent years. Some years ago the major grocers were advised to reduce their dependence upon short-term special offers, in favour of more stable pricing arrangements. However, other sectors have seen major temporal price changes, with seasonal sales reaching epidemic proportions in clothing and DIY (Betts and McGoldrick, 1996). This has brought a new rash of acronyms, such as 'HI-LO pricing', with EDLP or EDFP (everyday low/fair pricing) being the alleged cures. Indeed, while seasonal sales provide useful functions in clearing stock and generating some excitement at the end of seasons, their overuse can devalue hard-won retail images.

A number of countries have legislation that restricts the use of 'loss leader' or below cost pricing. From 1997, the Loi Galland prevented French retailers from using 'excessively low' prices. Similar restrictions were imposed from 1996 in Spain, plus a limit of only two 'seasonal sales' per annum (NatWest Securities, 1997).

Advertising and sales promotion

While much has been written about the alleged 'death of advertising', expenditure by UK retailers continues to grow apace. Expenditure by UK retailers grew from £285 million in 1985 to £1,079 million in 1996 (Nielsen, 1998). Table 28.10 shows a few of the major spenders, although it should be recognized that some of this expenditure is subsidized by manufacturers, in the form of 'co-operative advertising' deals. Neither do the figures take full account of discounts available to shrewd media buyers. In spite of these important caveats, which apply to both time periods, the data show a strong commitment by retailers to building their brands through advertising.

Indeed, there is a virtuous circle in the brand advertising of large retailers. As they increase their penetration within trading/

advertising areas, the cost-effectiveness of media advertising improves. As own brand development continues, the advertising builds both aspects of the brand: the store and the product. As store formats and ranges develop, the spread of advertising benefit increases still further.

With some notable exceptions, the advertising messages of retailers also appear to enjoy a greater degree of trust than those of manufacturers in general. The decision by the brand owners of Ariel to advertise in the stores and via the own-brand garments of leading retailers, such as Warehouse, is symptomatic of the greater degree of trust enjoyed by the retailer. Deals of this nature increase still further the scope of the retailers to build their brands.

Table 28.10 Retail advertising expenditures		
	1993 (£ millions)	1996 (£ millions)
Dixons Group	37.7	98.4
J. Sainsbury	24.9	31.7
Safeway	19.2	29.2
Comet	23.9	25.8
MFI	20.2	25.3
B&Q	22.9	25.2
Homebase	28.9	24.1
Asda	15.3	21.4
Boots	13.5	21.0
Woolworths	19.8	20.5
Source: Derived from Nielsen (1998)		

Retailers have many ways of communicating with their own regular customers, both in store and by mailings sent to account or loyalty/store card holders. Major objectives of media advertising are therefore to attract new customers, or to increase the visit frequency/expenditure of more marginal customers. Some retailers also make use of sponsorship as a promotional vehicle, which can avoid much of the 'clutter' in conventional media advertising.

Numeric and visual merchandising

Many innovations have occurred in the ways in which store space is designed and allocated. The store environment fulfils a number of objectives, seeking to achieve a balance between maximizing unplanned purchasing, offering a wide assortment of goods, holding adequate stock and offering a convenient, safe and pleasant place to shop. In pursuit of these aims, the store has become an excellent laboratory for the development and refinement of merchandising techniques.

At the most detailed level, models have been developed to allocate display or shelf space between categories and individual lines. Whereas some items are 'space elastic', with sales increasing in response to higher allocations of space, others are not. It makes sense therefore to study the response functions, which are rarely simple or linear, and allocate space to yield the best returns. To the equation, however, should be added measures of direct product profitability and estimates of shelf replenishment frequencies/costs; an overall view must also be taken of the impact of revised allocations upon images of the store.

In its earlier incarnations, the science of 'numeric' merchandising gave little impression of the 'look' of the displays. Improvements in computer graphics have facilitated the development of 'visual' merchandising, by which the calculated allocations can be vividly portrayed, such that the colours, sizes, shapes, etc. of individual items can be arranged both effectively and aesthetically. Visual merchandising also helps to convey the intended appearance of the displays to the individual stores.

Camera-based techniques, used by advertising agencies to track eye movements in response to advertising images, are now being used to examine responses to displays. Cameras are also used to track customer movements within the store as a whole, leading to major improvements in layout effectiveness. They pinpoint areas of high, possibly dysfunctional density, and 'cold' areas visited by few shoppers. They record where people stop to look, and where they tend to ignore the displays. Sometimes the store security system can provide sufficient detail: for more detailed analyses, small cameras can be built into the displays.

Retail atmospherics

At the broader level of store design, a blend of science and artistic creativity is also being achieved. The lack of success of some expensive refurbishments has given great impetus to the quest to establish sound principles to govern the choice of design components. The new science of 'atmospherics' is gaining momentum, as researchers seek to understand better the effects of environmental cues upon feelings and behaviours. Figure 28.8 offers a summary of the many components within the physical environment of a store, breaking these down into ambient, design and social factors.

Research has investigated in some detail the effects upon behaviour of different music levels and types, giving retailers various options to influence mood states, speed of movement through the store and general impressions of the store. The effects of colours have also been researched, from their use on individual packages and displays, to the decor of the store as a whole. Most recently, the use of scents has been tested by researchers, to understand better the influence of another factor that often operates at the subconscious level. Models developed in the broader field of environmental psychology have been applied extensively to the retail environment, measuring for example the effects of atmospherics upon the customer's level of pleasure and arousal.

Service and customer care

In spite of all that has been written and preached about service in recent years, the concept remains ill defined and, accordingly, difficult to

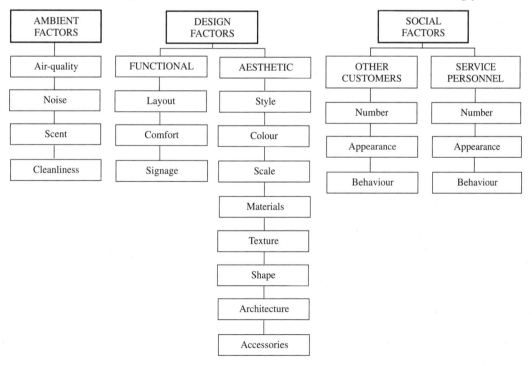

Figure 28.8   A classification of environment dimensions (developed from Baker, 1986)

measure. Part of the problem lies in the word itself, retailing involving service(s) at various different levels.

1 Retailing as a service industry, along with banking, catering, travel, etc.
2 Retailing as a service, bringing a combination of products together in a convenient location, within a pleasant environment, open long hours.
3 Services that retailers may or may not offer, such as free carriers, bag packing, credit/debit card payments, etc.
4 Quality of service provided, i.e., doing it well, reliability, etc.

At the second level of definition, the extension of hours has been a major development, driven in the case of Sunday opening by a change of legislation. Retailers are however experimenting with longer hours on other days, many stores now remaining open until 10.00 pm and other stores trying 24-hour trading. The problem with evaluation is the considerable time lag in the adjustment of consumers' spatial and temporal shopping patterns in response to newly available options.

At the third level, services have proliferated but competitive advantage is usually short lived if the service is easily copied. In modelling satisfaction with service, researchers have compared expectations with outcomes, to identify 'gaps' in service quality. The difficulty is that expectations shift rapidly as services lose their novelty and become rapidly institutionalized.

At the fourth level, retailers and shopping centres have instituted pledges and guarantees that they will 'do it well'. The law imposes liability for defective products but the returns policies of retailers such as Marks & Spencer go far beyond the requirement of the law. This removes much of the risk from the negative side of the value equation, discussed earlier. Centres such as Meadowhall near Sheffield have issued various detailed guarantees of service levels, for customers in general, for motorists, for families and for disabled shoppers. These contain spe-

cific promises, rather than vague platitudes about that ill-defined concept: service.

Human resources

With around 14 million people employed in retailing in Europe (Eurostat, 1997) and 2.3 million in Great Britain, it is clear that retailing is a 'people business'. Retailers also face the challenge that their lowest paid staff interface directly with their customers. Imagine how images of cars or chocolates would change if customers dealt directly with assembly line workers, rather than receiving these images through carefully crafted advertisements.

In retailing, the shelf packers, cleaners and checkout operators all represent key components of the service experience. This highlights the need for careful selection and training; overall, the need for an effective human resource function (see Marchington, in McGoldrick, 1994). Large retail chains also have the challenge of communicating their mission, values and expectations to a large and geographically dispersed staff.

There are of course some retail contexts within which staff hold highly creative selling roles. In the retailing of fashion goods, cars or other major durables, the sales staff are expected to combine extensive product knowledge with the skills of personal selling.

Information and logistics

The logistics role is largely unseen by most customers, becoming more apparent when it fails to maintain stock levels. Out-of-stock conditions may cause not only the immediate loss of item sales, they also undermine customer loyalty by increasing the need to shop elsewhere. The efficient management of the supply chain is therefore a key strategic function.

The benefits of checkout scanning equipment to supply chain management are starting to be fully realized. 'Efficient consumer response' developments include the sharing of live data with some major suppliers, with the effect of increasing stock availability, improving choice for customers, reducing stock levels and improving stockturns. At Asda, for example, the average rate of stockturn improved from 15 in 1992 to 23 in 1997.

Such systems require a high proportion of scanner equipped stores. By 1996, 7580 grocery stores in the UK used scanners, representing 88.6 per cent of grocery turnover (Nielsen, 1998). Scanning also offers direct benefits to customers in terms of faster service and itemized receipts. Further service enhancement is provided by the integration of electronics payment systems, accepting credit or debit payments and, in the latter case, offering customers the facility to request cash back. The same systems also capture individual customer purchase data, via the 50 million loyalty cards estimated to be in use in the UK by 1998.

Internationalization of retailing

In spite of the power and sophistication of large scale retailers, the process of internationalization has been slow and painful. In addition to the legal, linguistic and logistical problems, it is difficult to export even the most successful of retail concepts into other markets. As noted

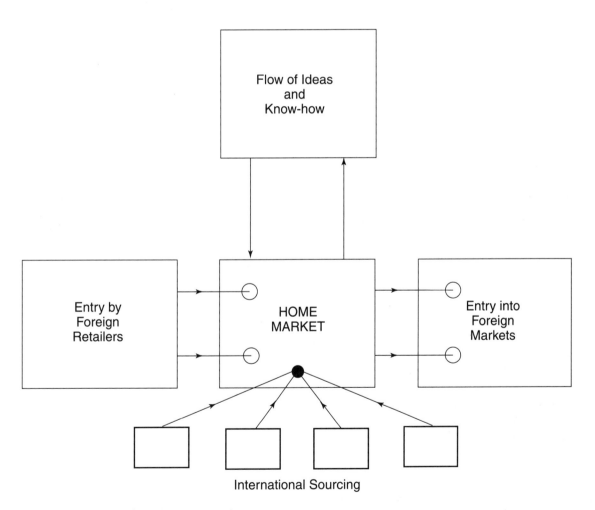

Figure 28.9   Facets of retail internationalization

earlier, competitive structures differ greatly and there are still major differences in consumer tastes and preferences (McGoldrick and Davies, 1995).

Difficult or not, the internationalization of retailing is gaining pace. Figure 28.9 summarizes the major facets of this process, including the arrival of foreign competition and entries into foreign markets. A view of internationalization should also recognize the flow of know-how and the import/export of retail concepts. International product sourcing has a long history in some companies but is becoming more widespread; for some retailers, it has facilitated the development of branches abroad. Table 28.11 summarizes the international activities of certain European retailers that derive a relatively large proportion of turnover from operations outside their home market.

Motives for internationalization

The pressures towards/reasons for internationalization are diverse, but may be summarized as 'push', 'pull' or 'facilitating' factors.

1 'Push' factors, including the maturity or saturation of home markets, domestic trading restrictions, unfavourable economic conditions, rising costs, adverse demographic changes and imitation of trading styles.
2 'Pull' factors, including more enlightened corporate philosophies, perceptions of growth opportunities abroad (niche or underdeveloped markets), established bridgeheads in other countries and imitative 'bandwagon' effects.
3 'Facilitating' factors, including the lowering of political, economic and perceived barriers between countries, the broader vision of senior management, an accumulation of expertise, the ability to assess other retailers' international moves and the improvement of communication technologies.

The particular mix of these factors often determines the most appropriate route to internationalization. Also relevant is the availability of capital, the level of understanding of market needs within other countries, and the compatibility of the domestic trading format(s) with

Table 28.11	Examples of international retailing in Europe			
Company	Country of origin	International turnover (M.U ECU)	Percentage of total turnover	Main activity
Ikea	Sweden	2 138	76.2	Furniture
Delhaize le Lion	Belgium	5 283	72.4	Food
Tengelmann	Germany	12 656	55.7	Food
Ahold	Netherlands	4 548	50.6	Food
Otto Versand	Germany	3 602	45.9	Mail order
Vendex	The Netherlands	2 808	35.3	Department store/food
La Redoute	France	879	35.0	Mail order
Metro	Germany	6 036	35.0	Department store/food
Promodes	France	5 506	34.4	Food
Carrefour	France	3 414	31.1	Food
Dixons	UK	726	30.6	Electrical

Source: Eurostat (1993).

those needs. It is clear that retailers have sometimes adopted the wrong approach to internationalization. There are several examples of leading retailers in domestic markets running into difficulties abroad.

Entry strategies

A number of alternative approaches are available, including the following.

1 Self-start entry, the chain being built up from scratch, or developed through organic growth from a very modest initial acquisition. Examples include Woolworths in the UK and Laura Ashley in the USA.
2 Acquisition, providing a quick entry route but at a cost, not least because companies available for acquisition may well be in financial difficulty. The approach has been used by many UK retailers, including the acquisition of Kings supermarkets and Brooks Brothers menswear in the USA by Marks & Spencer.
3 Franchising, avoiding much of the risk and demands upon capital; especially appropriate where a retailing concept can be readily exported. Notable examples include Italian manufacturer/franchiser Benetton, with over 6000 outlets in over 80 countries.
4 Joint venture, reducing time, cost and risk of entry by working with a partner already familiar with the market. In spite of their benefits at the outset, many joint ventures/partnerships have been terminated, having not met expectations.
5 Concessions (shops in shops), a relatively low cost/risk approach to exploring new markets, used for example by Burton in Spain and elsewhere.

Cross-border alliances have become a major element of international retail co-operation and expansion in recent years. There are four main types, namely, purchasing-led alliances, development alliances, skills-based alliances and multi-function alliances. Within this last category may be included the development of the European Retail Alliance (ERA) and Associated Marketing Services (AMS), linking retailers across Europe and opening opportunities for many forms of co-operation, including purchasing, sourcing, logistics, product development, promotion and political lobbying.

The internationalization of retailing has produced very diverse styles of operation, ranging from global to multinational. Global retailers such as Benetton vary their format very little across national boundaries, achieving the greatest economies of scale but showing the least local responsiveness. Multinationals, on the other hand, tend to develop or acquire a diversity of formats internationally, usually achieving rather lower benefits from integration. A middle course may be termed 'transnational' retailing, whereby the company seeks to achieve global efficiency while responding to national needs, opportunities and constraints. Some of the more recent developments by Marks & Spencer could best be described as transnational, recognizing that even the most successful retail formats within the domestic market may require adaptation to suit markets aboard.

Non-store retailing

In conclusion to this chapter, it is appropriate to mention potential and existing forms of non-store retailing. This category includes itinerant traders, a category for which little information is available, traditional 'home shopping' and various forms of electronic shopping.

Home shopping

In that telephone ordering has largely replaced the posting of orders, the term 'mail order' is giving way to 'home shopping'. In spite of numerous predictions that home shopping would take over a large share of retail trade, its role in Europe is still fairly modest. In Germany it holds the largest share, around 4.8 per cent of retail trade, the sector being dominated by Otto Versand and Quelle. This compares with 3.4 and 2.7 per cent in the United Kingdom and France

Table 28.12 Home shopping in Europe		
Country	Leading provides	Overall percentage of retail sales
Germany	Quelle Otto Versand (OV) Neckermann	4.8
United Kingdom	GUS Littlewoods Grattan (OV)	3.4
France	La Redoute Trois Suisses (OV)	2.7
Switzerland	Heine (OV) Quelle Vedia (GUS)	2.7
Belgium	Trois Suisses (OV) Quelle	1.5
Netherlands	Otto Versand La Redoute Wehkamp (GUS)	1.5
Portugal	La Redoute	0.8
Spain	Catalogo (OV) Quelle	0.4

Source: Derived from Redler (1995)

respectively, as Table 28.12 illustrates. Further afield, home shopping accounts for 2.9 per cent of retail sales in the USA, 3.4 per cent in Canada and 3.2 per cent in Australia (Redler, 1995).

The structure of home shopping in the United Kingdom is highly concentrated. Great Universal Stores (GUS) alone holds 24.5 per cent of the market, followed by Littlewoods at 15.5 per cent. At the European level too, the home shopping industry is highly concentrated. The top four companies, Otto Versand, Quelle, La Redoute and GUS, control around 47 per cent of the market (Redler, 1995). The sector has been the target of international acquisition, Grattan being sold to Otto Versand and Empire being acquired by La Redoute. Although holding a relatively modest share, the Next Directory represented a significant departure from traditional catalogues in the UK. Its style and design illustrated that home shopping could be tar-

geted towards younger, more affluent shoppers. In response, major operators introduced 'specialogues', designed for specific needs and groups.

Catalogues are not of course the exclusive domain of non-store retailers. Many retailers send or make available seasonal or specialist catalogues to their customers, to encourage pre-selection at home and to generate more store visits. The catalogue showroom represents a hybrid retail format, allowing selection at home from an extensive catalogue but usually requiring collection from a store. The advantage over conventional home shopping is that the item can be obtained without delay. Catalogue showrooms also display some of the seasonal or higher value items, allowing inspection before purchase. The format is well developed in the UK, the largest operators being Argos and Index (Littlewoods), and in The Netherlands.

Electronic shopping

Although logically a sub-set of home shopping, forms of electronic or teleshopping merit special attention, representing an area of future development in retailing. Existing offering systems include the following:

1 *Videotex services*—combining telephone transmission and television screen display of 'pages' of information. Experimental systems have used the Prestel system but with little commercial success; that technology is old and not especially user friendly. Major advances are however being made in the quality of images that can be transmitted down telephone lines.

2 *Shopping channels*—delivered by satellite or cable, thus providing high quality picture and sound, but usually requiring telephone ordering. Many such channels have failed in the USA but the QVC channel grew to a customer base of over four million by 1995; it started satellite broadcasting in Europe in 1993.

3 *Interactive cable television systems*—allow the customer to access more detailed information about specific products. J. C. Penney's 'Teleaction' claimed to be the first commercial system of this type in the USA.

4 *Internet-based sites*—providing both information and ordering facilities. Some companies also use their sites to encourage feedback from customers. In 1995, Barclays Bank launched Barclaysquare, which included J. Sainsbury, Toys'R'Us, Blackwells, Argos and Innovations (http://www, iti-net/ barclaysquare).

Projections for the future of home shopping include many possibilities, such as videophones, compact disc and multi-media. It is also possible that the technology of virtual reality, currently used to visualize kitchen layouts by some retailers, could be used at home to simulate the experience of browsing a store and touching the goods. With the history of failures and withdrawals from teleshopping, it is not surprising that most retailers are waiting for more widespread adoption of the relevant, home-based technologies. Estimates vary enormously but even a conservative forecast expects home shopping to more than double by 2010 (Corporate Intelligence, 1997). Only one thing is certain, technological developments, both in store and out of store, will continue to be a major driving force for change in this dynamic sector called retailing.

References

Aaker, D. A. (1991) *Managing Brand Equity*, Free Press, New York.

Baker, J. (1986) The role of the environment in marketing services: the consumer perspective, in J. A. Czepiel *et al.* (eds), *The Services Challenge: Integrating for Competitive Advantage*, American Marketing Association, Chicago, 79–84.

Betts, E. and McGoldrick, P. J. (1996) Consumer behaviour and the retail 'sales': modelling the development of an 'attitude problem', *European Journal of Marketing*, 30(8), 37–56.

Brown, S. (1987) Institutional change in retailing: a review and synthesis, *European Journal of Marketing*, **21**(6), 5–36. An incisive review of retail change theories; an extensive bibliography.

Brown, S. (1992) *Retail Location: a Micro-Scale Perspective*, Avebury, Aldershot. Examination and critique of retail location theory; many examples, maps and references.

Burns, K., Enright, E., Hayes, J., McLaughlin, K. and Shi, C. (1997) The art and science of retail renewal, *McKinsey Quarterly*, **2**, 100–113.

Chain Store Age Executive (1994) Retailing in the 21st Century, *Chain Store Age Executive*, **69**, 12 (Special Edition).

Corporate Intelligence (1997) Cyberlogues–the next generation of mail order? *Retail Report*, **97** (Nov.), 87–92.

Corporate Intelligence (1998) *The European Retail Handbook*, Corporate Intelligence, London.

Davidson, W. R., Bates, A. D. and Bass, S. J. (1976) The retail life cycle, *Harvard Business*

Review, **54**(6), 89–96. Classic article, relating the life cycle concept to retailing, with examples.

Euromonitor (1995) *Retail Trade International,* Euromonitor, London.

European Retail Digest (1997) Employment in retailing: trends and issues, *European Retail Digest,* **14** (Spring), 14–16.

Eurostat (1993) *Retailing in the Single European Market,* Statistical Office of the European Community, Brussels.

Eutostat (1997) *Retailing in the European Economic Area 1996,* Statistical Office of the European Communities, Brussels.

Institute of Grocery Distribution (1997) *The European Food Industry,* IGD, Watford.

Johnson, G. (1987) *Business Strategy and Retailing,* John Wiley, Chichester.

Key Note (1997) *Franchising,* Key Note, London.

Kotler, P. (1973) Atmospherics as a marketing tool, *Journal of Retailing,* **49**(4), 48–64.

Liu, H. and P. J. McGoldrick (1996) International retail sourcing: trend, nature and process, *Journal of International Marketing,* **4**(4), 9–33.

McGoldrick, P. J. (1990) *Retail Marketing,* McGraw-Hill, London.

McGoldrick, P. J. (1994) *Retail Management Cases,* London.

McGoldrick, P. J. (1998) Spatial and temporal shifts in the development of international retail images, *Journal of Business Research,* **42** (June), 189–196.

McGoldrick, P. J. and Andre, E. (1997) Consumer misbehaviour: promiscuity or loyalty in grocery shopping, *Journal of Retail and Consumer Services,* **4**(2), 73–81.

McGoldrick, P. J., Bosworth, D. L., Betts, E. J. and

Duffy, M. H. (1996) *International Retail Price Differences,* Office of Fair Trading, London.

McGoldrick, P. J. and Davies, G. (1995) *International Retailing: Trends and Strategies,* Pitman, London.

McGoldrick, P. J. and Greenland, S. J. (1994) *The Retailing of Financial Services,* McGraw-Hill, London.

McGoldrick, P. J. and Thompson, M. G. (1992) *Regional Shopping Centres,* Avebury, Aldershot.

Mitchell, J. (1978) *Marketing and the Consumer movement,* McGraw-Hill, London.

NatWest Markets (1998) *Store Wars,* NatWest Markets, London.

NatWest Securities (1997) Relevant legislation, *European Food Retailing,* February, 5–9.

Nielsen (1998) *Retail Pocket Book,* NTC Publications, Oxford.

Office of Fair Trading (1985) *Competition and Retailing,* OFT, London.

Redler, E. (1995) *Mail Order in Europe,* Pearson Professional, London.

Retail Review (1998) *Retail Review,* Co-operative Wholesaler Society, Manchester.

Rogers, D. (1996) Power retailers in Europe, *European Retail Digest,* **10**, 13–16.

Sopanen, S. (1996) Customer loyalty schemes: the bottom line, *European Retail Digest,* **11**, 12–19.

Samways, A (1996) *Private Label in Europe,* Pearson Professional, London.

Tordjman, A. (1993) *Evolution of Retailing Formats in the EC,* Groupe HEC, Jouy-en-Josas.

Tordjman, A. (1994) Toys'R'Us, in P. J. McGoldrick (ed.), *Cases in Retail Management,* Pitman, London, pp. 165–183.

CHAPTER 29

The marketing of services

ADRIAN PALMER

Introduction

The academic literature on marketing theory and applications has been dominated by the manufactured goods sector. This is probably not surprising, because marketing in its modern form first took root in those manufacturing sectors that faced the greatest competition from the 1930s onwards. However, the services sector has continued to grow in industrialized economies where it now forms the dominant part of many national economies. In growing, the services sector has become more competitive and therefore taken on board the principles of marketing. Deregulation of many services and rising expectations of consumers have had a dramatic effect on marketing activities within the sector.

But can we simply apply the established body of marketing knowledge, which is based on manufactured goods, to the services sector? Is the marketing of services fundamentally different to the marketing of goods? Or is services marketing just a special case of general marketing theory?

This chapter discusses the distinctive characteristics of services and the extent to which these call for a revision to the general principles of marketing. While many of the general principles can be applied to services, there are areas where a new set of tools need to be developed. Of particular importance are the effects of service intangibility on buyers' decision making processes; the effects of producing services 'live' in the presence of the consumer; and the crucial role played by an organization's employees in the total product offer.

There is debate about the significance of services to national economies, and indeed how services should be defined. Before discussing the distinctive marketing needs of services, this chapter offers a contextual background to the service sector. By the end of the chapter, the reader will be able to judge the extent to which services call for a distinct set of marketing principles, rather than simple adaptation of universal principles of marketing.

The importance of services to national economies

We have always had service industries, and indeed there are numerous biblical references to services as diverse as inn keeping, money lending and market trading. Over time, the service sector has grown in volume and in the importance ascribed to it.

Early economists saw services as being totally unproductive, adding nothing of value to an economy. Adam Smith included the efforts of intermediaries, doctors, lawyers and the armed forces among those who were 'unproductive of any value' (Smith, 1977) and this remained the dominant attitude towards services until the latter part of the nineteenth century. This is the continuing perception among some groups of people to whom service sector jobs are often considered second rate. Even today, different cultures at a similar level of economic development may view their service industries quite differently. In the UK and Germany, service is often associated with servitude while in the USA, being of service almost goes to the heart of the national culture.

Economists now recognize that tangible products may not exist at all without a series of services being performed in order to produce them and to make them available to consumers. So an agent distributing agricultural produce performs as valuable a task as the farmer. Without the provision of transport and intermediary services, agricultural products produced in areas of surplus would be of no value.

Today, there is little doubt that the services sector has become a dominant force in developed economies, accounting for about three quarters of all employment in the USA, UK, Canada and Australia. Between 1980 and 1992, it is reported that the EU created almost 1.3 million new jobs per year in the services sectors – twice the average for the rest of the economy (Eurostat, 1995). There appears to be a close correlation between the level of economic development in an economy (as expressed by its GDP per capita) and the strength of its service sector, although whether a strong service sector leads to economic growth or results from it is debatable.

Services have had a major impact on national economies and many service industries have facilitated improved productivity elsewhere in the manufacturing and agricultural sectors. As an example, transport and distribution services have often had the effect of stimulating economic development at local and national levels (e.g. following the improvement of rail or road services). One reason for Russian agriculture not having been fully exploited has been the ineffective distribution system available to food producers.

The text books have described what happened in England during the early part of the nineteenth century as the 'industrial revolution'. Visions of new technologies involving steam power, factory systems and metal production have led to the dominant view that England's development was primarily a result of progress in the manufacturing sector. But could the industrial revolution have happened without the services sector? Should it be better described as a service revolution? The period saw the development of many services whose presence was vital to economic development. Without the development of railways, goods would not have been distributed from centralized factories to geographically dispersed consumers and many people would not have been able to get to work. Investment in new factories called for a banking system that could circulate funds at a national rather than a purely local level. A service sector emerged to meet the needs of manufacturing, including intermediaries who were essential to get manufacturers' goods to increasingly dispersed markets. Today, we continue to rely on services to exploit developments in the manufacturing sector.

What are services?

It can be difficult to define just what is meant by a service because most products we buy contain a mixture of goods elements and service elements. A meal in a restaurant contains a combination of goods elements (the food) and service elements (the manner in which the food is served). Even apparently 'pure' goods such as timber often contain service elements, such as the service required in transporting timber from where it was produced to where a customer requires it.

Modern definitions of services focus on the fact that a service in itself produces no tangible output, although it may be instrumental in producing some tangible output. A contemporary definition is provided by Kotler, Armstrong, Saunders and Wong (1996):

A service is any activity or benefit that one party can offer to another which is essentially intangible and does not result in the ownership of anything. Its production may or may not be tied to a physical product.

In a more tongue-in-cheek manner, services have been described as 'anything which cannot be dropped on your foot'.

'Pure' services have a number of distinctive characteristics that differentiate them from goods and have implications for the manner in which they are marketed. These characteristics are often described as intangibility, inseparability, variability, perishability and the inability to own a service.

Intangibility

A pure service cannot be assessed using any of the physical senses – it is an abstraction which cannot be directly examined before it is purchased. A prospective purchaser of most goods is able to examine the goods for physical integrity, aesthetic appearance, taste, smell etc. Many advertising claims relating to these tangible properties can be verified by inspection prior to purchase. On the other hand, pure services have no tangible properties which can be used by consumers to verify advertising claims before the purchase is made. The intangible process characteristics which define services, such as reliability, personal care, attentiveness of staff, their friendliness etc. can only be verified once a service has been purchased and consumed. Measuring quality for services can be very different compared with goods. Goods generally have tangible benchmarks against which quality can be assessed (e.g. durability, reliability, taste). In the case of services, these benchmarks can often only be defined in the minds of consumers. So while there may be little doubt that a car which does not corrode within six years is of better quality than one which does, the same quality judgement cannot be made between say, a restaurant meal that takes one hour and another that takes two hours. In the latter case, the expectations of diners are crucial to an understanding of their perceptions of service quality, which may not be the same as the judgements of an outside observer.

The level of tangibility present in a service offer derives from three principal sources:

- tangible goods which are included in the service offer and consumed by the user,
- the physical environment in which the service production/consumption process takes place, and
- tangible evidence of service performance.

Where goods form an important component of a service offer, many of the practices associated with conventional goods marketing can be applied to this part of the service offer. Restaurants represent a mix of tangibles and intangibles and in respect of the food element, few of the particular characteristics of services marketing are encountered. The presence of a tangible component gives customers a visible basis on which to judge quality. While some services (such as restaurants) are rich in such tangible cues, other services provide relatively little tangible evidence (e.g. life insurance).

Intangibility has a number of important marketing implications. The lack of physical evidence which intangibility implies increases the level of uncertainty that a consumer faces when choosing between competing services. An important part of a services marketing programme will therefore involve reducing consumer uncertainty by such means as adding physical evidence and the development of strong brands. It is interesting to note that pure goods and pure services tend to move in opposite directions in terms of their general approach to the issue of tangibility. While service marketers seek to add tangible evidence to their product, pure goods marketers often seek to augment their products by adding intangible elements such as after sales service and improved distribution.

Inseparability

The production and consumption of a tangible good are two separate activities. Companies usually produce goods in one central location and then transport them to the place where customers most want to buy them. In this way, manufacturing companies can achieve economies of scale through centralized production and have centralized quality control checks. The manufacturer is also able to make goods at a time which is convenient to itself, then make them available to customers at times which are convenient to customers. Production and consumption are said to be separable. On the other hand, the consumption of a service is said to be inseparable from its means of production. Producer and consumer must interact in order for the benefits of the service to be realized. Both must normally meet at a time and a place which is mutually convenient in order that the producer can directly pass on service benefits. In the extreme case of personal care services, the customer must be present during the entire production process. A surgeon, for example, cannot provide a service without the involvement of a patient. For services, marketing becomes a means of facilitating complex producer–consumer interaction, rather than being merely an exchange medium.

Inseparability occurs whether the producer is human – as in the case of health care services – or a machine (e.g. a bank ATM machine). The service of the ATM machine can only be realized if the producer and consumer interact. In some cases, it has been possible to separate service production and consumption, especially where there is a low level of personal contact. This has happened, for example in the banking sector where many banks have replaced local branches (where there is face-to-face interaction between producer and consumer) with centralized telephone call centres (where interaction takes place through the medium of the telephone).

Inseparability has a number of important marketing implications for services. Firstly, whereas goods are generally first produced, then offered for sale and finally sold and consumed, inseparability causes this process to be modified for services. They are generally sold first, then produced and consumed simultaneously. Secondly, while the method of goods production is to a large extent (though by no means always) of little importance to the consumer, production processes are critical to the enjoyment of services.

In the case of goods, the consumer is not a part of the process of production and in general, so long as the product which they receive meets their expectations, they are satisfied (although there are exceptions, for example where the ethics of production methods cause concern, or where quality can only be assessed with a knowledge of production stages that are hidden from the consumer's view). With services, the active participation of the customer in the production process makes the process as important as the end benefit. In some cases, an apparently slight change in service production methods may totally destroy the value of the service being provided. A person buying a ticket for a concert by Madonna may derive no benefit at all from the concert if it is subsequently produced by Dusty Springfield instead.

Variability

Most manufactured goods can now be produced with high standards of consistency. However, when asked about the consistency of services such as railway journeys, restaurant meals or legal advice, most people would probably have come across cases of great variability in the standard of service that was delivered. For services, variability impacts upon customers not just in terms of outcomes but also in terms of processes of production. It is the latter point that causes variability to pose a much greater problem for services, compared to goods. Because the customer is usually involved in the production process for a service at the same time as they consume it, it can be difficult to carry out monitoring and control to ensure consistent standards. The opportunity for pre-delivery inspection and rejection which is open to the goods manufacturer is not normally possible with services. The service must normally be produced in the presence of the customer without the possibility of intervening quality control checks.

Variability in production standards is of greatest concern to services organizations where customers are highly involved in the production process, especially where production methods make it impractical to monitor service production. This is true of many labour intensive personal services provided in a one-to-one situation, such as personal healthcare. Some services allow greater scope for quality control checks to be undertaken during the production process, allowing an organization to provide a consistently high level of service. This is especially true of machine based services, for example telecommunication services can typically operate with very low failure rates (British Telecom claims that in over 99 per cent of all attempts to obtain service, customers are able to make a connection to their dialled number at the first attempt).

The tendency today is for equipment-based services to be regarded as less variable than those which involve a high degree of personal intervention in the production process. Many services organizations have sought to reduce variability – and hence to build strong brands – by adopting equipment-based production methods. Replacing human telephone operators with computerized voice systems and the automation of many banking services are typical of this trend. Sometimes reduced personnel variability has been achieved by passing on part of the production process to consumers, in the way that self-service petrol filling stations are no longer dependent on the variability of forecourt serving staff.

Variability can also be considered in terms of the extent to which a service can be deliberately customized to meet the specific needs of individual customers. Because services are created as they are consumed, and because consumers are often a part of the production process, the potential for customization of services is generally greater than for manufactured goods. The extent to which a service can be customized is dependent upon production methods employed. Services that are produced for large numbers of customers simultaneously may offer little scope for individual customization. The production methods of a theatre do not allow individual customers' needs to be met

in the way that the simpler production methods of a counsellor may be able to.

The extent to which services can be customized is partly a function of management decisions on the level of authority to be delegated to front line service personnel. While some service operations seek to give more authority to front line staff, the tendency is for service firms to 'industrialize' their encounter with customers. This implies following clearly specified standardized procedures in each encounter. While industrialization often reduces the flexibility of producers to meet customers' needs, it also has the effect of reducing variability of processes and outcomes.

The variability of service output can pose problems for brand building in services compared to tangible goods. For the latter it is usually relatively easy to incorporate monitoring and quality control procedures into production processes in order to ensure that a brand stands for a consistency of output. The service sector's attempts to reduce variability concentrate on methods used to select, train, motivate and control personnel. In some cases, service offers have been simplified, jobs have been 'de-skilled' and personnel replaced with machines in order to reduce human variability.

Perishability

Services differ from goods in that they cannot be stored. Producers of most manufactured goods who are unable to sell all of their output in the current period can carry forward stocks to sell in a subsequent period. The only significant costs are storage costs, financing costs and the possibility of loss through wastage or obsolescence. By contrast, the producer of a service which cannot sell all of its output produced in the current period gets no chance to carry it forward for sale in a subsequent period. A bus company which offers seats on a bus leaving Manchester for Bury cannot sell any empty seats once the bus has completed its journey. The service offer disappears and spare seats cannot be stored to meet a surge in demand which may occur at a later time.

Very few services face a constant pattern of demand through time. Many show considerable variation, which could follow a daily pattern (e.g. city centre sandwich bars at lunch time), weekly (the Friday evening peak in demand for railway travel), seasonal (hotels, stores at Christmas time), cyclical (mortgages) or an unpredictable pattern of demand (emergency building repair services following heavy storms).

The perishability of services results in greater attention having to be paid to the management of demand by evening out peaks and troughs in demand and in scheduling service production to follow this pattern as far as possible. It is not good enough to ensure that supply and demand are matched overall in the long term. They must match for each minute and for each place that service is offered. Pricing and promotion are two of the tools commonly adopted to resolve demand and supply imbalances.

Inability to own services

The inability to own a service is related to the characteristics of intangibility and perishability. In purchasing goods, buyers generally acquire title to the goods in question and can subsequently do as they wish with them. On the other hand, when a service is performed, no ownership is transferred from the seller to the buyer. The buyer is merely buying the right to a service process such as the use of a car park or an accountant's time. A distinction should be drawn between the inability to own the service act, and the rights which a buyer may acquire to have a service carried out at some time in the future (a theatre gift voucher for example).

The inability to own a service has implications for the design of distribution channels, so a wholesaler or retailer cannot take title, as is the case with goods. Instead, direct distribution methods are more common and where intermediaries are used, they generally act as a co-producer with the service provider.

Are services really a distinctive field for marketing?

It was noted earlier that the services sector has come to dominate the economies of most western countries. But this dominance has come about through a diverse range of services, so diverse that many have questioned whether the term services is too general to be of any use to marketers.

Many have pointed out that services and goods are very closely intertwined. Theodore Levitt argued that services contain many important elements common to goods, thereby making services marketing as a separate discipline obsolete:

'... there is no such thing as service industries. There are only industries where service components are greater or less than those of other industries' (Levitt, 1972).

On the other hand, many have pointed to the distinctiveness of services which makes the application of traditional marketing principles inappropriate. Examples of early work which sought to define the nature of services are provided by Gronroos (1978), Lovelock (1981) and Shostack (1977).

It can be very difficult to distinguish services from goods, for most products which we buy are a combination of goods and services. In this way, cars have traditionally been considered examples of pure goods. However, today, most cars are sold with considerable service benefits, such as an extended warranty, a maintenance contract or a financing facility. In fact, many car manufacturers now see themselves as service providers in which lease contracts provide all the services necessary to keep a car maintained, insured, financed and replaced. The idea of a manufacturer selling a tangible item (the car) and then not having any dealings with the customer until they are ready to replace the car is a rapidly disappearing goods approach to the marketing of cars.

Just as many pure goods may in reality be

quite service-like, so many apparently pure services contain substantial goods elements. A package holiday may seem like a pure service, but it includes tangible elements in the form of the airplane, the hotel room and transfer coach, for example.

Pure goods and pure services are hypothetical extremes, but which are nevertheless important to note because they help to define the distinctive characteristics of goods and services marketing. In between the extremes is a wide range of products which are a combination of tangible goods elements and intangible service elements. It is therefore common to talk about a goods–service continuum along which all products can be placed by reference to their service or goods dominance. Rather than talking about the service sector as a homogeneous group of activities, it would be more appropriate to talk about degrees of service orientation. In Figure 29.1, an attempt has been made to place a sample of products on a scale somewhere between being a pure service (no tangible output) and a pure good (no intangible service added to the tangible good).

A further useful approach to understanding the service–goods orientation of any particular product is provided by Shostack's 'molecular model' (Shostack, 1977). This attempts to analyse the elements of a service in terms of a molecular model of interrelated services and goods components. Thus an airline offers an essentially intangible service – transport. Yet the total product offer includes tangible elements, such as the airplane as well as intangible elements such as the frequency of flights, their reliability and the quality of in-flight services. When many of these intangibles are broken down into their component parts, they too include tangible elements, so that in-flight service includes tangible elements such as food and drink. The principles of services marketing have most relevance where the molecular structure is weighted towards intangible elements. A hypothetical application of the molecular model approach to the analysis of the complex output of a train service is shown in Figure 29.2.

It was noted above that the five characteristics of intangibility, inseparability, perishability, variability and lack of ownership have frequently been described as defining characteristics of services. However, many have argued that these characteristics are shared by many manufactured goods. For example, on the subject of variability, there are some non-service industries – such as tropical fruits – that have difficulty in achieving high levels of consistent

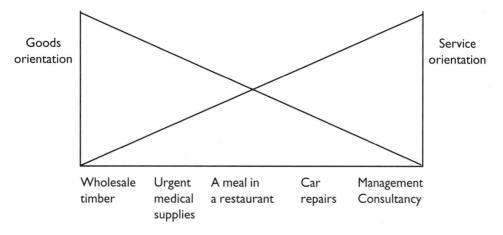

Figure 29.1   An illustration of the goods–services continuum

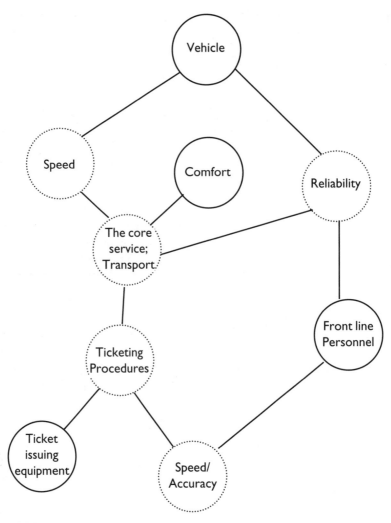

Source: Shostack, 1977

Figure 29.2 An analysis of the output of a train service using Shostack's 'molecular model'. Intangible elements of the service offer are represented by circles with broken lines; tangible elements by solid lines

output, whereas some service industries such as car parks can achieve a consistent standard of service in terms of availability and cleanliness etc. Similarly, many tangible goods share the problem of intangible services in being incapable of full examination before consumption. It is not normally possible, for instance, to judge the taste of a bottle of wine in a supermarket before it has been purchased and (at least partially) consumed.

Services marketers have learnt a lot from

the marketing activities in the goods sectors and vice versa. Some of the points of convergence are illustrated in Figure 29.3.

Classifying services

It should be clear from the above discussion that it is not possible to define a homogeneous group of products called services. Their diversity raises the question whether it is possible to talk about a body of knowledge known as services market-

Intangibility:	Services are increasingly augmented with tangible evidence (e.g. brochures, staff uniforms). Goods are increasingly augmented with intangible services (e.g. after-sales warranties).
Inseparability:	Service consumption is increasingly separated from production (e.g. telephone banking). Goods are increasingly produced in the presence of customers (e.g. while-you-wait bespoke tailoring).
Perishability:	Services are becoming better at storing tangible components of a service offer and in managing the pattern of demand (e.g. restaurants).
	Goods are now more likely to be supplied using 'just-in-time' principles (e.g. automotive car components).
Variability:	Industrialization of services allows levels of reliability to be achieved that matches those of goods.
Lack of ownership:	Addition of tangibles allows customers to 'own' evidence of service (e.g. a telephone 'calling card'. Goods manufacturers increasingly sell the services which a good provides, rather than passing on ownership (e.g. car leasing agreements).

Figure 29.3   **Points of convergence between the goods and services sectors**

ing which is universally applicable throughout the sector. A small jobbing plumber and a multi-national bank both belong to the services sector, but can they share a common body of knowledge about marketing? Because of the diversity of the services sector, marketing prescriptions will prove to be very weak unless smaller categories of services can be identified and subjected to an analytical framework which is particularly appropriate to that category of service.

The goods sector has traditionally developed classifications to describe the marketing needs of different groups of goods. Terms such as fast moving consumer goods, shopping goods, speciality goods, white goods, brown goods etc. are widely used and convey a lot of information about the marketing requirements of products within a category, for example with respect to buying processes, methods of promotion and distribution. The great diversity of services has made attempts to reduce services to a small number of categories difficult to achieve. Instead, many analysts have sought to classify services along a number of continua, reflecting the fact that products cannot be classified into dichotomous goods and services categories to begin with.

Traditionally, the most common basis for classifying services has been the type of activity that is performed. Statistics record service activities under headings such as banking, shipping, hotels, based largely on similarity of production methods.

Production-based classification systems are not particularly useful for marketers. A single production sector can cover a very diverse range of activities with quite different marketing needs. Small guest houses and international hotels may fall within the same sector, but their marketing needs are very different. The marketing needs of a particular production-based sub-sector may share more in common with another unrelated sub-sector rather than other areas within its own sector. Marketers should be more interested in identifying sub-sectors in terms of similarity of marketing requirements. In this way, the provision of banking services may have quite a lot in common with telecommunication services in terms of the processes by which customers make purchase decisions, methods of pricing and promotional strategies, for example.

The following sections identify some of the more commonly used bases for classifying services. It should be noted that many of these bases derive from the five fundamental characteristics of services which were noted earlier.

Degree of intangibility

Intangibility goes to the heart of most definitions of services. It was noted earlier that intangibility has consequences for the way in which buyers perceive risk in a purchase decision. The task of providing evidence that a service will deliver its promises becomes more difficult where the service is highly intangible. As a classification device, degree of intangibility has many uses and this will be returned to later in the context of the management of the marketing mix.

Producer versus consumer services

Consumer services are provided for individuals who use up the service for their own enjoyment or benefit. No further economic benefit results from the consumption of the service. By contrast, producer services are bought by a business in order that it can produce something else of economic benefit. An industrial cleaning company may sell cleaning services to an airport operator in order that the latter can sell the services of clean terminal buildings to airline operators and their customers.

Many services are provided simultaneously to both consumer and producer markets. Here, the challenge is to adapt the marketing programme to meet the differing needs of each group of users (for example, airlines provide a basically similar service to both consumer and producer markets, but the marketing programme may emphasize low price for the former and greater flexibility for the latter).

The status of the service within the total product offer

Given that most products are a combination of goods and service elements, the service elements can contribute to the total product offer in a number of ways. Many services exist to add value to the total product offer, as where a goods manufacturer augments its core tangible product with additional service benefits, such as after-sales warranties. Sometimes, the service is sold as a separate product that customers purchase to add value to their own goods (for example, a car valeting service is purchased to add to the resale value of a used car). A further group of services may add value to a product more fundamentally by making it available in the first place. Distribution services can facilitate delivery of a tangible good from the point of production to the place where it is required by the consumer. Financial services can provide the means through credit arrangements which allow tangible goods to be bought (for example, mortgages facilitate house purchase).

Extent of inseparability

Some services can only be provided in the presence of customers, whereas others require them to do little more than initiate the service process. In the first category, the production of personal care services, almost by definition, cannot be separated from their consumption. The involvement of consumers in the production process is often of an interactive nature, as where clients of a hairdresser answer a continuous series of questions about the emerging length and style of their hair. In such circumstances, the quality of service production processes can be just as important as their outcomes. Other services are more able to separate production from consumption, for example a listener to a radio station does not need to interact with staff of the radio station. Customer involvement in production processes is generally lower where the service is carried out on their possessions, rather than on their mind or body directly. The transport of goods, maintenance of a car or the running of a bank account can generally be separated from the customer, whose main task is to initiate the service and to monitor performance of it.

The marketing of highly inseparable services calls for great attention to the processes of production. Advertising claims about high standards of service will count for little if an organization does not have in place quality management procedures which are able to ensure consistently high levels of employee performance at the point of consumption. With separable services, there are greater opportunities for 'back-room' quality control checks before service delivery takes place.

The pattern of service delivery

Services differ in the ways that they are typically purchased. At one extreme, some services are purchased only when they are needed as a series of one-off transactions. This is typical of low value, undifferentiated services which may be bought on impulse or with little conscious search activity (e.g. taxis and snacks in cafes). It can also be true of specialized, high value services that are purchased only as required (e.g. funeral services are generally bought casually only when needed).

By contrast, other services can be identified where it is impractical to supply the service casually. This can occur where production methods make it difficult to supply a service only when it is needed (for example, it is impractical to provide a telephone line to a house only when it is needed – the line itself is therefore supplied continuously) or where the benefits of a service are required continuously (e.g. insurance policies).

A continuous service supply pattern is often associated with a relationship existing between buyer and seller. A long-term relationship with a supplier can be important to customers in a number of situations; where buyers face a novel purchase situation (here, the existence of a trusted relationship can help to reduce perceived risk); where the production/consumption process takes place over a long period of time (e.g. a programme of medical treatment); and where the benefits will be received only after a long period of time (many financial services); Ongoing relationships can also help to reduce transaction costs (for both buyer and seller) of having to re-order a service every time that it is needed (e.g. a subscription to a car breakdown recovery service avoids the need to find a garage each time that help is required). Increasingly, services organizations are seeking to move the pattern of delivery to customers from one-off and transactional to continuous and relational.

Extent of people orientation

For some services, by far the most important means by which consumers evaluate a service is the quality of the front-line staff who serve them. Service sectors as diverse as hairdressing, accountancy and law can be described as people-intensive. At the other extreme, many services can be delivered with very little human involvement – a pay and display car park involves minimal human input in the form of checking tickets and keeping the car park clean.

The management and marketing of people-based services can be very different from those based on equipment. While equipment can generally be programmed to perform consistently, personnel need to be carefully recruited, trained and monitored. The marketing of people-intensive services cannot be sensibly separated from issues of human resource management. For the marketer, people-based services can usually allow greater customization of services to meet individual customers' needs (although this is changing with the development of computer based delivery systems).

The significance of the service to the purchaser

Some services are purchased frequently, are of low value, are consumed very rapidly and are likely to be purchased on impulse with very little pre-purchase activity. Such services may represent a very small proportion of the purchaser's total expenditure and correspond to the goods marketer's definition of fast moving consumer goods (FMCGs). The casual purchase of a lottery ticket would fit into this category. At the other end of the scale, long lasting services may be purchased infrequently and when they are, the decision making process takes longer and involves more people. Life insurance and package holidays fit into this category.

Just as the marketing of FMCGs differs from that of consumer durables, so the marketing effort required to sell these two extreme types of services will need to be adapted. For more complex services, care must be taken to identify the decision making unit and to target it with appropriate messages. Risk is more likely to be perceived as a major issue with this type of service and must be addressed in a company's promotional programme.

Marketable versus unmarketable services

Finally, it should be remembered that many services are still considered by some cultures to be unmarketable. Many government services are provided for the public benefit and no attempt has been made to charge users of the service. This can arise where it is impossible to exclude individuals or groups of individuals from benefiting from a service. For example, it is not possible in practice for a local authority to charge individuals for the use of local footpaths.

A second major group of services which many cultures do not consider to be marketable are those commonly provided within household units, such as the bringing up of children, cooking and cleaning. While many of these services are now commonly marketed within western societies (e.g. child minding services), many societies – and segments within societies – would regard the internal provision of such services as central to the functioning of family units. Attempts by western companies to launch family based services in cultures with strong family traditions may result in failure because no market exists.

What was considered yesterday by a society to be unmarketable may be the opportunity for tomorrow. Firms who have been quick to seize the opportunities presented have often had to contend with an initially apathetic or hostile public, as has happened in the UK with the emerging market for privatized prison services, public water supply and toll roads.

Multiple classifications

The great diversity of services have now been classified in a way which focuses on their marketing needs rather than their dominant methods of production. It will be apparent that within any sector, there are likely to be major sub-categories of services which have distinctive marketing needs, and which may share a lot with other sectors. This commonality of marketing needs has provided great opportunities for companies who have extended their product range into services which are basically similar in their marketing needs if not in their production methods. Many of the UK grocery retailers have considered that the way people open savings accounts is similar to the way that they select groceries, so have extended their marketing expertise by applying it to the savings market.

Although a number of bases for classifying services have been presented in isolation, services are in practice, like goods, classified by a number of criteria simultaneously. There have been a number of attempts to develop multidimensional approaches for identifying clusters of similar services (for example, see Solomon and Gould (1991) who researched consumers' perceptions of sixteen different personal and household services).

An extended marketing mix for services

The marketing mix is the set of tools available to an organization to shape the nature of its offer to customers. The mix is not based on any theory, but on the need for marketing managers to break down their decision making into a number of identifiable and actionable headings. Goods marketers are familiar with the '4Ps' of product, price, promotion and place. Early analysis by Borden (1965) of marketing mix elements was based on a study of manufacturing industry at a time when the importance of services to the economy was relatively unimportant. More recently, the 4Ps of the marketing mix have been found to be too limited in their application to services. Particular problems which limit their usefulness to services are:

- The intangible nature of services is overlooked in most analyses of the mix – for example, the product mix is frequently analysed in terms of tangible design properties which may not be relevant to a service. Similarly, physical distribution management may not be an important element of place mix decisions.
- The promotion mix of the traditional 4Ps fails to recognize the promotion of services which takes place at the point of consumption by the production personnel, unlike the situation with most goods which are normally produced away from the consumer and therefore the producer has no direct involvement in promotion to the final consumer. For a bank clerk, hairdresser or singer, the manner in which the service is produced is an essential element of the total promotion of the service.
- The price element overlooks the fact that many services are produced by the public sector without a price being charged to the final consumer.

The basic list of 4 'Ps' also fails to recognize a number of key factors which marketing managers in the service sector use to design their service output. Particular problems focus on:

- the importance of people as an element of the service product, both as producers and co-consumers;
- the over-simplification of the elements of distribution which are of relevance to intangible services;

- definition of the concept of quality for intangible services, and identification and measurement of the mix elements that can be managed in order to create a quality service.

These weaknesses have resulted in a number of attempts to redefine the marketing mix in a manner which is more useful for the services sector. While many have sought to refine the marketing mix for general application (e.g. Kent, 1986; Wind, 1986), the expansion by Booms and Bitner (1981) provides a useful framework for the services sector. It should be stressed that these are not empirically proven theories of services marketing, but different authors' interpretations of the decisions that face services marketers in developing services to satisfy customers' needs. In addition to the four traditional elements of the marketing mix, it is common to recognize the importance of people and processes as additional elements. Booms and Bitner also talk about physical evidence making up a seventh 'P'.

Decisions on one element of the extended marketing mix can only be made by reference to other elements of the mix in order to give a sustainable product positioning. The importance attached to each element of the extended marketing mix will vary between services. In a highly automated service such as vending machine dispensing, the people element will be a less important element of the mix than a people intensive business such as a restaurant.

A brief overview of the extended services marketing mix ingredients is given below. In the case of the four traditional 'Ps', emphasis will be given to distinguishing their application in a services rather than a goods context.

Products

A product is anything that an organization offers to potential customers, whether it is tangible or intangible. After initial hesitation, most marketing managers are now happy to talk about an intangible service as a product. Thus bank accounts, insurance policies and holidays

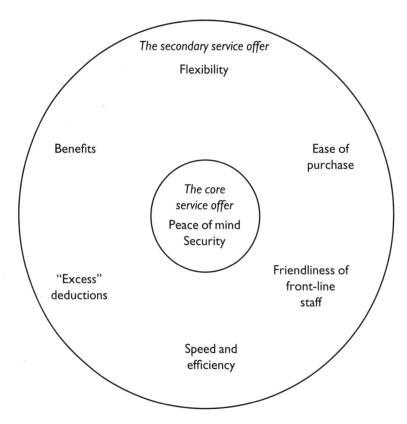

Figure 29.4   An analysis of the product offer of an insurance policy, comprising core and secondary levels of offer

are frequently referred to as products, sometimes to the amusement of non-marketers, as where pop stars or even politicians are referred to as a product to be marketed.

Marketing mix management must recognize a number of significant differences between goods and services. A number of authors (e.g. Kotler, 1997) have described a model comprising various levels of product definition. The model developed by Kotler starts from the 'core' level (defining the basic needs which are satisfied by the product), through a 'tangible' level (the tangible manifestation of the product), through to an 'augmented' level (the additional services which are added to the product). While this analysis is held to be true of products in general, doubts have been expressed about whether it can be applied to the service offer. Is it possible to

identify a core service representing the essence of a consumer's perceived need that requires satisfying? If such a core service exists, can it be made available in a form that is 'consumer friendly', and if so, what elements are included in this form? Finally, is there a level of service corresponding to the augmented product that allows a service provider to differentiate its service offer from that of its competitors in the same way as a car manufacturer differentiates its augmented product from that of its competitors?

Most analyses of the service offer recognize that the problems of inseparability and intangibility make application of the three generic levels of product offer less meaningful to the service offer. Instead, the product offer in respect of services can be more usefully analysed in terms of two components:

- the core service which represents the core benefit, and
- the secondary service which represents both the tangible and augmented product levels (Figure 29.4).

Sasser *et al.* (1978) described the core service level as the *substantive* service which is best understood as the essential function of a service. Gronroos (1984) uses the term *service concept* to denote the core of a service offering. Gronroos states that it can be general such as offering a solution to transport problems, e.g. car hire, or it can be more specific such as offering Indian cuisine in a restaurant.

The secondary service can be best understood in terms of the manner in which a service is delivered. For example, Little Chef and Brewers Fayre restaurants both satisfy the same basic need for fast, economical, hygienic food, but they do so in differing ways. This is reflected in different procedures for taking and delivering orders, differences in menus and in the ambience of the restaurants.

Services tend to be relatively easy to copy and cannot generally benefit from patent protection, as is often the case with goods. New product development often occurs in an incremental fashion, with a lot of variants of a basic service. The proliferation of mortgage products by a building society, all with slightly differing terms and conditions, but basically similar in their function, is an example of this.

Pricing

Within the services sector, the term price often passes under a number of names, sometimes reflecting the nature of the relationship between customer and provider in which exchanges take place. Professional services companies therefore talk about fees, while other organizations use terms such as fares, tolls, rates, charges and subscriptions. The art of successful pricing is to establish a price level which is sufficiently low that an exchange represents good value to buyers, yet is high enough to allow a service provider to achieve its financial objectives.

In principle, setting prices for services is fundamentally similar to the processes involved in respect of goods. At a strategic level, a price position needs to be established and implemented with respect to the strength of customer demand, the costs of production and the prices that competitors are charging. A number of points of difference with respect to services pricing are noted here: the effects of inseparability; the effects on pricing of cost structures; and the effects of distorted markets for services.

The inseparable nature of services make the possibilities for price discrimination between different groups of users much greater than is usually the case with manufactured goods. Goods can easily be purchased by one person, stored and sold to another person. If price segmentation allowed one group to buy a manufactured good at a discounted price, it would be possible for this group to buy the item and sell it on to people in higher priced segments, thereby reducing the effectiveness of the segmentation exercise. This point has not been lost on entrepreneurs who buy branded perfumes cheaply in the Far Eastern 'grey market' and import them to the UK where prices are relatively high. Because services are produced at the point of consumption, it is possible to control the availability of services to different segments. Therefore a hairdresser who offers a discounted price for the elderly segment is able to ensure that only such people are charged the lower price – the elderly person cannot go into the hairdressers to buy a haircut and sell it on to a higher price segment.

Services organizations frequently charge different prices at different service locations. The inseparability of service production and consumption results in services organizations defining their price segments both on the basis of the point of consumption and the point of production. An example of this is found in hotel chains, who in addition to using price to target particular types of customers, also often charge different prices at different locations. Some retailers with a combination of large superstores and small convenience stores can justify charging higher prices in their convenience stores.

A second major difference between goods and services pricing is based on the high level of fixed costs that many service providers experience. The marginal cost of one additional telephone call, one additional seat on an airplane or one additional place in a cinema is often very low. This can give service suppliers a lot of scope for charging different prices for what is basically the same product offer. High air fares in the peak period reflect a buoyant level of demand, as well as the amount needed to cover fixed costs at the peak. To encourage additional demand in quieter periods, airlines, like many other service industries, can reduce their prices. This is often referred to as marginal cost pricing. The price that any individual customer is charged is based not on the total unit cost of producing it, but only the additional costs that will result directly from servicing that additional customer. It is used where the bulk of a company's output has been sold at a full price that recovers its fixed costs, but in order to fill remaining capacity, the company brings its prices down to a level that at least covers its variable, or avoidable costs. Marginal cost pricing is widely used in service industries with low short term supply elasticity and high fixed costs. It is common in the airline industry where the perishability of a seat renders it unsalable after departure. Rather than receive no revenue for an empty seat, an airline may prefer to get some income from a passenger, so long as the transaction provides a contribution by more than covering the cost of additional food and departure taxes.

The final point of difference in managing the price element of the services marketing mix relates to the fact that services are more likely than goods to be made available in distorted markets, or in circumstances where no market exists at all. Public services such as museums and schools that have sought to adopt marketing principles often do not have any control over the price element of the marketing mix. The reward for attracting more visitors to a museum or pupils to a school may be additional centrally derived grants, rather than income received directly from the users of the service.

Services are more likely than goods to be supplied in non-competitive business environments. As an example, the high fixed costs associated with many public utility services means that it is unrealistic to expect two companies to compete. More importantly, much investment in services infrastructure is fixed and cannot be moved to where market opportunities are greatest. While a car manufacturer can quite easily redirect its new cars for sale from a declining market to an expanding one, a railway operator cannot easily transfer its track and stations from one area to another. The immobility of many services can encourage the development of local monopoly power.

Promotion

A well formulated service offer, distributed through appropriate channels at a price that represents good value to potential customers places less emphasis on the promotion element of the marketing mix. Nevertheless, few services – especially those provided in competitive markets – can dispense with promotion completely.

Although the principles of communication are similar for goods and services, a number of distinctive promotional needs of services can be identified, deriving from the distinguishing characteristics of services. The following are particularly important:

- The intangible nature of the service offer often results in consumers perceiving a high level of risk in the buying process, which promotion must seek to overcome. A number of methods are commonly used to remedy this, including the development of strong brands; encouragement of word-of-mouth recommendation; promotion of trial usage of a service; and the use of credible message sources in promotion (especially through public relations activity).

- Promotion of a service offer cannot generally be isolated from promotion of the service provider. Customers cannot sensibly evaluate many intangible, high perceived risk services, such as pensions and insurance policies, without knowing the identity of the service provider. In many cases, the service may be difficult to comprehend in any case (this is certainly true of pensions for most people), so promotion of the service provider becomes far more important than promotion of individual service offers.
- Visible production processes, especially service personnel, become an important element of the promotion effort. Where service production processes are inseparable from their consumption, new opportunities are provided for promoting a service. Front-line staff can become salespeople for an organization. The service outlet can become a billboard which people see as they pass by.
- The intangible nature of services and the heightened possibilities for fraud results in their promotion being generally more constrained by legal and voluntary controls than is the case with goods. Financial services and overseas holidays are two examples of service industries with extensive voluntary and statutory limitations on promotion.

Place

Place decisions refer to the ease of access which potential customers have to a service. For services, it is more appropriate to talk about accessibility as a mix element, rather than place.

The inseparability of services makes the task of passing on service benefits much more complex than is the case with manufactured goods. Inseparability implies that services are consumed at the point of production, in other words, a service cannot be produced by one person in one place and handled by other people to make it available to customers in other places. A service cannot therefore be produced where costs are lowest and sold where demand is

greatest – customer acce[...] designed into the service pro[...]

While services organiza[...] desire to centralize produ[...] achieve economies of scale, [...] seek local access to services, often at a time that may not be economic for the producer to cater to. Service location decisions therefore involve a trade off between the needs of the producer and the needs of the consumer. This is in contrast to goods manufacturers who can manufacture goods in one location where production is most economic, then ship the goods to where they are most needed.

Place decisions can involve physical location decisions (as in deciding where to place a hotel), decisions about which intermediaries to use in making a service accessible to a consumer (e.g. whether a tour operator uses travel agents or sells its holidays direct to customers) and non-locational decisions which are used to make services available (e.g. the use of telephone delivery systems). For pure services, decisions about how to physically move a good are of little strategic relevance. However, most services involve movement of goods of some form. These can either be materials necessary to produce a service (such as travel brochures and fast food packaging material) or the service can have as its whole purpose the movement of goods (e.g. road haulage, plant hire).

People

For most services, people are a vital element of the marketing mix. It can be almost a cliche to say that for some businesses, the employees are the business – if these are taken away, the organization is left with very few assets with which it can seek to gain competitive advantage in meeting customers' needs. For some organizations, the management of personnel can be seen as just one other asset to be managed. For others, human resource management is so central to the activities of the organization that it cannot be seen as a separate activity.

Where production can be separated from

consumption – as is the case with most manufactured goods – management can usually take measures to reduce the direct effect of people on the final output as received by customers. Therefore the buyer of a car is not concerned whether a production worker dresses untidily, uses bad language at work or turns up for work late, so long as there are quality control measures which reject the results of lax behaviour before they reach the customer. In service industries, everybody is what Gummesson (1991) has called a 'part time marketer' in that their actions have a much more direct effect on the output received by customers.

While the importance attached to people management in improving quality within manufacturing companies is increasing (for example through the development of quality circles), people planning assumes much greater importance within the services sector. This is especially true in those services where staff have a high level of contact with customers. For this reason, it is essential that services organizations clearly specify what is expected from personnel in their interaction with customers. To achieve the specified standard, methods of recruiting, training, motivating and rewarding staff cannot be regarded as purely personnel decisions – they are important marketing mix decisions.

People planning its widest sense has impacts on a firm's service offer in three main ways:

- Most service production processes require the service organization's own personnel to provide significant inputs to the service production process, both at the front line point of delivery and in those parts of the production process which are relatively removed from the final consumer. In the case of many one-to-one personal services, the service provider's own personnel constitute by far the most important element of the total service offering.
- Many service processes require the active involvement of consumers of the service and consumers therefore become involved as a co-producer of the service. At its simplest, this can involve the consumer in merely presenting themselves or their objects to the service provider in order for the service to be provided – for example, a customer might deliver their car to the garage rather than have it collected by the garage. In the case of services performed on the body or mind, the consumer must necessarily be designed into the production process.
- Other people who simultaneously consume a mass produced service can affect the benefits which an individual receives from the service in a number of ways. First, the characteristics of other users of a service can affect the image of the service, in much the same way as owners of certain brands of goods can lend them some degree of 'snob' appeal. In this way, a night club can build up an exclusive image on account of the high spending, high profile users who patronize it. Second, the presence of other consumers in the service production – delivery process means that the final quality of the service which any customer receives is dependent on the performance of other consumers. They in effect become co-producers of the service offering. Often fellow consumers have an important role to play in enhancing the quality of the service offering, as where a full house in a theatre creates an ambience for all customers to enjoy. On other occasions, fellow consumers can contribute negatively to the service production process, as where rowdy behaviour in a pub or smoking in a restaurant detracts from the enjoyment of an event for other customers.

Processes

Production processes are usually of little concern to consumers of manufactured goods, but can be of critical concern to consumers of 'high contact' services where the consumer can be seen as a co-producer of the service. A customer of a restaurant is deeply affected by the manner in which staff serve them and the amount of waiting which is involved during the production process. Issues arise as to the boundary between the producer and consumer in terms of the allocation of production functions – for example, a restaurant might require a customer to collect their meal from a counter, or to deposit their own rubbish. With services, a clear distinction cannot be made between marketing and operations management.

A lot of attention has gone into the study of 'service encounters', defined by Shostack (1985) as 'a period of time during which a consumer directly interacts with a service'. Among the multiplicity of service encounters, some will be crucial to successful completion of the service delivery process. These are often referred to as critical incidents and have been defined by Bitner, Booms and Tetreault (1990) as '. . . specific interactions between customers and service firm employees that are especially satisfying or especially dissatisfying'. While their definition focuses on the role of personnel in critical incidents, they can arise also as a result of interaction with the service provider's equipment.

Where service production processes are complex and involve multiple service encounters, it is important for an organization to gain a holistic view of how the elements of the service relate to each other. 'Blueprinting' is a graphical approach proposed by Shostack (1984), designed to overcome problems which occur where a new service is launched without adequate identification of the necessary support functions. A customer blueprint has three main elements:

- All of the principal functions required to make and distribute a service are identified, along with the responsible company unit or personnel.
- Timing and sequencing relationships among the functions are depicted graphically.
- For each function, acceptable tolerances are identified in terms of the variation from standard which can be tolerated without adversely affecting customers' perception of quality.

Services are, in general, very labour intensive and have not witnessed the major productivity increases seen in many manufacturing industries. Sometimes, mechanization can be used to improve the efficiency of the service production process, but for many personal services, this remains a difficult possibility. An alternative way to increase the service provider's productivity is to involve the consumer more fully in the production process.

As real labour costs have increased and service markets become more competitive, many service organizations have sought to pass on a greater part of the production process to their customers in order to try and retain price competitiveness. At first, customers' expectations may hinder this process, but productivity savings often result from one segment taking on additional responsibilities in return for lower prices. This then becomes the norm for other follower segments. Examples where the boundary has been redefined to include greater production by the customer include supermarkets who have replaced checkout operators with customer operated scanners and restaurants which replace waiter service with a self-service buffet.

While service production boundaries have generally been pushed out to involve consumers more fully in the production process, some services organizations have identified segments who are prepared to pay higher prices in order to relieve themselves of parts of their co-production responsibilities. Examples include car repairers who collect and deliver cars to the owner's home and fast food firms who avoid the need for customers to come to their outlet by offering a delivery service.

Despite handing over parts of the production process to consumers, many services remain complex, offering many opportunities for mistakes to be made. In many service sectors, giving too much judgement to staff results in a level of variability which is incompatible with consistent brand development. The existence of multiple choices in the service offer can make training staff to become familiar with all of the options very expensive. For these reasons, service organizations often seek to simplify their service offerings and to 'de-skill' many of the tasks performed by front-line service staff. By offering a limited range of services at a high standard of consistency, the process follows the pattern of the early development of factory production of goods. The process has sometimes been described as the 'industrialization' of services.

Physical evidence

The intangible nature of a service means that potential customers are unable to judge a service before it is consumed, increasing the risk inherent in a purchase decision. An important element of marketing planning is therefore to reduce this level of risk by offering tangible evidence of the promised service delivery. This evidence can take a number of forms. At its simplest, a brochure can describe and give pictures of important elements of the service product – a holiday brochure gives pictorial evidence of hotels and resorts for this purpose. The appearance of staff can give evidence about the nature of a service – a tidily dressed ticket clerk for an airline gives some evidence that the airline operation as a whole is run with care and attention. Buildings are frequently used to give evidence of service characteristics. Towards the end of the nineteenth century, UK banks outbid each other to produce grand buildings which signified stability and substance to potential investors, who had been frightened by a history of banks disappearing with their savings. Today, a clean, bright environment used in a service outlet can help reassure potential customers at the point where they make a service purchase decision. For this reason, fast food and photo processing outlets often use red and yellow colour schemes to convey an image of speedy service.

Tangibility is further provided by evidence of service production methods. Some services provide many opportunities for customers to see the process of production, indeed the whole purpose of the service may be to see the produc-

tion process (e.g. a pop concert). Often this tangible evidence can be seen before a decision to purchase a service is made, either by direct observation of a service being performed on somebody else (e.g. watching the work of a builder) or indirectly through a description of the service production process (a role played by brochures which specify and illustrate the service production process). On the other hand, some services provide very few tangible clues about the nature of the service production process. Portfolio management services are not only produced largely out of sight of the consumer, it is also difficult to specify in advance in a brochure what the service outcomes will be.

Managing the marketing effort

It was noted earlier that services marketing cannot sensibly be separated from issues of services management. The increasing dominance of the services sector has fuelled much of the current debate about the role of marketing within commercial organizations. While epitaphs for the marketing department are probably premature, there is considerable debate about the extent to which marketing should be fully integrated into everybody's job function, rather than left as a specialist function in its own right.

Should a service organization actually have a marketing department? The idea is becoming increasingly popular that the existence of a marketing department in an organization may in fact be a barrier to the development of a true customer centred marketing orientation. By placing all marketing activity in a marketing department, non-marketing staff may consider themselves to be absolved of responsibility for the development of customer relationships. In service industries where production personnel are in frequent contact with the consumers of their service, a narrow definition of marketing responsibility can be potentially very harmful. On the other hand, a marketing department is usually required in order to coordinate and implement those functions that cannot sensibly

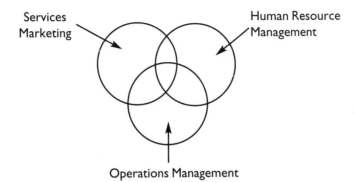

Figure 29.5   Services organizations' interfaces between marketing management, operations management and human resource management

be delegated to operational personnel – advertising, sales management and pricing decisions for example.

Services management has often been described as the bringing together of the principles of marketing, operations management and human resource management, in which it can sometimes be difficult – and undesirable – to draw distinctions between the three approaches (Figure 29.5). In this way, methods to improve the service provided by staff of a fast food restaurant can be seen as a marketing problem (e.g. the need to analyse and respond to customer needs for such items as speed and cleanliness), or an operations management problem (scheduling work in a manner which reduces bottlenecks and allows a flexible response to patterns of demand), or a human resource management problem (selecting and motivating staff in such a way that maximizes their ability to deliver a specified standard of service).

In marketing oriented organizations, the customer is at the centre of all of the organization's activities. The customer is not simply the concern of the marketing department, but also all of the production and administrative personnel whose actions may directly or indirectly impinge upon the customers' enjoyment of the service. In a typical service organization, the activities of a number of functional departments impinge on the service outcome received by customers:

- Personnel plans can have a crucial bearing on marketing plans. The selection, training, motivation and control of staff cannot be considered in isolation from marketing objectives and strategies. Possible conflict between the personnel and marketing functions may arise where – for example – marketing demands highly trained and motivated front-line staff, but the personnel function pursues a policy which places cost reduction and uniformity above all else.
- Production managers may have a different outlook compared to marketing managers. A marketing manager may seek to respond as closely as possible to customers' needs, only to find opposition from production managers who argue that a service of the required standard cannot be achieved. A marketing manager of a railway operating company may seek to segment markets with fares tailored to meet the needs of small groups of customers, only to encounter hostility from operations managers who are responsible for actually issuing and checking travel tickets on a day-to-day basis and who may have misgivings about the confusion that finely segmented fares might cause.
- The actions of finance managers frequently have direct or indirect impact on marketing plans. Ultimately, finance managers assume responsibility for the allocation of funds which are needed to implement a marketing plan. At

a more operational level, finance managers' actions in respect of the level of credit offered to customers, or towards stockholdings where these are an important element of the service offering can also significantly affect the quality of service and the volume of customers that the organization is able to serve.

Marketing requires all of these departments to 'think customer' and to work together to satisfy customer needs and expectations. There is argument as to what authority the traditional marketing department should have in bringing about this customer orientation. In a truly mature marketing oriented service company, marketing is an implicit part of everybody's job. In such a scenario, marketing becomes responsible for a narrow range of specialist functions such as advertising and marketing research. Responsibility for the relationship between the organization and its customers is spread more diffusely throughout the organization.

There is some evidence of the possibly harmful effect of placing too much authority in the marketing department of services organizations. In a survey of 219 executives representing public and private sector services organizations in Sweden, Gronroos (1982) tested the idea that a separate marketing department may widen the gap between marketing and operations staff. This idea was put to a sample drawn from marketing as well as other functional positions. The results indicated that respondents in a wide range of service organizations considered there to be dangers in the creation of a marketing department – an average of 66 per cent agreed with the notion, with higher than average agreement being found among non-marketing executives, and those working in the hotel, restaurant, professional services and insurance sectors.

Summary

The services sector is now a dominant part of the economies of most developed countries. However, defining just what is meant by a service has caused some debate and this chapter has reviewed some of the bases for classifying services into categories that are useful for the purposes of marketing management. Pure services are distinguished by the characteristics of intangibility, inseparability, perishability, variability and a lack of ownership. Increasingly however, goods and services are converging in terms of these characteristics. Few products can be described as pure goods or pure services – most are a combination of the two. There has been considerable debate about whether a new set of principles of marketing are required to understand services, or whether the established basic principles merely need adapting to the needs of services. The traditional marketing mix of the '4Ps' has been found to be inadequate for managers in the services sector and this chapter has discussed an alternative extended marketing mix of '7Ps' which recognizes the distinctive characteristics of services.

References

Bitner M. J., Booms, B. H. and Tetreault, M. S. (1990) The Service Encounter: Diagnosing Favorable and Unfavorable Incidents, *Journal of Marketing*, **54** (January), 71–84.

Booms, B. H. and Bitner, M. J. (1981) Marketing Strategies and Organization Structures for Service Firms, in J. Donnelly and W. R. George (eds), *Marketing of Services*, Chicago, pp. 51–67.

Borden, N. H. (1965) The Concept of the Marketing Mix, in Schwartz, G. (ed.), *Science in Marketing*, John Wiley and Sons, New York, pp. 386–397.

Eurostat (1995) *Europe in Figures*, Office for Official Publications of the European Communities, Luxembourg.

Gronroos, C. (1984) A Service Quality Model and its Marketing Implications, *European Journal of Marketing*, **18**(4), 36–43.

Gronroos, C. (1978) A Service Oriented Approach to Marketing of Services, *European Journal of Marketing*, **12**(8), 588–601.

Gronroos, C. (1982) *Strategic Management and Marketing in the Service Sector*, Swedish School of Economics and Business Administration, Helsingfors, Finland.

Gummesson, E. (1991) Marketing-orientation Revisited: The Crucial Role of the Part-time Marketer, *European Journal of Marketing*, **25**(2), 60–75.

Kent, R. A. (1986) Faith in the Four Ps: An Alternative, *Journal of Marketing Management*, **2**(2), 145–154.

Kotler, P. (1997) *Marketing Management: Analysis, Planning, Implementation and Control, 9th edn*, Prentice-Hall, Englewood Cliffs, NJ.

Kotler, P., Armstrong, G., Saunders, J. and Wong, V. (1996) *Principles of Marketing*, European edition, Prentice-Hall, London.

Levitt, T. (1972) Production Line Approach to Service, *Harvard Business Review*, **50**, Sept–Oct, pp. 41–52

Lovelock, C. (1981) Why Marketing Needs to be Different for Services, in J. H. Donnelly and W. R. George (eds), *Marketing of Services*, American Marketing Association, Chicago, IL.

Sasser, W. E., Olsen, R. P. and Wyckoff, D. D. (1978) *Management of Service Operations: Texts, Cases, Readings*, Allyn and Bacon, Boston, MA.

Shostack, G. L. (1977) Breaking Free From Product Marketing, *Journal of Marketing*, **41**, April, pp. 73–80.

Shostack, G. L. (1984) Designing Services That Deliver, *Harvard Business Review*, Jan/Feb, 133–39.

Shostack, G. L. (1985) Planning the Service Encounter, in J. A Czepiel, M. R. Solomon and C. F. Suprenant (eds), *The Service Encounter*, Lexington Books, Lexington, MA, pp. 243–54.

Smith, A. (1977) *The Wealth of Nations*, Penguin, Middlesex (first published 1776).

Solomon, M. R. and Gould, S. J. (1991) Benefiting From Structural Similarities Among Personal Services, *Journal of Services Marketing*, **5**(2), Spring, 23–32.

Wind Y. (1986) Models for Marketing Planning and Decision Making, in V. P. Buell (ed.), *Handbook of Modern Marketing*, 2nd edn, McGraw-Hill, pp. 49.1–49.12.

Further reading

There are now numerous texts which deal specifically with the marketing of services and the following are among the recent works which provide a comprehensive coverage:

Hoffman, K. D. and Bateson, J. (1997) *Essentials of Services Marketing*, Dryden, Forth Worth.

Mudie, P. and Cottam, A. (1994) *The Management and Marketing of Services*, Butterworth-Heinemann, Oxford.

Palmer, A. (1998) *Principles of Services Marketing*, 2nd edn, McGraw-Hill, Maidenhead.

Payne, A. (1993) *The Essence of Services Marketing*, Prentice-Hall, Hemel-Hempstead.

Woodruffe, H. (1995) *Services Marketing*, Pitman.

Zeithaml, V. and Bitner, J. (1996) *Services Marketing*, New York, McGraw-Hill.

The literature on services marketing has grown significantly during the past couple of decades, reflecting the growing importance of the services sector. The following article discusses the development of the literature.

Fisk, R. P., Brown, S. W. and Bitner, M. J. (1993) Tracking the Evolution of the Services Marketing Literature, *Journal of Retailing*, **69**(1), 61–103.

A number of articles appeared towards the end of the 1970s seeking to identify the nature of services and their distinctive marketing needs. The articles in the References by Lovelock (1981), Sasser, Olsen and Wyckoff (1978) and Shostack (1977) are worth revisiting. In addition, the following are still worth reading because they establish many of the basic principles of services marketing.

Bateson, J. (1977) Do We Need Service Marketing? *Marketing Consumer Services: New Insights*, Report 77-115, Marketing Science Institute, Boston.

Berry, L. L. (1980) Service Marketing Is Different, *Business*, May/June, **30**(3), 24–29.

Eiglier, P. and Langeard, E. (1977) A New Approach to Service Marketing, *Marketing Consumer Services: New Insights*, Report 77-115, Marketing Science Institute, Boston.

Levitt, T. (1981) Marketing Intangible Products and Product Intangibles, *Harvard Business Review*, 59, May/June, 95–102.

Zeithaml, V. A. (1981) How Consumers' Evaluation Processes Differ Between Goods and Services, in J. H. Donelly and W. R. George (eds), *Marketing of Services*, American Marketing Association, Chicago, pp. 186–90.

For a good selection of classic articles covering the breadth of services marketing issues, the following reader is useful.

Gabbott, M. and Hogg, G. (1997) *Contemporary Services Marketing Management: A Reader*, Dryden, London.

CHAPTER 30

The Internet: the direct route to growth and development

JIM HAMILL and SEAN ENNIS

Introduction

The last decade has witnessed the emergence of a powerful new alternative for conducting business activity that has major implications for marketers. The Internet lies at the forefront of the interactive multimedia formats. Key 'gateway' businesses such as CompuServe, Prodigy and America Online provide the necessary navigation assistance to allow end users to seek information about products, carry out comparative evaluations of brands and services, place an order and pay for the product through the vast electronic global network.

This chapter examines the role that the Internet has played thus far, and is likely to play in the future. The Internet has already presented a number of serious challenges for marketers as they are forced to re-think traditional methods for doing business. Over the next five years, as consumers increasingly gain easier and speedier access to the Internet – through platforms such as set-top boxes, television and screen-based telephones – it is anticipated that it will take on even greater strategic significance. The emergence of the aforementioned gateway providers, coupled with new handlers of information – infomediaries – will also challenge and define many industries' ability to create – and destroy – value (Hagel and Lansing, 1994).

This chapter considers the impact of the Internet on a number of critical marketing areas. The first section examines the challenge presented to conventional international research and practice by the popularity of Internet supported internationalization. The second section addresses the likely impact of the Internet on elements of the marketing mix: such as promotion, selling and channel management. The final part presents a case study that demonstrates how companies can develop the Internet as a strategic and important element of their overall business strategy.

The Internet: a challenge to conventional marketing wisdom

Although the mainstream academic literature has largely ignored the Internet's impact on the study and practice of international marketing, several recently published studies have pointed to revolutionary effects. Bill Gates (1996), for example, has argued that businesses worldwide will be transformed over the next decade or so as intranets revolutionize the way in which companies share information internally, and the Internet revolutionizes how they communicate externally. Similar comments have been made in recent papers by Quelch and Klein (1996) and by Hamill (1997) who argue that commercialization of the World Wide Web (WWW) will revolution-ize the study and practice of international mar-keting as we arrive at the new millennium. Hoffman and Novak (1995; 1996a, b) argue the need for new marketing paradigms to take account of the increasing importance of elec-tronic commerce; while authors such as Barnett (1995); Hammond (1996); Hagel and Armstrong (1997); Martin, (J.) (1996); Martin, (C.) 1997; and Tapscott (1996) call into question the continued relevance of existing business models and approaches to strategic marketing in a 'digital age'. Martin (C.) (1997), for example, argues that 'business concepts ingrained through past busi-ness school teachings and experiences collapse in the Net environment'. Martin (J.) (1996) argues that most organizations are structured for an age that is gone and that there is a need for developing new organizational forms to take full advantage of the networked economy.

Barriers to SME internationalization

The main barriers or obstacles facing SMEs when attempting to go international have been extensively examined in the literature (see, for example, Aaby and Slater, 1989; Abdel-Malek, 1978; Baker, 1979; Barker and Kaynak, 1992; Bilkey, 1978 and 1985; Bilkey and Tesar, 1977; Bradley, 1984; British Overseas Trade Board, 1987; Young and Hamill *et al.*, 1989).

Four main types of barrier have been identified:

Psychological barriers relating to SME perceptions concerning the costs, risks and profitability of exporting, including an ethnocentric rather than geocentric orientation; short- rather than long-term perspectives; the view that exporting is too risky, 'not for us', 'too much trouble', 'someone else's problem' and so on.

Operational barriers which refer to the problems encountered by SMEs in dealing with export paperwork, documentation, language prob-lems, delays in payment, etc.

Organizational barriers arising from having limited resources available to devote to the export

effort and the limited international experience of most SMEs.

Product/market barriers relating to the suitability (or lack of suitability) of the firms' product or ser-vice for foreign markets and the country selection decision, i.e. which country(ies) to enter and the decision regarding market con-centration versus market spreading.

The Internet does not provide a panacea for such problems. However, used effectively, it can be a very powerful tool to assist SMEs in over-coming the main barriers experienced, and there is growing recognition that one of the main impacts of the Internet will be a levelling of the corporate playing field and the more rapid inter-nationalization of SMEs (Ellsworth and Ellsworth, 1996a; Quelch and Klein, 1996; and Hamill, 1997). Thus the use of the 'Net' for mar-ket intelligence and to support international net-working can lead to a more positive, geocentric orientation towards the strategic importance of international markets. Electronic trading can overcome many of the operational barriers relat-ing to paperwork and export documentation, with Singapore's TradeNet system being a very good example (Turbin, McLean and Wetherby, 1996). The establishment and effective market-ing of a corporate web site can be used to over-come the product suitability/country selection decision allowing SMEs to develop global mar-ket niche strategies rather than country-oriented strategies. The implementation of an integrated Internet marketing strategy can provide SMEs with a low-cost 'gateway' to global markets; con-siderably improve communications with cus-tomers, suppliers and partners abroad; generate a wealth of information on market trends and developments world-wide; provide an 'ear to the ground' on the latest technology and R&D; and be a very powerful international promotion and sales tool.

Incremental internationalization

The more rapid internationalization of SMEs made possible by effective Internet marketing raises serious questions concerning one of the dominant and most commonly used paradigms in international marketing, namely, incremental internationalization. The view of internationalization as an evolutionary, incremental process was first developed by Johanson and Weidersheim-Paul (1975), based on the experiences of four Scandinavian companies. Since then a large number of other studies have applied the stages model to different samples of SMEs and the model has become one of the most widely used in international marketing teaching and research. Although there are some important differences in the various studies, most agree that internationalization is a step-wise process whereby companies gradually become more and more international over time with increasing knowledge and experience of foreign markets.

Given the comments made in the previous section, it is a legitimate question to ask whether this slow, evolutionary, stages of development model of internationalization remains valid when Internet technology and WWW provide SMEs with a low cost 'gateway' to global markets. The Internet's impact on internationalization processes will become a dominant research issue discussed in the international marketing literature as we arrive at the new millennium. New marketing paradigms will be needed as the 'stages of development' model loses much of its relevance in explaining internationalization processes in an on-line world.

Network and relationship marketing

In a number of recently published articles, the stages of development approach to internationalization has been linked to the growing volume of literature on business markets as networks of actor relationships (see, for example, Johanson and Vahlne, 1992; MCB Virtual Conference Site, 1996). According to such scholars, it is the knowledge and experience gained from business networks that help to break down the barriers to SME internationalization. Business networks, and the knowledge gained from them, evolve over time as partners build up

mutual trust in each other. Thus, the internationalization process is inherently linked to actor relationships in evolving international networks.

While the previous section questioned the continued relevance of the 'stages of development' model, the importance of developing effective network relationships is not in doubt. In an era of network or relationship marketing and just-in-time delivery, maintaining effective communications with foreign customers (actual and potential), suppliers, agents and distributors is critically important to successful internationalization. It is argued strongly by both authors that such relationships will increasingly be supported by electronic communications. This is a critical development that few mainstream network scholars have addressed. The Internet provides various low-cost tools for SMEs to improve on-going communications with the different actors in their international network including e-mail; Usenet; Listserv; Internet Relay Chat; MOOS and MUDS; video conferencing, etc. Effective use of these electronic communications tools will become increasingly necessary to support and develop international networks (see Poon and Jevons, 1997). As more companies go on-line, SMEs who are not connected face the danger of being shut out of international networks. In the near future, a business card without an e-mail address will be as useful as one without a telephone number.

The importance of electronic networks is the main theme of Hagel and Armstrong's (1997) book. According to the authors, competitiveness in an on-line world depends on the successful creation and management of virtual communities involving customers, suppliers, partners and competitors. Understanding how these virtual communities can be built and managed represents the biggest single challenge to senior management of existing companies and requires a mental model very different from that of the present. Virtual Communities of Common Interest (VCCI) would be an extremely valuable addition to the existing literature on relationship marketing.

Export market research

Marketing is essentially an information processing activity that links an organization to the external environment in which it operates. Processing information is now generally accepted as the fifth 'P' of the marketing mix, with effective management of information systems/information technology being a powerful source of competitive advantage. The need for effective management of information is particularly important in international marketing, where the firm will be dealing with a range of diverse and complex environments subject to rapid and often unexpected change. Empirical evidence shows that effective export marketing research is a 'critical success factor' discriminating successful from unsuccessful SME exporters. The key to success in entering new markets is often the systematic gathering and analysis of accurate and timely information. Sound marketing strategy and marketing management decisions cannot be made unless all relevant information is evaluated including the idiosyncrasies of the market, the needs and tastes of consumers, etc.

While the importance of export marketing research is generally accepted, the evidence also shows that few SMEs adopt systematic procedures in this respect. Several reasons have been suggested for this; including the view that export marketing is too expensive; the scope of the task is too complex and difficult; the SME is too concerned with day-to-day problems and has little scope for adopting a longer-term strategic perspective; and the fact that most SMEs lack in-house marketing research personnel, knowledge or resource.

The use of the Internet for marketing intelligence is one of the most important ways in which connectivity can improve SMEs' ability to develop international markets. Buying or commissioning market research reports can be a prohibitively expensive business. For a fraction of the cost, and in many cases free of charge, much of the same information can be gathered from the WWW.

The volume of relevant international marketing information available on the Web is too extensive to describe in detail here, but it includes numerous on-line newspapers and journals; an extensive list of individual country and industry market research reports; trade lists of suppliers, agents, distributors and government contacts in a large number of countries; details of host country legislation covering imports, agency agreements, joint ventures, etc; relevant international marketing listserv and discussion groups; and numerous other sources of information. A list of web sites useful in undertaking general country screening and export market research can be found at Internet Export Resources (http:/web.ukonline.co.uk/Members/jim.hamill/contents.htm).

Internet marketing strategies and management

Within the context of international marketing, the Internet will have a profound effect on international marketing strategies and management of the international marketing mix. Quelch and Klein (1996) present a concise summary of emerging trends in the paper. The authors predict that the Internet will allow greater facilitation of niche marketing on a global scale; lead to the increased standardization of prices across borders or at least a narrowing of price differentials; reduce the importance of traditional intermediaries in international markets and increase the importance of 'cybermediaries'; enhance the importance of networks supported by electronic communications; lead to improved customer interactivity and support; reduce global advertising costs and barriers to international market entry and development.

It is worth noting at this point that most authors agree that marketing on the Internet is different from traditional marketing and requires a radically different 'mindset' and different skills. The Internet is not a mass marketing or selling medium. It is a communications medium. A 'build it and they will come' approach will not work. A new Internet marketing 'mindset' is required; one, which empha-sizes mutual help, support and the establish-ment of long-term relationships as, opposed to the 'hard-sell' approach. (Ellsworth and Ellsworth, 1996a,b; Sterne, 1995; and Vassos, 1996).

The Internet: a new channel opportunity

As mentioned earlier, the Internet, because of its interconnected nature, presents many opportun-ities for companies to exchange both informa-tion about their products and services, as well as facilitate exchange. In this context, much debate is currently taking place about the role of the intermediary in this exchange process between the manufacturer and end user. This section examines this ongoing debate.

The rationale for using intermediaries has been articulated as far back as 1954, when Alderson provided the following observations:

- *Intermediaries provide economies of distribution,* by creating time, place and possession utility.
- *Intermediaries provide economies of scope,* by adjusting the discrepancy in assortment of goods and services held by the manufacturer and the assortment demanded by the end user.
- *Intermediaries provide routinization,* by minimiz-ing the cost of transactions by reducing them to routine exchanges.
- *Intermediaries structure information essential to consumers,* by facilitating consumers' search for information to satisfy their consumption needs.

Much has been written about the way in which information technology has impacted on organizations; in particular the linkages between manufacturers, suppliers and inter-mediaries. This is reflected particularly in the adoption of such tools as electronic data inter-change (EDI). This has allowed organizations to communicate electronically and achieve greater efficiencies in terms of cost savings (reduction in paper documentation, reduction in human error, instantaneous transfer of data, speedier order cycle times and ease of payment). These benefits have led many organizations to achieve a much tighter element of control of the man-agement of their supply chain activities.

The advent of the Internet affords an exten-sion of this electronic interconnectedness through the various activities of the supply chain and directly on to the end user. Prior to this, electronic communication occurred almost exclusively on an organization-to-organization basis. Thus the opportunity exists for companies to interact, on a one-to-one basis, with the indi-vidual potential consumer. Benjamin and Wigand (1995) provide ample evidence of the additional costs that intermediaries generate in the delivery of value to the end user. They cite the example of a manufacturer of high-quality shirts, where it would be possible to reduce the retail price by as much as 62% if wholesalers and retailers could be removed from the value chain. Companies such as Dell Corporation and Direct Line have clearly demonstrated the savings that can be made from eliminating intermediaries, and more importantly passed on to the end user. Producers, of course, also have the option of retaining these savings and reinvesting in other areas within the value chain. In such a situation, it can be argued that many traditional inter-mediaries will disappear, as companies re-engineer their supply chain in general and channel management activities in particular. Sarkar *et al.* (1996) describes this scenario as the 'threatened intermediaries hypothesis'.

Williamson was one of the first advocates of what is called the *transaction costs theory (TCT).* This suggests that a firm has two options for organizing its economic activities: by integrat-ing the various activities into its own manage-ment structure, or contracting these activities to external parties. It represents the classic 'make versus buy' decision.

Sarkar *et al.* (1996) argue that in the context of channel decisions, transaction cost theory can be applied in two ways: on the one hand, the

Internet, by extending directly into the home of the end user, lowers the transaction costs producers incur when marketing directly to such consumers. Conversely, the same theory can be used to suggest that producers will outsource intermediary functions, resulting in a greater reliance on intermediaries.

Clearly the biggest challenge facing the Internet, as companies evaluate its potential as a new channel alternative, is the lack of *personalization* attaching to the medium. If we examine the various roles played by intermediaries, it can be seen that intermediaries play an important task in terms of influencing purchases. For instance, many shoppers wishing to purchase a new VCR, may present themselves at an electrical store and entrust themselves to the sales assistant for appropriate advice and guidance. They may wish to reduce the perceived risk involved in spending a large amount of money on a product that they know little about (in terms of the various competitive offerings, features, prices and so on). The personalized contact, allied to the reassurance that accrues from advice provided by an 'expert' information source, reinforces the contribution that a traditional intermediary can provide.

It can be argued therefore that intermediaries perform a number of functions, some of which can be competently and cost effectively performed by electronic means. However for many products and services, particularly those that involve a combination of either a high level of pre- and post-sales service, high perceived risk, a desire to physically handle and experience the product, it may be difficult for the new so called 'cybermediaries' to perform such roles effectively and in a manner that is satisfactory to the end user. Sarkar *et al.* (1996) argue that

the coordination role played by intermediaries in the exchange process is, in fact, a multifaceted set of functions, which are quite likely to be differentially impacted by any electronic service provided over a network. Network-based services may do a particularly good job in facilitating product search, but less well equipped to offer product distribution (except of course for information and software products).

The new cybermediaries

Sarkar *et al.* (1996) provide a concise summary of the new cybermediaries. They can be summarized as follows:

- *Directories (general, commercial and specialized):* helping consumers find producers by categorizing web sites and providing structured menus to facilitate navigation. An example would be The All-Internet Shopping Directory that focuses on providing indices of commercial sites on the Net.
- *Search services:* helping consumers to conduct keyword searches of extensive databases of web sites or pages. Examples would be Alta Vista or Infoseek.
- *Malls:* referring to any site that has more than two commercial sites linked to it. It can be distinguished from commercial sites, because it provides infrastructure for the producer/retailer in return for a fee. An example would be the Pinnacle Mall.
- *Publishers:* playing the role of traffic generators that offer content of interest to consumers. They may appear more or less to be online newspapers or magazines. They become intermediaries when they offer links to producers through advertising or product listings related to their content. An example would be GNN.
- *Virtual resellers:* in contrast to the malls, the virtual reseller owns inventory and sells product directly. They are often product-focused, e.g. America's Shirt and Tie. They are able to obtain products directly from manufacturers, who may hesitate to go directly to consumers for fear of alienating retailers upon which they depend.
- *Web site evaluators:* where consumers are directed to a producer's site via new type of site that offers some form of evaluation. Some evaluation is based on the frequency of access; others carry an explicit review of the sites.
- *Auditors:* not direct intermediaries, but serve the same purposes as audience measurement services in traditional media. For instance,

advertisers require information on the usage rates associated with web advertising vehicles, as well as credible information on audience characteristics. An example if this form of indirect intermediary is the Internet Audit Bureau.

- *Forums, fan clubs and user groups:* again, not direct intermediaries, but can play a large role in facilitating customer-producer feedback and supporting market research. They may be created specifically to connect the producer with consumers, or they may be created by users to communicate with each other.
- *Financial intermediaries:* any form of e-commerce requires some mechanism for processing orders or payment. Intermediaries such as Digicash help consumers to pay in cash and First Virtual facilitates the consumer when sending secure electronic mail authorizing a payment.
- *Spot market makers and barter networks:* occurs where people exchange one good or service for another, however instead of paying with cash, they engage in a bartering arrangement. Examples include the news groups that act as markets for various products. Specialist groups can also operate (computer equipment, trading cards, etc.).
- *Intelligent agents:* software programs that begin with some preliminary search criteria from users, but can also learn from other past user behaviour to optimize searches.

Evolution versus revolution?

The arguments surrounding the future role of intermediaries remain unresolved. This is partly because a lot will depend on the degree of access to the Internet throughout the world. Estimates as to the value amount of purchases sold over the Internet vary and are inconsistent. Street (1998) calculates that around $2 billion dollars worth of business was achieved per annum over the Internet. This rises to around $10 billion per annum when business-to-business goods are included. It should also be noted that it is only

since 1996 that most companies established a web site page. Street (1998) also estimates that by the year 2001, approximately 10 per cent of the global population will have direct access to the Internet. A recent study in the US, carried out by Ernst and Young (1998), presents some interesting findings. Three major groups featured in this survey: over 850 consumers and 150 companies were interviewed. The main conclusions are summarized as follows:

Consumers
- 20 per cent of households have online access: 32 per cent of these have bought something online.
- 64 per cent research products online and buy them in traditional channels; 46 per cent fax or phone in orders.
- Web shoppers are multi-faceted; 40 per cent buy computer-related products online; 48 per cent are gardeners.

Retailers
- 34 per cent of retailers sell or plan to sell products on the Internet.
- 47 per cent say their products are ill-suited for web sales.
- Most will use uniform prices.
- Sales growth is the primary goal.

Manufacturers
- Only 21 per cent of manufacturers sell or plan to sell their products online.
- 88 per cent of web sellers believe the Net will strengthen their competitive position.
- One-third of web sellers say online commerce may strain retail relations.

These results suggest that while the Web is perceived by consumers as a viable channel option, a more cautious approach is adopted by manufacturers and retailers. Most companies are effectively 'testing the water' rather than adopting a proactive and aggressive strategy with regard to the Internet. Perhaps this is understandable given the differing projections about growth and adoption patterns.

The pace of change and development is largely dependent on the level of benefit accruing to the customer from purchasing product via the Internet, the degree of competitive activity (as companies veer to the more proactive adoption of the Internet as a viable channel of distribution) and economics. With respect to the latter point, the large supermarket operators will have to consider the enormous investment currently required to develop and open a new superstore (in UK terms, this can be conservatively estimated at around £60 million), versus the likely increase in the number of people wishing to purchase their products via the Internet. A recent study undertaken for the Coca-Cola Retail Research Group Europe (Coopers and Lybrand, 1996) suggested that roughly 5 per cent of food sales would be routed through new modes of shopping by the year 2005. However, at 1994 prices, this would mean a market opportunity estimated at $33 billion.

The strongest argument surrounding the concept of 'disintermediation' can be found if one considers the roles and responsibilities of travel agents or automobile dealers as working examples. Travel agents provide free vacation planning and make their money out of the ticket that they sell. Auto dealers maintain expensive showrooms and offer test-drives but do not make money until someone actually purchases a car. If people purchase such products on-line, via the Internet, the need for visiting or indeed utilizing such intermediaries will be eliminated. This scenario, if accepted, means that intermediaries will need to radically reappraise their activities and contribution to the delivery of value. Those intermediaries that do little more than act as 'order-takers' or 'go-betweens' are in a precarious position as a result of the developments with regard to e-commerce. In this context, intermediaries will need to consider their future role, as sales managers have had to reconsider the role of the sales representative. Those intermediaries that perform a more strategic role in the value chain, e.g. systems integrators, are in a stronger position to re-establish themselves in the 'new order'.

Change: not elimination

Given the uncertainty about future trends and developments that have been highlighted in the preceding section, it is more realistic to state that change rather than elimination of intermediaries is more likely to occur. For example, in the case of the travel agent, it is more likely that while a number of small, independent operators will disappear, the larger ones will join forces with the Internet. Customers can conduct routine transactions themselves over the Internet, while leaving the more complex itineraries for agents. Such agents can also send out customized bulletins through e-mail at significantly less cost than mail or fax. Such communications could alert customers to bargain fares. This kind of positioning of the travel agent as an intermediary between the producer and consumer should guarantee the more proactive agents a strategic role within the travel industry; albeit in a more rationalized and specialized way.

The global disparity of technological advancement and access between regions and countries will also mean that companies will face difficulties in establishing a globally integrated and coordinated distribution strategy. As mentioned earlier, the development of TV based links with the Internet, allied to improved technology, will lead to a much wider level of access among the population, allied to speedier download times. This will vary by region however.

From such a global perspective, it is more reasonable to observe that change will be imminent: not immediate.

Street (1998) notes that the process of buying itself is being unbundled. People may browse, seek product information and compare prices on the Internet, but the product could be purchased or picked up separately. The combined impact of these trends is creating a separate product selection, order and delivery process. This in turn poses a challenge for the company in that it will seriously have to consider multiple channels. For example, main UK supermarkets are experimenting with a number of options with their customer base: order at home, pickup at store; order at home, pickup at home; order at work, pickup at work. He argues that opportunities for companies to re-segment customers, categories and the process are 'immense' and that retailers are beginning to explore such possibilities.

In summary, the difficulties of predicting likely trends accurately means that firm predictions about the impact of the Internet are difficult. The evidence that was considered in the preceding paragraphs suggests that companies must reconsider the traditional channels that they utilize to deliver value to the end user. The next section examines the stages involved in preparing a strategy for interactive marketing

Designing an interactive marketing strategy

Kiertzkowski *et al.* (1996) have identified five critical success factors for successful digital marketers.

1   *Attract users:* The need to overcome the 'clutter' that currently exists on the Internet. It is unreasonable to assume that consumers will be attracted to the web page by their own volition. Instead, effective digital marketing must recognize the need to build 'traffic' by investing in advertising that promotes the web page. This can be achieved through a combination of newspaper/trade/billboard advertising, combined with links from other sites and promoting the web site on product packaging.

2   *Engage users' interest and participation:* There is a challenge here to provide a creative and interesting web site, allied to relevant content that engages the visitor to the page. An example of this is Saturn, the car company that attempts to engage users by allowing Saturn car owners to find and communicate with each other. It is not sufficient to develop a page and place the company's name on it. Instead companies need to go further and utilize the web site as an active selling and channel tool. The likely technical improvements should help companies to design interactive web pages that provide greater value to the customer.

3   *Retain users and ensure that they return to the application:* As is the case with basic promotion models, it is not sufficient to simply create awareness and interest. It is arguably more important to retain customers. This is essential if a company wishes to establish ongoing relationships and leverage more purchases from the customer base. In this respect, it is important the web page is continuously updated with fresh and relevant information.

4   *Learn about their preferences:* An interactive medium such as the Internet presents opportunities for companies to learn about customer attitudes, demographics and behaviours. This can come from e-mail communications to the company; opinions volunteered on bulletin boards or information collected from surveys or registration processes. Much of these benefits may not be fully accessible yet – given the reluctance of many consumers to part with a great deal of personal information; a perception that the Internet is not secure and that only a small percentage of a company's customers may be in a position to access this channel. This should not diminish the ability of the company however, to collect valuable information.

5   *Relate back to them to provide the sort of customized interactions that represent the true 'value bubble' of digital marketing:* This represents the opportunity to customize or tailor design the product or marketing communication to one customer at a time. In an era where mass customization is becoming a potential reality for many companies, the Internet can be utilized as a complementary mechanism for implementing such a strategy. The two-way capability for communication

(company to customer and customer to company) can allow the company to tailor a more focused and relevant product offering to the customer. It also allows the company (depending on the nature of the product offering) to inform the customer about new products, upgrades and so on. From the customer's point of view, this can be perceived as a highly personalized service – something that might not be expected from a large multinational company with a worldwide customer base in the normal course of events.

The preceding paragraphs demonstrate the potential that an interactive medium such as the Internet presents to companies. It more than fulfils many of the criteria required for effective relationship marketing, adding extra value to the product offer and presenting a tailor designed product for the individual consumer. Much depends of course on the category of product or service under consideration. Certain commodity purchases, such as gasoline for instance, would be very unsuitable. In the next section, we consider the example of Dell Computer Corporation and their recent adoption of the Internet as a viable channel alternative.

Case study: Dell Computer Corporation

Michael Dell founded Dell Computer Corporation in 1983. Spotting a market opportunity by selling PCs direct to the customer, and thereby eliminating the middleman, Dell has grown to a point where in 1997, it achieved world-wide sales of $16 billion. In May 1997, Dell launched its **www.dell.com/uk** web site. This new channel accounts for over 10 per cent of its sales. World-wide, sales from Dell's web sites generate $4 million to $5 million per day. The company believes that e-commerce, through the Internet, is a logical extension of its original Dell Direct strategy.

When designing the site, a number of basic rules were followed:

- It should be fast to download.
- Customers should never be more than three clicks from something interesting – and that includes making a purchase.
- The *Buy a Dell* icon should be visible at all times across the page.
- It should be able to be replicated across Europe, with multiple languages and local content.

Benefits to the customer?

The customer can browse through the pages, choose a configuration, place and pay for an order and consider add-ons that they might not have contemplated buying prior to visiting the site. It is convenient (open all hours). It allows a high level of interaction between the customer and Dell, resulting in a strong level of intimacy.

Benefits to Dell?

Lower transaction costs and scalability. Ability to acquire customers, retain all information about them online (every computer sold via the Internet can be traced to the individual customer), Dell can also use the Net to send information to purchasers about new product developments in hardware an software, possible add-ons, etc. No PC is manufactured until an order is received and paid for. Price changes can be made on the web page within three hours: this contrasts with a potential lead time of four to six weeks, if advertising space has to be booked in the national press and TV. Customized web pages can be designed by Dell and included on the intranets of individual companies. As a consequence, centralized purchasing facilities can be set up.

Summary

The Dell example demonstrates many of the virtues of using the Internet as a viable and cost-effective channel option. It adheres naturally to the Dell Direct concept. This has allowed Dell to operate on a *build to order* basis:

where every PC is built individually (customization) and less than seven days inventory is carried, with no finished stock at all, at its plants in the Republic of Ireland. The company also has a detailed record of every purchase order it has fulfilled via the Internet. This allows Dell to engage with its customers and send them information in a targeted and focused way about possible upgrades and so on. In this way, the company pursues a consistent form of relationship marketing. In addition, the Internet allows Dell to cost effectively manage its supply chain activities.

Of course there is also a downside. Only computer literate customers can use the web page with a strong degree of confidence. Dell do not actively encourage first-time buyers to use this channel option: the costs associated with handling telephone queries and sending out technical support personnel to address many mundane and simple problems, mean that the Internet is not an effective medium. Not every visitor to the site actually makes a purchase. The present conversion rate on the Dell UK web page is around 23 per cent (Hubbard, 1998). It is Dell's objective to raise this conversion figure to 33 per cent over the next three years.

Conclusions

This chapter has examined the major developments and trends with regard to the Internet. The first section has argued strongly that marketing practitioners and educators need to revisit many of the traditional conceptualizations regarding the internationalization of business. Preconceived perceptions about typical barriers to SME internationalization can be challenged as a consequence of using the Internet effectively. The traditional, and much used 'stages of international development' model also needs some revisionist thinking as a consequence of the Internet – where the development of a web site can mean that even the smallest business venture can become a global operator overnight. We argue that new marketing paradigms will be needed as such frameworks lose much of their relevance in explaining the process of internationalization in an on-line world.

The middle section places the Internet as a viable and innovative channel option under scrutiny. The debate over whether or not intermediaries will be displaced, eliminated or re-engineered was considered. There are no simple answers. Change in many industry sectors will be inevitable, but imminent rather than immediate. There are too many imponderables to allow for accurate prediction. A lot will depend on the extent to which individuals access the Internet. The associated costs and the technology improvements that will allow for speedier downloading times on the Net will influence this, in turn. This is likely to vary on a country by country basis. However the statistical evidence presented in this chapter suggests that by the middle of the next decade, the Internet will emerge as a viable and realistic channel of distribution as well as a route towards rapid internationalization.

The Dell Corporation case reinforces the view that the Internet is not simply a fashionable marketing tool. This company has managed to redefine it supply chain management activities and, in the process, has become even more competitive in its particular industry sector. This should suggest to readers that the Internet would play a significant role in the strategic planning activities of companies over the next number of years. In so doing, it will challenge existing conceptions about how value can be delivered to the customer and force companies to develop new paradigms for conducting business.

References

Aaby, N.-E. and Slater, S. F. (1989) Management Influences on Export Performance: A Review of the Empirical Literature 1978–1988, *International Marketing Review*, **6**(4), 7–26.

Abdel-Malek, T. (1978) Export Marketing Orientation in Small Firms, *American Journal of Small Business*, **3**(1), 7–26.

Alderson, W. (1954) Factors Governing the Development of Marketing Channels, in R. M. Clewett (ed.), *Marketing Channels for Manufactured Products*, Richard D. Irwin Inc., Homewood, Ill.

Baker, M. J. (1979) Export Myopia, *The Quarterly Review of Marketing*, Spring, 1–10.

Barker, S. and Kaynak, E. (1992) An Empirical Investigation of the Differences between Initiating and Continuing Exporters, *European Journal of Marketing*, **26**(3), 13–25.

Barnatt, C. (1995) *CyberBusiness: Mindsets for the Wired Age*, John Wiley, Chichester.

Benjamin, R. and Wigand, R. (1995) Electronic Markets and Virtual Value Chains on the Information Highway, *Sloan Management Review*, Winter, 62–72.

Bilkey, W. J. (1978) An Attempted Integration of the Literature on the Export Behaviour of Firms, *Journal of International Business Studies*, **9**(1), 33–46.

Bilkey, W. J. (1985) Development of Export Marketing Guidelines, *International Marketing Review*, **2**(1), Spring, 31–40.

Bilkey, W. J. and Tesar, G. (1977) The Export Behaviour of Smaller-Sized Wisconsin Manufacturing Firms, *Journal of International Business Studies*, Spring/Summer, 93–98.

Bradley, M. F. (1984) The Effects of Cognitive Style, Attitude Toward Growth and Motivation on the Internationalization of the Firm, *Research in Marketing*, **7**, 237–260.

British Overseas Trade Board (1987) *Into Active Exporting*, BOTB, London.

Coopers and Lybrand (1996) *The Future for the Food Store: Challenges and Alternatives*, Project VI, May 1996. A study conducted for the Coca-Cola Retailing Research Group, Europe.

Ellsworth, J. H, and Ellsworth, M. V. (1996a) *The New Internet Business Book*, John Wiley, New York.

Ellsworth, J. H, and Ellsworth, M. V. (1996b) *Marketing on the Internet – Multimedia Strategies for the WWW*, John Wiley, New York

Ernst and Young Report (1998) *Internet Shopping*, Stores, January, Section 2.

Gates, B. (1996) *The Road Ahead*, Penguin.

Hagel, J. and Armstrong, A. G. (1997) *net.gain:expanding markets through virtual communities*, Harvard Business School Press, http://www.hbsp.harvard.edu/netgain

Hagel, J. and Lansing, W. (1994) Who Owns the Customer? *The McKinsey Quarterly*, No. 4, 63–75.

Hamill, J, and Gregory, K. (1997) Internet Marketing in the Internationalization of UK SMEs, *Journal of Marketing Management*, Special Edition on Internationalization, Hamill, J. (ed.), **13**, Nos 1–3.

Hamill, J. (ed.) (1997) The Internet and International Marketing, *International Marketing Review*, Special Edition on Internet Marketing, **13**(1–3), 1–5.

Hammond, R. (1996) *Digital Business: Surviving and Thriving in an On-line World*, Hodder & Stoughton; available as an on-line book; http://www.hammond.co.uk

Hoffman, D.L. and Novak, T. P. (1995) The CommerceNet/Nielen Internet Demographics Survey: Is it Representative? Project 2000 Note, December 12th, http://www2000.ogsm.vanderbilt.edu/

Hoffman, D. L, and Novak, T. P. (1996a) Marketing in Hypermedia Computer Related Environments: Conceptual Foundations, *Journal of Marketing*, July.

Hoffman, D. L, and Novak, T. P, (1996b) A New Marketing Paradigm for Electronic Commerce, Project 2000 Working Paper, February 19th, http://www2000.ogsm.vanderbilt.edu/

Hubbard, P. (1998) Dell and E-Commerce: A Perfect Match. Presentation at Traditional & New Channels: Strategy, Selection and Management, National Materials Handling Centre, 26th March.

Johanson, J. and Vahlne, J.-E. (1992) Management of Foreign Market Entry, *Scandinavian International Business Review*, **1**(3).

Johanson, J, and Weidersheim-Paul, F. (1975) The Internationalization of the Firm – Four Swedish Case Studies, *Journal of Management Studies*, **12**(3).

Kiertzkowski, A., McQuade, S., Waitman, R.

and Zeisser, M. (1996) Marketing to the Digital Consumer, *The McKinsey Quarterly*, No. 3, 4–21.

Martin, C. (1997) *The Digital Estate: Strategies for Competing, Surviving and Thriving in an Internetworked World*, McGraw-Hill, http://www.mcgraw-hill.com/digitalestate

Martin, J. (1996) *Cybercorp: The New Business Revolution*, AMACOM.

MCB Online Conference Web Site (1996) http://mcb.co.uk/confhome.htm

Poon, S. and Jevons, C. (1997) Internet Enabled International Marketing – A Small Business Network Perspective, Special Edition of the *Journal of Marketing Management* on Internationalization. J. Hamill (ed.), **13**, Nos 1–3.

Quelch, J. A. and Klein, L. R. (1996) The Internet and International Marketing, *Sloan Management Review*, Spring, 60–75.

Sarkar, M. B., Butler, B. and Steinfield, C. (1996) Intermediaries and Cybermediaries: A Continuing Role for Mediating Players in the Electronic Marketplace, *Journal of Computer Mediated Communications*, **1**(3), 20–32.

Sterne, J. (1995) *World Wide Web Marketing: Integrating The Internet Into Your Marketing Strategy*, John Wiley, New York.

Street, R. (1998) Traditional and New Channels – Changing Routes to Market. Presentation at *Traditional & New Distribution Channels: Strategy, Selection and Management*, National Materials Handling Centre, 28th March.

Tapscott, D. (1996) *Digital Economy: Promise and Peril in the Age of Networked Intelligence*, McGraw-Hill.

Turbin, E., McLean, E. and Wetherby, J. (1996) *Information Technology for Management: Improving Quality and Productivity*, John Wiley, New York.

Vassos, T. (1996) *Strategic Internet Marketing*, Que Books; Author's web site at http://www.webdiamonds.com/~webdiamonds. Strategic Internet Marketing web site at http://www.mcp.com/que/desktop_os/int_market

Williamson, O. E. (1975) *Markets and Hierarchies: Analysis and Antitrust Implications*, Free Press, New York.

Young, S., Hamill, J., Wheeler, C. and Davies, J. R. (1989) *International Market Entry and Development*, Harvester Wheatsheaf, Hertfordshire.

Index